New

WITHDRAWN

Current Biography Yearbook 2004

EDITOR
Clifford Thompson

SENIOR EDITOR
Miriam Helbok

PRODUCTION STAFF
Gray Young (Manager)
Jeremy K. Brown
Richard J. Stein
Sandra Watson

ASSISTANT EDITOR
Peter G. Herman

CONTRIBUTING EDITOR
Kieran Dugan

STAFF WRITERS
Jennifer Curry
Karen E. Duda
Kaitlen J. Exum
Terence J. Fitzgerald
Hope Tarullo
Cullen F. Thomas
Lara Weibgen

CONTRIBUTING WRITERS
Dimitri Cavalli
Andrew I. Cavin
Kathleen A. D'Angelo
Christopher Mari
Paul B. McCaffrey
Geoff Orens
Liliana Segura
Luke A. Stanton
Selma Yampolsky

RESEARCHER
Verna J. Coleman

EDITORIAL ASSISTANT
Carolyn Ellis

THE H. W. WILSON COMPANY
NEW YORK   DUBLIN

SIXTY-FIFTH ANNUAL CUMULATION—2004

PRINTED IN THE UNITED STATES OF AMERICA

International Standard Serial No. (0084-9499)

International Standard Book No. (0-8242-1044-1)

Library of Congress Catalog Card No. (40-27432)

Table of Contents

PREFACE

The aim of *Current Biography Yearbook 2004*, like that of the preceding volumes in this series of annual dictionaries of contemporary biography, now in its seventh decade of publication, is to provide reference librarians, students, and researchers with objective, accurate, and well-documented biographical articles about living leaders in all fields of human accomplishment. Whenever feasible, obituary notices appear for persons whose biographies have been published in *Current Biography*.

Current Biography Yearbook 2004 carries on the policy of including new and updated biographical profiles that supersede earlier articles. Profiles have been made as accurate and objective as possible through careful researching of newspapers, magazines, the World Wide Web, authoritative reference books, and news releases of both government and private agencies. Immediately after they are published in the 11 monthly issues, articles are submitted to biographees to give them an opportunity to suggest additions and corrections in time for publication of the *Current Biography Yearbook*. To take account of major changes in the careers of biographees, articles are revised before they are included in the yearbook.

Classification by Profession—2004 and *2001–2004 Index* are at the end of this volume. *Current Biography Cumulated Index 1940–2000* cumulates and supersedes all previous indexes.

For their assistance in preparing *Current Biography Yearbook 2004*, I thank the staff of *Current Biography* and other members of The H. W. Wilson Company's General Reference Department, and also the staffs of the company's Computer and Manufacturing departments.

Current Biography welcomes comments and suggestions. Please send your comments to: The Editor, *Current Biography*, The H. W. Wilson Company, 950 University Ave., Bronx, NY 10452; fax: 718-590-4566; E-mail: cthompson@hwwilson.com.

Clifford Thompson

List of Biographical Sketches

ix

Current Biography Yearbook 2004

Current Biography Yearbook 2004

Aerosmith

Rock band

Hamilton, Tom
Dec. 31, 1951– Bassist; songwriter

Kramer, Joey
June 21, 1950– Drummer

Perry, Joe
Sep. 10, 1950– Guitarist; songwriter

Tyler, Steven
Mar. 26, 1948– Singer; songwriter

Whitford, Brad
Feb. 23, 1952– Guitarist

Address: c/o Mitch Schneider Organization, 14724 Ventura Blvd., Suite 410, Sherman Oaks, CA 91403-3504

"We believed that anything worth doing was worth overdoing," Steven Tyler has said. Tyler, the principal lyricist and lead singer of the phenomenally successful and long-lived rock group Aerosmith, may have been referring not only to the band's hard-driving music but also to its legendary intemperance both offstage and onstage. While selling more than 60 million albums in the U.S. alone in the last three decades, Aerosmith has experienced unusually pronounced highs and lows. On the strength of such hits as "Dream On," "Walk This Way," and "Sweet Emotion," the band's popularity soared in the mid-1970s; a few years later, riven by drug-fueled personality conflicts, it was widely considered beyond saving, even by some of its own members. Tyler and the group's lead guitarist, Joe Perry, were dubbed the "Toxic Twins," for their drug use and frequent quarrels. "The band's story was one of rock & roll excess," David Wild wrote for *Rolling Stone* (April 5, 1990), "complete with all the absurd trimmings: wives who incessantly bickered, band members who fell offstage with disturbing regularity, $100,000 room-service bills, contests to see how many things in a Holiday Inn room would fit through a television set, million-dollar budgets, nightmarish gigs at theme parks . . . and money that went who knows where." Unlike many other rock groups that found-ered on the shoals of superstardom, however, Aerosmith kept afloat. The group rebounded from near irrelevancy to release its multi-platinum comeback album, *Permanent Vacation*, in 1987, followed by *Pump* (1989) and *Get a Grip* (1993), which attracted millions of fans despite the popularity of grunge-rock, whose sludgy rhythms and morose themes differed markedly from Aerosmith's pop-tinged arena rock. On the verge of splitting apart yet again in 1997, the band released the aptly titled *Nine Lives*. Since then Aerosmith has remained, in the words of Jim Farber in the New York *Daily News* (September 6, 1993), "one of rock's most enduring, and successful, cases of arrested development." Their 2004 album is *Honkin' on Bobo.*

Aerosmith's high-energy live performances have contributed in no small measure to its commercial success. Tyler's sexual charisma, limber strutting, and mastery of playing to his audiences continue to draw crowds of all ages. So does the band's ability to reinvent itself repeatedly while retaining the core of the hard-rock identity it forged in the 1970s. Despite the enduring popularity of the music of the Beatles, the Rolling Stones, and other "elder statesmen" of rock, few radio stations other than those devoted to oldies or classic rock broadcast it; in contrast, Aerosmiths' songs, both old and new, are regularly scheduled on the play lists of radio stations that concentrate on modern alternative rock, whose audiences span several generations. And as its slew of music-video awards attests, Aerosmith has the ear of the MTV generation.

Born Steven Tallarico on March 26, 1948 in Yonkers, New York, on the northern border of the New York City borough of the Bronx, Steven Tyler hails from a long line of musicians. His paternal great-grandfather, Giovanni Tallarico, was a cellist who performed classical music in ballrooms and hotels. Tyler's father, Victor Tallarico, was a Juilliard-trained classical pianist who taught music in the New York City public-school system and once performed at Carnegie Hall. "I grew up under the piano," Tyler said in a 1990 interview for *Musician* magazine, as quoted by Martin Huxley in his book *Aerosmith: The Fall and the Rise of Rock's Greatest Band* (1995). "My father talked to me with his fingers, playing Debussy and Beethoven," he continued. "He didn't talk to me much one-to-one as a human being, but I'm glad he didn't. That's where my emotion comes from."

Aerosmith (left to right): Tom Hamilton, Steven Tyler, Joe Perry, Joey Kramer, Brad Whitford

For nine years while growing up, Tyler sang in the choir of a Bronx Presbyterian church. In many other ways, though, he was rebellious and disobedient. He was reportedly expelled from a public elementary school for chasing a girl while brandishing a broken lightbulb. As a teenager at Roosevelt High School in Yonkers during the early 1960s, Tyler joined a gang and experimented with drugs; the latter activity resulted in his arrest on a misdemeanor drug charge and his forced departure from Roosevelt. "An undercover nark [narcotics officer] infiltrated my high school ceramics class . . . ," Tyler told Ed McCormack for *Rolling Stone* (August 26, 1976). "The [expletive] sold lids of grass [marijuana] to me and some other kids, then busted us for possession." Tyler finished high school at Quintano's, a private school for disruptive but talented students. His arrest also led the local draft board to classify him as 1Y (youthful offender), which made him ineligible for military service at a time when many of his contemporaries were being drafted to fight in the Vietnam War.

Tyler's first excursions into entertainment occurred during his summer vacations, which he spent at Trow-Rico Lodge, his parents' 360-acre resort in Sunapee, New Hampshire. There, on Saturday nights, one of Tyler's aunts organized children's talent shows. "She had me up there doing a pantomime to 'Animal Crackers' and singing, 'There's a Hole in the Bucket, Eliza,'" Tyler recalled to Wild. Later, he played the drums in his father's swing band during gigs at another local hotel. In 1964, at age 16, Tyler formed his first band, the Strangeurs, for which he played drums and sang the lead vocals. Initially covering tunes made popular by the advance guard of the so-called British rock invasion—the Yardbirds, the Animals, and the Beatles, among others—the Strangeurs expanded their repertoire to include original songs written by Tyler and the band's keyboardist. Several of those songs were released as singles on the Date and Verve labels, but they garnered little attention. Through his work with the Strangeurs, later known as Chain Reaction, Tyler became a regular denizen of the Greenwich Village section of the New York City borough of Manhattan. There, he hooked up with the Left Banke, a band for which he sang backup vocals on the album *The Left Banke Too* (1968). Meanwhile, Chain Reaction had split up, after Tyler, during a gig at a Long Island, New York, resort, jumped from behind his drum set and began strangling the lead guitarist. After fronting a short-lived band called William Proud, Tyler returned to his parents' resort in 1969.

In New Hampshire Tyler met Joe Perry, the son of Anthony D. Perry, an accountant, and Mary (Ursillo) Perry, who taught physical education. Born on September 10, 1950 in Lawrence, Massachusetts, Anthony Joseph Perry was a misfit who spent countless hours during his teens practicing on his Sears Silvertone guitar in his bedroom. Worried about his lack of interest in his studies, his parents enrolled him in a prep school. As Perry told McCormack, "That's really where I learned to hate the system, 'cause the faculty was always hassling me to cut my hair and yelling every time I picked up my guitar." A month before graduation Perry dropped out of school and found a job at the Anchorage, a Sunapee ice-cream parlor, where he often ran into Tyler. "Steven would come up to Sunapee with all of his bands . . . ," Tyler recalled to Wild. "They were loud and obnoxious, behaving like rock stars are supposed to behave—especially when they're in a little town and nobody knows how not-so-big they really are. They'd come into the Anchorage and throw food . . . and I'd have to clean up after them."

In addition to working at the Anchorage, Perry played with the bassist Tom Hamilton (born to George and Betty Hamilton on December 31, 1951 in Colorado Springs, Colorado) in a weekend group called the Jam Band. One night Perry coaxed Tyler to attend one of the band's shows. Impressed by what he heard, Tyler decided to join. After briefly doubling on vocals and drums, Tyler soon settled into his position as the Jam Band's frontman; in addition to literally singing at the front of the band, he provided direction. In about 1970, after adding a second guitarist, Ray Tabano, a childhood friend of Tyler's and a former William Proud member, Tyler and the combo moved to Boston, Massachusetts, where Tabano owned and operated a leather-goods store. They were soon joined by the drummer Joey Kramer (born to Mickey and Dorris Kramer on June 21, 1950 in the Bronx), who had also attended Roosevelt High School in Yonkers and was then studying at the Berklee College of Music, in Boston.

For the next several years, Tyler shared an apartment in Boston with his fellow band members, who supported themselves with odd jobs (Perry as a janitor in a synagogue, Tyler as a bakery worker). After rejecting such names as the Hookers (which reflected Tyler's conception of musicians performing at a gig for pay), and Spike Jones (a nod to a famous, antic-loving bandleader of the 1940s and 1950s), the musicians settled upon "Aerosmith," a suggestion from Joey Kramer. (The name is not connected to *Arrowsmith*, a novel by Sinclair Lewis.) Having resolved to avoid the low-paying club circuit, Aerosmith arranged to have their debut gig at the Nipmuc Regional High School, in Upton, Massachusetts, for which they earned several hundred dollars. Roaring through a set that included such numbers as "Shapes of Things" by the Yardbirds, "Live with Me" by the Rolling Stones, and "Cold Turkey" by John Lennon, the band pleased their audience. As would become common during their tours, Tyler and Perry argued strenuously that night after the concert, after Tyler accused Perry of playing too loudly.

Aerosmith proceeded to gain a strong following throughout New England. By 1972, with Brad Whitford (born to E. Russell Whitford and Joyce Whitford on February 23, 1952 in Winchester, Massachusetts) having replaced Tabano on rhythm guitar, Aerosmith had also established a toehold in New York City. The president of the Columbia Records label attended a show at the city's legendary club Max's Kansas City (now defunct) and, soon after, signed Aerosmith to a $125,000 recording contract. The band's self-titled debut, eight-track album, released in January 1973, identified Steven Tyler (rather than Tallarico) as its frontman and included seven original songs that Tyler wrote or co-

wrote. A mixture of straight-ahead rock and funk-influenced blues, the album met with little initial commercial or critical success. Nonetheless, its first single, "Dream On," which was later recognized as having been among the first power ballads (along with Led Zeppelin's classic "Stairway to Heaven"), quickly became one of the most frequently requested songs on Boston-area radio stations. Unable to garner interest in their music outside the Northeast either through the radio or record sales, Aerosmith's manager sent the band on the road to win fans at the grassroots level. One of the first bands they opened for was the Mahavishnu Orchestra, a jazz-rock fusion ensemble led by the guitar virtuoso John McLaughlin, whose audiences did not respond favorably to Aerosmith's brand of gritty, straight-ahead rock. After a year-long tour in which Aerosmith opened for such groups as the Kinks, Mott the Hoople, and Sha Na Na, "Dream On" climbed to number 59 on the *Billboard* charts. (In 1976 the now-classic, reissued "Dream On" reached number six and proceeded to become Aerosmith's first million-selling single.)

Critical praise eluded the band in its early days, however, not least because of Tyler's physical resemblance to Mick Jagger of the Rolling Stones, whose blues-inflected rock Aerosmith was perceived to be imitating. Tyler took offense at such comparisons, which invariably cast his band in a bad light. "Sure, I've been affected by Jagger," Tyler told *Circus* magazine in 1974, according to Huxley. "What rock singer hasn't?" In the following year Tyler commented, as quoted by Huxley, "Anybody who says I'm a Jagger rip-off 'cause I look like him a little has no intelligence. . . . Joe Perry looks like Keith Richards a little. What are we supposed to do, get plastic surgery?"

During the next years of the 1970s, Aerosmith released a series of albums that solidified the band's position in the higher echelons of the rock-music world. *Get Your Wings* (1974) contained seven original tunes, including "Same Old Song and Dance," and a cover of "The Train Kept a-Rollin'," which had been popularized in the 1950s by Johnny Burnette & the Rock-'n'-Roll Trio and in the 1960s by the Yardbirds; the album hovered on the American charts for over a year, achieving certified gold status in 1975, by selling 500,000 copies. Although largely ignored by the music press at the time, the album is now considered a classic. "Comparing *Get Your Wings* to [Aerosmith's] 1973 debut is like night and day," Greg Prato wrote for the *All Music Guide Web* site. "It sounds almost like a completely different band—the playing is more aggressive, the songwriting succinct, and singer Steven Tyler had almost fully perfected his instantly recognizable yowl." During the support tour for *Get Your Wings*, one of Tyler's trademark stage props emerged: bunches of brightly colored scarves wrapped around the singer's microphone stand. The scarves initially provided a shield against objects hurled at the stage by impatient fans waiting for the headlining act; later, according to

Huxley, they hid compartments in which the singer would hide his stashes of narcotics.

Aerosmith's next album, *Toys in the Attic* (1975), proved to be the band's breakthrough effort, achieving platinum status (sales of one million) by the end of the year on the strength of such hits as "Sweet Emotion," "Big Ten Inch Record," and "Walk This Way," each of which has gone platinum six times over, according to the Record Industry Association of America (RIAA). The last song, featuring some of Tyler's sassiest double entendres, ascended to the number-10 position on the U.S. charts in 1977; the album itself, which spent a year on the charts, has sold about eight million copies. Despite such numbers, *Toys in the Attic* did not gain favor among critics at the time of its release. In *Rolling Stone* (July 31, 1975, on-line), for example, Gordon Fletcher acknowledged that "Aerosmith can be very good when they're on" but complained that the album was poorly produced and was flawed by "instances of directionless meandering and downright weak material."

The success of *Toys in the Attic* proved difficult for Aerosmith to match or sustain, even as the band's hectic touring schedule saw them headlining arena concerts in much of the country. The group's extended road trips provided Tyler with little fresh material for songs, and the heavy use of drugs and alcohol by all of Aerosmith's members made completion of the band's next album, *Rocks* (1976), an arduous task. Nonetheless, *Rocks*— which featured the singles "Back in the Saddle," "Last Child," and "Home Tonight"—rose to number three on U.S. charts and quickly went platinum.

Although between 1976 and 1979, tickets to Aerosmith concerts sold out at some of the nation's largest venues, including Madison Square Garden, in New York City, the band's drug use, excessive spending, and hotel mayhem began to take an increasingly heavy toll. "I was a garbage head," Tyler told a reporter for *People* (February 22, 1988). "Heroin, coke, Valium, anything that anyone came near with. . . . I got so clouded up I didn't know what this band was all about, didn't realize how great it was and what a statement it made." Two major overseas tours, to Europe and the United Kingdom in 1976 and to Japan in 1977, failed to produce the popular or media attention needed to justify the enormous costs of both ventures. The group's next album, *Draw the Line* (1977), which cost more than a million dollars to make, sold mainly on the strength of Aerosmith's reputation; it disappointed fans and critics alike. In 1978 the group released the double album *Live! Bootleg*; performed at the California Jam II festival, which was commemorated by a live album; and covered the Beatles' "Come Together" for the soundtrack to Robert Stigwood's film adaptation of their *Sgt. Pepper's Lonely Hearts Club Band* album, in which Aerosmith appeared as the Future Villain Band.

In 1979 Perry, who had contributed some material earlier in the year to Aerosmith's *Night in the Ruts*, left the band to produce his own projects. "Our realities weren't right. We'd explode at each other," Tyler later explained to Robert K. Oermann for *Celebrity* (May 28, 1988). "It was all over nothing. Your reality gets bent out of shape and you forget what you're there for." "We'd get in the dressing room and tear it apart," Perry told Wild, recalling the enmity he and Tyler felt, "but we never laid a hand on each other. But there was so much anger. If we were in a different space, we'd have killed each other." Perry released three albums under the auspices of the Joe Perry Project; the first album sold satisfactorily, but the next two attracted little interest. After running out of money, Perry lost his living quarters; he slept for a while on his manager's couch and then in a Boston boardinghouse. He was so out of touch with his former colleagues that he was unaware of Aerosmith's 1980 greatest-hits collection until a fan who noticed him in a grocery store asked him to autograph the album cover. (One of the most popular collections ever made, it sold 10 million copies.)

Meanwhile, Tyler's dependency on drugs had not ended. He had tried to hold the band together, but more members had defected. (The band's new recruits included Jim Crespo, on guitar, and Rick Dufay, on bass.) A drug-related motorcycle accident in 1980 left Tyler hospitalized for six months—one of the lowest periods in his career, as he recalled to David Fricke for *Rolling Stone* (November 3, 1994): "I was in the hospital with a cast up to my hip, and I remember hearing about the new band Van Halen with David Lee Roth. 'Who does this . . . guy think he is? He's standing in my limelight!' . . . People said, 'You idiot, you don't even have a band.' . . . But you don't miss your water till your well runs dry." Although Aerosmith's *Night in the Ruts*, which revived the Shangri-Las' 1964 hit "Remember (Walkin' in the Sand)," climbed to the 14th position on the *Billboard* charts, the group's next new album, *Rock in a Hard Place* (1982), rose only to number 32. In 1984 Perry returned to the band, and, without releasing a new record, Aerosmith commenced a tour dubbed "Back in the Saddle." Although the musicians had resolved to curb their harmful habits, they lapsed almost immediately into their familiar debaucheries. At one concert, in Springfield, Illinois, Tyler collapsed onstage, and the show had to be halted; to placate the audience and minimize any further bad press for the band, Aerosmith's manager arranged to have a free copy of their greatest-hits album sent to every attendee. In 1985 Aerosmith released the often-overlooked *Done with Mirrors*, its first album on the Geffen label; despite its echoes of earlier Aerosmith efforts, it climbed no higher than number 36 on the charts and sold only 500,000 copies—a poor showing by Aerosmith's standards.

In 1986 the rap group Run-D.M.C. recorded a lively rendition of "Walk This Way" to which members of Aerosmith also contributed. The video for the song, which received heavy play on MTV, brought Aerosmith back into the public eye. Among the first collaborations of a rap group and a heavy-metal act, it also helped to launch the rap-metal musical genre, which became extremely popular. Around this time Tyler's bandmates confronted him about his drug addiction. Their intervention proved beneficial: Tyler and his colleagues had become drug-free and sober by the time they released their next album, *Permanent Vacation* (1987). That was the first album for which Aerosmith hired outside lyricists, to complement Tyler's songwriting skills, and it had a distinctly more pop-oriented sound, as exemplified by its three Top 20 singles: "Dude (Looks Like a Lady)," "Angel," and "Rag Doll." A tour of the United States, Asia, and Australia, in which the musicians abstained from drugs and alcohol, followed in 1988. The album sold over five million copies.

In 1989 Aerosmith released *Pump*, which emphasized the band's bluesy roots in a string of radio-friendly tunes. The album sold about seven million copies and generated several hits, among them "Love in an Elevator," "The Other Side," and a song suggesting social awareness, "Janie's Got a Gun," about a girl who kills her sexually abusive father. On the *All Music Guide* Web site, Stephen Thomas Erlewine ranked *Pump* with *Toys in the Attic* and *Rocks*: "Where *Permanent Vacation* seemed a little overwhelmed by its pop concessions," Erlewine wrote, "*Pump* revels in them without ever losing sight of Aerosmith's dirty hard-rock core." With their "Janie's Got a Gun" video, Aerosmith won two MTV Video Music Awards, the Viewers' Choice Award and one for best metal/hard-rock video.

On the strength of *Permanent Vacation* and *Pump*, Aerosmith signed a highly publicized, six-album recording contract with Sony's Columbia Records worth about $50 million, one of the most lucrative contracts in music history up to that time. The deal surprised some observers because, as specified on their previous contract, the band owed Geffen two more albums and a greatest-hits compilation. With the Geffen-released *Get a Grip* (1993), Aerosmith continued to straddle the line between hard-rock and pop. *Get a Grip*, which contains the hits "Eat the Rich," "Livin' on the Edge," "Cryin'," and "Crazy," was the band's first album to reach number one; it sold seven million copies in the U.S. and an additional five million abroad.

Aerosmith released compilation albums in 1991 and 1994: *Pandora's Box* (on the Sony label) and *Big Ones* (Geffen), respectively. That evidence of member collaboration hid growing disagreements over musical direction. Working with the jazz-oriented producer Glen Ballard, the band produced an album of songs that redefined its sound and, according to Tyler, featured some of his best vocal performances. But when an early mix of the planned album, *Nine Lives*, was sent to Sony, it got a thumbs-down response. While Tyler was happy with the new material, the other members of Aerosmith agreed that the band should remain more faithful to its hard-rock origins. During the recording of the disk, a severe depression that had started earlier forced Kramer to stop working; Tyler and Perry opted to replace him with a new drummer. Meanwhile, a quarrel had erupted between Tyler and Aerosmith's longtime manager, Tim Collins, who publicly accused Tyler of resuming his drug use. Tyler heatedly denied the charge, but the other members of the band, not knowing whether to believe him, failed to rally to his side. In June 1996, finding themselves at a musical and personal impasse, the five members of Aerosmith agreed to work with a mediator at the California treatment center that had recently ministered to Kramer. After extensive counseling sessions the group fired Collins and re-recorded their album with the producer Kevin Shirley. *Nine Lives* was the first Aerosmith effort since the 1970s for which, for the most part, the musicians had played together in the same room; it glittered with the pop sheen that had characterized most of the group's albums since *Permanent Vacation*. Upon its release *Nine Lives* soared to the top of the *Billboard* 200 album chart, where it stayed for a week; the song "Falling in Love (Is Hard on the Knees)" made it to the Top 10.

In 1998 Aerosmith released the live album *A Little South of Sanity*, thus fulfilling its contractual obligations to Geffen. Preceded by the Top-10 song "Jaded," the band's next studio album, *Just Push Play*, was certified platinum within a month of its release, in 2001. Featuring funky guitar riffs, soaring choruses, and a sprinkling of sentimental ballads, the recording struck some critics as a return to form. "It's a sleek, classicist hard rock record that sounds good—better than Aerosmith has sounded in nearly a decade, as a matter of fact," Stephen Thomas Erlewine wrote for the *All Music Guide Web* site. In *Rolling Stone* (on-line), David Fricke wrote, "By now, after thirty years of big rock, hard drugs, wasted fortunes and seesaw chart rides, singer Steven Tyler, guitarists Joe Perry and Brad Whitford, bassist Tom Hamilton and drummer Joey Kramer should either be dead or babbling incoherently. Instead, Aerosmith are our most treasured and reliable warrior clowns. . . . They don't carry on with the dignity of old blues buddhas—Aerosmith just plain carry on." Aerosmith's most recent album, *Honkin' on Bobo*, released in March 2004, revisits the band's blues influences. Stephen Thomas Erlewine declared on the *All Music Guide Web* site, "It's been a long, long time since [Aerosmith has] sounded as good as they do here."

Aerosmith has won four Grammy Awards, each of them in the category "best rock performance by a duo or a group," for the songs "Janie's Got a Gun" (1990), "Livin' on the Edge" (1993), "Crazy" (1994), and "Pink" (1998). The group was voted best heavy-metal band of 1989 by the editors of

Rolling Stone, and in 1990 it was inducted into Hollywood's Rock Walk, on Sunset Boulevard. In the following year the group won two top honors at the American Music Awards and was named best band in the annual *Rolling Stone* Readers' Picks music awards. In 1994 the group won two American Music Awards, as favorite pop/rock band/duo/group and favorite heavy metal/hard rock artist, and a Right to Rock Award at Boston's Pepsi music awards, in recognition of their activities in support of the First Amendment. In December 1994 the band established the Boston nightclub Mama Kin, which bears the name of a song from their first album. In 1999 Aerosmith won an Artist Achievement Award at the *Billboard* Music Awards ceremony and an American Music Award for favorite pop/rock band. The group was inducted into the Rock & Roll Hall of Fame in March 2001. Tyler was awarded an honorary doctorate from Berklee College of Music, in Boston, in 2003. Aerosmith's music videos have earned numerous awards from MTV.

Steven Tyler lives in a home/studio in the Boston suburbs with his second wife, Teresa Barrick, and their two children, Chelsea and Taj. Tyler also has two daughters from previous relationships: Mia, the daughter of his first wife, Cyrinda Foxe-Tyler, and the actress Liv Tyler, the daughter of former model Bebe Buell. (Liv Tyler played a frolicking nymphet in her father's 1994 music video "Crazy.") Joe Perry and his wife, Billie Paulette Montgomery Perry, are the parents of Tony (born in 1986) and Roman (born in 1991). Perry's son Adrian, from a previous relationship, was born in 1981. Tom Hamilton and his wife, the former Terry Cohen, have two children, Julian Forrest and Dorothy Sage. Joey Kramer is married to April and has a son, Jesse Sky, and stepdaughter, Asia. Brad Whitford, who is divorced from Lori Phillips, is married to Karen Lesser, with whom he has three sons: Zachary, Graham, and Harrison. The members of Aerosmith are reportedly good friends. Joe Perry and Tyler, who live near each other, like to hang glide, water ski, shoot machine guns, and ride their motorcycles together. Tyler told David Fricke in 1994, "I'm looking to be the lounge act on the space shuttle so I can sing 'Walk This Way' on the ceiling. That's the kind of guy I am. My get-up-and-go has not gone up and went. . . . I don't buy into the idea that you're not supposed to rock-'n'-roll after a certain date."

—P.G.H.

Suggested Reading: *All Music Guide* (on-line); *Chicago Tribune* XIII p4 July 15, 1990, with photos; *Entertainment Weekly* p22+ Mar. 21, 1997, with photos; (New York) *Daily News* p29 Sep. 6. 1993, with photo; *New York Times* II p22 May 30, 1993; *Rolling Stone* p40+ Aug. 26, 1976, with photos, p46+ Apr. 5, 1990, with photo, p56+ Nov. 3, 1994; *Washington Post* F p1 May 30, 1976, with photos; DeCurtis, Anthony and James Henke, eds. *The Rolling Stone Album*

Guide, 1992; Huxley, Martin. *Aerosmith: The Fall and Rise of Rock's Greatest Band*, 1995; Rees, Dafydd and Luke Crampton, eds. *Rock Movers & Shakers*, 1991

Selected Recordings: *Aerosmith*, 1973; *Get Your Wings*, 1974; *Toys in the Attic*, 1975; *Rocks*, 1976; *Draw the Line*, 1977; *Live! Bootleg*, 1978; *Night in the Ruts*, 1979; *Aerosmith's Greatest Hits*, 1980; *Rock in a Hard Place*, 1982; *Done with Mirrors*, 1985; *Classics Live!*, 1986; *Classics Live! II*, 1987; *Permanent Vacation*, 1987; *Gems*, 1988; *Pump*, 1989; *Pandora's Box*, 1991; *Get a Grip*, 1993; *Big Ones*, 1994; *Box of Fire*, 1994; *Nine Lives*, 1997; *A Little South of Sanity*, 1998; *Just Push Play*, 2001; *Young Lust: The Aerosmith Anthology*, 2001; *O, Yeah! Ultimate Aerosmith Hits*, 2002; *Honkin' on Bobo*, 2004

Evan Agostini/Getty Images

Akers, Michelle

Feb. 1, 1966– Soccer player; writer

Address: c/o Soccer Outreach International, 10404 Oakview Pointe Terr., Gotha, FL 34734

After she graduated from college, Michelle Akers had a difficult time finding people with whom she could train in her chosen sport, soccer; she often ended up practicing with college- or high-school-age males. "The first couple of days were always a 'prove it' kind of competition between us—their challenging me to prove that I could play with them," she recalled in *Face to Face with Michelle Akers* (1996), written with Judith A.

Nelson. "Only after I beat them a few times or hung tough when they hammered me would they *just play*. It was a cool feeling each week to change kids' minds about the ability of a girl to play." Akers has changed many minds on that score, and in 2004 two prestigious honors served as testaments to her ability to play—and to the drive and determination she displayed in her 15-year career with the U.S. national women's soccer team, which ended in 2000. She and her former teammate Mia Hamm were the only two women, as well as the only two Americans, named to the Fédération Internationale de Football Association's (FIFA's) list of the 125 greatest living soccer players; and Akers was one of three inductees in the National Soccer Hall of Fame, receiving the greatest number of votes for the year. "Michelle is the first player that created universal acceptance of the women's game," Tony DiCicco, Akers's coach on the national team, told Jere Longman for the *New York Times* (May 18, 1999), two years before Akers's retirement. "People like [the male soccer stars] Pele and Franz Beckenbauer, they saw her play and realized that women could play the game as skillfully and tactically proficient as men could. . . . Her shot is incredibly hard with long-range accuracy. She can put a player onto the ball with 40-yard passes, right- and left-footed, and score a goal from 25 or 30 yards." Akers's soccer triumphs include two World Cup championships, an Olympic gold medal, and the FIFA Order of Merit, and she retired in 2001 as one of only four female players to score more than 100 goals in international competition. What makes Akers's achievements all the more remarkable is that, midway through her career, she was diagnosed with chronic fatigue syndrome. She has since become an active spokesperson for those suffering from the disorder.

Michelle Anne Akers was born on February 1, 1966 in Santa Clara, California. Her father, Bob Akers, was a meat cutter; her mother, Anne, stayed at home to raise Michelle and her younger brother, Michael. (After the couple's divorce, Bob Akers became a psychologist, while Anne joined the Seattle Fire Department as the city's first female firefighter.) The family moved to Seattle, Washington, when Akers was in fourth grade. The first sport she loved was football; she wore the jersey of the Pittsburgh Steelers great "Mean" Joe Greene and dreamed of scoring the winning touchdown in the Super Bowl. Her mother signed her up for a soccer team when she was eight; because her team lost quite a few matches, and she hated their pink and yellow uniforms, which she thought too girlish, the intensely competitive Michelle disliked the experience at first. By the end of the season, however, she had fallen in love with the game, and her dream was now to become either a professional soccer player in Europe or a paramedic.

Akers's turbulent adolescence threatened to derail such dreams. She was deeply affected by her parents' divorce, which occurred when she was 10. She was nearly expelled from high school for skipping classes and earning poor grades, and she also experimented with drugs. While she was popular among her peers and excelled in sports, lettering in soccer, basketball, and softball every year, her relationship with her family was tense and difficult. The one person with whom she could talk about her emotions was Al Kovats, who coached girls' basketball and boys' soccer at her high school and was instrumental in her religious development. In *Face to Face*, she recalled that once, after Kovats drove her home from basketball practice, she shared her feelings of pain and confusion with him, and the two prayed together. "From that moment forward, I was a different person," she wrote. "Nothing anyone would notice at first, but in time, that moment became a turning point in who I was and how I lived my life." She began attending church with Kovats and his family and studied the Bible.

After graduating in 1984 from Shorecrest High School, in Seattle, as a three-time All-American, Akers was sought by soccer programs at many universities. She attended the University of Central Florida on a scholarship and earned a degree in liberal studies and health in 1989. While there she was named ESPN Athlete of the Year in 1985; won the first women's Hermann Trophy, awarded to the top college soccer player in the nation, in 1988; was named the school's athlete of the year for 1988–89; and was a four-time All-American, twice leading the Golden Knights to the Final Four. Her college years were not free of difficulty, however. After breaking up with her first serious boyfriend, she sought to escape her anguish by partying almost every night; she began showing up at practice drunk and letting her grades slip to D's and F's, nearly losing her scholarship at the end of her junior year. Realizing that she had to shape up, she took summer classes to raise her grades, stopped drinking, and rededicated herself to soccer. She remains the school's record holder for career goals and assists, and her jersey number, 10, was retired in 1992. The school gave her a Distinguished Alumna Award in 1994.

Akers joined the U.S. women's national soccer team upon its founding, in 1985, scoring its first official goal on a trip to Italy that summer. "We didn't look like a national team," she told Kelly Whiteside for *Sports Illustrated* (June 5, 1995). "All we had were these lime-green and purple uniforms. No one was fit. It just felt like we were off to Italy on a vacation. We were just a bunch of kids, we didn't know what we were getting into." The team lost three of its four games during that trip and tied the other. At the time, instead of getting salaries, team members received $10 a day for meals and were housed in college dormitories. The U.S. players participated in one tournament per year and were routinely overwhelmed by the opposition. But the program slowly improved. Akers scored 15 goals in 24 games for the U.S. from 1985 to 1990; then, in 1991, she seemed to get better overnight, scoring 39 goals in 26 games. She was the U.S. Soccer Federation's female athlete of the year in 1990 and 1991. The national team came into its own in the latter year, winning the inaugural Women's World Cup event; Akers scored both U.S. goals in the final. The first came 20 minutes into the game, when she put in a goal off a header. Later, with the score tied 1–1 and two minutes left, she took control of a 50-50 ball (a loose ball than can be claimed by either team) outside the Norway penalty area and kicked in a shot from the end line that gave the Americans the win. She was the leading scorer in the tournament with 10 goals, including five in one game, and won the Golden Boot Award, as well as the Silver Ball award, given to the tournament's second-best player.

Despite having won U.S. soccer's first-ever world championship, for men or women, the team received little attention when they returned to the States. In *Face to Face*, Akers recalled that on the plane ride home she sat next to an elderly American woman who asked where she had been. "I told her I was representing my country at the first women's World Cup of soccer. 'How'd you do?' she asked. 'We won,' I replied proudly. 'That's nice,' she said. That was about the response we received from all of America. . . . This lack of recognition really stung." While the event had been covered in the press extensively overseas, there was not much mention of it in the U.S., and only a handful of people were waiting for the world champions when they arrived in New York. The financial rewards were meager as well. "It was really tough for us to train for the national team and eat, basically," Akers told Julie Phillips for the *Village Voice* (May 9, 1995). Each team member received a $1,200 bonus for the win, which, Akers said, did not even cover the airfare her family spent to see her play in China. Because of her experiences, she supports a federal Equal Pay Initiative, and at one point she and her teammates boycotted training to protest the disparities between their pay and those of the men's national team.

The years following the World Cup victory were busy ones for Akers. She became the first American female soccer player to have a paid product endorsement (for Umbro, a brand of athletic shoe). Speaking engagements, promotional appearances for Umbro, and invitations to assist at soccer camps enabled her to travel around the world. She competed for the Tyreso Football Club, in Sweden, in 1990 and 1992 and was the leading scorer among both men and women in that country in the latter year, with 43 goals. In addition, she played with the Orlando Calibre soccer club of Orlando, Florida, in 1993, when the team placed second in the U.S. Women's Amateur National Cup Finals.

That period of intense activity and success was interrupted in 1993, when Akers collapsed during a match in San Antonio, Texas. After several other diagnoses, she was told that she had chronic fatigue and immune dysfunction syndrome (CFIDS), also known as chronic fatigue syndrome. She had been fighting fatigue and illness since the World

Cup competition but had attributed her condition to her hectic schedule. The symptoms grew worse, however, and included migraine headaches, low blood pressure, memory loss, dizziness, and bouts of vomiting, and she was often so tired that she was unable to get out of bed. Adding to her troubles, her marriage of four years ended in 1994. (She and her ex-husband, Roby Stahl, a former professional soccer player, remain on good terms.)

For Akers one of the most difficult aspects of dealing with her illness was admitting that she could not do as much as she wanted. She had trained more rigorously than anyone else on the team, but now she worked out less than her teammates, often missed practices, and could play only 15 to 20 minutes of a 90-minute game. Some doctors told her that she would have to retire, and she wondered if she was hurting the team. With the encouragement of a friend, she began to attend church regularly, reaffirming and drawing strength from her religious faith.

Akers bounced back somewhat in 1994. While her playing time decreased considerably, the level of her performance did not. Originally a forward, she switched to the defensive midfield position to avoid some of the hard knocks that come with the forward spot, thus changing her role on the team from goalmaker to playmaker. She was named most valuable player (MVP) of the Confederation of North, Central American and Caribbean Association Football (CONCACAF) Qualifying Championship in Montreal, tying with her American teammate Mia Hamm as the second-leading scorer of the tournament, with six goals in four games. She also played again for Sweden's Tyreso Football Club. The Women's World Cup competition in 1995 did not turn out as she had hoped: she suffered a concussion and a knee injury six minutes into the opening game against China, and did not play again until the team's semifinal loss to Norway. Placing third in the tournament was disappointing for Akers. She was able, however, to come to terms with that outcome and with her illness. "As a Christian, you know that things don't happen without a purpose . . . ," she told Don Sider for *People* (November 10, 1997). "I think the challenge is to take these difficult and painful times and turn them into something beneficial, something that makes you grow." Shortly after returning to the U.S., she played in the 1995 U.S. Women's Cup tournament and was named to the all-tournament team. At the same competition the following year, she was named the team's most valuable player, scoring the winning goal in a 1–0 victory over China.

Meanwhile, Akers had tried various diets and health regimens to combat her energy-sapping disease, with moderate success. Shortly before the 1996 Olympic Games, in Atlanta, Georgia, in which women's soccer would make its debut, she decided to try the "elimination diet," which avoids gluten, dairy products, alcohol, caffeine, sugar, and beef and calls for drinking the juice of two pounds of carrots per day and taking a supplement to aid digestion. "It's a terrible diet. . . . It was disgusting, but I didn't care," she told Don Sider. "I said, 'I'm doing whatever it takes.'" The method paid off: while she was not completely cured, her energy level became higher than at any time since 1991. Akers also worked with the national team's doctor to find other ways of increasing her stamina during games and helping her to recover afterward. At halftime she drank coffee and ate cereal, granola bars, and fruit to boost her energy. After each game she received, via an IV needle, two to three liters of saline to replace depleted electrolytes. Although these changes helped, she still tired easily and felt exhausted after games. "The feeling is like running up a hill against a stiff wind with a 100-pound pack on my back," she told Tom Timmermann for the St. Louis *Post-Dispatch*, in a story posted on America On-Line's Total Sports Web page (July 8, 1999).

Nonetheless, Akers helped the U.S. team to win the gold medal at the 1996 Olympics. She started in all five of the team's matches, playing the full 90 minutes in four of them. She scored a crucial tying goal on a penalty kick in the team's semifinal game with Norway, sending the game into overtime; the U.S. won with a score of 2–1. Just as the popularity of women's soccer was increasing dramatically, Akers took most of 1997 off and maintained a light schedule in 1998 as well, starting 15 matches with the national team and making five goals and three assists. She helped the U.S. earn its first-ever Goodwill Games gold medal that summer, scoring in the semifinal victory over Denmark. On June 7, 1998 she won FIFA's highest honor, the Order of Merit, becoming the only woman and the only American to receive the prestigious award.

Because of the growing popularity of women's soccer in America, the World Cup was held in the U.S. in 1999. With more than one billion viewers worldwide, the competition was the most-watched women's sporting event in history. Akers struggled in the team's first game, against Denmark, but was able to play every minute of the quarterfinal match against Germany and the semifinal game against Brazil. She was instrumental in the 2–0 U.S. victory over Brazil, shutting down the opposition's star midfielder, Sissi, clearing a threatening shot in the first half, and scoring on a penalty kick. "No one could be disappointed by the way Michelle Akers has played in this tournament . . . ," Jere Longman wrote before the final match. "Akers, the first great star of this team . . . can still control a game in defensive midfield the way she once did at forward. At 33, she is the oldest player on the team, and perhaps the most indispensable." In the final, against China, Akers played for 90 minutes in 97-degree weather; after receiving a blow to the head, she had to leave the game, before the 30-minute overtime period that brought her team victory. Before her departure she played a crucial defensive role, closing off several possible scoring opportunities for China. She won FIFA's Bronze Ball Award for her performance in the championship, and in

December she was named "Women's Player of the Century" by a special FIFA commission. She was also named female player of the year by the U.S. Soccer Federation for the third time, and was CONCACAF's Century Player of the Year. Perhaps the most satisfying result of the 1999 World Cup triumph, for Akers, was its effect on the public consciousness. As she stated in *Face to Face*, "I was excited to change the *world's* mind about women's soccer."

Although she made the Olympic team in 2000, Akers retired from international competition before the Games began, citing fatigue and an ailing shoulder, which had required surgery in March and had been hurt again in the summer. The decision "was gut-wrenching," she said, according to Bill Buchalter in the *Orlando Sentinel* (August 25, 2000). "I wrestled with it all year. . . . I have cried every day, but it is a great sense of relief that this is over for now, that I can try putting my body together. . . . I am emotionally exhausted." (The women's team earned a silver medal at the Olympics, losing to Norway 2–3 in overtime.) The National Soccer Coaches Association of America (NSCAA) presented Akers with an Award of Excellence, and in December 2000 she was recognized as the "Best Female Soccer Player Ever" by the magazine *Futbol de Primera* at a ceremony in Los Angeles.

Akers played a season with the new Women's United Soccer Association (WUSA) professional league before retiring from the sport altogether, in October 2001. She ended her career as one of only four female players to reach at least 100 goals in international competition, with 105 goals in 153 international matches, and as the all-time leading scorer in World Cup competitions and the all-time leading scorer for both U.S. men's and U.S. women's national team programs, with 92 goals. The Women's Sports Foundation presented her with the Wilma Rudolph Courage Award in 2001 for her contributions to women's sports. That year she became an emergency medical technician and enrolled in a program to become a physician's assistant. Akers was already familiar with emergency rooms and hospitals in general, having endured about 20 knee operations, numerous stitches, strains, and bruises, and several lost teeth and broken bones in the course of her 16-year career.

Akers is the founder of Soccer Outreach International, an organization that helps people, churches, and agencies around the world integrate faith and sport into their daily lives. In addition to *Face to Face*, Akers has co-written two other books: *Standing Fast: Battles of a Champion* (with Tim Nash, 1997) and *The Game and the Glory* (with Gregg Lewis, 2000), both of which chronicle her battle with CFIDS, the importance of her religious faith, and how she overcame incredible obstacles to win Olympic gold. She has also written for the magazines *Sidekicks* and *Soccer Jr.* and the ESPN and WUSA Web sites. In addition, she has been active in raising awareness of CFIDS. To that end she delivered to Congress, for International CFIDS Awareness Day in May 1996, a statement about the disease's toll. Akers has provided TV analysis of soccer matches for ESPN2 and for the WUSA team the Atlanta Beat, and she has done motivational speaking for corporations, sports organizations, churches, and religious ministries. Akers is a member of the FIFA Soccer Committee and the NSCAA Women's Subcommittee.

During her playing career Akers encountered mixed opinions about the place of women in a traditionally male sport—and about her own drive and competitive spirit. "All the time I come across people—I call them 'normal women'—who are surprised by my intensity. . . . The men are a little surprised by it [too], but you're also proving that you can go out on the field with them . . . ," she told Phillips in 1995. "Some of the women feel uncomfortable around you." Since then, Akers has been widely credited with helping to change such attitudes and with popularizing women's soccer in the U.S.

The United States Olympic Committee named Akers Female Soccer Player of the Year (1990) and Athlete of the Year (1991) and presented her with the Jack Kelly Fair Play Award (1999). She received the Simon Sherman Leadership Award (1999) and the Henry Iba Citizen Athlete Award

(2000) for her humanitarian work. At five feet 10 inches, Akers was usually the tallest player on the field. Her teammates nicknamed the 150-pound soccer pioneer Mufasa, after a character in the Disney movie *The Lion King*, saying that her long, curly, golden brown hair resembled a lion's mane. Akers lives on a horse farm in Georgia. In addition to horseback riding, she enjoys hiking, water skiing, snow skiing, scuba diving, fishing, and watching movies and is an active churchgoer.

—K.E.D.

Suggested Reading: *America Online Total Sports* (on-line) July 8, 1999: ESPN Web site; *New York Times* D p2 May 18, 1999, with photo; *New York Times* (on-line) July 10, 1999, with photo; *Orlando Sentinel* C p1 Aug. 25, 2000, with photos; *People* p131+ Nov. 10, 1997, with photos; *Sports Illustrated* p73+ June 5, 1995, with photos; *Village Voice* p126 May 9, 1995, with photo

Selected Books: *Face to Face with Michelle Akers* (with Judith A. Nelson), 1996; *Standing Fast: Battles of a Champion* (with Tim Nash), 1997; *The Game and the Glory* (with Gregg Lewis), 2000

Applebaum, Anne

July 25, 1964– Journalist; writer

Address: Washington Post, 1150 15th St., N.W., Washington, DC 20001

Anne Applebaum won a Pulitzer Prize in 2004 for her book *Gulag: A History* (2003), a chronicle, unprecedented for a Western writer, of the vast system of forced-labor prison camps operated by the Soviet Union for most of the 20th century. From 1918 to 1989, tens of millions of Russians, mostly peasants and common workers but also political dissidents, intellectuals, and criminals, endured forced labor and inhumane conditions in the camps known collectively as the Gulag, many of them located in the coldest, most remote regions of the Soviet Union. In putting together her more than 600-page history, Applebaum used newly released Soviet archives, conducted numerous interviews with former guards and prisoners, traveled Russia, and studied the available literature by survivors and scholars. In addition to receiving the Pulitzer Prize, Applebaum's book has won widespread praise. In *Newsweek* (April 28, 2003), Andrew Nagorski called *Gulag* the "most authoritative—and comprehensive—account of this Soviet blight ever published by a Western writer." David Frum, writing for the *National Review* (May 5, 2003), described the book as a "titanic achievement: learned

Courtesy of Anne Applebaum

and moving and profound. . . . No reader will easily forget Applebaum's vivid accounts of the horrible human suffering of the Gulag." The *Economist* (April 5, 2003) opined that Applebaum's *Gulag* "should become the standard history of one of the greatest evils of the 20th century." In an article for *Capitalist Magazine* (November 7, 2003, on-line), Applebaum revealed that she wrote *Gulag* not to help ensure that such tragic, large-scale debasement of human beings would not happen again, "but because it probably will happen again. We need to know why—and each story, each memoir, each document is a piece of the puzzle." In the end, she wrote, "the more we know of the specific circumstances which led to each [historical] episode of mass murder, the better we will understand the darker side of our own human nature."

Applebaum's first book, *Between East and West: Across the Borderlands of Europe*, published in 1995, explored the tumultuous history of the region where eastern Europe meets western Russia and of the shifting nationalities of the peoples in the area. Applebaum, a conservative journalist who often writes about politics, returned to the U.S. in 2002 after 16 years in Europe, where she had served as an editor for the British magazines the *Economist* and the *Spectator*, among other publications. Applebaum has been a guest on many radio and television programs, both in Britain and the United States, including the BBC's *Newsnight* and programs on MSNBC, CNN, Sky News, and CBS. She is currently a columnist and member of the editorial board of the *Washington Post*.

The oldest of three daughters, Anne Applebaum was born to Harvey and Elizabeth Applebaum in Washington, D.C., on July 25, 1964. The family was upper middle class, liberal, and Jewish. Applebaum's father was a longtime partner in the Washington law firm Covington & Burling; her mother was a program coordinator at the Corcoran Gallery of Art. William F. Powers, writing for the *Washington Post* (December 13, 1994), described the Applebaums as having been "the kind of family that travels often, reads a lot, discusses ideas over dinner." Anne Applebaum attended Sidwell Friends School, in Washington, where she excelled academically. Discussing what she recalls as the somewhat sheltered, liberal atmosphere of Sidwell, Applebaum told Powers that despite its being a "great school," she found that to gain exposure to other ideas one had to "go across the river to Anacostia [a poorer section of the nation's capital], and that's very different and that changes your politics, or you go abroad." After graduating from Sidwell, which she attended from grade school through high school, Applebaum enrolled at Yale University, in New Haven, Connecticut, one of the most prestigious schools in the U.S., where she continued to perform well in her studies. She served as managing editor of the school's *New Journal*, which features articles on Yale and New Haven, and graduated summa cum laude with a double major in literature and history.

Applebaum applied for a Rhodes Scholarship but, as she has recalled, undermined her chances during the interview portion of the application process; Powers's explanation was that while success as a Rhodes scholar called for "subtle toady-ing," Applebaum is known as "a born provocateur." Instead she received a Marshall Scholarship, which allowed her to study for a year at the London School of Economics, in England. Following her time there she attended St. Anthony's College, at Oxford University. While at Oxford Applebaum began writing freelance articles for publications such as the *Economist*, which offered her a position as a freelance correspondent in Poland in 1988. Poland was then receiving international attention due to the political struggle between the dissident Solidarity movement and the entrenched Communist government. Applebaum began studying the Polish language and developing sources among the anti-Communist Polish dissident groups. Observers note that Applebaum's political views, which had been liberal during her college years, took a turn toward conservatism with her experiences in Poland. The reason stemmed in part from the fact that many of the Polish dissident groups about whom Applebaum wrote, and by whom she was influenced, idolized such staunchly conservative anti-Communist leaders as Ronald Reagan and Margaret Thatcher. Another factor cited in explaining her ideological shift is Applebaum's 1992 marriage to Radek Sikorski, a member of a minor aristocratic Polish family who, at 29 years of age, had served as a deputy defense minister of Poland in the early 1990s. Sikorski has written political commentary for many conservative newspapers and magazines in Europe and the U.S., and has hosted his own television show in Poland, on which he interviewed such heads of state and other potentates as Thatcher and Henry Kissinger.

In 1992 Applebaum returned to England, where she served briefly as an editor in the *Economist*'s London office before landing a job as foreign editor of the more than 150-year-old conservative British magazine the *Spectator*. Through that posting, and later as deputy editor of the *Spectator*, Applebaum worked her way into the inner circles of the British media. Recalling why the *Spectator*'s editorial style appealed to her sensibilities, Applebaum told Powers that the magazine allowed contributors "to write about serious things in a funny way. You know, high irony is permissible." At the time Applebaum described herself to Powers, who called her a "rising star of British journalism," as a "British writer. I write in the British style. My ideas are part of the British political debate . . . but I'm completely American." Applebaum later wrote a weekly column on British politics and foreign affairs that appeared at different times in the British newspapers the *Daily Telegraph,* the *Sunday Telegraph*, and the *Evening Standard*. As the political editor for the last-named newspaper, Applebaum covered the 1997 British general-election campaign, which resulted in a victory for the Labour Party leader Tony Blair, who became the youngest British prime minister in more than 150 years. For several years in the late 1990s, Applebaum wrote the "Foreigners" column for the American on-line publication *Slate*.

Applebaum told Powers that her goal in writing her first book, *Between East and West: Across the Borderlands of Europe* (1995), was to "get under the skin of this question of nationalism." In her attempt to do so, she traveled to different areas of Europe's eastern borders and to the western reaches of the former Soviet Union—Poland, Ukraine, Lithuania, and Belarus, among other countries—in 1991, just as the Soviet Union was about to break apart. With the waves of conquest that have rolled over those flat borderlands throughout the ages, the place names and rulers of the region have changed many times in the last 1,000 years. The result is that a traveler in that part of the world "can encounter a native Pole, a person raised in the Soviet Union, a citizen of the new Belarus—and they in fact may all be one man, an individual who has never set foot outside his father's village," as Marie Arana-Ward wrote for the *Washington Post* (November 20, 1994). In order to write the book, Applebaum roamed the region "intrepidly, suffering the hardscrabble existence of a traveler in these parts, looking up improbable witnesses, hitchhiking with drink-sodden peasants, arguing history with strangers on the street . . . ," Arana-Ward wrote. "Applebaum reveals an intelligence and sensibility that are rare in this brand of quick-sweep expeditionary journalism." Tina Rosenberg, in *New York Newsday* (November 27, 1994), found that the "rogue's gallery" of characters that Applebaum presented in the book—for example, an obese woman in Belarus who lives in a garbage-filled apartment and praises Adolf Hitler—makes Applebaum's introduction, in which she seems to defend the spirit of nationalism, "puzzling." Such characters, "aggressively nationalist, dedicated to proving that their own ethnic group was the most accomplished, suffered more and got here first," are emblematic of "the book's major flaw," in Rosenberg's view, as they "illustrate, over and over, the dead weight of the past but add few new insights." In his review of *Between East and West,* Robert D. Kaplan wrote for the *New York Times Book Review* (December 18, 1994) that although it "contains many poignant descriptions, the overall impression is of a region where rusted pipes are more conspicuous than ornate churches, and where rank prejudice is more obvious than compassion." He found "dull stretches of writing, and vignettes that don't add up to much. But these are faults attributable to Ms. Applebaum's apparent determination to show the reader exactly what it's like to travel in such places." Kaplan wrote that Applebaum's "inherent prediction—though never actually stated—is that the erasure of the past wrought by Communism will burden these already ambiguous new nations far into the future, bedeviling the search for political maturity among their inhabitants. . . . The Soviet Union may be officially dead, but *Between East and West* convincingly establishes the fact that it will go on dying." Despite such mixed reviews, *Between East and West* won an Adolph Bentinck Prize for European nonfiction in 1996.

For her next book project, Applebaum again entered the formidable world of Soviet and Russian history—specifically, the dark story of the prison-camp system known as the Gulag. ("Gulag" is an acronym of a Russian phrase meaning "main camp administration," as Applebaum explained to Ray Suarez for *NewsHour* [August 12, 2003, on-line].) The Soviet leader Vladimir Lenin arranged for the building of the first Gulag camps in the Soviet Union in 1918, the year after the Bolshevik revolution that ended the reign of the Russian czar. In the beginning, imprisonment in the camps was used chiefly as a way to suppress political dissidents, those suspected of disloyalty to the Soviet leadership, and members of Russian society who were deemed to be in need of Communist reeducation. The Gulag system grew until it became what Applebaum, in her article for *Capitalist Magazine*, called a "mass phenomenon," whose peak years were from 1929 to 1953, during the reign of the Soviet dictator Joseph Stalin. Applebaum and other scholars estimate that during that time some 18 million people entered the camps—where several million of them died—while another six or seven million, belonging to ethnic groups persecuted by the Soviets, were deported to barren regions of the Soviet empire. That means that the total number of people who experienced some form of imprisonment in the Soviet Union under Stalin may have been as high as 25 million, or about 15 percent of the total population. At thousands of camps spread over thousands of square miles, often in harsh climates, Stalin created a slave-labor economy, as staggeringly inefficient as it was cruel. Enduring brutally cold weather and ill treatment at the hands of overseers and fellow captives, the prisoners built railroads, power plants, weapons, furniture, factories, and even toys; they also dug coal, cut timber, and mined minerals using rudimentary tools, while subsisting on meager food rations and living in sparsely furnished barracks. One of the most notorious camps was located in Vorkuta, in the Arctic Circle, where temperatures regularly drop to −40 degrees Fahrenheit, the sun does not shine for six months of the year, and swarms of mosquitoes and flies form huge dark clouds in the air in summer. Over time the Gulag effectively became a country within a country, one with its own laws and folklore. Stalin's successor Nikita Khrushchev began to dismantle the Gulag system in the 1950s, but it continued in some form into the 1980s, when the reformist Soviet leader Mikhail Gorbachev brought it to an end.

For many years the history of the Gulag remained little-known in the West, and even today less is known about it than about other chapters of 20th-century barbarism such as the Holocaust, perpetrated by the Nazis under Adolf Hitler. The Gulag system was first, and most famously, detailed by the Russian writer Alexandr Solzhenitsyn, who himself had endured life the camps, in his seminal, multivolume work *The Gulag Archipelago*, published in the West in the early 1970s.

In researching her book, Applebaum used declassified Soviet archives, made available after the dissolution of the Soviet Union in 1991; the work of Russian historians; anecdotal material gathered from interviews she conducted over the course of several years; and autobiographical writings of Gulag survivors. Archives from individual camps, which included inspectors' reports, financial records, and letters from camp directors to government supervisors in Moscow, gave Applebaum a view of the Gulag's day-to-day administration. As a result, her work is the first by a Western scholar to combine the extensive documentary evidence now available and the personal stories of those who experienced the Gulag first-hand. "Anyone who wants to know about the darkest side of the Soviet Empire, and anyone who wishes to pursue other inquiries into the subject, will have to start [with Applebaum's book]," Michael Ledeen wrote for the *National Review* (May 6, 2003, on-line). Ledeen found that Applebaum had not used "colorful language" to convey the horrors of that episode of human history, but, instead, "with an almost bloodless detachment," had compiled a wealth of evidence, totaling nearly 700 pages, whose power needs no embellishment. "The result of all those pages and all that evidence is quite overwhelming, dizzying in fact," Ledeen wrote. "One is forced back into the dark hole of the past century, once again trying to cope with the amazing dimensions of totalitarianism." In the *Daily Telegraph* (May 10, 2003), Simon Sebag Montefiore called Applebaum's history a "magisterial work, written in an unflinching style that moves as much as it shocks, and that glistens with the teeming life and stinking putrefaction of doomed men and rotten ideals."

Some reviewers, however, found shortcomings in *Gulag: A History*. For example, Lars T. Lih for the *Washington Post* (April 13, 2003), while praising the book overall, concluded that Applebaum had not addressed sufficiently the "complicated questions surrounding the causes of the Gulag and its impact on Soviet society." Those very issues, including the question of why the history of the Gulag is "so seldom debated and discussed by Russians," as Applebaum wrote in *Capitalist Magazine*, continue to occupy her. Hers was not the only book on the Soviet Union to win a Pulitzer Prize in 2004: William Taubman also won for his biography *Khrushchev: The Man and His Era*.

Applebaum's opinion column for the *Washington Post* generally appears on Wednesdays. In recent articles she has written about sexual harassment at Yale University; her Jewish family's Christmas celebrations; and Secretary of State Colin Powell. She has expressed the opinion that American ideals will prevail only if the U.S. captures the minds and hearts of antagonists elsewhere, and that it was those ideals rather than the force of arms that won the Cold War. In the *New Republic* (June 28, 2004), Applebaum issued a plea for a change in tactics in the current war against Iraq. She maintained that the U.S. must "prove to Arabs that Western values, in some moderate Islamic form, will give them better lives" and must try to "rob radical Islam of its revolutionary glamour." She castigated the administration of President George W. Bush and, indeed, the president himself, for a "deep lack of seriousness" and complained that the administration "never had any interest in a dialogue with the Arab world. . . . For all its talk of universal human rights, this is not an administration that actualy perceives itself as part of something greater than the United States. For all of its talk about spreading American values to benighted foreigners, this is not an administration that even likes foreigners."

In 1992 Applebaum won the Charles Douglas–Home Memorial Trust Award for journalism about the former Soviet Union. Her work has appeared in the *New York Review of Books*, the *Wall Street Journal*, the *Financial Times*, *Foreign Affairs*, the London *Guardian*, the *Independent*, the *Weekly Standard*, *Newsweek*, the *National Review*, and the *Times Literary Supplement*, among other publications.

Applebaum and her husband, Radek Sikorski, have two children, Alexander and Tadeusz. They live in Washington, D.C.

—C.F.T.

Suggested Reading: Anneapplebaum.com; *First Things* p38+ Nov. 2003; *New Republic* p19+ June 26, 2004; (New York) *Newsday* p35+ Nov. 27, 1994; *New York Times Book Review* p11+ Dec. 18, 1994; *Washington Post* X p4 Nov. 20, 1994, B p1+ Dec. 13, 1994, with photos

Selected Books: *Between East and West: Across the Borderlands of Europe*, 1995; *Gulag: A History*, 2003

Ashwell, Rachel

Oct. 30, 1959– Interior designer; entrepreneur

Address: Rachel Ashwell Shabby Chic, 6330 Arizona Circle, Los Angeles, CA 90045

"A home can be truly lived in and still be lovely," the interior designer and entrepreneur Rachel Ashwell declared on her Web site, shabbychic.com. "I believe in cozy relaxed settings where kids are free to put their feet on the sofa and guests can place their cups on the coffee table without a care. For me, the secret to living well is to surround myself with beautiful things that are practical and deliciously comfortable." Ashwell is the founder and owner of Shabby Chic, a chain of six stores and a line of products for the home. Launched in 1989 with one store, in Santa Monica, California, Shabby Chic has grown into a mini-industry that, in 2003, grossed $15 million and encompasses the

Courtesy of Sally Fischer Public Relations

Rachel Ashwell

manufacture of furniture, bedding, household accessories, and clothing sold in hundreds of retail establishments in addition to the Shabby Chic shops; many items sell through the Internet as well. As of 2004 Shabby Chic had grown from a one-woman business to an operation with 125 employees, among them Brian Dell, the company's president; Ashwell still serves as the firm's sole designer and buyer. For a few years beginning in 1999, Ashwell hosted a television program, *Rachel Ashwell's Shabby Chic*, that was broadcast on the Style network, and she has written five coffee-table books: *Shabby Chic* (co-authored by Glynis Costin, 1996), *Rachel Ashwell's Shabby Chic Treasure Hunting and Decorating Guide* (1998), *The Shabby Chic Home* (2000), *Shabby Chic: The Gift of Giving* (2001), and *Shabby Chic: Sumptuous Settings and Other Lovely Things* (2004).

The apparently oxymoronic term "shabby chic" (which, as a proper name, she has trademarked) identifies Ashwell's style, which calls for decorating one's home with gently worn antique furnishings—or new tables, chairs, sofas, beds, bureaus, rugs, lamps, and other items constructed, as Ashwell specifies, to look like serviceable secondhand household effects reminiscent of bygone fashions. In the belief that a home should have a lived-in air and serve as a cozy "cocoon," she favors sofas with extra-puffy cushions (which one need not feel obliged to plump up after people have sat on them), tables with small dents and other imperfections, and lots of flowers—preferably, English roses, which add further to the ambience when they begin to wilt. The style "bespeaks old-money, upper-class pleasure . . . ," Amy Wilson wrote for the California *Orange County Register* (December

10, 2001). "It's eclectic, ostensibly mismatched and flea-market driven, but has been reworked by Ashwell to be the essence of comfortable wealth, without all that requisite priss, pretension or primogeniture." (Wilson added, parenthetically, "Which does not mean it's cheap.") In the *Los Angeles Times* (July 29, 1999), Mimi Avins observed, "Many of the women who want to own . . . Shabby Chic home furnishings are also, consciously or unconsciously, buying a piece of the image [Ashwell] projects: a hard-working mother who values beauty, comfort and practicality but has neither the patience nor inclination to insist on perfection."

To ensure that nonmatching furniture and accessories do not clash or look haphazard, Ashwell sticks to a palette of whites, creams, pale pinks, pale blues, and pale sea-foam greens. For simple, inexpensive maintenance, she advises covering wooden furniture with glossy or semi-gloss paint (white, preferably) and protecting upholstered chairs and sofas with washable slipcovers, made with the launder-friendly, vintage-style fabrics that Shabby Chic markets. "I think one of the secrets of [Shabby Chic's] success is that it's such an easy style to live with, and it's easy on the eye," Ashwell told Gabrielle Fagan for the *Irish News* (March 24, 2003). "The key ingredients are beauty, comfort and function. I believe nothing should be so precious that it can't be touched, and everything should not simply look lovely but should be useful. One should live in and around one's possessions and not be dominated by them."

Ashwell was born Rachel Greenfield on October 30, 1959 in Cambridge, England, and raised in London. Her father, Elliott Greenfield, is Jewish; her mother, Shirley, is Christian. She has an older sister, Deborah Greenfield, who has illustrated two of Ashwell's books. Deborah Greenfield is a prize-winning choreographer and flamenco dancer; she founded and directs the dance company Rosa Negra Flamenco. The sisters' father was a book dealer who specialized in rare, old editions; their mother bought, restored, and then resold antique dolls and teddy bears. While the girls were growing up, they accompanied their parents on hundreds of trips to flea markets, antique fairs, and other places where their father and mother bought most of their merchandise. In her mother's case, this included old lace and other materials necessary for constructing new but old-looking apparel for vintage dolls. "I saw [my parents] both treasure hunting, if you like, and turning it into an entrepreneurial thing," Ashwell explained to Mimi Avins. She told Rachel Bridge for the London *Sunday Times* (February 29, 2004), "Following my father around the markets taught me how to make quick decisions" about what was or was not worth buying. "My mother taught me how to restore without ruining the integrity of the piece, and without taking it so far that it was this slick unrecognisable new thing." In fixing antique dolls, Ashwell told Avins, her mother "knew just when to stop . . . , and I liked that she wouldn't make them quite perfect."

By the time she had entered her teens, Ashwell herself was selling antiques in London markets. She dropped out of school at 16 and, by age 19, had moved to Los Angeles, California. There, despite her lack of a high-school diploma, she found work as a wardrobe stylist and set designer for TV and film companies and producers of commercials. According to Mimi Avins, she specialized in period settings. "What she lacked in formal education she made up for with taste, grit and inventiveness," Avins wrote. Sometimes, Ashwell recalled to Bridge, she would "driv[e] around Sunset Boulevard in the sunshine, seeing big houses and cars, and thinking this is the land of opportunity."

During the 1980s Ashwell married a man who directed commercials. She was a full-time homemaker and mother, raising a toddler and an infant, when, during the second half of that decade, she and her husband divorced. Unwilling to take on jobs like those she had had earlier, because of the overly long hours they required, she cast about for another way to earn a living. Interior decorating struck her as a viable option. The attractiveness and practicality of the slipcovers with which she had covered her sofa and chairs after the birth of her first child had elicited compliments from her friends, some of whom had expressed the desire to own such slipcovers themselves. (Various sources imply that she herself made the slipcovers, but in an interview with Amy Wilson, she said, "I don't actually sew." She has also admitted that she isn't especially "handy" when it comes to refinishing furniture.) Banking on the appeal of her design ideas to a wider audience, in 1989 Ashwell borrowed $50,000 from her ex-husband (which she later repaid) and opened a home-furnishings shop in Santa Monica, California. She named the store Shabby Chic and stocked it with about $30,000 worth of items, primarily slipcovers and antique furniture that she had bought at flea markets and then had refinished and/or recovered, using fabric that she had "aged" by laundering them with tea-colored water in her washing machine. Everything sold within a few weeks. Recalling the beginnings of her business, she told Bridge, "I knew about fabrics, and vintage, but nothing about business, and my lessons have been my experiences. Now when I open a store I know I need [money for] expenses and working capital, but the first store I worked out on a piece of paper. If a table sold, it didn't occur to me that I needed another one. . . . In a funny kind of way the innocence of how I did it, rather than being big and slick, was what spoke to people."

By 1991 Ashwell had opened two additional stores, one in New York City and the other in San Francisco, California. Since then she has added three more, in Chicago, Illinois, and Malibu and Newport Beach, in California. Whereas she originally sold only secondhand goods, the necessity of replenishing stock quickly and her lack of sufficient time to accomplish that through flea-market purchases led her to turn to the manufacture of furniture and other "shabby-chic" items of her own design. She has steadily expanded her inventory to include such products as lampshades, chair cushions, ottomans, bedding, fabrics, and tote bags. Shabby Chic Baby offers such merchandise as cribs, changing tables, blankets, crib bumpers, lamps, and bibs. Also available, through Shabby Chic Studio, is slipcovered furniture that is less expensive than other Shabby Chic furniture. Shabby Chic and even Shabby Chic Studio prices might be described as upscale: as of late October 2004, according to its Web site, the price of one style of 16-by-12-inch Shabby Chic lampshade was $180; a small lampshade for a chandelier bulb, $56; a flowered, ruffled, standard-size pillowcase, $78; the baby bib, $20; and the changing table, $275 (with pad and pad cover costing an additional $50 and $78, respectively). In February 2004 Simply Shabby Chic, a collection of less costly Shabby Chic home furnishings and bedding that Ashwell designed exclusively for Target stores, became available.

Ashwell's celebrity devotées are said to include Madonna, Julia Roberts, Oprah Winfrey, and Anthony Hopkins. She has served as a decorator for the actress and singer Jennifer Lopez twice: in 2003, for Lopez's restaurant, Madre's, in Pasadena, California, and in 2004, for Lopez's wedding, held in her backyard, to the singer Marc Anthony. Although Ashwell has often been compared to the famous doyenne of interior decoration Martha Stewart, their philosophies and approaches differ significantly. In demonstrating home-decorating projects, for example, Stewart strived to hide any imperfections in the items she was working on; indeed, the goals of many of her projects were to hide defects in household articles. Ashwell, by contrast, believes that there is beauty in imperfection. She said to Mimi Avins, "That philosophical base can be applied to all kinds of things. Everything you do. What you wear. How you live." In addition, as Ashwell said to Amy Wilson, Martha Stewart "can tell you how to grow the wheat to make the bread that she puts on a plate; I can tell you to take things out of the freezer and how to arrange them beautifully on a plate."

Ashwell and her daughter, Lily, and son, Jake, live in Malibu, California. Photos of her house, which she remodeled several years ago, appear in her book *Shabby Chic Home*.

—K.J.E.

Suggested Reading: Bozzle.com; *Irish News* p34 Mar. 24, 2003; (London) *Sunday Times* p13 Feb. 29, 2004; *Los Angeles Times* E p1 July 29, 1999; *People* (on-line) July 26, 2004; Shabby Chic Web site

Selected Books: *Shabby Chic* (with Glynis Costin), 1996; *Rachel Ashwell's Shabby Chic Treasure Hunting and Decorating Guide*, 1998; *The Shabby Chic Home*, 2000; *Shabby Chic: The Gift of Giving*, 2001; and *Shabby Chic:*

Sumptuous Settings and Other Lovely Things,
2004

Selected Television Shows: *Rachel Ashwell's
Shabby Chic,* 1999–2004

Thos Robinson/Getty Images

Baitz, Jon Robin

Nov. 4, 1961– Playwright

*Address: c/o L.A. Theatre Works, 681 Venice
Blvd., Venice, CA 90291*

"It's so hard to write," the playwright Jon Robin
Baitz observed to Terry Byrne for the *Boston Herald* (June 12, 1996). "If you're going to do it, you
might as well hit the big themes." Baitz has expressed disapproval of such labels as "modern-day
moralist," as a *New York Times* headline described
him (May 7, 1992). Nonetheless, he has steadfastly
addressed serious moral and ethical questions in
his plays—but without moralizing—largely because of what he saw, heard, and experienced firsthand in the 1970s as an American adolescent living in South Africa, where the black majority had
long suffered the brutal oppression and racial segregation institutionalized by the white minority
through the nation's apartheid laws; indeed, most
of his plays are semiautobiographical. "I think
something kicked in for me in South Africa, something about feeling impotent to change things that
I found repugnant," he recalled to Misha Berson for
the *Seattle Times* (October 23, 1995). "And with
that came rage and a modified, complex liberal
guilt." In the *New York Times* (March 3, 1996), the

cultural critic Margo Jefferson wrote that Baitz has
focused on such questions as these: "How does the
home prepare one for the evils of the world? How
does the family and country we belong to shape us
for good or ill? And what do we do with all the
treacherous ambiguities in between; with the
choices that must be made and the catastrophes
that must be acknowledged?"

The first of Baitz's plays to be mounted, in 1985,
was the original version of his one-act comedy
Mizlansky/Zilinsky. The second, *The Film Society,*
opened in New York in 1988 and earned Baitz the
1989 George Oppenheimer Award (called the
Oppy), which honors the most impressive New
York debut of an American playwright. His later
works for the stage include *The Substance of Fire,
The End of the Day, Three Hotels, A Fair Country,
Ten Unknowns, Chinese Friends,* and *The Paris
Letter.* Known for his love of and sensitive ear for
language, Baitz has written screenplays and a contemporary version of Henrik Ibsen's *Hedda Gabler*
and has appeared in three films: *Last Summer in
the Hamptons* (1995), *One Fine Day* (1996), and
Sam the Man (2000). "I'll keep writing about the
decreasing power of the individual and the increasing responsibility of the individual," he once
said, as quoted on Virginia Commonwealth University's "Arts" Web site. "I'm in pursuit of something, and it's a long-term notion."

Jon Robin Baitz, called Robbie by friends and
relatives, was born on November 4, 1961 in Los
Angeles, California. His brother, Richard K. "Rick"
Baitz, born in 1954, is a composer and arranger
who has written scores for HBO and PBS presentations as well as for productions of works by his
brother. His father, Edward Baitz, now deceased,
was an executive with the international division of
the Carnation evaporated-milk company; his job
transfers dictated the family's subsequent moves.
For two years beginning when Robbie was eight,
the Baitzes lived in Brazil. In 1972 they set up
house in Durban, in the Republic of South Africa.
Explaining to Michael Lassell for *Interview* (April
1992) why, in his words, he "has always felt old,"
Baitz said, "You're so much on your own when you
live overseas as a kid of parents who are kind of doing their own thing. Being sad as a child makes
people grow up faster." He told a reporter for *New
York Newsday* (August 3, 1989), "Growing up as a
traveler, you learn to listen and observe in order to
determine what the rules of the game are going to
be in any given place." By the early 1970s in South
Africa, the black majority's plight under apartheid
had led to increasingly open and frequent rebellion. Some of the strikes, marches, and other protests ended in violence, with the police killing dozens of the participants. Baitz's first memory of
South Africa is of a sign reading "This door for
whites only" at the airport arrivals building. On his
first day at his all-white, Anglican boys' school, he
told William Grimes for the *New York Times* (May
7, 1992), after seeing all the students stand whenever a white adult entered the classroom, he alone

rose from his seat when a black janitor came in. He also remembers seeing blacks stopped on the streets of Johannesburg by white policemen armed with machine guns in 1976, after residents of the nearby black township of Soweto protested the national edict that instruction in black schools must be in Afrikaans, the language spoken by the descendants of South Africa's Dutch settlers. Once, when a heated argument between his mother and one of her black employees led her to summon a police officer, he heard the policeman advise her to buy a gun.

During the six years Baitz spent as an outsider in South Africa—in particular at his school, where he was the only Jew as well as the only American—he grew "increasingly comfortable, increasingly integrated, increasingly anguished, because as a teenager you get anguished. So the more comfortable I became, the less comfortable I was," as he recalled to William Grimes. Baitz told Misha Berson that he was "always struck by the kind of moral ambiguity that living in South Africa required." He told Grimes, "When one is confronted with such day-to-day evil, it should be very clear how to respond. And yet I found myself lacking—found myself, my peers, my parents, my parents' friends, the world lacking." He told Stephen Gaghan for *Bomb Magazine* (2004, on-line), "South Africa made me who I am. Being party to, not mere witness to, pure and simple state-run racism, the subjugation of entire peoples, [led to] my interest in how systems operate and how we lull ourselves into letting them operate with impunity. I write about that as much as I do parents and children; they're exactly the same thing." Baitz also told Gaghan that his mother "has contributed vastly to my personality; both of us struggling to understand, struggling to fit in . . . . She's not so much a muse as she is a half-me."

Baitz's family returned to Los Angeles in time for Baitz to spend his last year before college at Beverly Hills High School, where the students' disengagement from nearly all societal problems astonished him. He decided against continuing his education after his high-school graduation. "Because of the moving around, I'd never really focused on my schoolwork," he explained to Mervyn Rothstein for the *New York Times* (August 2, 1988). "Being a student seemed unreal, and going to college seemed evasive—a kind of sidestepping maneuver." Instead, he embarked on a series of "the usual drifter's jobs," as he put it to Rothstein, mostly in Israel and Europe.

At age 20 Baitz returned to Los Angeles. He got a job as a gofer with a producer of substandard films who was struggling to survive on Hollywood's margins. During this time he also worked as a salesclerk in a bookstore and started to attend plays. A turning point in his life came when he saw a production of Anton Chekhov's *The Cherry Orchard*, in which, because of debts and inattention, an old landowning family loses their property to Lopakhin, a former serf who has become a rich merchant. "The scene where Lopakhin says 'I told you this was going to happen,' I understood that moment of revenge," Baitz told Bruce Weber for the *New York Times* (October 30, 1994). "And I wanted revenge." He came to view the stage as "a forum to jumpstart something" and fight the "ever-present impulse to disengage," as he put it to Grimes.

For a while Baitz studied playwriting at the now-defunct Padua Hills Playwrights' Workshop and Festival, in Northridge, California. At 22 he wrote his first play and got his first rejection, from the Actors Theater of Louisville, in Kentucky, whose letter offered suggestions and encouragement. He next penned *Mizlansky/Zilinsky* (1985), inspired by his Hollywood employer's "byzantine, elusive business dealings," as Naomi Pfefferman wrote for the *Jewish Journal of Greater Los Angeles* (April 7, 2000, on-line). Referring to a writer of comedies and a tragedy by Arthur Miller, Baitz told Pfefferman that *Mizlansky/Zilinsky* was "like a Neil Simon version of *Death of a Salesman*, with all the little dramas of trying to get to the next good deal." Mounted in a storefront theater in Los Angeles, the play brought Baitz an *L.A. Weekly* Award. At the time, he told Pfefferman, "I had such an entitlement complex that my response was, 'This is right. What's next?'"

Baitz's next play, *The Film Society*, takes place in 1970 at a fictitious boys' school in Durban that resembles the one Baitz attended. Through his six characters, Baitz portrayed the school as a "fascinating microcosm of South Africa," as Mimi Kramer wrote for the *New Yorker* (August 8, 1988). The protagonist is a teacher who precipitates a crisis by inviting a black priest to speak at the school's centennial celebration. The possibility that the school will mistakenly be thought to be fomenting antiapartheid activity pushes some of the otherwise goodhearted characters "out of their amiable bumbling into fear-induced beastliness," as John Simon wrote for *New York* (August 1, 1988). In one of many complimentary reviews, Sylviane Gold wrote for the *Wall Street Journal* (August 2, 1988), "Baitz's South Africa is awash in moral ironies" and "full of betrayals, large and small. Mr. Baitz's understated writing . . . lets the point of the play slip out around the edges of the story: In a society based upon a lie, good faith is not possible. . . . In the end, we see that self-interest is the only creed that can survive in white South Africa." In Mimi Kramer's view, *The Film Society* "reverberates like the best work of [the renowned South African playwright] Athol Fugard."

Dutch Landscape, Baitz's next play, centers on an American family living in 1970s South Africa; the parents and their two sons have "lost touch with [their] roots in 1960s idealism . . . [and] are isolated and far away, not only from their home in America, but from each other," according to a blurb posted on kennedy-center.org. The play, which opened in late 1988 at the Mark Taper Forum, in Los Angeles, failed resoundingly. The harsh words of critics devastated its author, who grew angry, depressed, and confused. Afraid that the negative response to *Dutch Landscape* might paralyze Baitz professionally, Gordon Davidson, the artistic director of the forum's Center Theatre Group, persuaded him to start writing again immediately. Baitz described the negative reception to *Dutch Landscape* to Richard Stayton for the *Los Angeles Times* (January 17, 1993) as "the most seminal experience of my life." "Right after it I wrote *Substance [of Fire], Three Hotels*, and *End of the Day* in rapid succession," he said. "And I attribute all of that to *Dutch Landscape*, to learning from the extraordinary battle of that play. It fueled a great growth for me."

Baitz wrote *The Substance of Fire* with the actor Ron Rifkin, a friend of his, in mind for the leading role. At its premiere, at Playwrights Horizons, in New York City, in March 1991, Rifkin portrayed Isaac Geldhart, a refugee from Nazi Germany whose family perished during the Holocaust; he now owns a publishing company along with his adult children. In Act I, his children urge Isaac to bring out a trashy novel to bolster the firm's shaky finances. Instead, against their vehement objections and warnings of disaster, he insists on publishing a six-volume account of the medical experiments conducted by the Nazis on Jews and others deemed undesirable by the German dictator Adolf Hitler and his cohorts during the 1930s and World War II. Victimized by evildoers as a child, Isaac habitually attacks his own children verbally. In Act II, set three years later, his business is in the hands of a Japanese corporation; a now-retired, mentally unstable Isaac confronts his past from a different perspective when visited by a troubled psychiatric social worker sent by one son in hopes of having his father deemed incompetent. "For all his nastiness, it is hard to dislike Isaac . . . ," Frank Rich wrote for the *New York Times* (March 18, 1991). "Once Mr. Baitz ruthlessly challenges the premises by which Isaac has lived—examining the real meaning of his survival, the substance of his 'fire'—the audience is caught up in the sad reckoning facing him in late middle age. Is Isaac's proud insistence on holding onto his past the choice that allowed him to survive, or is it a burden that robbed him of any hope for happiness?" Rich also wrote, "It is the searing achievement of *The Substance of Fire* that it keeps chipping and chipping away at its well-worn, well-defended protagonist until finally he and the century that shaped him and then reshaped him are exposed to the tragic quick." Ron Rifkin starred in the film version of *The Substance of Fire* (1996), for which Baitz wrote the screenplay.

"On the heels of his daunting patriarch in *The Substance of Fire*, Baitz stacks up as a true American virtuoso" with *Three Hotels*, Jan Stuart declared in *New York Newsday* (April 7, 1993), expressing an opinion shared by many other reviewers. Baitz wrote *Three Hotels* for a presentation on the PBS television series *American Playhouse* in 1991 that he directed as well. Two years later the stage version opened at the Circle Repertory Theater, in New York City. *Three Hotels* has only two characters, Ken Hoyle and his wife, Barbara, and three acts, each set in a different hotel room overseas; in the first and third acts, only Ken is on stage (except for a moment at the very end, when a silent Barbara is seen); in the second act, only Barbara. Ken (born to a Russian-Jewish-American Communist) is a hard-nosed executive with a company that markets baby formula to underdeveloped nations, fully aware that the food is a poor and even dangerous substitute for breast milk, because in many areas the water necessary to prepare the formula is contaminated, and many users will not understand the proper way to mix it. (Baitz's father did not think that Hoyle's business tactics mirrored his. "I don't think I'm that venal a character," he told Bruce Weber. "I never thought [my son] was portraying me in that sense.") Ken is unaware that his wife, after two decades of seeming compliancy in her marriage, has become embittered and desperate. Barbara, who like Ken is a former Peace Corps volunteer, disapproves of his company's misleading sales tactics. In Act II she discloses that in a talk to company wives, she has not-so-subtly warned the women of the harm in store for them as appendages to their husbands in Third World environments. In Act III Ken reveals that his wife's subversive speech has cost him his job and that she has left him. The confident, combative corporate climber whom Ken presented to the world in Act I is barely discernible. "Kenneth and Barbara's alternating spiels reveal classic case histories of good liberal intentions gone awry," according to Jan Stuart. In the *New York Times* (April 18, 1993), David Richards wrote, "The playwright has not only painted a vivid picture of a marriage in collapse and a freewheeling career on the rocks, he's also indicted a whole society for which ethics is just a bothersome form of nit-picking."

Baitz took the title of *A Fair Country* from the poem "Refugee Blues," by W. H. Auden. A reworking of *Dutch Landscape*, the play opened at a Lincoln Center theater on February 19, 1996. It features Harry Burgess, an idealistic U.S. Foreign Service officer stationed in Durban; his wife, Patrice, a "walking nervous breakdown," as Vincent Canby described her in the *New York Times* (February 20, 1996), whose emotional turmoil is linked to her keen understanding of the horrors of apartheid and its damaging effects on her family; their adult son, Alec, a fiery, countercultural journalist who is visiting from New York; and their agonized, homosexual 17-year-old son, Gil, "the play's conscience," in Canby's words. Eager to remove Patrice and Gil from South Africa, Burgess succeeds in getting a job with the Voice of America in Europe—but with a string attached: he must divulge to the U.S. Central Intelligence Agency (CIA) the names of South African antiapartheid organizers who are Alec's friends. His acquiescence leads to the destruction of his family. *A Fair Country* left the *New York*

Times's Margo Jefferson with questions about the characters' inner lives and actions; nevertheless, she described what she called "Baitz's angry, intelligent new play" as "the best contemporary American play I have seen at Lincoln Center for some time."

In 1996 Baitz developed a life-threatening infection in one of his heart valves and underwent open-heart surgery. His illness left him "more fragile than I realized, with perhaps a diminished capacity for laughter, boldness and bravery," as he wrote for the *New York Times* (February 1, 1998). The Los Angeles Theater Works' request, in 1997, that he adapt *Mizlansky/Zilinsky* for broadcast on the radio helped him emerge from his gloom; "administering a kind of literary CPR on myself," as he put it in the *New York Times*, he made major changes in the play. Meanwhile, for about two years after his recuperation, Baitz worked on scripts for the silver screen—a lucrative but, for him, highly unsatisfying activity. "It left me feeling practically worthless as a writer," he told Bernard Weinraub for the *New York Times* (March 14, 1999). "The variables that I could not control just stymied me. I was left feeling impotent." A new project for the stage—adapting *Hedda Gabler* for contemporary audiences—enabled him to become "reacquainted with the exhilaration of writing," as he put it to Weinraub. Baitz's version of *Hedda Gabler* was mounted in Los Angeles in 1999 and at the Williamstown Theater Festival, in Massachusetts, in 2000.

Baitz's most recent plays include *Ten Unknowns* (2001), about the mysteries of artistic creation and corruption in the world of fine art. *Chinese Friends* (2004), set in 2030 in a dystopian U.S, amounts to a "jeremiad," as the playwright put it to Jason Zinoman for the *New York Times* (May 30, 2004), that grew out of his anger over the policies and actions of the administration of President George W. Bush. *The Paris Letter* deals with "the survivors, the benefactors and the victims of a sexual revolution," as Baitz, who is homosexual, put it to Stephen Gaghan. "I had been somewhat elliptical or cautious about sexuality in my work," he explained. "And it had started to bother me." *The Paris Letter* is scheduled to open in New York City in mid-2005.

For more than a decade, Baitz lived in New York City with the actor and director Joe Mantello, who directed some of his plays. He recently moved to Venice, California. His honors include the Playwrights USA Award from the Theatre Communications Group; the Humanitas Prize, from the Human Family Educational and Cultural Institute; and fellowships from the Rockefeller and Revson foundations, the American Academy of Arts and Letters, and the National Endowment for the Arts (NEA), which gave him a $15,000 grant in 1992. Later that year, to protest the refusal of the NEA's acting director to give grants to an arts center and a gallery despite the recommendations of the NEA's advisory panel, on the grounds that the funds would be used for exhibiting sexually explicit material, Baitz gave $7,500 each to the arts center and the gallery. He is a founding member of Naked Angels, a nonprofit New York City theater company of actors, writers, directors, designers, and producers. Baitz lamented to Gloria Goodale for the *Christian Science Monitor* (April 21, 2000) that theater is largely peripheral to contemporary American society. "The sense of futility, the feeling that the culture has passed you by is the most difficult part of being a playwright, that you're doing work that nobody knows about; most of the time I can't bear it," he told her. "I can't pretend I'm happy about it or reconciled or at peace with it, but I'm addicted [to writing]."

—H.T.

Suggested Reading: *Chicago Tribune* C p14 June 19, 1994, with photos; *Jewish Journal of Greater Los Angeles* (on-line) Apr. 7, 2000, with photo; *New York Times* C p15 Aug. 2, 1988, with photo, C p11 Mar. 28, 1991, with photo, C p1+ May 7, 1992, with photos, II p1+ Oct. 30, 1994, with photos; *Seattle Times* Tempo p12 Oct. 23, 1992

Selected Plays: *Mizlansky/Zilinsky*, 1985 (for theater), 1997 (for radio); *The Film Society*, 1988; *Dutch Landscape*, 1988; *The End of the Day*, 1993; *Three Hotels*, 1991 (for television), 1993 (for theater); *The Substance of Fire*, 1991; *A Fair Country*, 1996; *Ten Unknowns*, 2001; *Chinese Friends*, 2004; as adapter—Ibsen's *Hedda Gabler*, 1999

Selected Films: as screenwriter—*The Substance of Fire*, 1996; as actor—*Last Summer in the Hamptons*, 1995; *One Fine Day*, 1996; *Sam the Man*, 2000

Beers, Rand

Nov. 30, 1942– Democratic political adviser; former U.S. government official

Address: John F. Kennedy School of Government, Harvard University, 79 John F. Kennedy St., Cambridge, MA 02138

Rand Beers, who spent more than three decades in various positions in the National Security Council (NSC) and the U.S. State Department, has said that he has taken two major risks in his life. The first was as a Marine in Vietnam in the mid-1960s; the second came in March 2003, when, five days before the U.S. invaded Iraq, Beers abruptly quit his job as special assistant to President George W. Bush and senior director for combating terrorism. Several weeks later Beers joined the campaign of a presumptive Democratic presidential candidate, Senator John Kerry of Massachusetts, who later be-

Luis Acosta/AFP/Getty Images

Rand Beers

came that party's nominee and Bush's main opponent in the 2004 general election. During that year's presidential campaign, Beers served as one of Kerry's top national-security and foreign-policy advisers. Beers's departure from the Bush White House surprised domestic politicians and observers and made headlines. While he is a registered Democrat, Beers had never been known as an outspoken or ardent supporter of the Democratic Party, and he served ably in the NSC or U.S. State Department under the Republican presidents Ronald Reagan and George H. W. Bush before joining the staff of the George W. Bush administration. By most accounts Beers had been a dedicated and unassuming public servant, and he retained those qualities in his recent role as a Kerry adviser. "Randy's your model government worker," Wendy Chamberlin, a U.S. Agency for International Development worker in Iraq who was a colleague of Beers's in the NSC under George H. W. Bush, told Laura Blumenfeld for the *Washington Post* (June 16, 2003). "He works for the common good of the American people. He's fair, balanced, honest. No one ever gets hurt feelings hearing the truth from Randy."

Beers's defection from the second Bush administration stemmed from his growing frustration and disagreement with its policies and performance. "Counterterrorism is like a team sport. The game is deadly," Beers, who at the time of his resignation did not air his criticisms publicly, told Blumenfeld. "There has to be offense and defense. The Bush administration was primarily offense, and not into teamwork." As he explained further to Blumenfeld, he felt that the Bush administration was not "matching its deeds to its words in the war

on terrorism. They're making us less secure, not more secure. As an insider, I saw the things that weren't being done. And the longer I sat and watched, the more concerned I became, until I got up and walked out." In an interview with Juan Williams for the National Public Radio (NPR) program *Morning Edition*, as transcribed for the NPR Web site, Beers asserted that he is not "someone who would go out and simply be a critic. I want to be part of the solution." He thus brought to bear his considerable experience in foreign policy and national security to help Senator Kerry face George W. Bush in the presidential elections of November 2004.

Robert Rand Beers was born in Washington, D.C., on November 30, 1942. In 1964 he graduated from Dartmouth College, in New Hampshire, with a bachelor's degree in history. He then enlisted in the U.S. Marine Corps and spent the next four years in Vietnam, where the war between the Vietnamese Communist guerrillas (the Vietcong) and U.S. troops was escalating significantly. In 1967 Beers, then a desk officer at a Marine command post, was approaching the end of his tour of duty in Vietnam. Rather than leave the scene of the fighting, he requested that his tour be extended and that he be made the leader of a rifle company on the front lines. "I thought I was immortal," he told Massimo Calabresi for *Time* (March 15, 2004). Beers got his wish and became the commander of a rifle company. He returned to the U.S. in 1968. Soon afterward Beers enrolled at the University of Michigan, where he earned an M.A. degree in history in 1970. The next year he entered the foreign service, with a job in the State Department's Bureau of Politico-Military Affairs. During the 1970s his positions in that bureau included deputy assistant secretary for regional affairs and export control, with a focus on the Middle East and Persian Gulf; director of the office of security analysis and the office of international security policy; and deputy director of the office of policy analysis.

In the 1980s Beers replaced Oliver North as director for counterterrorism and counternarcotics in the NSC under President Ronald Reagan. (North became the public face of the Iran-Contra scandal, which refers to an illicit program of the Reagan administration in which money gained from arms sold to Iran were used to fund insurgents fighting the Communist Sandinista government of Nicaragua, as part of the U.S. government's larger Cold War strategy during that period to prevent the spread of communism in Central America.) From 1988 to 1998, under Presidents Reagan, George H. W. Bush, and Bill Clinton, Beers held a series of posts in the NSC, including director for counterterrorism and counternarcotics, director for peacekeeping, and senior director for intelligence programs.

From 1998 to 2002 Beers served as assistant secretary of state for international narcotics and law enforcement affairs. During that time he directed a U.S. plan, part of a long-term effort, to fight the production and trafficking of drugs in Colombia, a major producer of coca, the plant from which cocaine is processed. Colombia is the world's largest producer of cocaine, much of which is transported to and sold in the U.S. The money generated from Colombian drug trafficking has strengthened the country's notorious drug cartels and rebel groups. In a speech he delivered at a meeting of the United Nations General Assembly in October 1999, as posted on the United Nations Web site, Beers addressed the dangers posed by transnational crime, including drug trafficking, the trafficking of people, the smuggling of aliens, financial crimes, and the illegal manufacture and trafficking of firearms, among other transgressions. He stressed the importance of international cooperation, facilitated through the United Nations, to combat those ills.

While in that same State Department post, Beers played a part in a class-action lawsuit brought by thousands of Ecuadorians against the American company DynCorp, one of the State Department's largest contractors. At the State Department's request, and in conjunction with the Colombian government, DynCorp had been trying to destroy Colombia's coca fields, by covering them with plant-killing chemicals sprayed from planes. The Ecuadorians had argued that DynCorp's use of chemicals in Colombia, which borders Ecuador on the north, had led to the destruction of crops and serious health problems in their country. The State Department sought to have the suit dismissed on the grounds that it would disrupt the interdiction of Colombian drug production and trafficking and would therefore adversely affect the national security of the U.S. To make the State Department's case, Beers submitted to a federal court a statement, which he signed under oath, that listed dozens of reasons why the disruption of DynCorp's work in Colombia would pose a risk to American national security. Among the reasons given was that a major Colombian rebel group involved in narcotics trafficking had received training at Al Qaeda camps in Afghanistan and so, by extrapolation, might pose an international terrorist threat. No one has ever put forth evidence to corroborate that claim, however, and it was met by those involved in the case and other concerned parties with strong skepticism. Representatives for the plaintiffs publicly characterized the statement as a desperate attempt by the State Department to tie Colombia's woes to the post–September 11, 2001 hot-button issue of international terrorism. Beers admitted that the statement should not have been included in the documents given to the federal court, and he formally rescinded the controversial portion.

Critics have characterized the aerial crop-fumigation project and other actions connected with the U.S. government's drug-interdiction policies in Colombia as cruel and ineffective. The destruction of the coca crop, those critics argue, targets and hurts poor Colombian farmers while doing little to punish those who process the plant into cocaine or run the actual drug-trafficking operations. As the overseer and public face of those policies for several years, Beers himself was criticized by the policies' detractors. However, some sources, including the right-wing journalist Robert Novak in a syndicated column that appeared in the Augusta, Georgia, *Chronicle* (July 11, 2003), reported that Beers often urged caution in regard to U.S. policies in Colombia, and that that stance often put him at odds with those Republicans in Congress who were pushing for tougher action.

In August 2002 Beers accepted the post of special assistant to the president and, as part of the NSC staff, senior director for combating terrorism. Before September 11, 2001 the NSC usually met three times a week to discuss intelligence. After the deadly September 11 terrorist attacks, the NSC began meeting twice a day, at 7 a.m. and 3 p.m., to analyze intelligence reports coming from the CIA and other sources. Beers's main task was to evaluate the warnings his office received and to act on them when he deemed it necessary. On a typical day Beers sifted through and evaluated between 500 and 1,000 intelligence reports of possible terrorist threats. Those reports might relate to individuals who were observed suspiciously surveying a U.S. embassy or nuclear power plant, for example; a person holding a weapon who had been caught by airport security personnel; or an intercepted phone call between suspected terrorists. Beers's job also entailed planning for all imaginable contingencies and discussing worst-case scenarios with regard to threats to the country. "It's a monstrous responsibility," William Wechsler, who had served as the NSC's director for transnational threats during the Clinton administration, told Blumenfeld. "You sit around every day, thinking about how people want to kill thousands of Americans." That task began to wear on Beers. He had started out in his new post full of energy; after six months he felt enervated.

In an interview that appears on the American Patriot Friends Network Web site, Beers told Ted Koppel for ABC-TV News about the decisive moment in which he resolved to leave his counterterrorism post within the Bush administration. In March 2003, he recalled, five days before the United States began its second invasion of Iraq, Beers was staring down at the many files of classified documents on his desk, each of which contained information concerning "either a threat to the United States or a policy set that needed to be reviewed in order to try to deal with those threats." Beers had by then lost confidence in the ability of other members of the Bush administration to handle the urgent work on national security represented by those files, and decided to quit, as he told Koppel, because "I felt that the [Bush administration] team wasn't handling it and I alone couldn't do what was necessary to try to change that." In addition, Beers had grown disillusioned with President Bush's policies and handling of the issues; in particular, he faulted what he saw as the administration's rush to war with Iraq, an act that took the government's attention off the war on terrorism. Citing unspecified personal reasons, Beers tendered his resignation; he retired in April of that year. (Just a few months before Beers left his post, Richard Clarke, the government's so-called anti-terrorism czar, had left the Bush White House under similar circumstances.) At that time a number of journalists, including P. Mitchell Prothero of United Press International (March 19, 2003), reported that Beers was but one of a significant number of current and former intelligence officials who believed that the invasion of Iraq would divert much-needed resources from the war on terrorism. (Implicit in that belief is a refutation of the Bush administration's perspective that the removal of the Iraqi dictator Saddam Hussein was an essential step in the war on terrorism.) Prothero quoted one former intelligence official as saying, "I don't blame Randy at all [for his resignation]. This just reflects the widespread thought that the war on terror is being set aside for the war with Iraq at the expense of our military and [intelligence] resources and the relationships with our allies."

Eight weeks after leaving the White House, Beers reentered the political fray on the side of a Democratic presidential candidate, Senator John Kerry of Massachusetts, as Kerry's chief foreign-policy and national-security adviser. Rather than continue his public-service work as a lone individual, Beers had decided that "it was more important to become part of another team and help that team achieve what it would like to achieve, in terms of winning the presidency," as he told Koppel. Asked why he had made such a potentially risky move in terms of his career and the people in government whom his switch to the Democrats might alienate, Beers told Calabresi, "I wanted to defeat George Bush."

Before Kerry had all but been assured of winning the Democratic nomination for president, Beers had chosen to join Kerry's campaign because he felt that Kerry, out of all the Democratic candidates, had the most expertise in foreign affairs and security issues, and because both men had served in Vietnam. In Washington and among observers of American politics, the reaction to Beers's joining the Kerry campaign was one of shock and surprise. For example, Robert Novak wrote, "Resignation of a senior national security aide on policy grounds followed by defection to the political opposition is unprecedented." Adding to the surprise was that, although he was a registered Democrat, Beers had never been a public advocate for the party. "I can't think of a single example in the last 30 years of a person who has done something so extreme," Paul C. Light, a scholar at the Brookings Institution, a foreign-policy think tank, told Blumenfeld. "He's not just declaring that he's a Democrat. He's declaring that he's a Kerry Democrat, and the way he wants to make a difference in the world is to get his former boss out of office."

After his defection, the Republicans attacked Beers's record—in particular, his handling of a 1997 disclosure of attempts by Chinese intelligence agents to influence several U.S. congressional elections. Though the FBI had informed Beers, who was then President Clinton's senior intelligence assistant at the NSC, of the Chinese plans, Beers, his critics contended, failed to report the information to Anthony Lake, who then held the title of national security adviser. (According to Robert Novak, some White House aides had recommended to President Clinton that Beers be fired. Beers has defended his decision not to tell Lake about the Chinese operation on the grounds that it was not important enough to demand the attention of his superiors.)

Much of what Beers learned during his stint in the Bush administration is classified and cannot be discussed publicly. However, he has grown more vocal since his resignation and has aired his criticisms of the Bush administration's conduct of the current war on terrorism: he maintained to Blumenfeld that the mission of rooting out and eliminating Al Qaeda and the Taliban in Afghanistan was left half-done, as a result of which "Osama bin Laden could be almost anywhere in Afghanistan" and American forces would not know it; that the invasion of Iraq in the spring of 2003 was an "ill-conceived and poorly executed strategy"; and that the "difficult, long-term issues both at home and abroad have been avoided, neglected or short-changed and generally underfunded." The last criticism encompasses what Beers sees as the glaring lack of security at U.S. ports and chemical plants. In addition, Beers believes that while the creation of the Department of Homeland Security, into which many former agencies and bureaus were incorporated, was a positive step, the new department's actions have left "a great deal to be desired," as he put it to Koppel.

A note by Beers posted on John Kerry's official election Web site stated that the United States needs "to fix [the Bush administration's] go-it-alone policy that is making Iraq more dangerous for our soldiers and harder for them to secure the peace. I signed up with John Kerry because I know his values, experience and toughness will make peace a reality. Having worked with John for almost a year now, I feel confident he will restore America's leadership in world affairs." Beers has also cited Kerry's Vietnam experience as a factor in his decision to support him. As he told Juan Williams, Kerry "has experienced combat. He has experienced what it means to be shot at. I think that's an absolutely critical trait if you can have it in a president who has to make decisions about war and peace." Asked to elaborate on what a Kerry administration would do differently from the Bush administration, Beers told Koppel that a Kerry White House would be "much more willing to work with and find friends and allies and keep them on board, in pursuing our goals and objectives. I think you would find an administration that was more willing to use persuasion, as well as power, and not just rely upon the use of force to solve particular problems."

In his work for the Kerry campaign, Beers sat for numerous high-profile interviews with the media and created, as Calabresi reported, a "shadow national-security council that [held] press conferences nearly every Monday," during which members of the Kerry campaign discussed foreign affairs and domestic issues. Working with Beers to get Kerry elected were Kerry's longtime Senate aide Nancy Stetson, Beers's former deputy Jonathan Winer, and the lawyer Dan Feldman. Kerry's circle of advisers also included William J. Perry, a former U.S. secretary of defense; Richard Holbrooke, the U.S. ambassador to the United Nations under President Bill Clinton; former chairman of the Joint Chiefs of Staff John Shalikashvili; and Leslie H. Gelb, president emeritus of the Council on Foreign Relations, an independent think tank. With regard to Iraq, Beers and Kerry recommended that the United States turn over to the United Nations control of the political process of attempting to establish a sovereign Iraqi government, while the U.S. would maintain military control in the country for the time being. During a panel discussion on the ABC-TV program *This Week with George Stephanopoulos,* a transcript of which appeared on the ABC News Web site (April 11, 2004), Beers stated that the United States had been "unable to negotiate with the Iraqis. [Special United Nations envoy Lakdar] Brahimi has. It seems to me that we've got an issue here, we're the occupying power, we need to get that label off of us. We need to move to the UN to take a leadership role."

In an interview with Bernard Gwertzman on the Web site of the Council on Foreign Relations, for which Gwertzman is a consulting editor, Beers elaborated on crucial differences between Senator Kerry and President Bush: While Kerry expressed the belief that "this country always has to be prepared to use [military] forces, we should be very careful and use force only when necessary. . . . I'm not saying that George Bush doesn't care about American fighting men and women. But I think there is an important, if not fundamental, difference in attitude [between the two presidential candidates] about the approach to the use of force." Beers added that the "corollary to that, of course, is that you have to be prepared to use diplomacy and other means of persuasion other than the use of force to a much greater degree than this [Bush] administration is prepared to do." Beers also criticized the Bush administration's actions, or lack thereof, with regard to Iran's and North Korea's nuclear-weapon capabilities and ambitions. Another major concern, and another area where Beers drew a contrast between Bush and Kerry, was homeland security. Beers believed, as he told Gwertzman, that a Kerry administration "would pay much more attention to doing homeland security instead of simply paying lip service to the notion." Despite the concerted efforts of Beers and others involved

in Kerry's campaign, Bush won both the popular and the Electoral College votes in the 2004 presidential election.

Beers serves as an adjunct lecturer in public policy at the John F. Kennedy School of Government at Harvard University, in Cambridge, Massachusetts. He and his wife, Bonnie, a school administrator, live in Washington, D.C. The couple have two children.

—C.F.T.

Suggested Reading: (Augusta, Georgia) *Chronicle* July 11, 2003; Harvard University Web site; johnkerry.com; National Public Radio Web site July 15, 2003; *Time* p49 Mar. 15, 2004, with photo; United Press International Aug. 9, 2002, Mar. 19, 2003; *Washington Post* A p1 June 16, 2003

Courtesy of MoveOn.org

Blades, Joan and Boyd, Wes

Founders of the organization MoveOn

Blades, Joan
Mar. 18, 1956– Social activist; entrepreneur

Boyd, Wes
May 5, 1960– Social activist; entrepreneur

Address: MoveOn.org, P.O. Box 9063, Berkeley, CA 94709-0063

In 1998 a married couple, the software-industry entrepreneurs Joan Blades and Wes Boyd, found themselves weary of hearing about the scandal involving then-President Bill Clinton and the former White House intern Monica Lewinsky. Whether or not Clinton had had extramarital sexual relations with Lewinsky, and had lied about it under oath, Blades and Boyd did not consider those offenses to be deserving of impeachment, the measure then being discussed at great length by legislators. Rather, they thought that Congress—particularly the members of its Republican majority, who were more intent on pursuing the subject—needed to resolve the matter quickly and return to the more urgent business of government. On September 18, 1998 the pair sent to fewer than 100 of their friends and family members an E-mail petition consisting of one sentence: "The Congress must immediately censure President Clinton and move on to pressing issues facing the country." For a cost of $89.50, they also set up a Web site, which they called MoveOn.org. Within a week, more than 100,000 people had electronically "signed" the petition, a figure that doubled the following week. By the time the impeachment hearings began, 500,000 people had joined MoveOn, by signing up to receive E-mail newsletters, and the site had prompted more than 250,000 phone calls and one million E-mail messages to Congress. Blades, surprised and pleased by those results, commented to Chris Carr for the *Washington Post* (February 7, 1999, on-line), "We have sent a strong message that there are a lot of people out there who are unhappy with the impeachment trial." Since Blades and Boyd sent that first E-mail message, MoveOn has become one of the most prominent Internet-based grassroots organizations in the country, opposing many actions of the political right, in particular the administration of President George W. Bush. In an article for the *San Francisco Chronicle* (February 9, 2003), Charles Burress quoted the Columbia University journalism professor Todd Gitlin as calling MoveOn, which now boasts two million members (who receive E-mailed updates, make monetary contributions, and/or participate in MoveOn events), "the most effective Internet effort around, at least on the left side of center."

Prior to founding MoveOn, Blades and Boyd had co-founded Berkeley Systems, a California-based entertainment-software company. Although their original intent had been to develop software for the visually impaired, their company became best known for its computer screen savers depicting flying toasters and for the on-line game show *You Don't Know Jack*. Boyd served as chief executive officer of Berkeley Systems, while Blades was vice president of marketing and a member of the board. Under their leadership the company had grown to 150 employees and was earning $30 million in annual revenue before the couple sold it to Cendant Software in 1997 for about $13.8 million. Blades, a law-school graduate, is the author of several nonfiction books on divorce.

Wes Boyd was born on May 5, 1960 in Alaska. The son of a career military officer, he grew up in Ann Arbor, Michigan, and moved to Berkeley, Cal-

ifornia, at the age of 11. Within three years he had proven to be a computer whiz. Boyd attended the University of California at Berkeley but left without earning a degree. Joan Blades, born on March 18, 1956 and raised in Berkeley, attended the University of California and received a B.A. degree in history in 1977. She then enrolled at the Golden Gate University School of Law, in San Francisco, where she earned a degree in law in 1980. A member of the California and Alaska bar associations, she practiced mediation and taught the subject at Golden Gate University. She is the author of *Mediate Your Divorce: A Guide to Cooperative Custody, Property, and Support Agreements* and *Family Mediation: Cooperative Divorce Settlement*, both published in 1985, and co-wrote *The Divorce Book: A Practical and Compassionate Guide* (1984) with Richard Gosse, Peter D. Rogers, and Matthew McKay; the book was reprinted in 1999. Blades is an artist, too, with works published on greeting cards and as part of software packaging. She and Boyd met in the early 1980s and married in 1987.

Before co-founding Berkeley Systems, Boyd worked during the late 1970s and early 1980s at the University of California–Berkeley, as a senior staff programmer on research projects. Following the sale of Berkeley Systems, Boyd and Blades decided to focus on raising their children and developing educational software. The success of MoveOn's initial petition astonished the couple; Blades remarked to the KRON 4 Web site (June 27, 2003), "I was incredibly surprised originally and now I have this understanding that it's possible for people to do remarkable things online." Blades and Boyd decided that MoveOn, in order to realize those possibilities, should diversify its attempts to address important topics. The organization formed the MoveOn.org Political Action Committee (PAC) in the hope of affecting the outcome of the 2000 elections. While they urged people to vote in the presidential election, they focused a greater portion of their efforts on contests for the House of Representatives and Senate. That year the organization raised over $2 million to help elect five new members of the House and four U.S. senators. The PAC is currently focused on defeating President George W. Bush in the 2004 election. MoveOn.org Voter Fund exists primarily to run ads "exposing President Bush's failed policies," according to the MoveOn Web site. The MoveOn staff usually numbers about eight; as 2004 is a presidential-election year, there are currently twice as many employees. The size of the staff, however, does not reflect the scale of MoveOn's operations. Moreover, the employees do not prescribe the contents of its Web site; rather, its members determine (through their responses to on-line surveys, their E-mail messages, and their use of ActionForum software) which issues the organization should address and which strategies are preferred. "The main thing MoveOn does is help members become more effective in participating in public dialogue," Blades explained to Alan Lopez for the *Contra Costa* (California) *Times* (January 16, 2004). "I think what makes MoveOn different from traditional organizations is it's a very dynamic two-way conversation with the membership." Boyd said to Charles Burress that it is precisely this sort of communication that "keeps us honest. . . . We can't do anything our membership doesn't want us to do." As of early 2004 members considered the issues of energy, the environment, the war in Iraq, and the federal budget deficit to be the most important topics. Once members determine which issues are most important to them, they take action by making phone calls to congressmen and -women, having groups of constituents present their representatives with petitions in person, writing letters to the editors of prominent publications, and taking out ads on billboards, on television, in print, and on-line.

In early 2003 MoveOn raised $400,000 to air a television ad opposing a U.S.-led war with Iraq, a campaign undertaken ostensibly to rid that nation of weapons of mass destruction (which, as of late 2004, had not been discovered); the organization sponsored peace vigils and funded ads bearing the slogan "Inspections Work. War Won't." In September of that year, MoveOn launched a Web-based campaign to protest the recall of California's Democratic governor, Gray Davis, and to publicize allegations that the actor and former bodybuilder Arnold Schwarzenegger, who was running as a Republican to replace Davis, had sexually harassed a large number of women. (Schwarzenegger won election as governor the following month.) Other MoveOn projects have included a petition against the potential decision of the Federal Communications Commission (FCC) to relax guidelines on media ownership; a fund drive that generated $1 million in 48 hours in support of the Texas legislators who had fled the state to protest, and prevent passage of, a Republican-sponsored redistricting plan; and a gun-control campaign. Since April 2003 the Web site has called for Congress to censure President Bush for issuing "the misleading statements that pushed the country into war"; urged members to contact the Environmental Protection Agency (EPA) to combat mercury pollution; and provided links to a speech about global warming and the environment by former vice president Al Gore.

In June 2003 MoveOn hosted what was called the first Internet presidential primary. Speaking with Don Hazen and Tai Moses for *Yes* magazine (Fall 2003, on-line), Boyd explained the reason for the site's early involvement in the 2004 election process: "Pundits, pollsters, and big donors shouldn't be the only voices that count at this early and important stage of the process." In the first 48 hours alone, the number of "virtual votes" registered was greater than the number of ballots that would be cast in the 2004 primaries in Iowa, New Hampshire, and South Carolina combined; the on-line votes ultimately totaled 317,000. Howard Dean won the MoveOn primary with 44 percent of the vote, followed by Dennis J. Kucinich and John Kerry in distant second- and third-place positions, respectively. Some of Dean's opponents complained that MoveOn had unfairly advised Dean as to how he should present himself to its members. In response, Zack Exley, then MoveOn's organizing director, explained that the site had offered to advise the other candidates, too, but that only Dean had accepted the offer. Boyd pointed out that MoveOn was not designed to endorse any particular candidate unless the candidate received more than 50 percent of the on-line vote. "I don't spend any time figuring out who the right candidate is," he told Chris Taylor and Karen Tumulty for *Time* (November 17, 2003, on-line). "All I want to do is evangelize populism, so [candidates] go away thinking, 'Whoa—there's someone other than wealthy donors I have to impress?'"

Also in 2003 MoveOn sponsored a competition, entitled "Bush in 30 Seconds," to encourage people to create anti-Bush commercials. More than 1,500 entries were submitted and posted on the Web site. Two of these entries caused controversy by comparing President Bush to the German dictator Adolf Hitler. Boyd and Blades, who pointed out that the two ads in question were not finalists in the competition, issued a statement quoted by Alan Lopez: "We agree that the two ads in question were in poor taste and deeply regret that they slipped through our screening process. . . . In the future, if we publish or broadcast raw material, we will create a more effective filtering system." The commercials were narrowed down to 14 finalists, which were submitted to a panel of judges that included, among others, the singer Moby, the actor and comedian Janeane Garofalo, the actor and musician Jack Black, and the filmmakers Gus Van Sant and Michael Moore. The winning ad, "Child's Pay," depicted children working at a variety of low-level jobs, performing such tasks as washing dishes, repairing tires, and collecting trash, followed by the rhetorical question, "Guess who's going to pay off President Bush's $1 trillion deficit?" Although MoveOn members contributed enough money to pay for a time slot for the ad during the Super Bowl, CBS (which broadcast the event) refused to air the commercial, explaining that the network has a policy of not airing ads that comment on controversial issues. Instead, the winning commercial aired on CNN and is still posted on the Web site. Other MoveOn ads, too, have attracted attention. One (an updated version of an ad used by Lyndon B. Johnson in 1964, during his presidential election campaign), which protested the war in Iraq, was commonly known as "Daisy"; it featured images of a young girl counting the petals on a daisy, juxtaposed with scenes of conflict in the Middle East and, finally, a shot of a mushroom cloud from a nuclear bomb explosion. Another, called "Polygraph," played statements made by President Bush and showed them registering as false on a lie-detector test, thus suggesting that Bush had misled the public regarding the situation in Iraq. One of MoveOn's ads called for the firing of Secretary of

Defense Donald Rumsfeld for his alleged approval of a policy that, according to the Web site, allowed for the physical coercion and sexual humiliation of Iraqi prisoners. In March 2004 MoveOn published a book entitled *50 Ways to Love Your Country*, which contains tips on how to become an effective political activist. Later that year the organization collaborated with the nonprofit group Music for America to release a CD called *Future Soundtrack for America*, the proceeds from which were being donated to other nonprofits.

The MoveOn Web site expressed its support for the Democratic ticket in the 2004 presidential election. On the morning of November 3, about 12 hours after the polls had closed on the West Coast, the Democratic candidate, John Kerry, conceded the election to George W. Bush. Before he did, according to a message sent to everyone on MoveOn's list of E-mail recipients (November 3, 2004, on-line), he telephoned MoveOn's headquarters to thank MoveOn's members "for what we did to help his campaign." "That you put so much into this effort makes the loss [of the election] more painful in some ways," the E-mail message stated. "But the fact that so many of us were involved offers true hope for the future of democracy. In the campaign to defeat George Bush, you have proven that real Americans can have a voice in American politics. In the months and years to come, that revelation will change everything. . . . Our journey toward a progressive America has always been bigger than George Bush. The current leg is just beginning— we're still learning how to build a citizen-based politics together. But it's a journey our nation has been on for a long time. As Martin Luther King Jr. said, 'The arc of history is long, but it bends toward justice.'"

Although some label Blades, Boyd, and their MoveOn supporters as radical, especially in light of their opposition to the war in Iraq, Blades insisted to Alan Lopez that they are progressive, not extremist: "What's radical about us is [our] saying people should be involved in politics—and they should." In addition to the 2.4 million members, MoveOn has garnered the support of individuals such as the billionaire philanthropist George Soros, who, in conjunction with his business partner, Peter B. Lewis, pledged a $5 million matching grant (one dollar for every two raised by MoveOn members) toward an advertising campaign aimed at defeating President Bush's reelection bid. Al Gore is a fan of the organization, too: he has given several speeches to packed auditoriums of MoveOn members.

Blades and Boyd live in Berkeley with their son and daughter; they continue to operate MoveOn from their home. In 2003 *Ms.* magazine named Blades "Woman of the Year" for her efforts with MoveOn.

—K.J.E.

Suggested Reading: *Contra Costa* (California) *Times* F p4 Jan. 16, 2004; MoveOn.org; *Ms.* (on-line) Winter 2003; *San Francisco Chronicle* A p23 Feb. 9, 2003; *Yes* (on-line) Fall 2003

Selected Books: by Joan Blades—*The Divorce Book: A Practical and Compassionate Guide* (with Richard Gosse, Peter D. Rogers, and Matthew McKay), 1984; *Mediate Your Divorce: A Guide to Cooperative Custody, Property, and Support Agreements*, 1985; *Family Mediation: Cooperative Divorce Settlement*, 1985

Courtesy of the office of Kathleen Blanco

Blanco, Kathleen

(BLANG-koh)

Dec. 15, 1942– Governor of Louisiana (Democrat)

Address: Office of the Governor, Attn.: Constituent Services, P.O. Box 94004, Baton Rouge, LA 70804-9004

In November 2003 Kathleen Blanco, who has broken much ground for women in her more than 20 years of public service in Louisiana, became the first woman elected governor of the state. A conservative Democrat—who, for example, opposes abortion while seeking improvements in access to health care—Blanco is known for her nonabrasive and open governing style, and her rise has been greeted enthusiastically in Louisiana, where politics has often been marked by flamboyance and marred by corruption. Before becoming governor Blanco served two terms as Louisiana's lieutenant governor, during which she was often referred to as the state's "goodwill ambassador" and "tourism czar." The Louisiana state representative Sharon West Broome told John Hill for the *Advertiser* (January 11, 2004, on-line), "One of [Blanco's] biggest assets is her ability to engage people in a one-on-one and her open communications style. When you go in to talk to her, you know she is listening to you and your concerns." Referring to the moment that she began to think seriously about the role of women in politics, Blanco recalled to Louis Rom for the Acadiana, Louisiana, *Times* (January 8, 2003, on-line), "I was sitting around a table with elected men . . . I began to think of all the women I knew and I realized there were no women [officials] at that table. Women think of themselves as not being qualified for public office. The first thing a woman will tell you is, 'Oh, I don't have the qualifications. I don't have the background.' But what I found is there are no essential qualifications, it was just something in [those men's] eyes. And I realized that . . . the power was within us and if [women] wanted to step out we could, but if we never opened the gates we never would."

In characterizing the state that Blanco now governs, Michael Barone and Grant Ujifusa wrote in the *Almanac of American Politics 2000* of Louisiana's "charm and inefficiency, its communities interlaced by family ties and its public sector laced with corruption, with its own indigenous culture and its tradition of fine distinctions of class and caste." Barone and Ujifusa went so far as to write that Louisiana "often seems to be America's banana republic," a term usually suggesting a small country with a tropical climate and tyrannical rule. Blanco told Glynn Wilson for the *Christian Science Monitor* (November 17, 2003) that her gubernatorial victory "represents the desire for Louisiana people to really make a serious change and put our crazy politics of the past behind us," referring in part, no doubt, to the legacy of such past Louisiana politicians as the white supremacist David Duke, a former state legislator; the flamboyant former governor Edwin Edwards, who is in federal prison for racketeering and extortion; and the domineering former governor Huey Long. Her pronouncement notwithstanding, Blanco has taken on the same formidable difficulties that her predecessors have faced, in that among the 50 states, according to a CNN article dated January 12, 2004, Louisiana ranks sixth from last in per capita income, fifth from the top in terms of poverty, and third from the bottom in teacher salaries. Further, as quoted by Glynn Wilson, the Better Government Association ranked Louisiana 46th among the 50 states on its Capital Integrity Index.

Of Cajun heritage, Kathleen Babineaux Blanco was born to Louis and Lucille Babineaux in the Coteau settlement of Iberia Parish, Louisiana, on December 15, 1942. (Cajuns are Louisianans descended from French-speaking inhabitants of Acadia, a region of eastern Canada.) She grew up in Lafayette, Louisiana, the heart of Cajun country. Her father owned a carpeting business and once served as president of the Louisiana Association of Tax Administrators. Her mother, a homemaker, raised the Catholic couple's eight children. Blanco attended Coteau Elementary School, in New Iberia, before transferring to Mount Carmel Academy, also in New Iberia, where she completed her secondary education. She was reportedly an outgoing and confident child. One classmate at Coteau Elementary School recalled to Louis Rom that it was Blanco's encouragement that helped her to stand up to a bully who had continually tormented her. Blanco graduated from Mount Carmel Academy in 1960 and enrolled at the University of Louisiana at Lafayette, where she earned a B.S. degree in business education and met her husband, Raymond S. Blanco, then a football coach and teacher at Catholic High School in New Iberia. The two were married in 1964, the year she graduated from the university. Blanco then began teaching business classes at Breaux Bridge High School, near her birthplace, Coteau. Several weeks later, in an example of the prevailing attitudes of the period, she was forced to resign when she began showing signs of being pregnant with her and her husband's first child.

Before entering the world of public service, in addition to her teaching stint Blanco ran her own polling and marketing research firm, worked as a bookkeeper, and, from 1979 to 1980, served as a district manager for the state Census Office. In 1983 she ran successfully for the office of state representative of District 45, defeating her female opponent, Jan Heymann, with 60 percent of the vote, despite Heymann's having outspent Blanco by a large margin during the campaign. Blanco's victory made her the first woman elected to represent the people of Lafayette County in the state legislature. She served in that capacity from 1984 to 1989, during which time she was a member of the state legislature's house education committee and transportation, highways, and public-works committee. She chose to serve on the education committee "because it was what I knew," Blanco told Rom, and took a seat on the transportation committee "because I didn't know anything about it. That's how you learn." Rom described Blanco's state legislative career as "unremarkable," adding that she "proposed several bills with little fanfare and kept her differences with other representatives professional." Echoing the latter point, John Alario, a fellow Democratic representative, told Rom, "She disagreed with folks but understood to put it on the side when the fight was over."

In 1989 Blanco became the first woman elected to the Louisiana Public Service Commission (PSC), a powerful independent regulatory agency that works to ensure that utilities in the state provide the public with safe, reliable, and reasonably priced services. Blanco served as PSC chairperson from 1993 to 1994. As a public-service commissioner, Blanco helped to establish the state's Tele-Rely Center, which allows hearing-impaired people to communicate with the rest of society by receiving their messages via teletype, then relaying them to the intended parties—for example, relatives, delivery people, or bank employees. (That project had special significance for Blanco, as she has two nephews who are deaf.) Blanco left the PSC in 1995. Concurrently with her work for the PSC, from 1989 to 1995 she also sat on the Democratic State Central Committee.

Blanco was elected lieutenant governor, the state's second-highest office, in 1995. She served two terms in that office, winning her reelection bid, in 1999, by capturing the votes of an impressive 80 percent of the state's electorate. As lieutenant to Republican governor Mike Foster, Blanco was the direct supervisor of Louisiana's Department of Culture, Recreation and Tourism, which includes the offices of State Parks, State Museums, State Libraries, Cultural Development, and Tourism. In the *Almanac of American Politics 2000*, Michael Barone and Grant Ujifusa described Louisiana's economy as being "like that of an underdeveloped country, based on pumping minerals out of soggy ground, shipping grain produced in the vast hinterland drained by its great river, and increasingly dependent in recent years on businesses typical of picturesque Third World countries—tourism and gambling." In light of such conditions, one of Blanco's main tasks was to draw visitors to Louisiana by making the state an appealing travel destination. According to the Louisiana state Web site, during Blanco's stint as the state's tourism chief, tourism increased by 41 percent, leading to an extra $2.5 billion in the state's coffers and the creation of more than 20,000 new jobs. The state government invested in the hotel industry and in the development of a large, family-oriented state park system, which will eventually comprise a number of professional-quality golf courses to be known collectively as the Audubon Golf Trail. As lieutenant governor Blanco also served as the chief administrator of the Louisiana Serve Commission, which oversaw 64 national service projects across the state and involved more than 13,000 volunteer workers, and the Louisiana Retirement Development Commission, which promoted Louisiana as a good place for retirees to live.

Though many polls taken in the days before the 2003 gubernatorial election had her trailing, Blanco defeated her young Republican opponent, the Indian-American Bobby Jindal—a Rhodes Scholar who became Louisiana's secretary of health and hospitals at age 24—with 52 percent of the vote. History, among other things, seemed to work against Jindal, as Louisiana has had only three Republican governors since 1877. (Jindal would have been the first nonwhite governor in the Deep South since P.B.S. Pinchback, the son of an emancipated slave, served as acting governor of Louisiana for 35 days in 1872 and 1873.) Voter turnout for the election was unexpectedly high, as more than half of the state's 2.7 million registered voters cast ballots. As quoted on the Democratic National Committee Web site, the Baton Rouge *Advocate* gave as a reason for the high voter participation "Blanco's late appeal to women, especially on the health issues." In part, that appeal had been made through two large mailings, financed by the Democratic National Committee, which were sent out to voters in the final week of the campaign and specifically targeted women. Jim Brown, writing for the Web site politicsla.com (November 20, 2003), noted that Blanco had campaigned throughout the state for more than a year and a half, much longer than any of her opponents. "No one shook more hands, and made more individual contact than did Blanco," Brown wrote. "And she generally made a positive impression." Blanco even won a majority of votes in traditionally Republican northern Louisiana, in part, according to Brown, because she "wasn't threatening, she smiled a lot, and hey, she even had a hunting license." Many observers opined that the race had been decided only in the final two days before the election, and Blanco credited her final debate appearance with helping her to win. During that debate, when asked to identify the defining moment in her life, Blanco tearfully related the story of how her then–19-year-old son, Ben, died in 1997 after a large weight dangling from a crane fell on him as he was cutting up a barge as part of his summer job. "I've always felt or found in a big campaign, people eventually look for humanity," Blanco told Melinda Deslatte for the Associated Press (November 16, 2003), referring to her decision to share that personal tragedy with the public. (As of October 2004 there were eight other female governors in the United States: Democrats Jennifer Granholm of Michigan, Ruth Minner of Delaware, Janet Napolitano of Arizona, and Kathleen Sebelius of Kansas, and Republicans M. Jodi Rell of Connecticut, Linda Lingle of Hawaii, Judy Martz of Montana, and Olene S. Walker of Utah.)

In her inaugural address Blanco gave special mention to the goals of improving the state's health-care and education systems and its business climate. She has promised to continue the outgoing two-term governor Mike Foster's work of creating an accountability system for the state's public schools and investing in higher education. She said that her administration would differ from Foster's, however, in its emphasis on accessibility. Specifically, Blanco plans to travel around the state more than Foster did in order to make herself available to local civic leaders, and she stressed the importance of sending her staff and cabinet members out into the public domain to bring back ideas for improving the state's governance. "We have a lot of talent around Louisiana," the governor-elect told Hill. "Sometimes, we get so internally focused here in Baton Rouge that we forget there are people out there who may have answers, but they have never been engaged."

Whereas Foster had made many personnel changes when he took over for the four-term governor Edwin Edwards, Blanco has kept many of Foster's cabinet staff members, including Adam Knapp, policy director on economic development, and Andy Kopplin, Foster's chief of staff. Alex Aichinger, a political scientist at Northwestern State University, commented to Hill that Blanco is "going after competence in her staff. It seems she wants to surround herself with established figures in Louisiana politics, regardless of party affiliation—people who understand the system." Offering a similar observation, State Senator Don Hines told Hill that Blanco's choice of staff revealed that she is "trying to pick the best person and is neither partisan nor vindictive." In another comment that highlighted Blanco's inclusive, consensus-building governing style, Pearson Cross, a political scientist at the University of Louisiana at Monroe, told Hill, "I expect her to spend a great deal more time [than the former governor] bringing warring factions together. . . . Kathleen Blanco is more likely to create majorities on bills rather than only work [toward passing] those that already have majorities."

In January 2004, just days after being sworn in as governor, Blanco met at the airport President George W. Bush, who was making an appearance in New Orleans to honor the legacy of the civil rights leader Martin Luther King Jr. Riding into the city with the president, Blanco seized the opportunity to present him with a "wish list" for Louisiana. The list included requests for federal funding for coastal restoration in the state; the expediting of the transfer to Louisiana of 14,000 acres of federally owned land (site of the defunct Louisiana Army Ammunition Plant, near the town of Minden); and the federal government's assistance in improving or maintaining Louisiana's sugar, shrimp, and aerospace industries. As quoted by John Hill in the Shreveport, Louisiana, *Times* (January 16, 2004), commenting on his talk with Blanco, President Bush said, "We had a good discussion. She is not a shrinking violet in describing what she would like to see."

The economy of northern Louisiana suffered a setback in early 2004 when the State Farm Insurance Co., the largest private employer in that part of the state, closed its offices in the city of Monroe. In response, Blanco began to contact businesses and site-selection companies to inform them that the two office buildings formerly occupied by State Farm were available, and that the more than 1,000 former State Farm employees were ready to work. Reporting the story, John Hill wrote for the Shreveport *Times* (February 6, 2004), "The State Farm debacle is a lesson for the Legislature for the need to make Louisiana more business-friendly." Hill pointed to the state tax on corporate borrowing for capital and the state sales tax on machinery and manufacturing equipment as obstacles to achieving that goal. Blanco has repeatedly said that she intends to reduce the number of such obstacles to conducting business in the state.

True to her Louisiana roots, Blanco speaks the French-Canadian language of her Cajun ancestors and is said to love crab meat, especially boiled. She has named as the person she most admires the for-

mer U.S. representative from Louisiana and U.S. ambassador to the Vatican Lindy Boggs. Asked why, Blanco told Hill that Boggs's "compassion for those in need is always evident in all that she does." Blanco is a member of the American Association of University Women and the United Way. She is a former reporter, treasurer, and president of the University of Southwestern Louisiana Women's Club. Blanco's husband, Raymond, is the vice president of student affairs at the University of Louisiana. The couple have five surviving children—Karmen, Monique, Nicole, Ray, and Pilar—and five grandchildren.

—C.F.T.

Suggested Reading: (Acadiana, Lousiana) *Times* Jan. 8, 2003, with photo; *Advertiser* Jan. 11, 2004, with photo; *Christian Science Monitor* p2 Nov. 17, 2003, with photo; Louisiana state Web site; *Who's Who in America 2001*; *Who's Who in American Politics 2001–2002*

J. Henry Fair/Courtesy of ICM Artists

Blythe, Stephanie

1970– Opera singer

Address: c/o ICM Artists, 40 W. 57th St., New York, NY 10019

In writing an article for *Opera News* (October 2001), Ira Siff, the artistic director of the New York–based La Gran Scena Opera Company, recalled a moment during a performance of Benjamin Britten's opera *Peter Grimes* that he attended with a friend in 1996: "When the young mezzo performing the small role of Auntie began to sing, my friend and I both popped up in our seats, like two pieces of toast, and began leafing frantically through the program for the cast list. She and I both knew immediately that we were hearing an 'important' voice. The Met's Auntie that night was Stephanie Blythe." That same year Blythe completed the highly selective Lindemann Young Artist Development Program at the Metropolitan Opera House, in New York City. Three years later she won the Richard Tucker Award, the most coveted prize available to budding American singers and one that, when presented, "all but heralds the next great American opera superstar," as the Richard Tucker Foundation Web site puts it. Not yet 35, Blythe has joined the ranks of the most celebrated and popular mezzo-sopranos of her generation. (Occasionally she has been identified as a contralto.) She has earned enthusiastic critical praise for her vocal and dramatic interpretations of an unusual variety of operatic roles, ranging from that of the passionate, cigarette-smoking seductress in the title role of Georges Bizet's *Carmen*, to the vengeful, uncompromising Fricka, the goddess of hearth and family and the wife of Wotan, the king of the gods, in Richard Wagner's "Ring" cycle, to Maffio Orsini, a male carouser, in Donizetti's *Lucrezia Borgia*. (By her own account, Blythe loves to play so-called trouser roles.) In *Opera News* (June 2001), the magazine's editor in chief, F. Paul Driscoll, wrote of Blythe, "Her instrument is gorgeous—sunny in texture, generous in scope, noble in feeling—and her technique rock-solid, but in a mezzo-rich marketplace . . . what sets her apart is her particular brand of wit and intelligence. Blythe's brains are evident not only onstage (in her surgically precise comic timing, for example) but off, in her unerring ability to choose the correct role at the correct time." Two of Blythe's signature roles are those of Mistress Quickly in Giuseppe Verdi's *Falstaff* and Cornelia in George Frideric Handel's *Giulio Cesare*. She has also earned plaudits as a recitalist, offering exceedingly varied programs that display not only her prodigious gifts as a singer of operatic arias and other classical works but also her outstanding skills as a performer of popular songs. After she ended such a recital at the concert hall of the 92nd Street YM-YWHA in New York City in 2001, Driscoll reported, he overheard another attendee, a newspaper critic, say, "Can you think of any cabaret singer who could do what she just did? My God, if she ever decides to ditch opera, and I hope she doesn't, she could make a bloody fortune doing cabaret!" "Loving different kinds of music and wanting to sing it is no big deal, as far as I'm concerned," Blythe told Driscoll. "I mean, I worship and adore [the late American popular singer] Sammy Davis, Jr., and I think that [the Italian opera singer] Giulietta Simionato is fabulous, too."

A robust woman with a prototypical opera-singer's body, Blythe bucks the stereotype of the demanding, self-important opera diva, impressing interviewers with her openness, forthrightness, and down-to-earth perspective on her vocation. "I do my job. I sing, act and listen as best I can," she told Melinda Bargreen for the *Seattle Times* (January 4, 2004). When an interviewer from the Crane School of Music at the State University of New York (SUNY) at Potsdam asked her, "What advice would you give students interested in a performing career?," she answered, as quoted at potsdam.edu, "Get a good teacher. Find the right repertoire. Learn how to sing. Practice daily. Listen daily. Read about everything—art, history, music, great literature, everything. . . . Go see live performances as often as possible. Don't just say, 'I love it' or 'I hate it'—figure out why you love it or not. Don't take theory for granted, and for that matter, don't take any class for granted—be assured, someday it *will* come in handy. *Don't underestimate technique*—you will never be anything but 'good' without it. And my favorite—learn who you are."

Stephanie Blythe was born in 1970 in Mongaup Valley, a village in the Catskill Mountains, in New York State. (The "th" in her surname sounds like the soft "th" in "thin," not the hard "th" in "they.") Mongaup Valley is in the heart of what was once known as the borscht belt, an area dotted with resort hotels; most of them catered to Jewish urbanites, offering typical Jewish cuisine (borscht was a popular soup) and entertainment by such comics as Red Buttons, Henny Youngman, and Buddy Hackett. The singer's father, James Blythe, was a professional musician; he played clarinet, flute, and various horns as a member of a local hotel band. Her mother, Ingeborg, a native of Germany, was a professional translator of German to English. According to Blythe, her mother is tone deaf, but she enjoyed listening to recordings of classical music at home. Her mother has recalled that when, as a child, her daughter heard the renowned tenor Placido Domingo sing on a PBS TV broadcast, she exclaimed at the beauty of the sound. Since 1985 Blythe's parents have run a numismatics business, selling collector coins by mail order.

Blythe attended Duggan Elementary School in Bethel, near Mongaup Valley, whose curriculum included music classes in which the pupils learned songs. "It's incredibly important to be exposed to all that music," Blythe told Steve Israel for the *Times Herald-Record* (March 29, 2002), a Catskills newspaper. "It teaches you focus; it opens another world." As a student at Monticello High School, in a larger nearby town, Blythe benefited from an excellent music program and the guidance and encouragement of two teachers: Stephen Rovitz, who directed the program, and Martin Banner, the choral director. She played the flute in the student band and orchestra and sang in the school chorus. "She was a very quick learner, very good with foreign languages, and had a great flexibility in her style," Banner recalled, according to an article on the Monticello Schools Web page. "It was great to watch her vocal talents blossom." She also sang with a classmate's barbershop quartet and performed in school productions of such musicals as *Annie Get Your Gun, Carousel*, and *Hello, Dolly!* At 16, with her class, she attended an opera for the first time: a mounting of Giacomo Puccini's *La Bohème* at the Met. "I was completely blown away," she told Dinitia Smith for the *New York Times* (October 9, 2003). During that period she toyed with the idea of pursuing a career in musical theater; Banner and Rovitz suggested that, instead, she aim for the operatic stage.

After she graduated from high school, in 1987, Blythe enrolled at the Crane School of Music at SUNY–Potsdam (Banner's alma mater), where at first she concentrated in music education. A stint of student teaching at an elementary school convinced her that teaching young children did not suit her. After taking a class in creative writing, she changed her major to English, thinking that she might write professionally someday. A turning point came when she read "The Loss of the Creature," by the philosophical essayist and novelist Walker Percy, which contends that spontaneous and self-directed learning is incomparably more valuable than classroom instruction. (For example, according to Percy, a student in a school laboratory who is presented with the corpse of a fish for dissection, along with written instructions and suitable instruments, will discover far less about the creature than a person who, out of curiosity, closely examines the body of a fish of that species that has washed up on a beach.) Percy's argument awakened in Blythe new feelings about music and herself as a musician; as she wrote in an essay, as quoted by Dinitia Smith, it helped her to "break out of my restrictive learning pattern and discover the creature all over again. Music was no longer a technical exercise." She soon switched her major to music.

As she had in high school, Blythe benefited from "one-on-one nurturing" at Crane, as she put it in her interview for potsdam.edu. She also profited from listening to many recordings of famous singers in the collection of the school library and from participating in productions of the Crane Opera Ensemble. "The most important thing I learned about being in the theater is that I adore the process of putting something together," she told the interviewer for potsdam.edu. "Learning to work with colleagues is extremely important—collaboration is an art in itself. I also learned to be *prepared*. And believe me, I didn't learn that lesson the easy way. I learned to be proud of myself and what I can accomplish, as well as what a group can accomplish as a community. There are many things that must come together to do a successful production. At Crane, I learned about everything, from costumes to sets to acting to singing. One of the most important things I learned was to keep my ears and eyes open—watch, watch, watch. . . . I learned to believe in myself as a singing-actress—not every school affords a student that much time on the stage—and that's where you learn the most." In 1993 Blythe earned a B.M. degree from Crane. During the summers of 1993 and 1994, she was a Tanglewood Fellow at the Tanglewood Festival, in Lenox, Massachusetts.

Earlier, as an undergraduate, Blythe had studied with the voice teacher Patricia Misslin (who some years earlier at Crane had taught Renée Fleming, now a celebrated soprano). Under Misslin's tutelage, she began intensive study of five foreign languages and learned arias in each of them, to prepare for the Metropolitan Opera's National Council Auditions. The auditions, held every year, attract thousands of singers between the ages of 20 and 30 in 800 districts throughout the U.S. and Canada. District winners advance to any of 50 regional competitions. Those are followed by semifinals and then finals, at the end of which 10 singers remain. In 1994 Blythe was among those 10, all of whom performed with the Metropolitan Opera Orchestra in the ultimate contest, which was broadcast on the Met's radio network, and she emerged among the five grand winners. In addition to a $15,000 award, she gained entrance into the Met's Lindemann Young Artist Development Program, which provides training in music, languages, and the dramatic arts and funds private voice lessons. She also won the opportunity to perform at the Met.

Blythe made her Met debut during the 1994–95 season, when she sang the role of the offstage celestial Voice in a production of Wagner's *Parsifal* starring Placido Domingo. At a post-performance cast party, she recalled to Dinitia Smith, Domingo said to her, "Stephanie, when I hear how you sing at the end of the first act, I know how I must sing in the second." "I felt knighted," she told Smith. One day in 1996, while Blythe was still participating in the young-artist program, she replaced an ill Marilyn Horne in the role of Mistress Quickly in Giuseppe Verdi's *Falstaff* (which is based on Shakespeare's *The Merry Wives of Windsor*) at the Met. Blythe's outstanding performance soon led to her being cast in other roles, at both the Met and other opera houses, among them the title role in Jacques Offenbach's *La Grande Duchesse de Gérolstein*, Isabella in Gioacchino Rossini's *L'Italiana in Algeri*, Orsini in Gaetano Donizetti's *Lucrezia Borgia*, the Mother in Engelbert Humperdinck's *Hansel und Gretel*, Ludmilla in Bedrich Smetana's *The Bartered Bride*, Mamma Lucia in Pietro Mascagni's *Cavalleria Rusticana*, Baba the Turk in Igor Stravinsky's *The Rake's Progress*, Fricka in Wagner's *Das Rheingold* and *Die Walküre*, and Auntie in Benjamin Britten's *Peter Grimes*. "I've been very fortunate in that I've been able to develop and build my career at a pretty steady pace," Blythe told James D. Watts Jr. for the *Tulsa World* (October 10, 1999), an Oklahoma paper.

Two of Blythe's most celebrated roles are that of Cornelia in George Frideric Handel's *Giulio Cesare* and the title character in Bizet's *Carmen*. The plot of the former comes from Roman history, presenting the intertwining stories of the virtuous Caesar, his lover Cleopatra, and her evil brother Ptolemy; Cornelia is Ptolemy's noble wife. Blythe first played Cornelia in 1999 at the Met, in a breakthrough performance; the countertenor David Daniels was cast as Sesto, Cornelia's son. In a review for the *New York Times* (April 12, 1999), Bernard Holland wrote, "If there is a musical memory I shall take away from this season, it will be [Daniels] and Ms. Blythe in their duet of leave-taking at the end of Act I." Blythe described the production to Brian Kellow for *Opera News* (October 1, 1999) as a "life-changer. David Daniels and I had this wonderful chemistry. I love working with him. At the last two performances, when we sang that duet, it was so hot [that is, emotional] that when the curtain came down we just threw ourselves into each other's arms, you know? Because we felt that what was happening in the opera was really happening." Describing the same duet to Driscoll, she said, "That moment in the score really took us both . . . out of ourselves. I can't think of a better way of explaining it. The voices, our voices, the overtones, came together so completely that even I couldn't tell who was singing when. I couldn't even tell who was breathing." In *Opera News*, Ira Siff noted the "startling absence in the Met of coughing, purses clicking, candy wrappers or cell phones for five minutes" during the duet—"a tribute unto itself."

Blythe's first performance as Carmen took place at the Tulsa Opera House in 1999. Playing to packed audiences, both the singer and the production received rave reviews. Blythe's performance played a part in her receipt of the 1999 Richard Tucker Award (named for a legendary American tenor), which came with a cash grant of $30,000. (Blythe was not present at the award ceremony, held in November 1999; she was rehearsing for a production of the opera *Falstaff* in Paris, France.) Her portrayal of Carmen was so powerful that, when the general director of the Seattle Opera, Speight Jenkins, heard her sing at a matinee performance, he hired her on the spot to appear in the company's 2004 production of the opera. That production sold out all 12 performances before opening night, forcing the Seattle Opera to add on a 13th. "Carmen should become one of [Blythe's] signature pieces," the music critic R. M. Campbell wrote for the *Seattle Post-Intelligencer* (January 12, 2004). "Her singing is supple and seductive, rich in color and nuance. It is the rare singer who can play a part as fully in the voice as Blythe. The quietest of pianissimos are at her disposal, and she uses them, with great effect. She also has sheer power at her disposal. Blythe possesses genuine temperament, coupled with intelligence and wit." Almost without exception, Blythe has earned similarly superlative reviews of her performances of other roles.

Blythe has performed in concert in performances of Mendelssohn's *Elijah*, with the Atlanta Symphony; Mahler's Symphony no. 8, with the Minnesota Orchestra; Verdi's *Requiem*, with the Orchestra of the Age of Enlightenment; Bizet's *L'Enfance du Christ*, with the Orchestra of St. Luke's; Richard Danielpour's *American Requiem*,

with the Pacific Symphony Orchestra; Handel's *Messiah*, with the National Symphony (Washington, D.C.); and a song medley, with the Gay Gotham Chorus (New York City). Her debut album, *Handel and Bach Arias*, recorded with the Ensemble Orchestre de Paris with John Nelson conducting, was released by Virgin Classics in 2001; it includes duets with David Daniels. The composer Alan Louis Smith wrote *Vignettes: Ellis Island, A Song Cycle in Six Parts* (1999) specifically for Blythe.

Melinda Bargreen described Blythe as "a big, tall, voluptuous woman who probably is closer to the 19th-century ideal of beauty than are the size-2 actresses and celebrities who define our contemporary society's aesthetic." A natural comedian, she has often triggered belly laughs among her audiences during recitals. Blythe is married to David Smith-Larsen, a professional wrestler turned actor. The couple live on the Upper East Side of Manhattan. In her leisure time Blythe prefers to listen to recordings not of opera but of Cuban jazz, Brazilian music, and the singing of Ella Fitzgerald, Sammy Davis Jr., and Frank Sinatra. When F. Paul Driscoll asked her whether, having sung the role of Berta, a housekeeper, in Rossini's *Barber of Seville*, she might want to take on that of the female lead, Rosina, Blythe answered, "Nah. She's just not me. . . . She's just sitting there waiting for something to happen to her. And that's *really* not me."

—H.T.

Suggested Reading: (Catskills/Hudson Valley, New York State) *Times Herald-Record* (on-line) Mar. 29, 2002; FanFaire.com; *New York Times* E p1+ Oct. 9, 2003, with photos; *Opera News* p24+ June 2001, with photo; Richard Tucker Music Foundation Web site

Selected Operas: *Carmen*; *Falstaff*; *Giulio Cesare*; *L'Italiana in Algeri*; *Peter Grimes*; *The Rake's Progress*; *Das Rheingold*

Bontecou, Lee

(BON-tuh-coo)

Jan. 15, 1931– Artist

Address: c/o Michael Rosenfeld Gallery, 24 W. 57th St., New York, NY 10019

During the 1960s Lee Bontecou was one of the most talked-about young artists, and arguably the most influential woman, in the world of modern art. A regular at Leo Castelli's legendary New York gallery, she was best known for creating massive abstract wall sculptures made from welded steel and incorporating various fabrics and other materials; most of these sculptures featured menacing black holes that critics likened to the orifices of the

Josh Titus

Lee Bontecou

body. "The power of Bontecou's reliefs is remarkably single," the critic Donald Judd wrote in 1965, as quoted by Elizabeth A. T. Smith in *Art in America* (September 1993). "The three primary aspects, the scale, the structure, and the image, are simple, definite, and powerful. . . . The work asserts its own existence, form and power. It becomes an object in its own right." In 1971 Bontecou abruptly disappeared from the art scene, moving with her husband, the painter Bill Giles, to a farmhouse in rural Pennsylvania; as she explained recently, she wanted the freedom to create her art without the pressure of having to exhibit it on a regular basis. Although she continued to produce new work, it was not shown publicly, and for three decades after she left New York her only major exhibition was a mid-career retrospective at Chicago's Museum of Contemporary Art in 1972. In 2003, however, a major show featuring Bontecou's old and new work was launched at the UCLA Hammer Museum, in Los Angeles, California; from there it moved to the Museum of Contemporary Art and then to the Museum of Modern Art in New York City. The art critic Christopher Knight wrote for the *Los Angeles Times* (October 7, 2003) that the show "not only meets expectations—it actually exceeds them," noting that "Bontecou's art is a masterful tour de force, mesmerizing and poignant."

Lee Bontecou was born on January 15, 1931 in Providence, Rhode Island, and raised in Bronxville and various other towns in Westchester County, New York. Her father, Russell Bontecou, was in the aluminum-canoe business; during World War II her mother worked on submarine transmitters. Bontecou and her older brother, Hank, spent their summers in Nova Scotia, Canada, at the home of

their maternal grandmother. "The house was on a small island shaped like an 'H'," Bontecou told Calvin Tomkins in an interview for the *New Yorker* (August 4, 2003). "The roads were all dirt, and the cows were free to go anywhere they wanted. The dogs were free, the chickens were free, and the children were free." Bontecou attended Bradford Junior College, in Haverhill, Massachusetts; while there, she took several art courses and began to think seriously about becoming an artist. After graduating, in 1952, she studied with the artists John Havannes and William Zorach at the Art Students League, in the New York City borough of Manhattan. Her parents helped her out financially during her first year there, but thereafter she insisted on supporting herself. During this time she spent a summer at the Skowhegan School of Painting and Sculpture, in Skowhegan, Maine, on a scholarship.

In 1957 Bontecou traveled as a Fulbright fellow to Rome, Italy, where she was inspired by the earthy, fiery colors of the Spanish Baroque period. She created semi-abstract representations of birds, animals, and people out of terra cotta over reinforced-concrete bases, as well as several sculptures out of bronze. She also discovered a way to use an acetylene torch that caused it to emit a rich black soot, with which she began to experiment in several large drawings. Bontecou told Tomkins that she thought of those drawings as "worldscapes." "The black opened up something for me," she explained. "It was so deep—it gave you a feeling of outer space. I just knew where I was going, even though I didn't."

When she returned to the United States, in 1958, Bontecou moved into a loft on the Lower East Side of Manhattan with a friend from Skowhegan. A year later she received a Lewis Comfort Tiffany Foundation fellowship for her bronze sculptures of animals and birds, which she showed at her first solo exhibition, at Gallery G in Manhattan in 1959. Stuart Preston of the *New York Times* (February 8, 1959) described her as an "interesting young metal sculptor" and wrote of her work, "She abstracts from nature in an imposing, formal style of armor-plating which gives [the bird sculptures] a rigid, rather menacing, prehistoric appearance as well as lending them the ceremonial grace of ancient Chinese bronzes."

Bontecou next began making the abstract, canvas-and-steel wall sculptures for which she is best known. Consisting of beige, brown, and black canvas stretched across steel structures and held in place with wire, the pieces are best described as massive, three-dimensional wall reliefs punctuated by cavernous black spaces, which often enclose either bent band saws, giving the impression of teeth; army-surplus items she had found in second-hand stores; or other found items, such as fan blades. In a review of the 2003 retrospective for the *San Diego Union-Tribune* (October 19, 2003), Robert L. Pincus offered this description of her wall reliefs: "The shapes are both natural and mechanical.

Stitches in copper wire give them some bristle. And if you look closely, you'll discern faces within their forms, both from the front and the side. Perhaps their most dramatic features are dark cavities, black holes of seemingly limitless depth that are lined with soot." Viewers often found the gaping holes that punctuated the wall reliefs particularly unsettling, likening them to empty eye sockets or jagged mouths. As quoted in *Art in America* (September 1993), the critic Carter Ratcliff wrote in an essay for Bontecou's 1972 retrospective that one senses the "distinctively animal—not vegetable— quality of Bontecou's folded, nestled, layered forms. Hence the powerful specificity of the openings they reveal—eyes, mouths, vaginas." The artist's work was sought so enthusiastically by galleries and museums that she was forced to stop selling them in order to have enough available for her first exhibit at Leo Castelli's gallery, in the fall of 1960. In its review of the show, *Art in America* described the artist as "the find of the year," as quoted by Tomkins. A year later she put on a second exhibit at Castelli's gallery, and in 1962 she won second prize at the Corcoran Biennial in Washington, D.C. During that decade her work was featured regularly at Leo Castelli's and appeared in three of the Whitney Museum of American Art's annual exhibitions in New York. It was also shown at two of the most important and influential shows of the decade: "The Art of Assemblage" in 1961 and "Americans 1963," both at the Museum of Modern Art, in Manhattan.

Bontecou's pieces were unlike either minimalism or pop, the two dominant trends in the art world during the 1960s, and their huge scale, asymmetrical composition, fragmented forms, and often monochromatic palette also made them utterly unlike anything else being created at the time. Some critics thought the pieces alluded to aggressive female sexuality; others found them reminiscent of science fiction or suggestive of post-nuclear craters. As quoted in *World Artists 1950-1980* (1984), Bontecou offered this explanation in the catalogue for the "Americans 1963" group exhibition: "My concern is to build things that express our relation to this country—to other countries—to this world—in terms of myself. To glimpse some of the fear, hope, ugliness, beauty and mystery that exists in us all and what hangs over all the young people today. The individual is welcome to see and feel in them what he wishes in terms of himself."

In 1964 Bontecou created a 20-foot relief sculpture for the New York State Theater at Lincoln Center, in Manhattan. To fashion the piece, she welded pieces of metal to form a curved frame; she then attached canvas strips to the frame with wire. In order to create bulges in the work, she affixed to the canvas various fiberglass forms that were then covered with more canvas or with white paint. (The canvas came from random pieces she found in the street and from an old fire hose.) When the work was nearly completed, she covered various sec-

without throwing a dreaded "pick," as interceptions are often called. During the regular season Brady threw for 2,843 yards, while completing an outstanding 63.9 percent of his pass attempts (a Patriots team record), and recorded 18 touchdowns and 12 interceptions. His passer rating—a number that takes into account several key statistics and reflects a quarterback's overall performance—was an excellent 86.5. That year he played in the Pro Bowl, the NFL's equivalent of an all-star game. The team ended the regular season with 11 wins against five losses. In the play-offs the Patriots won a tough contest in the snow against the Oakland Raiders, then bested the Pittsburgh Steelers in the Conference Championship, earning the right to play the favored St. Louis Rams in Super Bowl XXXVI before more than 70,000 fans in New Orleans.

In the tightly fought championship game the Rams scored in the closing minutes to tie the score at 17. But Brady, responding superbly to the pressure, drove his team's offense 53 yards down the field, far enough for the Patriots' Adam Vinatieri to kick a winning field goal on the last play of the game. The Patriots had won the first Super Bowl in team history, and Brady had become, at 24 years of age, not only a star of the sport but the youngest quarterback ever to win an NFL championship. The previous record was held by Joe Montana, who in 1981 led the San Francisco 49ers to the championship at 25. Bill Walsh, Montana's former coach, has said that Brady's skills and game-time execution are the closest that he has seen to those of Montana. Brady himself, however, has downplayed such comparisons, telling Mike Lopresti for the Gannett News Service, as the article appeared on the Web site of the Asheville, North Carolina, *Citizen-Times* (February 2, 2004), "[Montana is] the benchmark for a quarterback in this league, and the way he succeeded and thrived in tight situations. There's no way I'm close to that. Hopefully one day I'm on that level. But no way now." Before Montana, the record for the youngest quarterback to win the Super Bowl was held by Joe Namath, who led the New York Jets to championship glory in 1969. Brady has also been compared by some sportswriters to Namath, who, like Brady, was a good-looking bachelor and a confident team leader.

Bill Beuttler wrote for *Boston Magazine* (August 2002, on-line) that in the wake of Brady's performance in Super Bowl XXXVI, the media focus on the young quarterback had been "pretty much nonstop. . . . Brady's pursuers include a relentless swarm of promoters, sponsors, reporters, and—assuming you believe the gossip columns—a parade of willing women." In the weeks that followed the Patriots' victory, among other signs of the quarterback's newfound celebrity, *People* magazine placed Brady on its 2002 list of the "50 Most Beautiful People"; a photograph of a bare-chested Brady was featured on the cover of *Sports Illustrated* (April 15, 2002) under the words "A Whirlwind Off-Season for the New Prince of the NFL"; he sparred playfully with the boxing legend Muhammad Ali at a fund-raiser; and the real-estate mogul Donald Trump flew Brady on his private jet to Gary, Indiana, so that the football star could help him judge the 2002 Miss USA contest. "These last few weeks have been a whirlwind, and I'm trying to learn as I go along," Brady told Silver. "I think I'm a pretty good quarterback, but there's all this other stuff that goes along with being a very recognizable person, and I suck at it. This is my new reality, I guess, and it's knocking me down." In the face of such potential distractions, Brady remained focused on football. "Why do some guys have one great year and then play so badly the next?" he asked Beuttler rhetorically. "Well, now I think I know why—because there are so many things that can take you away from what you need to do to focus on your job. My biggest fear is to end up being a one-hit wonder." The Patriots player Larry Izzo told Beuttler, "[Brady] works as seriously as anybody out here. He's here at seven in the morning throughout the off-season, with [backup quarterback] Damon Huard—throwing the ball, running. He works like he's a sixth-round draft pick out of Michigan still, not the Super Bowl MVP. And that's good. When you see a guy like that—a leader of your football team—doing all the hard stuff the hard way, you get a level of respect from everybody in the locker room."

Brady started all 16 regular-season games for the Patriots in 2002, again achieving excellent numbers, including a career-high 3,764 yards passing, completion of 62 percent of his pass attempts, a career-high 28 touchdowns, and just 14 interceptions. The Patriots as a team, however, did not fare well, stumbling to a 9–7 record and failing to qualify for the play-offs. In 2003, however, Brady and the Patriots returned to championship form, posting a league-best 14–2 regular-season record and recording a 15-game winning streak (which included the team's run through the play-offs and the Super Bowl game), the longest in the NFL in 31 years. In the regular season Brady threw for 3,620 yards, 23 touchdowns, and 12 interceptions. His passer rating was 85.9, 10th best in the league, which, while respectable, did not reflect the fact that Brady had led his team to victory more often than any other team's quarterback. On their march through the 2003 play-offs, Brady and the Patriots defeated the Tennessee Titans and the Indianapolis Colts, who were led by the quarterbacks Steve McNair and Peyton Manning, respectively, that year's NFL co-MVPs. (Brady finished third in the voting for league MVP.) The Patriots safety Rodney Harrison told Goodman, "No one ever puts [Brady] in a class of the Peyton Mannings and the Steve McNairs"—who are said to have stronger arms, to be better runners, and to be more talented overall. "But that's fine because when you keep taking him for granted, he keeps kicking you right in the butt." Speaking of Brady, Peyton Manning himself told Bill Williamson for the *Pioneer Press* (January 31, 2004), "He is one of the best quarterbacks in the game because of the way he does his job. He uses his head as well as anyone and just goes out and wins games."

In Super Bowl XXXVIII the Patriots again bested their opponents in a closely contested game, defeating the Carolina Panthers, 32–29, on another last-second field goal by Adam Vinatieri. Brady had played another superb game, completing 32 of 48 pass attempts, two of them resulting in touchdowns, for 354 yards. He had also made history again, this time as the youngest quarterback to win two Super Bowls, joining the rarefied company of quarterbacks who have won more than one NFL championship—a list that includes Joe Montana, Bart Starr, Terry Bradshaw, Troy Aikman, John Elway, and Roger Staubach, all of whom are either in the NFL Hall of Fame or among the strongest candidates for induction. Brady's career record in December and January, when the most crucial contests are waged, is an outstanding 17–2. With Brady leading them, the Patriots have made more than a dozen fourth-quarter comebacks, are 15–1 in games decided by seven points or fewer and 7–0 in overtime games, and have never lost a play-off game—all of which points to Brady's ability to perform at his best when the stakes are highest. In October 2004 the Patriots celebrated their 20th consecutive victory, an NFL record. With a 5–0 record for the 2004 season as of the end of that month, the team also broke the league record of 17 straight regular-season wins, set in 1933–34 by the Chicago Bears.

Brady enjoys playing golf and is rumored to be an Internet addict. He had a speaking part in the Farrelly brothers' movie *Stuck on You* (2003). Several weeks before the Patriots' Super Bowl victory in February 2004, Brady attended President George W. Bush's State of the Union address at the president's invitation. Over the years he has been linked romantically to a number of women, including the actress Tara Reid; as of February 2004 Brady was rumored to be dating the actress Bridget Moynahan.

Brady is six feet four inches tall and a lean, muscular 225 pounds. Photo- and telegenic, he has blue eyes, a bright smile, and a cleft chin. Referring to the methodical and precise way he goes about defeating his opponents on the football field, Jim Litke wrote, "Despite his boyish looks, Brady, at 26, already has the heart of an assassin."

—C.F.T.

Suggested Reading: Associated Press Jan. 25, 2004, with photo; *Boston Globe* Jan. 21, 2004; *Boston Magazine* (on-line) Aug. 2002; National Football League Web site; New England Patriots Web site; *Sports Illustrated* p52+ Nov. 19, 2001, with photos, p36+ Feb. 11, 2002, with photos, p34+ Apr. 15, 2002, with photos, p42 Feb. 9, 2004, with photos

---

Bravo, Rose Marie

Jan. 13, 1951– CEO of Burberry Ltd.

Address: Burberry Ltd., 18-22 Haymarket, London SW1Y 4DQ, England

Had it not been for the efforts of Rose Marie Bravo, the ubiquitous brown, red, white, and black plaid that is synonymous with the fashion house Burberry might still be glimpsed only in the linings of raincoats; today it adorns a wide variety of the company's very popular fashion accessories. After becoming chief executive officer (CEO) of Burberry Ltd. of London, England, in 1997, Bravo revived the company—turning the once-floundering firm into an upscale label with products perceived as symbols of both high socioeconomic status and "street cred," attracting a new, younger clientele without losing older, established customers, and helping to double the company's profits by the end of 2003. Previously, in over three decades in the fashion retail industry, Bravo had improved the images and business strategies of such stores as Saks Fifth Avenue and the Macy's-owned I. Magnin.

The fashion executive was born Rose Marie LaPila on January 13, 1951 in New York City. Her parents were immigrants; her father, Biagio, an Italian-American, owned a hair salon on 181st Street in the borough of the Bronx, and her mother, Anna Bazzano, was a Sicilian-born seamstress. Bravo attended the elite Bronx High School of Science, graduating in 1969. She then enrolled at the all-female Thomas More College, on the Rose Hill campus of Fordham University, also in the Bronx, where she earned a B.A. degree in English in 1971. The dean of Fordham College of Rose Hill, Reverend Jeffrey P. von Arx, told Michele Snipe for the Fordham Web site (May 20, 2000, on-line) that when Bravo "arrived on the Rose Hill campus . . . she was a young woman in a hurry," displaying "the energy and sense of direction that have distinguished her business career."

Following her graduation, Bravo began her career in retail at the now-defunct Abraham & Straus, in Brooklyn, New York, where she served as a department manager from 1971 to 1974. Later in 1974 she moved to the famed R.H. Macy & Co.—better known as Macy's—where she started out as an associate buyer and had ascended to the position of senior vice president of merchandising by 1988. During her time at Macy's, Bravo worked primarily in cosmetics, forming a high regard for the feminist sensibilities of major figures in the field. She told Kristina Zimbalist for *Time* (February 9, 2004, on-line), "In cosmetics, which is where I particularly grew up, we had these wonderful role models. Es-

AFP/Getty Images

Rose Marie Bravo

tee Lauder, Helena Rubinstein and Elizabeth Arden are all women who created companies. . . . If you've been given this road map and you see that others have gone before you and achieved, you never have in your mind the notion of failure. You have the notion that you can do it too, if you're good enough and smart enough and make the right decisions."

In 1988 Edward Finkelstein, then chairman of Macy's, promoted Bravo to chairman and CEO of I. Magnin, a no-longer-extant chain of specialty stores that Macy's had recently acquired. Bravo headed to San Francisco, California, to rejuvenate the stores' fading image. One of her first acts was to ask a local fashion reporter for a list of names and telephone numbers of women who frequented I. Magnin; she then invited the women to lunches, asking them for suggestions as to how to improve the store. When, for example, one woman proposed that I. Magnin might carry shawls to cater to tourists unused to San Francisco's variable weather, Bravo saw to it that shawls appeared in the accessory department before the end of the same week. To promote an air of exclusivity, she closed several I. Magnin locations and installed designer boutiques in the remaining stores. Bravo also arranged for a variety of personal appearances by designers, attracting the likes of Hubert de Givenchy, Emanuel Ungaro, Bob Mackie, Bill Blass, Gianfranco Ferre, and Oscar de la Renta, among others. While in that position, Bravo was known for her personal attention to designers, her pursuit of positive publicity, and her friendly but businesslike manner. According to Mandy Behbehani in *Mirabella* (December 1990), Robert A. Nielsen, chairman and president of Revlon at the time, called

Bravo "one of those very rare individuals who combine conceptual thinking with execution. If anyone can turn I. Magnin back to its former glory days, she can."

While Bravo was credited with making significant improvements at I. Magnin, Macy's as a whole was suffering. The company filed for bankruptcy in 1992. Only a few months later, in Los Angeles, California, riots broke out, sparked by the acquittal of four white police officers whose beating of a black man, Rodney King, had been captured on videotape; in the midst of the rioting, the Los Angeles I. Magnin store was looted. Bravo, who had just completed a $40 million renovation of that store, lamented to Richard Fletcher for the London *Sunday Telegraph* (October 5, 2003) that the rioters "looted everything except our rare books and our soaps. Every single thing." Later that year Bravo accepted the position of president of Saks Fifth Ave. Inc. In that capacity she was responsible for merchandising, overseeing the store's fashions, and developing private-label goods. "She's a brilliant merchant and a great leader of people," Philip Miller, who hired Bravo when he was vice chairman of Saks, said to Cathy Horyn and Suzanne Kapner for the *New York Times* (July 12, 2002). "She has a very good rapport with designers and the fashion market. She understands the whole world of luxury. And she works like a demon."

Demon-like determination may have been necessary for Bravo's next job: CEO of Burberry's Ltd., a post she assumed in 1997. (In 1999, for aesthetic reasons, the company dropped the apostrophe and "s" from its name.) Thomas Burberry, as a 21-year-old apprentice to a country draper, founded the brand in 1856 in Hampshire, England, where it became a favorite of sportsmen and hunters, who appreciated Burberry's new fabric—gabardine. Gabardine, which received a patent in 1888, was both breathable and waterproof and went into wide use, particularly once Thomas Burberry was commissioned to design the uniforms and trench coats for the British army, in 1901. In 1920, the famous Novacheck plaid lining was created. Since then, although such legendary figures as the Antarctic explorer Sir Ernest Shackelton had sported Burberry designs, the brand had lost its cachet, relying primarily on exports—ranging from suits to whiskey to biscuits—for its profits. Charged with injecting life into what was generally seen as a stodgy British raincoat company, Bravo found herself based in the company's seedy headquarters, located above its raincoat factory in Hackney, an unfashionable area of London's East End. When her parents went to visit her in London, they expressed concern for her well-being. Bravo recalled to *BusinessWeek* (January 12, 2004, on-line), "They said, 'You're leaving Fifth Avenue for this?'"

Within weeks of her arrival, Bravo secured the photographer Mario Testino and the model Stella Tennant for a fashion shoot that was meant to change the Burberry image; however, as no new clothes had yet been created for the brand, Bravo had to make do with what was available. "All we had [were] raincoats," she told Richard Fletcher. "I remember saying 'just get me some pretty pictures of the coat.'" Soon another model, Kate Moss, began endorsing the brand, which by that time consisted of more than just raincoats. By 2003, three fashion lines had been created: Burberry London, the basic collection, which accounts for 85 percent of the company's sales; Prorsum, a higher-end international line; and Thomas Burberry, a more casual collection geared toward younger consumers. Additionally, Burberry has marketed fragrances, a line of baby clothes and accessories, pet items, and other accessory collections, such as shoes and handbags. In 1999 Burberry held its first catwalk show in London. These successes allowed Bravo to relocate Burberry's head offices to a more presentable location—the newly converted flagship store in Haymarket, in London, which had originally opened in 1891. "The concept," Bravo explained to Horyn and Kapner, "is a British lifestyle, and we've stayed very committed to it for five years. It's family, friends, dogs, wit. Everybody getting together, in sort of this zany British setting."

Now that Burberry Novacheck plaid can be seen on items from baby carriages to dog coats to bowties, the question that some fashion pundits have pondered is whether Bravo has done her job too well. Imitations of Burberry goods are rampant, and some predict that, since the brand's identity is based so firmly on the easily identifiable plaid, the products' current position as status symbols might prove to be just a fad. Bravo sees such popularity in a positive light, though, as she told Matthew Goodman for the London *Sunday Times* (June 30, 2002): "By its very nature, the brand has broad appeal. It appeals to everyone from children to grandparents. I only see that as positive." Still, to avoid overdoing the emphasis on plaid, Bravo announced that less than 10 percent of the 2002 line of products would feature the Novacheck pattern. That decision may have been due to the revelation that some British pubs had banned Burberry-wearing customers because of U.K. gang members and fanatical soccer hooligans who had begun sporting the trademark plaid. While these developments might keep some harmless Burberry-wearers out of pubs, the phenomenon has also lent the brand further "street cred."

In 2002 Bravo became the highest-paid woman in Britain, when she was awarded a pay package that included a salary of £1 million per year; stock options; a one percent stake in the company (then valued at up to £14.5 million); use of a rent-free, furnished apartment in Kensington, in west London; a country-club membership; use of a car and chauffeur; and a wardrobe budget. In the following year about 30 percent of the company's non-majority shareholder votes were cast, without success, against an increased remuneration package for Bravo, which included a salary of £2 million per year and bound Bravo in a fixed-term contract until June 2005.

Under Bravo's guidance Burberry made a public stock offering in 2002. According to Nic Hopkins in the London *Times* (November 19, 2003), Bravo indicated that Burberry expected "mid-to-high single-digit sales growth for the spring-summer 2004 season." The company has reportedly expressed interest in acquiring the fashion and home-furnishings chain Laura Ashley.

Bravo has served on the board of directors of Tiffany & Co. since 1997 and of the Estee Lauder Co. Inc. since 2003. She is also on the advisory boards of the Fashion Group International and the Fashion Institute of Technology, in New York City. Bravo has been a trustee of Marymount University, in Arlington, Virginia, since July 1, 1998, and is also a trustee of Fordham University. In 2003 the Council of Fashion Designers honored Bravo with the Eleanor Lambert Award for her contributions to the field of fashion. She has also been honored for excellence in retailing by the National Italian American Foundation, of which she is a board member, the March of Dimes, and City of Hope. She was twice named one of the top women business executives in Europe by the *Wall Street Journal Europe*; in 2002 along with Sari Baldauf of Nikia Networks, she shared the number-one spot on the list; and in 2003 she headed it alone. She also won *Time*'s first Fashion Awards CEO of the Year honor in 2002. In 2004 *Fortune International* named her one of the 50 most powerful women in businesses outside the U.S.

Bravo married William Selkirk Jackey, a retired furniture-industry executive, in 1983. Her six-year marriage to Charles Emil Bravo ended in divorce in 1977. Bravo told Susan Lisovicz for CNN (September 9, 2001, on-line) that her family is very important to her and that her granddaughter, Grace Caroline, has been "an inspiration" for the Baby Burberry line and is "a delight."

—K.J.E.

Suggested Reading: *BusinessWeek* Web site; (London) *Sunday Telegraph* p12 Oct. 5, 2003; *Mirabella* Dec. p90+ 1990, with photo; *New York Times* W p1 July 12, 2002; *Time* (on-line) Feb. 9, 2004

Breen, Edward D.

1956– Chairman and CEO of Tyco International Ltd.

Address: Tyco International (US) Inc., 9 Roszel Rd., Princeton, NJ 08540

In 2002 Edward D. Breen, then the president of the thriving communications company Motorola, surprised industry analysts when he accepted the position of chief executive officer (CEO) of the troubled Tyco International Ltd., a Bermuda-based

Getty Images

Edward D. Breen

A Philadelphia, Pennsylvania, native, Edward D. Breen was born in 1956. He attended Grove City College, a Christian institution in Grove City, Pennsylvania, where he presided over the Beta Sigma fraternity, joined the wrestling team, and was inducted into the Delta Mu Delta business honorary society. In the fall of 1976, he met a fellow economics major, Lynn Branstner, in the campus dining hall; the pair began dating and married shortly after they graduated, in 1978. (Breen received a B.S. degree in business administration as well as economics.) Breen's bride organized the process of sending his résumé to hundreds of companies.

The cable television equipment manufacturer Jerrold Communications, a division of General Instrument (G.I.), hired Breen in 1978. Marketing pay TV and converters, he rapidly became one of the company's leading salesmen, eventually rising to the position of senior vice president of sales. In that position, from 1988 through 1994, he was in charge of worldwide sales operations and responsible for selling cable-TV boxes as well as the equipment that cable-TV stations required to provide programming to those boxes. He was then promoted to fill the roles of president of G.I.'s Broadband Networks Group, president of Eastern operations for the communications division, and executive vice president of terrestrial systems. In October 1997 Breen was promoted once again, this time to the positions of chairman and CEO of G.I. He also earned the admiration of both colleagues and employees, as well as a reputation for soliciting the opinions of those around him. Breen explained to Lee Wishing for the *Grove City College Alumni Magazine* (Winter/Spring 2000, on-line), "I want employees to make decisions. . . . Out of 10 decisions, if they make seven good ones and three not-so-good ones . . . that's okay. We'll learn from the bad ones, help customers with the good ones, capture market share and move on." For the same article, Edgar Ebenbach, who initially hired Breen, praised him, saying, "Ed makes critical decisions correctly and very fast. He has an uncanny ability to do the right thing. I've never seen anyone like him." In 1998 Breen won the National Cable Television Association's Vanguard Award for high achievers in the field of cable; in the following year he ranked in the top 15 of *CableFAX* magazine's 100 most influential people in cable. When Motorola acquired G.I. for $11 billion in January 2000, Breen became executive vice president of Motorola and president of Motorola Broadband Communications Sector (BCS). In only three months—half the time allotted by his supervisor—Breen succeeded in integrating the two companies' cable businesses, and the value of the company's stock rose by over 750 percent.

conglomerate whose products and services range from home-security systems to medical equipment. From Tyco's viewpoint, however, the move made sense: the company's former CEO, Dennis Kozlowski, had been charged with pilfering $400 million from the company and evading sales taxes on millions of dollars' worth of art, and the churchgoing, plain-living Breen—who had so boosted the fortunes of Motorola—seemed an ideal, indeed necessary, antithesis to his extravagant predecessor. Since he became CEO of Tyco, Breen has taken swift and decisive actions, such as replacing the entire board of directors, relocating the corporate office from an upscale New York City location to a less prestigious—and less expensive—spot in Princeton, New Jersey, and restructuring the company's $24 billion debt. He clarified his short-term goals to the *Chicago Tribune* (March 14, 2003), explaining, "The goal for this year is to clean the crap up. . . . I've got a zero-tolerance policy. If I find anything wrong, they're out of here, heads are rolling. We're not putting up with anything." Unlike Kozlowski, who oversaw Tyco's acquisition of 1,000 companies between 1994 and 2001, Breen announced that he would have the conglomerate acquire few or no new companies; instead, he has focused on strengthening Tyco itself, putting earnings back into the business rather than reporting them as profits or using them to acquire other businesses. Breen has suggested that Tyco will ultimately be able to return to acquisition mode, but not until its current problems have been solved. Although Tyco's leadership transition has not been seamless, Breen's efforts seem to be working, as Tyco's share price has tripled since he became CEO.

Breen assumed the titles of president and chief operating officer (COO) of Motorola on January 1, 2002. In those capacities he oversaw a major restructuring of the company, instituting a number of cost-cutting measures that led the flagging Motorola back to profitability. Dick Smith, corporate vice president of Motorola, assured Lee Wishing, "Where we are today is a direct result of Ed Breen's leadership!" Breen reportedly got along well with Motorola's chairman and CEO, Christopher Galvin, and was being groomed as his eventual successor.

Industry analysts were thus baffled when, on July 25, 2002, Breen quit Motorola to helm Tyco International Ltd., a struggling conglomerate. Founded in 1960, Tyco established an address in Bermuda, for tax purposes, in 1997. Edward Snyder, a senior analyst for J.P. Morgan, speculated to Barbara Rose for the *Chicago Tribune* (July 26, 2002) that Breen most likely "got a really good deal from Tyco, which is in desperate shape. My feeling is that Tyco probably made him an offer he couldn't refuse." For assuming control of Tyco, Breen received a pay package of $1.5 million in salary (twice his earnings at Motorola), a one-time signing bonus to compensate him for giving up his Motorola stock options, and options on about two million shares of Tyco stock. For the same article, the Morningstar Inc. analyst Todd Bernier suggested that Breen simply wanted to head a company, saying, "Clearly he's a leader and he may want to run his own ship." In the hour following the announcement of Breen's departure from Motorola, that company's stock fell almost 12 percent. (Michael Zafirovski, previously president of Motorola's cellphone division, assumed the vacated post.)

Breen has been consistently and favorably compared with the former CEO of Tyco, Dennis Kozlowski. For example, a *Chicago Tribune* article (July 27, 2003) explained, "While Kozlowski was Deal-A-Day Dennis, Wall Street's perception of Breen stood in stark contrast. He was 'Aw Shucks Ed,' as one investor put it." Likewise, analysts and commentators have often contrasted Breen's churchgoing, old-fashioned, moral persona to the spendthrift ways and extravagant tastes of his predecessor at Tyco.

In his own statement on the Tyco Web site (July 25, 2002, on-line), Breen expressed his happiness about his new position, asserting, "This is the opportunity of a lifetime. I could not be more excited about leading this great company, with its strong businesses and market-leading positions. Tyco and its employees have successfully weathered a very difficult few months, and I am confident that we will put the current issues behind us and begin to forge ahead. All of us at Tyco have a tremendous opportunity to build on the Company's operating strengths to realize the true value of this enterprise." In the same statement, he also promised to develop a specific plan of action that would address four main priorities, which he listed as: "restore confidence in Tyco with our employees, suppliers, customers and the financial community; enhance and strengthen the core businesses; ensure that we have the highest standards of corporate governance in place; and create value for shareholders." Breen promptly began accomplishing these goals. Within his first six months as CEO, he

replaced Tyco's entire board of directors, fired the whole corporate team, hired 80 new executives to fill those positions, and restructured the company's $24 billion debt. He also relocated the corporate headquarters from a posh Manhattan office overlooking Central Park to a commercial complex in Princeton. When Breen first saw the Manhattan Tyco office, complete with antiques, Persian carpets, marble floors, and fine china, he thought, as he recalled to Melanie Warner for *Fortune* (April 28, 2003), "This is embarrassing." Breen felt that for a company in such poor financial shape, a view of a New Jersey parking lot—that is, the reduced expense that such a view represented—was more appropriate than a Central Park vista. He also drew up long-term plans for the company's various departments and instituted a system of financial checks and balances.

While Kozlowski had been famous for his acquisitions, adding 1,000 companies over an eight-year period for a total cost of $63 billion, Breen told the *Chicago Tribune* (March 14, 2003) that Tyco "is not an acquisition machine anymore. . . . This is an operating company." Although he has emphasized that his focus is on refurbishing the existing divisions of the company, Breen proposed to Lou Whiteman for the New York *Daily Deal* (September 26, 2002), "It is a core competency of Tyco to do acquisitions, and at some point when we are comfortable I do see opportunities for us to do deals again."

In May 2003, only four months after an investigation conducted by the lawyer David Boies turned up no significant remnants of fraud at Tyco, Breen announced that his own audit had revealed an additional $1 billion in accounting discrepancies. As reported in the Salt Lake City *Deseret News* (May 1, 2003), Breen told investors, "I believe at this point we have identified all, or nearly all, legacy accounting issues."

By February 2004 Tyco's share price had more than tripled from its low of $8.21, the value when Breen assumed control. Breen has projected that the company's debt will be down to between $10 billion and $11 billion by 2006.

Breen and his wife, Lynn, have three children, Matthew, Leslie, and Ryan, and live in New Hope, Pennsylvania. Breen is on the board of trustees of Grove City College and was given the 2001 Jack Kennedy Memorial Alumni Achievement Award in 2001 for his contributions to his chosen field.

—K.J.E.

Suggested Reading: *Chicago Tribune* N p1 July 26, 2002, C p1 Nov. 17, 2002; *Fortune* p106+ Apr. 28, 2003; *Grove City College Magazine* (online) Winter/Spring 2000; Grove City College Web site; *Time* (on-line) Feb. 2, 2004; Tyco Web site

Ronnie Dunn (left) and Kix Brooks

Brooks and Dunn

Country-music duo

Dunn, Ronnie
June 1, 1953– Country-music singer and songwriter

Brooks, Kix
May 12, 1955– Country-music singer and songwriter

Address: c/o Richard De La Font Agency, 4845 S. Sheridan Rd., Suite 505, Tulsa, OK 74145

Kix Brooks and Ronnie Dunn are the best-selling country-music twosome in history. Calling their act Brooks and Dunn, they rank behind only one other pair—Paul Simon and Art Garfunkel—as the most commercially successful duo in any musical genre. For years before they became a team, in 1991, each singer/songwriter struggled in relative obscurity. Since then, they have sold a total of at least 25 million copies of their 10 albums, among them *Brand New Man, Hard Workin' Man, Waitin' on Sundown, Borderline, If You See Her, Tight Rope, Steers & Stripes,* and *Red Dirt Road*. They have also produced nearly two dozen number-one hits (written by both of them, by Dunn alone, or by or with others), among them "Brand New Man," "My Next Broken Heart," "Neon Moon," "Boot Scootin' Boogie," "She Used to Be Mine," "Little Miss Honky Tonk," "You're Gonna Miss Me (When I'm Gone)," "My Maria," "A Man This Lonely," "Only in America," and "Red Dirt Road"—songs that range from heart-tugging ballads to rolicking

expressions of joy. "You can't ignore the realities of everyday life when you write," Brooks told an interviewer for the Web site of the Richard De La Font Agency. "Average people is what country music is all about." He and Dunn have won 19 Academy of Country Music Awards, two Grammy Awards, the Country Music Association's duo-of-the-year award for eight consecutive years, and many awards from, among others, TNN/Music City News, *Billboard*, Blockbuster, BMI, and the magazine *Country Weekly*.

"From their first album as a duo in 1991 the pair wore a natural eclecticism on their sleeves," the cultural critic Carol Cooper wrote for the *Village Voice* (August 12, 2003). "Dunn's vocal tendency to slide from hillbilly yodel to blues moan and back paired well with Brooks's obvious affection for Memphis soul melodicism and Crescent City swing. . . . Kix was obviously born to reinvent the progressive country ballad, while Ronnie is synergistically called to sing redemptive parables rather than bitter rants." "The boundaries of country songwriting have expanded and I, for one, don't think that is dangerous at all," Brooks told the De La Font Agency's interviewer. "I don't think we had to stay in folk-music land. If you have a country lyric, I don't see what difference it makes whether you crank it up or rock a little bit on it. If the message is still there and the story is still something that people can relate to, then I think it's still a country song." Brooks and Dunn are known for their dissimilar personalities and voices: the former has a reputation for wild on-stage behavior, and his vocals have a drawling, conversational quality, while the latter is far more introverted, and his powerful tenor is considered one of the best voices among contemporary country musicians. "It doesn't bruise my ego a bit that Ronnie is such a great singer," Brooks told the agency's interviewer. "I love to hear him sing and I'm glad that radio likes it as much as I do." Dunn told the same source, "It is weird, but I think if we had been a lot alike it wouldn't have worked. We are so far the opposite in philosophy and personality. But we came to the table being as old as we are and knowing how to compromise." "I think we really appreciate the success we've been blessed with," Brooks told Richard Deitsch for *Sports Illustrated* (July 14, 2003). "We had 10 or 15 years of writing songs for other people and playing clubs and paying dues for a lot longer than most people probably do who have success. For lack of a better way of putting it, we just really appreciate how lucky we are, even after 12 or 13 years. We're just not inclined to let it go. We're still having the time of our lives."

The duo's primary guitarist, Leon Eric "Kix" Brooks III was born on May 12, 1955 in Shreveport, Louisiana. The frequent kicks his mother felt when she was pregnant with him are the source of his nickname. As a child he listened to a variety of music—Cajun, country, blues, and jazz; his parents' record collection also contained albums by the Rolling Stones and Eric Clapton. The Brookses' neighbors included the country and honky-tonk singer Johnny Horton and his wife, the widow of the singer Hank Williams, and Brooks became familiar with the work of both Williams and Horton from a young age. In sixth grade he played guitar with a band of his peers, called the Originals, and sang with one of Horton's daughters (her father had died in 1960); he wrote his own songs as well. Knowing that Williams and Horton had made their livings through songwriting and singing "made you think it was something people like you could do, though we were just doing it because it was fun, not because it was what you did when you grew up," as Brooks told an interviewer for an unsigned biographical article posted on several Web sites. Brooks attended a military school as a teenager and then studied speech and drama at a branch of Louisiana State University. He apparently left the college before he graduated, to work on the trans-Alaska oil pipeline, whose construction was completed in May 1977. He later moved to Maine, where he performed at ski resorts and other local venues. In 1979 he settled in Nashville, Tennessee, where within a few years he had found success as a country songwriter. His song "I'm Only in It for the Love" (co-written with Deborah Allen and Rafe Van Hoy) became a hit for John Conlee; the band Highway 101 co-wrote with him another popular tune, "Who's Lonely Now"; and the Nitty Gritty Dirt Band introduced his "Modern Day Romance." Brooks also recorded his own songs for little-known labels, scoring a moderate hit with "Baby, When Your Heart Breaks Down" in 1983. He released an eponymous album in 1989; it made little impact on the music scene. During this period he also took jobs with security squads at concerts.

Ronnie Gene Dunn was born on June 1, 1953 in Coleman, Texas, and grew up in Arkansas. Until adulthood, according to the Web site rons_hangout.tripod.com, he was "cripplingly shy." His father, a truckdriver, spent nine years in a federal prison. (Readily available sources do not indicate when.) The elder Dunn adored country music; he played the guitar and enjoyed singing honky-tonk tunes. Ronnie Dunn played the saxophone in the music program of one of the schools he attended. He has recalled that he honed his skills on the instrument by listening to recordings by the alto saxophonist Ace Cannon that his father bought. "My father never told me [he] loved me, but he brought me those records," Dunn has said, as quoted on the rons_hangout Web site. In high school he learned to play bass. Meanwhile, for some time, influenced in part by his unusually devout, churchgoing mother, he considered pursuing a career as a Baptist minister. Toward that end, he enrolled at Abilene Christian University (ACU), in Abilene, Texas. On weekends he guided the music programs at small rural churches; some nights he performed in area bars. After ACU administrators learned of the latter activity, he was forced to leave ACU—or chose to leave, according to rons_hangout.tripod.com, rather than abandon the

music he loved. "The ultimate religious message is that you are simply free to be human without restriction, but are completely loved and accepted in the end," he explained on that Web site. "There's no intellectual way to accept it . . . it just is."

With the intention of making music his full-time occupation, Dunn moved to Tulsa, Oklahoma. At that time, as the rons_hangout Web site put it, Tulsa was "a wild swing town"; others performing there then included Bonnie Raitt, the Gap Band, Eric Clapton, Joe Cocker, Ronnie and Ernie Isley, and Bonnie Bramlett. "The spectrum was so broad it really gave you an appreciation of what music could be," Dunn recalled during his induction into the Oklahoma Music Hall of Fame in 2003, as quoted on the Brooks and Dunn Web site. "And nobody worried about what it was, beyond good, so you picked stuff up from every kind of music being played and brought it to what you did." "Here I was this quiet church kid, hanging out with these wild ass rock & roll people," he has said, as quoted on rons_hangout. For a while he performed at the Caravan (formally, the Caravan Cattle Co.) with the fiddler Johnny Wills, a brother of the fiddler and bandleader Bob Wills. In the late 1970s he led a house band at Duke's Country, a Tulsa nightclub. By then music had become an all-consuming passion for him—"almost a damaging addiction," in his words. In the early 1980s he scored two modest hits with his singles "It's Written All Over Your Face" and "She Put the Sad in All His Songs," recorded for a local label. In 1989 he won a songwriting contest sponsored by Marlboro; the prize included a recording session in Nashville. There, he soon began working with the producer Scott Hendricks, who in 1990 gave samples of Dunn's music to his college friend Tim DuBois, who had been named vice president and general manager of the newly formed Arista Nashville the previous year. DuBois had already begun to work with Brooks, and, thinking that Brooks and Dunn might achieve greater success as a team, introduced the two. Although, despite their relative obscurity, both at first resisted giving up their solo careers, they soon realized they worked well together. Upon hearing some of their earliest joint efforts, DuBois signed the men to a recording contract.

Brooks and Dunn's debut album, *Brand New Man*, was released in 1991. With its title track (co-written by Don Cook, their producer) and the songs "My Next Broken Heart," "Neon Moon," and "Boot Scootin' Boogie," the pair became the first country act whose first four singles reached number one on the country charts. The album sold over four million copies and received generally positive critical reviews. "These guys practice a brand of honky-tonk rock similar to Travis Tritt and Mark Collie, and their songs . . . defuse the usual saloon self-pity with upbeat rhythms and a sly sense of humor," Geoffrey Himes wrote for the *Washington Post* (February 21, 1992). "When they describe love-on-the-rebound as '(Working on) My Next Broken Heart' or 'Cheating on the Blues,' you can tell they're chuckling good-naturedly at their own predicament. Coupled with catchy pop hooks and strong pop voices, this duo's refusal to whine is refreshing indeed." "Boot Scootin' Boogie," which had been recorded earlier by the group Asleep at the Wheel, has been credited with popularizing the country line-dancing fad.

Brooks and Dunn followed up with *Hard Workin' Man* (1993), which went quadruple platinum (selling four million copies) and produced five Top 10 hits: the number-one singles "We'll Burn That Bridge," "She Used to Be Mine," and "That Ain't No Way To Go," the number-two song "Rock My World (Little Country Girl)," and the title track, which hit number three. *Waitin' on Sundown* (1994), the pair's third album, produced three number-one songs—"She's Not the Cheatin' Kind," "Little Miss Honky Tonk," and "You're Gonna Miss Me (When I'm Gone)"—as well as the number-two song "I'll Never Forgive My Heart" and the number-three "Whiskey Under the Bridge." *Waitin' on Sundown* has sold over three million copies. *Borderline* (1996) went double platinum on the strength of three number-one songs: "My Maria," a cover of the 1972 B. W. Stevenson pop hit, "I Am That Man," and "A Man This Lonely." It also offered the single "Why Would I Say Goodbye," which climbed to six on the charts, and "Mama Don't Get Dressed Up for Nothing," which reached seventh place. The duo's *Greatest Hits Collection* (1997) sold two million copies. It contained three new songs: "He's Got You," which went to number one, "Honky Tonk Truth," which hit number two, and "Days of Thunder."

The following year saw the release of *If You See Her*. That platinum album had three number-one songs—"If You See Him/If You See Her," a joint effort with the singer Reba McEntire; "How Long Gone"; and "Husbands and Wives," a cover of a Roger Miller song. It also spawned the Top 10 hit "I Can't Get Over You." "Kix Brooks and Ronnie Dunn took the 'Ain't Broke, Don't Fix It' adage to heart, cranking out another album's worth of radio- and dancefloor-friendly country pop . . . ," Kevin Oliver wrote in a review for the Country Standard Time Web site. "This isn't the best [Brooks & Dunn] album yet, but . . . there is enough good material among the clunkers to get a head start on the second volume of their *Greatest Hits* collection."

With the exception of the Top 10 track "You'll Always Be Loved by Me," *Tight Rope* (1999) was an artistic disappointment and sold relatively poorly. After its release Brooks and Dunn found themselves the subjects of rumors about power struggles between them regarding songs, co-writers, and producers. (For the most part, Brooks wrote with his longtime collaborator and the pair's co-producer up until then, Don Cook; Dunn penned his songs with Byron Gallimore.) "There's always been that push-pull thing, you know," Dunn explained to Richard Harrington for the *Washington Post* (June 8, 2001). "There are so

many different factors to this business—the touring end, the entertainment aspect, the recording aspect—and Kix handles that stuff a lot better than I can. He's the more outgoing personality, and he can be more comfortable in that arena. I enjoy the recording process, love the singing, the song selection, the writing and all that."

Whereas with *Tight Rope* and its predecessors, Brooks and Dunn had usually written and recorded albums in three months, they devoted far more time on (and hired a new producer, Mark Wright, for) their next effort, *Steers & Stripes* (2001). "When we went in the studio, we were at a crossroads careerwise," Dunn recalled to Fred Shuster for the *Los Angeles Daily News*, as reprinted in the *Pittsburgh Post-Gazette* (August 3, 2001). "We needed to shake things up. We'd gotten too comfortable with a certain way of doing things and the results were getting a little lackluster. We sat there, looked at each other and said, 'What are we gonna do?' We had to show people what we're capable of, and we hadn't felt that way in a long time." *Steers & Stripes* debuted at number one on *Billboard*'s country-album chart and number four on the pop chart, and gave Brooks and Dunn three more number-one hits: "Ain't Nothing 'Bout You," "Only in America," and "The Long Goodbye." Later that year they launched a successful tour, dubbed the Neon Circus and Wild West Show. Inspired by a Cirque du Soleil performance they had seen in Las Vegas, Nevada, they included in their concerts such sideshow acts as a bubble-blowing goat, jugglers, clowns, comedians, hypnotists, fire-eaters, tattoo artists, and a contortionist. Also entertaining their audiences in the tour were the country singers Toby Keith, Keith Urban, and the duo known as Montgomery Gentry. With each show lasting an average of seven hours, the tour was enormously successful, grossing more than $17 million, attracting 600,000 fans, and winning the International Talent Buyers Association Country Tour of the Year Award. Brooks and Dunn's 2002 Neon Circus and Wild West Show tour featured Dwight Yoakam, Chris Cagle, Gary Allen, and Trick Pony; the lineup for the 2003 tour included Brad Paisley, Rascal Flatts, Aaron Lines, and Jeff Bates.

Brooks and Dunn released a holiday album, *It Won't Be Christmas Without You*, in 2002. With *Red Dirt Road*, which arrived the next year, they took "probably a little earthier approach . . . ," as Brooks told Steven Hyden for the Appleton, Wisconsin, *Post-Crescent* (April 24, 2003). "I think it sounds like us but it's a little more organic. A little more acoustic instruments and there's also full-blown rocking deals. It might be a little more reflective but it has plenty of party on it." With touches from an array of musical genres, the album pleased most critics. "They take a bluesier turn with *Red Dirt Road*," John Gerome wrote for the Associated Press, as published in the *Miami Herald* (July 16, 2003, on-line). "The songs are more soulful, with slide guitar, horns, organ and soaring gospel choruses. 'I Used to Know This Song by Heart,' for example, could have been plucked from a Leon Russell or Joe Cocker album, while 'You Can't Take the Honky Tonk Out of the Girl' echoes vintage Rolling Stones." In her *Village Voice* article, Carol Cooper described *Red Dirt Road* as "a provocative surprise" that offers "some of the best country rock in over a decade." "Galvanized by 9-11, these fortysomething singer-songwriters soberly reassessed how they grew up, then recorded 15 sociological portraits of unvarnished Americana . . . ," she wrote. "After 25 million albums sold, Brooks & Dunn may have thought there were no more career mountains to climb, no more battles to win. But that could change if they set themselves the task of gently diversifying the content and political discourse of mainstream country radio. It's a worthy, truly epic undertaking for two golden Teflon cowboys like them."

In addition to honors from the Academy of Country Music and the Country Music Association, Brooks and Dunn won Grammy Awards for best country performance by a duo or group with vocal in 1993 and 1997, for "Hard Workin' Man" and "My Maria," respectively; seven vocal-duo-of-the-year awards from TNN/Music City News (1993–99); five Blockbuster Entertainment Awards (1995, 1999, 2000, and two in 1998); two *Billboard* Entertainment Awards (1995 and 1998); an AMOA (Amusement and Music Operators Association) Jukebox Award (1992); two BMI (Broadcast Music Inc.) awards (1996 and 1998); and an award from Country Music Television (1997). In *Country Weekly*'s "Golden Picks," they were named favorite duo in 1995, 1996, 1997, and 1998, and "My Maria" was named favorite line-dance song in 1997; they also earned a Special Achievement Award from the magazine's editors in 1996. The industry newspaper *Radio and Records* named them best duo four times (1992–95) and their song "Boot Scootin' Boogie" best single in 1993. The presenters of the American Veteran Awards, which are associated with the Veterans Foundation Inc., honored Brooks and Dunn with the first annual Elvis Presley Patriotic Song Award, in 2002, for "Only in America."

Brooks and Dunn endorse and help design Panhandle Slim clothes. Both men are NASCAR fans and have sponsored Sterling Marlin's racecar in the NASCAR Winston Cup Series. Brooks serves on the board of directors of the Country Music Association. He and his wife, Barbara, have a son, Leon Eric (called Eric), and a daughter, Molly. They have homes in Los Angeles and Nashville. In his free time Brooks enjoys fishing, pool, and golf. In 2001 he drove a leg of the 50-state Drive for Hope, a fundraiser for the cancer-research group the Hope Foundation. Dunn and his wife, Janine, have three children—Whitney, Jesse, and Haley—and homes in Tulsa and Nashville. His hobbies include water skiing, playing tennis, and collecting Southwestern art.

—K.E.D.

Suggested Reading: *Billboard* B p1+ June 21, 2003, with photo; Brooks & Dunn Web site; *Country Music* p28+ Aug./Sep. 2001, with photo; countrystars.com (2003); Richard De La Font Agency Web site; *Village Voice* p54 Aug. 12, 2003, with photo; *Washington Post* WW p6 June 8, 2001

Selected Recordings: *Brand New Man*, 1991; *Hard Workin' Man*, 1993; *Waitin' on Sundown*, 1994; *Borderline*, 1996; *Greatest Hits Collection*, 1997; *If You See Her*, 1998; *Tight Rope*, 1999; *Steers & Stripes*, 2001; *It Won't Be Christmas Without You*, 2002; *Red Dirt Road*, 2003

Courtesy of David Brooks

Brooks, David

1961– Political commentator; social critic; columnist

Address: New York Times, *229 W. 43d St., New York, NY 10036*

"I think you need both liberals and conservatives," the political commentator David Brooks told Julia Keller in an interview for the *Chicago Tribune* (August 12, 2003). "If you had just one side in charge, they'd run the country off a cliff." In the fall of 2003, after more than 20 years in journalism, working with such publications as the *Wall Street Journal* and the *National Review*, David Brooks became a twice-a-week op-ed columnist for the *New York Times*, joining only a handful of comparatively conservative writers at the predominantly liberal newspaper. Because of his centrist ideology and his tolerance of opposing viewpoints, Brooks has been dubbed a "reasonable conservative," a label that has helped him reach diverse audiences. "I consider myself a Teddy Roosevelt conservative," Brooks told Keller, referring to the 26th president of the United States, a Republican who freely exercised his country's power abroad but also believed in regulating corporate interests, protecting common citizens, and conserving the environment. "I'm not a free market libertarian. I like an aggressive foreign policy. On domestic policy, I'm a neoconservative. I like welfare reform. I like vouchers and charter schools. I do support gay marriage, which I think comes from knowing a lot of gay people." Although Brooks has usually defended the administration of President George W. Bush, he has criticized the Republican Party for not having a clear overall philosophy. He has also written sensitively and sympathetically about Democratic voters and what he sees as their longing for a political leader dedicated to the pursuit of noble ideals. "Even if one doesn't quite see things Brooks' way—he recently termed President Bush 'a leader of the first order,' a judgment that might cause snarls of dissent among Democrats—one must concede that his courtesy and geniality are a welcome change from the high-decibel diatribes that constitute much political opinion-slinging these days," Julia Keller wrote.

Born in 1961, David Brooks was raised in New York City and Pennsylvania. His parents were liberal academics: his father taught English at New York University, in the New York City borough of Manhattan, and at Westchester University, in Westchester, Pennsylvania; his mother earned a Ph.D. in history from Columbia University, in New York City, and held various posts as a Western-civilization professor. One of Brooks's grandmothers, who was also quite liberal, ran a small art gallery in the city and often baked marijuana-laced "hash" brownies. When he was five his parents took him to a "be-in" in Central Park, where some hippies were throwing their wallets into a fire. Brooks recalled reaching up and grabbing a five-dollar bill that floated out of one of them, a sign of "early conservative tendencies," as he joked to George Gurley for the New York Observer (November 24, 2003). When he was 12 his family moved to a predominantly Republican suburb in Pennsylvania, where he was exposed to more conservative ideologies.

As an undergraduate at the University of Chicago, in Illinois, Brooks studied history with the intention of becoming an academic like his parents. Still a liberal at this point, he wrote for the campus newspaper a parody of the writer William F. Buckley, who founded the conservative magazine the National Review. Buckley learned of the article and was so impressed with it that, during a lecture at the University of Chicago, he asked the audience if Brooks was present and then offered him a job at his magazine. Brooks was in California at the time, preparing to debate on a local PBS show; he later learned of Buckley's offer but chose to ignore it.

After his college graduation, in 1983, Brooks tended bar at the university's alumni club and wrote articles for a small paper called the Chicago Journal, published on the South Side of Chicago. He subsequently worked as a police reporter for the City News Bureau, a wire service owned by the Chicago Tribune and the Chicago Sun-Times. On his first day on that job, he covered two tragic stories, one about a teenager who had committed suicide and another about a city official who had died in a car crash. He was soon assigned to cover life in Chicago's housing projects. "That part of life was eye-opening," he told Gurley. "You could just get your welfare check and you didn't have to do anything. . . . It seemed urban policy was broken, and it seemed to me the liberal policies just weren't working, so that began to make me think about the other side . . . . So I reacted against the culture that was being created there." Brooks gradually began to identify himself as a conservative rather than a liberal, so much so that he eventually called Buckley and asked if the job offer still stood. It did, and he subsequently spent several months writing articles for the National Review.

In 1984 Brooks left the National Review to write editorials and movie reviews for the Washington Times. He also worked at the Hoover Institution, a conservative think tank at Stanford University, in Stanford, California, before accepting a position as a book-review editor at the Wall Street Journal in 1986. Brooks later became a Brussels, Belgium–based foreign correspondent for that newspaper, covering Middle Eastern, South African, and European affairs; in time he was promoted to op-ed editor. In 1995 he was hired as a senior editor at the Weekly Standard, a conservative magazine that premiered in September 1995. A year later he edited the anthology Backward and Upward: The New Conservative Writing, published by Vintage Books, which contains articles by Danielle Crittenden, P.J. O'Rourke, Peggy Noonan, William Kristol, Charles Murray, Donald Kagan, and William Bennett, among others.

In 2000 Brooks published Bobos in Paradise: The New Upper Class and How They Got There, in which he argued that today's upper classes have merged the values of the bourgeois and the bohemians (the word "bobo" is a combination of the two). Brooks explained the premise behind the book to Dick Staub in an interview for Christianity Today (July 30, 2002, on-line): "The Bobos are the people who have these humongous new kitchens with Viking ranges that send up heat like a space shuttle rocket turned upside down. They're the people with the sub-zero refrigerators because zero just wouldn't be cold enough. They are like half hippies/half yuppies. They've got sort of the spirituality of the hippies but the moneymaking of the yuppies, and they merged these two opposite styles together." Brooks was inspired to write the book after he returned from Brussels and visited the town outside Philadelphia where his parents lived. "Suddenly it had six gourmet coffee shops," he told Staub. "And they've got one of these Great Harvest Bread Companies, which sell a piece of bread for $4.75. It had one of these organic food markets where you can get your vegetarian dog biscuits and your all-natural hair coloring, because if you're going to artificially color your hair, you want it to be all-natural." Throughout the book Brooks relentlessly and humorously criticized Bobos; nevertheless, he also praised them and admitted to being one himself. Noting their role as the nation's leaders and trendsetters, he wrote, "Wherever they have settled they have made life more enjoyable (for those who can afford it)," as quoted by Diane White in the *Boston Globe* (May 28, 2000). *Bobos in Paradise* became a *New York Times* bestseller and was enthusiastically received by critics. Janet Maslin, writing for the *New York Times* (May 4, 2000), described Brooks as "a thoughtful as well as an entertaining social critic" and called the book a "tartly amusing, all too accurate guide to the new establishment and its self-serving ways."

In the late 1990s Brooks had become an occasional contributor to the *New York Times*, writing articles for the Sunday magazine as well as the book-review and week-in-review sections. In the summer of 2003, Brooks was invited to become a twice-a-week op-ed columnist for the *Times*, a newspaper that, in its editorial columns, has generally taken liberal stances on political and social issues. "Has anybody ever said no to that question?" Brooks quipped to George Gurley. Some insiders believed the paper was looking for a successor to William Safire, the 74-year-old conservative columnist who has written op-ed pieces for the *Times* since 1973 and a weekly column on English usage for the Sunday magazine since 1979. As an anonymous source told Gurley, "I don't think there's been a date set, but you can just look at [Safire's] age and when columnists typically and reasonably have retired. There's not forced retirement for writers at *The Times*, only for editors, but I think it's been on their mind for some time who would succeed him. And I think that they've actually found the best possible person, in that he's a lovely guy and he's a good writer." Gail Collins, the editorial-page editor of the *Times*, told Julia Keller, "We look for someone who can add something different, and someone who is likely to develop a strong and distinctive voice. I was not looking for somebody who would be shrill or who would put people off. He's an inclusive writer. He makes people want to read him. That's a rare gift."

Brooks's first op-ed piece for the *New York Times*, published on September 9, 2003, asserted that even though President George W. Bush and his administration would not publicly admit that they had made mistakes in launching and carrying out the 2003 war against Iraq and President Saddam Hussein, they admitted to and made adjustments for mistakes in private. As proof, Brooks pointed to recent, significant policy shifts, such as the administration's asking the United Nations to play a larger role in rebuilding Iraq and agreeing to a timeta-

ble for handing power over to the Iraqis. "The leading Bushies almost never admit serious mistakes," he wrote. "They never acknowledge that they are listening to their critics. They never admit they are shifting course. They don these facial expressions suggesting calm omniscience while down below their legs are doing the foxtrot in six different directions. . . . Fortunately, while in public members of the administration emphasize their own incredible foresight, in private they are able to face unpleasant facts and pivot in response." In a letter to the editor published in the *Times* on September 10, 2003, a reader named David Hildebrand wrote, "David Brooks argues that while the Bush administration never acknowledges mistakes or valid criticisms, the lack of candor is absolved by the administration's hidden reassessments of bad policy choices. For many of us, however, evasiveness and dishonesty can't be forgiven so easily. . . . Mr. Brooks has pointed to, but hasn't admitted, that this administration allows political expediency to trump morality while taking a very painful human toll."

In a controversial column on December 13, 2003, Brooks maintained that the Bush administration had conducted itself with an almost radical degree of honesty and candor in international affairs. Describing the Bush administration as "drunk on truth serum," the columnist cited as an example of extreme forthrightness the president's openness regarding American preemptive action against Iraq. He wrote, "Until the Bush team came to power, foreign relations were conducted with a certain gentlemanly decorum. . . . The United Nations passed resolution after resolution condemning the government of Iraq, without committing the faux pas of actually enforcing them. The leaders of France and Germany announced their abhorrence of Saddam's regime, and expressed this abhorrence by doing as much business with Saddam as possible." President Bush, by contrast, shocked world leaders by announcing his intention of enforcing the resolutions and setting forth his doctrine of preemptive war. Brooks applauded the president for announcing his intentions regarding Iraq rather than acting in secret. Brooks concluded, "The administration's fundamental problem is that it is not very good at dealing with people it can't stand. The men and women in this White House are exceptionally forthright. When they come across someone they regard as insufferable, their instinct is to be blunt. They seek to be honest rather than insincere, to not sugar things up but to let these people know how they really feel." Brooks's piece outraged many readers who believed that the Bush administration had lied about its reasons for invading Iraq. One reader, Benjamin Rubin, wrote in a letter to the *Times* (December 16, 2003), "For Mr. Brooks to describe the Bush administration as 'drunk on truth serum' is truly astounding. Consider the administration's shifting rationales for an illegal war in Iraq; its misleading implications of Saddam Hussein's connection with [the Islamic terrorist organization] Al-Qaeda . . . and its penchant for putting corporate profits over public well-being. Does Mr. Brooks truly believe that such bold-faced lies can come from an honest administration?"

In a November 22, 2003 column that surprised conservatives and liberals alike, Brooks argued that gays should be allowed to marry. Given the current state of marriage—with many opting not to marry and half of those who do getting divorces—Brooks reasoned that the best way for conservatives to reinforce the sanctity and morality of marriage is to encourage as many people as possible to marry. "The conservative course is not to banish gay people from making such commitments," he opined. "It is to expect that they make such commitments. We shouldn't just allow gay marriage. We should insist on gay marriage. We should regard it as scandalous that two people could claim to love each other and not want to sanctify their love with marriage and fidelity."

In the spring of 2004, Brooks published *On Paradise Drive: How We Live Now (And Always Have) in the Future Tense.* "Essentially the question of the book is: if you drive around your basic fast-growing suburb in America, are these people as shallow as they look?" he told Joseph S. Lucas in an interview for the History News Network (August 25, 2003, on-line). "I hope to show that while there are many excesses of materialism and shallowness and complacency . . . some of the nobler impulses that Lincoln and Teddy Roosevelt talked about are still alive, if submerged, in these people." The book received mixed notices. Among the more positive of those was David Pitt's assessment for *Booklist*, as quoted on amazon.com: "As a satiric social commentator, Brooks is always looking for the humorous anomaly—there are more than 600 certified pet chiropractors in the U.S.—but along with exposing cultural absurdities, he offers acute observations on middle-class life, and he frequently takes us in previously unexplored philosophical directions. One way or the other, this book will give readers plenty of new things to think about."

Brooks has retained his position as a senior editor at the *Weekly Standard*. He is also a contributing editor at *Newsweek* and the *Atlantic Monthly* and a commentator on PBS's *NewsHour with Jim Lehrer*. He and his wife, Jane, live in Montgomery County, Maryland, with their two children.

—H.T.

Suggested Reading: *Chicago Tribune* C p1+ Aug. 12, 2003, with photos; History News Network (on-line) Aug. 25, 2003; *New York Observer* Front Page p3+ Nov. 24, 2003

Selected Books: as editor—*Backward and Upward: The New Conservative Writing*, 1996; as writer—*Bobos in Paradise: The New Upper Class and How They Got There*, 2000; *On Paradise Drive: How We Live Now (And Always Have) in the Future Tense*, 2004

Philip Scalia/Courtesy of Doubleday

Brown, Dan

June 22, 1964– Writer

Address: c/o Doubleday Broadway Publishing Group, 1745 Broadway, New York, NY 10019

What if Jesus Christ, the central figure of Christianity, had been married to the repentant prostitute Mary Magdalene, fathered a child, and spirited his family away to France in order keep them safe from his persecutors in the Middle East? That provocative question forms the basis of Dan Brown's blockbuster novel *The Da Vinci Code*. The book, whose action takes place over the course of 24 hours, traces the exploits of Robert Langdon, a Harvard professor and symbologist (an expert in symbols and their meanings) as he uncovers the mystery surrounding the secret lineage of Jesus and finds himself at odds with those who would die to keep it unsolved. Since its publication, in the spring of 2003, *The Da Vinci Code* has become an unqualified success, selling more than six million copies and making Brown a household name. Its popularity also attracted renewed interest in his previous three books, all of which have become best-sellers as well. In addition, it has sparked numerous debates among religious scholars and academics over its core theory. A number of books, including *Breaking the Da Vinci Code* (2004), have been written in response to Brown's book or inspired by the discussion it triggered, and in November 2003 ABC aired a television special, entitled *Jesus, Mary and Da Vinci*, that explored the story's ideas further.

Brown's books offer labyrinthine plots and focus on shadowy conspiracies and, most famously, secret societies. Each of his four novels—the others are *Digital Fortress* (1998), *Angels & Demons* (2000), and *Deception Point* (2001)—sheds light on a real-life group largely hidden from the public, be it the Priory of Sion, supposedly charged with concealing the bloodline of Jesus; the National Security Agency (NSA), a U.S. government organization that has the power to intercept personal E-mail messages and wiretap the phones of private citizens; or the Illuminati, a group of scientists (including Galileo Galilei) who swore vengeance on the Catholic Church for the persecution and execution of those who championed science over religion. "My interest [in secret societies] sparks from growing up in New England," Brown told an interviewer for his Web site, "surrounded by the clandestine clubs of Ivy League universities, the Masonic lodges of our Founding Fathers, and the hidden hallways of early government power." A former teacher of English at Phillips Exeter Academy, Brown also weaves many other historical elements into his stories. "One of the aspects that I try very hard to incorporate in my books is that of learning," he told Edward Morris for *BookPage* (April 2003, on-line). "When you finish the book—like it or not—you've learned a ton."

Dan Brown was born on June 22, 1964 in Exeter, New Hampshire, and grew up on the campus of Phillips Exeter Academy, one of the nation's most prestigious boarding schools, where his father was a Presidential Award–winning mathematics teacher. His mother performed sacred music—music rooted in spirituality and religion. The Brown house was filled with books; in addition, the family enjoyed working on puzzles and exchanging coded messages. Every Christmas, for example, Brown and his sister were given poems that provided clues to the locations of their gifts. At Phillips Exeter Brown was exposed daily to people of other races and cultures. His first baby-sitter was a student from Nigeria. "I grew up on a campus with kids from 37 countries," Brown told Julie Flaherty for the *New York Times* (June 25, 2003). "Racism just didn't occur to me." In addition, he would often spend time with some of the older students. "A lot of these guys missed their younger siblings, and plus it's a very high-pressure environment," he told Flaherty. "It's probably therapeutic on some level to stop and talk to some 9-year-old kid about Hot Wheels."

After graduating from Phillips Exeter, in 1982, Brown attended Amherst College, in Amherst, Massachusetts. While enrolled there he spent a semester in Seville, Spain, studying art history at the city's university. Brown graduated from Amherst with a B.A. degree in 1986; at that time, as he told Claire E. White for the Web site Writers Write (May 1998), he "had two loves—writing fiction and writing music." He moved to Hollywood, California, where he focused on writing songs and playing the piano. While in Hollywood he released four CDs of original material and toured the world with various singing groups. (In 1996 his song "Peace in Our Time" was performed at the Olympic Games in Atlanta, Georgia). In 1990, inspired by encounters with people in Los Angeles who struck him as strange, he penned a joke book entitled *187 Men to Avoid*; the book was published, with the subtitle *A Survival Guide for the Romantically Frustrated Woman*, by Berkeley Press in 1995.

Earlier, in 1993, Brown had returned to Phillips Exeter, where he taught English and creative writing. Two years later one of his students was briefly detained by the Secret Service, which was concerned that the boy posed a threat to national security. "As it turned out," Brown explained to Claire E. White, "the kid had been on the Internet the night before having a light-hearted political debate via E-mail with one of his friends and had made the comment that he was so mad at the current political situation he was ready to kill President [Bill] Clinton. The Secret Service came up to make sure he wasn't serious." The incident made an impression on Brown, particularly the notion that the Secret Service keeps such close tabs on private citizens. "I began wondering how the Secret Service knew what these kids were saying in their e-mail," he told D. Quincy Whitney for the *Boston Globe* (July 19, 1998), "and discovered the National Security Agency, an intelligence agency as large as the CIA that is home to the country's eavesdroppers. I realized it was a great backdrop for a novel."

Brown began conducting extensive research, communicating with two NSA cryptographers via anonymous remailers—Internet sites that forward E-mail messages to specified destinations without revealing the original sources of the messages. "At first, I was surprised with the information they were sharing," he noted during an interview for his Web site, "and I suspected, despite their obvious knowledge, that they were probably not who they said they were. But the more we spoke, the more I was convinced they were authentic. Neither one knew about the other, and yet they told almost identical stories."

The product of Brown's work, the novel *Digital Fortress*, was published in early 1998 to positive notices. "In this fast-paced, plausible tale," Sybil Steinberg wrote for *Publishers Weekly* (December 22, 1997), "Brown blurs the line between good and evil enough to delight patriots and paranoids alike." The story centers on a computer program that generates impenetrable codes, which could cripple U.S. intelligence, and on the efforts of a brilliant cryptographer, Susan Fletcher, to prevent such a disaster. The novel also provides the reader with a look inside the walls of the NSA and raises long-debated questions about the extent to which the federal government has invaded citizens' privacy. "The World Wide Web is anything but private," he noted on his Web site, as quoted by Whitney. "Many computer users still don't realize that the Web sites they visit will, in many cases, track their progress through the site, how long a user stays, what he lingers over, what files he downloads. If you're visiting sites on the Web that you don't want anyone to know you're visiting, you better think again."

Brown's second novel, *Angels & Demons*, introduced readers to Robert Langdon, the Harvard symbologist who would become the hero of *The Da Vinci Code*. The idea for *Angels & Demons*, which places its protagonist at the center of a wide-ranging conspiracy involving the Vatican and a secret society known as the Illuminati, came to Brown while he was vacationing in Rome, Italy. "I was beneath Vatican City touring a tunnel called il passetto—a concealed passageway used by the early Popes to escape in event of enemy attack," he recalled on his Web site. "According to the scholar giving the tour, one of the Vatican's most feared ancient enemies was a secret brotherhood known as the Illuminati—the 'enlightened ones'—a cult of early scientists who had vowed revenge against the Vatican for crimes against scientists like Galileo and Copernicus. I was fascinated by images of this cloaked, anti-religious brotherhood lurking in the catacombs of Rome. Then, when the scholar added that many modern historians believe the Illuminati is still active today and is one of most powerful unseen forces in global politics, I knew I was hooked. . . . I had to write an Illuminati thriller."

As was the case with *Digital Fortress*, Brown thoroughly researched the topics covered in *Angels & Demons*, which include the Vatican, the Illuminati, and the Conseil Européen pour la Recherche Nucléaire (CERN), a Swiss research facility that is credited with the invention of (among other things) the World Wide Web. *Angels & Demons* received solid reviews. "One of the best international thrillers of recent years, Dan Brown's *Angels & Demons* is both literate and extremely well researched, mixing physics with religion," Nancy Pearl wrote for *Library Journal* (November 15, 2000). Such praise notwithstanding, at the time of its initial publication, the book sold only 10,000 copies.

Brown continued writing, completing his third novel, *Deception Point*, in 2001. As he had with his two previous books, Brown revealed in the story the inner workings of a clandestine organization, in this case the National Reconnaissance Office (NRO), an intelligence agency that employs cutting-edge spy technology. The plot involves an asteroid, found beneath the arctic ice, that may contain evidence of extraterrestrial life, and the events that ensue when a female intelligence analyst attempts to uncover the conspiracy to keep the asteroid hidden. *Deception Point* received mixed notices from critics. Writing for *Publishers Weekly* (September 10, 2001), Jeff Zaleski called the book "an excellent thriller—a big yet believable story unfolding at breakneck pace, with convincing settings and just the right blend of likable and hateful characters. [Brown has] also done his research, folding in sophisticated scientific and military details that make his plot far more fulfilling than the norm." Offering a different take, in a review for *Booklist* (September 15, 2001), David Pitt wrote, "In the end, what does Brown's mixed bag add up to? Those who require only that thrillers deliver the requisite number of chills will have a good time here, but those looking for a little artistry, a little panache, are likely to be disappointed."

The idea for *The Da Vinci Code* came to Brown as he was researching *Angels & Demons*. Its seeds had been planted, however, during his college years. "I first learned of [the Italian artist, engineer, and architect Leonardo] Da Vinci's affiliation with the Priory of Sion when I was studying art history at the University of Seville," he told Edward Morris. "One day, the professor showed us a slide of *The Last Supper* and began to outline all the strange anomalies in [Da Vinci's] painting"; those oddities, such as the disembodied hand holding a knife and the feminine appearance of the figure who should have been John the Apostle, according to the teacher, suggested that Da Vinci had hidden messages in the painting. Knowing that a novel based on this idea would have to be complexly plotted, Brown began working out the details of the story during his morning exercise sessions. "I would go running with a Dictaphone and discuss the plot aloud with myself. I felt like a juggler who was trying to keep 13 balls in the air simultaneously," he told Aurelia C. Scott for *Audiofile* (June/July 2003, on-line). "Imagine if someone had found the Dictaphone. They would have heard a panting guy talking about Rome and Mary Magdalene's child and assassinations—and would have turned it in to the police!"

In writing the story Brown drew on a number of sources, including histories of the Knights Templar (a monastic military order founded in 1118, in the aftermath of the First Crusade, to help the new Kingdom of Jerusalem protect itself from its Muslim neighbors and ensure the safety of the large numbers of European pilgrims to Jerusalem); the Dead Sea Scrolls (hundreds of leather or papyrus scrolls and fragments, in Hebrew, Greek, or Aramaic, believed to have been written largely by a Jewish sect known as the Essenes between the third century B.C. and 68 A.D., which were discovered between 1947 and 1956 in caves near Qumran, near the Dead Sea); and the Holy Grail. Many passages in *The Da Vinci Code* suggest that history as many of us know it is false. According to the book, the Holy Grail is not, as Christian legend has it, the cup that Christ used at the Last Supper or the vessel that caught Christ's blood at the Crucifixion; instead, it is a series of documents that offer proof of Jesus's marriage to Mary Magdalene and of his royal bloodline, the so-called Merovingian Kings. While some may dismiss these notions as the ravings of a conspiracy theorist, Brown insists that there is historical evidence to support them. "Since the beginning of recorded time," he noted on his Web site, "history has been written by the 'winners' (those societies and belief systems that conquered and survived). Despite an obvious bias in this accounting method, we still measure the 'historical accuracy' of a given concept by examining how well it concurs with our existing historical record. Many historians now believe (as do I) that in gauging the historical accuracy of a given concept, we should first ask ourselves a far deeper question: How historically accurate is history itself?"

The Da Vinci Code arrived in bookstores in March 2003 and shot to number one on the *New York Times* best-seller list, a rare feat for an author with no previous successes to his credit. The enthusiastic public reception was expected, as there had been talk about the book in the publishing community since the summer of 2002. When 100 pages of the manuscript were circulated to the sales force at Doubleday, the response was uniformly positive. "There was a unanimous 'Oh my God' response," Stephen Rubin, the president of the Doubleday Broadway publishing group, which published the book, told Bill Goldstein for the *New York Times* (April 21, 2003). "If people [within the publishing house] are responding unanimously and rhapsodically, there's no reason to think that [other people] won't react the same way." For the most part, critical response was positive as well. "In this gleefully erudite suspense novel, Mr. Brown takes the format he has been developing through three earlier novels and fine-tunes it to blockbuster perfection," Janet Maslin wrote for the *New York Times* (March 17, 2003). "Not since the advent of Harry Potter has an author so flagrantly delighted in leading readers on a breathless chase and coaxing them through hoops." In *Entertainment Weekly* (March 28, 2003), in a somewhat less enthusiastic review, Scott Brown wrote that "the story is a straightforward, code-cracking mystery quest for the Sunday Jumble set. . . . The cliches click pleasantly into place, like the tumblers of an old, easy-to-pick lock." Writing for *Publishers Weekly* (February 3, 2003), Jeff Zaleski observed, "Brown sometimes ladles out too much religious history at the expense of pacing, and Langdon is a hero in desperate need of more chutzpah. Still, Brown has assembled a whopper of a plot that will please both conspiracy buffs and thriller addicts."

The success of *The Da Vinci Code* sparked a flurry of debate, among both religious leaders who challenged the veracity of Brown's claims and historians who called into question some of Brown's knowledge of Leonardo da Vinci. "How much does this murder mystery have to do with the real Leonardo?" Bruce Boucher asked in a *New York Times* (August 3, 2003) article titled "Does *The Da Vinci Code* Crack Leonardo?" "The short answer is not much, and the author's grasp of the historical Leonardo is shaky." In an article for *Crisis* (September 2003) called "Dismantling *The Da Vinci Code*," Sandra Miesel systematically picked the novel apart, concluding that Brown's knowledge of history as reflected in the book is at best questionable and at worst completely based on misperceptions. "So error-laden is *The Da Vinci Code*," she wrote,

"that the educated reader actually applauds those rare occasions where Brown stumbles (despite himself) into the truth."

In addition, much of the Christian community has expressed displeasure over the book. In an article in *Catholic New World,* as quoted by Mark O'Keefe in the *Houston Chronicle* (February 28, 2004, on-line), Francis Cardinal George called *The Da Vinci Code* "a work of bizarre religious imaginings" based on "a facade of scholarship" that takes advantage of readers' "gullibility for conspiracy." However, some have defended the book's assertions, arguing that, accurate or not, they might lead people to learn more about the life of Jesus. "It's only a threat if people read this fictional book naively, don't think critically about it and don't pursue truth," the Reverend Mark Roberts told O'Keefe. "Now that we have people thinking and talking, we can look at the real evidence of Jesus." Stephen Prothero, the chairman of the Religion Department at Boston University, told Ron Charles for the *Christian Science Monitor* (March 19, 2004) that the book "taps into a lot of longstanding stories about Jesus in America. Americans have been ruminating since the Colonial period about finding documents that would settle all the mysteries about Jesus."

As of November 7, 2004 *The Da Vinci Code* was number four on the *New York Times* hardcover best-seller list and had spent 84 weeks at or near the top spot. It has greatly spurred sales of Brown's earlier books; indeed, during one week in early 2004, all four of his novels appeared on the *Times* best-seller list. *The Da Vinci Code* has been translated into more than 40 languages and is scheduled to be made into a feature film, with Ron Howard directing.

Dan Brown makes his home in New Hampshire with his wife, Blythe, a painter and art historian. Due to the controversy that has surrounded *The Da Vinci Code,* he no longer grants interviews. Brown is currently at work on his next Robert Langdon novel, which will be set in Washington, D.C. "I was skeptical when I first started thinking of setting a book here that it could have the same sort of grandeur and punch as a place like Paris or Rome," he told Linda Wertheimer during an interview for the National Public Radio program *Weekend Edition* (April 26, 2003). "In fact, the more I researched about Washington's architecture and its history, the more I'm starting to think . . . it may surpass Rome in its secret history. What a fascinating place."

—J.K.B.

Suggested Reading: *Boston Globe* (on-line) July 19, 1998; Dan Brown Web site; *Houston Chronicle* (on-line) Feb. 28, 2004; National Public Radio Web site; *New York Times* C p11 Apr. 21, 2003, with photo, E p8 Mar. 17, 2003, with photo; Writers Write Web site

Selected Books: *Digital Fortress*, 1998; *Angels & Demons*, 2000; *Deception Point*, 2001; *The Da Vinci Code*, 2003

George Brainard/Courtesy of Telarc Records

Brown, Junior

1952– Country musician

Address: Thompson Brown Co., P.O. Box 690715, Tulsa, OK 74169-0715

When first confronted with the problem of how to play both the lead guitar and the steel guitar during his live shows, Junior Brown came up with a unique solution: he fused the two instruments, received a patent for the invention, and dubbed it a guit-steel. He found a similar solution to the problem of how to utilize all of the musical styles that had influenced him, which include traditional country, rock and roll, surf, Hawaiian hula songs, Western swing, blues, and more: he simply fused the styles into a unique signature sound. "I've done a lot of different things over the years," Brown told Lorraine Ali for *Gentlemen's Quarterly* (March 1999), "everything from playing Hawaiian luaus to performing with [ranchero accordion player] Flaco Jiminez. I'm trying to be real and present music that's part of me—and still have all this variety. It sounds like juggling, but that's what I've become— an amalgam of all this stuff. Country is just the center part of it. It's not the whole story." Brown sings in a laid-back, drawling baritone, often employing humorous lyrics and wordplay. His fiery guitar playing, influenced as much by the blues/rock legend Jimi Hendrix as by country pickers such as

Merle Travis, is full of surprises. Reviewing Brown's performance at a New York City club in 1994, Jon Pareles wrote for the *New York Times* (January 29, 1994), "He applies all the devices of country, blues and bluegrass guitarists: speedy bluegrass picking, plainspoken melodies, chicken-squawk repeated notes, melting steel-guitar chords, skidding fast runs and the deep twang of a bottom string being retuned downward. As if Mr. Brown could split his personality, the smooth tone of the steel guitar contested the wiry attack of the six-string; he didn't run out of ideas." With six full-length albums and countless performances to his credit, Brown is a music veteran, but it has only been in the past few years that he has attained significant commercial success. The outward signs of that success are now abundant: he has been nominated for four Grammy Awards, appeared or sung in advertisements for Gap clothing, Lipton tea, and Lee jeans, and toured with such prominent non-country acts as the Dave Matthews Band.

Jamison Brown was born in Cottonwood, Arizona, in 1952 (some sources say 1953). His father, Sam Brown, who was a musicologist and a piano player, encouraged his son to play as well, but Junior disliked the instrument. "He'd sit me down every day at the piano," Brown recalled to Ali, "and say, 'Why can't you do this?!' And I'd say, 'Dad, it's just not fun. It don't swing.'" Brown soon discovered a predilection for a different instrument. "I found a guitar with just a few strings on it in my grandparents' attic and I really took to it at a very young age," he told Chris Heim for the *Chicago Tribune* (January 14, 1994). "When I was about eight years old, I took lessons from a college student and learned about four or five chords. Aside from that, I learned it all myself."

When Brown was young his family moved around a great deal. After leaving Arizona, Brown lived in the backwoods of Indiana—in a town called Kirksville—and then in Annapolis, Maryland, from 1958 to 1965. In that year he and his family moved to Santa Fe, New Mexico, where Brown attended Santa Fe Prep School before dropping out of Santa Fe High School in his junior year. By that time he was already interested in music above all else. At 13 he had formed his first band, Harmonious Discord, which played mostly surf music. Next was Humble Harvey, a psychedelic band. Brown left home at 16, struggling to earn a living by performing at clubs around Santa Fe. He began appearing with country and honky-tonk bands, playing guitar and sometimes singing. (He did not write any of the music he performed during that period.)

In the 1970s Brown became serious about performing on the steel guitar, which is normally held face-up on the lap and played with a slide to produce smooth transitions between notes. He formed the Last Mile Ramblers, which became a staple of the Santa Fe music scene and opened for such acts as Willie Nelson, Waylon Jennings, and Dolly Parton when they came through town. In the mid-

1970s Brown moved to Colorado and joined Dusty Drapes and the Dusters. He next became a member of the Billy Spears Band, based in Lawrence, Kansas, then moved to Austin, Texas, in 1979 to team up with Alvin Crow's Western swing band. Around that time Brown also played briefly with Rank and File, Asleep at the Wheel, and Gary P. Nunn. Brown, who was more interested in traditional country music by the likes of Ernest Tubb than in country-pop music as played by bands such as the Gatlin Brothers, found his tastes at odds with those of the day. "People were in such a hurry to cover up that [traditional] stuff because it represented bigotry and what it was like to be a stupid hick," Brown told Joe Nick Patoski for *Texas Monthly* (June 1996). "I was a pariah. People made fun of me. As much money as I could've made doing Gatlin Brothers covers, I stuck with Ernest Tubb covers, and I was called all sorts of names."

In 1984 Brown was approached by a local Austin bass player, Speedy Sparks, who was starting his own record label and wanted Brown to record a single. Brown obliged with "Too Many Nights in the Roadhouse" and, on the record's B side, "Gotta Get Up Every Morning (Just to Say Goodnight to You)." Five hundred copies of the record were pressed. The following year Brown's vision for his hybrid guit-steel was finally realized, thanks to the work of the luthier Michael Stevens. For years Brown had been forced to switch back and forth between the lead guitar and pedal steel guitar, which interrupted the flow of his music, and in about 1980 a simple solution had come to him in a dream. "In this dream [the lead guitar and pedal steel guitar] just melted together and I was playing this double-necked instrument that was both," he recalled to Heim. "I woke up and arranged the two instruments on the bed and arranged the covers around them to form the shape of this thing and I thought it just might work." In the mid-1980s Brown moved from Austin to Oklahoma, where he was invited by Leon McAuliffe, a former pedal steel player for Bob Wills's Texas Playboys, to teach guitar at the Hank Thompson School of Country Music at Rogers State University, in Claremore. One of Brown's students there was Tanya Rae, whom he married in 1988.

The 1980s had been lean years for Brown. "I was very bitter for many years because I didn't do anything but play in club bands," Brown told Richard Harrington for the *Washington Post* (August 10, 2001). "I thought, 'I'm going to spend the rest of my life doing this in bars, playing for people who don't appreciate the music, learning songs that I don't particularly like.' It was dismal in the early '80s: Clubs started drying up and people got their entertainment elsewhere and a million bands showed up to undercut you. It didn't matter how good you were, they just treated you like a jukebox." Tanya Rae helped Brown to think in an organized way about his career. "I never could get a group together until I met Tanya Rae and really got serious about

it," he told Harrington. Brown began to branch out from country, incorporating his disparate influences—including surf, blues, Hawaiian, psychedelic rock, Texas swing, jazz, rockabilly, and bluegrass—into his music. He even made an extended trip to Hawaii, where steel guitar is prevalent in much of the music.

In 1990 (other sources say 1989 or 1991), Brown self-released a 12-song cassette called *12 Shades of Brown*. It featured a tune that alluded to his Hawaiian experience, "Hillbilly Hula Gal," and the crowd favorite "My Baby Don't Dance to Nothing But Ernest Tubb." In 1992 Curb Records, based in Nashville, Tennessee, took an interest in Brown after a talent agent named Bobby Cudd discovered the musician playing at the Continental Club in Austin. Brown's music "was so good, so profound, it was hard for me to believe," Cudd told Peter Cronin for *Billboard* (March 26, 1994). "His instrument is unique, his songwriting is unique, and his presentation is marvelous. Singing these songs with a twinkle in his eye and a snarl on his lip—you could tell it was real." In 1993 Curb Records reissued *12 Shades of Brown* along with a new album, *Guit with It*. On "Guit-Steel Blues" from that album, Brown demonstrated his prowess on his instrument with an extended jam that featured several riffs inspired by Jimi Hendrix. Brown's dry sense of humor is evident on several songs, including "My Wife Thinks You're Dead," on which he croons, as quoted by Ali, "Please go find another ex-sweetheart to hang around instead, cause you're wanted by the poe-lice, and my wife thinks you're dead." Brown, commenting on his penchant for humor, told Chris Heim, "There's a style of lighthearted, wise-guy country music that went out of style. People just didn't want to laugh at themselves. I think they were scared to be corny or whatever. But I don't care. I enjoy it." Reviewing *Guit with It* for *People* (October 25, 1993), Tony Scherman wrote, "Finally—a new country artist who doesn't sound like the result of market research! . . . His humor may be too bent and his sound insufficiently pasteurized for him to fit inside commercial country's confines, but Junior Brown will delight any true country-music fan."

By 1996 Brown was beginning to get a taste of the success he had long sought. He was selected by Country Music Television (CMT) as one of its rising stars for 1996, played with the house band on the television show *Saturday Night Live*, performed on the Grand Ole Opry, and appeared on *Late Night with Conan O'Brien* and the *Late Show with David Letterman*. The video for "My Wife Thinks You're Dead" won the video-of-the-year award at the 1996 Country Music Association (CMA) Awards ceremony and was nominated for best video by the Academy of Country Music. Brown also released *Semi Crazy* in 1996; on the title track he intoned, "Til I'm pushing up daisies, I'll be semi-crazy." The album contained Brown's usual mix of traditional country, rock and roll, and deadpan humor. It also featured a seven-minute medley of surf songs, which had become favorites in Brown's live shows. *Guitar Player* magazine chose *Semi Crazy* as its best country album of 1997; Brown also won that publication's vote for best pedal/lap steel guitarist and tied with Vince Gill for the best country guitarist award. A reviewer for the *CMJ New Musical Report*, as quoted on CDNow.com, wrote of Brown and *Semi Crazy*, "There's a certain artistry at work with this journeyman musician that's missing from so much of today's musical landscape. . . . We're lucky enough to have a few living legends in American music—James Burton, Willie Nelson, Johnny Cash, Merle Haggard, and such, and Junior Brown is quite simply another one in the making."

In 1997 Brown was nominated for Grammy Awards for best country song and best male vocal performance for "My Wife Thinks You're Dead." He also appeared on the television shows *Prime Time Country* and *CBS Sunday Morning* and was recruited for a Gap clothing-advertisement campaign. In 1998 he released his fourth major album, *Long Walk Back*, on which he had the chance to explore his Jimi Hendrix influence with "Stupid Blues," a nine-minute cut that also featured the work of Mitch Mitchell, Hendrix's former drummer. Brown also teamed up with Mitchell—and Noel Redding, the third member of the former Jimi Hendrix Experience—at the 1998 Bumbershoot Rock Festival, in Seattle, Washington, where the trio performed a rendition of Hendrix's "Stone Free." Brown expanded his media exposure further in 1998 by becoming a spokesman for Lipton tea (he is an avid tea drinker), appearing again on David Letterman's program, and making a guest appearance on *The X-files* on November 15, 1998.

Brown's eclecticism had always appealed to listeners who were not otherwise fans of country music, and as his popularity increased he was embraced by some high-profile bands decidedly outside the country-music scene. On the *Late Show with David Letterman* in 2000, he jammed with the alternative rock band Stone Temple Pilots, who had asked Brown to perform with them, and in 2001 he opened 12 concerts for the Dave Matthews Band and joined them on stage on several occasions. Also in 2001 Brown released *Mixed Bag*, which lived up to its title with songs ranging from the searing "Guitar Man" to the old-fashioned dixie swing of "Riverboat Shuffle" (on which Brown imitates a trombone with his guit-steel) to the offbeat "Cagey Bea," about a fantastical tryst with a seductive Soviet KGB spy. A reviewer for *Billboard* (August 11, 2001) called *Mixed Bag* "perhaps [Brown's] best ever, deftly melding jaw-dropping 'guit-steel' solos with authentic, Texas-style country." Reviewing *Down Home Chrome*, Brown's 2004 album, which includes the songs "Where Has All the Money Gone?," "Jimmy Jones," and "Two Rons Don't Make It Right," a critic for allmusic.com wrote, "Honky tonk, rockabilly, and the rich sound of Bakersfield country are leavened with a healthy sense of humor."

Junior Brown and his wife live in Oklahoma.

—P.G.H.

Suggested Reading: *Billboard* p30 Aug. 11, 2001; *Chicago Tribune* VII pR Jan. 14, 1994; *Gentlemen's Quarterly* p139+ Mar. 1999; *Newsweek* p57 July 15, 1996; *New York Times* Art p15 Jan. 29, 1994; *People* p35 Oct. 25, 1993; *Texas Monthly* p102 June 1996, with photo; *Washington Post* D p7 Oct. 23, 1993, WW p6 Aug. 10, 2001, C p8 Aug. 17, 2001

Selected Recordings: *12 Shades of Brown*, 1993; *Guit with It*, 1993; *Semi-Crazy*, 1996; *Long Walk Back*, 1998; *Mixed Bag*, 2001; *Down Home Chrome*, 2004

Dennis Pilsits, courtesy of Picador

Burroughs, Augusten

Oct. 23, 1965– Writer

Address: c/o St. Martin's Press, 175 Fifth Ave., Suite 401, New York, NY 10010-7703

"When I was 13, my crazy mother gave me away to her lunatic psychiatrist, who adopted me. I then lived a life of squalor, pedophiles, no schools and free pills." With those words, spoken to Claude Peck for the *Minneapolis-St. Paul Star Tribune* (November 16, 2003, on-line), the writer Augusten Burroughs summarized the contents of *Running with Scissors* (2002), a memoir of his turbulent teenage years. A critically acclaimed best-seller, *Running with Scissors* has been reprinted a dozen times and has been published in 10 languages in addition to English. "There have been a lot of authors writing about their screwed-up life—Tobias Wolff is a perfect example, with *This Boy's Life*," Dan Peres, the editor of *Details* magazine, told Peck. "The difference with Augusten is that he took an extremely intense and upsetting and traumatizing childhood and wrote about it in a way that doesn't necessarily make you feel sorry for him. He didn't write a tearjerker. He wrote a very honest book that makes you laugh." Similarly, Peter Neil Nason wrote for the *Tampa Tribune* (June 8, 2003), "Burroughs has the uncanny ability to do what so many authors strive for but few can accomplish with equal aplomb: He makes you laugh and then he tears out your heart." Burroughs, whose formal education ended with primary school, is also the author of *Sellevision* (2000), a well-received satirical novel based on his years as an advertising copywriter. His most recently published book, *Dry* (2003), a memoir that he wrote in the late 1990s, describes his addictions to drugs and alcohol, his treatment at a rehabilitation center that catered to homosexuals, and his struggles to remain sober after the death of his lover from AIDS. *Magical Thinking*, a collection of stories about himself, was published in 2004. Regarding Burroughs's success, Claude Peck commented, "It's the kind of career in writing that might make Burroughs the envy of classmates at his high-school reunion, if only he had gone to high school."

Burroughs was born Christopher Robison on October 23, 1965 in Pittsburgh, Pennsylvania. He has claimed to be a direct descendant of King James II of Scotland (1430–60). At age 18 he legally changed his name to Augusten X. Burroughs, because he thought it sounded literary. His father, John Robison, taught math and philosophy at the college level (he retired as head of the Philosophy Department at the University of Massachusetts at Amherst); he also suffered from alcoholism. His mother, Margaret Robison (called Deirdre in *Running with Scissors*), an aspiring poet, had bouts of manic depression and psychosis. As a child, in attempts to escape his parents' unending quarreling, Burroughs would fantasize of becoming an airline steward, a soap-opera star, or a hair-care-products tycoon. He yearned in vain for the sort of idealized happy life depicted on the 1950s sitcom *Leave It to Beaver*. "My parents had this relationship that was really terrifying," he recalled to Litsa Dremousis for Bookslut.com (October 6, 2003). "I mean, the level of hatred that they had, and the level of physical abuse—my mother would beat up my father, basically—and I think I was drawn to images on television that were bright and reflective. And shallow, very superficial." When he was quite young, his parents gave him a tape recorder as a gift. "Before I could write, I would talk into it," he told LoAnn Halden for the *Weekly News* (January 8, 2004, on-line), a Florida publication. "I would make up plays sometimes, but mostly what I would do is talk about my day."

During his adolescence Burroughs's parents divorced, and his father disappeared from his life for many years. When he was 13 his mother relinquished guardianship of him to her psychiatrist, Rodolph Harvey Turcotte (called Dr. Finch in *Running with Scissors*), who lived in Northhampton, Massachusetts, with his wife and three of their children. (Burroughs's older brother, John, nine years his senior, had already left home. He now owns a car dealership in Springfield, Massachusetts.) An assortment of the psychiatrist's patients and former clients also lived in the Turcottes' home for varying periods. All the while Burroughs maintained contact with his mother, who was repeatedly institutionalized for psychiatric treatment.

As Burroughs has described events, Turcotte physically resembled Santa Claus, but he was far from benign. Viewing himself as a "full-time theologist," he believed that God communicated to him through the shape of his feces. He also believed in what he called a "Bible dip": whatever word his finger happened to point to after he opened the Bible at random supposedly provided illumination into particular problems or questions. In addition, he and his wife apparently raised their daughters without rules. They did not object to the children's playing with an obsolete electroshock-therapy machine, for example; according to Burroughs, the girls strapped him into it during his first visit to the house. Further contributing to the strangeness of the household, Mrs. Turcotte ate dog food, and her husband had given legal guardianship of one daughter, who was then 13, to a tennis pro nearly 30 years her senior, who abused her during their ensuing three-year relationship. Dr. Turcotte also enabled the 13-year-old Burroughs to quit school, by helping him to fake a suicide attempt (by administering whiskey and Valium to the boy until he passed out); at the mental hospital where Burroughs was briefly held afterward, he was labeled psychologically unfit to attend school.

That year a man whom Burroughs called Neil Bookman, who was then in his 30s, began having sex with him. The relationship, which Turcotte and other adults in the house knew about, continued for several years, until Bookman vanished. Explaining why he submitted to Bookman, Burroughs told Colin Waters for the Scottish newspaper *Sunday Herald* (February 16, 2003), "I didn't have any adults in my life that were paying attention to me. My mother was crazy and my father wasn't around. Neil was an adult who was giving me a tonne of attention and time. It became sexual. I think what happened to me could happen to any kid, regardless of whether they're gay or straight. You get sucked into something like that because in order to get the attention and affection you crave, you have to pay the price, and that's sex. It's only years later you realise how horrible and wrong it was."

Burroughs received his GED (general equivalency diploma) at 17 and then enrolled at a community college, where he soon flunked out. At about that time his mother accused Dr. Turcotte of raping her, and Burroughs moved out of the Turcottes' home. Although, in light of his mother's mental problems, he was unsure whether to believe her charge of rape, "knowing Dr. Finch, I would say that he probably did rape my mother," as he told Waters. Finch, he said, had much in common with the American mass murderer Charles Manson, in that he "had charisma and was to some degree a leader. He was able to get vulnerable people to follow him. Finch had moments of clarity, possibly even brilliance, but these were heavily diluted with real madness." The doctor lost his medical license in 1986, when he was found guilty of insurance fraud; he died in 2000.

Burroughs lived in Boston, Massachusetts, and Chicago, Illinois, before moving to San Francisco, California, where he remained for five years. After working at a series of relatively unskilled jobs (waiter, dog trainer, candy-store clerk, and store detective), he attended a trade school with the intention of becoming a computer programmer. Then, by his own account, while watching TV one day, he saw a badly made commercial for the school; thinking he could do better, he rewrote every ad in a copy of *Fortune* magazine that happened to be at hand. (As a child he had loved the TV sitcom *Bewitched*, in which the main character's husband, Darren Stevens, was an advertising executive.) Soon afterward he landed a job with the advertising agency Ogilvy & Mather in San Francisco. "The only thing I could do was write ads, because it's manipulating people, telling them to look on the bright side—and I was good at that. I'd had a lot of practice," he told Jackie McGlone for the *Scotsman* (February 15, 2003). "I knew all about taking a situation that was [expletive] and finding the positive. Advertising is taking a wart and transforming it into a beauty mark."

Working in advertising is "pretty cushy in a lot of ways, but I hated it," as Burroughs told Litsa Dremousis. Nevertheless, in the early 1990s he took another job in the field, this time with an ad agency in New York City. During that period he began smoking crack cocaine and drinking to excess. Every night he would consume a bottle of whiskey; to disguise the smell of alcohol on his breath when he was at his office, he would spray his tongue with a men's cologne. "I had been very successful as an advertising copy writer, but I always felt like I had this horrible, dirty secret," he told James MacGowan for the *Ottawa Citizen* (July 28, 2002). "I really felt like my childhood, my past and my lack of any education was this extra, deformed leg I was dragging around behind me, trying to keep under my jacket. I was really ashamed of it and I felt like a prisoner of it. And try explaining it to someone on a third date who says, 'So, tell me about your parents.'"

Burroughs's drug and alcohol problems intensified until his co-workers persuaded him to enter a 30-day rehabilitation program specifically designed for homosexuals, at the Pride Institute, in

Eden Prairie, Minnesota, outside Minneapolis (dubbed the Proud Institute in *Running with Scissors*). In 2000 he quit drinking and within weeks wrote a novel, *Sellevision*. Published the same year, *Sellevision* focuses on a fictitious home-shopping network and several of the people associated with it. Burroughs described *Sellevision* to LoAnn Halden as a "total cheese popcorn of a book"—"which is exactly what he wanted it to be," as Halden reported. "Light and funny, with a bitter aftertaste," according to an assessment by Regina Marler for Amazon.com, *Sellevision* earned mixed reviews in *Publishers Weekly* and *Kirkus Reviews*, among other periodicals. As quoted on Amazon.com, more enthusiastic notices appeared in *People*, in which a critic called it "one of the hoots of this fall"; the New York *Daily News*, which labeled it "an absolute howl . . . wicked fun"; and *Booklist*, for which James Klise wrote, "As a bubbly soap opera, *Sellevision* is good company for the beach or the plane. Its literary value may be low, but the material sparkles."

At the suggestion of his agent, Christopher Schelling, Burroughs next began writing a memoir about his teen years. "I thought my childhood was a disgusting mess so I never thought anyone would be interested in reading about it, even with a gallows humour," he told Phillip McCarthy for the *Sydney Morning Herald* (April 5, 2003). "And so I never really thought about holding back. Should I tell about my pedophile relationship? Sure. Should I tell about eating dog food watching television? Why not." As reference, Burroughs used his extensive journals, which he began keeping at 14. "These journals were hilarious," he told Waters. "There I was, with a mother who was talking to the lampshades and eating peanut butter and cigarette sandwiches, and all I could think about was how I'd give myself an ulcer unless I started up my own line of hair-care products." Burroughs mined terrain already covered in countless childhood memoirs; what set his book apart from most of them was its combination of ghastliness and humor. "Hopefully the book isn't about self-pity and being a victim and whining and sniveling about how horrible my life was," Burroughs said to Waters. "Even at the time I saw how my life was so appalling it was funny." "*Running with Scissors* is—in every sense I can think of—a blast . . . ," Lynne Truss wrote for the London *Sunday Times* (February 2, 2003). "Burroughs is a likeable and wry narrator, and a born writer. . . . In the world of horrific and self-amazed childhood memoirs, *Running with Scissors* sets a new standard for, basically, getting over it and getting out more." Sara O'Leary, in a review for the *Vancouver Sun* (August 17, 2002), wrote that *Running with Scissors* "appears to do more than reinvent the genre [of personal memoir]—it completely obliterates it, or at least handily dispatches one of its many subgenres: the tell-all account of the dysfunctional family. After reading this memoir I don't see any point in anyone ever writing about an unhappy childhood again." According to O'Leary, Burroughs's "mix of cynicism, resilience, and self-deprecating humour . . . makes a highly readable book out of an often sickening story. . . . It's hard to believe that all his claims are literally true, but perhaps they are. At a certain point, if the story is good enough you just don't care." While several other reviewers also challenged the book's veracity, Burroughs told McCarthy that all of it was true. "I don't think you could really make up stuff like this," he asserted. "It would be too unbelievable. But I was writing it down in my journals my whole life . . . writing for four hours every day." Members of the Turcotte family have acknowledged the accuracy of some parts of *Running with Scissors*; other parts have led them to consider suing Burroughs. (As of November 2004 they had not taken any legal action.) Burroughs's mother has also taken issue with his depiction of some events, such as the scene in which he discovers her having sex with a minister's wife.

In his next book, *Dry* (2003), which was written before both *Sellevision* and *Running with Scissors*, Burroughs described his struggles with alcohol and drug addiction, his recovery, and his relationship with his best friend and lover George Stathakis (called Pighead in *Dry*), whom he helped care for when Stathakis was ill with AIDS. Burroughs had started writing *Dry* after his friend's death, in 1998, in an effort to stay sober. "I was like, 'What do I do all day?'" he told Jeff Baker for the *Oregonian* (June 6, 2003). "Everything was vibrating with intensity and I had all this energy. When I drank, I didn't keep a journal—I did some in rehab, but it didn't help at all—but when I got out I just wrote all day, every day." Burroughs explained to Claude Peck that after he completed rehab, "I was so exuberant, and so manic . . . I would stay inside on a beautiful day to write. I wasn't thinking about publishing, or that someone would read this someday; I just had to write. That's what *Dry* came from." The completed manuscript filled about 1,800 pages; with the help of Schelling and Jennifer Enderlin, an editor at St. Martin's Press, the author reworked it; the published book ends on page 293. Burroughs has said that in writing *Dry*, he took liberties with the truth, by combining characters, for example, and changing some details and time periods.

While critiques of *Dry* were favorable, they were not as positive as those for *Running with Scissors*. Among the most enthusiastic reviewers was Connie Ogle, who wrote for the *Miami Herald* (June 29, 2003), "What made *Scissors* so overwhelmingly enjoyable also makes *Dry* compelling: Burroughs can see himself at his lowest . . . and turn his pain into an unforgettable comic portrait. . . . The trick is that Burroughs can laugh at himself, and when he writes he reminds us that maybe we ought not to take ourselves and our problems so seriously. And he's more than just a garden variety wise guy: *Dry* takes a heartbreaking turn at the end, and the shift is perfect, moving and redemptive, an excellent counterpoint to the outrageous humor." By

contrast, Kim Hughes wrote for the *Toronto Star* (July 27, 2003), "While the slyly funny *Dry* might be as easy to knock back as Burroughs' preferred Ketel One martinis, it's relatively light on alcohol-fuelled disasters. Moreover, its rarefied setting . . . keeps us at an emotional distance. . . . Burroughs is to be commended for having the courage to examine his shortcomings publicly. And there's absolutely no doubt our man can sucker-punch the senses with a supple turn of phrase and many alert observations. But transparency is only as interesting as what lies beneath. In the case of *Dry*, the declarations of a privileged, well-heeled recovered alcoholic are only slightly more illuminating than avowals of a regular one."

In Burroughs's latest effort, *Magical Thinking: True Stories*, he continued to mine his life for literary material, which he set down this time in essay form. Although there were numerous favorable comparisons made between him and other essayists with a taste for the grotesque and amusing (among them David Sedaris, Jonathan Ames, and David Rakoff), Burroughs's collection struck some critics as flat, especially in light of the outsized carnival-sideshow attraction of *Scissors* and *Dry*. "Now comes the revenge of the quotidian," John Leland wrote about *Magical Thinking* for the *New York Times Book Review* (October 12, 2004). "After a few tales from his past, he muses here on the tamer oddities of life after rehab: his relative fame, his flirtation with steroids, telemarketers, moisturizer, tacky tourists in Key West, the stresses of buying a country house and, centrally, his happy Upper West Side domesticity with an art director named Dennis."

Burroughs has said that he learned much about writing during his career in advertising, including the importance of entertaining readers, cutting material that doesn't work, and writing even when one does not feel up to it. "You can't sit around waiting for inspiration or you'll never get anything done," he told Baker. "I write every day, whether I'm in the mood or not, and I got that from advertising." He reportedly signed a contract worth at least $1 million for *Magical Thinking*. Burroughs is also slated to publish a book in 2005; tentatively titled "Select Cuts," "it's all about myself," as he joked to Louise Roug for the *Los Angeles Times* (September 5, 2002). "If I go to Kmart and buy detergent— you'll read about it. If I wash the car—it's going to be a story." Burroughs has written frequently for the on-line magazine *Salon* and recently became a contributing editor at *Details* magazine. "He's one of the most prolific writers I know, and unbelievably fast," Dan Peres, the editor of *Details*, told Claude Peck. "We can agree on a column idea at noon, say, and by 2 o'clock he's filed it to me."

Peck described Burroughs as "tall and striking, with intense green eyes, sharp features, glasses and close-cropped reddish hair." Burroughs has included his E-mail address on his Web site; he spends about five hours a day answering his E-mail messages. He has named *A Confederacy of Dunces*, by John Kennedy Toole, and Todd Haynes's *Safe*, starring Julianne Moore, as his favorite book and film, respectively, and Elizabeth Berg as one of the writers he most admires. The relationship between Burroughs and his mother, who has been confined to a wheelchair since she suffered a stroke in 1989, has become strained; he has made peace with his father, who has remarried. In an essay in *Magical Thinking*, he described how he met Dennis Pilsits, who has been his partner for several years. He and Pilsits, who owns a corporate-communications firm, live in the New York City borough of Manhattan with their French bulldogs and are building a house in Amherst, Massachusetts. Their neighbors in Amherst will include Burroughs's brother, sister-in-law, and nephew.

—K.E.D.

Suggested Reading: Bookslut.com Oct. 6, 2003; *Minneapolis-St. Paul Star Tribune* (on-line) Nov. 16, 2003; *Oregonian* Arts and Living p10 June 6, 2003; *Ottawa Citizen* C p8 July 20, 2003, with photo; *People* p229 Sep. 23, 2002, with photos; *Sydney Morning Herald* Books p13 Apr. 5, 2003; *Weekly News* (on-line) Jan. 8, 2004, with photo

Selected Books: *Sellevision*, 2000; *Running with Scissors*, 2002; *Dry*, 2003; *Magical Thinking: True Stories*, 2004

Robert Mora/Getty Images

Cedric the Entertainer

Apr. 24, 1964– Comedian; actor

Address: c/o Visions Management Group, 4579 LaClede Ave., #402, St. Louis, MO 63108

Over the past decade the portly, dapper, bespectacled Cedric Kyles—better known as Cedric the Entertainer—has become a familiar presence on the comedy scene. He got his start in comedy clubs in the St. Louis, Missouri, area before landing a supporting role on the *Steve Harvey Show* and starring in his own program, *Cedric the Entertainer Presents*, which aired on the Fox network in 2002 and 2003. Beginning in the late 1990s he participated in the enormously successful *Kings of Comedy* tour, and he was seen in the 2000 Spike Lee film

of the same title. Other films in which he has performed include *Barbershop* (2002), *Intolerable Cruelty* (2003), and *Barbershop 2: Back in Business* (2004). In addition, Cedric's humorous TV ads for Bud Light beer have been seen by millions of viewers. In a profile of Cedric the Entertainer for *Ebony* (May 2002), Bobbi Roquemore wrote, "The name says it all. His routines as a stand-up comedian continue to make audiences double over with laughter. His acting takes on varying degrees of laughable . . . and dramatic. . . . Cedric 'the Entertainer' is well on his way to becoming known as a modern-day, Hollywood version of a Renaissance man."

The performer was born Cedric Antonio Kyles on April 24, 1964 in Jefferson City, Missouri, to Rosetta Kyles, a public-school reading specialist. As a child Kyles enjoyed entertaining his mother and her friends by dancing and singing, a talent that he hoped to develop later in life. Comedy was not his focus when he was young, even though he was voted "most humorous" and "most popular" by his high-school classmates. He told Tim Gordon for *Reel Images Magazine* (on-line), "I wasn't the class clown. My mom taught at the school district where I was being educated, so they weren't going to allow for no class clown! She would have clowned me!" As a student at Southeast Missouri State University, in Cape Girardeau, he joined the Kappa Alpha Psi fraternity and graduated with a bachelor's degree in communications; his minor was in theater. After college he worked for a time as a claims adjuster with the State Farm insurance company, while still hoping to be a singer.

All of that changed when Kyles was about 26, on the night his friends urged him to go on stage at a St. Louis comedy club. On that night regional tryouts for the Johnny Walker National Comedy Contest were being held; Kyles, impressing the contest's representatives by dancing, singing, and even reciting poetry, won the contest and walked away with $500. He went on to win the quarterfinals of the contest, in Chicago. Boosted by that success, he began to appear regularly at comedy clubs in and around St. Louis. It was during this period that he became known as Cedric the Entertainer. At one club, as he recalled to Mark Hinson for the *Tallahassee [Florida] Democrat* (November 14, 2003, on-line), "The emcee used to introduce the next act by saying, 'So-and-so the comedian will be out next.' He called everyone 'the comedian.' I told him not to call me 'the comedian' because I do more than that. I said, 'Call me The Entertainer.' And it stuck." The performer is known for a style of humor that is based on observation of everyday life and is relatively free of profanity. According to delafont.com, the Web site of the Richard De La Font Agency, Cedric attributes his clean style to his mother: "Mom came to many of my shows. So that affected a lot of what I said."

In 1992 Cedric the Entertainer made his first television appearance, on *Showtime at the Apollo*, a variety show filmed at the famed Apollo Theater in the Harlem section of New York City. The Apollo audience, known for voicing its opinions of performers—good or bad—in unambiguous terms, responded positively to Cedric's routine. That warm reception led to other TV appearances, on such programs as HBO's *Def Comedy Jam*, the *Tonight Show* with Jay Leno, and *Politically Incorrect* with Bill Maher. Cedric won the Miller Genuine Draft Comedy Contest in 1993; in the following year he was hired to host the BET cable network's program *Comic View*. Also in 1994 he won BET's Richard Pryor Comic of the Year Award.

In 1996 Cedric the Entertainer joined his friend and mentor Steve Harvey as part of the cast of the WB network's *Steve Harvey Show*. (Cedric had befriended Harvey in Dallas, Texas, years earlier, when the headlining comedian at Harvey's club failed to excite the crowd, which included Cedric—who persuaded Harvey to allow him to take the stage for free. The audience responded to his routine with a standing ovation.) On Harvey's sitcom Cedric played the lovable high-school sports coach Cedric Jackie Robinson, a role for which he won four consecutive NAACP Image Awards. Cedric parlayed his exposure on the successful *Steve Harvey Show* into a starring role on a short-lived WB sitcom, *Cedric the Coach*, in which he played the coach of the worst team in the National Basketball Association. Cedric's film debut was in the road movie *Ride* (1998); he later appeared in the comedy *Big Momma's House* (2000), starring Martin Lawrence.

The film *The Original Kings of Comedy* (2000), directed by Spike Lee, was shot entirely on location in Charlotte, North Carolina, and captured performances by the comedians in the *Original Kings of Comedy* tour, the highest-grossing comedy tour of all time: Harvey, Bernie Mac, D. L. Hughley, and Cedric the Entertainer. Michael O'Sullivan wrote for the *Washington Post* (August 18, 2000) that Cedric was "easily the best thing about *Kings*, especially when the dapper and roly-poly clown launches into an inspired parody of break dancing or when he delivers one of his wry nuggets inspired by the flotsam of pop culture."

On the merits of his success with *The Original Kings of Comedy*, the Anheuser-Busch brewing company chose Cedric to appear in the TV ad for Bud Light that aired during the 2001 Super Bowl. The ad, in which he played a man so excited to be on a date that he dances, accidentally shakes up his beer, then sprays it on his female companion, was so successful that *USA Today* (January 30, 2001) called the performer "Madison Avenue's MVP." Cedric was hired to tape several more commercials for Anheuser-Busch, which ran regularly and made him one of the most visible comedic personalities in the media.

As a result of that exposure, the Fox network offered Cedric his own TV show. The sketch comedy/variety program *Cedric the Entertainer Presents*, which premiered on September 18, 2002, co-starred Wendy Raquel Robinson, Shaun Majumder, and Amy Brassette and found Cedric playing a host of off-beat characters, including the outspoken Mrs. Cafeteria Lady and the Love Doctor, a smooth-voiced marriage counselor. Critics found the show to be uneven—wildly funny in some instances and plodding in others—with some suggesting the need for better writing. In June 2003 Fox executives decided not to renew the show for another full season, though new installments of it aired during the fall.

On the big screen Cedric played Ray Harris in the movie *Serving Sara* (2002), with Elizabeth Hurley. The film *Barbershop* (2002), which starred Ice Cube, found Cedric playing a barber named Eddie, an opinionated old-timer who never seems to give anyone a haircut. Ice Cube's character, Calvin, decides to sell the barbershop, a place that provides a group of inner-city Chicago residents with an oasis from their troubles; over the course of the day in which the movie is set, Calvin undergoes a spiritual awakening and realizes the value of the shop. *Barbershop* was the top-grossing film at the box office for two weeks in a row. It was also the focus of controversy, with several civil rights activists objecting to Eddie's comments about Martin Luther King Jr. and Rosa Parks. Cedric told *Jet* (September 16, 2002), "Eddie is very opinionated, usually shooting off his mouth with some half-truths or another. With that I saw a lot of comedic and dramatic opportunity, and I knew I'd have a lot of leniency with this character. Eddie has been there through generations and is the elder statesman of the shop. He's there to explain the significance of the barbershop in the neighborhood and to teach the young barbers. Basically, Eddie enjoys the social atmosphere of the place. It's his country club." The controversy, he told Mark Hinson, "was a little surprising, to say the least, and it did get a little out of hand. I didn't expect to end up on *Larry King Live* defending myself when I took the part." In 2003 Cedric appeared in Joel and Ethan Coen's film *Intolerable Cruelty*, which stars George Clooney and Catherine Zeta-Jones. Early the next year he starred in two movies, *Barbershop 2: Back in Business* and *Johnson Family Vacation*. In the former, which earned $25 million in its debut weekend, he returned to the role of the opinionated Eddie. The story includes a flashback in which Eddie, depicted as a young hustler, saves the barbershop from destruction during 1960s-era Chicago riots. Cedric has a featured role in *A Series of Unfortunate Events*, the $100 million adaptation for the silver screen of the Lemony Snicket children's books; that motion picture was due to open during the 2004 Christmas season. He will also be seen in the upcoming movies *The Honeymooners, Be Cool, Flash, Madagascar,* and *Back to School.* Cedric the Entertainer has lent his deep voice to several animated or nonhuman movie characters, such as those in *Dr. Doolittle 2* (2001), starring Eddie Murphy, and Disney's *Ice Age* (2002). He also has a recurring voice role as Bobby Proud in the Disney Channel's animated program *The Proud Family.*

Cedric the Entertainer is married to the former Lorna Wells, with whom he has a son, Croix Alexander, and a daughter, Lucky Rose; he also has a teenage daughter, Tiara, from a previous relationship. In 1995 he started the Cedric the Entertainer Charitable Foundation, which seeks to broaden the cultural horizons of inner-city youth. In 2002 he published *Grown-A$$ Man*, a collection of essays combining humor and social observation.

—L.A.S.

Suggested Reading: *Ebony* p90+ May 2002; *Entertainment Weekly* p39+ Feb. 2004; *Jet* p32 May 28, 2001, p58 May 12, 2001; *New York Times* E p5 Apr. 7, 2004; *Washington Post* III p1 Aug. 19, 2000

Selected Films: *The Original Kings of Comedy,* 2000; *Barbershop,* 2002; *Intolerable Cruelty,* 2003; *Barbershop 2: Back in Business,* 2004; *Johnson Family Vacation,* 2004

Courtesy of the office of Lincoln Chafee

Chafee, Lincoln

(CHAY-fee)

Mar. 26, 1953– U.S. senator from Rhode Island (Republican)

Address: U.S. Senate, 141A Russell Senate Office Bldg., Washington, DC 20510

The United States senator Lincoln Chafee of Rhode Island is something of an enigma to his colleagues on both sides of the aisle. He is a Republican who has voted against his party approximately 63 percent of the time, championing such liberal causes as preservation of the environment and opposing hefty, GOP-driven tax cuts; a descendant of one of Rhode Island's so-called five families (the state's original settlers), he spent seven years performing manual labor as a farrier; and although, as the son of a prominent politician—U.S. senator John Chafee—he might have been expected to enter national politics as a young man, if at all, he did so at age 46. Various sources present vastly differing views of his character: he has been described with adjectives ranging from "vacant" and "naïve" to "cagey" and "eccentric." Most of his colleagues in Congress, meanwhile, agree that Chafee is a "slow starter" who is "candid" and "thoughtful," unpretentious and shy. In light of his history and such assessments of him, it is both surprising and logical that Chafee often finds himself at the center of heated controversy.

The second of the six children of John Chafee and the former Virginia Coates, Lincoln Davenport Chafee (who calls himself Linc) was born on March 26, 1953 in Warwick, Rhode Island. His father, a decorated veteran of World War II and the Korean War, served as secretary of the U.S. Navy, as a representative in the Rhode Island state House, and as governor of Rhode Island, and won election four times to the U.S. Senate; he was known as a staunch environmentalist. Chafee's mother, too, fought to protect the environment; she was also a homemaker and a participant in the original organic-farming movement. One of Chafee's sisters, Tribbie, died as a teenager in a riding accident, when she was kicked in the head by a horse. His surviving siblings are his brothers, John Jr., Quentin, and Zechariah, and his sister Georgia Chafee Nassikas.

Chafee attended the prep school Phillips Andover Academy, in Andover, Massachusetts, where his classmates included the future Florida governor Jeb Bush. He went on to enroll at Brown University, in Providence, Rhode Island, where he was captain of the wrestling team and earned a B.A. degree in classics in 1975; in the same year he received the Francis M. Driscoll Award for leadership, scholarship, and athletics. Following his graduation from Brown, Chafee decided to "try something different before embarking on a high-pressure career," as he explained to Helen Dewar for the *Washington Post* (December 12, 1999). He attended a three-month course in horseshoeing at Montana State University, in Bozeman, then took jobs as a farrier, working primarily at harness racetracks throughout Canada and the United States. "It was a good life, learning a trade, working hard . . . ," he told Dewar. "It was far from 'dropping out.' It was just a different path." Chafee returned to Rhode Island in 1983 and entered the field of manufacturing management. He held several positions, including planner at the General Dynamics facility at Quonset Point and executive director of the Northeast Corridor Initiative, a nonprofit organization designed to promote the modernization of rail service throughout the eastern seaboard.

In 1985 Chafee embarked upon a political career when he was elected as a delegate to the Rhode Island Constitutional Convention. The following year he won the first of his two terms on the Warwick City Council. In 1990 Chafee ran for the office of mayor. He was defeated that year but succeeded two years later, winning by a margin of 335 votes to become the first Republican mayor of Warwick in 32 years. He was reelected in 1994, 1996, and 1998, gaining his fourth victory with 58 percent of the vote and carrying every ward in the city. According to the Web site chafee.senate.gov, Chafee's government home page, "As mayor, Lincoln Chafee had a strong record of fiscal management, environmental protection, open space acquisition, intergovernmental cooperation, economic development, labor relations, and significant increases in funding for schools." That assessment is generally corroborated by unbiased sources.

In 1999, when then-senator John Chafee decided not to seek another term, Lincoln Chafee announced that he would run for his father's vacated seat. During the campaign Chafee faced a challenge when asked if he had ever used illegal drugs. Having watched the press grill the presidential hopeful George W. Bush that year about his experiences with drugs, Chafee promptly admitted to having used marijuana and cocaine as an undergraduate. As reported by B. Drummond Ayres Jr. in the *New York Times* (August 25, 1999), Chafee explained, "Those were very tumultuous times. I'm not proud of it." He told a reporter for the *Providence Journal* (August 23, 1999), "I struggled with what's the politically correct answer. But in the end, honesty is the best policy. . . . People are tolerant and understanding. If you're forthright and honest with the public and you've got nothing to hide, I don't see why it's such a big story. If you try to cover it up, it becomes a problem." Although Ayres observed that in politics, responses such as Chafee's are "known not just as forthright honesty but also as 'inoculation,'" voters clearly appreciated Chafee's candor, and a subsequent Brown University poll showed that Chafee's approval rating among voters had shot up by 10 points.

The campaigns of the three major candidates for the office were cut short when the elder Chafee died of heart failure in November 1999, prior to completing his final term. Rhode Island's governor, Lincoln Almond, appointed Lincoln Chafee to finish the remaining 14 months of his father's term. As Matt Bai reported in the *New York Times Magazine* (March 23, 2003), Chafee is said to have nearly turned down the office, which he had wanted to win on his own. "When the day came for his swearing in," Bai wrote, "a Senate aide found Chafee seated at his father's desk on the verge of tears. 'I didn't want to get here this way,' he said." After completing the remainder of his father's term, Chafee campaigned again; he was elected to his first full term on November 7, 2000.

In the tradition of his maverick father, Chafee told Helen Dewar that as a senator he would "stand up for what I believe in," rather than simply adhere to party politics. That stance has produced some tension between Chafee and many of his colleagues in the Republican Party. Within his first three weeks in the Senate, for example, Chafee voted for a Democrat-sponsored bill proposing a $1 increase in the minimum wage. As a senator Chafee has alternately supported his own party and the Democrats. In July 2000 he was one of three Republicans in the Senate to back an unsuccessful Democratic plan to alter estate-tax regulations that would exempt all but one percent of the largest estates. The following year, Chafee and then-Republican senator James Jeffords of Vermont (who became an Independent in May 2001) opposed President George W. Bush's proposed massive tax cut and, in spite of enormous pressure from other Republicans, managed to effect something of a compromise by lowering the accumulated cuts from $1.6 trillion to $1.2 trillion. In addition, in 2002 Chafee was the only Senate Republican to vote against the U.S. invasion of Iraq, which took place the following spring. Similarly, he sided with government-employee unions in opposing President Bush's plan to reduce civil-service protections and dissolve collective-bargaining agreements for workers in the newly created Department of Homeland Security, when the president felt it necessary because of national-security concerns. Chafee butted heads with the Bush administration again in 2003 by sponsoring legislation designed to freeze at 38.6 percent (at least until the budget deficit is eliminated) the minimum tax rate for individuals in the top income bracket.

Following the defection of Jeffords from the Republican Party, there was much speculation that Chafee would be the next Republican to switch sides. Indeed, he has recently expressed a "never-say-never" attitude about leaving a party that has been accused of alienating its moderates. In *Newsweek* (January 20, 2003), Howard Fineman explained, "The GOP 'enjoys' a 51-48-1 edge in the Senate, giving inordinate clout to a tiny band of self-described 'centrists' that includes Chafee, [Arizona senator John] McCain, and Maine's Olympia Snowe and Susan Collins. . . . Given his position on the fault line of politics, Chafee could be a central player, in on every deal. But he refuses to take part in the Washington game." As an example of that refusal, Fineman reported that Vice President Richard B. Cheney and other White House officials had asked Chafee if they could do a favor for him or his state, in return for his vote in support of the president's tax plan. Chafee told them no, adding, "I just can't trade my vote. It's a dangerous path to go down." In Congress, Fineman observed, such behavior "is seen as a sign of stupidity—or at least malpractice." Some Republicans, convinced of Chafee's incompetence, refer to him as the "Missing Linc," because of stories such as one cited by Matt Bai: at one news conference those gathered were advised to "stick to the script," whereupon Chafee, with no evident irony, said, "Is there a script? I haven't seen it." Fineman, however, asserted, "Chafee's aura of obtuseness is deceiving—because it's deliberate." Matt Bai offered a slightly different interpretation of Chafee's character. "Two theories took hold and are often repeated: either the younger Chafee is a few votes short of a quorum or he's actually cagier than anyone realizes and enjoys being inscrutable. In fact, after you spend some time with Chafee, neither analysis seems right. He's not dim, nor does he have much capacity for guile or irony. He is, instead, a slow starter who learned early in life to ask questions, persevere, and wait his turn."

In an interview with Sheryl Gay Stolberg for the *New York Times* (October 4, 2004), Chafee made the startling revelation that he did not intend to vote for the reelection of President Bush. He traced his disillusionment with the current administration to a day in December 2000, a few weeks before Bush's inauguration, when Chafee and four other moderate Republican senators met with Vice President–elect Dick Cheney. Cheney's proposals for the introduction of huge tax cuts, the rejection of the so-called Kyoto environment accords, the bolstering of missile-defense programs, and other plans supported most enthusiastically by far-right Republicans shocked Chafee. "I literally was close to falling off my chair," he recalled to Stolberg. "It was no room for discussion." On Election Day 2004, he said, he would remain a devoted Republican but would cast his ballot for president for a write-in candidate rather than George W. Bush. "Mr. Chafee insists he has no intention of defecting" from the Republican Party, Stolberg reported.

"But it is no secret that Democrats would welcome him," and, she wrote, Senator Jim Jeffords of Vermont, who changed his political affiliation from Republican to Democrat in 2001, was "already . . . offering him counsel."

Chafee has served on a variety of Senate committees, including Environment and Public Works; Foreign Relations; Banking, Housing, and Urban Affairs; and the Joint Economic Committee. As of 2003 Chafee chaired the following subcommittees: Superfund, Waste Control, and Risk Assessment; Western Hemisphere, Peace Corps, and Narcotics Affairs; and Near Eastern and South Asian Affairs.

Chafee is married to the former Stephanie Danforth, an heiress to one of Rhode Island's largest family fortunes. The couple have three children—Louisa, Caleb, and Thea. Chafee lists his recreational activities as skiing and riding his horse, Trapper.

—K.J.E.

Suggested Reading: chafee.senate.gov; *New York Times* A p16 Oct. 4, 2004, with photo; *New York Times Magazine* p30 Mar. 23, 2003; newportthisweek.com; *Newsweek* p30 Jan. 20, 2003; prospect.org; *Washington Post* A p30 Dec. 12, 1999

Chapman, Steven Curtis

Nov. 21, 1962– Christian singer; songwriter

Address: P.O. Box 150156, Nashville, TN 37215

"God is God and I am not / I can only see a part of the picture He's painting / God is God and I am man / So I'll never understand it all / For only God is God." Those lines comprise the chorus of the song "God Is God," by the singer/songwriter Steven Curtis Chapman, a major figure in the Christian contemporary-music scene since the late 1980s. The words encapsulate the theme of nearly all of Chapman's 40 number-one hit songs and most of the others on his 14 albums: his deep, abiding faith in a higher power whose motives and ways will to some extent always remain mysteries to humans. Rather than preach, in his songs Chapman empathizes with others, describing his own struggles with his religious beliefs and his perplexity and unhappiness about the existence of pain and suffering in the world, but he still encourages people to retain—or develop—confidence in the wisdom and loving-kindness of God. As he explained to Dave Tianen for the *Milwaukee (Wisconsin) Journal Sentinel* (October 7, 2002), "I'm not going to stick a big spiritual Band-Aid on all this and pretend it's all OK. I'm still living with these questions and I'm going to continue to, but I'm going to trust [God]. If we're going to embrace [the Bible], and we're going to say we're believers in this book,

Kevin Winter/Getty Images

Steven Curtis Chapman

then I've got to have some kind of response to these things. I may not understand them, but I'm at least going to wrestle with them and grapple with them in my music." A reviewer for BPI Entertainment News Wire (October 15, 2001) wrote of Chapman, "Few [other] singer/songwriters have the ability to write songs that so exquisitely capture the essence of a faith-filled life, encompassing the joy, soul-searching, occasional bewilderment, and deep sense of wonder that are part of the Christian experience."

Chapman has often talked publicly about his attempts to accept, with what he considers proper humility, his fans' adulation and all the trappings of his enormous success. "Jesus Christ taught us that you should esteem others more than yourself," he told Lynn Van Matre for the *Chicago Tribune* (October 4, 1992). "In the music industry, though, you have to worry about promoting and marketing yourself and about your visibility. It's a struggle and a challenge to work that through and come to a place of clear conscience. I don't think it's right for me to say I don't want people getting excited at my shows. I know some of that is going to go on. . . . If someone is determined to put you on a pedestal, they will. . . . I think that as long as you are still struggling and praying about these questions, you're in a safe place spiritually. It's when you start walking off stage thinking you're pretty great stuff that it gets dangerous."

Inspired by such musical genres as rock and roll, gospel, gospel rock, and pop, Chapman has shown uncommon skill in composing catchy tunes as well as uplifting lyrics. Two of his albums—*Heaven in the Real World* and *Speechless*—have gone platinum (meaning that they sold at least a million cop-

ies), and seven have gone gold (half a million copies sold): *More to This Life, For the Sake of the Call, The Great Adventure, The Music of Christmas, Signs of Life, Greatest Hits,* and *Declaration.* Chapman has also earned four Grammy Awards, for best pop gospel album (1992–94 and 2000), and an unprecedented 47 of the Gospel Music Association's equivalent, the Dove Awards, nine of them the honors for songwriter of the year (1989–95 and 1997–98). "I Will Be Here," "The Great Adventure," "We Fall Down," "For the Sake of the Call," "Heaven in the Real World," "His Strength Is Perfect," "When You Are a Soldier," and other Chapman songs have become staples of Christian worship services and other religious events. Echoing the impression of many other reporters, Dave Tianen described Chapman in the *Milwaukee Journal Sentinel* (October 11, 2002) as "a warm, joyous and vibrant performer on stage." "Talent aside," Tianen declared, "part of what helps Chapman in concert is that he's an immensely likable guy—modest, boyish, open-hearted and blessed with a gentle and self-deprecatory sense of humor." Chapman told Mike Eisenbath for the *St. Louis (Missouri) Post-Dispatch* (December 3, 1992), "I have to ask myself sometimes, 'Is music what I love, or is it a deeper calling?' I believe God has called me to do this. He's given me the platform."

Steven Curtis Chapman was born on November 21, 1962 in Paducah, Kentucky, where he grew up. His father, Herb Chapman, owned a music store; he also wrote songs and served as guitarist in a folk and bluegrass band that performed locally on Friday nights. "My dad was a talented singer and player who took music very seriously, and all of my early influence came from my dad teaching me," Chapman told Jerry Wilson for *CCM (Contemporary Christian Music) Magazine* (on-line) in 2003. Early in his married life Herb Chapman had tried briefly to launch a career as a musician. According to one source, he abandoned that idea after seeing others in pursuit of the same goal living out of their cars on the streets of Nashville; according to another, he was dissuaded by the realization that being on tour might mean separation from his family for months at a time. Steven Chapman learned to play several instruments at his father's store, among them piano, mandolin, Dobro, lap steel guitar, and acoustic guitar, the last of which is the one he has come "closest . . . to mastering, " as he put it during a chat on prodigy.net. From his older brother, Herb Jr., he learned to play double bass. When he was seven his father gave him his own guitar.

As a young boy, Chapman has recalled, he was especially moved when the congregation at a local Baptist church sang the hymn "I Need Thee Every Hour." His mother, Judy, a full-time homemaker, brought him and his brother to services at the church every Sunday, while his father stayed home. One weekend when Steven was about seven, the church hosted a revival meeting, and one of the visiting preachers stayed with the Chapmans. The man was "very gentle" and "humble," Chapman recalled to Mike Eisenbath. "He told my dad his story of his faith, and my dad went to church that Sunday with us. . . . We started praying together as a family and reading the Bible. A year later, I became a Christian and committed my life to Christ. It became more than a religion for us and more than just being a good, moral person. I developed a personal relationship with Jesus." Although Chapman knew that his parents had struggled for years to resolve their conflicts, he felt both shocked and disheartened when, after 28 years of marriage, they divorced.

While growing up Chapman listened to recordings by a range of musicians, both black and white, among them the gospel singer Andrae Crouch and the gospel rock acts Dogwood, Dallas Holm, and the Imperials Quartet; the pop group the Archers; the folk and rock-and-roll singer/songwriter James Taylor; the blues and rock guitarist Stevie Ray Vaughan; the country/folk singer/songwriter John Denver; the rhythm-and-blues performer Billy Preston; and the rock bands the Eagles and the Doobie Brothers. By age 16 Chapman had started writing his own songs. "When I sat down with my guitar to write, gospel was what came most naturally," he told Lynn Van Matre for the *Chicago Tribune* (October 4, 1992). "There were love songs here and there about girls who broke my heart, but from the beginning I knew that Christian music was where my heart was." A later influence was the guitarist Harvey Jett, whom he met after Jett had left the band Black Oak Arkansas and was entertaining in churches. Jett "had a relaxed, conversational way on stage that really communicated with the people," Chapman told Thom Granger for *CCM Magazine* (on-line). "I also saw how humor would set people at ease, and how they would maybe believe you a little more when you became more vulnerable."

After he graduated from Heath High School, in Paducah, in 1981, Chapman enrolled at Anderson College (now a university) in Anderson, Indiana, which is affiliated with the Church of God. He spent the summer after his junior year traveling with an undergraduate singing group. Shortly after the start of his senior year, he learned that he had landed a job as a staff songwriter with Benson Music, in Nashville, Tennessee. He moved to Nashville and soon afterward, in the fall of 1984, married another Anderson student; his plan to earn a bachelor's degree at Belmont University, in Nashville, did not materialize. Early in 1986 he and his wife lost most of their possessions in an apartment-house fire. As Joan Brasher wrote for *Christianity Today* (Spring 1997, on-line), "Within the first years of their marriage, [they] learned that life's catastrophes were easier to deal with than life's daily routine. They differed significantly in their definition of 'normal family life,' and heated arguments over their conflicting expectations continually cropped up." Chapman's willingness to acknowledge the stresses in his marriage as well as the an-

guish he felt when his parents divorced have reinforced the image he has tried to project—that of an ordinary husband, father, son, and friend—and have informed some of his lyrics as well.

Later in the 1980s, according to Joan Brasher, Chapman's songwriting skills "were being noticed by artists such as the Imperials, Glen Campbell and Sandi Patty." During this period Chapman found work as an entertainer at Opryland USA, a Nashville theme park, and on a few occasions he performed on the *Grand Ole Opry*, which bills itself as the world's longest-running live radio show. "When I sang a song that I wrote myself," he told Lynn Van Matre, "I felt like that guy in the movie *Chariots of Fire*, the one who said that when he ran he could feel God's pleasure, because running was what God created him to do. I had a similar feeling when I played the music that was in my heart."

In 1987 Chapman signed a contract with Sparrow Records, a major Christian-music label. That same year he released his debut album, *First Hand*. His next, *Real Life Conversations* (1988), spawned two number-one hits and garnered Chapman his first two Dove Awards, for songwriter of the year and pop/contemporary recorded song of the year. His 1989 release, *More to This Life*, sold more than 500,000 copies—an extraordinary number in the genre of contemporary Christian music; the record spawned four number-one hits and won 10 Dove Awards. His fourth album, *For the Sake of the Call* (1990), which he described to Bob Darden for *Billboard* (March 23, 1991) as "the most honest, most representative record of my life" until then, established Chapman as a gospel superstar; the recording reached the number-one spot on the Christian albums chart and earned three Dove Awards and a Grammy Award.

Over the next five years, Chapman released *The Great Adventure* (1992), *The Live Adventure* (1993), *Heaven in the Real World* (1994), and *The Music of Christmas* (1995). Together, they produced 10 number-one hit songs and garnered 18 Dove and two Grammy Awards. For *Signs of Life* (1996), Peter York, Sparrow's president, gave Chapman a free hand; the result, Chapman told Mike Joyce for the *Washington Post* (November 15, 1996), was "the album I always wanted to make." Chapman told John Roos for the *Los Angeles Times* (February 15, 1997), "I needed to challenge myself and kind of fan the flames in my art and my life. I wanted to go back to my musical roots and also touch base with the places and influences where my faith in God was born. I don't think I was in a rut yet, but I sure was looking for a spark." Offering what Roos described as "a variety of musical textures, from rollicking, blues-tinged rockers to folk-tinged instrumentals to slower-paced, introspective ballads," the album marked a departure from Chapman's earlier work. As Roos wrote, "Chapman's prior abstract declarations of love, faith and redemption have given way to a more grounded, personalized approach to songwriting."

After the two-disk *Greatest Hits* (1997), Chapman released *Speechless* (1999). That record emerged after a short sabbatical he had from songwriting, during which he and his family experienced several emotional blows: the deaths of Chapman's friend and fellow performer Rich Mullins and a family friend's eight-year-old daughter, and shootings in 1997 at Chapman's high school that left three students dead and five others wounded. "When I first began writing for this record, I expected it to be introspective and reflective," Chapman told Shirley Armbruster for the *Fresno (California) Bee* (October 21, 1999). "As it turned out, it is an album filled with great joy and is, musically, pretty upbeat." Mike Joyce agreed: "Chapman's bedrock faith is the foundation for all the songs on *Speechless*, so that even when the lyrics are inspired by tragedy or self-doubt, they radiate a fundamental optimism and help shape some of the more engaging melodies and rhythms." Tom Roland wrote for the *Tennessean* (June 14, 1999) that the album "manages to balance mystery and brightness, awe and confidence, gentle pop and tough alternative sounds. Along the way, Chapman still comes across as that guy next door with a voice that's pleasant, sometimes pushed, but never overbearing." *Speechless* achieved platinum status, spawned seven chart-topping hits, and earned a Grammy Award.

Chapman had just completed the recording of *Declaration* (2001) when he discovered that he had lost the ability to sing the five topmost notes of his range. Doctors diagnosed the problem as a paralyzed vocal cord, caused, they believed, by a viral infection. Thanks to four months of treatment at the voice clinic at Vanderbilt University, in Nashville, and the healing effects of time, Chapman made a virtually complete recovery within a year. *Declaration*, meanwhile, earned enthusiastic critical praise and sold more than 500,000 copies.

For *All About Love* (2003), Chapman recorded 16 songs that explore the difficulties and rewards of marriage and other romantic relationships. "There are a ton of songs about falling in love and about break-ups, but in my opinion, there aren't enough songs that dive into what happens in relationships on a day-to-day basis . . . ," Chapman said to Tracey Evison for the Prince Edward Island, Canada, newspaper the *Guardian* (February 8, 2003). "That's something I wanted to explore with this project." Chapman dedicated *All About Love* to his wife, who served as executive producer. The album debuted at number one on *Billboard*'s Top Christian Albums chart and at number 12 on that magazine's Top 200 chart. *All About Love* and its title song won Chapman Dove Award nominations for pop/contemporary album of the year and song of the year, respectively; he was nominated in other 2004 Dove Award categories as well, including that of male vocalist of the year. Also in 2003 Hallmark sold its full run of 400,000 copies of Chapman's *Christmas Is All in the Heart*, which contained three new songs ("This Baby," "Going Home for Christmas," and the title song) and remixes of songs from Chapman's first Christmas album. (The second is not considered part of Chapman's official discography.) The singer's next recording, *All Things New*, on the Sparrow label, went on sale in the fall of 2004. "Steven Curtis Chapman has done it once again," Michael Lyttle wrote about that record for amazon.com. "Raising the bar to stratospheric heights and surpassing even his own lofty perch . . . Chapman has recorded and released a rich pop masterpiece full of insightful and relevant material in the form of *All Things New*. . . . As always, Chapman insists on keeping it real when it comes to where spiritual rubber meets the road. 'What Now' reminds Christians that how they care for fellow humanity is how they care for their savior. 'Last Day on Earth' is another track bound to challenge listeners to consider how well they are living their faith, especially if they knew today was their last. Chapman pulls no punches on *All Things New* as he issues a powerful and majestic-sounding call to arms for Christians to love the world around them as they love their God."

With his pastor, Scotty Smith of Christ Presbyterian Church in Nashville, Chapman wrote the quasi-memoir *Speechless: Living in Awe of God's Disruptive Grace* (1999). Arrangements in print for guitar, piano, and voice of many of his songs have been issued by the music publisher Hal Leonard. After the shootings at his high school, Chapman recruited the Christian filmmaker Ken Carpenter to make the antiviolence video *At the Edge*, which comes with a classroom discussion kit. "The goal of the video is to steer kids away from wrong choices and tragic endings. I want to help them see the warning signs in their peers . . . [and] intervene by getting help," Chapman, who appears at the end of the video offering a message of hope, told Michael Ross and Tom Neven for *Focus on the Family Magazine* (1999, on-line). In the 1990s Chapman volunteered with Prison Fellowship Ministries.

Chapman and his wife, born Mary Beth Chapman (the two shared a mailbox at Anderson College, where they met), have three biological children, their daughter Emily and their sons, Caleb and Will Franklin. They are also the parents of three girls born in China, whom they adopted as infants in 2000, 2003, and 2004, respectively: Shaohannah Hope (nicknamed Shaoey), Stevey Joy Ru, and Marie Sue. The family lives in Franklin, Tennessee, near Nashville. In 2000 Steven and Mary Beth Chapman set up a foundation called Shaohannah's Hope, which offers financial assistance to Christians who are already in the process of adoption. Chapman and his wife plan to write what is projected to be a series of children's books about Shaohannah; the first installment, *Shaoey and Dot: Bug Meets Bundle*, was scheduled for publication in November 2004. "I believe success is having those closest to you love and respect you the most," Chapman told John Roos. "The biggest compliment to me would be having my kids say,

'We saw our dad live the songs he sings about.' I don't think you can underestimate the importance of honesty and integrity in one's life."

—H.T.

Suggested Reading: *CCM Magazine* (on-line); *Chicago Tribune* Tempo C p1+ Oct. 4, 1992, with photos; *Christianity Today* (on-line) Spring 1997; CMCentral.com; *Focus on the Family Magazine* (on-line); *Milwaukee (Wisconsin) Journal Sentinel* Cue and Jump E p3 Oct. 7, 2002, News B p6 Oct. 11, 2002; *St. Louis (Missouri) Post-Dispatch* Everyday Magazine E p1 Dec. 3, 1992

Seleced Recordings: *First Hand,* 1987; *Real Life Conversations,* 1988; *More to This Life,* 1989; *For the Sake of the Call,* 1990; *The Great Adventure,* 1992; *The Live Adventure,* 1993; *Heaven in the Real World,* 1994; *The Music of Christmas,* 1995; *Signs of Life,* 1996; *Greatest Hits,* 1997; *Speechless,* 1999; *Declaration,* 2001; *All About Love,* 2003; *All Things New,* 2004

Scott Gries/Getty Images

Chappelle, Dave

(shah-PELL)

Aug. 23, 1974– Comedian; actor; writer

Address: c/o Marie Raubicheck, Press Central, 1775 Broadway, New York, NY 10019

In the tradition of George Carlin and Richard Pryor, the comedian Dave Chappelle has built his reputation by presenting controversial material in

a humorous light. The tag line for *Chappelle's Show,* now in its second season on the Comedy Central cable network, reads "Still Dave. Still Dangerous," and, indeed, the 30-year-old comedian has shown no signs of watering down his act. Since he began his career as a standup comedian, when he was 14, Chappelle, who is African-American, has focused mainly on race and, over the years, has touched on such subjects as reparations for the descendants of slaves, stereotyping of and by blacks, and drug use and crime in African-American communities. "The first season of *Chappelle's Show,*" Ellen Thompson wrote for the *New Paltz (New York) Oracle* (February 12, 2004, on-line), "managed to portray homeless blacks as crack addicts, minimize the historical seriousness of the 1977 [TV miniseries] *Roots,* mock the artistic ability of today's mainstream rappers and reinforce popular assumptions of urban blacks." Chappelle has not spared other races or shied away from addressing such emotional topics as sexual abuse in the Catholic Church or antidrug commercials. "He clearly gets a kick out of rattling the cage of cultural conformity," Mike Duffy wrote for the *Detroit Free Press* (April 4, 2003, on-line). Despite his concern with serious issues, Chappelle does not adhere to any high-minded comedic aesthetic. Often downright silly, he relies heavily on physical humor. In addition to starring in and writing (with Neal Brennan) *Chappelle's Show,* the comedian wrote and played a leading role in the drug-caper motion picture *Half Baked* (1998) and has appeared in such films as *The Nutty Professor* (1996), *Con Air* (1997), *You've Got Mail* (1998), and *Undercover Brother* (2002). He has also appeared as a guest on talk shows hosted by David Letterman and Conan O'Brien and on Bill Maher's series *Politically Incorrect,* and has performed in the company of Aretha Franklin, Richard Pryor, and Whoopi Goldberg, among many other celebrated entertainers. DVDs of the first season of *Chappelle's Show,* released in 2004, recently became the best-selling recorded television series up to that time; by November 2004, 1.9 million copies had been sold.

David Chappelle was born on August 23, 1974 in Washington, D.C., where he grew up. His father, William Chappelle, now deceased, taught music at Antioch College, in Yellow Springs, Ohio; his mother, Yvonne Seon, is an ordained Unitarian Universalist minister, an associate professor of African-American history at Prince George's Community College, in Largo, Maryland, and a vice chairperson of Africare, a nonprofit organization that provides many types of aid to people in Africa. Seon was the first African-American woman to be granted a fellowship as a Unitarian Universalist minister (in 1981) and was the first woman to hold the vice-chairperson position with Africare. She and her husband separated during Chappelle's early years but remained friends. The eldest of three children, Chappelle enjoyed a happy home life and often discussed racial and social issues with his parents around the dinner table. "We were like the broke Huxtables," he told Lola Ogunnaike for the *New York Times* (February 18, 2004, on-line), referring to the well-adjusted, affluent family on the hit TV sitcom *The Cosby Show*, which starred Bill Cosby.

Cosby figured heavily in Chappelle's decision to pursue a career in comedy. Fond of doing humorous imitations and other gags as a child, Chappelle did not believe he could support himself as a comedian until he read an article about Cosby in *Time* when he was about 13. "It hit me like a revelation," he told Bernard Weinraub for the *New York Times* (August 2, 1993). "It never occurred to me that being funny was a niche, something you could build a career on. I went out and bought [one of Cosby's books]. Here was a kid from the projects who dropped out of school, was bouncing around until he found comedy and became one of the richest men in the country. What's not to like?" Chappelle soon made his first standup appearance, at age 14, on an open-mic night at Garvins Comedy Club, in Washington. Because he was underage, his mother accompanied him. "It was the longest three minutes of my life," Chappelle told Jonathan Roslyn for the *Washingtonian* (July 1996), "but I was hooked. After that night, I wasn't a mediocre basketball player—I was an entry-level comedian. I thought if I could make a living at this I'd be the happiest man in the world."

From the earliest days of his act, the teenage Chappelle made jokes about race a staple of his repertoire. He presented a sketch about the lack of black characters on the TV show *Fantasy Island*, and he joked that if Batman tried to fight crime in a black neighborhood, his Batmobile would probably get stolen. His closing joke at the time, as he told Weinraub, was about Jesse L. Jackson, who was seeking the 1988 Democratic presidential nomination: "Jesse Jackson is running for President. Wow. Twenty years ago a black guy would say, 'I'm going to college, get my degree and be the best damn mailman you've ever seen.'" Chappelle's worst gig, as he recalled to Ryan Muldoon for the Death Valley Driver Web site (September 3, 2002), was at a restaurant in Virginia: "It was like an old Denny's that someone had bought. And these guys had actually put the stage right behind the salad bar. So anyone who came up to get salad was right in front of the stage. It was the worst possible thing you could think of."

After a three-year stay with his father in Ohio, Chappelle entered Eastern High School, in Washington, as a freshman. On the advice of his mother and grandmother, he transferred to the Duke Ellington School for the Arts, also in the nation's capital. When he was 17 he won a best-comedian contest in the city. Soon afterward he moved to New York City to try to make it as a standup comedian, having rejected the suggestions of some of his high-school teachers that he study acting and his grandmother's entreaties to attend college. With little more in his pocket than a check that his grandmother had given him as a farewell gift, he moved

into a small apartment in the New York City borough of Manhattan. On his first night in New York, he showed up at the Boston Comedy Club, in the city's Greenwich Village neighborhood, and demanded permission to perform. Reluctant at first to admit Chappelle, who looked even younger than his 17 years, the management relented. Chappelle's act impressed the club's owner, Barry Katz, and one of its doormen, Neal Brennan. A few days later Katz offered to manage Chappelle's career. Very soon afterward Chappelle began appearing on such nationally broadcast TV comedy shows as *An Evening at the Improv, Caroline's Comedy Hour*, and the *Arsenio Hall Show*. Meanwhile, Brennan, who is white, had provided Chappelle with some advice about his routine. Although his first response had been to reject Brennan's criticisms, the comedian soon acknowledged that they had merit. He and Brennan struck up a friendship, which blossomed into a long-term writing partnership.

Another important influence on Chappelle during his early years in New York was Charlie Barnett, a street comedian who performed in Washington Square Park, in Greenwich Village. Barnett, who later died of AIDS, according to the *TampaImprov* (April 20, 2004, on-line), took Chappelle under his wing and taught him, among many other things, the necessity of being fearless, particularly when working outdoors, where spectators come and go as they please and are not obligated to pay for the performance. In his interview with Muldoon, Chappelle noted that his youthfulness helped him to be as bold as he needed to be to succeed: "If I would have waited until I was older I may have never made it, because I get more humble as I get older. When you're young like that, you only think of when everything goes right. You don't think about, what if things go wrong." Chappelle has purchased the rights to Barnett's life story and plans to produce and star in a movie about him, tentatively titled "King of the Park."

Chappelle's career was bolstered in 1992, when he appeared at the 10th anniversary of the Montreal "Just for Laughs" Comedy Festival, which also commemorated the 350th anniversary of the founding of Montreal and featured the comedians Jerry Lewis, Drew Carey, Jon Stewart, Ray Romano, Lily Tomlin, and Adam Sandler, among others. His appearance in the high-profile festival helped him land both his first movie role, as Ahchoo in Mel Brooks's *Robin Hood: Men in Tights* (1993), and a television deal, to co-star in and also help create a new sitcom for ABC, called *Buddies. Buddies* was overseen by Carmen Finestra, Matt Williams, and David McFadzean, all of whom had been instrumental in the creation of the hit sitcoms *Home Improvement, Roseanne*, and *The Cosby Show*. The series, which co-starred Christopher Gartin, was about two aspiring filmmakers, one black and one white, who live next door to each other and run a videotaping business. Only six episodes of the series aired, in 1996, before its cancellation. Meanwhile, Chappelle had appeared in the movies *Un-*

dercover Blues (1993) and Getting In (1994) as well as in Comedy: Coast to Coast, an hour-long TV comedy show, and on Late Night with David Letterman, both in 1994. In 1996 he played a memorable role as the caustic comedian Reggie Warrington in The Nutty Professor, starring Eddie Murphy, and protrayed a cockroach in Joe's Apartment. In 1997 he appeared in Con Air, The Real Blonde, and the little-seen shorts Bowl of Pork and Damn Whitey, the latter of which he co-wrote with Gina Prince-Bythewood.

His being cast in The Nutty Professor benefitted Chappelle greatly, not only because it gave him the chance to act opposite Eddie Murphy, one of his idols, but also because Murphy encouraged him to try writing for the movies and TV. "He was really warm and supportive," Chappelle told Duffy. "He told me, 'I've been watching you on TV,' which really floored me. . . . It gave me a second career as a writer and I've realized that I'm not bad at it. When someone like Eddie Murphy tells you you can do something, it really helps to give you the confidence that you can do it." In 1998 Chappelle and Brennan teamed up to write the filmscript of Half Baked, about a group of potheads who try to raise bail for their imprisoned friend by selling marijuana. Chappelle played two roles in the film, those of the rapper Sir Smoke-a-Lot and Thurgood, who works as a janitor at a pharmaceutical lab and has access to prescription marijuana. The film has acquired a cult following, despite its being resoundingly panned by most critics, including Lawrence Van Gelder, who wrote for the New York Times (January 17, 1998, on-line), "Not very funny, intelligent or grippingly plotted, [Half Baked] is likely to appeal only to those who think that anything to do with marijuana—smoking, sharing, stealing or selling—constitutes the Everest of riproaring hilarity." Chappelle told Muldoon, "I felt a little guilty about that movie. It didn't turn out the way that I intended it, I'll be the first to admit that. . . . I think the jokes were good, but the way they did it, they kind of watered it down. I think at the time the studio was afraid of it. They freaked out a little bit. And I freaked out a lot when I saw it. I was like, '[Expletive]! I missed!'"

Also in 1998 a deal Chappelle made with the Fox network to create a sitcom fell through, after the network reportedly asked him to include additional white characters. Chappelle refused to comply and publicly lambasted the network, which he claimed had found his show "too black," according to the CNN Web site (July 9, 1998). He next appeared in the films Woo and You've Got Mail, in 1998, 200 Cigarettes and Blue Streak, in 1999, and Screwed, in 2000. In August 2000 he starred in his own one-hour, standup-comedy special on HBO. His next motion-picture performance came in Undercover Brother (2002), about a secret organization of African-American spies who fight against racial inequality. In his role as Conspiracy Brother, a paranoiac conspiracy theorist, Chappelle, in the opinions of some commentators, overshadowed the lead actor, Eddie Griffin.

In 2003 Chappelle, eager to create a comedy show free from the constraints of network television, signed a contract with the Comedy Central cable network to produce the Chappelle Show. "The timing was right," the comedian told James Verini for the Los Angeles Times (February 13, 2003). "I wanted to do a show of stuff I thought deserved to be seen but didn't have a venue, and Comedy Central wanted to court the urban market, as they say. But it didn't [initially] dawn on me . . . that people would actually be watching it. We created it in such a vacuum. Our philosophy was: Dance like nobody's watching." The first episode of the half-hour show aired at 10:30 p.m. in January 2003. It featured a fake documentary called "Blind Supremacy," about a blind African-American man, Clayton Bigsby, who is a leader in the white-supremacist group the Ku Klux Klan (KKK) and is known for his fiery anti-black speeches. Bigsby is unaware of his skin color, and because he wears the KKK's traditional white hood, his fellow members don't realize that he is black. Chaos ensues when Bigsby's race is revealed. In the New York Times (March 23, 2003), Elvis Mitchell lauded the skit as "as pointed a jab at American ambition as I've seen on television in years." In the next episode of his new show, Chappelle introduced Tyrone Biggums, a zany crack addict who, while speaking to schoolchildren on "Drug Awareness Day," expounds on the virtues of eating dog food and imparts other ridiculous advice. Biggums, whom Chappelle portrayed, became a fan favorite. Other controversial skits on Chappelle's Show include a takeoff on the MTV reality show Real World, which has sometimes been criticized for having only token representatives of non-white races in its casts; in Chappelle's version, "The Mad Real World," a white man moves into a housing project whose residents include a dozen, mostly hostile blacks, among them a pot addict and a former convict; the man's neighbors proceed to steal his girlfriend and stab his father. Chappelle kicked off the 2004 season of his show with a "racial draft" skit, in which separate teams of African-Americans, Jews, Latinos, Asians, and whites try to recruit into their ranks individuals of mixed or ambiguous ethnicity, such as Tiger Woods, Halle Berry, and Mariah Carey. The whites draft the U.S. secretary of state Colin Powell, while the African-Americans snare Tiger Woods, whose genetic inheritance is an African-American, Asian, native American, and Caucasian mix. After cheering, "So long fried rice, hello fried chicken," as quoted by Tony Norman in the Pittsburgh, Pennsylvania, Post-Gazette (January 27, 2004), Woods promptly loses his endorsement contracts.

Many commentators have praised Chappelle's Show for turning an unflinching eye toward the issue of race and for debunking racial stereotypes. Elvis Mitchell wrote that Chappelle's humor is fueled by "a kind of laid-back indignation, a refusal to believe that ignoring racial differences will make anyone's life better." On the Africana Web site (January 1, 2004), Armond White wrote, "Chappelle's satire [goes] from debunking Eminem to routines subverting racism, sexism and the clichés you might call blackism. Not just funny, but daring." Conversely, Matt Feeney argued in the online magazine *Slate* (March 4, 2004), "Chappelle doesn't 'subvert' [racism, sexism and blackism]— he exploits them. That is, he takes eager advantage of an obvious double standard: White comedians have either to avoid race or treat it with exquisite caution, but black comedians like Chappelle are able to extract laughs from America's racial hangups, not necessarily from a solemn underlying commitment to racial justice, but often with an unfettered and indiscriminate comic malice." Responding to questions about his use of black stereotypes, Chappelle told Adrienne Maree Brown for the Africana Web site (January 24, 2003), "We're in this holding pattern of political correctness, which is not gonna get anything done for anybody. . . . If you look, if you really look at what I'm saying, I can justify each and every thing. And before I do it, I pre-think it out: is this a disservice? And I don't think I'm doing a disservice to anybody. . . . If something like this can belittle us [African Americans], then what . . . kind of shaky ground are we standing on . . . ? With a black person, someone so much as says you like chicken, you'll flip out, and secretly, you probably do like chicken—I know I do. It doesn't make me less of a person—why can't we just be ourselves and do what we do? Don't let people kill your spirit or create this inferiority complex, trying to accommodate or apologize for who you are." Nevertheless, Chappelle felt compelled to explain his motives in the February 4, 2004 episode of his show (the third of its second season), in which, as reported by Thompson, Chappelle said that "he is being 'misunderstood' and that there is no room for 'subtlety' when undercutting racial stereotypes. He continued to explain that he is 'not advocating racial hatred, [he's] just making fun of cultures.'" Chappelle illustrated his point by debunking the myth that white people cannot dance, presenting a skit in which different types of music were played for white, Latino, and black spectators, and noting each group's culturally based musical preferences. After the skit he told viewers, "We are all part of the same human family; our differences are just cultural," according to Thompson.

In the summer of 2004, Chappelle signed a two-year, $50 million contract with Comedy Central for two more seasons of *Chappelle's Show*. The third season will begin airing in early 2005. The television special *Dave Chappelle: For What It's Worth* aired on the Showtime cable network in 2004.

Chappelle lives with his wife, Elaine, and two sons on a 65-acre farm in southwestern Ohio. He also spends much of his time in New York City.

— P.G.H.

Suggested Reading: Dave Chappelle Web site; Death Valley Web site; *Detroit Free Press* (on-line) Apr. 4, 2003; *Los Angeles Times* Calendar Weekend p24 Feb. 13, 2003; *New Paltz [New York] Oracle* (on-line) Feb. 12, 2004; *New York Times* C p11 Aug. 2, 1993, II p24 Mar. 23, 2003, with photo; *New York Times* (on-line) Feb. 18, 2004; *Progressive* (on-line) Nov. 2003; *Slate* (on-line) Mar. 4, 2004; *USA Weekend* (on-line) Apr. 20, 2003

Selected Films: *Robin Hood: Men in Tights*, 1993; *Undercover Blues*, 1993; *Getting In*, 1994; *The Nutty Professor*, 1996; *Joe's Apartment*, 1996; *The Real Blonde*, 1997; *Con Air*, 1997; *Half Baked*, 1998; *Woo*, 1998; *You've Got Mail*, 1998; *200 Cigarettes*, 1999; *Blue Streak*, 1999; *Screwed*, 2000; *Undercover Brother*, 2002

Selected Television Shows: *Buddies*, 1996; *Dave Chappelle: For What It's Worth*, 2004; *Chappelle's Show*, 2003–

NBAE/Getty Images

Cheeks, Maurice

Sep. 8, 1956– Basketball coach

Address: Portland Trail Blazers, One Center Court, Suite 200, Portland, OR 97227

Maurice Cheeks, the head coach of the Portland Trail Blazers, is one of the most respected figures in the National Basketball Association (NBA). Drafted in the second round of the 1978 NBA draft, he excelled in the point-guard position and helped win an NBA championship for the Philadelphia 76ers in 1983. He also became known for his stoic demeanor, crisp passing, and ability to steal the ball. When he retired, in 1993, Cheeks held the NBA record for most steals (2,310—currently third on the all-time list) and was near the top of the league in career assists. On June 27, 2001, after serving as an assistant coach for the 76ers for a half-dozen years, Cheeks was named head coach of the talented but troubled Trail Blazers. In his first two years at the helm, he has guided the team to the play-offs, despite the recurring behavioral problems of his players, who have been collectively dubbed the "Jail Blazers." Among other well-publicized incidents, various members of the team have been charged with marijuana possession, assault, and explosive arguments with referees.

Maurice Edward Cheeks was born in Chicago, Illinois, on September 8, 1956 and grew up in the Robert Taylor housing project on that city's South Side. During his senior year at Du Sable High School, where he played on the basketball team, several colleges offered him scholarships. He accepted one from the relatively unknown West Texas State University (since 1993, West Texas A&M University). With the West Texas State Buffaloes, he started in each of his four years and was named most valuable player (MVP) three times. He finished third on the Buffaloes' all-time scoring list, was twice an All-Lone Star Conference selection, averaged 16.8 points per game, and as a senior shot 56.8 percent from the field. Earlier, as a freshman, not anticipating the success he would go on to enjoy with the Buffaloes, Cheeks had considered quitting school. "My mother tried to reason with me to stay," he recalled to Ira Berkow for the New York Times (May 11, 2003, on-line). "I said, 'No, I'm leaving.' She said, 'Maurice, you quit school and you better not come home.' I stayed in school. I don't know what would have happened to me if I hadn't." In Cheeks's senior year the Buffaloes finished the season with a miserable record: eight wins and 20 losses. Nevertheless, the Philadelphia 76ers chose Cheeks (the 36th overall pick) in the second round of the NBA draft, largely on the strength of his performance in the 1978 college all-star game, in which he outplayed Butch Lee, who had led Marquette University's Warriors to the 1977 national championship. "Years ago, when NBA teams didn't blanket-scout schools the way they do now, a kid like Cheeks might have been missed," Phil Elderking, a former assistant coach with the 76ers, explained to Jack McMahon for the Christian Science Monitor (May 20, 1983). "The first time I watched Maurice play for West Texas State, all he showed me was quickness, plus he knew how to pass the ball. Even if the jump shot [could be made], he'd ignore it and try to get the ball inside to one of his teammates. After the game, when I asked a reporter if he knew why Cheeks didn't shoot more, he told me that the coach didn't consider shooting part of Maurice's job. Actually this coach had a rule that no one on his team could

take a jumper if he was more than 15 feet from the basket. It wasn't until I saw Cheeks in a post-season, all-star game that we decided to make him our second round draft pick."

As a rookie with the 76ers during the 1978–79 NBA season, Cheeks made an immediate impact by playing in all 82 regular-season games, leading the team in assists (431) and steals (174), and scoring in an impressive 51 percent of his shots. During the 1979–80 season he led Philadelphia in field-goal percentage (54 percent), steals (183), and assists (566) and helped the 76ers post a record of 59–23. They advanced to the NBA finals but lost to the Los Angeles Lakers in six games following a legendary, 42-point performance by the Lakers' rookie Earvin "Magic" Johnson. Cheeks continued to play well during the next two seasons, helping his team into the postseason both years—in 1981, to the Eastern Conference Finals, which they lost to the Boston Celtics (whose star Larry Bird had been named the 1979 College Player of the Year), and in 1982, to the NBA Finals, which they lost in six games to the Lakers, due in part to Kareem Abdul Jabbar's superior play at the center position. During the off-season the Philadelphia 76ers acquired the center Moses Malone from the Houston Rockets, thereby assembling one of the most dominant starting line-ups in NBA history—one that included Cheeks. In the 1982–83 season Cheeks averaged 6.9 assists per game and had 189 steals while helping the 76ers lead the league with a regular-season record of 65–17. The 76ers lost only one play-off game during their run toward the 1983 finals, in which they swept the Los Angeles Lakers. Cheeks's teammate Julius "Dr. J" Erving told Bill Lyon for the Sporting News (February 28, 1983), "[Cheeks] gets in a terrific rhythm and comes off the dribble just right. I think he has developed into just what you want in a point guard. If his man lays off him, he can hit the jumper; if his man crowds him, he can blow right by him and penetrate all the way. And he's a very creative passer, very efficient. Anyone can get you the ball, but the trick is to get to you when you're in the maximum scoring position." Cheeks, in turn, credited his fellow starters—Erving, Malone, Andrew Toney, and Bobby Jones—for the 76ers' success. "They made it easy . . . ," he told Phil Jasner for the Philadelphia Inquirer (March 13, 2003). "A lot of guys would have loved to have had [my] job, to have four guys like that who wanted to win."

The Cheeks-era 76ers never again reached the heights of their 1982–83 season; the team made the play-offs several more times but failed to advance to the NBA Finals. Still, Cheeks continued to perform well. During the 1984–85 season he achieved two remarkable shooting streaks—50 of 67 shots and 30 of 35—and during the 1985–86 season he set the franchise record for assists in a season: 753. Cheeks was traded to the San Antonio Spurs before the 1989 season and, after expressing interest in returning to the East Coast, was traded again the next year, to the New York Knicks. With the Knicks he competed for playing time with the young Mark

Jackson, then a promising but error-prone guard, and exhibited some of the maturity and insight that would later help him as a coach. "When I was about Mark's age with the 76ers, I had a rivalry with Henry Bibby and later with Lionel Hollins," Cheeks told Ira Berkow for the *New York Times* (February 26, 1990). "And I became friends with both of them. I found that there doesn't have to be animosity. And I also know that this is Mark's team, and they've been doing just fine. Remember, they're in first place in the division. My job is to come off the bench to spell him and to play X amount of minutes."

Cheeks was next traded to the Atlanta Hawks, in 1991, and then to the New Jersey Nets, in 1992. He retired as a player the following year. In addition to holding the NBA record for career steals and ranking near the top in career assists, he shared (and still holds) the NBA Finals record for most steals in a game (six) and shared (and still holds) the single-game play-off record for most steals (eight). He played in four All-Star games, was selected to four All-Defensive teams, led the 76ers in assists in all 11 seasons he played with them, led the team in steals in each of his first 10 years, and later, on February 6, 1995, became only the sixth player to have his number (10) retired by the Philadelphia franchise.

In the year of his retirement, Cheeks became an assistant coach with the Quad City Thunder, a team in the Continental Basketball Association (CBA). The Thunder won the CBA championship that season. The following season Cheeks was hired by the Philadelphia 76ers as an assistant coach. He soon gained a reputation for working well with the team's players, including its star, Allen Iverson. He was instrumental in helping them reach the 2001 finals, which they lost to the Los Angeles Lakers. "He's been a big part of the success we've had," Larry Brown, the 76ers' head coach, said of Cheeks, as quoted in the *Washington Post* (June 24, 2001). "A big part of [Iverson's] development as a player and a person."

In 2001, after spending seven years as an assistant coach in the NBA, Cheeks was hired as the head coach of the Portland Trail Blazers. That season he guided the team to a 49–33 regular-season record and into the play-offs, where they lost to the Los Angeles Lakers in the first round. "The Portland Trail Blazers have suddenly reemerged as championship contenders, and the credit goes to rookie coach Maurice Cheeks," Ian Thomsen wrote for *Sports Illustrated* (March 18, 2002). "The Trail Blazers have long been one of the NBA's most talented teams, and after an ugly 12-month hiatus, that talent is producing rebounds and defensive stops, not just points."

In the 2002–03 season Cheeks coached Portland to a record of 50–32 while also enduring a slew of off-court player-related problems, among them incidents of domestic violence, charges of marijuana possession, and fist fights among team members during practice. Cheeks coped with the stress by keeping a journal, a habit he had begun after the murder of his brother in 1991. "[Writing] helps," Cheeks told Jason Quick for the *Oregonian* (May 11, 2003), "because, say a player approaches you the next day [after an incident]. I might not be in the best of moods and I might snap at somebody. But if I wrote something down, I had already thought about the situation, and I would be better prepared to have a productive conversation." The Trail Blazers were eliminated from the play-offs during the first round in 2003 but impressed many by battling back from a three-game deficit to compete in a seventh game against the Dallas Mavericks, which they lost, 107–95. The Trail Blazers were the third team in NBA history to go from being three games down to tying a series; had they won game seven, they would have been the first NBA team to do so after a 0–3 deficit.

With one of the largest payrolls in the NBA and little in the way of postseason success to show for it, the Trail Blazers—and, inevitably, their head coach—came under fire from their fans and the press. But if Cheeks's reputation was ever in question, he did much to restore it with one simple gesture in April 2003, before the start of game three of Portland's play-off series against the Dallas Mavericks. Thirteen-year-old Natalie Gilbert, singing in front of more than 20,000 fans, forgot the words of the national anthem; Cheeks rushed to her aid, whispering the words in her ear and singing along with her to help her complete the song. Following this act, Cheeks received a vast amount of media attention. "Cheeks's moment of chivalry, replayed numerous times on television news and sports shows, touched the heart of some Americans in a most welcome and unexpected way," Ira Berkow wrote for the *New York Times* (May 11, 2003, online). "Ministers have written that Cheeks demonstrated the embodiment of the Good Samaritan, and spoke of him in their sermons. Coaches have expressed sentiments that it was the kind of message in sports they hope to convey—as opposed to the anger and rage and self-promotion that are so prevalent."

On November 13, 2003 the Trail Blazers signed Cheeks to a one-year contract extension, securing his position with the team through the 2005–06 season. Despite a large payroll and talented players, the Trail Blazers finished the 2003–04 season with 41 wins and 41 losses. At the end of October 2004, when the team's record stood at 4–3, Cheeks expressed optimism about the players' performance during the remainder of that season. "I think last year, our defense was worse than our offense at this time of the year," he said, as quoted by Andrew Seligman for the Vancouver, Washington, *Columbian* (October 27, 2004). "I think we've made a more concerted effort to work on the defensive end."

—L.A.S.

Suggested Reading: *New York Times* III p5 Oct. 8, 1990, II p11 Oct. 3, 1991, II p12 Dec. 30, 1992; *New York Times* (on-line) VIII p2 May 11, 2003; *Sporting News* p3 Feb. 28, 1983, with photo, p39 Mar. 5, 1990, p49 Dec. 2, 2002; *Sports Illustrated* p44 May 24, 1982, p28+ May 23, 1983, with photo, p166 Oct. 29, 2001

Courtesy of RCA Label Group

Chesney, Kenny

Mar. 26, 1968– Country musician

Address: c/o RCA Label Group, 1400 18th Ave. S., Nashville, TN 37212

"My audience wears baseball caps and cutoff blue jeans," Kenny Chesney, currently one of country music's biggest stars, told John Swenson for *Country Music* (June/July 2002). "My audience drives pick up trucks. My audience goes out Friday and Saturday nights. They're proud of where they came from. My audience is probably very deep in family. My audience likes to have a good time, and that's how I am." Whether they are about the joys of high-school football, the pressures newlyweds face, the responsibility weighing on a teenage father, or the simple pleasure of being young and in love ("One bottle of wine and two Dixie cups / Three a.m. I fell in love," he sings in "Don't Happen Twice"), Chesney's songs address issues that resonate strongly with his listeners. It is perhaps his ability to relate to the cares of ordinary music fans that has made him not only a top-selling country artist over the last decade but one of the few Nashville musicians in recent times to appeal to those who do not ordinarily like country music. His live shows often feature covers of rock songs, and many rock and rap stars have sung with Chesney, both live and on records. Most recently, Uncle Kracker, formerly a deejay with the rock/rap musician Kid Rock and now a solo artist in his own right, made a guest appearance on Chesney's newest album, *When the Sun Goes Down* (2004). "My crowd and Kid Rock's crowd listen to a lot of the same things . . . ," Chesney told Keith Ryan Cartwright for *Music Connection*. "I think that music is universal. I think that's been the secret of our success all along."

Kenneth Arnold Chesney was born in Knoxville, Tennessee, on March 26, 1968 and grew up in nearby Luttrell. He was raised primarily by his mother, Karen Chandler, after she and Chesney's father, David Chesney, divorced. As a boy Chesney never entertained notions of country-music stardom, despite the fact that Luttrell was also the hometown of the country legend Chet Atkins. "I'm not one of these guys who can sit here and tell you that since I was four years old I knew I wanted to be a country singer," he noted in 1997 on the Web site *delafont.com*. "To be honest, I never dreamed about being a singer as a kid. Never once gave it a thought." Instead, Chesney focused his energy on athletics. "I was in sports ever since I was old enough to pick a ball up," he told Swenson. "I played baseball and basketball in high school. I only went out for the football team in college because somebody told me I couldn't make it. I was a mediocre football player; a pretty good athlete, but a mediocre football player."

After high school Chesney attended East Tennessee State University (ETSU) in Johnson City. There, while pursuing a degree in advertising and marketing, Chesney became interested in playing guitar after receiving the instrument as a Christmas gift. He started by taking an introductory guitar class at the school and soon began performing for tips at bars in and around the area. One of his first gigs was at Chuckie's Trading Post, a local Mexican restaurant. "I got $5 an hour plus as many enchiladas as I wanted," he recalled to Richard Jerome and Kelly Williams for *People* (May 27, 2002). "At first I didn't get a tip. I put my guitar in my truck and said 'Man, do I suck that bad?'" Chesney joined the ETSU Senior Bluegrass Band, which performed at the World of Bluegrass Festival in Owensboro, Kentucky. In 1990 he traveled with the band to Russia for the International Folk Arts Festival.

After graduation Chesney moved to Nashville, Tennessee, the center of the country-music world, where he parked cars for a living during the day and, in the evenings, honed his singing and songwriting skills at open-mic nights on Lower Broadway, the city's musical hotspot. He initially felt daunted by the level of talent that surrounded him. "I remember going to Douglas Corner one night when I heard Buddy Cannon, Dean Dillon and some other people play in the round. I sat and listened to those guys and I thought, 'I don't know if

I can do this,'" he told Peter Cooper for the *Tennessean* (November 6, 2002, on-line). Still, he remained undeterred in his course. "My friends I went to high school with, when I came to Nashville they all got jobs at credit unions,'" he told Cooper. "I think they and my family decided music was something I'd try and that I'd get out of my system and be at peace with myself. In college, I got a degree in advertising and marketing. If I'd gone back home, I guess I'd have been a bad advertising salesman or something."

During his early years in Nashville, Chesney befriended Clay Bradley, the head of publisher/writer relations at BMI (Broadcast Music Inc., a performing-rights organization). In 1992 Bradley secured an audition for Chesney at Acuff-Rose, a premier songwriting firm with a long history. Chesney impressed executives there and won a songwriting contract. At a songwriters' showcase one night in Nashville, Chesney was spotted by an artist-and-repertory representative from Capricorn Records, which was starting up a country-music division; after signing with the company, Chesney released his first record, *In My Wildest Dreams*, in 1993. The struggling label was unable to promote Chesney's music extensively, and the album sold just over 100,000 copies (a comparatively low figure to some in the industry). Not long afterward, Capricorn closed its doors.

Other Nashville labels expressed interest in Chesney, however, particulary on the strength of "The Tin Man," a song he wrote in 1994. Soon Joe Galante, the chairman of the RCA Label Group, offered Chesney a deal on the company's affiliated label, BNA Records. Chesney's debut on BNA, *All I Need to Know* (1995), sold 300,000 copies, a respectable but unexceptional figure in music-business terms. His next effort, *Me and You* (1996), at first did not show signs of being a hit either, based on the lackluster performance of the first single, "Back in My Arms Again." That song "died in the 30s on the charts," as Chesney told Kimmy Wix for the Web site *cmt.com* (July 22, 1997, on-line). "Then after we released the 'Me and You' single, we finally started seeing solid sales increases every single week." By the time the third single, "When I Close My Eyes," was released, Chesney's reputation had begun to grow, and the song shot to number two on *Billboard*'s country chart. *Me and You* ultimately went gold, meaning that it sold at least 500,000 copies.

Chesney's next album, *Everywhere We Go* (1999), proved to be his breakthrough effort. The record went double-platinum (indicating sales of at least two million copies)and spawned two hit singles, "You Had Me from Hello" and "How Forever Feels." The former song was inspired by a line spoken by Renée Zellweger to Tom Cruise in the 1996 film *Jerry Maguire;* for Chesney, that line of dialogue suggested an approach to a love song that avoided the clichés of country music. "When Renée Zellweger said that in the movie, it was like instant. I said, 'That could be a wonderful song,'" he told a reporter for *USA Weekend* (September 12, 1999, on-line). "There's only so many ways you can say 'I love you' and 'I hate you.'" "You Had Me from Hello" and "How Forever Feels" (about a young man ready to commit to marriage) earned Chesney a strong following among females who identified with the themes of love and romance in his music. "I saw the kind of stuff that my mom used to have to go through, so I'm sensitive to that," Chesney told Randy Lewis for the *Los Angeles Times* (May 28, 2002). "Conway Twitty used to say he was singing all the things that women wanted to hear from their husbands or boyfriends that they could never say. In a way I'm sort of continuing that tradition."

Although Chesney was winning fans rapidly, some critics derided his music as lacking substance and cited such songs as the novelty track "She Thinks My Tractor's Sexy," from *Everywhere We Go* (whose lyrics include "She likes the way it's pullin' while we're tillin' up the land / She's even kind of crazy 'bout my farmer's tan"), as examples of the artist's vapidity. His fans, however, saw such lightweight songs as indications that he was able to poke fun at both himself and critics' expectations of him. In recent years, looking back on such songs of his as "Tractor," he has viewed them as necessary stepping stones to his current level of success, because their popularity has brought him artistic freedom. "That song separated me, in a good or bad way," he told Jon Bream for the *Minneapolis Star Tribune* (January 19, 2003). "It definitely gave the fans something to hang on to. Someone asked me the other day, if I had to do it over again, would I cut 'Tractor' right now? I don't think my career would be the same without 'Tractor.' But my life is in a different place now, and I think my music is more mature." In 2000 Chesney continued his hot streak with the release of *Greatest Hits*, a career-spanning disk that also included several new tracks. The record was an immediate hit, selling 85,000 copies in its first week to debut at the top of the country chart. It ultimately sold more than two million copies, making it Chesney's second double-platinum effort.

Chesney's professional triumphs were temporarily eclipsed beginning on June 3 of that year, when he and fellow country star Tim McGraw found themselves in an altercation with police in Buffalo, New York. The incident took place at a George Strait Country Music Festival, at which the two men were appearing. During the evening, Chesney noticed the horse of a mounted police officer, James Coyle, and thought it would be amusing to ride it to where McGraw and his family's tour bus was parked. According to Erie County sheriff Patrick Gallivan, Chesney was given permission to sit on the horse, but not to ride it; as he rode off, several officers gave chase and tried to remove him forcibly from the animal. When McGraw intervened, a scuffle broke out, and McGraw was accused of grabbing an officer in a choke hold, a claim he vigorously denied. (Days later, in an appearance on the *Tonight Show,* Chesney tried to make light of the incident, entering the stage on horseback.) Rather than agreeing to settle the case outside the courtroom, Chesney and McGraw went to trial to fight the charges: obstructing governmental administration, menacing behavior and harassment, assault, and resisting arrest. The felony charges were later reduced to misdemeanors. Chesney noted to Jerome and Williams that though he and McGraw had the chance to plead guilty to lesser charges, "the public would've thought we were guilty, that we were a couple of rednecks" if they had done so. The trial concluded on May 23, 2001 with McGraw and Chesney found not guilty on all counts.

While enduring the strain of the trial, Chesney was also recovering from the painful breakup with his fiancée, Mandy Weals, which resulted partly from his grueling tour schedule. "The one thing you must do in a relationship is make someone feel secure," he told a writer for *USA Weekend* (August 30–September 1, 2002), "and in my profession it's even more so. I didn't understand that."

Those tribulations formed the building blocks for what would be regarded as Chesney's most mature record up to that time, *No Shirt, No Shoes, No Problems.* Released on April 23, 2002, the record was met with some of the best reviews of Chesney's career. "[The songs] show a newfound depth and appreciation of subtlety," Brian Mansfield wrote for *USA Today* (May 8, 2002). Bill Friskics-Warren noted in the *Washington Post* (May 8, 2002) that the record "mixes regular-guy ballads and heartland anthems like some on-the-verge cross between Alan Jackson and John Mellencamp." Chesney told Wendy Newcomer for *Country Weekly* (April 30, 2002), "This is a very reflective album. A lot's happened in three and a half years. There's a little bit of me in every one of these songs. My heart and soul are opened up like a book." One of the two songs he co-wrote for the album, "I Can't Go There," speaks directly about his split with Weals and refers to places he can no longer visit because they remind him of her. After breaking up with Weals, Chesney told Jerome and Williams, "I went down to the [Cayman Islands] by myself, which was a mistake—because that's where we always went. . . . That's when I realized that emotionally, mentally and physically I couldn't be there." Another sign of Chesney's maturing as an artist, and of his willingness to address difficult personal issues, was his decision to cover Bruce Springsteen's "One Step Up," a darkly reflective song about a disintegrating marriage. Chesney infused the song's lyrics with his own sense of loss. "I've always really loved the song, but I had no idea that one day I would painfully learn the lesson of it," he said to Randy Lewis. "I almost recorded it a couple of albums back, but I'm glad I waited until I had lived it."

No Shoes, No Shirt, No Problems debuted at the top of the country and popular charts and sold 235,000 copies its first week. The record's first single, "The Good Stuff," was a big hit. The album eventually sold more than two million copies and made for the highest-grossing country tour of 2002. "When we started this tour," Chesney told a writer for the Web site *livedaily.com,* "all I wanted was [to] have enough people show up so we could go back and play all these places that my heroes had played when I was growing up. I'd never headlined before, so I just wanted to not embarrass myself, do enough business that we could keep growing it! Obviously we did a little better than I'd hoped."

Chesney's 2003 road show, the "Margaritas n' Senoritas" tour, ran from March through late August and again made him the highest-grossing country act of the year. In May he brought home two Academy of Country Music awards, one for top male vocalist and the other for record of the year, for "The Good Stuff." Late in the year he released a gold-selling Christmas album, *All I Want for Christmas Is a Real Good Tan*, before taking a hiatus to work on his next album. *When the Sun Goes Down*, Chesney's eighth album, was released on February 3, 2004. Chesney himself penned four of the songs on the record, which took its themes from his life. "I'm still learning as a songwriter," he told Kay West for *Country Music Today* (March/April 2004). "This is the first time I've recorded anything I've written by myself. Having co-writers can be sort of like having a crutch or an excuse. You can pass the emotion off on someone else. For the first time in my life, I feel comfortable as myself, comfortable enough to say something about myself." For the album Chesney explored both the lighter and darker sides of life. "Keg in the Closet" is a wistful look back at his freewheeling college days, while "Some People Change" examines how people can conquer their inner demons, such as bigotry and alcoholism. "I Go Back" at first seems to be a joyous reflection on the songs that changed the singer's life—until the last verse, which refers to the death of a close friend. Perhaps the most personal song on the record is "Old Blue Chair," a solo acoustic number Chesney wrote about his favorite chair in his house on a Caribbean island. "I was at home, going through all that stuff that piles up, and I found a bunch of pictures," he told West. "I kept coming across pictures of me in that blue chair. There were so many of them over time. It occurred to me how much time I had spent in that chair. Just sitting, thinking, reading books, writing songs. One New Year's Eve, after my fiancée and I had broken up, I pulled the chair out to the water and plopped down in that chair with a big cup of Malibu rum and Diet Coke. It was biggie-sized. I drank that whole thing and passed out in the chair, my head back. When I woke up, the cup was between my legs, and I was covered with about a million mosquito bites. I let go of her in that chair. So, when I was back in Nashville, looking at those pictures, I remembered that night, and I sat down on the edge of my bed and wrote that song in about four hours." Buoyed by the lead-off single, "There Goes My Life," *When the Sun Goes Down* sold 1.3 million copies in its first six weeks of release. In addition, the record was warmly received by critics. "Chesney shows development here as a writer, and past success ensures him top-shelf material," Ray Waddell wrote for *Billboard* (January 31, 2004, on-line). "He knows exactly what to do with it, too, with a delivery that relies far more on charisma than vocal gymnastics." Chesney received two 2004 American Music Award nominations, for favorite male/female artist and favorite album, for *When the Sun Goes Down*, and in November 2004 the album brought him his first Country Music Association Award, for album of the year.

When he is not on the road, Chesney makes his home in a plantation-style home just outside Nashville. Despite his wealth and success, Chesney is known for keeping in touch with his roots, as well as his audiences. During the "No Shoes, No Shirt, No Problems" tour he would often sneak into parking lots to drink margaritas with surprised fans. Through all the years he has worked in the country-music business, Chesney has held firm to the belief that his music is for listeners rather than critics. "You can't worry about what's not happening, you can only worry about the things you can impact," he told Wendy Pearl and Andrew Van Huss for *CMA Closeup* (May/June 2002). "I try to cut music I think the people I know can relate to—and I *really* try to remember those fans, to remember how it felt."

—J.K.B.

Suggested Reading: *Country Music* p24+ June/July 2002, with photos; *Country Music Today* p45+ Mar./Apr. 2004, with photos; *Country Weekly* p20+ Apr. 30, 2002, with photos; *People* p59+ May 27, 2002, with photos; *USA Weekend* (on-line) Sep. 12, 1999

Selected Recordings: *In My Wildest Dreams*, 1993; *All I Need to Know*, 1995; *Me and You*, 1996; *Everywhere We Go*, 1999; *Greatest Hits*, 2000; *No Shirt, No Shoes, No Problems*, 2002; *When the Sun Goes Down*, 2004

Chieftains

Irish music group

Conneff, Kevin
Jan. 8, 1945– Bodhrán player; vocalist

Fay, Martin
1938– Fiddler

Keane, Seán
July 12, 1946– Fiddler

Molloy, Matt
Jan. 12, 1947– Flutist

Moloney, Paddy
Aug. 1, 1938– Uilleann piper

Address: c/o BMG, 1540 Broadway, New York, NY 10036

Hailed by *Billboard* magazine (March 9, 2002) as "quintessential minstrels of traditional Irish music," the Chieftains are the world's best known and most beloved exponents of the form. Since 1963, when the pipes player Paddy Moloney formed the group in Dublin, Ireland, the six-time Grammy Award–winning Chieftains have recorded more than three dozen albums, performed around the world, collaborated with a wide array of musicians, and achieved international stardom. The group's mostly instrumental music has often been called "otherworldly." "The musical lifetime of the Chieftains defies nature by only getting stronger as it endures," in the words of the *Billboard* writer, who noted that the group has provided a "transfusion of lifeblood for a gloriously rich musical tradition which was, for many years, secreted away, unheard by many, behind the closed doors of Ireland's clubs and private houses. They helped bring that tradition of singing, dancing, fiddling and whistling into the mainstream to become part of a globally recognized musical dialect."

The band's celebrated and award-winning albums include *Another Country* (1992), *An Irish Evening* (1992), *The Celtic Harp* (1993), *The Long Black Veil* (1995), *Santiago* (1996), *Down the Old Plank Road* (2002), and, most recently, *Further Down the Old Plank Road* (2003). The music the Chieftains contributed to the soundtrack of the 1975 film *Barry Lyndon* helped that score to win an Academy Award. In 1989 the Irish government bestowed on the Chieftains the collective title Musical Ambassador, in recognition of the group's contributions to Irish culture. In addition to their leader and founder, Moloney, who plays uilleann pipes and tin whistle, the present-day Chieftains consist of another original member, Martin Fay (fiddle and bones); Seán Keane (fiddle), who joined the outfit in 1968; Kevin Conneff (bodhrán drum and vocals), a bandmate since 1976; and Matt Molloy (flute), who became a Chieftain in 1979. Derek Bell (harp) was a Chieftain from 1972 until his death, in 2002. "We keep the humor going," Moloney told Richard Corliss for *Time* (March 20, 1995). "I grew up in an atmosphere where music was about happiness and song. . . . The great leaders of the world should learn the tin whistle and have a party. And the world will be a happier place."

Barry McCall/Courtesy of Arista Associated Labels

The Chieftains (left to right): Seán Keane, Paddy Moloney, Kevin Conneff, Matt Molloy. (Not pictured is Martin Fay, who no longer tours with the group.)

Paddy Moloney was born on August 1, 1938, in Donnycarney, Dublin, the capital of the Republic of Ireland. Moloney inherited his family's love of traditional Irish music; his grandfather was a flute player, and his uncle belonged to the Ballyfinn Pipe Band. The young Moloney's first instrument was a plastic whistle; by eight years of age he was learning to play the uilleann pipes, a kind of bagpipe, from the pipe master Leo Rowsome. "I always had an interest in all kinds of music," Moloney told *Billboard*. As a child Moloney listened to the national Irish radio station RTÉ (Radio Telefis Éireann), which at the time did not air much traditional Irish music. Rather, the station broadcast a good deal of pop and classical music, and Moloney trained his ear intently to everything he heard.

Traditional Irish music is a broad classification encompassing many different styles of Irish singing and instrumentation. In general, traditional Irish music is thought of as "oral" music, meaning that it has been used to transmit stories and folklore, for example (as the medium of writing does), so that they might be preserved in the memory of listeners. Rural in origin and played mostly for recreation, the music is passed on from one performer to another, from one generation to the next. Because it is an oral tradition, Irish music is fluid in that many variations of standard songs and tunes exist. According to the Irish Traditional Music Archive Web site, the bulk of traditional Irish instrumentation is fast-tempo dance music—jigs, reels, and hornpipes; instruments such as the fiddle, whistle, flute, pipes, concertina, and accordion predominate. (Traditional Irish music has often been referred to as Irish folk music. Most of the

standard repertory of traditional Irish music was current in the 18th and 19th centuries.) As Moloney recalled to *Billboard*, in his youth traditional Irish music was underappreciated. It was played in homes and schools, "but if you were seen walking in Dublin with a fiddle under your arm, you'd get an awful slagging [mocking] from your mates: 'That's hick music. You should be singing the popular songs.' It was rather sad."

The Moloney family spent their summers at a small farmhouse in Ballyfinn, where there was no running water and no electricity; in spite of the lack of such comforts, the house was crowded every weekend with friends and family members who sang, danced, and played music. As a young man Moloney led a number of different bands, including a barbershop quartet and a group called the Happy Wanderers. "I did all sorts of funny things, and I loved jazz," Moloney recalled for *Billboard*. Meanwhile, he worked for several years as an accountant for a building company. In 1968 Moloney went to work for Claddagh Records, a fledgling record label. During his eight years as a director with Claddagh, Moloney either produced, coproduced, or supervised production of some 45 albums of mostly traditional and classical music. (Claddagh served as the Chieftains' primary record company from 1964 to 1986.)

Martin Fay was born in 1938 in Dublin. As a boy he was inspired to take up the violin after seeing a film about Niccolò Paganini, a 19th-century Italian violinist and composer; he later won a scholarship to the Dublin School of Music. Fay's fiddle playing is distinguished by what Mike Joyce, writing for the *Washington Post* (March 18, 1998), referred to as "melancholy eloquence." Seán Keane, the son of two fiddlers, was born in Dublin on July 12, 1946 and began playing the instrument at a young age. He attended the Dublin School of Music and soon became recognized as one of the finest fiddlers in Ireland, winning first place in the All-Ireland Championships and the prestigious Fiddler of Dooney competition, which earned him the title "master fiddler." Kevin Conneff was born in Donore, a historic suburb of Dublin, on January 8, 1945. In his youth he was fond of jazz; he began to take an interest in traditional music in his late teens. He learned to sing in both Gaelic, the traditional Celtic language of Ireland, and English, and to play the bodhrán, a drum that was traditionally used in Ireland during religious ceremonies and times of war. Conneff was a co-founder of the Tradition Club at Slattery's, in Dublin, a meeting place for fans of traditional Irish music and a venue for its top performers. Matt Molloy was born on January 12, 1947, in Ballaghaderreen, in Roscommon County, Ireland, an area known for its flute players. (He is the only remaining member of the Chieftains born outside Dublin.) Molloy began playing the flute at eight years of age; by age 17 he had won the All-Ireland Flute Championship. After moving to Dublin, in the early 1970s, he co-founded the folk-rock group the Bothy Band.

The original members of the Chieftains were Moloney, Fay, Seán Potts (who played tin whistle, bones, and bodhrán), Michael Tubridy (flute, concertina, and whistle), David Fallon (bodhrán), and the composer Seán Ó'Ríada, who met in Ireland in the late 1950s as members of Ceoltóirí Cualann, a Celtic folk orchestra led by Ó'Ríada. In a biography of the Chieftains, Bruce Eder wrote for the All Music Guide Web site that Ceoltóirí Cualann, which specialized in instrumental music, "stripped away the pop music inflections from Irish music—the dances were played with a natural lilt and abandon that came from deep within the music's origins, and the airs, stripped of their worst modern inflections, came across with even greater poignancy than anyone had recognized them for in decades, and perhaps centuries. Tempos were changed in mid-song, from reel to polka to jig to slow air and back again." Through connections to the Dublin music world that Ó'Ríada had developed, Ceoltóirí Cualann were broadcast regularly on Radio Eireann and performed a number of public concerts in Dublin, sparking in many listeners a renewed interest in traditional Irish music. Seeking to take the musical vision and style of Ceoltóirí Cualann a step further, Moloney founded the Chieftains in 1963. Derek Bell, a former child prodigy in music and a harp instructor at the Belfast Academy of Music, in Northern Ireland, began playing with the Chieftains in 1972, when Moloney decided to incorporate the sound of a harp into the Chieftains' music. In addition to his contributions to the group, which also included his work on dulcimer and piano, Bell was an accomplished solo artist and composer. He remained a Chieftain until his death, in the fall of 2002.

Bruce Eder wrote that the Chieftains were "a success virtually from the beginning, their music weaving a spell around audiences in Ireland and later in England, where they quickly became popular as both a performing and recording act." Traditional Irish music, however, enjoyed only a relatively small following even in Ireland; therefore, the members of the Chieftains decided to keep their day jobs and remain semiprofessional as a band during the 1960s and early 1970s, playing concerts together frequently but recording albums only sporadically. Their first album, now commonly referred to as *Chieftains 1* (1964), which the band initially envisioned as a one-time enterprise, featured their skillful interpretations and arrangements of traditional Celtic songs. In a later review of that album, Genevieve Williams wrote for Amazon.com that the Chieftains' first album "reflects only a taste of what was to come. It's straightahead folk music; the selections consist of stalwartly traditional reels, jigs, and airs, all of which illuminate the debt that American folk traditions owed to old-school Irish and Celtic folk forms. Fairly restrained in its energy, these songs float by without the confidence of the Chieftains' later work." Soon after the release of *Chieftains 1*, Ó'Ríada and Fallon left the band.

In the late 1960s the Chieftains played in front of large audiences at the Edinburgh Festival, in Scotland, and the Cambridge Folk Festival, in England. In 1969 the Chieftains recorded *Chieftains 2*, and *Chieftains 3* followed two years later. Despite having chosen to keep a low profile, the band soon became regarded as leading exponents of Irish music. They played their first concert in the U.S. at the Irish Arts Theater, in New York, in 1972. (The musical luminaries John Lennon and Yoko Ono were in attendance.) By the time they released *Chieftains 4* (1973), the group had grown to include Derek Bell and Peadar Mercier (on bodhrán and bones) and had become a bona fide attraction in Britain. Bell's harp added a soft, lyrical tone that enhanced the group's sound. *Chieftains 4* contained the song "Mná na hÉireann" ("Women of Ireland"), a hauntingly beautiful air composed by Moloney and Ó'Ríada. Along with other music by the Chieftains, that song was included on the Academy Award–winning soundtrack of Stanley Kubrick's movie *Barry Lyndon* (1975), which brought the Chieftains recognition in the U.S. "Women of Ireland" received a fair amount of airplay on American radio and even made the play lists of some Top 40–oriented radio stations. Around that time the group made a number of appearances on American television, mostly early-morning network programs. *Melody Maker* named the Chieftains group of the year in 1975.

Buoyed by that success, the members of the Chieftains declared the band a full-time enterprise and saw their international reputation grow. Their first concert as a full-time act was at Royal Albert Hall, in London, England, during which the band received a highly enthusiastic response from the audience. "As the band's celebrity grew and their collaborations became broader, their audience evolved fairly radically," David Weyner, a veteran record-industry executive, told Steve Graybow for *Billboard* (March 9, 2002). "Originally, their audience in the United States were sort of a hippy, folk audience who were enamored with the band because they were the beginning of what is now termed 'world music.' . . . Today you can find the broadest audience imaginable at a Chieftains concert."

Chieftains 5 (1975) was the group's first release on a major record label, Island Records, which also arranged to re-release the band's four earlier albums, previously available only from the Claddagh label in Ireland. Finding a growing audience of admirers for their music, the Chieftains were praised by the likes of Mick Jagger, Eric Clapton, Emmylou Harris, and other major music stars. In 1976 Kevin Conneff replaced Mercier, the group's principal bodhrán player, and in 1979 Matt Molloy, on flute, filled the place of the departing original member Michael Tubridy. Seán Potts, another founding member, also left the group in 1979. According to critics, Moloney's skillful arrangements enabled the Chieftains to retain their fresh sound despite those changes in personnel.

In quick succession the band released *Bonaparte's Retreat* (1976); *Chieftains Live* (1977); *Chieftains 7* (1977), which garnered the group's first Grammy Award nomination, for best ethnic recording; *Chieftains 8* (1978); and *Chieftains 9: Boil the Breakfast Early* (1979), which earned the group another Grammy nomination. Reviewing *Chieftains 8*, Jason MacNeil wrote for the Web site popmatters.com, "The album's collection of jigs, reels and occasional laments aren't lost on the listener, but it's the toe-tapping jigs which seem to get the listener's ear and foot immediately." In a review of *Chieftains 9* found on the Microsoft Network Entertainment Web site, Richie Unterberger, in All Music Guide, praised the band for "mixing up the reels, hornpipes, and more gentle airs, with an energy and deftness equaled by few." During Pope John Paul II's visit to Ireland in 1979, the Chieftains performed in Phoenix Park, Dublin, in front of an estimated 1.3 million people. (The band later played a concert at the Vatican.) The Chieftains released *The Chieftains 10: Cotton-Eyed Joe* in 1981. In 1983 the Chieftains made a historic tour of China, becoming one of the first Western groups to perform with a Chinese folk orchestra and the first to perform on the Great Wall of China. That musical adventure resulted in their album *The Chieftains in China* (1987) and a video that documented the group's trip; that documentary has been broadcast worldwide. "Moloney, . . . an instinctive musicologist, takes his greatest pleasure in joining the sometimes invisible dots that connect folk with jazz, classical, Eastern and other musical styles," *Billboard* noted. "And he has taken an unparalleled lineup of fellow musicians, from superstars to new discoveries, along for the ride."

Also in 1983, at the invitation of U.S. speaker of the House Thomas "Tip" O'Neill and Senator Edward Kennedy, the Chieftains became the first group to give a concert in the U.S. Capitol, in Washington, D.C. In the 1980s, during their live performances, the Chieftains began to employ Irish step dancers, including Michael Flatley and Jean Butler, both of whom later achieved fame in *Riverdance*, an elaborate Irish dance-and-music extravaganza that has toured the world and been the subject of a film. The group also continued to create music for television and films. Moloney created the score, which was performed by the Chieftains and Ireland's RTÉ Concert Orchestra, for the joint RTÉ/French television production of the miniseries *The Year of the French* (1982). (The Chieftains appeared in that program as musicians.) In addition, the group provided the soundtrack for the National Geographic special *The Ballad of the Irish Horse* (1985).

The 1987 album *Celtic Wedding*, on which the Chieftains explored the music of Brittany—a region in the north of France with a Celtic past—was nominated for a Grammy Award in the category of best ethnic recording, as was *Irish Heartbeat*, the Chieftains' 1988 collaboration with the Irish-born recording star Van Morrison. During the same period the band released two albums featuring their collaborations with the classical Irish flute player James Galway: *James Galway and the Chieftains in Ireland* (1987) and *Over the Sea to Skye: The Celtic Connection* (1990).

In the 1990s the Chieftains continued to make award-winning music and capture an ever-widening audience. *Reel Music* (1991), a compilation of their contributions to movie soundtracks, included music for *Treasure Island*, *Three Wishes for Jamie*, *Tristan and Isolde*, and *The Grey Fox*, whose score won a Genie Award, the Canadian equivalent of an Oscar, in 1983. *The Bells of Dublin* (1991), a Christmas album featuring contributions by Elvis Costello, Marianne Faithfull, Nanci Griffith, Ricki Lee Jones, and Jackson Browne, became the Chieftains' first gold album (meaning that it sold at least 500,000 copies). "There are many resplendent performances here," Martin Keller wrote in a review of *The Bells of Dublin* that appears on Amazon.com. "Like a banquet of traditional Irish fare with some updating to accommodate individual guests, *Bells* is the kind of holiday record you don't want to end." In 1992 the Chieftains put out two award-winning albums. *Another Country*, on which the band demonstrated the influences of traditional Irish music on American country music, won a Grammy Award for best contemporary folk album. Recorded live with Nanci Griffith and Roger Daltrey at the Grand Opera House in Belfast, Northern Ireland, *An Irish Evening* was nominated for three Grammy Awards and won in the category of best traditional folk album, making the Chieftains the first group to win two Grammy Awards in the same year (1993) for two different albums. (A video of the performance at the Grand Opera House in Belfast is also available.)

"While there's nothing quite like seeing the Chieftains live in concert, *An Irish Evening* marks the next best thing. . . . The disc captures the group's eclectic, fun, and loving approach to traditional Irish music," Roch Parisien wrote in a review for All Music Guide, as it appears on the Microsoft Network Entertainment Web site. *The Celtic Harp: A Tribute to Edward Bunting* (1993), a collaboration with the Belfast Harp Orchestra, brought the group another Grammy Award for best traditional folk album. (Edward Bunting helped to preserve harp playing as an art form in Ireland in the 18th century.) Offering interpretations of traditional and contemporary songs from Ireland and the United States and featuring contributions by Mick Jagger, Sinead O'Connor, and Sting, among other guests, the Chieftains' album *The Long Black Veil* (1995) continued their impressive run, achieving gold status just five weeks after its release and being named album of the year by both the *New York Post* and the *Los Angeles Times*. That album's track "Have I Told You Lately That I Love You," a collaboration with Van Morrison, captured a Grammy Award for best pop vocal collaboration, beating records by fellow nominees Mariah Carey and Michael Jackson. Richard Corliss called *The Long Black Veil* a "lovely introduction to this musical Irish institution, with a cogent, eclectic choice of material and Moloney's smart matching of song to singer."

Film Cuts (1996) features songs from eight different movie soundtracks to which the Chieftains have contributed over the years, including *Far and Away* (1992), *Circle of Friends* (1995), and *Rob Roy* (1995). (In addition to their film scores, the Chieftains have provided music for ballet and theatrical productions.) On their 1996 album *Santiago*, the Chieftains delved into the connection between Celtic songs and the music of Galicia, a province in the northwest of Spain, an area that Celtic peoples once inhabited; *Santiago* features guest artists Ry Cooder, Los Lobos, and Linda Ronstadt. In 1997 that recording brought the Chieftains another Grammy Award, for best world-music album. For *Tears of Stone* (1999) Moloney assembled a diverse group of female performers, among them Joni Mitchell, Bonnie Raitt, and the Corrs, an Irish family group that includes three sisters. Moloney told Roberto Gatti for the Web site mybestlife.com, "To realize *Santiago*. . . I had invited a wonderful bagpipe player whose name was Carlos Nunez. Well, in an old Nunez album, there was a wonderful Spanish song called just 'Tears of Stone.' I thought it would fit perfectly what I was up to." *Tears of Stone*, he added, is "all focused on love, and its several meanings and ways, from joy to sadness, from passion to hate, from mystic ecstasis to the hell of senses." In December 1998, a month before the release of *Tears of Stone*, the Chieftains played a concert with some of the guest artists on that album at the historic Dublin Castle. In addition to those already mentioned, the band's well-received albums from the late 1990s include *Fire in the Kitchen* (1998) and *Long Journey Home* (1998), and from 2000, *Water from the Well*. In a review of the last-named album for All Music Guide, which appears on the Web site artistdirect.com, Stephen Thomas Erlewine wrote, "Not only do the Chieftains have a great time embracing traditional dances and ballads, but their [musical] guests invigorate them, resulting in a very strong listen. It's the kind of record that only a seasoned band could make; it might not be groundbreaking or definitive, but it is an accomplished yet enthusiastic set of songs where the joy is in the little details." In 2002 the Chieftains celebrated their upcoming 40th anniversary with *Down the Old Plank Road: The Nashville Sessions*, the group's second collaborative recording with American country-music artists, and *The Wide World Over: A 40-Year Celebration*, a compilation of some of the Chieftains' best-known songs and collaborations. The next year the group released *Further Down the Old Plank Road*, which included guest vocal performances by Roseanne Cash, Emmylou Harris, John Hiatt, Patty Loveless, and Don Williams, among other singers.

The Chieftains' massive body of work also includes the albums *Tailor of Gloucester* (1988), *A Chieftains Celebration* (1989), *Best of the Chieftains* (1992), *The Magic of the Chieftains* (1992), and *Christmas in Rome* (1998), among others. Collections of the group's music include *From the Beginning: The Chieftains 1 to 4* (1999), a boxed set, *The Very Best of the Claddagh Years* (1999), and *The Very Best of the Claddagh Years Vol. 2* (2000).

In addition to his work with the Chieftains, Moloney has played as a solo artist with many top performers and has been featured as a guest artist on numerous albums in various musical genres. In 1982 he played whistle on the song "Rain Clouds," which was released as the flip side of Stevie Wonder and Paul McCartney's hit single "Ebony and Ivory." Moloney was awarded an honorary doctorate degree in music from Trinity College, in Dublin, in 1988. He chose the music for the Public Broadcasting Station (PBS) special *The Irish in America* (1998). Seán Keane's work apart from the Chieftains includes the solo albums *Gusty's Frolics* (1978) and *Jig It in Style* (1989). Matt Molloy owns a pub in Westport, Ireland, in Mayo County, where live music is featured. Kevin Conneff released his first solo album, *The Week Before Easter*, in 1989.

Among the many artists with whom the Chieftains have performed are Bob Dylan, Eddie Vedder, Pete Townshend, Roger Waters, Vince Gill, and Willie Nelson. The group has played all over the world and still tours the U.S. about twice a year. "They are an acoustic band," David Weyner explained to Steve Graybow, "so they can play anywhere, making them the ultimate portable act." Despite Derek Bell's death and the advancing ages of the group's remaining members, the Chieftains show no sign of slowing down. In the winter of 2003, they embarked on a U.S. tour, which culminated with a concert at Avery Fisher Hall, at New York City's Lincoln Center, on March 17, St. Patrick's Day. The Chieftains have made many television appearances, including spots on the long-running show *Saturday Night Live*, in 1979, and NBC's *Today Show*, in 1986. In 1988, the year of the group's 25th anniversary, the Chieftains were honored on the popular Irish program *The Late, Late Show* for their contributions to Irish culture. *Irish Music Magazine* honored the Chieftains with a lifetime achievement award in 2000.

When asked about the group's considerable legacy, Moloney told James Bickers for the Louisville, Kentucky, *Courier-Journal* (February 24, 2002, on-line), "We went out and spread the gospel about what this music was about. It didn't all finish with 'Danny Boy'! There was something else that I just thought the world should hear. It's quite an honor now to be given all this recognition. We set on a mission, spreading the gospel of this great music. And my dream came true."

—C.F.T.

Suggested Reading: *All Music Guide* (on-line); artistdirect.com; *Billboard* p49+ Mar. 9, 2002, with photos; *Time* p79+ Mar. 29, 1995, with photo; *Washington Post* D p6 Mar. 18, 1998; Glatt, John. *The Chieftains*, 1997

Selected Recordings: *Chieftains 1*, 1964; *Chieftains 2*, 1969; *Chieftains 3*, 1971; *Chieftains 4*, 1973; *Chieftains 5*, 1975; *Bonaparte's Retreat*, 1976; *Chieftains Live*, 1977; *Chieftains 7*, 1977; *Chieftains 8*, 1978; *Chieftains 9: Boil the Breakfast Early*, 1979; *Chieftains 10: Cotton-Eyed Joe*, 1981; *The Chieftains In China*, 1987; *Celtic Wedding*, 1987; *James Galway and the Chieftains in Ireland*, 1987; *Irish Heartbeat*, 1988; *Tailor of Gloucester*, 1988; *A Chieftains Celebration*, 1989; *Chieftains Collection*, 1989; *Reel Music*, 1991; *The Bells of Dublin*, 1991; *An Irish Evening: Live at the Grand Opera House, Belfast*, 1992; *Another Country*, 1992; *The Best of the Chieftains*, 1992; *The Magic of the Chieftains*, 1992; *The Celtic Harp*, 1993; *The Long Black Veil*, 1995; *Film Cuts*, 1996; *Santiago*, 1996; *Christmas in Rome*, 1998; *Tears of Stone*, 1999; *From the Beginning: The Chieftains 1 to 4*, 1999; *The Very Best of the Claddagh Years*, 1999; *The Very Best of the Claddagh Years Vol. 2*, 2000; *Water from the Well*, 2000; *The Wide World Over: A 40-Year Celebration*, 2002; *Down the Old Plank Road*, 2002; *Further Down the Old Plank Road*, 2003

Coldplay

British rock band

Martin, Chris
Mar. 2, 1977– Singer; songwriter; pianist

Champion, Will
July 31, 1978– Drummer

Berryman, Guy
Apr. 12, 1978– Bassist

Buckland, Jon
Sep. 11, 1977– Guitarist

Address: c/o Capitol Records, 1750 North Vine St., Hollywood, CA 90028

"Because the world will eventually end, I would really like it if on some alien planet, in a million years' time, you were able to purchase a CD called *The Best of the Earth—Ever!* and we were on it," Chris Martin, the lead singer of the British band Coldplay, told Wes Orshoski for *Billboard* (August 17, 2002). Judging from recent trends, Coldplay would be as likely as any other musical group to be featured on such a recording. The band's first full-length release, *Parachutes* (2000), has sold some eight million copies worldwide, and it won a 2002 Grammy Award for best alternative album. Their second disk, *A Rush of Blood to the Head* (2002), has been certified double platinum (over two million copies sold) in the U.S.; it also won two 2003 Grammy Awards (for best alternative music album and best rock performance by duo or group with vocal) and reached number five on the *Billboard* 200 album chart (a list on which, as of early November 2004, it remained). Coldplay, which also includes Jon Buckland on guitar, Guy Berryman on bass, and Will Champion on drums, is the first band to win the Grammy Award for best alternative music album two years in a row. In Great Britain the group have enjoyed at least as much success as in the U.S. Their recordings have topped various album and singles charts and garnered a host of awards, among them Brit Awards for best British group and best British album in both 2001 and 2003. The band's two full-length albums have been certified gold or platinum in more than 25 countries. While Coldplay's music is passionate and soulful, most of it is also mellow. Deeply committed to controlling their own music, the band have never allowed their music to be used in any advertisements or on any film soundtracks. "[Our success has] been all on our own terms," Will Champion wrote for Coldplay's official Web site. "We have 100 per cent control over any aspect of whatever we do, and that's really important to who we are and the music we make. We take control of the recording, the videos, the artwork. We're not a band that can be pushed around, although we do have some amazing advisors." By their own account, the members of Coldplay contribute 10 percent of their earnings to charitable causes.

Kevin Westenberg/Courtesy of Capitol Records

Coldplay (left to right): Jon Buckland, Guy Berryman, Chris Martin, Will Champion

Chris Martin is Coldplay's pianist and main songwriter as well as lead singer. The eldest of the five children of an accountant and a teacher, he was born on March 2, 1977 and grew up in Devon, England. He began playing piano at age five and continued to pursue his musical interests at the Sherbourne public school. There, he met Coldplay's future manager, Phil Harvey, and found a mentor in a music teacher who approved of his pop-music leanings. At Sherbourne, Martin struggled for a time with his sexuality and often wondered whether he was gay. Something of an outcast, he was booed off stage at 15 while performing one day with his band, the Rockin' Honkies.

All the members of Coldplay met as students at University College, in London. During his first week of attendance there, in 1996, Martin met Jon Buckland and started playing music with him. Buckland, who was born in northern Wales on September 11, 1977, began playing guitar at age 11; he has cited Jimi Hendrix and Eric Clapton as being among his musical influences. Next, Martin and Buckland were joined by Guy Berryman, who was born on April 12, 1978 and spent his childhood first in Scotland and then in Kent, England. Buckland and Martin accepted him as a member of their band at his request, after he approached them at a campus bar. Unlike the other two, Berryman was an aficionado of funk and soul music. Will Champion, who was born on July 31, 1978, became acquainted with Martin through the University College hockey team, for which both played. Originally a guitarist, Champion switched to drums to accommodate the needs of the band.

Martin and his bandmates initially called their group Starfish. They became Coldplay when they swapped names with a local band that had tired of that moniker. Coldplay spent a little over a year refining their sound and playing in local venues before making their first recording, the three-song EP *Safety*, in 1998. Although they had intended it to serve as a demo for record companies, the band and its management were so pleased with *Safety* that they produced 500 copies at their own expense.

On December 7, 1998 Coldplay appeared at the Camden Falcon, a London pub. Their strong performance attracted the interest of a representative of the Fierce Panda record label, which signed them soon afterward. Their first recording with Fierce Panda was the EP *Brothers and Sisters* (1999), whose tracks are "Brothers & Sisters," "Easy to Please," and "Only Superstition." Before the release of their next EP, *Blue Room*, later in 1999, Coldplay signed with Parlophone, a division of the United Kingdom arm of EMI Records. The pressure produced by the switch to a major label led to serious tension between Martin and his bandmates—something that had never occurred before. In particular, Martin clashed with Will Champion, whom he accused of subpar drumming and then kicked out of the band. "Things were going wrong in the studio and I told Will it was his fault . . . ," Martin recalled to an interviewer for *Q Magazine* (August 2002, on-line), as posted on the Easy to Please Web site. "It was an awful time. For a week Coldplay didn't exist." The clash brought about a change in the band's organization that has persisted to this day: though Martin comes up with the seeds of the songs and writes all the lyrics, each band member receives equal credit for every song, and all profits get split equally. "I don't want any more than the others," Martin told *Q Magazine*. "Do I really want to spend two weeks in court some way down the line arguing with my closest mates about who wrote what? Not all bands work that way and I've got into arguments with some about it. But going through that experience [the brief breakup] made me realise that our chemistry is special. I can't do it without them—all of them—and vice versa."

The consequences of their new financial arrangement soon became evident, as royalties from sales of their recording "Yellow" began to pour in. Released on June 26, 2000, the haunting and atmospheric single rose to number four on the British charts and raised expectations for *Parachutes*, which arrived in stores in July 2000. In addition to "Yellow," the album contains the songs "Shiver" and "We Never Change," to mention the ones that became best known. Immediately after its release *Parachutes* entered the U.K. album charts at number one, superseding Eminem's *Marshall Mathers* disk and remaining in the Top 10 for another 33 weeks. Melancholic and introspective, the album offers mostly low- and mid-tempo songs. Musically, the focus is on Martin, whose voice, heavy with emotion, slides seamlessly into and out of a crooning falsetto. Buckland added sparkling, atmospheric guitar lines, Berryman contributed hypnotic bass grooves, and Champion kept the beats simple and solid. In his lyrics, Martin tended toward the impressionistic, writing songs that, as he told Dorian Lynskey for *Blender* (September 2002, on-line), are about "what every album's about: Your fear of death, your love of girls and your anger at the [expletive] that politicians talk. Mainly about girls, though."

Despite being publicly branded "music for bedwetters" by the British rock-music guru Alan McGee, whose words were widely quoted on the Internet, *Parachutes* elicited mainly positive critical reviews. In a review for the Barnes & Noble Web site, Jem Aswad wrote, "Although *Parachutes* isn't the sort of album to throw on at your next kegger [a rowdy party involving a lot of beer drinking], the songs have a melodic strength and quiet beauty that belies the group's youth and elevates Coldplay to 'one to watch' status." "[This] debut album's secret arsenal," Mark Blake wrote for *Q Magazine* (October 2000, on-line), "comprises frontman Chris Martin's voice—prematurely aged for someone in their early twenties—and some supple, persuasive melodies. That and a great big side order of melancholy." Andy Greenwald complained in the *Washington Post* (January 14, 2001), "Coldplay's unfaltering devotion to melancholia eventually does begin to grate," but added, "*Parachutes* somehow manages the neat trick of being neither challenging nor quickly forgotten." In addition to a 2002 Grammy, *Parachutes* earned two Brit Awards in 2001 (for best British group and best album) as well as several *NME* (*New Music Express*) and *Q Magazine* awards.

Coldplay's highly anticipated sophomore album, *A Rush of Blood to the Head*, was released in August 2002, after much anxiety on the part of the band. Coldplay had started working on it in October 2001 and by December judged it to be complete. But they soon had misgivings about its readiness for release. "There was a feeling it was almost going too smoothly," Buckland recalled on the band's Web site. "We were pleased with it, but then we took a step back and realised that it wasn't right. It would have been easy to say we'd done enough, to release an album to keep up the momentum, but we didn't. And I'm glad because now we have something we'll be happy to tour with for two years." While its subject matter resembled that of *Parachutes*, *A Rush of Blood* was more highly orchestrated and included a greater number of up-tempo tracks. Among other songs, it contains "The Scientist," "Clocks," "Politik," "God Put a Smile Upon Your Face," and "In My Place." The release of *A Rush of Blood* prompted critics to express a new level of respect for Coldplay's work. In *Q Magazine* (November 2002, on-line), Dorian Lynskey asserted that the band had achieved the vaunted status of the United Kingdom's rock behemoths U2 and Radiohead: "Those who enjoy burrowing for hidden depths will find there is little here that won't be grasped within a handful of airings. But for everyone else, this is pretty much the apotheosis of post-Radiohead guitar-rock, a collection of vastly moving songs that will render stadiums as intimate as bedrooms. U2, Radiohead . . . Coldplay? It would seem so." David Browne, in *Entertainment Weekly* (September 6, 2002), agreed that, with their new album, Coldplay had become full-fledged stars. "Displaying a cohesion rarely heard in albums these days, *A Rush of Blood* bobs from one majestic little high to another. . . . At a time when so many bands, Brit or American, are intent on cramming as many genres as possible into each song, it's a relief to hear music that revels in the joys of a simple, graceful melody. The overall effect is tuneful and hypnotic—ambitious, but in the sneakiest, quietest way."

As soon as it went on sale, *A Rush of Blood* topped the U.K. and Canadian album charts. It entered the *Billboard* Top 200 chart at number five and has remained in the Top 100 since its release. In February 2003 Coldplay won Brit Awards for best British album and best British band. Two Grammy Awards followed later that month. In August 2003 Coldplay's "The Scientist" won three MTV Music Video Awards, for best group video, breakthrough video, and best direction (Jamie Thraves). For a while after the announcement of the MTV honors, *A Rush of Blood* again entered the Top 10 of the *Billboard* Top 200 album chart.

At about this time, the public learned that Martin had been dating the actress Gwyneth Paltrow, a revelation that made both of them fixtures in the tabloids. The media attention intensified after Paltrow became pregnant and the couple married in secret, in December 2003. (Paltrow gave birth to a daughter, Apple Blythe Alison Martin, on May 14, 2004.) Meanwhile, Martin and the other members of Coldplay had become more politically active, campaigning for AIDS relief in South Africa, for example, and in support of fair international-trade policies affecting farmers. Among other motives, according to Martin, he and his partners wanted to talk about matters of substance during conversations with the media. "We're not Mother Teresa or anything; our primary concern is to make music," Martin told Mark Brown for the *Ventura County Star* (May 29, 2003). "But we learned on the first album. We did so many interviews and so much TV, and we didn't really have anything to say. We were scared to say what we thought about things." In February 2003 Martin traveled to Haiti and the Dominican Republic in support of the British charity Oxfam's campaign to help those maintaining small farms receive fair prices for their produce. In September Martin and the other members of Coldplay took time out from their tour in Mexico to support the same cause. "When I came back, I had a feeling of elation, of being home but a new awareness," Martin told Cary Darling for Knight Ridder Newspapers, as quoted on mvonline.com in 2003. "We only tour in rich countries. We just don't see stuff like that. We live in a bubble." Along with such celebrated performers as Paul McCartney and Bono, Martin lent his voice to a re-recording of the song "Do They Know It's Christmas?" for a single marking the 20th anniversary of the humanitarian effort Band Aid. Proceeds from the single, which was scheduled to be released in Great Britain toward the end of 2004, were to be donated to famine-relief efforts in Sudan and other parts of Africa.

In July 2003 the normally mild-mannered Martin had an altercation with a photographer in Byron Bay, Australia, where Coldplay had come on tour. Martin became angry when, while surfing, he noticed the photographer snapping photos of him. When the photographer refused to erase the images in his digital camera, Martin broke the windshield of a car belonging to the man's employer (a contractor for a London newspaper) and deflated the car's tires. Martin was charged with malicious damage and was ordered to make a court appearance in October. In November, however, Australian police dismissed the case, explaining that Martin had "admitted his guilt . . . , expressed his contrition . . . [and] paid reparations for the damage," as quoted on BBC News (November 21, 2003, online).

On November 7, 2003 Coldplay won an MTV Europe Award for best group. Two weeks later the band released *Live 2003*, a two-disk DVD/CD set connected with the band's two concerts at the Horden Pavilion, in Sydney, Australia, in July 2003; the set contains an audio CD recorded at the performances, band commentaries, a documentary, and a tour diary. Plans for their next album have yet to be announced. "We're only on our second record . . . ," Martin told Edna Gundersen for *USA Today* (February 13, 2003, on-line). "I can't predict

the future, except that I'll always be the loudmouth frontman."

—P.G.H.

Suggested Reading: All Music Guide Web site; *Billboard* p1+ Aug. 17, 2002; (London) *Guardian* (on-line) July 7, 2000; *New York Times* B p14 Apr. 14, 2001; *USA Today* (on-line) Feb. 13, 2003; *Ventura County Star* G p20 May 29, 2003; *Village Voice* p122 Sep. 24, 2002; *Washington Post* G Jan. 14, 2001

Selected Albums: *Blue Room*, 1999; *Brothers and Sisters*, 1999; *Parachutes*, 2000; *A Rush of Blood to the Head*, 2002; *Live 2003*, 2003

Courtesy of the office of Senator Norm Coleman

Coleman, Norman

Aug. 17, 1949– U.S. senator from Minnesota (Republican)

Address: 320 Hart Senate Office Bldg., Washington, DC 20510

Norman Coleman—whose motto, as reported by newsmax.com, is "I just like to get things done"—completed a highly successful eight-year stint as the mayor of St. Paul, Minnesota, before becoming a U.S. senator. A former lawyer and public prosecutor in the Minnesota state attorney general's office, Coleman made his political reputation early on as a pro-business Democrat; he has since become a Republican who advocates low taxes as a means of facilitating economic growth, among other conservative positions. Since he won election to the Senate, in November 2002, Coleman has served on the Senate Foreign Relations Committee, the Small Business and Entrepreneurship Committee, and the Governmental Affairs Committee.

Of Jewish descent, Norman Coleman, known as Norm, was born on August 17, 1949 in Brooklyn, New York, the third of the eight children of Norman Coleman Sr. and Beverly Coleman. His father ran a construction company. Coleman has said that he was prepared for a life in politics by sitting around the large family kitchen table with his many relatives, who held good-natured yet impassioned debates about the issues of the day. As was common in the Flatbush section of Brooklyn, where Coleman grew up, he played stickball, enjoyed egg creams (a drink consisting of milk, seltzer, and chocolate syrup), and mixed with the numerous people of Jewish, Italian, or Irish descent who populated the area during the 1950s and 1960s. Coleman's first political victory came in sixth grade, when he was elected class treasurer. He graduated from James Madison High School in 1966.

As an undergraduate student at Hofstra University, in Hempstead, on Long Island, New York, in the late 1960s, Coleman was elected student-body president. During that turbulent decade, which saw many demonstrations in support of civil rights and against the Vietnam War, Coleman—sporting the long hair associated with the period—was active in such causes. A leader in the student antiwar movement, Coleman helped students to shut down the Hofstra campus briefly in 1970. After graduating from Hofstra, with a bachelor's degree in political science, in 1971, Coleman was eligible for the military draft. (At the time the U.S. government was drafting thousands of young Americans to fight in Vietnam.) Standing six feet tall and weighing just 135 pounds, however, Coleman failed a physical examination and therefore was not drafted. He next enrolled at the University of Iowa College of Law, where he was also student-body president; he earned a law degree and graduated with highest honors. Then, lured by a job opening, Coleman joined the staff of the Minnesota state's attorney general's office, where he served, in different capacities, for 17 years. As a prosecutor and then solicitor general, Coleman prosecuted cases all over Minnesota and participated in public-policy debates, in particular those related to drug abuse and civil rights in the state.

Running as a conservative Democrat, Coleman was elected mayor of St. Paul in 1993, defeating the candidate endorsed by the Democratic Farm Labor Party. One of Minnesota's "twin cities" (the other is Minneapolis), St. Paul is located on the Mississippi River, next to Minneapolis; at the time of the 2000 population census, St. Paul had a population of 287,151. One of Coleman's first legislative actions as mayor was to reject a proposed contract with city workers because it included a provision for retirement benefits for which no funds were available. That stand, while controversial initially,

ultimately saved city taxpayers tens of millions of dollars. In 1994 Coleman and the mayor of Minneapolis, Sharon Sayles Belton, published an op-ed article in the New York Times (August 9, 1994) that served to publicize City Vote, which was to take place in dozens of U.S. cities that November, before the Iowa caucuses, and which the mayors called "the first national urban Presidential primary." In their article Coleman and Belton called for a "national policy recognizing that for America to compete in the international marketplace it needs vibrant urban centers. We need national policies that give cities the flexibility to use our limited resources where they are most needed, on keeping our streets safe and clean and our neighborhoods strong."

When Coleman took office St. Paul was facing several glaring problems, including an economic downturn and an increase in crime. Seeking to address that problem, Coleman put forth the motto "Hope plus confidence equals investment." He reduced taxes and fostered business partnerships between the public sector and private companies and individuals. He also brought together the top 20 chief executive officers (CEOs) of the region to form the Capital City Partnership, which is dedicated to developing and marketing the city of St. Paul as a site for business. Coleman's efforts proved highly effective, as the city received more than $3 billion in private-sector investments during his tenure as mayor. In recognition of those efforts, in 2002 Coleman was honored with the U.S. Conference of Mayors' highest award for excellence in public-private partnership. That same year the conservative Web site newsmax.com hailed Coleman as a "hero of urban renewal," mentioning, among other successes, that during his eight-year tenure as mayor property taxes in St. Paul never rose and that property values increased in every neighborhood in the city. In addition, under Coleman's watch as mayor, 18,000 new jobs were created in St. Paul; Lawson Software, Minnesota's largest software developer, moved its offices to downtown St. Paul; and Harriet Island Park and other public lands along the Mississippi River were rehabilitated through the planting of more than 30,000 trees, among other ameliorations. Other improvements that Coleman helped to bring about included the construction of the $90 million Science Museum of Minnesota and the presence, once again, of a National Hockey League (NHL) team—this time, the Minnesota Wild—in Minnesota. The team plays in the Xcel Energy Center, a state-of-the-art arena built during Coleman's time as mayor.

Meanwhile, disillusioned with the Democratic Party, in 1996 Coleman switched to the Republican Party, believing, as his Web site states, that the latter would be better able to effect job growth, improve the state's education system, and achieve greater public safety. Coleman's Senate Web site further explains his change of party allegiance, stating that Coleman had been frustrated that the

"Democratic party he had been a part of from his youth had assumed the role of defenders of the status quo." In the *New York Times* (December 20, 1996), Dirk Johnson wrote that while Coleman's switch was somewhat surprising in that Minnesota has traditionally been a strongly Democratic and liberal-leaning state—Minnesota last supported a Republican candidate for president in 1972—Coleman had always been a relatively conservative politician. Johnson added that before going over to the Republican Party, Coleman "had been under fire" from Democrats, "especially by members of organized labor, who lustily booed [Coleman] at the Democratic-Farmer-Labor convention" in Minnesota in 1994. Political expedience was also cited in the press as a reason for Coleman's defection. As Johnson wrote, "It is widely believed that Mr. Coleman, who is considering running for governor in 1998, would have a difficult time in a Democratic field already crowded with famous Minnesota names." Running as a Republican, in 1997 Coleman was elected to a second term as mayor of St. Paul, winning 59 percent of the vote and becoming the first Republican mayor of the city in more than 25 years. In 1998 Coleman ran for governor of the state. In a closely watched race, Coleman and Attorney General Hubert H. Humphrey III, son of the former vice president, were narrowly defeated by the independent candidate and former professional wrestler Jesse "The Body" Ventura. As a testament to his focus and dedication, Coleman's Web site states that at 8: 00 on the morning after his electoral defeat, he was back at his desk in St. Paul.

When his second term as mayor came to an end, Coleman decided to run for one of Minnesota's seats in the U.S. Senate. His campaign platform included his pledge of economic assistance to Minnesota's rural and agricultural-based communities. Coleman and the incumbent Democratic senator, Paul Wellstone, were locked in a close race when, just 11 days before the election, Wellstone died in an airplane crash. The Democratic former vice president Walter Mondale replaced Wellstone on the ballot. The subsequent election drew one of the largest voter turnouts of all the 2002 congressional elections in the country. Coleman, who had been publicly backed in his bid for the Senate by President George W. Bush (some sources, including David Rubenstein in the *Nation* [January 27, 2003], stated that Coleman had actually been handpicked by the Bush administration to take on Wellstone), defeated Mondale by a slim margin, receiving 50 percent of the votes against Mondale's 47 percent. Coleman was sworn in as a United States senator on January 7, 2003.

Toward the fulfillment of his campaign promises, Coleman gained a seat on the Senate Agriculture Committee, and in the fall of 2003, he introduced to the Senate the Rural Renaissance Act, which called for $50 billion in federal grants to revitalize the country's rural economy. Coleman founded the bipartisan Senate Biofuels Caucus, which he now co-chairs. Through the caucus's activities and other efforts in the Senate, Coleman has advocated greater development of the country's renewable fuels. As chairman of the Senate Governmental Affairs Committee's Permanent Subcommittee on Investigations, he has supported in principle the recording industry's efforts to prevent the illegal downloading of music over the Internet, while publicly disagreeing with some of the industry's methods for doing so; put pressure on defense contractors delinquent in their tax payments; and investigated fake tax shelters arranged by the accounting industry, which, according to Coleman's Web site, have cost taxpayers more than $80 billion.

Coleman is a member of the Senate Foreign Relations Committee. After visiting regions of Africa devastated by high rates of HIV and AIDS among the local populations, Coleman has supported major long-term initiatives in Africa to combat the virus and the disease. He also serves as chairman of the Foreign Relations Subcommittee on the Western Hemisphere, a capacity in which he has traveled through Central and South America and the Caribbean, meeting with local government officials and leaders to discuss issues of concern to both their nations and the U.S. Coleman is also a member of the Small Business and Entrepreneurship Committee.

Senator Coleman supported the Bush administration's Medicare reform bill, which, upon its passage in 2003, became the first major reform of Medicare since the inception of the program. The new law offers senior citizens a limited, federally subsidized prescription-drug tax benefit, for which seniors and Democrats had been calling for years, as prescription-drug prices in the U.S. had become prohibitively high. (The Medicare reform bill, though passed into law, remains the subject of contentious debate; among other controversies surrounding the legislation, it has been revealed that the reforms will cost $100 billion more than the Bush administration initially told Congress.) Coleman also voted in favor of the Bush administration's Jobs and Growth Act, which passed into law in May 2003 and represents the third-largest tax-relief legislation in U.S. history. At that time the official White House Web site announced that through the Jobs and Growth Act, in 2003 "91 million taxpayers [would] receive, on average, a tax cut of $1,126." In addition, Coleman voted in favor of banning partial-birth abortion, and he authored legislation that covered the return-travel costs of American servicemen on leave from Iraq. Coleman introduced the Veterans Benefits Outreach Act of 2004, which aimed to educate disabled veterans about their eligibility for federal benefits.

Coleman has won a number of honors for his work in the Senate. The organization Americans for Tax Reform gave Coleman its Hero of the Taxpayer Award; the Small Business Survival Committee named him a Small Business Advocate in 2004; and the American Chiropractic Association has recognized Coleman with its Health Care Leadership Award. He has won the U.S. Chamber of Commerce's Spirit of Enterprise Award and the Family Research Council's True Blue Award.

Coleman and his wife, Laurie, an actress, have two children, Jacob and Sarah.

—C.F.T.

Suggested Reading: *New York Times* A p23 Aug. 9, 1994, A p27 Dec. 20, 1996; U.S. Senate Web site; *Who's Who's in American Politics 2001–02*

Eric Cabanis/Getty Images

Coleman, Steve

Sep. 20, 1956– Jazz saxophonist; composer

Address: c/o M-Base Concepts, P.O. Box 114, Allentown, PA 18105-0114

As stated on the Web site of the Roy and Edna Disney/CalArts Theater in Los Angeles, California, a venue for cutting-edge arts, Steve Coleman is "one of the most restless and intrepid explorers of jazz." A saxophonist, composer, and bandleader, known for melding jazz improvisation with various other musical forms, Coleman has assembled and led a number of bands over the years, including Five Elements, the jazz-funk group with whom he began recording albums in the mid-1980s; Metrics, which plays a fusion of hip-hop and jazz; and the Mystic Rhythm Society, which features an Afro-Caribbean sound. Also in the 1980s Coleman co-founded the loose jazz collective M-Base, the conceptual goal of whose members was, as the saxophonist told E. R. Shipp for the *New York Times*

(December 4, 1988), to create a "modern musical language common to us all, a modern version of what [the legendary jazz saxophonist] Charlie Parker did in the 1940s." As either a sideman or bandleader he has recorded dozens of albums and has played with many accomplished and famous musicians and singers, including Dizzy Gillespie; the brothers Branford and Wynton Marsalis; Bobby McFerrin; Dave Holland; Cecil Taylor; Sam Rivers; and Sarah Vaughn, along with many standouts of the younger generation of jazz musicians. Coleman has played at jazz clubs and festivals around the world. As Peter Watrous wrote in a 1987 *Village Voice* piece available on the Europe Jazz Network Web site, "The first time you hear [Coleman's] music, it's a blur; the synapses don't fire, nothing fits . . . The power lies in its ambiguity, and after the oddness wears off, the music is addictive. It's unmistakable: an attempt to resist obvious uses, virtuosic."

Through jazz, Coleman, whose work has often been referred to as avant-garde, has sought to explore the influences of the African diaspora on musical forms that have since emerged; capture the rhythms of nature, observable, for him, even in the way that people walk or talk; and experiment musically with concepts of spirituality and ancient occult philosophy. Thom Jurek, writing for the *All Music Guide* (on-line), called Coleman a "renaissance man for the left wing of jazz." Though he brings a vast, even cryptic, array of concepts and influences to his craft, Coleman's music "really doesn't require studious attention," Ben Ratliff opined for the *New York Times* (August 18, 2002). "It's hard, funky, buoyed by Mr. Coleman's clear, beautiful alto saxophone tone; it is rhythmically and contrapuntally orderly. Feeling it with your body is easy."

The fourth of five children, Steve Coleman was born on the South Side of Chicago, Illinois, on September 20, 1956. In an interview for the Web site Soundzimpossible.com, Coleman recalled to Thomas Stanley that while he was growing up, his mother and father "listened to music all the time," and he heard "all kinds of music. All kinds of black music anyway." His father was a devoted fan of Charlie Parker, and his two older sisters listened to the music of the group Funkadelic and to the blues-inflected rock of the guitarist and singer Jimi Hendrix. As Coleman told Stanley, he was aware of differences between the music traditionally played by white people and that performed mostly by African-Americans, and he concluded that "what people call today blues, jazz, funk, r&b, whatever, that whole thing is just black music." Even before he took up an instrument, Coleman was in "these little singing groups, imitating the Jackson 5, or . . . singing in church or something like that," as he recalled to Stanley. As a freshman in high school, he briefly played violin in the school orchestra; he switched to the alto saxophone soon afterward. Though Coleman's father encouraged him to emulate the musical style of Charlie Parker, at first Coleman was attracted more to the playing of Maceo Parker, the celebrated saxophonist who played with the soul-music legend James Brown. Coleman was soon playing in local bands that covered songs by Brown.

In the early to mid-1970s Coleman attended Illinois Wesleyan University, in Bloomington, Illinois, where, according to a biography of Coleman found on the VH1 Web site, he was the only African-American in the school's music department. Coleman says that he became truly serious about his playing at that time, when he was around 17 or 18 years old. Referring to jazz saxophone greats, he said to Stanley, "That's when I started to check out the music of people like Charlie Parker, Sonny Rollins, and [John] Coltrane and all these people, because I realized that what they were doing was on another level than what most people were doing." (Coleman has since said that Parker's music has had the greatest influence on him.) In the mid- and late 1970s, when popular music was dominated by disco, Coleman found himself bored by much of what was being played on the radio and released on records. "Specifically, at that time I remember I didn't like the rhythms. I didn't like that boom-boom-boom thing," he told Stanley. Instead, he drew inspiration from such soul artists as Stevie Wonder and Marvin Gaye, whose songs were complex and addressed a variety of subjects, as well as from jazz performers. After college (he did not earn a degree) Coleman returned to Chicago, where he began playing with the renowned tenor saxophonist and music teacher Von Freeman. Freeman taught him a great deal about jazz improvisation and bebop—the harmonically complex form of jazz pioneered by Charlie Parker and others.

In 1978 Coleman moved to New York, which he knew to be a center of artistic creativity and a magnet for many of the musicians he admired. There, he played his saxophone for money on the street for several years. He eventually earned a spot playing saxophone in a number of big bands, including the somewhat mainstream Thad Jones–Mel Lewis Orchestra and, later, the more cutting-edge big bands of Slide Hampton, Sam Rivers, and Cecil Taylor. As he told Fred Jung for an article posted on Coleman's Web site, m-base.com, Coleman appreciated playing with big bands, as "there's a certain discipline that you get, especially a phrasing thing and learning how to play with large groups of people. . . . That carries over to what you do with a smaller group."

In the early 1980s Coleman formed the group Five Elements, which has been called his "flagship ensemble." In its more than 20 years of existence, Five Elements' changing roster of musicians has, at one time or another, included the bass players Reggie Washington and Anthony Tidd; the guitarist David Gilmore; the drummers Marvin "Smitty" Smith and Sean Rickman; the keyboard player James Weidman; the trumpet players Graham Haynes and Ralph Alessi; and the pianist Andy Milne, among others. A few years after the birth of

Five Elements, Coleman co-founded, along with the alto/soprano saxophonist Greg Osby and others based in and around the New York borough of Brooklyn, a jazz collective called M-Base. The name is an acronym for Macro-Basic Array of Structured Extemporization. Coleman himself has, in interviews, played down the significance of the term M-Base and even the word "jazz." In his circuitous way of speaking, he told Jung that M-Base was "just a philosophy . . . just something that we used, only to differentiate what we were doing in our time, as opposed to what somebody else was doing in another time. . . . I don't like terms like jazz or whatever because they don't mean much to me. People have preconceived notions of what that is and then, when you fit that or don't fit it, then they feel they can say, 'Oh, well, that's not the way jazz is supposed to be played or you're not playing jazz.'"

In addition to Coleman and Osby and the members of Five Elements, at various times the M-Base collective included the vocalist Cassandra Wilson, the keyboardist Geri Allen, the saxophonist Gary Thomas, and the trombonist Robin Eubanks. Coleman told Daniel King for jazztimes.com, "The concepts of M-Base are based primarily on music from Africa and creative music of the African diaspora." In the *Village Voice* (June 16, 1998), John F. Szwed wrote, "M-Base's repertoire is largely made up of original compositions which begin by skittering along the rhythm floor until they reach air speed and rise like elaborately decorated kites. . . . Leaving aside the surface stylishness of M-Base, their real achievement is that they have found a way to reinvigorate bebop, returning precisely to the point where its originating figures left off in the late 1940s." According to Coleman, M-Base's creative journey was obstructed when some music critics, seeking tidy labels, characterized M-Base's music as a style and not as the broader philosophical venture Coleman and his colleagues had intended. "The original idea was to make music that keeps evolving," Coleman told Nicky Baxter for the Web site metroactive.com. "But the press made it a style of music. But there's never been any card-carrying [M-Base] members—just musicians who think along similar lines." Baxter wrote that if there was one unifying element among all the artists associated with the M-Base collective, it was "their willingness (compulsion?) to embrace the entire spectrum of African Diasporan music made in America," including hip-hop, soul, and funk, in addition to jazz. Recalling his time with Coleman and the collective in the 1980s, Greg Osby told Baxter, "Remember this was during the era of the 'young lions,'" a group of jazz musicians, including Wynton Marsalis, Terence Blanchard, and Donald Harrison, whose sound harkened back to an earlier period. "And the vibe was really retro. It was encouraged that younger musicians play [neo-bop]. We *respected* that music, but we didn't want to be restricted to that." The various M-Base proponents, including Coleman, often played live together in New York City and elsewhere and contributed to each other's recordings.

With Five Elements Coleman explored the intellectual concepts of M-Base. Since the mid-1980s he has toured extensively with Five Elements and recorded more than a dozen albums, mostly on the RCA and BMG record labels. The heavily funk-influenced *On the Edge of Tomorrow* (1986) contains one of Coleman's earliest and most celebrated compositions, "Nine to Five." His other albums from that time include *Motherland Pulse* (1986), *World Expansion* (1987), and *Sine Die* (1988). On *Rhythm People* (1990) Coleman attempted to meld pop music's glossy sensibilities with jazz improvisation and polyrhythmic funk. Peter Watrous wrote in the *New York Times* (November 25, 1990) that the album, like Coleman's earlier work, had its limitations: "For one, the compositions often sound similar." On two tracks Coleman tried rapping and, according to Watrous, "falls flat on his face, both because he can't do it and because he seems to completely misunderstand the genre." Watrous found, however, that the album's tracks "Ice Moves" and "Rhythm People" revealed an "intimacy and vulnerability" that had not been heard in Coleman's earlier recordings. *Black Science* (1991) featured the much-praised Coleman composition "Beyond All We Know," performed with the singer Cassandra Wilson. In the mid-1990s Natalie Bullock made a 22-minute documentary film, entitled *Black Science*, about Coleman and M-Base. As quoted on Soundzimpossible.com, Bullock called Coleman a "rebel in the truest sense. He refuses to adhere to convention. He follows his own rhythm, both literally and figuratively." Only one album has been made under the M-Base name: *Anatomy of a Groove*, which was released on the independent Rebel-X label in 1992. Coleman both performed on and produced the album.

In the 1990s Coleman began recording music that revealed the influence of Latin rhythms. Describing those albums, John F. Szwed wrote, "Though this music may at first seem to be Latin- or funk-driven, a kind of cerebrally hip dance music, its melodies move so obliquely and unpredictably, even against the rhythm, that it would take a harmolodic dancer to follow them." Coleman's offerings from early in that decade included *Drop Kick* (1992), which is full of his trademark complex, edgy rhythms, and *The Tao of Mad Phat* (1993). Reviewing a live performance in England by Coleman and Five Elements, John Fordham wrote in the London *Guardian* (November 3, 1993) that Coleman's "brittle, jolting New York music" was some of the "most striking" of all the manifestations of forward-looking jazz. Fordham also observed that Coleman's "powerful, fearless" music drew from the audience a reaction "far more gleeful and uninhibited than the earnest concentration that sometimes greets new jazz." In 1994 Coleman formed the sextet Renegade Way, with which he toured Europe the following year. Also in 1995 Coleman and Metrics released the album *A Tale of 3 Cities*, which represented a hybrid of jazz and hip-hop. *Def Trance Beat* (1995) offered more of Coleman's irregular meters and heavy grooves.

Coleman and Five Elements recorded the live album *Curves of Life* at the Hot Brass Club in Paris in 1995. Baxter wrote that *Curves of Life* "superbly illustrates the M-Base beat manifesto. Here, we find Coleman and company—keyboardist Andy Milne, bassist Reggie Washington and drummer Gene Lake—assaying modern black music in all its flamboyantly manifold shadings." Coleman and his bandmates were joined on the album by the rappers Black Indian, Sub-Zero, and Kokayi. "On the two tracks showcasing rhyming," Baxter wrote in regard to the hip-hop influence on the album, "there's no sense of disjunction, of culture clash. Rather, word and song both have power, and the mesh is infinitely satisfying." That same year Coleman also teamed with his bands Metrics and the Mystic Rhythm Society for live shows at the Hot Brass Club; those performances were recorded for the Metrics album *The Way of the Cipher* and the Mystic Rhythm Society's *Myths, Modes and Means*. (All three of those Paris sessions are contained on a three-CD boxed set, entitled *Steve Coleman Live in Paris at the Hot Brass Club*.) Gary Giddins, in the *Village Voice* (June 10, 1997), called the sound produced by Coleman and the Mystic Rhythm Society a "fascinating blend of chant and swing."

As part of his musical and spiritual quest, Coleman has traveled to a number of countries, including, most significantly for him, Ghana, Cuba, Egypt, Brazil, and India. "Basically, when I go to these places, I check out the belief systems of the people, the lifestyles, how they translate that into being, and, of course, how they translate it into music," he told Stanley. He said to Jung, "If you're a person with any kind of depth at all, [then] you're still checking things out. You're still checking yourself out. You're still checking out the world, what it means to be alive, what your relationship is with the universe. All of this is something that should keep going. The music is really just a reflection of that." Interested in exploring the Yoruba traditions of West Africa—which have had a deep influence on the spiritual practices found in the Caribbean, among other places—in 1996 Coleman traveled to Havana, Cuba, where he and the Mystic Rhythm Society collaborated with the native group AfroCuba de Matanzas. That musical adventure is captured on the album *The Sign and the Seal* (1996) and on a documentary film shot by Eve-Marie Breglia, tentatively titled "Elements on One," which had not been released as of early November 2004 but was scheduled for release in the near future.

In 1998 Coleman released in a two-CD boxed set the albums *The Opening of the Way* and *Genesis*. The latter, dealing with themes of the storied seven days of the world's creation, was recorded with the large group Council of Balance, which featured a string section and a number of percussionists. At that time, commenting on the path taken by Coleman's M-Base movement while reviewing the saxophonist's performance during the Texaco New York Jazz Festival, Peter Watrous of the *New York Times* (June 6, 1998) wrote, "Over the last decade some members have fallen away, others have become stars and Mr. Coleman and Mr. Osby have slipped into a bit of popular neglect. . . . One can deal with the music's coldness, its sameness, its emphasis on a textural hardness that sometimes seems like a retreat from emotionalism, or one can't; it still sounds like nothing else in music." Coleman and Five Elements' album *The Sonic Language of Myth: Believing, Learning, Knowing* (1999) features the jazz stars Ravi Coltrane (John Coltrane's son) and Jason Moran. Reviewing the album, Adam Shatz wrote for the *New York Times* (May 2, 1999) that Coleman "makes fascinatingly cryptic art that gives off more than a slight chill." The track "Ausar" features droning voices, recitations, and wailing notes from the instruments. Coleman recorded his part for "Ausar" in the Great Pyramid of Egypt. Shatz opined that the result is "intriguingly scary music—hard to love, perhaps, but impossible to ignore." Coleman's more recent releases include *The Ascension to Light* (2000), *Resistance Is Futile* (2002), *Alternate Dimension Series 1* (2002), *On the Rising of the 64 Paths* (2003), and *Lucidarium* (2004).

As a sideman Coleman has played and recorded with David Murray, Abbey Lincoln, Mike Brecker, and Doug Hammond, the drummer and composer with whom Coleman recorded the albums *Spaces* and *Perspicuity*, both in 1982. In the mid- to late 1980s Coleman was a member of the bassist Dave Holland's quartet and contributed, both as a composer and saxophonist, to a number of Holland's albums, including *Jumpin' In* (1983), *Seeds of Time* (1984), *The Razor's Edge* (1987), *Triplicate* (1988), and *Extensions* (1989). Peter Watrous wrote in 1990 that those five albums contain "some of the most impressive music recorded over the last decade. . . . Part of Mr. Holland's success on his albums has been due to Mr. Coleman's playing. More than on his own records, Mr. Coleman allows himself to show emotion and a reserved tenderness that makes him a powerful soloist; his reading of the compositions, especially the ballads, is often breathtaking. Over the last decade he has become one of jazz's most distinctive soloists . . ." Also as a sideman, Coleman played on albums by Branford Marsalis (*Scenes of the City*, 1984); one-time Five Elements' member Smitty Smith (*Keeper of the Drums*, 1987; *The Road Less Traveled*, 1989); and M-Base co-founder Greg Osby (*Man-Talk for Moderns, Vol. X*, 1991). Coleman can also be heard on Cassandra Wilson's record *Traveling Miles* (1999).

As a producer Coleman has worked on several albums by Cassandra Wilson, including *Point of View* (1986), *Days Aweigh* (1987), and *Jump World* (1989). In addition, he produced Geri Allen's *In the Middle* (1987); Steve Williamson's *A Waltz for Grace* (1990); his own albums *Phase-Space* (1991),

on which he teamed with Dave Holland, and *Rhythm in Mind* (1992); two albums by Strata Institute, a Coleman and Osby project: *Cipher Syntax* (1989) and *Transmigration* (1991); Ravi Coltrane's *Moving Pictures*; and two albums by Sam Rivers's Rivbea All-Star Orchestra, *Culmination* and *Inspiration*, both released in 1999.

Concurrently with his recording and performing, from 1985 to 1991 Coleman was on the faculty of the Banff School of Fine Arts, in Banff, Canada, serving in his final year there as artistic head. During that time he taught courses in improvisation, saxophone, composition, ensemble, computer-music applications, and music business. (In the late 1980s he created basic computer software that improvises music. Once, during a live concert in Paris, Coleman featured the computer program as a member of Five Elements.) In addition, Coleman served as a guest artist in residency at the Stanford Jazz Workshop, from 1995 to 1996. In that capacity, the jazzman, in collaboration with his group Metrics, held free community workshops, demonstrations, and lectures throughout the San Francisco Bay Area. Over the course of the following three years he conducted many music workshops around the world. From 2000 to 2002 Coleman held the position of associate professor in music at the University of California at Berkeley. His views on teaching are, in some ways, as unorthodox as his playing. He told Mark Faulkner for the Florida *Times-Union* (November 20, 2002), "You can't teach somebody to think, but you can create an environment which promotes that kind of activity. I think that's not happening in most schools. [The educational system] seems to be more interested in indoctrinating people into a certain sort of system instead of promoting students to think for themselves. This is across the board; I'm talking about music, but it's the same for music as anything else." He often tries to help students to experience or learn music "intuitively," through their senses and bodies rather than their minds. As quoted by Ben Ratliff, Coleman has said, "In school, they only talk about understanding things with your mind. But you can also understand things with your body. It's a fallacy of Western civilization that the mind is doing all the thinking."

Resisting the lures of fame and commercialization, Coleman has turned down invitations to play in high-profile settings and groups, including the house band of the *Tonight Show* with Jay Leno. He once, however, went on tour with the pop superstar Sting. Afterward, commenting on that experience, he told Jamie Kastner for the Toronto *Sun* (June 22, 1995), "Pop musicians always make a big deal when an album comes out—'Oh, I was going through this really hard time . . .' but having seen it up close, I can say that the only thing Sting or them think about when they write a song is 'Will this make money?'" Coleman has posted to his personal Web site downloadable MP3 files of most of his albums, virtually giving his music away for free. That action is explained somewhat by comments Coleman made to Kastner: "Records aren't that important. They're just a snapshot of you on a day, or two days, of your life. Albums can't catch the moments that happen over countless gigs. I play 150 gigs in one year. An album, generally, won't get the best moments or the worst moments—it'll wind up somewhere in the middle." He gave a further explanation to Fred Jung, saying, "I'm making a good living. . . . I'm not a millionaire or any of this kind of thing. I've never had a record that went anywhere near gold [500,000 copies sold] or anything like that, but . . . I'm not at all unhappy with where I am and I'm not jealous of people who have the Bill Gates style of money."

In 2000 Coleman was honored with the Herb Alpert Award in the Arts. For his work he has received commissions and grants from the Lila Wallace–Reader's Digest Fund and the National Endowment for the Arts, among others. Over the years he has launched several business ventures, including the music-publishing companies Goemon Publishing and M-Base Concepts, which is also involved in musical software development. He is also the president of two record labels, Time Lord Records and C&M Music Productions Inc.

Coleman is an avid fisherman. He lives in Allentown, Pennsylvania, and travels often. "The idea for a great musician would be to leave something for others to work on, like John Coltrane did, like Charlie Parker did—they became so radically different—like Steve Coleman might do," the respected jazzman Bunky Green told Faulkner. "That's where he's headed, I'd say. He's concerned about the music, nothing else. We need something like that to come [along] once in a while."

—C.F.T.

Suggested Reading: bsharp.org; m-base.com; metroactive.com; *New Grove Dictionary of Music and Musicians*, 2001; *New York Times* II p27+ Sep. 27, 1987, with photo, II p1+ Dec. 4, 1988, with photo, II p28 Nov. 25, 1990, with photo, C p13 June 6, 1994; soundzimpossible.com; *Toronto Sun* June 22, 1995; Mandel, Howard. *Future Jazz*, 1999

Selected Recordings: *On the Edge of Tomorrow*, 1986; *Motherland Pulse*, 1986; *World Expansion*, 1987; *Sine Die*, 1988; *Rhythm People*, 1990; *Black Science*, 1991; *Anatomy of a Groove*, 1992; *Drop Kick*, 1992; *The Tao of Mad Phat*, 1993; *Def Trance Beat*, 1995; *Curves of Life*, 1995; *The Way of the Cipher*, 1995; *Myths, Modes and Means*, 1995; *The Sign and the Seal*, 1996; *The Opening of the Way*, 1998; *Genesis*, 1998; *The Sonic Language of Myth: Believing, Learning, Knowing*, 1999; *The Ascension to Light*, 2000; *Resistance Is Futile*, 2002; *Alternate Dimension Series 1*, 2002; *On the Rising of the 64 Paths*, 2003; *Lucidarium*, 2004

Cooper, Chris

July 9, 1951– Actor

Address: c/o Paradigm Talent Agency, 10100 Santa Monica Blvd, Suite 2500, 25th Fl., Los Angeles, CA 90067

The Academy Award–winning actor Chris Cooper has distinguished himself in more than three dozen big-screen and television movies. Often referred to as a consummate character actor, Cooper got his start in stage productions in New York and London in the early 1980s. Thanks to his rugged looks and restrained, tough-guy demeanor, Cooper has often been cast as a cowboy, as in the television miniseries *Lonesome Dove* (1989); as a soldier, on the silver screen in *Pharaoh's Army* (1995) and *The Patriot* (2000); as a lawman, in *A Time to Kill* (1996) and *Lone Star* (1996); and as a strict father, as in *October Sky* (1999) and *American Beauty* (1999). The writer and director John Sayles, a friend of Cooper's since the actor co-starred in Sayles's film *Matewan* (1987), told Pam Lambert for *People* (August 5, 1996) that Cooper possesses "a kind of haunted quality. He has got this ability to seem like he has a past—and that it was a rocky one." Cooper broke out of the molds of his previous characters with his memorable performance in the critically acclaimed movie *Adaptation* (2002) as a toothless, brilliant wild-orchid hunter, which earned him an Oscar for best supporting actor. He also had a prominent supporting role as a horse trainer in *Seabiscuit* (2003). Despite his newfound fame and recognizability, the firmly grounded Cooper told Lambert that he always wanted to be "an actor, not a star."

Christopher Cooper was born on July 9, 1951 in Kansas City, Missouri, to Charles Cooper, a physician who had served in the U.S. Air Force, and Mary Ann Cooper, a homemaker, both of whom were originally from Texas. Cooper and his older brother, called Chuck, grew up on their parents' 1,000-acre cattle ranch. Cooper has drawn from his upbringing in his portrayals of cowboys, ranchers, and other hardworking outdoor types, but, as he told Louis B. Hobson for the *Calgary Sun* (February 13, 1999), he has "too much respect for real cowboys to ever call myself a cowboy." Cooper's interest in theater derived from his having enjoyed singing at elementary-school functions and in school choral groups and, when he was in his late teens, designing and constructing sets for a community theater group. (As he recalled to Hobson, "I had this great love of architecture and I was good at designing things.") That involvement also kept Cooper from wandering too far from the straight and narrow. As he recalled to Lambert, at about

Carlo Allegri/Getty Images

Chris Cooper

that time he and his friends were "starting to get into some serious trouble—let's just say petty theft. And it kind of frightened me."

In an interview with Jeff Jensen for *Entertainment Weekly* (March 21, 2003), Cooper recalled that his mother once responded to his budding interest in live performance by saying to him, "But honey, you don't have any imagination." "I understood what she meant—I just wasn't outgoing," Cooper, who struggled to overcome his adolescent bashfulness through singing, told Jensen. "But I knew what was in my head, and it was full of imagination." In time he came to see humor in his mother's comment. Cooper made his stage debut, a small role in a local theater's production of *A Streetcar Named Desire*, when one of the actors, Tom Berenger, failed to show up for a scheduled performance one day. Shortly thereafter Cooper temporarily left the theater world to serve in the U.S. Coast Guard Reserves. He later worked construction jobs and, as he had in his youth, helped his father on the cattle ranch. "My dad was the kind of father who insisted you do what you love to do and put all your energy into it," Cooper told Hobson. "He thought that meant ranching or construction. When I told him I wanted to study acting, it scared the hell out of him, but he threw his support behind me. That's the kind of man he was."

Cooper attended the University of Missouri at Columbia, where he studied agriculture and acting. As an undergraduate he also took ballet classes at Stephens College, a nearby school for women. "Probably the best thing that ever happened to me was taking dance," he told Lambert, "because I made a total fool of myself every day in front of a classroom full of women. It helped to break through the shyness that I'd always had." After graduating from the university with a bachelor's degree in general studies, in 1976, Cooper moved to New York City in the hope of furthering his acting career. He studied under Wynn Handman, the artistic director of the American Place Theater, and the legendary acting teacher Stella Adler. After struggling to support himself for a time, Cooper landed roles in stage productions of several plays, among them *Sweet Bird of Youth* (1985), co-starring Lauren Bacall and directed by Harold Pinter in London, England, and *Cobb* (1989), in which Cooper starred.

Cooper had made his movie debut earlier, in the British melodrama *Bad Timing: A Sensual Obsession* (1980). His first substantial role did not come until seven years later, with *Matewan*, an independent film written and directed by John Sayles. In *Matewan* Cooper played Joe Kenehan, a union organizer who attempts to unite a disparate group of coal miners in their opposition to a West Virginia coal company's abuses. "Sayles' characters and their portrayal, particularly by [James Earl] Jones, [Will] Oldham, and Cooper (the last as a cross between Sam Shepard and Harrison Ford), give *Matewan* a larger-than-life presence," Desson Howe wrote for the *Washington Post* (October 16, 1987). While *Matewan* earned critical plaudits, it attracted little interest among moviegoers. The year 1987 also marked the birth of a son, Jesse, to Cooper and his wife, Marianne Leone, who had met in 1979 in Wynn Handman's acting class and married in 1983. Jesse suffers from cerebral palsy, a term that describes various chronic abnormalities in movement and muscle coordination, which result from damage to the brain shortly before or at birth. When Jesse reached school age, in the early 1990s, Cooper and his wife moved to Massachusetts, where it is far easier than in other states to enroll children with disabilities in regular schools.

In 1991 Cooper appeared in another film written and directed by John Sayles: *City of Hope*, a depiction of political and economic greed and corruption in a fictitious modern city. In the little-seen *Thousand Pieces of Gold* (1991), directed by Nancy Kelly, Cooper portrayed a kind-hearted man who falls in love with a Chinese woman sold into slavery in a 19th-century Idaho town. For that performance Cooper won a best-actor award from the Cowboy Hall of Fame; the film also received a Western Heritage Award, in 1992.

In 1995 Cooper appeared in *Money Train*, playing a psychotic man who sets token-booth clerks on fire; the role proved controversial, as some observers blamed the movie for inspiring two real-life murders that mirrored the fictional killings committed by Cooper's character. *Money Train*, which co-starred Woody Harrelson, Wesley Snipes, and Jennifer Lopez, did not fare well in critical reviews or at the box office.

Cooper appeared in three movies released in 1996: *Lone Star, Boys,* and *A Time to Kill.* The writer and director of *Lone Star,* John Sayles, created the leading character—the laconic Sheriff Sam Deeds, who suspects that his father may have committed an old, unsolved murder—specifically for Cooper. Louis B. Hobson described the actor's work in the film as as a "breakthrough performance that proved [he] could carry a movie and hold the screen with his dynamic presence." Cooper earned an Independent Spirit Award nomination for best actor for his performance in *Lone Star. Boys,* a romantic drama, starred Winona Ryder and Lukas Haas, and *A Time to Kill* (a movie adaptation of a John Grisham novel of the same name) starred Matthew McConaughey and Sandra Bullock.

Cooper had a small yet significant role in *Great Expectations* (1998), a heavily altered abridged adaptation for film of Charles Dickens's mid-19th-century novel. Dickens's tale, set in early Victorian England, centers on a boy, Pip, who is raised in poor circumstances but is given the chance to improve his standing in life. As an adult he pursues the love of an unattainable woman whom he met when both were children. In the 1998 film version, which was directed by Alfonso Cuarón, Finn (the revised Pip character, played by Ethan Hawke) becomes an artist who enters the 1980s New York art world, all the while pining for the love of the young woman (Gwyneth Paltrow) he adored as a child. Cooper played Finn's sister's boyfriend, with whom the young man lives early on. "The scene where Joe (a very touching Chris Cooper), the man who raised Finn, attends [Finn's] New York opening is so acutely painful that I had to force myself to watch the screen," Charles Taylor wrote for the on-line publication *Salon* (December 30, 1998). The scene embodies "those horrible moments when we betray the people closest to us because, seen outside familiar surroundings, they embarrass us." Though the film attracted some positive reviews, it fared poorly at the U.S. box office, taking in less than $30 million.

In the 1998 drama *The Horse Whisperer* (adapted from the best-selling novel by Nicholas Evans), Cooper played a Montana cattle-ranch owner named Frank Booker, whose brother, Tom (Robert Redford, who also directed and produced the movie), has a gift for healing troubled or injured animals. The movie focuses on Tom's relationships with a young girl (Scarlett Johansson) and a horse, who were both badly injured in a riding accident. *The Horse Whisperer* earned a respectable $75 million at the box office, though reviews of the film were decidedly mixed, with many critics praising the beauty of the cinematography more than the story line or acting.

Cooper appeared as the West Virginia coal-mine superintendent John Hickman, who struggles to understand and accept his son's dream of becoming a rocket scientist, in *October Sky* (1999), which is based on the memoir *Rocket Boys,* by Homer H. Hickam Jr. In portraying Hickman, Cooper relied heavily on his relationship with his own father, which resembled in some ways the father–son relationship depicted in the movie. (Cooper's father lived long enough to see his son in *Matewan,* which made the older man very proud.) Cooper drew far more attention for his role in the Academy Award–winning *American Beauty,* which was also released in 1999. Cooper played Colonel Frank Fitts, a stern and repressed Marine Corps veteran, who comes to suspect his neighbor (Kevin Spacey), a suburban family man in the throes of a midlife crisis, of forming an inappropriate relationship with his son. Critical response to the film was largely positive. Writing in *Rolling Stone* (September 30, 1999), Peter Travers called *American Beauty* a "triumph of acting, writing and directing that defies glib description." Cooper and the rest of cast (which included Annette Bening, Mena Suvari, Thora Birch, Wes Bentley, and Peter Gallagher) shared a Screen Actors Guild Award in 2000 for best performance by a cast; the guild also nominated Cooper for a best-supporting-actor award.

Also in 2000 Cooper ventured into the genre of comedy, taking a role in Peter and Bobby Farrelly's movie *Me, Myself & Irene,* which starred Jim Carrey and Renée Zellweger. Though the film received mixed reviews, it proved popular among audiences, bringing in nearly $100 million in box-office receipts. Cooper filled the part of Colonel Harry Burwell of the Continental Army in *The Patriot* (2000), a drama, set during the American Revolution, starring Mel Gibson as a conflicted father who is driven to take up arms and lead the colonists in battle after British soldiers kill one of his sons. *The Patriot* received a number of critical plaudits and made more than $110 million at the box office.

Cooper next received critical acclaim for his turn in the award-winning movie *Adaptation,* directed by Spike Jonze, written by Charlie Kaufman, and based on the book *The Orchid Thief,* by Susan Orlean. The movie pleased critics with its house-of-mirrors narrative, in which a character named Charlie Kaufman (Nicolas Cage, who also played Charlie's fictional twin brother, Donald) tries to write a screenplay based on *The Orchid Thief.* (Meryl Streep played Orlean.) The book *The Orchid Thief* is about orchids, the concept of obsession, and people who are obsessed with collecting wild orchids—in particular a man named John Laroche. As depicted in the film by Cooper, Laroche is an idiosyncratic, crazed-looking botany lover whose hunting grounds are Florida swamps. A bizarre yet compelling character, Laroche dodges alligators, formulates a plan to start a pornography business, and gives intriguing discourses on love, among other subjects, to Orlean. For Cooper the role was a welcome departure from those of the emotionally restrained men and overbearing fathers with which he had become associated. "I was looking for something to get away from that caricature," Cooper told Jensen, "and *Adaptation* was the opportunity." Spike Jonze allowed the actors great leeway in deciding how to play individual scenes. According to Louis B. Hobson in the *Calgary Sun* (January 21, 2003), he shot multiple takes of nearly every scene that featured Cooper. "One take I'd be more reserved, the next I'd be more colorful, more over the top," the actor told Hobson. "It gave us the chance to be experimental, because the movie is kind of that way." As quoted on the MSN Web site, Sandra Brennan wrote for the *All Movie Guide* that Cooper's performance "was in turns hilarious, sad and poetic, providing the perfect showcase for his impressive range." Writing for *Rolling Stone* (November 28, 2002), Peter Travers called Cooper's turn a "bust-out star performance that brims with magnetism (not easy if you're acting with no front teeth). *Adaptation* is about obsession: for an orchid, for writing, for finding something or someone to obsess about. . . . Few scripts toss more challenging balls in the air, and Jonze juggles them all with artful, light-stepping ease. It's magic." Similarly, while praising the actors' performances, Roger Ebert for the *Chicago Sun-Times* (December 20, 2002) described *Adaptation* as "bewilderingly brilliant and entertaining" and "some kind of filmmaking miracle, a film that is at one and the same time (a) the story of a movie being made, (b) the story of orchid thievery and criminal conspiracies, and (c) a deceptive combination of fiction and real life." Despite glowing reviews such as these, *Adaptation*'s box-office receipts barely surpassed the $19 million spent in making it.

For his part in *Adaptation* Cooper won an Academy Award, a Golden Globe Award, and awards from the Broadcast Film Critics Association, the National Board of Review, and the Los Angeles Film Critics Association. In his Oscar acceptance speech, according to a transcript posted on Oscar.com, Cooper said that making *Adaptation* was the "most enjoyable job I ever had." He also thanked Meryl Streep for making the movie such a success: "Working with [Streep] was like making great jazz."

In the highly anticipated movie *Seabiscuit*, based on Laura Hillenbrand's best-selling nonfiction book about the horse who ran its way to the top of the horseracing world and into the hearts of Depression-era Americans, Cooper played Seabiscuit's real-life trainer, Tom Smith. In approaching the role Cooper had the advantage of the familiarity with horses he had gained as a boy, but a book on the day-to-day lives of cowboys helped him most. "My wife found it at a yard sale, just in time," Cooper recalled to Jane Stevenson for the *Toronto Sun* (July 22, 2003). "[It was] this great book written by a Canadian cowboy, at the turn of the [20th] century, right at the time that Tom Smith was doing his thing." Co-starring Jeff Bridges as Seabiscuit's owner, Charles Howard, and Tobey Maguire as the jockey Red Pollard, *Seabiscuit* was nominated for seven Academy Awards. For his work in the film, Cooper was nominated for two Screen Actors Guild Awards—one presented to him and his fellow actors in the movie, for out-

standing performance by a cast, and the other for outstanding performance by a male actor in a supporting role. Reviews of the film were generally positive. A. O. Scott, however, writing for the *New York Times* (July 25, 2003), faulted the film for a perceived "surfeit of reverence. It turns the thrilling celebration of a collection of rambunctious, maverick characters into an exercise in high-minded responsible sentimentality." Scott praised the actors, however, writing of Cooper's portrayal of Smith, "He speaks in an affectless, hesitant drawl, and his distant manner suggests a wisdom that cannot be translated into human language. Smith is the link between the modern world of racing and the all-but-vanished world of the frontier, and Mr. Cooper's performance, the least showy in the film, is also the most resonant." *Seabiscuit* earned more than $120 million at the box office.

In *Silver City* (2004), a political satire directed by John Sayles, Cooper starred as a bumbling gubernatorial candidate. (It was rumored that his character was based on President George W. Bush.) Although the film was widely panned by critics, Cooper himself received accolades for his performance. Also in 2004 he gave an uncredited performance in *The Bourne Supremacy*, reprising the role of a CIA project director that he had played in the suspense film *The Bourne Identity* (2002), starring Matt Damon. Other movies in which Cooper has acted include *Guilty by Suspicion* (1991), *This Boy's Life* (1993), *The 24 Hour Woman* (1999), and *Interstate 60* (2002). The actor is slated to appear in the upcoming films *Syriana*, *Capote*, *Miller*, and *Conquistadora*.

Cooper has played many parts for television. He made his small-screen debut as a member of the cast of the soap opera *Edge of Night*, and in the late 1980s he appeared in episodes of *The Equalizer* and *Miami Vice*. In 1996 he made a critically acclaimed appearance as a lawyer with connections to the Ku Klux Klan in an episode of the hit series *Law & Order*. Since the late 1980s Cooper has also appeared in more than 10 made-for-television movies. He portrayed Louis Halladay in *Journey into Genius* (1988), which centered on the early life of the great playwright Eugene O'Neill (Matthew Modine), and was seen as the cowboy July Johnson in the mini-series *Lonesome Dove* (1989), an adaptation of the Western novel by Larry McMurtry, which co-starred Robert Duvall and Tommy Lee Jones. Cooper reprised that role in the follow-up mini-series *Return to Lonesome Dove* (1993).

Other television movies in which Cooper appeared include *To the Moon, Alice* (1990), *A Little Piece of Sunshine* (1990), *In Broad Daylight* (1991), *Darrow* (1991), *Bed of Lies* (1992), *Ned Blessing: The True Story of My Life* (1992), *One More Mountain* (1994), *The Deliverance of Elaine* (1996), and *Alone* (1997). In the HBO movie *Breast Men* (1997), Cooper and David Schwimmer, who became famous as an actor on the television series *Friends*, co-starred as creators of the silicone breast implant. In 2003 Cooper was nominated for an Emmy and a Golden Satellite Award for his turn in the HBO movie *My House in Umbria*, which was based on the novel of that name by William Trevor; the film, which co-starred Maggie Smith, told the story of a group of travelers in Italy brought together by tragedy.

In an interview with Michael Joseph Gross for *Boston Magazine* (June 2003), Cooper described a career in acting as resulting in "a kind of gypsy's life. It's a very intense working relationship [with the other members of a particular cast and crew] when you're doing the job, and then people have the tendency to move on to other projects and become intensely involved with the people on those projects."

The actor lives with his wife, Marianne Leone, and son in Kingston, Massachusetts. Leone, an actress and screenwriter, has appeared in the docudrama *The Thin Blue Line* (1988) and in several other movies, including *Goodfellas* (1990) and, along with Cooper, *City of Hope*. In 2002 she appeared on the hit HBO series *The Sopranos*. Leone has written a screenplay, tentatively entitled "Conquistadora," that is based on her and Cooper's struggles to ensure that their son received a high-quality education. Cooper is slated to act in the film. Leone, recalling the early days of her courtship with Cooper, told Pam Lambert, "We'd sit and talk for hours, and I'd think, 'Well, this is great, but is this guy ever gonna make a move on me, or what?' It dawned on me that he was the last of the nice guys."

—C.F.T.

Suggested Reading: *Calgary Sun* p49 Feb. 13, 1999, with photos, p33 Jan. 21, 2003, with photos; *Entertainment Weekly* p48 Mar. 21, 2003, with photos; Hollywood.com; *People* p103 Aug. 5, 1996, with photos; *Toronto Sun* (on-line) July 22, 2003

Selected Films: *Matewan*, 1987; *Guilty by Suspicion*, 1991; *Thousand Pieces of Gold*, 1991; *City of Hope*, 1991; *This Boy's Life*, 1993; *Money Train*, 1995; *Pharaoh's Army*, 1995; *A Time to Kill*, 1996; *Lone Star*, 1996; *Great Expectations*, 1998; *The Horse Whisperer*, 1998; *October Sky*, 1999; *American Beauty*, 1999; *Me, Myself & Irene*, 2000; *The Patriot*, 2000; *Interstate 60*, 2002; *The Bourne Identity*, 2002; *Adaptation*, 2002; *Seabiscuit*, 2003; *Silver City*, 2004

Selected Television Films: *Journey Into Genius*, 1988; *To the Moon, Alice*, 1990; *A Little Piece of Sunshine*, 1990; *In Broad Daylight*, 1991; *Darrow*, 1991; *Bed of Lies*, 1992; *Ned Blessing: The True Story of My Life*, 1992; *One More Mountain*, 1994; *The Deliverance of Elaine*, 1996; *Breast Men*, 1997; *Alone*, 1997; *My House in Umbria*, 2003

Selected Television Shows: *Lonesome Dove*, 1989; *Return to Lonesome Dove*, 1993

Matthew Peyton/Getty Images

Cox, Lynne

Jan. 2, 1957– Long-distance ocean swimmer

Address: 10791 Los Alamitos Blvd., Los Alamitos, CA 90720

"If you look at the marine mammals in Antarctica, the whales, the walruses, the seals all have body fat to stay warm," the long-distance ocean swimmer Lynne Cox told Scott Pelley, as quoted on CBSNews.com (September 17, 2003). She made that observation a few months before becoming, in 2002, the first person in history to swim one mile (or swim at all—intentionally, at least) in the ice-cold waters of Antarctica. "Their blubber is very dense whereas mine will be more like a cotton sweater," she said. "But I'm not going to be in [the water] as long·as they are." As Shelby Murphy pointed out in WomenOf.com (2002), "Not many women in this culture that abhors fat are courageous enough to compare themselves to whales. But that is what sets Lynne apart. She understands that even though her body doesn't conform to the rail-thin standards set by the fashion industry, she's not in her swimming suit to model it. Her purpose is higher than that." Cox's purpose—in addition to "exploring my own outer limits," as she told Matt Dellinger for the *New Yorker* (January 27, 2003, on-line)—is actually twofold. She strives to parlay her extraordinary feats as a swimmer into a way "to bridge the distance between peoples and nations," as she wrote in her memoir, *Swimming to Antarctica: Tales of a Long-Distance Swimmer* (2004). She also seeks to "expand the notion of the possible," as JoAnn C. Gutin wrote for *Newsday* (February 15, 2004, on-line)—that is, to inspire people to believe that they are capable of far more than they may think, both as individuals and as members of communities and nations. In 1987, during the Cold War, her five-mile swim in 40-degree water across the Bering Strait—which separates eastern Russia from North America—was a symbolic plea for peace between the U.S. and what was then the Soviet Union. "There are no borders in the oceans," Cox said to Bill Donahue for *Sports Illustrated Women* (November 2002), "just imaginary lines dividing countries. People might believe in those lines less if I swim across them." When she swam across the Gulf of Aqaba, in the Red Sea, from Egypt to Israel to Jordan, in 1994, she was "motivated by idealism," as she said to Dellinger. "Some of my past swims . . . have helped open borders, so I believed that a swim that traced the process of peace and celebrated it could have a similar effect. I believe that sometimes just by seeing something small happen, something that is positive, other people realize that they can do something, too, something larger."

Among various other feats, Cox set two records in crossing the English Channel as a teenager (in 1972 and 1973) and two more in swimming between Norway and Sweden and between Denmark and Sweden (1976); she became the first woman to cross the Cook Strait, in New Zealand (1975), the first person to cross the Strait of Magellan, in Chile (1976), and the first to swim across three channels in the Aleutian Islands (1977). She swam around the Cape of Good Hope, at the southern tip of South Africa (1979), and around Jogashima Island, in Japan (1980), and crossed each of the five lakes that ring the snow-capped cone of Mount Fuji, in Japan (early 1980s). In 1985, in a project that she called "Around the World in 80 Days," she swam across Lake Myvatn, in Iceland; the Strait of Gibraltar, between Spain and Morocco (becoming the first woman to do so); the Strait of Messina, between southern Italy and Sicily; the Bosporus Strait, in Turkey, which connects the Mediterranean with the Black Sea; Lake Kumming, in China; and a half-dozen additional bodies of water. She crossed Lake Baikal, in what is now Russia (1988), the Beagle Channel, between Chile and Argentina (1990), the Spree River, between the newly united parts of Germany (1990), and Lake Titicaca, which straddles Peru and Bolivia and, at an altitude of 12,500 feet, is the world's highest navigable lake. (While Cox has swum in colder waters for longer durations than anyone else in recorded history, the record—still unbroken—for the longest distance covered by a swimmer in any ocean was set in 1979 by Diana Nyad, when she swam 102.5 miles from the island of Bimini, in the Bahamas, to Florida.)

On her long-distance ocean swims, Cox wears nothing other than a bathing suit, a swim cap, and goggles, and, except for areas of her body subjected to friction—the tops of her thighs, for example, at the leg holes of her bathing suit—she swims without petroleum jelly, lanolin, or any other protection on her skin (except, occasionally, for sun-

screen on her face). She is regarded as something of a medical anomaly for her ability to endure cold in which most people would die (from heart failure) within minutes, and she has been the subject of many experiments that scientists hope may help them better understand the mechanisms of homeothermy (warm-bloodedness, or the maintenance of a constant body temperature distinct from that of the surrounding environment) and hypothermia (subnormal body temperatures). William Keatinge, a University of London specialist in hypothermia who has studied Cox in the laboratory and also accompanied her on swims, "thinks Cox has somehow trained her body to keep most of her blood at her body's core and away from the skin where it's exposed to the cold," as Scott Pelley reported. Cox's five-foot six-inch, 180-pound frame is well-insulated with fat, and, as Keatinge told Pelley, the fat is distributed unusually evenly throughout her body, "going right down the limbs"—"an ideal set-up" for a swimmer like Cox, as he put it. Moreover, with fat accounting for 36 percent of her weight (in the average woman of normal weight, the figure is 20–25 percent), Cox is virtually the same density as sea water. Her fat thus gives her unusual buoyancy, which means that she expends nearly all her energy on moving forward and keeping sufficiently warm in frigid water rather than diverting some of it to keep afloat. Since her childhood Cox has spent countless hours acclimating herself to the cold, both physically and psychologically. She trained herself to push from her mind the painful sensations that very cold temperatures produce. "If you focus on the cold, then you're focusing on something that's not helping you get to where you need to get," she explained to Scott Pelley. In addition, her upper body is exceptionally strong—a huge advantage in rough waters, where swimmers must battle tides, currents, winds, and waves created by ocean-going vessels. Even her method of kicking, which might be described as restrained, is an asset; kicking draws blood toward the legs and feet, away from the core of the body, thus allowing heat to escape. (Polar bears swim much like Cox, using their legs as rudders rather than a means of locomotion.)

Cox's father, Albert Percy Cox, a radiologist, and her mother, Estelle Marie Cox, have always supported her wholeheartedly and encouraged her to strive toward her goals, however unconventional or unattainable they might have seemed to others. The second of their four children, Lynne Elaine Cox was born on January 2, 1957 in Boston, Massachusetts. She is related to the Hollywood cinematographer Allen Daviau, whose credits include *E.T.: The Extra-Terrestrial, The Color Purple,* and *Bugsy.* Cox's older brother, David, attended college on a swimming scholarship and held the record time for swimming the Catalina Channel (between Catalina Island and Los Angeles, California) until Lynne broke it, in 1974; early in her swimming career, he sometimes acted as her coach. Her younger sisters, Ruth and Laura, swam competitively and as teenagers played water polo. Her maternal grandfather, Arthur Daviau, was a powerful swimmer who swam across many lakes in Maine. He and his wife owned property on Messalonskee Lake (also called Snow Pond), in Maine, where the Coxes spent summers. Estelle Cox taught her children to swim there; Lynne learned at the age of three. Cox's parents often took their children to swim in the Atlantic Ocean, too.

Once, when she was nine years old, Cox remained in a swimming pool during a storm, after all her companions had run for shelter. As cold raindrops pelted the water, as she recalled in *Swimming to Antarctica*, the pool no longer struck her as "a flat, boring rectangle of blue; it was now a place of constant change, a place that I had to continually adjust to as I swam. . . . That day, I realized that nature was strong, beautiful, dramatic, and wonderful, and being out in the water during that storm made me feel somehow a part of it, somehow connected to it." Soon the raindrops turned to pea-sized hailstones. "As I pulled my arms through the water, I felt as if I were swimming through a giant bowl of icy tapioca . . . ," she wrote. "I realized that by putting myself in a situation different from everyone else's, I had experienced something different, beautiful, and amazing."

In 1969, when Cox was 12, her parents moved the family from New Hampshire, where Cox had lived since infancy, to Los Alamitos, California, so that she and her siblings could swim all year round. Cox trained at the Phillips 66 Swim Club with Don Gambril, who coached California State University (CSU) swimmers and later, in 1984, the U.S. Olympic swim team. Two CSU athletes, Hans Fassnacht, a native of Germany who later set many European records, and Gunnar Larsson, who later became an Olympic gold medalist for Sweden, sometimes practiced at the club, where they thrilled and inspired Cox. As the months passed under Gambril's solicitous and insightful tutelage, Cox began to feel uncomfortably confined in the pool. (In the following years she also began to feel intolerably hot in pools. "I overheat—sweat profusely and turn bright lobster red . . . ," as she told Dellinger. "I just really enjoy swimming on my own in wide-open waters, where a lap is one mile or as long as I want it to be.") Gambril, meanwhile, had come to realize that Cox would probably never become a champion speed swimmer in pools, but that with her rare stamina, she might excel in distance swimming. Since, to this day, the longest distance for women in the Olympics is the 800-meter freestyle (for men, it is 1,500 meters), Gambril suggested that Cox enter the Seal Beach Rough Water Swim, a set of ocean races. She did so soon afterward, in 1971, swimming in both the three-mile and two-mile races; competing against adults as well as younger swimmers of both sexes, she came in third and second, respectively. She then joined the Seal Beach Swim Team and began training to swim the Catalina Channel. Either her mother or father would awaken hours before dawn to drive

her to the beach; as one or the other walked along the shore, she would swim long laps in the ocean.

That year, at age 14, she swam across the Catalina Channel—a straight-line distance of 21 miles that, because of strong currents, stretched into 27 miles for Cox and the three other teenagers who completed the swim; her time was 12 hours and 36 minutes. (She did not swim as fast as she felt she could have, because the teens had resolved to swim as a team.) The next year, as a student at Los Alamitos High School, after having trained individually with Ron Blackledge, the coach of the Seal Beach team, and then Don Gambril, she set a record, for men as well as women, by swimming across the English Channel—from a beach near Dover, England, to Cape Gris-Nez near Wissant, France. Her time was nine hours and 57 minutes, 26 minutes faster than the previous record-holder; because of currents, her trip was significantly longer than the official 21-mile width of the channel at that location, and for at least an hour into her swim, she was forced to sprint to avoid getting caught in the lane of an oil tanker. Her parents provided the thousands of dollars necessary to fund that project (as they did with some of her later swims), which entailed, among many other expenses, the cost of hiring a so-called swimming pilot in Dover. Such a pilot must be intimately familiar with the currents and other conditions that prevail in the channel; he or she keeps close track of the weather, to determine when it is good enough for a channel crossing, selects the precise start and end points, and accompanies the swimmer during the crossing, to guide him or her away from any sort of danger and to provide encouragement. For Cox's channel crossing, her mother and a deckhand also made the trip, in the pilot's boat. Three weeks after Cox swam the channel, Davis Hart beat her record by 13 minutes. In 1973 Cox set another, for both sexes, by crossing the same waterway in nine hours and 36 minutes. (The current record, seven hours and 17 minutes, was set in 1994 by the American Chad Hundeby.)

In 1975 Cox became the first woman to cross Cook Strait, between the two main islands that comprise New Zealand (North Island and South Island). Before her attempt there had been 20 others, in which only three men had succeeded. Because no organizations exist to help with the exhaustive research required for long-distance swims, Cox had corresponded with specialists at universities and oceanographic institutes as well as local New Zealand experts to help her gauge the dangers posed by the strong surf and tides and marine creatures such as sharks. Unexpectedly, because of storms hundreds of miles away that her advisers had erroneously predicted would not affect the area in which she was to swim, powerful winds and waves as high as eight feet lengthened what she had thought would be a five-hour, 12-mile trip into one that lasted 12 hours and 2.5 minutes and many more miles. Indeed, after the first five hours of strenuous swimming, she found herself further from the finish than when she started. She was about to give up when one of her crew members relayed word to her that a local New Zealand radio station that had been broadcasting news of her adventure was flooded with calls of support from all over the country. That encouragement gave Cox the strength to continue for another two hours. Later, when she again felt that she could swim no longer, pods of dozens of dolphins appeared. For an hour the intelligent, friendly mammals accompanied her and her human companions (who were in boats), "chattering, squeaking, clicking, whistling, calling," as she recalled in *Swimming to Antarctica,* and sometimes leaping out of the water and pirouetting in the air before nose-diving back into the water; a few of them even "danc[ed] on their tails across the bright blue sea," in Cox's words. When, with land in sight, she again felt as if she "had hit a brick wall," the dolphins reappeared. "I knew they were guiding us in to shore," she wrote. After noting in her book that church bells had rung throughout New Zealand both when she finished her swim and at noon the next day, Cox wrote, "More than anything I now understood that no one achieves great goals alone. It didn't matter to New Zealanders that I wasn't from their country. It only mattered that I was trying to swim their strait. They had cheered me on for hours, and in doing so, they had cheered the same human spirit within themselves. . . . During the Cook Strait swim, we were united in a human endurance struggle that surpassed national borders."

In 1976 Cox became the first human to swim across the Strait of Magellan, the narrow waterway that separates the southernmost end of the South American mainland and Tierra del Fuego, an archipelago. Whirlpools and ferocious tides and currents in the strait had proved fatal to many of the ships that, before the completion of the Panama Canal, in 1914, attempted to cross from the Atlantic Ocean to the Pacific (or vice versa) rather than journey around Cape Horn. Despite the tremendous effort of sprinting through 44-degree water that at times seemed, in Cox's words, "like a raging river," and conditions that imperiled not only the success of her swim but her life, the experience struck Cox, as she wrote in her memoir, as "wonderful . . . and fun" as well as "wild" and "frightening." In the following years, with the eventual goal of crossing the bitterly cold Bering Strait—a project her father had suggested to her after her Cook Strait swim, when, as she wrote in her memoir, "he knew that once again I was searching for what to do next"—she planned swims that she "hoped would be progressively colder and farther," in her words. In Glacier Bay, Alaska, for example, in which she swam one mile in 28 minutes in 1985, she found herself navigating a 38-degree obstacle course of pans and chunks of ice and small icebergs.

Earlier, in about 1975, Cox had entered the University of California at Santa Barbara; in 1979 she earned a B.A. degree in history there. To earn her living during the following years, she worked as a reference librarian, gave swimming lessons, assisted a group of physical therapists, and wrote magazine articles. Meanwhile, starting in the mid-1970s, she had started planning her swim across the 2.7-mile channel in the Bering Strait that lies between Little Diomede Island, in U.S. territory, and Big Diomede Island (also known as Ratmanov Island), which at that time was territory of the Soviet Union. It took Cox nearly a dozen years to overcome the many hindrances that prevented her from getting permission from the U.S. and the Soviet governments to swim across the strait, and thus across the watery boundary from one country to the other. As she recounted in *Swimming to Antarctica*, she finally began making preparations for her swim and set a tentative date for it even before the Soviet government gave her its approval, both out of desperation and in the hope that she would push the Soviets to agree to her request. Her scheme worked, and in early August 1987 she made the swim—accomplishing what, as far as is known, no other human had ever done before. The temperature of the water when Cox entered was 42 degrees; two hours and five minutes later, when she crawled out of the sea, it had dropped to 38 degrees. Her core temperature had sunk to the point of hypothermia, 94 degrees; with the help of medics, it returned to normal in an hour. Her swim made her famous throughout the Soviet Union. In Washington, D.C., on December 8, 1987, when President Ronald Reagan of the U.S. and President and General Secretary Mikhail Gorbachev of the Soviet Union signed the Intermediate-Range Nuclear Forces (INF) Treaty, the first nuclear-arms-control agreement that reduced existing quantities of nuclear arms, Gorbachev said, as quoted in *Swimming to Antarctica,* "Last summer it took one brave American by the name of Lynne Cox just two hours to swim from one of our countries to the other. We saw on television how sincere and friendly the meeting was between our people and the Americans when she stepped onto the Soviet shore. She proved by her courage how close to each other our peoples live." Soon afterward she was honored by Pope John Paul II at the Vatican and President Reagan at the White House.

Cox began preparing for her Antarctic swim in 2000; she trained in a gym, her backyard pool, and the ocean for three or four hours a day, five days a week. A year later, to build her strength even further, in part so as to be able to keep her head above the water to conserve heat, she began vigorous workouts with Jonathan Moch, a former wrestler; her regimen included doing crunches with 30-pound weights, doing curls and flies with 15-pound dumbbells, and throwing and catching a 10-pound medicine ball. Inspired by the multilayered insulation of penguins, she grew her hair long so that she could pile it up in layers inside her swim cap. She also put on 12 pounds to increase her natural insulation and had dental treatments to fill the pores of her enamel and thus protect her teeth from cracking in the cold. Unlike speed swimmers, who typically shave the hair from their entire bodies, she shaved none of it, as another way to retain heat.

In November 2002 Cox and her companions—among them a group from the polar-cruise company Quark Expeditions, a CBS film crew, and an entourage of doctors and navigators—sailed to Admiralty Bay, in Antarctica, so that she could complete a practice swim. The water that day was 33 degrees, the air temperature 34 degrees. "The water was searing cold," Cox recalled in an article for the *New Yorker* (February 3, 2003). "I felt as if I were naked, standing still, and being sprayed with ice water from a high-pressure hose, and it took all my focus to move. I swam with my head above water, panting. It was incredibly difficult to catch my breath; my lungs felt as if they were being squeezed in a tight corset. . . . As my breathing evened out, I began to notice other sensations. The water felt different from any other water I'd swum in, as if it were more solid than fluid, as though I were swimming through a liquid Sno-Kone. I checked my hands. They were red and swollen and, like my feet, had become numb and achy. . . . A wave shattered in my face. I choked, and started to panic. I knew I had to keep swimming; it was too cold to stop. I kept spinning my arms, trying to swallow and clear my throat. Another wave slammed into my face. I was choking harder, and feeling even more panicked. I couldn't breathe. I considered rolling over onto my back, but decided it was too cold and this would slow me down too much." Cox decided to stray from her plan and dip her head into the water. "My body flattened," Cox wrote in her article, "and I began swimming through the water instead of climbing up against it. . . . As I moved across the sub-Antarctic sea, I looked at the glaciers that encircled the harbor. My torso and head felt warm on the inside, and I relaxed just a little. . . . When I glanced at my watch again, I saw that I had reached my goal of ten minutes."

A couple of days later, Cox and her team readied to enter the Antarctic waters at a harbor a few miles north of her practice run. This time both the air and water temperatures were slightly colder, but to Cox it felt warmer, because she had sustained nerve damage during her practice swim. (Years earlier, she had suffered nerve damage during an experiment in which she held one hand in 32-degree water for 30 minutes. Her recovery took three months.) Cox began her swim at a pace much faster than normal for her. Her navigators guided her to and fro across the bay, making sure that she covered at least one mile, as she intended. About 200 yards from shore, a flock of chinstrap penguins dove in and began surging through the water around her. Cox reached the beach in 25 minutes, having swum 1.22 miles. In addition to becoming the first person known to swim a mile in the Antarctic, Cox may have become the first to swim with penguins. "I couldn't endure the cold like a penguin or a seal or a whale, but, having entered their world for a brief time, I had been able to experience something extraordinarily beautiful and harsh,"

Cox wrote for the *New Yorker*. She later told Kelli Anderson for the Web site sportsillustrated.cnn.com (February 17, 2003) that she swam in the Antarctic because she "wanted to do something extraordinary." "To do it," she added, "I had to draw on everything I had ever known and everything [I] didn't. It was like going to Mars." In early 2004 she told JoAnn C. Gutin that she was considering three new swims, which she described as "risky."

Cox, who still lives in Los Alamitos, gives motivational speeches and swimming lessons. She has written articles for *Women's Sports & Fitness*, *European Car Magazine*, and the series *Travelers' Tales*. Cox has appeared on television, on the programs *60 Minutes II* and the *Late Show with David Letterman* and on the Discovery Channel. In a blurb that appears on the back cover of her memoir, the neurologist Oliver Sacks, referring to Antoine de Saint-Exupéry, the author of several classic accounts of his experiences as a pilot (as well as of *The Little Prince*), wrote, "Lynne Cox writes about swimming the way Saint-Exupéry wrote about flying, and one sees how swimming, like flying, can stretch the wings of the spirit. Lynne is an extraordinary achiever, but it is her enthusiasm and warmth, along with her respect for others, that come across above all in her writing, which is as easy and natural as her swimming ability. *Swimming to Antarctica* is thrilling, modest, vivid, and lyrical, an inspiring account of a life of aspiration and adventure." The *Los Angeles Times* named Cox Woman of the Year in 1975, as did *Glamour* magazine in 2003; in 2000 she was inducted into the International Swimming Hall of Fame. According to the SwimInfo Web site (October 5, 2004), the San Francisco, California, Board of Examiners named October 2, 2004 "Lynne Cox Day."

—P.G.H./M.H.

Suggested Reading: *BBC News* (on-line); *Chicago Tribune* I p3 August 8, 1987, with photo; *Current Science* p10+ Aug. 29, 2003; International Swimming Hall of Fame Web site; *New Yorker* p160+ Aug. 23–30, 1999, p66+ Feb. 3, 2003; *Sports Illustrated* p54+ Feb. 3, 1975, with photos, p16+ Feb. 17, 1975, with photos; *Sports Illustrated Women* p65 Nov. 2002; *Women's Sports & Fitness* p36+ Apr. 1993, with photos; Cox, Lynne. *Swimming to Antarctica*, 2004

Selected Books: *Swimming to Antarctica*, 2004

Courtesy of Mississippi State University

Croom, Sylvester Jr.

Sep. 25, 1954– Football coach

Address: MSU Football, P.O. Box 5327, MSU, MS 39762

American colleges and universities are traditionally viewed as bastions of opportunity. Statistics, however, do not always bear this perception out, particularly when one looks at an institution's high-profile endeavors, such as athletics. According to a National Urban League press release dated December 5, 2003, fewer than 800 African-American men and 200 African-American women occupy the National Collegiate Athletic Association's (NCAA) nearly 14,000 head-coaching positions at schools other than historically black colleges. The percentage is even smaller when it comes to big-time college sports. Of the 117 NCAA Division I-A football programs, four had black head coaches during the 2003 season, the same number as the year before. Only 21 African-Americans have ever been in charge of a I-A football team. Still, every major football conference has had at least one black coach. Until recently there was an exception: in the 71-year history of the Southeastern Conference (SEC), among U.S. colleges' most storied athletic organizations, never had an African-American been given a chance to run a football team—until December 2003, when Mississippi State University hired Sylvester Croom Jr.

"It took 50 years after Brown vs. Board of Education, nearly 40 years after the Civil Rights Act, more than 30 years after black players started getting scholarships in the SEC, for Croom to get his chance," Steve Wilstein noted for the Associated Press (December 4, 2003). In the meantime, in over a quarter-century as a position coach, Croom helped coach teams to two national college championships, guided a number of National Football League (NFL) running backs to personal-best seasons, directed one of the NFL's most potent offenses ever, and was widely praised as a great student and teacher of the game. In the spring of 2003, he was considered for the head-coaching job at his alma mater, the University of Alabama, but the position went to a less experienced white candidate, who went on to guide the perennial powerhouse to one of its least successful seasons. While years of unrewarded achievement might make others bitter, Croom has demonstrated patience, persistence, and poise, traits he developed as a witness to, and participant in, social change in the U.S.

The great-grandson of slaves, the grandson of sharecroppers, and the son of teachers, Sylvester Croom Jr., known to his friends as "Sly," was born on September 25, 1954, in racially segregated Tuscaloosa, Alabama. His father, Sylvester Sr., taught secondary school, and his mother, Louise, taught elementary school. Croom's younger brother Kelvin told Harvey Araton for the *New York Times* (December 3, 2003, on-line) that their parents "taught us to strive to be leaders, not judge people on their race and never use race as an excuse." As he revealed to his children, Sylvester Croom Sr. had had the experience of being judged because of his skin color. One day, while growing up in the 1930s, he went rabbit hunting with his brothers; while they were away, a white girl was raped and claimed that her assailants were black. Sylvester Sr. and his brothers, returning from the woods with blood on their clothes from hunting, were immediately jailed. As a lynch mob was forming, a local minister convinced the authorities that the boys could not have committed the crime. The boys were rushed out of town to Birmingham, where their names were cleared.

Although he never suffered such harrowing incidents, Sylvester Croom Jr. grew up with the indignities of segregation. "When you were in your black neighborhood and your black churches, that wasn't a problem," he told Lori Nickel for the *Milwaukee Journal Sentinel* (September 23, 2003, on-line). "When you needed to get some food, stop for gas, that's when it hit you in the face. They always had three bathrooms. Men, women, colored, and it was usually so filthy." Croom did not attend school with white students until he reached the ninth grade, when he was part of his junior high school's first integrated class. On the first day of school that year, a white boy hit him in the face with a spitball. Though the boy seemed to forget what he had done, Croom never forgot him. The two later became football teammates. "I never said a word to him, but I hit him extra hard, every day [at practice]," Croom admitted to Frank Schwab for the Appleton, Wisconsin, *Post-Crescent* (June 29, 2003). "I couldn't tell you his name, but I can still see his face. That spitball caused him a lot of grief."

That recollection notwithstanding, Croom, a Baptist clergyman like his father and brother, prefers not to dwell on the slights he experienced in junior high school. As he explained to Schwab, "If 99 people of the same race mistreat me badly, No. 100 may be the guy that makes a change in my life. But I don't know who No. 100 is, so you have to be fair to everybody." He points, instead, to those who risked the scorn of other whites by extending a hand to him, such as the mother of Stan Bradford, a white quarterback on his ninth-grade team. Their spring practices were held three miles away, at the high school. The black players walked to their first practice, because all of their parents had to work, while the white players had someone available to drive them. The next afternoon, a car pulled up beside them as they walked. In it were Bradford and his mother, offering a ride. "And they took us to practice every day the rest of that spring," Croom recalled to Schwab. "I have never met her since that time, but she doesn't know how much that meant to me. Because I know she took on that one. That was hard. You appreciate that."

Croom again found himself part of a school's first integrated classes when he entered Tuscaloosa High School. Tom Danner, Tuscaloosa's football coach, saw in Croom leadership skills that matched his on-field talent. "He came into our program with certain goals and objectives, because of who he was he felt like he needed to succeed and he needed to be a role model for other kids to follow," Danner said to Ralph D. Russo for the Associated Press (December 2, 2003). "Other kids in the same situation saw how he acted and they mimicked him."

As children Croom and his brother dreamed of attending the University of Alabama in Tuscaloosa and playing football for its team, the Crimson Tide—never believing, however, that they would really do so. The elder Sylvester (who would become the Tide's team chaplain) had attended and played for historically black Alabama A&M University, where he was named All-American, and his sons assumed that they would follow in his footsteps. But in 1971, eight years after Alabama governor George Wallace made the state's flagship public university a symbol of the civil rights movement by standing in the doorway of Foster Auditorium to stop two African-American students from registering for classes, Sylvester Croom Jr. enrolled at the University of Alabama. One year after Alabama awarded its first football scholarship to a black player, Croom was among the Crimson Tide's third class of African-American recruits.

Though he was again on the front lines of integration, Croom found a less racist atmosphere at Alabama, due in part to the tone set by legendary coach Paul "Bear" Bryant and in part to the meritocratic nature of football. "It wasn't a big deal," he told Russo. "When you line up in a three-point stance and hit another guy in the mouth you forget what color he is real fast." Standing six feet tall and weighing 235 pounds, Croom was small for an offensive lineman, but he established himself on the field with good blocking technique and even better leadership skills. The Hall of Fame tight end Ozzie Newsome, a former teammate of Croom's and a trailblazer himself, as the first minority to be hired as general manager of an NFL franchise, told Michael Wilbon for the Washington Post (December 3, 2003): "In my career I've been around a lot of great leaders. And he led that huddle, trust me. He was impressive at a lot of things, but mostly [as] a leader." In Croom's two seasons as starting center (1973-74), the Crimson Tide compiled a record of 22–2 and won a national championship in 1973. A year later Croom was named All-American by the American Football Coaches Association and voted team captain by his peers. "You look back, and from the number of black guys on the team, there weren't many. So the white guys were voting for them," Croom's friend, agent, and Alabama co-captain Rick Davis told Frank Schwab, referring to the Tide's first three black captains, John Mitchell, Wilbur Jackson, and Croom. "And it was based on respect, the guys that your teammates respected and felt like they were a leader, and Sly was."

Croom graduated in 1974 with a bachelor's degree in history. He intended to follow his parents into teaching, but he first wanted to play in the NFL for a few years to save money for graduate school. He was picked up as an undrafted free agent by the New Orleans Saints. Before leaving for training camp, he sought out Coach Bryant to ask his advice about graduate schools. Bryant's response took Croom by surprise. As Croom recalled for Lori Nickel, Bryant said, "Croom, if things don't work out for you in the pros, I want you to come work for us." The offer would come in handy. Croom arrived at the Saints' training camp and promptly impressed the coaching staff, winning the starting-center job from a second-round draft pick from Auburn University. His lack of size, however, caught up with him in his first pro game. Washington's defensive tackle Diron Talbert manhandled Croom as the Redskins routed the Saints, 41–3. Croom was cut from the team the next day. He returned to Alabama to become Bryant's graduate assistant and begin work toward a master's in educational administration, which he completed in 1977.

That year Bryant surprised Croom again, by naming his former player linebackers coach. "I discovered Coach Bryant never let you coach your own position," Croom told Nickel. "His philosophy was, if you can coach, you can coach anything. He wanted you to learn the details and technical aspects of the entire game so that you could understand the whole concept." Croom held that post under Bryant until his mentor retired, in 1982, having led Alabama to back-to-back championships, in 1978 and 1979. Bryant's successor, Ray Perkins, asked Croom to stay on in the same capacity, and he agreed. When the NFL's Buccaneers lured Perkins away from Alabama in 1987, he offered Croom the same job in Tampa Bay. The linebackers coach initially declined, preferring to stay at the university; he changed his mind once he learned that Alabama's new head coach, Bill Curry, wanted to change Croom's duties with the Crimson Tide. Perkins had already filled the linebacker-coaching position in Tampa Bay, but he was willing to create a new post, running-backs coach, for Croom. "I gave Sylvester the playbook, and he knew it from front to back within a week," Perkins told Rick Cleveland for the Jackson, Mississippi, *Clarion-Ledger* (December 2, 2003, on-line). "He's smart and, just as importantly, he will work at it."

Croom coached in Tampa Bay through the 1990 season. Following a one-year stint with the Indianapolis Colts, he was hired by Bobby Ross in 1992 to coach running backs for the San Diego Chargers. Croom coached the star Chargers running back Natrone Means to his best season (1,350 yards rushing) en route to a 1995 Super Bowl appearance. When Ross accepted an offer to be head coach of the Detroit Lions, in 1997, he, like Ray Perkins, wanted Croom to follow, this time as coordinator of Detroit's entire offense. The Lions already had potent weapons in place before Croom's arrival, but he made better use of them than any prior coach. In Croom's first season as offensive coordinator, Barry Sanders ran for 2,053 yards and receivers Herman Moore and Johnnie Morton caught passes for more than 1,000 yards. That was the first time in NFL history that teammates led the league in rushing and receiving in the same season. Consistent with the peripatetic life of the coach, however, Croom was forced to move on after a turbulent 2000 season in Detroit. Burned out and embarrassed by a mid-season loss to the Miami Dolphins, Ross resigned and assistant head coach Gary Moeller took over. Moeller immediately accepted a three-year contract, led the team to the play-offs, and was then fired along with the rest of the coaching staff at the end of the season. The Green Bay Packers sought Croom's expertise as a running-backs coach in 2001. In his first season as a Packer, Croom tutored his lead pupil Ahman Green to career highs in rushing yards (1,387) and total yards from scrimmage (1,981). The next season, Croom's corps of backs rushed for an average of 120.8 yards per game, the most by a Packers team since 1985. The fruits of Croom's coaching efforts peaked in 2003, when Green shattered his personal bests with a franchise-record 1,883 rushing yards (tied with Barry Sanders for seventh most rushing yards in a single NFL season) and a league-leading 2,250 yards from scrimmage.

Croom's proven ability to coax such performances from players consistently, as well as his—in the words of one reporter—"touched-by-the-bear" pedigree (an allusion to Bryant), led the University of Alabama to consider him for their newly vacated head-coach position in May 2003. The once-proud program had recently fallen on hard times. The Crimson Tide had not won a national championship since 1992, which was also their first since 1979. Threatening the team's immediate

prospects for success, the NCAA cited the Tide in 2002 for illegal recruiting by team boosters. Sanctions included a two-year ban on postseason bowl appearances, which are a significant source of revenue for major programs; a reduction of 21 scholarships over three years; and a five-year probationary period, during which the program undergoes constant, intensive scrutiny. Further humiliation came in the form of Mike Price, who was hired in December 2002 to turn the program around but was fired four months later for questionable behavior during and after a drunken night in a Florida strip club.

Also being considered for the Crimson Tide's head-coaching job were Richard Williamson, who, like Croom, had played and coached under "Bear" Bryant and had NFL coaching experience, and Mike Shula, the son of Don Shula, the "winningest" coach in NFL history, and the Crimson Tide's quarterback during Croom's last three years on the Alabama coaching staff. Of the three job candidates, it was generally agreed, Croom was the best: he had more experience than Shula and better credentials than Williamson, and his filling the job would represent what most thought was a much-needed change for the SEC. It was not surprising, therefore, when Alabama's announcement of Mike Shula as its next head coach drew criticism from many quarters, including the civil rights activist Jesse Jackson, who called for an investigation of hiring practices at Alabama and all SEC schools. In the following months, however, the controversy subsided, and Croom resumed his work in Green Bay. Shula, meanwhile, led the Crimson Tide to an overall record of four wins and nine losses and a conference record of 2–6, just ahead of Mississippi State University (MSU) at the bottom of the SEC West division.

That ranking does not tell the whole story about MSU, which, though not as steeped in tradition as Alabama, is thought by some scouts to have the best concentration of gridiron talent in the United States. Its football team, the Bulldogs, has not always been able to take advantage of the talent in its own state; competing against such wealthy SEC rivals as the University of Florida and the University of Tennessee, both of which often raid Mississippi's talent pool, MSU, for many years, rarely threatened to take the SEC title. But when Jackie Sherrill took over the program, in 1991, the Bulldogs' fortunes seemed to turn. Within eight seasons the veteran coach made MSU a contender, leading them to the brink of the SEC title in 1998. The following season they won 10 games, matching the school's record, set in 1940. All told, under Sherrill the Bulldogs were awarded six invitations to bowl games and several top-25 national rankings, making them one of the SEC's most successful programs in the last decade of the 20th century. That legacy is marred, however, by recruiting violations. On October 27, 2004 the NCAA infractions committee found two of Sherrill's assistants and several school boosters guilty of breaking recruiting rules. MSU was placed on four years' probation and stripped of eight football scholarships that would have been awarded during the next two seasons. In addition, the team was banned from postseason play for 2004. That penalty has proved to be effectively meaningless: as of the date of the NCAA's decision, the Bulldogs had a 2–5 record and were unlikely to be selected for a bowl game even if they were eligible. Furthermore, the Bulldogs ended each of Sherrill's last three seasons at MSU at the bottom of the SEC West, compiling a record of eight wins and 27 losses in that time.

Within weeks of Sherrill's retirement, Mississippi State University asked Croom to be its new head football coach. By accepting, Croom joined Fitz Hill at San Jose State University, Tyrone Willingham at the University of Notre Dame, Tony Samuels at New Mexico State University, and Karl Dorrell at the University of California at Los Angeles as the only African-American head coaches in Division I-A football. In his new position, for which he signed a four-year contract, Croom will earn between $870,000 and $900,000 per season. "The state of Mississippi is perceived as the deepest of the Deep South and the place where change is most likely to be resisted in racial matters," William Ferris, of the University of North Carolina's Center for the Study of the American South, noted to Kelly Whiteside for USA Today (December 1, 2003, on-line). "For this change to happen there makes it more dramatic." Mississippi State's decision was similarly hailed across the nation, although some, such as C. Keith Harrison, founder and director of the Paul Robeson Research Center for Academic and Athletic Prowess at the University of Michigan, were quick to assert that it had been too long in coming. "It's significant but also a little sad," he told Harvey Araton. "To think of all the African-American athletes who have played for these schools [in the SEC] and we've just had the first head coach."

In 1987 the Alabama coach Bill Curry honored Croom by instituting the Sylvester Croom Commitment to Excellence Award, which is given to a deserving member of the Crimson Tide at the conclusion of each spring's practices. That honor would prove to be a new source of tension between Alabama and Croom. In March 2004 Mike Shula decided to rename it the Bart Starr Commitment to Excellence Award, after a Tide Quarterback from the 1950s. Shula explained that he thought it inappropriate for Alabama to have a player award named after a rival SEC coach. Many considered Shula's decision to be an insult, including Croom, who admitted publicly that he was hurt by it and argued that Alabama appeared to be taking away from his on-field accomplishments because of what he has achieved as a coach. A week after the decision, amid a storm of bad press, Shula reinstated Croom's name to the award. Shula also called his Mississippi State counterpart. "He assured me that it was not personal, that he meant no disrespect toward me," Croom told Gentry Estes for the

Decatur Daily (April 6, 2004, on-line). "He was looking at it strictly from a recruiting standpoint. . . . I assured Mike that there were no hard feelings on my part, and I think we both look forward to putting all this behind us."

Croom and his wife, Jeri, who met in high school, have built a home in Starkville, also home to MSU. Their daughter, Jennifer, and her husband, Ira Bates, have a daughter named Ryan. in June 2003 the University of Alabama honored Sylvester Sr., who died in 2000, for his work as a civil rights leader.

—T.J.F.

Suggested Reading: (Appleton, Wisconsin) Post-Crescent B p1 June 29, 2003; Associated Press Dec. 2, 2003, Dec. 4, 2003; Atlanta Journal-Constitution (on-line) May 7, 2003; (Biloxi, Mississippi) Sun Herald B p1 Dec. 3, 2003, with photo; Decatur Daily (on-line) Apr. 6, 2004; (Jackson, Mississippi) Clarion-Ledger (on-line) Dec. 2, 2003; Milwaukee Journal-Sentinel (on-line) Sep. 23, 2003, with photo; New York Times VIII p1+ July 18, 2004, with photos; New York Times (on-line) Dec. 3, 2003, with photos; USA Today (on-line) Dec. 1, 2003, with photo; Washington Post D p1 Dec. 3, 2003

Cummings, Elijah E.

Jan. 18, 1951– U.S. representative from Maryland (Democrat); chair of the Congressional Black Caucus

Address: 1632 Longworth House Office Bldg., Washington, DC 20515; 1010 Park Ave., Suite 105, Baltimore, MD 21201

"As a people, Americans of color continue to face unacceptable 'equality gaps' in education, income, wealth, home ownership, and business opportunities," the Democratic U.S. congressman Elijah E. Cummings of Maryland wrote in an article posted on the Web site Urban Spectrum. "We continue to suffer from disparities in our access to health care, discrimination in federally financed health programs, racial profiling, and inequitable sentencing in our criminal justice system." Cummings, who has been a member of the House of Representatives since 1996, was chosen to head the Congressional Black Caucus (CBC) in December 2002. During his two-year term, he announced, the CBC would hold a series of fact-finding forums, centering on economic and social-policy issues, in the home districts of its members; the group is also developing a questionnaire for presidential candidates to inform black voters about their positions on various issues. In addition, since he took on his new role, Cummings has been vocal about the inability of the Congressional Black Caucus to obtain

Stefan Zaklin/Getty Images

Elijah E. Cummings

a meeting with President George W. Bush. "The thing that drives me is a desire to fulfill a mission," Cummings told Alice Bernstein for the *East Texas Review* (September 11–18, 2003, on-line). "My religion teaches me that God has perhaps taken me, a young man like many others—poor, not having a whole lot to hope for—and lifted me up to be an example, to strengthen other people. That's how I view my life."

Elijah Eugene Cummings was born on January 18, 1951 in Baltimore, Maryland, to Robert and Ruth Cummings. His parents, who had been sharecroppers in South Carolina, were both Baptist preachers, despite their lack of formal education—neither had attended school past first grade. In Baltimore Cummings's mother worked at a pickle factory and later as a maid, while his father was a laborer at Davidson Chemicals. Although his parents struggled financially themselves, they believed in helping others and instilled that belief in their son. "When we were little, my daddy used to go to the orchard and pick fruit for canning—apple preserves, peaches," he told Bernstein. "We actually made jelly—it's incredible when I think about it! Then they took almost half and gave it to other people. . . . Even in the hard life, they were constantly giving." Cummings's desire to become a lawyer stemmed from his wish to help others. "Many young men in my neighborhood were going to reform school," he told Bernstein. "I used to watch [the TV courtroom drama] *Perry Mason.* Though I didn't completely know what reform school was, I knew that Perry Mason [a defense attorney] won a lot of cases. I also thought that these young men probably needed lawyers. So back when I was, I guess, around ten I decided to be a lawyer to help people. "

As a young man Cummings worked in a small drugstore in South Baltimore whose proprietor, a Jewish man named Albert Friedman, encouraged his aspirations. "[Friedman] introduced me to this concept: You, Elijah, must live in two worlds, able to relate to your own people and relate to all people. You have to have an education, he used to say, then go out in the world and change it," Cummings told Bernstein. "He thought I'd make a good politician. Doc Friedman gave me the funds to apply to Howard University, and every few weeks he'd send a ten dollar bill with a note 'Hang in there.'"

Cummings graduated with honors from Baltimore City College High School in 1969. He then enrolled at Howard University, in Washington, D.C., where he served as student government president and graduated Phi Beta Kappa in 1973, with a degree in political science. He earned his law degree from the University of Maryland in 1976, passed the Maryland Bar that December, and maintained a general-law practice for 19 years. Meanwhile, he served in the Maryland House of Delegates (the lower house of the state's General Assembly) for 13 years, from 1983 to 1996. There, he chaired the Legislative Black Caucus (he was the youngest person to have held that position) and in 1995 became the first African-American in the state's history to be named speaker pro tem, the second-highest position in the House of Delegates. As a delegate he focused on such issues as education, health care, and reform of the justice system. Among those who had influenced his decision to run for public office were Albert Friedman and the civil rights leader Martin Luther King Jr., whose radio addresses he had listened to as a high-school student.

Cummings was elected to the United States House of Representatives in April 1996, in a special election for Maryland's 7th Congressional District, which includes low-income neighborhoods in West Baltimore and part of Baltimore County's middle-class southwestern suburbs. About 59 percent of the district's residents are African-American, while 35 percent are white and the remainder primarily Asian or Hispanic. Problems such as crime, drug abuse, teen pregnancy, and unemployment are prevalent in parts of the district. The main industries there are health care, manufacturing, and technology. Cummings serves on the House Government Reform Committee, the Wellness and Human Rights Subcommittee, the House Transportation and Infrastructure Committee, the Subcommittee on Highways & Transit, the Subcommittee on Railroads, and the Criminal Justice, Drug Policy and Human Resources Subcommittee (on which he is the ranking member). A member of the Democratic Policy Committee, he is also the co-chair of the House AIDS Working Group, and is a member of the House Task Force on Health Care Reform.

In September 2002 Cummings joined Eddie Bernice Johnson, then head of the CBC, to issue a statement opposing congressional authorization of military action in Iraq, which had been requested by

President George W. Bush for the stated purpose of ridding Iraq of "weapons of mass destruction." "I am convinced that there is not enough information out there for us to send our young people off to war and thereby place their lives in harm's way . . . ," he told Vicki T. Lee for the *Baltimore Afro-American* (October 4, 2002), approximately six months before the U.S. military struck Iraqi targets. "In order to effectively deal with terrorism, we must have the cooperation of friendly countries. If we go into Iraq unilaterally, are we doing damage to relationships of other countries that refuse to be a part, and therefore diminishing our capability for war on terrorism?" He also told Lee that a war could detract attention from pressing problems within U.S. borders. "We have to refocus our domestic agenda. Not to say that we shouldn't address terrorism, but there are too many issues inside the country. I'm afraid that with the intensity of the war effort, not only will those things be pushed to the back burner, but off the stove."

In December 2002 the African-Americans in the House chose Cummings over Illinois representative Bobby Rush to lead the Congressional Black Caucus. He assumed the post (which is limited to one, two-year term) when Congress convened in the following January. The CBC was formed in 1969 by the 13 black members of the House of Representatives then serving. It has often been called "the conscience of Congress," and its priorities include creating new jobs and businesses, granting all Americans access to health care, achieving equal access to education, and strengthening civil rights. The CBC, which currently boasts 39 members, is considered the most formidable and active minority political organization in Congress. Cummings took over leadership of the group after it had been weakened by Democratic election losses and at a time when Republicans held a majority in both houses of Congress. (He is the third representative of Maryland's District 7 to fill the post, following in the footsteps of Parren Mitchell and Kweisi Mfume.) "I think he has the skills to do the job," University of Maryland political science professor Ron Walters told Charles Brooks for the New York *Amsterdam News* (December 25, 2002). "He's an aggressive leader, and that's what's needed right now in the CBC. He's coming in at a time when the Black community is looking for aggressive leadership from the Congressional Black Caucus. Blacks expect the CBC to exercise some leadership and not drag its feet." Hillary Shelton, director of the Washington bureau of the National Association for the Advancement of Colored People (NAACP), told Brooks, "I think he'll do a fabulous job. . . . He has a proven track record in addressing the concerns of African-Americans and people of color. . . . He thinks strategically; he's assertive and articulate. I think you're going to see the progressive tradition going forward."

In August 2003 Cummings urged President Bush to send troops to Liberia to bring order to the politically volatile African country. Founded by people of African descent who had been freed from slavery in the U.S., Liberia has suffered 23 years of civil war. "President Bush is dragging his feet," he told Dwight Lewis for the *Tennessean* (August 3, 2003). "The U.S. needs to put a peacekeeping force of between 2,000 and 3,000 troops in Liberia immediately, and we're calling on the United Nations to join us in helping to stabilize Liberia." He supported Bush's demand in June of that year that Liberian president Charles Taylor step down to avert further clashes between rebels and government forces in the country. Several U.S. ships, carrying 2,300 Marines, were sent to positions on the coast of Liberia in August, but only 200 soldiers went ashore, for just 10 days, and their tasks were limited to coordinating logistics and communications for 700 Nigerian troops. Many commentators believe that the presence of troops from a Western nation will be required to stabilize the country. A peace agreement in August ended the latest fighting, but U.N. officials have said that in order to maintain peace they must collect weapons from the estimated 14,000 soldiers (former government fighters or members of rebel groups) roaming the country. In September the U.N. Security Council approved the dispatching of 15,000 peacekeepers to Liberia; the first 4,500 arrived in October, and the rest of the troops were deployed in early 2004.

Improving public education is one of Cummings's top legislative priorities. "It is very important that we get more funds into our schools," he told Alice Bernstein for the *East Texas Review* (September 18–25, 2003, on-line). "In most schools it's a luxury to have one computer for every 5 children; many have one for every 100 children. The greatest threat to our national security is the failure to educate our children. The very person who could be finding the cure to cancer, or who could be defending this country, may be sitting right now in jail. The one who could create works like Picasso, is dead at an early age." Cummings has criticized the Bush administration's education policies, including proposed changes to Head Start, a program that was begun in the 1960s and helps millions of low-income children prepare for grade school by providing academic skills as well as health care, mental-health assessment, parent education, and other services. The Bush administration has proposed that the program be funded by state block grants rather than by federal funds. This change would mean that close to 3,000 children currently eligible for the program would not be guaranteed inclusion. "This proposal does exactly the opposite of the Administration's promise to leave no child behind," Cummings said in a July 15, 2003 news release posted on his Web site. He also pointed out that one study had found that every dollar invested in the program saved between $4 and $7 spent later on remedial education or other compensatory programs. "As we consider the future of one of the most effective federal programs in this country, we also will be determining the future of this nation's most important resources—our children," Cummings told Nisa Islam Muhammad for the *Final Call*, as posted on the *Sacramento Observer* Web site (August 4, 2003). "What gets lost in the countless number of policy papers, press releases, facts and figures, is who these children really are. All too often, we lose sight of the fact that each child in Head Start has the potential to be a future doctor, lawyer, teacher, or even president." Along with other lawmakers, he feared that placing responsibility for the program with the states could result in the shifting of money to other programs instead, which would weaken Head Start.

Cummings supports provisions for prescription drugs under Medicare and universal, affordable long-term health insurance. He introduced legislation that would make 20 million federal employees eligible for a long-term insurance program. The Long Term Care Security Act, based on his original proposal, was signed into law in September 2000. Cummings has also called for an increase in the number of federally licensed health centers that provide treatment even for those who are without health care and cannot pay for services; such centers currently serve 11 million Americans. He has backed the REACH Initiative, which would develop 1,200 new or expanded health centers, and also co-sponsored the Health Care Safety Net Improvement Act, to reauthorize the federal Health Centers program and the National Health Service Corp. In addition, he came out in favor of the Medicare Safety Net Access Act, which would expand services available to Medicare patients in federally qualified community health centers. He co-sponsored legislation that created the National Center on Minority Health and Health Disparities, part of the National Institutes of Health. He has also fought for famine relief for Africa and increased U.S. funding of the Global AIDS and Health Fund.

In July 2003 Cummings proposed the Dawson Family Community Protection Act, to provide up to $1 million annually to cities fighting severe epidemics of drug abuse and violent crime. The bill was named for a Baltimore family who perished in a house fire believed to have been set by drug dealers after the family had called the authorities to report their presence in the neighborhood. The congressman co-sponsored the Congressional Resolution on Voting Rights, to guard against voter disenfranchisement and intimidation, which included a provision allowing the U.S. Commission on Civil Rights to gather data and investigate reports of voting irregularities in the 2000 presidential election. (That legislation failed to pass in the 107th Congress.) He also co-sponsored the Racial Profiling Prohibition Act of 2001, to prohibit the use of racial profiling in patrolling highways; the Local Law Enforcement Hate Crimes Prevention Act, to provide state and local governments with funds for prosecuting hate crimes (legislation that still awaits committee action); and the Accuracy in Judicial Administration Act of 2001, to provide a temporary moratorium on the death penalty.

Meanwhile, in April 2003, Cummings was chosen to deliver one of the House Democrats' weekly radio addresses. In it he criticized the Bush administration's budget priorities, saying that the White House placed more emphasis on cutting taxes for wealthy Americans than on creating jobs or funding health care and education programs. "According to the Republican budget, cutting taxes that disproportionately benefit wealthy Americans is the single most important thing that we can do during these difficult economic times and while our country is at war," he said, as quoted on the Democratic National Committee Web site (April 19, 2003). "The Republican budget says that cutting taxes that disproportionately benefit wealthy Americans is more important than educating our children or assuring that all American children have health insurance. . . . Families can only spend money that they have earned, but the Republicans in Congress passed a budget that spends money we don't have. The Republicans passed a budget that puts our country further into debt, mortgaging our future. We need to get America's families back to work— earning the money to pay for their homes, their health care, their children's education and their retirement."

In July 2003 Cummings turned down an invitation to hear a report from President Bush on his recent trip to Africa, because the president had not met with the Congressional Black Caucus since January 31, 2001 (the date of his only meeting with the group so far); Bush had denied the CBC's request for another meeting at least four times since then. "I wanted to make sure he was clear that if he wanted to meet with me, he needed to meet with the Caucus," Cummings told Tavis Smiley for the *Tavis Smiley Show* on National Public Radio (July 17, 2003). "After all, these are 39 brilliant men and women representing over 670,000 people each, and we represent a constituency that needs to be heard by this president because much of what he has been doing over the last two and a half years has been destructive to our community." He said to Gebe Martinez for *Congressional Quarterly* (July 16, 2003), "We want to talk to [the president] about the 11.8 percent black unemployment rate; we want to talk about Africa with regard to the Republicans trying to slash the AIDS funding that he just talked about in Africa; we want to talk about his efforts with regard to anti-terrorism."

Cummings has urged the Department of Homeland Security to develop a plan to ensure railroad security. "It is unfortunate that a year-and-a-half after the September 11 terrorist attacks, the administration has still not made substantial progress in addressing the security of the nation's rail system," he and three other House members wrote in a letter to the Homeland Security and Transportation departments, as quoted by John B. O'Donnell intto the *Baltimore Sun* (May 24, 2003). At a news conference, as reported by O'Donnell, Cummings said, "We want to see action. We've got to start somewhere. We just cannot sit around and wait for an incident to happen or to say to ourselves that it could never happen." In December 2003, during the race for the Democratic Party's presidential nomination, Cummings endorsed the early front-runner, former Vermont governor Howard Dean. After Massachusetts senator John F. Kerry secured the nomination, Cummings campaigned energetically for the Democratic ticket.

Cummings was reelected in 1998 and 2000, both times with 87 percent of the vote; also both times, his opponent was Kenneth Kondner, a Republican. In 2002 he won 73 percent of the vote, beating Republican challenger Joseph E. Ward; in 2004 he defeated the Republican Tony Salazar with 74 percent of the vote. Among the groups who have supported Cummings are the Alliance for Retired Americans, which gave him a 100 percent rating in 2002, and the NAACP, which gave him an "A" rating in July 2002. He has encouraged African-American students to get involved in politics and community issues. "It is easy to stand on the sidelines and complain about what is wrong with life," he said in a speech at the University of Maryland, as reported by Adam Guttentag for the *Eclipse* (April 21, 1998, on-line). "In the city of Baltimore, there are over a thousand monuments, and not one monument is erected to memorialize a critic. Every one of the monuments is erected to memorialize one who was severely criticized."

Cummings is a member of the Morgan State University Board of Regents, the Baltimore Zoo Board of Trustees, the Baltimore Aquarium Board of Trustees, the board of directors of the Baltimore

Area Council of the Boy Scouts of America, and the Dunbar-Hopkins Health Partnership Executive Board. He writes a bi-weekly column for the Baltimore *Afro-American* newspaper and is an active member of New Psalmist Baptist Church. He has chaired Maryland's Governor's Commission on Black Males since its founding, in 1990, and founded the Maryland Bootcamp Aftercare Program in 1991. In addition, he is the president of the Bancroft Literary Society and chief judge of the Maryland Moot Court Board. He received an honorary doctor of laws degree from Howard University in 2003 and a Distinguished Alumni Award from the school in 2000.

The legislator, who is separated from his wife and has two daughters, ages 21 and nine, lives in the Madison Park community in Baltimore. In his free time he enjoys listening to jazz and growing plants. "The thing I love about plants is that they turn to the light," he told Bernstein (September 18–25, 2003). "Deep in our hearts most of us want to turn to truth. The politician who puts his finger in the air to figure out which way the wind is blowing, and then says 'This is what I'm for,' is least respected. People want truth!"

—K.E.D.

Suggested Reading: Congressman Elijah E. Cummings Web site; *East Texas Review* (on-line) Sep. 11–18, 2003, Sep. 18–25, 2003, Sep. 25–Oct. 2, 2003, with photo; (New York) *Amsterdam News* p3 Dec. 25, 2002, with photo; National Public Radio July 17, 2003

Curry, Ann

Nov. 19, 1956– Broadcast journalist

Address: NBC News, 30 Rockefeller Plaza, New York, NY 10112

"I've been asked if I'm Iranian, Eskimo, Hispanic," Ann Curry, the news anchor of the *Today Show*, NBC's popular morning program, told Jeffrey Zaslow for *USA Weekend* (December 18–20, 1998, on-line). "The Currys of South Carolina, a black family, invited me to their family reunion. They said, 'You're black, aren't you?'" Curry, whose father is white and mother was Japanese, attributes such questions to people's desire to see those of their own ethnic and racial backgrounds represented on television. She understands that desire, recalling that she looked noticeably different from those around her, and saw few faces like hers on television, when she was growing up. "When you're a child and you don't see people like you doing something, it doesn't enter your mind you could do it," she told Zaslow. "It's like looking through a shut glass door into a room that seems so

tantalizing, but the door isn't open to you." Being an Asian-American on the country's most-watched morning show is a source of pride for Curry, who joined the *Today Show* in 1997, after working for NBC and CBS affiliates on the West Coast and hosting *NBC News at Sunrise* in the early 1990s. Curry views her position with the show as an opportunity not only to keep viewers informed about important events worldwide, but also as a chance to influence their lives. "NBC News pays my salary, but I feel as if I work for the viewers, helping them make sense of the world," she told Daniel Levine for *Reader's Digest* (March 2000).

The oldest of five children, Ann Curry was born on November 19, 1956 in Agana, on the Pacific island of Guam, a U.S. territory, to Robert Paul and Hiroe (Nagase) Curry. Her father, known as Bob, was a career officer in the U.S. Navy, who retired as chief petty officer after 27 years of service; he met her mother, the daughter of a rice farmer, when stationed in Japan in the late 1940s, and they married in 1953. Curry's family moved around a great deal when she was young, spending about three years in Norfolk, Virginia, where Curry began high school, before settling in Ashland, Oregon. Describing the intolerance that her parents faced be-

Evan Agostini/Getty Images

Ann Curry

cause of their marriage, Curry told Jeremy Helligar, Cynthia Wang, and Jennifer Wulff for *People* (October 12, 1998) that her father's "commanding officer told him, 'Your eyes are going to slant and you're going to turn into a bamboo American.' It took great courage to stay with their love despite those pressures." Curry's mixed-race background caused her, while she was growing up, to feel different from other people. Her parents had differing responses to the challenges faced by their children. "It was very difficult to be Japanese here" in the 1950s, Curry told Zaslow. "People were still angry about the war"—World War II, one of whose key events was Japan's attack on the U.S. military base at Pearl Harbor, in 1941. "So [my mother] raised me to be American. She wouldn't even let me speak Japanese." It was her father who encouraged her to take pride in her Asian heritage. "He told me, 'Never forsake either world. In fact, if you have to choose, choose your Japanese side.' He gave me permission to embrace the samurai side, the side of strong people he'd come to admire," she said. Zaslow reported that in raising her own children, whose father is white, Curry "repeats words her father once spoke to her: 'You are the best of both worlds.'"

When Curry and her siblings were children, their father challenged them to talk about serious issues. "I remember having long, lively discussions about the Vietnam War and Watergate with my father as we ate dinner," Curry told Larry Bonko for the *Virginian-Pilot* (October 5, 1999). "I'd state an opinion, and then my father would come back with, 'How could a daughter of mine say that about our government?' He taught me to be passionate about the news. He also instilled a sense of duty

and service in his five kids." Although he had hoped she would follow in his footsteps and join the military, she was instead inspired to pursue journalism. (Her two brothers joined the military, however.) Following her graduation from high school, in Ashland, she took various jobs to pay for her college education, including one as a hotel maid and another in which she made maps for the U.S. Forest Service. She graduated from the University of Oregon School of Journalism in 1978.

While she originally thought about becoming a newspaper journalist, Curry began her career in 1978 at KTVL, an NBC affiliate, in Medford, Oregon. There, she quickly encountered sexist attitudes. "The executive producer said, 'You're a woman. You can't carry the camera. If you were smart you wouldn't take this job,'" she told Helligar, Wang, and Wulff. She remained at the station until 1981, when she became a reporter and anchor for KGW, the NBC station in Portland, Oregon. In 1984 she moved to Los Angeles to work as a reporter for KCBS. At that station she earned two Emmy Awards—one for her live coverage of the October 1987 Los Angeles earthquake, and another for her coverage of the explosion of a gas pipe in San Bernardino.

Curry rejoined NBC in June 1990. She began broadcasting nationally, becoming the network's Chicago news correspondent that October and anchoring *NBC News at Sunrise* from July 1991 to July 1996. She became news anchor for the *Today Show* in March 1997, two months after Matt Lauer became one of the program's co-hosts (replacing Bryant Gumbel) and Al Roker took over as the morning weatherman. Katie Couric has been a co-host of the program since 1991. The *Today Show* has been the number-one-ranked network morning program for the past eight years, earning NBC $350 million a year in revenue and attracting about 6.5 millions viewers daily. (ABC's *Good Morning America* is a distant second, with 4.5 million viewers, while *CBS This Morning* averages 2.7 million.)

Among the high points of Curry's career at NBC to date was an exclusive on-air interview, for the evening program *Dateline,* with Bobbi and Kenny McCaughey of Iowa—parents of septuplets born in 1997. Curry was the only reporter whom the family allowed full access at the hospital and in their community, and she has conducted a follow-up interview with the family each year. In April 1999 Curry became the first network news anchor to cover the refugee crisis in the Balkans, following Serbian aggression against Albanians in Kosovo. She reported extensively from "ground zero" after the September 11, 2001 terrorist attacks on the World Trade Center, in New York City, interviewing victims, city officials, firefighters, and other emergency workers. In November 2001 she carried out a weeklong assignment aboard the USS *Theodore Roosevelt*, stationed in the Arabian Sea, culminating in an exclusive interview with General Tommy Franks at Ramstein Air Force Base. On

May 14, 2003 Curry switched jobs with the soccer star Mia Hamm as part of the *Today Show*'s week-long "Trading Places" feature; while Hamm took on Curry's duties on *Today*, Curry attempted to fill Hamm's place as a member of the Washington Freedom, part of the Women's United Soccer Association. (Curry had trained with the team for a week in preparation for the day's activities, which included a scrimmage.) While Curry covers a mixture of hard news and lighter stories, she has said that the common denominator in her work is a desire to change people's lives for the better and to encourage them to make a difference in the world. "I report on real people, and many have suffered greatly," Curry told Diane Clehane for *TV Guide* (January 12–18, 2002). "If there is a prejudice I bring to a story it is this: I want you to care."

Curry arrives at NBC's studio in Rockefeller Center, in New York, at 5: 00 a.m. each weekday. Her first task is to check the newswires for breaking stories. Her job entails reading, editing, and fact-checking every news story that comes in; during the three-hour news and entertainment program, which begins at 7: 00 a.m., Monday through Friday, she relates those items deemed important. In addition to her *Today Show* duties, she serves as a daytime anchor on the MSNBC cable network and has hosted its *Special Edition* program; contributes reports to *Dateline NBC;* co-anchors *Dateline International* for NBC Europe; and is a substitute anchor for the Sunday edition of *NBC Nightly News.*

When Couric's contract expired in May 2001, some industry observers speculated that if Couric were to leave NBC, Curry might take over her co-hosting role. (In December 2001 Couric signed a $65 million, five-year contract to stay with the show, making her the highest-paid television journalist in history.) Curry has said that while she enjoys filling in for Couric on occasion, she is happy with her current role and would rather be known for covering news stories. "I'm not looking for Katie's job," she told Zaslow. She added, referring to the longtime anchor of *NBC Nightly News*, "I want Tom Brokaw's job." In the meantime, she appears content to be part of such a successful show; the camaraderie among the four on-air *Today Show* personalities is often noted, and Curry has said that it is based on a genuine affection for one another. "I work in a creative, fast-paced, lively, enjoyable and incredibly invigorating environment and I can't wait to get to work each morning," she told Marc Berman for *Daily Variety* (January 14, 2002). "At times I have to pinch myself—I really do feel like Cinderella at the ball."

Curry is a four-time winner of the Golden Mike award from the Radio & Television News Association of Southern California and a recipient of an NAACP Award for excellence in reporting (1989). Her other honors include Associated Press Certificates of Excellence (1987, 1988), a Certificate of Excellence from the Greater L.A. Press Club (1987), and Emmy Awards in 1987 and 1989. (She was also nominated for Emmys in 1985, 1986, and 1988). She is a member of the Asian American Journalists Association and an honorary board member of the Multiple Myeloma Research Foundation, and *People* magazine named her one of the world's "50 most beautiful people" in 1998. She is also an advocate for breast-cancer prevention, research, and treatment and a supporter of the Susan G. Komen Breast Cancer Foundation. (Her younger sister Jean was diagnosed with the disease in 1998.) She was honorary chair of the survivor celebration at the Komen Foundation's National Race for the Cure in Washington, D.C., and has been a presenter for the foundation's annual awards luncheon. She was also a panelist on a *Larry King Live* segment about breast cancer and has appeared in public-service announcements focusing on early detection. Curry wrote the foreword to *Fighting for Our Future: How Young Women Find Strength, Hope, and Courage While Taking Control of Breast Cancer* (2002), by Beth Murphy.

The five-foot six-inch news anchor, who practices yoga, lists *The Sound of Music* as her favorite film. "I was nine when I first saw it, and I've probably seen it 20 times since," she told Kate Coyne for *Good Housekeeping* (May 2003). "I love the story of a young woman who struggles to discover who she really is and finds happiness." Among her prized possessions is a copy of *Webster's New World Dictionary* she received from her father upon earning straight A's when she was 12. She married Brian Wilson Ross, a computer consultant whom she met in college, in the late 1980s; the couple have a daughter, Anna McKenzie, 11, and son, William Walker, nine. The family lives in New York City, in the borough of Manhattan.

—K.E.D.

Suggested Reading: *People* p109+ Oct. 12, 1998, with photos; *USA Weekend* (on-line) Dec. 18–20, 1998, with photo; *Virginian-Pilot* E p1 Oct. 5, 1999, with photo

---

Davidson, Richard J.

Dec. 12, 1951– Neuroscientist; educator

Address: W. M. Keck Laboratory, Waisman Center, University of Wisconsin, 1500 Highland Ave., Madison, WI 53705

Like many of his colleagues in the field of neuroscience, Richard J. Davidson has spent much of his career studying the brain activity of individuals suffering from depression, anxiety, or phobias. Unlike most other neuroscientists, however, he has also investigated the brain patterns of people who appear to be happy. Davidson is a pioneer in affective neuroscience, the study of the relationships between the brain and emotions: that is, the links

Courtesy of Richard Davidson

Richard J. Davidson

as compassion, kindness, and forgiveness and has cited Davidson's work in his book *The Art of Happiness* and elsewhere. Davidson has conducted extensive research on the effects of meditation on veteran Tibetan Buddhist monks—"the Olympic athletes, the gold medalists, of meditation," as he described them to Stephen S. Hall for the *New York Times Magazine* (September 14, 2003)—and novice monks. His other subjects have included people of all ages, among them those considered normal as well as those who have been diagnosed as having psychological, neurological, or genetic disorders. Davidson is the William James and Vilas Research Professor of Psychology and Psychiatry at the University of Wisconsin at Madison, where he was instrumental in founding the W. M. Keck Laboratory for Functional Brain Imaging and Behavior, which he has directed since its opening, in 2001. In recognition of his vital role in advancing psychology and neuroscience, he has received many honors, among them, in 2000, the highest tribute of the American Psychological Association: the Distinguished Scientific Contribution Award, for lifetime achievement.

Richard J. Davidson, called Richie by all who know him, was born on December 12, 1951. He attended Midwood High School, in the New York City borough of Brooklyn, a public school for academically gifted teenagers. During his years there he worked as a volunteer in the sleep laboratory at Maimonides Medical Center, also in Brooklyn; his assigned task was to clean the electrodes that had been affixed to subjects' scalps, torsos, arms, and legs as a means of studying their neurological and other physiological activity while they slept (or tossed and turned) at night. As Daniel Goleman pointed out in his book *Destructive Emotions*, "Just such electrodes have been a basic tool of his trade ever since." In 1968 Davidson enrolled at New York University, in New York City. While there, along with Judith Rodin, a fledgling assistant professor of psychology (she is now the president of the University of Pennsylvania), he conducted research on mental imagery. After he earned a B.A. degree, in 1972, he entered the graduate program in psychology at Harvard University, in Cambridge, Massachusetts. He had chosen Harvard in part because he wanted to study with Gary E. Schwartz, an expert in psychophysiology, and learn from Daniel Goleman, who had just returned to Harvard's graduate program after 15 months of travel in India, where he had interviewed Hindu yogis and other practitioners of meditation; Davidson had read Goleman's accounts of his research in India in the little-known *Journal of Transpersonal Psychology*. On his first day at Harvard, in a seminar given by Schwartz, Davidson met Goleman; the two became friends immediately. The photos of Indian spiritual teachers that Goleman had pasted on the dashboard of his car, and the realization that he and Goleman shared an identical fascination with meditation and its physical, emotional, and intellectual effects, "just shattered my mind," Davidson

between the activities of the billions of neurons that make up the brain and the intangible positive and negative feelings that humans define as emotions: excitement, distress, happiness, anger, and a myriad of others. Among his most significant findings, he has discovered that the left frontal cortex is associated with feelings of good will and happiness, and it is more active in the brains of people who are generally optimistic, cheerful, and enthusiastic than in those of individuals who are usually pessimistic, gloomy, and dispirited; it is also more active in men and women who meditate than in those who do not. Moreover, he has found, activity in those areas of the brain indicates in babies as young as 10 months the nature of their apparently inborn temperaments. He has also discovered that training in meditation can lead to measurable changes in the brain, along with increases in a person's feelings of well-being and confidence and decreases in feelings of stress and insecurity.

Davidson became interested in the physiology of mental processes and emotions years before he earned his doctoral degree, in 1976. He persisted in his experimentation and data gathering at a time when psychological research was firmly in the grip of behaviorists, who "scorned the study of any internal experience and argued that only actions that could be observed should be the subject of scientific investigation," as Daniel Goleman wrote in his book *Destructive Emotions: How Can We Overcome Them?: A Scientific Dialogue with the Dalai Lama* (2003). Davidson has worked closely with the current Dalai Lama, Tenzin Gyatso, the spiritual leader of the Tibetan people and winner of the 1989 Nobel Peace Prize, who has written and spoken extensively on such aspects of human nature

said years later, as quoted by Goleman. His ride in Goleman's car that day, according to Goleman, "symbolized for Richie the beginning of his alternative graduate education."

Among those influential in Davidson's traditional graduate education was Harvard's pathbreaking behavioral neurologist Norman Geschwind, whose work included observations of brain-injured people whose trauma had resulted in marked changes in their emotions. Davidson also studied with a Massachusetts Institute of Technology professor, Walle J. H. Nauta, a leading authority on the brain's anatomy. Among the many structures that comprise the human brain are the brain stem, a stalklike structure that connects nerves inside the skull to those outside it (most importantly, those in the spinal cord); the cerebellum, a relatively small part that lies in back of the brain stem and controls balance and coordination; and the largest part, the cerebrum, which is divided into left and right hemispheres. The topmost layer of each hemisphere is the cerebral cortex, which has multiple folds and four lobes: the frontal, the parietal, the temporal, and the occipital. (The frontal cortex is sometimes referred to as the prefrontal cortex.) In the early 1970s conventional wisdom held that emotion was under the control of the oldest parts of the brain, evolutionarily speaking: the limbic system, which is deep within the brain and is present in amphibians, fish, and reptiles as well as humans, and the brain stem. Walle Nauta's research, however, had led him to believe that connections existed between those parts of the brain and the frontal cortex—a possibility that fascinated Davidson.

Working with Goleman and Schwartz at Harvard, Davidson conducted experiments on attentional ability—the power to concentrate on a particular task, idea, or anything else despite distractions. He discovered that training in meditation can help people improve their capacity to focus their attention and keep their minds from wandering. During his stint in graduate school, he took a leave of absence from Harvard to travel in Sri Lanka and India, to learn firsthand about Eastern meditation techniques. He earned his Ph.D. in 1976. Before he left Harvard he received from his mentor, the psychologist David C. McClelland, advice that helped him keep his spirits up during the next decade, when he often tried in vain to obtain research grants or find journals willing to publish his papers: in Goleman's words, McClelland told him that "if he felt he was on to something, he should trust his scientific intuition, believe in himself, and not worry about what the rest of the world thought—eventually they would catch up."

After he completed graduate school, Davidson obtained a teaching position at the State University of New York at Purchase. During the next eight years or so, he accumulated evidence connecting brain-activity patterns and moods. (As has often happened in science, researchers elsewhere were making similar discoveries—in this case, Don M.

Tucker and his co-workers in the Department of Psychology of the University of Oregon. "Probably neither one of us would have believed it if we observed it just in our own lab," Tucker told Daniel Goleman for the New York Times in 1991. "No one expected that there should be such a tie between activity in the frontal lobes and emotions.") In 1984 Davidson joined the faculty of the University of Wisconsin at Madison, where, in a welcome change, "the scientific climate was very open to his research interests," according to Goleman. He currently holds professorships in both the medical school and the Department of Psychology. Assisted by others at the college, he raised sufficient funds ($10 million) to build the W. M. Keck Laboratory for Functional Brain Imaging and Behavior (named for one of the donors, a petroleum-industry executive and philanthropist). The laboratory is affiliated with two other facilities at the university: the Waisman Center, which is devoted to research into developmental difficulties, and the HealthEmotions Research Institute, where scientists investigate the links between emotions and illness or health.

Davidson has studied the relationships between brain activity and emotions in a wide range of adults and children, both those judged to be normal and those suffering from any of a variety of abnormalities or maladies, such as autism or fragile-X syndrome in children, and mood, anxiety, or personality disorders in adults. To record patterns of and changes in brain activity, he uses state-of-the-art electroencephalographs, which produce records known as EEGs; functional magnetic resonance imaging (fMRI), which records changes in the chemical composition of brain areas or changes in the flow of fluids occurring over timespans ranging from seconds to minutes; and positron emission tomography (PET), in which the distribution of positrons (a type of elementary atomic particle) from a radioactive substance illuminates the biological processes occurring within tissue, also over a period of time.

Davidson's studies have revealed a striking relationship between brain activity and emotional well-being. In one experiment, in which he analyzed the brain activity of 99 women who were sitting quietly, he compared the 15 women whose left frontal cortexes showed the most pronounced activity with the 15 whose right frontal cortexes were most active. As revealed afterward by a "personality scale," a psychological test used to determine an individual's behavioral and emotional characteristics, the former group had a more positive outlook on life than average, while the latter had a relatively negative outlook. Davidson and his colleagues repeated similar experiments with other females and males of various ages and states of mental health. In one, he showed that he could predict which 10-month-old babies would cry when their mothers left the room for one minute, based on whether their left or their right frontal cortexes were generally more active. Without exception, all those with more activity on the right cried, while none of those with more activity on the left did. In another experiment, described in the *Journal of Abnormal Psychology* (November 1991), Davidson compared the brain patterns of people who had recovered from depression after professional treatment with those of people who had never been depressed (that is, *persistently* sad or unable to feel pleasure or interest in daily life for more than a couple of weeks) and knew of no family members who had suffered from depression. Those who had been depressed showed less activity on the left side of the brain and more on the right than those who had never been depressed. Moreover, as Davidson explained to Daniel Goleman for the *New York Times* (February 12, 1991), "You find similar brain patterns in people who are depressed, or who have recovered from depression, and in normal people who are prone to bad moods. We believe that in the face of life stress like losing a job or a divorce, they are likely to be particularly susceptible to depression. Someone with more left frontal activity, though, would be more resilient to the same stress."

In the July 28, 2000 issue of *Science*, Davidson and his co-workers released the results of a research project that focused on people with a history of violent behavior. They examined data concerning 500 violent individuals, some of whom suffered from antisocial personality disorders (in particular, they exhibited unusual levels of aggression on personality tests) and childhood brain injuries, and compared that information with data on people who had rarely if ever behaved violently. The researchers discovered distinct differences in the two groups' brains. Davidson believes that in the latter group, who were representative of most people, the brain is hardwired to prevent overreaction to fear, anger, and other negative emotions. In violent people, that control mechanism is somehow short-circuited. The study also found dysfunction in the same regions of the brain in 41 murderers and in groups of people unable to control their aggressive impulses. In addition to the frontal cortex in violent subjects, the activity of the amygdala (a small, almond-shaped, evolutionarily ancient structure deep within the brain that produces automatic responses to threats and has been linked to the emotion of fear) "essentially ran out of control, while other brain regions could calm it down in normal people," Davidson and his colleagues found.

Davidson has also investigated the effects on brain activity of meditation, which, "in Buddhist tradition . . . ," as he explained to Stephen S. Hall, "is a word that is equivalent to a word like 'sports' in the U.S. It's a family of activit[ies], not a single thing," and each requires a particular skill. Since 1992, at the invitation of Tenzin Gyatso, the 14th Dalai Lama, he and his co-workers have conducted experiments involving Tibetan Buddhist monks in India, where the Dalai Lama and his followers currently reside in exile, and in the U.S.

The researchers have focused on three forms of meditation: focused attention, in which one tries to concentrate on one thing for a long time; the cultivation of the feeling of compassion, in which one thinks of an event that sparks negative feelings and then tries to "transform it and infuse it with an antidote, which is compassion," as Davidson put it to Hall; and "open presence," which he defined as "a state of being acutely aware of whatever thought, emotion or sensation is present, without reacting to it." Davidson has found signs of unusually high activity in several areas of the monks' left frontal cortexes.

The beneficial results of meditation were also revealed in an experiment Davidson performed in collaboration with Jon Kabat-Zinn, the founder of the Mindfulness-Based Stress Reduction Clinic at the University of Massachusetts Medical School, in Worcester. In that study he measured the effects of an eight-week, 45-minute-a-day course in Buddhist-style meditation on a group of employees from a high-pressure biotechnology firm. The electrical activity of the subjects' brains was measured before they began the course; they were also given flu shots, to ascertain whether the training would affect their immune systems. At the end of the eight weeks, the researchers measured the participants' brain activity while the subjects wrote about negative and positive life experiences. They then compared those data with data obtained before the course. Davidson and his colleagues found that not only did the subjects report feeling less anxious about day-to-day stresses, but, in addition, their brains showed a marked shift of activity from the right frontal cortex to the left. Measurements of the subjects' antibodies indicated that their immune systems had grown stronger.

Davidson has published more than 150 articles in professional journals and edited or co-edited 12 books, among them *Consciousness, the Brain, States of Awareness, and Alternate Realities* (1979); *Psychobiology of Affective Development* (1984); *The Nature of Emotion* (1994); *Anxiety, Depression, and Emotion* (2000); *Visions of Compassion: Western Scientists and Tibetan Buddhists Examine Human Nature* (2002); and *The Asymmetrical Brain* (2003). His many honors include a National Institute of Mental Health (NIMH) Research Scientist Award; an NIMH Merit Award; an Established Investigator Award from the National Alliance for Research in Schizophrenia and Affective Disorders; and the Hilldale Award from the faculty of the University of Wisconsin at Madison, for distinguished professional accomplishment. In 2004 Davidson and his colleagues at the University of Wisconsin earned a $10.7 million grant from the NIMH to research emotions in people during difficult periods of their lives.

For many years Davidson has practiced Vipassana meditation, which, according to various sources, focuses on mindful self-awareness or "self-transformation through self-observation" and aims to help people see things as they really are or recognize that the self and all other objects, thoughts, and phenomena are impermanent. In 1996 he turned down an offer to chair Harvard's Department of Psychology. In offering the reasons for his decision, he told Samara Kalk for the *Capital Times* (December 13, 1999), a Madison, Wisconsin, newspaper, "One of the things which is so important about the work I do, and so characteristic of the work I do, is that it is highly interdisciplinary. They don't grow egos as large in the Midwest as they do in Cambridge, Massachusetts. It allows people to get together and work together without all the obstacles that I think would have been present had I moved." He also said that his family loved living in Madison; their happiness, he said, "was too precious a thing to disrupt."

—H.T./M.H.

Suggested Reading: *American Psychologist* p1193+ Nov. 2000; *New York Times* C p1+ May 22, 1984, C p1+ Feb. 12, 1991, F p2+ Feb. 4, 2003; *New York Times Magazine* p46+ Sep. 14, 2003, with photo; W. M. Keck Laboratory Web site

Selected Books: as editor or co-editor— *Consciousness, the Brain, States of Awareness, and Alternate Realities*, 1979; *Psychobiology of Affective Development*, 1984; *The Nature of Emotion*, 1994; *Anxiety, Depression, and Emotion*, 2000; *Visions of Compassion: Western Scientists and Tibetan Buddhists Examine Human Nature*, 2002; *The Asymmetrical Brain*, 2003

Marion Ettlinger, courtesy of Debra Dickerson

Dickerson, Debra

1959– Writer

Address: c/o Pantheon/Random House, 1745 Broadway, 20th Fl., New York, NY 10019

Once "a little girl from the ghetto," as she described herself to Robert Fleming during an interview for *Publishers Weekly* (July 17, 2000), the African-American writer Debra Dickerson went on to become, successively, an air-force captain in charge of intelligence at an American base in Turkey; a Harvard Law School graduate; a journalist; and what has come to be known as a "public intellectual." In her memoir, *An American Story* (2000),

she described her insatiable curiosity and desire for reading, learning, and understanding, which enabled her to overcome her father's beatings, her own rape, and the anti-female discrimination in the military. Her extraordinary ability to analyze and transcend her past experiences led her to write *The End of Blackness* (2004), a controversial book in which she urged her fellow African-Americans to stop defining themselves in terms of white people's perceptions or expectations and to participate fully in society. Dickerson explained to Tavis Smiley in an interview for National Public Radio (January 22, 2004), "When I think about how to live my life . . . is this a struggle against white people? No, it's a struggle . . . to live up to the legacy that I've inherited." She included in that legacy the work of the black activists Frederick Douglass, W. E. B. Du-Bois, and Martin Luther King Jr. as well as white participants in the civil rights struggle.

The writer was born Debbie J. Dickerson in St. Louis, Missouri, in 1959 to Johnnie Florence Gooch, a waitress, and Eddie Mack Dickerson, an ex-marine who worked as a laborer. She grew up under harsh circumstances. Her father, in spite of his fundamentalist Christian beliefs, beat Dickerson, her five siblings, and her mother. Dickerson later came to believe that her father, who struggled against poverty and racism, "needed to fight; he needed an enemy, something to defeat or at least resist, so he wouldn't feel helpless," as she told Linton Weeks during an interview for the *Washington Post* (August 29, 2000). Needing an escape, she "listened to a junk-pile radio that had no tuning knob," Weeks reported, quoting Dickerson as writing that to change stations, "you could either pick it up and shake it just right or use a pair of pliers. In neither case could you control where you landed." Her main refuge, however, was the library. Weeks quoted her as writing, "Going to the library was like happening upon the keys to the enemy's storehouse. I couldn't believe they just gave them to me." She treasured books, arranging and rearranging them by subject, author's name, and publication date.

Talented academically, Dickerson was sent to a secondary school for gifted children, where she learned to appreciate the works of Shakespeare and Dickens and to use stories from *Treasure Island* and *The Three Musketeers* to entertain her friends and family. Because she was one of the few black students in that school, however, her insecurity and sense of inferiority were reinforced. "I had learned," she wrote, as quoted by Weeks, "to be ashamed of who and what I was, what we [her family and other blacks] all were." She had been influenced by her parents' "congenital lack of a sense of entitlement," as Maureen Corrigan phrased it in a review of *An American Story* for the *Washington Post Book World* (September 17, 2000). Corrigan quoted Dickerson as writing, "We Dickersons didn't fight the power, we sought the shadows. We were oriented toward evading blows, not striking them . . . we didn't see ourselves as served by the government, but rather as subservient to it. Taxes, for us, were a form of protection money; all we asked in return was not to be crushed under the boot heel of government. We expected, demanded, nothing, and that's exactly what we got." Her mother found the resolve to remove herself and the children from her husband's orbit when Dickerson was 14. Still, the family's feelings of powerlessness remained, contributing in Dickerson's case to her dropping out of Florissant Valley Community College and then the University of Missouri at Columbia. Linton Weeks quoted her as writing that she feared being "found out as the unworthy upstart I was." To avoid being asked to leave school, acting on her low self-esteem, she left on her own.

In 1980 Dickerson enlisted in the United States Air Force and was stationed in South Korea. Explaining her attraction to the military, she wrote in *An American Story*, as quoted by Weeks, "Nerdiness, love of detail, and hyperorganization are valued traits in the service. They make you cool." She then returned to the United States and worked for a year at the Pentagon. Her initial training in the military, she has recalled, instilled confidence as well as conservative values in her; it also led her to downplay the role of race in her life and in society—made her, as she put it, "fiercely incog-Negro." Her confidence received a serious setback, however, when she was raped by a member of her own unit in Korea in 1981. Although her attacker had confessed to the crime, others in the unit came to his defense, and he received only a light sentence, while Dickerson was ostracized. For years afterward, she avoided—as much as possible—thinking about the incident. "I blamed my commander for everything," Dickerson wrote in an op-ed piece for the *New York Times* (March 18, 2003). "But I refused to hold the Air Force complicit. Why? Desperation, I guess. A need to believe that the Air Force truly did consider me one of its own. At that point in my life the service was all I had; I didn't have any other choice but to persevere. I didn't deal with the rape for a decade. " She was later to conclude, however, that "I was never one of the Air Force's own. My rapist was," and that it "was infinitely more difficult to be female in uniform than to be black."

While she continued to perform her duties in the air force following the rape, she also began to rethink her conservatism, having been repelled by what she referred to in *An American Story* as "the intellectual shamelessness and moral clay feet" of the right; she came to feel that she had based her conservative views on her "own self-hatred." At the same time, she disliked what she termed the "intellectual dishonesty of the left." In this lonely time, Dickerson also began to long to embrace the black community in a way she had not done before. Linton Weeks cited a passage in *An American Story* in which Dickerson recalled going to a bar in East St. Louis, where, observing a host of black people enjoying themselves, she felt "wistfulness because I wasn't a part of it."

Performing well despite her emotional confusion, Dickerson was singled out for promotion and given a chance to complete her college education, with tuition paid by the air force. Majoring in government and politics, she received her B.A. degree in 1984 from the University of Maryland at College Park and was commissioned as an officer in 1985. She went on to obtain an M.A. degree in international relations from St. Mary's University, in San Antonio, Texas, in 1988. Starting in 1989, Dickerson, by that time a captain, served for two years as chief of intelligence at Ankara Air Station, in Turkey. She left the military in 1992.

Dickerson then worked on Bill Clinton's first successful campaign for the presidency. Afterward, she attended the law school of Harvard University, in Cambridge, Massachusetts. The two experiences taught her that she had "no stomach for elective politics" or for the law, as she put it on her Web site. She resolved her quandary over which career path to pursue by following a dream that had taken hold during her law-school days: that of being a writer. Her essay "Who Shot Johnny," about an attack on her nephew that left him paralyzed, was published in the *New Republic* (January 1, 1996) and then chosen for the annual *Best American Essays* collection. After her graduation from law school, she found a job at *U.S. News & World Report*. When James Fallows, the editor who had hired her, was fired, Dickerson left and wrote for the on-line publication *Salon* for a year. Fallows then helped her obtain a one-year fellowship at the New America Foundation, whose mission, as stated on its Web site, is "to bring exceptionally promising new voices and new ideas to the fore of our nation's public discourse." Meanwhile, she worked as a freelance journalist, contributing to such publications as *Mother Jones*, the *Village Voice*, the *Washington Post*, and *Good Housekeeping*. In addition, she began to attract notice as a commentator on television and on National Public Radio.

Dickerson's memoir, *An American Story*, "started as a thinly disguised autobiographical novel, but that soon changed," as she told Robert Fleming. *An American Story* traces Dickerson's life, from her difficult childhood, to her time in the military, to the point at which she became an independent thinker. Upon its publication, a reviewer for *Publishers Weekly* (July 17, 2000) commented, "Rarely does a memoir strip away so much emotional armor to expose so many defects as well as strengths. . . . If Dickerson is ruthless in her appraisal of others, she is twice as hard on her own shortcomings, especially the views about poor and lower-working-class blacks trapped in poverty and despair she held as a young woman. Her display of courage following a rape, along with her gritty determination to excel at Harvard, attests to the complexity and resilience of this chameleon of a woman." Corrigan felt that Dickerson's memoir placed her in the tradition of Ralph Waldo Emerson, "our bard of the idiosyncratic," because "it embodies the solitude often borne by American free thinkers."

In her next book, *The End of Blackness: Returning the Souls of Black Folk to Their Rightful Owners* (2004), Dickerson argued that black Americans should pay tribute to the martyrs of the civil rights movement by moving on from complaints about racism and pursuing their goals without heed to the attitudes of whites. She also expressed the opinion that the civil rights movement has not fully accomplished its goals, as long as blacks refuse to take responsibility for their own self-definition. Janet Maslin, the reviewer for the *New York Times* (January 29, 2004), called the book "a dazzling diatribe" and "a furious, bitterly funny indictment," adding that even "readers whom she enrages—and there will be many—cannot ignore the range and ferocity of her attack. . . . Why, she asks, should whiteness even be a point of reference for a black self-image? Blacks have the power to cease being hamstrung by history and to transcend the grievances of the past." Maslin quoted an analogy from *The End of Blackness* that Dickerson applied to the plight of African-Americans: "[The escape artist] Harry Houdini once famously struggled for hours picking a jail cell lock, only to lean against it in exhaustion and have the door swing open. It had never been locked at all. All that confined him was in his own head." While expressing the view that Dickerson "leaps too quickly to generalizations, suffers a weakness for black-and-white debating dichotomies and resorts to oversimplifications that are more wisecracking than profound," Maslin felt that the strengths of the book outweighed its weaknesses, and that "the provocations presented . . . are often incontrovertibly formulated."

Like some other reviewers, Elisabeth Lasch-Quinn, writing in the *Washington Post Book World* (January 18, 2004), judged Dickerson to have fallen short of her own exhortations by burying her arguments in contradictory statements: "Dickerson's entire argument—that blacks need to let go of old notions of black identity and the forms of identity politics and racial grievance at their core—is subverted early in the book by a surprising chapter on 'white intransigence' in which she presents a litany of complaints against whites. . . . Earlier faulting blacks for wrongly feeling excluded from America, she later says that blacks 'find themselves defined out of America.' Well, which is it?" Nonetheless, Lasch-Quinn observed that Dickerson "exhibits a praiseworthy independence of mind." She noted that to "Dickerson, true loyalty to the civil rights movement's heroes and heroines, both black and white, would lead to full 'civic self-actualization'—full participation in the benefits and responsibilities of American citizenship—in place of outsidership status."

Debra Dickerson lives in Washington, D.C., with her husband, an architect, and their children.

—S.Y.

Suggested Reading: *New York Times* (on-line) Mar. 18, 2003, Jan. 29, 2004; *Publishers Weekly* p182 July 17, 2000; *Washington Post* C p1 Aug. 29, 2000; *Washington Post Book World* p7 Sep. 17, 2000, p6 Jan. 18, 2004

Selected Books: *An American Story*, 2000; *The End of Blackness: Returning the Souls of Black Folk to Their Rightful Owners*, 2004

Dickinson, Amy

Nov. 6, 1959– Advice columnist

Address: "Ask Amy," Chicago Tribune, TT500, 435 N. Michigan Ave., Chicago, IL 60611

"My first reaction was I wanted to go straight to bed and stay there. My second reaction was, 'I am the great and powerful Oz!' . . . ," Amy Dickinson joked to Seth Mnookin for the MSNBC Web site, speaking of her response to having become an advice columnist for the *Chicago Tribune* in the summer of 2003. "I know who I am and what I'm doing. And when I answer a letter, I think I'm talking to just 'Busted in Baltimore,' not the whole world. If you approach anything that way you can do it. I also don't take myself that seriously, and I think that helps." Dickinson's column has received considerable publicity, since she is filling the space left vacant by the death of Eppie Lederer, better known as Ann Landers—for nearly 50 years the author of one of the world's most popular advice columns, with syndication in 1,200 newspapers worldwide and 90,000 daily readers. "Ask Amy: Advice for the Real World by Amy Dickinson" currently appears in 53 newspapers, among them the *Los Angeles Times*, *Newsday*, the *Seattle Times*, the *Boston Herald*, the *Baltimore Sun*, the *Charlotte Observer*, the *Orlando Sun Times*, and the

Courtesy of Amy Dickinson

Amy Dickinson

Philadelphia Enquirer, in addition to the *Chicago Tribune*. After the *Tribune* chose her to succeed Lederer, Dickinson told reporters that her column would be more inclusive than Lederer's—in particular, that it would devote more space to men's concerns—and that her style would be different from her predecessor's. "My column is a general advice column, as hers was, but I'd say my responses to people are probably edgier and a little funnier, lengthier and contain more reporting," she told *Current Biography*. "I'm a pretty avid consumer of pop culture and am more likely to make a cultural reference. I'm also 'in the trenches' of raising a child as a single parent and I draw on my own experiences as a starting point in my answers." Like Lederer, Dickinson adopts a more serious attitude when writing about complicated or significant problems, and she often points readers to books or Web sites for further information.

The youngest of four children, Amy Dickinson was born on November 6, 1959 on a dairy farm in Freeville, New York, a town of 450 people in the Finger Lakes district of the state. Both her mother's and her father's families have lived in the region, or in New England, since about the turn of the 17th century; her distant relatives include the 19th-century poet Emily Dickinson. Her parents, Jane Genung and Charles Lee Dickinson, divorced after her father left the family, when Amy was 12. She and her siblings—her brother, Charles, and sisters, Rachel and Anne—continued to live on the farm with their mother for some time, but, having "lost all of our livestock" and "auctioned off the contents of the barn and all our equipment," as Dickinson told *Current Biography*, they rented the land to neighbors; later, they sold it to relatives. "It was re-

ally a hardscrabble life there and eventually the farm went the way of many small farms, out of business," she told Rick Kogan for the *Chicago Tribune* (July 9, 2003). Her mother got a job as a typist at Cornell University, in Ithaca, New York; at age 50 she returned to school, earning a master of fine arts degree at Cornell and becoming a teacher of writing there and then at Ithaca College. She is now retired and lives in Freeville. Dickinson has said that her mother is the person she most admires and the one to whom she most often turns for advice. Dickinson's father is a beekeeper and beehive inspector in rural Pennsylvania.

Dickinson began college at Clark University, in Worcester, Massachusetts, in 1977; she completed her junior and senior years at Georgetown University, in Washington, D.C., where she earned a B.A. degree in English in 1981. Her college activities including playing varsity field hockey and singing in school choirs and chamber groups; once, she sang in a choir at a papal Mass in Washington. ("For a Presbyterian that was quite a big deal," she told *Current Biography*.) After she graduated Dickinson worked in a bicycle shop on Block Island, Rhode Island, and sang with a local rock band before returning to Washington, where she held a series of menial jobs and also worked as a lounge singer in a bar. Thanks to the intervention of two of the bar's patrons, she landed an entry-level job at NBC-TV's Washington bureau; she worked first at the news desk and then on the overnight shift as a desk editor. While there, she told *Current Biography*, she impressed the television anchor Roger Mudd by answering a "newsroom trivia question" about the musical *Paint Your Wagon*. In 1983 she moved to New York City, where the *New Yorker* hired her as a receptionist. She left that job when Mudd hired her as an associate producer for NBC in New York. In that position she helped to produce stories for several short-lived newsmagazine shows, among other assignments.

In 1986 Dickinson married the CBS News correspondent Anthony Mason. The following year she moved with him to London, England, where, in 1988, their daughter, Emily, was born. The couple divorced in 1990, and the next year Dickinson moved with her daughter to Washington, D.C., where she took a temporary job at National Public Radio (NPR), filling in for an employee who was on maternity leave. In time she secured a part-time job at NPR as a commentaries editor and producer. In 1996 she started writing and producing stories for the NPR weekday program *All Things Considered* and writing a weekly column for the American Online Web site's news channel. Meanwhile, she had established herself as a freelance writer; her pieces appeared in the *Washington Post, Esquire, Allure,* and *Vanity Fair*, among other publications, and she wrote several commentaries for the TV series *CBS Sunday Morning*. She also worked as a substitute nursery-school teacher and as a Sunday-school teacher ("experiences which I cherish," she told *Current Biography*). In 1999 the Washington bureau chief of *Time* magazine, who had heard several of her stories on NPR, hired her to write a column about family life. The column appeared for more than two years.

In her pieces for *Time*, in addition to describing aspects of her life as a single parent and experiences with her large extended family, Dickinson frequently offered advice. She wrote of the importance of maintaining good relationships with all the grandparents of one's child, even when no longer involved with the child's other parent; counseled parents on raising children who appreciate the value of money; and recommended that people who are planning to get married find out first about the family, friends, and future plans of those they intend to wed. Other topics she covered were ways to help children deal with death; the problems parents face due to a lack of affordable, quality child care; video games that do not contain excessive violence; the Million Mom March for gun control; ways to persuade children to do chores; eating disorders among boys; and lessons in table manners for children. She sometimes angered her readers with her advice, as in a 2000 column in which she defended the idea of a co-ed sleepover party for teenagers, provided the party is held in one large room; she wrote that teens would be less likely to engage in sexual behavior if they lacked privacy. Dickinson's employment at *Time* ended after the September 11, 2001 terrorist attacks on New York City and the Pentagon. During the next months, because of the worsening economy, she found freelance jobs scarce.

Soon after Esther "Eppie" Lederer died, on July 22, 2002, editors at the *Chicago Tribune* began the search for another writer to offer solutions to readers' problems. Dickinson, who had done some freelance writing for the paper, commented jokingly in an E-mail message to one of the paper's editors that she would love to have such a job; a month later she was invited to try out for the post. Along with nine other candidates, she was sent sample questions by E-mail and given a week to answer them. "It was so fun, I got started and really enjoyed it, and I e-mailed back literally within two or three hours," she told Mnookin. "[The editor] told me to take the full week, but I said no, this is it, this is my answer, if you want me, I'm right here on the page. . . . I knew to do the job I'd have to work very quickly, and I feel like that's one of my assets." She told *Current Biography*, "The moment I answered those questions, I knew that I could do the job and that I wanted to do the job." As reported by the *New York Post* (July 9, 2003, on-line), the *Tribune* editor Ann Marie Lipinski said that Dickinson quickly distinguished herself from her competitors: "Amy just kept answering questions with tremendous common sense, some from the head, some from the heart and that, combined with her reporting skills, to me, made a very potent candidate." As soon as she was offered the job, Dickinson telephoned a Freeville diner where she knew her mother and a dozen other members of her family were having breakfast. The family "were all quite stunned, I assure you," she told *Current Biography*.

The daily column "Ask Amy: Advice for the Real World by Amy Dickinson" debuted in the *Chicago Tribune* on July 20, 2003 and was picked up for syndication by Tribune Media Services on September 1 of that year. "I am tremendously excited by this opportunity but the other night I had a dream about being buried under envelopes," she said, as reported by Kogan. "And I worry about trying to fill Eppie Lederer's pumps. She was really skilled at taking the national pulse, and her column over the years reflected the hopes, dreams, fears and concerns of the great wide majority of the American public. . . . I really want my column to reflect this moment in time and to give people a place to turn for a humane hearing of their problems and to offer accurate and helpful advice."

Dickinson revealed that she had read the Ann Landers column while growing up. "Reading her column allowed me to listen to the national dialogue," she told Kogan. "People in Dallas, Iowa City, Savannah, Boston, Portland and upstate New York were worried about the Vietnam War and alcoholism and, oh, yes, meddling mothers-in-law. Sometimes her column was just really entertaining, but reading that there are strangers out there who shared problems and concerns, that was a tremendous value. Ann Landers was a person of her time, and I'm a person very much of my time."

In her first column Dickinson gave advice to a gas-station clerk on how to tell if a regular customer was interested in him romantically, then urged him not to undervalue himself because of his unprestigious job. She also recommended to the mother of a 20-year-old man with no job or initiative that she charge him rent if he moved back home, and provided a teen with ways to tell whether or not a boy had a crush on her. A July 24 column advised a woman not to alter a ring given to her as a keepsake by her grandmother, and told a long-married couple trying to cope with the anger in their relationship to seek marriage counseling.

Dickinson has covered weightier topics in her column as well. Her August 6 column included a letter from a married man who had had an affair with a woman in his neighborhood and believed that he, not the woman's husband, was the father of the woman's two-year-old son. The writer of the letter, already a father, wanted to have a hand in raising the child. "You mention that you have a family, yet don't seem interested in the effect this will have on them. In fact, you seem more interested in punishing this child's mother and taking him from the only father he has known, than in being a father to the boy," Dickinson responded. "That having been said, now that you're in this mess, you do need to deal with it. If you are this boy's father, he needs to know soon; there are emotional as well as genetic implications here, and he is an innocent party who deserves the truth." She urged the man to get in touch with a professional mediator with a background in family law to explore his options; to learn about paternity laws in his state; and to talk to the child's mother to work out a solution "that hopefully revolves around the best interests of this child."

In her August 10 column, in response to a letter from a widowed 78-year-old woman who complained about being left out of family activities and ignored because of her age, Dickinson chastised her own generation for failing to respect and value its elders. "If we don't start listening to and learning from our elders, we're going to be the most self-absorbed, demanding and difficult older generation imaginable," Dickinson wrote. "So partly, I'd like to make a plea for younger people to spend less time yammering about their jobs and kids and more time listening to their older relatives and friends. But I also would urge all the elders out there who feel similarly frustrated to please get together with one another, form social clubs and book groups, go on outings and spend time volunteering or just watching videos together. Don't wait for my generation to become less self-absorbed and more respectful—that's going to take time, and you deserve to feel honored and useful right now." In her August 14 column she responded to a letter from a 32-year-old man who believed that he would be more comfortable living as a woman but was afraid to explore hormone therapy or surgery for fear of his family's reaction. Dickinson recommended that he read the book *She's Not There: A Life in Two Genders*, by Jennifer Finney Boylan, and that he further research the issue and seek a qualified therapist to help him work through his feelings before undergoing surgery, as his friends had suggested. "Being transgender doesn't mean you're gay or straight," she wrote, addressing the man's confusion about his sexuality. "Gender is often separate from sexual orientation; but once you work the gender thing out, your sexual orientation might become clearer. . . . What you must do is act now to try to explore who you really are so you can make your own informed decisions."

"Amy is not only a terrific reporter but someone with a common sense approach to dealing with life and with life's questions," Anne Marie Lipinski told Kogan. "She is also a delight to be around. It is rare to find people who on paper are the same as they are in person. Amy is just that and I think readers will immediately sense it." Dickinson and her daughter, Emily, live in Chicago. She has described herself as a voracious reader and passionate fan of old movies. She also enjoys singing and running along the shore of Lake Michigan. "My favorite way to start the day is to run along the Lake as the sun is coming up," she told *Current Biography*. "I run toward the beautiful Chicago skyline and still can't believe how lucky I am to be here. Sometimes I feel as if I've come a very long way from where I started, but most of the time I don't. I feel like exactly the same person I've always been—my concerns and my dreams and aspirations don't seem to have changed all that much."

—K.E.D.

Suggested Reading: *Chicago Tribune* Tempo p1 July 9, 2003, with photos; CNN (on-line) July 20, 2003; MSNBC (on-line) July 9, 2003, with photo

---

Dimon, James

(DYE-mon)

Mar. 13, 1956– President and chief operating officer of J.P. Morgan Chase & Co.

Address: J.P. Morgan Chase & Co., 270 Park Ave., New York, NY 10017

In 1998 James Dimon was ousted from his position as president of the financial conglomerate Citigroup by the company's chief executive officer (CEO), Sanford Weill, Dimon's longtime mentor and friend, with whom he had built up the company. Many insiders expected Dimon to attempt to avenge himself by taking over a similarly high-profile financial firm and competing against his former boss. He therefore surprised analysts when, two years later, he accepted a position as the head of Bank One, a floundering financial-services firm based in Chicago, Illinois. Dimon's brilliant cutting-costs strategies and willingness to take risks helped return the bank to profitability, and its stock prices had risen by over 80 percent by the beginning of 2004. That was when Dimon made a deal to sell Bank One to the New York–based investment-banking powerhouse J.P. Morgan Chase for $58 billion, creating the second-largest bank in the United States, after Citigroup. Dimon is scheduled to become head of the company when J.P. Morgan's current CEO, William Harrison, steps down in 2006—the same year that Weill will step down as CEO of Citigroup. "The timing is delicious," Michael Holland, a fund manager and former Bank One shareholder, told Landon Thomas Jr. for the *New York Times* (January 15, 2004). "Sandy exits stage right and Jamie takes center stage. Jamie built a franchise for himself and the people around him. In the back of his mind I guess he always wanted to come back to New York."

Of Greek heritage, James Dimon was born on March 13, 1956 in Astoria, a working-class neighborhood in the New York City borough of Queens. Both his grandfather and father worked as stockbrokers in the borough of Manhattan, and as a teenager Dimon worked for his father on Wall Street. At Tufts University, in Boston, Massachusetts, he studied psychology and economics, graduating summa cum laude in 1978. As a student Dimon

Ron Wurzer/Getty Images

James Dimon

firm and one of the most powerful men on Wall Street. In 1993 Weill again promoted Dimon, this time to the position of chief operating officer (COO); Weill explained to reporters, as quoted on *PR Newswire* (November 4, 1993), "Jamie Dimon provides a range of talents and depth of knowledge of all our businesses from which everyone on the management team at Primerica benefits. His contributions to the efficient operation of the parent company . . . are virtually immeasurable. This new title, therefore, is simply well-deserved recognition for, and a formalization of, the myriad responsibilities he assumes and executes so exceedingly well throughout the organization."

Later in 1993 Primerica acquired Travelers Corp., a high-profile insurance company, for $4 billion and changed its own name to Travelers Group, thus becoming one of the largest and most diverse financial-services companies in the world. Dimon continued in his capacity as president and COO; in 1994 he was given the additional title of head of brokerage operations at Smith Barney, which offered brokerage, investment banking, and asset-management services to corporations, individuals, and governments. Dimon continued to rise through the ranks at Smith Barney until he became chairman and chief executive officer there, in 1996. A year later Travelers acquired the investment bank Salomon Brothers and merged it with Smith Barney, resulting in a company called Salomon Smith Barney Holdings Inc. Dimon then shared the title of CEO of Salomon Smith Barney with Salomon's Deryck C. Maughan.

In the spring of 1998, Travelers Group purchased Citicorp, the second-largest bank in the U.S., for $70 billion. Known as Citigroup, the merged concern immediately became the world's largest financial services corporation up to that time. Weill shared the post of chief executive officer with John Reed, who had served as Citicorp's CEO and was expected to retire within a few years. Dimon was named president of Citigroup, and most saw him as Weill's heir apparent. Tensions between the two men had been mounting for years, however, and in November 1998 Dimon succumbed to internal pressure and left the company. The move shocked many industry insiders. "Both internally and to the outside world, people had viewed Jamie Dimon as professionally, the perfect foil to Sandy Weill, and personally, almost like a son to him," Carla D'Arista, managing director of bank research for Friedman Billings Ramsey, in Arlington, Virginia, told Randi Feigenbaum for *Newsday* (November 3, 1998). "I feel that while no one is irreplaceable, the Wall Street perception is Jamie was as close as it got." Many traced Dimon's departure to his clash with Weill's daughter, Jessica M. Bibliowicz, a senior executive at Smith Barney whom Dimon had refused to promote. (Bibliowicz herself later left the company, much to Weill's displeasure.) Others speculated that Weill saw Dimon as a threat and as having grown too powerful and influential under his tutelage. In a public state-

wrote a thesis on one of Sanford Weill's earliest takeovers of another company at Shearson Lehman Brothers Inc., the company Weill helped found in 1960 and sold to American Express in 1981; the paper won him a summer internship with Weill. In 1982 Dimon earned an M.B.A. degree from Harvard University, in Cambridge, Massachusetts. As a favor to Dimon's father, who worked as a stockbroker at Shearson, Weill hired James Dimon as his assistant at American Express. Over the next several years, the two developed a strong relationship, with Weill serving as Dimon's mentor. When Weill was ousted from American Express, in 1985, Dimon left with him.

A year later Weill took over as chairman and CEO of Commercial Credit Co., a struggling, Baltimore, Maryland–based consumer-finance company that sold insurance and offered loans to middle-income Americans; he named Dimon chief financial officer and senior vice president. Weill, Dimon, and several other Commercial Credit Co. executives subsequently took the firm public with an enormous initial public stock offering, after which the company began to flourish. Throughout his career with Weill's company, Dimon played a central role in the mergers and acquisitions that would turn Commercial Credit Co. into one of the most powerful financial services companies in the world. In 1988 the company purchased Primerica Corp., a Greenwich, Connecticut–based financial-services and specialty retailing firm, for $1.7 billion. Commercial Credit Co. then changed its name to Primerica Corp. Two years later Dimon was promoted from executive vice president to president, making the 34-year-old one of the youngest presidents of a major financial-services

ment, as quoted by Randi Feigenbaum, Dimon offered this explanation for his departure: "I know Citigroup is well poised for growth, so this is the perfect time for me to leave and regenerate with some new opportunities."

Dimon spent the next two years as an independent investor. In 2000 he was hired as chairman and CEO of Bank One, then the country's fourth-largest bank. At the time the Chicago-based company was suffering from poor returns, excessive costs, and customer losses. Dimon was brought in to restore the bank's profitability; his biggest challenge was to revive the bank's credit-card operation, the second-largest in the U.S., after Citigroup's. Some insiders questioned whether Dimon was up to the task, pointing to his lack of experience in retail banking. Dimon, however, believed he could turn the bank around. To prove it, he purchased $2 million worth of stock immediately upon being hired. "I want to build one of the best financial services companies in America," he told Mark Tatge for *Forbes* (May 13, 2002). "Something everybody who works here can be proud of, something the people who built it can hand off to another generation and say, this is a great thing we did."

Dimon's strategy was to slash costs, reduce the number of bank branches, and tighten lending standards in order to produce more profitable loans. He also linked all of the company's branches together in the same computer system, so that operations would be carried out in a consistent manner. Other strategies focused less on profit and more on employee satisfaction, with an eye toward the hourly workers in particular. He paid those employees $1,000 for each money-saving idea they generated and redistributed to employees, in the form of Bank One shares, money saved from cutting management perks. Dimon's work paid off: by 2004 Bank One stock had increased in value by over 80 percent. Morningstar Inc., a global investment research firm, named Dimon as its 2002 CEO of the Year, an honor that recognizes a chief executive who, through independent and creative thinking, has increased shareholder wealth. "Jamie Dimon has transformed what once was considered one of the most poorly run banks in the country into a solidly profitable firm with a bright future . . . ," Patrick Dorsey, director of stock analysis for Morningstar, said in a press release quoted by *PR Newswire* (January 3, 2003). "He has made Bank One a much better financial institution by focusing on basic business principles—keep costs low, serve customers, and focus on profitability rather than growth at any cost."

On January 14, 2004 Bank One and the investment-banking firm J.P. Morgan Chase merged, after the latter bought the former for $58 billion. The transaction produced the second-largest banking franchise in the country, after Citigroup, with combined assets of $1.1 trillion, 2,300 branches, and a strong presence in the Northeast and Midwest. With a market value of $132 billion, versus Citigroup's $255 billion value, the new conglomerate,

which will assume the name J.P. Morgan Chase & Co., must find new areas of growth in order to compete against its rival; specifically, analysts say that Dimon has to make a bid for a brokerage firm with a chain of retail brokers in order to close the gap (neither Bank One nor J.P. Morgan Chase currently owns a brokerage network). Nevertheless, observers have spoken optimistically about the company's future. As Dimon noted in a J.P. Morgan Chase press release (January 14, 2004, on-line), "The merger of Bank One and JPMorgan Chase makes tremendous sense strategically, operationally and financially. . . . Our combined company will have the size, scale, product mix, customer base, distribution channels, and earnings stability to achieve outstanding results, and enhanced shareholder value for many years to come." Dimon will serve as the company's president and chief operating officer until 2006, when J.P. Morgan Chase's current chief executive, William Harrison, steps down. According to several reports, Weill was one of the first to call and congratulate Dimon after the merger.

Dimon serves on the board of directors of Tricon Global Restaurants Inc. and is a member of the Council on Foreign Relations. He also serves on the board of the Center on Addiction and Substance Abuse and on the board of trustees of Mount Sinai-New York University (NYU) Medical Center and Health Systems. In addition, he is a vice chairman of the NYU School of Medicine Foundation Board. The James and Judith K. Dimon Foundation, established by Dimon and his wife, known as Judy, has supported organizations involved with education, children's aid, and conservation of natural resources, among other endeavors. The couple have three daughters; they currently live in Chicago and are planning to move to New York City. In 2004 the on-line trade periodical *American Banker* named James Dimon "banker of the year."

—H.T.

Suggested Reading: *Forbes* p64 May 13, 2004; *International Herald Tribune* Finance p11+ Jan. 19, 2004; *New York Times* C p1+ Jan. 15, 2004, with photo; *Newsday* (on-line) Jan. 15, 2004; *Time* p36+ Jan. 26, 2004

D'Onofrio, Vincent

(dah-NOFF-ree-oh)

June 30, 1959– Actor

Address: c/o RiverRun International Film Festival, 202 W. Third St., Winston-Salem, NC 27101

"In your career as an artist, any kind of artist, if you're lucky, you'll do one or two classics in your life," the actor Vincent D'Onofrio told Liz Braun

Evan Agostini/Getty Images

Vincent D'Onofrio

for the *Toronto Sun* (April 24, 2002). "The rest is fluff anyway. I never shot for the stars. I never tried to be a movie star. I just wanted to act." A character actor with considerable physical and emotional range, D'Onofrio has appeared on Broadway, on popular television shows, and in more than 50 films since 1983, among them *Full Metal Jacket*, *JFK*, *The Player*, *Malcolm X*, *Ed Wood*, *The Whole Wide World*, *Men in Black*, *Steal This Movie*, and *The Salton Sea*. He earned a 1998 Emmy Award nomination for his guest appearance in *Homicide: Life on the Street*. During the past three years, he has starred as a shrewd New York City detective on another successful television series, *Law & Order: Criminal Intent*. "[D'Onofrio]'s an artist in the best sense of the word," Robert Greenwald, who directed him in *Steal This Movie*, told Mark Kennedy for the Associated Press (August 21, 2000). "He commits to the creative process, wherever it takes him, whatever the toll it will take. He just won't let go of the muse." "When he's in character, he's a completely different person . . . ," Dan Ireland, the director of *The Whole Wide World*, told Tim Townsend for *Velocity Magazine* (November 2000, online). "When we were filming . . . , sometimes I'd forget to call 'Cut!' because I'd be so lost in what Vincent was doing. He took it beyond the point of getting it right. He made it painfully real."

The first of the three children of Gennaro "Gene" D'Onofrio and his wife, Phyllis, Vincent Phillip D'Onofrio was born in the New York City borough of Brooklyn on June 30, 1959. He has two sisters: Elizabeth, who teaches acting, and Toni, who teaches culinary arts. His father reportedly worked as an interior decorator when his children were young; more recently, he has worked as an ac-

tor, director, and professor of film studies at Brevard College, in North Carolina. Vincent D'Onofrio and his siblings grew up in Hawaii, Colorado, and Florida. In a profile of the actor for a Web site devoted to information about him, Barbara Chabai, the editor and publisher of *What*, a Canadian magazine for teens, reported that D'Onofrio's father and mother divorced when their son and daughters were quite young; afterward, his father as well as his mother remained an active presence in the children's lives. According to Chabai, D'Onofrio has recalled that as a boy he was so shy that, on the day he turned six, he hid under his bed in an attempt to avoid appearing at his own birthday party. He enjoyed working behind the scenes at a community theater his father organized. Immediately after young Vincent's first communion at a local Catholic church, Gene D'Onofrio told Tim Townsend, the boy—still wearing his white communion suit—went to the theater to help operate the stage lights for a production of *A Streetcar Named Desire*. In Miami, Florida, in his early teens, D'Onofrio became friendly with Cuban street magicians, who taught him some of their tricks. By performing them himself in public, he began to lose his diffidence and to gain confidence in his abilities. Soon he started to win roles in plays mounted at his father's community theater. "Anytime I would get involved in a play, the kinds of roles that interested me were never the leads, always the supporting parts," he has said, according to Chabai. "The interesting characters that Tennessee Williams wrote, the characters on the periphery."

D'Onofrio graduated from Hialeah–Miami Lakes Senior High School in 1977. He spent the next year or two studying at a college in Colorado and acting with a nearby community-theater troupe. He then moved to New York City, to study acting at the American Stanislavsky Theatre with Sonia Moore and at the Actor's Studio with Sharon Catten. "I did what most actors do in class," he told Tim Townsend. "I sat there and only listened to what made sense to me. But I do use everything I learned every time I act." He also told Townsend that he never feels as if he has prepared for a role completely. "Preparing for a role is like cramming for a test," he explained. "You overcompensate—you learn more than you need to, lots more—so that when you need it, it's [available in your memory]. . . . You can never overdo it. Even the stuff you think you don't use is useful. Maybe it informs the way you walk or talk—some detail. Because when something's missing, you have to *act* "—with unconvincing results. During this period D'Onofrio appeared in several New York University student films and supported himself by working as a bouncer at various clubs in New York City and as a bodyguard for Yul Brynner and other actors. In 1984 he became a full member of the Stanislavsky Theatre and performed in its productions of Robert Sherwood's *The Petrified Forest*; David Mamet's *Sexual Perversity in Chicago*; Israel Horovitz's *The Indian Wants the Bronx*; and *Of*

Mice and Men, the stage adaptation of John Steinbeck's classic novel. That same year D'Onofrio made his Broadway stage debut, in *Open Admissions*, a Tony and Drama Desk Award–nominated play by Shirley Lauro, which centers on the interactions between an unhappy, distracted female professor of speech at an urban college and a brilliant but illiterate young black student who is desperate to better himself. D'Onofrio's ability to maintain an authentic-sounding Brooklyn accent during his audition won him the role, that of another student.

Earlier, in 1983, the actor had launched his film career, with a part in the sophomoric teen comedy *The First Turn-On!!* Next, he was cast in another little-noticed movie, *It Don't Pay to Be an Honest Citizen* (1984). With his third appearance on the silver screen, in Stanley Kubrick's gritty *Full Metal Jacket* (1987), which follows a group of Marines from the rigors of basic training to the horrors of battle during the Vietnam War, he captured the attention of moviegoers and critics alike. To prepare for his role, that of an unstable, overweight recruit, D'Onofrio—at Kubrick's request—gained more than 50 pounds (60 or 75, according to some sources), by increasing his daily intake to 10,000 calories. (He later lost the extra weight with the help of a personal exercise trainer.) "The impressive Vincent D'Onofrio . . . ," Rita Kempley wrote in a review of *Full Metal Jacket* for the *Washington Post* (June 26, 1987), "goes over the edge. . . . His unfortunate Pvt. Leonard (Gomer) Pyle [is] a fat, slow-witted boy whose stupid grin becomes a psycho's secret smile when something snaps under the rigors of war games. It is a broad, scary and skilled performance." Writing for the *New York Times* (September 23, 1987), Thomas McElroy found D'Onofrio's characterization "chilling."

D'Onofrio was next cast in two light-hearted movies: the formulaic *Adventures in Babysitting* (1987), starring Elisabeth Shue, and *Mystic Pizza* (1988), a romantic coming-of-age comedy featuring Julia Roberts. In *The Blood of Heroes* (1988), a science-fiction film about a brutal sport played in a post-apocalyptic world, he portrayed one of the athletes; in *Signs of Life* (1989), a drama set on the coast of Maine, he depicted a boatyard worker committed to caring for his retarded brother.

In the 1990s D'Onofrio appeared in three movies per year, on average. He starred as a killer in the ill-received *Naked Tango* (1990), which disappointed fans of its writer and director, Leonard Schrader, the co-writer of the screenplay for *Kiss of the Spider Woman*. His credits in 1991 included roles in Joel Schumacher's *Dying Young*, a sentimental romantic drama about a woman (Julia Roberts) who falls in love with a man (Campbell Scott) who is terminally ill, and in the highly publicized and exceedingly controversial *JFK*, the director Oliver Stone's interpretation of the events surrounding the assassination of President John F. Kennedy, in 1963. D'Onofrio portrayed Bill Newman, a real eyewitness to the killing, whose testimony about what he thought he saw is part of the official record of the investigation into the assassination. While a fair number of critics roundly dismissed *JFK* as the product of paranoia and conspiracy theories, others found it exciting, skillfully made, and emotionally powerful. D'Onofrio appeared in two of the most highly praised films of 1992: *The Player* and *Malcolm X*. In *The Player*, director Robert Altman's biting satire of the Hollywood movie industry, he portrayed a frustrated screenwriter who, mistakenly thought to have threatened the life of a duplicitous Hollywood movie-studio executive (Tim Robbins), is murdered himself. D'Onofrio again depicted the Kennedy-assassination witness Bill Newman in Spike Lee's acclaimed biopic *Malcolm X*, which starred Denzel Washington as the charismatic Nation of Islam minister, who was murdered 15 months after the killing of John Kennedy. In 1993 D'Onofrio had roles in the movies *Household Saints*, *Mr. Wonderful*, and *Being Human*.

In the director Tim Burton's film *Ed Wood* (1994), about the idiosyncratic, cross-dressing, real-life Edward D. Wood Jr., regarded as "the worst director of all time," D'Onofrio played a young Orson Welles, a towering figure in American cinema and one of Wood's heroes. In the *Washington Post* (October 7, 1994), Hal Hinson described as "magnificent" the scene in which Wood (played by Johnny Depp) meets Welles; D'Onofrio, he wrote, portrayed Welles with "uncanny accuracy"—a sentiment shared by a number of other critics, who also singled out that scene for praise. In 1996, in addition to other film appearances, D'Onofrio co-produced and starred in *The Whole Wide World*, Dan Ireland's directorial debut, in which he played Robert E. Howard, the prolific 1930s pulp-fiction writer who created the well-known characters Conan the Barbarian and Red Sonja. The screenplay was based on a memoir by Novalyne Price Ellis, a close friend of Howard's, played by Renée Zellweger in the film. "Vincent D'Onofrio is commanding as Robert," James Berardinelli wrote for his ReelViews Web site, "presenting him as a 'morose, ungainly misfit among men' [as Howard once described one of his characters] whose shy, gentle nature is occasionally ripped apart by brief, psychotic episodes." After describing D'Onofrio's performance as "wildly eccentric," Jack Mathews wrote for the *Los Angeles Times* (December 23, 1996, on-line), "Howard is so loud at times, you'll be wishing you could get your hands on his volume control. But at other times, when Howard's desperation for Novalyne leaves him literally tongue-tied, D'Onofrio's expression melts your heart." For his work in *The Whole Wide World*, D'Onofrio won the award for best actor at the 1996 Seattle International Film Festival. At the 2004 Academy Awards ceremony, Zellweger, who won an Oscar for best supporting actress for her role in *Cold Mountain* in 2003 and who to date has appeared on the silver screen with him only in *The Whole Wide World*, thanked D'Onofrio "for teaching me how to work."

D'Onofrio also co-produced and starred in *Guy* (1997), directed by Michael Lindsay-Hogg from a screenplay by Kirby Dick. *Guy* is about a young woman (Hope Davis) who, determined to document the life of a complete stranger, follows a young man (D'Onofrio) everywhere with her camera. The woman, whose name is not revealed, never asks Guy for permission to film him. "Guy is taken aback by this intrusion into his life," Greg Lee wrote for boxoffice.com. "He responds sequentially with bewilderment, anger, resignation and ardor. D'Onofrio portrays Guy's range of emotions—and his general manner—with such surprising realism it's easy to forget about the movie projector's buzz." Lee also wrote, "Vincent D'Onofrio's talent as a character actor is indisputable. With last year's *The Whole Wide World*, D'Onofrio showed he had a knack for producing as well, even as he carried a lead role; *Guy* is no different." Like *The Whole Wide World*, *Guy* attracted few moviegoers.

By contrast, D'Onofrio's next film, Barry Sonnenfeld's science-fiction comedy *Men in Black* (1997), was a smash hit, grossing more than $250 million in box-office receipts. Adapted from a comic-book series by Lowell Cunningham, *Men in Black* follows two special agents (Will Smith and Tommy Lee Jones) who hunt for "immigrants" from space who masquerade as humans. D'Onofrio played an irascible farmer named Edgar who becomes the agents' target after a flying saucer collides with his truck and an alien (in the form of a giant cockroach) usurps his body. "Stumbling around with his head at an odd angle and folds of skin hanging off him, [D'Onofrio] doesn't do much more than snort and drool whenever he's on screen," Charles Taylor wrote for Salon.com (July 4, 1997), "but he made me laugh a lot anyway. He's like a cross between something from *The Texas Chainsaw Massacre* and a haywire carnival ride." For his performance in *Men in Black*, in 1998 D'Onofrio was nominated for a Blockbuster Entertainment Award and won a Saturn Award for best supporting actor from the American Academy of Science Fiction, Fantasy & Horror Films.

In *The Newton Boys* (1998), an ensemble film directed by Richard Linklater, D'Onofrio starred alongside Matthew McConaughey, Ethan Hawke, and Skeet Ulrich, as brothers who escape their hand-to-mouth farmers' lives by becoming bank robbers. D'Onofrio executive produced and acted in the universally panned AIDS-themed drama *The Velocity of Gary* (1998), directed by Dan Ireland. The next year D'Onofrio appeared in *The Thirteenth Floor*, a science-fiction thriller; *Spanish Judges*, a crime caper; and *That Championship Season*, a made-for-television remake of a 1982 movie (adapted by Jason Miller from his Pulitzer Prize–winning stage play of 1972) about four former high-school basketball champions who, in the course of a reunion with their onetime coach, discover some long-buried truths about themselves. Paul Sorvino played the coach and also directed.

D'Onofrio portrayed the 1960s countercultural icon Abbie Hoffman in *Steal This Movie* (2000), which he also co-executive produced; Janeane Garofalo was cast as Hoffman's wife, Anita. Abbie Hoffman, who died in 1989, was active in the civil rights and anti–Vietnam War movements; he was a co-founder of and major figure in the Youth International Party (whose acronym is the source of the term "Yippies," as Hoffman and his fellow activists called themselves) and attracted much attention for his public criticisms of American corporate culture. When Stephen Lemons, who interviewed D'Onofrio for Salon.com (August 18, 2000), asked the actor whether he found portraying a fictional character or a real person more difficult, D'Onofrio answered, "There's a lot of shame that goes on when you're playing someone who has really lived and has passed. You're struggling with it all the time. I am, anyway. When I played Robert Howard in *The Whole Wide World*, I was struggling with it. There's this dual thing where you feel real good about being able to play this juicy part, and then there's constant shame. Who am I to pretend to know who this guy was? Who am I to represent this guy for people who never knew him? The pressure is unbelievable." "Despite the film's obvious fondness for its subject and for the era, *Steal This Movie* . . . doesn't sanctify either the '60s or the main character, whom Vincent D'Onofrio plays with an appealing, self-conscious gusto," Stephen Holden wrote for the *New York Times* (August 18, 2000, on-line). "Strapping and heroic, D'Onofrio may not physically resemble the more diminutive Hoffman. And the actor's odd Boston-meets-Brooklyn accent sounds somewhat forced. Yet his portrayal of this excitable, mischievous proponent of the 'politics of joy' still emerges as a reasonable enough facsimile."

Also in 2000 D'Onofrio was cast as a serial killer in *The Cell*, a science-fiction horror film that co-starred Jennifer Lopez. The actor told Lemons that he and Lopez deliberately avoided discussing any of their scenes before the actual shooting, in part because, with the permission of the director, Tarsem Singh, he ad-libbed much of the dialogue rather than following the script precisely. "The cool thing about doing a film like that, unlike the *Steal This Movie* part, is you don't have to be social at all. I prefer that. That's more my personality. . . . I don't want anyone to know what I'm going to do." For his work in *The Cell*, D'Onofrio earned nominations for two 2001 prizes, one from the MTV Movie Awards, in the category of best villain, and the other from the Blockbuster Entertainment Awards, for favorite supporting actor in a science-fiction film.

In 2002 D'Onofrio appeared in two television movies—*A Case of Evil*, in which he played Professor Moriarty, the nemesis of Arthur Conan Doyle's famous fictional detective, Sherlock Holmes, and *The Red Sneakers*, which Gregory Hines directed, about a boy (Dempsey Pappion) who gets a magical pair of sneakers from a junk dealer (Hines). Hines had starred with D'Onofrio in an earlier film, the largely forgotten inspirational comedy *Good Luck* (1996), directed by Richard LaBrie. During the shooting of an emotional scene in *Good Luck,* Hines recalled to Tim Townsend, he watched D'Onofrio as the camera operator focused on his face. "Vincent's eyes fill up with tears, but the tear doesn't fall. The scene plays out and the director yells, 'cut!' I said, 'Vincent, what happened, you almost had it. . . . All you had to do was blink and the tear would've fallen.' He said, 'But it didn't come. It wasn't real. It's gotta be a real tear.' So we did it until the tear came."

Also in 2002 D'Onofrio had parts in four feature films: the futuristic *Impostor,* directed by Gary Fleder and co-starring Gary Sinise; the little-noticed *Bark,* with Lisa Kudrow and Lee Tergesen; *The Dangerous Lives of Altar Boys,* about mischievous adolescents in a repressive 1970s Catholic school, in which D'Onofrio played a priest; and D. J. Caruso's exceedingly dark revenge thriller, *The Salton Sea,* in which he played Pooh-Bear, a psychotic drug lord who has "snorted so much [crystal methamphetamine] his nose had to be replaced by a plastic one . . . ," as Peter Travers wrote in a review for *Rolling Stone* (May 9, 2002). "With Pooh-Bear, who lets his pet badger nibble on the [private parts] of his enemies and re-enacts the JFK assassination with pigeons, D'Onofrio creates a rock-the-house villain. He's the fire in the belly of this cool groove of a movie." "Over the years I've played so many [emotionally disturbed] people that I have a whole library of psychology and psychopathy and sociology books in my house," D'Onofrio told Liz Braun. "I've never screwed around when I've played bad guys . . . I want to know what their brain propensity is."

For his guest appearance as a commuter trapped under a subway car in a 1998 episode of the award-winning television series *Homicide: Life on the Street* (1993–99), D'Onofrio was honored with an Emmy Award nomination. He has starred in the NBC drama *Law & Order: Criminal Intent* since its premiere, in 2001. (Like *Law & Order: Special Victims Unit,* the series is an offshoot of the Emmy Award–winning series *Law & Order.*) Steve Vineberg, in the *New York Times* (March 3, 2002), described *Criminal Intent* as a "more cerebral version of *Law & Order* in which the psychology of the perpetrator and the modus operandi of the detective are given equal attention." On the show D'Onofrio plays Robert Goren, a New York City police detective with unusual intuition and brilliant powers of deduction. A writer for *People* (October 29, 2001) credited D'Onofrio's "mesmerizing" performances on *Criminal Intent* with enhancing "the value of the [*Law & Order*] brand." "Bobby Goren takes you through a different story every week," the actor was quoted as saying on the Web site allyourtv.com. "Sometimes it's a 'who-dunnit' or sometimes a 'why-dunnit.' The fun and interesting thing about our show is that the audience knows things my character doesn't and, as the story moves

along, will realize that I know things that they don't. The whole story is a game and we all get to play." Vineberg wrote, "No television cop show has ever put forth a hero as unorthodox as Vincent D'Onofrio's Detective Bobby Goren . . . He's a show-off, and he's a nerd on a mission, fascinated by even the most banal details of police procedure. . . . What really turns him on, though, is the chance to rattle suspects and shake loose their secrets." The role of Goren is a departure for D'Onofrio, who, as a character actor, has usually switched from one character and project to the next. "It's the first time I've ever had to return to a character, which is a little strange," he told Kate O'Hare, as posted on the Web site tv.zap2it.com. "I guess I've gotten used to it, but it's still a bit odd to play the same guy all the time." *Law & Order: Criminal Intent* was nominated for a 2002 People's Choice Award as favorite new television dramatic series.

In 1998, in collaboration with his father and sister Elizabeth, D'Onofrio launched the RiverRun International Film Festival, in Brevard, North Carolina, to promote new directors and screenwriters; since 2003 the festival has been affiliated with the School of Filmmaking at the North Carolina School of the Arts, in Winston-Salem. More than 10,000 people attended the 2003 festival, which offered screenings of 65 films, workshops, panel discussions, and other events.

D'Onofrio met his first wife, the actress Greta Scacchi, on the set of the film *Fires Within* (1991). From their marriage, which ended in divorce in 1993, he has a daughter, Leila. D'Onofrio fathered a son, Elias, with his second wife, the model and photographer Carin van der Donk, whom he married in 1997. According to Ann Oldenburg in *USA Today* (October 17, 2003, on-line) and several other sources, the couple have separated and plan to divorce.

—C.F.T.

Suggested Reading: allyourtv.com; Associated Press Sep. 23, 1987, Aug. 21, 2000; *Chicago Sun-Times* Oct. 7, 1994; hollywood.com; imdb.com; *New York Times* II p37 Mar. 3, 2002; *People* p32 Oct. 29, 2001; Salon.com July 4,1997, Aug. 18, 2000; *Toronto Sun* (on-line) Apr. 24, 2002; *Velocity Magazine* (on-line), Nov. 2000; *Washington Post* June 26, 1987

Selected Films: *Full Metal Jacket,* 1987; *Adventures in Babysitting,* 1987; *Mystic Pizza,* 1988; *The Blood of Heroes,* 1988; *Naked Tango,* 1990; *Dying Young,* 1991; *Fires Within,* 1991; *JFK,* 1991; *The Player,* 1992; *Malcolm X,* 1992; *Household Saints,* 1993; *Being Human,* 1993; *Ed Wood,* 1994; *The Whole Wide World,* 1996; *Guy,* 1997; *Men in Black,* 1997; *The Newton Boys,* 1998; *The Velocity of Gary,* 1998; *Happy Accidents,* 2000; *The Cell,* 2000; *The Salton Sea,* 2002; *The Dangerous Lives of Altar Boys,* 2002; *Impostor,* 2002

Selected Television Programs: *Law & Order: Criminal Intent*, 2001–

Mike Smith/Courtesy of jerrydouglas.com

Douglas, Jerry

May 28, 1956– Guitarist

Address: Jerry Douglas World Headquarters, P.O. Box 58034, Nashville, TN 37205

Jerry Douglas is a master of the Dobro, a descendant of the guitar. Highly in demand in the bluegrass and country-music scenes since the 1970s, he has more than 1,000 recording credits to his name, as a session player, band member, and solo artist skilled in styles ranging from bluegrass to rock to country to jazz. Now, after years of lucrative session work, he has turned his back on such projects to spend more time on his critically acclaimed—if not always commercially successful—solo efforts. "I just turned down a record date with Lynyrd Skynyrd," Jerry Douglas remarked in an interview with Andy Ellis for *Guitar Player* (July 1, 2002). "It freaks me out to say 'no,' but if I want to have a solo career, I can't be perceived as a session guy who jumps at everything that's thrown at him. That's what I've always done, but now when I dish out my licks, they'll go on my albums."

Gerald Calvin Douglas was born on May 28, 1956 in Warren, Ohio, to a West Virginia couple who had moved to Ohio to find work in the local steel mills. His father, John Douglas, performed with a bluegrass band on weekends. Early on Jerry listened to recordings of the Dobro player Burkett Graves (known as Buck Graves, Josh Graves, and

Uncle Buck), who joined Lester Flatt and Earl Scruggs's band, the Foggy Mountain Boys, in the late 1950s. "I loved the sound," he told Nick Barraclough for BBC Radio 2 (July 24, 2002, on-line). As a youngster Douglas began playing a "cheap Sears and Roebuck guitar," as he described it to Barraclough, whose strings—possibly in order to create a sound like a Dobro's—were raised so high above the guitar, and were therefore so tight, that he had difficulty pushing them down with his small fingers. When he was about seven, his father took him to a concert of the Foggy Mountain Boys, where for the first time he saw Graves's innovative picking technique. At home after the concert, his father "just took this piece of wood and raised the strings on the guitar just a little bit more than they already were . . . ," as he recalled to Barraclough. "That worked really well until one day I came home from school and my guitar had exploded from all the tension! So I had to go in search of a real Dobro. The exploding guitar is really what gave me the start!" Although he had enjoyed singing "all the time," as he told Barraclough, he stopped singing entirely when he took up the Dobro, because, as he explained, he thought that the Dobro was "what my voice should be."

The Dobro guitar was invented in 1926 by John Dopyera, a Slovakian immigrant. With his brother Rudy, Dopyera developed the first metal-bodied National guitar and soon afterward the Dobro (derived from **Do**pyera **bro**thers), whose body is made of wood or steel. The Dobro has been described as looking as if a hubcap is attached to the body under the strings, where the opening to the soundwell is in ordinary acoustic guitars. The "hubcap" is the coverplate of a cone-shaped resonator, which allows the guitar to have great volume and sustain; those qualities made it a very popular band instrument in the 1920s and 1930s, since its sound was not drowned out by the horns, as that of acoustic guitars was. Like the slide guitar, the Dobro rests horizontally on the player's lap; instead of pressing the strings to the fretboard with the left hand, the player uses a small tube, usually made of metal, and touches the strings lightly, so that they do not reach the fretboard. The player uses a fingerpick on the right hand to pluck the strings. A trademarked name, "Dobro" is now owned by the Gibson Guitar Corp.; similar instruments are known as resonator or resophonic guitars. Douglas once helped design a new Dobro for Gibson.

By the age of 13, Douglas was performing with his father's band, the West Virginia Travelers. When he was 17, the group appeared at a local festival alongside the Country Gentlemen, an esteemed ensemble of bluegrass musicians. Douglas's playing so impressed the members of the Country Gentlemen that, then and there, they asked him to join their band. The Country Gentlemen opened doors to new opportunities for the teenage Douglas. He recalled in his BBC interview going to New York City with the band for his first recording session: "I'd never been to New York, I'd never been on an aeroplane. . . . I fly to New York City, and you know, it's a culture shock! Before I'd even played a note I was already in a completely different world to anything I'd ever been in. . . . We stayed in a legendary hotel called The Chelsea Hotel, which was at that time really a home for avant-garde artists and a lot of rich junkies! I remember walking into the hotel, getting my key, going to the elevator and the first thing that steps out of the elevator is a lady with this huge fruit design on her head, like a Carmen Miranda. It just started off so strange. Making the record was the simple part! But my first impressions of New York City were that it was wild! It was completely crazy!"

After a year or so with the Country Gentlemen, Douglas joined J.D. Crowe and the New South, a bluegrass group led by the banjoist James Dee Crowe. Douglas's Dobro work is said to have contributed significantly to the group's highly acclaimed, eponymous 1975 long-playing record (LP). He left the band in 1976 to form, with Ricky Skaggs and Vince Gill, the band Boone Creek, which introduced a new generation to bluegrass music. After Boone Creek released an eponymous album, in 1977, and One Way Track, in 1978, Skaggs disbanded the group to join the Hot Band, fronted by Emmylou Harris. In 1979 Douglas felt confident enough to record his first solo album, Fluxology, whose title refers to his nickname, Flux. "Somewhere in my 20's, I began to play like myself, not like someone else," he told Daniel Menaker for the New York Times Magazine (January 27, 2002). The unique sound of the Dobro was not easily captured in a studio setting in 1978, when Douglas arrived in Nashville to make his recording. "Most engineers didn't know how to record a Dobro," he recalled in his interview with Andy Ellis. "They'd just set up a [mike] and hope for the best. At that point, it was a novelty instrument—something thin and whiney that producers used to label a track as a country song. But I was playing the Dobro differently from the guys they'd recorded before. I approached it as a lead instrument, and engineers had to learn to dig out the sound. Eventually, they found the sweet spot: It's on the treble-string side, right between the screen and the coverplate." For the All Music Guide (online), Ken Dryden called Fluxology a "marvelous original."

In the late 1970s Douglas became a member of the Whites, a family band made up of the legendary mandolin player Buck White and his two daughters, Sharon and Cheryl, who provided vocal harmonies. Meanwhile, Douglas was also making a name for himself as a session musician, contributing to such albums as Emmylou Harris's Roses in the Snow (1980) and Ricky Skaggs's Don't Get Above Your Raising (1981). Indeed, he became something of a cottage industry in Nashville as a session guitar player. All told his name appears on upwards of 1,000 recordings; he has played with such diverse artists and groups as Joan Baez, Garth Brooks, Mary Chapin Carpenter, Glen Campbell,

Rosanne Cash, Ray Charles, the Chieftains, Bill Frissell, Art Garfunkel, Vince Gill, Amy Grant, Waylon Jennings, George Jones, Led Kaapana, Alison Krauss, Lyle Lovett, Martina McBride, Reba McEntire, the Nitty Gritty Dirt Band, Mark O'Connor, Phish, Michelle Shocked, Paul Simon, James Taylor, Travis Tritt, Tammy Wynette, Trisha Yearwood, and the New York City–based Orchestra of St. Luke's. With the last-named ensemble, he joined the violinist Joshua Bell, the Scottish composer Patrick Doyle, and the composer/instrumentalists Edgar Meyer and Wynton Marsalis in providing music for the album Listen to the Storyteller: A Trio of Musical Tales from Around the World (1999), which was narrated by Marsalis, the British actress Kate Winslet, and the Native American actor Graham Greene. Listen to the Storyteller won the 2000 Grammy Award for best children's spoken-word album.

In 1982 Douglas recorded his second solo album, Fluxedo; a year later, as a member of the group New South, he earned his first Grammy Award, for best country instrumental, for "Fireball." His next solo albums were Under the Wire (1986), Changing Channels (1987), and Plant Early (1989). With the mandolin player Sam Bush, the violinist Mark O'Connor, the bassist Edgar Meyer, and the banjoist Bela Fleck, in 1988 he formed the short-lived bluegrass quintet Strength in Numbers. Their album, The Telluride Sessions (1989), was highly lauded. During the next decade Douglas recorded such notable solo efforts as Slide Rule (1992), Skip, Hop & Wobble (1994), and Yonder (1996). The year 1996 also saw the release of the genre-bending experimental album Bourbon and Rosewater, on which he performed with the Indian slide guitarist Vishwa Mohan Bhatt; Bhatt's instrument, which he modified himself and dubbed the Mohan vina ("vina" being the name for several Indian plucked stringed instruments), has been described as a cross between the guitar and the sitar. Despite that joint effort and his growing solo oeuvre, Douglas had not yet received mainstream recognition for his work outside Nashville music circles and longed to be recognized as an artist, not merely as a session musician (though one so valuable that he received double-scale pay). As he told Jim Bessman for Billboard (May 4, 2002), "At the end of the day, everything you've done that day, every note you play, goes into someone else's column, and you have a faceless identity. I want to change that and do something for myself." Toward that end Douglas released his solo album Restless on the Farm (1998). In one of the enthusiastic reviews the recording earned, Geoffrey Himes wrote for the Washington Post (November 6, 1998), "Jerry Douglas can do some amazing things on the dobro, but his best moments come not on his solos but in his dialogues with other musicians. For it's his ability to echo someone else's vocal or instrument phrase and then recast it in the sliding, shimmering shapes of the metallic, resonating instrument in his lap that makes him special."

In 1998 Alison Krauss asked Douglas to fill in on a tour with her band, Union Station; the collaboration proved so rewarding that she asked him, without success at first, to join Alison Krauss and Union Station on a permanent basis. His refusal "was never really a serious issue, but it did get awkward after a while," he told Daniel Menaker. "One day I was sitting in the bus and the other guys were sort of looking at me, and Alison just got up and came over to where I was sitting and said, 'Jerry, please join the band.' So I did." He has been a full-time member since then, but since Union Station works only six months a year, he still has time for other projects. One involved the soundtrack for Ethan and Joel Coen's film *O Brother, Where Art Thou?* (2000), a comic takeoff on Homer's *Odyssey* that is set in the 1930s rural American South. Because Douglas knew many mountain-music players personally, T-Bone Burnett, who produced the music for the film, asked him to gather the best ones to record some old standards. Among the musicians who recorded songs for the soundtrack were James Carter, Harry McClintock, Norman Blake, Alison Krauss, Emmylou Harris, Leah Peasall, the Fairfield Four, and the Stanley Brothers. Douglas also played on three tracks, among them "I Am a Man of Constant Sorrow," performed by the Soggy Bottom Boys. The soundtrack was hugely successful—the album made from it remained in the upper reaches of *Billboard*'s charts for more than 80 weeks—and it led to a revitalized interest in mountain and bluegrass music.

In his most recent solo effort, *Lookout for Hope* (2002), Douglas combined a variety of genres. "I tried to think of what to call it, 'country-punk-disco,' or something. But it's more like 'new acoustic,'" he explained to Jim Bessman. "That's a vague term, but it's what I'm doing: bluegrass music with a rock 'n' roll/jazz attitude." Most of the album's tracks are instrumentals; the two with vocals offer James Taylor singing "The Suit" and the Irish crooner Maura O'Connell singing "Footsteps Fall." To promote the album, Douglas assembled a band and toured in late 2002 and early 2003.

At the 2003 Grammy Awards ceremony, Douglas won two prizes for his work with Union Station, for best bluegrass album for *Live* and best country instrumental performance for "Cluck Old Hen"—bringing his total number of Grammys to eight. (He won four in 2001 alone, for his collaborations with various other artists.) He and his wife, Jill, live in Nashville. The couple have two daughters and a son.

—C.M.

Suggested Reading: *All Music Guide* (on-line); BBC Radio 2 (on-line) July 24, 2002; BBC Radio 2 Country Features (on-line); *Guitar Player* p39 July 1, 2002; Jerry Douglas Web site; *New York Times Magazine* p26+ Jan. 27, 2002, with photo; *Philadelphia City Paper* (on-line) Mar. 19–26, 1998; *Washington Post* B p6 Feb. 4, 1991, N p18 May 3, 1996, N p11 Nov. 6, 1998

Selected Recordings: *Fluxology*, 1979; *Fluxedo*, 1982; *Under the Wire*, 1986; *Changing Channels*, 1987; *Everything Is Gonna Work Out Fine*, 1987; *Plant Early*, 1989; *Slide Rule*, 1992; *Skip, Hop & Wobble*, 1994; *Yonder*, 1996; *Restless on the Farm*, 1998; *Lookout for Hope*, 2002

Duesberg, Peter H.

Dec. 2, 1936– Molecular biologist; virologist

Address: 229 Stanley Hall #3206, University of California, Berkeley, CA 94720-3206

In persevering as a scientist and as a so-called AIDS denialist or AIDS dissenter, the molecular biologist and virologist Peter H. Duesberg has been guided by an article of faith expressed by the preeminent physicist Albert Einstein: "The important thing is to not stop questioning." During the 1960s and 1970s, Duesberg gained prominence as a researcher specializing in retroviruses—viruses whose genetic, or hereditary, material is in the form of RNA (ribonucleic acid) rather than DNA (deoxyribonucleic acid). On the strength of his discoveries, he earned tenure as a professor at the University of California at Berkeley (UC–Berkeley) in 1973 and was elected to the prestigious National Academy of Sciences in 1986. Ironically, several years before he received that honor, Duesberg—who had had no trouble obtaining ample funding for his projects and had enjoyed the near-universal respect of his colleagues—saw his standing in the professional community begin to decline. That process began in 1983, when he publicly questioned the widely held theory that cancer is caused by mutations in genes; instead, he had come to believe, the culprit is the presence of abnormal numbers of chromosomes. His reputation plummeted to new lows in 1988, after he published a paper in the professional journal *Science* stating his conviction that AIDS does not result from infection with HIV, the human immunodeficiency virus; in other words, he rejected the cause-and-effect relationship of HIV and AIDS, which all but a tiny number of experts in the field have long considered as virtually beyond doubt. Rather, he contended, and still maintains, in the United States AIDS can be traced in large part to damage to victims' immune systems from the overuse of recreational drugs of the sorts popular among homosexuals (in particular, aphrodisiac nitrite inhalants, or "poppers"), since severely weakened immune systems make people highly vulnerable to a host of illnesses—some of them potentially fatal—whose symptoms

Courtesy of Peter H. Duesberg

Peter H. Duesberg

mirror those of maladies that have been linked to HIV infection. Moreover, according to Duesberg, many supposed victims of AIDS die not from a virus-caused illness but from what he and other AIDS dissenters refer to as "death by prescription": the effects of anti-HIV drugs (also called anti-AIDS drugs or anti-retrovirals) such as AZT; originally formulated to kill cancer cells, AZT is highly toxic and, he believes, leads to death when taken indefinitely. Duesberg has also asserted that what has been called an epidemic of AIDS in Africa is a misnomer on two counts, because the numbers of people who are ill are not extraordinary, and because those individuals, who often suffer from severe malnutrition as well as parasitic and other infections, are victims not of a newly emergent disease but of the array of diseases that have afflicted people in parts of Africa that lack clean drinking water. In support of his position, as detailed in his most recent paper on the subject, in the *Journal of Bioscience and Bioengineering* (June 2003), published by the Society for Biotechnology, in Japan, Duesberg and his two co-authors wrote that the "virus/AIDS hypothesis . . . is burdened with numerous paradoxes," which they listed in the form of questions: "Why is there no HIV in most AIDS patients, only antibodies against it? Why would HIV take 10 years from infection to AIDS? . . . Why is there no vaccine against AIDS? . . . Why is AIDS in the US and Europe not random like other viral epidemics? Why did AIDS not rise and then decline exponentially owing to antiviral immunity like all other viral epidemics? . . . Why would only HIV carriers get AIDS who use either recreational or anti-HIV drugs or are subject to malnutrition?" Their own investigations, Duesberg and his

co-authors wrote, show that "AIDS is not contagious, . . . not treatable by vaccines or antiviral drugs, and HIV is just a passenger virus." A "passenger virus"—a term seldom used except in articles by Duesberg or about his theories—is a virus that accompanies other microorganisms but is itself harmless.

Duesberg's theories about AIDS, as presented in his 1988 and 2003 papers and many other articles as well as in his books, speeches, and interviews, have appalled and angered many other scientists, some of whom have warned that the dissemination of his ideas might seriously hamper efforts to control the spread of the HIV virus, and in some cases has already done so. As an example, they have cited the stance taken until recently by Thabo Mbeki, who in 1999 was elected president of South Africa, where at least 10 percent of the population is HIV-positive: based partly on what he had read on Internet postings by Duesberg and other AIDS denialists, Mbeki questioned the existence of AIDS as a distinct disease, expressed his doubts about the HIV/AIDS connection, and declared that prescribing anti-HIV drugs to people said to be infected with the virus would be irresponsible, in light of such drugs' toxicity; those urging their distribution, he charged, were waging a "campaign of intellectual intimidation and terrorism" akin to "the racist apartheid tyranny we opposed," as he put it in a letter to then-President Bill Clinton, as quoted by Agence France-Presse (April 19, 2000, on-line). Mbeki therefore would not allow South Africa to accept such drugs, even if they were free, and recommended instead the use of traditional remedies to fight the illnesses attributed to HIV. Critics of Mbeki's AIDS policy, who are also critics of Duesberg's theories, have noted, according to the London-based Medical Research Council, that between 1998 and 2003 the number of known deaths of people aged 15 to 49 in South Africa rose 68 percent, from 272,000 to 457,000, as reported in *Medical News Today* (March 3, 2004, on-line), and that AIDS was responsible for most of the increase. Had Mbeki allowed AZT and other anti-retroviral drugs to be administered, these critics have said, far fewer people would have died.

In response to the assertions of Duesberg and other AIDS-denialists, the National Institute of Allergy and Infectious Diseases (NIAID), a division of the National Institutes of Health (NIH, an arm of the U.S. Department of Health and Human Services), has posted on its Web site a multipage fact sheet entitled "The Evidence That HIV Causes AIDS." The first among the pieces of evidence offered on the site is that the AIDS virus is strongly associated with HIV: the blood of AIDS patients contains antibodies to HIV, which indicates HIV infection; the virus can be isolated from their blood and reproduced in the laboratory (thanks to state-of-the-art microbiological techniques); and when uninfected people become infected with HIV, through sexual intercourse, a blood transfusion, or another routes, they develop AIDS if not treated with anti-AIDS drugs. In those ways, the virus fulfills conditions described by the pioneering pathologist Robert Koch (1843–1910) and known as Koch's postulates, which for many years scientists have used to determine whether a given bacterium or virus can be considered the cause of a particular disease. The next piece of evidence on the NIAID site is that "the occurrence of AIDS in human populations around the world has closely followed the appearance of HIV. . . . In every region, country and city where AIDS has appeared, evidence of HIV infection has preceded AIDS by just a few years." The next is that "many studies agree that only a single factor, HIV, predicts whether a person will develop AIDS." Thus, a person may develop one of the otherwise rare infections that have become common among AIDS victims, but if that person's blood does not contain HIV, he or she will not develop AIDS. Among other evidence, the NIAID Web page states that "newborn infants have no behavioral risk factors for AIDS, yet many children born to HIV-infected mothers have developed AIDS and died," and when twins are born to an HIV-infected mother, if one twin is born infected with HIV but the other is not, "the HIV-infected twin develops AIDS while the uninfected twin does not."

The NIAID Web site also offers responses to various AIDS-dissenter arguments, which it labels "myths." One myth, according to NIAID, is that in Africa, "AIDS is nothing more than a new name for old diseases." In refuting that belief, the NIAID acknowledges that many of the diseases seen in African AIDS patients have afflicted Africans for many years, but stresses that only since the appearance of HIV have such diseases become common not only in the very young, the elderly, and the malnourished but among previously healthy young adults and well-nourished members of the middle class as well. The NIAID also labels as a myth the belief that "AZT and other antiretroviral drugs, not HIV, cause AIDS," pointing out that "the vast majority of people with AIDS never received antiretroviral drugs," and it offers evidence against the beliefs that "AIDS among transfusion recipients is due to underlying diseases that necessitated the transfusion, rather than to HIV" and that "high usage of clotting factor concentrate, not HIV" causes AIDS in hemophiliacs.

Since Duesberg's emergence as an AIDS denialist, in 1988, his colleagues in the scientific community, with rare exceptions, have denounced or ignored him, and funding for his work has dried up. Nevertheless, in his book *Inventing the AIDS Virus* (1996) and elsewhere, he has continued to propound his theories vigorously. He has also continued to respond to the many critics who have tried to refute his theories. Those critics include Robert C. Gallo, hailed as the co-discoverer (with Luc Montagnier of France) of the causal link between HIV and AIDS, who, for 30 years, directed the Laboratory of Tumor Cell Biology at the National Cancer Institute, a division of the NIH. Duesberg, Gallo

charged in an interview with Jeff Miller for *Discover* (June 1988), was "confusing people. The public has no way of judging that Duesberg's claims are totally unfounded." In a special report in *Science* (December 9, 1994) that was devoted to an evaluation of Duesberg's theories, Jon Cohen quoted Warren Winkelstein Jr., an epidemiologist then associated with UC–Berkeley, as saying that to describe HIV as harmless was "irresponsible, with terribly serious consequences." Another of Duesberg's detractors is Robert A. Weinberg of the Massachusetts Institute of Technology, a leading researcher into the origins of cancer in humans, who, in a conversation with Michelle Locke for the Associated Press (May 27, 2000), likened Duesberg to a "man who is shipwrecked on a desert island, looks around, asks if there's a government on the island and if so, he announces himself to be against it." His critics have noted that Duesberg and other AIDS denialists have conducted little or no hands-on research on HIV or AIDS and have had little or no clinical experience with AIDS patients; rather, they have arrived at their theories by reviewing the research or reports of others. In doing so, according to his critics, they have often misinterpreted or misrepresented others' conclusions and dismissed or ignored studies that do not support their views, that contain inconsequential weaknesses, or that do not meet their impossible-to-satisfy standards of definitive proof.

Most reviewers of *Inventing the AIDS Virus*, which Duesberg wrote for the general public, also found his arguments unconvincing. In the *New York Times Book Review* (April 7, 1996), for example, the microbiologist June E. Osborn, a former chairperson of the National Commission on AIDS, wrote, "Mr. Duesberg's credentials make his assertions both distracting and disabling of preventive response. Denial has always been the most devastating social and political dynamic of the AIDS epidemic—and his book feeds it abundantly. In sum, this book is destructive of personal morale, prevention efforts and public understanding of both HIV/AIDS and of biomedical science in general. It has the potential to wreak serious harm at a crucial point in the AIDS epidemic, which has been judged by many to be one of the greatest public health challenges of our time."

Duesberg is not without defenders. Among them is Harry Rubin, a specialist in cell and tumor biology and a colleague of his at UC–Berkeley, who told Jeff Miller in 1988, "I don't necessarily agree with everything that Peter is saying. But I *do* support his questioning the simplistic idea that this very complex syndrome is caused by this one virus." Rubin also said, "He has the right to dissent, and I feel that what he says deserves to be taken seriously." According to Christoph Lengauer, an assistant professor of oncology at the Johns Hopkins University School of Medicine, Duesberg has provided a valuable service: as Lengauer told Michelle Locke, "I think [Duesberg] has a tendency to polarize, which is good because that's what science is lacking nowadays. It's lacking a discussion." The summer of 2004 saw the publication of *Oncogenes, Aneuploidy and AIDS: A Scientific Life and Times of Peter H. Duesberg,* by Harvey Bialy, a defense of Duesberg's work that argues that his theories and accomplishments have been distorted by others. Another of Duesberg's champions is Kary B. Mullis, who won the 1993 Nobel Prize in chemistry for his invention of the polymerase chain reaction (PCR), an immensely useful technique for multiplying DNA fragments millions of times in a matter of hours. In his introduction to *Inventing the Aids Virus,* Mullis wrote, "I like and respect Peter Duesberg. I don't think he knows necessarily what causes AIDS; we have disagreements about that. But we're both certain about what doesn't cause AIDS. We have not been able to discover any good reasons why most of the people on earth believe that AIDS is a disease caused by a virus called HIV. There is simply no scientific evidence demonstrating that this is true."

Mullis's last sentence is discussed in a thought-provoking essay posted by Johan "Jo" van Schalkwyk, a South African–born physician, on his Web site anaesthetist.com. Under the essay's title, "Duesberg's Dismal Failure," the author added in parentheses, "And why we should perhaps, just perhaps, be grateful for him!" Van Schalkwyk wrote that personal attacks on Duesberg or Mullis because of their views on HIV and AIDS are "inappropriate," since the men "seem to be really bright people, at least formerly at the cutting edge of their disciplines." In the contradictory arguments about HIV and AIDS presented by Duesberg and his critics, van Schalkwyk identified a "clash of philosophies" regarding the very nature of scientific proof. Early in the essay he defined "scientific proof" as "an accumulated body of evidence that proves 'beyond reasonable doubt' (or possibly, as Mullis has put it, 'at least with a high probability') that a scientific theory is true." Van Schalkwyk then referred to ideas of the Scottish philosopher David Hume (1711–76), who described what is called the "Problem of Induction": "Can we, knowing what has gone before, ever be sure in our knowledge of what is to come?" He then explained why, as he put it, "unfortunately for us, it turns out that the answer is 'no!'" Van Schalkwyk next turned to the writings of the Austrian-British philosopher Karl Popper (1902–94), who rejected the belief that knowledge of any phenomenon can be 100 percent certain. Indeed, as he explained, Popper showed "quite convincingly" that "as the information content of a scientific theorem increases, so its *probability* [that is, the probability that every statement in it is true] must decrease, for the probability of two assertions taken together must be less than the probability of each on its own, but clearly the information content of two assertions *must* together be greater than that of each alone." In summary, Van Schalkwyk wrote, "Hume tells us that, however many observations we make, we cannot be sure that we will in the future never make an observation that refutes

our pet theory! And Popper shows us that, the more 'likely' a theory is to be true, the more trivial it is!"—that is, the less information there is to support it. Van Schalkwyk then presented another definition of science: "Science is the body of assertions that can be disproved!" In other words, all theories must contain statements that can be tested, either by means of observation or experiment. The attacks on the HIV/AIDS hypothesis made by Duesberg and others who share his views, he wrote, "are almost invariably based on 'inadequacy of proof' rather than 'falsification'" (the latter being demonstrations of the falsity or incorrectness of any statements); he then showed in what ways representative contentions of the AIDS denialists are irrelevant, incorrect, illogical, or emotional rather than scientific. Van Schalkwyk also asserted that it is equally vital for those who support the HIV/AIDS hypothesis to reformulate all statements in their own theories to make them testable and refutable.

Van Schalkwyk concluded, "We cannot simply make bland statements like 'HIV causes AIDS.' We must provide practical, relevant, and testable (*falsifiable*) assertions that should allow 'dissident scientists' to attack our standpoint using the scientific approach of falsification. Needless to say, we should welcome *well-formulated* attacks, for science can only proceed by the identification of problems, the creation and refinement of explanatory hypotheses, and the testing of these hypotheses for their ability to withstand the sharpest arrows we can shoot at them. In this sense, and this sense alone, we should welcome criticism from Professor Duesberg and his colleagues. We should perhaps be grateful to Prof. Duesberg for providing us with an opportunity to explore the nature of science, and see how badly one can go off the rails if one concentrates on 'proof of causation' rather than 'falsification.'"

Peter H. Duesberg was born to Richard Duesberg and Hilde Saettele on December 2, 1936 in Münster, Germany. His mother was a physician, his father a professor of internal medicine. With the exception of a year at the University of Basel, in Switzerland (1958–59), Duesberg received his formal education, from primary school through postgraduate work, in what was then West Germany. He earned an intermediate degree in chemistry from the University of Würzburg in 1958, and a diploma (equivalent to a bachelor's degree) in chemistry from the University of Munich in 1961. In 1963 he completed his Ph.D. in chemistry at the University of Frankfurt. That year Duesberg also served as a postdoctoral fellow at the Max Planck Institute for Virus Research, in Tübingen, Germany.

Duesberg recalled to Tom Bethell for the *American Spectator* (June 2000) that at that time he was looking for "a hot issue in molecular biology that I could work on before I settled down in some drug company to make fertilizers. Everybody said 'go west.' Everybody was saying that they had recently found viruses that cause cancer. That would be important." That advice spurred him to write to Wendell Stanley, the first scientist to win a Nobel Prize for discoveries about viruses and a professor of biochemistry at UC–Berkeley, expressing his wish to work at that school. With Stanley's help, he succeeded in getting a job as a postdoctoral fellow and assistant research virologist at UC–Berkeley in 1964. He earned promotions to assistant professor in residence in 1968, assistant professor in 1970, associate professor in 1971, and professor in 1973. Since 1989 he has been a member of UC–Berkeley's Department of Molecular and Cell Biology.

Earlier, in 1970, Duesberg had announced his discovery that the virus that causes influenza (commonly called "flu") is not like most viruses, whose genes are linked in one molecule of nucleic acid made of RNA or DNA. Instead, the flu virus is among the few viruses that have a segmented genome; its seven or eight segments are composed of RNA. "This would explain its unique ability to form recombinants by reassortment of subgenomic segments," as Duesberg explained on his Web site. Also in 1970, through his investigations of retroviruses, Duesberg became the first person to isolate a cancer-causing gene and map its structure and components. The importance of that work was recognized by the California Science Center (the largest hands-on science facility for the general public on the West Coast), which named Duesberg the California Scientist of the Year in 1971. His achievements in illuminating the characteristics of retroviruses then and in the following years brought him the first annual American Medical Center Oncology Award, in 1981, and an Outstanding Investigator Award in 1986 from the NIH, which also gave him a seven-year grant and named him the Fogarty scholar-in-residence in 1986–87. Also in 1986 he was made a member of the National Academy of Sciences.

Duesberg has traced the first signs of a decline in his reputation to an article he published in the journal *Nature* (July 21–27, 1983) about his research on oncogenes, or "retroviral transforming genes," which theoretically cause mutations in genes that are supposedly predisposed to such changes; the oncogenes, or onc genes, thus transform a normal cell into a cancerous one. The article was entitled "Retroviral Transforming Genes in Normal Cells?" As W. Wayt Gibbs noted for *Scientific American* (August 2001), "In Duesberg papers the question mark often signals that he is about to yank on the loose threads of a popular theory." In this case Duesberg described findings from his research that, he believed, weakened the oncogene theory of the origin of cancer. Instead, that research and his subsequent investigations have led him to conclude that a far more likely cause of cancer is the presence of abnormal numbers of chromosomes within cells, a condition called "aneuploidy." The descendants of an aneuploid cell are all mutants, with each generation differing from its predecessor. After many divisions, with a corre-

sponding number of changes in the chromosomes, the cell may acquire the ability to reproduce uncontrollably anywhere in the body—that is, it may become cancerous. Duesberg has found some evidence to support this theory and is continuing to search for more—a difficult task, given the paucity of his funding and resources—but so far, he has not convinced many other cancer researchers of the correctness of his theory. Martyn T. Smith, for example, a professor of toxicology at UC–Berkeley, told Lisa M. Krieger for the *San Jose Mercury News* (January 26, 2004, on-line) that Duesberg's theory was too simplistic. "That's not to say that aneuploidy is not important to cancer," he said. "It just means that it is not the only potential mechanism. It could be one of many ways the genome is destabilized. There are many genetic changes. Aneuploidy could be one of them."

Years ago UC–Berkeley officials forced Duesberg to move to a laboratory one-fifth the size of the one he had long used on the school's campus. Despite his inability to secure government or (with one major exception) private funding for his research, and despite the ostracism to which he has been subjected, Duesberg has kept his laboratory operating, albeit with only one assistant. In an interview with Garry Abrams for the *Los Angeles Times* (May 21, 1991), he explained why he had continued to propound his unpopular theories about HIV and AIDS: "Sometimes you have to be cranky and speak up, if social responsibility means anything."

From his first marriage, Duesberg has three adult daughters. With his second wife, he has a son who is now in elementary school. In his spare time he likes to roller skate.

—M.H.

Suggested Reading: *American Spectator* June 2000; Associated Press May 27, 2000; (London) *Times* (on-line) May 11, 1992; *Los Angeles Times* p1+ May 21, 1991, with photos; *San Jose Mercury News* (on-line) Jan. 26, 2004; *Science* p1485+ Mar. 25, 1988, with photos, p1642+ Dec. 9, 1999; *Scientific American* p30+ Aug. 2001; Bialy, Harvey. *Oncogenes, Aneuploidy and AIDS: A Scientific Life and Times of Peter H. Duesberg*, 2004

Selected Books: *Infectious AIDS: Have We Been Misled?*, 1995; *Inventing the AIDS Myth*, 1996

Courtesy of the office of John Edwards

Edwards, John

June 10, 1953– U.S. senator from North Carolina (Democrat); 2004 Democratic vice-presidential nominee

Address: United States Senate, 225 Dirksen Office Bldg., Washington, DC 20510

The 2004 presidential campaign began uneasily for the Democratic Party. Its unofficial launch was the Florida Democrats' April 2002 conference, whose slate of speakers was crowded with high-office hopefuls. The country was still grappling with the effects of the September 11, 2001 terrorist attacks on the World Trade Center and the Pentagon, and President George W. Bush held high approval ratings, with the country having rallied behind him in the wake of the attacks. His identification in his 2002 State of the Union address of Iraq, Iran, and North Korea as an "axis of evil" and as the greatest threats facing America was still fresh in the public's minds. Faithful Democrats gathered in Orlando, some out of curiosity to see if former vice president Al Gore, who had been defeated by Bush in the 2000 presidential election, would announce that he intended to run again. Chief among them was Senator Joseph I. "Joe" Lieberman of Connecticut, Gore's running mate, who vowed that he would not enter the presidential primary if Gore sought the nomination again. Other contenders included such veteran Democratic politicians as Massachusetts senator John Kerry, former House minority leader Richard Gephardt of Missouri, and Senate minority leader Tom Daschle of South Dakota. The person who generated the most buzz, however, was a freshman U.S. senator: John Ed-

wards of North Carolina. After two decades spent building an exceptionally successful career as a trial lawyer, Edwards entered public life in grand style, winning a contentious 1998 battle for one of North Carolina's U.S. Senate seats. As a senator Edwards has championed public education, children's rights, and improved health care; by the time he had finished his first year in office, he was already being mentioned on the short list of possible running mates for Gore in 2000. Just two years later, he threw his hat into the ring, seeking his party's backing for the nation's highest office. In the primaries he captured more delegates than all but one of his more-experienced congressional colleagues: John Kerry, who in July 2004 announced that he had chosen Edwards to run with him as the Democratic vice-presidential nominee as he faced President Bush in the general election.

The oldest of three siblings, John Reid Edwards was born in Seneca, North Carolina, on June 10, 1953 to Wallace R. Edwards, who worked in textile mills, and Catherine ("Bobbie") Edwards, who ran a small furniture-refinishing shop. His parents had to take out a $50 loan to pay the hospital bill stemming from their first-born's delivery. John Edwards grew up primarily in the small town of Robbins, in the Piedmont region of North Carolina. As a boy he held summer jobs at a local textile mill. When he entered Clemson University, in Clemson, South Carolina, in 1971, he became the first person in his family to attend college. A talented football player in high school who also lettered in three other sports, Edwards hoped to become a gridiron star— and win an athletic scholarship—and earned a spot on Clemson's team as a walk-on. When the scholarship failed to materialize, he transferred to the less expensive North Carolina State University, in Raleigh. Edwards, who attended the school's College of Textiles and majored in textile technology, received a B.S. degree with honors in the spring of 1974. He entered law school at the University of North Carolina at Chapel Hill the following fall. In 1976 he took a summer internship at the Securities and Exchange Commission in Washington, D.C. There, after boarding a city bus for the first time in his life, he discovered, to his embarrassment, that he did not know how to pay his fare. "I was such a hillbilly!" he admitted to James Carney for *Time* (July 13, 1998).

In 1977 Edwards graduated with honors from law school. That year he married a fellow law student, Mary Elizabeth Anania (called Elizabeth). The couple had passed the North Carolina bar exam the day before their wedding and subsequently served clerkships with federal judges. For about three years beginning in 1978, they practiced law in Nashville, Tennessee, having passed that state's bar exam in 1978; John Edwards was an associate with the firm Dearborn & Ewing. In 1981 the Edwardses moved to Raleigh, where John Edwards joined the firm of Tharrington Smith & Hargrove, which primarily represented defendants in criminal cases. As an associate there, Edwards took on a medical-malpractice lawsuit on behalf of an alcoholic man who had sustained severe brain damage from a drug overdose administered at a hospital. (The man could no longer walk or speak.) Edwards created a stir among members of the North Carolina bar when he turned down an initial settlement offer of $20,000. The case went to trial, and as the jury deliberated, the hospital made a second offer, this time amounting to $350,000; Edwards declined that one, too. The jury decided in favor of Edwards's client and awarded him a then-record $3.7 million in damages. In the years afterward, on the strength of his capacity to charm and persuade, to familiarize himself with complex details and intricate medical subjects, and to create illuminating graphic exhibits, Edwards won many subsequent lawsuits of a similar nature. He was named a partner at Tharrington Smith & Hargrove in 1984 and remained with the firm until 1992.

In 1993 Edwards and David Kirby, a classmate from law school, set up their own practice, which gave both men greater control over the types of cases they would accept. While Kirby concentrated on product-liability suits, Edwards specialized in malpractice and persona-injury cases—usually representing families in suits against corporations. As he had from the first, he took calculated risks in many of his cases, often rejecting settlements in favor of trials. Reinforcing his confidence in his ability to win was the information he gained from the many intensive-care nurses and other specialists whom he contacted and what he learned from focus groups that he formed before particular trials, to give him insight into how juries might respond to his arguments. "When he took a case, you knew it was going to be prepared better than you'd ever seen," Robert A. Wicker, a former president of the North Carolina state Bar Association, who represented a defendant in one of Edwards's cases, told Joan Biskupic for *USA Today* (July 27, 2004, on-line). "And there was a very high probability that he was going to prove to a jury just what he wanted to prove." According to Biskupic, "During the 1980s and '90s, [Edwards] . . . won more than $200 million for his clients" and "won 54 verdicts and settlements that totaled more than $1 million each." By working on contingency and receiving about a third of awarded damages (but nothing in cases that he did not win), Edwards grew wealthy.

Meanwhile, in the early 1980s, Edwards and his wife had become the parents of a son, Lucius Wade (called Wade), and then a daughter, Katherine Elizabeth (called Cate). On April 4, 1996, while Wade was driving to the family beach house, where his parents and sister were to join him later in the day, a gust of wind caused him to lose control of his Jeep; the car flipped over, and Wade, age 16, was killed. For several months afterward John and Elizabeth Edwards remained in seclusion to repair their lives. (Later, after talking with Cate about the possibility, the couple decided to have more children. With the help of fertility treatments, Elizabeth, who is several years older than her husband,

gave birth to another daughter, Emma Claire, and then another son, Jack.) When he returned to work, Edwards continued his winning ways in court. He secured a record $25 million personal-injury judgment for a five-year-old girl who had been sucked into the defective drain of a swimming pool and suffered acute intestinal damage, and then a record $23 million malpractice ruling for a child who was brain-damaged at birth because signs of fetal distress on a monitoring device had been ignored. During this period Edwards set up an after-school program as a way to memorialize his son. (Also in remembrance of Wade, he always wears his son's Outward Bound button on his suit lapel.) At the same time his long-held interest in pursuing public office grew stronger.

In 1998, despite having no substantive political experience, Edwards launched a campaign for a United States Senate seat from North Carolina. He easily defeated his rivals in the Democratic primary. He then faced the incumbent junior senator, Lauch Faircloth, an extremely conservative Republican with close ties to business who had often been overshadowed by the state's senior senator, Jesse Helms, also a conservative Republican. In his campaign Edwards used strong populist language in stressing standard Democratic Party issues—education, health care, and Social Security. He repeatedly promised to push for a patients' bill of rights, to give people the right to choose their own doctors, to have greater access to specialists, and to have doctors explain treatment options more openly. "I think it just infuriates people that medical decisions, things that affect their lives and their children's lives, are being made by some bureaucrat sitting behind some computer screen up in Hartford, Connecticut," he said in one TV ad, as quoted by Barry Yeoman in the *Nation* (October 19, 1998). Among issues on which Democrats disagreed, he strongly supported the death penalty and firmly opposed charter schools and the North American Free Trade Agreement (NAFTA), the latter of which he felt was hurting American workers.

The race between Edwards and Faircloth was close. Edwards's strong challenge forced Faircloth to accept some populist proposals, such as a patients' bill of rights, and the incumbent began to call attention to what he claimed were his attempts to protect the environment. He also accused Edwards of helping to raise the cost of health insurance and medical care by suing hospitals and family doctors. Edwards made no apologies for his legal history. "I've spent the last twenty years representing people against powerful institutions: insurance companies, banks," he told Barry Yeoman. "These are the people I have the strongest feelings about, and they're 98 percent of all North Carolinians. These are the people who are left out of the process." Edwards was helped by his good looks and charm. Advocating cleaner politics, he stated that he would not accept money from political action committees (PACs) or lobbyists, and he contributed $4 million of his own money to his campaign.

On Election Day, Edwards came out the victor, earning 51 percent of the vote to 47 percent for Faircloth.

"Edwards hit the Senate like he was running the 100-yd. dash," Senator John Breaux, a Democrat from Louisiana, told Michael Duffy for *Time* (July 19, 2004). Ambitious in his new role as legislator, Edwards quickly became known for his ability to make backroom deals and focus on issues that concerned his constituents. He also championed the modernization of schools. "Providing a solid public education for all students in good school buildings should be a national priority," he declared in a press release. "Building a stronger partnership between the federal government and the states and local school districts would help us afford the schools that all of our children deserve. One of the best ways to help young students learn more is to put them in smaller classes with better-trained teachers who can provide more individual attention." The National Education Association and the Children's Defense Fund gave him 100 percent approval ratings for his support in the Senate to improve schools and work for children's rights. Edwards also co-sponsored legislation to improve health care for senior citizens who lived in rural communities, through a process that, according to another press release from his office, would combine "cutting edge computer technology with high-tech medical care." Because crime and the cultivation of marijuana in federal forests in North Carolina had increased in recent years, Edwards wrote an amendment to a bill funding the Interior Department; adopted by the Senate in July 2000, the bill allocated $500,000 for law enforcement in North Carolina's national forests, set aside $1 million for the purchase of property around Lake Logan, in North Carolina, and put another $1 million toward the protection of undeveloped land around Lake James, also in the state. "This is for every hiker, biker, hunter, camper, logger and fisherman who spends time on our public lands," Edwards stated in a press release. The Sierra Club, a leading environmental group, gave him a 100 percent approval rating for his environmental votes. Motivated by the widespread destruction Hurricane Floyd wreaked in his state in 1999, Edwards co-formed the Natural Hazards Caucus with Alaskan Republican senator Ted Stevens, which, according to a press release, "promote[s] ways to reduce the loss of life and property when disasters strike and to streamline aid for victims." "For far too long, federal, state and local officials and private agencies have survived with a piecemeal approach to disasters," Edwards stated in the release. "We can do a better job preparing for natural disasters and we can do a better job helping innocent victims of hurricanes, tornadoes, earthquakes and other calamities."

As a senator representing a large tobacco-growing state, Edwards opposed the lawsuit against tobacco companies for damages connected with the high cost of medical care of people with smoking-related illnesses. He stated in an article reprinted on his Web site, "I simply do not believe in the legality or validity of such a suit . . . that is fundamentally unfair on its merits and can only bring further economic hardship to North Carolina." Vowing to support North Carolina farmers, Edwards continued, "I promised that I will oppose increasing excise taxes on tobacco and tobacco products. I oppose funding social programs with further taxes on tobacco because I feel such strategies are misguided and short-sighted."

Edwards has also campaigned in the Senate for the funding of research on the genetic defect known as Fragile X, which is the leading cause of inherited mental retardation. In collaboration with the organization MADD (Mothers Against Drunk Driving), he has pushed for stronger national drunk-driving laws. North Carolina and 17 other states currently have a legal blood-alcohol limit of .08, which Edwards would like to see imposed nationally. He also introduced the Abducted Young Adults Act, which gave the National Center for Missing and Exploited Children legal authority to aid law-enforcement officers in finding abducted people ages 18 through 21. At the same time, he introduced a bill that became known as Kristen's Law, named for a student from North Carolina State University who disappeared at age 18 after visiting a San Francisco beach. The law authorizes the U.S. attorney general to provide grants to non-profit organizations and public agencies that help locate missing adults. Edwards also proposed legislation on privacy issues, and in 1999 the Senate passed a bill co-sponsored by Edwards that regulated sweepstakes promotions, which had often been deceptive.

Edwards's ambition and knack for tackling domestic issues quickly brought him national attention and notice from Democratic Party leaders— enough that by 2001 he had begun to contemplate seeking higher office. His legislative record, though impressive, was still thin for such aspirations, however. He held seats on the Senate's Banking, Government Affairs, and Small Business Committees—all of which, while important, are of regional interest or usually fail for other reasons to attract the public's attention. Looking toward a possible presidential run, he sought and gained seats on the nationally prominent Commerce Committee and on the Select Committee for Intelligence, thus bolstering his expertise in foreign policy. In January 2003 Edwards officially announced that he was running for the presidency. He accrued substantial funds for his campaign, mostly from fellow trial lawyers grown tired of the attempts by President George W. Bush and other Republicans to place dollar limits on lawsuits. For more than a year, Edwards was overshadowed by the sudden emergence into the spotlight of two Democratic hopefuls, retired U.S. general Wesley Clark and former Vermont governor Howard Dean. Regardless, Democrat voters responded positively to his populist message, which was both upbeat and combative. Rather than attacking his rivals in the Democratic primary, he presented his philosophy and outlook as a sharp contrast to those of the Bush administration. His speeches offered scathing indictments of the president's record, coupled with images of his own vision for America. "Today, under George W. Bush," he proclaimed in a December 29, 2003 stump speech in Iowa, "there are two Americas, not one: One America that does the work, another America that reaps the reward. One America that pays the taxes, another America that gets the tax breaks. One America that will do anything to leave its children a better life, another America that never has to do a thing because its children are already set for life. One America—middle-class America—whose needs Washington has long forgotten, another America—narrow-interest America—whose every wish is Washington's command. One America that is struggling to get by, another America that can buy anything it wants, even a Congress and a President."

As Edwards's campaign gathered momentum and those of most of his rivals began to deflate, his fortunes rose radically. Heading into the 10-state March 2, 2004 primaries, in what is known as "Super Tuesday," Edwards was the last viable challenger standing between John Kerry and the Democratic presidential nomination. Of the 2,162 delegates needed to secure the nomination, Kerry then held 562 to Edwards's 204, with more than 1,150 delegates in a total in 10 states—California, Connecticut, Georgia, Maryland, Massachusetts, Minnesota, New York, Ohio, Rhode Island, and Vermont—up for grabs. When the March 2 ballots were counted, Kerry emerged as the victor in all 10 states, and his delegate count had risen to about two-thirds of the number necessary for the party nomination. In light of that development, Edwards ended his run for the presidency.

As a sign of his commitment to his presidential campaign, Edwards had declined to run for a second term in the Senate. Thus, to prevent the probable end of his short political career, his next best hope was to be tapped by Kerry as a running mate. The field of vice-presidential candidates was even more crowded than the race for the presidential nomination. In addition to all of his former rivals, Kerry also considered Joseph R. Biden, his Senate colleague from Delaware; former Georgia senator Max Cleland, a friend and fellow decorated Vietnam War veteran; and Iowa governor Tom Vilsack, whose midwestern appeal, it was thought, might help secure votes. Among all of them, Edwards commanded prime consideration, because of his impressive victory in his debut election, his gifts as a speaker, his boyish good looks (which suggest clean living), his knack for fund-raising, and his residency in a region hotly contested between Republicans and Democrats. Perhaps most important of all, Edwards had proved himself by running a largely positive, populist primary campaign that had clearly resonated with voters. Also, Edwards had apprenticed in the Senate under Kerry's senior

colleague in Massachusetts, the Democrat Edward M. "Ted" Kennedy. Ultimately, as reported by many sources, it was his ability to craft a message—to connect with voters the way he had once connected with juries—that swayed Kerry. On the morning of July 6, 2004, Edwards called his wife and immediately handed the phone over to six-year-old Emma Claire, who, like four-year-old Jack, was with him. "Senator Kerry picked daddy!" Emma Claire called into the phone, according to *People* (July 19, 2004). (Jack then shouted out, "Mommy, I learned to swim above the water!")

During their ensuing joint campaign, Kerry and Edwards worked to distinguish themselves from George W. Bush and his vice president, Richard B. "Dick" Cheney, not only on such issues as the war in Iraq and high jobless rates but also with regard to their political partnership. According to many accounts, Cheney has had unprecedented influence on the commander in chief since he became vice president—and his influence on Bush began even earlier than that: before Bush's official nomination at the 2000 Republican National Convention, Cheney, who headed a group advising Bush on his choice of a vice-presidential running mate, suggested himself to fill that role. Alluding to Bush's relationship with Cheney, Kerry told Karen Tumulty for *Time* (July 19, 2004) that Edwards would have "a very powerful position, properly utilized," in a Kerry administration. "I don't think it has been properly utilized in this [Bush's] administration. I think it's been excessive, and I intend to be a President who is on top of what's happening in every regard. On final decisions, I'm not going to be pushed into them the way I sense this President was." "We will talk constantly about issues," Edwards said to Tumulty. "He'll know what I believe and what I think needs to be done. But at the end of the day, the President of the United States has to make the final decision. The American people expect that, and I expect that. And both of us understand that."

As polls nationwide closed on the night of November 2, 2004, thus ending one of the most expensive, bitter, and tightly contested national elections in U.S. history, it became evident that the election rested on the decisions of the voters of Ohio, one of a handful of "battleground" states (those whose electorates were evenly divided in their choices for president). By the following morning, the Bush-Cheney ticket had secured 254 and the Kerry-Edwards ticket held 252 of the 270 Electoral College votes needed to claim victory, and Bush held a six-figure lead in Ohio, which has 20 electoral votes. At that point the total in Ohio did not include the tally of provisional ballots (paper ballots cast by people denied a choice in the voting booth because of various registration errors or other problems), and the Kerry-Edwards camp considered requesting a recount. At about 11:00 a.m. on November 3, though, after the team had determined that statistically, their candidates could not surmount their opponents' lead in Ohio, Kerry conceded the election to Bush. As of November 5, 2004, with a few precincts still unreported, the total popular vote stood at about 59,460,000 for Bush-Cheney and about 55,950,000 for Kerry-Edwards, or about 51 percent to about 48 percent, respectively, with approximately 59.6 percent of eligible voters having cast ballots. The Electoral College total came to 286 for Bush-Cheney and 252 for Kerry-Edwards.

With John Auchard, a professor of English at the University of Maryland, Edwards wrote *Four Trials* (2003), in which, along with detailed descriptions of four personal-injury cases in which he represented the plaintiffs, he offered glimpses of his personal life, including the indelible influence his

son Wade had on him. His daughter Cate, who graduated with honors from Princeton University in 2004, campaigned actively for her father during his bid for the vice presidency.

—T.J.F.

Suggested Reading: John Edwards 2004 (on-line); John Edwards's U.S. Senate Web site; Kerry/Edwards campaign Web site; *Nation* p19+ Oct. 19, 1998; *New York* (on-line) Feb. 23, 2004, with photo; *New York Times* I p10 July 5, 1998; *New Yorker* p58 May 6, 2002; *Newsweek* p20+ July 19, 2004, with photos; *Time* p34, p46 July 19, 2004, with photos

---

Julie Cordeiro/Courtesy of the Boston Red Sox

Epstein, Theo

Dec. 29, 1973– General manager of the Boston Red Sox

Address: Boston Red Sox, Fenway Park, 4 Yawkey Way, Boston, MA 02215

On November 25, 2002 the Boston Red Sox announced that the 28-year-old Theo Epstein would be their new general manager (G.M.), making him the youngest general manager in the history of baseball. The Red Sox had been without a G.M. since a group headed by John W. Henry bought the team, in February 2002, and then fired Dan Duquette from that position. Because of his youth, the appointment of Epstein—whose primary responsibilities include assessing talent, recruiting new players, and negotiating contracts—generated con-

troversy as well as enthusiasm. "Age is an arbitrary matter . . . ," the Red Sox's president, Larry Lucchino, said, as quoted on the Hometown Channel Web site (November 25, 2002). "Theo is young, but he is much older than he was when this process began. And I think that he will handle himself with great dignity and great respect for the Red Sox franchise." During the same press conference, Epstein, who at the time already had more than 10 years of experience in baseball, seconded this opinion, explaining, "I think relative youth and relative inexperience is only dangerous when the person in question thinks he has all the answers."

On October 27, 2004 the Red Sox won their first World Series in 86 years, thus ending the infamous (and mythical) "curse of the Bambino," which attributed the team's longtime inability to capture a world-championship title to its sale of the legendary hitter and pitcher Babe Ruth to the New York Yankees in 1918. In a feat that made history, the Red Sox went from being three games down to beat the Yankees in the American League Championship Series (ALCS) and went on to capture the World Series in four straight wins over the St. Louis Cardinals. Many commentators and fans (as well as John W. Henry) have credited much of the team's recent success to Epstein, who also holds the title of Red Sox senior vice president.

The youngest of three children, Theo N. Epstein was born on December 29, 1973 in New York City to Leslie D. Epstein and Ilene Epstein. His paternal grandfather, Philip Epstein, and granduncle, Julius Epstein (who were twins), won the 1943 Academy Award for best screenplay for their work on the classic wartime love story *Casablanca* (1942), which starred Ingrid Bergman and Humphrey Bogart. His older sister, Anya Epstein, has written screenplays and scripts for such TV series as *Homicide: Life on the Street* and *The Beat* and is married to the actor Dan Futterman. His fraternal twin brother, Paul, who was born one minute before him, is a social worker and soccer coach at Brookline High School, in Massachusetts. His father, a former Rhodes Scholar, is an educator and writer; among other books, he wrote the acclaimed novels

King of the Jews, Pinto and Sons, Pandaemonium, and *San Remo Drive: A Novel from Memory.*

When Theo was four his father left his job at Queens College, in New York, to join the faculty of Boston College, in Massachusetts, as a professor of English and director of the school's Creative Writing Program. The family settled in Brookline, an upscale Boston suburb, where, for the past 25 years, Ilene Epstein has run the Studio, a women's clothing store, with her twin sister and a friend. Despite his tender age when he moved to the Boston suburb, Theo Epstein was already a Red Sox fan, because his father preferred the Sox to the New York Yankees. "I was probably a Red Sox fan before I even knew it," he told Bella English for the *Boston Globe* (December 5, 2002, on-line), as quoted on the Brookline High Alumni Association Web site. As a small child Epstein showed talent as a baseball player. When he was three, his parents would pitch wiffle balls to him in Central Park, in Manhattan, where, as he recalled to English, "I'd hit them over the fence. People would gather to watch the little kid." He also competed daily with his twin brother; as he told John Tomase for the *Eagle-Tribune* (November 26, 2002), a Massachusetts newspaper, "Sports were our whole form of interaction. There was a long hallway in our apartment and we used to compete in racing, jumping, baseball, all different stuff. I don't know how many ceiling light fixtures we broke or how many times the downstairs neighbors banged on the heating pipe for us to chill out." Epstein pitched well until he strained the muscles in his arm after learning to throw curveballs. As he got older he continued to play baseball—he made the Brookline Little League All-Stars and pitched for Brookline High School—but by that time he had turned out to be, by his own admission, a second-rate athlete. During his adolescence and early teens, he also played soccer. "Theo wasn't the most talented player on the team," Harvey Soolman, Epstein's high-school junior-varsity baseball coach, told John Tomase, "but no one understood the game better." Samuel H. Kennedy, a high-school teammate of Epstein's who is now a Red Sox vice president, told Tomase, "Everyone knew he was the smartest kid on the team. He could figure out your batting averaging, slugging percentage and on-base percentage in about four and a half seconds." Brad Cohen, who coached Epstein when the latter was a high-school senior, told Tomase, "I used Theo like a bench coach. That's the proper analogy. He was that smart."

After graduating from high school, in 1991, Epstein enrolled at Yale University, in New Haven, Connecticut, where he became the sports editor of the *Yale Daily News.* In 1994 he focused an editorial spotlight on the dissatisfaction of members of Yale's football team with their coach, Carm Cozza, who had worked at the university for 30 years; although Cozza was among the most successful coaches in Ivy League history, the players wanted him to retire. Epstein discussed the athletes' argu-

ments in a special section of the newspaper, titled "Cozza Must Go," which was also a preview of the 111th Harvard–Yale football game. The Yale team went on to win the game and afterward presented Epstein with the game ball for inspiring them to victory. Epstein earned a bachelor's degree in American studies from Yale in 1995.

Earlier, during summers, he had worked as a public-relations intern for the Baltimore Orioles. He soon caught the attention of Larry Lucchino and other Orioles executives, by conceiving and organizing a tribute to players from the Negro Leagues as part of the 1993 All-Star Game festivities, which were held at Oriole Park. After Lucchino became president of the San Diego Padres, in 1995, he recruited Epstein to work for that franchise. While with the Padres, Epstein earned a law degree at the University of San Diego School of Law. In 2000 he was named the Padres' director of baseball operations, with responsibility for keeping track of the team's inventory, ordering supplies, and overseeing concessions and cleaning, among other tasks.

In February 2002 Lucchino joined the Florida financier John W. Henry as part of the group that bought the Red Sox. He brought Epstein with him and made him the team's assistant general manager. Lucchino, the team's president and CEO, promptly fired the Red Sox's G.M., Dan Duquette, named Mike Port as the interim G.M., and began looking for a replacement. The Oakland Athletics' Billy Beane accepted the job, then withdrew his acceptance, having decided to stay in Oakland for reasons having to do with his family. Ultimately, Lucchino settled on Epstein, who became only the 11th Red Sox G.M. since 1933. In explaining his choice, Lucchino told Murray Chass for the *International Herald Tribune* (November 27, 2002, online), "There's a certain philosophy we have that Theo embodies . . . , a more innovative way of looking at player development." During the press conference at which the Red Sox announced his promotion, Epstein said, as quoted on the ESPN Web site (November 26, 2002), "I was a Red Sox fan from Day 1. . . . Growing up in New England, you never lose the Red Sox from your blood. Being here, being general manager of this club, it just feels right." The Blue Jays' general manager, J. P. Ricciardi, told John Tomase, "The Red Sox haven't discovered a diamond in the rough. They've discovered a diamond."

In order to support their young G.M., the Red Sox surrounded him with a group of experienced aides, including three former G.M.s. "It fits my management style . . . ," Epstein said to Chass. "I tend to solicit opinions from all those around me. I like to hear opinions and the rationale behind [them] from everybody in the room. Perhaps it's the result of going to law school and using the Socratic method." Epstein has used a variety of tactics in an attempt to "turn the Red Sox into a championship organization that has a chance to win year in and year out," as he told John Donovan for *Sports Illustrated* (March 7, 2003, on-line). A key element of his approach has been the recruitment of young new players through the Boston minor-league teams, rather than the luring of established stars with the promise of huge salaries. "Our goal for player development and scouting is to develop a constant flow of impact talent through our farm system," which entails recruiting primarily "low-risk, high-reward" college players, Epstein said in an on-line chat for the Boston Dirt Dogs Web site (February 6, 2003). The alternative, he said, is fiscally irresponsible and is "the single quickest way to hamstring a franchise for a decade." He explained to John Donovan, "The days of giving up first-round picks for star players and overspending just to make the fans happy in January or February [the off-season] . . . are over. The Red Sox want to please their fans in late October [during the playoffs], not December."

The following year the Red Sox again qualified for the ALCS, but after three straight losses to the Yankees, their prospects seemed dismal. Then, in an astonishing reversal of fortune, the Red Sox won the next four games, becoming the first baseball team in history to win the league championship after being down 3–0. The team proceeded to capture the World Series, triumphing over the St. Louis Cardinals in four straight games. Their victory, Epstein declared to Tyler Kepner for the *New York Times* (October 28, 2004, on-line), was "for anyone who ever played for the Red Sox, anyone who ever rooted for the Red Sox, anyone who ever saw a game at Fenway Park. This is bigger than the 25 guys in the clubhouse. This is for all of Red Sox Nation, past and present." While enjoying the team's victory with a beer-and-champagne–soaked postgame celebration in the clubhouse, Epstein remained focused on the future. "We need to keep a major Red Sox team together," he told Nick Cafardo for the *Boston Globe* (October 28, 2004, on-line). "I'd love to be able to tell every one of these guys they'll be back next year. We have to be consistent in our approach and put the team first. We have to take into consideration the whole sum of the parts and formulate a plan for next year."

In order to scout players and make trading decisions, Epstein relies partly on the rather unconventional practice of sabermetrics—"the search for objective knowledge about baseball," according to the coiner of the term, the respected baseball writer Bill James. Devotees of sabermetrics use the creative analysis of baseball statistics as a guide to understanding and making decisions about the game. In *Newsweek* (March 24, 2003), Mark Starr explained that Epstein "is turning to sophisticated computer analyses of baseball statistics to evaluate players, rather than relying on century-old standards like batting average, home runs and runs batted in." Among the more basic statistics that Epstein and other practitioners of sabermetrics consider are on-base percentage (which, unlike batting average, factors in a player's walks) and slugging percentage (a measure of a player's extra-base hits). In 2002 the Red Sox, partly in response to Epstein's

suggestion, hired Bill James as an adviser. Attitudes toward the application of sabermetrics are varied: while a few teams, such as the Oakland Athletics and the Toronto Blue Jays, have embraced it, others are skeptical of or opposed to the practice.

Epstein has been an exceptionally active G.M. For example, in a two-month period during the summer of 2003, he made four widely praised trades to secure new pitching talent. That was done partly to tackle problems with the Red Sox's relief-pitching staff, whose dismal performance in the early part of the season cost the team many games. The pitching trouble aroused even more controversy than it ordinarily would have, because it was attributed by many to sabermetrics-inspired managerial practices: the Red Sox had opted to defy conventional thinking about relief pitching by allowing relievers to share various pitching duties, rather than giving them restricted roles, and putting them into games at unconventional times, a technique that was derisively dubbed "closing by committee." Though Epstein maintained in an on-line chat for the Boston Dirt Dogs Web site (February 8, 2003) that the closer-by-committee concept was simply a way "to put the best pitcher in the game to get the most critical outs," the tactic was soon abandoned. On the whole, however, both players and management have spoken positively about Epstein's performance. Indeed, the team was more successful during the 2003 season than it had been in several years. According to Encyclopedia4U.com, that year the Red Sox accumulated more runs and achieved a higher total batting average (.289) than any other team in Major League Baseball; their slugging percentage, .491, set a baseball record, bettering the previous record, set by the 1927 Yankees, by .002 percent, and their 238 home runs set a team record. The Red Sox performed well enough to play in the American League Championship Series in October 2003, in which the New York Yankees defeated them in extra innings in game seven. Refusing to dwell on that defeat, Epstein told Ian Browne for the Major League Baseball Web site (November 10, 2003, on-line), "As far as for the Red Sox, we look at the winter as an opportunity to get better . . . . We're going to explore every single possibility to get better to put another winning team on the field in 2004. We're hoping to get better and improve on last year, to set us up to have consistent, perennial, contending teams."

Epstein, who is single, lives in an apartment building in Boston that is located "a block and a half from [Fenway Park's] Gate D," as he told Bella English. When English interviewed him, he was working an average of 100 hours a week during the baseball season and 80 hours a week at other times. To relax, he enjoys playing his acoustic guitar, surfing the Internet, running, and lifting weights.

—K.J.E.

Suggested Reading: *Eagle Tribune* (on-line) Nov. 26, 2002; *Esquire* p169 Dec. 2003, with photo; *Newsweek* p48+ Mar. 24, 2003, with photo; *Sports Illustrated* p60+ Dec. 23, 2002, with photo; *USA Today* (on-line) Nov. 30, 2002, with photo

Courtesy of Hyperion Books

Everett, Percival

Dec. 22, 1956– Writer

Address: Dept. of English, University of Southern California, University Park, Los Angeles, CA 90089

Like the protagonist of his satirical 2001 work *Erasure*, Percival Everett is an African-American writer of books that are difficult to categorize but have at least one thing in common: they contrast sharply with the many stereotype-filled contemporary novels by and about blacks. "Of course my experience as a black man in America influences my art; it influences the way I drive down the street," Everett told an interviewer for the University Press of New England Web site. "But certainly John Updike's [writing] is influenced by his being white in America, but we never really discuss that. I think readers, black and white, are sophisticated enough to be engaged by a range of black experience . . . just as one accepts a range of so-called white experience." In his 16 novels and short-story collections, Everett, a former graduate student in philosophy, has turned a ruthlessly analytical eye and acid humor on subjects ranging from race to families to Greek myth to government to the publishing

industry, featuring characters who include a baseball player, a retired doctor, a hydrologist, a racist cowboy, and the god Dionysus. Jabari Asim noted for the *Washington Post Book World* (October 2, 2001) that in Everett's works, "'conventional' narrative passages abruptly give way to philosophical speculations." "I've never had a bestseller, and I'm not going to have one," Everett told Ed Newton for the University of Southern California's *Trojan Family Magazine* (Spring 1999, on-line). "I watch our culture, and I see what sells. That's not what I write. I do make demands on the reader."

Percival L. Everett was born on December 22, 1956 in Fort Gordon, Georgia, near Augusta, to Dorothy Stinson Everett and Percival Leonard Everett, a sergeant in the U.S. Army who later became a dentist. He has a sister, Vivian. Shortly after his birth the family moved to Columbia, South Carolina, where Everett grew up, and where his childhood was "filled with books," as he told Ed Newton. After graduating from A.C. Flora High School, he attended the University of Miami, in Florida, where he received a B.A. degree in philosophy, with a minor in biochemistry, in 1977. He went on to study the philosophy of language from 1978 to 1980 at the University of Oregon in Portland. Everett intended to become a professor of philosophy, having been "seduced completely by [Ludwig] Wittgenstein," as he told Ed Newton, and agreeing with Wittgenstein's "theory that most philosophical problems were semantic—misunderstandings caused by imprecise language," as Newton put it. He ultimately grew disillusioned with philosophy, however, having lost the belief that it "could be a genuine intellectual pursuit instead of an academic game," as he told an interviewer for the *Houston Chronicle* (June 30, 1985). Instead of completing his dissertation, Everett sent some of his fiction to the creative-writing department at Brown University, in Providence, Rhode Island. He was accepted to the well-regarded graduate program there and received an M.A. degree in 1982. At the same time he maintained his interest in Wittgenstein. "He still informs my way of thinking," he told Newton. "The root for me is matters of language."

While journalists have written of Everett's varied career as a jazz musician, sheep-ranch hand, and high-school teacher, he devoted only a few years to those pursuits before joining the creative-writing faculty at the University of Kentucky, in 1985. He went on to teach at Notre Dame University and at the University of California at Riverside. In 1999 he became a professor of English at the University of Southern California in Los Angeles.

Meanwhile, Everett's master's thesis at Brown University was published as *Suder*, his first novel, in 1983. *Suder* portrays the flight of the title character, a third baseman for the Seattle Mariners, from marriage, parenthood, and his botched career. As Suder becomes involved with cocaine smugglers and a small runaway girl, among others, flashbacks return him to his childhood in the rural South, where he was mentored by a jazz pianist who helped relieve the stress brought on by his dysfunctional family. Carolyn See, assessing *Suder* for the *Los Angeles Times Book Review* (July 31, 1983), called it "a mad work of comic genius, combining symbols and myths from ancients and moderns, white culture and black, juxtaposing heartbreak with farce." Jabari Asim commented in the *Washington Post Book World* (November 7, 1999) that "although *Suder* is about a black character, rarely does race influence the outcome of his adventures." Asim noted the "lack of heavy-handedness and the absence of an overt sociological approach" in *Suder*. With "sly matter-of-factness, in language and dialogue impressively devoid of the deadly earnestness that frequently burdens" such explorations, Asim commented, Everett examined "stereotypical images of black men—jock, musician, sexual threat—while putting his hero through a series of comic misadventures, leavening his subtle social commentary with dry irony." *Suder* won Everett a D.H. Lawrence fellowship from the University of New Mexico.

In the years that followed, Everett proved himself to be a prolific novelist and short-story writer. His second novel, *Walk Me to the Distance* (1985), tells of a Vietnam War veteran who, unsettled by his experiences in combat, flees his family in Georgia and winds up in the fictional Slut's Hole, Wyoming, where he gets a surer grip on his life. In his 1986 book, *Cutting Lisa,* which Richard Eder—in the *Los Angeles Times Book Review* (November 26, 1986)—termed "a bleakly survivalist story," a widowed, semi-retired physician, John Livesey, "embittered . . . by what he sees as the failure of honor and loyalty in the world around him," becomes "the judge of this world and, in a manner of speaking, its executioner," in Eder's words. Everett, he wrote, "has the uncommon skill to work his story up into an ending of genuine though troublesome shock, even while broadcasting it all along." After the publication of *The Weather and Women Treat Me Fair* (1987), a short-story collection, Everett turned to futurist fantasy for the novel *Zulus,* published in 1990. Set in a time after nuclear holocaust, *Zulus* is the story of an obese woman who has eluded mandatory sterilization, thus becoming the only fertile woman on Earth. Impregnated by a rapist, she attracts the interest of rebels who oppose the nihilist regime and want to restart the human race. *Zulus* was followed later in the year by *For Her Dark Skin* (1990), a reworking of Greek myth.

The One That Got Away (1992), illustrated by Dirk Zimmer, represented Everett's entry into the world of children's literature. In it, cowboys rope number ones—represented as figures with faces and limbs—corralling nine of them. While the captors are asleep, however, the biggest number one escapes, and the cowhands go looking for it. "This offbeat but endearing little book exhibits a congenial marriage between text and illustration, at once whimsical and humorous," the *School Library Journal* (May 1992) reviewer, Ann Welton, wrote.

God's Country, Everett's 1994 novel, is his foray into the "unspoiled" and untamed American West of the 1870s. Curt Marder, the central character, is a Union Army deserter homesteading land in "God's country." When marauders dressed as Indians kidnap his wife, loot and pillage his farm, and kill his dog, he hires a "tracker," a black man named Bubba, and sets off looking for vengeance. Noting that at one point, Marder complains to Bubba, "Man, it's 1871, ain't you people ever gonna forget about that slavery stuff?," David Bowman, writing for the *New York Times Book Review* (June 5, 1994), called *God's Country* "Everett's extended answer to that question." The novel, Bowman wrote, "starts sour, then abruptly turns into Cowpoke Absurdism, ending with an acute hallucination of blood, hate and magic. It's worth the wait. The novel sears." Eric Miles Williamson, writing for *American Book Review* (February 1995), disagreed strongly: "Rather than illuminating an aspect of America's grisly past, and rather than presenting an allegory from the past in order to enrich the present, and rather than aspiring to the condition of Art or Literature or even entertainment, Mr. Everett has given us an angry essay. Mr. Everett is a fine writer of prose. Perhaps his next book will be a novel. We hope so."

The stories in *Big Picture,* Everett's 1996 collection, "chart the inexplicable moments when life takes unexpected turns," according to Maggie Garb in the *New York Times Book Review* (September 15, 1996). "There are no shattering epiphanies here, just the casual comment or quirky object that can set off a rumble of change through a habitually dreary life." The characters in the book include "an unlikely assemblage of cowboys and painters, veterans and veterinarians," Garb wrote.

Further expanding his range, Everett made the central character of his 1996 novel, *Watershed,* a hydrologist. As Everett told the interviewer for University Press of New England, "I love research and it never stops. Reading, as with many writers, is what usually leads me to my characters and stories. My characters force research. . . . I knew nothing of hydrology, but I needed [the main character] to have a job that put him in touch with his landscape and water being so important in the west. I wanted to think like a hydrologist, so I had to attempt to internalize some of the knowledge he would possess." He told the interviewer that he had read books on hydrology and then "created a fictitious landscape for the character to know. I drew topographical maps of this place and wrote hydrologic reports about the watershed, of which one appears in the novel." Everett's hydrologist, Robert Hawks, a black man from Virginia, although not particularly involved in politics, is caught up in a dispute between the FBI and a fictional Native American tribe in Colorado. After beginning a romantic relationship with the mysterious Louise Yellow Calf, Hawks uncovers a toxic dumping ground, together with a dam built to divert water from that area into the reservation where Louise's people live. Recalling his grandfather and father, who became activists in the civil rights movement despite themselves, he joins the struggle against the government.

Watershed received a mixed response. The *Publishers Weekly* (March 4, 1996) review referred to the "bumpy ride" the novel offered readers, with its "leaden excerpts from secondary sources (ranging from topographical reports to a 1916 treaty granting water rights to the Plata Indians). . . . It's an ambitious novel, but Everett's dolorous subplots about broken families and failed relationships lack the nuance of the cultural background he gives them, one of black and Native American communities waging turf battles against rogue cops and racist whites." In the *New York Times Book Review* (December 1, 1996) James Polk presented the opposite viewpoint: "Illuminating his novel with excerpts from broken Indian treaties, F.B.I. memos and hydrologists' reports hinting at the scope of what Hawks has stumbled into, . . . Everett builds a taut story." The *Small Press* (February 1997) reviewer, Joseph Ferguson, agreed: "Everett syncopates his text between events, past and present, and direct quotations from Indian treaties, hydrology reports, and other documents. Small details and matter-of-fact dialogue lend credibility to the plot while serving to define even minor characters. The result is not only a high-quality, fast-paced mystery, but an empathetic portrait of a man and how he came to be what he is."

Frenzy, Everett's 1997 novel, is the story of Dionysus, the ancient Greek god of wine and pleasure, as related by his mortal assistant Vlepo. The central character in *Glyph* (1999) is the unnaturally intelligent Ralph, age four, who narrates the story of the first years of his life—during which he has not spoken but has written poetry and read adult-level books, including complex philosophical works, insatiably. Ralph is kidnapped on separate occasions, and for varying reasons, by a mad child psychologist, a Pentagon officer, and a married couple desperately seeking a child, among others. The *Washington Post Book World* (November 28, 1999) critic, Steven Moore, deemed *Glyph* to be "a strange novel, but not strange enough. The premise of an infant with full linguistic capacities but little life experience should yield a defamiliarized language, yet too often Ralph sounds like . . . well, like Professor Percival Everett of the University of Southern California." Nevertheless, he concluded that since "*Glyph* is a farce, it's probably a mistake to get too literal-minded. . . . Everett is a clever writer with a gift for parody and a formidable library in his head. *Glyph* is obviously written for a small, select audience." David Galef, writing for the *New York Times Book Review* (November 28, 1999), praised Everett's "sendups of everything from semiotics to military intelligence, deconstruction and cognitive psychology. . . . Here his omnivorous intelligence and wordplay match Ralph's imperiled intellect perfectly." In *Grand Canyon Inc.*, a short novel published in 2001,

"Rhino" Tanner, a greedy and violent man not terribly concerned with truth, sets out to turn the Grand Canyon into a theme park. Jabari Asim in the *Washington Post Book World* (October 2, 2001) found the book to be "slight, absurd and consistently funny" and filled with "semiotics, signifying and fun with names."

Ironically, it was his next novel, a scathing satire about the book-publishing business, that brought Everett more than his previous share of recognition in the literary world. In *Erasure* (2001) Everett parodied literary accounts of black ghetto life that are written by people with little or no knowledge of their subject and embraced by the mostly white-controlled book industry, which has often ignored other kinds of writing by African-American authors. The main character, Thelonious "Monk" Ellison, is a Harvard University graduate and the author of a number of ill-selling highbrow novels, which some critics have pronounced "not black enough." Monk leaves his California university teaching job to go home to Washington, D.C., where he tries to help the members of his family: his mother, who has been stricken by Alzheimer's disease; his brother, who has abandoned his wife and children for a gay lifestyle; and his sister, a doctor who performs abortions and is later murdered for her work. Among his sister's possessions Monk finds a copy of *We's Lives in Da Ghetto*, a best-seller supposedly detailing life in Harlem, which both appalls him and gives him an idea for how to support his family. Taking the pseudonym Stagg. R. Leigh, Ellison pens his own "ghetto" tale, *My Pafology* (included in its entirety in *Erasure*), which becomes a runaway best-seller and is nominated for the country's top literary award. "Monk's experience is very much my own, though he of course is not me at all," Everett told the University Press of New England interviewer. "Yes, I have been hit with the 'not black enough' complaint, but always from white editors and critics. I find that curious."

Everett's "stinging satire enables him to take deadly aim at . . . the narrow categories and bookstore shelves to which black novelists are often confined; some blacks' obsession with 'ghetto fabulous'-ness and 'keeping it real'; and the still-stupefying ignorance of publishers who can't or won't conceive of black authors who may be more interested in ideas than in 'gritty' urban drama," Jabari Asim wrote in his review of *Erasure* for the *Washington Post Book World* (October 2, 2001). David McGoy noted in Bookreporter.com (2001), "With multiple layers of satire, *Erasure* takes no prisoners in its assault on the publishing industry and its notions of 'African American literature.' Percival Everett thumbs his nose at the literary snobs and the commercial hounds alike. Television is also a target for his wrath, as he dedicates several unforgettable scenes to exposing the adverse role it can play in literature and the stereotyping of Black people."

Everett published two novels in 2004: *American Desert* and *A History of the African-American People [Proposed] by Strom Thurmond,* the second written with James Kincaid. These books, according to Sven Birkerts, writing for the *New York Times Book Review* (May 9, 2004), confirm Everett's "standing as one of the wilder of our wild-card satirists." In *American Desert*, Theodore Street is on his way to end his unhappy life by drowning himself when he is decapitated in a traffic accident. Street's head is crudely sewn back on his body for his funeral, at the close of which he sits up in his coffin. Medically deceased but seemingly alive, he returns home to his wife and children, only to be abducted by a religious cult and find himself in other bizarre situations. The full title of *A History* refers to the real-life U.S. senator and onetime segregationist (who after his death, in 2003, was revealed to have fathered a child with a black woman); the novel takes the form of letters between Thurmond's assistant and members of a publishing firm. The result, a *Publishers Weekly* (April 26, 2004) reviewer wrote, "is a truly funny sendup of the corrupt politics of academe, the publishing industry and politics, as well as a subtle but biting critique of racial ideology." Everett's story collection *Damned If I Do* was scheduled for publication in late 2004.

Everett has been the recipient of the New American Writing Award in 1990, the PEN/Oakland-Josephine Miles Award in 1996, and the Hillsdale Prize for Fiction, presented by the Fellowship of Southern Writers, in 2001. He served as a fiction judge for the 1991 PEN/ Faulkner Award and the 1997 National Book Award. Everett is married to Francesca Rochberg, a professor of ancient history at the University of California at Riverside. The couple live on a farm and raise horses in a bucolic setting not far from Los Angeles. Everett also has a home in British Columbia.

—S.Y.

Suggested Reading: *Bomb* (on-line) Summer 2004; *Boston.com* Dec. 9, 2001; *Callaloo* p62+ Winter 2001; *Houston Chronicle* p4 June 30, 1985; *Poets & Writers* p32+ May/June 2004; University Press of New England Web site; *USC Trojan Family Magazine* (on-line) Spring 1999; *Washington Post Book World* p8 Oct. 2, 2001

Selected Books: Fiction—*Suder,* 1983; *Walk Me To the Distance,* 1985; *Cutting Lisa,* 1986; *The Weather and Women Treat Me Fair,* 1987; *Zulus,* 1990; *For Her Dark Skin,* 1990; *God's Country,* 1994; *The Big Picture,* 1996; *Watershed,* 1996; *Frenzy,* 1997; *Glyph,* 1999; *Grand Canyon Inc.,* 2001; *Erasure,* 2001; *American Desert,* 2004; *A History of the African-American People [Proposed] by Strom Thurmond* (with James Kincaid), 2004; Children's books—*The One That Got Away* (illustrated by Dirk Zimmer), 1992

Falls, Robert

Mar. 2, 1954– Stage and theater director

Address: Goodman Theatre, 170 N. Dearborn, Chicago, IL 60601-3205

The award-winning stage and theater director Robert Falls has been the artistic director of the Goodman Theatre in Chicago, Illinois, one of the finest regional theaters in the United States, since 1986. Under Falls's direction, in 1992 the Goodman won the Tony Award for outstanding regional theater—a term for the mounting of professional theatrical productions in places in the U.S. other than New York City. During the 1970s and early 1980s, as the artistic director of the Wisdom Bridge Theatre, also in Chicago, Falls attracted notice for his vibrant intellectual energy and his willingness to experiment on the stage. His successful productions include, at the Wisdom Bridge Theatre, *Of Mice and Men, In the Belly of the Beast: Letters from Prison,* and *Mother Courage and Her Children,* and at the Goodman, *Galileo, The Misanthrope, The Iceman Cometh, The Young Man from Atlanta,* and *The Night of the Iguana.* In 1999 his nationally acclaimed staging of Arthur Miller's *Death of a Salesman,* which Falls mounted first at the Goodman and later on Broadway, won four Tony Awards. In 2003 his Broadway staging of Eugene O'Neill's *Long Day's Journey into Night* was nominated for a slew of honors and won several, including a Drama Desk Award for best director and a Tony Award for best revival of a play. "What I've always striven for is that larger theatrical consciousness," Falls told Hilary DeVries for the *Christian Science Monitor* (December 4, 1985), "those plays that have larger ideas, that challenge our ideas about who we are and how we got here."

The oldest of the four children of Arthur Joseph Falls and the former Nancy Stribling, Robert Falls was born in Springfield, Illinois, on March 2, 1954. He spent most of his childhood in nearby Ashland, Illinois, a town with fewer than 2,000 residents. His maternal relatives farmed in the area. His father, an Irish-Catholic native of New York, was a Republican politician; he ran unsuccessfully for the office of Illinois state treasurer in 1966, won election as the state's assistant secretary of transportation in the early 1970s, and, along with Richard Ogilvie, managed Gerald Ford's presidential campaign in Illinois in 1976. Robert Falls remembers attending the theater in downtown Chicago with his family during his childhood and performing for his own amusement the song-and-dance routines he had seen in such shows as *The Music*

Frank Micelotta/Getty Images
Robert Falls

Man and *Mame.* Always interested in "making stories happen," as he told Richard Christiansen for the *Chicago Tribune Magazine* (September 28, 1986), he created plays with puppets and, when he was about 10 years old, publicly staged his own version of the classic science-fiction movie *The Day the Earth Stood Still*, using friends of his as actors. "I moved the audience around from scene to scene in the town park," Falls recalled to Christiansen regarding that production, "and I had the Alien enter Earth by climbing down the ladder of the town water tower with a silver bag over his head."

When Falls was in seventh grade, his father was hired as director of admissions and scholarships at the University of Illinois at Urbana, and the Falls family moved to that college town. In a new environment and without his Ashland friends, young Robert became "withdrawn from real life," as he recalled to Christiansen. He spent much of his free time at the movies, sometimes watching as many as three or four a day on Saturdays and Sundays; he supported this pastime by working a paper route. "It was movie mania . . . ," he told Christiansen. "I had no friends; I lived totally at the movies." He also became interested in Broadway musicals, collecting albums featuring the original casts of popular shows, memorizing song lyrics, and staging imaginary scenes in his head.

During his sophomore year at Willowbrook High School, in Villa Park, Illinois, Falls, though fearful of auditioning, won a small part in a school production of *Inherit the Wind*, a drama based on the so-called Scopes monkey trial of 1925, in which a Tennessee schoolteacher was prosecuted for teaching the theory of evolution. At around this time Falls began making weekend trips to Chicago to see professional theater. Using material he culled from Broadway shows, the radio, and comedy albums released by Second City, Chicago's foremost sketch-comedy troupe, he also started writing, acting in, and directing his own full-length plays on his own. He acted in a number of school productions as well, among them Joseph Kesselring's black comedy *Arsenic and Old Lace*, about two sweet, elderly sisters who poison a dozen old men to relieve them of loneliness, and Arthur Miller's tragedy *Death of a Salesman*, about a decent, ordinary family man who has never realized his ambitions. James Harms, a drama coach at Willowbrook who taught Falls, recalled to Christiansen that Falls was a "tall, gangly, skinny kid, so responsive and enthusiastic in what he was doing and so self-motivated that he made you look good, no matter what you told him to do. He was just the kind of student you hope you'll get if you go into teaching." Falls's passion for the theater seemed to cure him of his detachment from others. In his junior year he won election as president of his class; as a senior he was elected president of the student council.

Falls considered preparing for a career in law, which would have pleased his father; instead, after he graduated from high school, in 1972, he opted to study theater at the University of Illinois at Champaign-Urbana on a Shubert Foundation scholarship for playwrights. Falls told Christiansen that after he made that choice, his father "wrote me one of his rare letters, saying that he loved me and that he had faith in me and in what I had decided to do. But because as a politician he knew what it was to be out of a job, he was pretty damn nervous about how I was going to make a living." At the University of Illinois, Falls continued to write plays and act. "I was told I was too tall to be an actor," he recalled to Christiansen, "which left me empty and hurt, so out of spite I did as much acting as I could." He also directed plays. In Falls's view, the university's theater department could not compare to professional schools when it came to hands-on training. But, as he told Carol Kleiman for the *Chicago Tribune* (April 6, 1979), the department had "incredible energy. Many of us were touched by it." With the help of two classmates, Stuart Oken and Jason Brett, Falls mounted, in an old railroad station, a well-received presentation of *Moonchildren*, a play by Michael Weller about students during the Vietnam War in the mid-1960s. (The material was close to home: Falls's high-school and college years coincided with the period of protest and heated debate regarding the United States' involvement in the Vietnam War, which came to an official end in 1975.) When Christiansen asked Oken what Falls was like at that time, Oken said, "When it came to the theater, [Falls] had a creativity that made him seem much older than he was. He had a strong sense of casting, and he was very inventive and cinematic in his direction. . . . He was an extremely bright, overgrown kid, terrifically funny and with tremendous energy, but outside the theater he was completely disorganized and never had any money. He was always staying at somebody else's house." Falls graduated from the University of Illinois with a bachelor of fine arts degree in theater in 1976.

After a brief period of study with the acting coach Edward Kaye Martin in New York City, Falls returned to Chicago, where, to support himself, he worked as a shoe salesman for $60 a week. In the mid-1970s Chicago was teeming with playwrights, directors, designers, and actors—among the latter, such future stars as John Malkovich, Gary Sinise, and Joan Allen. Many new theaters had been established on the city's North Side. At one of those new spaces, the St. Nicholas Theater, founded by the award-winning playwright David Mamet, Falls again directed *Moonchildren*, which proved to be a hit. He also took small parts in plays at the St. Nicholas Theater, including one as a roller-skating panda in Mamet's children's play *The Revenge of the Space Pandas; or Binky Rudich and the Two-Speed Clock*. Offered the opportunity to direct any play he wanted—as long as the production did not cost anything—at the then nearly defunct Wisdom Bridge Theatre, also in Chicago, in early 1977 Falls mounted a production of John Steinbeck's *Of Mice and Men*; that, too, was a critical and popular hit. At the invitation of members of Wisdom Bridge, Falls became the artistic director of the small theater, which was deeply in debt. Despite the difficult circumstances, Falls and his Wisdom Bridge colleagues felt confident in their abilities to create noteworthy theater. He boldly mounted productions of such challenging plays as *The Idiots Karamazov* (1977), a satire by Christopher Durang and Albert Innaurato; *Travesties* (1980), by Tom Stoppard; and *Mother Courage and Her Children*, by Bertolt Brecht. "I look back at that period in wonder," Falls told Christiansen. "We were convinced we could do anything, lick anybody." Christiansen reported that among those who knew Falls during his tenure at Wisdom Bridge, "the word 'genius' comes quickly when speaking of him." Regarding his own impressions of Falls, Christiansen wrote, "[Falls's] personal style is disheveled, his conversation crackles with instantly recalled facts, passionately held opinions and remarkably sharpened insights." In 1981 *Standing on My Knees*, John Olive's powerful story of a female poet suffering from schizophrenia, premiered at Wisdom Bridge. After its successful run in Chicago, Falls and his crew brought *Standing on My Knees* to the Manhattan Theatre Club, in New York City, where the production received a decidedly negative assessment from Frank Rich of the *New York Times* (October 25, 1982) as well as poor critical notices from other reviewers. "I was overwhelmingly depressed at the time," Falls recalled to Christiansen, "but it was the best thing that ever happened to me. I had spent all this time trying to please New York. Now I had to ask myself, 'What do you really want?'"

Back at Wisdom Bridge, Falls's direction of *In the Belly of the Beast: Letters from Prison*, an adaptation for the stage of the autobiographical writings of the convicted murderer Jack Henry Abbott, marked a turning point for the young director. Starring the actor William L. Petersen, a longtime collaborator of Falls's, *In the Belly of the Beast* was a resounding success in Chicago, and Falls and his company went on tour with the play to the Kennedy Center, in Washington, D.C., and to theaters in Glasgow, Scotland, and London, England. Another of Falls's productions from that time, *Kabuki Medea*, a mélange of Greek tragedy and stylized Japanese theater, enjoyed similar international success. Falls had by then attained a reputation as one of the most respected young theater directors in the country. He has credited much of his success at Wisdom Bridge to his chief collaborator and confidant, Jeffrey Ortmann. "I learned a certain courageousness from Jeffrey," Falls told Christiansen. "He was the radical, and I was the conservative. It was Jeff who urged me to go ahead with my visions on *Mother Courage* and *In the Belly of the Beast* when I was timid."

According to Stephen Kinzer in the *New York Times* (December 4, 2000), when Falls applied, in 1986, for the job of artistic director of the Goodman Theatre, the largest and oldest of Chicago's resident theaters, he told the theater's board of directors that he would accept the position only if the board members were willing to "spend lavishly" so that he could attract top talent and stage big-budget productions. "I was impressed by his youth and at the same time by his maturity in the theater," Irving J. Markin, the president of the board of Goodman Theatre, told Christiansen. "He had a candor and enthusiasm in expressing his particular theatrical vision, and he projected a very strong sense of energy. . . . And, of course, we all were impressed by his record of performance at Wisdom Bridge."

Falls set about making the Goodman, already a respected theater, into one of the country's finest. Along with the Guthrie Theater, in Minneapolis, Minnesota, and the MacArthur Theater, in Princeton, New Jersey, the Goodman is widely considered to be among the top regional theaters in the United States. The Goodman was founded in 1925 by a couple whose son, an aspiring playwright, had died young, of influenza. The theater began its rise to prominence in the 1970s and 1980s, when David Mamet's work was performed there. In 2000 the doors to a new, $46 million home for the Goodman Theatre were opened in Chicago. "It's just a building," Falls told Kinzer, "but it's something we've always wanted because it means that now we can do anything from an epic to a three-character new play. It's certainly reinvigorated me and the artists who make this place their home. We've got resources now that very few theaters anywhere in America have, and we're going to make full use of them."

After assuming the artistic direction of the Goodman, Falls set about putting up ambitious productions of well-known works. "Now is the time for testing ourselves in the great classical roles," Falls told Christiansen. "We've shown how well we can do in contemporary works, and Chicago has built its reputation as a theater town in these dramas." The time had come, Falls felt, "[to go] back to the classics: Shakespeare, Molière, Brecht, Ibsen, the Greeks—the big plays." The Goodman's first offering under Falls's direction was a $400,000 production of the German playwright Bertolt Brecht's epic *Galileo*, in which Brecht drew parallels between both the relationship of the 17th-century Italian physicist and astronomer Galileo to the religious authorities of his day and the relationships of scientists during World War II to the government officials in Nazi Germany and the United States. Falls's production received plaudits.

In 1989 and 1990, first at the La Jolla Playhouse, in La Jolla, California, then at the Goodman, Falls directed an updated version of the 17th-century French playwright Molière's comedy *The Misanthrope*, about a man smitten by a beautiful woman who is a product of the superficial society he loathes. Whereas Molière set his tale in the royal court of 17th-century France, Falls placed the action of the play in contemporary Hollywood. In 1990 Falls and the Goodman oversaw the premiere of Scott McPherson's play *Marvin's Room*, which centers on a woman who, while caring for her ill father, learns that she herself has leukemia and reconciles with her estranged sister. The play later traveled to New York and won several Off-Broadway awards. That same year Falls led a highly praised production of one of the American playwright Eugene O'Neill's best-known works, *The Iceman Cometh*, which focuses on a motley group of failures who pass their time drinking and dreaming in a seedy bar. The production starred the stage and screen actor Brian Dennehy, who has contributed to many of Falls's theatrical successes at the Goodman and on Broadway. In 1992 Falls was invited to remount *The Iceman Cometh* at the Abbey Theatre in Dublin, Ireland.

In presenting new works, however, Falls had not always been as successful as he had with venerable and contemporary classics. His mountings of Steve Tesich's plays *The Speed of Darkness*, in 1989, and *On the Open Road*, in 1992, along with *Riverview: A Melodrama with Music*, also in 1992, were greeted with mixed reviews. As quoted by Peter Marks in the *New York Times* (March 17, 1996), Richard Christiansen said of *Riverview*, "It was kind of a dark film noir musical about the old Chicago amusement park. I did not like it. It just did not work. And Bob [Falls] was extremely disillusioned and unhappy about it." Falls told Christiansen that criticisms of the "rich, ambitious, perhaps inherently flawed new works by writers I cared about" left him feeling wounded and "much more vulnerable." But thanks in part to Falls's success in broadening the Goodman Theatre's audience base,

in 1992 the theater was awarded a $1 million grant from the Resident Theatre Initiative of the Lila Wallace–Reader's Digest Fund (now called the Wallace Foundation). When Falls began as artistic director in 1986, the Goodman was more than $500,000 in debt, but thanks in part to private grants, by the following year the theater had a $500,000 cash reserve. Christiansen reported that in 1992 the Goodman under Falls was still in the black. Falls spent the 1992-93 theater season reading new plays, watching other productions, and taking time to "replenish and get a little distance," as he told Christiansen. His colleagues Frank Galati, the Goodman's associate director, and Michael Maggio, its resident director, filled in for him during his absence.

Earlier, in about 1981, the playwright Tennessee Williams, having enjoyed seeing a production of his play *A Streetcar Named Desire* directed by Falls in Chicago, had invited Falls to his home in Key West, Florida, to read a new script to him—a tremendous honor for Falls, who was then only 27 years old. In early 1994 (11 years after Williams's death), on the Goodman's main stage, Falls directed a revival of Williams's *The Night of the Iguana*, a story of midlife emotional and psychological decay and spiritual redemption. Set in a shabby hotel on the west coast of Mexico in 1940, the play centers on a group of lost souls who meet on a stormy night. "There are no stylized, outrageous moments in his *Night of the Iguana*, but Mr. Falls has nonetheless put his stamp on the play," Peter Marks wrote. Indeed, *The Night of the Iguana* held personal meaning for Falls: as he explained to Marks, when he had first read the play, it helped him to recover from the breakup of an eight-year romantic relationship. "I was overwhelmed with the sense of healing and love that are in this play," Falls said to Marks. "The play became almost a bible on the healing process for me. It's about how one gets through the night." Falls restaged *The Night of the Iguana* for the New York City–based Roundabout Theater Company in 1996.

Falls received an Obie Award (which honors Off- and Off-Off-Broadway plays) for his direction of Eric Bogosian's *subUrbia* at the Mitzi Newhouse Theater, in Lincoln Center, in New York City, in 1995. Also that year his Broadway production of Tennessee Williams's *The Rose Tattoo*, staged at the Circle in the Square Theater, received a Tony Award nomination for best revival. In 1996 Falls directed a Goodman Theatre production of Eugene O'Neill's *A Touch of the Poet*, set in Massachusetts in 1828, in which Brian Dennehy played a bar owner haunted by his former glory as a British officer in the Napoleonic Wars. Reviewing the play for *Variety* (May 20–26, 1996), Lewis Lazare wrote, "In one of his finest Chicago directing efforts in several years, Robert Falls has put together a straightforward, honest production." The following year Falls mounted a production of Horton Foote's Pulitzer Prize–winning play *The Young Man from Atlanta*; after its highly successful run at the Goodman, he brought it to Broadway, where it was nominated for a Tony Award for best production of a play.

In 1999 Falls teamed with the producer David Richenthal and Brian Dennehy to mount at the Goodman a highly successful production of *Death of a Salesman*, in which Dennehy played the hero, Willy Loman; later, on Broadway, it won four Tony Awards, including those for best director and best revival of a play. The production was subsequently filmed and broadcast on the Showtime cable channel. Also in 1999 Falls's production of Elton John and Tim Rice's musical *Aida*, for Walt Disney Theatrical Productions, opened at the Cadillac Palace Theatre in Chicago; its success there propelled the musical, in March 2000, to Broadway, where it garnered several Tony Awards, including those for best original score and lighting design. As of December 2003 *Aida* was still running on Broadway.

In 2002 Falls staged Eugene O'Neill's *Long Day's Journey into Night* at the Goodman Theatre; he brought the production to Broadway the next year. (According to the *Playbill* Web site, his was the fourth revival of *Long Day's Journey into Night* to appear on Broadway.) Falls's version featured Dennehy as James Tyrone, an aging actor who has sacrificed artistry for monetary gain; Vanessa Redgrave as his wife, Mary, who became a morphine addict following the difficult birth of her second son, Edmund; Robert Sean Leonard as the sickly Edmund, an aspiring writer; and Philip Seymour Hoffman as the trouble-making firstborn son, Jamie, an alcoholic. The production received rave reviews and was nominated for five Drama Desk Awards, with Falls winning for best director. Of its four Tony Award nominations, it won three, including the one for best revival.

Among Falls's other directing credits are productions of the plays *House and Garden*, by Alan Ayckbourn; *Three Sisters*, by Anton Chekhov; and *Landscape of the Body*, by John Guare. At the end of every year, Falls and the Goodman stage a production of Charles Dickens's *A Christmas Carol*. In addition, Falls has directed revivals of *Getting Out*, *Hamlet*, and *Pal Joey*, for which he wrote a new book, and the American premiere of *Pravda*, a play by Howard Brenton and David Hare, about a megalomaniac media magnate, which Falls mounted at the Guthrie Theatre in 1989. Among other venues, Falls has directed at the Remains Theatre in Chicago; the Ahmanson in Los Angeles; and the Westside Theatre and the Joseph Papp Public Theater in New York City. He has directed operas at the Lyric Opera of Chicago, the Metropolitan Opera, in New York City, and the Grand Théatre de Genève, in Switzerland.

Among other honors, Falls has won several Joseph Jefferson Awards, which honor excellence in professional theater in the Chicago area, and the 1999 Illinois Arts Council's Governor's Award for the Arts. For his work at the Goodman in 1994, the *Chicago Tribune* named Falls a Chicagoan of the Year in the Arts.

A large, bearded man who stands six feet four inches tall, Falls married Kathleen Moynihan, a writer from Chicago, in the mid-1990s. The couple have one child.

—C.F.T.

Suggested Reading: *Chicago Tribune* XIII p6+ July 12, 1992, with photos; *Chicago Tribune Magazine* p10+ Sep. 28, 1986, with photos; Goodman Theatre Web site; *New York Times* II p8 Mar. 17, 1996, with photos, E p1 Dec. 4, 2000; *Playbill* Web site; *Variety* p47 May 20–26, 1996; *Who's Who in America, 2001*

Courtesy of Lucas Digital

Fangmeier, Stefen

Dec. 9, 1960– Film visual-effects supervisor

Address: Industrial Light & Magic, 3155 Kerner Blvd., San Raphael, CA 94901

In a sense, Stefen Fangmeier makes movie stars. He is not a talent scout, a public-relations agent, or an acting coach, but a visual-effects supervisor, responsible for creating the nonhuman phenomena at the center of many action-oriented films—such as the tornadoes in *Twister* (1996), the ocean tempest in *The Perfect Storm* (2000), and the dinosaurs that rampage through *Jurassic Park* (1993). Critics and fans alike agreed that the focus of those successful films was not on the human performers but, rather, on the computer-generated elements that were integral to all those productions; that is the domain of Fangmeier, an employee of George Lucas's San Rafael, California–based special-effects company, Industrial Light & Magic (ILM), and one of the most prominent individuals in the visual-effects industry. In an interview with Anne Thompson for the *New York Times* (January 27, 2004, on-line), Lorenzo DiBonaventura, who oversaw production of *The Perfect Storm*, said of Fangmeier, "Some are good at executing, some are good at innovating. Stefen Fangmeier is that rare breed of creative talent who can innovate and execute." He also told Thompson, "With *The Perfect Storm*, if the wave doesn't work, the movie doesn't work. We sold *Perfect Storm* on the wave and *Twister* on the tornado." A recipient of a variety of awards and nominations, Fangmeier was most recently nominated for an Academy Award for the visual effects in the sea-adventure movie *Master and Commander: The Far Side of the World* (2003).

The middle child in his family, Stefen M. Fangmeier was born on December 9, 1960 in El Paso, Texas, the son of Heinz Fangmeier, an officer in the German Air Force, and Ursula Fangmeier, a modern dancer turned homemaker. His older sister, Undine, who currently lives in Los Angeles, California, was also born in El Paso; his younger brother, Thomas, was the only sibling born in Germany, where he currently lives. In the summer of 1961, Heinz Fangmeier's duties took the family to Germany, where they remained until Stefen was 16; they then moved back to El Paso. When Heinz Fangmeier was again transferred to Germany two years later, his elder son decided to stay in the United States. Stefen Fangmeier moved to Los Angeles and attended California State University at Dominguez Hills, where he received a bachelor's degree in computer science in 1983. Although he had originally been interested in music, having played the piano and guitar since about the age of 12, he discovered that he enjoyed playing the instruments more than learning about music theory, a necessary pursuit for a serious student of music. When choosing a course of study in college, he kept in mind the advice of one of his father's friends, who worked at IBM and had suggested that Fangmeier consider the field of computers. As Fangmeier told *Current Biography*, he liked the idea of technology that was constantly changing and would enable him to continue learning. He thus began taking classes in logic, computer science, programming, and computer graphics, which he enjoyed most.

After his graduation, Fangmeier held various jobs. He worked as a systems programmer and image-processing analyst at the Aerospace Corp. in El Segundo, California, for about a year and a half, then became a technical director for Digital Productions in Los Angeles. Next, after having lived in Los Angeles for almost eight years, he relocated to Illinois, for a position as a scientific visualization program manager at the National Center for Supercomputing Application at the University of Illinois at Champaign. In 1989 Fangmeier went back to Berlin to serve as director of production at Mental Images, a 3-D imaging company. In an interview with *Current Biography*, he described the year he spent in that position as "the most frustrating work experience I ever had," as the company was struggling and Fangmeier routinely put in 16-hour days. The following year an employee of Industrial Light & Magic, the wife of one of Fangmeier's former colleagues at Digital Productions, asked Fangmeier if he would be interested in joining ILM. He went to work in the computer-graphics department at the company in November 1990. Founded by George Lucas in 1975, ILM is the largest and one of the most advanced visual-effects facilities in existence; it has created the special effects for such films as the *Star Wars* series, *Schindler's List* (1993), the *Indiana Jones* chronicles, *Titanic* (1997), *Pirates of the Caribbean* (2003), and the *Harry Potter* movies. According to the ILM Web site, the company has won 14 Academy Awards for best visual effects and 16 awards for technical achievement for its work on an assortment of films.

Fangmeier's first major project at ILM was *Terminator 2: Judgment Day* (1991), which starred Arnold Schwarzenegger, Linda Hamilton, and Edward Furlong. The first sequel to the highly successful 1984 film, *Terminator 2* followed the further exploits of the murderous cyborg (played by Schwarzenegger). As a computer-graphics shot supervisor, Fangmeier was largely responsible for creating the look of the movie's T-1000 character, a shape-shifting cyborg played, in its human form, by the actor Robert Patrick. Fangmeier next worked as the computer-graphics supervisor for *Hook* (1991), a live-action reworking of J. M. Barrie's classic book *Peter Pan* that starred Robin Williams, Dustin Hoffman, and Maggie Smith. In 1993 Fangmeier moved up to the position of lead computer-graphics supervisor for the movie *Jurassic Park*, based on Michael Crichton's novel of the same name, about a dinosaur theme park in which the genetically engineered creatures wreak havoc after the park's security system breaks down. Although Sam Neill, Laura Dern, Richard Attenborough, and Jeff Goldblum starred in the film, which was directed by Steven Spielberg, the computer-generated dinosaurs stole the show. *Jurassic Park* was the first feature-length film in which dinosaurs were created solely through computer graphics. Brian Webster wrote for *Apollo Guide* (1993, on-line), "Despite the ridiculous premise, *Jurassic Park* does an incredible job of showing us what dinosaurs might have looked and acted like. The skill with which these amazing fake beasts were created is directly responsible for this becoming the largest grossing film of all time." Talking with Barbara Robertson for *Animation Magazine* (Spring 2003), Richard Edlund, another visual-effects artist, said that the dinosaurs in *Jurassic Park* "represent significant points in the development of CG [computer graphics]."

For many years on-screen dinosaurs were represented by lizards, magnified to appear enormous and superimposed into scenes. These were soon replaced by miniature dinosaurs that could be manipulated into different positions and shot in stop-motion animation, one frame at a time, so as to create the illusion of continuous motion. Prior to *Jurassic Park*, ILM had relied on a technique dubbed go-motion, in which tiny computer-driven motors controlled the movements of model dinosaurs. This method proved effective in films such as *Dragonslayer* (1981), and Spielberg had planned to use the same technique in *Jurassic Park*; however, after seeing a demo of ILM's computer-generated dinosaurs, Spielberg was sufficiently impressed to incorporate computer animation throughout the film. (Some close-ups of dinosaurs were animatronics.) In the course of providing realistic dinosaurs, Fangmeier and his fellow effects engineers scanned small models of dinosaurs into computers; over this digital skeleton (the joints of which could be moved by clicking a mouse) was added representations of muscles and skin. Furthermore, effects designers could digitally incorporate additional elements—wetness, shadows, reflections, or dirt on the creatures' skins—thus creating dinosaurs that were groundbreaking in their realism.

In 1995 Fangmeier served as digital-character co-supervisor for the film *Casper*, starring Christina Ricci and Bill Pullman, and in 1996 he was the visual-effects supervisor for *The Trigger Effect*, which starred Kyle MacLachlan and Elisabeth Shue. Both films received mixed reviews. Also in 1996 Fangmeier served as visual-effects supervisor for *Twister*, starring Helen Hunt and Bill Paxton. *Twister*, like *Jurassic Park*, was based on a story by Michael Crichton (in this case, co-written by his wife, Anne-Marie). As in the earlier film, the plot was widely panned while the visual effects earned accolades and official recognition. For his work on *Twister*, Fangmeier received an Academy Award nomination and won the British equivalent of an Oscar, a British Academy of Film and Television Arts (BAFTA) award, for his visual-effects supervision. *Twister*, Fangmeier told Barbara Robertson, contained one of his favorite computer-generated sequences, "the cow in the tornado. In *Twister*, the moment that's memorable to everybody is the cow flying by. [Director] Jan de Bont created such a playful moment. The tornado is surrounding you and yet there's a cow flying by. A couple of seconds later another cow flies by in another direction. It was slapstick in the face of a life-threatening force of nature; a nice touch that plays with the human reaction that in the face of danger, we want to have a bit of a laugh. We even put a little moo in the sound track. It was a perfect moment for the use of CG."

Since 1996 Fangmeier has worked almost exclusively in the position of visual-effects supervisor. He contributed his talents to *Speed 2: Cruise Control* (1997), with Sandra Bullock and Jason Patric, and *Small Soldiers* (1998), which starred Kirsten Dunst and Dennis Leary and featured the voices of Ernest Borgnine, Tommy Lee Jones, and Sarah Mi-

chelle Gellar. Also in 1998 Fangmeier worked on Steven Spielberg's World War II film *Saving Private Ryan*. The movie, which starred Tom Hanks and Matt Damon, showcased what were considered to be among the most realistic extended battle sequences ever presented on film. Fangmeier, who designed "war enhancement" effects to portray action in battle scenes that would have been too dangerous or complicated for live actors to perform, received his second BAFTA award for his work on the film. For *Galaxy Quest* (1999), a science-fiction spoof that featured Tim Allen, Sigourney Weaver, and Alan Rickman, Fangmeier served not only as visual-effects co-supervisor but as the second-unit director, as well. (The second unit is responsible for shooting the less crucial scenes in a film, once the first unit has shot scenes with the principal actors.)

For his work on *The Perfect Storm*, in 2000, Fangmeier was again nominated for an Academy Award and won another BAFTA award. The film, which was based on the true story of a boat called the *Andrea Gail* and her crew, portrayed by George Clooney and Mark Wahlberg, presented some unique difficulties from a visual-effects perspective. Fangmeier explained for an article on the International Cinematographers Guild (ICG) Web site that the task of depicting an ocean storm through computer graphics was complicated by the very reality of what was being portrayed. "This is not a made-up world like *Small Soldiers* or *Galaxy Quest*," he said. "Everyone knows (or thinks they know) what real water looks like." In order to make the storm convincing, Fangmeier and his team had to take into account a such factors as lighting conditions, the effects of wind, the presence of sea foam, mist, and fog, the wake created by the boat, and different types of wave motion. In a complicated process, Fangmeier and his colleagues manipulated digital water molecules to form the ocean waves. He explained for the ICG article, "The water surface itself wasn't the most difficult—the combination of the elements became the challenge. There are capillary waves, smaller waves and foam that forms, changing the surface even more. Then, of course, there is the wind that tears across the waves and whips that foam off, making it interact with the air." They approached the problem of creating a massive wave, which ultimately capsizes the boat, in stages; as he joked in his interview for the ICG Web site, "It went from 'Woody Allen' to 'Jack Nicholson.' We began creating a character that whimpered and ended up with a full-blown rage." In his interview with Barbara Robertson, Fangmeier cited the wave from *The Perfect Storm* as "an iconic image . . . a singular image that described the whole struggle. A death moment, and also very beautiful. It represents the defiance and struggle of mankind against nature, of men who go out to sea and find their grave out there."

Fangmeier followed *The Perfect Storm* with the Spanish and German film *Aizea: City of the Wind* (2001), *The Bourne Identity* (2002), starring Matt Damon and Franka Potente, and *Signs* (2002), which was written by M. Night Shyamalan and starred Mel Gibson. Fangmeier expressed particular excitement about his work on *Dreamcatcher* (2003), a science-fiction thriller based on Stephen King's novel of the same name, about four psychic friends who, on their yearly pilgrimage to a remote cabin in the woods, must fight off an alien invasion. King wrote the book while recovering from a near-fatal car accident; Fangmeier noted in an interview with Ron Magid for *American Cinematographer* (April 2003), "I think [King] was probably dealing with a lot of fears related to his own body. The alien has a very organic, very grotesque design, one with Freudian undertones." Fangmeier was initially taken aback when the director, Lawrence Kasdan, showed him the designs of the creatures by Mark "Crash" McCreery; the designs depicted the aliens as "basically giant penises running through the land," Fangmeier observed. Fangmeier nonetheless declared himself pleased with the final result: "We were able to give them a rather unique surface quality because our goal wasn't to be too realistic. . . . We were able to make our aliens' skin slightly translucent, very slimy and very specular, with a jellyfish-like quality. That, along with their design and movement, gave them a very different feel." The movie earned little praise, save for Fangmeier's effects.

Fangmeier's next project was *Master and Commander: The Far Side of the World* (2003), starring Russell Crowe and Paul Bettany and based on the sea-adventure novels by Patrick O'Brian. Initially, 20th Century Fox hired Asylum Visual Effects, not ILM, to create the special effects, but during mid-production ILM was called in to perform what has been called "a 911," or emergency work on the film. Even after 20th Century Fox turned over the special-effects duties to ILM and Fangmeier, the film's release was five months late, due to visual-effects-related delays. As with *The Perfect Storm*, the action in *Master and Commander* is set on the open seas—this time during the Napoleonic Wars; thus Fangmeier had to deal with concerns of historical authenticity in addition to creating believable special effects. The film boasted more than 700 special-effects shots and brought a third Oscar nomination for Fangmeier. He is currently serving as the visual-effects supervisor for a movie based on Lemony Snicket's *A Series of Unfortunate Events* novels. The film will star Jim Carrey and Meryl Streep and is due in theaters near the end of 2004.

Fangmeier has an 11-year-old son, Dylon, and a nine-year-old daughter, Rubye, both from a seven-year marriage that ended in divorce. In his free time he enjoys playing the guitar and piano, cooking, and collecting wines, pursuits that he has said enable him to express his creativity when he is off the set. While he might have been the last person expected to do so, Fangmeier has expressed disapproval of the ubiquity of special effects in films. "There's a lot of excess going on," he said to Anne Thompson. "It puts too much burden on the films, makes them too expensive, puts more demand on them to make their money back and cater to the lowest common denominator."

—K.J.E.

Suggested Reading: *American Cinematographer* p66 Apr. 2003; *Animation Magazine* p38+ Spring 2003; International Cinematographers Guild (on-line); *New York Times* (on-line) Jan. 27, 2004

Selected Films: *Terminator 2: Judgment Day*, 1991; *Jurassic Park*, 1993; *Twister*, 1996; *Saving Private Ryan*, 1998; *The Perfect Storm*, 2000; *Master and Commander: The Far Side of the World*, 2003

Courtesy of Deadria Farmer-Paellmann

Farmer-Paellmann, Deadria

Nov. 25, 1965– Social activist

Address: c/o National Coalition of Blacks for Reparations in America, P.O. Box 90604, Washington, DC 20090-0604

Deadria Farmer-Paellmann made history in March 2002, when she became the lead plaintiff in a class-action suit against the insurance company Aetna, the railroad company CSX Corp., and Fleet-Boston Financial Corp. over the profits those firms had reaped from slavery in the United States. Although others had unsuccessfully sued the federal government for reparations for slavery, Farmer-Paellmann's lawsuit marked the first time anyone had sought reparations from companies that had supported or made money from the practice. While some have called Farmer-Paellmann's lawsuit frivolous, arguing that it is misguided to hold companies responsible for actions that took place before slaves were freed by the Emancipation Proclamation, in 1863, legal experts maintain that her novel approach has a better chance of succeeding than any previous attempt to win financial restitution for the wrongs committed against African-Americans. The lawsuit filed by Farmer-Paellmann was dismissed by a federal judge on January 26, 2004. U.S. district judge Charles Norgle ruled that there was no clear connection between the plaintiffs and the companies being sued; he also stated that the issue of slavery reparations was one to be decided by the legislative and executive branches of the government, not the judiciary. However, by dismissing the case "without prejudice," he left the door open for future reparations lawsuits. Since she filed the suit, Farmer-Paellmann, a law-school graduate, has received messages from supporters as well as hate mail. Her ultimate goal is a financial award to be used for economic development in black communities as well as the creation of affordable housing and access to quality education and health care for blacks; nonetheless, she has said that she is pleased by the dialogue the lawsuits have begun.

One of six daughters of a single mother, Wilhelmina Farmer, the activist was born Deadria Farmer on November 25, 1965. She grew up in the predominantly white neighborhood of Bensonhurst, in the New York City borough of Brooklyn, where she experienced racism first-hand. "We didn't go outside to play," she told Christina Cheakalos for *People* (October 28, 2002). "It was too dangerous." She traces her interest in reparations for slavery to her childhood, when she listened to her grandfather Willie Capers talk about their family's history. Many of the tales dealt with the horrors of slavery, including one about her great-great-grandmother Clara Hinds, who escaped from a rice plantation in South Carolina and hid in swamps for weeks on her journey north to freedom. Her grandfather also spoke of the restitution that was promised when slavery ended but was never delivered. (At the close of the U.S. Civil War, the Union general William Tecumseh Sherman ordered that former slaves each be given a 40-acre plot of land and a mule to work it, but following the assassination of President Abraham Lincoln, the order was rescinded by President Andrew Johnson.) Intrigued, young Deadria began asking her mother questions about slavery. "I couldn't answer them all, so she started reading books in the library," Wilhelmina Farmer told Larry Neumeister for the Associated Press, in an article available on the Savannah Now Web site (April 7, 2002). "She started studying about slavery. . . . I always knew she'd do something that was great."

Farmer-Paellmann received her undergraduate degree in political science from Brooklyn College, part of the City University of New York, in 1988. After graduating she became engrossed by the writings of Malcolm X, who argued that the U.S. government owed African-Americans compensation for the enslavement of their ancestors. She earned a master's degree from the George Washington University Graduate School of Political Management, in Washington, D.C., in June 1995. That August she enrolled at the New England School of Law, in Boston, Massachusetts, where she examined previous efforts, all unsuccessful, to win slavery reparations from the federal government. "I started doing research about the possibility of a lawsuit against the government," she told Tamar Lewin for the *New York Times* (June 4, 2001). "But I turned to corporations, after finding how difficult it would be to win a claim against the government, given sovereign immunity, the statute of limitations, and an opinion by a relatively liberal court rejecting the idea. If you can show a company made immoral gains by profiting from slavery, you can file an action for unjust enrichment." Realizing, too, that going after corporations would prove less inflammatory to the general public than would taking on the U.S. government, in 1997—in a law-school course called Race and the Law—she began researching corporate ties to slavery. "I don't think people are very sympathetic toward multibillion-dollar corporations that profited from slavery," she told James Cox for *USA Today* (February 21, 2002). "People don't put up a wall when you talk about reparations from companies." She went to law school with the goal of eventually fighting for the cause of reparations. (She earned her Juris Doctorate degree at the New England School of Law in 1999, but has not yet passed the bar exam.)

While doing research for a presentation for her Race and the Law class, Farmer-Paellmann learned about Aetna's practice, during the 1800s, of issuing insurance policies on the lives of slaves with slave owners as beneficiaries. Upon her request, the company provided her with records of those transactions. "I got a package from Aetna in January of 2000," she told Dennis Duggan for *Newsday* (March 27, 2002). "I was standing in my kitchen when I opened it. When I saw what was in it I broke down and cried." The package contained a copy of a document for the policy of a New Orleans man, Thomas Murphy, insuring three of his slaves (22-, 23-, and 28-year-old brothers) for $2,900. During her research Farmer-Paellmann also discovered the long history of the struggle for reparations. Beginning in the 1890s and continuing through the 1920s, about 600,000 emancipated slaves lobbied for pensions, and a suit filed in the early 1900s tried to force the government to pay former slaves out of the profits made from cotton during the last few years that slavery was legal. Every year since 1989, when the federal government announced restitution to Japanese-Americans detained in internment camps during World War II, the Democratic representative John Conyers Jr. of Michigan has introduced a measure calling for a comprehensive study of reparations; it has never come close to passing.

In March 2002, after Farmer-Paellmann had researched the issue for five years, three federal lawsuits based on her research were filed in Brooklyn, with her as the lead plaintiff; in seeking financial compensation, the lawsuits targeted corporations that allegedly contributed to the economic system that allowed slavery to continue. The groups named were Aetna, FleetBoston Financial Corp., and the railroad giant CSX Corp. Those companies were accused of conspiracy, human-rights violations, unjust enrichment from their role in the slave trade, and conversion of the value of slaves' labor into profit. (Aetna had insured slaves, while CSX is a successor to numerous railroads that were built or run partly by slave labor. FleetBoston was formerly Providence Bank of Rhode Island, which was founded by the slave trader John Brown and allegedly financed him in that practice.) In March 2000 Aetna publicly apologized for selling policies on slaves; the company has also given over $36 million to programs benefiting the black community and hosts an annual symposium on race. Farmer-Paellmann has said, however, that such actions do not absolve a company of responsibility for its past actions. "These are corporations that benefited from stealing people, from stealing labor, from forced breeding, from torture, from committing numerous horrendous acts, and there's no reason why they should be able to hold onto assets they acquired through such horrendous acts," she said, as reported by Peter Viles for CNN.com (March 27, 2002).

While many observers have accused Farmer-Paellmann and other reparations activists of pursuing unrealistic goals, there are several significant cases in which governments have paid funds to victims of brutal actions, or their descendants, many years after wrongs were committed. In accordance with the terms of the Alaska Native Claims Act of 1971, Native Alaskans (defined as those with at least one-fourth Native ancestry) received nearly $1 billion and approximately one-ninth of the state's land, and in the 1980s the U.S. and Canadian governments began paying Eskimos and Native Americans for the abuses their ancestors suffered at the hands of white settlers and the government. In 1989 the U.S. government agreed to pay $20,000 to each Japanese-American imprisoned in World War II internment camps (a total of $1.2 billion), and since 1995 the state of Florida has paid about $2 million in reparations to the victims and the descendants of the victims of a 1923 race riot in the black town of Rosewood, in which eight blacks were killed by a white mob, others were injured, and property was damaged. In March 2001 an Oklahoma commission recommended that survivors (and their descendants) be compensated for the Tulsa race riots of 1921, in which at least 40 people were killed and numerous homes and businesses were destroyed. Outside the U.S., the German government has provided compensation to Holocaust survivors, including a recent settlement promising to establish a $4.8 billion fund to compensate forced labor during World War II.

Farmer-Paellmann's class-action suit did not specify the amount sought, but she said that any money awarded would go toward paying for education, housing, and jobs for the 35 million Americans who are descendants of African slaves. The suit estimated the worth of the labor performed by slaves between 1790 and 1860 at $40 million; in current values that could be as high as $1.4 trillion (a figure equal to 14 percent of the U.S. gross domestic product in 2001). While the suit was ongoing, Farmer-Paellmann said she would name up to 100 additional companies in lawsuits. Among the businesses named in similar lawsuits filed by others to date are the insurance companies Lloyd's of London and New York Life; the financial institutions AFSA Data Corp., Brown Brothers Harriman, JPMorgan Chase, and Lehman Brothers; the tobacco companies R.J. Reynolds, Brown & Williamson, Liggett Group Inc., and Loews Corp.; the railroad companies Canadian National, Norfolk Southern, and Union Pacific; and the textile company Westpoint Stevens. Municipal governments, which do not enjoy the same sovereign immunity as the federal government, could also be targeted, and some reparations activists have said they would file suits against newspapers that published ads for runaway slaves and colleges whose founders or benefactors were slaveholders. Farmer-Paellmann hopes that the companies sued will become strong advocates for reparations from the government. "My interest in this is to get these corporations, once they are aware of their own connections, to be our chief lobbyists in Washington for other forms of restitution," she told Lewin. "Apologies aren't enough."

Critics of these actions have said the lawsuits are unfair, contending that the companies targeted are vastly different from what they were before U.S. slavery was abolished, and that the companies' shareholders should not be held responsible for actions that took place generations before they were born. "The real problem is they are publicly-traded companies, and they cannot afford the publicity," the conservative author and commentator David Horowitz said, as reported by Kelley Vlahos Beaucar for Fox News (March 27, 2002, on-line). "[The lawsuits are] a form of shakedown, extortion. The companies today are completely different from the companies they are talking about in the past; the people who will get the money are people who aren't slaves." (In the case of reparations from the U.S. government, Horowitz and others have argued that taxpayers would foot the bill unfairly, since most Americans are not the descendants of slaveholders; they also maintain that reparations have already been made in the form of affirmative action, and that reparations would hurt the African-American community and race relations in the long run, by fostering resentment on the part of whites.) Other observers say that although such lawsuits have little chance of success, the true intention behind them is to foster a public dialogue on the centrality of slavery and racism to the American way of life. "These lawyers—and they are some of the finest legal minds in America—know that this is basically a frivolous lawsuit that will not succeed, but to the extent that they can stir the pot and get us to talk about this and maybe create this fund for scholarships and maybe get an apology from Congress, they will have accomplished their purpose," the Fox News senior judicial analyst Andrew Napolitano told Vlahos Beaucar.

The lawsuits were prepared by some of the same lawyers who helped Holocaust survivors win $8 billion from Swiss banks that held Nazi assets taken from Jews during World War II. In working with Farmer-Paellmann, the lawyers filed the first class-action suit seeking reparations from companies for profiting from American slavery. The suit used the same argument employed in the Nazi case, that labor is property and can thus be stolen if people are forced to work against their wills; unlike in the Nazi case, however, the money is being sought not for the people who performed slave labor but for their descendants. Another difference and potential stumbling block is that many African-Americans cannot identify the parties who enslaved their ancestors 140 years ago. Some lawyers, however, note that the Nazi Holocaust case was weak legally but was settled out of court because it was damaging to the reputations of the German companies involved; the U.S. government helped to mediate the agreement.

While each company named in the U.S. lawsuits prepared its own defense, most of them—though acknowledging the wrongfulness of benefiting from slavery—emphasized that such actions were not illegal under U.S. law at the time. Additionally, many of the companies pointed out that they did not exist until after slavery was outlawed and are being named in lawsuits only because they have purchased older companies with ties to slavery. Many historians say that slavery was such an integral part of the American economy until after the Civil War that most large companies benefited from it in some way. "The entire economy of this country was based on slavery, North as well as South," Eric Foner, a professor of history at Columbia University, told Lewin. "New York had a stranglehold on the cotton trade, which made up half the total value of U.S. exports in 1850. Brooks Brothers supplied a lot of clothing to plantation owners. Merchants, manufacturers, everyone felt the economic ripples."

While some proponents of reparations argue that the federal government should pay (among them the Reparations Coordinating Committee, which includes the renowned defense attorney Johnnie Cochran), most legal scholars say that Farmer-Paellmann's tactic of targeting corpora-

tions has a far greater chance of eventual success. A 1995 lawsuit against the government asked for $100 million in reparations and an apology, but a judge ruled that the government had immunity and the statute of limitations had run out. On the other hand, the success of Holocaust survivors in winning reparations from banks and insurance companies in recent years indicates that individual companies are seen as a legitimate target in the quest for slavery reparations. "I think there's a lot less sympathy for corporations. I think it is important for white Americans not to feel like they have to pay for something somebody else did. The corporations are the ones who did it," Farmer-Paellmann told Larry Neumeister. Robert Ward, one of Farmer-Paellmann's law-school professors and now dean of the Southern New England School of Law in Dartmouth, Massachusetts, told Neumeister, "The challenge for Deadria was to find a legal vehicle that will allow a discussion of the issues. That's the beauty of this. Part of what this lawsuit does is show in a concrete way that African-Americans were part of the economic fiber of this country."

Farmer-Paellmann's activities spawned a California law, which went into effect in 2001, stating that insurance companies operating in the state must reveal their histories with respect to slavery. The following year the Chicago City Council passed the Slavery Era Disclosure Ordinance, requiring companies doing business there to make public their past investments or profits based on business transactions involving slaves. Chicago, Los Angeles, Detroit, and Washington, D.C., have adopted resolutions urging the federal government to study the case for reparations. In August 2003 a crowd of 10,000 descended on Washington for a rally demanding reparations. Farmer-Paellmann has also inspired others—including Cochran, the Harvard University law professor Charles Ogletree, and George Washington University's associate dean Alfreda Robinson—to pursue reparations from corporate entities. Ogletree, who heads a group seeking to file reparations lawsuits, believes that Farmer-Paellmann will deserve the lion's share of the credit if any corporations are forced to pay for past actions involving slaves. "The idea of corporate involvement has always been raised in the reparations movement," he told Cox. "But I don't think anybody has been as conscientious or as thorough as Deadria. She is the key factor in making these [legal] claims come to life."

Americans are deeply divided along racial lines over the issue of reparations. Only 10 percent of whites responding to a CNN/USA Today/Gallup poll believed that the government should pay reparations for slavery, while 55 percent of African-Americans thought the government should pay. Thirty-two percent of whites and 68 percent of blacks thought corporations that profited from slavery should be required to apologize to African-Americans, and 35 percent of whites and 75 percent of blacks thought such companies should set up scholarship funds for descendants of slaves.

While most major African-American organizations support reparations, some black leaders and scholars do not. "If the government got the money from the tooth fairy or Santa Claus, that'd be great," Walter E. Williams, chairman of the Department of Economics at George Mason University, told Lewin. "But the government has to take the money from citizens, and there are no citizens alive today who were responsible for slavery. The problems that black people face are not going to be solved by white people, and they're not going to be solved by money. The resources that are going into the fight for reparations would be far more valuably spent making sure that black kids have a credible education." Farmer-Paellmann has said that her lawsuit was not frivolous, since the legacy of slavery continues in America today, manifesting itself in housing discrimination, racial profiling, and police brutality, as well as in more subtle ways. For example, she has said that while she is routinely asked to produce proof of her identity when using a credit card, her husband, who is white, is almost never asked for identification when doing so. "We're still living with the vestiges of slavery," she told Cox. "Most black folks, unless they're living in la-la land, could tell you about an incident every day of their lives." As for her reaction to the January 2004 dismissal of her suit, she informed *Current Biography* that she is "disappointed" but "not surprised." In April 2004 Farmer-Paellmann was one of eight plaintiffs who filed a lawsuit in federal court in New York City seeking reparations of $1 billion from Lloyd's of London, FleetBoston Financial, and R. J. Reynolds for allegedly "aiding and abetting the commission of genocide" against their ancestors. In an action unprecedented in a suit involving slave reparations, she submitted DNA evidence connecting her to the Mende tribe of Sierra Leone, who suffered documented atrocities during the slave trade. As of the fall of 2004, the case was tied up in litigation.

Farmer-Paellmann has worked on the reparations issue with groups including the Congressional Black Caucus, the National Coalition of Blacks for Reparations in America (N'COBRA), and the Reparations Coordinating Committee as well as with the New York State assemblyman Roger L. Green. She is executive director of the Restitution Study Group. She and her husband, a German-born executive, have a three-year-old daughter, Sabina. The family lives in the Gramercy Park area of Manhattan, in New York City.

—K.E.D.

Suggested Reading: *People* p95+ Oct. 28, 2002; Savannah Now (on-line) Apr. 7, 2002, with photo; *USA Today* (on-line) Feb. 21, 2002, with photo

Farmer, Paul

Oct. 26, 1959– Physician; educator; organization founder; social activist; writer

Address: Partners In Health, 641 Huntington Ave., Boston, MA 02115

"So passionate is [Paul] Farmer's desire to minister medicine to the poor that he maintains a mind-boggling schedule—shuttling between the shacks of Haiti; the barrios of Lima, Peru; and the slums of Roxbury, Massachusetts, to treat patients stricken with TB [tuberculosis], AIDS, and other ills," Ira Hellman wrote for *Biography* magazine (September 2001). Working tirelessly to bring quality health care to destitute people around the world is the primary but not the only item in Farmer's crowded calendar; in addition, he serves as chief of the Division of Social Medicine and Health Inequalities at Brigham and Women's Hospital, as the Maude and Lillian Presley Professor of Medical Anthropology at Harvard Medical School, and as co-director of the school's Program in Infectious Disease and Social Change, all in Boston, Massachusetts. One of the world's leading authorities on the treatment and control of tuberculosis, Farmer has spent a substantial part of every year since the early 1980s in rural Haiti, working through the medical organization Zanmi Lasante ("Partners in

Courtesy of Partners in Health

Health" in Creole, Haiti's main language), which he helped to found in the mid-1980s. Hundreds of thousands of Haitians, most of them rural farmers, have come to rely on Zanmi Lasante, which, among other facilities, runs Clinique Bon Sauveur, one of the largest charity hospitals in the country. In poor areas of other countries, too, among them Peru and Russia, Farmer, along with his colleagues, has been successful in implementing community-based health networks to treat victims of HIV, tuberculosis, and other infectious diseases. The World Health Organization (WHO) has lauded Farmer's community-based treatment programs and has adopted his model for them.

Farmer's other accomplishments include the co-founding, in 1987, of the Boston-based nonprofit organization Partners In Health (PIH), an offshoot of Zanmi Lasante whose mission is to provide health care to impoverished individuals everywhere. The Pulitzer Prize–winning writer Tracy Kidder, whose latest book is *Mountains Beyond Mountains: The Quest of Dr. Paul Farmer, A Man Who Would Cure the World* (2003), told Ira Hellman of Farmer, "I've never seen anybody who goes through the world with his nerve endings more exposed. Particularly when it comes to people who are sick, injured—underdogs—it takes almost nothing to arouse his sympathy. It doesn't seem to matter how tired he is or how busy. . . . It comes way before intellectual analysis and all the other stuff. Compassion that seems to flow naturally from him, that's what keeps him going." Farmer has written extensively about matters of health and human rights for various journals and in several acclaimed books: *AIDS and Accusation: Haiti and the Geography of Blame, The Uses of Haiti, Infections and Inequalities: The Modern Plagues*, and *Pathologies of Power: Health, Human Rights, and the New War on the Poor*. His honors include a MacArthur Foundation "genius award" (1993) and the American Medical Association's Outstanding International Physician's Award (2002). When she presented to him the 2003 Heinz Award for the Human Condition, Teresa Heinz Kerry, chairwoman of the Heinz Family Foundation, stated, as quoted on the Partners In Health Web site, "Dr. Farmer and his extraordinary organization have been a force in making the world confront the health care needs of those who historically have never had access to proper care. Because of his dedication and compassion, critical health care services are now being administered around the globe to people who previously would have been left untreated." Echoing that sentiment in the *New York Times* (September 10, 2003), Patricia Cohen wrote, "Dr. Farmer does not have anywhere near the name recognition of, say, Albert Schweitzer or Mother Teresa. But if any one person can be given credit for transforming the medical establishment's thinking about health care for the destitute, it is Paul Farmer."

Known to his family as P.J., for Paul Jr., Paul Edward Farmer Jr. was born in western Massachusetts on October 26, 1959. He is the second of the six children of Paul Edward Farmer Sr., a salesman and teacher, and the former Ginny Rice, who became a librarian at the University of Central Florida after raising her sons and daughters. Paul Farm-

er Sr. was a talented athlete who once turned down an opportunity to play professional baseball; he died in 1984, while playing a game of pickup basketball. He was "a very educated man," Ginny Farmer told Hellman, "but also a strict disciplinarian and a bit of a gypsy. His dream was to live on an island and have the children around him in a compound setting. So we did have some very strange adventures." Chasing a sales job, Hellman reported, Paul Sr. moved the family to Birmingham, Alabama, where he ended up teaching at a school for a salary of only $5,000 a year. He and his family lived in two old buses that he had outfitted as campers.

In 1971 the Farmers moved to Florida. They lived on a boat that Paul Sr. had bought and named the *Lady Gin*; later they settled in a bayou north of Tampa. Struggling to feed her family on her husband's meager income, Ginny Farmer would cook "hot dog bean soup," Farmer's sister Katy recalled to Hellman, and she would buy dented cans of food at discount prices from the Winn-Dixie grocery store where she worked. Hot water was scarce, so the Farmers bathed in a river. Among the family's minor luxuries was a small television, on which they watched mostly educational programs. Indeed, Paul Sr. pushed his children to excel and encouraged their interests in the arts and academics. Gifted artistically and academically, Paul Jr. often made charcoal drawings of animals, using them to explain various aspects of each creature's anatomy and biology to the rest of the family, who, under orders from Paul Sr., would listen attentively. The Farmers' relatively difficult circumstances also helped to instill in Paul and his siblings a strong sense of compassion. "My parents clearly believed in helping the underdog," Farmer told Hellman. "My father was always collecting lost causes and wounded types. My mom is the same way." Ginny Farmer told Hellman, "Empathy is one of Paul's strongest qualities. He's always saying, 'You don't know how that shoe feels or how it pinches until you have it on your foot.'" Farmer is an adherent of liberation theology, introduced within Catholicism through various movements in the 1960s, which calls for freedom from oppression of all kinds, including the economic exploitation of less developed countries, sexual prejudice against women, racial discrimination, and political tyranny. In his article entitled "On Suffering and Structural Violence: A View from Below," in *Daedalus* (Winter 1996), Farmer called liberation theology an "interesting meeting place between economics and theology/social philosophy."

Farmer attended Duke University, in Durham, North Carolina, on a scholarship; as an undergraduate he also volunteered at a hospital emergency room. He earned a bachelor's degree in anthropology from Duke in 1982. Eight years later he received, simultaneously, a medical degree and a Ph.D. degree in anthropology from Harvard University, in Cambridge, Massachusetts. Earlier, in 1983, after graduating from Duke, Farmer had visited Haiti, which along with the Dominican Republic makes up the Caribbean island of Hispaniola. With more than 80 percent of the population living in poverty, Haiti is the poorest country in the Western Hemisphere. According to Hellman, in the year 2001—some 18 years after Farmer's first visit—98 percent of all Haitians had no electricity; 70 percent of adults were unemployed; and half of all deaths occurred among children ages five or less. The U.S. Central Intelligence Agency (CIA) reported on its Web site in 2003 that life expectancy at birth in Haiti is only 52 years. Moved by the plight of the poor and appalled by the unavailability of even basic health care for a population with high rates of tuberculosis, HIV, typhoid fever, and malaria, Farmer began practicing medicine in Haiti before he received his medical license. (Tuberculosis, a disease of the respiratory system, is spread through an infected person's coughing or sneezing; no effective vaccine exists for the illness, which kills more than two million people a year. An estimated 42 million people now living have been infected by the virus that causes AIDS, the world's leading infectious killer. Typhoid fever is caused by a bacterium that lives in a person's bloodstream and intestinal track and enters the body via food or water that has been contaminated by human feces. Malaria is characterized by fever, muscle aches, and vomiting and is caused by a parasite that spreads among humans through malaria-infected mosquitoes. The World Health Organization estimates that malaria kills over a million people a year.)

In around 1985 Farmer helped to found Zanmi Lasante, with the aim of bringing health care to, and treating infectious diseases among, impoverished Haitians; it provides such services as prenatal and postnatal care for poor women and the administration of vaccines to children. Early on, according to Hellman, Farmer and his fellow PIH founder, Jim Kim, had no funds to purchase medical supplies for the sick people they hoped to treat; in desperation, they took a microscope and powerful drugs from Harvard Medical School and Brigham and Women's Hospital. (Soon afterward, a Boston businessman who became a benefactor to PIH paid the hospital and the school for the supplies.) Using money he had raised, Farmer then arranged for the construction of a medical facility, named Clinique Bon Sauveur, in Cange, a small town located on the Central Plateau, Haiti's poorest region. Clinique Bon Sauveur is supported mainly by private donors and foundations. For some time the hospital had only several dozen beds, half of which constituted a tuberculosis ward; it employed 10 Haitian physicians and a large staff of community health workers. In 2003 more than 340,000 patients received treatment at Clinique Bon Sauveur, which, despite its considerable growth, has a theoretical capacity of no more than 25,000 visits per year. (According to Hellman, more than one million Haitians rely on the facility for medical care.) Patients who require advanced

treatments are taken to Port-au-Prince, Haiti's capital, or to Boston, where some of them have stayed at Farmer's apartment.

Haiti's troubles are myriad. In 1994, when the Reverend Jean Bertrand Aristide, Haiti's first democratically elected president, returned to power (having spent three years in exile after his ouster by a military coup in 1991), the United States and multinational organizations promised the country $500 million in development aid, in the form of grants and loans. Because of alleged irregularities during the Haitian legislative elections in 2000 and the nation's supposed failure to take appropriate steps to foster democracy, however, the administration of U.S. president George W. Bush withheld the promised U.S. funds and placed an embargo on $146 million in loans that the Inter-American Development Bank had previously approved and earmarked for efforts to improve Haiti's health and education sectors.

In an article for the *Boston Globe* (December 12, 2002), Farmer and Mary C. Smith Fawzi wrote, "During the past several years, Haiti's life expectancy has continued to decline. Can this decline in life expectancy be attributed directly to the embargo? This question is difficult to answer, but it is clear enough that our affluent and powerful country is failing once more to help the Haitian people achieve decent conditions for themselves and their families." Farmer and Smith Fawzi also wrote, "In the 19 years that Zanmi Lasante has been working in Haiti, we have seen U.S. aid flow smoothly and generously during the years of the Duvalier dictatorship and the military juntas that followed. The current embargo has been enforced during the tenure of a democratically elected government, a situation inconsistent, in our view, with the articulated U.S. policy and the views of the American people, and is on the face of it immoral." In an interview that appeared in *Satya* (April 2000), Farmer said, "I would argue that a social justice approach should be central to medicine. . . . But no matter how you slice it, the only way to deal with global public health problems is to move resources from places in which they are concentrated, where there is little disease, to those where resources are limited and shrinking. It is in the latter settings, of course, that one finds the greatest burden of disease."

At Clinique Bon Sauveur Farmer began treating pregnant women who had tested positive for HIV with the drug AZT to prevent the transmission of HIV to the women's unborn babies. For his patients with serious illnesses such as AIDS and tuberculosis, which are considered tantamount to death sentences in the developing world, he devised a treatment program in which teams of community-health workers closely monitored AIDS and TB patients every day to ensure that they were following the complicated drug regimens prescribed for them. Due in part to such daily monitoring, the patients' responses to the therapies provided by Zanmi Lasante in Haiti have been excellent—better than those among patients in many inner-city clinics in the U.S. A community-based treatment program that Farmer and his colleagues established in Peru halted the spread of a highly resistant strain of tuberculosis in that nation—over 80 percent of the TB patients they treated in Peru were cured—and in prisons in Tomsk, Russia, where Farmer was the chief medical consultant to the Tuberculosis Treatment Project. According to the Partners In Health Web site, because of the success of Farmer's community-based treatment program in Haiti, that country was among the first group of nations that qualified in 2002 for donations from the Global Fund to Fight AIDS, Tuberculosis, and Malaria. Furthermore, impressed by the success of Farmer's program, the World Health Organization (WHO), a United Nations agency, despite its earlier conviction that highly infectious diseases such as AIDS and TB could not be effectively treated in poor areas, adopted Farmer's treatment methods. Subsequently, Farmer was instrumental in establishing the WHO's Working Group on Multi-Drug Resistant Tuberculosis, and he has been a member of the WHO's Working Group for the Global Tuberculosis Programme. In addition, he has served as the chief adviser to tuberculosis programs of the Open Society Institute, a New York City–based grant-making foundation.

Working with Zanmi Lasante, Farmer still spends up to 10 months a year in Haiti, where his accommodations are spartan: a small house that lacks hot water. He continues to make house calls to minister to the ill, often trekking for hours over Haiti's dry mountains to reach his patients. "Haiti keeps me centered," he told Hellman. Zanmi Lasante's facilities have expanded over the years and now include a primary school, an infirmary, a surgery wing, a training program for community health workers, a 104-bed hospital, a women's clinic, a pharmacy, a blood bank, and a pediatric-care facility. In addition to his other efforts, Farmer has collaborated with local Haitian authorities in the Central Plateau region to improve the quality of drinking water, build new schools, and establish microcredit programs. As Farmer told the *Satya* interviewer, "In an era of failed development projects, and economic policies gone bad, I sometimes feel very lucky as a physician, since my experience in Haiti has shown me that direct services are not simply a refuge of the weak and visionless, but rather a response to demands for equity and dignity."

Farmer's work as head of the Division of Social Medicine and Health Inequalities at Brigham and Women's Hospital (which *U.S. News & World Report* has consistently listed among the finest hospitals in the country) involves "fostering the support and coordination of training, research, and service" to reduce the disproportionately high occurrence of disease among poorer people and "to improve treatment outcomes both at home and abroad," according to the hospital's Web site. The division's staff use insights gleaned from anthropology, sociology, statistics, history, economics, and other disciplines to "introduce clinical social medicine to [Brigham and Women's Hospital] and thereby to improve medical care."

AIDS and Accusation: Haiti and the Geography of Blame (1992), Farmer's first book, was hailed as the first full-length ethnographic study of AIDS in a poor society. In the book Farmer offered evidence showing that racism has played a part in American attitudes toward the AIDS crisis in Haiti, one of the first countries to experience the devastation caused by the disease. The *Medical Anthropology Quarterly* called *AIDS and Accusation* a "superbly crafted volume" and an "outstanding scholarly contribution to the 'anthropology of suffering,'" as quoted on the University of California Press Web site. The book won the Wellcome Medal of the Anthropological Institute of Great Britain and Ireland. An updated version of Farmer's next book-length work, *The Uses of Haiti* (1994), was published in 2003. On the Web site Haitiaction.net, Farmer noted that almost 10 years earlier, "when *The Uses of Haiti* was first written, I noted that it was written to serve as a tool for activism. It has been updated for the same reason: to fight for an end to the racist and mean-spirited policies that have characterized [the United States'] official policies toward Haiti for almost 200 years." Those policies, he declared, were inextricably related to the health crisis that has engulfed Haiti. As quoted on Haitiaction.net, the linguist and political philosopher Noam Chomsky wrote in the introduction to *The Uses of Haiti* that the book "tells the truth about uncomfortable matters—uncomfortable, that is, for the structures of power and the doctrinal framework that protects them from critical scrutiny. . . . It tells the truth about what is happening in Haiti, and the U.S. role in its bitter fate."

Along with Margaret Connors and Janie Simmons, Farmer co-edited the collection *Women, Poverty, and AIDS: Sex, Drugs, and Structural Violence* (1996), which won the Eileen Basker Memorial Prize for Studies in Gender and Health from the Society for Medical Anthropology. He also co-edited *The Global Impact of Drug-Resistant Tuberculosis* (1999). In his book *Infections and Inequalities: The Modern Plagues* (1999), Farmer showed that diseases such as tuberculosis, malaria, and AIDS are most prevalent among the poor and examined the local and global forces that to a great extent determine why some people get sick and others do not. He also argued against the prevailing notion that poor countries must develop economically before lasting health improvements can take root. As quoted on the Web site informedpremed.com, the London *Guardian* book reviewer Phil Whitaker called *Infections and Inequalities* a "powerful and rigorously argued critique of economic and health care inequality." Farmer's most recent book is *Pathologies of Power: Health, Human Rights, and the New War on the Poor* (2003).

Farmer has written or co-authored more than 100 scholarly articles dealing with issues related to health and human rights. He has been a member of the International Conference on AIDS, a project of the International Scientific Committee, and of the Commonwealth of Massachusetts' Bureau of Communicable Disease Control, as well as a coordinator of the International Working Group on Multidrug-Resistant Tuberculosis. In addition to his other honors, Farmer has won the Margaret Mead Award from the American Anthropological Association and the Duke University Humanitarian Award.

While working at his clinic in Haiti in the early 1990s, Farmer met Didi Bertrand, whose mother was one of Farmer's patients. The daughter of the local school headmaster, Bertrand became Farmer's assistant at the clinic. They married in 1996. Their daughter, Catherine, was born in 1998. Mother and daughter split their time between Haiti and Paris, France, where Bertrand is studying at the Sorbonne for a doctorate in medical anthropology. In 2002 Farmer joined them in Paris, taking a temporary post as visiting professor of anthropology at Collège de France. "When you hang out with Paul you begin to think that altruism is normal," Tracy Kidder said to Hellman, "and the other stuff we tend to think of as part of human nature—greed, selfishness, mendaciousness—that those are the things that are abnormal. It's just another way of seeing the world tilt around."

—C.F.T.

Suggested Reading: *Biography* p82+ Sep. 2001, with photos; *Boston Globe* A p15 Dec. 12, 2002; Brigham and Women's Hospital Web site; Haitiaction.net; Harvard University Web site; *New York Times* A p1+ Nov. 30, 2003; *New Yorker* p40+ July 10, 2000; Partners In Health Web site; *Satya* (on-line), Apr. 2000; Kidder, Tracy. *Mountains Beyond Mountains: The Quest of Dr. Paul Farmer, A Man Who Would Cure the World*, 2003

Selected Books: *AIDS and Accusation: Haiti and the Geography of Blame*, 1992; *The Uses of Haiti*, 1994; *Infections and Inequalities: The Modern Plagues*, 1999; *Pathologies of Power: Health, Human Rights, and the New War on the Poor*, 2003; as co-editor—*Women, Poverty, and AIDS: Sex, Drugs, and Structural Violence*, 1996; *The Global Impact of Drug-Resistant Tuberculosis*, 1999

Fawcett, Joy

Feb. 8, 1968– Soccer player

Address: c/o WUSA, 6205 Peachtree Dunwoody Rd., 15th Fl., Atlanta, GA 30328

The term "soccer mom" usually connotes a suburban wife who does the lion's share of shuttling her school-age children to and from their various extracurricular activities. Joy Fawcett, however, gives the words a different meaning. At one time the oldest member of the U.S. national women's soccer team, Fawcett helped lead the squad to World Cup Championships in 1991 and 1999 and to gold medals at the 1996 and 2004 Olympic Games, in the process building a reputation as one of the best defenders not only in the U.S. but in the world; she accomplished those and other feats while raising three young daughters. Fawcett, Mia Hamm, Kristine Lilly, Julie Foudy, and Brandi Chastain—teammates on the U.S. national squad beginning in 1988—composed the so-called "Fab Five" of American women's soccer. While Fawcett is not as well-known as some of her Fab Five cohorts, she played in more games (239) and scored more goals (27) than any other defender in U.S. women's soccer history. Along with the other stars of the women's national team, Fawcett has helped to bring attention and prestige to women's soccer in particular and women's sports in general, becoming a role model to a generation of young fe-

Thom Vollenweider/Courtesy of Joy Fawcett

male athletes. In addition to those impressive accomplishments, Fawcett was a founding player in the Women's United Soccer Association (WUSA), the first women's professional soccer league in the United States, which was established in 2000 (and as of November 2004 was inactive but still in existence). Playing for the San Diego Spirit, currently one of eight teams in the league, in 2002 Fawcett was named her team's most valuable player (MVP). In 2003 Fawcett helped the Spirit reach the play-offs, won the WUSA Defender of the Year Award, and was named First-Team All-WUSA. In the fall of 2004, she announced her retirement from professional soccer.

The athlete was born Joy Lynn Biefeld in Inglewood, California, on February 8, 1968. She has four brothers and four sisters. Fawcett began playing soccer in the American Youth Soccer Organization in Huntington Beach, California, when she was five years old. During an informal interview with several young female soccer players and fans of Fawcett's, recorded on the Web site soccer.org, Fawcett said that the biggest challenge she has faced in her life is learning to be "confident with myself." As a child, she added, she was "really shy and didn't want to try out for teams, and people had to drag me to go try out and stuff." By her teens she had evidently moved beyond that stage; at Edison High School in Huntington Beach, Fawcett ran track and continued to play soccer, leading the girls' soccer team to four consecutive league championships. She has credited Edison's soccer coach, Colleen Silva, with teaching her to be disciplined. Fawcett attended the University of California (UC) at Berkeley, where she played on the women's soccer team from 1987 to 1989 and was named a First-Team All-American. She led the team to third-place finishes in both 1987, the year she also joined the U.S. women's national soccer team, and 1988. She remains UC–Berkeley's all-time leading scorer, with 55 goals and 23 assists. Fawcett earned a bachelor's degree in physical education from the school in 1990.

In 1991 Fawcett traveled to China to compete with the U.S. women's national team in the first-ever women's soccer World Cup. The U.S. team won the tournament, at a time when many Americans were not even aware that the U.S. had a women's soccer team. As the U.S. had no professional women's soccer league at that time, Fawcett next lent her athletic talents to the Ajax of Manhattan Beach, California, an amateur team. With her help, the Ajax won the U.S. Women's Amateur National Cup in 1992, 1993, and 1998. In 1993 Fawcett became the first coach for women's soccer (as well as the first female coach for soccer) at the University of California at Los Angeles (UCLA), a post she held until 1997. In her last year as coach, she led the UCLA team to a 19–3 record, its first Pac-10 championship, and a berth in the quarterfinals of the National Collegiate Athletic Association (NCAA) soccer tournament, in which the team was ultimately defeated by Notre Dame. Fawcett was honored as the Pac-10 coach of the year in 1997. (The Pacific-10, commonly referred to as the Pac-10, is a geographical grouping of the athletic programs of Division 1 universities and colleges; other Pac-10 schools include Stanford University and Oregon, Washington, and Arizona State Universi-

ties.) Fawcett resigned as coach following the 1997 season in order to focus more on her family—by that time she had given birth to two daughters and was also serving as the coach of a youth soccer team—and her own career as a player. After she announced her resignation, Chris Umpierre wrote for the UCLA newspaper, the *Daily Bruin* (December 3, 1997, on-line), that Fawcett would be "remembered as the coach [who] brought UCLA women's soccer to national recognition. Throughout her five year tenure, Fawcett helped transform the program from a little known team into a legitimate national contender." Fawcett's record as head coach over those five years was 65–24–7.

Even while coaching at UCLA, Fawcett had continued playing for the national team. At the World Cup in 1995, played in Sweden, Fawcett and the American team placed third. While playing in the 1995 U.S. Olympic Festival, in Denver, Colorado, she broke her right leg during a match, but through her willpower and discipline, she made a complete and relatively quick recovery. In front of more than 70,000 fans in attendance during the women's soccer tournament of the 1996 Olympic Games, held in Athens, Georgia, Fawcett helped to lead an inspired American team to the gold medal. In the championship game, against China, she assisted on the game-winning goal. Fawcett was named MVP of the Nike U.S. Women's Cup in 1998; also in 1998 she was a member of the gold medal–winning team at the Goodwill Games, which were held in New York that year and for the first time featured women's soccer. In 1999 Fawcett played in 27 games for the U.S. women's national team, scoring four goals and notching four assists while placing second on the team in minutes played (2,280).

As quoted on the Web site soccer.org, Fawcett called the U.S. women's team's victory at the 1999 Women's World Cup her proudest accomplishment, because "we did a lot of good on and off the field. We had to go out and sell [the tournament] to the fans"—by such means as public appearances, advertising, and interviews with media representatives. "People didn't know a lot about American women's soccer. And we won on the field as well." In that tournament Fawcett scored a crucial goal against Germany in the quarterfinals, hitting with her head a corner kick for a 3–2 come-from-behind victory. In the following year Fawcett led the national team in minutes played, with 2,712 in 31 games. At the 2000 Olympic Games, the U.S. women's team lost to Norway in the title match and brought home the silver medal. At the 2003 World Cup, which was played in the United States, the U.S. team—ranked number one in the world, with Fawcett as newly named co-captain—lost 3–0 to the eventual champion, Germany, in the semifinals. That match was Fawcett's 23d, and last, World Cup contest.

Fawcett was a founding team member of the WUSA, which played its first season in 2001. The league features many of the best women players from the U.S. national team as well top foreign players. Fawcett's participation during the 2001 season was abbreviated due to the birth of her third child; her first full season in the league was 2002, when she started 19 games for the San Diego Spirit and was named the team's MVP. She anchored the Spirit's defense, which was the second-best in the league in terms of goals allowed in 2003. That year the Spirit posted the third-best record in the league—eight wins and six losses, with seven ties—and qualified for the play-offs, in which they were eliminated before reaching the championship game.

At the 2004 Summer Olympics in Athens, Greece, Fawcett helped propel the U.S. women's soccer squad to the championship match, where they defeated Brazil, 2–1, to win the gold medal. After participating in the team's victory tour, Fawcett announced her retirement.

In addition to her other honors, Fawcett was named U.S. soccer's Chevrolet Female Athlete of the Year in 1988, and in 1997 the University of California inducted her into its hall of fame. Fawcett has served as a spokesperson for a number of organizations and products, including the California Milk Advisory Board, Nokia, and Full90 Sports Inc., a global soccer company and the inventor of a protective, padded headband. She has contributed articles on parenting and post-pregnancy workout regimens to the Web site momsteam.com, which offers, among other topics, "youth sports information for parents," and she has, along with other WUSA players, contributed personal journal entries to the WUSA Web site.

Fawcett is often called the "ultimate soccer mom" in the press and was referred to as "Mama Joy" by her teammates. She and her husband, Walter, have three children, Katelyn, Carli, and Madilyn, who often went to their mother's practices and home games and even accompanied her on road trips. (The children have been to China, Portugal, and Australia, among other countries.) The family lives in Huntington Beach. During some periods in Fawcett's career, her husband gave up jobs outside the home in order to care for the children. Fawcett was able to regain her strength and speed quickly after the birth of each of her children and return to her world-class level of play. She continued to exercise, including lifting weights and running stadium stairs, months into each of her pregnancies, and resumed practicing with the national team as quickly as three weeks after giving birth. In light of this, Fawcett has often been mentioned in the press in the context of women's health and fitness as they relate to childbirth. As quoted on the Web site fifaworldcup.com, Fawcett's fellow national team standout Julie Foudy called Fawcett "superwoman." Explaining why, she said: "She comes to [soccer training] camp with Madi in her arms, holding Carli's hand, diaper bags hanging off her, carrying a baby seat on her head and pushing a stroller. That's Joy." During the interview that appeared on soccer.org, when asked if she had any advice for young girls who want to become professional soccer players, Fawcett replied, "Whatever you want to do, it just takes a lot of hard work and dedication. And it takes getting up early and working out. You know there are times when I just don't want to get out of bed early in the morning and go kick the ball. But I do it anyway, because I love the game. . . . But the most important thing is you've got to have fun! That's really what got me this far."
—C.F.T.

Suggested Reading: joyfawcett.com; *New York Times* VIII p1 May 9, 1999, D p6 Oct. 10, 2003; *People* p171+ July 5, 1999, with photos; *Redbook* p62+ Jan. 2000, with photo; soccer.org; *Working Mother* p62+ Aug./Sep. 2002, with photo; *Who'sWho in America 2001*

Joe Pugliese for *USC Trojan Family Magazine*, courtesy of Caleb E. Finch

Finch, Caleb E.

July 4, 1939– Neurobiologist

Address: Andrus Gerontology Center, University of Southern California, 3715 McClintock, Los Angeles, CA 90089-0191

If one considers only officially authenticated public records, the longest-lived person known was Jeanne Calment, a Frenchwoman who died in 1997 at the age of 122, infirm but "spirited and mentally sharp until the end," as CNN.com (August 4, 1997) reported. According to CNN, "Calment credited her longevity to Port wine, a diet rich in olive oil, and her sense of humor." Scientists who specialize in gerontology, the study of the processes of aging, however, believe that the secrets to her remarkably long life were far more complex. The neurobiologist Caleb E. Finch, a pioneer in gerontology, has been working for more than three decades to discover the secrets of longevity—particularly those connected to the physiological aspects of aging. When he began his research, in the early 1970s, the accepted wisdom was that aging was "an intractable area, just a bunch of diseases," as Finch told Jane E. Brody for the *New York Times* (May 20, 1997). Even if illness were avoided, it was widely assumed, human cells could divide or replenish themselves only a finite number of times, and metabolism could continue only for so long; thus, every person was in effect programmed to die at a certain age. Once, when Finch was a graduate student at Rockefeller University, the Nobel Prize–winning pathologist Peyton Rous, a longtime Rockefeller researcher, asked him why he was "wasting [his] time" looking into the processes of aging, according to *AARP Magazine* (March/April 2003). "Everyone knows that aging is mainly about cancer and vascular disease!" Rous declared to him. But Finch disagreed; as the same magazine quoted him as saying, "I had already convinced myself to the contrary." As he recalled to Jane Brody, he had come to believe that "there were colossal questions [regarding aging] that had not been approached precisely and aggressively." "Clearly there are multiple forces and mechanisms at work in determining life span," he told her. Paraphrasing Finch, Brody wrote, "The rate of aging is most likely a function of gene expression [that is, detectable effects of genes] interacting with the environment"—"environment" in the broadest sense, ranging from weather and air pollution to working conditions, foods eaten, and, for women, the physiological conditions associated with pregnancy.

Finch has even questioned the widely held idea that declining physically after several decades is the fate of all living creatures (other than one-celled organisms, which, by repeatedly and endlessly dividing, may be said to have limitless life spans). Among plant species, individual giant sequoias, bristlecone pines, and creosote bushes have survived for thousands of years; among animal species, scientists have found 220-year-old quahog clams, 200-year-old giant tortoises and bowhead whales, 150-year-old orange roughy (a type of fish), and 120-year-old turkey buzzards, to name just a few of those capable of reaching highly advanced ages. Moreover, rockfish and painted turtles, among other very long-lived creatures, remain vigorous and fertile into their 70s and beyond. Finch has suggested that such organisms might escape altogether the deterioration associated with aging—and perhaps even death, were it not for fires and deforestation by humans, in the cases of trees, and predation, accidents, or environmental destruction, in the cases of animals. "We're finding new examples of this phenomenon all the time," Finch told Linda Marsa for the *Los Angeles Times* (January 5, 2004).

In a 1997 conversation with Jane Brody, John W. Rowe, who was then president of the Mount Sinai Hospital and Mount Sinai School of Medicine and had worked with Finch on the MacArthur Foundation's project on aging, noted three of Finch's outstanding characteristics as a scientist: first, "his vision. He can almost see around corners in terms of the direction in which aging research is going." Second, "his openness to new ideas. Scientists tend to have very closed channels in which they work." And third, "his remarkable capacity to translate basic science and evolutionary biology into the everyday life of an older person by linking basic research to clinical needs." Finch has worked at the University of Southern California (USC), one of the world's leading private research universities, since 1972; he has held an endowed chair there for 20 years and the highly prestigious title of University Professor for 15. An internationally renowned researcher into the causes of Alzheimer's disease (now also called Alzheimer disease), since 1984 he has directed or co-directed the Alzheimer Disease Research Center, which is funded by the U.S. National Institute of Aging and located on the USC campus. Referring to Finch by his nickname, Edward L. Schneider, who was then the dean of the Ethel Percy Andrus Gerontology Center at USC, told Eric Miller for *USC Trojan Family Magazine* (Spring 2002, on-line), "Tuck is the world's most recognized scientist in the field of aging research. I don't know of anyone working in the science of aging—or in any science, really—who has a broader knowledge base than he does. If you have a question about anything from molecular biology to the longevity of fish to the evolution of aging, call on Tuck."

Finch has written or co-written more than 350 scientific papers and three books—*Longevity, Senescence, and the Genome* (1990), *Aging: A Natural History* (with Robert E. Ricklefs, 1995), and *Chance, Development, and Aging* (with Thomas B. L. Kirkwood, 2000); he has edited or co-edited 17 other books, among them *Biology of Aging* (1978), *Between Zeus and the Salmon: The Biodemography of Longevity* (1997), *Clusterin in Normal Brain Functions and During Neurodegeneration* (1999), *Cells and Surveys: Should Biological Measures Be Included in Social Science Research?* (2001), and *Brain and Longevity* (2003). He has contributed to *The Encyclopedia of Aging: A Comprehensive Resource in Gerontology and Geriatrics*, which has appeared in three editions, most recently in 2001. Finch is an accomplished fiddler and has performed and recorded traditional Appalachian mountain songs as a founding member of the Iron Mountain String Band.

Caleb Ellicott Finch was born on July 4, 1939 to American parents in London, England, where his father's employer, City Bank of New York, had posted him. Following the outbreak of World War II, two months later, his mother, the former Faith Stratton, returned with her infant son to the United States. His father, Benjamin Finch, rejoined his wife and child in the U.S. in 1941, after contracting tuberculosis; the disease led to his death a few years later. Caleb Finch was raised in the Hudson River Valley, in southern New York State, and Connecticut. In the *Scientist* (January 25, 1988, online), Finch recalled that even as a young child he felt curious about the process of growing old. His curiosity was sparked in large part by the presence of an unusual number of very elderly people among his relatives (one of his great-uncles, for example, lived to the age of 103) and the tales some of them told about their lives in the previous century and about their (and his) ancestors from as far back as the 1770s and '80s. His mother, who was still physically active and mentally alert at 90, as he told Jane Brody, "fostered my omnivorous appetite for bizarre knowledge." In about 1957 Finch entered Yale University, in New Haven, Connecticut, where he majored in biophysics. Thanks to a "scholarship job" on campus, as he put it in the *Scientist*, he became friendly with several accomplished professors in the Biophysics Department, among them the microbiologist Carl Woese, the structural biologist and crystallographer Donald Caspar, the biophysicist Richard Setlow, and the physicist Ernest C. Pollard. "They included me in many free-wheeling discussions about the remarkable prospects for moleclar biology that made me boil with excitement. In one session, . . . Carl said, 'Why don't you study aging? Nothing is known, and you are crazy enough to try.'" Finch continued, "I was also much influenced by two courses, Pollard's on thermodynamics and Setlow's on atomic physics, which stressed how crucial assumptions are to building theories. Like many others, I hoped that rigorous and comprehensive theories on molecular biology could emerge by using approaches that were so effective in physics."

After Finch earned a B.S. degree from Yale, in 1961, he entered Rockefeller University, in New York City, to pursue a Ph.D. in cellular biology. Within the next two years or so, he began working there in the laboratory of Alfred Mirsky, whose wide-ranging research then focused on gene regulation, about which the first discoveries were being made; one of his fellow lab workers was the young cell biologist Eric H. Davidson. Mirsky and Davidson "greatly helped to formulate my ideas about aging," Finch wrote for the *Scientist*. After a number of attempts, he succeeded in breeding a particular strain of mice whose members were long-lived and resistant to illness; these mice resembled one another genetically far more closely than they did unrelated mice. (He has used later generations of the same colony of mice in his research to this day.) When the oldest of the mice were no longer young (in mouse years), he set about studying aspects of their cellular activities. Having remembered seeing, as a child, elderly relatives shivering in temperatures in which he himself did not feel cold, he devised an experiment in which he exposed both old and young mice to cold, with the goal of determining whether their physiological reactions to

the cold differed and, if so, whether the differences could be attributed to changes in genetic expression in the older mice. He did so by measuring the presence in each mouse's blood of an enzyme, produced in the liver, called tyrosine aminotransferase. It was already known that production of that enzyme is sparked by the presence in the blood of particular hormones that are secreted by endocrine glands (in this case, the pituitary and adrenal glands) as needed—for example, to warm the body when its temperature falls below a certain point. Finch showed that when he induced the production of the enzyme not by exposing the mice to cold but by manipulating the hormones so that they acted directly on the liver, young mice and old mice produced the enzyme at the same speed. By contrast, when the mice were exposed to cold and experienced what scientists refer to as cold stress, the younger mice produced the enzyme significantly faster than the older ones. (The older mice would thus feel cold long before the younger mice did.) Since the actions of hormones are regulated by genes, Finch's experiment showed that the same genes had caused different effects in the two sets of mice. He reported his results in 1969, shortly after another scientist, the biochemist Richard C. Adelman, had reported similar results with experiments involving a different enzyme. Finch's finding that "gene functions could change with age," as he wrote for the *Scientist*, suggested to him "the hypothesis that neuroendocrine age changes could cascade to many other cells." He added, "Adelman and I were lucky to report similar results within a few months [of each other] . . . , because we few researchers often waited years before data were replicated."

Finch remained at Rockefeller as a guest investigator until 1970, then spent two years as an assistant professor at Cornell University Medical College, also in New York. In 1972 he joined the faculty of the University of Southern California as an assistant professor of gerontology. He served as an associate professor from 1975 to 1978, when he was promoted to professor of biological sciences and neurology; since 1985 he has held the title Arco and William F. Kieschnick Professor of the Neurobiology of Aging (named for the Atlantic Richfield oil company and one of its former executives), and since 1989, that of University Professor (an honor currently held by only a dozen others at USC).

At USC Finch has investigated the anatomical and functional relationships between the brain and the endocrine system. Using rats and mice as well as human subjects of various ages, he studied changes in the rates and quantities of catecholamines (for example, epinephrine and norepinephrine, which are produced in the brain and transmit signals between nerve cells) to help to explain why some neurological diseases in adults usually occur at particular ages. Through the years Finch has also given much thought and devoted many of his research hours to trying to determine the causes, understand the progression, and find ways of preventing or slowing the ravages of Alzheimer's disease, which currently affects roughly 4.5 million Americans and consumes more than $100 billion a year in health-care costs in the U.S.—figures that may quadruple within a few decades, according to Linda Bren in *FDA Consumer* (July/August 2003, on-line), as the more than 60 million Americans ages 45 to 64 in 2002 grow older and survive to more advanced ages than previous generations. Currently, nearly half of people ages 85 and over suffer from Alzheimer's, which is marked by memory loss and mental confusion and is invariably fatal. One symptom of Alzheimer's (as determined through microscopic analysis of the brain after death, which is the only way to diagnose the disease with certainty) is the formation within the brain of plaques (dense, sticky accumulations of a protein called beta-amyloid) in spaces between nerve cells, and tangles (snarled masses of threads, or fibrils, of a protein called tau) inside nerve cells; another symptom is the overabundance of the enzyme cholinesterase and the resulting deficiency in the neurotransmitter acetylcholine. Finch discovered yet another: the presence of so-called inflammatory proteins (which scientists previously thought did not occur in the brain) that produce a new form of amyloid (a type of protein) called amyloid β derived diffusible ligands, or ADDLs (pronounced "addles"), which can spread throughout the brain and appear to be toxic. Further experiments showed that a substance known as APO-J, or clusterin, could prevent ADDLs from forming plaques, but it also disrupted neurons' capacity to transmit signals to one another. Along with the molecular pharmacologist and biochemist Grant A. Krafft and the neurobiologist William L. Klein, Finch set up a company called Acumen Pharmaceuticals, whose goal is to create a vaccine to prevent Alzheimer's; the company recently formed a partnership with the giant pharmaceutical company Merck. Finch has also found evidence that people who have taken anti-inflammatory drugs, such as aspirin or ibuprofen, for long periods (in the hopes of preventing heart attacks, for example) are less likely than others to develop Alzheimer's. Other studies conducted by Finch have tentatively linked antioxidants to Alzheimer's-related neurological deterioration and have revealed connections between hormone replacement therapy—specifically, the hormone estrogen—and the possible delay of onset of, or even prevention of, Alzheimer's.

One factor that makes research in longevity inherently difficult is plain: studying long-lived animals as they grow older requires an investment of many years. Others are less obvious. As Finch explained to an interviewer for *Living Longer and Loving It* (Spring 2001, on-line), published by the Alliance for Aging Research, "We know that there are families with a rare genetic history of early-onset Alzheimer's, diabetes, cancer and heart disease—families whose carriers of these strong genes die before 50. Some of these diseases show up later

in the general population as well, and when they show up later, we don't know if there is a strong genetic effect. There also are people who have two copies of a 'bad' gene who live into their 80s, 90s and more without ever getting the disease. So we don't know if the absence of disease is due to lifestyle or the effect of some other gene or genes. There are many complicated questions that must be answered before we really understand the relationship between genetics and disease." When the interviewer asked him, "How is longevity related to genes, and how much can be attributed to environmental and lifestyle factors?" Finch responded, "If you look at longevity itself, and not disease, you find that identical twins, by the time they're 80, have no closer life spans than other members of the general community in which they live. So you might draw the conclusion that after a certain age, genes have a relatively weak effect on life span. On the other hand, there are families whose members seem to have an unusually long life span despite environmental factors. Overall, about one-third of life span within a species can be associated with particular gene differences between individuals. We don't know what the other two-thirds is yet. Is it the environment interacting with genes? We just can't tell yet."

Finch has contributed more than 350 articles to professional journals; in 1991, according to *Science Watch* (May 1991, on-line), as measured by the number of times other researchers cited papers of his that were published from 1981 to 1990, he ranked among the top one-half of one percent of scientists internationally. Among other honors, Finch has won the USC Associates Award for Creativity in Research and Scholarship, the Robert W. Kleemeier Award of the Gerontological Society of America, and the Brookdale Foundation Award for Distinguished Contributions to Gerontology through Research in Biology (all in 1985); the Allied-Signal Inc. Award for Achievement in Biomedical Research on Aging (1988); the Arthur Cherkin Memorial Award, from the University of California at Los Angeles (1991); the Sandoz Prize, the premier award of the International Association of Gerontology (1995); and the Irving Wright Award of the American Federation of Aging Research (1999).

A serious fiddler for 44 years, Finch formed the Iron Mountain String Band with Eric H. Davidson, who plays banjo, and others in the 1960s; since the early 1970s, the band has been a trio, with Brooke Moyer as guitarist and singer. Three of the group's albums—*The Iron Mountain String Band: An Old Time Southern Mountain String Band* (1973), *Walkin' in the Parlor* (1975), and *Someday We'll Meet Again* (1981), are Folkways releases; the fourth, *Songs of Old Time America* (1998), recorded in 1981, came out on the Peach Bottom label. Much of the inspiration for the group's music comes from their collection of field recordings, made by Davidson, Finch, and others in Virginia and North Carolina for 30 years ending in the

1980s; a dozen of those recordings, released on the Folkways/Asch label, are now distributed by the Smithsonian Institution. The band has performed widely, at festivals, colleges, clubs, and bars and on the radio; it played the music (composed by John Rubinstein) for *The Dollmaker*, a 1984 made-for-television movie that starred Jane Fonda.

In 1975 Finch married Doris Nossaman, a fabric artist; he is stepfather to her two adult sons, Michael Tsongas and Alec Tsongas. Finch told Jane Brody that he has "an excellent intellectual navigation system" and enjoys "exuberant stress." "I believe in going hell-bent for leather," he said, "as long as you don't do yourself in if you feel tired or sick."

—M.H.

Suggested Reading: *Los Angeles Times* View p1+ Jan. 12, 1986, with photo; *Natural History* (on-line) Sep. 1999; *New York Times* C p4 May 20, 1997, with photo; *Science Watch* (on-line) May 1991, with photo; *Scientist* (on-line) Jan. 25, 1988; University of Southern California Web site; *USC Trojan Family Magazine* (on-line) Spring 2002, with photo; *Who's Who in America, 2001*

Selected Books: *Longevity, Senescence, and the Genome*, 1990; *Aging: A Natural History* (with Robert E. Ricklefs), 1995; *Chance, Development, and Aging* (with Thomas B. L. Kirkwood), 2000; edited or co-edited—*Biology of Aging*, 1978; *Between Zeus and the Salmon: The Biodemography of Longevity*, 1997; *Clusterin in Normal Brain Functions and During Neurodegeneration*, 1999; *Cells and Surveys: Should Biological Measures Be Included in Social Science Research?*, 2001; *Brain and Longevity*, 2003

Robert Laberge/Getty Images

Finch, Jennie

Sep. 3, 1980– Softball player

Address: c/o Octagon Worldwide, 1270 Ave. of the Americas, 7th Fl., New York, NY 10020

"Blessed with a howitzer arm and a bombshell mien to match," as Patrick Hruby wrote for the *Washington Times* (June 15, 2004), the softball star Jennie Finch has won legions of fans since the mid-1990s as, successively, a high-school softball phenomenon, a collegiate national champion, and an Olympic athlete. During her college career the six-foot-tall Finch set numerous softball records as a formidable batter and a dominating—indeed, often unhittable—pitcher, leading the University of Arizona Wildcats to the National Collegiate Athletic Association (NCAA) softball championship in 2001. She set a dazzling NCAA record with 60 consecutive victories as a pitcher and won the Honda Softball Award, which honors the nation's best player, in both 2001 and 2002. Finch also helped the U.S. women's national softball team to win gold medals at the 2002 International Softball Federation (ISF) World Championships, the 2003 Pan American Games, and the 2004 Summer Olympic Games, continuing the team's dominance in international play.

In terms of the public's interest, the combination of Finch's good looks and athletic prowess has helped her to transcend her sport's relatively small confines. She has co-hosted the Fox television program *This Week in Baseball* and has appeared in *Vanity Fair* and *Glamour*, among other magazines. In 2004 *People* magazine included Finch in its annual list of the world's 50 most beautiful people. "She's become an ambassador for our sport," her fellow Olympic softball-team member Leah O'Brien-Amico told Hruby. "She's well spoken. She's beautiful. And she does her talking on the field. Everything she's gotten is well-deserved." Concerning the fans that sometimes clamor around her when she is seen in public, Finch told Sol Tucker for pointedmagazine.com that she has to "stop and realize that these people are lined up for my autograph and all of these girls show up screaming Jennie Finch, it's pretty crazy. . . . I am just a softball player, but it's great, it just shows you how far women's athletics have come."

Softball differs from baseball in that the ball is larger and softer and is pitched underhand, in a kind of abbreviated windmill motion, rather than overhand, as in baseball. Softball games are seven innings long, not nine, as in baseball. (Games in both sports go into extra innings if the score is tied at the end of seven or nine innings, respectively.) Also, in softball a pitcher throws from a mound 43 feet away from home plate, where the batter stands, whereas in baseball the distance is 60 feet six inches. Finch, who throws right-handed, has a number of different pitches in her wicked repertoire, including curveballs; changeups, which fool batters because they look fast coming out of pitchers' hands but are actually traveling more slowly; and riseballs. Many consider the last-mentioned pitch to be Finch's deadliest. The riseball is more or less a fastball that is on the rise as it passes a batter. Finch can throw her riseball 70 miles per hour, which is the equivalent of a Major League Baseball pitcher's 90-mile-an-hour fastball.

The third child of Doug and Beverly Finch, Jennie Finch was born in La Mirada, California, on September 3, 1980. She has two older brothers, Shane and Landon. Finch began playing softball at the age of five. Part of her motivation was her mother's interest in baseball. Beverly Finch was a passionate fan of the Los Angeles Dodgers and held season tickets to their games. Finch's father helped teach his daughter how to pitch—she started pitching at age eight—and set up a batting cage for her to use in the family's backyard. Doug Finch recalled to Patrick Hruby, "People came up to us when Jennie was with her first major travel team, 10 and under, and would tell us that our daughter was really talented." Finch's parents knew that their daughter had talent, but they did not realize its magnitude. In 1993, when she was 12, Finch helped to lead her team to the 12-and-under national title in Chattanooga, Tennessee. (Later, while in high school, Finch played on the teams that won the 14-and-under and 18-and-under national championships, in 1995 and 1997, respectively.) "My family vacations were softball tournaments," Finch recalled to Hruby. "Seeing the sacrifices [my parents] made . . . , understanding what they did for me and how hard it was and seeing the benefits I have from it, it's amazing." In honor of her parents, at 10 Finch chose to wear the number 27, the date on which they began dating, and has worn it ever since.

In 1994 Finch began attending La Mirada High School, where her athletic talent became evident immediately. She set a slew of impressive records as the star pitcher of the school's women's-softball team; she also played first base and shortstop. With Finch propelling them, La Mirada's women's-softball team won four straight Suburban League championships. Her career high-school pitching record was 50–12. Among her victories were six perfect games (that is, contests in which the pitcher faces the minimum number of batters possible [21], does not walk any batters, and does not surrender

any hits); 13 no-hitters (games in which a pitcher plays the entire game without giving up a hit); and 14 one-hitters. Using her powerful fastball or riseball, Finch struck out 784 batters in 445 innings and finished her high-school career with an astounding 0.15 earned-run average (ERA)—evidence that her pitches were all but unhittable. She was named the team's most valuable player (MVP) three years in a row, and was the Suburban League MVP in her final two seasons, 1997 and 1998. She was also named to the first team All-Suburban League three years in succession. The *Long Beach Press-Telegram*, a local newspaper, named Finch to its Softball Dream Team in 1997 and 1998. In addition to softball, she played on the volleyball and basketball teams at La Mirada in her junior and senior years; she was the captain of the basketball team and was named MVP of the team in both years. She captained the volleyball team as well in her senior year. In 1998 Finch was named the La Mirada High School female athlete of the year, and the *Long Beach Press-Telegram* named her player of the year. According to her Web site, she was also honored with the Athletic Directors Association Female Athlete Award. When she graduated, *Jump* magazine named Finch the number-one high-school softball prospect in the country.

Finch chose to attend the University of Arizona, in Tucson, because it was relatively close to her parents' home and boasted a fine athletic department, including what was arguably the best women's softball team in the country. The Arizona Wildcats women's softball team had won the NCAA College World Series four times between 1993 and 1997. In 1999, Finch's first year playing for the Wildcats, she helped the team to reach the Women's College World Series again. (They lost the championship.) Although, by her own account, she felt somewhat timid at first in the competitive arena of college athletics, Finch won 24 games as a starting pitcher that season, the second-highest total ever by a Wildcats' rookie. On the offensive side she led the team with 21 extra-base hits, including a team-high 14 doubles, and was second on the team in home runs (seven). Her fielding percentage at first base was an outstanding .990. (Fielding percentage measures the number of errors a fielder committed against the total number of fielding chances she had; the figure .990 reveals that Finch was nearly flawless in fielding the ball.) During the 1999 championship tournament, Finch had performed beautifully under pressure, posting a 3–0 record as a pitcher, including a no-hitter against Southwest Texas State University's team. She was subsequently named the NCAA Regional most outstanding player. For her performance for the year, Finch earned honorable mention as an All-Pac-10 player. (The Pac- or Pacific-10 is a grouping of schools in the NCAA. Other Pac-10 schools include the state universities of Oregon, Washington, and California.) Behind Finch's dominant play in 2000, the Wildcats again had a successful regular season and advanced to the women's College World Series. Finch's overall pitching record was a superlative 29–2 with a .79 ERA. She had also performed well at the plate, hitting for a .327 batting average with 16 home runs, tying for the most on the team in that category. Playing first base when not pitching, Finch again showed her finesse with the glove, earning a .983 fielding percentage. As a pitcher, Finch once again posted a 3–0 record and another no-hitter in the championship tournament. For the second year in a row, she was named the NCAA Regional most outstanding player. Her other honors for her performance during the 2000 season included First-Team All-Pac-10 and National Fastpitch Coaches Association (NFCA) First-Team All-American selections.

In 2001 Finch guided the Wildcats to the College World Series title. She was unbeatable that year, posting a 32–0 record, thereby setting an NCAA mark for most wins in a season without a defeat. She twice struck out 14 batters in a single game—against South Carolina and Stanford, respectively—tying her career high. When not pitching, Finch played first base or served as the team's designated hitter (one who does not take the field but who has a regular batting spot in the team's lineup). At the plate Finch posted a .309 batting average and hit 11 home runs, including three grand slams. In a game against the University of Oregon's women's softball team, Finch drove in nine runs, tying the second-best single-game NCAA mark for runs batted in (RBI). She was named the Pac-10 pitcher of the year. In the championship tournament Finch was just as overpowering; she was selected to the NCAA Regional All-Tournament Team and named the most outstanding player of the Women's College World Series. In addition, she was an NFCA First-Team All-American, First-Team All-Pac-10, and All-Pacific Region selection.

In her senior year, in the 2002 season, Finch and the Wildcats finished second in the College World Series. Finch had notched a total of 60 consecutive victories, an NCAA record. For the second consecutive season, Finch was selected as the Pac-10 pitcher of the year. She made the NCAA Regional All-Tournament Team and the Women's College World Series All-Tournament Team. Finch was also named to the First-Team All-Pac-10, First-Team All-Pacific Region, and NFCA First-Team All-American. In addition, she was one of three finalists for the U.S.A. Softball collegiate player-of-the-year award. She was co-winner of the 2002 Ruby Award, which is presented annually to the University of Arizona's outstanding female senior student-athlete. In recognition of her outstanding college career, the University of Arizona retired her jersey number, 27, in a pregame ceremony on May 9, 2003.

Finch has also been a star in international play. In 1998 she was a member of the U.S. women's national softball team, which beat the Australian women's team to win the gold medal at the inaugural Junior Superball international competition.

The following year Finch and the U.S.A. national softball team won the silver medal at the Junior Women's World Championship. Finch played with the U.S.A. Blue Team at the Pan American Games qualifying tournament in Maracay, Venezuela, in 2001. During that tournament Finch pitched two games, winning both; in one, she threw a perfect game against Guatemala. She did not surrender a single run during her two starts, while striking out 27 batters. At the 2001 Canada Cup, played in Surrey, British Columbia, Finch and the U.S.A. Blue Team finished a disappointing fifth. "I hate losing," the competitive Finch was quoted as saying on the Web site askmen.com. "I mean I love winning, but losing is a much more intense feeling. When I lose, I take it very personally."

The year afterward Finch was a member of the U.S. national team that won the International Softball Federation (ISF) World Championships, by defeating Japan 1–0 in the deciding game; the victory marked the women's team's fifth consecutive world-championship title. (The ISF World Championships are played once every four years.) In an earlier game in that tournament, Finch pitched a one-hitter, with 11 strikeouts, in guiding the U.S. to a 4–0 win over Canada. At the 2003 Pan American Games, played in Santo Domingo, capital of the Dominican Republic, Finch won a gold medal as a member of the U.S. women's team. (During the team's advance in the tournament, Finch struck out 15 batters in leading the American women to victory in a semifinal match against the host country's team.) The win brought the U.S. women's softball team its fifth straight gold medal at the Pan American Games. (Though the national teams of other countries are steadily catching up to the high level of play of the U.S. women's national softball team, the American women have not lost a major international tournament in the last 20 years.)

In 2003 Finch was selected to play on the U.S. women's 2004 Olympic softball team. As a teenager Finch had watched the U.S. women's team win gold medals in the 1996 and 2000 Olympic Games, played in Atlanta, Georgia, and Sydney, Australia, respectively. Regarding playing in the Olympics, Finch told Sol Tucker that a gold medal would be her ultimate accomplishment and that "wearing USA across your chest is the highest honor you can achieve as a softball player. It definitely has been my goal since I was a little girl." The U.S. National Team has been ranked number one in the world for the last 18 years. (The 1996 Olympics were the first to feature softball as a sport.) The U.S. women's team's dominance notwithstanding, Finch explained to Tucker that on any given day "anyone can win. . . . You have to go in there and prepare, because one swing or one pitch can change the game. You prepare and hope that you get lucky." Finch was one of four starting pitchers on the team that represented the U.S. in the Games held in Athens, Greece. The others were Lisa Fernandez, a key member of both of the previous gold medal–winning Olympic teams and one of the best players in the world; the left-handed Lori Harrigan, another two-time Olympic gold medalist; and Cat Osterman, a powerful hurler from Texas and the youngest player on the team. The 2004 Olympic team included only six players from the 2000 squad.

As a pre-Olympics warm-up, the national softball team played against college teams from around the country. The national team was undefeated in dozens of such contests. In late May 2004, in a game played in Arizona, Finch led her team to a 6–1 victory against her alma mater's squad, the Arizona Wildcats. Finch recorded 13 strikeouts and was the winning pitcher; a home run by a Wildcats player broke her streak of 43 1/2 straight scoreless innings. When Tucker asked her about the ending of the streak, Finch declared, "I'm mad. I don't like giving up runs. I have expectations higher than that when I take the field and you have to learn from it and move on." Overall, Finch's record on the national team's pre-Olympics tour, which ended in mid-July, was a flawless 15–0; she gave up an average of only .27 runs per game.

In Greece the American female softball players lived up to all expectations, thoroughly dominating the competition and extending the national team's unbeaten streak to 79 consecutive games. In the opening game of the eight-team Olympic tournament, Finch led the U.S. to a 7–0 victory over Italy, striking out five of the 10 Italian batters she faced. The Americans won the fifth game, too, by a score of 7–0, thanks to Finch's one-hit shutout, with eight strikeouts, against Canada. With their 5–1 victory over the Australian women's team in the gold-medal contest, on August 23, the U.S. women had won the last of their nine games and their third-straight Olympic gold medal. They set an Olympic record—one of more than a dozen they broke in Athens—by outscoring their opponents by a total of 51–1. Writing for the Associated Press (August 23, 2004), Tom Withers called Finch and her colleagues "America's newest golden girls" and stated that fans were "unlikely ever to see a team as good as this red-white-blue Dream Team of power and speed."

Finch has served as a softball analyst for ESPN and has hosted the Fox network program *This Week in Baseball*. On the latter she has interviewed such Major League Baseball (MLB) stars as Barry Bonds, Mike Piazza, Albert Pujols, and Larry Walker. To the delight of viewers, after the interviews the major-league stars would try to hit Finch's pitches. In nearly every challenge Finch struck them out. (In their defense, MLB players are not used to riseballs.) Sol Tucker wrote that Finch's "killer pitch" had earned her the respect of some of baseball's best.

Recently, in an ESPN poll, Finch was voted the "hottest" female athlete by a wide margin over former favorite Anna Kournikova, a professional tennis player and popular sex symbol. Finch's focus, however, is not on her looks, as she explained to

Tucker: "I want to be a good person and good player and hopefully be one of the best players to play the game of softball. . . . I want to be known as an athlete." Still, she has acknowledged that the attention she is receiving is beneficial for women's softball, which has not always had a large following. (Indeed, in 2002 the International Olympic Committee's program commission recommended that softball be dropped from the Olympic Games, in part because of a lack of interest in the sport.) "Our sport needs exposure," Finch told Hruby, "so any we can get, positive exposure, is a good thing."

Finch has a signature line of softball equipment, made by the company Mizuno. She also markets a fitness apparatus, called the Finch Windmill, which, among other purported benefits, strengthens one's pitching arm. (Finch's Web site offers photos of her at various ages using the device.) She has signed an endorsement deal with Bolle sunglasses.

Finch has bright blond hair and blue eyes. She owns several small dogs, among them two toy poodles, named Misty and Hershey, and a Yorkshire terrier named Prada. She is engaged to Casey Daigle, who pitches for the Arizona Diamondbacks' Triple-A team. The December 2004/January 2005 issue of *Modern Bride* featured her on its cover. Among Finch's goals is competing for another Olympic gold medal in 2008.

—C.F.T.

Suggested Reading: Askmen.com; *Charlotte Observer* (on-line) June 15, 2004; Jenniefinch.net; pointedmagazine.com; usasoftball.com; *Washington Times* C p1 June 15, 2004, with photos

---

Firth, Colin

Sep. 10, 1960– Actor

Address: c/o International Creative Management, Oxford House, 76 Oxford St., London W1N OAX, England

Although he had never been out of work since his professional debut, in 1983, and had appeared—sometimes in the lead role—in more than two dozen plays and films in his native Britain, Colin Firth turned 35 believing that he would never be considered anything more than a character actor. "I felt I was reaching an age where the romantic leading man was passing out of my scope," he told Gabrielle Donnelly for *Real Magazine* (August 13–26, 2002, on-line). "I was thinking it was time to . . . embrace the pleasures of being a middle-aged oddity, and joyfully get fat." Then, in 1995, Firth was cast in a TV miniseries as Mr. Darcy—the brooding and emotionally repressed but secretly compassionate, loving, and gentle hero of Jane

Frazer Harrison/Getty Images

Colin Firth

Austen's classic novel *Pride and Prejudice*—and he became an instant heartthrob. "Each night during the run of *Pride and Prejudice*, the streets and stores of Britain were void of women," Helen Fielding, the author of the novel *Bridget Jones's Diary* and an admitted Firth admirer, told Louis B. Hobson for the *Calgary Sun* (April 23, 2001, online). "They were all madly in love with Colin's Mr. Darcy." The series aired in the United States a few months later, in early 1996, and became wildly popular there as well, largely because of Firth; as Sharon Maguire, who later directed the actor in his role as another Darcy, in the movie version of *Bridget Jones's Diary*, told Liana Messina for *La Repubblica* (October 16, 2001, on-line), "He makes haughty so darned sexy." Among his subsequent film roles are those of a good-natured, cuckolded pilot in *The English Patient* (1996), the irascible Lord Wessex in *Shakespeare in Love* (1996), and the brilliant 17th-century Dutch painter Johannes Vermeer in *Girl with a Pearl Earring* (2003). Oliver Parker, who directed Firth in the most recent movie version of *The Importance of Being Earnest* (2002), told Alona Wartofsky for the *Washington Post* (May 19, 2002, on-line), "Colin conveys a quiet reserve and strength of character. There's a natural humility matched with intelligence and wit to sustain the person that appears onscreen. The more time you spend with him onscreen, the more interested in him you become." Two other assessments of his skills appear in reviews of *Girl with a Pearl Earring*: in the *New Republic* (February 2, 2004), Stanley Kauffmann described Firth as "an actor who keeps holding us because he keeps turning his talent like a prism, displaying different facets of credibility"; and in the *New Statesman* (Janu-

ary 19, 2004), Mark Kermode praised him for "pulling on the period pants with the ease of one who knows he's in his element without ever descending to the narcissistic soft-pedalling demanded of his 'sex symbol' status."

Colin Firth was born in Grayshott, Hampshire, England, on September 10, 1960. (Several sources have reported his birthplace as being in Africa.) According to Susie Steiner in the London *Guardian* (March 31, 2001, on-line), his parents are "staunchly leftwing . . . and concerned about the social issues of the day." His mother, Shirley Firth, lectured on comparative religion at the Open University (which maintains more than 300 "study centers" in the United Kingdom and overseas); his father, David Firth, taught history at King Alfred's College, in Winchester. Firth has a younger sister, Kate, who is a voice coach, and a younger brother, Jonathan, an actor, whose credits include the BBC-TV series *Middlemarch*. For several years after his birth, Firth's family lived in Nigeria, where his parents taught as participants in an exchange program; according to some sources, his grandfather and grandmother, who were missionaries, also lived in Nigeria then. When Firth was about five and ready to enter elementary school, his family returned to the U.K. During the next half-dozen years, they moved several times within England. Firth has often described his schoolboy memories as unremittingly unhappy. In 1972, the year he turned 12, his family spent a year in the United States, where he attended a junior high school in St. Louis, Missouri. In a conversation with William Leith for the London *Observer* (April 9, 2000), he described the experience as miserable; he felt out of place and conspicuously British in an environment in which kids his age wore T-shirts printed with anti–Vietnam War slogans and appeared to him "like something out of Woodstock"—a reference to the huge three-day music festival where thousands of hippies cavorted on a field in New York State in 1969. He dealt with his discomfort by adopting an attitude that made him unapproachable. "Someone would say, 'What's your name?'" Firth recalled to Leith, "and I'd say, 'Mind your own business.'" Thus, according to Leith, "the first serious acting he did was to pretend he was tough, when he was not." Reflecting on his childhood, Firth told Alona Wartofsky, "I am an outsider. I have always been. I'm not lamenting that fact. It does create confusion, and it is a little painful . . . but I think it's been enormously beneficial to me." He added, "I suppose I got into feeling a little bit different. . . . I saw other perspectives."

Back in England, by age 14 Firth had fallen far behind his classmates in math and science proficiency; by his own account, he once received a grade of 3 percent on a chemistry exam. He was far more successful in English and music courses at Montgomery of Alamein, a state-run, all-boys secondary school in Winchester; in a conversation with Garth Pearce for the *Times Educational Supplement* (September 13, 2002, on-line), he cited several of his English and music teachers as outstanding. He also earned praise for his acting in school plays. After he completed secondary school, in 1979, he worked for six months for the Shaw Theatre in London, handling phone calls, and the next six months as a wardrobe assistant (or cloakroom attendant, according to one source) at the National Theatre, also in London. During that time he successfully auditioned for admittance, in 1980, to the Drama Centre London, now a division of the Central Saint Martins College of Art and Design, part of the London Institute; the center's curriculum, according to its Web site, is based upon a synthesis of the Stanislavski method of acting (which emphasizes the importance of creating characters who have interior lives, by drawing upon one's own memories, emotions, and experiences) and the study of movement as developed by Rudolf Laban. One of Firth's instructors, the director Christopher Fettes, remembered Firth as a "conspicuously intelligent" and gifted student. "It is very rare to have the privilege of training people for the theatre who are by nature poets," he told Leith. "And Colin is." Yat Malmgren, a co-founder of the Drama Centre, told Karen S. Schneider for *People* (February 8, 1999) that Firth "was the kind of student who almost never occurs. He had everything I expect and rarely find: imagination, intelligence, logic, common sense." In his senior year at the Drama Centre, Firth earned plaudits for his performance of the title role in Shakespeare's *Hamlet*—a production mounted especially for him at the school, where the drama had never before been staged.

Soon afterward Firth landed his first professional role, in the award-winning West End production of Julian Mitchell's drama *Another Country* (1981), based on the true story of Guy Burgess and Donald Maclean, schoolboy friends who as adults became spies for the Soviet Union. Firth was one of several successive replacements for the actor Rupert Everett in the role of Guy Bennett (the Burgess character), a privileged homosexual who becomes a traitor-in-the-making after befriending another boy, Tommy Judd (the Maclean character), a staunch Marxist who refuses to conform to the repressive, snobbish culture of their upper-crust, 1930s British boarding school. In the film version of *Another Country* (1984), directed by Marek Kanievska, Everett reprised the role of Bennett while Firth took on that of Judd.

After his stint on the West End, more roles came Firth's way, and he did not return to the Drama Centre. He appeared on stage in George Bernard Shaw's *The Doctor's Dilemma* in 1984, Arthur Schnitzler's *The Lonely Road* in 1985, and Eugene O'Neill's *Desire Under the Elms* in 1987. He was also seen on television, in the movie *Nineteen Nineteen* (1984), which starred Paul Scofield, whom he later named in an interview with Annarita Caroli for *Caffe Europa* (July 12, 2002, online) as "the actor I learnt most from." He also had parts in such TV miniseries as *Lost Empires* (1985)

and *The Secret Garden* (1987), and in plays broadcast on radio, he read the part of the 14th-century British king Richard II in Anthony Minghella's *Two Planks and a Passion* (1986) and that of the 20th-century British poet Rupert Brooke in *The One Before the Last* (1987). He was nominated for a London *Evening Standard* Award for his portrayal of Tom Birkin, a shell-shocked survivor of World War I, in the feature film *A Month in the Country* (1991), directed by Pat O'Connor and co-starring Kenneth Branagh.

In 1987 Firth starred as Robert Lawrence in *Tumbledown,* a fiercely controversial BBC-TV drama written by Charles Woods, about a real-life Scottish army officer who suffered severe brain damage during the Falklands War of 1982, in which Great Britain rebuffed an attempt by Argentina to gain control of the Falkland Islands by force. The story of the once happy-go-lucky, battle-loving soldier, whose alleged mistreatment by the military during his rehabilitation filled him with bitterness, gripped Firth powerfully. The actor's portrayal of Lawrence, which Giuliana Mercorio described in *Films & Filming* (September 1989) as "intelligent, brutally honest, and utterly devoid of sentimentality," earned Firth the Royal Television Society's award for best actor in 1989 and a BAFTA (British Academy of Film and Television Arts) nomination in the same category. Firth, who found *Tumbledown* "the most exciting film script" he had worked from until then, told Mercorio, "It's rather difficult to be objective about [*Tumbledown*] as a drama. I got to know Robert Lawrence [who was often present during shooting] very closely, and it was a very strange relationship because he's not someone I think I would have become friends with under normal circumstances. Seeing [the movie], all I could think of was, 'is that all, is that all that's made it onto the screen?' After what I learnt, what I went through, what we all went through—it's just a film, that's all it is."

Firth was next cast as an emotionally disturbed movie buff named Adrian LeDuc in Martin Donovan's dark psychological/political thriller *Apartment Zero* (1988), which was set in Buenos Aires, Argentina. The actor told interviewers that he became obsessed with the country's recent history, in particular the so-called dirty war (1976–83), in which thousands of Argentinians (now known as the disappeared) were killed during the ruling military junta's campaign to wipe out leftist dissidents and others. Some of the army officers responsible for the murders were later convicted of their crimes, but all were pardoned by a subsequent government, and the bodies of the vast majority of the victims were never found. Firth told Giuliana Mercorio that he and his co-star, Hart Bochner, talked about Argentina "constantly." "We were both very nervous and frightened a lot of the time," he said. Firth won the Seattle Film Festival's 1988 award for best actor for his work in *Apartment Zero*.

During the next half-dozen years, Firth appeared on television in the movies *Out of the Blue* (1991), *Hostages* (1992), *Master of the Moor* (1993), and *The Deep Blue Sea* (1994); on stage in Harold Pinter's *The Caretaker* (1991) and *Chatsky* (1993), a translation by Anthony Burgess of an early 1800s Russian tragicomedy; and, on the silver screen, in *Valmont* (1989), *Wings of Fame* (1989), *Femme Fatale* (1990), *The Hour of the Pig* (1993), *Good Girls* (1994), and *Circle of Friends* (1994). For about three years during that period, he lived with the actress Meg Tilly (one of his co-stars in *Valmont*) and their son, William, who was born in 1990, in a remote part of British Columbia, Canada, that he described to William Leith as "serious wilderness . . . really the middle of nowhere." "I had a kind of reclusive impulse at the time, but not that reclusive," he said. He and Tilly separated amicably in 1993.

Firth reportedly had some misgivings before he accepted the role of Fitzwilliam Darcy in the TV miniseries *Pride and Prejudice*, a joint BBC/A&E venture directed by Simon Langdon; nevertheless, he later told Alona Wartofsky, "Whatever way you look at it, I think that story does make him sort of irresistible." He explained to Lesley O'Toole for the London *Times* (April 9, 2001, on-line), "It was Mr. Darcy's obstacles and problems which appealed to me, not the fact that I was going to play a wonderful romantic man." He added, referring to the moment when Darcy, overwhelmed by repressed feelings of sexual passion and affection for the main female character, Elizabeth Bennet (played by Jennifer Ehle), jumps fully clothed into a pond, "I wouldn't have been able to do that famous scene coming out of the pond with the wet shirt unless it was about a man who's absolutely paralysed with embarrassment. It's not about a man saying, 'All right girls, here's the shirt.'" Referring to the repeated images of Darcy "looking down his nose at everyone," Firth said to O'Toole, "It reminds me of high-school parties where you'd stand there, feeling all hung-up and repressed. And the only way you can deal with that is to pretend it's because you're superior and enigmatic. So that's what you hide behind to deal with the paralysing situations." Firth told Jenny Cooney Carillo for *Australian TV Week* (July 6–12, 2002, on-line) that when he began hearing about female viewers' intense devotion to Langdon's *Pride and Prejudice*, "I didn't believe it at first because it was my mother who was trying to convince me . . . but then it astonished me to discover that there really was a phenomenon going on around the whole series." Firth next starred in several television movies or miniseries, including *The Widowing of Holroyd* (1996), *Nostromo* (1997), *Donovan Quick* (1999), *The Turn of the Screw* (1999), and *Conspiracy* (2001), in which he was cast opposite Kenneth Branagh. He appeared on the silver screen in, among other films, *Shakespeare in Love* (1998), in a "dastardly hilarious" performance as the "villain" Lord Wessex, as John Larsen wrote for lightviews.com

(2002); *Fever Pitch* (1997), as a fanatical, clumsy-looking soccer buff who becomes romantically involved with a fellow teacher who detests the game, in an adaptation of an unusual memoir by Nick Hornby; *A Thousand Acres* (1997), as a seductive hippie, in an adaptation of a Jane Smiley novel that has been called a feminist farm-belt version of Shakespeare's *King Lear*; *My Life So Far* (1999), as a cheerful inventor and father in early 1900s Scotland who falls in love with his brother's French fiancée; and several movies that received virtually no press in the United States: *Secret Laughter of Women* (1999), *Blackadder Back and Forth* (2000), *Relative Values* (2000), and *Londinium* (2000).

In a role tailored for him (or, more accurately, his Mr. Darcy), Firth played Mark Darcy, a dull, wooden lawyer who belatedly recognizes the charms of the title character (portrayed by Renée Zellweger) in the comedy *Bridget Jones's Diary* (2001), which also co-starred Hugh Grant as Bridget's boss and sometime lover. In Oliver Parker's *The Importance of Being Earnest* (2002), based on Oscar Wilde's 1895 farce (which Wilde subtitled "A Trivial Play for Serious People"), Firth was cast as Jack Worthing, a member of Parliament, who, like his ne'er-do-well friend Algernon (Rupert Everett), pretends to be a man named Ernest; both Jack and Algernon fall in love with women determined to marry someone with that name. "I framed this adaptation in a way that Jack was central to the emotional narrative," Parker told Alona Wartofsky. "So I was looking for somebody who has a certain sympathetic quality, who could be at once vulnerable and complex. And Colin, I think, is very skillful at creating an active inner life while sustaining the comedic requirements of the piece." In a review for *Newsweek* (May 27, 2002), David Ansen wrote, "Firth's comic timing is subtle and seductive, and plays nicely off Everett's jaded foppery." "There is nothing more intoxicating for an actor and nothing sets you on fire more than good language," Firth told Jenny Cooney Carillo. "So, when the language vibrates as it does with Oscar Wilde, it becomes a very enjoyable experience. . . . You actually have to process it through your intellect and be equal to it, which makes it an incredible intellectual challenge." In 2003 Firth starred in the perky teen comedy *What a Girl Wants*, as a stuffy, wealthy British politician, the long-lost father of a 17-year-old American girl (played by Amanda Bynes) who pays him a surprise visit. Also in 2003 he co-starred with Minnie Driver and Heather Graham in the little-noticed romantic comedy *Hope Springs*, in which he played an English artist who moves to Vermont to mend his broken heart. Firth's other 2003 films include *Girl with a Pearl Earring*, in which he gave a critically acclaimed performance as the painter Johannes Vermeer, and *Love Actually*, a romantic comedy that follows the intersecting lives of eight Londoners during the month before Christmas one year.

Firth has often told interviewers that he considers comedic acting to be considerably more demanding than drama. Also difficult for him has been the task of establishing an identity in the public imagination outside the Fitzwilliam Darcy mold, despite the years and many roles separating him from Darcy's jodhpurs and chin-length sideburns. As William Leith exclaimed in his 2000 profile of the actor, "Colin Firth! Mr. Darcy! You cannot mention one of these names without the other following immediately." Firth may be helped in his task by the attention he has drawn in recent years for activities not related to acting. In 2000, for example, at the invitation of Nick Hornby, he wrote a story for *Speaking with the Angel*, a collection of tales by such writers as Dave Eggers, Helen Fielding, Melissa Bank, Zadie Smith, Roddy Doyle, Irvine Welsh, and Hornby himself. (Hornby edited the book, a portion of whose profits were to benefit the British school for autistic children that his son attends.) Firth's piece, entitled "The Department of Nothing," a first-person account in which an 11-year-old boy describes his relationship with his ailing grandmother, earned praise from British reviewers. On another front, in 1999 Firth joined politicians and religious leaders in a protest outside the Parliament buildings in London to condemn the government's policies on political-asylum seekers. More recently, he publicly criticized Prime Minister Tony Blair's support of the U.S.-led war against Iraq.

In November 2004 Firth again appeared on the silver screen as Mark Darcy, in *Bridget Jones: The Edge of Reason*. Comparing himself with Jane Austen's Mr. Darcy, Firth told an interviewer for *People* (May 14, 2001), "I have far more of a sense of humor, and physically I am much more animated." The actress Embeth Davidtz, who appeared in *Bridget Jones's Diary*, described the actor to the *People* interviewer as "bright and funny and sparky." "At rest," according to William Leith, "Firth's face is set in a sort of handsome grimace, he looks easily haunted. The mouth turns slightly down; the bones of the face cast shadows. But his expressions change with almost no effort; as an acting tool, this is a highly strung face. One slight touch on the happy pedal and he beams; an iota of misery and he glowers." Firth told Leith, "I never saw myself as Mr Ugly, but I'm not that handsome. I can sort of be made to look quite a lot better or quite a lot worse." Firth was scheduled to star in three films in 2005: *Nanny McPhee*, *Where the Truth Lies*, and *Toyer*.

In 1997 Firth married Livia Giuggiolo, a native of Italy who, when the two met, on the set of *Nostromo*, was working in the film industry. The actor, who speaks Italian fluently, lives with his wife and their two sons—Luca, born in 2001, and Mateo, born in 2003—in London; the family regularly spends time in Italy. Firth has said that his visits in California with his eldest son, Will, serve as welcome periods of relaxation for him.

—L.S.

Suggested Reading: *Films & Filming* p18+ Sep. 1989, with photos; (London) *Evening Standard* (on-line) May 8, 2003, with photo; (London) *Guardian* (on-line) Feb. 24, 1999, Mar. 31, 2001, with photo; (London) *Observer* (on-line) Apr. 9, 2000, with photo; *Repubblica* (on-line) Oct. 16, 2001, with photo; *Washington Post* (on-line) May 19, 2002; *International Who's Who*, 2000

Selected Films: *Nineteen Nineteen*, 1984; *Apartment Zero*, 1988; *Valmont*, 1989; *Wings of Fame*, 1989; *Femme Fatale*, 1990; *A Month in the Country*, 1991; *The Hour of the Pig*, 1993; *Master of the Moor*, 1993; *The Deep Blue Sea*, 1994; *Good Girls*, 1994; *Circle of Friends*, 1994; *The English Patient*, 1996; *Fever Pitch*, 1997; *A Thousand Acres*, 1997; *Shakespeare in Love*, 1998; *Secret Laughter of Women*, 1999; *Blackadder Back and Forth*, 2000; *Relative Values*, 2000; *Londinium*, 2000; *Bridget Jones's Diary*, 2001; *The Importance of Being Earnest*, 2002; *Girl with a Pearl Earring*, 2003; *Love Actually*, 2003; *What a Girl Wants*, 2003; *Hope Springs*, 2003; *Bridget Jones: The Edge of Reason*, 2004

Selected Plays: *Another Country*, 1981; *The Doctor's Dilemma*, 1984; *The Lonely Road*, 1985; *Desire Under the Elms*, 1987; *The Caretaker*, 1991; *Chatsky*, 1993

Selected Television Movies, Series, or Miniseries: *Lost Empires*, 1985; *The Secret Garden*, 1987; *Tumbledown*, 1987; *Out of the Blue*, 1991; *Hostages*, 1992; *Pride and Prejudice*, 1995; *The Widowing of Holroyd*, 1996; *Nostromo*, 1997; *The Turn of the Screw*, 1999

Foner, Eric

Feb. 7, 1943– Historian

Address: 620 Fayerweather Hall, Columbia University, New York, NY 10027

For Eric Foner, the DeWitt Clinton Professor of History at Columbia University, in New York City, and a specialist in the Civil War, Reconstruction, slavery, and other aspects of 19th-century America, history is not a monolithic, unidirectional tale. Rather, it is a story that can change over time, depending on whose version one hears and the circumstances under which the telling occurs. As Daniel Snowman wrote for *History Today* (January 2000), "Foner eschews any single-thread approach to the complex warp and weft of history. His method, rather, is to hold up a particular conceit, personality, party or event and then turn it around and examine its multifarious facets from various perspectives, like a diamond in the light." Through his

Courtesy of Eric Foner

Eric Foner

and engaging to those outside academia. In addition to the 17 books he has written or edited since 1970, he has penned numerous articles, essays, reviews, and op-ed pieces for such popular and academic publications as the *New York Times*, the *Washington Post*, the *New York Review of Books*, and the *Journal of American History*. He has also co-curated two museum exhibitions focusing on the Civil War period and served as a historical consultant for several National Parks Service sites and museums, as well as for the 1999 Broadway musical *The Civil War*. In 1993, to the chagrin of some fellow historians, he rewrote the five-minute history of the United States that introduces the Hall of Presidents exhibit at Disney World. Shrugging off criticism from colleagues who deemed his collaboration with Disney inappropriate, Foner told *Publishers Weekly*, "History ought to be good history, whether it's on TV or in museums or at Disney World."

Eric Foner was born on February 7, 1943 in New York City and grew up in Long Beach, Long Island, New York. His mother, Liza Kraitz Foner, was a high-school art teacher. Two of his uncles, Moe Foner and Henry Foner, were prominent union leaders. Before his birth his father, Jack Donald Foner, and his uncle Philip S. Foner taught history at the City College of New York. In 1941, in what, 40 years later, the city Board of Higher Education termed an "egregious violation of academic freedom," both were fired (along with 58 other staff members) under suspicion of being Communists—in Jack Foner's case, largely because of his active support for, among other causes, the struggle for civil rights for African-Americans, according to an obituary of him posted on the Web site of the University of Pennsylvania English Department (December 16, 1999). For the next three decades, Jack Foner supported his family mainly as a freelance lecturer on current affairs. From 1969 to 1976 he taught at Colby College, in Maine, where he established one of the nation's first black-studies programs. As children, Eric Foner and his younger brother, Tom, were consistently exposed to the left-wing political convictions of their parents and uncles, for whom history and current events were favorite topics of conversation. In his 2002 book, *Who Owns History? Rethinking the Past in a Changing World*, as excerpted on-line, Foner recalled, "Only gradually did I realize that other families did not discuss the intricacies of international relations and domestic politics over the dinner table, or follow election returns in France, India, and Guatemala as avidly as those in the United States."

In 1957, at the age of 14, Foner attended the first civil rights march on Washington, D.C. That occasion was not the first on which a member of the Foner family expressed an interest in African-American politics. Philip S. Foner had devoted much of his academic career to publishing and writing about the works of the ex-slave and early abolitionist Frederick Douglass, and Jack and Liza Foner had made a point of opening their children's

pioneering archival research and writings, Foner has analyzed traditional narratives with an eye toward the roles of gender, class, and especially race in American history. Above all, Foner insists that "good history" must take into account the diverse experiences of minorities, women, and laborers in addition to the activities of political and financial leaders. In an interview with *Publishers Weekly* (October 26, 1998), Foner remarked, "There is virtue, I think, in trying to see history whole and not excluding large groups of people."

The concept of freedom has been of especial interest to Foner, so much so that it has become, in Snowman's words, a "rondo theme" for the historian. In particular, Foner has explored the different ways in which Americans experience and think about freedom, which, he believes, have much to do with the legacy of racial inequality left by slavery. As he explained to *Publishers Weekly*, "The existence of slavery has so shaped our idea of freedom. Freedom is so often defined by its opposite rather than as an idea. . . . Whites seem to feel freedom is something you're born with and that someone is trying to take it away. Blacks see it as something you're aspiring to, working toward, that is never quite achieved." Indeed, Foner's "particular contribution," Snowman wrote, "has been to illustrate the chameleon-like quality of freedom and to suggest the diverse, elusive, mercurial nature of the concept. What 'Freedom' has meant, to whom, when and where—these themes run through the entire skein of American history, and they inform and inspire much of Eric Foner's work."

In keeping with his belief in the power of the past to illuminate the present, Foner has demonstrated a commitment to making history accessible

eyes to the history and ongoing plight of black Americans. In an interview with Brian Lamb for the C-SPAN television program *Booknotes* (November 15, 1998), Foner recalled, "I grew up, well before the civil rights movement, just knowing that the condition of black Americans was sort of a standing test of the . . . truth of the professions of this country about liberty and equality. And I also learned very early that some of the rhetoric about freedom in our country doesn't always measure up to reality."

In 1959 Foner enrolled as a freshman at Columbia with the intention of pursuing a major in astronomy, his interest since early childhood. Meanwhile, the interest in social progress that he had absorbed from his family persisted, and he soon became involved in a number of pro–civil rights activities. During his undergraduate years, in solidarity with blacks who staged sit-ins at segregated department-store lunch counters in the South, he joined picket lines in front of Woolworth's department stores in New York City. He also served as the first president of ACTION, a student political party that issued newsletters about civil rights, sponsored folk-music concerts, and fought against the discriminatory renting policies of local landlords. In his junior year his political concerns took the form of a preoccupation with the Civil War era, which has since become his passion. The catalyst for Foner's switch from astronomy to history was his enrollment in a seminar on the Civil War period taught by James P. Shenton (who later wrote the foreword and conclusion to Jack Donald Foner's book *Blacks in the Military in American History* [1974]). In Shenton Foner found an intellectual role model to complement the early example of his father, from whom Foner had, as he wrote in *Who Owns History?*, "imbibed a way of thinking about the past in which visionaries and underdogs—Tom Paine, Wendell Phillips, Eugene V. Debs, and W.E.B. Du Bois—were as central to the historical drama as presidents and captains of industry, and [learned] how a commitment to social justice could infuse one's attitudes toward the past." Under Shenton's tutelage Foner came to an understanding of the connections between history and politics; in particular, he began to appreciate the links between 19th-century black history and the current experiences and hardships of African-Americans. By the end of his junior year, Foner had given up astronomy in order to pursue a history major.

Foner wrote his senior thesis on the Free Soil Party of 1848 under the supervision of the historian Richard Hofstadter. (Ironically, Hofstadter had replaced Jack Donald Foner at City College in 1941; he had begun to teach at Columbia in 1959.) The project, an exploration of antebellum Republican ideology, was Foner's first foray into archival research and a reflection of his interest in the ties between Civil War–era history and civil rights. "The fact that the civil rights movement was then reaching its crescendo," Foner wrote in *Who Owns His-*

tory?, "powerfully affected my choice of subject: the racial attitudes of those who opposed the expansion of slavery." Upon his graduation from Columbia, in 1963, Foner was awarded membership to the Phi Beta Kappa society and a Kellett Fellowship to study at Oriel College, at Oxford University, in England. He had just enough time to attend the landmark March on Washington that occurred on August 28 of that year before setting off for Oxford, where he would spend the next two years studying for his second bachelor of arts degree.

At Oriel, under Oxford's tutorial system, Foner was required to write a paper every week and read it aloud to a tutor. The experience served as a crash course in writing clear expository prose very quickly, and Foner has since attributed his prolificacy as a writer to those assignments. The Oxford program "taught [him] how to write very fast, not to worry about it, and not to obsess about it," he told *Publishers Weekly*, and in *Who Owns History?* he added, "I probably owe it to my years at Oxford that writer's block has never been one of my problems."

Foner finished his program at Oriel in 1965 and returned to New York to enroll in Columbia's doctoral history program. That decade saw the escalation of U.S. involvement in the Vietnam War; Foner, political as ever, became active in the antiwar movement, and in 1968 he took part in the famous Columbia student uprising, during which student protesters ransacked the university president's office and occupied several university buildings, bringing classes to a virtual standstill. Also during his years of doctoral study, he taught a summer course in African-American history for Double Discovery, a Columbia-affiliated program for minority high-school students. Under Hofstadter's supervision, he wrote his dissertation on the Republican position in the years before the Civil War, returning to the subject on which he had written his undergraduate thesis. He was awarded his Ph.D. by Columbia in 1969, and his paper served as the basis for his first book, entitled *Free Soil, Free Labor, Free Men: The Ideology of the Republican Party Before the Civil War*. The book was published in 1970 and greeted with positive reviews; David Donald, writing for the *New York Times Book Review* (October 18, 1970), described it as "a useful and fair-minded summary of what Republicanism meant in the 1850's, and . . . especially valuable as a corrective to older historical stereotypes," and William W. Freehling, writing for the *New York Review of Books* (September 23, 1971), called it "the best guide yet written to the Republican position in the years before the Civil War."

From 1969 to 1973 Foner served as an assistant professor of history at Columbia. During this period he taught Columbia's first course in African-American history, drawing objections from some black students, who felt that the class ought to be taught by a black scholar. In 1971 he published *Nat Turner*, a biography of the slave-rebellion leader, and served as the editor of *America's Black Past: A Reader in Afro-American History*. From 1972 to 1973 he held an American Council of Learned Societies fellowship.

In 1973 Foner left Columbia to pursue an associate professorship at City College. Two years later he was awarded a prestigious Guggenheim fellowship. He published his third book, *Tom Paine and Revolutionary America*, in 1976, and his fourth, *Politics and Ideology in the Age of the Civil War*, in 1980. Of the latter, J. H. Silbey wrote for *American Historical Review* (October 1981), "[Foner] is excellent at delineating the dominant ideologies and linking them to political events." In the *New Republic* (November 22, 1980), C. V. Woodward praised Foner's treatment of the connection between economic concerns and race politics, claiming, "The author is dead right in fixing on control of black labor as the basic issue of Reconstruction."

Foner returned to Columbia University in 1982 to accept a position as the DeWitt Clinton Professor of History, the same chair that his mentor Richard Hofstadter had once held. In 1983 he published *Nothing but Freedom: Emancipation and Its Legacy*, and from 1985 to 1992 he served as the consulting editor of the *American Century* series, a collection of books about American history, society, and politics published by Hill and Wang. In 1988 he published his sixth book, *Reconstruction: America's Unfinished Revolution 1863-1877*, a massive work of research and synthesis that had taken nearly a decade to complete. For source material Foner used a number of archives that had never before been tapped by historians, demonstrating a breadth of scholarship the likes of which, Theodore Rosengarten wrote for the *Nation* (May 28, 1988), was "not likely to be repeated for a generation." The book, generally regarded as the authoritative history of Reconstruction, examined the economic, political, and social forces that shaped the postbellum period and explored the ways in which the ultimate failures of Reconstruction had established an enduring legacy of racism in America. David Herbert Donald, writing for the *New Republic* (August 1, 1988), noted that Foner had "performed a real service in bringing blacks front and center in the Reconstruction drama, where they belong." Daniel Snowman echoed Donald's sentiment, remarking, "Foner finally placed the black community centre stage, not in the passive role of slaves but as active participants after emancipation in a series of complex social and political processes. The book was thus a major act of historical reassessment—one, moreover, that accorded precisely with the temper of the times." Foner received numerous awards for his work, among them the Bancroft Prize, the Parkman Prize, and the *Los Angeles Times* Book Award.

Between 1990 and 1993 Foner published four books: *A Short History of Reconstruction* (1990), *The New American History* (1990), *The Reader's Companion to American History* (1991), and *Free-dom's Lawmakers: A Directory of Black Officeholders During Reconstruction* (1993). In 1990 he acted as co-curator, with Olivia Mahoney, of *A House Divided: America in the Age of Lincoln*, an exhibition at the Chicago Historical Society. In 1993 and for some years thereafter he served as consulting editor for Hill and Wang's *Critical Issues* series, and in 1995 he collaborated again with Mahoney to curate *America's Reconstruction: People and Politics After the Civil War*, a traveling exhibition that opened at the Virginia Historical Society. Also in 1995 Foner was named Scholar of the Year by the New York Council for the Humanities.

Foner's 1998 book, *The Story of American Freedom*, was nominated for a National Book Award. An examination of the ways in which the meaning of freedom has evolved and been contested throughout American history, *The Story of American Freedom* addressed the diverse experiences of previously marginalized people, particularly women and people of color. "Over the course of our history," Foner wrote in his preface, "American freedom has been both a reality and a mythic ideal—a living truth for millions of Americans; a cruel mockery for others." Writing for *Commonweal* (November 6, 1998), Alan Wolfe called the book "an impressive challenge to the postmodern suspicion of master narratives."

Foner served as president of the American Historical Association in 2000. Two years later, in 2002, Hill and Wang published *Who Owns History?*, Foner's consideration of the historian's relationship to the world of the past, present, and future. According to the Hill and Wang Web site, Michael Kammen of Cornell University, in Ithaca, New York, expressed admiration for Foner's ethical approach to history, claiming, "Above all, the book carries and conveys what I call 'moral weight,' which is one of Eric Foner's notable gifts as a historian." What Kammen called Foner's "moral weight" was interpreted by others in a more negative light; Ronald Radosh, writing for the conservative *National Review* (July 10, 2002, on-line), complained, "In Foner's writing, the probing analysis of a scholar like Hofstadter gives way to the ranting of a left-wing polemicist."

Foner continues to teach history at Columbia, where he is admired by students and colleagues alike; he was the recipient of the Society of Columbia Graduates' Great Teacher Award in 1991. His most recent book, *Give Me Liberty! An American History*, was published in 2004, along with a companion volume of documents called *Voices of Freedom: A Documentary History*. On June 20, 1965 Foner married Naomi Achs, a graduate of Barnard College in New York and an associate producer with the Children's Television Workshop; the couple divorced in 1977. Foner lives in Columbia's faculty housing with his second wife, the dance historian and critic Lynn Garafola, and their daughter, Daria Rose, to whom *The Story of American Freedom* was dedicated.

—L.W.

Suggested Reading: *Booknotes* (on-line) Nov. 15, 1998; *History Today* p26+ Jan. 2000; *Publishers Weekly* (on-line) Oct. 26, 1998; Cimbala, Paul A. and Robert F. Himmelberg, editors. *Historians and Race: Autobiography and the Writing of History*, 1996

Selected Books: *Free Soil, Free Labor, Free Men: The Ideology of the Republican Party Before the Civil War*, 1970; *Nat Turner*, 1971; *Tom Paine and Revolutionary America*, 1976; *Politics and Ideology in the Age of the Civil War*, 1980; *Reconstruction: America's Unfinished Revolution 1863–1877*, 1988; *Thomas Paine*, 1995; *The Story of American Freedom*, 1998; *Who Owns History? Rethinking the Past in a Changing World*, 2002; *Give Me Liberty! An American Hsitory*, 2004; as editor—*Voices of Freedom: A Documentary History*, 2004

Amanda Edwards/Getty Images

Frum, David

(fruhm)

June 30, 1960– Writer; political commentator; foreign-policy pundit

Address: c/o American Enterprise Institute, 1150 17th St., N.W., Washington, DC 20036

From 2001 to 2002 the conservative ideologue, writer, and political commentator David Frum served as special assistant for economic speech-writing under President George W. Bush; it is Frum whom some credit—and others deride—as the

coiner of the now famous phrase "axis of evil," which President Bush first used in his 2002 State of the Union address, referring to the nations of Iran, Iraq, and North Korea. In that speech, given only a few months after the September 11, 2001 terrorist attacks on the U.S., Bush characterized those countries as supporters of international terrorism and as admitted enemies of the United States, and the phrase he used to do so took on a life of its own, cited often in the press as a symbol of the Bush administration's foreign policy of preemptive military strikes and vigorous war against terror. Among other works of nonfiction, Frum is the author of the best-selling book *The Right Man: The Surprise Presidency of George W. Bush* (2003), which was the first insider's look at the Bush administration, and the co-author, with Richard Perle, of *An End to Evil: How to Win the War on Terror* (2003). In addition, Frum contributes opinion pieces and articles on foreign policy to publications including the *New York Times,* the *Wall Street Journal,* the *Weekly Standard,* and Canada's *National Post,* and he writes a daily column, "David Frum's Diary," for the Web site of the *National Review.* He is an advocate of limited federal governance; economic conservatism; and the preemptive use of military force to protect the U.S. and to effect positive change in the world. In his writings Frum has supported the 2003 U.S. invasion of Iraq and the Bush administration's methods for prosecuting the war on terror. In doing so he has at times alienated journalists and members of the foreign-policy community, including fellow conservatives, with his sometimes harsh criticisms of those with differing opinions. Frum is a *Readers Digest* Fellow at the American Enterprise Institute. He also serves as a panelist on the National Public Radio (NPR) program *Left, Right, and Center* and has provided commentary for the NPR segment *Morning Edition.* In 1996 the *Wall Street Journal* described Frum as "one of the leading political commentators of his generation," and in 2001 Judge Richard A. Posner's book *Public Intellectuals: A Study of Decline,* listed Frum as one of the 100 most influential minds in the United States.

David Frum was born to a prominent family in Toronto, the capital of the Canadian province of Ontario, on June 30, 1960. His father, Murray Frum, was a wealthy real-estate developer in the Toronto area. His mother, Barbara Frum, who died in 1992, was one of Canada's most respected and influential journalists. In addition to writing columns for Canadian national newspapers such as the *Globe and Mail* and the *Toronto Star,* in the 1970s she co-hosted a highly successful Canadian Broadcasting Corp. (CBC) radio interview program, *As It Happens,* and in the 1980s she co-hosted the CBC television newsmagazine the *Journal.* Barbara Frum won many awards, including the National Press Club of Canada Award for outstanding contribution to Canadian journalism (1975) and the Order of Canada (1979).

Frum and his sister, Linda, who, like her brother, later became a conservative journalist, grew up in the rarefied air of the family household. As Malcolm Gladwell described it for *Saturday Night* (December 1994/January 1995), during the 1970s the Frum home "became a kind of eighteenth-century salon for literary figures and intellectuals passing through Toronto." Barbara Frum was, as her son described her to Gladwell, a "fifties liberal." When asked to explain how he came to hold political convictions so different from those of his parents, Frum pointed to the respective eras in which he and his parents came of age. "My parents are from the Depression," he explained to Gladwell. "They remembered the victory in World War II. They both remembered the extraordinary spell of good fortune that befell Canada from the forties to the seventies." By contrast, he said, his and his sister's "formative experience was the great recession of the 1970s, the catastrophe of government social-welfare programmes, the American military defeat in Vietnam, then the inexorable growth of Soviet military power all over the world."

Frum received, simultaneously, B.A. and M.A. degrees in history from Yale University, in New Haven, Connecticut, in 1982. In 1986 he was appointed a visiting lecturer at Yale. The following year he graduated cum laude from Harvard University Law School, in Cambridge, Massachusetts, where he also served as president of the school's Federalist Society. From 1989 to 1992 Frum worked as an assistant editor of the *Wall Street Journal*, for which he has written many opinion pieces. In 1992 he was a columnist for *Forbes* magazine. While serving from 1994 to 2001 as a fellow of the Manhattan Institute for Policy Research—which is described on its official Web site as a think tank dedicated to "new ideas that foster greater economic choice and individual responsibility"—he continued writing for newspapers and magazines and began to write books.

Frum's first book, *Dead Right*, a look at conservative politics and ideology in America, was published in 1994—the year in which the Republican Party took control of both houses of Congress for the first time in more than 40 years and the new Speaker of the House, Newt Gingrich, presented the controversial Contract with America, the new Republican majority's political and social agenda for the country. In *Dead Right* Frum enumerated what he saw as the shortcomings of the Republican Party: that it had, in his view, lost sight of its core conservative values in the 1980s in order to become more centrist. He also found fault with the administrations of the Republican presidents Ronald Reagan (1981–89) and George H. W. Bush (1989–93), during both of which, contrary to basic conservative prescriptions, the federal government grew. Frum urged fellow conservatives to fight for a smaller federal government, which would limit its expenditures, including its funding of social-welfare programs. Pointing to the ironies surrounding the highly publicized book, Malcolm

Gladwell observed, "What has propelled *Dead Right* . . . is not so much the arguments it makes but who has been making them. It is an unabashedly patriotic book on partisan American politics by a Canadian. It is an attack on Ronald Reagan by a conservative. It is a book by a young man animated not by the angry passion of youth but by the despairing sigh of old age. All of these incongruities . . . have combined to give Frum's message an urgency and freshness it would not otherwise have." As quoted on the Web site elephanthost.com, the conservative icon William F. Buckley Jr. called *Dead Right* "the most refreshing ideological experience in a generation." In the *New York Times* (November 20, 1994), Frank Rich praised Frum's work as "the smartest book written from the inside about the American conservative movement." Frum's next book-length efforts were *What's Right: The New Conservative Majority and the Remaking of America* (1996) and *How We Got Here: The 70's: The Decade That Brought You Modern Life—For Better or Worse* (2000). Commenting on the latter book, Mark Rozzo wrote for the *New Yorker* (March 6, 2000) that Frum argued that the 1970s "ushered in nearly every problematic aspect of modern life, from irony and radical feminism to divorce and raspberry-flavored vinegar."

From 2001 to 2002 Frum was a special assistant to President George W. Bush for economic speechwriting. He was instrumental in creating the phrase "axis of evil," which, after being used by President Bush during his 2002 State of the Union address, was splashed across newspaper headlines and discussed exhaustively in the media. As Frum wrote in *The Right Man*, his involvement in crafting the phrase began when President Bush's chief speechwriter, Michael Gerson, asked Frum for his help in creating a sentence that would best make the case for a U.S. attack on Iraq. The existence of a number of foreign governments perceived to be hostile toward the United States had reminded Frum of the Axis powers—Nazi Germany, Italy, and Japan—aligned against the United States and its allies during World War II. Scouring the speeches of the wartime president Franklin D. Roosevelt for inspiration, Frum settled upon the phrase "axis of hatred," which Gerson amended to "axis of evil." Frum told Elizabeth Wasserman for the *Atlantic* (February 12, 2003, on-line) that the phrase reaffirmed "that good and evil are valid concepts by which to evaluate what goes on in the world." Though the president himself stopped using the phrase publicly around mid-2002, it had already come to represent, in many people's minds, his administration's post–September 11 foreign policy, which was marked by an aggressive stance toward any perceived enemy of the U.S. Supporters of the administration saw the words "axis of evil" as signaling a much-needed embrace of realpolitik—which in this case meant recognizing the dangerous state of the world and the threatening nature of regimes such as those of Iraq's Saddam Hussein and North Korea's Kim Jong Il. Critics of the Bush administration, however, have argued that the labeling of an "axis of evil" has actually worked against the United States' goals by setting back the reformist movement in Iran, spurring North Korea toward further nuclear brinkmanship, and spoiling any chance that existed for avoiding war with Iraq.

Frum found himself at the center of controversy—and, some observers suggested, out of favor in the White House—when an E-mail message sent to friends by his wife, the journalist and novelist Danielle Crittenden, wound up in the hands of the press. In the message Crittenden had boasted that her husband was responsible for creating the phrase "axis of evil." Traditionally, presidential speechwriters maintain relative anonymity, as the ideas, policies, and political vision of a given administration are thought to be more important than the writer's role in articulating them; thus, some White House observers suggested, Frum had angered his colleagues by stealing part of President Bush's thunder, however inadvertently. While he left his post at the White House shortly after the episode, Frum insisted that his colleagues in the government were amused rather than resentful and that his departure had nothing to do with his wife's E-mail message or the words "axis of evil." Frum claimed that he had simply grown weary of his job. "As thrilling as it was," he told Julian Borger for the London *Guardian* (January 28, 2003), "speechwriting is ultimately frustrating for someone who wants to be a writer."

Published in 2003, Frum's book *The Right Man: The Surprise Presidency of George W. Bush* was considered the first insider's account of the Bush administration. Though Frum's view of the president is, as the title suggests, positive overall, it was not always so. When he first accepted the job as presidential speechwriter, Frum's "faith in Bush was not deep. But my curiosity was," he wrote in *The Right Man*, as quoted by Elizabeth Wasserman. "I had been looking in from the outside for a very long time. If only for a little while, I would like to look out from the inside." In the book Frum discussed the view that prior to the epoch-making events of September 11, 2001, President Bush and his administration seemed destined for mediocrity and relative historical insignificance. According to Frum, the terrorist attacks on the World Trade Center, in New York City, and the Pentagon, outside Washington, D.C., redefined the country and Bush's job. Frum wrote of his strong belief that President Bush's responses to the challenges of a new era—the launching of the war on terror, the strengthening of homeland security, and the marshaling of forces to oust Saddam Hussein—have proven him the right man to lead the country in such trying times. In the *Right Man* Frum also explained that the September 11 attacks had renewed his own sense of loyalty to the country and the administration. As quoted by Wasserman, he wrote, "I don't know what I was ready to do—whatever it is that speechwriters do in times of war. Type, I suppose—but type with renewed patriotism and zeal."

As quoted by Borger, Frum offered a sometimes critical portrait of President Bush, describing him as "sometimes glib, even dogmatic; often uncurious and as a result ill-informed; more conventional in his thinking than a leader should be. . . . Bush was a sharp exception to the White House code of niceness. He was tart, not sweet. In private, he was not the easy, genial man he was in public. Close up, one saw a man keeping a tight grip on himself." Frum also described the White House under Bush as being influenced to a significant degree by Christian evangelism. Frum concluded that Bush, like most individuals, is an amalgam of strengths and weaknesses, and that "taken all in all, he's a pretty impressive character, the right character [to lead the United States] for now," as he told Wasserman. "That doesn't make him faultless. And it doesn't mean that people should dismiss his faults as unimportant." He further asserted to Wasserman that "misunderstanding about [Bush's] character has become a very important part of political debate. A lot of the objections to this war [the 2003 invasion of Iraq] rest on personal opposition to [Bush]."

As to whether the Bush administration and the Pentagon failed to prepare adequately for the aftermath of the U.S. invasion of Iraq—carried out for the stated purpose of ridding that nation of weapons of mass destruction—Frum has said that mistakes are inevitable in war. According to Frum, one development the Bush administration did not anticipate with regard to Iraq was the campaign of sabotage, meant to cripple Iraq's infrastructure, that Saddam Hussein had organized before he was captured by U.S. forces. Frum viewed the war itself, however, as necessary. "The fact is that this problem of Islamic extremism was one that the United States ignored for a long time. And we lost a lot of time," Frum stated in an interview for the Institute of International Studies at the University of California at Berkeley (UC–Berkeley), as it appeared on the university's Web site. "Now it's thrust upon us, and we have to make the best resolution of it that we can." Though Frum is a strong advocate of an aggressive U.S. foreign policy, he does not rule out nonmilitary options. In the same interview he said, "Diplomacy, in my view, is not the art of smoothing relations. Diplomacy is the art of getting your way through words. Sometimes the right words are 'please, please, please.' And sometimes the right words are 'do it again and we'll knock your teeth out.'" He believes that the U.S. is entitled to demand from other countries, especially those in the Middle East, complete cooperation in the war against terrorism, a view summed up by saying that other countries are either "with us or against us," as Frum phrased it in the interview—an approach that has to an extent driven the Bush administration's foreign policy. When asked during the interview what he thought would emerge as the legacy of the Bush administration, Frum answered that the battle against terrorism would be its defining theme. As to how the administration has performed in that area, Frum said, "We don't yet know the answer to that. I think on the whole, taken all in all, they've done a reasonably good job, but there's so much more to go and we need to work so hard."

Frum has said that he hopes *An End to Evil: How to Win the War on Terror* (2003), which he co-wrote with Richard Perle, the former chairman of the Defense Policy Board and an influential policy maven allied with the Bush administration, will serve as a manual for U.S. foreign policy for the post–September 11 era. A quoted on Amazon.com, *Publishers Weekly* described *An End to Evil* as advocating a "new commitment to security at home, a new audacity in our strategy abroad, and a new boldness in the advocacy of American ideals." In his interview for the UC–Berkeley Institute of International Studies, Frum stated that *An End to Evil* represents an attempt to show the U.S. government and the public that winning the war against terror is "not a futile task. It is an achievable task." The book offers a prescription for how to accomplish that objective. The United States, according to the authors, should be steadfast in its support of Israel; work to overthrow the government of Iran; end any support for a Palestinian state; blockade North Korea; rely little on European countries as allies; sever relations with Saudi Arabia; and reform the intelligence agencies that failed to prevent the 2001 terrorist attacks. "Despite the authors' insider resumes, little here is groundbreaking," the *Publishers Weekly* reviewer wrote. "Many of their opinions and arguments are those debated daily in the media. The book is also highly partisan. . . . Nevertheless, this is a comprehensive, no-nonsense primer on the conservative approach to handling the terrorist threat." Gary Kamiya's review for the on-line magazine *Salon* (January 30, 2004) was less forgiving: "Undaunted by the Iraq debacle, uber-hawks David Frum and Richard Perle air their fevered wet dream of a national-security superstate that slaps down uppity Muslims, bombs North Korea, slices and dices civil liberties and scatters the Palestinians like birdseed. . . . With its trademarked combination of chipper propaganda, bullying bluster, intellectual dishonesty and radical policy prescriptions, *An End to Evil* offers a guided tour of the mind of George W. Bush, as filtered through the higher-grade neurons of its authors."

Frum ruffled feathers on both ends of the political spectrum, and not for the first time, when he penned an article for the *National Review* (April 7, 2003) entitled "Unpatriotic Conservatives: A War Against America." That piece presented a list of conservative journalists, politicians, and others who in Frum's estimation, through their criticism of the war on terror and the U.S. invasion of Iraq, had shown themselves to be "anti-American." Frum accused the columnist and former presidential candidate Pat Buchanan and the syndicated columnist Bob Novak, for example, of having "made common cause with the left-wing and Isla-

mist antiwar movements in this country and in Europe. They deny and excuse terror. They espouse a potentially self-fulfilling defeatism. They publicize wild conspiracy theories. And some of them explicitly yearn for the victory of their nation's enemies." In an article for the *Chicago Sun-Times* (March 24, 2003), Novak responded to Frum's charges, writing that Frum "represents a body of conservative opinion that wants to delegitimize criticism." More than a few political commentators reacted negatively to what they saw as Frum's equating of dissent with a lack of patriotism.

Frum has served as a contributing editor to the *Weekly Standard* since 1995 and as a columnist for Canada's *National Post* since 1998. He has also written for the *Daily Telegraph*, a British publication.

Frum and his wife have three children. They live in Washington, D.C.

—C.F.T.

Suggested Reading: American Enterprise Institute Web site; *Atlantic* (on-line) Feb. 12, 2003; (London) *Guardian* p6 Jan. 28, 2003; Manhattan Institute for Public Policy Research Web site; *Saturday Night* p35+ Dec. 1994/Jan. 1995, with photo

Selected Books: *Dead Right*, 1994; *What's Right: The New Conservative Majority and the Remaking of America*, 1996; *How We Got Here: The 70's: The Decade That Brought You Modern Life—For Better or Worse*, 2000; *The Right Man: The Surprise Presidency of George W. Bush*, 2003; *An End to Evil: How to Win the War on Terror*, 2003

Gagne, Eric

(gahn-YAY)

Jan. 7, 1976– Baseball player

Address: Los Angeles Dodgers, 1000 Elysian Park Ave., Los Angeles, CA 90012

"I'm me on the mound," the Los Angeles Dodgers closing pitcher Eric Gagne told Daniel G. Habib for *Sports Illustrated* (June 2, 2003). "I like to show my emotion, be real aggressive and give everything I've got for one half inning." At his best in pressure-filled situations, Gagne has embraced the closer's do-or-die ethos with gusto. His intensity has paid enormous dividends for the pitcher, who has emerged as one of the foremost closers in the game. In 2003 the Baseball Writers Association of America named Gagne as the year's National League Cy Young Award winner—marking the first time a relief pitcher had been so honored since the great Dennis Eckersley captured the prize, in 1992. The award recognized Gagne's two-year as-

Eliot J. Schechter/Getty Images

Eric Gagne

cent from the category of borderline major-league starters to the ranks of baseball's most feared hurlers. During that time he set records by becoming the first closer to achieve more than 50 saves in each of two seasons; tying John Smoltz's National League record for saves in a season, with 55 in 2003; and setting the mark for most consecutive saves, with 84. Moreover, with his goatee and goggle-like eyeglasses, signature fist pump, and devastating pitching arsenal, the burly Gagne is not only one of baseball's greatest throwers, but one of the sport's most distinctive.

Eric Serge Gagne was born on January 7, 1976 in Montreal, Quebec, Canada, to Richard Gagne, a bus driver, and Carole Gagne. He grew up in Mascouche, a Montreal suburb. Like many French Canadians, from an early age Gagne loved ice hockey, especially the Montreal Canadiens, a team in the National Hockey League (NHL). He was also a passionate devotee of the Montreal Expos, idolizing the baseball club's longtime third baseman Tim Wallach. Encouraged by his parents, Gagne pursued his interest in sports, playing both baseball and hockey, the latter as a defenseman. "I was a good skater, bigger than everybody else, had a good slap shot," he told Ken Gurnick for the Major League Baseball Web site (May 14, 2002). "Not great hands for dribbling. I played junior hockey, which is like minor leagues in baseball." "He played to win ever since he was young," his father told Brian Daly, as quoted on ottawalynx.com (November 12, 2003). "He didn't play because he wanted to make millions of dollars when he grew up. He just wanted to win." His father also told Daly that his son is "not a guy who is going to give up. He wasn't pushed, he made the steps by him-

self, one stage at a time." As a youth Gagne developed a reputation as an enforcer, a player whose often threatening presence dissuades opposing players from intimidating the less-imposing yet more skillful scorers on the enforcer's team. His career as a hockey enforcer left its mark on his knuckles, which bear scars from his many fights. His goggle-style eyeglasses protect the site of a long-ago injury near his eye.

Gagne attended the Polyvalente Edouard Montpetit High School, in Montreal, which specializes in training gifted athletes. (A dozen of its alumni are currently on the rosters of Major League Baseball teams.) The year he turned 15, Gagne left his parents' home to live in his own, school-provided apartment in Montreal. Throughout high school he struggled to decide whether to pursue baseball or hockey exclusively. As a Montreal-area French Canadian, he felt strongly drawn to the national pastime; his ability to throw blistering fastballs and other particular talents, however, suggested that baseball was his true calling. For two years Gagne was a starter on Team Canada's junior world-championship baseball team. In 1995 he moved to the national team; since it already had more than enough starters (among them the future major-league hurler Ryan Dempster), he began serving as closer for the first time.

Meanwhile, Gagne had attracted the interest of major-league scouts. In 1994 the Chicago White Sox drafted him, in the 30th round. As a high-school senior, he faced choices that included playing baseball for the White Sox organization, accepting a hockey scholarship to the University of Vermont, or remaining in Canada and possibly pitching for Canada in the next Olympic baseball competitions. Gagne decided to focus on baseball (and a possible Olympic appearance); he matriculated at Seminole State Junior College, in Seminole, Oklahoma, a school recommended by one of his Team Canada colleagues. At Seminole State, Gagne, a native speaker of French with minimal command of English, learned the latter language by attending twice-a-day tutoring sessions, taping class lectures and listening to them repeatedly, and watching such American sitcoms as *Everybody Loves Raymond* and *Mad About You*. On the baseball diamond he perfected his fastball, slider, splitter, and other aspects of pitching under Lloyd Simmons, the Seminole State coach at that time. At over six feet and nearly two hundred pounds, Gagne had an imposing presence, and Simmons encouraged him to look and act intimidating on the mound and to throw high and tight when the situation called for it—for example, when he faced a power hitter, or when a batter crowded the plate. Simmons influenced him greatly. "He turned me around," Gagne recalled to Gurnick. "He showed me discipline, how that makes you a better player, to give 100 percent all the time."

Later in 1994, due to a technicality, Major League Baseball declared Gagne an amateur free agent; thus, the White Sox no longer had a claim to his services. In the spring of 1995, Claude Pelletier, a Canadian-born baseball scout with the Los Angeles Dodgers who had been following Gagne's development for several years, offered him a contract with the Dodgers. With his heart set on the Olympics, Gagne hesitated, until Pelletier pointed out, according to the JockBio Web site, that the Canadian national baseball team "had yet to qualify for the Atlanta Summer Games, while a deal with the Dodgers guaranteed him a shot at pro ball." Gagne then joined the Dodgers, earning a $75,000 signing bonus.

Gagne began his career in the Dodgers organization with the Class-A Savannah Sand Gnats of the South Atlantic League, in the spring of 1996. In his first year he won seven games, lost six, and piled up an impressive 131 strikeouts over 115 innings. He missed the entire 1997 season because of a torn ligament in his right elbow; the injury led him to undergo "Tommy John" surgery, in which the ligament was replaced with a nonvital tendon harvested from elsewhere in his body. (The procedure is named for another Dodgers pitcher, who was the first person to have the operation, in 1974.) Gagne's convalescence was difficult mentally as well as physically; as he told Gurnick, "I was concerned about being able to [throw] the ball at all, about ever playing baseball again. You have to start all over. I couldn't throw from here to the wall. For six months, I couldn't pick up a ball. I couldn't wash myself." He told Marc Goldin for the Associated Press (September 27, 2003), "I thought about going back to play hockey. . . . I thought about going back to school for a psychology degree at McGill University in Montreal." Those misgivings notwithstanding, Gagne returned to organized ball in the spring of 1998, with Class-A Vero Beach of the Florida State League, with whom he began to rebuild his pitching repertoire. Given the fragility of his elbow, he was not permitted to throw splitters or sliders. Instead, he focused on his fastball and added the change-up to his arsenal. He completed the season with nine wins and 144 strikeouts. Gagne began the 1999 season with the Double-A San Antonio Missions of the Texas League. With a devastating change-up and scalding fastball, Gagne pitched two perfect innings in the Double-A All-Star Game, held at mid-season. He maintained his dominance through the rest of the season, notching at least 10 strikeouts in five consecutive starts; he was the first minor leaguer in three years to accomplish that feat.

Leaping straight from Double-A to the big leagues, Gagne made his debut with the Dodgers on September 7, 1999. He performed outstandingly on the mound, pitching six scoreless innings and recording eight strikeouts in a game won by the Florida Marlins, with no decision for either him or the Marlins' pitcher, Ryan Dempsey. In the next weeks he won one game and lost one, compiling an earned-run average (ERA) of 2.10, with 30 strikeouts and 15 walks in 30 innings. At the end of the season, with 185 strikeouts in 167 innings and a

12–4 record with the Missions, he was named the Dodgers' minor-league pitcher of the year.

Gagne did not live up to expectations in the 2000 season. After spring training, in which he compiled an ERA of 15.63, he failed to make the big-league roster; instead, he was optioned to the Triple-A Albuquerque Dukes of the Pacific Coast League (PCL). But after several of the Dodgers' starting pitchers suffered injuries during the early weeks of the season, Gagne was again called up to the big-league club. Control continued to elude him, however, and he was shuttled back and forth between the Dukes and the Dodgers throughout the season. When he returned to the Dodgers in September, he succeeded in making some satisfactory starts. In the majors that year, Gagne pitched a bit over 101 innings and started 19 games; his record also included four wins and six losses, an ERA of 5.15, 79 strikeouts, and 60 walks. His numbers in Albuquerque were more impressive: Gagne won five games and lost one and posted a 3.88 ERA. He also shone in the postseason, pitching to a semifinal-round victory for Aubuquerque in the PCL play-offs against the Memphis Redbirds.

Gagne performed inconsistently in the opening months of the 2001 season, and he again traveled back and forth between the Dukes and the Dodgers before earning his spot on the big-league roster permanently in July. That same month the Dodgers' general manager, Dave Wallace, proposed to others within the organization the possibility of using Gagne as a closer, but no action was taken toward implementing his suggestion. Near the end of the season, the Dodgers found themselves with an unusually large number of pitchers in their starting rotation but a leaky bullpen as they battled for a wild-card spot. Consequently, the team's manager, Jim Tracy, began using Gagne as a long reliever. Gagne proved to be effective in that role, but the Dodgers were unable to clinch a play-off berth, finishing the season with a record of 86 wins and 76 losses. At season's end, Gagne had compiled six wins, seven losses, and an ERA of 4.75. He notched 130 strikeouts, 46 walks, appeared in 33 games—in 24 as a starter—and pitched, in total, a little more than 151 innings.

In the 2002 season Gagne found his footing in the major leagues, establishing himself as one of the game's premier closers. To prepare for that year's campaign, he undertook a strenuous exercise regimen, working out in Montreal with several hockey players. By the time he reported to spring training, he had increased the velocity of his fastball from 93 to 97 miles per hour (mph). At the same time, his already impressive change-up strengthened. When Tracy tested Gagne in the bullpen during spring training, the pitcher played well. At the start of the regular season, Tracy announced that he would try a "closer-by-committee" system involving Giovanni Carrara, Paul Quantrill, and Gagne; whoever performed best would become the team's full-time closer. Just a week into the season, Tracy assigned Gagne to that position. A "turning point" in his career, as Gagne told a *Sports Illustrated* (June 17, 2002) writer, came on April 11, 2002, during a contest with the San Francisco Giants. The Dodgers held a one-run lead when, in the bottom of the ninth inning, Tracy—showing "a lot of confidence in me," as Gagne told the *Sports Illustrated* writer—sent him to the mound. Gagne pitched his way into trouble, putting runners on first and third with one out. Tracy then visited the mound, telling Gagne, "I should bring in [the lefthander Jesse] Orosco, but I'm not. It's your game." Gagne struck out the next batter and got the final out on a fly to center field. During the rest of April, Gagne performed outstandingly, racking up nine saves with an ERA of 0.69. He continued in that mode in May and June. "The stuff [Gagne is] featuring now is the best stuff I've ever seen . . . ," his teammate Shawn Green said to Mike DiGiovanna for the *Los Angeles Times* (June 22, 2002). "He's throwing a 97-mph fastball wherever he wants it. He could hit a gnat right now. And his changeup moves so much he can throw it for strikes or in the dirt so hitters will chase it. It's incredible to watch and fun to play behind. I'm glad I don't have to face him." In a contest with the Cincinnati Reds on August 1, Gagne was ejected from the game for hitting a batter with the ball; in the ensuing verbal confrontation between Gagne and the umpire, the former bumped into the latter while arguing his case. A day later Major League Baseball officials ruled that the umpire had been at fault, that his dismissing Gagne from the game had been unwarranted, and that the league would not punish Gagne for the incidental contact. In the following games Gagne pitched just over 82 innings in 77 games, in which he notched 52 saves out of 56 chances and posted a record of four wins and one loss. His save total for the season ranked fifth in baseball history and set a Dodgers record. Perhaps his most spectacular statistic that season was his strikeout-to-walk ratio: Gagne struck out 114 batters while walking only 16, a ratio of over seven to one. He earned the National League's pitcher-of-the-month award for June and was named to the All-Star Team, which played on July 9, 2002. (That game ended in a tie.) After the season the Canadian Baseball Hall of Fame and Museum named him and Larry Walker, of the Montreal Expos, the co-winners of the annual Tip O'Neill Award (named for the 19th-century Canadian ballplayer James "Tip" O'Neill), which honors the player "judged to have excelled in individual achievement and team contribution while adhering to the highest ideals of the game of baseball," according to the Canadian Baseball News Web site.

Gagne's success as a closer stems not only from his physical abilities but also from his mental fortitude, which enables him to withstand the constant tension that comes with his position. When a closer enters a contest, there is little margin for error. If a starting pitcher gives up runs, his teammates have the chance to improve the score in subsequent innings, but a closer has no such luxury;

his job exists at the juncture of victory and defeat. In addition, a closer must be able to shake off a dramatic loss and return the next day to a similar pressure-filled situation; what has been described as "the closer's quick turnaround and the amnesia that is essential to the job" are among Gagne's notable assets. Carrying out his responsibilities as a closer gives him "the best feeling in the world," he has said, according to the JockBio Web site. "The game's on the line, and you're the guy in the spotlight." Jim Tracy told Mike DiGiovanna for the *Los Angeles Times* (July 6, 2002) that Gagne "has shown time and time again that he has the poise and guts of a burglar." Of his comparative lack of success as a starter, Gagne explained to Daniel G. Habib for *Sports Illustrated* (June 2, 2003), "Being a starter, you have to be more mellow, more relaxed. It was boring. I'm not that kind of guy." The days of waiting between starts, the study of filmed play, the constant emphasis on mechanics—all essential to a starter's success—apparently do not suit Gagne's temperament.

Prior to Gagne's historic 2003 campaign, the pitcher and the Dodgers organization wrangled over a contract in the preseason before reaching a deal. There was fear in spring training that Gagne's fastball, which clocked in regularly at 97 mph during the 2002 season, might have lost some its pep, but those fears quickly proved unfounded. Entering home games to Guns N' Roses' "Welcome to the Jungle" issuing from the stadium's loudspeakers, Gagne pitched extraordinarily well, showing that his 2002 performance had not been a fluke and inspiring Dodger fans to don T-shirts emblazoned with the words "Game Over." During the regular season, he achieved 55 saves in 55 chances—an unprecedented accomplishment. His total tied the all-time National League record, set by John Smoltz of the Chicago White Sox in 1990, and fell only two short of the all-time major-league record, set by Bobby Thigpen of the White Sox, also in 1990. (Thigpen achieved his 57 saves in 65 chances.) Gagne pitched 82.1 innings in 77 games, won two contests while losing three, and compiled an amazingly low ERA—1.20. With 137 strikeouts and 20 walks, Gagne again demonstrated overpowering pitching and tremendous control. He also set the major-league record for consecutive saves converted: 63, accrued over the 2002 and 2003 seasons. (In his second All-Star Game, in 2003, Gagne pitched the game-deciding home run, to Hank Blalock, which gave the American League the lead. The statistics compiled in All-Star Games are not applied to players' regular season totals, so Gagne's consecutive-saves streak remained intact.) At season's end Gagne was considered a prime candidate for the Cy Young Award, even though the Baseball Writers Association of America, which chooses its recipients, has traditionally shied away from honoring relievers, believing that they are too specialized and log considerably fewer innings than starters. As Gagne's landslide victory in the Cy Young voting showed, the writers found him to be eminently deserving of the 2003 award. Steven Hirdt of the Elias Sports Bureau, which compiles baseball statistics, said of Gagne's performance to Ross Newhan for the *Los Angeles Times* (September 28, 2003), "I'm sort of in awe, like everybody else. . . . I mean, averages, statistics, calculations and things like that generally are not designed to deal with perfection, and what we have here is a unique situation."

Gagne continued his save streak well into the 2004 season, converting his first 21 chances. Then, on July 5, in a home game against the Arizona Diamondbacks, Gagne yielded two runs in the top of the ninth inning, thus ending his streak at 84. Nevertheless, he remained one of the best closers in the game, finishing out the year with 45 saves, the third-best mark in the National League. During the 2004 season Gagne appeared in 70 games, pitching a total of 82.1 innings. He struck out 114 batters, walked only 22, notched seven victories and three losses, and held opposing batters to a .181 batting average. At the end of the regular season, having finished at the top of their division, the National League West, the Dodgers advanced to the first round of the play-offs, where they faced the St. Louis Cardinals. In the second game, on October 7, Gagne pitched a scoreless inning, yielding one walk with two strikeouts; in the fourth game, held three days later, he struck out one and allowed one

hit over two scoreless innings. Gagne's fine performance failed to propel the Dodgers into the next round, however, as the Cardinals defeated them three games to one in the best-of-five series.

In exchanging vows during his wedding ceremony, according to the JockBio Web site, Gagne said to his wife, Valerie, "I pledge you my heart and my arm." The couple have a daughter, Faye, who was born in 2000, and a son, Maddox, born in 2004. In the off-season Gagne enjoys playing golf, although at times, out of frustration, he has broken clubs and thrown several into ponds. Gagne works actively in various charities and regularly visits hospitalized children. "I'm weak for kids," he told T. J. Simers for the *Los Angeles Times* (June 19, 2003). "I knew a youngster when I was younger who died from leukemia, and . . . I learned so much from watching him. . . . I'm in a position to do some things now, and I'd just like to give these kids something else to think about for a week or so instead of what they have to go through every day."

—P.B.M.

Suggested Reading: ESPN Web site; Jock Bio Web site; *Los Angeles Times* IV p2 June 19, 2003, with photo, IV p1 Aug. 5, 2003, with photo, IV p7 Sep. 28, 2003, with photo; Major League Baseball Web site; *Sports Illustrated* p81 June 17, 2002, with photo, p56 June 2, 2003, with photo

Gardner, Rulon

Aug. 16, 1971– Wrestler

Address: c/o USA Wrestling, 6155 Lehman Dr., Colorado Springs, CO 80918

When the super heavyweight Rulon Gardner stepped onto the mat for the Greco-Roman wrestling finals at the 2000 Olympic Games, in Sydney, Australia, he had already far outstripped everyone's expectations. The affable Wyoming farm boy, who had never previously placed higher than fifth in the World Championships, would earn the silver medal even if he lost the match. That outcome was, nonetheless, what most observers expected. To get to the gold, Gardner would have to defeat a legend, Alexander Karelin of Russia, whose chiseled six-foot three-inch, 286-pound frame stood in sharp contrast to his own, which looked as though it carried leftover baby fat. If Karelin's physique was not enough to terrorize most opponents, his sunken, unblinking eyes certainly were. Undefeated in international competition for 13 years, Karelin was seeking his fourth consecutive Olympic gold medal, a feat unprecedented in Greco-Roman wrestling. What set him so much apart from the rest of the competition was his freakish strength.

Pierre-Phillippe Marcou/AFP/Getty Images

Karelin's trademark maneuver was the reverse lift, also dubbed the "Karelin Lift"—in which he would clamp his arms around his opponent's torso in a rib-cracking bear hug, and then, using his back and legs, hoist the challenger over his shoulder and back in one fluid motion, sending him crashing to the floor behind him. Gardner knew Karelin's signature move well: the last time they had met on the mat, in 1997, Karelin flipped him onto his head three times en route to a 5-0 thrashing—a performance so dominant only pinning could have topped it. But Gardner, who came to Greco-Roman wrestling later than most, brought to the 2000 match his own unorthodox technique. He thought that if he could wriggle enough, he could keep his feet set, secure his balance, and stop Karelin from getting a firm grip around him. The tactic worked. With five seconds left in the third, overtime period, an exhausted Karelin, who had failed to uproot his opponent, walked away, leaving Gardner to celebrate one of the most unlikely upsets in the history of sport. Four years later Gardner ended his storied wrestling career with a bronze medal at the Olympic Games in Athens, Greece.

Rulon Gardner was born on August 16, 1971, the fifth son of Reed and Virginia Gardner and the youngest of their nine children. He was raised on the family's 250-acre dairy farm in Afton, in Wyoming's Star Valley, which his great-great-grandfather Archibald Gardner—a sawmill builder and Mormon polygamist—settled in 1889 with his 11th wife, Mary. (It has been said that Rulon looks strikingly like her.) Rulon had a troubled relationship with his father, who was never one to coddle his sons, and as the youngest child often had to take on the worst chores. "Either you're the one who gets to shovel the manure with a pitchfork or a shovel," Gardner told Allan Donnelly for *Men's Fitness* (February 1, 2002), "or you're stacking hay down in the pit and your brothers and sisters are trying to throw hay bales on you and trying to hurt you." He could not even find refuge in school, where his classmates called him "fatso" and his teachers chastised him for being a poor student. "I was a slow reader," he told *People* (October 16, 2000). "I had to push myself past what anybody said I could do." The year 1979 was a difficult one for the family; a fire destroyed the farm's milking barn, and aplastic anemia claimed the life of Ronald, Rulon's elder brother by five years. "It was hard on everybody," Reed Gardner told Jack McCallum for *Sports Illustrated* (October 9, 2000). "Maybe it made us tougher in the long run."

Rulon's brother Reynold, who is 16 months older, was Wyoming's 1988 high-school wrestling champion and went on to capture two Pac-10 Conference championships as a wrestler for Oregon State University. Rulon captured the state high-school championship a year after his brother. Then, despite having been told by his counselors that he would never attend college, he enrolled at Ricks College, in Rexburg, Idaho. He became the 1991 National Junior College Athletic Association national champion and was awarded a wrestling scholarship by the University of Nebraska, where he earned his bachelor's degree in physical education in 1996. Meanwhile, he placed fourth in the National Collegiate Athletic Association's 1993 national championship.

It was at about that time that Gardner, who had wrestled freestyle, in which competitors can attack each other by the legs, was introduced to Greco-Roman competition. In that form of wrestling, one of the two sports in the modern Olympic Games known to have taken place in the ancient Olympics, competitors are not allowed to execute takedowns by attacking the legs. Strength, therefore, is a prized commodity, as wrestlers try to score points by lifting or throwing their opponents while grappling only the torso. Lifts and throws are commonplace in the lower weight classes, in which the wrestlers' strength is greater in relation to body mass. Few in Gardner's class—super heavyweights, who routinely exceed 280 pounds—are strong enough to throw their equally massive rivals, even on the world-class level. But when Gardner learned about Greco-Roman wrestling, he also learned of the wrestler who was the exception to that rule: Alexander Karelin.

Gardner spent the bulk of the 1990s making the transition from freestyle to Greco-Roman wrestling. He caught on quickly. He went from being the 1994 University Nationals freestyle champion to taking the same title the following year in both styles. In 1995 Gardner also took the U.S. Nationals Championship, which he followed with a second-place showing in the World Team Trials behind Matt Ghaffari, who until his retirement from wrestling, in 2000, was the most successful U.S. Greco-Roman heavyweight, with three World Championship medals, a bronze and two silvers, and an Olympic silver won in 1996. Two years later Gardner returned as U.S. Nationals champion, a title to which he added, later that year, that of first-place finisher at the World Team Trials—the first time he had captured that distinction. His breakout year was 1998. He took championships at international competitions in Colorado, Hungary, Finland, and Cuba, which he topped off with a gold medal at the Pan American Games. That momentum carried him through the subsequent seasons as he seized his second U.S. Team Trials championship—this time for the 2000 Olympics.

At the Sydney Games Gardner was blessed with a relatively easy preliminary draw leading up to the medal matches—that is, his draw was not populated with wrestlers who were clearly superior. This, coupled with the tremendous stamina he had built throughout his life by working on the dairy farm, left him fairly fresh throughout the medal rounds.

In Gardner's gold-medal match against Karelin at the 2000 Olympic Games, the first three-minute period passed without a score. In the second period, Karelin began to look frustrated as he repeatedly tried and failed to clamp onto Gardner. Each time, Gardner pressed into him, wiggled, and settled his stance, and the clinch ended in a stalemate. Twenty-nine seconds into the round, Karelin tried once again. This time, Gardner added a twist:

he flexed his back, which caused Karelin to release his grip, an uncharacteristic mistake that cost him a point. Now up on the scorecard, Gardner could wrestle even more conservatively and force Karelin to try to come from behind, a role in which the Russian had almost never found himself. "He made a mistake, and I got a lucky call," Gardner told Joel Stein for *Time* (October 9, 2000). "He was the one who had to go out and win the gold medal. I would have been tickled pink to win the silver." The second period ended 1-0. As mandated by Greco-Roman rules, any match that ends with a score differential of less than three goes into a third, overtime round. Gardner had to survive three more minutes with Karelin, but the extra time played to one of Gardner's strengths. Karelin's uncanny power meant that he had rarely had to exert himself for this long. Meanwhile, Gardner, no weakling himself, had a knack for wearing out opponents through his tenacity. When Karelin walked away five seconds before the end of the period, Gardner—confused at first by his opponent's actions and wary of a ruse—stayed crouched and ready. When he realized what was happening, he cartwheeled across the mat in celebration of his victory.

Following his stunning success, Gardner made personal appearances and traveled the talk-show circuit before settling back into training. "You don't really picture yourself a celebrity when you're sweating all over each other on the mat," he quipped to John Canzano for the *Portland Oregonian* (August 26, 2004). In an encore to his Olympic win, he was victorious at the 2001 World Championships, capturing a title that reportedly means at least as much to him as his win in Sydney, because it represented his best wrestling performance up to that time.

The Championships that year were originally scheduled to take place September 26–29 at Madison Square Garden, in New York City. Because of the attacks on the World Trade Center, they were moved to December 6–9 in Athens, Greece. This time, Gardner had a much tougher draw. Leading up to the gold-medal match, he had to face four of the world's top-ranked wrestlers—Israel's Yuriy Yevseychyk, the Ukraine's Georgiy Soldadse, Russia's Yuri Patrikeev, and Bulgaria's Sergej Moreyko—all of whom had at some point in their careers gone through the vaunted Russian Greco-Roman system that produced Karelin. Against Patrikeev, Gradner overcame a three-point deficit to pin the Russian and advance. Finally, he had to face the Hungarian Mihaly Deak-Bardos, who had won the European Greco-Roman championships and had defeated Gardner twice before in that same year. After a hard-fought stalemate, Gardner took the gold from the Hungarian in overtime with a 2–0 victory.

His plans to return to the Olympics in 2004—indeed, his very life—were placed in grave jeopardy on February 14, 2002, when Gardner and two of his friends took a snowmobile trip in the Bridger-

Teton National Forest, in Wyoming. Two and a half hours into their afternoon ride, one friend left to attend his daughter's basketball game, inadvertently taking the trio's only survival kit with him. Two hours later Gardner separated from the other friend, who was unwilling to tackle some of the steeper terrain Gardner wanted to explore. Before long Gardner became lost. He spent the night in below-zero temperatures, wearing only five thin layers of clothing, some of it wet, because he had sunk into deep water holes. By the time his rescuers arrived, at 9: 00 a.m. the next day, Gardner's core body temperature had dropped to 80 degrees (at which most people would slip into a coma), and his toes were frozen; in the hospital, doctors had to amputate the middle toe of his right foot. Gardner has preserved the toe in his refrigerator. "People always ask about what happened to it, so I have a show-and-tell," he told Brian Cazeneuve for *Sports Illustrated* (May 19, 2003). "It's also a reminder about how far I've come since [the ordeal]."

Gardner missed the entire 2002 wrestling season, but he was back in training by October of that year. In his absence, the U.S. Army sergeant Dremiel Byers captured the world title. Still heavily bandaged and tentative on his feet, Gardner returned to competition in the following May, at the 2003 U.S. National Championships. He wrestled well, dominating his opponents through the preliminary rounds, before losing in the semifinal round to his former training partner, Corey Farkas. "It's hard to push and react with the confidence I had when I have to go up on my toes," he told Cazeneuve, "but I have no complaints. There's no reason I should be alive after that night." A month later he faced off against Farkas in the finals of the U.S. team trials to compete in the World Championships. This time he defeated him handily to earn a place on the team. He went on to place 10th in the competition.

Gardner kept his sights on a return to the Olympics in 2004. His continuing recovery was not helped when he and his motorcycle flipped over a car that had cut in front of him, on March 30, 2004. "I almost landed on my head," he quipped to Brian Cazeneuve for *Sports Illustrated* (May 31, 2004), "but some days I wrestle without it anyway." Gardner walked away from the accident with minor scrapes. Three days later he dislocated his wrist in a pickup basketball game. He put off surgery and competed a week later at the U.S. National Championships, at which he lost in the finals to Byers. He also dislocated his wrist seven more times during the tournament—and two more times, by shaking hands with well-wishers. He had three pins inserted and removed from his wrist prior to the U.S. team trials to qualify for the Olympics. Byers, in taking the national title, had earned the right to be seeded directly into the finals at the trials; it seemed unlikely that Gardner's wrist would hold up well enough for him even to advance to face Byers, much less defeat the 2002 world champion. But Gardner had confronted long odds before. He started the tournament by pinning Farkas, who decided to attack Gardner's injured wrist. Gardner retaliated by pulling his hand away and smacking Farkas in the head repeatedly—a legal maneuver, as long as the hand is open. He then advanced to the finals—a best-of-three-match elimination format—against Byers. Gardner swept the first two matches to claim the U.S. team's top super heavyweight slot for the Olympics. More importantly, he won the majority of his points in the clinch, which should have exposed any weaknesses in his wrist.

In the 2004 Athens Olympics, Gardner moved steadily through his preliminary matches. Although his injuries had initially placed him, once again, in the role of underdog, he looked increasingly like the super heavyweight to beat. Heading into his semifinal match against Georgiy Tsurtsumia of Kazakhstan, Gardner had every reason to be confident. Tsurtsumia had placed third in the previous World Championships—the one in which Gardner placed 10th—but Gardner had easily controlled the wrestler, who was 10 years younger, in a match the year before. The first round ended in a 1–1 tie, and Gardner could sense Tsurtsumia tiring. But then Gardner himself had a brief lapse in concentration as he attacked Tsurtsumia, who slipped behind the American and brought him to the mat, scoring a three-point takedown. Tsurtsumia took the match to earn the right to challenge Karelin's successor on the Russian team,

Khasan Baroev, who eventually won the gold medal. Gardner, meanwhile, was left to vie for the bronze medal against the surprise semifinalist Sajad Barzi; he handily defeated the Iranian, 3–0. Then, according to wrestling tradition, he left his shoes on the mat, signifying his retirement from competition. "I was a wrestler today," Gardner said, according to John Canzano, "but tomorrow, I'll be a husband."

Rulon Gardner lives in Colorado Springs, Colorado, with his second wife, Lisa, whom he married a month before the 2004 Games. He hopes to make his home again in Afton, where he was honored, following his bronze-medal performance, with a parade and a holiday named for him. Afton had honored him in 2000 by naming the road leading to his alma mater, Star Valley High School, after him. Gardner's other plans include burying his amputated toe with his deceased dog, Bo. "That way part of me will always be with him," he told George Kimball for the *Irish Times* (September 2, 2004).
—T.J.F.

Suggested Reading: *GQ* p204 Oct. 2002, with photos; *Sports Illustrated* p50 Oct. 9, 2000, with photos, A p21 Mar. 18, 2002, with photos, p56 June 3, 2002, with photos; *U.S. News & World Report* p58 Oct. 9, 2000, with photos

---

Garrels, Anne

July 2, 1951– Journalist

Address: National Public Radio, 635 Massachusetts Ave., N.W., Suite 1, Washington, DC 20001-3752

A senior foreign correspondent for National Public Radio (NPR), Anne Garrels earned international attention as one of only 16 American journalists who remained in Baghdad, the capital of Iraq, during the American-led invasion of that country in the spring of 2003. As the U.S. and British forces converged on Baghdad in their mission to oust the Iraqi dictator Saddam Hussein from power, Garrels described for millions of NPR listeners the scenes on the city's streets and the reactions of people she encountered. She later described those experiences in her book *Naked in Baghdad: The Iraq War As Seen by NPR's Correspondent* (2003). A former foreign correspondent for ABC News and U.S. State Department reporter for NBC News, Garrels joined NPR in 1988. Since then she has filed stories from several war zones in addition to Iraq, among them the West Bank, Chechnya, Bosnia, Kosovo, and Afghanistan. "I didn't look for the wars, the wars found me," she told Mark Herman for the *Dartmouth* (November 4, 2003, on-line), a Dartmouth College campus news-

Christopher Little/Courtesy of NPR

paper. As she said to *Resonance* (Fall/Winter 2003), a publication of the organization Women in Public Radio, "With the breakout of ethnic wars, I inadvertently became a war reporter." In Garrels's view, the fact that she is performing a high-risk job traditionally associated with brave men is not particularly noteworthy; in war zones, she explained to Ron Franscell for the *Denver Post* (September 14, 2003), "the dangers are basically the same whether you are male or female. Bullets don't discriminate." When Tim Clark asked her for *Yankee* magazine (Summer 2002) if being a woman had been a hindrance or a help to her work as a journalist, Garrels responded, "Initially being a woman was a distinct hindrance. There were few women foreign correspondents and no role models. However, once I broke the barrier and started working in the field, I have found being a woman a huge advantage. In Afghanistan, for instance, I have had no trouble interviewing men, but I also have access to the women's quarters, from which male reporters are banned." Garrels's reports air on the NPR programs *All Things Considered, Morning Edition, Weekend Edition Saturday,* and *Weekend Edition Sunday.* As quoted on Amazon.com, David K. Shipler, a former Jerusalem bureau chief for the *New York Times,* has said of Garrels, "Whether from Baghdad or Moscow, Jerusalem or another place of crisis, Anne Garrels infuses her reporting on warfare and politics with lucid, human accounts of lives caught in conflict. Every time her voice comes on NPR, it's a signal that you are about to hear a story with exceptional clarity and rigorous respect for the highest standards of journalism." In 2003 the International Women's Media Foundation (IWMF) presented Garrels with a Courage in Journalism Award in recognition of her work in Iraq.

Anne Longworth Garrels was born on July 2, 1951 to John C. Garrels Jr., a retired chairman and managing director of Monsanto Ltd., the London, England, division of a leading American agricultural-products and -chemicals company, and Valerie Garrels, who is now deceased. She attended Harvard University, in Cambridge, Massachusetts, where she majored in Russian. After she earned a bachelor's degree, in 1972, she found work with a publishing company. Then, she recalled to the *Resonance* interviewer, "the world began to change, opportunities began to open up, and I guess I was pushy enough to take advantage of them and one thing led to another and I became a journalist."

Garrels began her journalism career in 1975, as a production assistant for ABC News; she worked for ABC in various positions for the next 10 years. In 1978 ABC chose Garrels over higher-paid, more experienced reporters to fill the post of Russian-speaking correspondent in what was then the Soviet Union. "I was cheap," she told Herman regarding her selection. Garrels spent three years as ABC News's Moscow correspondent and bureau chief. At an October 2003 public forum co-sponsored by Connecticut Public Radio and the Connecticut Historical Society, in Hartford, Garrels recalled, as quoted by Alice Tessier in the Litchfield, Connecticut, *County Times* (October 10, 2003), "The first night in the apartment in Moscow, I sobbed. The apartment was bugged [with listening devices

planted by Soviet authorities]. . . . It was all very tense . . . because of the psychological pressure." Garrels also said at that forum that it took her many years to learn how to deal with the pressures of her job and that she has become "more mellow" as well as "more crafty" as a foreign correspondent. Nevertheless, she admitted, she still becomes frightened and even cries at times when she finds herself in dangerous places or tense situations.

In her acceptance speech at the 2003 Courage in Journalism Awards, Garrels said that during her stint in Moscow, her interviews with the Nobel Prize–winning human-rights crusader Andrei Sakharov and his dissident colleagues served as an education in journalism, because it taught her "how to be a witness," as quoted on the IWMF Web site. Garrels had difficulty persuading Soviet citizens to speak with her on camera; as she recalled to Mark Herman, "Raising a camera was a bit like raising an M16—everybody would scatter." Getting film past Russian censors also proved troublesome; often, government agents confiscated the rolls of film her ABC crew shot. Garrels focused her reporting on "how the Soviet Union worked—or didn't work—as the case may be," as she told Herman.

In 1982 the Soviet news agency Tass released an English-language attack on Garrels after it became known that she had voiced her suspicions that the KGB, the Soviet secret police, had been involved in the theft of her purse while she was on a street in Kiev. (According to John Carmody in the *Washington Post* [February 29, 1988], she had gone to Kiev on a private visit to some Soviet Jewish friends.) On the day that Tass released its statement, in which it charged that Garrels had fabricated details of the purse-snatching incident, Garrels, driving in Moscow during a heavy rainstorm, accidentally struck and killed a woman and injured a man, both of whom were Russian citizens. Shortly after those events ABC recalled Garrels to the United States. Garrels has said that her experiences in the Soviet Union, which was then a police state, prepared her well for what she faced decades later in Iraq.

Also as an ABC News reporter, Garrels covered the Eastern Bloc, in particular the rise of the Solidarity movement and the imposition of martial law in Poland. From 1984 to 1985 she served as the network's correspondent in Central America. While on that assignment Garrels endured what she has called the scariest moment of her career: coming under fire, for the first time in her life. While she was sleeping on the porch of a hut in El Salvador, Garrels and the hut suddenly came under attack by a group of guerrillas. "Tracer bullets lit up the night sky, coming straight at me," she told Tim Clark. "I started shaking so uncontrollably I was a moving target. The next thing I remember, I had taken refuge in a bread oven along with a family of pigs."

In 1986 Garrels left ABC for NBC News, where for about two years she served as the network's State Department correspondent. In 1988 she became a foreign correspondent for NPR. NPR is a respected nonprofit producer and distributor of noncommercial news, talk, and entertainment programming; its programs air on more than 750 independent, public radio stations around the country. In her interview with John Carmody around the time she made the decision to leave NBC, Garrels said, "I want to get back into daily journalism. NBC has 60 correspondents out there around the country fighting for maybe three spots every night [on *NBC Nightly News with Tom Brokaw*]. That's a very hard system to break into." In an interview for NPR, as posted on the Web site of the North Carolina–based radio station WUNC, Garrels said, "I think that I certainly enjoy being a reporter far more at NPR" than at commercial news outlets such as ABC or NBC. "It's a far greater challenge, because [with NPR] I'm given the time to explore issues far more in-depth than I was at the networks."

Garrels reported from Tiananmen Square, in Beijing, China, in June 1989, when scores (hundreds, according to some sources) of pro-democracy demonstrators were gunned down by Chinese soldiers. In 1990 Garrels reported from Saudi Arabia on events leading up to the Persian Gulf War, in which an American-led coalition fought the armies of Iraqi dictator Saddam Hussein, after they had invaded neighboring Kuwait without provocation. For her reporting during the Gulf War, Garrels and the other members of NPR's news team won an Alfred I. DuPont–Columbia University Award in 1992. Another foreign assignment for NPR took Garrels to Chechnya (formerly a republic within the Soviet Union), where, in the mid-1990s, she observed firsthand and reported on that region's horrific secessionist war with Russia. In the NPR interview posted on WUNC's Web site, Garrels said that the conflict in Chechnya was a "far more chaotic war" than the 2003 Iraqi war. "There was indiscriminate carpet-bombing by the Russians. The soldiers on the ground were drunk and out of control. The Chechens increasingly loathed us [the press], so we became targets for the Chechens over the years." For her coverage of the former Soviet Union, in particular the former Soviet-controlled Central Asian Republics, Garrels won her second DuPont–Columbia Award, in 1996. In Bosnia in the mid-1990s, Garrels witnessed the brutal ethnic and religious fighting that tore apart the Balkan region. She also reported from Kosovo, the site of feuding and violence between Serbians and Kosovo's ethnic Albanian population, and Israel, which has been locked in a periodically violent struggle with Palestinians since the late 1940s.

Between 1996 and 1997 Garrels spent a year as an Edward R. Murrow fellow at the Council on Foreign Relations, an independent, national organization dedicated to study and discussion of the foreign policies of the United States and other countries. Following the terrorist attacks of September 11, 2001, Garrels spent much of her time reporting from Pakistan, Afghanistan, and the Middle East.

In 2002, after having branded the regime of then–Iraqi president Saddam Hussein part of an "axis of evil" (the others being those in North Korea and Iran), the administration of U.S. president George W. Bush began preparing for a preemptive invasion of Iraq. Garrels began reporting intermittently from Iraq in the fall of 2002. In March 2003 she began filing daily reports from Baghdad. That month U.S. forces invaded Iraq, overthrowing Hussein and his government and occupying the country. Garrels had paid $1,000 to the Iraqi ambassador in Amman, Jordan, to obtain an Iraqi visa. Referring to that man, Garrels told Tamara Wieder for the Boston *Phoenix* (September 26–October 2, 2003), "Thank God for his greed," because it allowed her to get into the country and get her stories after another reporter for NPR had already been expelled from Iraq. Describing for Wieder the situation in Iraq immediately before the war, Garrels called the country a "world you just couldn't predict." Every journalist in the country seemed to have heard a different rumor. "Somebody had spoken to someone who said, 'You're going to get taken hostage,'" she recalled to Wieder, "[while] other officials were saying, 'No, you're not; stay.' Nobody knew what to believe, and everybody was sort of walking up to each other saying, 'Are you staying? Are you going? What are your bosses saying? Are you being pulled? Are you not?' And then suddenly one network left in the middle of the night. It was like *Ten Little Indians*: and then suddenly there were 16 [American journalists remaining]." (Correspondents from the *New Yorker*, the *New York Times*, and the *Washington Post*, among other publications, were among those who remained in Baghdad.) Garrels took the calculated risk of staying in Baghdad. She was the only U.S. network staff member to remain in the Iraqi capital until after U.S. forces reached the city. (Contrary to some reports, Garrels was not the only female American journalist to remain in Baghdad: an American woman reporting for *Newsweek* also stayed, as did women from European publications and television stations.) Discussing how she was able to remain in the country when other journalists were not, Garrels explained to Wieder, "I think the networks certainly felt that they were just too high-profile. I didn't suffer from that. It was just me, there was no big team, I didn't have a fancy office. I mean, I *thought* I was below the radar [of the Iraqi authorities], although as I have since come to find out, I was not as much under the radar as I thought." According to Garrels, a man named Qadm, who was in charge of daily operations at the Iraqi Information Ministry before the war, had a file on her but for undivulged reasons had kept it from being passed on to others who might have taken action to detain or deport Garrels.

Garrels roamed Baghdad to the extent that Iraqi authorities allowed her to do so, speaking with Iraqi officials and ordinary residents. She had to contend with bombs, the threat of snipers, and looting on the streets, among other perils. "It was all bad," she told Susan Stamberg in an NPR interview posted on the NPR Web site. "After a couple of days of the bombing, you realized how accurate it was—and it wasn't scary, curiously. It was more dealing with the Iraqi security apparatus and the worrying that they were going to arrest us, use us as hostages. That was the fear. At the very end, the scary part was when the ground fighting started, because you had no idea where it was going to erupt and if you were going to be in the middle of it." Garrels gave on-air reports by means of a satellite phone in her room on the 11th floor of Baghdad's Palestine Hotel. As a strategy for buying time if security forces from the Iraqi Information Ministry were to come looking for her, she wore no clothes while using the phone. "If someone knocks," Garrels wrote in her book, as quoted by Wieder, "I can pretend they have woken me up, beg for a few minutes to get dressed, and then perhaps have enough time to dismantle the phone and hide it. Not a great plan, but the only one I could come up with." As of December 2003, 18 journalists had died in the war in Iraq. Several journalists were killed the previous April when the U.S. military fired on the Palestine Hotel. Garrels was not injured in that attack.

While she condemned the brutality of Saddam Hussein's police state, Garrels was skeptical of the merits of the American invasion. She told Wieder, "Like Iraqis, I never fully understood what the rush was. . . . I certainly didn't understand the need [for the U.S. to invade] so fast, nor did I believe, talking to U.S. officials, that they were fully prepared for what we've now seen. There was so little planning for the aftermath. . . . By allowing the looting and the destruction, which did *not* come from the bombing, the U.S. in essence sat by. So Iraqis' own abilities to help rebuild went up in smoke in those early days [of the war]. And it made it just that much easier for them then to say [to the Americans], 'Hey, you're the occupiers: you do it.'" Garrels told Wieder that the Iraqis she had spoken to "knew *exactly* what was going to happen, whether it was the looting in the immediate aftermath of the war, to the violence and attacks that we're now seeing. They know themselves pretty well." Garrels left Iraq at the end of April 2003, when most major U.S. combat operations ceased; she returned in the summer to report on American and coalition efforts to establish stability and begin reconstruction. Those efforts have been badly retarded by unremitting guerrilla-style attacks on American troops. "I've been asked, why is the press giving us such a negative view of what's happening on the ground [in Iraq]," Garrels told Ken Gewertz for the Harvard University *Gazette* (October 1, 2003). "Well, if things are going so well, why are the civilian officials hunkered down behind

barbed wire? Why haven't nongovernmental organizations come in to help? Why hasn't the United Nations sent more people in? The answer is, it's just too damned dangerous. For Iraqis, the problem is very simple—security, security, security."

Garrels did not get a sense of her audience's reactions to her broadcasts until after she returned to the U.S. "I was in a cocoon for the entire time I was [in Iraq]," she told Wieder. Waiting for Garrels in the U.S. were presents, cards, and what she described to Wieder as "enormously personal messages" from NPR listeners—far more feedback and recognition than she was accustomed to. The enthusiastic responses of NPR listeners to her reports were among the factors that led her to write *Naked in Baghdad*. In the book Garrels—who acknowledged to Wieder that "all of us covering the war saw just one part of it"—offered an account of her daily activities in the chaotic Iraqi capital and her observations about what was transpiring around her. Using her satellite phone, Garrels spoke daily to her husband, James Vinton "Vint" Lawrence, a former Central Intelligence Agency (CIA) operative and political cartoonist for the *New Republic,* who was at home in the U.S. Lawrence regularly wrote E-mail messages to family and friends, sharing with them what Garrels had told him over the phone. Vint referred to his messages as "Brenda Bulletins," an allusion to the comic-book reporter and heroine Brenda Starr, whom Garrels had idolized as a child. "Brenda Bulletins" are included in *Naked in Baghdad*. Garrels dedicated the book to her husband and to Amer, an Iraqi taxi driver who became her helper and friend while she was in Baghdad. "The foreign correspondent's secret," Garrels told Ken Gewertz, "is that wherever we work we have to have someone like Amer. Having someone like that makes a huge difference because they help you understand the society and get to the people you need to speak to. When you arrive in a new place, you've got to find them fast." Ron Franscell called *Naked in Baghdad* "intimate, authentic and blunt, without much literary decoration. . . . Despite NPR's reputation for news with a liberal bias, Garrels' account is scrupulously impartial." Vanessa Bush, writing for *Booklist,* as posted on Amazon.com, called *Naked in Baghdad* a "fascinating look at how [Garrels] manages . . . to cover the build-up to the war and the war itself. Readers looking for details and background on the war will appreciate Garrels' account." According to a less laudatory review of Garrels's book, by *Publishers Weekly,* also on Amazon.com, "This account works well as a personal narrative of courage under fire, suffering and survival, but unfortunately, it lacks in insightful commentary and summing up of events." *Naked in Baghdad* is also available on audiotape.

For her coverage of the former Soviet Union and her series of reports on water-related issues around the world, Garrels was honored with Overseas Press Club awards in 1996 and 1999, respectively. She received an Alumni Recognition Award from

Harvard University in 2002. That same year Garrels served as the Joe Alex Morris Jr. Memorial Lecturer at her alma mater's Nieman Foundation for Journalism. For her work in Iraq, in 2003 Garrels was presented with InterAction's Award for Excellence in International Reporting. She sits on the board of the Committee to Protect Journalists and is a volunteer emergency medical technician.

Garrels and her husband live in Norfolk, Connecticut, with their chocolate Labrador retrievers and several cats. The couple have no children. "[Having] a family and being a foreign correspondent is still a very difficult thing to do for a woman," Garrels said during the NPR interview. As quoted in an article dated April 23, 2003 and posted on the NPR Web site, Garrels said, referring to the dangers of reporting from war zones, "I can't do it to my husband again. I'll never do it to him again." In January 2004 she was on assignment in Iraq, reporting on, among other topics, the plight of the Marsh Arabs, whose 5,000-year-old way of life in the country's vast marshlands was almost destroyed during the reign of Saddam Hussein.

—C.F.T.

Suggested Reading: *Dartmouth* (on-line) Nov. 4, 2003; *Denver Post* (on-line) Sep. 14, 2003; (Harvard University) *Gazette* (on-line) Oct. 1, 2003; (Litchfield, Connecticut) *County Times* (on-line) Oct. 10, 2003; National Public Radio Web site, with photos; *Washington Post* B p10 Feb. 29, 1988

Selected Books: *Naked in Baghdad: The Iraq War as Seen by NPR's Correspondent*, 2003

Justin Sullivan/Getty Images

Gates, Melinda

1964– Philanthropist

Address: Bill & Melinda Gates Foundation, P.O. Box 23350, Seattle, WA 98102

In January 2000, when its assets rose to $21.8 billion, the Bill and Melinda Gates Foundation surpassed the London-based Wellcome Trust to become the wealthiest foundation in the world. At the end of 2002, its assets were worth more than $24 billion, almost two and a half times that of the second-largest grant-making foundation in the U.S. (the Lilly Endowment), more than two and a half times that of the Ford Foundation (ranked third), and nearly nine times that of the Rockefeller Foundation (ranked 15th). By the end of 2004, the foundation's assets had risen to about $27 billion, nearly all of which had come from the contributions of its founders, the world's richest couple. Indeed, the Microsoft Corp. co-founder and chairman Bill Gates (formally, William H. Gates III) and his wife, Melinda, have made charitable donations exceeding those of any other individuals in history. Melinda Gates, a former general manager of information products at Microsoft—where she worked for about nine years, from 1987 to 1996—has played an active role in decisions regarding the foundation's allocation of grants. According to Justin Gillis in the *Washington Post* (October 1, 2003, on-line), the hands-on approach Bill and Melinda Gates have adopted in their philanthropic activities is unusual. "Most people in the world with billions of dollars to give away, and there aren't many, would set broad guidelines, hire experts and trust them to use the money sensibly, while continuing to run whatever business enterprise produced the fortune," Gillis wrote. Referring to the foundation's health- and medicine-related grants, he continued, "The Gateses have hired experts, for sure, but they have also steeped themselves in the scientific details. They have read textbooks on immunology and infectious disease. They routinely interrogate doctors and [foundation] staffers about the smallest points of controversy or uncertainty." They have also educated themselves by visiting poverty-stricken communities and medical facilities in Asia and Africa, where they have talked with victims of disease and their caregivers, and by reading about and observing conditions in American high schools. (Education is another of the foundation's main concerns.) In addition, they have spoken before many professional groups, describing existing problems, proposing solutions, and attempting to enlist the help of others in turning those solutions into reality.

With a few minor exceptions, grants from the Bill and Melinda Gates Foundation support endeavors in four categories: Third World medicine and health; the American educational system—in particular, high schools; libraries in the U.S. and Canada; and assistance for people in the Pacific Northwest, where Microsoft is located. The Gateses have said that they hope to supervise the foundation for as long as they are able and plan to leave to it in their wills whatever remains of their fortune (minus relatively small bequests to each of their three children). "Who knows why we're in the situation we're in?" Melinda Gates told Gillis, referring to the couple's wealth (about $48 billion in mid-October 2004). "I don't think either of us can explain that. Yes, Bill worked really hard and he's been incredibly smart about some things, but also very, very lucky. Given that, we both feel a huge responsibility to do what we can with that resource."

Gates was born Melinda French in 1964 in the Dallas, Texas, area, where she was raised by her father, Raymond French, an engineer, and her mother, Elaine Amerland French. She has credited one of her teachers at the Catholic parochial high school that she attended with making her "think about broader opportunities" regarding career choices, as she recalled in a speech to the National Conference of State Legislatures in July 2003, as recorded on the Gates Foundation Web site. Gates said that her teacher, Mrs. Bauer, "encouraged me to take classes in math, science, and computer science when there were very few girls pursuing those areas." Thanks to Bauer's influence, Gates chose to major in computer science after she enrolled at Duke University, in Durham, North Carolina, where she was a member of the Kappa Alpha Theta sorority. She earned a bachelor's degree in computer science and economics in 1986 and an M.B.A. from the university's Fuqua School of Business in 1987.

Upon completing her studies Gates joined Microsoft, where, in time, she supervised more than 100 employees in the consumer group, serving as both product manager and general manager for such multimedia products as the on-line encyclopedia *Encarta* and the movie guide *Cinemania*. She also assisted with the development of software programs, among them Microsoft Word for MS-DOS and Windows, Microsoft Works, and Microsoft Publisher. She continued working for Microsoft after her marriage to Bill Gates, in 1994. In May 1996, about a month after the birth of the couple's first child, she left the company.

Gates has traced her interest in global-health issues to a 1993 vacation in Africa that she took with her future husband and some of their friends. "We had a wonderful safari, seeing the African countryside and the animals," she told Geoffrey Cowley, *Newsweek*'s health-and-medicine editor, in an E-mail exchange published in *Newsweek* (February 4, 2002). "What I didn't expect was how moved I would be by the people. I came back and told a close friend that Africa changed me forever. It's a place that gets under your skin. Seeing the women walking, walking, walking really struck me. We would go for miles and miles and see these women walking, and we'd always look to see if any had shoes. They didn't." The safari was in Zaire, which was suffering from governmental corruption, political instability, and inflation; in many of the towns, shops were closed, and once-thriving markets were nearly deserted. "Seeing such destitution and the plight of women—that certainly touched me," Gates told Cowley. Several years later, she recounted, she read a piece in the *New York Times* about which diseases kill the most children worldwide. "It was stunning," she told Cowley. "We just don't face many of those diseases in the U.S. It's the first time I remember talking with Bill about how tragic these diseases are for children: We asked ourselves what we could possibly do."

The couple's first philanthropic endeavors were carried out by the William H. Gates Foundation (set up in 1994 and named after Bill Gates's father) and the Gates Learning Foundation (called the Gates Library Foundation at its inception, in 1997). Some of their more notable activities included launching, in 1997, a five-year, $250 million initiative to help bring Internet access to all libraries in the U.S., in fulfillment of which the Bill and Melinda Gates Foundation later provided funds for the installation of 40,000 computers in 10,000 libraries and the training of 50,000 librarians; giving $5 million, in 1999, to the Nonprofits' Insurance Alliance of California, which offers liability insurance to nonprofit organizations; donating $26 million, in 1999, to the United States Committee for Unicef, an American group supporting the United Nations Children's Fund; contributing $50 million, in 1999, toward a campaign to eradicate polio; and announcing, in 1999, gifts to the foundations of the former South African president Nelson Mandela and his wife, Graça Machel. A gift of $10 million was granted to the Nelson Mandela Foundation, and $5 million was given to Machel's organization, the Foundation for Community Development; both foundations promote health care and education in Africa.

The Bill and Melinda Gates Foundation was established on January 1, 2000, when the Gateses merged the William H. Gates Foundation and the Gates Learning Foundation. The Bill and Melinda Gates Foundation is co-chaired by Bill's father, William H. Gates II, who also serves as CEO, and Patty Stonesifer, a former senior vice president for Microsoft's Interactive Multimedia Division, who also holds the title of foundation president. The foundation's top priority is to improve the health of the billions of people living in poor countries, where the so-called disease burden—the occurrence of malaria, tuberculosis, AIDS, and myriad other diseases—is far greater than it is in developed nations, and where such illnesses kill millions of children and adults annually. To lower the incidence of disease in the developing world, the

Gates Foundation has supported, on a massive scale, research into the development of new vaccines, widespread vaccination programs for those vaccines already in existence, expanded programs of prenatal and postnatal care, and programs in population control.

Among the Bill and Melinda Gates Foundation's first major actions, in July 2000 it joined the American pharmaceutical firm Merck & Co. Inc., the Merck Foundation, and the government of Botswana (which has a higher incidence of HIV/AIDS than any other country) to found the African Comprehensive HIV/AIDS Partnerships (ACHAP). Along with Botswana's National AIDS Coordinating Authority, ACHAP manages that government's anti-AIDS program. The Gates Foundation committed $50 million to ACHAP over five years. In July 2002 the foundation released its "Blueprint for Action" on the worldwide HIV and AIDS crisis. The Gates Foundation and the Henry J. Kaiser Family Foundation gathered 40 experts to evaluate UNAIDS (the Joint United Nations Programme on HIV/AIDS) and determine what resources are needed for an effective global HIV-prevention campaign. The experts found that the prevention programs of most nations did not receive support from the highest levels of government and did not involve all sectors of society. In November 2002 the Gates Foundation announced that it would give $40 million over 10 years to slow the spread of HIV and AIDS in India—the largest single amount focused on a specific country in the foundation's history. India has an estimated four million cases of HIV (many believe the actual number is higher), but, with its population of more than a billion people, the rate of infection is still relatively low. In October 2003 the amount of aid was increased to $200 million. In March 2003 the foundation announced a gift of $60 million to the International Partnership for Microbicides, a nonprofit organization whose goal is to develop and distribute a topical means—such as foams or gels—of preventing HIV transmission. The $60 million grant was the largest ever for microbicide research and development. Topical products would most likely be used by poor women in sub-Saharan Africa, who make up 90 percent of new AIDS cases among women; drug companies have reportedly had little interest in developing such products because they would provide little or no profits. Several of the foundation's other health initiatives also focus on Africa. In December 2000 it gave $15 million to develop drugs to treat sleeping sickness and leishmaniasis, diseases that kill thousands of Africans every year. In September 2003 the charity awarded $168 million to projects for the treatment and prevention of malaria in Africa. In the U.S., it donated $150,000 in 2004 to the Oregon-based Cascade AIDS Project's Kids' Connection program, which helps HIV-infected children and their families.

Other foundation projects are aimed at stamping out diseases that remain prevalent in the Third World despite being almost nonexistent in industrialized nations. (Currently only 10 percent of medical research is devoted to diseases responsible for 90 percent of the world's health burden; most research is focused on diseases that are concerns primarily of richer nations.) The foundation has committed $750 million over five years to help vaccinate children in developing countries and in March 2001 awarded $10 million to the United Nations Development Programme (UNDP)/World Bank and the World Health Organization to develop new tests for tuberculosis, which kills two million people each year, primarily in poor nations. In May 2002 the organization pledged $50 million toward the $70 million budget of the Global Alliance for Improved Nutrition, which fortifies with vitamin supplements basic foods including rice, flour, and edible oils. In January 2003 the foundation gave $200 million to identify ways of decreasing the most common causes of death in developing countries—prominent among them malaria, tuberculosis, and malnutrition. The foundation also committed $55 million in September 2003 to develop an effective vaccine against the dengue virus, contributing the money to a consortium called the Pediatric Dengue Vaccine Initiative, which involves research institutions, public-health organizations, and industrial firms. In fall 2000 the charity gave nearly $8.9 million to the International Planned Parenthood Federation to improve reproductive health care worldwide. The foundation has also offered incentives to pharmaceutical companies to develop and distribute a vaccine against meningococcal meningitis, which killed an estimated 100,000 people between 1988 and 1997, donating $70 million to such efforts in June 2001. In August 2004 the foundation gave the World Health Organization a grant of $5 million to begin a program called Health Leadership Service, which is designed to train the next generation of leaders in health care.

Thus far, despite the millions of dollars spent to find cures for fatal diseases, no new vaccines or drugs have been developed through research supported by foundation funds. Programs funded by the foundation, however, have helped poor countries gain access to existing vaccines. "Ours is an approach to philanthropy that requires taking risks . . . ," Melinda Gates said in a speech at the Washington Women's Foundation annual meeting, on April 5, 2000, as posted on the Gates Foundation Web site. "I think the success my husband achieved in business was achieved on the basis of taking risks. And that's one reason he's willing to go out there and take some big risks with our philanthropy. Our approach is that we'll test a number of things, figure out what works and doesn't and then go back and try again. The only thing we know for sure is that our philanthropy will continue to grow out of who we are and where our hearts are."

Education is another area in which the foundation concentrates its energies, providing large grants to develop smaller high schools and make college scholarships available to low-income minority students. Citing the national high-school graduation rate of only 70 percent (the figure is 55 percent among African-Americans and 53 percent among Latinos) as a primary reason that smaller schools and more teachers are needed, the foundation has dedicated enormous sums to decrease the populations of individual high schools and lower student-teacher ratios. In June 2000 the foundation awarded 4,100 scholarships to low-income minority students to promote their studies in education, math, science, and engineering; this was the first step in fulfilling a pledge to give at least $1 billion over the next 20 years for such scholarships. (The United Negro College Fund, the Hispanic Scholarship Fund, and the American Indian College Fund are administrating the disbursal of $50 million a year for the program.) In June 2001 the foundation committed $100 million to improve the training of school administrators throughout the country, including $7.5 million for computer training for superintendents, principals, and other school supervisors in New York State. In March 2002 the foundation granted $40 million to help disadvantaged students enter college, by creating 70 high schools that offer college-level courses, thus enabling students to earn both a high-school diploma and an associate's degree or two years' worth of college credit. (The Ford, Carnegie, and Kellogg foundations also contributed funds to the project.) In February 2003 the Gates Foundation gave $31 million to various nonprofit groups to start small, alternative high schools for 36,000 pupils. Troubled students have often been placed in alternative schools; the intent of the grant was to ensure that such schools were academically rigorous and fostered closer relationships between students and teachers.

The foundation has also given funds to replicate the innovative program at Cristo Rey Jesuit High School, in Chicago, which offers college-prep courses and part-time jobs that help urban students earn money for college tuition. The foundation pledged $10 million in May 2003 to help expand the model to 12 additional schools; the Cassin Educational Initiative supplied an additional $9 million. The following September the foundation gave $51.2 million to seven nonprofit organizations in New York City—the largest single gift ever given to the city's schools—to create within the next five years 67 small public high schools, each with a maximum of 500 students. (Many city schools have several thousand students, only a tiny percentage of whom have close contacts with their teachers.) City officials said that at least 10 of the schools would open in September 2004, and they expect the others to open within three to five years. The next month the foundation donated $22 million to the New Schools Venture Fund to help build up to 100 new charter schools around the country. Other education-related grants the foundation has administered include, in April 2000, $10 million toward the construction of a $265 million underground visitors' center on Capi-

tol Hill in Washington, D.C.; in the spring of 2003, $30 million to support a new science building and extracurricular programs at Duke University; and, in October 2003, $6.8 million to the City University of New York for the creation of 10 high schools in which students would complete two years of college-level work before their graduations, when they would earn associate degrees.

Regarding library funding, the foundation has concentrated primarily on providing Internet access for public libraries. In 2002 the foundation gave $3.1 million to Wisconsin libraries to buy computers and provide training to increase public use of the Internet. The Gateses have also sought to improve libraries in other ways; for example, the Bill and Melinda Gates Foundation Access to Learning Award includes a $1 million gift and is given to a public library outside the United States every year. Past winners were BibloRed of Bogota, Colombia, and the Smart Cape Access Project of Cape Town, South Africa.

On her quest to improve health conditions in poor countries, Melinda Gates has traveled around the world; she visited Thailand and India in 2002 and, with her husband, Botswana, Mozambique, and South Africa in 2003. Melinda and Bill Gates received the Council of Chief State School Officers' (CCSSO) Distinguished Service Award in 2002 and Africare's John T. Walker Distinguished Humanitarian Service Award in 2003. A dinner honoring the couple was held by the United Nations Association-USA on May 8, 2002, at which U.N. secretary general Kofi Annan praised their efforts to improve medical care in Third World nations. "[Bill] and Melinda, when they first established their Foundation, immediately saw that the shameful gap between the haves and have-nots in health, and in access to medical care, is one of the greatest challenges to philanthropy in our time. And ever since, they have been determined to do something about it," Annan said, as reported in a September 5, 2002 U.N. news release posted on the organization's Web site. The Gateses also received the UNA-USA Global Leadership Award.

Melinda Gates joined the board of trustees of Duke University in 1996 and is currently serving her second five-year term. From 1988 to 1991 she sat on the school's alumni admissions-advisory committee. She is a former board member of the Mount Rainier, North Cascades, and Olympic Fund, a group that raises money for those national parks, and a former board member and contributor to the capital campaign for the Village Theater in Seattle. She has also served on the advisory committee of SeniorNet.org, a computer community for senior citizens; co-chaired an early-learning commission in Washington State; and served on the board of directors of the Internet start-up Drugstore.com, a health-product Web site.

Bill and Melinda Gates have three children: Jennifer Katherine (born in April 1996), Rory John (born in May 1999), and Phoebe Adele (born in September 2002). The family lives in a $75 million mansion on Lake Washington in Medina, Washington, near Seattle, but their lifestyle has been described as unpretentious. Because she is seldom recognized when in public, Melinda Gates is able to take her children to McDonald's, drop them off at school, and shop in the local grocery store without interference. "I try to maintain a low profile so we can lead as normal a family life as possible," she told Cowley. "That said, I also care deeply about the work we are doing with the foundation, so maintaining a balance between these two is a challenge. As our children become older, I do envision increasing my role with the foundation. If a microbicide or AIDS vaccine comes along, if I feel I could really make a difference in furthering the distribution of these for the developing world in some way, I would likely give up even more anonymity to do so."

—K.E.D.

Suggested Reading: *Duke Magazine* (on-line) May/June 2002; *Fuqua Exchange* Winter 1996; *Newsweek* p46+ Aug. 30, 1999, with photo, p50+ Feb. 4, 2002, with photos; *Washington Post* (on-line) Oct. 1, 2003, with photos

Mike Theiler/Getty Images

Gerberding, Julie Louise

(GER-ber-ding)

1955- Director of the Centers for Disease Control and Prevention

Address: Centers for Disease Control and Prevention, 1600 Clifton Rd., Atlanta, GA 30333

Julie Louise Gerberding, the first female director of the federal Centers for Disease Control and Prevention (CDC), has become "the face and the voice of public health," as Anita Manning wrote for *USA Today* (June 11, 2003, on-line). "Easily recognizable, with that dramatic streak of gray hair that partially frames her face and her give-it-to-you-straight delivery, [she] projects a sense of calm rationality in the face of menacing microbes." The CDC is an arm of the U.S. Department of Health and Human Services (HHS); according to its Web site, its mission is to "promote health and quality of life by preventing and controlling disease, injury, and disability." It attempts to do so by providing the U.S. public at large and the medical community in particular with up-to-date, credible information about health threats ranging from industrial and agricultural dangers (stemming from the use of various types of equipment or chemicals, for example), to epidemics of flu and other infectious diseases, to obesity in growing numbers of children and adults and the consequent rise in the rates of such maladies as diabetes. "We live in a society that values disease care far more than it values prevention," Gerberding said to Bruce Haring for the Associated Press (June 13, 2003). "The time to change that is now."

Since the September 11, 2001 terrorist attacks on the U.S., the CDC's responsibilities have grown. As Gerberding explained to Lois A. Bowers for *CWRU Magazine* (Spring 2003), a publication of Case Western Reserve University, the CDC must try to ensure that all aspects of the American healthcare system are prepared for a possible bioterrorist attack—that is, the intentional release into the atmosphere, water supply, or elsewhere of harmful microorganisms or toxins in quantities capable of killing or injuring large numbers of people. As Gerberding told Bowers, the CDC must "make sure that, should a threat occur, we have the appropriate measures to take care of exposed or affected people." Before she began working for the CDC, in 1998, Gerberding spent 17 years at the University of California at San Francisco and its medical center, first as a student and then as a physician, educator, and administrator. She has headed the CDC since July 2002. In a conversation with Anita Manning, C. Charles Stokes, the president and CEO of the CDC Foundation (a private, nonprofit group that supports the work of the CDC), praised Gerberding's "natural managerial ability" and "calming, reassuring personality." "People want to believe they're getting a straight answer and the right answer, and Julie conveys that," Stokes said. "When you combine her interest in the very best science and her belief that the CDC ought to communicate straight with the public, it's a great mixture, and it's what the country needs in this time when there is so much fear out there."

The daughter of a police chief and a teacher, Julie Louise Gerberding was born in 1955 in South Dakota and grew up in Estelline, a tiny town near the state's eastern border. She has told interviewers that by the age of four, she knew that she wanted to be a doctor. She attended high school in Brookings, South Dakota, about an hour's drive from Estelline, and then entered Case Western Reserve University, in Cleveland, Ohio, where she majored in both chemistry and biology. As an undergraduate she won the Hippolyte Gruener Prize for merit in chemistry and the George Talbot Hunt Award for high academic standing and leadership; she was also elected to the national honor society Phi Beta Kappa. After she earned a B.A. degree, magna cum laude, in 1977, she entered the same university's medical school. There, she was elected a member of Alpha Omega Alpha, the medical honor society. When she graduated, with an M.D. degree, in 1981, she received the Alice Paige Cleveland Prize, given to a woman who has shown strong leadership capabilities. Gerberding next moved to California, to undertake an internship in internal medicine at the University of California at San Francisco (UCSF) School of Medicine, one of the top medical schools in the U.S. Her arrival coincided with the appearances of the earliest cases of a mysterious disease among gay men in San Francisco that, in 1982, the CDC linked to an unknown agent in blood; that same year, the CDC dubbed the illness "acquired immune deficiency syndrome," or AIDS. In her third year at UCSF (1983–84), Gerberding served as chief medical resident at San Francisco General Hospital, which is linked to the UCSF School of Medicine. She then completed a National Institutes of Health (NIH) training fellowship in infectious diseases and clinical pharmacology, also at UCSF. "My clinical training really evolved with the AIDS epidemic, and it was natural to get started in the infectious disease area during that time," she told Lois A. Bowers.

For the next half-dozen years, Gerberding served as a physician at San Francisco General Hospital and taught courses in infectious disease at UCSF's medical school. In 1990 she earned a master's degree in public health from the University of California at Berkeley. That year she was named director of the Prevention Epicenter at UCSF, which the CDC Web site described as "a multidisciplinary service, teaching, and research program that focused on preventing infections in patients and their health care providers." In that post, Gerberding pioneered studies on HIV infections in nurses, physicians, and other health-care workers (contracted primarily via needlesticks: pricks with needles contaminated with the blood of HIV carriers or AIDS patients). She also helped set up guidelines for employers of people diagnosed as HIV-positive, bearing in mind the fears

and needs of both the affected workers and their bosses. "From the beginning of her career, she had thrust upon her a responsibility to think through something that affected not just an individual patient, but something that affects a community, the larger society," Julius R. Krevans, a chancellor emeritus of UCSF, told Anita Manning.

In 1998 Gerberding left UCSF to join the CDC as director of the Hospital Infections Program, now known as the Division of Healthcare Quality Promotion. She specialized in patient safety and worked on initiatives to prevent the spread of infections and the commission of medical errors in health-care facilities. By 2001 she had been named acting deputy director of the CDC's National Center for Infectious Diseases. In that position Gerberding played a leading role in the federal response to the anthrax bioterrorism attacks that had occurred that fall: specifically, the mailing of seemingly ordinary envelopes that contained spores of anthrax in the form of what appeared to be a white powder. (Anthrax is an acute infectious disease that, historically, has been confined primarily to cattle; the spores can be fatal in humans, especially when inhaled.) The envelopes arrived in the offices of various news organizations and two U.S. senators in the nation's capital. Gerberding acted as a spokesperson for the CDC, holding daily teleconferences for journalists and briefing HHS staff members. The media later revealed that the FBI, who had U.S. Army laboratories analyze the anthrax-laden envelopes, had neither invited nor permitted any CDC staff members to be present during the analyses and had not permitted anyone from the CDC to examine the envelopes or their contents. Almost a year and a half later, in the *Nation* (March 18, 2002), Marc Siegel paraphrased Gerberding, who by then had become the CDC's acting deputy director of the National Center for Infectious Diseases, as saying that CDC scientists should have had access to the anthrax "before the CDC rendered public health predictions." She told him that the CDC might then have been able to determine, in her words, "the concentration of the bacteria, and the chemicals that have been added to the powder to aerosolize it," factors that "affect the impact of the anthrax on humans." The CDC did not know, for example, that in at least one case, the anthrax spores were small enough to pass through the molecules-wide holes in the envelopes and contaminate postal equipment; thus Gerberding and other CDC spokespeople passed along inaccurate information. Indeed, two Postal Service employees who worked in the Brentwood postal facility, in Washington, D.C., died from anthrax infections. (As of late 2004, the identity of the person or people responsible for the anthrax mailings remained unknown.)

In late February 2002 the epidemiologist Jeffrey Koplan, who had headed the CDC since October 1998, announced that he would step down from his post on March 31, 2002. The following July 3, Tommy G. Thompson, the secretary of HHS, announced that Gerberding had been named director of the CDC and administrator of the Agency for Toxic Substances and Disease Registry (ATSDR). According to various sources, public-health organizations, among other entities and individuals, had lobbied for her appointment. "Dr. Gerberding knows public health, she knows infectious diseases, and she knows bioterrorism preparedness . . . ," Thompson said, as quoted on the CDC Web site. "She brings the right mix of professional experience and leadership skills to ensure the CDC continues to meet the nation's public health needs." Jeffrey Koplan told M. A. J. McKenna for the *Atlanta Journal-Constitution* (July 3, 2002, on-line) that he believed Gerberding's appointment was "a great choice. . . . Amongst the many very talented people at the CDC, she is a real star: smart, hardworking, thoughtful, compassionate and well-respected."

Headquartered in Atlanta, Georgia, the CDC employs nearly 8,600 people in the U.S. and three dozen other countries. In addition to the office of the director, its components include seven national centers, which focus on birth defects and developmental disabilities; chronic disease prevention and health promotion; environmental health; health statistics; HIV, sexually transmitted diseases, and tuberculosis prevention; infectious diseases; and injury prevention and control. Other divisions of the CDC are the National Immunization Program, the National Institute for Occupational Safety and Health, the Epidemiology Program Office, and the Public Health Practice Program Office. The ATSDR's mission, according to its Web site, is "to prevent harmful exposures and disease related to toxic substances"—for example, by assessing the risks to humans of hazardous-waste disposal sites and the presence in the environment of hazardous substances from other sources.

In the past two years, Gerberding has dealt with such potential threats to the U.S. population as SARS (severe acute respiratory syndrome), an apparently new form of pneumonia that struck thousands of people worldwide in 2002 and 2003 and killed about 10 percent of them; in response, the CDC issued travel alerts for Beijing and other parts of mainland China, Hong Kong, Toronto, and Taiwan. Another recently identified threat is the West Nile virus, which spreads to humans via mosquito bites. In most people, the virus has no apparent effect; about 20 percent of those infected get mildly ill, with such symptoms as fever, body aches, and nausea; a small percentage become severely ill and may suffer permanent neurological damage, and an even smaller percentage die. In 1999, the first year in which doctors in the U.S. reported seeing people infected with the virus, the CDC recorded 62 cases; the figure for 2002 was 4,156 reported cases, with 284 deaths (6.8 percent), and for 2003, 9,862 cases, with 264 deaths (2.6 percent).

Microorganisms, whether emanating in nature or from the labs of bioterrorists, are far from the only threats to the health and well-being of the populace. Chronic illnesses, among them heart disease, all types of cancer, emphysema and other lung diseases, and diabetes, kill more than 1.7 million people in the U.S. every year; stated another way, chronic disease—much of which is preventable—is the cause of seven out of every 10 deaths annually in the U.S. Moreover, such diseases have disabled some 25 million of the 90 million people who suffer from them. In a section called "Cost-Effectiveness of Prevention" in an article titled "Chronic Disease Overview" on the Web site of the National Center for Chronic Disease Prevention and Health Promotion, the center noted that "for every $1 spent on water fluoridation, $38 is saved in dental restorative treatment costs," and "the direct medical costs associated with physical inactivity was $29 billion in 1987 and nearly $76.6 billion in 2000." In 2002 Gerberding told the CDC Foundation, as reported on the CNN Web site, "Right now our nation's demographics are changing dramatically. Our population is aging. There is an obesity epidemic. Our racial and ethnic diversity is growing. . . . These create new challenges for the public health system, because we must provide relevant services that meet the needs of all people."

Gerberding is a tenured associate professor of medicine, epidemiology, and biostatistics at UCSF, where she is currently on a leave of absence, and an associate clinical professor of medicine (specializing in infectious diseases) at Emory University, in Atlanta, Georgia. She is a member of the American Society for Clinical Investigation, the American College of Physicians, and the Society for Healthcare Epidemiology of America, on whose board she served for three years. Gerberding has served on the editorial board of *Annals of Internal Medicine* and as an associate editor of the *American Journal of Medicine*. She has written or co-authored more than 140 professional papers and textbook chapters. In 2002 she won an International Health and Medical Media Award (known as a FREDDIE Award) for Outstanding Medical Communication.

Gerberding lives in Atlanta with her husband, David A. Rose, a software engineer and information-technology specialist, and their three cats. She is stepmother to Rose's daughter, Renada Rutmanis, who in 2004 was on assignment with the Peace Corps in Romania. In her free time Gerberding enjoys scuba diving, gardening, hiking, and reading on the beach.

—K.J.E.

Suggested Reading: CDC.gov; *CWRU Magazine* (on-line) p28+ Spring 2003, with photos; CWRU.edu; *Modern Healthcare* p6+ July 22, 2002; *Science* p173+ July 12, 2002; *Time* p102 Apr. 26, 2004, with photo; *Wall Street Journal* B p1+ June 4, 2003

Frank Micelotta/ImageDirect/Getty Images

Goldsman, Akiva

July 7, 1962– Screenwriter

Address: c/o Writers Guild of America, 7000 West Third St., Los Angeles, CA 90048

The screenwriter and producer Akiva Goldsman won an Academy Award for his screenplay for *A Beautiful Mind* (2001), the biopic based on the real-life Princeton University mathematician and economist John Nash, who suffered from delusional schizophrenia and won a Nobel Prize in 1994. In addition to the high praise and honor it brought Goldsman, the screenplay for *A Beautiful Mind* marked a dramatic departure for him in three salient ways: first, the story did not center on superheroes, the supernatural, or fictional intrigue, as all of Goldsman's previous scripts had; second, in terms of theme, it was his most serious script to date; and third, it was his first script to feature a protagonist based on a real-life person. The movie, directed by Ron Howard and starring Russell Crowe as Nash, won the Academy Award for best picture and took in more than $170 million at the box office. Goldsman has also written or co-written the scripts for two installments of the popular Batman movie franchise, *Batman Forever* (1995) and *Batman & Robin* (1997), and the big-screen adaptations of two best-selling novels by the lawyer-turned-novelist John Grisham, *The Client* (1994) and *A Time To Kill* (1996). His most recently produced screenplay is his 2004 adaptation of Isaac Asimov's science-fiction novel *I, Robot*, which Goldsman co-wrote with Jeff Vintar.

Akiva Goldsman was born in New York City on July 7, 1962 and grew up in Brooklyn, one of the city's boroughs. His father, Tev Goldsman, a therapist, and his mother, the well-known child psychologist Mira Rothenberg, turned the family home into one of the country's first centers for what were then called emotionally disturbed children. (The conditions from which those children suffered, mainly schizophrenia and autism, are now referred to as pervasive development disorder or conduct disorder.) He told Richard Natale for an article posted on the Writers Guild Web site that early in his life, because of what he had been exposed to at home, "I had come up with the notion that people who were bad were without reason. I'm no expert on mental illness or mental health, but this much I know: Nothing we do is without reason." The children his parents treated, he said, "had reasons" for their actions. "We just didn't understand them."

In the early 1980s Goldsman attended Wesleyan University, in Middletown, Connecticut, where he became friends with Paul Schiff, who would later produce more than a dozen Hollywood movies, including *Young Guns* (1988) and *Mona Lisa Smile* (2003). Goldsman and Schiff shared a student house which was later part of the inspiration for the college-themed film comedy *PCU* (1994). After graduating from Wesleyan, in 1983, Goldsman studied creative writing at New York University, in Manhattan. During that time he began writing screenplays. According to a number of sources, including the MSN Entertainment Web site, Goldsman's first script to be produced was the dramatic comedy *Indian Summer*. In 1994 he wrote an original film entitled *Silent Fall*, which was informed by Goldsman's early exposure to his parents' work and centered on a psychologist who treats an autistic boy, the witness to a crime. *Silent Fall*, which starred Richard Dreyfuss and Linda Hamilton, garnered very little attention.

At about the same time, Goldsman adapted for the screen two novels by the best-selling author John Grisham: *The Client*, which reached theaters in 1994, and *A Time To Kill*, released in 1996. (Those movies followed on the heels of earlier screen adaptations of Grisham's novels *The Firm* and *The Pelican Brief*, both released in 1993.) *The Client* told the story of a streetwise 11-year-old boy (Brad Renfro) who enlists the help of a lawyer (Susan Sarandon) when his life is endangered because of his knowledge about certain mobsters and politicians. Though *The Client* received mixed reviews overall, *Rolling Stone* (August 11, 1994, on-line) called it the "best and certainly the liveliest, tensest and most emotionally involving film yet of a Grisham novel." Theatergoers seemed to embrace the movie, as it grossed in excess of $90 million at the box office. *A Time to Kill* was an even larger commercial success, earning more than $100 million in box-office receipts. Its story centered on a lawyer (Matthew McConaughey) and his assistant (Sandra Bullock) who fight to save a man on death row (Samuel L. Jackson). Barbara Shulgasser, writing for the *San Francisco Examiner* (July 24, 1996), found fault with the number—and handling—of secondary characters in the movie: "Director Joel Schumacher and screenwriter Akiva Goldsman seem incapable of emphasizing what's important and relegating the rest to secondary status." Peter Travers registered a similar complaint in *Rolling Stone* (August 8, 1996), writing that in *A Time to Kill* Schumacher and Goldsman "cram in too much, including Grisham's polemics about racism, the resurgence of the Ku Klux Klan and the moral dilemma of the death penalty." Having received many negative reviews, the movie also attracted the notice of those who present the Razzie Awards, given each year to what are deemed abysmal movies. *A Time to Kill* was the winner in the Razzie category of worst-written film to gross over $100 million.

Goldsman next turned his talents to the *Batman* movie franchise. A popular comic-book superhero created by Bob Kane in 1940, the caped, crime-fighting Batman character had previously inspired a number of animated and live-action movies and television series, including the hit movies *Batman* (1989) and *Batman Returns* (1992), both starring Michael Keaton and directed by Tim Burton. Goldsman co-wrote the script for the next installment, *Batman Forever* (1995), with Lee Batchler and Janet Scott Batchler. Their script was turned into an action-packed movie starring Val Kilmer as Batman, Tommy Lee Jones and Jim Carrey as the colorful villains Two-Face and The Riddler, respectively, Nicole Kidman as a flirtatious psychologist smitten with Batman, and Chris O'Donnell as Batman's newly recruited acolyte, Robin. Directed by Joel Schumacher, the movie earned mostly positive notices and proved an enormous commercial success, taking in more than $180 million in theaters nationwide. Christine James wrote for the Web site boxoffice.com that *Batman Forever* "exemplifies big-budget grandeur gone right." "I liked the look of the movie and Schumacher's general irreverence toward the material," Roger Ebert wrote for the *Chicago Sun-Times* (June 16, 1995). "But the great Batman movie still remains to be made." Continuing the series, Goldsman next wrote the script for the Schumacher-directed 1997 movie *Batman & Robin*, which saw George Clooney replacing Kilmer in the Batman role, Alicia Silverstone stepping in as Batgirl, Arnold Schwarzenegger playing Batman's enemy Mr. Freeze, and Uma Thurman portraying the sexy, villainous Poison Ivy. Critical responses were mixed. A common complaint about the movie was summed up by Barbara Shulgasser for the *San Francisco Examiner* (June 20, 1997), who wrote, "Too often this movie, written by Akiva Goldsman, seems like a big collection of Vegas acts strung together." In the online publication *Salon* (June 20, 1997), Robin Dougherty was even harsher, writing sarcastically that there was "something almost maniacally heroic about packaging the fourth sequel of a superhero action series without resorting to the old standbys of good writing, capable acting or inspired directing." (For *Batman & Robin* Goldsman earned a second Razzie Award, this one for worst screenplay.) While the movie was more popular among general audiences than critics, its box-office gross—$107 million—was less than the cost of making it.

In 1998 Goldsman took on a double role, writing the screen adaptation of *Lost in Space*, based on the hit science-fiction television series of the 1960s, and producing the movie from his script as well. His next script, adapted from a novel of the same name, was for the movie *Practical Magic* (1998), a romantic comedy about two sisters (Nicole Kidman and Sandra Bullock) who use their magical powers to aid their search for love. Neither film was particularly successful with critics or moviegoers.

Goldsman's screenplay for the movie *A Beautiful Mind* (2001) was based on a biography by Sylvia Nasar of the brilliant mathematician and economist John Forbes Nash Jr. Nash was a professor at Princeton University who made amazing discoveries in the mathematical worlds of game and number theory but who, suffering from delusional schizophrenia, also descended into madness. Nash believed, for example, that Russians were sending him coded messages on the front page of the *New York Times* and that he was being pursued by a federal agent. Later in his life his mental condition went into remission, and in 1994 he was awarded the Nobel Prize in economic sciences. (The game-theory concept developed by Nash has become a foundation of modern economics, influencing global trade negotiations, labor relations, and the field of evolutionary biology.) Because Goldsman had been exposed early in his life, through his parents' work, to children with schizophrenia, Nash's story was close to his heart. Also, as he told Richard Natale, "When I read the story of John Nash in *Vanity Fair* and then Sylvia Nasar's biography, I fell in love with its architecture. It's as good a story as god will give to a human. Genius. Madness. Nobel Prize. It doesn't get much better than that." Through his screenplay Goldsman sought to "use this man's journey to give some insight into what it might feel like to suffer from this disease," as he told Natale. "In movies about mental disease there is the person who has the disease and the person who points to the person who has the disease. It's voyeuristic. With John's life, there seemed to be an opportunity to build a structure wherein the audience might have some hint of what the experience of the illness was like."

In *USA Today* (December 20, 2001), Mike Clark described *A Beautiful Mind* as "one inspiring movie" and as being "among the most affecting ever made about co-existing with mental demons." Despite that glowing assessment, and the many awards the film won, *A Beautiful Mind* received a fair number of negative reviews as well. Among those who found fault with it was A. O. Scott of the

New York Times (December 21, 2001), who argued that the finished film, while praiseworthy in some respects, hewed closely to Hollywood formula and presented a sanitized and highly selective portrait of Nash's life. Scott wrote that "anything that would dilute our sympathy by acquainting us with the vicissitudes of Mr. Nash's real life has been air-brushed away, leaving a portrait of a shy, lovable genius." Nevertheless, in 2002 *A Beautiful Mind* won the Academy Award for best picture. Also honored by the Academy of Motion Picture Arts and Sciences were the film's director, Ron Howard, and the actress Jennifer Connelly, for her turn as Nash's long-suffering wife, Alicia. Russell Crowe won high praise from critics, and earned an Academy Award nomination as best actor, for his portrayal of Nash. Goldsman took home the Academy Award for best screenplay based on previously published material. In addition to the Oscar, Goldsman's screenplay for *A Beautiful Mind* won a Golden Globe Award and a Writers Guild of America Award. His script was also nominated for honors from the American Film Institute, the British Academy of Film and Television Arts, the Chicago Film Critics Association, and the Broadcast Film Critics Association.

A film version of *I, Robot*, inspired by Isaac Asimov's same-titled, futuristic 1950 book and directed by Alex Proyas from Goldsman and Jeff Vintar's screenplay, was released in July 2004. In it Will Smith is seen as Del Spooner, a police detective in the year 2035, who distrusts the human-like robots who, as envisioned by the filmmakers, perform many tasks. Spooner investigates a mysterious death that may have been the work of such a machine. In the *New York Times* (July 16, 2004, on-line), A. O. Scott pronounced *I, Robot* to be "a straightforward genre exercise" that is "one of the smarter dumb movies I've seen in a while"; in the *Chicago Tribune* (July 25, 2004), Michael Wilmington called it a "compromised but exciting" movie—one that is less than faithful to the original material but works well as entertainment. Goldsman's upcoming projects include three screen adaptations of best-selling novels: *The Cinderella Man*, *Memoirs of a Geisha*, and *The Da Vinci Code*. All three were scheduled for release in 2005.

In addition to *Lost in Space*, Goldsman has produced more than a half-dozen movies, including the thriller *Deep Blue Sea* (1999) and *Starsky & Hutch* (2004), a lighthearted film version of the popular TV show from the 1970s. He will also earn credit as a producer of the upcoming movies *Mindhunters*, *Constantine*, *Mr. and Mrs. Smith*, and *The Exec*. Goldsman made a brief, uncredited appearance as a guest at a party held at the Playboy Mansion in the movie *Confessions of a Dangerous Mind* (2002). According to the Internet Movie Database, the writer has appeared on screen only one other time: in a 2001 episode of the popular teenage TV series *Felicity*. Goldsman's nickname is Keevie, a playful version of his first name.

—C.F.T.

Suggested Reading: Internet Movie Database; Writers Guild Web site

Selected Screenplays: *Silent Fall*, 1994; *The Client*, 1994; *Batman Forever*, 1995; *A Time to Kill*, 1996; *Batman & Robin*, 1997; *Lost in Space*, 1998; *Practical Magic*, 1998; *A Beautiful Mind*, 2001; *I, Robot*, 2004

Courtesy of Random House

Groopman, Jerome

Jan. 11, 1952– Physician; writer

Address: Beth Israel Deaconess Medical Center, 330 Brookline Ave., Boston, MA 02215

"A doctor's words are like a scalpel," Jerome Groopman, a leading physician in AIDS and cancer treatment, told Rachel K. Sobel for *U.S. News & World Report* (January 26, 2004). "If they are applied precisely at the right time and in the right place, they can be amazingly beneficial. But if they are misdirected and misapplied, they can be terribly harmful." Groopman's words have not only comforted and educated his patients, they have provided him with a second career; since 1997, when his first book, *The Measure of Our Days: New Beginnings at Life's End*, was published, he has been a prolific writer. His books, which focus on the human side of medicine, have been lauded for their clarity, insight, and humanity. His essays appear frequently in the *New Yorker* —Groopman was named a staff writer in 1998—and have been similarly praised.

Jerome Groopman was born on January 11, 1952 and grew up in the New York City borough of Queens. His father, Seymour, was a dentist, and his mother, Muriel, was a secretary at Columbia-Presbyterian Medical Center. Groopman, interested in literature from an early age, graduated from Bayside High School. He then entered Columbia University, in New York City; in 1972 he earned a bachelor's degree in 19th-century political philosophy, and four years later he earned his medical degree from the university's College of Physicians and Surgeons. Groopman served his internship and residency at Massachusetts General Hospital, in Boston. He then participated in specialty fellowships in hematology and oncology at the University of California and at the Children's Hospital and Sidney Farber Cancer Center, in Boston. (The last has since been renamed the Dana-Farber Cancer Institute.)

Groopman is currently the chief of experimental medicine at Beth Israel Deaconess Medical Center (a Harvard Medical School teaching hospital), where he is also director of the AIDS oncology program and director of the Robert Mapplethorpe Laboratory for AIDS Research. In these capacities, he has conducted seminal research to find ways to improve the immune systems of those with AIDS and to treat AIDS-related cancers, including Kaposi's sarcoma, which afflicts a large percentage of AIDS patients. Groopman performed the first clinical trials using genetically engineered proteins to increase the production of blood cells in immunodeficient patients and was an important participant in developing many effective AIDS-related therapies, including the well-known drug AZT and protease inhibitors. (Protease inhibitors block the body's production of the protease enzyme, which HIV needs in order to create new viruses. When protease inhibitors were introduced in combination with other drugs, the percentage of AIDS patients who contracted opportunistic infections and died fell sharply.)

Celebrated for his work with AIDS, Groopman has also studied breast cancer and neurobiology. Under his direction, for example, in 1997 scientists at his laboratory discovered a gene, CHK, that appeared to slow the growth of breast cancer. (The gene and its application to treatment of the disease are still being explored.) In the field of neurobiology, the laboratory's scientists have identified a previously undiscovered gene family that appears to regulate the growth of neurons. Research is being conducted on the genes' role in such degenerative neurological diseases as multiple sclerosis, Lou Gehrig's disease, and Alzheimer's.

Renowned in medical circles for his research, Groopman is perhaps best known to the general public as a writer. Having witnessed numerous patients facing their own mortality with varying degrees of grace, Groopman wrote up eight case histories, including that of Kirk, an aggressive financial whiz desperate to try any experimental therapy to fight his disease, and of Elizabeth, a commanding older woman humbled by the experience of being ill. Their stories appear in *The Measure of Our Days: New Beginnings at Life's End* (1997), in which Groopman wrote about the spiritual lives of patients with serious illnesses and the opportunities for fulfillment they sometimes find. The book was serialized in both the *New Yorker* and the *Boston Globe Sunday Magazine*. "In *The Measure of Our Days* this prominent Harvard researcher offers an unflinching portrait of terminal illness as seen through the eyes of a compassionate physician," Stephen Fowle wrote for *People* (January 12, 1998). "The result is a moving story of a doctor and patients grappling with cancer and AIDS." In the *New Republic* (November 17, 1997), John W. Krakauer called the volume "a thoughtful and impassioned book about the complex terrain that must be negotiated between the physician and the dying patient. . . . With rare perceptiveness, Groopman manages to capture the sudden plunges and upturns that occur on a minute-to-minute basis in the encounter between the physician and the patient."

Shortly after the book was serialized in the *New Yorker*, Groopman was hired as a staff writer for medical and biological topics. His essays for that periodical have examined such topics as the line between persistent behavior and obsessive-compulsive disorder; whether or not fibromyalgia is really a disease; heart surgery; electrical implants to help the blind; genetic screening for the BRCA gene, which has been linked to breast cancer; hepatitis C; the drug Celebex; bone-marrow transplants; the genetic similarities between humans and dogs; and the physiological aspects of a Mars mission. (His work has also appeared in other publications, including the *Wall Street Journal*, the *New Republic*, and the *New York Times*.)

Groopman's next book, *Second Opinions: Stories of Intuition and Choice in a Changing World of Medicine*, was published in 2000. The book focuses, through specific case histories, on how doctors diagnose illness and the decisions that affect their patients' treatments. Writing for the *Anglican Theological Review* (Summer 2001), David K. Urion described the work as "an elegant and countercultural book about the role of intuition in medical decision-making. . . . Dr. Groopman reminds us of the roles those most mysterious entities, intuition and choice, play in the care of patients. . . . Dr. Groopman offers us examples of choice, intuition, and prayer from his own life and practice that are, by turns, compelling, frightening, heartrending."

Groopman and his wife, Pamela, who is also a doctor, learned the importance of seeking a second opinion and trusting their intuition when their first child, Steven, became severely ill at nine months of age. They were visiting relatives in Connecticut at the time and took him to an older, experienced doctor who dismissed his troubles as a minor gastrointestinal upset. However, on the ride back to their Boston home, the couple saw that their son was becoming much sicker. They rushed him to a hospital emergency room, where a young resident correctly identified the problem as an intestinal blockage, but then told the anxious parents that surgery could wait until the next day. Groopman and his wife insisted on seeing a senior doctor for another opinion; their son underwent an operation immediately and recovered fully.

Partly as a result of that experience, Groopman urges people to respect their intuition and not blindly trust doctors' diagnoses. He told Alexis Jetter for *Health* (July–August 2000), "[Doctors] are not gods. We are not infallible. And particularly when dealing with complicated and life-threatening situations, we should be seeking help and input."

Groopman's first two books were used as the basis for the critically acclaimed ABC television series *Gideon's Crossing*, which aired from October 2000 to April 2001. In it Andre Braugher starred as Ben Gideon, Groopman's alter ego, the head of an experimental oncology ward at a fictitious New England hospital.

Groopman's third book, *The Anatomy of Hope: How People Prevail in the Face of Illness* (2004), is about the power of hope to heal illness and relieve pain. It includes many accounts of seriously ill patients Groopman has known who were either cured or came to terms with their illnesses and died in peace with the help of positive thinking. Michael Dirda wrote for *Inc.* (January 2004), "In all these stories, Groopman builds narrative suspense like a good thriller writer, while revealing again and again how emotional outlook affects a patient's prognosis. He closes this fine book by pointing out that true hope recognizes the realities of a medical condition but 'tempers fear so we can recognize dangers and then bypass or endure them.'"

Groopman knew firsthand the benefits of a hopeful attitude. In 1979, while training for the Boston Marathon, he had ruptured a lumbar disk. Surgery to correct the condition failed, and he lived in pain for 19 years. Finally, when he could not walk more than four or five blocks at a time, a rehabilitation doctor at New England Baptist Hospital in Boston prescribed new exercises that he acknowledged would initially cause more pain, but would ultimately work. Infused with a new sense of hope, Groopman performed the prescribed exercises; the results seemed miraculous, leading him to wonder if a hopeful attitude might also be part of the recovery process. He told Nora Seton for the *Houston Chronicle* (February 27, 2004, on-line), "[That doctor] realized that I had bought into others' incorrect assumptions. He told me that the narrative I had been living for nearly two decades—that there was no hope for me and that I would be constrained to live in a very debilitated state—was wrong."

Groopman believes that emotions can change brain chemistry. He has written that experiments have shown that hope causes the brain to release enkephalins and endorphins, substances that affect the body in the same way the drug morphine does. Groopman stresses, however, that he does not advocate simply trying to wish pain away, saying that hope is not "a magic wand, which by itself is going to melt a cancer or purge H.I.V. from the blood," as he told Dinitia Smith for the *New York Times* (March 16, 2004). "True hope is clear-eyed. It sees all the difficulties that exist and all the potential for failure, but through that, carves a realistic path to a better future."

Groopman is on the scientific board of Onconova, a biopharmaceutical company focused on the identification, development, and commercialization of drugs for the treatment of patients with cancer; he has also served on the scientific advisory board of Vertex Pharmaceuticals. He has served on the Advisory Council of the National Heart, Lung and Blood Institute (NHLBI) for AIDS-related diseases and has worked on several committees for the U.S. Food and Drug Administration (FDA). In 2000 Groopman was elected to the Institute of Medicine of the National Academy of Sciences; he was an original member of the organization's committee on AIDS. Groopman is a popular speaker and frequent guest on TV and radio talk shows. He also serves on many scientific editorial boards and has published more than 150 scientific articles. He contributed a chapter to the ninth edition of *Technology and the Future* (2002), criticizing the work and views of Leon Kass, the chair of President George W. Bush's Council on Biomedical Ethics. Groopman has also been active in community education projects, fostering AIDS awareness in teenagers and young adults.

Groopman and his wife have three children: Steven, Michael, and Emily. He typically starts his day between 4:00 and 4:30 in the morning, dictating his books into a tape recorder until 7:00 a.m. After an hour-long workout at the gym, he starts his work at Beth Israel Deaconess Medical Center and his teaching at Harvard Medical School, where he is currently Dina and Raphael Recanati Professor of Medicine.

Groopman has assisted many prominent patients, including King Hussein of Jordan, who died of lymphoma in 1999. An observant Conservative Jew who attends synagogue regularly and does not work on the Sabbath, he has said that his religious faith has a significant impact on his work. "I believe God created the universe, but that the universe works according to natural laws," he told Dinitia Smith. "It's not as though God is intervening to give cancer or to take it away, [but] one of the great gifts of God is the capacity of hope . . . in human character." Groopman was awarded an honorary doctorate from the Jewish Theological Seminary in 2002.

—K.E.D.

Suggested Reading: *Health* p119+ July–Aug. 2000; *Houston Chronicle* (on-line) Feb. 27, 2004; jeromegroopman.com; *New York Times* F p5 Mar. 16, 2004

Selected Books: *The Measure of Our Days: New Beginnings at Life's End*, 1997; *Second Opinions: Stories of Intuition and Choice in a Changing World of Medicine*, 2000; *The Anatomy of Hope: How People Prevail in the Face of Illness*, 2004

Courtesy of Samuel Gruber

Gruber, Samuel H.

May 13, 1938– Shark expert

Address: University of Miami, RSMAS/MBF, 4600 Rickenbacker Causeway, Miami, FL 33149-1098

The marine biologist Samuel Gruber sees sharks not as sources of culinary delicacies or medicinal materials, or as the man-eating monsters depicted in such films as *Jaws*, but as members of a beautiful, endangered species that needs to be protected. Although Gruber, a professor at the University of Miami's Rosenstiel School of Marine and Atmospheric Science and Division of Marine Biology and Fisheries, has studied sharks in general, he specializes in the study of lemon sharks (*Negaprion brevirostris*), a species named for the trademark yellow coloring of its belly. Lemon sharks, Gruber has explained, remain among the most mysterious of all sharks. For an article on the Web site at-sea.org (1999), he explained his passion for learning about the creatures: "Sharks are magnificent predators, and I want to poke into their private lives. These animals are wild, free, and one of the few creatures left that can challenge man. Because they are so formidable and mysterious, sharks have become shrouded in myths, portrayed as villains,

and worshipped as gods. The question that drives me is, 'What's the real truth?'" His 40-year search for that truth has led Gruber to become one of the world's foremost shark experts.

Samuel Harvey Gruber was born in Brooklyn, New York, on May 13, 1938 to Sidney Gruber, a financier, and Claire Gruber, a homemaker. The family, which also included Samuel's older brother, Herbert, and sister, Sandy, later moved to Florida, where Samuel attended elementary school in Miami Beach. He then went to Riverside Military Academy, a boarding school in Gainesville, Georgia, after which, in 1956, he entered Emory University, in Atlanta, Georgia, with the goal of studying medicine. During this period Gruber first felt the allure of marine biology. He has traced his interest in sharks to the day in 1958 when he went spearfishing and "had a close encounter with a 2000 foot long hammerhead. At least it *seemed* that big at the time!" as he said, according to the at-sea.org site. Soon thereafter, he transferred to the marine-biology program at the University of Miami, in Florida, where he received his B.S. degree in zoology and M.S. and Ph.D. degrees in marine sciences in 1960, 1966, and 1969, respectively.

Gruber focused his research on lemon sharks, as they thrive in captivity, survive in tanks, and are easily transported, but are not as small and docile as the often-studied dogfish shark. The lemon shark belongs to the family Carcharhinidae (commonly called requiem sharks, for obscure reasons), which includes the better-known tiger shark and milk shark. Lemon sharks average eight to 10 feet in length and inhabit relatively shallow coastal waters; they live in the Pacific Ocean off the coasts of Latin American countries and in the Atlantic off the coasts of South America and West Africa, as well as in the Gulf of Mexico. The lemon shark is, as Gruber said to *Current Biography*, an "impressive, rapacious, aggressive animal" that thus fits the popular image of the shark in many ways and makes a fascinating subject for study. From 1960 through 1976 Gruber primarily studied the anatomy, physiology, and psychophysics of the visual system of the lemon shark. Based at the Rosenstiel School, he continued to investigate shark vision through 1981. Although it was commonly believed, when Gruber began his research, that sharks were nearly blind, Gruber's studies proved otherwise, offering evidence of their "exquisitely adapted visual system," as he told at-sea.org. The studies revealed that sharks' eyes allow them to distinguish colors, have lenses seven times as powerful as those in human eyes, and contain tapeta, which function as mirrors behind the retinas and reflect images, thereby increasing visual power. In 1976 Gruber devoted himself to field research to understand better the role of sharks in tropical marine ecosystems. This preliminary research, which he conducted during ocean outings, served as the basis for a decade-long study, supported by the National Science Foundation (NSF), on the early life of the lemon shark. Gruber is currently summarizing the results of the NSF study.

Gruber grew increasingly alarmed about the depletion of shark populations, due to overharvesting and widespread killing by those seeking shark fins as a culinary delicacy or shark liver oil, touted for its medicinal properties. His concern led him, in 1990, to establish the Shark Specialist Group as a branch of the preexisting World Conservation Union. Gruber has pointed out that, although some sharks may live to 100 years of age, as a species they are vulnerable to extinction, because they grow slowly and mature late in life; many are killed before reproductive age. Moreover, they breed only once every two years and produce few offspring. (He hypothesized that the slowness of the lemon shark's digestive system, which can take up to four days to process one meal, causes very slow growth, which in turn may account for this sluggish maturation process.) Gruber lamented to William K. Stevens for the *New York Times* (December 8, 1992), "The hammering that sharks are taking simply cannot be sustained. There's so much that's fascinating about sharks that to have them killed off before we've explored the wonders of their biology and ecology, especially in ignorance and just to make a quick buck, is a crime." Gruber and his colleagues have continued to protest the depletion of shark populations.

In the late 1990s Gruber and his team, an international group of students and researchers, embarked upon one of his best-known studies when they boarded the research vessel *Sea Diver* on a quest to learn about lemon sharks' breeding habits. For the at-sea.org Web site, Gruber explained the logic behind the mission: "Nothing at all is known about the breeding strategy of requiem sharks like the Lemon Shark . . . and they are the most evolutionarily successful kinds of sharks. They are apparently [among] the most modern sharks as well. And they are the most heavily targeted group—fished and overfished for fin and flesh. So do we want to see them go extinct before we even know how they go about reproducing?" The research produced several interesting results, revealed in 2002. DNA testing and tagging allowed the team to track sharks so that they could be caught repeatedly. Gruber and his colleagues then determined that female lemon sharks practice polyandry, or the practice of mating with more than one male per breeding cycle, and that, although females breed only once every two years, they always return to the same lagoon to give birth. This finding held particular significance, as it suggested that biologists might have to locate and protect such nursery grounds, in addition to the sharks themselves.

As of 2003 Gruber had begun the preliminary research on a new study to determine if lemon sharks gather before mating, in what he calls a "precourtship aggregation," and to obtain more information on their physical characteristics and behavior. Thus far Gruber has theorized that only the female sharks always return to the same breeding grounds, recruiting different males every year (which ensures the genetic diversity of their offspring). The main impetus for this pending mission is a phenomenon occurring every winter in the deep water off Jupiter, Florida. Since 2000 large groups of lemon sharks, sometimes as many as 80, have been seen congregating in the waters just outside the Jupiter Inlet. Randy Jordan, a diving instructor in Jupiter, told the *Jupiter Courier* (February 9, 2003) that he solicited Gruber's input on the shark gatherings. "Everybody who goes out there gets overcome with a childlike excitement," Jordan asserted. "When Dr. Gruber saw it for the first time, I asked him for a scientific opinion on what was causing the sharks to gather like that. All he could say was 'holy crap.'" After his first sighting of the shark gathering, Gruber returned to dive into the midst of the sharks. "Here, in one afternoon, I saw more adult sharks than I've seen in my 42-year career," he told Susan Cocking for the *Miami Herald* (March 9, 2003). "It was stunning, fabulous. I was drawn like a magnet. I looked at their faces and their bodies and I felt like I was at home. It was like being with your family." Gruber received funding the following year to study the phenomenon, but so far in 2004 few sharks have shown up at the location. Currently, he is conducting tests to determine the efficacy of A-2, a newly created shark repellent derived from extracts gleaned from the bodies of dead sharks.

Even after over 40 years of researching sharks (during half of that time, he simultaneously battled lymphoma, which has been in remission since 1989), Gruber remains energetic and devoted to his vocation. According to Ed "Redwood" Ring, writing for the EcoWorld Web site, "Though he's in his . . . sixties, in spite of or perhaps because of his lifelong devotion to his passion, Dr. Gruber appears a much younger man." Colleagues have said that he still expresses awe and enthusiasm about his work. "My favorite thing to do is discover something new about how sharks work—and to transmit that information to the public," he said for the at-sea.org article. "No myths—only facts and quantitative models of the lifestyle of this great fish!!! Someday, when your daughter or son asks about sharks, perhaps you won't have to rely on myths and propaganda. There are a lot of new facts out there, and because of this, I have seen a real change in the public's perception of sharks. I feel personally good about this change. In some small way I feel like I have been able to spread the 'truth.'"

In 1983 Gruber founded the American Elasmobranch Society (AES), over which he presided for four years. Five years later he established the Samuel Gruber Endowment Fund, designed to encourage excellence in research and in scientific papers by AES student members. The fund is the source of the Gruber Award, given to the student member who delivers the best oral paper at the annual AES meeting. Gruber has written more than 175 scientific articles and edited the 1991 book *Discovering Sharks*, a collection of scientific papers. A popular speaker at scientific conferences, he has appeared on numerous television shows, on the BBC, PBS, the Discovery channel, and the National Geographic Society channel.

Gruber (or Doc, as he is often called) has been married since 1969 to Mariko Hirata, a former fashion designer. They have two daughters, Meegan, a surgeon, and Aya, an attorney and law professor. Gruber and his wife live in Miami but spend much of their time at his field-research station in Bimini, in the Bahamas.

—K.J.E.

Suggested Reading: at-sea.org; EcoWorld Web site; *Jupiter (Florida) Courier* A p3 Feb. 9, 2003; *Miami Herald* (on-line) Mar. 9, 2003; *New York Times* C p1 Dec. 8, 1992; University of Miami Web site

Selected Books—as editor: *Discovering Sharks*, 1991

Gregory Allen/Courtesy of Pantheon Books

Guillermoprieto, Alma

(gee-yare-moh-pree-AY-toh)

May 27, 1949– Journalist

Address: c/o Pantheon, 1745 Broadway, New York, NY 10019

Alma Guillermoprieto, who was born and raised in Mexico and taught dance in Cuba, has drawn on her background to write, in English, reports from Central and South America that delve into the complexities of Latin American society. In *Samba* (1990) she recounted her immersion in the life of a Brazilian favela, or shanty town, exposing the misery as well as the joys experienced by poor people in Rio de Janeiro. Her books *The Heart That Bleeds: Latin America Now* (1994) and *Looking for History: Dispatches from Latin America* (2001) examine conditions in a number of Latin American countries, while her memoir, *Dancing with Cuba* (2004), tells of the time she spent as a young woman in that country, a decade into the rule of Fidel Castro. Guillermoprieto, who has served as a contributing writer for the *New Yorker*, was awarded a MacArthur "genius" grant in 1995 for her unbiased and compassionate reporting. Sarah Kerr wrote of her in the *New York Times Book Review* (July 22, 2001, on-line), "Guillermoprieto has set the standard for elegant writing in English on Latin America." In the *New York Times* (February 6, 2004), Richard Eder called Guillermoprieto's "some of the most sophisticated and steely writing about Latin America's revolutionary and postrevolutionary travails available to the American reader."

Alma Guillermoprieto was born in Mexico on May 27, 1949 and grew up in Mexico City. At the age of 12, she committed herself to training and performing as a dancer, so much so that at 16 she moved to New York City, where she came under the tutelage of three luminaries in the dance world—Martha Graham and, later, Merce Cunningham and Twyla Tharp. In *Dancing with Cuba*, Guillermoprieto described the struggles that she and other young dancers faced, as they trained rigorously, held daytime jobs to make ends meet, and strove to attain success before they passed their physical prime. "We were the oldest young people in the world: our time was already running out," she wrote, as quoted by Richard Eder. A sign that "hers had," as Eder put it, came when Cunningham informed her of a job opening for a dance instructor in Cuba. "If I were you, I would take it," Tharp told her, according to Eder. "You're not going to get anywhere hanging around here."

It was thus that Guillermoprieto, in 1970, became a dance teacher at the National Schools of Art, a government-run institution in Havana, Cuba, which had for a decade been under the rule of the Marxist-Leninist dictator Fidel Castro. At that point, Guillermoprieto wrote in *Dancing with Cuba*, as quoted by Sarah Kerr in the *New York Review of Books* (May 27, 2004), "My political attitude toward the world I lived in, if I had one at all, was, I believe, a mixture of sincere elements of antiauthoritarianism, anticlericalism, horror of torture, revulsion at social inequality, defense of animals, terror of any type of violence, and distrust of anything related to big business, especially advertising." In Havana Guillermoprieto encountered a dozen enthusiastic if ill-trained students and a lack of even the most basic teaching tools, such as mirrors and phonographs. She also observed the rigid and repressive nature of the government and its representatives in postrevolutionary Cuba. After six months, disillusioned by conditions in that country and weary of dance, Guillermoprieto returned to New York "in a painful limbo . . . ," as Sarah Kerr put it. "She no longer aspire[d] to incarnate truth in her body, in a single perfect gesture. . . . She [had] started on a journey toward stories and words."

Later in the 1970s Guillermoprieto became a reporter, covering a subject she had already begun to know first-hand: life in Latin American countries. At the start she filed reports from Central America for the Manchester *Guardian*. Guillermoprieto's assignments involved physical hardship and danger. In 1979, on assignment in Managua, Nicaragua, she wrote for the *Guardian* (June 21, 1979, online) a dispatch entitled "An Air Raid on Octopus City." (Managua was called Octopus City because it "lies like an octopus along the Managua Lake.") As she wrote, a struggle was being waged by the Sandinistas against Nicaragua's dictator, Anastasio Somoza; Guillermoprieto was living in a hotel with other foreign journalists whose activities the Somoza regime was trying to curtail; and Managua, which had been largely destroyed in a 1972 earthquake, was being bombed. "The sound is maddening," she wrote in the dispatch. "The slow insistent buzzing never quite fades away but circles and circles again. Then there is a second of silence, a whooshing sound and a deafening noise like a hundred tin roofs being clattered together. To the people of Managua hiding under tables or lying on the floor of their flimsy houses that is what Anastasio Somoza's air raid on his own country feels like." Guillermoprieto later wrote about war-torn El Salvador for the *Washington Post*. In 1989 she became a contributing writer for the *New Yorker*, writing "Letters," which Sarah Kerr called "elegant," from a number of Latin American countries and attracting a readership. Guillermoprieto's most recent piece for the *New Yorker* appeared in the February 2003 issue.

Guillermoprieto published her first book, *Samba*, in 1990. In it, she combined her love for and knowledge of dance with her deep understanding of life in Latin America to produce an account of a year in a favela in Rio de Janeiro, Brazil. In the favelas live the poorest of Rio's citizens, descendants of the slaves who were freed only in 1888, when sugar production was mechanized and it was no longer economically viable to maintain slaves as cheap labor. Guillermoprieto went to live in a favela, where she was able to join its samba "school," one of the groups competing for the best costumes, floats, and dancers in the annual Mardi Gras carnival. In *Samba* she wrote, as quoted in the *Globe Corner Bookstore* (on-line), "There was no possibility of sleep in the narrow room Dona Esmeralda's family had vacated for me. The walls were burning. The fan, churning full speed, could not make the air move. Eventually, I joined my hosts on the cooler rooftop, dozing uneasily to the train-track rattle of the drums below, soon woken by a swollen red sky that announced yet another day in flames. It was carnival weather." In addition to describing the carnival, Guillermoprieto shed light on the social fabric of the favela, explaining the religious practices of candomble (a religion based on Afro-Brazilian beliefs) and giving an account of the violent drug subculture.

Samba was acclaimed by reviewers as being one of the very few accounts written in English of the lives of poor Brazilians. John Ryle noted in the London *Times Literary Supplement* (July 13, 1990) that *Samba* has "a gusto that bespeaks deep involvement with [its] subject" and "a proper sense of balance; between the brute reality of the lives of the poor and the joy of their transcendent moments, between participation and detachment, between the obligations of a guest and the demands of reportage." He concluded that Guillermoprieto "has mastered the trick of being moved and staying still, the literary equivalent of the art of samba." The *New York Newsday* (February 11, 1990) reviewer, David Lida, termed *Samba* "an informative and always entertaining book that is part memoir, part history, part sociology and part journalistic account of Brazil's black culture. . . . The prevailing impression one gets from *Samba* is that of the sympathy and affection that only an insider can feel. . . . Guillermoprieto . . . has given a long-unexplained topic its due." In 1990 Guillermoprieto received a Maria Cabot Moore Prize for journalism, an award established to recognize work that advances inter-American understanding. Four years later her *New Yorker* article on the Shining Path guerrillas in Peru won a National Magazine Award.

Guillermoprieto's second book, *The Heart That Bleeds: Latin America Now* (1994), is a collection of 13 essays culled from the *New Yorker*, originally published between 1989 and 1993. Guillermoprieto drew from observations of the garbage pickers in Mexico, the drug cartels in Colombia, the Shining Path guerrillas, the life of Manuel Noriega of Panama, and the love lives of the presidents of Brazil and Argentina a portrait of a region "where people long to change their lives even as they relish the pain of their 'bleeding, burning, conquered, crunched, roasted, ground, blended, anguished hearts,'" as Marie Arana-Ward wrote for the *Washington Post Book World* (March 6, 1994). "It's enough to make you weep." Other critics, too, responded favorably to *The Heart That Bleeds*. "Whether she's talking about violence and drug traffic in one country, or guerrilla activity in another, . . . her overarching theme is why these countries find the clothes of late-twentieth-century modernity ill-fitting and what that discomfort portends for their particular futures," Brad Hooper wrote of the volume in *Booklist* (February 15, 1994). "Guillermoprieto offers no easy answers, simply appreciating the largeness of the question."

Guillermoprieto was the first recipient of the Samuel Chavkin Prize for Integrity in Latin American Journalism. She also won, in 1995, a

MacArthur Fellowship, popularly known as a "genius grant," in recognition of her "accomplishments in journalism, which demonstrate originality, creativity, and ability to make a contribution to our life" and, in particular, of her being one of the first journalists to report on the massacres in the villages of El Mozote, El Salvador. The amount of her grant was $285,000.

Guillermoprieto's 2000 series of articles in the *New York Review of Books* analyzed conditions in Colombia and the United States' involvement in what Dennis Hans, in Mediachannel.org (June 14, 2000), described as "Colombia's four interrelated wars: civil, dirty, propaganda and drug." Colombia, Guillermoprieto pointed out, is the third-largest recipient of U.S. aid after Israel and Egypt; U.S. government spokespersons have described the aid as being given to fight the war against illegal drugs in that country and, in turn, to protect Americans from the depredations wrought by international sales of such drugs. The Colombian civil war is being fought between government forces and the FARC (Fuerzas Armadas Revolucionarias de Colombia, or Revolutionary Colombian Armed Forces), the country's largest guerrilla group, with the government supported by paramilitary forces. The civil war and drug war intersected when the United States began supplying arms and financing for the Colombian government's fight against drug trafficking. Colombia, however, according to Guillermoprieto, as quoted by James North in the *Nation* (July 2, 2001), "had found what most developing countries lack, a cheap crop that can produce the levels of employment, return on investment, and national growth that only industrial goods normally provide." That crop is coca, the basis for cocaine. When the coca plantations were sprayed with herbicide by the United States and the governments of Peru and Bolivia, growers turned to the almost uncharted territories of Colombia. The FARC guerrillas, seeing an opportunity to make money, began to tax the sale and transport of coca in return for protecting the growers. The other major source of income for the FARC derives from abduction or threats of abduction, which is effective only against the rich—many of whom, in Colombia, are drug lords. The FARC thus began kidnapping relatives of drug lords, who turned for help to paramilitary groups organized by Fidel Castaño (whose father became a victim of the FARC), among others. At the time of Guillermoprieto's report, the Castaño army was said to have 11,200 troops. As Guillermoprieto reported, at one point "a group of men under orders from Fidel Castaño moved like a scythe through the riverside villages near Segovia where Castaño believed his father had been held, pulling babies out of their mothers' arms and shooting them, nailing a child to a plank, impaling a man on a bamboo pole, hacking a woman to pieces with a machete." This level of violence and counterviolence has marred life in Colombia since the 1980s. Although the United States aid package is ostensibly directed at opposing every-

body "who's in the drug business—guerrillas, autodefensas, or drug traffickers," Guillermoprieto wrote that Pentagon statements "raise the strong possibility that this is really an antiguerrilla package disguised as an antidrug package." In other words, there are indications that the money ostensibly intended to fight drugs is actually meant to oppose the guerrillas' Socialist agenda.

Guillermoprieto's next book, *Looking for History: Dispatches from Latin America* (2001), combines essays about three countries, according to Mark L. Grover in *Library Journal* (March 15, 2001): "Cuba, where revolutionary idealism had to face reality; Colombia, where revolutions have always failed; and Mexico, a land of political fantasy." Grover termed the book a collection of "perceptive and insightful observations of Latin American politics and society that help illuminate this important part of the world." The *Publishers Weekly* (March 12, 2001) reviewer praised Guillermoprieto's objectivity, noting that "she excoriates the violence of the left (the murderous guerrilla brigades of Colombia) and of the right (the murderous Colombian paramilitary forces)." Most of all, the reviewer observed, Guillermoprieto "displays an insightful grasp of the absurdities and chaos (one of the root causes of which is the U.S.'s inexhaustible appetite for drugs) that, in her view, permeate Latin American politics." In the opinion of the *Economist* (April 21, 2001) reviewer of *Looking for History*, Guillermoprieto's skill lies in combining wide reading and sympathetic understanding of Latin American perceptions with a knack for the illuminatingly off-beat interview—with, for example, an expert practitioner of electoral fraud in Mexico, and a Colombian woman who was once a guerrilla but has joined the right-wing paramilitary force, who seek to install their own military dictatorship.

Guillermoprieto's *Dancing with Cuba: A Memoir of the Revolution* (2004), which she wrote in Spanish, was translated into English by Esther Allen. In it Guillermoprieto recounted her six months of teaching dance to young people, some of whom had been brought from remote villages in the belief that children could be forced to become artists. Guillermoprieto, who had been impressed by the rhetoric of the Cuban revolution, found her enthusiasm dampened as she witnessed the ineptitude of lower-echelon administrators. In the book, the "implications . . . are reflected upon by the mature Ms. Guillermoprieto while she recounts—with the odd mix of pain and dispassion that makes her book both diffuse and piercing—the confusion of the young Alma torn by personal doubts and longings," Richard Eder observed. He noted that Guillermoprieto had only increased her credibility with her disclaimer that she may not remember every event accurately: "As a journalist she has disentangled too many botched and elided memories not to know that 'this was' must always be less truthful than 'this may have been.'" In *Foreign Affairs* (February 2004), Kenneth Maxwell called

Dancing with Cuba a "marvelous book" in which, as with Guillermoprieto's other works, the "political analysis is sensitive to culture and history and punctuated by telling details that illuminate larger dilemmas." Sarah Kerr, in the *New York Review of Books* article, observed that the "young woman at the end of *Dancing with Cuba* has yet to learn how to make us feel in our bones what happened. . . . But at least she has quit being a frustrated apprentice to masters, imitating dance genius while stuck three rungs down from it on the ladder. . . . She has begun to think about a different approach to truth, one that still seeks beauty but now bears responsibility, and risks despair. Giving up on a certain idea of greatness, she has won her freedom. She will become an artist after all."

Guillermoprieto won the George Polk Award for Foreign Reporting in 2001. Sarah Kerr reported that Guillermoprieto has based herself in Mexico in recent years and that she has taught "the art of literary reporting" to students at the Foundation for New Iberoamerican Journalism in Cartagena, Colombia, established by the novelist Gabriel García Márquez. In an interview with Esther Allen for *Bomb* (Spring 2004), Guillermoprieto said that her "main topic" is "Latin Americans navigating an enormously stressful transition into a not very successful version of modernity."

—S.Y.

Suggested Reading: *Bomb* p74+ Spring 2004; *Boston Globe* p48 Mar. 2, 1990; *Economist* p95 May 14, 1994, p79+ Apr. 21, 2001; *Foreign Affairs* p177 Feb. 2004; *Mediachannel.org* June 14, 2000; *Nation* p31+ July 2, 2001; *New York Newsday* p22 Feb. 11, 1990; *New York Review of Books* p16+ May 27, 2004 with portrait; *New York Times Book Review* (on-line) Mar. 20, 1994, July 22, 2001; *Publishers Weekly* p394 Jan. 17, 1994, p74 Mar. 12, 2001; *San Francisco Chronicle* p8 July 1, 1990

Selected Books: *Samba*, 1990; *The Heart That Bleeds: Latin America Now*, 1994; *Looking for History: Dispatches from Latin America*, 2001; *Dancing with Cuba: A Memoir of the Revolution* (translated by Esther Allen), 2004

Guinier, Lani

(gwih-NEAR)

Apr. 19, 1950– Lawyer; educator; writer

Address: Griswold 503, Harvard Law School, 1563 Massachusetts Ave., Cambridge, MA 02138

"I am a law professor who teaches students the best way is not to go to court; I am a law professor who teaches students that lawyers should not be leaders. It is lawyers and judges who have been asking us to ignore race. We need to think race, not ignore it," Lani Guinier said during a 2002 lecture at the University of California at Los Angeles (UCLA) Center for African American Studies, as reported by Elizabeth C. Dowdy for the *Precinct Reporter* (April 25, 2002). Guinier is probably best known for her ill-fated 1993 nomination for assistant attorney general in the Civil Rights Division of the U.S. Department of Justice; during the ensuing scrutiny of her career, Guinier was harshly criticized by commentators of various political persuasions over the views she expressed in her scholarly writings, and President Bill Clinton withdrew the nomination before Guinier had a chance to defend herself at a confirmation hearing. While that episode represents the peak of her exposure to the public, it does not reflect the breadth of her professional accomplishments. Guinier, who was a very successful lawyer for the Legal Defense and Educational Fund of the National Association for the Advancement of Colored People (NAACP) in the 1980s, is the first African-American woman to re-

Courtesy of the Harvard University Press

ceive tenure at Harvard Law School and has authored several books on the subjects of race, gender, and political power. She believes that the Voting Rights Act of 1965 should not only give members of minority groups a chance to elect minority lawmakers but also oblige legislatures to enact policies that reflect the interests of those groups. In her articles in law journals, she has suggested that areas with records of proven abuses of the Voting

Rights Act employ a system of proportional representation, as well as cumulative voting, in which citizens could vote for more than one candidate for an office or use all of their votes during an election season for a single candidate. "Lani is very good at pushing people's hot buttons," Colin Diver, dean of the University of Pennsylvania Law School, told Dale Russakoff for the *Washington Post* (January 29, 1995). "She has such a wonderfully soft-spoken style in the flesh that you sort of marvel at how she can go out and provoke people the way she does. She's somebody who says, 'Look, I'm seeing what I see and I'm calling it as I see it.'"

Carol Lani Guinier was born on April 19, 1950 in New York City to Ewart and Genii Guinier; she grew up in that city's borough of Queens. Because her father was African-American and her mother Jewish, race was a frequent topic of dinner conversation for the family, which included Lani's three sisters. Guinier has said that she began to dream of being a lawyer when, in 1962, she watched on television as Constance Baker Motley—a lawyer for the NAACP—escorted James Meredith, the first African-American admitted to the University of Mississippi, through a hostile crowd. She told Nancy Waring for the *Harvard Law School Bulletin* (Spring 1999, on-line), "I said to myself, 'I can do that, I can be a woman lawyer in the cause of civil rights.'" She was also inspired to fight for civil rights due to the experiences of her father, who had had to drop out of Harvard Law School because of financial difficulties, despite working several jobs; the school had given another African-American student a scholarship and would not provide funds for a second black student. In addition, because he was black, he was not allowed to live in school housing, and after he left Harvard, the only job he could find was as an elevator operator for the *New York Times*. (In spite of those obstacles, he eventually graduated from New York University Law School. He went on to become a union organizer and, later, the first chair of Afro-American Studies at Harvard University.)

Guinier graduated from high school third in her class of more than 1,000 students. She then went to Cambridge, Massachusetts, to attend Radcliffe College (now a part of Harvard University), where she earned a B.A. degree in 1971. Three years later she received a law degree from Yale University, in New Haven, Connecticut, where her classmates included Bill Clinton; his future wife, Hillary Rodham, currently a U.S. senator; and Clarence Thomas, who would become an associate justice of the U.S. Supreme Court. Guinier was a law clerk for Judge Damon J. Keith of the U.S. Court of Appeals, Sixth Circuit (in Detroit, Michigan) from 1974 to 1976, then served for a year as juvenile court referee in the Wayne County Juvenile Court in Detroit. From 1977 to 1981 she was special assistant to Assistant Attorney General Drew S. Days in the U.S. Department of Justice's Civil Rights Division; her job included ensuring that state and local governments abided by the Voting Rights Act.

Guinier left government employment in 1981 to work as assistant council for the NAACP Legal Defense and Educational Fund, winning all but two of the 32 cases she argued as head of the Voting Rights program. She became known as a coalition builder, finding common ground between opposing factions. After four years in the post, she was eager for a change. "Once I practiced at the Legal Defense Fund, I realized that it might not be entirely appropriate for lawyers to be leading a social justice agenda or a movement," she told Vanessa E. Jones for the *Boston Globe* (February 26, 2002). "The law gives you certain tools, but it also cabins and constrains your analysis and your ability to think boldly about significant social progress." She was an adjunct professor at the New York University School of Law in New York City from 1985 to 1989; in 1988 she began teaching at the University of Pennsylvania Law School, in Philadelphia.

On April 23, 1993 President Clinton nominated Guinier for assistant attorney general in the Civil Rights Division of the U.S. Department of Justice, the top civil rights position in the Justice Department and the post Drew S. Days had held when Guinier worked as his special assistant in the late 1970s. (Guinier and Clinton had maintained a friendship since law school, despite the fact that in the late 1980s, while working for the NAACP, Guinier had successfully sued Clinton in his role as governor of Arkansas for failing to enforce the Voting Rights Act in the southeastern part of the state.) Based on articles she had written for law journals, Guinier was quickly attacked by many conservatives for her ideas on achieving racial equality and called a "quota queen" because of her proposals for increasing minority representation in government. (She has supported affirmative action but staunchly condemned quota systems.) "While advancing novel and intellectually challenging ideas is rewarded within the academic audience that Guinier was addressing, her articles were dynamite in the political arena," as Michael Isikoff observed in the *Washington Post* (June 4, 1993).

In her articles Guinier stated that the ideal of a truly representative American government had not been achieved despite advances in voting rights, and she introduced ideas for experimental solutions to that problem, many of them designed to give minorities greater power than they currently enjoy. Most of her proposals are rooted in the language of the Voting Rights Act, and several were used, before she discussed them, in specific instances. She was criticized for her advocacy of the proportional representation voting system used in most other democracies in the world, in which citizens vote for political parties rather than individual candidates, and the number of seats each party has in the legislature is proportional to the percentage of the vote the party receives. According to that model, party members then elect members for various posts. Guinier's support of cumulative voting also proved to be unpopular. In this system, each voter is given the same number of ballots but can distribute them as he or she chooses, and can vote for one candidate more than once. In this way, minorities can use all their votes to select a single candidate and give that candidate an edge over others, which could increase the likelihood of minorities' being elected in some cases. (Thirty states require or permit corporations to use such a system to elect boards of directors.) Guinier's advocacy of a "minority veto" in certain situations was also assailed as ignoring the will of the majority. (Several commentators pointed out that a filibuster in Congress, in which a minority of representatives can block legislation approved of by the majority by refusing to relinquish the floor, effectively functions as a minority veto.) Lally Weymouth, writing for the *Washington Post* (May 25, 1993), was among the commentators who felt that Guinier's prescriptions for increasing minority participation and influence in the electoral system were extreme and undemocratic: "In recent articles, [Guinier] spells out her goal: to do away with the contemporary American electoral system. 'We ought to question the inherent legitimacy of winner-take-all majority rule,' she writes in the November 1991 *Virginia Law Review*. When Guinier says 'question,' she really means 'abolish.' And in this instance, she intends to abolish one of the cornerstones of American democracy—majority rule. . . . Guinier . . . seeks a society in which a minority can impose its will on the majority." David S. Broder wrote for the *Washington Post* (June 16, 1993), "It is [her] hunger for a qualitative test of representation that Guinier's critics rightly challenged. . . . Her record and the examples she cites . . . clearly indicate her belief that government should keep tinkering with the process until the results are what she would consider 'right.' . . . What pervades Guinier's essay [an op-ed piece in the *Post*] is an assumption that the dynamics of the political process are so stacked against blacks and other minorities that the rules of the game must be constantly rewritten to ensure that they are not victimized."

Guinier had her defenders as well. "I think this is one of the most vivid examples of the dumbing down of American politics I've ever seen," Randall Kennedy, a noted author and professor at Harvard Law School, told David Von Drehle for the *Washington Post* (June 4, 1993). "She asked very tough questions about our democracy . . . and we're supposed to be against somebody for asking questions. . . . She's addressing herself to a situation where black people have been marginalized, and she's asking, 'How can we make marginalized people more a part of the system?' She has been attacked for trying to destroy the system when all she wants to do is make minorities more involved in the system." In an article for the *Washington Post* (June 20, 1993), Elaine R. Jones wrote, "From its inception, the Voting Rights Act has focused on the responsiveness of elected representatives to their African American constituents. The Senate Judiciary Committee listed nine factors that may be considered by the federal courts in determining whether a Voting Rights Act violation has occurred, including 'whether there is a significant lack of responsiveness on the part of elected officials to the particularized needs of the members of the minority group.'" She also pointed out that the Voting Rights Act prohibits practices that result in fewer opportunities for racial minorities than for other citizens to participate in the electoral process and elect representatives of their choice. "The act is explicitly race-conscious and focuses on the results of the political process," Jones wrote. "Although we all aspire to colorblindness, this aspiration does not mean ignoring the racial discrimination that persists."

Guinier was instructed by the White House not to respond to what she thought were misrepresentations of her ideas by the press, and she did not, believing she would have a chance to answer questions at her confirmation hearing. That hearing was canceled, however, as the attacks against her complex proposals led Clinton to withdraw the nomination on June 3. In doing so, Clinton said that when he began to read through Guinier's published articles after the controversy arose, he was disquieted by what he found. "They clearly lend themselves to interpretations that do not represent the views that I expressed on civil rights during my campaign," he said, as quoted by Isikoff. On June 4, 1993, the day after her nomination was withdrawn, Guinier held a news conference clarifying her viewpoints. She recounted her father's negative experience in law school at Harvard, which would not give scholarships to more than one African-American. "He was the victim of a racial quota, a quota of one. I have never been in favor of quotas. I could not be, knowing my father's experience," she said, in a transcript reprinted by the *Washington Post* (June 5, 1993). Later in her statement, she said, "I have always believed in democracy, and nothing I have ever written is inconsistent with that. I have always believed in one man, one vote, and nothing I have ever written is inconsistent with that. . . . I am a democratic idealist who believes that politics need not be forever seen as an 'I win, you lose' dynamic in which some people are permanent, monopoly winners and others are permanent, excluded losers." (Guinier has not spoken to Clinton since her nomination was withdrawn. She was reportedly angered and hurt that he called her views "anti-democratic" in a nationally televised address.)

After her name was pulled from consideration for the civil rights post, some commentators pointed out that Guinier had never had a chance to defend her ideas in detail before Congress or the American people; others accused the media of giving undue weight to the accusations against her. "In the media smear campaign against Lani Guinier . . . her views were not only distorted, but in many cases presented as the exact opposite of her actual beliefs," Rob Richie and Jim Naureckas wrote for *Extra!* (July/August 1993, on-line), a publication of the organization Fairness and Accuracy in Reporting. They pointed out, for example, that Guinier had been said to support the shaping of electoral districts to create black majorities, whereas she had actually criticized such practices, believing that districts created in this way isolate blacks and prevent cross-racial coalitions.

Guinier has written widely on such topics as voting rights, democratic theory, affirmative action, race and gender issues, political representation, educational equity, and political and legal education. Her books include *The Tyranny of the Majority: Fundamental Fairness in Representative Democracy* (1994), *Becoming Gentlemen: Women, Law School, and Institutional Change* (co-authored with Michelle Fine and Jane Balin, 1997), *Lift Every Voice: Turning a Civil Rights Setback into a New Vision of Social Justice* (1998), and *Who's Qualified?* (with Susan Sturm, 2001).

Becoming Gentlemen grew out of an article Guinier published in 1995 in the *University of Pennsylvania Law Review*, which reported that in the school's 1990 and 1991 law program, men were three times as likely as women to be in the top 10 percent of the class by the end of the first year, and twice as likely as women with comparable credentials to be in the top 10 percent at graduation. The report upset many, but Guinier said that that was not her intention. "Some people think I'm trying to incite a riot, but that's not what I'm doing," she told Russakoff. "I'm trying to speak truth to power and to use the fact that I have a voice to speak on behalf of those who may not, or may feel their voice is silenced." A separate study of 6,000 students at 90 law schools conducted by the Law School Admission Council backed Guinier's findings. While the gender gap between men's and women's performances was small, it appeared consistently across law schools and gave male students an edge in landing prestigious jobs after graduation. While interviewing law students in the course of researching *Becoming Gentlemen*, Guinier and her co-authors found that many women felt alienated from their professors and the classroom environment, which typically rewards students who are aggressive and self-promoting. Women were more likely to see classroom exchanges as conversations than as opportunities to distinguish themselves. Guinier has maintained that the sexes can learn from each other. "Women can learn from men how to 'play the game,' and men can learn from women that there is a value to coming to class with the goal of listening and of making a contribution building on what other people are saying," she said in a speech at a Harvard Law School event, as quoted by Waring. "That goal has the potential of making you an excellent lawyer. It was my experience as a trial lawyer, it was my experience as a government lawyer, and certainly is my experience as an academic, that those who listen are in a better position to take criticism and use it to move forward in a constructive fashion." (The title of her book is a reference to Guinier's own years as a law student at Yale, where one professor always welcomed his class with the phrase "Good morning, gentlemen" and told the female students not to feel excluded by this greeting, since in his mind the term "gentlemen" included them as well.)

In 2002 Guinier and Gerald Torres, a law professor at the University of Texas, published *The Miner's Canary: Enlisting Race, Resisting Power, Transforming Democracy*. The book advanced a view of race based on ideas rather than biology. "What Gerald and I are trying to do in this book is to move beyond just racial identity as either skin color or some sense of cultural allegiance, to really talk about race as a political choice that people make," she said in an appearance after the book was published, as quoted by Etelka Lehoczky for the *Chicago Tribune* (February 27, 2002). "It's a form of critique and mobilization. We're trying to move from the idea of race as a biological or cultural identity, to thinking of it as a political project." The title of the book refers to the former practice of taking canaries into coal mines: because the birds are more sensitive to toxic gases than humans are, their reactions served as early warning signs when conditions were unsafe, thus enabling workers to escape danger. Guinier thinks that racial minorities can act in a similar capacity in the United States, and that the particular problems that affect them may be harbingers of things to come among the general population. "The experience of the canary can alert us to toxins in our political atmosphere," she said, as reported by Lehoczky. "Problems that converge around racial minorities affect us all." The book calls on people of color and poor and working-class whites to join together to fight the social injustices they often share.

"Based on a series of lectures, *The Miner's Canary* is a carefully structured and thoroughly researched argument . . . that the best way to transform the American democracy into something closer to its original intent . . . is to enlist race, not ignore it," Michael Brosnan wrote for *Independent School* (Summer 2003). "Along with challenging the shortsightedness of colorblind policies, the authors believe that, through greater attention to race in America, we can reshape the political landscape, develop a more just model for sharing power, and ultimately turn democracy toward the problems it was intended to solve." The book spawned the Web site Miner's Canary, which includes articles by site founders Guinier, Torres, and Susan Sturm on race, gender, and class issues, as well as contributions by other authors and a bulletin board. Miner's Canary is Guinier's second online project; in 1996 she and Sturm launched RaceTalks Initiatives with funding from the Mott and Ford Foundations. RaceTalks is "an ongoing interdisciplinary project that seeks to develop new paradigms for linking racial and gender justice to the project of building more inclusive institutions," according to its Web site.

Guinier is a sought-after speaker and commentator on legal cases. She disagreed with the U.S. Supreme Court's 2000 decision, in Bush v. Gore, to award the presidency to George W. Bush after a disputed election in which many Florida voters claimed that they had been disenfranchised. She took issue with the claim of five of the nine justices that the decision was based on the equal protection clause of the Fourteenth Amendment. "In Bush v. Gore, the majority granted to a single candidate with a privileged pedigree rights that the Court has yet to accord the average voter," Guinier wrote for the *Loyola University Chicago Law Journal* (Fall 2002). "The opinion was clear on this distinction—the protections afforded applied only to George W. Bush in this instance. . . . The Court majority vindicated the rights of a powerful individual. Yet, in other contexts, the same majority has ignored the needs of the people as a whole to exercise their power through equal and meaningful participation in political decisions that shape their lives. The implicit message of the Court's intervention was that democracy is a domain of governing elites, not robust and engaged citizens."

Weighing in on two cases before the Supreme Court dealing with affirmative action policies at the University of Michigan, Guinier told Tavis Smiley for National Public Radio (NPR) on April 2, 2003 that there was no reason the law school had to make a choice between academic excellence and racial diversity. She said that the cases, initiated by white students who were not admitted into the undergraduate program and the law school, respectively, highlighted the ways in which racial divisions still lingered in universities and colleges. (The plaintiffs contended that the school's admittance procedures gave more points to members of racial minorities and were therefore discriminatory.) "The issue of resentment among whites is an important one, and I think that it has been misunderstood," she told Smiley. "That is many whites resent the fact—especially poor working-class whites—that there are not enough slots at these elite public institutions to accommodate everyone who can actually do the work. The problem is that they have focused their resentment on the wrong target. They resent or at least have been encouraged to resent the beneficiaries of affirmative action who are actually not the ones monopolizing these scarce slots. It's the affluent population that is dominating access to the University of Michigan, the University of Texas, the University of California, and so the fight really is between working class and poor whites on the one hand and more affluent whites on the other. But because of the role that race plays in this society, race becomes the convenient scapegoat, even though it's not really the relevant factor." After the Supreme Court upheld the admission policy at the law school but struck down that of the undergraduate college, Guinier told Juan Williams for NPR's *Morning Edition* (June 23, 2003), "Considering the two decisions together . . . the Supreme Court has affirmed the use of race and has acknowledged that race still matters in this country. So in that sense, I think that the decisions are a net plus."

Guinier believes that a student's economic class affects his or her performance on standardized tests and that, therefore, admission to colleges and universities should not be based solely on merit as measured by scores on such tests. "SAT scores] correlate with your parents' socio-economic status," she said in a September 2002 lecture at the University of Wisconsin, as quoted by Michelle Diament for the *Daily Cardinal* (September 18, 2002). "Those who were already privileged are gaining." She cited programs at the University of Texas and Texas A&M University in support of her belief that "underachieving" students can do well in college. Both schools admit all students graduating in the top 10 percent of their high school classes, regardless of test scores. "Those who come in under [the program] have higher freshman GPAs than those with SATs 200 and 300 points higher," she said, as quoted by Diament. She has praised the program for increasing the percentage of minority students as well as white students from low-income brackets, who were previously underrepresented at the institutions. She has said that a student's grade-point average gives a better indication of how he or she will fare in college than SAT scores, and that the LSAT (a prerequisite for law-school admission) is not a reliable predictor of future success in law school, proving only 9 percent better than random guessing at foretelling performance.

Guinier began teaching at Harvard Law School as a visiting lecturer in 1996, and in 1998 she became the first black woman appointed to a tenured professorship at the school. "What I'm really most excited about is joining a faculty in which other members don't shrink from speaking out publicly, particularly on issues affecting women and people of color," she told Ethan Bronner for the *New York Times* (January 24, 1998). "When Harvard speaks, the world listens. I feel the one real domain for leadership in the 21st century is the universities because the political arena has abdicated its responsibilities." She has been Bennett Boskey Professor of Law at the school since 2001.

Guinier is the founder of Commonplace, a national nonprofit organization aiming to transform public discourse and encourage democratic decision-making by fostering connections among citizens, communities, and ideas. Her honors include outstanding service awards from the U.S. Department of Justice in the late 1970s and early 1980s, as well as the Crisis Torch of Courage Award from the NAACP Convention, the Champion of Democracy Award from the Center for Voting and Democracy, the Chauncy Eskridge Distinguished Barrister Award from the Southern Christian Leadership Conference, and the Congressional Black Caucus Chairman's Award, all in 1993. In 1994 the graduating class of the University of Pennsylvania presented her with the Harry Levin Teaching Award, and that year she also received the Rosa Parks Award from the American Association of Affirmative Action. Her other honors include the Champion of Democracy Award from the National Women's Political Caucus (1995), the Margaret Brent Women Lawyers of Achievement Award from the American Bar Association (1995), an Alumnae Recognition Award from Radcliffe (2001), and the Sacks-Freund Teaching Award from Harvard Law School (2002). She holds 10 honorary degrees, including those from the University of Pennsylvania, Smith College, Spelman College, Swarthmore College, Hunter College, and the University of the District of Columbia.

In 1986 Guinier married Nolan A. Bowie, a lawyer and adjunct lecturer in public policy at the John F. Kennedy School of Government at Harvard University. The couple have a teenage son, Nikolas. She has named Martin Luther King Jr., Supreme Court justice Thurgood Marshall, and Judge Constance Baker Motley as her heroes. "Lani is the kind of person you want at your children's birthday party, because when the kids start fighting over a game, she will figure out a new game," Dana Cunningham, who worked with Guinier at the NAACP Legal Defense and Educational Fund, told Von Drehle. "A game nobody loses and everybody loves."

—K.E.D.

Suggested Reading: *Boston Globe* E p1 Feb. 26, 2002, with photos; *Chicago Tribune* Woman News p3 Feb. 27, 2002, with photo; *Washington Post* C p1 June 4, 1993, with photo

Selected Books: *The Tyranny of the Majority: Fundamental Fairness in Representative Democracy*, 1994; *Becoming Gentlemen: Women, Law School, and Institutional Change* (with Michelle Fine and Jane Balin), 1997; *Lift Every Voice: Turning a Civil Rights Setback into a New Vision of Social Justice*, 1998; *Who's Qualified?* (with Susan Sturm), 2001; *The Miner's Canary: Enlisting Race, Resisting Power, Transforming Democracy*, 2002

Courtesy of the office of Chuck Hagel

Hagel, Chuck

Oct. 4, 1946– U.S. senator from Nebraska (Republican)

Address: U.S. Senate, 248 Russell Senate Office Bldg., Washington, DC 20510

In the late 1960s, serving in the U.S. Army during the Vietnam War, Chuck Hagel was twice decorated with the Purple Heart—after suffering a shrapnel wound in his chest, and, on another occasion, when he had received burns on his face that would take a decade to heal. He also saved the life of a fellow soldier, his brother Tom, during his tour of duty. As he explained to Frank Bruni for the *New York Times* (August 9, 1999, on-line), "You can't help but carry that experience around with you every day—every day—for the rest of your life. . . . It's buried in your subconscious. You don't pull it out all the time. But it's there." His experiences in Vietnam have served as the basis for the views that Hagel, now a Republican U.S. senator representing his native Nebraska, has espoused since he was first elected, in 1996. With an appreciation for "the high stakes of international relations," in Bruni's phrase, Hagel is a leading proponent of trade with foreign nations, even those known for human-right abuses, arguing that shutting down trade relations with such countries "further isolates them and isolates us," as he said to Bill Kelly during an interview available on the Nebraska Public Television Web site. "How does that help the people [whose] rights are being violated?" His belief in fostering cooperation among nations has led to his frequent criticism of President George W. Bush and the U.S.-led war in Iraq, which has been conducted, in his view, without the international support crucial for its success. In keeping with his passion for foreign relations, Hagel chairs the Subcommittee on International Trade and Finance and the Subcommittee on International Economic Policy, Export, and Trade Promotion. Prior to his career in the Senate, Hagel enjoyed considerable success as a businessman, cofounding Vanguard Cellular Systems and serving as president of an investment-banking firm; those ventures, his support of international trade, and his opposition to certain measures aimed at combating global warming have earned him a reputation as pro-business—and the ire of many environmentalists. He has taken conservative positions with regard to several other political issues, opposing abortion and greater gun control while favoring the death penalty.

A fourth-generation Nebraskan, Charles Timothy Hagel was born on October 4, 1946 in North Platte, Nebraska, the eldest son of Charles Hagel, a trouble-shooter for lumber companies, and the former Betty Dunn, a secretary. Chuck Hagel spent his childhood moving with his family from one western Nebraska town to another. By the age of nine, he had begun working as a carhop at a drive-in restaurant. On Christmas morning, 1962, he awoke to find that his father had died of a brain aneurysm, leaving the 16-year-old with a great deal of responsibility for his family. Displaying the maturity that his mother often praised in him, Hagel helped with his father's funeral arrangements. While his mother worked both days and nights to support the family, Hagel, then a student at St. Bonaventure High School in Columbus, Nebraska, took odd jobs to pay for his own clothes. He also helped his mother to raise his three younger brothers: Jimmy, who died in a car accident in 1969; Tom; and Mike. In 1964 Hagel won a football scholarship to Wayne State University, in Nebraska. After he lost the scholarship, because of an injury, he transferred to Kearney State College (renamed the University of Nebraska at Kearney in 1991). Also in 1966 he attended the Brown Institute for Radio and Television, in Minneapolis, Minnesota. Hagel took a break from school and went to work for a radio station in Lincoln, Nebraska. Soon afterward he was contacted by the draft board. Given the option of returning to college within six months or serving in the military during the Vietnam War, Hagel entered the U.S. Army in 1967. Hagel, then 21, and his brother Tom, 19, were assigned to the same unit in the Ninth Infantry Division. Both were wounded, earning five Purple Heart medals between them. Hagel was discharged in 1968, with the rank of sergeant.

Following his military service, Hagel resumed his work in radio as a newscaster, reporter, and talk-show host at stations KBON and KLNG, both in Omaha, Nebraska. At the same time, he worked as a bartender and attended the University of Nebraska, in Omaha, from which he earned a B.A. degree in history in 1971. From 1971 to 1977 he was an administrative assistant to U.S. representative John Y. McCollister, a Nebraska Republican. He then went to work in Washington, D.C., as a lobbyist for the Firestone Tire and Rubber Co. Hagel held his first position of political prominence in 1980 and 1981, when, following Ronald Reagan's election as president, he served as vice chair of the inaugural committee. Also in 1981 President Reagan nominated him to serve as deputy administrator of the Veterans Administration, a post that made him the highest-ranking Vietnam War veteran to serve in the Reagan White House; he resigned after one year. From 1982 to 1985 Hagel was the director and

president of Collins, Hagel and Clarke Inc., a management consulting company he co-founded. More notable was his co-founding, in 1984, of the Greensboro, North Carolina–based Vanguard Cellular Systems Inc. Hagel served as director and executive vice president of the publicly traded firm, which became the nation's second-largest independent provider of cell-phone service and made Hagel a multimillionaire. After leaving the company, in 1987, Hagel held a succession of other positions, serving as president and chief executive officer (CEO) of World United Service Organizations from 1987 to 1990, as president and CEO of the Private Sector Council of Washington, D.C., from 1990 to 1992, and as president of McCarthy and Co., an Omaha–based investment-banking firm, from 1992 to 1996. In 2001 Hagel received the Horatio Alger Award, which honors people who have overcome adversity to become self-made business leaders.

In 1996, when Senator Jim Exon decided to retire and a Senate seat became vacant in Nebraska for the first time since 1978, Hagel ran against the popular two-term, Democratic governor, Ben Nelson. Despite their different party affiliations, the candidates shared a number of positions, such as their opposition to abortion and support of school prayer, school vouchers, and a constitutional amendment to balance the budget. In addition, both were wealthy and described as charismatic. Robynn Tysver observed for the Associated Press (November 1, 1996) that with so many similarities between Hagel and Nelson, the race seemed "like a powder-puff derby." "People, I don't think, are desperately afraid of either one winning," Robert Miewald, a political scientist at the University of Nebraska, told Tysver. However, in a state with five Republicans for every four Democrats, Hagel's party affiliation proved to be an advantage. On November 5, 1996 he won the race, his first run for elective office, with 56 percent of the vote. He was reelected in 2002 with 83 percent of the ballots.

During Hagel's first term as a senator, one of his areas of concern was a United Nations treaty on global warming then being negotiated by President Bill Clinton. The 1997 plan, known as the Kyoto Protocol, called for the U.S., by the year 2012, to reduce emissions of greenhouse gases to 7 percent below 1990 levels, while exempting many Third World and developing nations—such as China—from the requirement. According to Patrice Hill in the *Washington Times* (November 24, 1997), although Clinton suggested that he would insist upon "meaningful participation" in the plan by developing countries, only Argentina agreed to the proposal. In the face of so little support, Hagel and Senator Robert C. Byrd, a West Virginia Democrat, authored a resolution opposing the exclusion of developing countries, a measure approved unanimously in the Senate. Hagel explained, as quoted by Hill, "If their objective is to cut greenhouse gas emissions, it is complete lunacy and fallacy to believe they will do it by leaving out" developing nations, which he projected would be "the biggest emitters in 15 or 20 years." As reported by *Washington Dateline* (December 13, 1997), Hagel claimed that the treaty would devastate the U.S. economy, because the regulations would hamper the activities of businesses, and protested, "I don't believe the American people are willing to sacrifice their own economic security, their jobs and their children's futures for a U.N. treaty on global warming." In the next year Hagel attracted attention by running against the incumbent, Mitch McConnell of Kentucky, for the position of chairman of the National Republican Senatorial Committee, which raises campaign money and attempts to put more Republicans in office. Hagel lost to McConnell by a vote of 39–13.

In 1999, in the midst of the investigation into President Clinton's having lied about his sexual relationship with the former White House intern Monica Lewinsky, Hagel voted to convict Clinton on both Articles of Impeachment. Hagel's closed-door statement, as posted on CNN.com (February 12, 1999, on-line), clarified his reasoning: "The Impeachment clause of our Constitution is there to ensure the fitness of an individual to hold high office. President Clinton's conduct has debased his office and violated the soul of justice—truth. He has thereby debased and violated the American people." On other issues, in 1998 he unsuccessfully opposed bringing to a vote a bill designed to increase restrictions on the tobacco industry and raise taxes on tobacco products. He supported the 2001 proposal, which became law, to cut federal income taxes by $1.35 billion through the fiscal year 2011. Never an advocate for environmental issues, in 2002 Hagel voted to postpone the implementation of stricter automobile fuel-efficiency standards and to permit drilling for oil in the Arctic National Wildlife Refuge. (The first motion was adopted, the second rejected.)

In August 1999 Hagel and his brother Tom returned to Vietnam for the first time in 30 years to attend the opening of a new U.S. consulate in Ho Chi Minh City. The trip was, as Chuck Hagel had predicted, an emotional experience for the brothers. The senator told Paul Alexander for the Associated Press (August 16, 1999), "When you look back on [having served in the Vietnam War], you realize you were half-sick and delirious most of the time and how tough it was. The heat and humidity pounded at you. The stress of a possible ambush at any time was there." Despite the upsetting memories that the trip brought to mind for him, Hagel saw the positive aspects of his journey to the country with which the U.S. had made peace: "The bottom line is there is hope for the world when we can piece together a relationship like the one between the United States and Vietnam, that people can deal with each other in a way other than at the point of a gun."

Hagel attracted national notice in 2000, when he publicly sided with, and acted as a spokesman for, another Vietnam War veteran—the Republican presidential hopeful John McCain, a senator from Arizona with whom he has been friends for more than two decades. Hagel was one of only four Republican senators in McCain's camp, as opposed to the 41 who supported then–Texas governor George W. Bush in his presidential bid. McCain ultimately lost the nomination to Bush in the Republican primaries, after which Bush reportedly considered Hagel as his running mate. As a social conservative and opponent of abortion, Hagel had embraced values that were consistent with Bush's; seen as strikes against him, however, were his dependably Republican constituency, which suggested that he might not appeal to a large enough number of voters nationwide; his ties to big business, which might cause some to view him as a pawn of industry; and the likelihood that he would be a target for environmentalists. In the end Bush chose Richard B. "Dick" Cheney as his running mate.

McCain and Hagel's names were linked again the following year, this time as opponents, when the senators introduced separate bills aimed at campaign-finance reform. Hagel advised Margaret Carlson of *Time* magazine (March 26, 2001), "Don't make this into a Shakespearean struggle. . . . This is not an issue between John and me personally. We've always known the day would come when we would go different ways." The legislation sponsored by McCain and Russell Feingold, a Wisconsin Democrat, called for a ban on all "soft money" donations (funds donated to political parties) in federal elections, greater disclosure of donations by independent groups, and a ban on issue ads during the final 60 days of each campaign; by contrast, the bill authored by Hagel and Mary Landrieu, a Democrat from Louisiana, would have capped soft-money donations at $120,000 per donor per two-year election cycle and raised the limit on "hard money" (funds donated to individual candidates) to $6,000 per donor (up from $1,000) for each election cycle. Hagel's proposal was defeated in a Senate vote, 60–40, and a version of McCain's bill passed in 2002.

Hagel next found himself opposing President Bush on the matter of war with Iraq, undertaken in the spring of 2003, ostensibly to rid that country of weapons of mass destruction and as part of a wider war on terrorism. He took issue with the February 2002 speech in which the president used the phrase "axis of evil" in describing Iraq, Iran, and North Korea as countries that harbored and abetted terrorists. As John J. Miller reported in the *National Review Online* (August 12, 2002, on-line), Hagel said in reference to the speech, "Our potential to lead the world at such a critical time in history calls for creativity, boldness, and vision rather than nostalgia and dividing the world into simplistic categories." Although Hagel does not describe himself as a pacifist, he expressed his reluctance about the use of force by the U.S., as quoted in the same article: "America must be about enhancing its relationships in the world, not just its power." Hagel's frequently expressed skepticism earned him television airtime and a good deal of print coverage. He lamented the United States' having waged war in Iraq without the United Nations' support and found fault with the process of rebuilding Iraq. He asserted that the war and the rebuilding process had been poorly planned and had succeeded in increasing the number of terrorist cells. "It's harder to deal with [terrorists] because they're not as contained. Iraq has become a training ground," he complained to James Sterngold for the *San Francisco Chronicle* (July 1, 2004, on-line). Hagel also felt that, in general, the president had been given too much latitude in conducting foreign policy after the September 11, 2001 terrorist attacks on the U.S. and during the subsequent war in Afghanistan. Hagel objected in an Associated Press article (October 22, 2003) to Bush's apparent disregard for the lack of international support for U.S. intervention in Iraq: "The one great mistake that America made in those 58 years [since World War II] . . . was we tried to do something alone. That was Vietnam."

Throughout Hagel's tenure in the Senate, he has held foreign relations and international trade to be of the utmost importance. In 2001 he was one of only two senators who voted against extending the Iran-Libya Sanctions Act of 1996, which banned investment in either Iran or Libya, both of which have supported acts of international terrorism, and imposed sanctions on any foreign company that invested over $40 million in either country. He favors U.S. trade relations with China, which, though improving, have long been strained because of U.S. disapproval of China's Communist government. Hagel also strenuously opposes the 42-year-old trade embargo against Cuba (implemented in 1962 in hopes of weakening the country's dictator, Fidel Castro), to the extent that he was the only lawmaker whom former president Jimmy Carter invited to accompany him to Havana in 2002. (He was not able to go.) Hagel stated during a speech titled "Defining a Foreign Policy for the 21st Century," delivered on October 29, 2003 and available on his Web site, "Trade is a major catalyst for economic growth, at home and abroad. America must remain the global champion of free, fair, and open trade."

Hagel serves on the Senate Committee on Banking, Housing, and Urban Affairs, the Senate Committee on Foreign Relations, the Senate Select Committee on Intelligence, and various subcommittees. He chairs both the Subcommittee on International Trade and Finance and the Subcommittee on International Economic Policy, Export, and Trade Promotion and co-chairs the Congressional-Executive Commission on China.

Hagel, an Episcopalian, is married to the former Lilibet Ziller. The couple have a daughter, Allyn, and a son, Ziller. For fun on Halloween each year, Hagel usually dresses as a different well-known Washington figure.

—K.J.E.

Suggested Reading: Associated Press Nov. 1, 1996, July 11, 1998; hagel.senate.gov; *National Review Online* Aug. 19, 2002, Sep. 25, 2002; *New York Times* (on-line) Aug. 9, 1999; *Time* (on-line) Mar. 26, 2001

Hamm, Paul and Morgan

Gymnasts

Hamm, Paul
Sep. 24, 1982–

Hamm, Morgan
Sep. 24, 1982–

Address: c/o Ohio State University, Men's Gymnastics, Woody Hayes SE Tower, Columbus, OH 43210

In 2000 Paul and Morgan Hamm became the first set of twins ever to be selected for the U.S. men's Olympic gymnastics team. Four years later the 140-pound, five-foot six-inch brothers made history again, by helping the United States win its first Olympic team medal in men's gymnastics since 1984 and only its second since 1932. Paul, a three-time all-around national champion who has generally maintained a slight competitive edge over his brother, skyrocketed to international celebrity when he emerged as the first American male gymnast ever to claim an Olympic gold medal in the individual all-around event. He was also awarded a silver medal for his performance on the high bar. Though Morgan, the older twin by 20 minutes, did not receive any individual medals at either Olympics, he is a two-time national champion in floor exercise. During an interview for the *Today* show (May 31, 2004), Miles Avery, the U.S. men's Olympic team coach, praised the Hamm twins for their contribution to U.S. gymnastics, commenting, "I wish they were triplets."

While the Hamm brothers resemble one another very strongly, from their compact, muscular builds to their red hair and freckles, they have never had a DNA test to determine whether they are identical or fraternal twins, a fact that has caused some consternation among journalists. The brothers and their parents have all expressed the belief that Morgan and Paul are fraternal twins, but none of them seems particularly eager to settle the question. "We don't care at all. It's immaterial," the twins' father, Sandy Hamm, said during an interview for *Slate* (August 19, 2004, on-line). Olympic teammates have described Paul as the more outspoken and

Peter Kramer/Getty Images

Morgan (left) and Paul Hamm

frigerator. At the age of six, following in the footsteps of his older sister, who was then nine, Paul took up gymnastics lessons. Not wanting to be left behind, Morgan enrolled a few months later.

Dedicated to their sport from the outset, Paul and Morgan practiced gymnastics regularly outside the gym, training on makeshift equipment. At first they attempted to perform pommel-horse routines on a boulder, but they scraped their legs so badly that their father decided to build a pommel horse by covering the stump of a maple tree with foam padding and leather taken from the upholstery of a car. He also hung a set of still rings in the attic, put a trampoline in the barn, and fashioned a set of parallel bars from a pair of staircase railings and a steel high bar from an old metal rod. Sandy Hamm saw such promise in his sons that he approached Stacy Maloney, a former world-class gymnast, and asked him to become the twins' personal coach. Maloney, who was then pursuing a fledgling career as a rock musician, was reluctant to take on the responsibility, but Sandy eventually persuaded him to do so. For over a decade afterward, Morgan and Paul received private lessons from Maloney at least once a week, a fact to which their father has attributed their enormous success. "Aside from their talent and whatever, I think that's the singlemost contributing factor," he told Eddie Pells during an interview for the Associated Press (September 14, 2000).

By age 11 Morgan and Paul were working out five days a week at Swiss Turners Gymnastics Academy, in West Allis, Wisconsin. Around that time they became captivated by the gymnasts from the former Soviet Union whom they had seen performing on television, particularly Vitaly Scherbo of Belarus, who captured six gold medals at the 1992 Olympic Games, held in Barcelona, Spain. Determined to introduce his sons to their idol, Sandy Hamm arranged for Scherbo to participate in a clinic and exhibition at Swiss Turners in 1993 and invited the famous gymnast to stay with the family at the farm during his visit. Shortly thereafter, Konstantin Kolesnikov, a former member of the Soviet national team, was hired as an assistant coach at Swiss Turners. He lived with the Hamms for an entire year, contributing significantly to the twins' gymnastics education. During an interview for *USA Today* (August 11, 2004), Sandy Hamm emphasized the role that Scherbo and Kolesnikov played in his sons' development as gymnasts, remarking, "Paul and Morgan are products of the Russians. That's why the international judges like them so much—they have the elegance, poise and grace of the Russian gymnasts."

daring twin, a characterization with which both Morgan and Paul have expressed agreement. "Paul is a gymnastics genius and he's almost always the guinea pig in the gym," Morgan has said, according to the NBC Olympics Web site. Paul, in turn, has described Morgan as more of a thinker. Although the brothers are often pitted against one another in competition, they have a close relationship that has been strengthened rather than strained by their intense commitment to gymnastics. "A lot of people ask us if we have sibling rivalry. But the truth is we don't," Morgan said during the *Today* show interview. "We always are rooting for each other to do well in a competition." Paul echoed Morgan's sentiment during an interview with Brian Heyman for the *Journal News* (August 13, 2004), saying, "We've pushed each other since we were young kids. It's great to have someone with you who's going through the exact same thing that you are."

The sons of Sandy and Cecily Hamm, Paul and Morgan Hamm were born on September 24, 1982 in Ashland, Wisconsin, and grew up on a farm in Waukesha, Wisconsin, 20 miles west of Milwaukee. Their family was one of unusual athletic prowess. As a youth Sandy Hamm had been an All-American diver. The twins' older sister, Betsy, was a successful gymnast who competed for Iowa State University and was the 1998 National Collegiate Athletic Association (NCAA) balance-beam champion. Two of their cousins were also gymnasts, and a maternal great-grandfather once coached Eric Heiden, the five-time Olympic speed-skating gold medalist. Physically active from a young age, Morgan and Paul often amused themselves by jumping from rafter to rafter in the family barn, running around the house and backyard, and scaling the re-

By 1999 the Hamm brothers had developed the strength and skills they needed to compete at the national level. That year Paul finished 11th all-around at the U.S. Championships, earning a spot on the national team. Morgan lagged slightly behind his brother, earning his place on the team the following February and, along with Paul, qualifying for the 2000 Olympic trials. Paul finished second all-around at the trials, guaranteeing himself a spot on the Olympic team. Morgan finished sixth, and although only the top four American gymnasts were supposed to compete in the Games, held that year in Sydney, Australia, U.S. coaches and officials named him to the team on the strength of his vault scores and his performance in floor exercises. The brothers made the Sydney team just as they were about to enter their senior year of high school, becoming its youngest members and two of the youngest Olympic athletes that year. Although the American male gymnasts did not win any medals that year, finishing fifth as a team, Morgan made it all the way to the finals in the floor exercise. (The all-around event measures gymnasts' skills in the full range of gymnastics events offered in a competition. The floor event, which usually lasts about a minute for each competitor, involves exercises that combine maneuvers demonstrating strength and flexibility, and is performed on a mat.) On the twins' 18th birthday, Paul, who finished 14th all-around, watched Morgan perform a respectable floor routine that would earn him the seventh-place spot in the event.

In 2001 both Morgan and Paul suffered injuries. Paul broke his right ankle and had to have it repaired with a screw, a procedure that caused him to miss six weeks of training. Morgan, who had recently become almost as strong a gymnast as his brother, surpassing Paul on floor, vault, and still rings, had an even more serious injury. A damaged nerve casing in his left shoulder sidelined him for five and a half months, causing him to miss the 2001 U.S. National Championships as well as the 2001 World Championships in Ghent, Belgium. At the latter, despite having hit his face against the high bar, badly cutting his lip, Paul had the highest U.S. finish in the men's all-around, coming in seventh. The American men won the silver medal in the team event, giving the best U.S. men's performance at a World Championship in history. Just as Morgan was trying to decide whether to have surgery that might well have ended his athletic career, doctors told him that the damaged nerve was healing on its own.

By the time of the 2002 U.S. Championship competition, Morgan claimed to be "85 percent healthy," according an article on the NBC Olympics Web site. While his left shoulder proved to be permanently weakened, making competition on the parallel bars and still rings difficult, he is once again one of the world's best floor gymnasts, and he rivals Paul on vault and pommel horse. Working through his injury at the Nationals, Morgan placed fourth all-around and first in floor exercise, earning his first U.S. title. Paul placed first all-around, defeating the five-time national champion Blaine Wilson. He also won the pommel-horse and vault titles. Later that year, at the 2002 World Championships, Paul won his first medal on the international stage. He finished fourth in the floor-exercise event but moved up to claim the bronze when the silver medalist, Gervasio Deferr, from Spain, tested positive for marijuana use and was obliged to relinquish his title.

At the 2003 Nationals Paul captured his second consecutive all-around and pommel-horse national titles and also won in the high-bar event. Morgan repeated his achievements at the 2002 Nationals, reclaiming the floor-exercise title and once again placing fourth all-around. Having proven themselves repeatedly in competitions, Morgan and Paul were both selected as members of the 2003 World Championships team. Together they helped the United States win a silver medal in the team event—the best finish for a U.S. men's team in 24 years. In the individual all-around, Paul completed a difficult high-bar routine to defeat China's Yang Wei, whom he had been trailing in the judges' scoring by less than five one-hundredths of a point. He thus became the first American male ever to win the all-around gold medal for gymnastics. He also claimed the gold medal on the floor, tying with Bulgaria's Jordan Jovtchev. Impressed with his achievements, the International Gymnastics Federation (FIG) named Paul its 2003 Gymnast of the Year.

In October 2003, two months after Paul claimed the all-around world title, the Hamm twins decided to end their tutelage under Stacy Maloney, their longtime coach, in order move to Columbus, Ohio, where they could train alongside their 2003 World Championship teammates Raj Bhavsar and Blaine Wilson under the guidance of the Ohio State University coach Miles Avery. Although some members of the gymnastics community questioned the twins' decision to leave Maloney so soon after Paul's major triumph and less than a year before the Olympics, both of the Hamm brothers adapted well to the change and expressed satisfaction with their decision. "We needed a spark, an atmosphere to train in that's very motivating," Paul said, according to the NBC Olympics Web site. "It is motivating to train with Blaine Wilson. He's a very high-energy guy."

At the 2004 Nationals Morgan placed third all-around, as well as third on vault, pommel horse, and high bar, and fourth in the floor event. Paul placed first in the all-around, floor-exercise, and high-bar events. During the 2004 Olympic trials, Paul finished first all-around, guaranteeing himself a spot on the team for the second time in a row. Morgan performed well in several events, including the high bar, in which he landed a double-twisting double layout (a sequence of two twisting flips), to score a 9.675 out of a possible—but rarely achieved—10. Waiving the possibility of catching up to Brett McClure, who came in second, he opted to skip the rings event in the fourth rotation, retaining the third-place position that he had earned at the Nationals. That same night the selection committee named Morgan, along with Jason Gatson, to the team, despite its original plan to name only the top two all-around gymnasts to compete in the 2004 Olympic Games, held in Athens, Greece.

The 2004 U.S. men's Olympic gymnastics team was widely regarded as the country's strongest since 1984. Together with Jason Gatson, Brett McClure, Blaine Wilson, and Guard Young, as well as Raj Bhavsar and Stephen McCain as alternates, the twins helped the United States secure a silver medal in the team event, outstripping Romania and coming in second to Japan. Although Morgan failed to reach the finals in any individual events, Paul took a silver medal on high bar and finished fifth on floor and sixth on pommel horse. Paul's most stunning achievement at the 2004 Olympics, however, was his performance in the all-around, during which he pulled off one of the most spectacular comebacks in Olympic history. During the vault event, he attempted a difficult move, called a Kasamatsu, that requires a total of nearly three full airborne twists and a blind landing (one in which the gymnast must alight without seeing where he or she will end up). Although he had never before missed the vault in competition, he landed short, stumbling off the mat and into the judges' table. His score of 9.137 pushed him all the way down to 12th place, with only two events to go. Then, to the astonishment of his fellow gymnasts, the judges, and spectators all over the world, he performed two of the most impressive routines of his career, to win the all-around gold medal by the closest margin ever. The comeback began with an outstanding routine on the parallel bars, during which Paul flipped from one handstand into another and nailed a perfect dismount. His score, a 9.837, in combination with a series of unexpected failures among his competitors, pushed him all the way up to fourth place in the standings. Despite his debacle on vault, Paul suddenly had a shot at the gold medal. In order to tie with Kim Dae-eun of South Korea, who was in the lead, he needed to pull off a 9.825 on high bar, the next and last event in the all-around. Executing three straight release moves and a perfect dismount, he scored another 9.837, finishing with a total of 57.823 points. With that score he clinched the contest, beating Kim by just 1.2 one-hundredths of a point and becoming the 2004 Olympic gold medalist in men's gymnastics.

Paul owed his victory, in part, to an error made by three judges, who failed to give Yang Tae Young, from South Korea, the correct start value for his parallel-bars routine. Had Yang been scored properly, he would have come in first rather than third, bumping Paul down to the silver-medal spot. South Korean officials lodged a complaint, but failed to do so right away. Although representatives from the FIG acknowledged that Yang should have been awarded more points for his routine and suspended the erring judges, the organization followed its rule, which states that objections must be filed immediately in order for scores to receive official review. Therefore, despite protests from the South Koreans, the Romanians (whose top gymnast, Ioan Suciu, finished fourth, narrowly missing a bronze-medal win), many journalists, and even

the president of the FIG, Bruno Galdi, Paul retained his gold medal.

Paul and Morgan Hamm live in Columbus, Ohio. In August 2004, in recognition of their performance at the 2004 Olympics, town supervisors in Waukesha renamed a municipal park in their honor. The twins have also been named two of *People* magazine's 50 most eligible bachelors of the year. Between August 31 and October 2, 2004, the Hamm twins took part in the Rock & Roll Gymnastics Championships Tour, visiting 12 cities across the United States. They plan to enroll at Ohio State University in the winter quarter of 2005. When asked how he felt about "living in his brother's shadow," as Nancy Armour put it in an article for the Associated Press (August 14, 2004, on-line), Morgan Hamm said, "It doesn't really bother me, for some reason. . . . I'm proud of him for what he's done, and I just try and stay up to his par."

— L.W.

Suggested Reading: Associated Press Sep. 14, 2000; Hamm Twins Web site; *Los Angeles Times* A p1+ Aug. 19, 2004; (Minneapolis) *Star Tribune* Aug. 10, 2004; NBC Olympics Web site; *USA Today* (on-line) Aug. 11, 2004

Harper, Ben

Oct. 28, 1969– Musician; songwriter

Address: c/o Virgin Records, 150 Fifth Ave., New York, NY 10011-4311

"Eclectic" is undoubtedly the word most frequently used to characterize the music of Ben Harper, who regularly incorporates blues, folk, reggae, rock, gospel, and other styles into his repertoire. As Harper jokingly explained to Jeff Zillgitt for the *Tweak* Web site (1996), "You can't put my music in a general music section. It needs a section all by itself. Call it the Ben Rack." While far from mainstream, Harper boasts a large and devoted following and has earned respect and accolades from critics for such albums as *Welcome to the Cruel World*, *Burn to Shine*, and *Diamonds on the Inside*.

Of African-American, Cherokee, and Lithuanian descent, Harper was born on October 28, 1969 and raised in the Inland Empire region of southern California. From his earliest years he was surrounded by music. His mother, Ellen, sang and played guitar; his father, Leonard, was a luthier and percussionist; and his grandparents, Charles and Dorothy Chase, founded the Claremont Folk Music Center, a music and rare-instrument store and museum, in 1958. Although he did not receive formal training, Harper could scarcely avoid cultivating an interest in music. As he told Austin Scaggs for *Rolling Stone* (February 25, 2003, on-line), "Me and my dad sitting around the house listening to Stevie

Giuseppe Cacace/Getty Images

Ben Harper

Wonder's *Talking Book* is my first memory as a kid, period. He must have played it until the grooves wore out." Harper's parents also took him and his two brothers, Joel and Peter, to see a variety of concerts and performers, including the blues legend Taj Mahal, when Harper was six. At the age of seven, Harper was given his first guitar. When he was about nine, he and his father went to see Bob Marley in concert at the Starlight Bowl, in Burbank, California. That experience was one of the defining moments of Harper's young life; by the end of the concert, he knew that he wanted to be a musician.

For a short time, with the emergence of such hip-hop groups as the Sugarhill Gang and Grandmaster Flash, Harper strayed from his folk and blues roots, a period that he referred to as "my own rebellion" in an interview with Will Hodgkinson for the London *Guardian* (February 14, 2003, online). But he soon returned to traditional music, because, as he told Hodgkinson, "there was no getting around what was part of my DNA." During his adolescence Harper worked at his grandparents' music store for five years, restoring guitars. Of the Folk Music Center, Harper told Heather Lalley for the VH1 Web site (August 26, 2000), "It's my musical lifeline. In a very important way, it's where I grew up. It's where I wrote my first song. It's just a very important musical environment for me." During this period, he developed a passion for playing both antique and modern instruments, particularly guitars. He initially favored the acoustic guitar, then gravitated toward the bottleneck slide guitar and the lap-steel guitar. The instrument that later became Harper's signature, however, was the Weissenborn guitar, a type of lap slide guitar made

by Hermann Weissenborn only between 1920 and 1930. Made of Hawaiian Koa wood, with a hollow neck and body, the instrument produces a unique, dynamic sound that sparked Harper's creativity.

Dipping into his blues repertoire, Harper performed his first real show at Patrick Brayer's Starvation Café, in Fontana, California. He told Scaggs, "I remember that after the first gig I said, 'I am never going to do this again.' It was a coffeehouse series. I didn't even know if I could play a full song from the beginning to the end. I was in a time warp from the first song to the last. When I was done, I was like, 'What was that?' But I kept wanting and needing to feel that way I did onstage." Eventually, Harper learned to channel his nervousness and excitement about performing into a stage presence that can be beguiling to his fans. Describing the atmosphere of Harper's shows, Pieter Hofmann wrote for *Drop-D Magazine* (September 6, 1996, on-line), "The 'Church of Ben,' as an acquaintance likes to say, can be a breathtaking exploration event. . . . Harper seems to rise to the occasion and embrace the audience with an almost religious conviction *sans* any snake oil salesman hollowness."

In 1992, with the help of his frequent co-writer and co-producer, J. P. Plunier, Harper recorded a little-known blues album called *Pleasure and Pain*. Chris Darrow also appeared on the album, of which only 1,500 copies were released, all on vinyl. In the fall of 1992, one of Harper's idols, Taj Mahal, invited Harper to join him on tour. The tour, which continued until early 1993, garnered much attention for Harper, gave him the opportunity to open for the blues legend John Lee Hooker, and eventually led to his headlining his own concerts. Furthermore, he attracted the notice of Virgin Records, which released Harper's first major album, *Welcome to the Cruel World*, in 1994. This album boasted a greater mix of styles and genres than did *Pleasure and Pain* and featured Harper's signature Weissenborn. Among its most notable songs were "I'll Rise," a comment on racism that was based on Maya Angelou's poem "And Still I Rise," and "Like a King," which concerned both Martin Luther King Jr. and Rodney King, the black man whose beating by the police—who were later acquitted—set off the Los Angeles race riots of 1992. Although Geoffrey Himes, in the *Washington Post* (March 18, 1994), called the album "underwhelming," "dreary," and "heavy-handed," with "vocals [mumbled] with so little articulation and within such a narrow range that [Harper] makes Bob Dylan sound like Al Green by comparison," most critics viewed it as a promising, if unpolished, first entry.

Harper's second major album, *Fight for your Mind* (1995), demonstrated his evolution as an artist and incorporated the influences of Jimi Hendrix, Bob Marley, and Bob Dylan. The album included such songs as the reggae-influenced, pro-marijuana crowd favorite "Burn One Down," the stinging breakup ballad "Please Me Like You Want to," and the socially conscious "Excuse Me Mr." Harper's follow-up album, *The Will to Live* (1997), was the first in which he played the electric guitar, though he did not abandon his signature Weissenborn. The song "Roses from My Friends" blazed with the sound of a dozen Weissenborns tracked backward, overdubbed by a slide guitar played forward for a unique sound. The album also included the poignant "Widow of a Living Man" and the delta-blues number "Homeless Child."

Burn to Shine (1999) was the first of Harper's albums to receive significant play on mainstream radio stations. Particularly successful was the playful "Steal My Kisses," which, as Harper related to Lalley, was based on the fact that his scratchy beard would make his young son run away when he tried to kiss him. "That song is my son's song as much as mine," Harper said. Other popular songs on the album included "Suzie Blue," a bluesy number backed by the Real Time Jazz Band, the spiritual "Two Hands of a Prayer," and the Motown-inspired "Show Me a Little Shame." While some critics saw *Burn to Shine* as a surrender to pop sensibilities, it generally enjoyed a warm critical reception. "*Burn to Shine* presents proof positive that you can always distill the essence of rock & roll down to a solitary man alone with his guitar and conscience . . . ," Chris Slawecki wrote for the *All Music Guide* Web site. "[The album] is a minor masterpiece that may prove to be not so minor."

In 2001 Harper released *Live from Mars*, a two-CD compilation of Harper's live performances. The first disc featured Harper and his backing band, the Innocent Criminals, while disc two consisted of solo performances. Reviews of *Live from Mars* were mixed: most of Harper's fans were enamored of the album, but critics generally concurred that the two-disc set might have been preferable as a single disc.

Harper's next album, *Diamonds on the Inside* (2003), is considered by many to be his finest to date. Alan Sculley, in the Everett, Washington, *Herald* (August 22, 2003, on-line), called it "every bit as eclectic and uncompromising as his earlier work," and Darryl Sterdan, in the *Winnipeg Sun* (March 7, 2003, on-line), praised the album as a "mind-expanding hour-long beauty" and called "Touch from Your Lust" a song "Lenny Kravitz would give his nipple rings to write." In the *CMJ New Music Report* (March 2003, on-line), Doug Levy wrote, "Capturing rock, reggae, soul, gospel and funk in a chrysalis of unique design, the hybrid sonic creations that Ben Harper unleashes have consistently left him as an artist without contemporary peer."

In 2004 Harper released *There Will Be a Light*, a project with the Blind Boys of Alabama, a seven-man southern gospel group founded in 1939. (The group includes three founding members, all of whom are in their 70s.) Harper had intended to collaborate on two songs, but after an eight-day session, he and the Blind Boys had recorded 11 songs together. The resulting album is a blend of gospel, blues, folk, and rock with a heavy emphasis on religious themes. "Listen to this [disc]," Jeff Miers wrote for the *Buffalo (New York) News* (October 22, 2004); "it can't promise you eternal salvation, but it will give you a temporary dose."

In addition to performing live and recording albums, Harper has contributed to films and television. He collaborated with Taj Mahal on the soundtrack for the children's video *Follow the Drinking Gourd* (1992), a documentary about Harriet Tubman and the Underground Railroad; composed music for the film *For Ever Mozart* (1996); and performed a cover of "Strawberry Fields" for the film *I Am Sam* (2001). Harper appeared in the television special "VH1's 100 Greatest Rock Stars" and in the documentaries *Last Party 2000* (2001), *Standing in the Shadows of Motown* (2002), and *Pearl Jam: Live at the Garden* (2003). *Pleasure & Pain*, a documentary about Harper during his U.S. and European tours, was directed by Danny Clinch and released in 2002. (One of the highlights of the film is a scene in which Harper and his mother play a Bob Dylan tune together.)

The lineup of Harper's band, the Innocent Criminals, has changed over the years. The current members are Leon Lewis Mobley (drums), Oliver Charles (drums), Jason Yates (keyboards), Marc Ford (guitar), and Juan Nelson (bass). Harper has appeared on records or in concert with Beth Orton, Government Mule, Pearl Jam, Radiohead, Marilyn Manson, the Roots, and the Dave Matthews Band, among many others. He also has his own record label, Inland Emperor Records. Harper supports taping at his shows and plans to release live recordings of many of his performances because, as he explained to Neal Weiss for *Rolling Stone* (May

7, 2003, on-line), "It's not about the bread, it's about getting out quality versions . . . . If you're gonna have your mistakes out there, they may as well sound good."

As is evident from his music, Harper is an extremely spiritual man, although he does not subscribe to one particular religion. He has written songs about Jesus, attended Native American sweat lodges, visited places of worship around the world, been tattooed with spiritual Maori designs in New Zealand, and wears a Lion of Judah ring, a symbol of Rastafarianism. He told an interviewer for *Lift Magazine* (January, on-line) that music is "the strongest form of inspiration amongst humanity. . . . Music is the spirit. Anything that can move people to act is the spirit." Harper told Randy Grimmett for the American Society of Composers, Authors and Publishers (ASCAP) Web site, "Music to me is not a joke. I don't want to be overly clever or cute. I take songwriting seriously because I love it so much and respect it so much and I want to bring something new to it. It's a blessing to be able to do this for a living."

Harper, who is intensely private about his family, has a son and a daughter from his first marriage and another son, Ellery Walker (born on August 21, 2001), with his current girlfriend, the actress Laura Dern. He lives in California and in his free time enjoys skateboarding and collecting guitars.

—K.J.E.

Suggested Reading: *Drop-D Magazine* (on-line) Sep. 6, 1996; (London) *Guardian* (on-line) Feb. 14, 2003; *Rolling Stone* (on-line) Feb. 25, 2003; *Washington Post* Weekend p18 Mar. 18, 1994

Selected Recordings: *Pleasure and Pain* (with Chris Darrow), 1992; *Welcome to the Cruel World*, 1994; *Fight for Your Mind*, 1995; *The Will to Live*, 1997; *Burn to Shine*, 1999; *Live from Mars*, 2001; *Diamonds on the Inside*, 2003; *There Will Be a Light* (with the Blind Boys of Alabama), 2004

Selected Films: *Pleasure & Pain*, 2002

Harris, Eva

Aug. 6, 1965– Molecular biologist; social activist; educator

Address: University of California, Berkeley, Division of Infectious Diseases, 239 Earl Warren Hall, Berkeley, CA 94720-7360

The molecular biologist Eva Harris has likened her vision of a just society to the internal workings of a living cell. When one studies a cell, "if you understand how all the molecules work," it becomes clear that "there's this incredible energy conservation," Harris told Harry Kreisler for the Conversations with History interview series. In the same interview, as posted on the Web site of the Institute of International Studies at the University of California (UC)–Berkeley, she said, "There's a feedback loop that actually works. All the elements work together for the greater good of the whole. All of these really beautiful principles are played out, and that's how we are able to exist, all organisms. There are so many kinds of mottoes that we dream about in a just, human world, [which] are actually being played out every instant in our own bodies." Dubbed the "Robin Hood of biotechnology" by Claudia Dreifus in the *New York Times* (September 30, 2003), Harris has devoted herself to a practice that she calls "appropriate technology transfer": bringing cutting-edge technologies in molecular biology to developing countries, not as they were originally patented but in simplified and less expensive forms. Chief among her exports is polymerase-chain-reaction (PCR) technology, which, among other applications, can be used as a

Courtesy of Eva Harris

powerful diagnostic tool. In 1993 she founded and became director of the Applied Molecular Biology/Appropriate Technology Transfer (AMB/ATT) Program, which has brought life-saving technologies and knowledge to such countries as Nicaragua, Cuba, Guatemala, Ecuador, and Bolivia. According to the Web site of the Sustainable Sciences Institute, to date Harris and her co-workers have trained more than 500 scientists in Central and

South America in basic molecular-biology techniques for the diagnosis of infectious diseases.

In 1998 the AMB/ATT program became an arm of the Sustainable Sciences Institute, which Harris set up with money awarded to her as a MacArthur Foundation fellow. She has also brought her humanistic approach to science to UC–Berkeley's School of Public Health, where she became an assistant professor of infectious diseases in 1998. "I see science as a social contract," Harris told Dreifus. "I do it to understand the biological functioning of cells and to understand disease to eradicate it. To me, science is about making a better world." At the conclusion of her interview with Kreisler, Harris said, "You have to be good [at what you do], but if you believe in something, follow your passion. I think that that's the most important thing. Don't let go of values, because that's what's going to matter. You're the one who's going to live with it for the rest of your life. If you can hold on to good values and make a positive impact on the world, then everybody else is going to benefit."

An only child, Eva Harris was born on August 6, 1965 in New York City. Her father, Zellig Sabbettai Harris, who immigrated with his family to the U.S. from the Ukraine at four years of age, was an internationally renowned linguist who founded the first linguistics department in the U.S., at the University of Pennsylvania, in Philadelphia, his alma mater; students of his whom he profoundly influenced include the linguist and political dissenter Noam Chomsky. Originally a specialist in Semitic languages, Zellig Harris wrote more than a dozen books related to linguistics. Speaking of her father, Eva Harris told Harry Kreisler, "I spent a lot of time conversing with him about many, many things." Harris's mother, Naomi Sager, is a professor of computer science and linguistics at New York University.

Eva Harris spent her childhood shuttling between New York City and Paris, where her parents had many interesting friends. "One of the women who helped raise me fought in the Russian Revolution," Harris recalled to Kreisler. She noted that among her parents' other friends were people who had been members of the French Resistance, which fought Nazi Germany's occupation of France during World War II, and the German syndicalist movement, which advocated the union of all workers and governance of the nation by such a union. "I was very struck by their hearts of gold," Harris recalled. "People had given everything and risked their lives for other people. That made a big impression." In addition to being influenced politically by the liberal views of her parents and their friends, Harris, whose family did not own a television, began forming her political opinions at an early age through extensive reading. "When I was ten or so, I read all the classics—Orwell, and *All Quiet on the Western Front*. I always felt that even though I had a lot of politics around my life, I came to my own conclusions that, essentially, war is bad, and money's bad; you know, things like that.

That was from my perspective as a six-year-old. I feel like I came to that on my own, even though, of course, it was within this context of [my parents and their friends]." She also told Kreisler, "My parents believed in me and let me do everything I wanted. I was an overachiever on my own, so they were always hoping I would fail at something once in a while." As a child she also spent much time engaged in crafts projects, constructing "tons of things," as she put it.

Harris attended Harvard University, in Cambridge, Massachusetts, where, struggling to choose a major, she enrolled in many classes in the humanities—political economy, French literature, and art history, for example—before committing herself to biochemistry. During a summer project she met Jeff Schatz, a scientist from the University of Basil, whose efforts to bring advanced laboratory technologies to Guatemala impressed her. Harris received a B.S. degree from Harvard in 1987. She had been accepted to UC–Berkeley's graduate program in biology and had secured a National Science Foundation predoctoral fellowship when, in the same year, she decided to postpone graduate studies and instead travel to Nicaragua to teach biochemistry through a program that normally placed computer scientists. "They didn't really have any place to put me," Harris told Marcia Barinaga for *Science* (November 25, 1994). "They literally just dropped me off at the Ministry of Health in Managua. There were roosters running everywhere. I barely spoke Spanish; nothing had prepared me for this. It was the most frightening experience of my life." Soon, however, Harris became fluent in Spanish (she had learned a variant of the language during an earlier visit to Spain). She taught a course in technical English and a seminar on molecular biology and helped to perfect a test for detecting endotoxins in blood plasma at a plasma factory. She also began working on a method for identifying the various strains of the Leishmania parasite, a protozoan that grows in the guts of sandflies and infects humans through sandfly bites. Depending on the particular strain (at least 21 species are known to affect humans), the resulting disease, leishmaniasis, has various manifestations, ranging from relatively benign skin lesions to acute systemic infections that may prove fatal, particularly in people whose health is already compromised because of malnutrition or other conditions. Each type of leishmaniasis must be treated differently.

After three months in Nicaragua, Harris returned to the U.S. to attend graduate school at UC–Berkeley. Working with Jeremy Thorner, she conducted research in yeast genetics; on her own, she continued to investigate Leishmania. The following summer Harris returned to Nicaragua and applied her newest research to the Leishmania problem. Once again, she was unable to find a reliable method for identifying different strains of the parasite. It was in connection to Leishmania that Harris got the idea for using PCR technology. Back in

Berkeley, at her request, Christian Orrego, the director of the DNA lab at Berkeley's Museum of Comparative Zoology, taught Harris the PCR technique. With Orrego's help, Harris put together a five-day lab course in PCR and, after soliciting funding, began teaching it in Nicaragua in the summer of 1991. Working in very primitive labs, Harris succeeded both in reliably executing the PCR technique and in applying it to the identification of Leishmania strains. "I was on a high for months," Harris told Barinaga. "To see that this stuff was actually applicable and appropriate just blew my mind."

PCR involves isolating a string of DNA and placing it in a solution of DNA building blocks and other materials, where it can reproduce billions of times. In this way the DNA sequence is "amplified," and scientists can easily identify it, sequence it (that is, determine the exact order of the building blocks that make up that string), or clone it. Because the DNA of every species—including viruses, bacteria, and protozoans—is peculiar to that species, PCR is a relatively simple and accurate way of diagnosing illnesses caused by invasive organisms. According to thinkcycle.org, "PCR can capture epidemiological information on strains and subtypes while simultaneously diagnosing a patient. . . . The speed of PCR and its utility in capturing finer data on the infectious agents make it an incredibly useful technique." After she returned to Berkeley, Harris continued work on her Ph.D. thesis while investigating ways of using PCR to identify other disease organisms, such as the tuberculosis bacterium, several strains of diarrhea-causing E. coli, and a parasite implicated in malaria. After she completed her doctorate, in 1993, Harris was accepted as a postdoctoral fellow to work under Stanley Falkow, a professor of microbiology, immunology, geographic medicine, and infectious diseases at Stanford University. However, she decided at the last minute not to enter the program. "I thought, 'Well, I can't just go on with my career and ignore all this excitement that we've engendered, so I'll take a year and make good on my promises, and then go back to my scientific life,'" Harris told Kreisler. Harris returned to Ecuador, where, with the help of her Latin American colleagues, she created the AMB/ATT program through the University of California at San Francisco. For several years the program kept afloat by means of an ill-funded core of volunteers. Harris's perennial worries about how she would scrape together enough money to continue its operations ended in 1997, when whe won the $210,000 MacArthur grant. "It's like a fairy godmother appearing out of nowhere and saying, 'You can keep doing this work,'" Harris told Diana Walsh for the *San Francisco Examiner* (June 17, 1997). "It makes everything possible. I can continue to do this while I build up the research as well." With the grant money, Harris formed the Sustainable Sciences Institute of San Francisco to carry on her work in technology transfer.

From 1997 to 1998 Harris continued her work in Latin America while also serving as an assistant adjunct professor at UC–San Francisco. In 1998, in collaboration with Nazreen Kadir, she published *A Low-Cost Approach to PCR: Appropriate Transfer of Biomolecular Techniques*, in which she outlined her simple and inexpensive methods for applying PCR technology to the field of public health. PCR and its associated supplies are often sold to laboratories in kits that make the process easier and more convenient but are also expensive and do not require an understanding of PCR's underlying concepts. Harris's knowledge-based technology transfer, as outlined in the book, involves teaching the fundamental principles of PCR so that practitioners need not rely on expensive kits to use the technology. For example, Harris explained to Dreifus that a silica substance often provided in kits to purify DNA samples normally sells for about $100 for a few milliliters: "The substance is essentially ceramic dust. So what we've done is buy a 20-pound bag of ceramic dust for $5 at the hobby store. And you wash the stuff in nitric acid and sterilize it, and then you have thousands of tubes of that substance. We're not violating anything because the commercial manufacturers have their way of doing this, and we have ours." (Harris added that adopting patented technologies is not a violation of intellectual property rights if you do not charge a fee for your services; in the U.S., however, many laboratory supplies are protected by patents, and it is illegal to use homemade versions of those products in hospitals.) Harris's handbook on transferring PCR technology is considered a useful and clear guide for practitioners in the public-health field. "What distinguishes this book from other manuals is its simple and practical approach to introducing the reader to the general principles and the theoretical basis of the technique, the practical details of the specific protocols, and the various ways to adapt PCR to a low-cost method," Olga Rickards wrote for *Human Biology* (August 2000). "Harris's worthy idea was not only to compile an essential work of reference for use as textbook and practical benchtop manual, but also to provide a model for the transfer of other technologies to laboratories working in vastly different situations."

Harris joined the faculty of UC–Berkeley in 1998. She is a member of the university's Graduate Group in Infectious Diseases and Immunity. She also serves as a co-director of the Fogarty International Emerging Infectious Diseases Training Program, an activity of the National Institutes of Health. In the 2003–04 academic year, she taught graduate-level courses in infectious-disease research in developing countries and in molecular parasitology. She has published articles in such professional publications as the *Journal of Virology*, the *Journal of Parasitology*, the *American Journal of Tropical Medicine and Hygiene*, the *Journal of Clinical Microbiology*, *Clinical and Diagnostic Laboratory Immology*, and *Emerging Infectious Diseases*, a journal of the Center for Disease Control and Prevention, an arm of the U.S. Department of Health and Human Services. Through the Sustainable Sciences Institute, she has continued to bring PCR and other technologies to countries throughout Latin America. Currently, she is conducting research on, among other subjects, the dengue virus, which is transmitted by mosquitoes and infects roughly 100 million people annually. Harris herself contracted dengue fever in 1995 in Nicaragua; according to the Web site of UC–Berkeley's Health Sciences Initiative, she diagnosed the disease in its early stages. (Unlike Harris, the vast majority of victims do not have access to treatment.) She decided to study the virus because of its pervasiveness. She recalled to Kreisler, "Everyone said, 'Eva, work on this. You always said you were going to follow the urgency.' I said, 'I'm not a virologist'; then I said, 'Well, I guess, I'm going to become one.'" The "basic science" aspect of her work involves, as she explained to Kreisler, "testing certain anti-viral compounds to see if they are effective against dengue virus. If we understand how the virus replicates, we can identify pieces of the virus which are important to knock out, to create an attenuated strain for a vaccine."

Eva Harris is a member of the American Association for the Advancement of Science (AAAS) and the American Society for Microbiology (ASM). In 2001 she won an investigator's award from the Pew Scholars Program in the Biomedical Sciences. The next year she won the Prytanean Faculty Award, which honors an outstanding UC–Berkeley female assistant professor. Also that year the Ellison Medical Foundation pledged up to $750,000 to support Harris's attempts to develop a so-called mouse model for study of the dengue virus. In 2003 she and her UC–Berkeley colleague P. Robert Beatty won a Doris Duke Innovation in Clinical Research Award to support their development of an "ImmunoSensor" for HIV infections.

Harris has one son, Paolo Harris Paz, who was four years old in late 2004.

—P.G.H.

Suggested Reading: Berkeley Institute of International Studies Web site; *Human Biology* p722+ Aug. 2000; *New York Times* F p3 Sep. 30, 2003; *San Francisco Examiner* A p4 June 17, 1997; *Science* p1317 Nov. 25, 1994

Selected Books: *A Low-Cost Approach to PCR: Appropriate Transfer of Biomolecular Techniques* (with Nazreen Kadir), 1998

Heymann, David L.

1946– Epidemiologist; World Health Organization program director

Address: World Health Organization, Avenue Appia 20, 1211 Geneva 27, Switzerland

"David L. Heymann has had an extraordinary career," the physician Lawrence K. Altman wrote for the *New York Times* (August 12, 2003). "The epidemiologist has helped discover two new diseases (Ebola and Legionnaire's), rid the world of an old one (smallpox) and stop [the] spread of the newest"—SARS, which stands for "severe acute respiratory syndrome." Unlike many other epidemiologists, who specialize in one or two diseases, Heymann is an expert in many; indeed, he is a world leader in epidemiology, the branch of medical science that deals with the incidence, distribution, and control of diseases in populations. In July 1998 he was appointed the executive director of the communicable diseases program of the World Health Organization (WHO), a specialized agency of the United Nations (U.N.) that is headquartered in Geneva, Switzerland. Five years later WHO's new director general, Jong Wook Lee, named him the organization's representative for polio eradication, in which position he directs activities aimed at wiping out that disease. Referring to the importance of Heymann's work, Jong Wook Lee, who has

AFP/Getty Images

worked in various WHO positions since 1983, told Altman, "No job today, including the director general's job in WHO, is more important than leading this polio campaign." Lee stated that Heymann is not only the "most important communicable disease control expert in WHO, but truly in the world."

Earlier, as an employee of the U.S. Centers for Disease Control and Prevention (CDC) beginning in the late 1970s, Heymann spent a dozen years working as an epidemiologist in sub-Saharan Africa. During that time he investigated the first outbreak of Ebola hemorrhagic fever (so-called because its symptoms include internal and external bleeding); among the deadliest viral diseases known to humankind, Ebola causes death in 50 to 90 percent of cases. In 2003 Heymann was instrumental in the international effort to stop the SARS epidemic, which affected thousands of people and killed hundreds. In arresting the spread of the disease, Heymann and his WHO team combined traditional methods of epidemiology with use of the World Wide Web. Referring to such innovations, the doctor told Altman, "It was a new way of thinking about monitoring emerging diseases, and we realized the fruits of that vision in stopping SARS."

"The tools used to control one disease often can be used to control another," Heymann told Altman. "What makes epidemiology such an important and useful science is that it can be applied to any disease anywhere." Heymann has been engaged in work that has saved the lives of countless people and may save or improve the lives of millions—and, in years to come, even billions more. That work includes the surveillance and control of tropical, emerging, and communicable diseases, among them measles; German measles; malaria (which many estimate has killed more people than all wars combined); tuberculosis (which kills about two million people every year); HIV/AIDS (from which about three million people die every year); leprosy; polio; and onchocerciasis, or river blindness, which is caused by a parasitic worm spread by the black fly and affects at least 18 million people in Africa and Central and South America. Since it was established, in 1988, WHO's polio-eradication program has made great strides toward eliminating the disease, which affects the body's central nervous system and can lead to paralysis and death. While polio has become extremely rare in the U.S., it remains common in India, Nigeria, and Pakistan and, to a lesser extent, Egypt, Afghanistan, Niger, and Somalia. Infectious diseases such as polio, malaria, tuberculosis, and HIV/AIDS are the world's leading killers of children and young adults, accounting for more than 13 million deaths a year, according to the U.N. Integrated Regional Networks Information Web site. "This suffering—and its social consequences—should not be happening," Heymann has said, as quoted on the U.N. Web site. "We are the first generation ever to have the means of protecting the world from the most deadly and common infectious diseases. Today, we possess the knowledge and the drugs, vaccines and commodities to prevent or cure tuberculosis, malaria, HIV, diarrhoeal diseases, pneumonia, and measles practically anywhere on our planet."

David L. Heymann was born in Pennsylvania in 1946. He earned a B.A. degree in science from Pennsylvania State University in 1966 and a medical degree from Wake Forest University School of Medicine (then the Bowman Gray School of Medicine of Wake Forest University) in 1970. Heymann's interest in public health began when he worked for Project Hope in Tunisia, in 1969, during his years at Wake Forest. Project Hope ("Hope" stands for "health opportunities for people everywhere") is a medical philanthropic organization founded by William B. Walsh in Washington, D.C., in 1958. Since its establishment more than 5,000 health-care volunteers have worked with the project's staff to conduct programs in more than 70 countries, bringing medical aid to millions of people. On the mission to the port city Tunis, the capital of Tunisia, Heymann worked aboard the S.S. Hope, the organization's 15,000-ton ship, which contains three operating rooms, a pharmacy, an isolation ward, a radiology department, and closed-circuit television, which enabled local doctors and students who visited the docked ship to observe operations. After he returned from Tunisia, Heymann began an internship at Washington Hospital Center. In the early 1970s, when young Americans were being drafted to serve in the Vietnam War, he fulfilled part of his military duty as a doctor on a Coast Guard icebreaker in the Antarctic.

In considering his options for a career in medicine, Heymann concluded that he could do greater good as a public-health specialist than as a practicing physician working for a hospital or in private practice. With that in mind, he enrolled at the London School of Hygiene and Tropical Medicine, in England, where he earned a diploma in tropical medicine and hygiene in 1974. Heymann spent the next two years in India as a medical officer with WHO's Smallpox Eradication Programme, a highly successful venture that later, in 1980, achieved its goal of ridding the world of smallpox. (Smallpox, which left its victims scarred and sometimes blinded and killed more than 10 percent of them, has afflicted humans for thousands of years. An estimated two million people died from smallpox annually in the decades preceding its eradication—which marked the first and only time that a naturally occurring disease has been completely wiped out.) Continuing his far-flung travels as a doctor, Heymann then ministered to workers constructing the oil pipeline on the North Slope of Alaska. After that he joined the Epidemic Intelligence Service, the epidemiology program office of the U.S. Centers for Disease Control and Prevention, in Atlanta, Georgia. Later, through the CDC, he completed his epidemiology training.

In his first assignment with the CDC, in 1976, Heymann investigated what was then a mysterious respiratory illness that had afflicted members of the American Legion who had attended a state convention in Philadelphia, Pennsylvania. Heymann and his fellow investigators were the first to study the new illness, which became known as Legionnaire's disease. (It is caused by the Legionella bacterium, which can spread through air-conditioning systems.) Heymann then spent 13 years, from 1976 to 1989, on assignment with the CDC in sub-Saharan Africa, specifically in Cameroon, the Ivory Coast, Malawi, and Zaire (which is now the Democratic Republic of the Congo and borders the far smaller Republic of the Congo). At the beginning of that stint, Heymann traveled to Yambuku, in Zaire, to participate in the investigation of the outbreak of a hemorrhagic fever. The fever was later traced to a previously unknown virus dubbed Ebola. Heymann collected blood samples from local residents so as to conduct laboratory tests to determine how many people had been infected with the disease. He later helped to investigate the second Ebola outbreak, in Tandala, also in Zaire, in 1977; nearly two decades later, in 1995, Heymann faced the disease again, when he directed the concerted international response to the Ebola outbreak in Kikwit, in the same nation. Due to the unknown nature of the Ebola virus, news of its appearance initially created considerable fear and concern. The work of Heymann and his colleagues indicated that Ebola occurred sporadically but was not likely to become epidemic. (The largest number of people known to have died in a single outbreak—425—was recorded in Uganda in 2000–01.)

From 1977 to 1980 Heymann also investigated a number of diseases in Cameroon, where Pygmies had been infected with a disease related to that caused by the Ebola virus. He also conducted surveys in Cameroon on the paralysis caused by the polio virus, in order to determine the effectiveness of polio immunization programs. In Malawi Heymann studied cases of drug-resistant malaria, a disease caused by a parasite that is spread among humans through the bites of infected mosquitoes. His team's investigative method, inspired by one used by car manufacturers who check production quality by testing samples from various lots or batches, was very effective in helping to guide subsequent treatment programs. Whereas most previous tests of the drug-resistant strains of malaria had been conducted in laboratories, Heymann had his team perform clinical tests in the field, on patients infected with the disease. For example, he and his fellow epidemiologists would test a select group of several dozen malaria patients, collecting their blood to determine the disease's resistance to drugs that the patients had been given earlier. If all of the selected patients had responded to the antimalarial drugs, Heymann's team concluded that the strain's level of resistance was less than one percent. If one or more of the patients had not responded to the drugs, the team would select and conduct blood tests on a new group of malaria patients to try to determine the level of resistance. WHO still uses this method of malaria testing.

In about 1989 Heymann joined WHO as chief of research activities for the U.N.'s Global Programme on AIDS, which also encompasses other sexually transmitted diseases. He worked in Geneva, the site of WHO's headquarters. Internationally, an estimated 42 million people are suffering from HIV/AIDS; it is currently the world's leading infectious killer, having surpassed tuberculosis in the late 1990s. In the early to mid-1990s Heymann was named director of WHO's Programme on Emerging and Other Communicable Diseases, before becoming executive director of the communicable diseases program in 1998. Since early 2003 Heymann has directed WHO's program to eliminate polio, which is caused by a virus that enters a victim's mouth, attacks the central nervous system, and can cause paralysis and even death.

Polio has certain characteristics that make it one of the few infectious diseases that are potentially eradicable: namely, it affects humans, not animals; it produces no asymptomatic carriers—those who show no outward signs of having the disease and so could silently spread the microbes that cause it; and it is preventable by vaccines (developed by Jonas Salk in 1952 and Albert Sabin in 1963). However, polio is difficult to diagnose, because many diseases besides polio can cause paralysis. In addition, only half of one percent of polio victims develop paralysis; most exhibit only diarrhea and other gastrointestinal symptoms, which can be caused by any number of ailments. Since its founding, in 1988, WHO's polio program, which to date has cost over $5 billion, has reduced the incidence of paralysis caused by the disease by over 90 percent. According to the WHO Web site, in 1988 more than 350,000 children in 125 countries were newly afflicted with paralytic polio; in 2003 fewer than 2,000 cases in seven countries were recorded. Though WHO has gone a long way toward achieving its goal, a single case of polio can lead to its spreading to thousands of other individuals. Heymann told Lawrence Altman for the *New York Times* (July 27, 2003) that since 1998 polio had been exported 12 times into areas that had previously been polio-free. WHO initially set 2000 as the year by which it hoped to have completely eliminated the scourge of polio, but civil strife in many countries where the disease is prevalent, as well as other obstacles, both logistical and cultural, have forced the organization to push that date back to 2005. Heymann has stressed that time is of the essence. As he told Altman, "We know that if we don't accomplish [complete eradication] within the next two years, it may never be accomplished."

On March 15, 2003, before he assumed his current post, as WHO's representative for polio eradication, Heymann made the first global-health-emergency warning in the 55-year history of the U.N. agency: he announced the appearance of a new, fatal kind of pneumonia, known as SARS, which is caused by an airborne virus—one that spreads through an infected person's coughing or sneezing, for example, and infects an individual's lungs. The virus had killed people in East Asia and had been carried unwittingly by infected individuals to dozens of countries, among them Canada and the United States. As the epidemic neared its end, Rob Stein reported in the *Washington Post* (June 7, 2003) that more than 8,000 SARS cases had been recorded in 30 countries and that more than 700 victims had died. The failure of the government of mainland China, where the outbreak of the disease apparently began, to acknowledge publicly the reality of the SARS epidemic for several months after its appearance prevented WHO or any other organization from taking steps immediately to prevent the further spread of the disease.

After alerting the world to the SARS crisis, Heymann and other WHO workers scrambled to coordinate, with local health providers in areas with infected residents, the critical process of identifying and isolating individuals infected with the disease. By April 2003, through the work of its network of 12 international laboratories, WHO had determined with 99 percent certainty the cause of SARS, as Heymann told Lawrence Altman for the *New York Times* (April 16, 2003). By conducting experiments with monkeys—which was necessary, as Altman explained, because "the lack of an effective treatment for SARS and the relatively high death rate make it unethical to conduct such experiments on humans"—WHO scientists had identified as the cause of the disease a previously unknown coronavirus that infected the lungs. That discovery made possible the first step in halting the spread of the virus: namely, the development of a reliable diagnostic test to determine who was infected. By the summer of 2003, Heymann and his colleagues, along with the many health-care workers around the world who had treated those infected, had effectively contained SARS.

In late 2003 and early 2004, an upsurge of polio cases in western and central Africa, beginning in Nigeria, prompted WHO to intensify its efforts to immunize children against the disease. The new, $4.6 billion initiative, which included sending WHO representatives door-to-door to immunize newborns and infants, was at first met with apprehension from some Nigerian political and religious leaders, who believed that the vaccine would render girls infertile. Although the Nigerian government eventually agreed to allow WHO to proceed with its anti-polio campaign, by June 2004 the polio virus had spread from Nigeria to 10 other African countries, including three that had previously become entirely polio-free. In the *International Herald Tribune* (October 28, 2004), in an article co-authored by Julie Louise Gerberding (the head of the CDC), Carol Bellamy (the executive director of UNICEF), and Glenn Estess Sr. (president of Rotary International), Heymann expressed both optimism and apprehension about the future of polio-eradication efforts: "We are within sight of a milestone in human history. But these final steps are the toughest and require the greatest commitment—at the country level, to immunize the poorest and hardest to reach children, and from the global community, to fast-track funding to this initiative and safeguard the enormous investments that have been made over the past 15 years."

When asked what he has learned about epidemics through all his experiences, Heymann told Madeline Drexler for the journal *Biosecurity and Bioterrorism: Biodefense Strategy, Practice, and Science* (2003), "What's become clear to me is that there's always a reason why an infectious disease amplifies or spreads. These organisms, these infectious diseases, can find weak points wherever they are and amplify. AIDS found sexual behavior and amplified after it got into urban areas. Ebola finds improper hospital practices and spreads to health workers and then to their families. SARS found health practices that permitted it to spread into hospitals and then out into the community through health workers. . . . Microbes are always outsmarting humans."

WHO's limited ability to pressure countries to cooperate with its investigations and to warn nations of possible epidemics (by issuing travel alerts, for example, as it had regarding SARS—an unprecedented action) had compounded the difficulties of combating the spread of SARS. During the SARS crisis Heymann and his WHO colleagues fought for and won from the World Health Assembly, WHO's governing body, the power to investigate health crises even in countries whose governments have not admitted the existence of such problems. In future crises WHO will thus be able to exert more pressure on individual nations when the health of people all over the world may be at stake. In addition, WHO's new powers have led to the establishment of the first global emergency communications hotline, to enable WHO to coordinate its international efforts more effectively and receive health information as fast as possible, which is vital when dealing with infectious diseases.

Heymann and his colleagues have staunchly advocated various changes to the International Health Regulations, the only treaty-based international law governing what a country or agency can or cannot do to protect populations from disease while at the same time respecting the national sovereignty of foreign nations and their determination to protect their economic interests. The process of revising the International Health Regulations has been ongoing since the 1990s. The SARS outbreak and WHO's role in combating it have brought the issues at stake into greater focus. "I'm optimistic that a solution can be found to everything," Heymann told Madeline Drexler. "If you lose your optimism, you can't do your job. Someone once told me that when you start in public health, there's a whole series of candles that are lit. Those who succeed in public health continue to let at least some of those candles remain lit."

Heymann is married and has three children.

—C.F.T.

Suggested Reading: *Biosecurity and Bioterrorism: Biodefense Strategy, Practice, and Science* p233+ Vol. 1 No. 4, 2003; Centers for Disease Control and Prevention Web site; World Health

Organization Web site; *New York Times* A p6 Apr. 16, 2003, with photo, July 29, 2003; *New York Times* (on-line) F p7 Aug. 12, 2003, with photos; *Washington Post* A p10 May 18, 2003, A p27 June 15, 2003

Hill, Andrew

June 30, 1937– Jazz pianist; composer

Address: 167 Wayne St., #307G, Jersey City, NJ 07302-3401

Underappreciated for many years, the jazzman Andrew Hill is now often compared to such luminaries of the genre as Thelonious Monk, for his creativity and skill as both a piano player and composer. During the 1960s Hill blurred the boundary between melodic, percussion-driven hard bop and experimental jazz, which featured irregular rhythms, complex harmonies, and occasional dissonance. Writing for the *Village Voice* (October 30, 1984), Stanley Crouch noted that Hill's albums for the Blue Note record label in the 1960s "provide perhaps the richest range and originality of any pianist then associated with the avant-garde." Hill's 1964 album *Point of Departure* is thought to have been ahead of its time and has inspired generations of jazz musicians. Continuing to evolve over the next four decades, Hill's music—which has included works with a choir, pieces incorporating Afro-Cuban rhythms, and moody solo recordings—has defied easy categorization. "His piano style is a patchwork of approaches—ringing chords and quick jabs and stride piano oom-pahs, skittering runs and skewed be-bop lines, melodies fractured by pauses and asides—cobbled together in asymmetrical fits and starts," Jon Pareles wrote for the *New York Times* (January 29, 1989), adding that Hill's "themes are just as eccentric, barely announcing themselves as ballads or hard-bop before veering away." Following a 10-year absence from recording studios, in 2000 Hill released the critically lauded album *Dusk*, which he followed in 2001 with *Les Trinitaires*; in 2002 with *A Beautiful Day*; and in 2004 with *Day the World Stood Still*. In the last several years his classic records from the 1960s have begun to appear in new editions, and in 2003 he won the prestigious Jazzpar Prize, given annually to an internationally recognized jazz artist. As James Hale wrote of him in *Down Beat* (July 8, 2000), "Andrew Hill has made a career of confounding expectations and intermingling styles, inventing his own in the process."

The son of Haitian immigrants, Andrew Hill was born on June 30, 1937 in Chicago, Illinois, and raised on the city's predominately African-American South Side. (For years it was widely believed that he was born in Haiti.) Early on, Hill demonstrated talent as a pianist and as an accordionist. As a boy he often listened outside his neighborhood's jazz nightclubs, sometimes playing the accordion or even dancing; it was in that way that he met the great jazz pianist Earl "Fatha" Hines, who encouraged him and gave him piano lessons. Hill also took lessons with the jazz trombonist and arranger William Russo, who introduced him to the German classical composer and music theorist Paul Hindemith. Hill met with Hindemith about a half-dozen times from 1950 to 1952; he shared his compositions with Hindemith, who "showed me things about extended composition," as Hill told Stanley Crouch. In 1953, at age 16, Hill played at the Graystone Ballroom in Chicago, accompanying the legendary jazz saxophonist and bebop pioneer Charlie Parker. (Bebop, a style of jazz that emerged in the 1940s, is characterized in part by rapid melodies and solos and complex chord progressions.) As a teenager Hill also played or rehearsed with such jazz giants as Miles Davis and Coleman Hawkins. In 1955 he released his debut album, *So in Love With the Sound of Andrew Hill*, on the Warwick label.

In 1961 Hill moved to New York City to work with the singer Dinah Washington; he also accompanied the vocalists Al Hibbler and Johnny Hartman and worked with the group led by the saxophonists Johnny Griffin and Eddie "Lockjaw" Davis. After a brief stint in Los Angeles, California, with Rahsaan Roland Kirk's jazz band, Hill returned to New York and, during a recording session for the saxophonist Joe Henderson's album *Our Thing*, attracted the notice of Alfred Lions of the prestigious jazz record label Blue Note. Signing with Blue Note, Hill recorded with some of the most talented, experimental "post-bop" jazz musicians of the day, including the reedmen Henderson and Eric Dolphy, the trumpeters Woody Shaw and Freddie Hubbard, and the drummer Tony Williams. In an interview with Fred Jung for *Jazz Weekly* (on-line), Hill called the jazz scene of the early 1960s "budding," noting that "it was the zenith of jazz as a popular music. It came from a period where everyone who played music had heard music in their neighborhoods from black theaters where they had bands." Hill's first record for Blue Note as a leader was *Black Fire* (1963), which merged avant-garde stylings with firm melodic structures and hard bop; that record featured Joe Henderson as well as the trumpeter Kenny Dorham. Writing for the *All Music Guide* (on-line), Stephen Thomas Erlewine called *Black Fire* an "impressive statement of purpose that retains much of its power decades after its initial release." Hill's next record, *Smoke Stack* (1963), was made up entirely of his own compositions and featured the unorthodox quartet of a piano, two basses, and drums. Writing for *All Music Guide*, Erlewine noted that the record was a "dense, cerebral set of adventurous post-bop" that "is in the middle ground between hard bop and free jazz—it isn't as loose and dissonant as free, but with its long, winding modal improvisations and hazy song structures, it's a lot less accessible than bop." Hill returned in

Courtesy of Palmetto Records

Andrew Hill

1964 with *Judgment*, which, like *Smoke Stack*, was notable for the absence of horns and offered subdued yet experimental post-bop.

Later in that year Hill released his best-known album, *Point of Departure*, which Stanley Crouch singled out as "probably his masterpiece." That harmonically sophisticated record featured Henderson and Dolphy on reeds, Tony Williams on drums, Dorham on trumpet, and Richard Davis on bass. Hill concluded the year with the nearly as lauded *Andrew!!!* He moved further into the avant garde with such releases as *Cosmos* and *Compulsion* (both 1965) and *Involution* (1966). In 1968 he released *Grass Roots*, on which he emphasized traditional rhythms to a greater extent than on his previous records, to please the increasingly commercial-minded Blue Note executives. Hill and his collaborators did not abandon more complex music, however; rather, they used the more mainstream sound as a starting point for further experimentation. That same year Hill recorded *Dance with Death* (which was not released until 1980, as Blue Note initially found it to be too experimental to market). In 1969 Blue Note put out Hill's *Lift Every Voice*, featuring seven vocalists and a jazz quintet. That same year Hill recorded *Passing Ships*, a disc featuring a nine-piece band, which was released—to much acclaim—34 years later. During the late 1960s Hill also composed a jazz opera, *The Golden Spoon*, which he has been reworking over the years.

In the early 1970s, as jazz-rock fusion became popular and interest in experimental jazz declined, Hill turned to academia to earn a living. He served as composer in residence at Colgate University, in Hamilton, New York, from 1970 to 1972. For the next three years, he participated in the Smithsonian Institution's touring program, performing with his wife, Laverne Hill, who died of cancer in 1989 and whom Hill has named as the person who most inspired and nurtured him. In the mid- and late 1970s, the Hills moved first to San Francisco, California, and then to nearby Pittsburgh, California; that period saw him teaching in public schools and prisons. Hill later went to Oregon to teach at Portland State University, where he established the school's Summer Jazz Intensive. He also recorded during that time. Hill's albums of the 1970s often were received well, if not with the same acclaim and renown as his 1960s albums. Among his records from that time are *Invitation* (1974); *Freedom* (1974); *Divine Revelation* (1975), which featured the 25-minute title track; *Nefertiti* (1976); and *From California with Love* (1978). Influenced by the rhythms of his parents' native country, Haiti, Hill released *Faces of Hope* in 1980. After *Strange Serenade*, which he recorded as part of a jazz trio later that year, Hill would not release his next album until 1986, the year *Shades* and then *Verona Rag* appeared. Hill next recorded two well-received records on Blue Note—*Eternal Spirit* (1989) and *But Not Farewell* (1990).

The remainder of the 1990s found Hill performing but not recording, with the exception of an appearance on *The Invisible Hand*, a 1999 record by Greg Osby (who had played on *Eternal Spirit* and *But Not Farewell*). Hill's prowess as a performer apparently did not diminish during the hiatus. Reviewing a 1998 show by Hill's sextet at the Knitting Factory, in New York City, Peter Watrous wrote for the *New York Times* (June 8, 1998), "It became clear that [Hill] was producing the equivalent of a perfect game in baseball. . . . The music, filled with long written passages, riffs and solos that were barely contained by the material, reached a point where its idiom wasn't important; it was music, played at an extremely high level." Working with most of the musicians from the New York dates—Ron Horton on trumpet, Marty Ehrlich on saxophones, Scott Colley on bass, and Billy Drummond on percussion—Hill released *Dusk* (2000) on the Palmetto label, a record inspired by *Cane*, the 1923 collection of stories and poems by the African-American writer Jean Toomer. Pronounced to be as successful as Hill's music from the 1960s in terms of its unorthodox rhythmic and harmonic structures, *Dusk* was named the best album of the year by *Down Beat* and *Jazz Times*. "If Andrew Hill's *Dusk* . . . sounds like state-of-the-art jazz, that's because the jazz world has finally caught up with the 63-year-old pianist and not vice versa," Ed Hazell wrote for the *Boston Phoenix* (June 8–15, 2000). Writing for the *Atlantic Monthly* (April 2000), Bob Blumenthal observed that *Dusk* "delivers the beauty and spark of [Hill's] best early work" and is filled with "complex, limber, and rarely predictable music." Hill was awarded the 2000–01 Best Composer Critics' Choice Award by the Jazz Journalist Association. *Les Trinitaires* (2001), a melancholic solo album recorded in a small French club in 1998, was followed by the live album *A Beautiful Day* (2002), which captured Hill's work with a large ensemble at Birdland, in New York. Writing for the *All Music Guide*, David R. Adler called *A Beautiful Day* "remarkable." In 2004 Hill released *Day the World Stood Still*, recorded in Denmark the previous year.

Hill remarried several years ago and lives in New Jersey. He has received the Lifetime Achievement Award from the Jazz Foundation of America and was among the first recipients of the Doris Duke Foundation Award for jazz composers.

—G.O.

Suggested Reading: *Jazz Times* p52+ July/Aug. 2000, with photo; *Jazz Weekly* (on-line), with photos; *New York Times* p11 Jan. 28, 1989, with photo, I p5 Jan. 29, 1989, with photo, E p3 June 8, 1998; *Village Voice* p93 Oct. 30, 1984, with photo

Selected Recordings: *So in Love with the Sound of Andrew Hill*, 1955; *Black Fire*, 1963; *Smoke Stack*, 1963; *Judgment*, 1964; *Point of Departure*, 1964; *Andrew!!!*, 1964; *Compulsion*, 1965; *Involution*, 1966; *Grass Roots*, 1968; *Lift Every Voice*, 1969; *Invitation*, 1974; *Spiral*, 1974; *Blueback*, 1975; *Homage*, 1975; *Divine Revelation*, 1975; *Nefertiti*, 1976; *From California with Love*, 1978; *Faces of Hope*, 1980; *Dance with Death*, 1980; *Strange Serenade*, 1980; *Shades*, 1986; *Verona Rag*, 1986; *Eternal Spirit*, 1989; *But Not Farewell*, 1990; *Dusk*, 2000; *Les Trinitaires*, 2001; *A Beautiful Day*, 2002; *Passing Ships*, 2003; *Day the World Stood Still*, 2004

Mark Heitoff/Courtesy of Steven Holl Architects

Holl, Steven

(hall)

Dec. 9, 1947– Architect

Address: Steven Holl Architects, 450 W. 31st St., 11th Fl., New York, NY 10001

"Architecture needs to learn all the lessons of tradition and transform them and come forward to create in the present moment," the architect Steven Holl told Carol Polsky for *Newsday* (January 13, 2003). "It's not about reproducing a once hand-carved wooden molding in fiberglass. When you make something [that reflects] your time, you give a gift to the generation that inherits it. It says we had hope about what we could do today. We didn't have to ape an earlier generation as if we were ashamed of our moment in time." Holl is widely considered one of the most innovative practitioners of his craft in the U.S. "His best work combines virtues of 1920s European rigor and 1980s American charm, of [Walter] Gropius and [Michael] Graves," Kurt Andersen wrote for *Time* (March 20, 1989). "His designs tend toward the ascetic, and he is determined to invent, not simply revive old styles." In the *Seattle Times*'s magazine, *Pacific Northwest* (December 3, 2000, on-line), staff writers reported that Holl "is known worldwide for the value he places on finding a metaphor to guide design, and for how faithfully he will stick with that metaphor once he's found it." He is also renowned for what has been called his poetic use of natural light in buildings designed to capture every available ray of the sun, at all times of the day or year. Holl has designed institutional, commercial, and large residential buildings as well as private houses. His works in the U.S. include the offices of D. E. Shaw & Co. (1992), in New York City; an extension of the Cranbrook Institute of Science, in Bloomfield Hills, Michigan (1992–95); four houses and a chapel in Port Ludlow, Washington (1992); an addition to the College of Architecture and Landscape Architecture (1996) in Minneapolis, Minnesota; the Chapel of St. Ignatius (1995–97), on the campus of Seattle University, in Washington State; the Bellevue Art Museum (1997), also in Washington; Simmons Hall (2000–03), a dormitory for Massachusetts Institute of Technology (MIT) students; and a partially completed addition to the Nelson Atkins Museum of Art, in Kansas City, Missouri. Buildings he has designed for locations overseas include the American Memorial Library (1989), in Berlin, Germany; the Palazzo del Cinema (1990) in Venice, Italy; the Makuhari housing complex (1996), for commercial and residential uses, in Chiba, Japan; and Kiasma, the Museum of Contemporary Art (1993–98), in Helsinki, Finland. A show of his work at the Museum of Modern Art in New York City in 1987 helped to solidify his reputation in the United States and abroad.

According to the architecture critic Paul Goldberger, writing for the *New York Times* (February 12, 1989), Holl "is able to bestow upon primal, basic geometric form a level of poetic meaning. His shapes are fundamental ones—he relies particularly on proportion, and makes frequent use of multiple squares and rectangles proportioned according to the golden section of Classical antiquity. His materials and his details are spare and can often be quite harsh. But Mr. Holl's harshness resonates: his work is, in a sense, a struggle to bring Modernism out of its muteness, to force it to speak to us." "The feeling of space, light, material is not an academic process," Holl told a *Pacific Northwest* writer. "For me, the experience that you get from a building is the measure. It's a feeling. Like how you feel riding on the ferry when the incredible Northwest sunlight washes over Elliott Bay"—a waterway connected to Puget Bay, in Washington State, where he grew up. Most of Holl's designs have earned one or more honors, among them the Progressive Architecture Award, sponsored in part by the American journal *Architecture*; New York and U.S. design awards; and various American Institute of Architects (AIA) awards, as well as prizes from organizations and nations overseas.

The first of the two children of Myron and Helen Holl, Steven Holl was born on December 9, 1947 in Bremerton, Washington, a ferry ride away from Seattle. His father, a skilled draftsman, managed a sheet-metal shop that specialized in the installation of furnaces; when Steven got old enough, he sometimes helped his father at the shop, "getting a feel for building and an appreciation for pure materials," as *Pacific Northwest* put it. Like their father, Steven and his younger brother, James "Jim" Holl, demonstrated uncommon artistic abilities early on. Jim Holl made art his career; recently, he

contributed to Steven Holl's designs for part of the reconstruction and expansion of the Museum of Modern Art in New York City. As children, the brothers played a game they called Property, making roads, buildings, and treehouses in their backyard from wood and stone; they even dug some underground forts. During his youth Holl got pleasure from viewing the Seattle skyline from the ferry to and from Bremerton. He also remembers how impressed he felt by the design of the Space Needle, constructed for the 1962 Seattle World's Fair and now a symbol of the city.

After he graduated from high school, Holl studied architecture at the University of Washington at Seattle. One of his professors was Hermann Pundt, a specialist in the history of architecture and art, who, according to *Columns* (December 2000, online), the university's alumni magazine, strived to impart to his students "a love of the past, as well as a desire to create new, exciting buildings." Holl regarded Pundt as an exception among the faculty; indeed, for a while he considered dropping out of college, because he found most of his architecture courses uninspiring. Instead, acting upon Pundt's advice, he spent his junior year as a student in the architecture program of the university's Rome Center, in Italy. He made many visits to the Pantheon, an extraordinarily well-preserved Roman temple built in the second century A.D.; he especially enjoyed the effects of light on the interior at different times of day and in different types of weather. "Rome was the first time that I was truly inspired by architecture," he recalled to a *Pacific Northwest* reporter. Holl returned to the University of Washington for his senior year. He earned a bachelor's degree in architecture in 1971.

Earlier, Holl's drafting skills had landed him his first job in his field, in the summer of 1970. After he graduated from college, he left the Seattle area, in part because he felt that those involved in the building boom there had little or no interest in high-quality architecture or sensible urban planning. He settled in San Francisco, California, where he worked for several years as an architectural intern. During that period he designed, free of charge, a house for his parents on a waterfront site near Bremerton. Myron Holl, a perfectionist, found fault with half a dozen different drafts before he approved the blueprints, in the face of his son's threats to abandon the job. Holl told a *Pacific Northwest* writer that whenever he was asked if he regretted anything about any of his completed projects, he would answer, "I made my mother's kitchen too small. It's been 25 years and it's still too small." In 1976 he studied and taught at the Architectural Association of London, in England.

In about 1977 Holl moved to New York City, where he set up his own firm, Steven Holl Architects; at present two dozen people work with him there. His first projects were primarily designs for apartment renovations and new private homes, among them a small pool house and sculpture studio in Scarsdale, New York (completed in 1981), and the Berkowitz-Odgis house in Martha's Vineyard, Massachusetts (1988). In his book *Stretto House* (1996), Holl wrote that the design of the Martha's Vineyard house was inspired by Herman Melville's classic novel *Moby-Dick* and aimed to evoke the image of a whale skeleton; the house has a "bonelike, linear structure," he explained, and an outer "skeleton" of wood posts that frame a veranda and other structures. Another of his projects during this period was the American Memorial Library in Berlin, Germany (1989). According to his Web site, stevenholl.com, the library has open stacks throughout, to make possible "the unobstructed meeting of reader and book." The library was designed to be "analogous to a city gate"; thus the children's library, erected above the original building, "elevates children to caretakers of the city." Sloped floors in that section enable youngsters to read comfortably while lying on their bellies.

As a young architect, Holl also designed dinner plates and candlesticks for Swid Powell, a company that commissions architects and designers to create patterns for china and similar products. In 1977, along with the San Francisco architect William Stout, he founded the innovative series Pamphlet Architecture, as "an alternative to the mainstream architectural press," according to its Web site. Holl and Stout's goal was to encourage young architects, designers, and urbanists to offer their "designs, manifestos, ideas, theories, ruminations, hopes, and insights," and challenge the philosophies, assumptions, and methods of their predecessors, for publication in "modest, affordable booklets that could be easily produced and purchased, to ensure a continuous, serious debate and discussion about architecture." The series' influence, its Web site declared, has "far exceeded the ad-hoc nature of these humble publications" and has launched the careers of various architects, among them Lebbeus Woods and Zaha M. Hadid. The most recent, 26th pamphlet, "13 Projects for the Sheridan Expressway" (2004), by Jonathan Solomon, whose title refers to a highway in New York City, reexamines "the urban expressway as a political, physical, and mythic manifestation of American culture," as the Pamphlet Architecture Web site put it.

In 1989 Holl's designs, along with those of Emilio Ambasz of Argentina, were featured in a show at the Museum of Modern Art in New York City. In "Two Architects Who Tap into Our Deepest Moods," Paul Goldberger wrote for the *New York Times* that both had "an attitude toward architecture that is poetic, even mystical. This is not architecture that is about other architecture, or at least not primarily; it is architecture that seeks to be about human experience. . . .This architecture is powerfully evocative. Yet for all its determination to inspire an emotional response, it is blissfully free of sentimentality. And for all its idealism, it is completely free of naïve utopianism."

That same year Holl began work on one of his most admired projects, a 28-apartment housing complex in Fukuoka, Japan, which was completed in 1991. Pools in what Holl termed "void space" between the four buildings in the complex reflect light into the interiors, which he described as "hinged space," a reference to the colorful, movable panels that enable residents to change the configurations of their apartments, to enlarge living space during the day and bedrooms at night, for example, or to accommodate changing numbers of occupants. Another of Holl's famous projects from that period is the Stretto House (1990–92), near Dallas, Texas, which *Architectural Record* (April 1991) included in an issue devoted to what its editors deemed the "most significant examples of residential architecture" of 1990. A reviewer of Holl's book *Stretto* (1996) for ecampus.com explained, "The need for protection from the scorching Texas sun led the architect to explore the ideas of shadow and overlap," which in turn led him to apply to his design the musical concept known as "stretto" (the overlapping of particular parts of a fugue), in particular as it occurs in the orchestral piece *Music for Strings, Percussion, and Celeste*, by Béla Bartók. In Pamphlet Architecture number 16, "Architecture as a Translation of Music" (1994), Elizabeth Martin discussed the Stretto House as an example of layered relationships.

Architecture critics have said that Holl's use of color and light in his buildings is almost painterly. An outstanding watercolorist, Holl always carries a small sketchbook with him. Before he starts a particular design, he makes paintings in watercolor of the site where it will be built as seen from different angles, experimenting with light, form, and atmosphere. His approach to architecture is phenomenological: he does not start with ideas of what the structure will look like but, rather, thinks about what will best co-exist with buildings already at the site and the surrounding landscape. "We have all experienced inspiring conditions in nature where . . . the moonlight on the snow glows and one walks through a landscape and feels uplifted and euphoric over this condition of space and light and movement and textures," he said in the video *Steven Holl: The Body in Space*, according to the Michael Blackwood Productions Web site. "I think that architecture really is the one art that has the opportunity to add this to our daily lives. . . . I see it as an urgent mission on this level." On arcspace.com (July 8, 2002), he was quoted as saying, "In each project, we seek new ways to integrate an organizing idea with the programmatic and functional essence of a building. Rather than a 'style' carried to different sites and climates, or pursued regardless of different programs, we seek the unique character of a program and site, local and global, as the starting point for an architectural idea." In his book *Stretto House*, he wrote, "A . . . consideration of materials always enters our design process from the very beginning. Even before the idea has been settled upon, we work on various models in different materials"—for example, small wooden sticks, chipboard, clay, wire, and cast plaster. "In building these sketch models, a direction is already beginning in the project. In other words, the conceptual process or idea—sketching, making watercolors, writing down sentences—is formed simultaneously with this material exploration. It is important that they run parallel." While he uses computers in some aspects of his work, he strongly opposes designing solely on computers and other digital devices, deploring such practices as antithetical to the spirit of architecture. "I believe in the analog as the beginning of architecture," he told Joseph Masheck for *Bomb* (Spring 2002). "There's a whole school of architecture now that speaks about composing on the computer, which I think is completely wrongheaded. . . . The very first thought, the meaningful first diagram, the 'concept' for the building, is a combination of eye and mind and hand, and, one hopes, the spirit. . . .The subtleties and qualities of the role of intuition in conception are best begun directly in the idea/mind/hand/eye. With this directness I feel a fusion of idea-space-conceptions and what I could only describe as spiritual meaning. After, the work can be digitally supercharged . . . it can take off."

Holl's winning design for Kiasma, the Museum of Contemporary Art in Helsinki, was chosen from among 516 proposals and was the first by a non-native of Finland to win a major competition there since 1917. "Undoubtedly any architect who was able to comprehend the nature of museum spaces in such a manner had to understand a great deal about art itself," Tuula Arkio, the museum's director, was quoted as saying on the Web site of Gingko Press, which published the book *Kiasma* (2001). Curved and tapered, the building overlooks Töölö Bay and neighbors the Finnish Parliament building and Finlandia Hall, the last work of the renowned Finnish architect Alvar Aalto. Holl won the Alvar Aalto Medal, Finland's highest architectural honor, for his design for the museum, which makes optimal use of both reflected light from the bay and daylight. The glass planks with translucent insulation that comprise the museum's western wall "trap and diffuse light from the sun, which hovers near the horizon for half the year," as Michael Webb wrote for *Metropolis Magazine* (May 1998, on-line). In Webb's opinion, "Holl's understanding of the subtleties and psychological impact of light is nowhere more evident than in his design for the Kiasma museum."

Holl's design for the 195,000-square-foot Simmons Hall, an undergraduate dormitory at the Massachusetts Institute of Technology (2003), received much praise. In planning its construction, Holl found inspiration in the structure of natural sponges (for reference, he bought real sea sponges for himself and his staff) and was guided by what he has termed the "sponge" concept. The façade of the 10-story, 330-foot-long dormitory consists of a grid of more than 3,000 small windows, each about two feet square, with nine operable windows, in rows of three, in each of the 350 single-occupancy dorm rooms. The building, which also houses a small theater, a night café, and a dining room with outdoor seating, illustrates various energy-conservation techniques (the 18-inch-deep outer walls, for example, retain heat in winter and provide shade in summer) and is unusually well ventilated, thanks to such innovations as elevators with porous, grillwork walls and several canyon-like, four-story atria with large skylights. "Since the building opened in August 2002, residents have likened living in Simmons Hall to living in a piece of art," Julian Astbury, Leroy Le-Lacheur, and Mark Walsh-Cooke reported for the *Arup Journal* (February 2003, on-line). "This building . . . is also a work of science to be studied and advanced in the future." Simmons Hall won the 2000 Progressive Architecture Award, the 2002 New York Design Award, the 2003 National Design Award, and the 2003 AIA Honor Award.

In July 2002 a Holl design was selected for the expansion and renovation of the Natural History Museum of Los Angeles County, California. His recent projects also include designs for the new, $75 million Tyler School of Art, at Temple University, in Philadelphia; a contemporary-art exhibition hall in Nanjing, China; a residential/commercial building complex in Beijing, China; a new building for the Department of Art and Art History at the University of Iowa in Iowa City; and a marina, public space, and 80-unit apartment building in the old harbor of Beirut, Lebanon. Holl and the American sculptor Jene Highstein worked together on a project titled *Oblong Voidspace* for the Snow Show, an installation of 30 snow and ice structures in two cities in the Finnish part of Lapland, held in February–March 2004. Holl's proposal for the rebuilding of the World Trade Center site, on which he collaborated with the architects Richard Meier, Charles Gwathmey, and Peter Eisenman, was among seven finalists; it was rejected in favor of Daniel Libeskind's. In 1999 Holl finished second to the Dutch architect Rem Koolhaas, ahead of 24 other applicants, in the competition for the design of Seattle's new central library. The building opened to wide acclaim in 2004.

Holl has discussed his philosophy of architecture and his work in several books, among them *The Alphabetical City* (1980), *Anchoring: Selected Projects 1975–1991* (1991), *Questions of Perception* (1994), *Intertwining: Selected Projects 1989–1995* (1996), *The Chapel of St. Ignatius* (1999), *Parallax* (2000), *Steven Holl: Idea and Phenomena* (2002), and *Steven Holl: Written in Water* (2002), a collection of his watercolor sketches. He and his designs are also the subjects of Kenneth Frampton's *Steven Holl, Architect* (2003) and Yukio Futagawa's *Steven Holl* (1996). He is a professor in the Department of Architecture, Planning, and Preservation at Columbia University, in New York City, whose faculty he joined in 1981. For several years before that, he taught at the Parsons Institute of Design, also in New York. In 2002 he received the Cooper Hewitt National Design Award in Architecture, from the Cooper Hewitt Museum's parent, the Smithsonian Institution. His firm's many honors include the 2001 gold medal from the French Academy of Architecture.

In 1989 Holl struck Kurt Andersen as "opinionated, uncompromising and, concerning architectural details, fussy to the point of fanaticism." He "seems to thrive on challenging settings and complex programs," John Morris Dixon wrote for *Architecture* (May 2003). Holl's wife, the artist and architect Solange Fabião, has worked with him on several projects. The couple live in the Greenwich Village section of New York City and also own a house in Rhinebeck, New York, about 90 miles north of the city.

—K.E.D.

Suggested Reading: arcspace Web site; *Bomb* p24+ Spring 2002, with photos; *Newsday* II B3 Jan. 13, 2003, with photo; Steven Holl Web site; Frampton, Kenneth. *Steven Holl, Architect*, 2003; Futagawa, Yukio. *Steven Holl*, 1996; Garofalo, Francesco. *Steven Holl*, 2003

Selected Projects: Zollikerberg Residential Complex, Zurich, Switzerland, 1993; Amsterdam Manifold Hybrid, 1994; Chapel of St. Ignatius at Seattle University, Washington, 1997; Samsung Project office building, Seoul, South Korea, 1995; Sarphatistraat Offices, Amsterdam, the Netherlands, 1996–99; addition to the College of Architecture and Landscape Architecture, Minneapolis, Minnesota, 1996; Knut Hamsun Museum, Hamaroy, Norway, 1996; Museum of the City, Cassino, Italy, 1996; rebuilding of the Higgins Hall School of Architecture, Pratt Institute, Brooklyn, New York City, 1997; Bellevue Art Museum, Bellevue, Washington, 1997; an extension of the Museum of Modern Art, New York City, 1997; Y House, a private residence, Catskill Mountains, New York State, 1997; Whitney Waterworks Park and water-treatment facility, Hamden, Connecticut, 1998; hotel. Guadalajara, Mexico, 1998; Simmons Hall, dormitory at the Massachusetts Institute of Technology, 2000–03; central library building, Seattle, Washington, 2004

Selected Books: *The Alphabetical City*, 1980; *Anchoring: Selected Projects 1975–1991*, 1991; *Questions of Perception*, 1994; *Intertwining: Selected Projects 1989–1995*, 1996; *The Chapel of St. Ignatius*, 1999; *Parallax*, 2000; *Steven Holl: Written in Water*, 2002

Hondros, Chris

Mar. 14, 1970– Photojournalist

Address: Getty Images, 601 N. 34th St., Seattle, WA 98103

"Photography is an art, a craft . . . ," the award-winning photojournalist Chris Hondros told *Current Biography*, adding, "ultimately you have to communicate people's suffering." Hondros is a staff photographer for Getty Images, one of the world's leading providers of pictures for newspapers, magazines, advertisers, television programs, book publishers, and Web sites in the U.S. and abroad. In the last five years, he has photographed many images of suffering and brutality in nearly a dozen war-torn countries, among them Iraq, Afghanistan, and Sierra Leone. His poignant and graphic photographs frequently appear in the *New York Times*, the *Washington Post*, the *Los Angeles Times*, the *Economist*, *Newsweek*, *Time*, and other major publications. "The task is to draw people in," Hondros told *Current Biography*, "and you do that by creating work with a certain amount of beauty. And beauty in the face of terror, in the face of pain, is nothing new." In April 2004, for a series of photographs he took in the West African nation of Liberia, where civil war has raged for more than 10 years, Hondros was named a finalist for a Pulitzer Prize in the category of breaking news photography.

A first-generation American, Christopher E. Hondros was born in New York on March 14, 1970. He has a younger brother, Dean. His father, Christopher Sr., a Greek immigrant, and his mother, Inga, a German immigrant, met in the United States in the 1960s. Chris Sr. owned and operated a Greek diner; Inga was a full-time homemaker. The family lived in New York for the first four or five years of Hondros's life, then moved to Fayetteville, North Carolina.

"I did realize rather early that I wanted to be a photographer," Hondros told *Current Biography*. "I'd always liked photography, but I'd never really shot 35-mm. I'd always had those cheap point-and-shoot type cameras." While attending a Fayetteville high school, Hondros has recalled, he was impressed by the quality of the snapshots taken by a friend with a newly bought 35-mm camera. Inspired, Hondros bought himself the same kind of camera and began experimenting with it. "I would pan it; I would move it around and see how the pictures would look blurry. I would try things like time-exposures, self-portraits of various kinds. I tried different colors of light. I pushed that camera to the limit," he recalled to *Current Biography*. Later, when he became a professional photographer, Hondros began using Nikon cameras; he now prefers those made by Canon.

Courtesy of Chris Hondros

Chris Hondros (middle) on assignment in Liberia

After he graduated from high school, in 1988, Hondros attended North Carolina State University, in Raleigh, where he earned a bachelor's degree in English literature in 1993. He then moved to Troy, Ohio, where he took his first job in journalism, as a photographer, at the *Troy Daily News*. Having decided that he wanted to study photography formally, in 1994 he left Troy and enrolled in the graduate program in photojournalism at Ohio University's School of Visual Communications. After he completed the two-year program, in 1996 (because he did not fulfill all the requirements, he did not earn a master's degree from the university until years later), Hondros moved back to North Carolina, where he was hired as a staff photographer for the *Fayetteville Observer* and covered everything from local features to sports. During the next year and a half, as he recalled to *Current Biography*, Hondros "came to a little bit of a thinking point about my work. I wanted to move in a different direction. I don't even know if I articulated it at the time, where I wanted to go." Acting on that vague impulse, in 1998 Hondros moved to New York, where he became a photo editor with the Associated Press (AP). As a photo editor Hondros was charged primarily, in his words, with "managing the stream of photos" that came into his office from all over the world. He spent a small part of his time toning photos or touching them up.

When *Current Biography* asked him how he came to cover news stories in foreign countries, Hondros replied that he has "always loved to travel. I've always had a certain amount of wanderlust. In high school I used to drive cross-country every year with a friend." Furthermore, Hondros had always admired the work of such well-traveled,

award-winning photojournalists as James Nachtwey and Christopher Morris, both of whom are members of the photographers' collective Seven, and Carol Guzy of the *Washington Post*. In 1999 Hondros was awarded a $25,000 grant from the United States Agency for International Development (USAID) to photograph in Kosovo, a province in southern Serbia, which was then wracked by ethnic violence between Serbs and the province's ethnic Albanians. (Kosovo is currently under the administrative control of the United Nations.) During that trip Hondros photographed grieving family members who had lost relatives in the fighting; ethnic Albanian soldiers; and some of the hundreds of thousands of Albanian refugees in neighboring Macedonia and Albania. Some of his photos were displayed at the USAID gallery, in Washington, D.C.

In the fall of 1999, Hondros traveled on his own to Angola, in West Africa. There he captured in pictures the hardships endured by starving, infirm, and displaced Angolan civilians in the town of Malanje, which was surrounded by rebels. In December 1999 Hondros took a job as a staff photographer for Getty Images, a global company founded in 1995 that has customers in more than 50 countries. According to its Web site, Getty Images "employs some of the world's most renowned photographers, artists, photojournalists, and creative researchers, keeping the company on the cutting edge of creating relevant and unique imagery that helps shape the visual world." Getty employs approximately 90 full-time photojournalists, who cover a range of topics and events, from breaking news stories and politics to sports and entertainment. Photographs from Getty Images are ubiquitous in print media in the United States. In the year 2003 alone, the company's Web site recorded nearly 51 million visits and close to 1.3 billion Getty Web pages viewed. "Most of my [Getty] assignments have started out with a conversation like, 'You know, West Africa is looking kind of interesting right now,'" Hondros told *Current Biography*. "'Looks like there's a civil war brewing there; that might be a big story.'" He will then learn about the locale under discussion, its history, and the logistics of getting there. "You fly to this or this place, then you have to go across the border by taxi; you need a visa from here or from there. It costs this much. This and this is happening. And then you propose it [to Getty editors]," he told *Current Biography*. Hondros also seeks out advice and information on his destinations from knowledgeable friends and colleagues. An average assignment abroad lasts six weeks to two months. Using a digital camera, as do most professional photographers now, he shoots between 500 and 1,000 pictures on a busy day. Hondros does not submit all of them to his editors at Getty; rather, he selects the ones that, in his view, best depict the events.

In the summer of 2001, Hondros traveled on assignment to Sierra Leone, which was nearing the end of a brutal, decade-long civil war. In late 2001 and early 2002, he took pictures in three regions that have been plagued by violence of political, ethnic, and religious origin: Afghanistan, Pakistan, and Kashmir (the last of which India and Pakistan each claim as its territory). In the early spring of 2002, Hondros recorded images of Camp X-Ray, the controversial American-run prison at Guantanamo Bay, Cuba, which has been used for nearly three years to hold men accused of being members or active supporters of the Taliban (the faction that ruled Afghanistan from 1996 to 2001) or the terrorist network Al Qaeda. Later that year he completed an assignment for Getty in the West Bank, disputed territory in the Middle East; annexed by Jordan after the 1948 Arab-Israeli War and captured by Israel during the Six-Day War of 1967, it has been the site of many bloody clashes between Israeli soldiers and Palestinian nationalists and militants. Hondros's photographs included shots of a forlorn Palestinian boy staring through the bullet-riddled bars of a gate; destroyed refugee camps; and a pensive Yasir Arafat, the Palestinian leader, at his headquarters in the town of Ramallah.

Journalists are often an unwelcome presence in war zones, as their documentation and publicizing of events may not be in the best interests of one or another of the warring parties. It is not uncommon for journalists to be fired upon by those waging armed conflict, either to disable them and thus prevent them from doing their work or simply to scare them away. As people all over the world have become more familiar with Western media, Western journalists' jobs have become even more dangerous. That is especially true in areas in which, unlike U.S. and Israeli soldiers, the combatants have not undergone "shot discipline," training in directing bullets toward specific parts of a target's body with the object of disabling the person temporarily rather than killing him. Israeli soldiers in the West Bank sometimes shoot journalists, "though they tend to shoot journalists at least with rubber bullets, and they tend to try not to kill journalists," shooting them in the legs mainly, as Hondros explained to *Current Biography*. In contrast, in Hondros's experience, in West Africa, Iraq, and Afghanistan, among other places where armies are not as well trained, many of the fighters are "terrible shots; they're extremely undisciplined soldiers; they just run up, spray bullets, and run back."

Hondros has often put himself in harm's way in the course of carrying out his assignments. His closest brush with injury or death occurred in Iraq in March 2003, when the United States invaded that nation with the aim of toppling the regime of the dictator Saddam Hussein. On the third or fourth day of the war, the sports utility vehicle in which Hondros was riding with several other journalists in southern Iraq was ambushed by an Iraqi militiaman loyal to Hussein. When the journalists got within about 20 yards of him, the man walked into the road and sprayed their vehicle with bullets as Hondros and the others drove past. Although the man succeeded in damaging the car, no one inside was injured. Later in 2003 Hondros returned to Iraq to record with his camera some of the ongoing attempts to stabilize and reconstruct the country. Among the images he captured were those of the hole in the ground in which U.S. soldiers found Saddam Hussein; the comedian Robin Williams entertaining American troops; an American helicopter flying above the golden dome of a mosque; and a car destroyed by a bomb blast.

In the summer of 2003, Hondros spent five weeks taking photographs in the West African country of Liberia, where a civil war has raged for over a decade. He found himself in the midst of the fighting as rebel groups struggled to wrest control of Monrovia, the nation's capital, from armed militias loyal to the Liberian government. In a statement he penned in conjunction with an exhibit of his work from Liberia, mounted at the Half King, a restaurant and art space in New York City, Hondros wrote, as posted on the Half King Web site, "Stray bullets zinged and deadly mortars fell indiscriminately, indifferent to whether they landed on a miserable refugee camp, the US embassy compound, or the press hotel. Sharing the fear and terror of the Liberians was important to creating an empathetic and intimate report of what it was like to live in such madness." The exhibit included photos of the bloody bodies of Liberian civilians killed by mortar shells, child militia fighters, and a Liberian man in a church praying for peace. For his photographs from Liberia, Hondros was named a finalist for a Pulitzer Prize and received the Overseas Press Club's John Faber Award for best photographic reporting from abroad in newspapers or wire service. He also earned first- and second-place honors, in the magazine-news category of its annual photojournalism contest, from the National Press Photographers Association (NPPA). The NPPA also gave Hondros a third-place prize in its magazine-news picture-story category. The photograph that captured the NPPA's first-place honor shows a young, shirtless Liberian militia leader in a celebratory half leap with both arms raised, his rocket-propelled grenade launcher clutched in one hand. Behind him, smoke rises; debris and spent shell casings are scattered on the bridge from which he has been shooting. He seems almost to be enjoying the frenzy of battle. According to Hondros, that fighter was fairly typical of the young Liberian militia members he encountered. As he told *Current Biography*, the Liberian pro-government fighters defending Monrovia were unique among warriors whom he has met in that they showed no hostility toward him or other foreign journalists. Indeed, they would greet him warmly and then turn around to resume shooting at the enemy.

Hondros has also covered stories within the United States. In Pennsylvania in the fall of 2003, he compiled a photographic portrait of members of the Amish, a religious group that resists many of the trappings of modern life. In the first half of 2004, he took photographs to illustrate the effects of job losses in the manufacturing sector in Ohio. He also photographed scenes from the ultimately successful campaign of Senator John Kerry of Massachusetts to win the Democratic nomination for president.

From January to May 2001, Hondros was a fellow at the Pew Center for International Journalism. The fellowship enables selected journalists to study at the Paul H. Nitze School of Advanced International Studies (a division of Johns Hopkins University), in Washington, D.C., before traveling abroad to work in countries of the fellows' own choosing. Hondros chose Nigeria, in West Africa—in particular, the southern part of the country, the source of Nigeria's enormous oil wealth. Because of the highly unequal distribution of oil revenues in Nigeria, most of the people living in that area remain impoverished.

In addition to his other awards, Hondros won both a third-place prize and honorable mention in the 2004 Pictures of the Year International contest, sponsored by the Missouri School of Journalism, and he has received honorable mention in the World Press Photo Contest.

Hondros is single and, when not on assignment, lives in New York. "One of the ongoing themes in my work, I hope, and one of the things I believe in, is a sense of human nature, a sense of shared humanity above the cultural things we put on ourselves," he told *Current Biography*. "Clearly we are all quite similar. We put all these layers of ethnicity and culture on ourselves and it really doesn't mean that much compared to the human experience." On June 3, 2004 Hondros returned to Iraq on assignment.

—C.F.T.

Suggested Reading: Christopher Hondros Web site; Getty Images Web site; National Press Photographers Association Web site

---

Hounsou, Djimon

(HOON-soo, JY-mun)

Apr. 24, 1964– Actor

Address: c/o Kami Putnam, Gersh Agency, 232 N. Canon Dr., Beverly Hills, CA 90210

When the director Jim Sheridan was casting the part of Mateo, a reclusive black painter dying of AIDS, for his 2003 film *In America*, which told the semiautobiographical story of a family of illegal Irish immigrants during their first year in New York, he was faced with a predicament. As he told Lola Ogunnaike for the *New York Times* (December 3, 2003), Sheridan knew he was engaged in a search for someone rare: "a man who is genuinely gentle and has rage." When the Benin-born actor Djimon Hounsou auditioned for the role, Sheridan realized that he had found precisely what he sought. Hounsou "had a different, almost spiritual quality about him," Sheridan told Ogunnaike; moreover, due to Hounsou's striking good looks and muscular build, "Every single woman in my office was screaming at me to cast him." Judging from the reactions of audiences, critics, and the Academy of Motion Picture Arts and Sciences, Sheridan made an excellent casting decision: Hounsou's performance earned widespread praise and an Oscar nomination for best supporting actor. Marjorie Baumgarten enthused in the *Austin Chronicle* (December 19, 2003), "As Mateo, the story's dark cloud and ultimate agent of the family's emotional turnaround, Hounsou cuts a dramatic figure, veering between the extremes of howling rage and acute sensitivity. Although there clings to Mateo a bit of the new film stereotype of the mysterious black man who sets the white characters' moral agendas back on course, Mateo is too complex and Hounsou's performance too textured to be reduced to simple stereotyping." Such praise came several years after similar accolades for Hounsou's performance in Steven Spielberg's historical drama *Amistad* (1997).

Djimon Hounsou was born on April 24, 1964 in Cotenou, in the Republic of Benin, in West Africa, where he grew up with his three brothers and sister

Giulio Marcocchi/Getty Images

Djimon Hounsou

in the care of his mother, Albertine, while his father worked as a cook in the Ivory Coast. As a boy Hounsou would rummage through the garbage for the tops of laundry-detergent boxes, which he could exchange for admission to a Wednesday matinee at the local movie house. American Westerns, especially those starring John Wayne or Gary Cooper, were his favorites, and it was the popularity of these films that first inspired Hounsou to become an actor. "Once you were in [the theater], you couldn't move," he told Carol Day and Irene Zutell for *People* (January 12, 1998). "Every space was filled with people. That's when I knew I wanted to be an entertainer." At the age of 13, Hounsou moved to Lyons, France, to join two of his brothers, who were attending school there. (Benin, formerly known as Dahomey, was governed by France until 1960; its official language is French.) Hounsou originally planned to go to medical school, as his parents wanted, but he became restless after several years. "Stupidly, I decided to leave school," he told Joey Berlin for *Hollywood Online*. "[My brother] didn't like it at all and told me I had to move on and do my own thing and get out of the house." And so, when he was 20 years old, Hounsou left Lyons for Paris.

Alone and nearly penniless, Hounsou was homeless for more than a year, sleeping in the subway and bathing in public fountains. He also endured the indignity of being offered various material comforts in return for sex, offers that he declined. At one point he was approached by a passerby who claimed to know a photographer who wanted to take Hounsou's picture. Hounsou agreed to pose for him, and the photos made their way to the French fashion designer Thierry Mugler. Capti-

vated by his looks, Mugler featured Hounsou in an advertising campaign for his menswear collection. Suddenly, Hounsou was a sought-after fashion model, and he began to travel around the world for fashion shows and photo shoots.

In 1989 Hounsou moved to Los Angeles, where he performed in music videos for such recording artists as Madonna ("Express Yourself"), Steve Winwood ("Roll with It"), Paula Abdul ("Straight Up"), and Janet Jackson ("Love Will Never Do Without You"). He did not find his modeling and video work particularly satisfying, however, and was determined to achieve much more. "I never saw myself as a model," he explained to Day and Zutell. "I was just fortunate to be making a living." By his own account, Hounsou improved his English by watching the Learning Channel and the Discovery Channel on television, and as soon as he felt comfortable with the language, he enrolled in acting classes. In 1990 he began to land small parts in films and on television, beginning with Sandra Bernhard's movie *Without You I'm Nothing* and an episode of *Beverly Hills, 90210*. He had cameo roles in *Unlawful Entry* (1992) and *Stargate* (1994), both of which starred Kurt Russell, and a six-episode recurring role on *ER* as Mobalage Ikabo, a Nigerian refugee, also in 1994.

Discussing his audition for *Amistad* with Terry Lawson of the *Detroit Free Press* (December 11, 1997, on-line), Hounsou recounted, "I don't really know what [Spielberg] saw in my [audition] tape. He has never really explained that to me. I am just grateful he found what he wanted in me." In the film Hounsou played the role of Cinque, the leader of a group of West African slaves who rise up against their Spanish captors while en route to the New World, aboard the ship of the title. After they demand to be returned to their home continent, the ship goes wildly off-course, ending up in Connecticut, where the West Africans find themselves on trial in a case that winds up in the U.S. Supreme Court. Because Cinque speaks Mende, one of the languages spoken in Sierra Leone, Hounsou, in performing the role, had to rely heavily on body language and the few words of English that his character learns to deliver—an emotional testimony regarding personal freedom, pride, and justice in court. For the role of Cinque, Spielberg wanted an actor with a strong physical presence and a degree of charisma, in order to project authority. Spielberg also sought a native West African, because he wanted someone who could master the Mende dialect in a short time. And, although the director preferred to cast an unknown actor, it was necessary that he be accomplished enough to hold his own in scenes with such respected actors as Anthony Hopkins and Morgan Freeman.

Hounsou said that while he was elated to find out he had been cast in the role of Cinque, he was also somewhat frightened. "I had only 10 days to learn the Mende dialect that Cinque spoke," he told Lawson. "Even though both are West African, there is even less similarity between Benin and

Mende than between French and English." While some of Hounsou's lines in *Amistad* were broken down phonetically for him to memorize, he found it important to understand the meaning of his lines. "It was very hard," he told Lawson. "I would go home every night and work, work, work on the script, and then sometimes I would show up the next day feeling disappointed in myself. But everyone tried to help me all they could, giving me encouragement. Morgan Freeman gave me good advice. He said acting is like life, and that some days you are good at it and some days you just have to get through by doing the best you can."

Hounsou also said that understanding the film's historical context proved to be a profound learning experience. "I really didn't know much about the story before I began," he told Lawson. "But the script made it very clear to me and moved me very much. I did most of my research on how Cinque might have lived when he was in Africa, what kind of life he would have had there. I was feeling very proud of that, of what kind of people I came from, and then I show up on the set for the first day and they lock me in these chains and shackles, which were real, not phony. This made me understand what Cinque would have felt. I hated it so much. I wanted to quit the first day." Bob Curtright wrote for the *Wichita Eagle* (on-line), "Hounsou's expressive face is a fascinating canvas of both subtle and broad emotions. His eyes search for some glimmer of understanding; they implore and then turn defiant. His voice is calm and direct, but filled with intensity and power." For his performance in *Amistad*, Hounsou was nominated for a Golden Globe Award, and he won the NAACP Image Award for outstanding actor in a motion picture.

Since he appeared in *Amistad*, Hounsou has portrayed another African captive, in *Ill Gotten Gains* (1997), an independent art film written and directed by Joel Ben Marsden. While the subject matter of the two films—Africans captured for the slave trade—is the same, *Ill Gotten Gains* takes place mainly aboard an illegal slave ship and concerns itself primarily with the incitement of the Africans' revolt by a spirit. In the 1998 film *Deep Rising*, about a cruise ship that is attacked by a large squid-like creature in the South China Sea, Hounsou made an appearance as a pirate. Of this less momentous role, Roger Ebert wrote for the *Chicago Sun-Times* (January 30, 1998, on-line), "Hounsou turns in an effective supporting performance as one of the more fanatical members of the pirate gang . . . , although on the whole I'll bet he wishes the giant squid movie had come out before the Spielberg film."

In 2000 Hounsou starred as Russell Crowe's comrade in *Gladiator*, which won the Academy Award for best picture. He also narrated the French film *Passage du milieu* and appeared in one episode of the television show *Soul Food*. The following year, he starred in the virtually unnoticed film *The Tag*, and in 2002 he appeared in another French film, *Le Boulet*. Also in 2002 Hounsou ap-

peared as yet another African slave in *The Four Feathers*, a remake of the 1939 film of the same title, with Heath Ledger and Kate Hudson. (When Lola Ogunnaike asked him in 2003 if he would reject future offers of slave roles, the actor replied, "Hell yes.")

Critics heaped praise upon Hounsou's performance in his next film, *In America*. Written by Jim Sheridan (who also directed) and his two filmmaker daughters, Naomi and Kirsten, the movie tells the story of a couple of Irish immigrants—played by Paddy Considine and Samantha Morton—who, with their two young daughters (real-life sisters Sarah and Emma Bolger), immigrate to America. Hounsou played Mateo, a tortured African artist dying of AIDS. The role was particularly meaningful to Hounsou, as he explained to Lola Ogunnaike: "The essence of the story is very close to the way I came to this country, in search of quote unquote the American dream." Hounsou, who lost nearly 30 pounds for the part, was nominated for an Oscar for best supporting actor. (He lost to Tim Robbins, who took the award for his work in *Mystic River*.)

In 2003 Hounsou also starred in the short film *Heroes*, which was dedicated to Godsonou Pierre Hounsou, Djimon's father, who died while his son was shooting the film. That same year he appeared in *Biker Boyz*, with Laurence Fishburne, and *Lara Croft Tomb Raider: The Cradle of Life*, with Angelina Jolie. Hounsou recently completed work on *Blueberry*, a Western, which was released in 2004, and the as-yet-unreleased *Constantine*, which is based on the D.C./Vertigo comic-book series *Hellblazer* and will star Keanu Reeves. He is currently working on two films that are in production: *Beauty Shop*, with Queen Latifah, and *The Island*, with Ewan McGregor, Steve Buscemi, and Scarlett Johansson. He also has a recurring role on the television series *Alias*.

The muscular Hounsou, who speaks English with a French accent, is six feet two inches tall. He lives in Los Angeles. Now that he is steadily gaining prominence, Hounsou joked to Lola Ogunnaike that he hopes audiences will finally start pronouncing his name correctly: "I think people are getting used to it. Schwarzenegger had a hard time, too."

—K.J.E.

Suggested Reading: *Chicago Sun-Times* (on-line) Dec. 12, 1997; *Detroit Free Press* (on-line) Dec. 11, 1997; *New York Times* A p19 Dec. 6, 1997, with photo, II p17 Dec. 7, 1997, with photos; *New York Times* (on-line) Dec. 3, 2003; *People* p151+ Jan. 12, 1998, with photos

Selected Films: *Stargate*, 1994; *Amistad*, 1997; *Gladiator*, 2000; *The Four Feathers*, 2002; *In America*, 2003; *Lara Croft Tomb Raider: The Cradle of Life*, 2003; *Blueberry*, 2004

Courtesy of Steny Hoyer

Hoyer, Steny

June 14, 1939– U.S. representative from Maryland (Democrat)

Address: 1705 Longworth House Office Bldg., Washington, DC 20515; 6500 Cherrywood Ln., Suite 310, Greenbelt, MD 20770

"I happen to like the game," U.S. representative Steny Hoyer, a Maryland Democrat, told Jim Naughton for the *Washington Post* (August 3, 1989), referring to national politics. "I'm excited about the competition. I like to win. Beat the other guy. I'm just a competitive guy." First elected to Congress in 1981, Hoyer became the Democratic whip, the party's number-two position in the House of Representatives, in 2002. During his years as a representative of Maryland's Fifth District, he has earned a reputation as an astute politician, a master of consensus, and an effective provider for his constituents. According to Matthew Chin of the Capital News Service (October 23, 1998, on-line), Hoyer has been described as a politician who "doesn't just bring home the bacon, he brings home the entire pig." "Steny is a political animal, and his instincts are perfect," Maryland state senator Barbara A. Hoffman told R. H. Melton for the *Washington Post* (May 31, 1994). Although his voting record is liberal—in 2001 Americans for Democratic Action, a liberal lobbying group, approved of 95 percent of his votes, while the American Conservative Union agreed with only 9 percent—Hoyer is known for reaching out to diverse groups, including southern conservatives. His pro-military position (his district encompasses two military bases) and his ability to gain job open-

ings and federal funding for his constituents have helped him win reelection despite the significant conservative presence in his district. "I do politics reasonably well," he told Richard Wolf for *USA Today* (July 10, 1991). "Unambitious people, for the most part, don't get much accomplished."

Steny Hamilton Hoyer was born on June 14, 1939 in the New York City borough of Manhattan to Steen Hoyer and Jean (Slade) Hoyer, both immigrants from Denmark. His given name is a diminutive of his father's. When Hoyer was a teenager, he and his family moved to Prince George's County, in Maryland, where he graduated from Suitland High School, in Forestville. In 1959, while he was attending the University of Maryland at College Park, he heard John F. Kennedy, then a U.S. senator from Massachusetts, give a speech. Inspired by Kennedy, Hoyer changed his focus from public relations to politics and became more dedicated to his studies. In 1963 he earned a B.S. degree with high honors and was named an outstanding graduate. Three years later he received a law degree from Georgetown University, in Washington, D.C. By then he had been elected a member of two honor societies (Phi Kappa Phi and Omicron Delta Kappa), the Kalegathos Society (which honors students who have helped the University of Maryland's Greek community), and the law fraternity Delta Theta Phi. After passing the Maryland bar exam, in 1966, he practiced law with Haislip and Yewell for three years. In 1969 he established his own firm, Hoyer, Fannon and Johnson.

Meanwhile, Hoyer had strengthened his political skills and developed many contacts through various jobs. He worked as an intern in the office of U.S. senator Daniel B. Brewster, a Maryland Democrat, in 1963. In 1966 he was elected to the Maryland Senate, where he served from 1967 to 1979. During his last three years there, he held the post of Senate president; he was the youngest in Maryland history to do so. While serving in the Maryland legislature, Hoyer held the titles of vice chair of the Commission to Revise the Annotated Code of Maryland (1975–79), chair of the Task Force on Crime (1976–79), chair of the Maryland Commission on Intergovernmental Cooperation (1971–74), chair of the Legislative Council (1975–76), and co-chair of the Legislative Policy Committee (1976–79). He was also a member of the Rules Committee, the Joint Budget and Audit Committee, the State House Trust, the Maryland Historical Trust, and the Maryland Veterans Home Commission. In 1978 Hoyer unsuccessfully sought the Democratic nomination for lieutenant governor of Maryland. He spent the next couple of years concentrating on his law practice; he also served on the Maryland State Board for Higher Education. In May 1981 a special election was held to choose a legislator to represent Maryland's Fifth District in Congress; Gladys Spellman, a Democrat who had won the regular election in November 1980, had been only semi-conscious since suffering a possible heart attack or stroke shortly before her victory, and the following April the House voted to declare her seat vacant. Running against the Republican Audrey Scott, Hoyer won the special election with 55 percent of the vote.

Hoyer's leadership experience in the state legislature proved valuable in Congress, as he quickly cultivated friendships with key members of his party and landed a seat on the Appropriations Committee after just one year. He gained attention for calling on his colleagues in person to discuss legislation, rather than sending form letters or making telephone calls, as is usual. On New Year's Day 1985, Hoyer was chosen to deliver the Democratic response to President Ronald Reagan's weekly radio address, a rare honor for a member who had completed only one term in office. From 1987 to 1989 he served as deputy majority whip.

As a member of the powerful House Appropriations Committee—which commands more control over how federal money is spent than any other House committee—Hoyer serves on two of its subcommittees: the Labor, Health and Human Services, and Education Subcommittee and the Military Construction Subcommittee. He is the ranking Democrat on the Treasury, Postal Service and General Government Subcommittee, the House Administration Committee, and the Joint Library Committee and co-chairs the Federal Government Service Task Force. He was chair of the House Democratic Caucus (the fourth-highest leadership position within his party in the House) from 1989 to 1994 and is a member and former co-chair of the House Democratic Caucus Steering Committee. In addition, Hoyer was the chief candidate recruiter for House Democrats from 1995 to 2000 and served as a parliamentarian (rule-keeper) at the 2000 Democratic National Convention. He joined the Commission on Security and Cooperation in Europe (known as the Helsinki Commission) in 1985 and is currently its co-chair. In April 1999 he visited Albania as part of an official delegation of 18 members of Congress. While he defended the NATO bombing operation against Yugoslavia, he urged President Bill Clinton to consider sending ground troops to the area as well.

The 1992 election proved to be a challenging race for Hoyer, because the Maryland state legislature had redrawn the Fifth District in the previous year, and a majority of the constituents within its new borders were believed to be relatively unfamiliar with Hoyer and his record. (The district now includes Calvert, Charles, and St. Mary's counties and parts of Anne Arundel and Prince George's counties.) Furthermore, in its former configuration Hoyer's district had been overwhelmingly Democratic and liberal, while the new district included significantly more Republicans and conservative Democrats. Nevertheless, on Election Day Hoyer won 53 percent of the vote, defeating Larry Hogan Jr., a real-estate broker and son of a former congressman. Since then he has won each election handily against his Republic opponents: in 1994 he defeated Donald Devine, a former Reagan ad-

ministration official, with 58.8 percent of the vote; in 1996, John S. Morgan, a member of the Maryland House of Delegates, with 57 percent; in 1998, Robert B. Ostrom, a prominent lawyer, with 65.4 percent; in 2000, Thomas E. Hutchins, a member of the House of Delegates, with 65 percent; in 2002, Joseph T. Crawford, a business consultant, with 69 percent; and in 2004, Brad Jewitt, a local Maryland politician. In each campaign he outspent his competitors significantly, typically spending between $1.2 and $1.3 million. (In 1996 he was fined $15,000 for failing to report in a timely manner donations of over $140,000 during the 1994 campaign, according to the *Washington Post* [February 18, 1996].) He has often given some of the money he raises to other Democrats; in 2000, for example, he contributed $1.5 million to other candidates.

Twice in 1991 and once in 2001, Hoyer sought the post of Democratic whip in the House without success, the last time losing to Nancy Pelosi of California. In November 2002 his Democratic colleagues unanimously elected him to that position. The second-ranking member of the party, the whip must keep members of the party united, to ensure that the Democrats have enough votes to pass or defeat particular measures. One of the primary goals of Hoyer and the rest of the Democratic leadership is to win back control of the House, where, currently, there are 229 Republicans, 205 Democrats, and one Independent. Hoyer believes that collaboration and cooperation among House Democrats are improving. "We are creating consensus, and we are creating policy that a broad spectrum of the party can support, which will help us in those marginal districts where the control of Congress will ultimately be decided," he told Mark Wegner for *CongressDaily AM* (April 8, 2003). Hoyer listed Arizona, Colorado, Georgia, Iowa, and Texas as states in which Democrats ran competitively in 2002 but failed to win seats. Congressional Republicans have a financial advantage, raising nearly $22 million in campaign contributions during the first quarter of 2003, about $15 million more than was collected by the Democratic Congressional Campaign Committee.

"Steny represents the perfect blend of a person who has done an incredible job of representing his district and being a national leader on important issues," Ben Cardin, a Democratic member of the Maryland state legislature, told Etan Horowitz for the Capital News Service (October 25, 2002), as posted on the Maryland Newsline Web site. In Hoyer's view, his biggest legislative accomplishments to date include the passage in 1990 of both the Americans with Disabilities Act and the Federal Employee Pay Comparability Act, which restructured the pay system for federal workers; he has continued to push for pay raises for federal workers and military employees (about 95,000 of whom live in his district) to levels close or equal to those of their private-sector counterparts. In addition, he has secured funding to allow federal employees to work closer to home via telecommuting centers. In the fall of 2001, with Bob Ney, a Republican from Ohio, he introduced the Help America Vote Act, to overhaul the national electoral system. The legislation was drafted in an attempt to correct the massive problems that occurred in the 2000 presidential election, which remained undecided for weeks. "We must remove this stain from our democracy," Hoyer told Karen Foerstel for *Congressional Quarterly* (November 17, 2001). "This bill will significantly improve the integrity of our election process, improve voter participation and restore public confidence in our system." The law, which passed in 2002, sets minimum national election standards and provides federal funds to states for improving access to polling places and facilitating voter registration and ballot counting. Hoyer also helped write new security and evacuation procedures for the Capitol in the wake of the September 11, 2001 terrorist attacks.

Hoyer has faulted the recent Republican-introduced Medicare legislation, on the grounds that it prohibits the secretary of Health and Human Services from negotiating lower drug prices; that it will force the millions of senior citizens who spend more than $180 per month for their medications to pay a significant portion of their total expenses out of their own pockets; and that it will increase premiums for many seniors. Hoyer continues to support a federal prescription-drug plan in which Medicare would cover the costs of prescriptions; he does not believe health maintenance organizations (HMOs) should be involved. "I'm not prepared to put seniors at risk by relying on HMOs," he said in a debate during his 2000 reelection campaign, as quoted by Monte Reel in the *Washington Post* (October 19, 2000). "They understand Medicare, they rely on Medicare, and they know it works." He branded unconstitutional the new law that bans partial-birth abortions, and he supports the Food and Drug Administration's approval of RU-486, the so-called "morning after" contraceptive. Hoyer opposes school-voucher plans as proposed by the George W. Bush administration. "We need to make sure we have every dollar available that we can invest in public education and not divert that through vouchers to another system," he said, as reported by Reel. Hoyer opposes federal funding of elections but supports campaign-finance reform. He has supported antidiscrimination legislation to protect the rights of homosexuals and has advocated the inclusion of gays and lesbians as members of protected groups in hate-crimes legislation.

In a practice often referred to as pork-barrel politics, Hoyer has secured many lucrative projects and jobs for his district, which relies heavily on military bases for its economic well-being. He successfully lobbied for the construction of a $10 million aircraft-testing facility at Patuxent River Naval Air Station, secured $5 million for research on airplane ejection seats at Indian Head Naval Surface Warfare Center, and obtained $2 million for the establishment of a day-care center at Indian Head. He also succeeded in having 8,000 acres set aside for the partially federally funded Patuxent Wildlife Research Center, helped consolidate naval air operations to generate about 4,000 jobs in southern Maryland, saved a naval electronics base from closing in St. Mary's County, and was instrumental in having the National Archives II building and a Food and Drug Administration building constructed in College Park. "'Pork' is an epithet that applies to projects that are not in one's district," he told Kent Jenkins Jr. for the *Washington Post* (July 5, 1992). "It's politics. I'm trying to represent my area as effectively as I can. And I plead guilty to representing my area very effectively."

Hoyer has been extremely critical of President George W. Bush's economic-stimulus program. In a May 23, 2003 news release posted on the Democratic Whip Web site after a Republican tax proposal passed in the House of Representatives, he said, "Since the opening day of this 108th Congress, the president and Congressional Republicans have made clear that they have one legislative priority that trumps all others: enacting the largest possible tax cut, with no regard for the consequences. With no regard for the fact that just two years after enacting the largest tax cut in American history, the GOP has turned a record budget surplus of $236 billion in fiscal 2000 into a record deficit of more than $300 billion this year and deficits as far as the eye can see. With no regard for the fact that at the same time we debate this bill, the GOP demands the largest debt limit increase in American history. With no regard for the fact that these GOP tax cuts will steal every dime from the Social Security trust fund, add $1 trillion to the national debt, and pass the costs on to our children. And with no regard for the fact that the American people face pressing, unmet needs." According to Hoyer, the rich will benefit disproportionately from the new tax laws, with a millionaire receiving a tax cut of $94,000, or 9.4 percent, while a family earning $40,000 to $50,000 would receive only $450, or approximately 1 percent. He also maintained that the tax cuts would do little to help the nine million jobless Americans or the 45 million U.S. citizens who do not have health insurance.

Hoyer was named state official of the year by the Maryland Municipal League in 1971. In 1975 the Maryland Jaycees gave him its Outstanding Young Man Award, and he was named legislator of the year by the Maryland State's Attorneys' Association in 1977. In 1986 he was named congressman of the year by the National Multiple Sclerosis Association and congressional advocate of the year by the Child Welfare League. In 1988 the National Association of Homebuilders named him policymaker of the year, and *Washingtonian* magazine dubbed him Washingtonian of the year. He was named a "Rising Star in Congress" by the *National Journal* in 1990 and a champion of pediatric research by Children's National Medical Center in 1995, and received the Jack Niles Medal of Honor from the Public Employees Roundtable in 1999. Hoyer is a member of the St. Mary's College of Maryland board of trustees and is on the boards of directors of the Baltimore Museum of Art, the Baltimore Council of Foreign Relations, and the Prince George's County Mental Health Association. He has been inducted into the University of Maryland Alumni Association's hall of fame and has been on the board of regents of the University System of Maryland since 1999. The congressman has homes in Mechanicsville, Maryland, and St. Mary's County. His wife, Judy (Pickett) Hoyer, an administrator in the Prince George's County school district, died of cancer in 1997. He has three adult daughters—Susan, Stefany, and Anne—and five grandchildren.

—K.E.D.

Suggested Reading: Steny Hoyer Web Site; *USA Today* A p6 July 10, 1991, with photo; *Washington Post* D p1 May 31, 1994, with photo, M p1 Oct. 19, 2000

Courtesy of Cohn Davis Communications

Hunt Lieberson, Lorraine

(LEE-ber-son)

Mar. 1, 1954– Opera singer

Address: c/o Nonesuch Records, 1290 Ave. of the Americas, 23d Fl., New York, NY 10104

Lorraine Hunt Lieberson is widely regarded as one of the world's greatest contemporary opera singers and is, in the estimation of the *New Yorker* (January 5, 2004), "a mezzo with the most potent voice" since the late soprano Maria Callas. "Every phrase that Hunt Lieberson sings seems gorgeous of tone, perfectly controlled and mines perilously deep seams of emotion and expression," Charlotte Higgins gushed in the London *Guardian* (August 8, 2003). "But she is not a histrionic singer—rather, she boils emotion down until it is reduced to a powerful, concentrated essence." The mezzo-soprano, who is renowned for her interpretations of Baroque and contemporary music, did not begin singing professionally until she was 30; prior to that, she performed as a violist with orchestras in San Francisco and Boston. Since her professional singing debut, in 1984, Hunt Lieberson has appeared with the Metropolitan Opera, the New York City Opera, and the San Francisco Opera, as well as with numerous orchestras and ensembles. She is particularly known for her performance as Dido in Hector Berlioz's *Les Troyens*, in both Scotland and New York, and for her singing of two Johann Sebastian Bach cantatas staged by Peter Sellars. The vocalist has chosen an unusual path to success; she has never signed a long-term contract with a recording label nor apprenticed with an opera house. Rather, she has built her reputation by appearing at small but important music festivals with ensembles that specialize in period pieces. In this way, Hunt Lieberson has become something of a cult figure among opera aficionados and critics alike. Rupert Christiansen, writing for the London *Daily Telegraph* (March 27, 2001), called her "one of the few truly great singers of our time," and Andrew Clements proclaimed in the London *Guardian* (December 18, 2003), "There is no better mezzo-soprano in the world today." "Hunt Lieberson is the best singer around these days . . . ," Alan Rich wrote for *LA Weekly* (October 18, 2002), "for her command of melodic line, of course, but also for her ability to make language itself a thing of special beauty." In 2001 she was named Vocalist of the Year by the performing-arts newspaper *Musical America*.

The eldest of four siblings, the singer was born Lorraine Hunt on March 1, 1954 in San Francisco, California, and raised in the Bay Area. Her father taught music in local high schools and conducted a community orchestra in his spare time; her mother was an accomplished vocalist who taught singing and often performed with her husband's orchestra. As a child Hunt Lieberson began playing the piano and, later, the violin. Her father was a perfectionist, and under his influence she practiced constantly. "He was very controlling and, at the same time, he couldn't seem to control his own anger. He was single-minded in his desire to develop my gifts . . . ," she told Charles Michener in an interview for the *New Yorker* (January 5, 2004). "He made me practice everything excruciatingly slowly so that there wouldn't be any mistakes. Mistakes were not a natural phenomenon in our house." As Hunt Lieberson revealed to Michener, her father's nature left its mark on her own personality; citing an example, she recalled attending a birthday party that she has "never forgotten": "A parent put a waltz on, and the kids began dancing. For some reason, I tried to choreograph everyone, and I got really high-powered about it. Finally, the birthday girl's mother took me aside and said gently, 'Maybe you should let everybody just do what they want.' It was a terrible moment of self-awareness." At the age of 12, Hunt Lieberson took up the viola; she was soon playing the instrument in a youth orchestra. The viola, which was originally used as an accompanying—rather than solo—instrument, "suited me better," she told Michener. "I wasn't very ambitious at the time, and I liked being the inner voice in a group." She also sang in several choirs during that period.

At San Jose State University, in California, Hunt Lieberson continued her studies on the viola, financing her education by playing with the San Jose Symphony. She also enrolled in the opera program at the university, later dropping her voice studies in favor of her extracurricular musical work. She explained to Michener that at the time, "I didn't feel close to opera, particularly since my father had made me sit and listen to the [Metropolitan Opera's] Saturday-afternoon broadcasts, sometimes with a score on my lap. Between that and the bad radio reception and some of the wobbly singers, I was mostly turned off." After college Hunt Lieberson formed a lounge act with a boyfriend who played jazz guitar, performing music by Stevie Wonder, Joni Mitchell, Chicago, and others. When her boyfriend was arrested in Mexico on marijuana charges, she and several other women bribed the guards to let them live with their boyfriends and husbands in makeshift structures on the prison grounds. "The guards were so corrupt that you could buy all sorts of favours . . . ," she recalled to Charlotte Higgins. "The guys were in an open yard with no roof. But you could bribe the guards to let you bring in building materials. One of the American prisoners was a carpenter, so we built these little shacks along the walls, fantastic shacks with doors and lofts."

During the late 1970s Hunt Lieberson worked as the principal violist in the Berkeley Free Orchestra. When the orchestra decided to put on a free performance of Engelbert Humperdinck's *Hansel and Gretel* at the state prison in San Quentin, California, she volunteered to play the part of the boy Hansel. "It was my first serious singing in six years," she told Charles Michener. "I found a short-haired wig at a Goodwill store, and I put on a pair of ripped pants and a big flannel shirt, because I couldn't figure out how to flatten my boobs." After ending her relationship with the jazz guitarist, Hunt Lieberson began dating a man who played the French horn with the Vancouver Symphony Orchestra. When the Boston Symphony Orchestra hired him as a musician, she moved east with him, planning to earn her living as a violist while taking voice lessons. After applying unsuccessfully to the famous Juilliard School, in New York City, she enrolled at the Boston Conservatory.

An audition for Craig Smith, the artistic director of the Boston ensemble Emmanuel Music, landed her the role of Tamiri in a concert performance of Wolfgang Amadeus Mozart's *Il re pastore* at the Castle Hill Festival in the summer of 1984, which marked the beginning of her professional singing career. The following year she played Sesto, the child of the murdered Pompey, who vows to avenge his father's death, in a Peter Sellars production of Georg Frideric Handel's *Julius Caesar,* held at the Pepsico Summerfare Festival in Purchase, New York. The role represented a coup for Hunt Lieberson, as Sellars is widely regarded as one of the world's most important directors of theater and opera; his innovative approach to both Western and non-Western works has garnered him a number of major awards. Talking with Michener, the director recalled Hunt Lieberson's audition: "She started singing, and you were in the middle of this raging forest fire. Certain things were a *little* out of control, but what you got was sheer power, sheer concentrated energy." Her reputation grew rapidly. In an article he wrote for *Musical America* (2001, on-line), the music critic Richard Dyer recalled that when he introduced the *New Yorker* critic Andrew Porter to the mezzo-soprano after a 1985 performance, Porter said to her, "It's a pleasure to meet America's greatest singer." Three years later a series of events prompted Hunt Lieberson to give up the viola entirely; she recalled to Rupert Christiansen that "at a time when I was beginning to get more work as a singer, my viola was stolen and I took that as a sign. I still have the occasional pang, especially if I'm singing with a string quartet."

Rather than serving an apprenticeship with an opera house, Hunt Lieberson sang with various period-instrument performance ensembles, such as the Paris-based Arts Florissants and the San Francisco–based Philharmonia Baroque. These collaborations allowed her to develop a unique repertoire of Baroque pieces. Although she had never studied Baroque vocal technique or theory, Hunt Lieberson effortlessly picked up the vocal style of the period. "I've never been scholarly in the bookwormy sort of way," she told K. Robert Schwarz in an interview for the *New York Times* (January 21, 1996). "I got a wonderful exposure to a heartfelt way of expressing Baroque music. It wasn't what you'd call a purist early-music style. It wasn't about using no vibrato. It was about singing this music with passion and heart. When you do that you don't necessarily have to study the style. The style just comes." In fact, one of Hunt Lieberson's hallmarks as a singer is the ability to imitate the vocal style of virtually every historical period and region. As Steven Blier, pianist and director of the New York Festival of Song, told Schwarz, "Lorraine is definitely channeling something, and where it comes from I can't tell you. The first thing I did with her was a Spanish program, and when Lorraine started singing, it was as authentic as if she had just whipped up a paella in four seconds flat. The whole stylistic smell of it was so right, it was the kind of thing you could never show anyone how to do."

Beginning in the mid-1980s, Hunt Lieberson appeared with various symphonies, orchestras, and opera companies around the world, solidifying her reputation among music enthusiasts as one of the most brilliant mezzo-sopranos of her generation. Her concert highlights included Gustav Mahler's Symphony no. 3, with the Boston Symphony Orchestra under James Levine; Gunnar Berg's *Seven Early Songs,* with the Berlin Philharmonic under Kent Nagano; Hector Berlioz's *Les Nuits d'été,* with the Philharmonia Baroque Orchestra under Nicholas McGegan; and Berlioz's *L'Enfance du Christ,* with the Orchestra of St. Luke's under Sir Charles Mackerras. Hunt Lieberson also made appearances at the Tanglewood festival, in Lenox, Massachusetts, at Carnegie Hall, in New York, and with the Boston Symphony Orchestra and the Los Angeles Chamber Orchestra. Her operatic work included Ottavia in Claudio Monteverdi's *L'Incoronazione di Poppea,* with the San Francisco Opera; Sesto in Mozart's *La Clemenza di Tito;* the title role in Handel's *Xerxes,* with the New York City Opera; the title role in Benjamin Britten's *The Rape of Lucretia,* at the Edinburgh Festival; and Irene in Handel's *Theodora* in a Peter Sellars production at the Glyndebourne Festival. Hunt Lieberson made her Metropolitan Opera debut in 1999, appearing as Myrtle Wilson in John Harbison's *The Great Gatsby,* based on the novel by F. Scott Fitzgerald; Harbison had written the part expressly for her.

One of Hunt Lieberson's most celebrated roles is that of Dido in Berlioz's *Les Troyens.* The opera, based on Virgil's *Aeneid,* tells the story of the fall of Troy and the subsequent wanderings of the Trojan prince Aeneas. Dido is the Queen of Carthage, a city believed to have been located in northern Africa; she becomes Aeneas's lover and, after he leaves her, kills herself on a sword he has left behind. Hunt Lieberson first performed the role at the Edinburgh International Festival, in Scotland, in 2001. In the *Guardian* (August 20, 2001), Tim Ashley described Hunt Lieberson's work as "the greatest performance of the role I have ever heard. Its force derives from her ability to generate overwhelming emotion by the sparsest of means. A simple walk across the platform denotes tremendous majesty. The droop of her head indicates terrible anguish. Phrases and words are etched with immaculate restraint until she gets to the final scene, when Dido's cries of misery seem ripped from her and she delivers the final prophecy in a voice that both is and is not her own." A year later the mezzo-soprano performed the role at the Metropolitan Opera, where, according to one report, the cast lined up to applaud her. "The Met's new *Troyens* is a tour de force," Justin Davidson opined in *Newsday* (February 13, 2003), "not just because of its complexity and scale, but also thanks to Lieberson's absolute technical control over her voice and body. Her ability to extract a character's con-

flicts puts her in a class with [the Academy Award–winning actress] Meryl Streep, but no other contemporary opera singer I can think of."

In 2001 Peter Sellars staged two of Johann Sebastian Bach's cantatas for Hunt Lieberson to perform with the Orchestra of Emmanuel Music under Craig Smith. In the first, Cantata no. 199, *"Mein Herze schwimmt im Blut"* ("My Heart Swims in Blood"), an anguished woman confesses her sin and finds joy in the salvation she envisions from God. Dressed in an aqua-blue gown and a rose-colored scarf, Hunt Lieberson used mime, gestures, and facial expressions to dramatize her singing. The second, no. 82, *"Ich habe genug"* ("I Have Enough"), tells the story of a dying woman's acceptance of death. As in the other cantata, Hunt Lieberson used extensive gestures in her performance, singing the piece while lying in bed, dressed in a hospital gown with medical tubes attached to her body. Some purists loathed Sellars's dramatic, over-the-top staging; in Paris, for example, the audience booed Sellars when he took his bow. But critics and audiences alike were rapturous about Hunt Lieberson's performance. "I don't normally believe in channeling," Mark Swed wrote for the *Los Angeles Times* (September 30, 2003) of her performance at Royce Hall at the University of California, Los Angeles, "but when the first indescribably physical sounds come out of her mouth, I am ready to believe anything. So strong, so vibrant and so utterly communicative, they are as if tones were made flesh. For half an hour, Royce Hall and all in it were in the thrall of an amazing, hypnotic artist at the absolute peak of her powers."

In September 2003 Nonesuch Records released an album of Hunt Lieberson's renditions of the cantatas, along with her interpretations of several others of Bach's songs. T.J. Medrek wrote in a review for the *Boston Herald* (September 23, 2003) that the recording offered "proof that perfection is possible. The Nonesuch disk captures the glorious mezzo at her finest. Her heartbreakingly beautiful voice, so filled with emotional depth, carries us along on two of Bach's most powerful journeys to hell and back."

The songs held personal significance for Hunt Lieberson: in 1999 one of her younger sisters had died of breast cancer, and one month before her death, the singer herself had been diagnosed with the disease. The cancer had not spread far, however, and after she underwent surgery and various homeopathic therapies, no signs of the cancer remained. She told Rupert Christiansen that her illness had served as a "gentle wake-up call" for her—a signal to begin taking care of herself, both physically and emotionally. "I hadn't realized what a screwed-up state I was in," she explained to him. "My immune system hadn't been functioning properly for years. I kept canceling performances or singing over low-grade flu, thinking that short-term measures like massage or acupuncture would help sort it all out. Now I feel truly well for the first time in 20 years. Blessings emerge from these terrible situations: I don't think I could have sung *Ich habe genug* while I was in the thick of all the pain and grief and bereavement: now it's become part of the healing process."

The singer's work in 2004 has included Mahler's Third Symphony, performed with the Philadelphia Orchestra under Christoph Eschenbach, and a recital of Spanish songs as part of a series called "Latin Evenings." Hunt Lieberson's many recordings of songs include a recital disk of works by Handel and Gustav Mahler for BBC Recordings, a disk of Robert Schumann songs for Koch Classics, and a recording of the music of John Harbison for Archetype Records. Her discography also includes *Idomeneo* for EMI, *Hippolyte et Aricie* and *Médée* for Erato, and *Ariodante, Susanna, Theodora, Messiah, Dido and Aeneas*, and *Anna Magdalena* for Harmonia Mundi. Hunt Lieberson's recording of Britten's *Phaedra* with the Halle Orchestra was nominated for a Grammy Award. The singer was seen on the television broadcasts and subsequent video releases of three Peter Sellars productions: *Don Giovanni, Theodora*, and *Giulio Cesare*.

Hunt Lieberson and her husband, the composer Peter Lieberson, live in Santa Fe, New Mexico. The couple met in 1997, when she appeared in his opera, *Ashoka's Dream*. Recently, in live performances, Hunt Lieberson has sung a number of Rainer Maria Rilke's poems, set to music composed by her husband.

—H.T.

Suggested Reading: (London) *Daily Telegraph* p21+ Mar. 27, 2001; (London) *Guardian* p6+ Aug. 8, 2003; *New York Times* II p29+ Jan. 21, 1996, with photo; *New Yorker* p42+ Jan. 5, 2004, with photo

Selected Recordings: *Handel Arias*, 1994; *Bach Cantatas*, 2003; *Handel—La Lucrezia & Arias from Serse*, 2004

Chris Hondros/Getty Images

Immelt, Jeffrey R.

(IM-mult)

Feb. 19, 1956– Chairman and CEO of General Electric Co.

Address: General Electric Co., 3135 Easton Turnpike, Fairfield, CT 06431

On September 7, 2001 Jeffrey R. Immelt became chairman and chief executive officer (CEO) of General Electric Co. (G.E.), one of the world's largest corporations, with more than 300,000 employees in at least 100 countries. Best known to consumers for its popular line of home appliances, G.E. has numerous subsidiaries, including the National Broadcasting Co. (NBC), one of the "big three" broadcasting networks in the U.S.; G.E. Medical Systems; and G.E. Capital Corp., a financial-services company. Immelt took over his duties from Jack Welch, one of the corporate world's most accomplished executives, and has since faced a plethora of challenges—including a national economic downturn, recent scandals involving companies' reporting of their finances, and the September 11, 2001 terrorist attacks, which killed thousands of people and precipitated a sharp decline in the company's stock value. Immelt has addressed these crises by increasing security at G.E.'s facilities throughout the world, to counter the threat of terrorism; appointing independent members to G.E.'s board and opening the company's books to a higher level of scrutiny, in order to restore investor confidence; and increasing capital investment, or funds earmarked for research and development, part of his plan to bring about a double-digit increase in the value of the company's stock.

Immelt began his career with G.E. in 1982, holding a variety of positions in the company's plastics division over the next few years. In 1989 he advanced to the position of vice president for consumer services with G.E. Appliances; two years later came his appointment as vice president of worldwide marketing and product management. After serving successively over the next several years as head of G.E. Plastics Americas' Commercial Division, vice president and general manager of G.E. Plastics Americas, and head of G.E. Medical Systems, Immelt—emerging from a fierce internal competition—was elected the ninth chairman and CEO of G.E., the company founded in 1892 by, among others, the inventor Thomas Alva Edison. Immelt told Mike Boyer for the *Cincinnati Enquirer* (September 9, 2001) about G.E., "It's a great company. It's a company that's been a big part of my life. I love the company completely, and I think I have the best job on Earth."

The younger of two sons, Jeffrey R. Immelt was born on February 19, 1956 in Cincinnati, Ohio, to Joseph Immelt, an engineer in G.E.'s Aircraft Engines division, and Bonnie Immelt, a teacher. He told Mike Boyer, "My parents from the very earliest age said you can do whatever you put your mind to. I always had an environment around me that was never negative, that was always stretch." ("Stretch" is a term used by many at G.E. to refer to thinking positively and on a grand scale.) Immelt also said to Boyer that as a boy he was "a classic younger brother" who "always wanted to do everything [his] older brother did and wanted to compete with him." (Immelt's brother, Stephen, is now a lawyer.) Immelt attended Finneytown High School, where he distinguished himself as both a good student and all-around athlete and graduated in 1974. He then enrolled at Dartmouth College, in Hanover, New Hampshire; there, he became president of the Phi Delta Alpha fraternity, received an award for character, and earned a bachelor of science degree in economics and applied mathematics in 1978. Immelt, who is six feet four inches tall, also played offensive line on the school's football team. Buddy Teevens, the football team's quarterback, told Mike Boyer about Immelt, "He always had a knack when things were tense to crack a one-liner in the huddle that would relax everybody. You won't find anybody on the team who won't have a good thing to say about Jeff."

After graduating, Immelt worked for about two years at Procter and Gamble, maker of a wide variety of household and other products, which, he told Boyer, "gave me a great foundation. Great business discipline, and I met a lot of terrific people." Immelt then attended Harvard University, in Cambridge, Massachusetts, earning a master's in business administration. While there he worked on a consulting project for G.E., after which the company offered Immelt a position in its plastics division, in 1982. At the time, Immelt revealed to Boyer, "I figured I'd stay five years and figure out where I really wanted to go." Instead, Immelt began a steady rise in the company. As vice president for consumer services at G.E. Appliances, beginning in 1989, he helped organize a recall of more than one million malfunctioning G.E. refrigerator compressors—a highly difficult task that saw him, in his words, go "from being a boy to a man," as *Time* (September 10, 2001, on-line) reported. (In an echo of that comment, Len Vickers, Immelt's first boss at G.E., told Mike Boyer, "What separates the men from the boys, in my opinion, are imagination and willpower. I think [Immelt] has them both.") According to *Time*, during the recall Immelt helped

boost the spirits of employees by giving inspirational speeches from atop forklifts on the shop floor, and on some occasions he even put on a G.E. service uniform to accompany repair staff on visits to customers' homes. (A "nervous eater," as *Time* reported, Immelt temporarily gained a good deal of weight during that stressful period; when he left G.E. Appliances, his co-workers gave him a cartoon showing him in his office, "harried and surrounded by junk food.")

Next, in 1991, Immelt was appointed to the position of vice president of worldwide marketing and product management. In the following year he became vice president and general manager of G.E.'s Plastics Americas Commercial Division. In that job, Immelt was charged with raising the prices of products sold to customers including the General Motors Corp. His initial failure to persuade customers to accept the price hike led Jack Welch, the CEO of G.E., to put a great deal of pressure on him. As reported by Diane Brady in *BusinessWeek* (April 29, 2002), the situation grew so tense that Immelt "almost came to blows" with a General Motors executive before the automaker approved Immelt's plan to increase its productivity and agreed to the price hike. Immelt's then-boss, Gary L. Rogers, told Brady, "There were a lot of bruised feelings. Jeff learned that while it's important to be customer-friendly, sometimes the situation requires you to do things that aren't going to delight them." Immelt recalls, according to Brady, that the experience "toughened him up." In addition, his success greatly impressed Welch; in 1993 Immelt became vice president and general manager of Plastics Americas. Four years later he was named president of G.E. Medical Systems, a post in which he oversaw a $2 billion increase in sales of medical diagnostic equipment, to $7 billion. Discussing the variety of positions he had held in the company in previous years, Immelt told Mike Boyer, "It was a gas. I loved what I did. I had great bosses in a series of great jobs. That's what happens, you put your nose down, learn a lot, like what you do and success takes care of itself."

In November 2000 Immelt was appointed CEO and chairman-elect of the board of General Electric, a corporation ranked sixth on the *Fortune 500* list. He was to succeed Jack Welch, who had enjoyed a reputation as a highly effective chief executive. When Immelt took on his new duties, Michael Hammer, a management consultant, told Claudia H. Deutsch for the *New York Times* (September 6, 2001), "Jeff Immelt has to demonstrate quickly that G.E.'s excellent institutionalized management system, not Jack Welch, set G.E. apart from other conglomerates." In a talk with Peter Behr for the *Washington Post* (November 28, 2000), Noel Tichy, a University of Michigan business professor who heads G.E.'s leadership-training program, discussed Immelt's taking the reins of the highly successful company, comparing it to "taking over the Chicago Bulls [basketball team] at their peak. You have a high risk of slipping. It won't happen overnight, but in time [Immelt will] have to ratchet [G.E.] up to the next level of performance." For his part, Immelt expressed optimism and viewed G.E.'s strong position in a positive light, telling Claudia H. Deutsch, "I'm inheriting a company with no burning platform, no business sucking up cash, every business returning its cost of capital." Indicating that G.E. might well expand further, he added, "This isn't a $130 billion one-product company, but a group of businesses operating in growing industries."

On September 11, 2001, the third day of Immelt's tenure as CEO, terrorists attacked the World Trade Center, in New York City, and the Pentagon, outside Washington, D.C. Immelt immediately made a $10 million company donation to the families of rescue workers who died at the World Trade Center and sent G.E. medical equipment and mobile generators to the Trade Center site. When trading resumed at the New York Stock Exchange, six days after the attacks, G.E.'s stock value had fallen by 20 percent, which translated into an $80 billion decline in the value of the company. G.E.'s jet-engine business suffered a sharp decline in sales, and NBC sacrificed $50 million in profits to provide continuous, advertisement-free news broadcasts following the tragedy. The national economic downturn—to which the events of September 2001 contributed—hit the company's stock hard: a 39 percent decline in its value carried over into 2002, a year in which the company saw its smallest gain in net income since 1993.

To stimulate growth, Immelt directed G.E. to spend $2.6 billion on research and development in 2002 and made capital investments in its technology centers throughout the world, including $60 million to build a new center in Shanghai, China, $52 million for a research facility at the Technical University of Munich, in Germany, a multimillion-dollar investment in its Japanese research center, and a $100 million renovation of the company's Global Research headquarters, in upstate New York. As a result, G.E. was awarded more than 1,400 patents in 2002. Immelt told Ron Insana for *Money* (September 2002), "When you look at how G.E. has been put together, you'll see that we are a long-term player in every industry were in. We've really invented most of these industries. We haven't acquired our way into any specific business, except maybe for NBC; we've developed these businesses from the ground up, whether they're in G.E. Capital or the G.E. industrial businesses."

General Electric faces a host of other challenges, including negotiations with the unionized segments of its labor force. One subject of contention involves increases in co-payments for medical expenses; G.E. executives have sought to shift part of the rising costs onto employees, with union representatives insisting that they have already been hurt by the increases. In addition, the unions wish G.E. executives to remain neutral with regard to the recruiting of union members in newly acquired divisions of the company. Immelt, however, has directed management to signal its displeasure with employees' choosing union membership.

Following recent episodes in which large companies—most prominently, the energy company Enron—misrepresented the states of their finances, bankrupting investors as a result, Immelt implemented a disclosure plan for G.E. In addition, he filed a sworn statement with the Securities and Exchange Commission, affirming the accuracy of the company's recent financial statements. Henry T. C. Hu, a security and corporate law professor at the University of Texas at Austin, told Ben White for the *Washington Post* (August 1, 2002), "This certification is a big step. Immelt is putting his money where his mouth is." As for the financial picture at G.E., "the persistently sluggish economy has hurt sales of such disparate G.E. items as plastics and aircraft engines," as Claudia H. Deutsch reported in the *New York Times* (October 11, 2003). She added that while the company's revenue (or total earnings) in the third quarter of 2003 stood at $33.39 billion, 2 percent higher than in the same period in 2002, net earnings (or earnings remaining after expenses) had fallen from $4.09 billion in the third quarter of 2002 to $3.65 billion in the same period in 2003. A hopeful sign came in mid-January 2004, when the value of G.E.'s stock rose $1.18 a share, to $33.18. Meanwhile, G.E. had made acquisitions in the fall of 2003 aimed at long-term growth: the Medical Systems division purchased Instrumentarium, a Finnish maker of hospital equipment, and NBC merged with Vivendi Universal's entertainment assets, a deal that brought a large collection of films and new television shows under the ownership of G.E.

In October 2004 G.E. announced that its third-quarter earnings showed an increase in profits of 11 percent—the largest gain since Immelt assumed leadership of the company. Later that same month, Immelt announced G.E.'s plans to invest up to $100 million in Russia's railway and energy sectors.

Jeffrey R. Immelt met his wife, Andrea, while they were both working at G.E. Plastics in the 1980s; they have a teenage daughter, Sarah. Immelt often works seven days a week, sometimes as much as 20 hours a day, and spends approximately 70 percent of his time traveling to various G.E. facilities throughout the world. In his limited free time, he enjoys playing golf.

—L.A.S.

Suggested Reading: (Albany, New York) *Times Union* V p1 Feb. 16, 2003; *Business Week* p86+ Apr. 29, 2002; *Business Week* (on-line) Sep. 5, 2001; *Money* p67+ Sep. 2002; *New York Times* III p1 Sep. 6, 2001, with photo; *Washington Post* V p1 Nov. 28, 2000

Courtesy of RCA Label Group

Jackson, Alan

Oct. 17, 1958– Country singer; songwriter; guitarist

Address: c/o Arista Records, 6 W. 57th St., New York, NY 10019

The country singer, songwriter, and guitarist Alan Jackson seems the physical embodiment of the songs he sings: genuine, unpretentious, and traditional. "Jackson is low-key and relaxed, striving to balance career demands with his family life," Randy Lewis wrote for the *Los Angeles Times* (July 31, 1994). "He's not given to grand gestures or controversy, and he plays it straight and simple on stage. . . . And instead of cultivating celebrity with a high profile, he heads for the hills at every opportunity." Jackson's down-to-earth demeanor and accidental-heartthrob persona have only increased his appeal. In another article for the *Los Angeles Times* (November 19, 1994), Lewis proposed that qualities such as Jackson's "gawrsh-ma'am sincerity and [his] Gary Cooper-like decency . . . are every bit as important to Jackson's remarkable commercial success as his singing or his songwriting." By injecting his own brand of humor and sympathy, particularly toward women, into his music while still adhering to traditional country roots, Jackson has earned numerous fans and accolades. Over the 14 years since he made his debut, with the album *Here in the Real World* (1990), his recordings have enjoyed a position at or near the top of the country-music chart; among them are such albums as *Don't Rock the Jukebox* (1991), *Who I Am* (1994), *When Somebody Loves You* (2000), and *Drive* (2002). Jackson recently won his

first Grammy Award, for best country song of 2003, with "Where Were You (When the World Stopped Turning)," which expressed his emotional reaction to the terrorist attacks of September 11, 2001.

The youngest—and the only male—among five children, Alan Eugene Jackson was born on October 17, 1958 in Newnan, Georgia, the son of Eugene Jackson, a mechanic for the Ford Motor Co., and Ruth (Musick) Jackson, a homemaker. His sisters are Diane, Connie, and twins, Cathy and Carol. The Jackson children grew up in a house that their grandfather had converted from an old tool shed; many of their relatives lived on adjacent plots of land. Referring to the 1970s TV show about a large, rural Depression-era family, Jackson told Richard Cromelin for the *Los Angeles Times* (July 31, 1994), "We were like the Waltons kind of. The family and all my cousins lived around us, my grandmother lived next door. I feel like sometimes I grew up in a time warp where I was 30 years behind other people." Jackson's family was not particularly musical; his earliest memories related to music are of watching the television shows *Hee Haw*, a country-music and comedy program, and *Gospel Jubilee*. He recalled on countrystars.com (on-line), "My daddy watched *Hee Haw* religiously, every week. So I watched it, too. My daddy doesn't say much, but I remember one time when [the co-host] Buck Owens was playing he said, 'You ought to be one of them singers,' or something like that. I don't know why that struck me, but it did."

Jackson gave his first performance in a fourth-grade talent show, singing "Li'l Red Riding Hood," by the 1960s rock-and-roll band Sam the Sham and the Pharaohs. Jackson attended Newnan High School, where he formed a folk-country duo with a girl who played the guitar and sang harmony. At the age of 16 or 17, with an older boy who played guitar, he started a band that played at private parties and local pizza parlors. After graduating from high school, Jackson attended West Georgia College for a year before dropping out. He married his high-school sweetheart, Denise, on December 15, 1979; while she worked as a schoolteacher, he took a variety of jobs, such as forklift driver at Kmart, construction worker, and car salesman. He also played with a band called Dixie Steel in local clubs and attended country-music concerts, which inspired him to pursue a career in music. He said to Richard Cromelin, "I decided, 'I'm gonna move to Nashville and just give it a try.' A buddy of mine said he was gonna be an airplane pilot . . . and the next thing I know he was workin' for American Airlines. You know, he had a dream and he went for it and he made it. I said I need to at least give mine a shot. I'd never been to Nashville, or hardly anywhere. I told my wife I wanted to sell everything and move, and everybody thought I was crazy."

Jackson was further encouraged in his plan by a fortuitous chance encounter: while Denise was working as a flight attendant with the now-defunct Piedmont Airlines, she spotted the actor and country singer Glen Campbell in the Atlanta airport and asked for his help in fostering her husband's career. Campbell gave her his card and agreed to listen to a demo tape of Jackson's music. A week later the Jacksons moved to Nashville, Tennessee, the center of the country-music scene, where Jackson got a job working in the mailroom of the Nashville Network cable channel (TNN), which is now defunct. Within a year he was writing songs for Campbell's music-publishing company, but he was still having no luck in signing a record deal. After another four years, Jackson, nearly ready to give up, collaborated with a producer, Keith Stegall, on one final set of demos—recordings of a live performance. Those recordings attracted the attention of executives at Arista Records; when Arista's founder, Clive Davis, decided to open a Nashville office, he signed Jackson as the first artist on the Arista Nashville label. The president of Arista at the time, Tim DuBois, told Richard Cromelin, "I don't know why everybody passed, but I do know why I signed [Jackson]. . . . I saw in him a unique writing talent, coupled with an identifiable voice. . . . There was a simplicity in what he did and what he said as a writer that really attracted me. He hadn't been in Nashville so long that he had been polluted by the way we Nashville tunesmiths write things. . . . He was still doing things a little bit different. It was neat and it was fresh."

In February 1990 Arista released Jackson's first album, *Here in the Real World*, which was well received both critically and popularly. Reviewers praised Jackson's sincere, unshowy delivery, catchy tunes, and classic-country leanings, and by 1994 the album had been certified double platinum (meaning that it had sold more than two million copies). It also spawned five hit singles: "Chasin' That Neon Rainbow," "Blue Blooded Woman," "Here in the Real World," "Wanted," and "I'd Love You All Over Again." After the release of *Here in the Real World*, Jackson became quite prolific. His second album, *Don't Rock the Jukebox*, reached stores in 1991; it produced five number-one hits: "Someday," "Midnight in Montgomery," "Don't Rock the Jukebox," "Dallas," and "Love's Got a Hold on You." Jackson followed that album with *A Lot About Livin' (and a Little 'Bout Love)* in 1992, which boasted three number-one hits, including "Chattahoochee," a nostalgic rockabilly tune. Next came *Honky Tonk Christmas* (1993); *Who I Am* (1994), containing such hits as "Gone Country," which describes the then-trendy leanings toward country in pop music; *Greatest Hits* (1995); *Everything I Love* (1996); *High Mileage* (1998); *Super Hits* and *Under the Influence* (both 1999); *When Somebody Loves You* (2000); *Drive*, for which Jackson wrote the title song to honor his father, who died in 2000, and *Let It Be Christmas* (both in 2002); *Greatest Hits Volume II* (2003); and *What I Do* (2004). In total, 29 of Jackson's songs have reached the number-one spot on the country chart, 21 of them written by Jackson. In addition to releasing his own albums, he has contributed tracks to a variety of compilations and has performed with other artists, ranging from George Jones to Jeff Foxworthy to the Chipmunks. Occasionally, he has written songs for other performers, too; he wrote "I Can't Do That Anymore" for Faith Hill, for example. Jackson's popularity with audiences has held steady, while most critics have grown increasingly less enthusiastic about his work, characterizing it as inoffensive but shallow and bland. In a representative assessment, Mike Boehm wrote for the *Los Angeles Times* (November 21, 1993), "Jackson's success has been predicated on pleasantly catchy, mildly witty material that never seeks to dig beneath the surface of everyday human interactions." Similarly, Randy Black, in the *Los Angeles Times* (October 18, 1992), described Jackson as a performer who "continues to vacillate between being a writer who wants to tap his own experience and a singer who can't resist a catchy phrase, even at the expense of the truth."

One of Jackson's best-known songs is "Where Were You (When the World Stopped Turning)," a commentary on the terrorist attacks of September 11, 2001, in which nearly 3,000 people died. Although some critics considered it jingoistic and sentimental, "Where Were You" was immensely popular; a day after Jackson first performed it live, at the 2001 Country Music Association (CMA) Awards ceremony, requests for the song, which had not yet been released as a single, began pouring in to radio stations. The demand was so great that radio stations downloaded recordings of the live version from the awards ceremony in order to play it on the air. Jackson had not originally planned to release the song as a single at all, as he did not want to appear to be capitalizing on a tragedy. When "Where Were You" later won the CMA award for song of the year, Jackson commented, as reported by Richard Cromelin in the *Los Angeles Times* (May 23, 2002), "I've always felt uncomfortable about the attention this song has brought to me, and I guess I was always uncomfortable about what it was written about." The song also brought Jackson his first Grammy, for best country song of 2003.

In addition to enjoying Jackson's music, fans (especially female fans) value the sensitivity reflected in his music and—much to his puzzlement—regard Jackson as a sex symbol. In *USA Today* (July 6, 1993), David Zimmerman quoted Jackson as saying, "I never thought I was hideous, but I never thought I was good-looking. It's a mystery to me. I see myself loping across the stage in some of those videos and I'm embarrassed." To devotees, though, he is, as Zimmerman put it, "a pure-country torchbearer and undisputed heartthrob." The six-foot four-inch singer adopted his signature long, blond hair and white Stetson hat not out of vanity but for practical reasons, as he told Cynthia Sanz and Jane Sanderson for *People* (September 2, 1991): the hat covers scars above his left eyebrow ("reminders of childhood run-ins with a door and a coffee table," as Sanz and Sanderson reported), and the hair reflects aspects of his earlier years ("When I was playing in them dives, it got to where I just never did get my hair cut"). Jackson speculated to Zimmerman that his appeal to women may be related to his having four older sisters, and that his songs convey his ability to sympathize with them: "I watched them grow up and date their boyfriends and get married. I guess maybe I learned a little bit from that."

Jackson's fans are also enamored of his unassuming, sincere persona. He is a strong adherent to traditional country music and shows respect for his predecessors in the field; at the same time, he retains a sense of fun. For example, during the 1999 CMA ceremony, Jackson stopped in the middle of performing his own music and began playing the country legend George Jones's "Choices," in honor of Jones, who had declined to appear at the ceremony when asked to shorten his performance of the song there to under a minute. So noncompetitive is Jackson that he was reportedly regretful when his album *Drive* ousted an album by the music group Creed from the number-one spot on *Billboard*'s pop chart after a two-month reign in 2002. "Somebody said they were going for a record number of weeks or something, and I knocked 'em out. I kind of hated to do it. They're a new act, I guess, and it's probably a big thing for them," Jackson told Chris Willman for *Entertainment Weekly* (March 15, 2002). Jackson's live shows focus primarily on music rather than spectacle; backed by his band, the Strayhorns, Jackson does not dance or wear flashy, rhinestone-studded clothes, as many other country performers do. Similarly, the visual effects at his concerts are limited to screens that flash a mix of live concert footage and Jackson's music videos. Lorraine Ali, in *Newsweek* (February 18, 2002), quoted Jackson as saying, "I'm not a big showman. I'm a singer-songwriter kind of guy. They use big lights and video to try to make me look excitin', but it's still just me standing there in the end." While some critics have complained about what they see as the blandness of his concerts, many find Jackson's simplicity and straightforwardness to be refreshing and his performance style to be none the worse for lack of embellishment.

Jackson has contributed to the long-running radio show *Grand Ole Opry* since 1991. In addition to a Grammy, he has won more than 50 other major honors, including those from the CMA and the American Society of Composers, Authors and Publishers (ASCAP) as well as American Music Awards and TNN/Music City News Awards.

Jackson and his wife, Denise, live in Nashville with their three daughters, Mattie Denise, Alexandra Jane (called Ali), and Dani Grace. In his free time Jackson pilots airplanes and collects and refurbishes vintage cars.

—K.J.E.

Suggested Reading: alanjackson.com; countrystars.com; *Entertainment Weekly* p26+ Mar. 15, 2002, with photos; *Los Angeles Times* p4 July 31, 1994; *People* p76+ Sep. 2, 1991, with photos

Selected Recordings: *Here in the Real World*, 1990; *Don't Rock the Jukebox*, 1991; *A Lot About Livin' (And a Little 'Bout Love)*, 1992; *Honky Tonk Christmas*, 1993; *Who I Am*, 1994; *Greatest Hits*, 1995; *Everything I Love*, 1996; *High Mileage*, 1998; *Super Hits*, 1999; *Under the Influence*, 1999; *When Somebody Loves You*, 2000; *Drive*, 2002; *Let It Be Christmas*, 2002; *Greatest Hits Volume II*, 2003; *What I Do*, 2004

Stephanie Gross, courtesy of the University of Virginia

Jagger, Janine

1950(?)– Epidemiologist; inventor; educator

Address: International Health Care Worker Safety Center, P.O. Box 800764, Charlottesville, VA 22908-0764

The epidemiologist Janine Jagger began her work to prevent so-called needlestick injuries—those caused by accidental pricks with contaminated syringe needles or other medical equipment—in 1985, when the "first red flags were going up on exposure to AIDS," as she recalled in an interview with the MedTech1 Web site (February 15, 2001). Doctors, nurses, and other medical personnel had been at risk of contracting such diseases as hepatitis B and C from needle pricks for many years, but after the emergence of AIDS (Acquired

Immune Deficiency Syndrome), in the early 1980s, fears of the repercussions of such injuries intensified greatly. Yet the only advice for health-care workers was to be careful around "sharps" (needles, scalpels, and other sharp medical or surgical instruments that can pierce the skin). "There were even punitive policies in some hospitals," Jagger told *Needlestick Safety News* in a profile of her for the Needlestick Forum (May 21–27, 2002, on-line). "If you reported a needlestick injury more than once you were a problem, and there would be notes entered in your records." Drawing from her experience in designing products to reduce the risks of brain damage caused by automobile accidents, she suggested that needlestick problems stemmed not from workers' carelessness but from faulty medical devices. Because data for such injuries were unavailable at the time, Jagger created EPINet, a computerized system of collecting and sharing such information, and was soon designing safer medical products to reduce the rate of health-care workers' exposure to blood-borne pathogens. Some experts estimate that each year, more than 500,000 U.S. health-care workers are stuck by contaminated needles or other sharps. "These are people who take care of us when we are ill," she told William Carlsen for the *San Francisco Chronicle* (April 14, 1998). "And yet they are expected to put their lives and health in danger to do it. When I realized how preventable needle sticks were, I felt something had to be done." Jagger, who has patents for five safety needles, received a so-called genius grant from the MacArthur Foundation in 2002.

Janine Jagger was born in about 1950 and raised in New Jersey. One of her grandfathers invented and patented a submarine detector in 1917. Jagger received a bachelor's degree in psychology from Moravian College, in Bethlehem, Pennsylvania, in 1972 and a master's degree in public health from the University of Pittsburgh, also in Pennsylvania, in 1979. She worked as a research associate at Yale University, in New Haven, Connecticut, in 1978; the following year she joined the medical faculty at the University of Virginia at Charlottesville, where she received a Ph.D. in epidemiology in 1987. Jagger is currently the Becton Dickinson Professor of Health Care Worker Safety, professor of internal medicine, and director of the International Health Care Worker Safety Center at the University of Virginia School of Medicine.

Jagger has specialized in injury prevention and control since the beginning of her career. Prior to the mid-1980s, her research and advocacy focused on brain trauma and motor-vehicle safety; in particular, she studied air-bag design and use and the prevention of brain injuries. She shifted focus to preventing needlestick injuries after several health-care workers in the U.S. were infected with HIV (the human immunodeficiency virus, which causes AIDS) after accidentally sticking themselves with needles contaminated with the blood of infected patients. In the automobile industry, products that could potentially cause injury to drivers and passengers were altered to reduce that risk, but in the infection-control field, injuries were often blamed on "accident-prone" employees rather than on faulty or dangerous equipment. "I just took this bold leap into the dark," Jagger told a writer for the Associated Press, as reported by the Newport News, Virginia, *Daily Press* (October 1, 2002). "We looked at the design features of needles related to injury risk."

In 1985 Jagger began to chart relationships between needlestick injuries and the incidence of transmissible diseases among health-care employees, collecting data from hospitals, clinics, and other health-care facilities and assessing not only the transmission of blood-borne diseases such as AIDS and hepatitis but also the psychological effects of such injuries on workers. She carried out the first investigation of accidental needlestick injuries to uncover what circumstances precipitated the injuries. Conducted at the University of Virginia, the study noted the circumstances of each injury and the instruments involved. In August 1988 Jagger and her colleagues published a landmark paper in the *New England Journal of Medicine* that detailed characteristics of medical devices known to cause needlestick injuries among health-care workers; it also outlined criteria for protective needle designs. The paper concluded that a significant portion of needlestick injuries were caused by poorly designed needles and clinical tools rather than workers' carelessness. The article spurred the creation of a new generation of safer medical devices; since 1988 approximately 2,000 U.S. patents have been issued for safer needle devices.

In 1991 Jagger developed the Exposure Prevention Information Network (EPINet) surveillance system, a standardized computer system for health-care facilities to track needlestick injuries and workers' exposures to blood and other body fluids. The EPINet system became available to health-care facilities in 1992 and is currently used by more than 1,500 facilities in the United States and around the world. EPINet also provides a data-sharing network, in which participating hospitals (currently more than 50) make available information about needlestick injuries in their facilities. EPINet contains almost 12 years' worth of data from 84 hospitals; it is the largest continuous database to monitor the occurrences of needlestick injuries suffered by health-care workers in the United States. By keeping track of how needlestick injuries occur, Jagger has helped engineers develop better medical tools. In 1992, on a tiny budget, Jagger founded the International Health Care Worker Safety Center at the University of Virginia, to disseminate the findings of EPINet and to accelerate medical facilities' adoption of safety technology.

When Jagger began her research, the federal Centers for Disease Control and Prevention (CDC) and the Food and Drug Administration (FDA) were not collecting statistics on the epidemic of needlestick injuries, and even now the CDC does not keep track of the number of health-care workers who have contracted hepatitis C or HIV from sharps or the annual rate of needlestick injuries in the United States. Jagger lobbied for federal legislation requiring all health-care centers to provide safe medical devices and promote safe techniques for their staffs. The Needlestick Safety and Prevention Act, which became law in 2001, contains guidelines for accomplishing those ends. Its passage marked the first time since 1970 that Occupational Health and Safety Administration (OSHA) rules regarding measures to prevent the spread of blood-borne pathogens had been updated. Because hospitals undergo frequent inspections, most of them quickly adopted new safety measures and enforced the proper use of safety devices. According to Jagger, however, hospital administrators who "are very supportive of worker safety issues . . . are in the minority," as she told Rick Dana Barlow for *Materials Management in Health Care* (May 2001). Workers' compensation rules preclude employees from suing their employers for failure to buy better equipment. (Only manufacturers of devices that harm workers can be sued.) Clinics and doctors' offices are inspected less often than hospitals; thus, administrators and workers in those places are more likely to ignore the law or to delay implementing new procedures. Even in places that have made good-faith efforts to comply with the law, some health-care workers do not use safety devices properly; for various reasons, many anesthesiologists have refused to use safe IV catheters, for example, and in many cases the staffs of laboratories that analyze blood have resisted using new, safer equipment.

A particularly dangerous type of sharp is the suture needle, commonly used in surgery. According to Jagger, such needles could be replaced with blunt suture needles, surgical staples, or tissue adhesives. Also hazardous are glass capillary tubes—tiny glass tubes used to draw blood from patients' fingers. The tubes shatter easily; Jagger has estimated that each year, broken tubes cause about 2,800 injuries. Simple alternatives exist—plastic tubes or glass tubes wrapped in puncture-resistant film—but in part because they cost a little more than bare glass, three-quarters of the 110 million capillary tubes sold in the U.S. annually are the bare-glass type. Jagger also believes that medical personnel should wear two pairs of gloves while performing surgery, and that laboratory workers should wear long gloves and forearm covers, since standard lab coats and gloves, particularly when worn incorrectly, may fail to fully protect such employees from exposure to blood and other body fluids. Many phlebotomists (technicians who draw blood), preferring to locate veins with a bare index finger, cut off the tips of those fingers of their gloves, and workers often roll up the sleeves of their lab coats, both for ease of movement and to keep sleeves out of the way of equipment. In addition, most lab coats are made of cotton or a cotton/polyester blend, fabrics that may not provide an effective barrier to spilled fluids.

While there is evidence from clinical trials that using safer sharps reduces needlestick injuries significantly, Jagger does not have enough data from the field to form broad conclusions about the effectiveness of such equipment; among other problems, many facilities do not report all such injuries. "It is really hard to document in a sound epidemiological way because there were no surveillance systems before, and [documentation] only started in a collective way in 1993," she told *Needlestick Safety News*. A report in *Advances in Exposure Prevention*, however, offered evidence of a dramatic drop in needlestick injuries from 1993 to 2001. The rate of such injuries "is probably still going down, but there are other factors besides devices that play a role," Jagger told Sandy Smith for *Occupational Hazards* (July 1, 2003). "While the risk of American health care workers getting stuck by a device is lower, because of changes in the health care system, the length of hospital stays is shorter. Nurses and other health care providers see more patients in a shorter period of time and the intensity of care has increased. To some degree, these changes may offset the benefits of safer needle devices." In addition, one-third of health-care workers have not been vaccinated for hepatitis B, although OSHA requires that hospitals offer the vaccine to employees at no cost. Jagger has also warned that hepatitis C, a more deadly form of the disease and one for which no vaccine yet exists, is "the sleeping giant of occupational risk," as William Carlsen put it. Other diseases that can be transmitted through needlesticks include syphilis, malaria, tuberculosis, streptococcal and staphylococcal sepsis, Rocky Mountain spotted fever, herpes, hepatitis D and G, babesiosis, brucellosis, leptospirosis, arboviral infections, relapsing fever, Creutzfeld-Jakob disease, and fevers caused by the Ebola virus.

The potential for conflicts of interest has led to criticism of Jagger for accepting funding from medical-device manufacturers such as Becton Dickinson, which established a chair for her at the University of Virginia and underwrites EPINet. Critical of manufacturers years ago, Jagger now finds them sympathetic to her cause; thanks to growing awareness of the magnitude of the needlestick problem, many manufacturers have begun to sell safer products. "Hospitals have been the biggest barrier to the adoption of safety-engineered needles and sharp devices," she told the MedTech1 Web site. "The medical device industry has been ahead of the curve all the way back to the late 1980s. They were putting safer devices into the marketplace before the regulatory agencies acknowledged the devices and included them in their regulatory statutes. The medical device industry has been pushing this technology through their usual marketing methods. Many of the devices are more expensive than conventional devices—not all of them, but some of them. They have been pushing against hospitals' cost control resistance."

Under Jagger's direction the International Health Care Worker Safety Center staff has grown to six and conducts original field research, studies legal problems that result from needlestick injuries, and publishes a bimonthly journal, *Advances in Exposure Prevention*, of which she is editor in chief. She received a Distinguished Inventor Award from the group Intellectual Property Owners in 1988 and the President's Award from the American Academy of Pediatrics in 1989. Safety devices she designed were part of a display assembled by the U.S. Patent and Trademark Office for its 1990 Bicentennial Exhibit. Among her other honors are the Henderson Inventor of the Year Award from the University of Virginia Patent Foundation (1996) and an Excellence in Research Award from the Association of Operating Room Nurses (1998). Jagger was recognized as a "MedTech Hero" for March 2001 by the Advanced Medical Technology Association, the largest medical-technology trade association in the world. In 2002 she was named a MacArthur Foundation fellow; the prestigious MacArthur "genius" grant amounted to $500,000. Jagger announced that she would use the money to finance ongoing projects supported by the International Health Care Worker Safety Center and expand the center's work in other countries.

Jagger is married to Patrice Guyenet, a French-born professor of pharmacology at the University of Virginia School of Medicine. Jagger and Guyenet have patented several devices jointly. The couple, who have two children, live in Charlottesville, Virginia.

—K.E.D.

Suggested Reading: MedTech 1 Web site Feb. 15, 2001; *Needlestick Safety News* May 21–27, 2002; *San Francisco Chronicle* A p6 Apr. 14, 1998, with photo; University of Virginia Web site

Courtesy of ACTA Publications

James, Bill

Oct. 5, 1949– Baseball statistician and writer; senior baseball-operations adviser with the Boston Red Sox

Address: c/o Boston Red Sox, 4 Yawkey Way, Boston, MA 02215-3496

In 1977, while employed at a pork-and-beans plant, the baseball pundit Bill James self-published *The Baseball Abstract*, a photocopied, 68-page treatise on the game. Advertised in the back pages of the *Sporting News* and selling for $3 a copy, *The Baseball Abstract* offered offbeat observations derived from arcane baseball statistics, which James used as evidence to debunk some of the sport's time-honored assumptions. Within a few years James's annual abstract had become an unlikely best-seller, and over time his rigorous analytical approach to baseball caught on not only with readers but with players, coaches, and officials, making James perhaps the most influential baseball writer of our time. His books—most notably *The Bill James Historical Baseball Abstract* (1985)—spurred a widespread search for objective truth about baseball, or "sabermetrics," a term, coined by James, whose first two syllables echo the acronym for the Society for American Baseball Research. While James's theories gained currency in baseball and attracted many enthusiastic believers, they also aroused the ire of baseball traditionalists who felt that his emphasis on statistics took the romance out of the game and failed to take into account the human element that makes baseball unpredictable. Prominent among his detractors is the Baseball Hall of Fame manager Sparky Anderson, who once described the six-foot five-inch James as "a little fat guy with a beard . . . who knows nothing about nothing," according to Ben McGrath in the *New Yorker* (July 14, 2003). In assessing James's contributions to baseball, Ross Wetzsteon wrote for the *New York Times Book Review* (April 29, 1990), "James cultists claim that his annual 'Abstract' revolutionized baseball's simpleminded savvy with computer-generated statistics. James critics argue that his books destroyed the game's pastoral poetry with logarithmic formulas. But Mr. James hasn't so much deconstructed baseball's statistics or demythologized its lore as tested the links between the two. What both idolaters and detractors fail to see is the radical methodology behind his work—its common sense."

Sabermetrics has become an important guide in the decision-making of various Major League Baseball (MLB) teams, including the Oakland Athletics, the Toronto Blue Jays, and the Boston Red Sox, the last of which hired James as its senior baseball-operations adviser in 2002. Many of his theories have already gained the status of conventional wisdom. Regarding batters, for example, James has emphasized the importance of on-base percentage above batting average and has therefore advised that hitters who are well ahead in the count (having more balls than strikes) should look for a walk rather than swing for a hit. He has also argued against the idea that teams must trade outs for runs, using sacrifice flies, bunts, and stolen bases to advance runners along the base paths; while these methods, James found, can produce small clusters of runs, they tend to make less likely the big scoring rallies that can seal games. Some of James's observations may at first seem obvious, such as his assertion that a player's minor-league performance is highly indicative of the degree of success he will have in the big leagues. However, many scouts have had trouble in correlating minor- and major-league success, because, according to James, they fail to consider the most predictive combinations of statistics. James's scouting methodology has made him a valuable consultant to the Red Sox in their search for undervalued young players. "One of the problems in baseball is being able to judge a guy's value to the team," the TV announcer and baseball Hall of Famer Joe Morgan told Richard Zoglin for *People* (June 3, 1991). "A .260 hitter can be more valuable than a .300 hitter. A player who hits 35 home runs may not drive in 100 runs. All those things were brought into focus by Bill James."

The youngest of the six children of George L. James and Mildred (Burks) James, George William James was born on October 5, 1949 in Holton, Kansas, and grew up in the nearby small town of Mayetta. His father was a carpenter; according to one source, he sold cream. When James was six, his mother died. Although never an exceptional athlete (volleyball was his best sport), he was drawn to baseball from an early age. When he was 11 he began listening regularly to radio broadcasts of Kansas City Athletics and St. Louis Cardinals games and figuring out players' batting averages in his head. He has been hooked on baseball ever since. "I think about baseball every waking hour of my life," James once said, as quoted by Joe Posnanski in the *Kansas City Star* (October 23, 2001, on-line).

James attended the University of Kansas at Lawrence, where he studied English and economics. After his graduation, with a B.A. degree in 1973, he spent two years in the U.S. Army. He then taught for two years in small-town high schools in Kansas; according to different sources, he gave classes in English or special education. In the mid-1970s he earned another bachelor's degree from the University of Kansas, this one a B.S. in language-arts edu-

cation. The realization that he might parlay his baseball knowledge into a career came to him gradually. "There was a period when all of my friends were getting married and I was going to weddings and talking to people," he recalled to an interviewer for the *American Enterprise* (April/May 2004, on-line). "And it seemed like at every wedding I would run into somebody who was fascinated by my baseball analysis. Most of the world was trying to tell me I would never earn my keep by doing this. But I began to think, 'If these people are so interested in what I'm doing, how can it not be possible to make a living at it?'" Intent on recording his thoughts on baseball, he quit his teaching job to work as a night watchman and boiler attendant at the Stokely-Van Camp pork-and-beans plant, where he found plenty of time to write. (He had begun working there in 1974, while still teaching.) James contributed articles to several baseball publications and soon began working on his baseball almanac. He culled data from daily box scores and phone calls to each of baseball's major-league teams and reckoned all the statistics himself, without using a calculator. In 1977 he issued *The Baseball Abstract*, his first compilation. Although its tiny sales (70 copies) disappointed him, James decided to put together another one, if only to improve on his first effort; he published it in 1978. Later that year he received a letter from the writer and editor Dan Okrent (currently the *New York Times*'s public editor), who praised the abstract. In 1979 Okrent helped James get an assignment to write a baseball preview for *Esquire*. Thanks in part to Okrent, sales of *The Baseball Abstract* began to increase. (The writers Norman Mailer and William Goldman were among those who bought copies.) Then Okrent wrote a profile of James, entitled "He Does It by the Numbers," which appeared in the May 25, 1981 issue of *Sports Illustrated* and was widely read. "That article made me what I am," James told Michael MacCambridge for the *Sporting News* (July 7, 1997). "I've made a living off that article ever since then. The article didn't guarantee me a living, but it gave me the opportunity to get a book contract and made me credible as a media personality."

In 1982 Ballantine Books published the first installment of *The Bill James Baseball Abstract*, which became a national best-seller that year and in each of its six successive yearly incarnations. James wrote in the book that he wanted to approach the topic of baseball "with the same kind of intellectual rigor and discipline that is routinely applied, by scientists great and poor, to trying to unravel the mysteries of the universe, of society, of the human mind, or of the price of burlap in Des Moines," as quoted by Ben McGrath. Many readers were enamored not only with James's insights into baseball but also with his witty, unostentatious prose. "What set the writing apart," according to McGrath, was "the accessibility of the logic, the insistence on eliminating biases and ignoring illusions, the practical tone. James's approach seemed distinctly American, descended from the nineteenth-century pragmatist tradition exemplified by his namesake, the philosopher William James." Baseball devotees were greatly impressed by James's fresh and lucidly reasoned insights into the game. As the noted baseball writer Robert W. Creamer told MacCambridge, James "did miraculous things in analyzing and understanding baseball. He makes more sense about the game than almost anyone you could name—but a lot of people who admire him don't have Bill's intelligence and comprehension of what you can do with baseball statistics."

James soon attracted the notice of various baseball insiders, among them Sandy Alderson, a current Major League Baseball executive who in 1981 became the general counsel to the Oakland Athletics and later the team's general manager and president. Alderson, who helped develop the talents of the Oakland A's players Jose Canseco, Mark McGwire, and Walt Weiss, applied some of James's offbeat theories to managing the team. "I've never wanted to tout James and his theory because I subscribed to it so strongly that I didn't want anyone else to think about it, although as time goes by, more people have," he told Michael MacCambridge. Other major leaguers who openly subscribe to James's theories are Billy Beane, who read the abstracts as a player and then became the general manager of the A's in 1997, and J. P. Ricciardi and Theo Epstein, the general managers of the Toronto Blue Jays and the Boston Red Sox, respectively.

The year 1985 saw the publication of *The Bill James Historical Baseball Abstract*, in which James offered a historical analysis of the game from the 1870s to the 1970s and also ranked the men he viewed as the 100 greatest players of all time. Ben McGrath, in the *New York Times* (March 31, 2002), called the book James's "magnum opus"—"the definitive explanation of changing trends and patterns of play over the sport's history, bar none." The highly esteemed baseball writer Lawrence S. Ritter judged it to be one of the three best books ever written about baseball. While his readership was growing, James was also coming under fire from those who disagreed with his views; in addition, he was experiencing intense pressure from Ballantine to complete his almanacs earlier each year. Consequently, in 1988 he announced that he was discontinuing the series. He also expressed regret about the explosion of statistical information about baseball on TV broadcasts, in sports writing, and on the Internet—an "eyesore," as he later put it, that he himself had helped to develop.

In 1990 James published *The Baseball Book*, which includes contributions from Mike Kopf, Jack Etkin, and others. Its three sections, "Teams," "People," and "Players," are generally less bound by statistics than his earlier books. In the opinion of Ross Wetzsteon, James lacked his usual incisiveness in the first two sections but was "back at his best in the third section, the byte-sized summaries of every major-league player that were the most popular feature of the *Abstract*." New editions of *The Baseball Book* appeared in 1991 and 1992. In the three editions of *The Bill James Player Rating Book* (1993, 1994, 1995), James evaluated more than 1,000 major-league players and minor-league prospects. In *The Politics of Glory: How Baseball's Hall of Fame Really Works* (1994), James critiqued the selection procedures of the Baseball Hall of Fame and suggested other criteria for induction. "Baseball maven James . . . offers a witty, contentious examination of the Hall of Fame, covering its history and politics with typically incisive and outspoken commentary on who is in the Hall and who should be . . . ," *Kirkus Reviews* reported, as quoted on Amazon.com. "Another home run from baseball's most interesting iconoclast, guaranteed to fuel the kind of good-natured arguments that make baseball our most intellectually provocative sport." James turned his attention to the game's decision makers in *The Bill James Guide to Baseball Managers: from 1870 to Today* (1997), giving Bobby Cox of the Atlanta Braves the nod as possibly baseball's greatest manager.

The New Bill James Historical Baseball Abstract (2001) is a revision of his celebrated 1985 work, with updated player and team histories and amended interpretations. In the 2001 book he introduced his new player-evaluation system, called Win Shares, which enables him to compute a numerical value for ranking a player's overall worth, including his defensive abilities, which had previously eluded James's and others' attempts at quantification. "Sports fans have been attempting to compile lists like these since long before Abner Doubleday did or did not invent baseball in Cooperstown, N.Y.," Ben McGrath wrote in his *New York Times* piece, "and James's effort here is the most ambitious to date, sure to touch the nerves of everyone who's ever called himself a fan." In McGrath's view, the 2001 book was even better than the original, and other critics tended to agree. "If you add just one baseball book to your collection this year, make it this one," Wes Lukowsky wrote for *Booklist*, as quoted on Amazon.com. Two books by James appeared in 2003: *The Bill James Handbook* and a second edition of *The New Bill James Historical Baseball Abstract*. The year 2004 saw the publication of a new edition of *The Bill James Handbook* and *The Neyer/James Guide to Pitchers*, co-written with the noted baseball columnist Rob Neyer.

While his influence on the game of baseball had become enormous by the end of the 20th century, some observers—and even he himself, to some extent—regarded James as an outsider, content to scrutinize and debunk baseball's myths from his office in Lawrence, Kansas. James had once written that baseball's front offices and managerial staffs were filled with "an assortment of half-wits, nincompoops, and Neanderthals like Don Drysdale and Don Zimmer [who] are not only allowed to pontificate on whatever strikes them, but are actually solicited and employed to do this," as quoted by McGrath in the *New Yorker*. It thus came as somewhat of a surprise when, in 2002, James was approached by John Henry, the new owner of the Red Sox, and Theo Epstein, who was then assistant manager, to serve as an adviser to the Sox. Few people knew that, in secret, James had already consulted for three major-league teams and worked with the agents of several players, providing statistics to be used in salary arbitrations. He now decided that the time was right to become an acknowledged, full baseball insider. For his first assignment, he produced an 86-page assessment of the team along with suggestions for its improvement, a document that the club's president, Larry Lucchino, has said is "never very far from my right hand," as quoted by Tyler Kepner in the *New York Times* (November 28, 2002).

One of the most unorthodox of James's proposals was that the Red Sox restructure its pitching bullpen, particularly with regard to its relief pitchers. Normally, in close games, baseball managers bring in a reliever called a setup man to play in the sixth or seventh inning until the ninth, when the closer, often one of the team's strongest pitchers, replaces him, to protect a lead or a tie. James considered this arrangement inefficient, arguing that a team's ace reliever ought to be in the game earlier, especially if the score is tied, so as not to waste his talent. "Using your relief ace to protect a three-run lead is like a business using a top executive to negotiate fire insurance," James has written, as quoted by Mel Antonen in *USA Today* (February 14, 2003, on-line). On the advice of James, Epstein restructured the Red Sox pitching staff, a process that included trading the closer Ugueth Urbina, despite Urbina's 40 saves with the team. Some managers disagreed with James's actions; Tony La Russa, of the St. Louis Cardinals, for example, who had popularized the use of one-inning closers while managing the Oakland A's in the late 1980s, told Antonen, "In my opinion, a three-run lead is one of those classic situations. If you lose that game, it is more harmful than losing the one-run lead. It's a tougher loss than getting beat by 10. It would have an effect for the next day or days."

On the opening day of the 2003 season, Boston led the Tampa Bay Devil Rays, 4–1, going into the ninth inning, thanks in part to a great performance by their star pitcher, Pedro Martinez, but two innings and three pitchers later, they lost, 6–4. The defeat seemed like a bad omen for James and the Red Sox, who in the final two innings could certainly have used Urbina, who had been their best closer. That spring Red Sox relievers racked up a huge earned-run average (ERA), routinely giving up multiple runs in the final innings of games. James—who at the time told McGrath for the *New Yorker*, "I'm trying desperately to avoid comparing our bullpen to a festering sore"—compiled an exhaustive statistical profile of every pitcher in the league, to help make the Sox management's acquisition of new relievers more effective. The Red Sox front office then signed the closer Byung-Hyun

Kim, from the Arizona Diamondbacks; later, during the 2003 off-season, they acquired an ace reliever, Keith Foulke, from Oakland. "Many writers considered [the signings] to be a rejection of James' ideas . . . ," *Wikipedia* (on-line) reported in its article about James. "Others, however, argue that the Boston pen was simply not very talented and that the outcome doesn't necessarily undermine James' arguments."

The Red Sox's batting, by contrast, was outstanding in the 2003 season. By August the team led the league in batting average (.294), on-base percentage (.361), and slugging average (a measure of a hitter's extra-base hits, or those beyond a single). (James helped bring the latter two categories into public focus.) The Red Sox posted a win–loss record of 95–61, finishing second in their division, then advanced past the Oakland A's in the American League Division Series to meet their arch-nemeses, the New York Yankees, in the American League Championships. They lost in the final game of that series, after the Sox's manager, Grady Little, made the decision to leave a flagging Pedro Martinez on the mound in the eighth inning, with the Sox leading 5–2; Martinez gave up three runs, sending the game into extra innings, and the Yankees scored in the bottom of the 11th on a solo home run to capture the American League Championship.

In 2004 the Red Sox improved their record to 98 wins and 64 losses, finishing second in the American League East to the New York Yankees and advancing into the postseason after clinching the American League Wild Card spot. The Red Sox swept the Anaheim Angels in the first round to bring about another matchup with the Yankees. After losing the first three games, the Red Sox became the first team in baseball history to come back from such a deficit, winning the next four games and the pennant, while handing their rivals one of the most shocking defeats in sports history. In the 2004 World Series, the Red Sox swept the St. Louis Cardinals to capture their first world championship since 1918.

Recently James revealed some new, major proposals for changing the game of baseball. To reverse the recent increases in the average numbers of home runs, strikeouts, and walks achieved each year, he has suggested returning to the sorts of thick-handled, harder-to-grip bats used in the 1950s and moving the batter's box farther away from home plate, to make it harder for batters to hit outside pitches. He has also advocated limiting the numbers of walks and intentional walks permitted, as he told the *American Enterprise* interviewer: "I suggest a batter should be able to decline a walk. Not only an intentional walk, but any walk. The batter's team should able to say, 'No thanks, I don't want that walk.' And if you walk him again, he goes to second base and anybody already on moves up two bases. The reason that should be the rule is because the walk was created to force the pitcher to throw hittable pitches to the batter. That is the walk's natural function. To allow the walk to become something the defense can use to its advantage with no response from the offense is illogical and counterproductive."

In 1978 James married Susan McCarthy, an artist, who has designed some of his book jackets. The couple live in Lawrence, Kansas, and have three children: Rachel, Isaac, and Reuben. Regarding his unusual association with the Red Sox, James told Kepner, "It will have a lot more significance if we succeed than if we fail. If I'm not able to succeed and the relationship is terminated after a couple of years, it's just a footnote. If we're able to make it work and have success as an organization, it could become something more than that."

—P.G.H.

Suggested Reading: *American Enterprise* (online) Apr./May 2004; *New York Times Book Review* p32 Apr. 29, 1990, p12 Mar. 31, 2002; *New Yorker* (on-line) July 14, 2003; *People* p93 June 3, 1991, with photos; *Sporting News* p15+ July 7, 1997; *USA Today* (on-line) Feb. 14, 2003

Selected Books: Annual editions—*Baseball Abstract,* 1977–81; *Bill James Baseball Abstract,* 1982–88; *The Baseball Book,* 1990–92; *The Bill James Player Rating Book,* 1993–95; Single editions—*The Bill James Historical Baseball Abstract,* 1985; *The Politics of Glory,* 1994; *The Bill James Guide to Baseball Managers,* 1997; *The New Bill James Historical Baseball Abstract,* 2001; *The Bill James Handbook,* 2003 and 2004; *The Neyer/James Guide to Pitchers,* 2004

Courtesy of the University of Colorado

Jin, Deborah

Nov. 15, 1968– Physicist

Address: JILA, University of Colorado, 440 UCB, Boulder, CO 80309-0440

In 1999 the world-renowned journal *Science* named as one of the top 10 scientific breakthroughs of the year an ingenious experiment conceived and executed, with some assistance, by the physicist Deborah Jin. Overcoming formidable obstacles connected with the nature of fundamental particles, Jin and her graduate student Brian DeMarco succeeded in cooling atoms of an isotope of the ele-

ment potassium to a temperature significantly closer to absolute zero than had ever been done before with any material of its kind. Absolute zero is defined as minus 459.67 degrees Fahrenheit, or minus 273.15 degrees Celsius (or centigrade), or zero degrees on the Kelvin scale; at absolute zero all the elementary particles that constitute matter are at what David H. Freedman, in *Discover* (February 1993), described as "the stillest possible state," with no motion "except for a minimum residual buzz." By lowering the temperature of their experimental material to less than one-millionth of a degree above absolute zero on the Kelvin scale, Jin and DeMarco made possible a better understanding of fundamental particles and paved the way for the creation of ever more accurate and useful atomic clocks and other devices. Jin's work earned her several prestigious honors, among them, in 2000, the Presidential Early Career Award for Scientists and Engineers, the highest honor given by the U.S. government to young scientists; in 2002, the Maria Goeppert-Meyer Prize, from the American Physical Society, and the National Academy of Sciences Award for Initiatives in Research; and in 2003, a $500,000 MacArthur Fellowship.

Jin, who has worked at the Joint Institute for Laboratory Astrophysics (JILA), in Boulder, Colorado, since 1995, has continued to refine and improve her techniques. In January 2004 she and two of her colleagues announced their successful cooling of their experimental material to a temperature of 50 billionths of a degree above absolute zero on the Kelvin scale and the resultant formation of a so-called fermionic condensate—"a long-sought, novel form of matter," according to a news release (January 28, 2004, on-line) from the University of Colorado at Boulder (UC–Boulder), which helps to support JILA. The news release continued, "Physicists hope that further research with such condensates eventually will help unlock the mysteries of high-temperature superconductivity, a phenomenon with the potential to improve energy efficiency dramatically across a broad range of applications." In November 2002 the popular science magazine *Discover* included Jin in its list of the 50 most important women in science.

Deborah Shiu-lan Jin was born on November 15, 1968 and raised in Florida. In an interview for the *Princeton Alumni Weekly* (November 19, 2003, online), she said that, as a scientist, she has had several mentors, but only one among them was female: her mother, who held a master's degree in engineering physics and worked as an engineer. Jin attended Princeton University, in Princeton, New Jersey. She spent the summer following her sophomore year as a federal-government researcher at the Goddard Space Flight Center, in Greenbelt, Maryland. "That summer pretty much settled things," she told T. R. Reid for *Newsbytes* (October 7, 2003). "I think I knew from that point on that I was going to be a physicist." In her senior year Jin won Princeton's Allen G. Shenstone Prize for her exemplary academic performance in physics. She graduated magna cum laude from the school in 1990, with an A.B. degree in physics. From 1990 to 1993 she held a National Science Foundation Graduate Fellowship in Physics. She earned a Ph.D. from the University of Chicago, in Illinois, in 1995; her dissertation was entitled "Experimental Study of the Phase Diagrams of Heavy Fermion Superconductors with Multiple Transitions."

Also in 1995 Jin secured a position as a National Research Council research associate at the Joint Institute for Laboratory Astrophysics. That same year her supervisor at JILA, Eric Cornell, and his colleague Carl Wieman announced that they had created a new state of matter called a Bose-Einstein condensate (BEC). (In 2001 Cornell and Wieman, along with the Massachusetts Institute of Technology physicist Wolfgang Ketterle, who had formed a BEC independently, shared the Nobel Prize in Physics for their work.) BECs are named for the Indian physicist Satyendra Nath Bose and the German-born physicist Albert Einstein; according to a UC–Boulder news release (November 20, 2003, online), "BECs have been described as a magnifying glass for quantum physics, the basic laws that govern the behavior of all matter." In 1925, building upon Bose's work, Einstein predicted that if a dense gas were cooled to absolute zero, the atoms would clump into a sort of superatom in which the identities of the individual atoms would disappear. The superatom, Einstein predicted, would constitute a new form of matter, with properties unlike those of any known substance. Essential to the concept of BECs is the division of all fundamental particles (particles with no internal substructure) into two types: bosons (named in honor of Bose) and fermions (named for the Italian-born physicist Enrico Fermi). The characteristics that distinguish bosons from fermions are described in terms connected with the theory of quantum mechanics (the science of physics at the scale of atoms), according to which all fundamental particles have wavelike properties, and, conversely,

light waves sometimes exhibit particle-like properties; particles emit and absorb energy in discrete packets, called quanta; and, in revolving about the nucleus of an atom, electrons can move from one orbit to another, with each orbit associated with a specific energy level. According to quantum theory, all particles have spin, a highly complex, intrinsic property associated with the angular momentum of the particle. The spins of bosons (which include photons, the carriers of light; gluons, the particles that bind quarks to one another; liquid helium; and W and Z bosons, the carriers of what is known as the weak nuclear force) are measured in terms of integers (for example, one, two, three); the spins of fermions (which include quarks, the building blocks of the subatomic particles neutrons and protons; leptons; and neutrinos) are measured in terms of odd numbers of half-integers (for example, $1/2$, $3/2$, $5/2$). Bosons are said to exhibit what is called Bose-Einstein statistics: they can have the same quantum state in the same place at the same time; fermions, by contrast—constrained by what is known as the Pauli Exclusion Principle—cannot co-exist in the same state at the same time and location. Bosons, as the January 28, 2004 UC–Boulder news release put it, "are inherently gregarious; they'd rather adopt their neighbor's motion than go it alone," while fermions "are inherently loners." In their natural states, to offer crude analogies, bosons may behave like two dozen cupcakes stuffed into a child's lunchbox; fermions, by contrast, resemble people standing on separate steps of a narrow staircase. When cooled sufficiently, Enrico Fermi predicted, fermions would create "stacks" of quantized energy states and form a vapor, called a Fermi gas; in that state, the atoms would "degenerate" and act more like waves than like particles.

In creating Bose-Einstein condensates, Eric Cornell and Carl Wieman worked with atoms of an isotope of the element rubidium (rubidium-87). First, they cooled the rubidium to 20 millionths of a degree above absolute zero by means of a laser trap (a weave of light waves generated by a half-dozen lasers); then they cooled the atoms even further, to 20 billionths of a degree above absolute zero on the Kelvin scale, by means of a magnetic trap. Thanks to their bosonic properties, when the atoms were subjected to Cornell and Wieman's supercooling techniques and reached the lower temperature, they behaved as Bose and Einstein had predicted: they all descended into the same quantum state (a near standstill), thus losing their separate identities and coalescing into a superatom—a Bose-Einstein condensate. Aiming for a similar though theoretically far more difficult result, Jin and Brian DeMarco (currently an assistant professor of physics at the University of Illinois at Urbana-Champaign) chose to work with a gas made up of potassium-40 atoms, which exhibit fermionic rather than bosonic properties. Brilliantly adapting and building upon the methods used by Cornell and Wieman, they first supercooled room-temperature potassium-40 gas by means of a magneto-optical trap, which consists of both laser beams and a magnetic field. Then, using a highly sophisticated microwave technique, they separated atoms with higher energy levels from those with lower energy levels; the former were forced to fly away, so to speak, leaving the others at a lower temperature: less than one-millionth of a degree Kelvin above absolute zero. At that point, as Jin explained on her personal page on the UC–Boulder Web site, "quantum mechanics starts to dominate the properties of the gas." It is not yet possible to provide visual evidence of the stacked molecules, but after the magnet was turned off and the gas expanded, it became possible to measure certain effects: what Jin termed "the thermodynamics and collisional dynamics." Those effects constituted evidence of the degenerate state of the gas. In *Science* (September 10, 1999), in a paper entitled "Onset of Fermi Degeneracy in a Trapped Atomic Gas," Jin and DeMarco described the result of their experiments. "The creation of a Fermi degenerate gas is a major scientific achievement and a lot of scientists have been trying to make it ever since we created the Bose-Einstein condensate," Carl Wieman declared, according to a UC–Boulder news release (September 9, 1999, on-line). He then predicted, "It will probably be at the top of the list of important physics news for this year." In addition to being named one of the top 10 scientific achievements of the year by *Science*, Jin's work was honored by the Office of Naval Research, which in 1999 named Jin an ONR Young Investigator. In 2001 she won the National Institute of Standards and Technology's (NIST's) Samuel W. Stratton Award for "her pioneering creation of a degenerate Fermi gas in a dilute atomic vapor, a microscopic model for important scientific and technological materials."

On the Web site of *Nature* on November 26, 2003 (and in the December 4, 2003 print version of the journal), Jin and her colleagues Cindy A. Regal and Markus Greiner announced their successful formation of the world's first "molecular Bose-Einstein condensate from a Fermi gas," as the title of their paper described it. Working again with gaseous potassium-40, they manipulated the atoms so that the attractions between pairs of atoms increased. When this was done at a sufficiently low temperature (150-billionths of a degree Kelvin above absolute zero), loosely bound bosonic molecules formed, constituting a Bose-Einstein condensate. Five months later Jin created and observed a Bose-Einstein condensate of those molecules. The results of Jin's research were submitted for publication on the same day that a group of physicists at the University of Innsbruck at Austria announced that they had accomplished the same thing using lithium atoms; the Innsbruck group's paper appeared one month earlier than that of Jin's. "Both of these papers represent a very large step in what people have wanted to do for a long time," Eric Cornell told Kenneth Chang for the *New York Times* (November 25, 2003). Cornell described the

transformation of fermion atoms into bosonic molecules as "a lovely unification of two things that in the physics world we're used to thinking of as different as male and female."

About two months later, in *Physical Review Letters* (January 24, 2004), Jin, Regal, and Greiner reported yet another achievement: instead of using magnetic fields to bind two fermions into a molecule and condense them into a BEC, they used the field to create an attractive force that could not cause two fermions to form ordinary molecules but that nonetheless caused the fermions to form a condensate. This condensate more closely resembled what happens in a superconductor (in which electrons form what is known as Cooper pairs) than what happens in a BEC. Their experiment—which Eric Cornell called "a technological and scientific tour de force," according to Charles Seife in *Science* (January 28, 2004)—proved that a condensate can have properties related to both a superconductor and a BEC. "The strength of pairing in our fermionic condensate, adjusted for mass and density, would correspond to a room temperature superconductor," Jin explained, according to the January 28, 2004 UC–Boulder press release. "This makes me optimistic that the fundamental physics we learn through fermionic condensates will eventually help others design more practical superconducting materials."

On September 28, 2004 Jin received the Service to America Medal in the category of "science and the environment." The medal, created in 2002 by the nonprofit organization Partnership for Public Service and the Atlantic Media Group, brings with it a $3,000 award. Jin currently holds three titles: she is a JILA fellow; a physicist with the Quantum Physics Division of NIST (the arm of the U.S. Department of Commerce that, together with UC–Boulder, supports JILA); and an associate professor adjoint with the Physics Department of UC–Boulder. Since 1996 she has lectured as an invited speaker at more than 50 conferences or other events, at sites ranging from college campuses in California, Oregon, and Oklahoma to sites in Mallorca, Spain, Florence, Italy, and Yatsugatake, Japan. Jin is married to the physicist John Bohn, a JILA fellow and a research scientist in the University of Colorado's Physics Department. Bohn's work is closely connected with Jin's, and, along with others, they have co-authored several professional papers together. By her own account, Jin is glad that, although she works on the campus of a university, she is not required to teach; as she explained to T. R. Reid, "I'm sort of isolated from the academic politics, and being a federal employee frees you up from the teaching load and the other requirements they have for [university] faculty. I don't have to wait the six years to find out if I'm going to get tenure. The government just leaves you alone to do your work." Jin and Bohn, who live in Boulder, have one child—a daughter, Jaclyn, born in October 2002; photos of her with her parents appear on Bohn's personal page on UC–Boulder's

Web site. "Having an infant around, I don't spend as much time at work [as I used to], when possible," Jin told the *Princeton Alumni Weekly* interviewer. "And gosh, when you have an infant, no other job seems as difficult! There's so much at stake, and it's really hard. It gives you perspective. Like physics, it's very challenging, at least for me. I'm not a natural at it. But, like physics, it's also very rewarding."

—H.T.

Suggested Reading: Jin Group Web site; MacArthur Foundation Web site; *Princeton Alumni Weekly* (on-line) Nov. 19, 2003; University of Colorado at Boulder Web site; *Washington Post* Newsbytes Oct. 7, 2003

Courtesy of HarperCollins

Jones, Edward P.

Oct. 5, 1950– Writer

Address: c/o Amistad Press, HarperCollins Publishers, 10 E. 53d St., New York, NY 10022

Having grown up in numerous neighborhoods in predominantly black Washington, D.C., Edward P. Jones crafted tales of that world: his story collection *Lost in the City* (1992) describes the lives of those ordinary residents of Washington, mostly women, capturing them in their struggles, foibles, and occasional heroism. While that volume brought Jones awards and critical acclaim, it was his 2003 novel, *The Known World*, that placed him in the public eye. In the novel Jones depicted the decay of the slave society in the years preceding the Civil War, evoking a time and place in which even black people born slaves could be corrupted by the desire to own their fellow human beings. Gene Seymour wrote in *Newsday* (August 24, 2003), "Jones' novel is a significant contribution to the growing body of work by such African-American novelists as Toni Morrison (*Beloved*) and John Edgar Wideman (*The Cattle Killing*) who are seizing imaginative autonomy over their shared history." In his novel, as in his stories, Jones did not set out to teach a moral lesson; as he told Mary Ann French during an interview for the *Washington Post* (July 22, 1992), "Whatever lessons there are, somebody else has to do those. . . . I can't do that myself. . . . Ultimately, what I'm doing, what I'm trying to do, I'm trying to write literature."

The oldest of three children, Edward Paul Jones was born on October 5, 1950 in Arlington, Virginia, to Aloysius and Jeanette Majors Jones. He was raised in nearby Washington, D.C., which was then racially segregated. Jones had a difficult, impoverished childhood; early on, his father left the family, and his mother, who could not read or write, supported her children by cleaning houses and working at various menial jobs in an upscale hotel restaurant. "I don't even pretend to begin to say what my mother went through when she went out to work each morning," Jones told Mary Ann French. "She could have gotten up one morning and gotten on the bus and never come back. But she didn't. She always came back in the evening." Jones's younger brother was mentally retarded and was eventually institutionalized. When Jones was about 14, his younger, more extroverted sister, with whom he was very close, was sent to live with relatives in Brooklyn, New York, to give her a chance for a better life. By Jones's count, the family moved within Washington on some 18 occasions, "for one reason or another—the roof would leak or there would be some other defect," as he recalled to an interviewer for the *Washington Post Book World* (August 24, 2003). The frequent relocations made it very difficult for him to maintain friendships. He described his childhood summers in an article for the *Washington Post Magazine* (August 7, 1994), "Moving Pictures: In Search of Summers Past." Of the summer of 1964, he wrote, "I am unable to make friends with the children on Sixth Street because my heart is unable to take it anymore, unable to extend itself, knowing that in a few months or a year we will move again and the friends will be lost and I will have to start all over." Reflecting on what his life was like when he was an older teenager, he noted, "Though I am close to friendless, in a way it is not a great hurt. It may well be what saves my life, saves me from being devoured by the streets, saves me from the shaky love of a girl who would have given me a baby and sent me bumbling off into a raw kind of manhood." A saving grace of the poor neighborhoods where Jones lived, he has recalled, was the sense of community conveyed by the adult residents. While his mother washed dishes in a restaurant all night when he was about three, in "a house of neighbors who treat us like their own children, my sister and I sleep without fear alone in our room until our mother returns in the early morning."

As a boy Jones found solace in reading. With money he earned by running errands or collecting empty soda bottles, he bought comic books, with *Archie, Richie Rich,* and *Casper the Friendly Ghost* among his favorites. (The rise in the price of comic books from 10 to 12 cents "broke his heart," as Linton Weeks wrote in the August 16, 2003 issue of the *Washington Post.*) As a 13-year-old Jones began to read more sophisticated works, such as Richard Wright's novel *Native Son* and the autobiography of the singer and actress Ethel Waters, books that impressed him with the richness of experience and the sense of human possibility they reflected. Jones attended Cardozo High School in Washington, where he became an honors student in English. He revealed to Rachel L. Swarns for the *New York Times* (October 16, 2003) that he had to sign his mother's name to his report cards, since she could not do so.

During high school Jones had a chance encounter with a Jesuit teacher at the College of the Holy Cross, in Worcester, Massachusetts, who was bicycling through the boy's neighborhood. Their conversation led to a friendship; at the teacher's suggestion, Jones applied to Holy Cross, where he was admitted and received a scholarship. Jones originally majored in mathematics there, but switched to English when he did not do well in a calculus course. (The reason, he later found out, was that he had needed glasses and was not seeing the numbers on the blackboard properly.) "It surprised me that I was competitive" at Holy Cross, Jones said to Linton Weeks. "The public schools in Washington had given me a pretty substantial education." He graduated in 1972; in his sophomore year he had begun to write fiction.

After college, Jones returned to Washington and took care of his mother, who was then ill, while working sporadically. After her death, in January 1975, Jones continued to have trouble finding work and stayed for a time in a shelter for homeless people. The year 1976, however, saw two positive developments: *Essence* magazine accepted one of his short stories and paid him $400 (the magazine's staff had trouble locating him to send him the check); and he found steady work, answering telephones at the American Association for the Advancement of Science, where he spent three years. At a writers' conference at George Mason University, in Virginia, Jones met the novelist John Casey, who encouraged him to pursue creative writing in graduate school. Jones chose the program at the University of Virginia, because it was close to Washington and because James Alan McPherson, whose short stories Jones had enjoyed in college, taught there. Jones studied there from 1979 to 1981, earning an M.F.A. degree. He told Lawrence P. Jackson for an interview in the *African American Review* (Spring 2000) that he learned more from the literature courses he took than from writing courses. Since then, teaching creative writing from time to time at various colleges, he has tried to do as "thorough a job as I can, point by point, almost line by line if there's time, because I didn't think that I got that when I was in graduate school." In 1983 Jones landed a job at Tax Analysts, a nonprofit company based in Arlington, Virginia, that assists tax professionals in understanding changes in regulations; he remained there for nearly two decades as a writer and proofreader for the organization's publication *Tax Notes.*

Meanwhile, Jones continued to publish short stories in magazines including *Essence* and *Callaloo.* His book *Lost in the City,* a collection of 14 short stories, appeared in 1992. The city of the title is Washington, D.C., where black people from the Deep South have come to improve their lot. There, they make modest gains in security and prosperity but still struggle to hold their families together. Most of the stories are told from a female point of view. "Jones has near-perfect pitch for people," Michael Harris noted in the *Los Angeles Times Book Review* (July 12, 1992). "A motherless girl who raises pigeons, old women stirred by a lightning storm to remember the dark rural past, a boy whose demanding lady boss at a grocery store becomes his best friend, a man who finds a new lifestyle knocking on strangers' doors in search of his runaway daughter, a woman whose father, imprisoned 25 years for killing her mother, wants to get back into her life—whoever they are, he reveals them to us from the inside out." As Jonathan Yardley wrote in the *Washington Post Book World* (June 21, 1992), when a woman in one of the stories tells her daughter, "God don't put no more on us than we can bear," Jones "puts that proposition to the test. Though there are many themes in his work, none is more important than the daily struggle of ordinary people against terrible odds. Some of these are imposed from without: Discrimination and segregation, though only occasionally brought to the forefront, are stunting, inescapable realities. But so too are those imposed from within, by people who have ignored or forgotten a grandfather's advice: 'Don't get lost in the city.'" Jones's collection was nominated for a 1992 National Book Award and won the PEN/ Hemingway prize for first fiction. In 1994 Jones received a Lannan Literary Award, with a stipend of $50,000; he was also awarded a $20,000 grant from the National Endowment for the Arts.

In early 2002 Jones's job at Tax Analysts was phased out. That development, as Jerome Weeks wrote in the *Dallas Morning News* (October 6, 2003), gave Jones "the jolt" he needed to finish the novel he had begun years earlier; the money from his awards—and his frugal lifestyle—allowed him to concentrate on his writing full-time. Since college, when he had learned that some African-Americans had owned slaves, Jones had nurtured the idea of writing a novel on the subject. Over the years he had collected and read many books on the slave era but had made a conscious decision not to become overly influenced by historical facts; he told Linton Weeks that he "didn't want the research to get in the way of the people and the world I had already imagined."

The Known World was published in 2003 to great acclaim. The novel suggests that slavery corrupts absolutely, exempting no one, whether slave or master. The novel focuses on Henry Townsend, who was born a slave but whose parents have purchased the family's freedom; he acquires his own plantation and slaves and is mentored by Robbins, his former master. By the time of his early death, Henry has acquired more than 30 slaves, who are left to his wife. Henry watches from beyond the grave as the overseer Moses, who has begun an affair with Henry's widow, plots to betray his family and the other slaves. Meanwhile, news of slave revolts and escapes lead the whites in the novel to doubt even their seemingly devoted slaves, with the result that "cozy certainties become unmoored," as Gene Seymour phrased it in *New York Newsday* (August 24, 2003). "Justice, love and the sanctity of life are worn away and ultimately disfigured by the habit of treating people of color as property."

Jones's unusual choice of subject attracted reviewers' attention, but it was the quality of his writing that drew praise. Ron Franscell noted in the *Denver Post* (August 31, 2003) that the "biblical rhythms" of Jones's prose "lend depth to a story about profound moral confusion." In the *New York Times* (August 14, 2003), Janet Maslin pronounced the novel to be "stunning" and added, "In no way is Mr. Jones's work morally black and white. Racial lines here are intriguingly tangled and not easily drawn. . . . With its eloquent restraint and simplicity, *The Known World* penetrates a realm of contradictions and takes the measure of slavery's punishments." In March and April 2004 Jones won the National Book Critics Circle Award and the Pulitzer Prize for fiction, respectively, and in September of that year he was awarded a $500,000 MacArthur Fellowship (widely referred to as a "genius grant," but not by the MacArthur Foundation itself). The large increase in his bank account notwithstanding, Jones told Deborah Solomon for the *New York Times Magazine* (October 10, 2004) that he did not intend to change his lifestyle much. "I don't want to own anything that I can't fold up and bring into my apartment," he declared.

Jones lives in Washington, D.C. He is unmarried and spends many solitary hours reading and watching television. (One of his favorite programs is *Judge Judy*.) Rachel L. Swarns reported that when reviews of *The Known World* began to appear, Jones "had no car, no cellphone and no fax machine to cope with the flurry of interview requests. Now he has a driver to ferry him to literary events and a fax machine, all courtesy of his publisher. He has decided against buying a cellphone, fearing it could seem too pretentious." An explanation for that attitude was perhaps provided by a co-worker of Jones's at Tax Notes, Shirley Grossman, who told Swarns that the novelist "saw the world divided when he was very small into folks who didn't have jobs and folks who did. His feeling for the common man, instead of the guy who's gotten there, is very strong." Jones is currently at work on a second book of short stories. "I refuse to write about ignorance, despair and weakness, [or] about people going to clubs and doing dumb things . . . ," Jones told Robert Fleming during an interview for *Publishers Weekly* (August 11, 2003). "I want to write about the things which helped us to survive: the love, grace, intelligence and strength of us as a people."

—S.Y.

Suggested Reading: *African American Review* p95+ Spring 2000; *Denver Post* (on-line) Aug. 31, 2003; *Los Angeles Times Book Review* p6 July 12, 1992; *New York Times* C p18 June 11, 1992; *New York Times* (on-line) Aug. 14, 2003; *New York Times Magazine* p17 Oct. 10, 2004, with photo; *Newsday* D p32 Aug. 24, 2003; *Publishers Weekly* p254 Aug. 11, 2003; *Washington Post* G p1 July 22, 1992; *Washington Post Book World* p3 June 21, 1992; *Washington Post Magazine* p8+ Aug. 7, 1994

Selected Books: *Lost in the City*, 1992; *The Known World*, 2003

Jones, Elaine

1944– Lawyer; former president of the NAACP's Legal Defense and Educational Fund

Address: NAACP LDF, 99 Hudson St. #16, New York, NY 10013

"People call me an optimist," Elaine Jones, the recent president of the NAACP Legal Defense and Educational Fund, told Michael Paul Williams for the *Richmond (Virginia) Times Dispatch* (February 5, 2003). "But I have a lot of confidence in the American people. If people have the information, they invariably make the right decision." Jones has spent the past 34 years trying to persuade judges and legislators to make what she views as the right decisions on matters affecting equality. As an African-American child who experienced racism and segregation first-hand while growing up in pre–civil rights era America, she decided to dedicate her life to fighting for equal rights; since 1970 she has been a member of the NAACP Legal Defense and Educational Fund (LDF), leaving the organization only for two years in the mid-1970s and serving from 1993 to 2004 as president. Jones has a reputation as a skillful negotiator and a passionate voice for those who have been cut off economically, politically, or socially from mainstream so-

Stefan Zaklin/Getty Images

Elaine Jones

ciety. "Elaine has always had an acute realization of the unfair disadvantages that people suffer by reason of race, economic circumstance and the general behind-the-eight-ball-ism that have-nots face in this society," Tony Amsterdam, a law professor at New York University and Jones's former colleague at the LDF, told Michael A. Fletcher for the *Washington Post* (June 23, 2003). "She has a remarkable combination of legal talent, a powerful moral compass and a dedication and willingness to give of herself. . . . She was born for this kind of work." Jones stepped down from her position as president on May 1, 2004. She has said that she will continue to be an "active presence" in LDF programs and fund-raising and has vowed to continue to fight for equality for all before the law. Her resignation followed complaints that she acted unethically in attempting to stall the confirmation of a judicial nominee who she thought would rule unfavorably in an affirmative-action case on which the Legal Defense Fund had worked.

Elaine R. Jones was born in Norfolk, Virginia, in 1944. Her mother was a teacher; her father worked on the railroad as a Pullman porter and was a member of the nation's first black-run trade union (the Brotherhood of Sleeping-Car Porters). Her brother is now the pastor of a large Baptist church in Philadelphia, Pennsylvania, while her sister is a district court judge in Norfolk. From the age of eight, Jones knew that she wanted to be a lawyer in order to pursue justice, having already experienced the effects of racial discrimination in her daily life. "What really drove it home . . . my father was a Pullman porter and traveled quite a bit," she told Williams. "He took the three of us, my sister, brother and me to New York and Chicago . . . and on

those trips we walked the streets. We couldn't find a place to stay. That was America. That was the mid-'50s. And that shouldn't be. I said to myself, 'There's something wrong.'" She was further inspired to fight for racial equality by Aline B. Hicks, her chemistry teacher at Booker T. Washington High School, in Norfolk, who had filed a lawsuit against the school district in 1939 over the fact that she and other African-American teachers earned less than their white counterparts. Hicks's case had been taken up by the black attorney and future U.S. Supreme Court justice Thurgood Marshall, and was about to be argued before the Supreme Court, when the school system's administrators decided to settle the case, agreeing to phase in a salary adjustment. Hicks taught Jones more than 20 years later, in the 1960s, but her fight against inequality remained relevant in the eyes of her students. "Every once in a while she would get contemplative," Jones told Leslie Anderson Morales for *Footsteps* (March/April 2003, on-line). "She talked about the lawsuit. She wasn't bitter. She knew there was power in numbers. She opened my eyes to the law."

Jones attended Howard University, in Washington, D.C., where she earned a degree in political science, with honors. She then spent two years teaching English in Turkey as a Peace Corps volunteer before becoming the first black woman to enroll in—and graduate from—the University of Virginia School of Law. (John F. Merchant became the first black to graduate from the school, in 1958.) Pointing to the common assumptions about race at that time, Jones recalled that during her first week there a secretary mistook her for a cleaning woman. "She saw the color. She didn't notice the books," Jones told Williams.

Upon her graduation, in 1970, Jones accepted an offer to join the prestigious Wall Street law firm of Mudge, Rose, Guthrie & Alexander but later changed her mind. Instead, she went to work for the National Association for the Advancement of Colored People (NAACP) Legal Defense and Educational Fund, where she has been ever since, with the exception of two years spent as special assistant to the U.S. secretary of transportation. The LDF was created in 1940 by Thurgood Marshall as an independent arm of the NAACP, the nation's oldest civil rights organization, founded in 1909; the two groups separated entirely in 1957, and LDF's lawyers have argued before the U.S. Supreme Court more frequently than any other group of legal advocates except those at the U.S. Justice Department.

Jones was one of the first black women to defend death-row inmates, arguing capital cases throughout the South. At that time, she has said, it was not unheard of for black defendants to be sentenced to death in the Deep South for crimes such as nighttime burglary (as distinguished from breaking and entering in daytime), and she has recalled once arguing for a change of venue for a black defendant in Alabama as a group of Ku Klux Klansmen ringed the courthouse in full regalia. (She won the argument.) She was counsel of record in *Furman v. Georgia*, a landmark U.S. Supreme Court case that abolished the death penalty in 37 states, and overturned the sentences of 629 death-row defendants, in 1972. (Reworked death-penalty statutes would gain the court's approval in the mid-1980s. The LDF continues to oppose the death penalty on the grounds that it is carried out disproportionately against minorities and the poor.) She was the organization's managing attorney from 1973 to 1975, when she was named special assistant to U.S. secretary of transportation William T. Coleman Jr. Among her accomplishments in that capacity was taking the lead in crafting policy that opened the U.S. Coast Guard to women.

Jones returned to the LDF in 1977 as legislative advocate in its Washington, D.C., office. In that role, while continuing to litigate, she took on other responsibilities, among them providing briefings and expert testimony for congressional staffs and committees; monitoring the nominations of federal judges and working for or against their confirmation; seeking to extend the benefits of civil rights victories to women and other groups; and working to expand civil rights through legislation. Among the legislative milestones in which she had a hand were the Voting Rights Act Amendments of 1982, the Fair Housing Act of 1988, the Civil Rights Restoration Act of 1988, and the Civil Rights Act of 1991. She has argued numerous employment-discrimination cases, several of them class-action cases against some of the country's largest employers, including *Patterson v. American Tobacco Co.*, *Stallworth v. Monsanto*, and *Swint v. Pullman Standard*. Her work has been instrumental in ensuring that the federal judiciary includes more members of racial minority groups and more judges committed to equal rights.

In 1993 Jones became the first woman to head the NAACP's legal arm, and only the fourth person to do so since it was founded. As director she oversaw 28 lawyers, a $9.5 million annual budget, and more than 300 cases. In addition to pursuing the organization's original aims of fighting for educational equity, fair employment and housing practices, and the unbiased administration of criminal justice, Jones broadened the LDF's mission to include encouraging blacks to participate in the political process and to seek economic empowerment. She singled out environmental justice as a priority, pointing out the high percentage of black children in inner cities who are affected by lead poisoning, which can cause learning disabilities, among other illnesses. She has also cited as new targets for legal action impediments to health care for blacks and hazardous-waste sites, which she believes affect African-Americans disproportionately. Under her leadership the LDF undertook cases demonstrating the negative effects of mandatory minimum sentencing guidelines and the fact that the high incarceration rate of African-Americans crosses social and economic bound-

aries. One example of the Legal Defense Fund's work in this area was its call for clemency for Kemba Smith, a 24-year-old woman who was sentenced in 1994 to 24 and a half years in prison after pleading guilty to distributing cocaine. Smith was a student at Hampton University from a middle-class background; though her boyfriend was the head of a drug ring, she herself had never used or sold drugs. The LDF appealed the case for four years, until President Bill Clinton granted Smith clemency, in his final months in office. In addition, LDF and other civil rights groups represented 38 people, nearly all African-American, who were convicted on drug charges in Tulia, Texas. Some of the defendants were serving sentences of 90 years despite the fact that the one-man police investigation leading to the 1999 arrests uncovered no drugs, guns, or large sums of money. The convictions were overturned in April 2003.

The organization played an important role in the U.S. Supreme Court's decision in June 2003 to preserve the use of race as one factor in admission to the University of Michigan's law school, following a challenge to that policy by white students who had been denied admission. The LDF maintained that a policy of affirmative action was necessary at the school to counteract the effects of its past racism as well as many other economic and social factors working against black and Latino applicants. Jones called the case "the Brown vs. Board for higher education," an allusion to *Brown v. Board of Education of Topeka, Kansas*, the landmark 1954 Supreme Court decision that struck down segregation in public schools in the United States. The Supreme Court ruled on two cases dealing with affirmative-action policies at the University of Michigan—one concerning undergraduate admissions, the other focusing on admittance to the law school; the court returned split decisions on the cases, upholding the admission policy at the law school in a 5–4 vote but striking down that of the undergraduate college, 6–3. The undergraduate policy was ruled illegal because it gave too much weight to an applicant's race, rather than considering it as one of many factors, as the law-school admission policy does. Many civil rights advocates and supporters of affirmative action considered the decisions a victory. "The court has said something that is absolutely phenomenal and wonderful," Jones told Tavis Smiley for the *Tavis Smiley Show* on National Public Radio (June 24, 2003). "The Supreme Court said in unmistakable terms that it rises to a level of constitutional significance that institutions of higher education have a diverse student body." She said that the decision had laid out a blueprint for ways in which undergraduate schools, including the University of Michigan, could have affirmative-action programs within the limits of the law.

December 2003 brought allegations that Jones had acted unethically in asking U.S. senator Edward M. Kennedy of Massachusetts to stall the confirmation of Julia S. Gibbons, a nominee for the

Sixth U.S. Circuit Court of Appeals, until after that body had ruled on the affirmative-action case involving the University of Michigan. (That ruling came before the Supreme Court decision on the same matter; the Senate Judiciary Committee confirmed Gibbons, 5–4, several weeks after the appeals court upheld the university's policy.) The charges against Jones arose from an April 17, 2002 memo to Kennedy from his staff, advising him of Jones's telephone call and request. Several groups, including the Center for Individual Freedom, the Coalition for a Fair Judiciary, Project 21 (an African-American leadership network), and the Congress for Racial Equality filed a complaint with the Virginia State Bar (an administrative agency of the Supreme Court of Virginia) and asked that Jones be disbarred. "It's manipulating the outcome of a case to which you are a party," Jeffrey Mazzella, director of the Center for Individual Freedom, told Charles Hurt for the *Washington Times* (December 4, 2003) about Jones's actions. "It's no less than tampering with a jury or bribing a judge." In April 2004 the Virginia State Bar rejected the complaint. (The conservative legal watchdog group Judicial Watch filed a formal Senate ethics charge against Kennedy and Illinois senator Richard Durbin, both Democrats and members of the Senate Judiciary Committee, for acting improperly in the matter.)

After serving as the organization's head for 11 years, Jones announced her resignation as president and director-counsel of the LDF, effective May 1, 2004. Without mentioning the ethics allegations against her, she said that she had made her decision after the Supreme Court upheld affirmative action at the University of Michigan law school. "It was clear when I took this job that the Supreme Court was going to look at an affirmative action case," she said, as quoted in *Jet* (February 9, 2004). "We had to make sure it was the right one. Michigan was it, and it ended in a slam-dunk victory affirming the principles we have been fighting for. After that I knew I could go." Theodore M. Shaw, formerly the group's associate director-counsel, was named to succeed her.

Jones contends that the country's perception of racial matters has not altered significantly in recent years. While LDF lawyers and other civil rights groups set out to dismantle segregation through strategic lawsuits, conservative legal groups have followed a similar strategy in seeking to outlaw affirmative action, often stating that it runs against the concept of a color-blind society. "A colorblind society? I wish it was so, but it's not," she told Fletcher. "We got to realize that we've got a heavy racial inequality in this country and it didn't just spring forth from the head of Zeus." Jones views affirmative action as a way of redressing past wrongs and achieving racial justice in a nation with a long history of discrimination.

One challenge for Jones and her colleagues at the Legal Defense Fund is the need to ensure that past legal victories are not eroded. "The law is not static," Jones told Fletcher. "If you win it one day, it doesn't mean you got it. You can't rest on your laurels. They'll take it away from you." She added, referring to persistent inequality of access to decent education in the U.S., "We won Brown 50 years ago . . . but look at us now." Among her concerns are the high percentage of African-Americans involved in the criminal justice system as defendants and the fact that over the last 30 years black and Latino students have more than ever been effectively segregated into poor school districts.

In 1989 Jones, who has been described as vivacious and outspoken, became the first African-American elected to the American Bar Association's board of governors, on which she served a three-year term. She continues to sit on the organization's Council of Individual Rights and Responsibilities. She has been active in the National Bar Association, which singled her out as the first female recipient of its Founder's Award, and has served as co-chair of its Judicial Selection Committee. She has also contributed her time and energy to the Old Dominion Bar Association, based in Virginia. She is a former board member of the Mexican American Legal Defense Fund, a member of the executive committee of the Leadership Conference on Civil Rights, and a board member of the National Women's Law Center.

In 1998 Jones received the University of Virginia Women's Center's Distinguished Alumna Award. In 2000 she received both the Eleanor Roosevelt Award for Human Rights, presented by President Bill Clinton, and the Oliver W. Hill Freedom Fighter Award, and she was named one of the "10 Most Powerful Blacks" by *Ebony* magazine in 2001. She holds nine honorary degrees as well as the Jefferson Medal of Freedom from the University of Virginia, and has been recognized by the Sara Lee Foundation, the National Newspaper Publishers Association, the Southern Christian Leadership Conference, the Olender Foundation, the National Association of Black Women Attorneys, the National Legal Aid and Defender Association, the National Bar Association, the American Bar Association Commission on Women in the Profession, the Southern Christian Leadership Conference, the National Council of Jewish Women, and the National Association of Black Women Attorneys. Jones has been a fellow at Harvard University's Institute of Politics and a guest lecturer at the law schools of American University, Georgetown University, the College of William and Mary, and Oxford University, in England.

Jones is a self-described workaholic who enjoys reading mystery novels.

—K.E.D.

Suggested Reading: *Richmond (Virginia) Times Dispatch* E p1 Feb. 5, 2003, with photo; *Washington Post* C p1 June 23, 2003

Courtesy of Henry Holt & Co.

Judson, Olivia

1970– Evolutionary biologist; writer; educator

*Address: Imperial College London, South
Kensington Campus, London SW7 2AZ, England*

The evolutionary biologist and prize-winning
journalist Olivia Judson is the author of the best-
selling book *Dr. Tatiana's Sex Advice to All Creation: The Definitive Guide to the Evolutionary Biology of Sex* (2002). Written in the style of a sex-
advice column to animals, the book details the variety of sexual practices in the natural world and
provides the reader with an overview of the evolutionary biology of sex. Judson's opus became a
best-seller in both the United States and Britain,
and it was short-listed for the Samuel Johnson
Prize, a British honor for excellent nonfiction writing. "For me, writing this book has changed the
way I look at nature; the more I learn the more
amazed and absorbed I am by the diversity and
complexity of life," Judson explained in an interview for *Readers Read* (April 2003, on-line). "If
I've managed to impart even a fraction of my own
enthusiasm for biology . . . I'll consider myself to
have succeeded."

Olivia Judson was born in 1970 in England. At
the age of 10, she moved to Baltimore, Maryland;
her father, Horace Freeland Judson, had been invited to join the faculty at Johns Hopkins University.
The elder Judson was a historian of molecular biology and the author of a seminal book on the subject, *The Eighth Day of Creation* (1979). Olivia Judson recalled to Ken Ringle for the *Washington Post*
(May 28, 2003) that her father had "a little tube of
DNA he showed me as a child and there were al-

ways biologists about. I did have an idea of doing
something in science." She later attended Stanford
University, in California, where she originally
planned to major in physics. She changed her
mind quickly, however, when she found herself
"in a three-hour, open-book exam where I couldn't
begin to do any of the problems," she told Ringle.
After switching to biology, Judson spent the spring
semester of her junior year working as a biological
field assistant, and studying European starlings, at
Oxford University in the United Kingdom. She
won a Fulbright scholarship, as well as a three-year
National Science Foundation fellowship, and later
returned to Oxford to pursue a doctoral degree in
biological studies. In her spare time, she wrote
freelance science articles for the *Economist* and
Nature.

In 1995, after finishing her dissertation on asex-
ual reproduction, Judson joined the staff of the
Economist for a two-year stint as a science writer.
Dr. Tatiana's Sex Advice to All Creation grew in
part out of a prank she played on an *Economist*
business-affairs editor: one day, Judson disguised
herself in a pink miniskirt, high heels, and a blond
wig. She gave her name as "Dr. Tatiana" and interviewed for a position in the business section of the
magazine; the interview lasted until the editor's
questions became too exacting for a science journalist to answer. After Judson's editor assigned her
to a piece about animal sexuality for the Christmas
issue, she drew on the quirky persona of Dr. Tatiana because, as she recalled to Ken Ringle, the
piece would otherwise have been boring. A conversation with colleagues at a party inspired her,
however: "We were talking in particular about the
queen bee and how she flies off trailing thousands
of drones," Judson explained. "The odds are
25,000 to 1 against any one of them having sex with
her. But those who do go out with a bang. Their penises explode, leaving their genitalia in place in
her body. Then someone said, 'What if [the late advice columnist] Ann Landers got a letter saying,
'My lover has just exploded! What do I do?' And
suddenly, hey! The light went on." The resulting
article—"Sex Is War!"—was published in the December 18, 1997 issue of the *Economist* and offered
queries to Dr. Tatiana from a queen bee, a male spider, and a fruit fly, among others. "Sex Is War!"
won the Glaxo Wellcome/British Association of
Science Writers' Award.

The positive reaction to the article prompted
Judson to turn the piece into a book. She left her
post at the *Economist*, although she continued to
freelance for other publications, and set to work for
four years, fighting a case of writer's block so persistent that she felt the need to flee her home in
London for the sunnier climate of southern France.
"Picture the scene," she recalled to *Readers Read*.
"I was living and working in a tiny apartment in
central London, it was winter, with all the rain and
gloom that winter in London entails, and I was
badly stuck. Worse, the lease on my apartment was
about to come to an end. The whole situation was

demoralizing. Then, I discovered that it was cheaper to live in a hotel in southern France than it was to rent my apartment in London. . . . I intended to go for two months; I stayed for five. I snapped out of depression, and of writer's block, and I made enormous progress. I had a fabulous time: going there was the best decision I've made in about ten years."

Dr. Tatiana's Sex Advice to All Creation: The Definitive Guide to the Evolutionary Biology of Sex was published in both Britain and the United States in the summer of 2002. Modeled on Judson's piece for the *Economist* and written in the form of a sex-advice column for animals, the book explores the myriad ways in which animals mate with one another. Each question launches "Dr. Tatiana" into a thorough and humorous explanation of the sex life of the species in question. "Dear Dr. Tatiana," one letter begins, as quoted on the Amazon Bookseller's Web site, "My name's Twiggy, and I'm a stick insect. It's with great embarrassment that I write to you while copulating, but my mate and I have been copulating for ten weeks already. I'm bored out of my skull, yet he shows no signs of flagging. He says it's because he's madly in love with me, but I think he's just plain mad. How can I get him to quit?" Dr. Tatiana replies, "Your paramour is mad, though not with love but with jealousy. By continually copulating he can guarantee that no one else will have a chance to get near you. It's a good thing he's only half your length, so he's not too heavy to carry about."

Through her replies, Judson-as-Dr.-Tatiana manages to overturn several stereotypes about what constitutes "normal" sexual behavior in the animal kingdom, with implications for the human world as well. One of these is the notion that females prefer to mate with very few partners. In her reply to the above query, as quoted on Amazon, Judson noted that the male stick insect has good reason to be jealous: "In most species, girls are more strumpet than saint. Rather than just mating once, they'll mate with several fellows, and often with far, far more than necessary just to fertilize their eggs." She further explained that in the animal kingdom, females are rarely faithful to just one male and that "rampant promiscuity is no malfunction. Rather, females benefit from it." She pointed out that in most cases, females who copulate with many partners have higher rates of reproductive success—in other words, they have more offspring. Judson also debunked the myth that monogamy is the norm, and cited numerous cases illustrating how much more common it is for animals to have multiple partners. The author's larger message is one of tolerance. "Beyond the basic fact that males make sperm and females make eggs, there are no rules, not even in what appear to be the most stereotypical gender-related areas," she wrote, as quoted in the *San-Diego Union Tribune* (September 8, 2002).

Readers in both the United States and Britain initially ignored *Dr. Tatiana's Sex Advice to All Creation* despite largely positive critical reviews. A highly publicized book tour in the U.S., however, which included an appearance on CNN, soon propelled the book onto best-seller lists on both sides of the Atlantic. Mary Carmichael opined for *Newsweek* (August 5, 2002): "Easy to understand and hard to resist, it's sex education at its prime—accurate, comprehensive and hilarious." "'Simultaneous' is one of the great words in the human sexual lexicon, and here Judson has achieved a most rare synchronicity of a different kind—between science and humour," Margie Thompson wrote for the *New Zealand Herald* (September 21, 2002). "If you've nothing better to do one evening soon, Dr. Tatiana could keep you amused, safely, for hours." In a review posted at the Brothers Judd Web site (September 17, 2002), however, Orrin Judd argued that Judson's willingness to transfer her open-mindedness about sexual practices in the animal world to the human world resulted in oversimplification: "Assuming evolution is sound science, animals respond to an overwhelming force of nature; they don't pick and choose sexual behaviors because they seem like fun; only humans have this privilege. . . . Ultimately, Ms. Judson overreaches her material, but not before she's made reading the book worth our while." Judson's book was translated into 16 languages and short-listed for the Samuel Johnson Prize. "I wanted to give people not only a sense of the incredible richness of natural history, but also a sense of how much we have still to discover," she told Ken Ringle. "There is just so much out there that's fascinating, much of it still a dark, unexplored realm."

Judson lives in London, where she is a research fellow at Imperial College. She has recently written science essays for the *Prospect*, a British magazine, and the *New York Times*. On June 17, 2004 the Zoological Society of London presented Judson with its Biosis Award, in recognition of her work in disseminating zoological information. According to a Web site devoted to Judson's book, a series of three one-hour television programs inspired by *Dr. Tatiana's Sex Advice* was scheduled to air in the U.S. and U.K. in the fall of 2004 and winter of 2005.

—H.T.

Suggested Reading: (London) *Daily Telegraph* p15+ May 13, 2003; *New York Times* F p3+ Nov. 5, 2002, with photo; *Readers Read* (on-line) Apr. 2003; *Washington Post* C p1+ May 28, 2003

Selected Books: *Dr. Tatiana's Sex Advice to All Creation: The Definitive Guide to the Evolutionary Biology of Sex*, 2002

Courtesy of jacksonkatz.com

Katz, Jackson

May 7, 1960– Anti-sexism activist

Address: c/o Lordly & Dame, 51 Church St., Boston, MA 02116

One of the leading anti-sexism activists in the United States, Jackson Katz is recognized for his work in the field of gender-violence prevention, particularly violence directed against women, in the arenas of academia, the military, and sports. Jackson is the founder and director of MVP (Mentors in Violence Prevention) Strategies, an organization that offers gender-violence prevention education and materials to universities, high schools, law-enforcement agencies, the U.S. military, community organizations, and corporations. Katz has given lectures at hundreds of universities and high schools and conducted hundreds of professional training programs, seminars, and workshops both in the U.S. and abroad. His MVP Program, which Katz co-founded in 1993, is the most widely used gender-violence prevention program in college athletics in the U.S. One of the goals of the program, and Katz's organization as a whole, is to foster an awareness of how depictions of men, women, sex, and violence in sports culture, advertising, television programs, movies, popular music, and other media contribute to gender violence and other social ills. Although he wants to awaken all segments of society to the reality of gender violence, he especially hopes to influence males, who are responsible for the vast majority of the rapes, sexual assaults, incidents of battering and domestic abuse, and other violent crimes that plague American society. Most men, Katz tells his audi-

ences, have a female relative, spouse, or friend who has been the victim of some form of sexism or gender violence. He works to inspire men to take a stand against violence committed by other men and the potentially harmful models of masculinity that much of popular culture peddles. "The goal is to create a male peer culture, an atmosphere whereby the abuse of women by some men will be seen as completely unacceptable by the male peer culture," he told Eric Ostrem for the the *Daily Californian* (October 22, 2002), the campus newspaper of the University of California at Berkeley.

Katz, a former all-state high-school football player and college athlete, is a member of the Task Force on Domestic Violence set up by the U.S. secretary of defense; from 1998 to 2000 he served on the American Bar Association's Commission on Domestic Violence. "Jackson's dynamic theories and teaching style have had a profound impact on audiences in the programs he has done for us," Roberta Valente, another member of the commission, has said, as quoted on Katz's Web site (jacksonkatz.com). "We count on him to open the eyes and ears of lawyers and judges as we try to spread the word that violence against women is everybody's business." For use in his lectures and seminars, Katz has created educational films on the topics of gender violence and sexism. Among them is *Tough Guise: Violence, Media, and the Crisis in Masculinity* (2000), considered the first educational video for high-school and college students that examines the relationships between images from popular culture and the construction of masculine identities. The American Library Association named *Tough Guise* one of the top 10 young-adult videos of 2000. As quoted on Katz's Web site, Susan McGee Bailey, the director of the Wellesley Centers for Women, said, "Jackson has a rare gift for applying feminist insights about gender and power to the real life experience of boys and men. He does this in a way that helps men think critically without becoming defensive, while offering women valuable new perspectives into masculinity." Katz has been quoted widely in the media and has appeared on the television programs *Good Morning America*, the *Oprah Winfrey Show*, *Montel Williams*, *MSNBC*, *20/20*, and the *CBS Evening News*.

Jackson T. Katz was born on May 7, 1960. Katz told an interviewer for the feminist on-line magazine *Merge* (January 2001) that people have often asked him how he came to care about issues of gender violence and whether a specific event in his life pushed him in that direction. "I'm asked this not just because of my sports background but just because I'm a guy," he said. "My typical response is to ask people to think about it for a minute. When people get involved in environmental activism—the degradation of the water, endangered species—people don't question their motives or wonder why they're doing it. They assume that the ecosystem is important enough to take care of. If someone is a civil rights activist, people don't question their motives; they just assume some people seriously question the supposed values of our country, and want to fight for equal treatment for all. With any major issue, it's the same. Yet when a man speaks out against men's violence against women, people wonder what is going on. There must have been something that happened to him, he must have been a child witness to domestic violence, or a woman close to him must have been assaulted." He added, "We need to turn the question around and ask why are so few men, who have women and girls they supposedly care about in their lives, working on these issues." Katz told Alexis Kindig for the *Daily Forty-Niner* (April 15, 2002), a campus newspaper of the California State University at Long Beach, that his desire to stop sexual abuse and gender violence stems in part from the physical abuse he and his siblings experienced as children at the hands of their stepfather, who had been abused by his own father. Katz played several sports competitively and was an all-state football player in high school. By his own account, he grew up in what he has labeled a "jock-ocracy," as quoted by Kindig. A literature course he attended as an undergraduate at the University of Massachusetts (UM) at Amherst sparked his interest in the women's movement and other social movements of the 1960s and 1970s, as well as issues of gender violence. At UM–Amherst Katz played three sports and became the first man in the school's history to earn a minor in women's studies. After he earned a bachelor's degree, in 1982, he received a master's degree from the School of Education of Harvard University, in Cambridge, Massachusetts, where his research focused on the social construction of violent male role models in sports and the media.

In 1993 Katz co-founded the Mentors in Violence Prevention Program at the Center for the Study of Sport in Society at Northeastern University, in Boston, Massachusetts. He is the primary author of MVP's teaching materials. Funded in part by the U.S. Department of Education, MVP is among the first large-scale projects to enlist high-school, college, and professional athletes in the fight against all forms of male violence against women. The MVP Program spawned MVP Strategies, through which Katz has expanded his efforts. Having been introduced to thousands of student athletes at more than 85 U.S. colleges, the MVP Program is the most widely used gender-violence prevention program in college sports. Addressing on his Web site the question of why his work has often focused on male student athletes, Katz explained that school rape-crisis and battered-women centers have faced serious challenges due to the "apathy, defensiveness—and sometimes outright hostility—of male athletic directors, coaches, and student-athletes." Further, male student athletes often "occupy a privileged position in school culture and particularly in male peer culture. As such, male student-athletes—especially in popular team sports such as football, basketball,

hockey, baseball, wrestling, and soccer—tend to have enormous clout when it comes to establishing or maintaining traditional masculine norms. Their support or lack of support for prevention efforts can make or break [those efforts]." In other words, male student athletes can be very effective leaders and so can help to change attitudes and create at their schools environments in which women and their rights are treated with more respect. Another reason that Katz has singled out student athletes for special attention is that, as studies have shown, although male student athletes make up only a small percentage of the total male student population at most schools, they account for a high percentage of sexual assaults on campuses. Along with other MVP staff members, Katz has trained players, coaches, and front-office personnel of the New England Patriots of the National Football League (NFL).

Since 1997 Katz has directed a gender-violence prevention program in the U.S. Marine Corps—the first such program ever instituted in that branch of the military. He and his colleagues have reached thousands of marines on more than a dozen bases in the U.S. and Japan. According to his Web site, the U.S. Navy has tested Katz's program among sailors on the aircraft carrier *USS Carl Vinson*. Katz has lectured at more than 650 colleges, preparatory schools, high schools, middle schools, professional conferences, and military installations in more than 40 states in the U.S. He brings to the attention of his audiences the well-documented fact that over 99 percent of rapes are committed by men. In his lectures, writings, and elsewhere, he has often posed this rhetorical question: If over 99 percent of rapes are committed by men, why is rape considered a women's issue? Since rape, domestic abuse, sexual harassment, and related crimes are considered "'women's issues,' men think they can ignore [them]," he told Katy Hogan for the Lowell, Massachusetts, *Sun* (April 11, 2002). He urges young men to stand up for the dignity of women and girls despite the possibility that they may find themselves labeled as feminine or as lacking masculinity. As quoted on the Web site of Rollins College, where he has lectured, Katz is quoted as having said, "If you really care for these girls in your life, whether it be your mom, sister, niece[,] girlfriend, cousin, best-friend, or aunt, [then] the time is now [to take a stand against all forms of abuse of women], and if you can hold your head up high [then] it does not matter what your male friends say." He added, "Being one of the guys is easy, it doesn't take strength. What takes strength is speaking up when men demean women." Katz tells women that, contrary to the beliefs of many, they should not avoid adopting a feminist stance. In encouraging women to fight for respect when necessary, Katz (as quoted on the Rollins College Web site) has shared with audiences a quotation from the former first lady Eleanor Roosevelt: "You can't be made to feel inferior without your consent."

Katz has developed four major lecture series. One is based on his award-winning educational video, *Tough Guise: Violence, Media, and the Crisis in Masculinity,* in which he argued that widespread violence in American society, including school violence (the 1999 massacre at Columbine High School in Littleton, Colorado, being only one example, albeit among the most horrific), needs to be understood as part of an "ongoing crisis in masculinity," in his words. *Tough Guise* systematically examines the relationships between images in popular culture and American society's concepts of what a man is or should be. The video has been shown as part of many college communication, sociology, gender-studies, psychology, and criminology courses and is used by educators and counselors in such fields as rape and domestic-violence prevention. In an appraisal of *Tough Guise* for *Video Reader,* as quoted on Katz's Web site, Randy Pitman, a librarian who specializes in videos, wrote, "Many programs released over the past few years have offered self-evident observations about America's violence problem—especially the disturbing uptick in deadly school violence—but . . . *Tough Guise,* hosted by Jackson Katz, is the first title to make my relatively savvy mental wheels turn. . . . His general arguments are very persuasive. . . . Highly recommended." Mary Atwater, a violence prevention coordinator for Jefferson County, Colorado, wrote, as quoted on the same site, "Violence prevention begins with a fearless look at the cultural factors that encourage violence, especially school violence. *Tough Guise* needs to be watched by every high school and middle school student in America."

Katz's presentation *My Gun's Bigger Than Yours: Images of Manhood and Violence in the Media* consists of a slide show and lecture during which Katz discusses images in Hollywood films, the world of sports, advertising, and music videos. In *More Than a Few Good Men: A Lecture on American Manhood and Violence Against Women,* he addresses such subjects as rape, sexual harassment, abusive relationships, and other forms of gender discrimination, and discusses the ways in which homophobia prevents men and women from dealing with issues of sexism. *It's the Masculinity, Stupid: White Males, Iconic Images, and Presidential Politics* is another of Katz's illustrated lectures.

In addition to *Tough Guise,* Katz's highly regarded educational videos include *Wrestling with Manhood: Boys, Bullying, and Battering* (2002), made by Katz and Sut Jhally, a professor in the Department of Communication at UM–Amherst, it examines professional wrestling's popularity among young males and looks at its relationship to real-life violence. Katz and Jhally argued that the entertainment professional wrestling offers is related to homophobia and sexual assault. As examples, they included clips from televised wrestling events in which male wrestlers graphically describe physically harming women, literally stomp on women

and throw them to the ground, and even simulate rape. In making the educational video *Spin the Bottle: Sex, Lies, and Alcohol,* Katz worked with Jean Kilbourne, an award-winning pioneer in the study of the damage to women and society as a whole that is caused by advertising and other media. *Spin the Bottle* addresses the pervasive depiction of alcohol consumption as attractive or beneficial, despite estimates that, among students, alcohol abuse contributes to more than one thousand deaths, half a million injuries, and more than 50,000 sexual assaults every year.

In his writings, many of which appear on his Web site, Katz has discussed such controversial figures from popular culture as Larry Flynt, who founded a pornography empire and has been lauded by some as a champion of free speech; the rapper Eminem, whose lyrics contain statements frequently described as misogynistic, sexist, or hostile to homosexuals; and Kobe Bryant, the basketball superstar who has been charged with raping a 19-year-old woman. Katz warns that Flynt's degrading portrayals of women and young girls may be having harmful psychological effects on American society, in which rape, sexual assault, and battering, among other crimes, occur at high rates. (For example, according to the book *Rape and Sexual Assault: Reporting to Police and Medical Attention, 1992–2000* [2002], published by the U.S. Department of Justice, during those years there were on average 140,990 rapes, 109,230 attempted rapes, and 152,680 sexual assaults committed in the United States against individuals age 12 or older. In more than 85 percent of those incidents, the victims were female. Those statistics do not tell the whole story, as many rapes and crimes of sexual assault go unreported.) Concerning Eminem, in the article "8 Reasons Eminem's Popularity Is a Disaster for Women," which appeared on his Web site, Katz asked how it was possible to "reconcile a concern for women's physical, sexual, and emotional well-being with admiration for a male artist [Eminem] whose lyrics consistently portray women in a contemptuous and sexually degrading manner." He told readers that the "most powerful lesson" to be gleaned from the Bryant case, regardless of whether or not the sports star is guilty as charged, is "Don't ever force a woman (or a man) to have sex with you."

Katz's list "10 Things Men Can Do to Prevent Gender Violence," as posted on his Web site, includes the exhortations, "Have the courage to look inward. Question your own attitudes. Don't be defensive when something you do or say ends up hurting someone else. Try hard to understand how your own attitudes and actions might inadvertently perpetuate sexism and violence, and work toward changing them. . . . If you are emotionally, psychologically, physically, or sexually abusive to women, or have been in the past, seek professional help NOW. . . . Recognize and speak out against homophobia and gay-bashing. Discrimination and violence against lesbians and gays are wrong in and of themselves. This abuse also has direct links to sexism. . . . Don't fund sexism. Refuse to purchase any magazine, rent any video, subscribe to any Web site, or buy any music that portrays girls or women in a sexually degrading or abusive manner. Protest sexism in the media."

Katz's published work includes the articles "Put the Blame Where it Belongs: On Men," written with Sut Jhally for the *Los Angeles Times* (June 25, 2000); "The Price Women Pay for Boys Being Boys," for the Seattle *Post-Intelligencer* (May 13, 2001); and "Big Trouble, Little Pond: Reflections on the Meaning of the Campus Pond Rapes," written with Sut Jhally for the University of Massachusetts *UMass Magazine* (Winter 2001), the last of which discussed several incidents of alleged sexual assaults on the school's campus in late 1999. His essays and articles have been included in a number of books, among them *Rape 101: Sexual Assault Prevention for College Athletes* (1994), edited by Andrea Parrot, Nina Cummings, and Timothy Marchell; *Gender, Race and Class in Media: A Text Reader* (1995), edited by Gail Dines and Jean M.

Humez; *Sport in Society: Equal Opportunity or Business as Usual?* (1996), edited by Richard E. Lapchick; *Readings for Diversity and Social Justice* (2000), edited by Maurianne Adams and others; and *Masculinities at School* (2000), edited by Nancy Lesko.

Katz has served as a consultant for the Liz Claiborne Co.'s award-winning domestic-violence awareness and educational campaign, called Women's Work.

—C.F.T.

Suggested Reading: *Daily Californian* Oct. 22, 2002; jacksonkatz.com; *Los Angeles Times* VI p6+ Dec. 9, 2001; mergemag.org; Rollins College Web site; *Santa Barbara Independent* p36+ May 15, 2003

Selected Videos: *Tough Guise: Violence, Media, and the Crisis in Masculinity*, 2000; *Wrestling with Manhood: Boys, Bullying, and Battering*, 2002; *Spin the Bottle: Sex, Lies, and Alcohol* (with Jean Kilbourne), 2003

Keegan, Robert

1947– Chairman and CEO of Goodyear Tire & Rubber Co.

Address: Goodyear Tire & Rubber Co., 1144 Market St., Akron, OH 44316

A proven success as a leader in the consumer-products industry, Robert J. Keegan became chairman of the board and chief executive officer (CEO) of the Goodyear Tire & Rubber Co., the world's biggest tire maker, in 2003. Keegan described himself to Marcia Pledger for the Cleveland, Ohio, *Plain Dealer* (September 15, 2000) as someone who "really enjoys consumer markets." "I'm very happy in the consumer market space," he told Jim Mackinnon for the *Akron (Ohio) Beacon Journal* (September 15, 2000). "Every decision you make starts from the consumer." Before joining Goodyear, Keegan worked for more than 25 years with the Rochester, New York–based Eastman Kodak Corp., the photographic-products company that is perennially number one in U.S. film sales. At Kodak Keegan held a variety of positions, including director of finance for Kodak's Photographic Products Group and executive vice president, in addition to separate stints as general manager of Kodak New Zealand and Kodak Spain. He is credited with helping to revitalize Kodak's slumping sales in the late 1990s, when he ran Kodak's Consumer Imaging division, which is responsible for roughly half of the company's total sales of more than $10 billion a year. "He's a genius when it comes to figuring out what customers want and how best to get it to them in new ways," Ed Wagner of *Photo Industry*, a trade

Goodyear/Getty Images

publication, told Mary Ethridge for the *Akron Beacon Journal* (September 17, 2000) regarding Keegan. When Keegan joined the tire giant Goodyear as president, in 2000, then–Goodyear chairman and CEO Samir Gibara told the Associated Press (September 14, 2000), "The breadth and depth of Bob Keegan's global sales, marketing and business operating experience over more than two decades in the consumer products industry should prove of great value to Goodyear."

As chief strategist for Goodyear—which was founded more than 100 years ago, has plants and offices in 28 countries, and employs nearly 100,000 workers—Keegan has been entrusted with changing the company's marketing strategies in order to make it a more consumer-focused business, and thereby help it recover from the decline in profits and stock value it has suffered since the late 1990s. In 2001 Goodyear posted its first yearly loss in nearly a decade; two years later the company's stock reached a 40-year low. Despite the difficult task he faces, Keegan remains optimistic about his chances of restoring Goodyear's prosperity. "You don't lead by telling people what to do," Keegan told John Russell for the *Akron Beacon Journal* (September 30, 2001). "You get them energized by telling them you're open to new ideas and you're with them in terms of trying to drive success."

Robert J. Keegan was born in Rochester, New York, near Lake Ontario, in 1947. His father, Robert Keegan Sr., played professional baseball as a pitcher for the Chicago White Sox; in 1957 he pitched a no-hitter against the Washington Senators. The Keegan children took five weeks off from school every spring in order to be with their father during professional baseball's annual spring training. In the summers Robert Jr. and his siblings lived in a rented house in Chicago, Illinois, the home of their father's team, watching the White Sox's games on television and spending time around the team's players. "I wanted to be a ballplayer my whole life," Robert Jr., who played Little League baseball as a shortstop and pitcher, told John Russell, "until I was 14 and concluded I didn't have the talent." A tall boy, Keegan switched to basketball, which he played competitively in high school and college and as a hobby into his 40s.

In 1969 Keegan earned a bachelor of science degree in mathematics from LeMoyne College, in Syracuse, New York. He was awarded an M.B.A. in finance from the University of Rochester in 1972. That same year Keegan began his career with Kodak. At that company—founded by George Eastman in 1880—he started as an employee in the distribution and marketing divisions in Rochester, then held a series of positions in marketing and finance in the United States and Europe, spending nine years in London. He was named general manager of Kodak New Zealand in 1986.

Keegan returned to Rochester in 1987 and was named director of finance for Kodak's Photographic Products Group. In 1990 he was appointed general manager of Kodak Spain, and the following year he was named general manager of the Consumer Imaging unit for Kodak's European, Middle Eastern, and African divisions. (The Consumer Imaging unit deals primarily with film, cameras, and digital products.) In November 1993 Keegan was elected a corporate vice president.

Keegan left Kodak in 1995 to become the executive vice president and global strategy officer at the Pasadena, California–based Avery Dennison Corp., a leader in pressure-sensitive and self-adhesive materials, office products, and specialized labels. According to Ulysses A. Yannas, a business analyst, as quoted by Marcia Pledger, Keegan's main goal in leaving Kodak to join Avery was to have a chance eventually to run a large company. "He was looking for a place where he could be the top banana," Yannas told Pledger. When Avery did not offer Keegan the top spot in the company, Keegan returned to Kodak.

In July 1997 Keegan became president of Kodak Professional and was reelected to the position of corporate vice president. Later that same year he was appointed president of Consumer Imaging, replacing David P. Biehn, and elected a senior vice president. Consumer Imaging is Kodak's largest and most lucrative division; according to the Associated Press (September 14, 2000), it accounted for more than half of Kodak's $14 billion in annual sales. In the months prior to Keegan's return, Kodak had lost market share to the Tokyo, Japan–based Fuji Film, and Kodak's new digital division was losing money due to its struggles in trying to market new photographic technologies. The magazine *M2 Presswire* predicted in 1998 that digitization–the word used to describe the combining of traditional photography with emerging technological tools such as scanners, the Internet, and cell phones–would increase the global photo industry's revenues from $80 billion a year to nearly $100 billion within three years' time. Accordingly, Keegan's efforts at the time were aimed in part at increasing the digitization of consumer film and photographs. To that end, Kodak aligned itself with digital and computer-based companies such as America Online (AOL) and Intel. Keegan led a joint project in 2000 with the computer giant Hewlett-Packard to develop photo-finishing equipment for digital photography, a development that Mary Ethridge called a "major technological step" for Kodak. "Because of digitization," Keegan told *M2 Presswire* (September 18, 1998), "there is no need for any consumer to fall behind on technology adoption." He also said that with the use of digital technologies such as the Internet, through which digital photos can be sent by E-mail, "all of a sudden a photo that might have gone straight to the shoe box has a digitized life of its own. Sometimes five or six new lives." Keegan offered *M2 Presswire* the example of a wedding photographer who can now post his pictures of a wedding on a Web site, which would enable all the event's attendees to see the pictures and order prints through a service such as Kodak PhotoNet On Line. Keegan was largely responsible for Kodak's breakthrough deals with the Walt Disney Co. and the retail chain Toys "R" Us. After talking to customers, who told him that they wanted a simpler way of shopping for photography-related merchandise, Keegan helped Kodak to move aggressively to manufacture and promote disposable cameras and new, easy-to-understand, color-coded packages for its products.

Keegan told Marcia Pledger that during his three years as the head of Consumer Imaging, Kodak held its market share in the United States, improved market share worldwide, and succeeded in selling more premium-priced film. In 2000 Ethridge reported that Kodak's revenue was up 5 percent from the previous fiscal year, compared to declines of 8 and 9 percent the previous two years, and that sales of digital products were up 46 percent over the year prior, accounting for 17 percent of the company's total revenue. "He was determined to turn Kodak around," Ed Wagner told Ethridge regarding Keegan. "He's a very strong leader, very action oriented. He embraced change, welcomed it for the good of the company." Mitchell Goldstone, president of 30 Minute Photos Etc., a large California photo shop, told Ethridge that Keegan is "passionately interested in employees and customers—in people. Everyone tells me he turned morale around at the company and engendered a lot of affection among employees."

In January 2000 Keegan became an executive vice president of Kodak, but in October of that same year he left the company to become president, chief operating officer (COO), and director of the Goodyear Tire & Rubber Co., based in Akron, Ohio. Goodyear is the world's largest tire maker and operator of commercial truck services and a major retailer of tires and automotive services. The company owns more than 2,000 auto, tire, and service centers. Goodyear helped to woo Keegan by offering him an $800,000 base salary, the possibility of bonuses that would put his yearly earnings well over $1 million, and a contractual guarantee that he would be made CEO within three years' time or be entitled to millions more. Referring to the fact that Keegan had no prior history with Goodyear, Russell called him "the first outsider in a century to be named president" of the company. Most essential for Keegan was his learning the tire business—in particular, the process by which tires are made. From the start, though, Keegan knew that he wanted Goodyear to be focused on the needs of its customers. John Russell summed up one of the challenges facing Keegan, writing, "First fact: Tires are a critical part of cars, trucks and airplanes. Second fact: Most people don't care about their tires." Keegan told Russell, "Any good marketing man can't help but gravitate toward that kind of challenge. The more I thought about it, the more excited I got."

Optimistic about Keegan's chances to improve sales and market share for Goodyear, Saul Ludwig, an analyst at McDonald Investments in Cleveland, Ohio, told Pledger, "With film, just like tires, it may be difficult to differentiate quality among competing brands, and Mr. Keegan did a terrific job in arresting the decline of the Kodak brand to Fuji over the last two years." Keegan, too, compared his new company to Kodak, telling Pledger, "Both are No.1 in their industries and share market. Both have envied brand franchises, and both have strong trade partnerships and the highest quality of state-of-the-art technology. Both face global competition and are in very competitive markets."

Still, Goodyear faced serious challenges in 2000. Russell quoted *Businessweek Online* as having stated on the occasion of Keegan's hiring, "The world's largest tire maker needs all the help it can get because slow growth and inefficient management have kept Goodyear well under top speed lately." Part of the decline was attributable to the loss of sales to competitors such as Michelin and Bridgestone, an increase in raw material costs, and the general economic downturn in the United States. In response, before Keegan's arrival Goodyear was attempting to integrate its three major tire brands—Goodyear, Dunlop, and Kelly—into one, and was overhauling and unifying its North American tire and auto-service stores under a single new name, Gemini. "To some degree, if I look at my role," Keegan told Russell, "I see myself as a change agent. I think Sam [Gibara] and the board brought me in to do that. I need our people, throughout the organization, to accept the fact that business as usual is slow death."

The changes Keegan enacted early in his tenure at Goodyear included replacing the company's longtime advertising agency, J. Walter Thompson of Detroit, Michigan, whose advertisements for Goodyear focused on tire tread patterns, traction, and other technical features, with Goodby, Silverstein & Partners of San Francisco, California, who launched an emotional, safety-focused advertising campaign for Goodyear in the wake of the Bridgestone/Firestone tire recall. (According to the National Bureau of Economic Research Web site, in August 2000 Bridgestone/Firestone and the Ford Motor Co. jointly announced the recall of more than 14 million tires that were deemed to be defective and to create safety liabilities. The following month the National Highway Traffic and Safety Administration found that faulty Firestone tires had been a factor in hundreds of traffic fatalities.) In addition, according to Russell, Keegan instructed his top managers to issue him reports monthly instead of quarterly, as had been the practice before, and insisted on beginning every executive meeting by talking about Goodyear's customers. Keegan also encouraged junior executives by meeting with them to hear their ideas and suggestions regarding the company's operations.

Despite Keegan's changes, Goodyear did not rebound financially. The company's "On the Wings of Goodyear" advertising campaign, which Keegan had overseen, failed to attract customers or excite tire dealers; the company continued to lose market share and was forced to cut back on tire production. John Russell reported for the *Akron Beacon Journal* (October 2, 2002) that in 2001, with revenues stagnating at $14 billion, Goodyear lost more than $200 million, its first yearly loss in nine years. In 2002 Goodyear reported a record $1.1 billion annual loss, and its stock fell by more than 60 percent. Despite the fact that six of Goodyear's seven major units had performed well in 2002, Goodyear's North American Tire division, the company's largest unit, had continued to lose market share, causing the whole company to suffer. (Michelin and Bridgestone, Goodyear's major competitors, gained market share in 2002 and saw their stock prices drop only slightly.)

As Goodyear's losses continued, some questioned the wisdom of bringing in a man who had no prior experience with tires as the second-most-powerful executive in the company. "[Keegan is] not a tire man. He's been involved in a lot of the decisions in the last two years," Don Headrick, a pipe fitter with Goodyear for more than 25 years, said to Betty Lin-Fisher for the *Akron Beacon Journal* (October 2, 2002). "There's no rubber people left in the company. They make bad decisions and compound them instead of selling tires." Other business observers have noted that the origins of many of Goodyear's financial and operational problems predate Keegan's arrival at the company. For example, as reported by John Russell in the *Akron Beacon Journal* (June 23, 2003), Samir Gibara's tenure at the helm of Goodyear left the company with the "highest cost structure among the global 'Big Three' in the [tire] industry" and more than $5 billion in debt.

Replacing Gibara, on January 1, 2003 Keegan became CEO of Goodyear. In an attempt to halt the decline of the company's fortunes, he cut more than 700 salaried jobs, arranged a $3.3 billion debt restructuring with lender institutions, and put Goodyear's profitable chemical division up for sale. "Last year was one of the toughest in the history of our company," Keegan told Russell for the *Akron Beacon Journal* (February 12, 2003). "Softness in the market, combined with missteps on our part in both strategy and execution, hurt us." Keegan affirmed that Goodyear needed to shift its focus to work more closely with the many independent tire dealers who drive tire sales. Establishing good working relations with independent dealers is critical to Goodyear's success, as independent dealers, who often stock a wide variety of tire brands, "sell about two-thirds of all passenger replacement tires in North America and can often sway car owners on which kind of replacement tires to buy," Russell wrote. "In the past, Goodyear hasn't always listened to its dealers," Keegan told Michael Hooper for the Topeka, Kansas, *Capital-Journal* (February 27, 2003). "We need to take advantage of their knowledge." Keegan's primary goals include a more than $1 billion reduction in costs by the end of 2005; a 4 percent increase in revenue per tire; a reduction of debt; and a two-point market share increase in North America by 2005. "I relish the challenge. I don't underestimate the substantial hurdles that confront us," he told M. R. Kropko for the Associated Press (May 8, 2003).

Keegan was elected chairman of the board of Goodyear on July 1, 2003. A month later *Forbes* (August 1, 2003, on-line) listed Keegan as fourth-best among automotive executives in terms of approval ratings, computed by using readers' votes. (William C. Ford Jr. of the Ford Motor Co. was first, with a rating of 67 percent; Keegan was given a rating of 30 percent.)

The six-foot three-inch Keegan enjoys playing golf and attending theater performances. He is said to have an amiable and down-to-earth demeanor. He and his wife, Lynn, have two children. According to Russell, before relocating from Rochester to Akron, Keegan changed the tires on his BMW sedan to Goodyear. His wife's car already sported Goodyear line Dunlop tires. "There was no way in the world I was going to drive into Akron with anything but Goodyear or Dunlop tires on these cars," he quipped to Russell.

—C.F.T.

Suggested Reading: *Akron (Ohio) Beacon Journal* E p1 Sep. 15, 2000, G p1 Sep. 17, 2000, with photo, B p1 Sep. 30, 2001, with photos, A p10 Oct. 2, 2002, A p1 Feb. 12, 2003, A p1 June 23, 2003; (Cleveland, Ohio) *Plain Dealer* C p1 Sep. 15, 2000; Goodyear Web site; *M2 Presswire* Sep. 18, 1998

Keith, Toby

July 8, 1961– Country-music singer; songwriter

Address: c/o DreamWorks Records, 1516 16th Ave. S., Nashville, TN 37212

Toby Keith has been many things, including a rodeo hand, a football player, and a worker in oil fields. He spent the 1990s as a solid but often unnoticed country-music singer, songwriter, and guitarist, releasing such albums as *Toby Keith*, *Boomtown*, and *Dream Walkin'*, all of which sold well but were largely overlooked by the country-music industry when it came time to hand out awards. After almost a decade of relatively modest successes, Keith burst into prominence—some might say notoriety—with the release of his song "Courtesy of the Red, White, & Blue (The Angry American)," his reaction to the terrorist attacks on the U.S. on September 11, 2001. Instantly, he found himself in the eye of a storm of controversy over the single, which some called patriotic, others jingoistic. Amid the opinions of Keith and his music, one thing is certain—he no longer slips under the radar of the music industry: *Unleashed* (2002), the album that contains his controversial song, received 15 award nominations. Keith is known for his unabashedly traditional honky-tonk country style and his refusal to make his songs more mainstream by veering toward pop sounds or infusing his lyrics with so-called political correctness. "He sticks to topics that a rowdy crowd can easily get behind: drinking, smoking, partying and hanging out with friends," Jim Harrington wrote for the *Oakland*

Courtesy of DreamWorks Records

Toby Keith

(California) Tribune (August 31, 2004, on-line). "His choruses are built to be sung by thousands of people and his lyrical punch lines are often quite clever." The success of such albums as *How Do You Like Me Now?!*, *Pull My Chain*, *Unleashed*, and *Shock 'N Y'all* offers evidence of how well Keith knows, and caters to, his audiences.

The singer was born Toby Keith Covel on July 8, 1961 in Clinton, Oklahoma, and grew up on a farm in Moore, a town on the outskirts of Oklahoma City. Even as a boy he was a music fan; he listened to his father's records by the country stars Merle Haggard and Bob Wills and loved spending time at his grandmother's supper club, which featured live musicians. He recalled to Jack Hurst for the *Chicago Tribune* (January 14, 1994) that his grandmother would let the young Toby sit in with the band one day a week and play a percussion instrument. "I'd wait all week for that one chance, just to get up there and stand with them and let everybody look up at you," he said. "I think I got the bug on that at an early age." Keith, who had spent much of his time since the age of five playing football, took up the guitar when he was eight and later developed an interest in songwriting. He was 11 when his grade-school homeroom teacher announced that her class would write short stories every Friday. While most of the class disliked the assignment, Keith found that he enjoyed it. "I'd write about anything, just let my imagination run wild and free as it could. That's the earliest sign I can ever remember of wanting to be a writer," he told Hurst. Keith wrote songs in his spare hours; he spent most of his time, when not attending school, working on the farm and as a rodeo hand, test-riding newly purchased bulls and broncos. After graduating from high school, he got a job in nearby oil fields. In 1984 he formed a band called Easy Money, which played in local bars and nightclubs, mainly covering songs by the country group Alabama. Later they began performing some of Keith's original compositions, too.

When, after Keith had been working in the oil fields for about three years, the oil industry took a downturn, he attempted a new career: playing football. He spent two years as a defensive end for the Oklahoma City Drillers, a semi-professional team, and later tried out successfully for the Oklahoma Outlaws of the United States Football League (USFL). When the USFL folded, in 1985, Keith decided to take a risk and concentrate on his music full-time. He and the other members of Easy Money went on the road, with Keith focusing more than before on writing. Although they did not have a recording contract, Keith and the band managed to support themselves as live performers. Keith made a few records with local independent labels but did not receive any major attention until 1992, when, during a flight, a friend who worked as an airline attendant gave one of Keith's demo tapes to Harold Shedd, the president of the label Polydor Nashville. Shedd was so impressed by the tape that he later flew to Oklahoma City to hear Keith perform in person. Over breakfast the next morning, he signed the singer to Mercury/Polygram Records.

Keith released his eponymous debut album in 1993. In February of the same year, his first single, the tongue-in-cheek "Should've Been a Cowboy," reached the number-one spot on the country-music chart. (Keith found inspiration for the song in an observation he made while touring with his band; he explained to Hurst, "When I got to playing music, everybody had a [cowboy] hat on, whether you were from a high-rise in New York City or a high-rise in Dallas or the country. Everybody was a hat act, so I quit wearing mine, even though I've probably been on more bucking stock than any of them. It was the norm to wear a hat, and we wanted to be the abnorm.") Two other songs on the record, "Wish I Didn't Know Now" and "A Little Less Talk and a Lot More Action," also went to number one, and "He Ain't Worth Missing" made it to the Top Five. *Toby Keith* stayed on the charts for a year, eventually going double platinum (meaning that it sold at least two million copies). *Billboard* magazine named Keith the top new country artist of the year, and many considered him a shoo-in for one of the industry's newcomer-of-the-year awards; to the surprise of those people, he was not even nominated. While Keith admitted to being hurt by the slight, he remained philosophical. "I'm the wealthiest person with my last name ever in my roots, as far as we know," he told Jack Hurst for the *Chicago Tribune* (November 6, 1994). "I've got all the material things I could want. If the rest of it [industry recognition] comes, OK. By the time it gets here, there'll probably be somebody else out there sitting and watching [the awards show] that's more deserving that day than I am."

In 1994 Keith released the single "Who's That Man," about a woman moving to her first apartment, which was another number-one hit. *Boomtown*, the album that featured "Who's That Man," came out the same year and soon went gold (selling at least 500,000 copies); it also included the Top 10 hits "Upstairs Downtown" and "You Ain't Much Fun." The next year came *Christmas to Christmas*, which contained Keith's versions of popular holiday songs. *Blue Moon*, released in 1996, boasted two Top 10 singles, "A Woman's Touch" and "Does That Blue Moon Ever Shine on You," and another number-one song, "Me Too." Keith himself produced *Blue Moon*, which went platinum. His next album, *Dream Walkin'* (1997), marked the beginning of his professional relationship with the producer James Stroud. That gold record, a collaborative effort between Keith and Stroud, contained the number-one hits "Dream Walkin'" and "We Were in Love" as well as "I'm So Happy That I Can't Stop Crying," a Grammy-nominated duet with Sting that reached number two on the country chart. The following year Keith released *Greatest Hits, Volume I*.

Pleased with his collaboration with Stroud and increasingly dissatisfied with Mercury Records' promotional efforts, Keith left the label and joined the Nashville division of DreamWorks, which was led by Stroud, in 1999. Although he had done relatively well on his previous label, Keith was convinced that he was destined for greater things. "I was confident in what I was doing and I have a strong spiritual belief that spurred me on," he remarked on his Web site, tobykeith.com. "Believe it or not, that was a peaceful time for me." Keith's late 1999 DreamWorks debut, *How Do You Like Me Now?!*, was a smashing success, attaining platinum status. Its title track reached both number one on the country chart and the Top 40 on the pop chart, marking the first time that any of Keith's songs had cracked the pop market. The record also contained the number-one country tune "You Shouldn't Kiss Me Like This" and the Top Five hit "Country Comes to Town." *How Do You Like Me Now?!* finally garnered Keith the industry recognition that he had long sought, when, in 2000, the Academy of Country Music (ACM) named him male vocalist of the year and picked the record as album of the year. He also received nominations for music video of the year and single of the year (both for "How Do You Like Me Now?!") from the Country Music Association (CMA). Keith interpreted his success as proof that he had made the right choice in maintaining his traditional, twangy style as a musician rather than conform to more commercial standards. "I wouldn't have been happy with compromise, and I never gave up," he stated on his Web site. "I did my last album the way I did my first—my way. It never entered my mind to change or try to conform just to stay afloat."

In 2001 Keith released *Pull My Chain*. That second album for DreamWorks surpassed the first, going double platinum, topping the country charts, and—in a first for Keith—reaching the Top 10 on the pop chart. *Pull My Chain* contained three number-one singles, "I'm Just Talkin' About Tonight," "I Wanna Talk About Me," and "My List," and earned Keith more CMA award nominations and the award for male vocalist of the year. It was his next record, however, and one of its singles in particular, that secured his fame among the general public. Shortly following the September 11, 2001 terrorist attacks on the United States, which had come soon after Keith's father, a military veteran, died in a car accident, Keith wrote on a piece of scrap paper what he was feeling; his notes turned out to be the starting point for the song "Courtesy of the Red, White, & Blue (The Angry American)," released in the summer of 2002. Reactions to the song were as varied as they were fierce. While many embraced it, others thought that Keith was capitalizing on the tragedy, and still others criticized what they felt were Keith's insensitivity and arrogance—exhibited, in their opinion, in such lines as "And you'll be sorry that you messed with / The U.S. of A. / 'Cause we'll put a boot in your ass / It's the American way." That particular line led to a conflict when Keith was scheduled to appear on ABC's *World News Tonight* on the Fourth of July; the program's anchor, Peter Jennings, reportedly objected to the lyric, and Keith's appearance was canceled. (ABC maintained that Keith's performance had never been officially confirmed, but Keith claimed otherwise.) The song proved controversial even among the country-music community, as evidenced when Natalie Maines, a member of the group the Dixie Chicks, criticized it, sparking a feud between the two musicians. Keith responded to the criticism by showing, at one of his concerts, a fake picture of Maines with the Iraqi dictator Saddam Hussein, and Maines retaliated by wearing to the 2003 ACM Awards ceremony a T-shirt that read "F.U.T.K."

Keith's song had its defenders as well as its detractors. Jim Harrington argued in the *Oakland (California) Tribune* (October 13, 2002), "Toby Keith is a patriot. He bleeds red, white and blue. That the song went to No. 1 on the country charts, thus introducing a little more green into the equation, doesn't change that fact. . . . 'The Angry American' is just Keith being real. And that's something that we simply don't get enough of in country music today." The single shot to the number-one position on the country chart and made it into the Top 25 on the pop chart; *Unleashed*, the album that contained "Courtesy of the Red, White, & Blue (The Angry American)," debuted at number one later that year, on both the country and the pop charts, ultimately reaching the quadruple-platinum mark. The album also featured the number-one song "Who's Your Daddy?" and a Top 10 duet with Willie Nelson, "Beer for My Horses." Due to the success of *Unleashed*, Keith won the 2003 ACM entertainer of the year award, and the next year he received more CMA and ACM nominations (seven and eight, respectively) than any other artist. In

2003 Keith released *The Millennium Collection*, a compilation of some of his hits. He titled his next album, released in November of the same year, *Shock 'N Y'all* (a pun on "shock and awe," a term with which the administration of President George W. Bush has referred to the 2003 U.S. air strikes on Iraq). His tour promoting the record was immensely popular, and *Shock 'N Y'all* netted Keith seven CMA nominations and another ACM "entertainer of the year" honor. Keith's latest album, a compilation entitled *Greatest Hits, Volume II*, was released in November 2004. It featured a duet in which Keith sang with his daughter Krystal.

Earlier, in May 2003, Keith performed "Courtesy of the Red, White, & Blue" at a Kansas homecoming parade for Patrick Miller, a former prisoner of war in Iraq, who had taunted his captors by singing the song to them. Keith told Roxana Hegeman for the Associated Press, as quoted on the London *Independent*'s Web site (May 11, 2003), that his decision to appear at the parade was an easy one to make: "After finding out he [Miller] was singing the 'Red White and Blue' to the Iraqis—how can you say no?" Twice in 2003 Keith gave performances, at the request of the White House, for troops at U.S. military bases.

The singer has dabbled in television, too, appearing in TV ads for the long-distance telephone company 10-10-220, a TV movie based on the popular series *The Dukes of Hazzard*, and an episode of *Touched by an Angel*. He also contributed the song "Humanity" to the 1998 animated film *The Prince of Egypt*.

Keith lives outside Norman, Oklahoma, with his wife, Tricia, his daughters, Krystal and Shelley, and his son, Stelen. He is in the process of completing Dream Walkin' Farms, a Thoroughbred-horse breeding and training facility. He has also teamed with Harrah's Las Vegas Casino and Hotel to open a country-themed bar, restaurant, and entertainment venue in the same city. That restaurant is slated to open during the summer of 2005; another is in development at Harrah's North Kansas City location.

—K.J.E.

Suggested Reading: Artist Direct Web site; *Chicago Tribune* p3 Jan. 14, 1994, with photo, p23 Nov. 6, 1994, with photo; delafont.com; *Oakland Tribune* (on-line) Oct. 13, 2002; tobykeith.com

Selected Recordings: *Toby Keith*, 1993; *Boomtown*, 1994; *Blue Moon*,1996; *Dream Walkin'*, 1997; *Greatest Hits, Volume I*, 1998; *How Do You Like Me Now?!*, 1999; *Pull My Chain*, 2001; *Unleashed*, 2002; *Shock' N Y'all*, 2003; *Greatest Hits, Volume II*, 2004

Keller, Marthe

(mart)

Jan. 28, 1945– Actress; opera director

Address: c/o Metropolitan Opera House, 30 Lincoln Center Plaza, New York, NY 10023-6922

If a writer were to base a character on Marthe Keller, the person might be described as "a strong, slim woman of indeterminate age with ash-blonde hair, an elegant profile and a musical voice; a director who moves easily from country to country and language to language; an award-winning film and stage actress who hates Hollywood; a cultured European who doesn't have e-mail or know how to 'google,'" Helen Sheehy wrote for *Opera News* (March 2004). "In other words, a rare creature who sounds entirely fictional. In person, however, Marthe Keller is warmly real." For nearly four decades, the Swiss-born Keller has enjoyed a successful career as an international stage, film, and television actress and spoken-word performer. By the time she debuted in an American-made film—*Marathon Man*—in 1976, when she was 31, she had appeared in 17 movies emanating from France, Germany, Italy, or the former Yugoslavia or Czechoslovakia. A classically trained dancer and actress, she had also performed in many stage

Paul Hawthorne/Getty Images

plays, among them works by Shakespeare, Molière, and Chekhov and other staples of legitimate theater. For six years beginning in 1983, she performed annually in the role of Buhlschaft in the morality play *Jedermann* at the influential Salzburg Festival, in Austria. That job led to her being cast, in 1984, as the title character in Arthur Honegger's dramatic oratorio *Jeanne d'Arc au bûcher* (*Saint Joan at the Stake*), a nonsinging role that she has made "fully her own," as James R. Oestreich wrote for the *New York Times* (March 8, 1994). In 1999, after adding another 18 European-made movies and additional stage credits to her résumé, she tried her hand at directing, but not in the milieus with which she was most familiar; rather, marshaling her diverse talents, skills, and the knowledge and insights born of her wide professional and personal experiences, she joined the ranks of the world's few female directors of operas. Her direction in 1999 of Francis Poulenc's *Dialogues des Carmélites* earned a French critics' award for best operatic production of the year. She has since directed a well-received mounting of Donizetti's *Lucia di Lammermoor* and what Anthony Tommasini, in the *New York Times* (March 3, 2004, on-line), hailed as a "triumphant" new production of Mozart's opera *Don Giovanni*. "I always like to discover," Keller told Helen Sheehy. "I like the unknown. I want to learn every day. I am never satisfied with myself."

Descended from Germans on her father's side and Hungarian Jews and Roma (formerly known as Gypsies) on her mother's, Marthe Keller was born on January 28, 1945 in Switzerland. She was raised on a farm outside Basel, in the German-speaking part of the country, where her father bred horses and ran a school for equestrians. As a child Keller loved to ride horses. Starting at about age seven, she studied classical dance at the Basel Opera School of Ballet. She made her first stage appearance at eight, in a local production of Honegger's *Jeanne d'Arc au bûcher*. "I was one of the little girls dancing and singing," she recalled to Richard Dyer for the *Boston Globe* (August 6, 1989). "Even now, I am shaken by that scene—all the words come back. The things you do for the first time, you remember your whole life." In her mid-teens she damaged a knee in a skiing accident, which ended her chances of becoming a principal ballerina. Unwilling to make a career as a member of a corps de ballet rather than as a soloist, she applied successfully to the Stanislavsky School of Dramatic Arts in Munich, Germany, where she studied with the help of a scholarship from a Basel sponsor. Her background in ballet has helped her as an actress; as she told Dyer, "I approach my work like a dancer. I work out my muscles, and then I wait to see what will happen. My method is no method at all."

After she graduated from the Stanislavsky School, Keller remained in Germany. She performed with the prestigious Berliner Ensemble, founded by the playwright Bertolt Brecht, and then, for two years, with the Schiller Theater drama company, also in Berlin. At the Schiller Theater, Lloyd Shearer reported in *Parade* (July 18, 1976), she specialized in Shakespearean roles. During this period she also enrolled in college courses in philosophy and sociology.

Keller made her film debut in 1966, with an uncredited appearance in the British spy drama *Funeral in Berlin*. She next appeared in several French television productions; for several years beginning in 1969, she starred in a very popular French TV series, *La Demoiselle d'Avignon*, in the role of a princess who works as an au pair. Earlier, in 1968, she had landed a part in the French film *Le Diable par la queue* (The Devil by the Tail). She became romantically involved with the film's director, Philippe de Broca; they separated before the birth of their son, Alexandre, in 1971. The second de Broca–directed film in which Keller appeared, *Les Caprices de Marie*, was released in the U.S. in 1970 as *Give Her the Moon*. Also in 1970 Keller won a prize for her role in a production in Paris of Peter Nichols's play *A Day in the Death of Joe Egg*, which had premiered two years before. "Prizes mean nothing but they give you hope . . . ," she told Ken Ringle for the *Washington Post* (September 17, 2002). "And I [thought] maybe now I can be a serious actress. Because I had thought movies were superficial." She also continued to act in French films, among them *La Vieille fille* (*The Old Maid*, 1972), *La Chute d'un corps* (*Fall of a Body*, 1973), and *Toute une vie* (*And Now My Love*, 1974), the last of which, directed by Claude Lelouch, earned an Academy Award nomination for best screenplay. Partly as a result of the attention the last-named film brought Keller among Hollywood insiders, in 1976 the American director John Schlesinger asked her to try out for a small role in the suspense thriller *Marathon Man*, which was to co-star Dustin Hoffman, Laurence Olivier, and Roy Scheider. By her own account, Keller, who knew little English, spent a sleepless night before the audition and, in the morning, fortified herself for it by drinking a large quantity of wine. She won the part, that of the double agent cum girlfriend of a graduate student (Hoffman) who unwittingly becomes entangled in the nefarious activities of a Nazi fugitive (Olivier). Keller learned her lines phonetically and, in addition, embarked on an intensive self-study course to learn English; her approach worked well, just as it had when she had taught herself to speak French a few years earlier. (She is now fluent in German, French, English, and Italian.) Her performance in *Marathon Man* earned Keller a Golden Globe nomination for best supporting actress. Lloyd Shearer, who interviewed her a few months before the movie's U.S. premiere, described her then as "one of Europe's top stars, immensely talented, free-wheeling, free-loving, talkative beyond description, uninhibited, colorful, yet marvelously disciplined and thoroughly trained."

Hollywood beckoned again in 1977, when Keller won the part of an Eastern European terrorist in John Frankenheimer's *Black Sunday*, an adaptation of a novel by Thomas Harris. Also in 1977 Keller appeared opposite Al Pacino in *Bobby Deerfield*, directed by Sydney Pollack. In that poorly received film, Pacino played a reckless, self-absorbed race-car driver who falls in love with a woman (Keller) who helps him to recognize the joys of everyday life although, unbeknownst to him, she is fatally ill. During the shooting of *Bobby Deerfield,* Pacino and Keller developed an intimate relationship; they remained romantically linked for much of the next half-dozen years and have remained close friends.

After appearing in Billy Wilder's *Fedora* (1978) and John G. Avildsen's *The Formula* (1980), both of which flopped, Keller moved back to Europe with her son. Since the 1980s she has had roles in more than 30 films made in France, Germany, Italy, or the U.S., most notably as Marcello Mastroianni's lover in Nikita Mikhalkov's *Oci cironie (Dark Eyes,* 1987), based on several stories by Anton Chekhov; the mother of the German-born Russian czarina in TNT's *Young Catherine* (1991); a concert pianist in *Mon amie Max* (My Friend Max, 1994); and a German-Jewish woman in pre–World War II Europe, again opposite Mastroianni, in *According to Pereira* (1995). Keller told Helen Sheehy that Mikhalkov's approach to direction, which required the actors to improvise to some extent, influenced her greatly. "After *Dark Eyes,* I always asked myself, 'How would Nikita direct that?' He was so inspiring, like a living Chekhov." Keller also maintained her stage career, mainly in Berlin, Paris, and Munich, with roles in such classics as Shakespeare's *Romeo and Juliet,* Goethe's *Faust,* and Harold Pinter's *Betrayal.* Her only Broadway appearance occurred in 2001, when she played the wife of a German general in *Judgment at Nuremberg,* an adaptation by Abby Mann of his screenplay for the same-titled 1961 film, which was based on the trials (1945–49) of Nazi officials accused of war crimes and "crimes against humanity" perpetrated during World War II. Keller's performance garnered her a Tony Award nomination for best supporting actress.

Keller branched out professionally in 1983, when she made the first of six annual appearances in *Jedermann* (Everyman), Hugo von Hofmannsthal's musical play, which is based on a medieval morality tale; written for Austria's annual Salzburg Festival in 1911, it became the centerpiece of the event. Having seen her in *Jedermann,* William Bernell, the artistic director of the Boston Symphony Orchestra, recruited her for the title role in the orchestra's planned performance of Honegger's *Saint Joan at the Stake.* (She replaced Meryl Streep, who had bowed out because of a prior commitment.) As soon as she accepted the part (which requires almost no singing), Keller told Nan Robertson for the *New York Times* (December 11, 1984), she immediately quit smoking. "I became like a hysterical diva, protecting my voice and getting enough sleep and working 10 hours a day," she said. She also immersed herself in accounts of Joan's life, repeatedly viewed Carl Dreyer's silent film *The Passion of Joan of Arc* (1928), and listened many times to a recording of the Honegger work. "I've never been so happy in my life as the time I've spent with that girl, Joan," she told Robertson. "She was a miracle, a mystery, a mixture of peasant sanity and high, high poetic sensitivity." Her part demanded that she speak in specific rhythms in accordance with Honegger's score—a difficult task, as she explained to Richard Dyer: "In a movie, you are an object— other people move you around, decide which parts of your work the audience will see. In the theater, once you are onstage, you are the subject. In a concert piece, you are neither the subject [n]or the object, but part of the music. . . . If you make an extra little pause, you will fall behind the music, and that is like running behind a train—you will never catch up. . . . You must always be thinking about technique, while an actor must leave the technique behind." She told Robertson, "My training as a dancer sharpened my instinctive sense of rhythm, and that really helps me. . . . Also, my first contact with art was music. Classical music, all my life, has been my psychiatrist, my jogging, my health food, my religion. . . . It gives me a lot of strength, a lot of energy." Presented by the Boston Symphony Orchestra under the direction of Seiji Ozawa at Carnegie Hall, in New York City, on December 12, 1984, *Saint Joan at the Stake* received warm reviews, with Keller singled out for special praise. In the *New York Times* (December 14, 1984), Donal Henahan declared that the actress had "turned the evening into a personal triumph." After noting that he had seen such celebrated performers as Vera Zorina, Ingrid Bergman, Dorothy Maguire, and Irene Pappas in the role, he wrote, "No previous Joan in my experience has found more in the part than Miss Keller. Her Joan seemed rather faunlike at first but it soon became apparent that this was a faun with a spine of iron. Though the piece is . . . heavily orchestrated and brings to bear an immense chorus of men, women and children, Miss Keller's husky voice penetrated well into the hall, and into the listener's bones, as well. As the Paul Claudel libretto requires, she conveyed the mystical ecstasies and transports but balanced it at times with an affecting girlish charm." Keller's performances of the same role five and a half years later, with the Boston Symphony Orchestra under Ozawa at Tanglewood, in Lenox, Massachusetts, and nearly five years after that, with the New York Philharmonic under Kurt Masur at Avery Fisher Hall, in New York City, again earned superlative reviews. She has also appeared in the Honegger work in Europe.

During a press conference after one of her performances, when asked if she would ever consider directing an opera, Keller responded, "Are you kidding?," as she recalled to Ken Ringle. "But something start[ed] working in my mind." In 1999, after rejecting other offers to direct operas in major cities, where she felt she would be subjected to intolerable pressure, Keller accepted an invitation to direct a production of *Dialogues des Carmélites,* by the 20th-century French composer Francis Poulenc, to be mounted by the Opéra national du Rhin, in Strasbourg, France. Set during the French Revolution, the opera begins with Blanche, a fearful young woman from an aristocratic family, announcing to her father that she plans to enter a Carmelite convent, to protect herself from the turmoil that grips France. But even as a nun she cannot escape the revolutionaries' brutality, because they regard the Catholic Church and its representatives as symbols of the old order that must be destroyed. In the end Blanche chooses martyrdom, by joining her fellow nuns at the scaffold. The production, in which the Orchestre Philharmonique de Strasbourg was conducted by Jan Latham-Koenig and Anne Sophie Schmidt sang the role of Blanche, earned high praise; it later traveled to the Royal Albert Hall, in London, England. In a review of a DVD of a 1999 performance in Strasbourg, released in 2000, the film critic Kevin Filipski wrote, as quoted on family-movie-review.com, "Marthe Keller does a superlative job of conveying Poulenc's intentions. Her spare staging effectively evokes the austere world of the cloistered nuns, and there are many striking images, notably the opera's final tragic moments when the women literally drop, one by one, to the musical sound of the guillotine's blade."

In 2001, at the invitation of the legendary tenor Placido Domingo, the artistic director of the Washington National Opera, in the U.S. capital, Keller directed the company in a production of Gaetano Donizetti's opera *Lucia di Lammermoor*. Based on Sir Walter Scott's novel *The Bride of Lammermoor*, the opera tells the story of Lucia, a Scottish maiden whose beloved, Edgardo, is an enemy of her father's. Leading her to believe, by means of a forged letter, that Edgardo has been unfaithful, Lucia's brother dupes her into marrying the man her father has chosen for her. When, on her wedding day, she discovers the truth, she kills her husband, and, apparently insane, dies of a broken heart. Keller set the opera in the mid-19th century rather than the late 17th century, scrapped the traditional use of kilts in favor of period garments, and added to the score the sounds of rain and thunder. Keller also took a novel approach to the characterization of Lucia, portraying her not as a victim but as an angry woman who seeks justice for herself. "She's very excited by fear," Keller told Donna Perlmutter for the *Los Angeles Times* (November 16, 2003). "Raised like a boy, with men all around her, she's a strong woman, a fighter, not a victim like in the book. I see her capable of being livid, with the blood draining out. Did she go mad because she killed her husband? Or did she kill her husband because she was mad? We don't know." The production, which starred Elizabeth Futral in the title role, opened on September 16, 2002 for a nine-performance run. In 2003 Keller staged another production of *Lucia di Lammermoor* for the Los Angeles Opera, for which Placido Domingo serves as general director.

When Metropolitan Opera decision-makers chose to retire Franco Zeffirelli's staging of *Don Giovanni,* Mozart's two-act opera about an extraor-

dinarily successful womanizer, they hired Keller to create the new production. Keller told Cori Ellison for the *New York Times* (February 29, 2004) that she wanted audiences to see the title character through the eyes of the women he seduced. "I've seen so many productions where the women were victims," she said. "The thing I want to bring across is that Giovanni is completely contagious. We know how bad he is, but we know how wonderful he is too. Everybody becomes more alive through his presence. You get drunk from him, and you know it's bad, and the next day you're sorry. But what is life without wine?" Michael Yeargan, who designed the sets for the production, told Helen Sheehy, "Before Marthe could definitely commit to direct *Don Giovanni* . . . she had to analyze the piece from the inside out. It was thrilling to be part of that exhaustive examination. Rather than starting with the visual world, we spent a great deal of time analyzing the characters and situations. . . . Marthe's experience as an actress has made the design process a true revelation of the opera as a contemporary experience, not just a period costume drama." Keller's production, which opened on March 1, 2004 with Thomas Hampson in the title role, René Pape as Giovanni's servant, Leporello, and Christine Goerke as Donna Elvira, received mixed reviews. Detractors included Howard Kissell, who wrote for the New York *Daily News* (March 3, 2004), "At times . . . [Keller] gives the characters vivid ideas, but mostly her direction is static and lifeless, too small to fill the huge Met stage"; similarly, Alex Ross, writing for the *New Yorker* (March 29, 2004, on-line), described the production as "nondescript" and "lacklustre" and complained, "The best that can be said of [it] is that it has none of the bombast of the affair that preceded it, by Franco Zeffirelli." By contrast, Peter G. Davis, who remembered Zeffirelli's staging as "a lumbering, decadently decorated affair," wrote for *New York* (March 22, 2004, on-line), "Perhaps the most refreshing aspect of the . . . new staging . . . is its lack of pretension, a desire to challenge an audience with the piece itself rather than a production team's bright new idea of it. . . . Keller has seen to it that all the characters onstage are developing personalities who move with a fluidity that is always rooted in the theatrical reality and absorbing musical perspectives the composer has provided"; the staging, he felt, was "as notable for its beauty of design . . . as for its thoughtful insights into the opera's characters." Anthony Tommasini agreed; in his *New York Times* review, he wrote that Keller had drawn "tellingly nuanced and touchingly honest performances from a fine cast."

Keller has never married, "because I don't believe in divorce. And if I married, there would inevitably be a divorce," as she told Donna Perlmutter. She maintains apartments in New York and Paris and a home in Switzerland. When Sheehy asked her about her plans, the actress answered, "I go like the wind." "In my life, the question is always more important than the answer," she told

Perlmutter. "The process is better than the result."
—H.T.

Suggested Reading: *Boston Globe* Arts & Film p71 Aug. 6, 1989, with photos; filmos.actricesdefrance.org; Hollywood.com; *Los Angeles Times* E p44 Nov. 16, 2003, with photos; (New York) *Daily News* III p1 Mar. 13, 1977, with photo; *New York Times* C p17 May 18, 1977, with photo, II p23 Feb. 29, 2004, with photos; *Opera News* p38+ Mar. 2004, with photos; *People* p53+ Nov. 28, 1977, with photos; *Washington Post* C p1+ Sep. 17, 2002

Selected Films: *Funeral in Berlin*, 1966; *Le Diable par la queue* (*The Devil By the Tail*), 1968; *Caprice de Marie* (*Give Her the Moon*), 1969; *La Vieille fille* (*The Old Maid*), 1972; *La Chute d'un corps* (*Fall of a Body*), 1973; *Toute une vie* (*And Now My Love*), 1974; *Per Le antiche scale* (*Down the Ancient Staircase*), 1975; *Marathon Man*, 1976; *Black Sunday*, 1977; *Bobby Deerfield*, 1977; *Oci cironie* (*Dark Eyes*), 1987; *Young Catherine*, 1991; *Mon amie Max* (*My Friend Max*), 1994; *Sostiene Pereira* (*According to Pereira*), 1995; *K*, 1996; *Nuits blanches*, 1996; *Os três desejos* (*Elles*), 1996; *Le derrière* (*From Behind*), 1998; *L'école de la chair*, 1998; *Fri-fri*, 1998; *Par amour*, 2002; *La nourrice*, 2003

Selected Plays and Spoken-Word Performances: *A Day in the Death of Joe Egg*, 1970; *Jedermann* (*Everyman*), 1983–89; *Joan of Arc at the Stake*, 1984; *Judgment at Nuremberg*, 2001

Selected Television Series: *Charterhouse of Parma*, 1982

Selected Operas: as director—*Dialogues de Carmélites*, 1999; *Lucia di Lammermoor*, 2001; *Don Giovanni*, 2004

Dennis Clark/Getty Images

Keller, Thomas

Oct. 14, 1955– Chef; restaurant owner; cookbook writer

Address: The French Laundry, 6640 Washington St., Yountville, CA 94599-1301

"Eating at chef Thomas Keller's famed Napa Valley restaurant The French Laundry makes me think of watching Fred Astaire," the food critic Patricia Wells wrote for her eponymous Web site (February 24, 2004). "When you watch the master dance, you only think about how much fun he must be having, it all looks so easy, so natural. It never crosses your mind that he is working about as hard as a human being can work. The truth is, no matter how hard the modest, talented Thomas Keller works, you can be sure he is having fun at it." According to *Food & Beverage International Magazine* (April 10, 2000, on-line), he is "the most respected American-born chef cooking in this country today." The 48-year-old Keller began his career at the age of 17 at the Palm Beach Yacht Club, in Florida, when, with virtually no experience, he began cooking for club members. He has never attended a culinary school; rather, he gained his expertise as a restaurateur while on the job at various eating places in the United States in addition to the yacht club and while working as an apprentice in a half-dozen restaurants in France. He also learned a great deal as the co-founder/co-owner/chef of a restaurant in Florida, which closed after a short time in the early 1970s, and of another in New York City—the much-praised Rakel, which opened in 1985 and closed in 1990. His skills, knowledge, boundless culinary creativity, and perfectionism have turned the French Laundry into a restaurant that many publications (among them *Esquire, Gourmet, Bon Appétit, USA Today, Food & Wine,* the *New York Times,* the *Los Angeles Times,* the *San Francisco Chronicle,* and *Wine Spectator*) have ranked among the finest in the United States. Keller "never tires of coming up with new, surprising, and well-executed variations of the possibilities of something as simple as an egg or a tomato," Dana Cowin, the editor in chief of *Food & Wine,* told Peter Kaminsky for *New York* magazine (January 5, 2004, on-line). "He explores every facet of an ingredient in every possible way—playfully yet intellectually and dramatically. I get the sense that he tries new flavors and dishes because he wants to please himself." Keller is the only person to be honored two years in succession by the James Beard Foundation, whose awards are known as the Oscars of the culinary industry: in 1996, when he was named the best chef in California, and in 1997, when he won the Outstanding Chef of the Year Award. *The French Laundry Cookbook* (1999), which he wrote with Michael Ruhlman, has won awards as well. Within the past half-dozen years, relinquishing some of the hands-on control for which he had become well known, Keller has opened two bistro-style restaurants, both called Bouchon (one in Yountville, California, a short walk from the French Laundry, and the other in Las Vegas, Nevada), and a bakery (also in Yountville). In February 2004, in what has been described as his most ambitious project to date, he opened another restaurant, Per Se, in the new Time Warner Center, in New York City. "The kitchen is such an athletic place," he told Joel Stein for *Time* (September 17, 2001, on-line). "At some point you have to stop being, say, a running back and become a coach."

Thomas Keller was born on October 14, 1955 in Oceanside, California, to Edward Keller, a U.S. Marines drill instructor, and his wife. During his childhood his parents divorced; his mother then raised him and his siblings (he has several older brothers and a sister) in southern Florida, where, according to different sources, she owned or managed restaurants or clubs, among them the Palm Beach Yacht Club. "If I wanted to see my mom after school, I went to the yacht club . . . ," Keller told Florence Fabricant for the *New York Times Magazine* (December 11, 1988). "I wound up washing dishes or peeling potatoes. Otherwise, it was go home and eat chili dogs with my older brothers. I hated the kitchen." After he graduated from high school, Keller took a dishwashing job at the yacht club. When its cook quit, his mother "moved him to the stoves," as Joel Stein put it. Keller prepared simple fare—hamburgers, sandwiches, salads, eggs. Sometimes, when a customer wanted something he had never cooked before, he would call his brother Joseph for guidance. (Joseph Keller is also an esteemed chef.) During this period, according to Stein, Keller attended a Florida college for two years, majoring in psychology. Feeling that he was "in a rut," as he put it to Fabricant ("I'm easily bored," he told her. "That's one of the reasons I keep trying different things"), he ended his employment at the club.

Keller next worked in a succession of restaurants in various places, among them Newport, Rhode Island; Lake Park, Florida; New York City; and the Catskill Mountains region of New York State. In some of them he got hands-on instruction. "It was very mechanical, learning how to make hollandaise [sauce] . . . ," he told Dave Welch for Powells.com (October 18, 2000). "But it was a challenge, trying to make it perfect every day." He also learned "by asking stupid questions," as he re-

called to Marian Burros for the *New York Times* (October 16, 1996). In a restaurant in the Catskills, every night for three summers, he singlehandedly cooked for 80 people; he thereby "learned great organizational skills because I had to do it all myself," as he told Burros. His approach to and understanding of cooking began to change in about 1977, after he met Roland G. Henin, who was then the chef at a private club in Rhode Island and is now the corporate executive chef for the companies that manage the restaurants and other concessions in Yosemite National Park, California. Through Henin, who became his mentor, he came to realize that cooking is not "about mechanics" but "about a feeling, wanting to give someone something, which in turn was really gratifying," as he told Dave Welch. "That really resonated for me. I wanted to learn everything I could about what it takes to be a great chef. It was a turning point for me."

Earlier, at age 21, Keller, along with two men who had no experience in the field, opened a restaurant in southern Florida. "It was my first taste of responsibility, managing people and being critiqued and learning the why of cooking," he told Burros. The venture failed after 18 months. "I became more focused after that and . . . I understood that I needed to know much, much, much more," Keller told Hattie Bryant for PBS's Small Business School Web site. In the early 1980s he worked at Raoul's, an expensive French restaurant in New York City, then moved to the Westbury Hotel's Polo Lounge, also in New York, which had been set up shortly before by the now-celebrated chef Daniel Boulud. Later, in a conversation with Peter Kaminsky, Boulud described the young Keller's way of working as "boom, boom, get the job done, like clockwork." Next, Keller spent one and a half years in France, serving as an apprentice in the kitchens of such top-ranked restaurants as Guy Savoy, Gerard Besson, Taillevent, Le Toit de Passey, Chiberta, and Le Pré Catalan.

In 1985, back in New York, after working for others (among them La Reserve and Raphael) for a year or two, Keller opened the restaurant Rakel, in collaboration with Serge Raoul (the owner of Raoul's), in a former factory building in Lower Manhattan. Rakel soon attracted wide attention for what John Mariani, in *Wine Spectator* (November 30, 1995, on-line), labeled Keller's "highly individualized work" and Florence Fabricant described as "his daring flights from the ordinary." Fabricant's article, published in the "Food" section of the *New York Times Magazine*, includes Keller's recipes for four items on the Rakel menu: rosemary tuiles (a type of cookie that is usually sweet rather than seasoned with herbs, as is Keller's version); medallions (small round or oval servings) of monkfish with lentils (preferably "imported French green lentils," as Keller advised); breast of lamb, braised, deboned, and grilled in the French manner; and lemon sabayon tart with pine-nut crust, a shell of baked dough filled with a whipped lemony mixture. Frequented by many Wall Streeters, Rakel fared well until the stock-market crash of October 1987. With its clientele shrinking, Raoul felt that the restaurant had to lower its prices by altering its menu. Keller, however, would not agree to cost-cutting measures that required a drop in standards; instead, in about 1989, he ended his partnership with Raoul. "It was heartbreaking, confusing," he told Burros. "It was torture. I was sad, depressed, embarrassed. Now I feel it was a great accomplishment to gain that experience at that age." In 1990 the restaurant went broke. "My credibility was low after Rakel failed," Keller told Terry McCarthy for *Time* (February 1, 2004, on-line). "I was labeled the chef who couldn't control food or labor costs."

At around this time Keller moved to Los Angeles, California, to assume the post of executive chef at the Checkers Hotel. His experience there was "disastrous," as he told Bryant, mainly because his many duties did not include cooking: "I found out that I was more miserable . . . in a kitchen environment and not being able to cook than I was not cooking." After 17 months Keller left Checkers. With a partner, he founded a small company, called Evo, that sells bottled olive oil. He also began seeking another opportunity to produce the kinds of meals he wanted to serve the public.

While visiting Napa Valley, in California, in the late 1980s or early 1990s, Keller discovered the French Laundry, a restaurant surrounded by lush gardens and set up in a 19th-century, two-story stone building that had once housed a French steam laundry. "It was a magical place," he told Burros. "It reminded me of France." After its owners, Don and Sally Schmidt, put the restaurant up for sale, Keller told them that he wanted to buy it. For the next year and a half to three years (sources differ on how much time elapsed), the Schmidts waited patiently while Keller struggled to raise the $1.2 million purchase price. He achieved that goal by borrowing thousands of dollars on credit cards and in bank loans to finance his 70 percent share and by setting up a limited partnership with 48 others, who invested the remaining 30 percent.

The French Laundry reopened in 1994, with seating for 62 people; recently, the staff numbered 28. The restaurant serves lunch on Fridays, Saturdays, and Sundays between 11: 00 a.m. and 1: 00 p.m. and dinner every day, from 5: 30 p.m. to 9: 30 p.m. There are three prices for dinner: $125 for the all-vegetable menu, $135 for the regular menu, and $150 for the "chef's tasting menu." Those figures do not include "supplements" ($20 or $25) for especially extraordinary dishes, the costs of wines, or the 18 percent service charge automatically added to each bill.

A typical meal at the French Laundry includes six to 12 courses, each of which consists of a very small, beautifully presented portion of a meticulously prepared dish. The meal is meant to be consumed slowly, over the course of two and a half to four hours. "Our philosophy is simple," Keller told Bryant, explaining that it is based on "the law of diminishing returns—the more you have of something the less you want of it. So we want to give you just enough to where you get to the point where you've had that last bite and it's at the pinnacle of flavor, because your taste buds have reached that. They've gone through the kind of initial acceptance of the flavor, to the realization of the flavor, . . . to the point where all of a sudden, [your mouth] becomes saturated with the flavor and then it starts to go down. Well, we want to keep you at the top of the bell curve of your taste buds. . . . I want you to say, 'God, I wish I had one more bite.'"

The menu on the French Laundry's Web site on April 28, 2004 listed such appetizers as "chilled English pea soup infused with white truffle oil and served with a parmesan crisp," "salad of jumbo green asparagus, pickled ramp bulbs, toasted pine nuts, and 'fines herbes' vinaigrette," and "fruit-wood smoked Atlantic salmon 'tiede' [warm], russet potato 'gnocchi' [dumplings], marinated English cucumber, California white sturgeon caviar, pickled onion vinaigrette." Main dinners included "sweet garlic crusted Catham Bay cod, thyme roasted fingerling potatoes, carmelized spring garlic and Italian parsley 'coulis' [thick sauce]" and "sautéed sirloin of Cloverdale Farms rabbit, ragoût [mixture] of baby garlic, fava beans, French Laundry chorizo, green almonds and Fubbiano extra virgin olive oil." The desserts included "sweet polenta cake with port marinated cherries, port sorbet and yogurt 'foam'" and "field rhubarb tart 'à l'ancienne' with 'crème fraîche' ice cream and balsamic vinegar reduction." John Mariani, in an assessment representative of many, wrote, "Every item on the menu seems to have a reason for being there, with each dish balancing another, each flavor enhancing the last, each texture leading to the next. This is the true, modern fusion cuisine—a fusion of seasonal elements into perfect balance, every dish a coalescence of herbs, spices, meat or seafood into a splendid whole." Most of the ingredients for Keller's recipes come from local farms, the French Laundry's gardens, and specialty growers and producers, among them a commercial pilot who raises hearts of palm and a scholar who sends Maine lobsters by Federal Express.

While Keller is deeply serious about his craft, he maintains that preparing and eating high-quality foods should not be elevated into a quasi-religious experience. To set diners at ease, the menu at the French Laundry often contains such familiar-sounding dishes as bacon and eggs, chips and dip, coffee and doughnuts, and macaroni and cheese, though each is far from the usual. The macaroni and cheese, for example, consists of orzo in coral oil with mascarpone cheese topped with lobster and a parmesan chip, while the coffee and donuts, Keller's signature dessert, is cappuccino semifreddo, a flavored mousse, topped with steamed milk and served with tiny cinnamon-sugar donuts. "Coming to a restaurant like this can be intimidating," Keller told Stein. "And that's the last thing I want. I don't want people to come here afraid, like it's some kind of temple of gastronomy. It's just a restaurant. Coffee and doughnuts on the menu should make you smile. It gets everyone laughing and in a good mood."

In 1999 Keller published *The French Laundry Cookbook*, co-authored by Michael Ruhlman, with photographs by Susie Heller and Deborah Jones. The book won an unprecedented three awards from the International Association of Culinary Professionals in 2000, for best book of the year, best first book (the Julia Child Award), and best-designed book. In addition to instructions for preparing 150 dishes served in the French Laundry, the book includes essays in which Keller discussed techniques, his love of particular foods, experiences that helped him develop as a chef, and his relationships with his food suppliers. As of February 2004 the book had sold 243,000 copies and had been reprinted 16 times. According to a review on the Global Gourmet Web site, Keller's "creative process, reverence for ingredients, and deep respect for his purveyors, not to mention his wit and whimsy, come to life in a series of recipes and essays that make *The French Laundry Cookbook* more than just a cookbook. . . . This is a book driven by passion, a very personal book that reveals the soul of a chef." The recipes in Keller's second cookbook, *Bouchon* (2004), are based on the less complex dishes prepared in his bistro-style restaurants, also called Bouchon. (The word means "cork" or "stopper" in French.)

In 1998 Keller opened the first Bouchon, down the street from the French Laundry. Five years later he opened a bakery on the same street and a second Bouchon, in the Venetian, a Las Vegas resort, hotel, and casino. In 2001 the offer of a site for a restaurant at the Times Warner Center lured him back to New York City. The center, which was then under construction, is at Columbus Circle, on the southwest corner of Central Park. As part of the deal, Keller secured a prime location for his restaurant, overlooking the park, and veto power over the installation of other potential eateries in the center. Built at a cost of $12 million, Per Se, as his new, 16-table restaurant is called, offers a menu and service on a par with those of the French Laundry. Six weeks after its debut, in February 2004, a kitchen fire forced Per Se to close temporarily; it reopened on May 1.

Keller spent 18 months training members of his French Laundry staff for the move to New York. With the second Bouchon and Per Se, he will likely be more than doubling his annual receipts, but he is determined to do so without sacrificing the high quality for which he has become known. Toward that end, he set up a six-member advisory board (which includes two bankers, an attorney, a restaurant consultant, an accountant, and a psychologist) and has increased staff training. In addition, he has installed a live video link between the kitchens of the French Laundry and Per Se, so that he can view the food preparation in either restaurant from the opposite coast. A $1.8 million renovation of the French Laundry that began in January 2004 was completed within six months.

The French Laundry is unusual for the calm and extreme neatness of its kitchen and the politeness that prevails among its workers—a far cry from the noise and frenzy commonly associated with restaurant kitchens. Keller himself, an acknowledged perfectionist with an obsession for even the smallest details, has checked his tendency to explode in anger. He has connected his once-frequent outbursts to his father, who "used to tear people apart and then build them up again," as he told McCarthy. "I used to be like that. But now if I shout at someone, I get embarrassed." With professional help, he has also learned to temper his desire to control the behavior of others. That change has proved invaluable with the opening of Per Se and a second Bouchon, since Keller now spends much of his time as an adviser rather than a chef. He assumed that role not only because of the distance between his eating establishments but also because of his knee problems, which stem from years of standing for 16 or 17 hours every day. Although he has had two knee operations and, much like a professional athlete, typically tapes his knees at the start of the day, they still ache much of the time.

In addition to his awards from the James Beard Foundation, Keller has won *Restaurants & Institutions'* Ivy Award (1996) and the World Master of Culinary Arts Award (2002), and he was dubbed "America's Best Chef" by *Time* magazine. The French Laundry received the Smithfield Foods Outstanding Service Award in 2003 and occupied the top spot on *Restaurant Magazine*'s list of the "world's 50 best restaurants" that year.

Keller has been described as soft-spoken, gracious, and thoughtful. He has admitted that he sometimes enjoys dining at such relatively lowbrow eateries as In-N-Out, a California burger chain; Roscoe's Chicken and Waffles; and the Chinese restaurant Yang Chow in Los Angeles. He and his girlfriend of 10 years, Laura Cunningham (the general manager of the French Laundry), live in Yountville, in a house in back of the restaurant. Keller has served as a spokesperson for the California Milk Advisory Board and appeared in the advertising campaign of the California Raisin Board. If he were not a chef, he has said, he would love to play shortstop for the New York Mets baseball team. Keller has attributed his drive to his desire to make his mark on the world, even beyond his lifetime. "Most people's legacy is their kids," he told McCarthy. "I don't have any kids, so my legacy is the restaurant. And to keep the continuity, the key is picking the right people and training them."

—K.E.D.

Suggested Reading: *Gourmet* p118+ Oct. 1999, with photo; *Modern Maturity* p26+ 88 Nov./Dec. 2000, with photos; *New York* p38+ Jan. 5, 2004, with photos; *New York Times Magazine* p97+ Dec. 11, 1988, p57+ Aug. 31, 1997; Powells Web site Oct. 18, 2000, with photo; *Small Business School* (on-line), with photos; *Time* (on-line) Sep. 17, 2001, Feb. 1, 2004

Selected Books: *The French Laundry Cookbook*, 1999; *Bouchon*, 2004

Kevin Winter/Getty Images

Kennedy, Robert F. Jr.

Jan. 17, 1954– Environmental advocate; lawyer

Address: Riverkeeper, P.O. Box 130, Garrison, NY 10524

"To me, the environment cannot be separated from the economy, housing, civil rights and human rights," Robert F. Kennedy Jr., a noted environmental lawyer, told Roger Rosenblatt for *Time* (August 2, 1999, on-line). "How we distribute the goods of the earth is the best measure of our democracy. It's not about advocating for fishes and birds. It's about human rights." Kennedy's father was a U.S. attorney general and U.S. senator, and his uncle John F. Kennedy was the 35th U.S. president; since he became a lawyer for the environmental organizations Riverkeeper and the National Resources Defense Council (NRDC), in 1984, Kennedy has used his legal expertise, his extensive contacts, his understanding of environmental issues, and his famous name to further his cause: protecting New York's waterways. He and his colleagues have built Riverkeeper into a powerful environmental watchdog group that has not only helped in decreasing the pollution of the Hudson River and the rest of the New York City watershed but has also served as a model for similar groups throughout the country. Kennedy has brought more than 150 legal actions against polluters of the Hudson River and helped in other environmental battles throughout North America. He is also credited with raising public awareness of water-preservation issues. "A decade ago nobody knew there was a water supply, they just knew you turned on your tap and got water," Peter Lehner, an NRDC senior attorney and the director of its Clean Water Program, told Robert Worth for the *New York Times* (November 5, 2000). "Bobby Kennedy's drumbeat of enforcement cases on the watershed has brought the issue much more attention than it would have gotten otherwise."

Robert Francis Kennedy Jr. was born on January 17, 1954, the third of the 11 children of Robert F. Kennedy and Ethel (Skakel) Kennedy. His paternal grandfather, Joseph P. Kennedy, amassed a fortune in various businesses before serving successively, during the administration of President Franklin Delano Roosevelt, as the first chairman of the Securities and Exchange Commission, chairman of the Maritime Commission, and ambassador to Great Britain. Kennedy's uncle Edward M. "Ted" Kennedy has represented Massachusetts in the U.S. Senate since 1963. His older sister, Kathleen Kennedy Townsend, served two terms as the lieutenant governor of Maryland (1995–2003); his older brother, Joseph P. Kennedy II, who represented a Massachusetts district in Congress for six terms (1987–99), is the founder, chairman, and president of the nonprofit Citizens Energy Corp., which provides affordable heating oil to needy households. His younger sisters are Courtney Kennedy Hill, a former representative for a United Nations AIDS foundation; Kerry Kennedy, who has served on human rights delegations to more than 20 nations and who set up the Robert F. Kennedy Center for Human Rights, which supports defenders of human rights worldwide; and Rory Kennedy, a documentary filmmaker. His younger brothers are Christopher Kennedy, who manages the Merchandise Mart, in Chicago, the world's largest commercial building, and also assists the Chicago Food Depository; Max Kennedy, a former Philadelphia assistant district attorney who has taught at Boston College; and Douglas Kennedy, a print and TV journalist who currently hosts the series *Douglas Kennedy's American Stories* on the Fox News Channel. His younger brother David died of a drug overdose in 1984, at age 28; his younger brother Michael, who managed the Citizens Energy Corp. and fought for gun control, died in a skiing accident in 1997, at age 39.

Kennedy's father attracted much notice during the mid-1950s as the chief counsel for the U.S. Senate subcommittee investigating labor racketeering, particularly within the Teamsters Union. A few years later he managed the successful presidential campaign of his older brother John F. Kennedy. In 1961, at age 35, he joined Kennedy's Cabinet as the nation's attorney general; in that post he vigorously prosecuted civil rights cases. He was also the president's closest adviser in foreign as well as domestic affairs. He remained attorney general until a few months after John Kennedy's assassination, on November 22, 1963. In 1964, as a new resident of New York State, he was elected to the U.S. Senate, where he became known as a passionate advocate for social justice and the rights of minorities. In March 1968 his growing opposition to President Lyndon B. Johnson's continuation of the Vietnam War, among other motives, led him to announce his candidacy for the Democratic nomination for the presidency. On June 5, 1968, immediately after a campaign speech in a California hotel, while live-action images of him were being broadcast on TV, he was shot at point-blank range; he died the following day. Robert F. Kennedy Jr. was then 14. "At home someone told me Daddy had been shot," he wrote in his book *The Riverkeepers* (1997), as quoted by Elisabeth Bumiller in the *New York Times* (November 24, 1998). He and his siblings flew to Los Angeles, where their father was on life support. "Each of us spent time with him that night, holding his hand, praying, saying good-bye, listening to the pumps that kept him breathing. In the morning, my brother Joe came into the ward where all the children were sleeping and told us, 'He's gone.' We all cried." "I feel like my father's still part of my life," he told Bumiller. "I feel like he's still helping me when I have trouble or when I'm trying to make a decision. He's very much a presence in my life."

As a child Robert Kennedy Jr. loved nature and dreamed of becoming a veterinarian. He often brought home snakes, raccoons, and other wild creatures; when he was 12 his father gave him a hawk, which became another of his pets. He also enjoyed such activities as hiking with his father and Supreme Court justice William O. Douglas and whitewater rafting with the astronaut John Glenn. His father's death led him to pursue a career in public service. He received a bachelor's degree in history and literature from Harvard University, in Cambridge, Massachusetts, in 1977; the topic of his senior thesis was Alabama politics and the civil rights movement. He had gone to Alabama in 1976, with the intention of dedicating himself to the cause of civil rights. There he became close friends with Frank Johnson, a federal judge who spent years fighting the racist, segregationist policies of Governor George C. Wallace. Johnson became the subject of Kennedy's first book, *Judge Frank M. Johnson, Jr.: A Biography* (1978), which grew out of his senior thesis.

Kennedy next studied at the London School of Economics, in England, and at the University of Virginia School of Law, in Charlottesville, where he earned a law degree in 1982. He then attended the Pace Law School, in White Plains, New York, which awarded him a master's degree in environmental law. In the same year he accepted an appointment as an assistant district attorney in the office of the Manhattan district attorney, Robert M. Morgenthau. (He had interned in Morgenthau's office in the summer of 1979.) He left that job in early 1983. Also in 1983 he passed the New York State bar exam; he was admitted to the state bar in 1985.

During the early 1980s Kennedy began to use illegal drugs. In 1983 he was arrested in South Dakota for heroin possession. After he pleaded guilty, in 1984, he was ordered to take periodic tests for drug use and receive treatment for drug addiction, and he was sentenced to 1,500 hours of community service and two years' probation. He fulfilled his community-service obligation as a volunteer with the National Resources Defense Council, which had provided legal counsel to Riverkeeper since 1970. Founded in 1966 by Robert H. Boyle as the Hudson River Fishermen's Association, Riverkeeper is an advocacy organization of fishermen and others who monitor the ecological health of the 315-mile-long Hudson River, its many tributaries, and its watershed (which encompasses more than a quarter of the area of New York State); the group also takes steps to clean the waterways and keep them free of pollution, in part by aggressive legal challenges to polluters. Boyle, who was then Riverkeeper's president, became a mentor to Kennedy, taking him on fishing trips and walks in the Hudson Valley. By the end of 1984, Kennedy had been hired as Riverkeeper's chief prosecuting attorney. He has worked as an NRDC lawyer as well since that year.

One of Kennedy's first victories with Riverkeeper came in 1985, in connection with a seven-mile creek in Newburgh, New York. While walking its length, he compiled a list of two dozen businesses and government agencies that were using the creek as a dumping ground; he then filed lawsuits against all of them. His action attracted the attention of the state Department of Environmental Conservation and led to the cleanup of the creek. In 1989 he successfully sued New York City to stop it from adding Hudson River water containing chlorine (an element essential to many chemical processes) and alum (a chemical used in papermaking and the preparation of leather) to the West Branch Reservoir, one of the two main sources of drinking water for half the state's residents. In July 1992 Kennedy and a coalition of environmental groups filed suit against the U.S. government and the National Parks Service for violating federal statutes by failing to remove an estimated 500 tons of lead at the Blue Mountain Sportsman Center in Cortlandt, part of the 1,500-acre Blue Mountain Reservation, a Westchester County park; the lead, from countless bullets fired during the previous 30 years, had accumulated in the soil at levels hundreds of times greater than the federal limit and thus posing a serious danger to wildlife and humans, especially children. After dangerously high levels of lead were found in the bodies of two children of a sportsman-center employee whose family lived on the property, the state Environmental Protection Agency (EPA) ordered the center to rid the site of the metal. Riverkeeper also forced the Indian Point Nuclear Power Plant to install $25 million worth of equipment to prevent the contamination of fish, and in 1994 the group successfully sued to make the EPA set official safety standards for power plants. Riverkeeper has so far failed in its efforts to persuade the Nuclear Regulatory Commission, a federal agency, to shut Indian Point completely, on the grounds that as a potential target of a terrorist attack, it poses an intolerable risk to the 20 million people who live within a 50-mile radius of the plant.

In 1997 Kennedy was the chief architect of the New York City Watershed Memorandum of Agreement, which obligated the city to spend $1 billion over 10 years to ensure the safety of water in its 19 upstate reservoirs. In response to the agreement, the city purchased land around its reservoirs, constructed new storm sewers and septic systems, and updated sewage plants in the watershed. In addition, the city worked with farmers in upstate New York to limit pollution and paid $140 million to local governments and businesses in the watershed area to preserve their lands' capacity for natural water filtration. (The city also has the power to condemn watershed land and regulate its development even if it does not own it.) The billion-dollar price tag of these initiatives was far less than the estimated $6 billion to $8 billion cost of a new filtration plant, which could have been required if the EPA had determined that steps were not being taken to protect the city's water supply. The agreement is considered an international model for sustainable development, because rather than addressing the problem reactively, by requiring the building of a filtration plant, which would require constant upkeep and might eventually become outdated, it employs a variety of proactive steps that— if followed—are likely to keep the natural water supply clean into the foreseeable future.

In 1999 Kennedy criticized New York City's then-mayor, Rudolph W. Giuliani, for jeopardizing the city's water supply in order to gain political favor from upstate Republican leaders and developers, in preparation for a planned Senate run. Specifically, he accused Giuliani's administration of failing to control development along the upstate reservoirs that supply drinking water for the city. In a 1999 Riverkeeper report on the city's response to the 1997 agreement, Kennedy charged that the engineering staff of the city's Department of Environmental Protection had allowed itself to become "an agent of destruction in the New York City watershed," as reported by Elisabeth Bumiller in the New York Times (November 10, 1999). In July 2000 Hudson Riverkeeper announced that it would sue the city for failing to keep its end of the agreement.

In June 2000 Robert H. Boyle and seven other members of Riverkeeper's board resigned, in protest of Kennedy's hiring as a staff scientist a man who had served time in federal prison in the 1990s. Kennedy refused to fire the man, who had been convicted of smuggling rare birds from Australia into the U.S. Kennedy justified his actions by saying that the man deserved a second chance; as an example of learning from one's mistakes, he pointed to his own drug conviction and subsequent activism. The board members argued that Kennedy

had put the organization in the embarrassing position of promoting environmental protection while employing someone who had flouted environmental laws. "Riverkeeper has always had clean hands when it went into court," Boyle told Robert Worth. "It calls into question very strongly the reputation of the organization." In addition to that issue, insiders revealed that for years, there had been tension and disagreements among Boyle, Kennedy, and John Cronin, Riverkeeper's executive director until February 2000; some contended that Kennedy bore lingering resentment of the board's refusal, in 1998, to approve his use of the Riverkeeper name for a bottled-water product that he introduced in 1999. (The label bears the name Keeper Springs; Kennedy donates all the after-tax profits to the Waterkeeper Alliance, an association of more than 100 local groups.) According to various sources, some of the board members who resigned had grown unhappy with the public's identification of Riverkeeper with Kennedy, who had raised its profile and helped attract such celebrities as Alec Baldwin and Lorraine Bracco as supporters. Kennedy is currently vice president of Riverkeeper's board of directors.

In the spring of 2000, Kennedy visited the Puerto Rican island of Vieques, the site of U.S. Navy and Marine Corps bombing drills and other military maneuvers since the 1940s. (The navy and Marine Corps own two-thirds of the island.) Many observers have characterized what happened at Vieques as an ecological disaster. The navy initially denied but later admitted that it had tested depleted-uranium weapons on the island. Blasting has destroyed coral reefs; other activities have decimated breeding grounds for mammals and sea turtles; and tons of unexploded ammunition lies on the ocean floor. The soil is contaminated with toxic heavy metals, underground water is polluted, and the island has the highest rates of infant death, cancer, and lung and skin diseases in Puerto Rico. "In all my years of environmental activism, in all my travels throughout the world, I have never witnessed such a pitiless aggression against any ecosystem as I have been able to see here," Kennedy said, as quoted by James Ridgeway in the Village Voice (May 9, 2000). "The Navy's activities in Vieques have had a disastrous effect on the health and the quality of life of all Viequeans. It must be stopped from extending that damage, immediately and permanently." Kennedy was among those sentenced to 30 days in jail for trespassing on government property while protesting the damage. With his help, the NRDC prepared two lawsuits against the navy, one protesting the bombings on environmental grounds and the other taking the form of a class-action suit in which health problems of Vieques residents were traced to the navy's activities. A short while before the lawsuits went to trial, President George W. Bush ordered that the bombing be halted by 2003.

Kennedy has also spoken out about the dangers of polychlorinated biphenyls (PCBs), synthetic organic chemicals widely used in industry until 1977, when, after scientists linked them to cancer and other diseases, the U.S. banned their manufacture and use. Without human intervention, PCBs break down into their components extremely slowly, so they have remained in the environment, especially in soil and waterways. PBCs accumulate in the tissues of fish and crustaceans (lobsters and crabs, for instance) and, in turn, in the fat cells of humans who eat contaminated creatures. General Electric, which released more than a million pounds of PCBs into the Hudson River between 1947 and 1977, has opposed the efforts of the EPA and other groups to hold the company financially responsible for cleaning up sites with high PCB levels. Among those sites are large parts of the Hudson, and for that reason Kennedy does not let his children eat anything they catch on family fishing trips on the river. "It's a tragedy that any parent has to worry about the safety of what their children are eating," he told W. Reed Morgan and Stephen A. Shoop for *USA Today* (September 24, 2001). "And it's even harder to explain to them why the fish they catch could cause life-long health risks." "No one has any right to put chemicals in our bodies or those of our children," Kennedy told Morgan and Shoop. "Our message to [General Electric] and other polluters is a simple one: 'Clean up after yourself.' It's a lesson we all learned in kindergarten."

Kennedy, along with many others, has charged the administration of President George W. Bush with proposing and instituting policies that favor corporate polluters. New Clean Air Act rules, for example, make it easier for factories to upgrade without having to install more pollution controls, and the EPA is trying to relax mercury-pollution controls for coal-burning power plants. In a critique of Bush's environmental record for *Rolling Stone* (December 11, 2003), Kennedy wrote, "George W. Bush will go down in history as America's worst environmental president. In a ferocious three-year attack, the Bush administration has initiated more than 200 major rollbacks of America's environmental laws, weakening the protection of our country's air, water, public lands and wildlife. Cloaked in meticulously crafted language designed to deceive the public, the administration intends to eliminate the nation's most important environmental laws by the end of the year. . . . Furthermore, the deadly addiction to fossil fuels that White House policies encourage has squandered our treasury, entangled us in foreign wars, diminished our international prestige, made us a target for terrorist attacks and increased our reliance on petty Middle Eastern dictators who despise democracy and are hated by their own people."

In an interview posted on the NRDC's Web site, Kennedy noted that it is easier to hold industry accountable for environmental degradation than the government. "For one thing, governmental agencies charged with the enforcement of environmental law are extremely reluctant to prosecute other governmental agencies," he said. "The E.P.A., for example, actually has a policy that does not allow it to prosecute sister governmental agencies. In New York State there is a written policy that requires the Department of Environmental Conservation to go through a labyrinthine negotiation process before it actually files suit against a sister agency. In truth, it just never happens." As an alternative, Riverkeeper has brought lawsuits against government agencies to force compliance, and Kennedy has advised other groups and citizens to do the same. The environmental movement received a major blow when, in 1992, the U.S. Supreme Court ruled, in *United States Department of Energy v. Ohio et al.*, that in lawsuits brought by citizens, federal agencies cannot be penalized even if they are found guilty of violating environmental laws. "Sure, we can still sue them to force compliance," Kennedy said in the NRDC interview. "But without any penalties, the incentive for every government agency is to continue to break the law until they're caught and prosecuted and there's a judgment against them. In other words, there is now a definite economic incentive for government agencies *not to comply* with the law until they're forced to. We literally end up having to sue every single agency for every single facility that violates the law."

Kennedy has impressed government officials and environmental activists with his ability to back his legal cases with scientific facts. "I have rarely come upon a person who could ferret out scientific information and present it so persuasively," Peter Skinner, a staff scientist with the New York State attorney general's office, told Worth. Albert F. Appleton, a senior fellow at the Regional Plan Association and a former New York City commissioner of environmental protection, told Jacques Steinberg for the *New York Times* (February 13, 1995) that Kennedy is "relentless. He is very dedicated to his goals, always keeps coming at you and is not easily put off." Others have remarked on his singlemindedness and resistance to compromise. "Intellectually, I think his arguments are often good and provocative," Marilyn Gelber, the executive director of the Independence Community Foundation and also a former New York City commissioner of environmental protection, told Steinberg. "However, as a practical matter, he is not a consensus builder. He is not someone who wants to see more than one side of an issue."

In 1997 Kennedy and John Cronin co-authored *Riverkeepers: Two Activists Fight to Reclaim Our Environment as a Basic Human Right*, which is part history and part memoir. In a review for the *New York Times* (November 16, 1997), the noted science writer James Gorman asserted that while the work of the two men and their organization was admirable, the book was poorly written. By contrast, most of the 19 readers who had posted their opinions on the Amazon.com Web site by November 2004 praised the pair's account. In August 2004 Kennedy published *Crimes Against Nature: How George W. Bush and His Corporate Pals Are Plundering the Country and Hijacking Our Democracy*, a condemnation of the Bush administration's record on environmental and other issues. Kennedy's book for young readers, *St. Francis of Assisi: A Life of Joy*, was scheduled for publication in 2005.

Kennedy teaches at Pace University in White Plains, New York, where he founded the Environmental Litigation Clinic, which works almost exclusively with Riverkeeper. He is also the supervising attorney for the clinic's law students, who are granted the status of lawyers under an agreement with New York State. In 1992 he and the Riverkeepers launched the National Alliance of River, Sound and Baykeepers, now called the Waterkeeper Alliance; he serves as its president. In addition to his work in New York State, he has assisted indigenous peoples in Latin America and Canada to negotiate treaties protecting their traditional homelands and involved himself with logging issues in Clayoquot Sound, in British Columbia. Kennedy recently signed on as a weekend host on Air America, a major progressive radio network that was launched in April 2004.

From his first marriage (1982–94), to Emily Ruth Black, Kennedy has a son, Robert F. Kennedy III, and a daughter, Kathleen Alexandra Kennedy. He lives with his second wife, Mary Richardson, an architectural designer, their three sons (born in 1992, 1997, and 2001), and their daughter (born in 1993) in a house located on 10 acres bordering a 30-acre lake in Bedford, New York. Kennedy, who has said that his children provide much of his motivation for trying to protect the environment, enjoys camping with them on the banks of the Hudson. In his free time he also water-skis, fishes, and scuba dives in the river. His hobbies include falconing with his two Harris hawks.

—K.E.D.

Suggested Reading: *E: the Environmental Magazine* p10+ Nov./Dec. 1995, with photos, p34+ Nov./Dec. 2003, with photo; *New York* p42+ Nov. 27 1995, with photos; *New York Times* B p1 Feb. 13, 1995, with photos, B p2 Nov. 24, 1998, with photo; *Rolling Stone* p133+ Dec. 10–24, 1992, with photo; *Time* (on-line) Aug. 2, 1999, with photo; *Wildlife Conservation* p68+ Jan./Feb. 1994, with photos

Selected Books: *Judge Frank M. Johnson, Jr.*, 1978; *Riverkeepers: Two Activists Fight to Reclaim Our Environment as a Basic Human Right* (with John Cronin), 1997; *Crimes Against Nature: How George W. Bush and His Corporate Pals Are Plundering the Country and Hijacking Our Democracy*, 2004

Kerry, John

NOTE: An earlier article about John Kerry appeared in *Current Biography* in 1988.

Dec. 11, 1943– U.S. senator from Massachusetts (Democrat); 2004 Democratic presidential nominee

Address: 304 Russell Senate Office Bldg., Washington, DC 20510

United States senator John Kerry's acceptance of the Democratic Party's nomination for president, in late July 2004, was a milestone in one of the most prominent American political careers of recent times. In the November general election, Kerry lost a close race to President George W. Bush, whose administration he had sharply criticized for its environmental policy, tax-cut policy, and handling of the war in Iraq.

Kerry first came to national attention in the early 1970s, when, as a 27-year-old, decorated but disillusioned veteran of the Vietnam War, he led others in opposing U.S. military involvement in Southeast Asia. Following an unsuccessful run for Congress in 1972, Kerry earned a law degree and served as an attorney in both the public and private sectors before winning election as lieutenant governor of Massachusetts and, in 1984, as the state's junior U.S. senator. In his 20-year career in the Senate, he has fought against government corruption—it was Kerry, for example, who in the 1980s brought to light the actions of President Ronald Reagan's administration that came to be known as the Iran-Contra affair. He has also sought to protect the environment, supported campaign-finance reform, and proposed methods of improving public education on a national scale. His fellow Democratic Massachusetts senator, Edward M. Kennedy, said to Paul Alexander for *Rolling Stone* (April 11, 2002), "[Kerry] has demonstrated his courage and commitment in wartime. He's a leader on environmental issues. . . . I think John is qualified for any job he puts his mind to."

John Forbes Kerry, born on December 11, 1943 in Denver, Colorado, is the second of the three children of Rosemary (Forbes) Kerry and Richard John Kerry. His mother was a member of one of New England's wealthiest and most prominent families. His father, a lawyer, joined the United States Foreign Service and spent many years in Europe. As Louise Sweeney wrote for the *Christian Science Monitor* (July 18, 1985), "John Kerry grew up in an atmosphere in which politics was passed around the table like mashed potatoes." One of Kerry's earliest memories is of helping his older sister collect money for the Democrat Adlai E. Stevenson's presidential campaign in 1952.

John Kerry

Kerry was raised as a Roman Catholic, but when his father was posted to West Berlin, West Germany, in about 1954, his parents enrolled him at St. Paul's School, an exclusive Episcopalian preparatory school in Concord, New Hampshire. His classmates have recalled that politics was Kerry's ruling passion even at that early age. The walls of his dormitory room were decorated with campaign posters, and one of his favorite pastimes was arguing politics. When his boyhood idol and fellow New Englander John F. Kennedy was elected to the White House, in 1960, Kerry began emulating him, to the extent that he took to signing his papers with the initials "J.F.K.," which he happened to have in common with the president. "His election was a real catalyst," Kerry told Lois Romano for the *Washington Post* (February 21, 1985). "He kind of touched chords for all of us."

Following his graduation from St. Paul's, Kerry enrolled at Yale University, in New Haven, Connecticut. He "hit Yale running," as Lois Romano put it, "displaying the same kind of single-mindedness that would follow him for two decades." His interest in politics continued unabated, so much so that classmates began calling him "Little J.F.K." One student, David Boren, who went on to become a Democratic U.S. senator from Oklahoma, met Kerry as a result of their mutual involvement in the Yale Political Union, a student debating society. Boren, who was ahead of Kerry at Yale, recalled for Lois Romano that Kerry was a politically active "go-getter" who ran for and won a Political Union office. Despite their age difference, Boren and Kerry became friends; Boren later wrote a letter of support for Kerry when he was invited to join Yale's secret Skull and Bones Society.

After winning varsity letters in soccer and lacrosse, Kerry graduated from Yale in 1966 with a B.A. degree. Although he had criticized the draft and the Vietnam War when he made the senior oration, he deferred his plans to attend graduate school abroad and enlisted in the United States Navy rather than wait for his impending draft notice. He did so, Kerry has said, because he has always believed strongly "in a code of service to one's country." Intrigued by his first, brief visit to Vietnam, Kerry volunteered to return as a commander of a "swift boat"—one of the small, high-speed boats used to patrol coastal waters. He told Lois Romano that his time in Vietnam was "a major, major, formative experience in my life." Although he so distinguished himself in combat that he won a Silver Star, a Bronze Star, and three Purple Hearts, Kerry became disillusioned with America's involvement in the war. Taking advantage of a navy regulation that allowed him to return home, he took a job in March 1969 in New York City as an admiral's aide. Even after he did so, Kerry's feelings about the Vietnam War continued to haunt him. Determined to act on them in a positive way, he obtained an early release from the navy to run for Congress on an antiwar platform from his home district, the Third Congressional District in Massachusetts. A month later, though, he withdrew from the Democratic primary race in favor of the Reverend Robert F. Drinan.

When, while campaigning for Drinan, Kerry had appeared on Dick Cavett's television talk show, leaders of an antiwar group called Vietnam Veterans Against the War (VVAW) saw him and asked if he would join their cause. Kerry agreed and became the national coordinator of VVAW. In 1971 he was one of the organizers of Operation Dewey Canyon III, a much-publicized VVAW demonstration in Washington, D.C., that was staged by 1,000 veterans and named as a reminder of the 1969 incursions into Laos by South Vietnamese and U.S. forces; VVAW leaders caustically termed the demonstration "a limited incursion into the country of Congress." On April 22, 1971 about 200 of the veterans crowded into the Senate Foreign Relations Committee hearing room to listen as Kerry delivered a ringing indictment of U.S. involvement in Southeast Asia. Clad in army fatigues, his chest festooned with his combat decorations, Kerry articulated the anger and sense of betrayal that he and other Vietnam veterans felt and argued that the Vietnam conflict was really a civil war in which the United States had little reason to be involved. Kerry went on to criticize the motives of President Richard Nixon's administration for pursuing the war. Pronouncing U.S. involvement in the conflict to be a terrible mistake, he demanded, "How do you ask a man to be the last man to die for a mistake?"

Kerry's Capitol Hill appearance thrust him into the national spotlight. In a nation hungry for heroes, in the years following the assassinations of such beloved leaders as Martin Luther King Jr. and

Robert F. Kennedy, Kerry seemed to many to be ideal for the role. In the words of Helen Dudar, writing for the *New York Post* (April 30, 1971), television viewers had been naturally drawn to that "lean, elegant figure, with beautifully barbered long hair, whose face evoked Hollywood and whose inflections, complete with a broad A, recalled Kennedy's."

Encouraged by the public reaction to his speech and to a book of photos about Operation Dewey Canyon III entitled *The New Soldier* (1971), for which he supplied the text, Kerry resigned from his VVAW position to run for political office—driven, as he later admitted, by the idea of being the first Vietnam veteran to win a seat in Congress. When a seat became available in the Fifth Congressional District in Lowell, Massachusetts, he succeeded in winning his party's nomination. Given his national profile, the election battle attracted a lot of attention, and liberals around the country had high hopes that Kerry would be elected. Rather than risk splitting the conservative vote, the independent candidate, Roger P. Durkin, withdrew, leaving the race a two-way fight between Kerry and the Republican Paul W. Cronin. The Vietnam War took a back seat to bread-and-butter issues in the district, and on voting day blue-collar support helped Cronin to win by a margin of 18,000 votes.

The election loss was a crushing blow for Kerry, who dropped out of the limelight for the next decade. He returned to academic life to study law at Boston College. Following his graduation, he spent three years, from 1976 to 1979, working as the first assistant district attorney for Middlesex County, Massachusetts. In 1979 he went into private practice as a partner in the Boston law firm of Kerry & Sragow. At the same time he became involved in business, with the Kilvert & Forbes Cookie Co., taught part-time at the Fletcher School of Law and Diplomacy at Tufts University and at the Georgetown School of Foreign Service, and provided occasional commentary for broadcast news programs.

Still harboring political aspirations, in 1980 Kerry entered the Democratic primary in Massachusetts' Fourth Congressional District, only to withdraw before voting day because he thought it was better for the party; Barney Frank won the primary and the general election as a result. In 1982 Kerry successfully ran for the position of lieutenant governor of Massachusetts on a liberal ticket with Governor Michael Dukakis. Tempering his delight at finally winning an election was the emotional devastation caused by the breakup of his 12-year marriage. To the surprise of some skeptics, Kerry transcended his personal problems and became an effective lieutenant governor.

Two years later, in January 1984, the junior Democratic senator from Massachusetts, Paul E. Tsongas, decided to resign for health reasons. Sensing that the time had come for him to reach a position of political importance, Kerry declared himself a candidate for his party's nomination and took 41 percent of the vote to edge out Representative James M. Shannon in the Democratic primary. The subsequent Senate election campaign was a classic bare-knuckle, liberal-versus-conservative battle between Kerry and his Republican opponent, Ray Shamie, an ultraconservative, self-made millionaire in his 60s. Despite the fact that Democrats outnumbered Republicans in Massachusetts by four to one, polls indicated that the race was much closer than many people anticipated. Boosted by squads of veterans calling themselves Kerry's Kommandos, Kerry captured 55 percent of the vote to defeat Shamie on Election Day.

That Kerry had been tabbed for big things by Democratic Party officials was made clear when he secured a seat on the powerful Senate Foreign Relations Committee less than three months after his arrival on Capitol Hill—becoming the only freshman to win a seat there. Making full use of his position to advance his neoliberal philosophy, Kerry emerged during his first term as what Louise Sweeney termed "a large thorn in the paw" of the Republican administration of President Ronald Reagan.

Kerry compared the arms race and White House policies in Central America to early American involvement in Southeast Asia. Intent on seeing that "the mistakes of Vietnam" were not repeated, he steadfastly opposed aid to the Nicaraguan Contras. It was an October 1986 report by Kerry's staff that first exposed the involvement of Lieutenant Colonel Oliver North in the setting up of a private network to deliver military equipment to the Contras. The report also suggested that the Reagan administration may have secretly, and illegally, sold arms to Iran and funneled the profits to the Nicaraguan rebels. Kerry's report kicked off a storm of controversy, and the subsequent investigations and televised hearings became known as the Iran-Contra affair.

In the wake of the scandal, Kerry continued his investigations, focusing this time on the international drug trade, and the Panamanian dictator Manuel Noriega in particular. He began investigating reports that Noriega, who had aided the Contras, was involved in drug trafficking, with the complicity of the United States government. Kerry formed an unlikely alliance with Senator Jesse Helms, a hardline conservative from North Carolina, and drafted a resolution that proposed to cut by 50 percent the aid to Panama that had not already been given. Both Helms and Kerry stated that Panama had become a center for drug shipments and the laundering of drug money. Although the resolution was largely symbolic (it passed two days after the deadline Congress had set to take such action under terms of the U.S. foreign assistance program), Kerry and Helms maintained that it had sent a message to those countries that received U.S. aid but refused to cooperate in the war on drugs.

In 1988 Jose Blandon, a former aide to Noriega, testified to the Senate Foreign Relations Subcommittee on Terrorism, Narcotics and International Operations that the National Security Council and the Central Intelligence Agency had been supplying Noriega with classified information on Kerry, as well as on other U.S. senators. Kerry was outraged by Blandon's account, calling it, as quoted in the *San Francisco Chronicle* (February 10, 1988), "as disturbing a revelation as I've heard in the course of a lot of disturbing revelations." In 1990 Noriega was removed from power by a U.S. incursion into Panama known as Operation Just Cause.

In the wake of Noriega's ousting, Kerry launched an investigation into the Bank of Credit and Commerce (BCCI), a London-based institution that Kerry accused of having laundered drug profits in excess of $10 million. The bank initially pleaded guilty and agreed to forfeit more than $15 million in assets to the United States. Kerry was displeased with the settlement, which he felt was not harsh enough and which, in an interview with Douglas Frantz for the *San Francisco Chronicle* (January 17, 1990), he called "a sad commentary on a country that is supposed to be taking money laundering extremely seriously." Kerry's probe continued, eventually revealing that BCCI was involved in bribery and income-tax evasion as well as the support of arms trafficking, smuggling, and illegal immigration. On July 5, 1991 BCCI was shut down by the Bank of England.

In 1990 Kerry easily secured a second Senate term, with 57 percent of the vote. In 1992 he was selected to investigate allegations—made by many Vietnam veterans and by the billionaire and independent presidential candidate Ross Perot—that numerous soldiers were still missing in action (MIA) in Vietnam or being held there as prisoners of war (POWs). Kerry was named head of the POW-MIA committee, which produced evidence that as many as 2,200 servicemen may have been left in captivity in Vietnam, despite the official contention that all POWs had been released in 1973, during Operation Homecoming. Kerry persuaded the Pentagon to declassify more than one million pages of records, many of which hinted at the possibility of POWs' still being held in captivity. "The information available to the committee does constitute evidence that some Americans remained alive in Indochina after Operation Homecoming," Kerry told Donna Cassata for the *New Orleans Times-Picayune* (June 25, 1992). "We cannot prove they were alive."

Together with Senator John McCain of Arizona, Kerry headed to Vietnam, in hopes of discovering the truth about the men left behind. The pairing with McCain, himself a Vietnam War veteran who had spent six years in the infamous "Hanoi Hilton" POW camp, surprised many, as McCain, a Republican, had often opposed Kerry on legislative matters. The two had reached an understanding, however, during a long plane flight, discussing their experiences in the war. Kerry and McCain, along with other senators including Tom Daschle, Bob Smith, and Hank Brown, made more than a dozen fact-finding trips to Southeast Asia. The 1,223-page report they compiled, issued in January 1993, stated that there was "no compelling evidence" to suggest that soldiers were still in captivity in Southeast Asia. Many former POWs and supporters of their cause were outraged by the report, accusing Kerry of destroying documents and obscuring other evidence during his investigation. Most people, however, considered the matter settled, and in January 1994 a Senate resolution to lift the trade embargo placed on Vietnam in 1975 passed by a vote of 62 to 38. On February 3, 1994 President Bill Clinton officially lifted the embargo. "In the end," McCain told Paul Alexander in 2002, "we would not have had the normalization of relations with Vietnam and a free trade agreement had it not been for the work that John Kerry did."

Kerry was reelected to the Senate in 1996, after finding himself in a dead heat with his opponent, William F. Weld, then governor of Massachusetts. The Senate race with Weld, a Republican, was later described by John Aloysius Farrell in the *Boston Globe* (June 21, 2003) as "a campaign for the ages, the marquee Senate contest in the country." Weld, who had been elected governor with 71 percent of the vote, challenged Kerry's legislative record and faced off with him in seven televised debates. In the end, Kerry defeated Weld by 191,508 votes, or 7.5 percent of the ballots cast.

The year after the election, Kerry found himself one of only five Senate supporters of the proposed Clean Money, Clean Elections Act, which would have placed limits on the amount of money accepted or spent by candidates for elective office and called for candidates to solicit donations from ordinary voters as well as organizations. In addition, he supported the motion put forth by Illinois senator Dick Durbin to shut down the School of Americas, a U.S. Army–run institution in Fort Benning, Georgia, designed to train military officers from Latin American countries in combat, counterinsurgency, and methods of fighting the illegal drug trade; the school had been established for the ultimate purpose of fighting Communist uprisings in Latin America. Durbin argued that many of the school's graduates, including Manuel Noriega, had gone on to take part in atrocities, and both senators believed that the school was teaching techniques of torture and assassination. Despite their protests, the motion received only 20 votes. The school, which changed its name in 2001 to Western Hemisphere Institute for Security Cooperation, has since been the subject of several investigations. In 1998 Kerry proposed an overhaul of public education, suggesting that each public school in the country become a charter school, which would be run not by the government but by an independent, government-approved organization and would be free from bureaucratic control. In speeches in Washington and Boston, Kerry challenged school systems nationwide, saying that the existence of tenure protected incompetent teachers and that under the current system parents had few choices when it came to their children's education. That same year he voted in support of the Iraq Liberation Act, which sought to ease the suffering of the Iraqi people under the regime of Saddam Hussein by providing humanitarian assistance and urging a transition to democracy there.

Kerry, who opted not to run in the 2000 presidential election, made the short list of potential running mates for the Democratic nominee, Al Gore. (Gore ultimately chose Connecticut senator Joseph Lieberman). Also in 2000 Kerry helped organize the 30th annual Earth Day celebration, further demonstrating his commitment to environmental protection. A year later he helped lead the fight against attempts by President George W. Bush's administration to open the Arctic National Wildlife Refuge to oil drilling. The administration argued that oil from the Arctic region was essential to end America's dependence on Middle Eastern oil, a dependence seen by many as contributing indirectly to the September 11, 2001 terrorist attacks against the U.S. Those who opposed drilling pointed out that the Arctic oil would not be ready for use until 2010 and would, even then, amount to only about 18 months' supply. "I've learned a few lessons about national security as a soldier and a senator," Kerry told Matthew Engel for the London *Guardian* (April 19, 2002), "but the mathematics I learned in elementary school prove that Arctic drilling won't make a difference for national security." The Bush proposal was defeated in the Senate in 2002. Kerry's next bid for the Senate was not even challenged by the Republican Party. His only competition came from the Libertarian candidate, Michael Cloud, whom Kerry trounced with 81 percent of the vote.

In 2003 Kerry announced that he would seek the presidency in the following year's election. As he and the other Democratic candidates prepared for the primary elections, Kerry was endorsed by several prominent Democrats, including Senator Edward M. Kennedy and former Georgia senator Max Cleland. Nonetheless, he initially trailed former Vermont governor Howard Dean, who signed up more than 600,000 volunteers for his campaign. With the Iowa caucuses, on January 19, 2004, however, Kerry steamed ahead, capturing 38 percent of the vote; his closest competitor, Senator John Edwards of North Carolina, got 31.9 percent, and Dean, 18 percent. He went on to win state after state, easily surpassing Edwards, Dean, and the other Democratic candidates, Wesley Clark, Dennis Kucinich, Carol Moseley-Braun, Richard Gephardt, Joseph Lieberman, and Al Sharpton. On March 16 Kerry won the Illinois caucus with 72 percent of the ballots, unofficially sealing his nomination for president.

Kerry's military record became a key focus of his campaign during the early part of 2004. In particular, he made veterans' issues of prime importance, noting on several occasions his belief that the Bush administration had not protected the interests of those it had sent to war in Afghanistan and Iraq. In addition, Kerry called Bush's own military service into question. (In May 1972 Bush, who served in the Texas Air National Guard, received permission to transfer to the Alabama National Guard so that he could participate in a U.S. Senate campaign; his whereabouts between then and the following May, when he returned to Houston, have been disputed.) Referring to Republicans' efforts to label him as a "Massachusetts liberal" who is weak on defense, Kerry said on *Good Morning America*, as quoted by Adam Nagourney and Jodi Wilgoren in the *New York Times* (April 27, 2004), "The Republicans have spent $60 million in the last few weeks trying to attack me, and this comes from a president and a Republican Party that can't even answer whether or not he showed up for duty in the National Guard. I'm not going to stand for it."

Meanwhile, Kerry made clear his stances on other key issues. He proposed tough measures against crime, supporting the Community Oriented Policing System Act, which he hoped to expand by placing an additional 100,000 police officers in community-policing assignments around the country. In addition, although he had opposed the death penalty in the past, he stated during the campaign that he would support it in the case of convicted terrorists; that qualification was a reversal of his previous argument that having a death penalty for terrorists might make more difficult the extradition of suspects to the United States for trial. (Many nations refuse extradition if a suspect is facing possible execution.)

Such reversals provided a target for Kerry's opponents. The Bush administration labeled Kerry a "waffler" and accused him of repeated "flip-flops" on various issues. For example, in 1991, Kerry supported most-favored trade status for China. In later interviews, however, he criticized the Bush administration for trading with China, in light of that nation's human-rights abuses. He also voted for the Patriot Act, which allows the federal government access to medical records, financial information, and even library transactions in its efforts to root out terrorist cells. The bill passed 98–1 in the Senate and 357–66 in the House. During the campaign, however, Kerry became an outspoken critic of the legislation, saying that it violates basic civil liberties.

Another hot-button issue of the 2004 election was that of gay and lesbian rights. Kerry is a co-sponsor of the Hate Crimes Prevention bill, which would strengthen existing hate-crimes laws by targeting crimes committed because of a victim's real or perceived sexual orientation, gender, or disability, and he supports the reauthorization of the Ryan White Comprehensive AIDS Resources Emergency (CARE) Act, first enacted in 1990, which supports a wide range of community-based services for people with AIDS. He also expressed belief in equal rights for homosexual couples and supported same-sex civil unions. He said, however, that he believes that the term "marriage" should apply only to heterosexual couples, due to its religious association.

Kerry stated his belief that the costs of the current health-care system in the U.S. are unacceptable. Many Americans, he contended, cannot afford adequate health-care coverage due to rising premiums, which have gone up an average of $2,700 per family in the past four years. "Health care in the richest country on the face of this planet is not a privilege, it's a right," he told Carla Marinucci for the San Francisco Chronicle (May 28, 2003). "We need to guarantee [that health care] is available to all Americans in a cost-effective, efficient and openly accessible, affordable way." Kerry's proposed health-care plan aimed to make coverage available to 95 percent of Americans, as well as create an enforceable patients' bill of rights and pursue ways to reduce medical errors.

In the late spring of 2004, another incendiary issue arose, which many thought would have ramifications for the presidential race. On April 28 60 Minutes II, a CBS-TV news program, broadcast shocking photos of Iraqi prisoners of war being tortured and humiliated by U.S. troops. (The troops had overthrown the Iraqi dictator Saddam Hussein the previous year in a war whose purpose, the Bush administration had asserted, was to rid Iraq of weapons of mass destruction. As of early November 2004, none had been found there.) The Iraqi POWs were being held at the infamous Abu Ghraib prison, the site of the detainment and execution of many political dissidents during the reign of Saddam Hussein. Almost immediately following the release of the photos, a public outcry arose, with many calling for the resignation of Secretary of Defense Donald Rumsfeld and blaming the Bush administration overall. "They are sickening, appalling, depraved and sad," Kerry said of the pictures, speaking with Jodi Wilgoren for the New York Times (May 15, 2004). He added that the existence of the photos and what they depicted provided evidence of "a lack of command control." He also noted that the scandal had "put American troops at greater risk, put Americans at greater risk, tarnished all of us and, I think, been a great disservice to the effort that we have been engaged in over there." Following the revelations about Abu Ghraib, 40 percent of Americans surveyed said that they approved of the president's handling of the situation in Iraq, down from 55 percent in January 2004.

As U.S. military activity in Iraq continued, Kerry came under fire for his stance on the war, with some critics noting that the senator, who has criticized the Bush administration's handling of the conflict, himself voted for a resolution authorizing the use of force to remove Saddam Hussein from power. In 2003 he voted against the administration's request for $87 billion for operations in Iraq and Afghanistan, after suggesting that the money be raised by increasing taxes on the wealthy. An explanation of his reasoning led Kerry to make the often-cited statement, "I actually did vote for the $87 billion before I voted against it"—a quote on which Republicans seized as an example of Kerry's

"flip-flopping." Kerry, however, as quoted by Mark Kasindorf in USA Today (April 13, 2004), said, "It is the president who flipped and flopped and squandered his promise to Americans to go to war as a last resort and misled Americans with respect to weapons of mass destruction." Kerry said that when he supported the 2003 invasion of Iraq, he believed, as many had been led to, that Iraq contained such weapons—but that the aftermath of the invasion revealed the war to be both misguided and poorly planned. Referring to previous U.S. military campaigns abroad, Kerry said in an interview with Philip Gourevitch for the New Yorker (July 26, 2004), "I have a thirty-five-year record of making it clear what my foreign policy is. I supported Bosnia. I supported Kosovo. I supported Haiti. I supported Panama. I support military action when I think it is appropriate."

On July 6, 2004 Kerry announced that he had chosen Senator John Edwards as his running mate. The choice was well-received by Democratic Party officials, many of whom had placed Edwards at the top of their lists of the most eligible candidates, despite his having been in the Senate for only five and a half years. Edwards, a self-made millionaire and personal-injury lawyer, was seen as a potential draw for voters who could better relate to Edwards's humble roots than to Kerry's rather privileged upbringing.

Kerry formally accepted his party's nomination on July 29, 2004 at the Democratic National Convention, held in Boston, Massachusetts. At the climax of a convention that had emphasized his military heroism, in a speech that pundits called one of his best, Kerry outlined his plan for the nation. "My fellow Americans: we are here tonight united in one simple purpose: to make America stronger at home and respected in the world," he said, as quoted on his official Web site. He went on to criticize the Bush administration's handling of domestic and foreign affairs, saying, "I will be a commander in chief who will never mislead us into war." Implicitly criticizing actions by Bush's vice president, Richard B. Cheney; secretary of defense, Rumsfeld; and attorney general, John Ashcroft, he added, "I will have a Vice President who will not conduct secret meetings with polluters to rewrite our environmental laws. I will have a Secretary of Defense who will listen to the best advice of our military leaders. And I will appoint an Attorney General who actually upholds the Constitution of the United States."

In his three, televised debates with Bush, on September 30, October 8, and October 13, respectively, Kerry was generally thought to have outperformed the president. While Bush accused Kerry of being inconsistent in his positions with regard to the war in Iraq, Kerry repeatedly criticized the president for failing to bring Osama bin Laden—the architect of the 2001 terrorist attacks on the U.S.—to justice; for "rush[ing] to war in Iraq without a plan to win the peace"; and for pursuing a tax-cut policy that favored the wealthiest Americans. Opinion polls indicated that the debates had hurt the president, who had enjoyed a surge in polls after the Republican National Convention, while helping Kerry. Observing what was called the most divisive election campaign in recent memory, many predicted a contest so close that it might take days or even weeks to resolve, as had been the case with the 2000 election. Nonetheless, on Election Day, November 2, President Bush won 286 electoral votes to Kerry's 252 and 51.07 percent of the popular vote to Kerry's 48 percent. In conceding the election the following day, Kerry told a gathering in Boston, as quoted by the *New York Times* (November 3, 2004, on-line), "My friends, it was here that we began our campaign for the presidency. And all we had was hope and a vision for a better America. It is a privilege and a gift to spend two years traveling this country, coming to know so many of you. . . . I thank you from the bottom of my heart. . . . I want to especially say to the American people: In this journey, you have given me the honor and the gift of listening and learning from you. I have visited your homes. I've visited your churches. I've visited your community halls. I've heard your stories. I know your struggles. I know your hopes. They are part of me now. And I will never forget you and I'll never stop fighting for you."

The six-foot four-inch John Kerry currently makes his home in a six-floor brownstone in Beacon Hill, an upscale suburb of Boston. He has two daughters, Alexandra and Vanessa, from his marriage to Julia Thorne, which ended in divorce. In 1995 he married Teresa Heinz, the widow of Pennsylvania senator John Heinz and heiress to the H. J. Heinz food empire. Teresa Heinz Kerry has three sons, John, Andre, and Christopher. In his leisure time Kerry enjoys skiing, snowboarding, sailing, and windsurfing. He is also an avid hockey player and a Harley-Davidson enthusiast and flies a twin-engine Cessna, sometimes between stops on the campaign trail. In addition, he is a voracious reader, who has cited James Bradley's book *Flags of Our Fathers* and *Undaunted Courage*, by Stephen Ambrose, as being among his favorite books. The books he read while on the campaign trail include Clyde Prestowitz's *Rogue Nation* and Barbara Ehrenreich's *Nickel and Dimed*.

—J.K.B.

Suggested Reading: *Atlanta Journal-Constitution* A p15 Feb. 22, 2004; *Christian Science Monitor* p1+ July 1985; *New York Times* p4 Apr. 23, 1971, A p13 May 15, 2004; *New Yorker* p50+ July 26, 2004, with photo; *Rolling Stone* p53+ Apr. 11, 2002, with photos; *Washington Post* D p1+ Feb. 21, 1985

Kilbourne, Jean

Jan. 4, 1943– Educator; author; social activist

Address: Wellesley Centers for Women, Wellesley College, 106 Central St., Wellesley, MA 02481

In the U.S., according to Jean Kilbourne, the average person is exposed to more than 3,000 advertising images and sound bytes every day—through radio and television, magazines, newspapers, junk mail, the Internet, billboards, posters in public places, T-shirts, hats, jackets, and other items and places. "I'm not saying that people are brainwashed," Kilbourne told Clea Simon for *Ms.* (December 2000/January 2001). "I'm not saying that advertisers have absolute control or anything like that. I'm just saying it is a powerful influence and we need to take it seriously. It's a powerful influence that's increasing in the culture." An internationally recognized public speaker, writer, and filmmaker, Kilbourne is best known for her critical analyses of the advertising industry, especially tobacco and alcohol advertisers and ads aimed at women, and her efforts to teach people to be media literate. Though Kilbourne has acknowledged that most adults are aware that the purpose of advertisements is to sell products or services, she has warned that the effects of advertising are cumulative and mostly unconscious. She has argued that

Courtesy of Jean Kilbourne

many advertisements portray women as objects, make violent behavior against women seem normal or even erotic, depict sex as a trivial act, foster addictions to alcohol and tobacco, and induce eating disorders, mostly in women and girls who attempt to conform to unachievable ideals of beauty.

Kilbourne's lectures have become key parts of award-winning educational films, including *Killing Us Softly: Advertising's Image of Women* (1979), *Still Killing Us Softly* (1987), and *Slim Hopes: Advertising and the Obsession with Thinness* (1995), which, like her books, among them *Can't Buy My Love: How Advertising Changes the Way We Think and Feel* (2000), have helped to develop and popularize the study of gender representation in advertising. Kilbourne served as an adviser to the former U.S. surgeons general C. Everett Koop and Antonia Novello and has testified before the U.S. Congress. She has also advised an attorney general of Massachusetts and once served as keynote speaker at a conference on gender bias that was attended by all the judges in that state. Since 1993, as an appointee of Donna Shalala, who was then the U.S. secretary of health and human services, she has served on the National Advisory Council on Alcohol Abuse and Alcoholism, which provides information and advice to the National Institute on Alcohol Abuse and Alcoholism, a division of the National Institutes of Health (NIH). She has delivered more than a thousand lectures at high schools and colleges around the country and has twice been named lecturer of the year by the National Association of Campus Activities. "Smoking, obsession with thinness and image, alcohol, obesity, binge drinking and prescription drugs should all be addressed as public health issues," Kilbourne told Sandy Spears for the *Daily Illini* (November 7, 2002, on-line), a University of Illinois campus newspaper. "Public health issues can only be solved by changing the environment." "The most important thing we can do is teach media literacy in our schools," she told Clea Simon. "Most other nations do. A truly critical audience would be less easily manipulated." Among other honors, Kilbourne was once named woman of the year by the National Organization for Women and received the Women's Image Now Award from the American Federation of Television and Radio Artists (AFTRA) in 1995. "Kilbourne's work is pioneering and crucial to the dialogue of one of the most unexplored yet most powerful realms of American culture—advertising," the feminist writer Susan Faludi has said, as quoted on Kilbourne's official Web site. "We owe her a great debt."

Jean Kilbourne was born on January 4, 1943 in Kansas and grew up near Boston, Massachusetts. She earned a bachelor's degree in English from Wellesley College, in Wellesley, Massachusetts, in 1964. To some degree Kilbourne has traced her interest in the issues on which her life's work is based to her experiences in the fashion industry. "I had done some modeling after I graduated from college—those were the days when it was very hard for women to get work," she recalled to Simon. "I really hated modeling. At that time, there were no words like objectification and sexual harassment, but I knew that was what was happening

to me. That left me with a real interest in the power of beauty." She began collecting print advertisements and talking to people about how those ads may have affected them. Because she had been addicted to alcohol and tobacco for a number of years beginning in her mid-teens, she focused on the ways in which those products were marketed. She found that the overwhelming majority of ads indicated that people's lives would generally improve if they would simply purchase the products in question. Also during the 1960s Kilbourne received an award from Wellesley that allowed her to spend three years in Europe, where she worked for the British Broadcasting Corp. (BBC) in London and for a French film company in Paris.

In 1972 Kilbourne earned a master's degree in education from Boston University. A few years later she began her career as an educator, lecturing to students about gender stereotypes and the underlying messages in media images. She began lecturing full-time in 1977. In 1979 she appeared in her first educational film, *Killing Us Softly: Advertising's Image of Women*, which was directed by Margaret Lazarus and Renner Wunderlich and featured footage of Kilbourne lecturing on the effects of advertising on women, with illustrations interspersed. In a review of the film for the *Boston Globe*, as quoted on Kilbourne's Web site, Jay Carr wrote, "Ads continue to teach men contempt for women and the feminine side of themselves. All encourage people to think that life's problems are best solved with products. . . . With skill, humor and acuteness, Kilbourne encourages action against these society-weakening images." After receiving her doctorate in education from Boston University, in 1980, Kilbourne revisited the themes in *Killing Us Softly* in the films *Still Killing Us Softly* (1987) and *Killing Us Softly 3: Advertising's Image of Women* (1999).

In her work Kilbourne has noted that advertisers often hire psychologists to conduct group studies to determine what consumers want and how advertisers can best influence them. A key strategy is to target the "leaders," or trend-setters, in the general population, who presumably impel "followers" to purchase the same products. Advertisers, according to Kilbourne, also conduct psychological research on children to learn how to lure them to their products. (Many countries prohibit advertisers from targeting children. The U.S. does not.) To defend against the influence of advertisers, Kilbourne advises parents, as she told Simon, to "start a mother-daughter group and lobby for the schools to teach media literacy. Lobby for campaign finance reform. Run for office. Support the feminist groups that exist now, the battered women's centers and the rape crisis centers. Every single thing that people do in that regard is important. What will bring about the change is a critical mass of people who are seeing things differently."

According to Robert Coen of the advertising agency Universal McCann, as quoted in *Yellow Pages & Directory Report* (December 26, 2003, on-line), the U.S. advertising industry spent nearly $250 billion in 2003. (By comparison, the 2005 fiscal-year budgets for the U.S. Departments of Homeland Security, Energy, Justice, Interior, Agriculture, Veterans Affairs, Housing and Urban Development, and Labor total $239.3 billion.) In her lecture-based documentary *Pack of Lies: The Advertising of Tobacco* (1992), which she made with an associate, Rick Pollay, Kilbourne vehemently criticized the tobacco and advertising industries. "There's a myth in this culture that smoking is rebellious and defiant, but the truth is that smokers smoke for a manipulative and unbelievably callous industry," she told an audience of students and faculty at the University of Utah, as quoted by Adam Benson in the *Daily Utah Chronicle* (March 31, 2003). In *Pack of Lies* she stressed that tobacco killed more people in the 20th century than wars and that in the U.S. nearly half a million people die every year from smoking-related illnesses. Kilbourne has been involved in national campaigns to stop tobacco advertisers' practice of marketing their products to young people. As an example of the results of the tobacco industry's aggressive advertising practices, Kilbourne has noted that some elementary-school students in the U.S. are more familiar with the character Joe Camel, seen in advertisements for Camel cigarettes, than the internationally known Walt Disney character Mickey Mouse.

Returning to the theme of advertising's effects on women, Kilbourne, along with the media critic George Gerbner, made the illustrated film *The Killing Screens: Media and the Culture of Violence* (1994). In it they argued that media images affect not only women's sense of themselves but also the way men and societies as a whole treat women; the film tried to show that the objectification of the female form in ads is a gateway to violence. Narrowing the scope of her exploration of advertising and women, Kilbourne focused on the role of the media in shaping women's body images in the film *Slim Hopes: Advertising and the Obsession with Thinness* (1995). Kilbourne asserted that advertisers' constant use of images of "perfect"-looking women—many of which are airbrushed or doctored in other ways to achieve a kind of artificial perfection—can be very harmful to teenage girls and young women, the vast majority of whom cannot achieve the ideal and often suffer a loss of self-esteem or become depressed. Early in life, "girls get the message" from advertisers about how they should look, Kilbourne told an audience at the University of Nebraska, as quoted by Crystal Weaver in the *Daily Nebraskan* (March 5, 2003). "Self-esteem plummets once they reach adolescence; they just hit a wall. One in five girls in America have an eating disorder, and I would suggest that four in five have unhealthy attitudes toward food and their bodies." *Slim Hopes* won the award for creative excellence at the 1996 International Film and Video Festival. As quoted on Kilbourne's Web site, Francis Berg, the editor of *Healthy Weight*

Journal, judged *Slim Hopes* to be "extremely important. . . . [Kilbourne's] message is timely, persuasive, and thought provoking."

In her recent films, Kilbourne has returned to the topic of the alcohol and tobacco industries. In *Deadly Persuasion: The Advertising of Alcohol & Tobacco* (2003), she examined how those industries use advertising to keep consumers addicted to their harmful products. She asserted that the alcohol and tobacco industries are well aware of the addictiveness of their dangerous products and that they exploit addiction to increase profits. In *Spin the Bottle: Sex, Lies & Alcohol* (2003), Kilbourne and her fellow media critic Jackson Katz discussed teenage binge drinking and the ways in which alcohol marketers manipulate the fragile gender identities of young men and women to promote the consumption of alcohol. They also showed how alcohol abuse has been made to seem normal by ads, movies, and television, despite the fact that every year such abuse leads to thousands of deaths, injuries, and sexual assaults, especially among college students. Many of the advertisements that Kilbourne has cited as examples seem to encourage reckless behavior or depict women and men who drink or smoke as more sexually desirable than those who do not. On her Web site, a print ad for a type of tequila shows a woman suggestively licking the ear of a smiling man; the ad's text reads, "The tequila is pure. Your intentions don't have to be."

In addition to making films, Kilbourne has published books. After years of rejections from other publishers (which she has attributed to their fears of promoting books critical of the advertising industry), her book *Deadly Persuasion: Why Women and Girls Must Fight the Addictive Power of Advertising* was published by Simon & Schuster in 1999. It was reprinted in paperback the following year under the title *Can't Buy My Love: How Advertising Changes the Way We Think and Feel*. Kilbourne has contributed chapters to several other books, among them *TV and Teens: Experts Look at the Issues* (1982), edited by Meg Schwarz, and *Feminist Perspectives on Eating Disorders* (1993), edited by Patricia Fallon and others. In addition, articles by Kilbourne have appeared in such publications as the *New York Times*, *USA Today*, and the *Journal of the American Medical Women's Association*. Some of those articles are in the textbooks *Gender, Race, and Class in Media* (1994), edited by Gail Dines and Jean M. Humez, and *Impact of Mass Media* (1995), edited by Ray Eldon Hiebert. Kilbourne has been interviewed by reporters from major American and Canadian newspapers, among them the *New York Times*, the *Wall Street Journal*, the *Washington Post*, and the Toronto *Globe and Mail*. She has appeared on *The Oprah Winfrey Show*, *Today*, and *20/20*.

Kilbourne has been a visiting scholar at Wellesley College since 1984 and has sat on the boards of directors or advisory councils of the Junior League, the Women's Action Alliance, the Media Education Foundation, and the Marin Institute for the Prevention of Alcohol and Other Drug Problems. In addition to her other honors, Kilbourne has received a special-recognition award from the Academy of Eating Disorders and the Leadership in Action Award from the Women's Action Alliance.

Kilbourne, who is divorced, lives with her teenage daughter, Claudia, in Boston.

—C.F.T.

Suggested Reading: *Daily Nebraskan* Mar. 5, 2003; Jean Kilbourne Web site; *Ms. Magazine* p54+ Dec. 2000/Jan. 2001, with photo; Wellesley Centers for Women Web site; Signorielli, Nancy. *Women in Communication*, 1996

Selected Films: *Killing Us Softly: Advertising's Image of Women*, 1979; *Still Killing Us Softly*, 1987; *Pack of Lies: The Advertising of Tobacco*, 1992; *The Killing Screens: Media and the Culture of Violence*, 1994; *Slim Hopes: Advertising and the Obsession with Thinness*, 1995; *Killing Us Softly 3: Advertising's Image of Women*, 1999; *Deadly Persuasion: The Advertising of Alcohol & Tobacco*, 2003; *Spin the Bottle: Sex, Lies & Alcohol* (with Jackson Katz), 2003

Selected Books: *Deadly Persuasion: Why Women and Girls Must Fight the Addictive Power of Advertising*, 1999 (reprinted in 2000 as *Can't Buy My Love: How Advertising Changes the Way We Think and Feel*)

Alex Wong/Getty Images

Kilpatrick, Kwame M.

June 8, 1970– Mayor of Detroit (Democrat)

Address: Mayor's Office, Coleman A. Young Municipal Center, 2 Woodward Ave., Suite 1126, Detroit, MI 48226

During his successful run for mayor of Detroit, in 2001, Kwame M. Kilpatrick made a rap song a signature of his campaign and quoted lyrics of others; for years—except during part of that campaign—he has also worn a diamond stud earring. Those are among the reasons that, though not with his wholehearted approval, he has been referred to as "America's hip-hop mayor." Kilpatrick, who was sworn in as mayor on January 4, 2002, is the

youngest person ever to win election to Detroit's highest office; currently, at age 34, he is also the youngest mayor of any major U.S. city. Shortly before he hosted the Detroit Hip-Hop Summit, in 2003, Kilpatrick said in a speech, as quoted on PR Newswire (April 18, 2003), "Detroit moves the world, and in many cases, we have done it on the backs of young people without them realizing it. Detroit is rebuilding and resurging, and young people are beginning to understand that they have a place and a role in changing the world, right here from their city. Hip-hop artists and managers can begin to utilize their talents and platforms to actually change the things in urban America that they describe as troubling in the music." An All-American football star in college and a law-school graduate, Kilpatrick served as a Michigan state representative from 1998 to 2002. During his tenure in the state legislature, he played a major role in the launching of the Clean Michigan Initiative, among other achievements. As Detroit's mayor, Kilpatrick has worked to revitalize an economically devastated city, whose population shrank from close to two million in 1950 (when it was the nation's fifth largest city) to less than one million in 2000 (by which year it had dropped to 10th place). Among other actions, he has instituted a plan to demolish many dilapidated buildings in Detroit's virtually abandoned urban center and has encouraged the development of the downtown area, securing millions of dollars in investments and raising millions more by means of a controversial arrangement with the city's three gambling casinos. A former teacher, he has been a highly visible proponent of after-school programs and improved classroom instruction. Kilpatrick was the inspiration for the main character in the film *Head of State* (2003), about a black, streetwise Washington, D.C., alderman who finds himself running for the presidency of the United States. According to Kevin Chappell in *Ebony* (December 2002), Kilpatrick "often greets men with a chest-bump, embraces women with a hug, and tells those looking to talk business to 'hit' him up on his cell phone or two-way pager." "People can see themselves in the mayor's vision for the city," Detroit's police chief, Jerry A. Oliver Sr., a Kilpatrick appointee, told Chappell. "This is not some abstract vision that you can't really get a hold on, that you can't get your mind around. He can make a vision real in his comments to people. He can energize them to want to accomplish it. That's his strength." In his 2003 State of the City message, the mayor cited as "the Kilpatrick team attitude" words that the U.S. senator Robert F. Kennedy borrowed from the writings of George Bernard Shaw: "Some men see things as they are and ask, Why? I dream of things that never were and ask, Why not?"

Kwame M. Kilpatrick was born on June 8, 1970 in Detroit. He has one sibling—a sister, Ayanna. His mother is Carolyn Cheeks Kilpatrick, a Democrat who has served in the U.S. Congress since 1997 as the representative of Michigan's 13th Congressional District; among other assignments, she serves on the powerful House Appropriations Committee. His father is Bernard Kilpatrick, who formerly served as a Wayne County, Michigan, commissioner; in 2003 Kwame Kilpatrick appointed him to the Detroit–Wayne County Community Mental Health Board. Politics has been a part of Kilpatrick's life since his childhood; he has recalled playing in the state capitol building as an eight-year-old while his mother, then a state legislator, worked in the legislative chamber. When he was 11 his parents divorced.

Kilpatrick was a rambunctious boy. "I got a lot of whippings," he told Kevin Chappell. "My mother had to come to school a lot for me. I was talking, running my mouth, playing. But I always got good grades." Kilpatrick attended Pelham Middle School and graduated from Cass Technical High School with a 2.87 grade-point average in 1988. He then enrolled at Florida A&M University, in Tallahassee. He joined the Alpha Phi Alpha fraternity and became captain of the school football team, which won a conference championship in 1990. In 1992, after helping his team to its first Division I-AA top-10 national ranking since the late 1970s, he was named an All-American. Kilpatrick's hope of becoming a pro was dashed after he injured his back as a senior. "I was a typical football player, hung out, partied, had a good time," he told Kevin Chappell. "I had a lot of fun in college." He also performed well academically; he graduated with a B.S. degree cum laude in political science, and a teaching certificate, in 1992. He then taught briefly at Rickards High School, in Jacksonville, Florida, before returning to Detroit to teach social studies to seventh- and eighth-graders at Marcus Garvey Academy, a public school. "Kwame was good for the children's souls," Harvey Hambrick, the principal of the academy, told Robert Alan Glover for the *Michigan Chronicle* (January 1, 2002), "cutting the boys' hair, taking the students on outings, coaching basketball and becoming our first Boy Scout leader." During that time Kilpatrick also attended the

Detroit College of Law, from which he earned a J.D. degree in 1998.

Earlier, in 1996, at age 26, Kilpatrick was elected to represent Detroit's Ninth District in the Michigan state House of Representatives—the seat vacated by his mother, who won election to the U.S. Congress on the same day. (Michigan has a bicameral legislature, with a 38-member Senate in addition to the 100-member House.) In 1998 Kilpatrick played a key role in designing the Clean Michigan Initiative, which earmarked 60 percent of $675 million in funds for the cleanup and redevelopment in Detroit of numerous "brownfields" (former commercial or industrial sites, many of them polluted), waterfront areas, and parks. In November 1998 Kilpatrick became the first African-American floor leader of Michigan's House Democratic Caucus, a position that made him his party's second in command in the legislature. As a state representative he also secured $7 million for the prevention of lead poisoning and joined in efforts to strengthen personal-protection orders (court orders that seek to protect victims of domestic violence, stalking, and other forms of abuse), pass environmental legislation, and expand health-care benefits for retirees. In 2001 Kilpatrick became the youngest person and first African-American to serve as the House Democratic leader in the Michigan state legislature.

On April 17, 2001 Dennis Archer, who had been Detroit's mayor since January 1993, announced that he would not seek reelection. One month later Kilpatrick announced his candidacy for the position, which, like those of the nine-member City Council, is filled by means of a nonpartisan election. The names of 20 other people joined that of Kilpatrick on the ballot in the primary, held on September 11 of that year. Kilpatrick's main competitor in the race was Gilbert R. "Gil" Hill, the 69-year-old president of Detroit's City Council and a former homicide detective. (Hill also appeared in the *Beverly Hills Cop* movie series, as the irate boss of Detective Axel Foley, played by Eddie Murphy.) Kilpatrick emerged from the primary 15 percentage points ahead of Hill, who came in second, and the two faced each other again in the general election. As had occurred before the primary, Kilpatrick and Hill waged strongly negative campaigns. Hill pointed to Kilpatrick's relative inexperience and questioned the legality of some of the funds Kilpatrick had raised, such as a $50,000 donation from a tax-funded homeless shelter. Kilpatrick, who campaigned with the slogan "Our future . . . right here, right now!," characterized Hill as a symbol of the status quo and Hill's career as the city's top homicide inspector as lackluster; he also emphasized his own youthfulness and energy to great effect. On Election Day, November 6, 2001, with less than 25 percent of registered voters going to the polls and despite a controversy concerning the counting of absentee ballots, Kilpatrick triumphed with 54 percent of the vote.

Kilpatrick recalled to Kevin Chappell that when he began his four-year term, on January 4, 2002, "we didn't know how bad" conditions in the city were. "We had a $170 million deficit," he explained. "There was very little accountability in place. Our equipment hadn't been maintained in years. The infrastructure, a lot of it, from transportation to public lighting, had not been cared for in years. We came into something that was not working. We had 48 labor unions. All of the contracts had expired. We had to negotiate these contracts as soon as we walked in the door." In order to raise revenue, Kilpatrick instituted cost-cutting measures (without laying off any city employees), oversaw an unusually successful amnesty program for delinquent taxpayers, and negotiated an agreement for casino development that generated $285 million for the city. Within his first six months as mayor, the city had wiped out a budget deficit of $169 million. He also launched the "Motor City Makeover," in which Detroit residents collected 11,000 tons of trash and demolished 2,000 vacant houses. Abandoned houses, he told Jodi Wilgoren for the New York Times (July 7, 2002), are "where drugs dealers stash their drugs, . . . where people stash guns, . . . where girls get abused. It's also a pride issue. If you don't have community pride, if you don't have a safe, clean city, you don't have a world-class city."

On the educational front, Kilpatrick initiated Mayor's Time, a program that has provided afterschool programs for thousands of schoolchildren. In his February 12, 2003 State of the City message, as posted on the city's Web site, he announced that the Robert Wood Johnson Foundation had pledged $3.8 million to support Mayor's Time. In addition, he said, the Intel Corp. would help Detroit set up four computer-equipped clubhouses where "youngsters can work on projects . . . and become involved with technology." He also called for city agencies and the public-school system to work together "to build communities" rather than building new houses and new schools "in a vacuum," and he directed his newly appointed board of education to develop ways to improve the involvement of parents in their children's education.

Kilpatrick has also reformed the Detroit police department, by implementing new technologies and aggressively recruiting minority candidates to become officers. In an effort to involve the community in policing, he expanded an annual three-day volunteer event known as "Angels Night," which occurs each year around Halloween and was launched to counteract Detroit's "Devil's Night," when people traditionally committed arson or other acts of vandalism. With Kilpatrick's encouragement, more than 40,000 volunteers turned out in 2002 to guard city streets. "This type of turnout for 'Angels Night' is further proof of the tremendous spiritual movement that is taking place in our city," Kilpatrick told a reporter for PR Newswire (November 1, 2002). "When the efforts to take back our neighborhoods were initiated some 17 years ago, people dreamed of a day like this where our children and grandchildren wouldn't have to worry about arson during a national period of family fun."

In the wake of the September 11, 2001 terrorist attacks on the U.S., Kilpatrick has sought to strengthen security in Detroit, focusing particularly on the city's shared international border with Windsor, Canada. "I think we need to see some improvements," he told Robert Alan Glover for the Michigan Chronicle (January 1, 2002), "especially in the area of manpower, and put more customs people at the border while also working with all the Canadian law enforcement agencies, such as the Royal Canadian Mounted Police, to secure the crossings and keep that security up." Kilpatrick's antiterrorist program also emphasizes the sharing of information by city agencies.

Kilpatrick suffered a setback in the elections of November 2004, when voters defeated a proposal that would have given the mayor's office more authority over the public-school system. Earlier in 2004 former bodyguards of his and a former deputy chief of police publicly accused him of engaging in extramarital affairs—charges that he has denied. He has also dismissed criticism from some quarters about his alleged overuse of a city-funded expense account.

Kwame Kilpatrick is a member of the National Association for the Advancement of Colored People, the Wolverine Bar Association, and the Michigan State Bar. His wife, Carlita, is a violence-prevention counselor. The couple have three sons—Jalil and Jelani, who are twins, and their younger brother, Jonas.

—L.A.S.

Suggested Reading: Ebony p60+ Dec. 2002; Los Angeles Times I p1 May 11, 2003; Michigan Chronicle p1 Jan.1, 2002, p1 Nov.12, 2002; New York Times I p10 July 7, 2002

Klein, William

1928– Photographer; filmmaker; painter

Address: 5 Rue de Medicis, Paris, France 75006

The career of the expatriate photographer, filmmaker, and painter William Klein has spanned half a century and produced works as celebrated as they are provocative. After serving in World War II and beginning his artistic career as a painter in France, Klein turned to photography; for a decade starting in the mid-1950s he worked for *Vogue* magazine, taking photos whose tongue-in-cheek nature startled the fashion world, and during the same period he published his first book of photographs, *Life Is Good and Good for You in New York: Trance Witness Revels*, a groundbreaking

AFP/Getty Images

William Klein

straphanger's eye made him a master of crowd shots, of enduringly animated in-your-face pictures," as Mary Blume wrote for the *International Herald Tribune* (June 8, 2002). Klein's penchant for visual art led him to spend a great deal of time at New York City's Museum of Modern Art; he also read voraciously. He graduated from high school at the age of 14, then enrolled at the City College of New York, where he studied sociology. In 1945, during World War II, Klein—a year away from graduation, "dreaming of a life as a painter in Paris," as one writer put it—joined the U.S. Army, serving as a cartoonist for *Stars and Stripes*.

After the war, through the G.I. Bill, he attended the Sorbonne, in Paris, France. Also in France he studied under the noted painter Fernand Leger. During this period he created large works, embracing what he described to Michel Guerrin in the Manchester *Guardian Weekly* (July 24, 2002) as "an increasingly abstract and geometrical form of painting." Some of those works were shown at the Galleria Il Milione, in Milan, Italy, in 1952. Afterward, Klein was commissioned to paint similar works, which would be mounted on revolving panels. Klein decided to capture the movement of the works, an idea that led to his "first serious contact with photography," he said, as quoted by Jane Livingston in *The New York School: Photographs, 1936-1963*. According to Livingston, as quoted on the Master of Photography Web site, Klein added, "At one point I photographed the turning panels. While they revolved, using long exposures, the geometrical forms blurred. It seemed to me that blur gave another dimension to the lines, squares and circles we were all playing with and was a way out of a hard-edged rut. I was intrigued by what could be done with a camera—or even without a camera. I saw how I could go one step further creating forms in the darkroom. I cut out basic figures in black paper, projected light through them and literally drew with light on photographic paper. The results were then photographed, blown up and used wall size." Around the same time, Klein began to take a multidisciplinary approach to art, as did other artists studying in France at the time, including his friends Ellsworth Kelly and Jack Youngerman. Citing one example of such an approach, Klein told Tobias Grey for the London *Financial Times* (June 1, 2002), "The whole idea of the Russian constructionists was that they were multi-disciplinarians: they would be painting, they would do typography, interior design, sculpture, movies and so on and I thought that's cool, I would do the whole thing. And then, there was one area, reportage, where I thought nothing's really happening and it's very sedate, old-fashioned . . . painting was going in every different direction and photography [wasn't], and I thought, 'well, not only will I go back to New York, I'm going to do a book of photographs on New York.'"

Meanwhile, an exhibition of Klein's was seen by Alexander Liberman, then the art director of all Condé Nast magazines, including *Vogue*. Liber-

volume for which Klein "broke half the rules of photography and ignored the other half," as Jim Lewis put it in *Slate Magazine* (April 25, 2003). The photos in that book, which was initially overlooked in the U.S. but highly popular in Europe, set the tone for the other cityscapes he would produce, with their seemingly spontaneous and unposed shots and their sometimes blurred images. As a filmmaker Klein is perhaps best known for *Muhammad Ali: The Greatest, 1964-74*, which captured the atmosphere surrounding some of the heavyweight boxing champion's most legendary fights; his other films include bitterly satirical, antiwar movies of the 1960s as well as *Messiah* (1999), an homage to George Frideric Handel's most famous composition. Klein's most recent book of photographs is *Paris + Klein*. His work, for which he has won numerous prizes, continues to be exhibited in museums and galleries in the U.S. and abroad.

The son of Jewish immigrants, William Klein was born in New York City in 1928. (According to one source, he was born in Hungary.) He was raised in a poor, rough area, 108th Street and Amsterdam Avenue, after his father's clothing business failed with the stock-market crash of 1929. When he was a boy, as he told David D'Arcy for National Public Radio's *Morning Edition* (May 6, 2003), " [I never] thought that I'd be able to take photographs, because I was a very clumsy little Jewish kid and I had no money. I had friends who had darkrooms; it would knock me out. I'd go to see them putting out prints from the chemicals and I was amazed. I thought, 'I'll never be able to do that.'" Still, as he rode crowded subway trains to and from Townsend Harris High School, "his

man offered Klein the opportunity to be a fashion photographer for *Vogue*; Klein worked for the publication from 1955 to 1965. He told Sophie Berrebi for *Eyestorm* (February 28, 2001, on-line), "Liberman had this thing about me; he thought I could jazz up the magazine. . . . I was an outsider to fashion photography, to say the least. For instance, I found the fashion shows a drag, and I never went to them. I was only interested in photographic ideas. The editors would bring in the clothes and I would find a way to photograph them." In addition, Klein told Ruth La Ferla for the *New York Times* (April 1, 2003), "My photographs [for *Vogue*] are mostly parodies. The intention was to show how phony the poses were. But nobody complained. I always made sure that you could see the dress." As quoted on the Masters of Photography Web site, Alexander Liberman wrote of Klein, "In the fashion pictures of the fifties, nothing like Klein had happened before. He went to extremes, which took a combination of great ego and courage. He pioneered the telephoto and wide-angle lenses, giving us a new perspective. He took fashion out of the studio and into the streets."

At the beginning of Klein's tenure with *Vogue*, Liberman had arranged for the photographer to travel back to New York, where Klein embarked on his mission of photographing the city. "I saw New York differently after being in Paris for a few years. I saw it from two points of view—one part of me was the wiseass New Yorker, the other was a snotty Parisian," he recalled to Kevin West for *Women's Wear Daily* (March 24, 2003). "Everything I saw knocked me out. I went into crowds and shot point blank. I was like an anthropologist with the Zulus. They need[ed] to be studied and indexed." His resulting book of photos, *Life Is Good and Good for You in New York: Trance Witness Revels* (1956), contained strikingly unusual shots of the city. According to Master of Photography, "Klein's visual language made an asset out of accident, graininess, blur, and distortion." Jim Lewis wrote about the book, "The title shares a certain attitude with the pictures inside and the streets they capture: a celebratory stance coupled with a wiseass smile; a cityboy cockiness; a makeshift, grabbed beauty; and a sense that if two of anything is a pleasure, then a dozen must be an epiphany." *Life Is Good and Good for You in New York* failed to attract much notice—or even a publisher—in the United States, but it sold very well in Europe, where it was published, and won the prestigious Prix Nadar prize there. Kline told Mary Blume, "I don't make a big deal about taking photographs, I just take it. Although I am not invisible, people very often don't see me. This is something I developed from my New York book because New Yorkers think there is nothing more natural and deserving than for them to be photographed. I went to crowded parts of New York, like the place on 46th street where they sell discounted theater tickets, and people saw the sign and probably thought there was a new TV show they were going to be in and they smiled."

Among the images in Klein's first book is "Gun 1, New York," possibly his most famous photograph. Jane Livingston quoted the photographer's explanation for the image of what appears to be an enraged boy pointing a gun at the camera while another boy looks on: "The picture of the two boys . . . is a self-portrait. Because for me, those two boys are myself. On the one hand, I could play with the gun. On the other hand, I could be the very angelic-looking boy who is holding his hat." (According to Kevin West, Klein took the photo after spotting two boys playing in a doorway and shouting at the one with the toy pistol, "Look tough!") Klein, as quoted by Jane Livingston, described the photo as exemplifying "the fake violence which, in New York, can become real violence in two seconds." *Life Is Good and Good for You in New York* was reissued in 1996, on the 40th anniversary of its publication.

Klein next turned to film, directing the 12-minute *Broadway by Light* (1958), which, in David D'Arcy's description, "shifted between a nighttime documentary tour and a rhythmic abstraction of marquees and neon advertising." During this time he also produced three more photo books about cities: *Rome* (1958), *Moscow* (1961), and *Tokyo* (1961). Jane Livingston wrote: "Together, these works fully express Klein's strikingly original achievement as a still photographer, and presage what was to come in his films. Their lush printing in photo-gravure, far from mitigating the ominous, excessively dark and contrasty nature of the photographic prints, enhances these qualities. Klein cultivates extreme, sometimes obliterative, *black tones* in his work in the same way other photographers go for richly variegated detail." In 1963 an international jury at Photokina, an annual festival, voted Klein one of the 30 most important artists in the medium's history.

Klein explained to Kevin West that the release of his feature-length film *Who Are You Polly Maggoo?* (1966) "was the beginning of my split with *Vogue*," as it included thinly disguised portraits of figures at the magazine in its satire of the fashion industry. Even more daring was the 1967 film he co-directed with Jean-Luc Godard and several others: *Far from Vietnam*, a scathing attack on the United States' involvement in the country of the title. In 1969 Klein angered many Americans when he released *Mr. Freedom*, a blistering satire on the United States' policies, both foreign and domestic. Klein then directed two French-language films, *Festival Panafricain* (1969) and *Eldridge Cleaver, Black Panther* (1970).

The year 1974 saw the release of Klein's most celebrated film, *Muhammad Ali: The Greatest, 1964-74*, about the boxer some have called the greatest heavyweight champion of all time. When that project was begun, a decade earlier, Ali was not its central subject. Klein had boarded an airplane to Miami, Florida, to film a heavyweight boxing match between the then-champion, Sonny Liston, and the young underdog Cassius Clay. On the flight Klein sat next to the fiery black leader and Nation of Islam minister Malcolm X, who advised him, as Peter Lennon reported in the London *Guardian* (February 6, 2002), "Target Clay. He will surprise you at the match and he will surprise you after the match." Clay surprised Klein and many others, first by defeating Liston to become champion and then by announcing his conversion to Islam and the changing of his name to Muhammad Ali; Klein, who had heeded Malcolm X's advice, was present at both occasions. In 1974, by which time Ali had been stripped of his title for refusing induction into the U.S. Army during the Vietnam War and had emerged as a symbol of black pride and the 1960s counterculture, Klein flew to Africa to record Ali's fight with the younger, stronger champion, George Foreman. Ali won the match, again stunning observers. Among other notable segments, *Muhammad Ali: The Greatest, 1964-74* features an interview with Malcolm X, who was assassinated three weeks after being filmed. Klein's documentary is widely considered to be the finest treatment of Ali's lasting cultural impact.

Klein's subsequent films include *Le Couple Témoin* (1977), *The Little Richard Story* (1980), *The French* (1982), *Mode in France* (1984), and *Messiah* (1999); the last-named movie is an ambitious effort to capture many different performances of the 18th-century musical work by George Frideric Handel, and to explore the lives of some of the performers. In 2003 *Muhammad Ali: The Greatest, 1964-74* was released on DVD and shown in theaters around the U.S.

In the late 1970s, meanwhile, Klein had returned to photography after a renewed public interest in his early works. He published more books of photographs, including *William Klein* (1982), *Common Knowledge* (1984), *Close Up* (1990), and *In & Out of Fashion* (1994); his works began to be seen regularly in many galleries and museums around the world. Most recently, in 2002, Klein released *Paris + Klein*, a book of mostly never-before-shown photographs of the city where he has lived for more than 50 years. A writer for Amazon.com described *Paris + Klein* this way: "In his signature color and black-and-white compositions, jostled to the brim with more information than a single camera lens was ever expected to take in, we find: men in the street, celebrities, demonstrations, fashion, the police, politics, races, the métro, soccer, death. . . . The whole life of a capital seen through the lively, acidic, melancholic, humorous, ironical, and moving eyes of William Klein." The following year saw something of a Klein revival: Gallery 292, in New York City, exhibited his photographs of Tokyo; Klein's photographs of various cities were shown at the Museum of Art in Philadelphia, Pennsylvania; a retrospective of his short films was held at the French Institute, in New York; and an exhibition of photographs from *Paris + Klein* took place at Hermes, the New York headquarters of a French institution.

Among his many honors, Klein has received the International Prize from the Hasselblad Foundation, in Sweden, a Guggenheim Foundation grant, the French Grand Prix National de la Photographie, and the German Agfa Bayer Award. Peter Lennon reported in 2002 that Klein lives in a flat overlooking the Jardin du Luxembourg in Paris. He is married to Jeanne Florin; the couple have a son. In the 1984 book *William Klein: Photographs*, John Heilpern described the photographer, filmmaker, and painter this way: "[Klein] has a knack of offending people, particularly those who might help him. He possesses a breezy combination of principle and opportunism. A maverick by nature, Klein puts up a show of taking the rough with the smooth, as if to take life and the tangled subject of photography too seriously would be to betray the street-wise image he likes to project. 'Photography—it's no big deal,' he likes to say in his flip way, while giving the impression of half hoping that's he's wrong. It isn't that he is frivolous about photography. He prefers to demystify it, which is refreshing."

—L.A.S.

Suggested Reading: *Christian Science Monitor* (on-line) Oct. 20, 1997, with photos; *Financial Times* IX p7 June 1, 2002; *International Herald Tribune* p22 June 8, 2002; *New York Times* II p33 Oct. 18, 1992, V p29 May 18, 2001; *Slate Magazine* Apr. 25, 2003; *Village Voice* p111 Apr. 15, 2003

Selected Books: *Life Is Good and Good for You in New York: Trance Witness Revels, 1956*; Rome, 1958; *Moscow, 1961*; *Tokyo, 1961*; *Close Up*, 1989; *Paris + Klein*, 2002

Selected Films: *Broadway by Light*, 1958; *Who Are You Polly Maggoo?*, 1966; *Mr. Freedom*, 1969; *Eldridge Cleaver, Black Panther*, 1970; *Muhammad Ali: The Greatest, 1964-74*, 1974; *Messiah*, 1999

Koff, Clea

Sep. 14, 1972– Forensic anthropologist

Address: c/o Random House, 1745 Broadway, New York, NY 10019

"I have an innate excitement about bones. They speak to me," the forensic anthropologist Clea Koff told Jane Perlez for the *New York Times* (April 24, 2004). Between 1996 and 2000 Koff was a member of two United Nations forensic missions in Rwanda and five in the former Yugoslavia, where she and other experts exhumed and examined the remains of hundreds of innocent people killed during the brutal violence that ravaged those countries

Sam Brown/Courtesy of Random House
Clea Koff

Koff documented some of her experiences in her critically acclaimed memoir, *The Bone Woman: A Forensic Anthropologist's Search for Truth in the Mass Graves of Rwanda, Bosnia, Croatia and Kosovo* (2004). In a review of the book for the *Washington Post* (May 9, 2004), Laura Secor described Koff as "hard-working, physically strong and emotionally resilient; she has a capacity for stoicism, a desire for justice, and the ability to respond with equanimity to the sight and smell of maggot-ridden, decomposing flesh. . . . If at the start of *The Bone Woman*, Koff's fascination with bones and decomposition strikes the reader as macabre, by the end it's hard not to appreciate that something like a love for humanity, as well as simple acceptance of the mortality of our flesh, lies at its core."

One of the two children of David Koff and Musindo Mwinyipembe, Clea Koff was born in England on September 14, 1972. Her mother, a native of Tanzania, and her father, an American, are independent documentary filmmakers concerned with human rights issues. As a child Koff traveled widely in Africa—mainly in Kenya, Tanzania, and Somalia; her parents, as Perlez wrote, "believed that taking their two children to the gritty reaches of Africa was the best preparation for life." When she was six or seven, Koff was left in England while her father and mother pursued a lawsuit in the U.S. David Koff had sued the Boston public television station WGBH, which had commissioned him to make a documentary about race in Great Britain and then had edited the film, *Blacks Britannica*, in ways that he found highly objectionable. Though she was too young to understand fully the issues involved in her parents' court case (which they lost), her exposure to it taught Koff something about standing up for one's rights.

Koff attended primary school in London, England, before moving to the United States. She first lived in Washington, D.C.; in 1988 her family moved to Los Angeles, California, where she graduated from Ulysses S. Grant High School. Beginning at the age of seven, she told Jennifer Byrne, she would bury in plastic bags the dead birds, squirrels, or rodents that she found in the family's yard. When she was a bit older, she not only buried such corpses but also, after a time, would dig them up, so as to examine their states of decay—something that both repulsed and fascinated her. "As a girl, I always had a sense that things from the past were important," she told Christopher Bantick for the on-line Australian publication the *Age* (April 22, 2004). "For me, bones were interesting because, if they came from the past, even the recent past, then it was something that had been left behind. It struck me that you could actually tell stories from them. For me, this is the ultimate insight."

In about 1990 Koff enrolled at Stanford University, in Stanford, California, where she began studying for a degree in English. She soon changed her major to archaeology and then to anthropology.

in the early to mid-1990s. As defined on the Web site of the Forensic Science Society, forensic science is "the application of science to the law" in both criminal cases (for the purpose of identifying the victim or perpetrator of a crime, for example) and civil cases (to resolve disputes connected with, say, an industrial accident for which damages have been claimed). In forensic anthropology, a subdivision of forensic science, methods of analyzing skeletal remains (rather than skin, muscle, or other soft tissue) are applied to cases of legal importance. Koff is fond of explaining the discipline she practices by quoting the pioneering forensic anthropologist Clyde Snow: "Bones don't lie." By examining the bones of a dead individual, a forensic anthropologist may be able to determine if, how, and when the person was killed, the person's age and sex, and what he or she was doing at the moment of death, among other pieces of information. Applying forensic anthropology to human remains recovered in Rwanda and Yugoslavia, Koff and her colleagues acquired physical evidence of genocide, crimes against humanity, and war crimes. That evidence has been used to convict dozens of the perpetrators of those crimes at special international tribunals arranged by the United Nations. Koff explained to Jennifer Byrne for the Ninemsn.com.au *Bulletin* (2004) that part of her motivation for her work is her aversion to "people getting away with bad things." "But I'm not the sort of person who believes in revenge—like an eye for an eye," she continued. "I like the idea that somebody's done something, they think they've gotten away with it, and the way in which they're found out is not through video-tape or a co-conspirator betraying them, but it's the very person they silenced" who reveals the crime.

A major reason for that switch was her discovery of the work of Clyde Snow, as described in the book *Witnesses from the Grave: The Stories Bones Tell* (1991), by Christopher Joyce and Eric Stover. In the 1980s Snow performed trailblazing work in Argentina, gathering evidence from mass graves that was used to prosecute members of the government who had aided in the killing of thousands of innocent civilians. Snow's work made a powerful impression on Koff; as she told Byrne, "It was real and it was affecting people's lives. It was shedding light on things no one else could explain and was being denied, and, in addition, was potentially incriminating people." Koff graduated from Stanford with a bachelor's degree in anthropology, then entered the master's degree program in forensic anthropology at the University of Arizona, in Tucson. While there she completed an internship at a local medical examiner's office, thereby acquiring some of her first hands-on experience with human remains. Koff left Arizona before completing her course of study in order to work in Rwanda. Later, in 1999, she earned a master's degree in anthropology from the University of Nebraska at Lincoln.

Earlier, in 1996, Koff, then 23 years old, joined a team of 16 experts working for the United Nations on massacre sites in Rwanda, a small, landlocked country in East Africa. The vast majority of those killed were Tutsis, members of the smaller of Rwanda's two main ethnic groups; nearly all their killers were from the majority tribe, the Hutus. Hostility between the Tutsis and the Hutus has existed for centuries; between 1990 and 1992, hundreds of thousands from both tribes died in a civil war. When, on April 6, 1994, a plane carrying the president of Rwanda, a Hutu, was shot down over the nation's capital, extremist Hutu militias immediately launched an organized, systematic massacre of Tutsis in all parts of the country. Within 100 days, the Hutus had murdered an estimated three-quarters of a million Tutsi men, women, and children, along with moderates in their own tribe. The first acts since World War II that the U.N. officially labeled genocide, the mass killings in Rwanda became one of the worst human disasters of the 20th century, in large part because not one nation or international body intervened to try to prevent the slaughter. The mission of Koff and the other forensic experts sent to Rwanda under U.N. auspices was to gather evidence for the U.N. International Criminal Tribunal for Rwanda, which sought to bring to justice those who had perpetrated or incited the violence in Rwanda in 1994. Specifically, the team sought to determine whether the victims were noncombatants—in other words, innocent civilians—and not soldiers or warriors engaged in conflict. Most of the killing had been carried out with crude weapons, most commonly machetes. Many of the bodies had been mutilated and dismembered, making the job of identification all the more difficult.

Wearing overalls, protective gloves, and boots, Koff, the youngest member of the team, and her colleagues located mass graves by searching for places where the color and consistency of the soil differed from those of the surrounding land. They then dug up the bones and decaying flesh of those buried there. Next, Koff and the rest of the team carefully cleaned the remains, scraping dirt from bones and clothes; painstakingly reconstructed what had been retrieved of individual skeletons; tried to determine the age and sex of each victim; and documented everything in detail. Much of a person's physical profile and history can be gleaned by a careful examination of the individual's bones—for example, evidence of trauma, such as a bone broken years before; the effects of malnutrition or illness; and the effects of repetitive actions connected with labor of one kind or another. In their attempts to identify victims, the U.N. team also used—in addition to remains of clothing, jewelry, keys, and other personal belongings—whatever medical and dental records existed; they also extracted tissue for DNA analysis, to be compared with the DNA of possible family members. In cases for which they had access to a lot of evidence, Koff and her colleagues could not only determine who the people were but also the manner of their deaths and the position of the victims in their final moments. "The bodies exhibit clues to people's behavior as they approached death," Koff explained to Jane Perlez. "They are not telling us about their political beliefs. They're telling us about themselves." In an overwhelming majority of the victims Koff examined, evidence revealed that the individuals had been defenseless and cut down in cold blood. For example, from the marks left by machete blades on heel bones, Koff and the other experts determined that in many cases, the killers had cut the Achilles tendons of their victims in order to disable them before murdering them. "These are not situations where there is an argument about self-defense, about what happened in combat," Koff told Jennifer Byrne, "but where innocent people are just being executed."

Despite the chilling and gruesome nature of her work, Koff kept her composure by continuously reminding herself that the evidence of crimes that she unearthed would help to bring the perpetrators to justice; that an explanation of how their loved ones had died, and the knowledge that someone was going to be punished for their deaths, might bring a sense of closure to the victims' families; and that a proper burial would bring dignity to the dead. "The emotional self-mastery required by her work was perhaps the greatest challenge for Koff, and she met it not with steeliness but with buoyancy of spirit," Laura Secor wrote. Koff told Secor, "I find it inordinately satisfying to lift bodies I've excavated out of the grave. These are people whom someone attempted to expunge from the record, the very bodies perpetrators sought to hide." In the Toronto *Globe and Mail* (May 7, 2004), the anthropologist Dawnie Wolfe Steadman wrote that the importance of the evidence Koff and other forensic anthropologists gather is that it helps to "establish an objective and accurate historical record of controversial events that will nullify propaganda, derail revisionist subterfuge and provide the victims [with] a permanent voice."

With the help of the evidence obtained by Koff and the other forensic scientists working under U.N. auspices, as of early October 2004, the U.N. tribunal for Rwanda, which opened in Arusha, Tanzania, in 1996, had convicted 20 individuals for their involvement in the 1994 Rwandan genocide, as Farhan Haq, a U.N. spokesman, informed *Current Biography*. In the process the court has achieved several landmarks: it was the first court in history to convict a former head of government of the crime of genocide—namely, Jean Kambanda, the prime minister of the Hutu government at the start of the massacre, who was given a life sentence; the first to determine that rape had been used as an act of genocide; and the first to conclude that journalists who had, through the media, incited hatred and violence were also guilty of genocide. More than three dozen people still face criminal charges at the U.N. tribunal for Rwanda in relation to their roles in the genocide.

In 1996, after working in Rwanda earlier that year, Koff participated in five U.N. forensic missions to the former Yugoslavia, the sight of horrific ethnic and religious bloodshed that had occurred earlier that decade. From 1991 to 1995 Serbs, Bosnian Muslims, and Croats, among other groups in the breakaway republics of Croatia, Bosnia and Herzegovina, and other areas of Yugoslavia, waged violent war against one another, in the course of which many of the participants committed atrocities. As in Rwanda, the U.N. forensic team's task was to find the dead and search for evidence of genocide and crimes against humanity; also as in Rwanda, it became painfully clear to Koff and her colleagues that many of the victims had been unlawfully and mercilessly murdered. For example, many of the dead exhumed in Bosnia had their hands tied behind their backs, wore blindfolds, and had many gunshot wounds. That particular information was presented as part of the evidence against the former Yugoslavian president Slobodan Milosevic, who since 2002 has been on trial at the U.N. International Criminal Tribunal for the former Yugoslavia for crimes against humanity and genocide. (The tribunal, which operates in The Hague, the Netherlands, has conducted trials since 1994.) More than 100 people, including many of the former leaders of the Yugoslavian government, have been indicted by the tribunal for their involvement in war crimes and crimes against humanity. More than three dozen people have been convicted and sentenced to prison.

Some relatives of Rwandan and Serb, Croat, or Bosnian murder victims find little solace in the U.N. forensic scientists' work. In *The Bone Woman*, Koff wrote about a woman in Rwanda who, when Koff tried to present her with the only part of her uncle's body that had been recovered—his skull—stood at a distance from Koff and wept. In another case, in Vukovar, Croatia, the wives and mothers of some victims resented the U.N. forensics team's attempts to show them proof of their loved ones' deaths; they preferred to believe that the missing people were still alive and being held as prisoners of war.

The most recent of the U.N.'s forensic missions in which Koff participated took place in 2000 in Kosovo, a small, former Yugoslavian province. In the two years before Koff's arrival, Kosovo had been wracked by ethnic violence, with Serbs murdering thousands of ethnic Albanians and then being subjected to retaliatory killings. Koff told Jennifer Byrne that the atrocities she has witnessed left her "broken-hearted; there's something awful about the enormity of it, as well as the individual stories." On the plane leaving Kosovo, Koff wept: "Instead of pushing emotions down, kind of zipping things up to go back to work the next day, this time my body was telling me to step back and take a look," she recalled to Byrne. Koff has estimated that during her seven missions for the U.N. she disinterred or examined close to 1,000 bodies. Despite having seen, smelled, and felt evidence of some of the worst horrors of the 20th century, Koff told Byrne that she still believes that "there's as much capacity in people for good as for evil." Koff revealed to Byrne that she keeps a file she has titled "look here for inspiration," into which she puts "articles about people who have done good things."

Using as reference the journals she had kept, Koff took time off from her work and, in Melbourne, Australia, wrote *The Bone Woman*. She told Jane Perlez that one reason she wrote the book was to show Western readers that individuals in foreign countries are not simply savages who are prone to mindless violence and murder. Simply because the genocide in Rwanda "didn't happen with weapons of mass destruction but with machetes, doesn't mean it happened without a policy"—that is, that these are cases not of wanton, spontaneous killing but of premeditated murder on a massive scale. In her book Koff described the human skeleton and how body parts are bagged and tagged. She also wrote of the guilt of the survivors of these massacres; how she herself was affected by what she saw; who was prosecuted based on the evidence she and her co-workers obtained from their work; and what her experiences taught her about the world. One complaint of Koff's about the U.N. forensic missions was that they seemed to be carried out, to some extent, in isolation from the local people. Koff also recalled in her memoir how, despite her ability to control her emotions during her work, she at times broke down and wept. One such occasion occurred in Srebrenica, when she handled the bullet-riddled bones of a very young male—the remains of one of the roughly 8,000 Bosnian Muslim men and boys massacred in 1995 by Serbian fighters who had overrun what the U.N.

had designated as a safe haven. Koff also wrote about her nightmares, such as one she suffered repeatedly in Rwanda, in which she was sharing her bed with a mess of tangled, dismembered legs. The publication of *The Bone Woman*, in 2004, was timed to coincide with the 10th anniversary of the genocide in Rwanda. In her review Laura Secor found that as a memoir *The Bone Woman* is "less than fully realized"; the author's self-knowledge, Secor found, comes only "in flickers, rather than driving her narrative." Secor also faulted the author for devoting large parts of some chapters to her relations with her colleagues on the U.N. team—which Secor found to be something as mundane as office politics. "At times like these," Secor wrote, "Koff seems to be narrating an ordinary tale of a young woman's first work experiences, rather than the truly extraordinary story that's hers alone to tell." But when Koff tells of "crouching over a mass grave, untangling limbs, scraping dirt from a corpse's clothes," as Secor wrote, and finding not horror but "something human that speaks," the beauty and significance of her work is clear. "Fortunately, that alone is enough to make this book surprising, compelling and worth reading." In another review, Dawnie Wolfe Steadman lamented that Koff's explanations of the bloody history of the places in which she worked were "too shallow in places," but she described the book as a "must-read for students of forensic science, political science,

international law and other disciplines that study or directly contribute to human rights investigations." As quoted in a blurb on TheBoneWoman.com, the British publication the *Herald* declared that Koff's book—"indeed her life—is a testament to an idealism that shines through a grim, bloody reality."

Koff, who in recent years has lived in Melbourne and London, plans to settle in the United States. She has considered establishing a private agency that will identify some of the thousands of unidentified corpses lying in morgues in many U.S. cities, thereby, perhaps, bringing closure to some families with missing relatives.

—C.F.T.

Suggested Reading: bulletin.ninemsn.com.au; *New York Times* A p4 Apr. 24, 2004, with photo; theage.com.au Apr. 22, 2004; TheBoneWoman.com; (Toronto) *Globe and Mail* (on-line) May 7, 2004, with photos; United Nations Web site; Koff, Clea. *The Bone Woman: A Forensic Anthropologist's Search for Truth in the Mass Graves of Rwanda, Bosnia, Croatia and Kosovo*, 2004

Selected Books: *The Bone Woman: A Forensic Anthropologist's Search for Truth in the Mass Graves of Rwanda, Bosnia, Croatia and Kosovo*, 2004

Kripke, Saul

(KRIP-kee)

Nov. 13, 1940– Philosopher; logician

Address: Graduate Center, City University of New York, 365 Fifth Ave., New York, NY 10016

Saul Kripke, a professor of philosophy at the Graduate Center of the City University of New York (CUNY), in New York City, and professor emeritus of Princeton University, in Princeton, New Jersey, is known internationally for his pioneering work in the fields of abstract mathematical theory, linguistics, and the philosophy of language. In particular, his philosophy of modal logic (a branch of symbolic logic that deals with concepts of necessity and possibility), his theories regarding the relationships between names and the objects that they designate, and his controversial interpretation of writings by the Austrian-born philosopher Ludwig Wittgenstein (1889–1951) have been widely regarded by fellow academics and students as significant contributions to the field of philosophy. Kripke's examinations of the relationship between names and their referents have led him to advance theories of meaning based on social constructions of language use, that is, to assert that a person's un-

derstanding of language is inextricably linked to his or her role as a social creature. While these ideas have been highly influential among scholars, Kripke's attempts to use Wittgenstein's later work to support them have been denounced by a number of critics. In an article for the *Yale Law Journal* (April 1998), Ahilan T. Arulanantham referred to Kripke's famous 1982 book, *Wittgenstein on Rules and Private Language*, as "Saul Kripke's infamous misreading of Wittgenstein."

Saul Aaron Kripke was born on November 13, 1940 in Omaha, Nebraska. His father, Myer S. Kripke, was a rabbi, and his mother, the former Dorothy Karp, was a children's-book author with degrees from Hunter College, Columbia University, and the Jewish Theological Seminary of America, all in New York City. In addition to Saul, the Kripkes had two daughters, Madeline and Netta. Even as a young child, Saul Kripke demonstrated exceptional intelligence. At age three he asked his mother if the idea that God was everywhere implied that when he, Saul, entered the kitchen, he was squeezing part of God out. When he was five years old, he taught himself Hebrew. Because the grade schools he attended did not approve of accelerated education, he began, with the help of his parents, to study several subjects independently. While his classmates were still learning to add and subtract, Kripke was already teaching himself to multiply.

Robert Matthews/Courtesy of Princeton University

Saul Kripke

As a fourth-grader he read all of William Shakespeare's plays, and by the time he reached the seventh grade he had moved on to philosophical works by the 17th-century French philosopher René Descartes and the 18th-century Scottish philosopher David Hume. In the eighth grade, having already mastered algebra, Kripke began to study calculus, and by age 15 he was convinced that some of his ideas about mathematical logic had never before appeared in print. During his senior year in high school, Kripke published his first scholarly article, "A Completeness Theorem in Modal Logic," in the *Journal of Symbolic Logic*.

After graduating from high school, Kripke enrolled at Harvard University, in Cambridge, Massachusetts. He graduated summa cum laude in 1962, after which he went on to study at Princeton University; Oxford University, in Oxford, England; and Rockefeller University, in New York City. Although he has never obtained a doctoral degree, he has been awarded honorary doctorates by the University of Nebraska; Johns Hopkins University, in Baltimore, Maryland; and the University of Haifa, in Israel. He has also been honored with a Fulbright scholarship and two Guggenheim fellowships, as well as grants from the National Science Foundation, the American Council of Learned Societies, and the National Endowment for the Humanities. Furthermore, he is a fellow of the American Academy of Arts and Sciences and the British Academy, and he has served on the editorial boards of *Philosophia: Philosophical Quarterly of Israel* and the *Journal of Philosophical Logic*.

From 1963 to 1966 Kripke was a junior fellow at Harvard University. During the first year of his tenure there, he published his second major contribution to the field of modal logic, an article entitled "Semantical Considerations on Modal Logic," in *Acta Philosophica Fennica*, a publication of the Philosophical Society of Finland. From 1964 to 1966, concurrent with his fellowship at Harvard, he held a position as a lecturer and junior professor at Princeton University. He was a lecturer at Harvard from 1966 to 1968, after which he became an associate professor at Rockefeller University in 1968 and a full-fledged professor there in 1972.

Also in 1972, Kripke published *Naming and Necessity*, a series of three lectures that he had delivered at Princeton in 1970. The lectures first appeared in print in *Semantics of Natural Language*, a collection of academic papers edited by the philosophers Donald Davidson and Gilbert Harman and published by Reidel Press, and were reprinted in 1980 as a stand-alone volume by Harvard University Press. In this influential work, Kripke offered a refutation of the descriptivist theory of referential meaning, which, having originated in the work of the philosophers Bertrand Russell and Gottlob Frege, was the prevailing theory of reference in analytic philosophy at that time. According to the theory, a name (that is, a proper noun) refers to an object by virtue of the name's association with a particular description or set of descriptions that the object, in turn, satisfies. (By that definition, an object is a specific place or something else identified by a proper noun, rather than a table, fruit, or any other object that is identified by a lowercase noun.) Instead, Kripke proposed a causal theory of reference, arguing that a name is not a term that applies to an object's description, but a "rigid designator" that refers directly to the object itself and to the same particular object in all possible worlds. The connection between a name and the object that it designates, Kripke contended, is direct and historical, or causal. In other words, people are able to appreciate the meaning of a name not because the name is related to a list of qualities that its referent possesses, but because a chain of usage leads back to the object, designating it directly. As Simon Blackburn explained in an article for the *New Republic* (February 7, 2000), "The 'rigidity' in question means that when you use a name, even to talk about strange and different possibilities, you are still interpreted as talking about whatever it is to which the name actually refers. So if I say, 'Had the political boundaries been slightly different, the people of Konigsberg might have spoken Latvian,' I am still talking about that very town, Konigsberg. But if I say, 'Had his parents moved south, Kant's hometown might have been Berlin,' the description 'Kant's hometown' has become detached, as it were, from Konigsberg. For I am not trying to say that had Kant's parents moved south, Konigsberg might have been Berlin. I am saying that Berlin is where he might have been born and raised. This is what is meant by saying that descriptions are not rigid, whereas names are rigid."

On the basis of these semantics, Kripke went on to suggest that, contrary to ideas set forth in earlier theories of knowledge, necessary truth is not essentially related to the *a priori* (that which can be determined independently of experience). It is possible, he maintained, to arrive at some necessary truths by way of empirical discoveries rather than *a priori* logical deductions, as in the case of certain identity relations. For example, while it is known that the names "Hesperus" and "Phosphorus" both designate a single body (the planet Venus), direct observation is required to determine that Hesperus, the evening star, is indeed the same object as Phosphorus, the morning star. It is possible to imagine a world in which the two names would not coincide, and would instead designate two distinct bodies, but direct observation proves that this is not the case. Thus, "Hesperus is Phosphorus" is an example of an "*a posteriori* necessity," a fact that is necessarily true even though it can be ascertained only through empirical investigation.

The ideas that Kripke set forth in *Naming and Necessity* elicited a mixture of praise and criticism from other philosophers. As a reviewer for the *London Review of Books* wrote, according to the Harvard University Press Web site, "When these lectures were first published . . . they stood analytic philosophy on its ear. Everybody was either furious, or exhilarated, or thoroughly perplexed. No one was indifferent." Some critics have noted that Kripke's ideas concerning causal reference and *a posteriori* necessities are similar to those presented some time earlier in the works of the philosopher and logician Ruth Barcan Marcus, and both Marcus's and Kripke's works have been compared to the subsequent writings of the philosopher Hilary Putnam. Further parallels have been drawn between Kripke's arguments against identity materialism in the philosophy of mind (the view that every mental fact is identical with some physical fact) and similar ideas defended by the philosopher David Chalmers.

In 1976 Kripke's article "Is There a Problem about Substitutional Quantification?" appeared in *Truth and Meaning: Essays in Semantics*, a collection of essays edited by Gareth Evans and John Henry McDowell and published by Oxford University Press. In 1977 Kripke became the James Mc-Cosh Professor of Philosophy at Princeton University, having been associated with the school for several years as a visiting lecturer. That same year, his article entitled "Speaker Reference and Semantic Reference" appeared in *Contemporary Perspectives in the Philosophy of Language*, an anthology edited by Peter A. French, Theodore E. Uehling Jr., and Howard K. Wettstein and published by the University of Minnesota Press. From 1977 to 1983, concurrent with his tenure at Princeton, Kripke was the A. D. White Professor-at-Large at Cornell University, and in 1979 he contributed the essay "A Puzzle about Belief" to *Meaning and Use: Papers Presented at the Second Jerusalem Philosoph-*

ical Encounter, edited by Avishai Margalit and published by Reidel Press.

During the mid-1980s Kripke delivered a set of lectures at Princeton, popularly referred to as "The Nozick-Bashing Lectures," in which he presented arguments against the ideas of Robert Nozick, a professor of philosophy at Harvard University. While Kripke's objections to Nozick's work have been widely disseminated and discussed amongst academics and philosophy students, they have never been published.

In 1982 Kripke published his second major work, entitled *Wittgenstein on Rules and Private Language*. The book was an examination and interpretation of *Philosophical Investigations*, a text that Ludwig Wittgenstein had written during the latter part of his career. Kripke attributed to the earlier philosopher a social theory of meaning and rule-following, arguing that it is communities, not isolated individuals, that establish the nature of meaning in language. According to Kripke's understanding of Wittgenstein, while people can be credited with possessing and understanding ideas, it is impossible to identify any particular rule that governs the way in which they use terms. Rather, they can be credited with comprehension simply by virtue of their belonging to a community whose members have agreed upon a certain set of semantic relationships. In short, membership in a group with a shared set of reactions to word stimuli is all that the notion of comprehension can ever mean. As Consuelo Preti explained in an article for *Philosophical Forum* (Spring 2002), "Kripke reads Wittgenstein as claiming that no one by herself can determine meaning—there is no such thing as a private language, understood as a language whose content is specified by me and me alone—on pain of paradox. . . . Rather, as Kripke claims, Wittgenstein's view about the nature of meaning, meant to solve the skeptical paradox, is that meaning is established by public criteria. The community with which we, as it were, play the language game that we play is that which determines, in a strict sense, what we mean by our words."

Kripke's study of Wittgenstein, while influential among students and scholars of Wittgenstein's work, has been widely criticized as a misinterpretation of the earlier philosopher's arguments. Many of Kripke's contemporaries refer to the text jokingly as "Kripkenstein," alluding to their belief that the version of Wittgenstein that Kripke presents, like the monster in the 1818 novel *Frankenstein*, by Mary Shelley, is a grotesque invention that bears only a distorted resemblance to the man it is supposed to represent. According to Consuelo Preti, "Kripke misconstrues the very nature of Wittgenstein's project. . . . He attributes a view to Wittgenstein that does not (cannot, perhaps, given the nature of the misconstrual) accurately represent the investigation that Wittgenstein was explicitly engaged in." Similarly, in his 1990 book, *Wittgenstein on Meaning*, the philosopher Colin McGinn wrote, "Kripke is . . . disarmingly aware that he is foisting onto Wittgenstein's text what is not to be found inscribed on its surface," according to the *"Wittgenstein on Rules and Private Language* Ultimate HomePage" Web site. Furthermore, Kripke has been faulted by some critics for not giving due credit to other authors, such as the philosopher Robert J. Fogelin, who have interpreted Wittgenstein in a manner similar to his own.

In 1988 Kripke was presented with the Behrman Award for distinguished achievement in the humanities at Princeton University. He left Princeton in 1998, becoming a professor emeritus, and in 2001 he was awarded the Rolf Schock Prize in Logic and Philosophy by the Royal Swedish Academy of Sciences for his contributions to the fields of modal logic, metaphysics, and the philosophy of language. In 2002 he was named a visiting professor at the CUNY Graduate Center, where he continues to teach, having accepted a full-time professorship there in 2003. In 1976 he married Margaret Gilbert, a professor and writer who specializes in what she calls philosophical social theory. He lives in Princeton, New Jersey.

—L.W.

Suggested Reading: *Philosophical Forum* p39+ Spring 2002

Selected Books: *Naming and Necessity*, 1980; *Wittgenstein on Rules and Private Language*, 1982

Courtesy of Don LaFontaine

LaFontaine, Don

Aug. 26, 1940– Voice-over actor

Address: c/o Steve Tisherman Agency, 6767 Forest Lawn Drive, Los Angeles, CA 90068

Don LaFontaine, nicknamed "Thunder Throat" and "The King," has been the definitive voice of Hollywood movie trailers for 40 years. LaFontaine fell into the work in the 1960s, when trailers, as the short previews for upcoming feature films are known, were just becoming a common advertising tool for drumming up the public's interest ahead of a given movie's release. LaFontaine and others estimate that he has provided the voice-overs for more than 4,000 motion-picture trailers and helped to coin some of the well-worn, melodramatic phrases that accompany the promotional highlights of so many films—for example, "In a world where . . ."; "From the bedroom to the boardroom . . ."; "Nowhere to run, nowhere to hide . . ." According to LaFontaine, the ability to read advertising copy—much of it ham-handed and hackneyed—with flair and rhythm is as crucial as a compelling voice in making a riveting trailer voice-over. "A voice is a small part of it," he explained to *People* (December 9, 1996). "It's what you do with it." Bob Israel, chief executive officer of Aspect Radio, a motion-picture advertising agency, told *People* that LaFontaine's plangent baritone is "the voice of God. He's got a great ear, and he can act." Eric Silver, an ad copywriter who has worked with LaFontaine, told Regina Oberlag for *Shoot* (August 14, 1998) that LaFontaine's "voice is so distinctive he could say, 'Pass the cole slaw,' and it would always sound dynamic."

Don LaFontaine was born in Duluth, Minnesota, on August 26, 1940. He moved to New York City in the 1960s. At that time, most movie trailers were still made at studios by the films' editors, and not much time or attention went into them; trailers were not broadcast often on television or radio at the time. Those that existed "all followed the same basic formulas, and used the same voice for almost every trailer," LaFontaine recalled for the Web site thetrailertrash.com. In 1962 LaFontaine, then a young recording engineer, went to work for the radio producer Floyd Peterson at National Recording Studios, in New York. At the time Peterson was working on several radio advertising segments for the movie *Dr. Strangelove*. LaFontaine found himself making several suggestions to Peterson, which were well received. Peterson then enlisted LaFontaine to help him put together the radio spots, and soon afterward LaFontaine was handling all aspects of making the trailers. "My job . . . consisted of writing, directing, recording, creating music and effects 'beds' for the spots," he recalled to thetrailertrash.com. He also took care of the sound mixing and mastering of the trailers: he played with the trailers' audio component, rearranging such aspects as the sequence, volume, and tone of sounds and creating the final audio tape (the master) for the trailer. He even handled the mailing of the packages containing the finished products to radio stations, once they were accepted and purchased by the film studios. "As a writer, I was one of maybe five people in the business, Floyd included," LaFontaine recalled to thetrailertrash.com. In 1963 LaFontaine and Peterson formed a two-man movie-trailer company. Within several years they had moved their operations into their own building and had 40 employees working for them. LaFontaine's main tasks at that time were writing and producing radio spots for movies.

One night in the mid-1960s, LaFontaine was busy working on six different trailer projects, including one for the little-known movie *Gunfighters of Casa Grande,* when the announcer he had hired to record the copy for that trailer failed to show up. LaFontaine went into the sound booth and recorded it himself. (The copy, which LaFontaine had written himself, read, "In a blur of speed, their hands flashed down to their holsters and came up spitting fire.") To the surprise of LaFontaine, who had had no acting training and had never before done a voice-over, Columbia Pictures bought the spot the next day. "I took the eighty dollar payment and ran like a thief," LaFontaine recalled to thetrailertrash.com. "Over the next few years I did more and more radio [voice-overs], and eventually TV and [movie-theater] trailers. Because I had written the copy, I knew how I wanted it to sound, so I had a distinct advantage."

LaFontaine moved to Los Angeles, California, in 1982 to establish his own movie-trailer production company. A few days after his arrival, a friend introduced him to the agent Steve Tisherman, who persuaded LaFontaine to make voice-over work for movie trailers his full-time job. His career took off after he did the voice-over for the comedy *Bachelor Party*, starring Tom Hanks, in 1984. In attempting to create trailers that described the plots of movies in just a few sentences, LaFontaine was one of the first to deliver such standard trailer phrases as "In a world where . . ." Regarding that locution in particular, LaFontaine told thetrailertrash.com that "even though it's sort of recognized as a cliché, when it plays in a theater, it's rarely greeted with hoots of derision. It just goes to show you how conditioned the audience is to accept it as a standard way to set the scene of a trailer." His job, as he told Joshua S. Burek for the *Christian Science Monitor* (March 9, 2001, on-line) is to "bring as much veracity and freshness [as possible] to whatever the copy is, regardless of how cliched, trite, or stale it may be." Summing up LaFontaine's path to success, Burek wrote, "With his copy-writing background, he combined a knack for penning tasty pitches with his signature sound to quickly dominate the burgeoning movie-trailer industry." The industry's other highly recognizable voices belong to Hal

Douglas, Ashton Smith, Lex Lang, and Howard Parker. Some of the better-known films among the thousands for which LaFontaine has recorded the trailer voice-overs are *Doctor Zhivago* (1965), *2001: A Space Odyssey* (1968), *The Godfather* (1972), *Ghostbusters* (1984), *The Terminator* (1984), *The Untouchables* (1987), *Die Hard* (1988), *Field of Dreams* (1989), *Batman* (1989), *Home Alone* (1990), *Independence Day* (1996), *L.A Confidential* (1997), *There's Something About Mary* (1998), *Office Space* (1999), *Shrek* (2001), and *Rush Hour 2* (2001). (By the time he began focusing on voice-overs, in the 1980s, LaFontaine no longer wrote much if any copy for trailers.) Mastering the quick, full-blast nature of the trailer has become a craft in itself. Trailers usually feature several lines of dramatic exposition, which can be heard over a fast-moving montage of select scenes from the not-yet-released movie. In the view of LaFontaine and other observers of popular culture, movie trailers have had a significant influence on advertising in general and on other media. As LaFontaine commented to Burek, the rapid-fire style of trailers "has had a trickle-down effect on everything, from the way they sell television shows to the ways they sell soap to certainly MTV."

When asked if he adjusts his normal speaking voice when doing a voice-over, LaFontaine told thetrailertrash.com that his movie-trailer sound is "my voice, only bigger. I don't mean louder, although that certainly is the case sometimes. I emphasize certain elements of my voice—adding an edge or a cushion of air, and then slightly overemote." LaFontaine admitted in the same interview, "If I used that voice in normal conversation, people would look at me and wonder who the pompous ass was."

A voice-over for a trailer takes from five minutes to a half-hour to record. LaFontaine often has a dozen or more recording sessions in a day, with an average of 60 per week. He either shuttles from one Los Angeles movie studio to the next in his own chauffeured limousine or works from home in his personal state-of-the-art studio. Voice-over work has become its own industry, as trailers have developed into a vital part of movie marketing campaigns. According to the Australian publication the *Age* (November 29, 2003), LaFontaine estimates that there are at least 35 voice-over companies that employ more than 60 actors each. The more successful of these individuals can earn up to $2,000 per recording session and can easily earn six- or seven-figure incomes each year. LaFontaine himself earns "millions a year," as he told *People* (December 9, 1996). Asked by fadeinmag.com whether he does anything special to protect his voice, LaFontaine said, "I don't abuse it. I don't smoke and I don't drink too much. I don't go places where I have to shout and scream. But I don't wrap stuff around my throat or drink tea either." When asked by thetrailertrash.com if, after having recorded more than 4,000 movie trailers, he still found the work challenging, LaFontaine answered in the affirmative. "I'm constantly trying to come up with new ways to 'bend' a phrase or 'color' a word." In addition, being able to work on all genres of movies "keeps the work reasonably fresh and exciting for me. I'm like any other actor—I'm always looking forward to the next role." On a similar note, he stated in his interview with fadein-mag.com, "No matter what picture I do, it's somebody's favorite picture. And that makes me feel good. Even though [a movie may be] a critical failure in the world, it's somebody's banana cream pie!"

LaFontaine lives with his wife, Nita Whitaker, and their two daughters, Skye and Elyse. He told thetrailertrash.com that when he retires he is "just going to relax, play golf, travel, read and make passes at my wife. I have been able to do virtually everything I've ever wanted to do over the course of the years, including sky-diving, scuba, . . . traveling behind the iron curtain, attending great Broadway shows, marrying the best and the most beautiful woman on the planet and fathering great kids." He told *People* (December 9, 1996), "I live a fantasy life. I have money, a beautiful house, a beautiful family. It's like living an enchanted existence."

—C.F.T.

Suggested Reading: *Age* A p2 Nov.29, 2003; *Christian Science Monitor* (on-line) Mar. 9, 2001, with photo; *People Weekly* p92 Dec. 9, 1996, with photos; thetrailertrash.com

---

Courtesy of the office of Representative Barbara Lee

Lee, Barbara

July 16, 1946– U.S. representative from California (Democrat)

Address: 1724 Longworth House Office Bldg., Washington, DC 20515-2661

In the wake of the September 11, 2001 terrorist attacks against the U.S., the deadliest such attacks in the nation's history, polls indicated that Americans overwhelmingly favored swift and decisive action against those responsible for the tragedy. On September 14 of that year, Congress voted on whether to give President George W. Bush unprecedented power to use military force against the perpetrators. Only one member of Congress voted against doing so: Representative Barbara Lee, a Democrat representing California's Ninth District. Lee was widely vilified and attacked for her action—the noted conservative David Horowitz, for example, called her an "anti-American communist"—but also gained the respect and admiration of peace activists worldwide. Lee has said that while she is an American patriot and ardently believes that terrorists should be brought to justice, she could not in good conscience support a policy open to such broad interpretation. "It was a blank check to the president to attack anyone involved in the Sept. 11 events—anywhere, in any country, without regard to our nation's long-term foreign policy, economic and national security interests, and without time limit," she wrote for the *San Francisco Chronicle* on September 23, 2001, as quoted on the Wildness Within Web site. "In granting these overly broad powers, the Congress has failed its responsibility to understand the dimensions of its declaration." Other areas of concern for Lee, a former social worker who was first elected to Congress in 1998, include affordable housing and health care and the prevention and treatment of AIDS worldwide.

Barbara Lee was born on July 16, 1946 in El Paso, Texas. Her father, a colonel in the U.S. Army, served in the Korean War; because of her father's career, the family lived in a number of places, including England, while Lee was growing up. They moved to San Fernando, California, in 1960. Upon her graduation from San Fernando High School, Lee received the Rotary Club Music Award and the Bank of America Achievement Award in the field of music. She married at age 16; by 20 she was the mother of two young sons and had divorced. She received welfare payments for a time before receiving a B.A. degree from Mills College, in Oakland, California, in 1973 and an M.S. degree in social welfare from the University of California at Berkeley (UC–Berkeley) in 1975. She then made her living as a social worker in blue-collar communities in and around San Francisco. She has said that the difficult family situations she encountered in her work have led her, since that time, to consider problems carefully before leaping to judgment.

Lee's first brush with politics came in 1972, when, as chairwoman of the Black Student Union at Mills College, she invited the U.S. congresswoman and presidential candidate Shirley Chisholm to speak at the school. "[Chisholm] convinced me that if I really wanted to make a significant impact, that I should get involved in politics," Lee told the *California Journal Weekly* (March 21, 1994). She became a Northern California coordinator of Chisholm's campaign. While working toward her graduate degree, Lee founded a community mental-health center in Berkeley. She began her political career in 1975, as an intern in the office of Congressman Ron Dellums, eventually becoming his senior adviser and chief of staff. She worked for him until 1987, when she started a small business.

Lee served from 1991 to 1997 in the California State Assembly, winning seats on the Ways and Means Committee and the Rules Committee; in 1997 and 1998 she was a member of the California State Senate. During that time, among other issues, she worked on raising awareness of the problems faced by African-American males and encouraging businesses to see Africa as a new market and trading partner. She voted against the "three strikes" law, which mandates that those convicted of three felony offenses serve prison time for the third and any subsequent offense regardless of their severity.

Lee was first elected to the U.S. House of Representatives from the Ninth District of California on April 7, 1998, in a special election to fill the seat of Congressman Ron Dellums, who was planning to retire; she won with 67 percent of the vote. One of the most politically liberal districts in the nation, the Ninth District includes Oakland, Berkeley, Piedmont, Emeryville, Albany, Ashland, Castro Valley, Cherryland, and Fairview. Lee's constituency is largely blue-collar, although it also includes many academics, as UC–Berkeley falls within its boundaries. She serves on the Committee on Financial Services (as well as on its Domestic and International Monetary Policy, Trade, and Technology Subcommittee and Housing and Community Opportunity Subcommittee) and on the Committee on International Relations (for which she is a member of both the Africa and Europe Subcommitteees). She is co-chair of the Progressive Caucus, chair of the Congressional Black Caucus (CBC) Task Force on Global HIV/AIDS, whip for the CBC, and a member of the CBC Minority Business Task Force.

Lee has worked to form bipartisan coalitions to seek affordable health care and housing, equal access to quality education, and jobs, and she is a leader in the fight against HIV and AIDS, having helped to secure over $5 million for HIV/AIDS services in Alameda County, California. She has also been successful in passing legislation to initiate international efforts to fight the disease, and with Jan

Shakowsky, a Democratic representative from Illinois, she introduced the Global Access to HIV/AIDS Medicines Act of 2001, to increase the affordability of AIDS drugs worldwide and to link international debt relief to a given country's HIV/AIDS prevention and treatment programs and social and health infrastructures. As a member of the subcommittee on housing, she helped secure for Oakland a $34 million grant from the Department of Housing and Urban Development. She also convened the Western Regional Summit on Housing and Wealth Accumulation, as part of which Fannie Mae, a federally backed organization that promotes home ownership, contributed $500,000 to the Northern California Land Trust for low-cost housing.

In 2000 Lee traveled to Cuba with Representative Maxine Waters, a fellow California Democrat, to find out how the people there felt about the case of the five-year-old Elían González. González's mother and stepfather had died during the boat trip that brought the boy illegally to the U.S. from Cuba; Lee supported returning González to his father, whom she deemed a fit parent. (The boy later returned to Cuba with his father.) Also that year Lee sponsored an education bill aimed at making young people from poor urban areas into better prospective parents.

In March 2001 Lee denounced a lawsuit brought by 39 pharmaceutical companies against the South African government over its Medicines Act of 1997, which sought to limit the cost of drugs in that country. "I stand firm in my belief that by denying the basic human right to medical care, this lawsuit in itself was criminal," she said, as quoted on the Truth Out Web site (April 19, 2001). "Through this lawsuit the pharmaceutical companies jeopardized the lives of millions of South Africans living with AIDS." The companies dropped the suit in April. Lee pointed out, however, that there was still a threat of litigation against India, Brazil, and other developing nations that were trying to implement strategies for supplying their populations with expensive AIDS medications at reduced costs.

Three days after the September 11, 2001 terrorist attacks on New York City and Washington, D.C., Lee cast the lone dissenting vote against authorizing the president to use "all necessary and appropriate force" to retaliate. (Military action was later taken to oust the Taliban, then the governing group of Afghanistan, which had allegedly given aid to Osama bin Laden, the head of the terrorist group Al Qaeda and the chief suspect in the planning of the attacks.) Lee was accused by many of being insensitive to the families of those who had died on September 11; some even accused her of treason and claimed that she was siding with the terrorists. Because of her vote, she became the target of hate-mail campaigns and death threats. (The Washington, D.C., police provided her with 24-hour protection for a while.) "This was the most painful vote I have taken in Congress, really in all 12 years that

I've been in elected office," she told KMEL-FM talk-show host David "Davey D" Cook in a September 22, 2001 interview, as posted on the Progressive Austin Web site. "It was a grueling experience for me. . . . I was in the Capitol when the plane went into the Pentagon, and we had to evacuate. It's been a nightmare. I went through the intellectual process, through the fact-gathering, through the policy analysis, looking through the foreign policy and intelligence and military implications of our move. It weighed heavily on me. I was not going to the National Cathedral for the prayer service . . . because I wanted to continue in my discussions, and reflect on the resolution that was coming up. But at the last minute, I decided to go, that I had to pray over this. . . . It was a very powerful, very beautiful prayer service, very painful. . . . One of the clergy very eloquently said, in his prayer, 'As we act, let us not become the evil that we deplore.' And at that moment, I knew what the right vote was, and what I had to do." Although other Democrats had initially resisted the resolution, a slight change in its language changed their minds. "We talked about it in our caucus meeting and there were several members who spoke very aggressively about the reasons we should not support this type of resolution . . . but of course, then the anger and the sadness of the moment took over and I believe that what happened was that people went with the flow," she told Fergal Keane for the *Independent* (February 4, 2003, on-line). Paraphrasing Lee's arguments for opposing the authorization of the measure, Keane wrote, "Pared down to its essentials, it ran like this: Congress represented the rational. It was a body that had to remain above the fray. What decisions it made had to consider the lasting good and not respond to the emotion of the moment."

Lee has said that she did not agree with the decision to hold the vote so quickly, a move that amounted, in her view, to Congress's abdicating its power to the executive branch. While her stance brought her negative publicity, it also brought her donations and support from like-minded citizens, including the comedian and actor Bill Cosby and the musician Bonnie Raitt. In addition, a rally of 3,000 of her supporters gathered outside Oakland's City Hall. Her vote did not affect her popularity with her constituents, either, as she won reelection with a very comfortable margin in 2002. (She had been reelected with 85 percent of the vote in 2000.) Among those groups endorsing her in the 2002 election were the John George Democratic Club, the East Bay Gay and Lesbian Democratic Club, the Alameda County Central Labor Council, the Alameda County Democratic Committee, the Oakland East Bay Democratic Club, the Teamsters Union, the Sierra Club, the Latino Democratic Club, and the American Federation of State, County, and Municipal Employees, AFL-CIO.

September 2001 was not the first time that Lee was a lone dissenter. In 1999 she was the only member of the House of Representatives to vote against supporting NATO's bombing of military targets in the former Yugoslavia, carried out to halt Serbian aggression against Kosovar Albanians. The previous year she had been one of only five members to vote against renewed bombing against Iraqi military and security targets as punishment for its refusal to allow weapons inspections by the United Nations.

Lee has not hesitated to point out that any war disproportionately affects minorities in the U.S., as they compose a large part of the U.S. armed forces. "Around 40 per cent of the military is African-American and Latino, so in any war you're going to see some very dramatic numbers of troops from communities of colour throughout our country," she told Keane. While her harshest attacks have come from right-wing politicians and commentators, some members of the hard left have criticized Lee for voting to give huge amounts of funding to strengthen U.S. security. "It's very important that we deal with terrorism and bring terrorism to justice," she told Keane. "You cannot allow the world to be taken over by people who want to destroy it."

In September 2002 Lee introduced a resolution calling for the United States to forego immediate military action against Iraq and instead work with the United Nations to determine, through inspections, if Iraq had weapons of mass destruction. She opposed the resolution to give President Bush permission to launch a military attack against the country. "Nuclear weapons are pointed in all directions," she told Ross McGowan in a September 23, 2002 interview for KTVU in San Francisco, as quoted on the Web site On Lisa Rein's Radar. "We must seek peaceful resolutions to conflicts in the world. I think we need to understand right now what is the purpose of this resolution and the United States' Administration policy. Is it regime change or is it to rid the world of weapons of mass destruction? Everyone agrees the world would be a safer place without Saddam Hussein. However, does that justify us going in and using this new doctrine of pre-emption. . . . If China believes Taiwan is an imminent threat. . . . Is it okay for China to nuke Taiwan? We have India and Pakistan. This doctrine of pre-emption is a very dangerous doctrine. We've supported and continue to support a doctrine of deterrence, disarmament and prevention." She spoke at the "No War on Iraq" march in San Francisco on January 18, 2003 and has been active in the global peace movement, frequently speaking at peace rallies and marches. Lee has insisted that she is not a pacifist, but she once introduced a bill to establish a Department of Peace and has often been compared to Jeanette Rankin, the first woman elected to Congress, who voted against the United States' entry into World War I in 1917 as well as against declaring war on Japan after the bombing of Pearl Harbor in 1941.

The congresswoman criticized Bush's budget for the 2005 fiscal year, particularly plans to perpetuate tax cuts that favor wealthy citizens, despite the fact that the budget, if approved, would boost the national deficit to $521 billion, the largest in

U.S. history. She also criticized proposed cuts to social services, including housing, environmental, health-care, and education programs. "This budget reflects the priorities of an Administration out of touch with its own people," she said in a February 2, 2004 press release available on her official Web site.

Lee admires and has often quoted the civil rights leader Martin Luther King Jr. and has named Dellums as her role model and mentor. Another of her heroes is Senator Wayne Morse of Oregon, a Republican turned Democrat, who was one of two senators to vote against the 1964 resolution that allowed the United States to enter the Vietnam War.

Lee is on the boards of directors of the California Coastal Conservancy; the District Export Council; the East Bay Conversion and Reinvestment Commission; the Bay Area Black United Fund; and the California Defense Conversion Council. In 2001 she received a perfect rating from Peace Action for her votes on military issues (she was the only member of Congress to get a perfect rating from the group, the largest peace organization in the country). She has a 100 percent rating from the AFL-CIO, the League of Conservation Voters, and the Human Rights Campaign, and received an "A" rating from the NAACP. Lee has served as a board member of the California State World Trade Commission, the California State Coastal Conservancy, and the District Export Council, and as a member of the California Defense Conversion Council. She created and presided over the California Commission on the Status of African American Males, the California Legislative Black Caucus, and the National Conference on State Legislatures Women's Network, and served as a member of the California Commission on the Status of Women. She is on the advisory board of the Alameda Boys Club and is also a member of Black Women Organized for Political Action, the Commission on the Status of Women, the League of Women Voters, the Niagara & John George Democratic Clubs, and the National Women's Political Caucus, as well as an ex officio member of the California State World Trade Commission.

In 2002 Lee won the Wayne Morse Integrity in Government Award, was awarded the Sean Mac-Bride Prize from the International Peace Bureau, and was named a local hero by the Web site Best of the Bay. The following year she was named Public Elected Official of the Year by the National Association of Social Workers "for her vital role in reconnecting the social work profession to its activist roots." The congresswoman, who has been described as quiet and soft-spoken, lives in Oakland with her husband, the Reverend Michael Millben, an Oakland-based pastor.

—K.E.D.

Suggested Reading: *California Journal Weekly* March 21, 1994; *Independent* (on-line) Feb. 4, 2003; *Mother Jones* (on-line) Sep. 20, 2001, with photo; *Progressive Austin* (on-line) Sep. 22, 2001

Courtesy of Carl Levin

Levin, Carl

June 28, 1934– U.S. senator from Michigan (Democrat)

Address: 269 Russell Office Bldg., U.S. Senate, Washington, DC 20510

Carl Levin of Michigan is one of the most influential members of the U.S. Senate. Long considered to be a liberal Democrat, Levin is also known for taking stances atypical of liberals and for working well with other members of Congress, regardless of their political affiliations. Early in his political career, he gained a reputation for his boldness in dealing with such federal agencies as the Department of Housing and Urban Development (HUD), the Environmental Protection Agency (EPA), and the Federal Trade Commission (FTC), which he criticized for wastefulness, abuses of power, and arrogance. "When he tackles legislation, he is not in the game to make a point," Levin's former press secretary told a reporter for the *Detroit News* (January 13, 1999). "He's in the game to get something done. That puzzles a lot of people who look at politicians as a class of people who are in it for their own glory or for scoring political points." The ranking Democrat and a former chairman (from June 2001 to January 2003) of the Senate Armed Services Committee, Levin is an expert on defense issues and has "impressed everyone by mastering the arcana of defense policy," as Will Marshall of the Progressive Policy Institute told Michael Crowley for the *New Republic* (October 7, 2002). Republican senator John S. McCain of Arizona said during his unsuccessful campaign for the presidency in 2000 that if elected he planned to consult with

Levin on defense-related matters; many of Levin's colleagues have often deferred to him on questions related to the military. Described as the "conscience of the Senate " by the pollster Ed Sarpolus, as quoted by Richard A. Ryan in the *Detroit News* (November 6, 2002), Levin has a longstanding interest in government ethics and oversight and serves on the Subcommittee on Oversight of Government Management and the Permanent Subcommittee on Investigations. His work ethic, fairmindedness, and legal expertise have won him respect in Congress, on both sides of the aisle.

A son of Saul Levin and the former Bess Levinson, Carl Levin was born in Detroit, Michigan, on June 28, 1934. His father was an attorney whose specialties included immigration law; during part of his career, he served on the Michigan Corrections Commission. Levin's paternal uncle Theodore Levin was a distinguished federal judge; the U.S. courthouse in Detroit is named for him. Levin's older brother, Sander "Sandy" Levin, has represented Michigan's 12th Congressional District in Congress as a Democrat since 1983. Carl Levin told Martin Tolchin for the *New York Times* (April 28, 1983) that his father was "sensitive to human causes, to social and economic injustice. I got involved in prison work because of my father, and my brother became involved in helping migrant workers." Levin attended Central High School, in Detroit, where, as he recalled to Tolchin, he was elected president of his class after "running around with a piece of matzoh"—unleavened bread, which is made without yeast—telling other students, "This is what happens to bread without Levin." Levin attended Swarthmore College, in Swarthmore, Pennsylvania; he earned a B.A. degree with honors in political science in 1956. He received a J.D. degree from Harvard University, in Cambridge, Massachusetts, in 1959. He then began practicing and teaching law. In 1964 he was appointed assistant attorney general of Michigan; in that position he became the first general counsel for the Michigan Civil Rights Commission, created in 1963 by the Michigan Constitution as a means of protecting citizens from discrimination because of race, color, religion, or national origin.

In 1969 Levin was elected to the Detroit City Council, thanks to a substantial number of votes cast by blacks as well as whites. According to the *Almanac of American Politics, 2000*, he was virtually the only member of the council to win the support of people of both races, in that election as well as the next, held four years later. He soon found himself embroiled in a battle with the federal Department of Housing and Urban Development (HUD) over housing conditions in Detroit, where between 10,000 and 15,000 houses owned by HUD had been abandoned. Unwilling to spend the money to either renovate or tear down the buildings, the agency left them to decay; the properties became targets for arson and the settings of other crimes, which spurred many Detroit residents to move away from the city. Unable to obtain permis-

sion from HUD to destroy any of the buildings, Levin proceeded anyway, arranging to have two buildings leveled in spite of HUD's threats to prosecute him for destroying government property. The charges were dropped when the agency realized its chances of winning a lawsuit were minimal. In 1973 Levin was reelected to the City Council; because he earned more votes that any other candidate running for a seat on the council, he automatically became its president. In that post Levin tangled with other federal officials, including those working under the Comprehensive Employment and Training Act (CETA) and with the food-stamp program. "I saw those federal programs so poorly administered, administered with such inflexibility, with such disregard for congressional intent, with such arrogance," Levin recalled to Jerry Flint for *Forbes* (November 12, 1979). Fighting government corruption and inefficiency became one of Levin's chief concerns.

In 1978 Levin ran for a seat in the U.S. Senate. The incumbent, Robert P. Griffin, a Republican, had announced that he planned to retire at the end of his term, and he began to miss roll-call votes. He then changed his mind about leaving the Senate, but his many absences proved fatal; after repeatedly reminding voters of Griffin's seeming lack of interest in his job, Levin won the Senate seat with 52 percent of the ballots cast. The first committee assignment he secured after being sworn in, in January 1979, was to the Governmental Affairs Committee. Later that year he established and became the chairman of the committee's Subcommittee on Oversight of Government Management, the mission of which, as described on Levin's Web site, is "to improve the efficiency and effectiveness of federal programs and eliminate federal waste, fraud and abuse." In that capacity he has introduced many bills that have become law. Among them are the Competition in Contracting Act of 1984, which required the General Services Administration (GSA) to "acquire supplies and services, including leased space, through the use of full and open competitive procedures," according to the GSA's Web site; the Social Security Disability Benefits Reform Act of 1984, which aimed to make more humane the review of individuals' disability benefits and to standardize the criteria used in such reviews; the Anti-Kickback Enforcement Act of 1986, designed to close loopholes in earlier statutes pertaining to government contractors and subcontractors and their employees; the Whistleblower Protection Act of 1989, which aimed to establish mechanisms within the federal government to protect and thus, indirectly, encourage whistle-blowers; the Ethics Reform Act of 1989, which dealt with long-overdue pay raises for federal judges and other employees; the Great Lakes Critical Programs Act of 1990, which aimed to make existing Environmental Protection Agency programs affecting the Great Lakes more effective; the Negotiated Rulemaking Act of 1990, which authorized the Federal Mediation and Conciliation Service to improve government operations by means of its facilitation services; the Lobbying Disclosure Act of 1995, which listed criteria indicating whether an organization or company must register their employees as lobbyists; the Reports Elimination Act of 1995, which identified as no longer needed scores of previously required reports from governmental agencies and aimed to reduce unnecessary paperwork; and the False Statements Accountability Act of 1996, which designated as punishable offenses not only the making of false statements, written or oral, regarding matters within the purview of the legislative, executive, or judicial branches of government but also attempts to "falsify, conceal, or cover up a material fact by trick, scheme, or device," in the words of the law.

Levin is also a longstanding member of two other subcommittees of the Governmental Affairs Committee: the Permanent Subcommittee on Investigations and the International Security, Proliferation and Federal Services Subcommittee (ISPFS), whose duties include the oversight of nuclear and biological weapons in all parts of the world. As the ranking member of the ISPFS in 1997 and 1998, Levin helped the Senate keep abreast of nuclear proliferation and technologies classified as secret that are related to satellites and high-performance computers. He also led an investigation into the deceptive practices of mail-order companies that use sweepstakes to entice people to purchase products, with such statements as "You may be a winner!"; a large number of people, many of them senior citizens, have lost money through those schemes.

As described on Levin's Web site, the Subcommittee on Investigations "has jurisdiction to conduct complex investigations into financial crime, organized crime, offshore jurisdictions, and federal waste, fraud, and abuse, among other issues." In 1999 Levin directed the subcommittee to look into the banking and securities industries for possible money laundering, which involves concealing the true sources of funds and investments. Hearings were held that year and in 2001, and further investigations are under way. Some of the subcommittees' findings were incorporated into the money-laundering provisions of the U.S.A. Patriot Act of 2001. Levin became chairman of the Subcommittee on Investigations in May 2001, after Senator James Jeffords of Vermont defected from the Republican Party to become an Independent, thus giving Democrats the majority of seats in the Senate. Among his first acts as chairman was the launching of an investigation into gasoline and crude-oil pricing. Based on hearings in the spring of 2002 and March 2003, the subcommittee concluded that industry mergers were a leading cause of gas-price fluctuations and that the existence of the government's vast oil reserves contributed more to increases in oil prices than they did to ensuring energy security. In 2002 Levin led an investigation into the activities of the Enron Corp., which had declared bankruptcy in December 2001 amid scandals of illegal accounting methods and other financial irreg-

ularities. After finding that not only the Enron board of directors but also some U.S. financial institutions had played a role in Enron's deceptions, the subcommittee helped write and pushed for the passage of the Sarbanes-Oxley Act (July 2002), the goal of which, as it stated, was "to protect investors by improving the accuracy and reliability of corporate disclosures." The legislation ordered the creation of an oversight board; spelled out rules for ensuring the independence of auditors and the accuracy of financial disclosures and preventing improper corporate interference with audits, among other goals; and called for penalties for those found guilty of committing or conspiring to commit criminal fraud or other offenses. Levin lost his post as chairman of the subcommittee in January 2003, when, as a result of the November 2002 elections, the Republicans regained control of the Senate. As the subcommittee's senior Democrat, however, he has continued to lead investigations, including a look into the tax-shelter industry in 2003.

Early in his Senate career, through his seat on the Armed Services Committee, Levin became involved in U.S. military issues. One of his areas of interest has been curtailing waste in government defense spending. (Reducing wasteful spending was one of the goals of the Competition in Contracting Act of 1984.) During President Ronald Reagan's terms of office, Levin repeatedly voiced disapproval of what he viewed as the overly generous allocation of tax dollars to the Department of Defense and some of the ways in which the money was spent. In an op-ed article for the *New York Times* (September 5, 1984), he complained that, for an enormous price, an already glutted nuclear-weapons supply had been expanded at the expense of much-needed conventional weapons and supplies. "The Pentagon's budget has increased by $116 billion, or 40 percent, in constant dollars," he wrote. "Yet the unwise spending of these sums has led to unsatisfactory readiness and sustainability. . . . This administration has spent too much for fancy aircraft, vulnerable surface ships and redundant strategic nuclear weapons, while spending too little on the nuts, bolts and staying power of conventional-forces readiness." He also criticized Reagan's "Star Wars" missile-defense system, arguing that its creation would be a breach of the 1972 Anti-Ballistic Missile (ABM) Treaty with the Soviet Union. (He has also questioned President George W. Bush's missile-defense plan, saying that more testing must be done to determine its effectiveness before taxpayers begin to bear the huge cost of its implementation.) In 1994 the senator helped to gain passage of the Federal Acquisition Streamlining Act, another piece of legislation regulating defense spending. He has repeatedly pressed for increasing the pay of U.S. soldiers.

Levin has also emphasized the importance of ensuring U.S. security through international diplomacy, including the negotiating of treaties to reduce nuclear-weapons stockpiles. He has supported the Nunn-Lugar Cooperative Threat Reduction program, which seeks to deactivate and destroy weapons of mass destruction (WMDs) and help scientists who have developed these weapons devote their talents to other projects. (It is estimated that the program has spurred the deactivation of almost 6,000 nuclear warheads.) Levin opposed the Persian Gulf War of 1991, on the grounds that it could provoke instability in the Middle East (he has since said that his position was wrong) and voted against the ultimately successful 2002 Senate resolution granting power to the president to attack Iraq. He argued that even if Iraq's then-leader, Saddam Hussein, possessed WMDs (the official rationale for U.S. military action), there was still little evidence that he intended to use them; Hussein, according to Levin, could be counted on to act in his own self-interest and would therefore not risk taking any actions, such as deploying WMDs, that would spur retaliation from other countries. "The result of our attack would be his using the very weapons we are trying to deter," Levin said on the ABC news program *Nightline*, as quoted by Michael Crowley in the *New Republic* (October 7, 2002). Faced with the seeming inevitability of war with Iraq, Levin urged that the U.S. make every effort to work with the United Nations; he offered an alternative to the 2002 Senate resolution, suggesting that the president be authorized to use military force only if it was sanctioned by the U.N. Security Council. "It is very clear to me that the best way to avoid war—or if necessary, if war becomes in fact in the cards, to reduce the risks of war—is if the world community endorses that kind of effort," he told Tony Snow and Brit Hume on the TV news program *Fox News Sunday*, as quoted in the *Detroit News* (February 11, 2003). After the fall of Baghdad and the U.S. occupation of Iraq, where, as of early November 2004, no evidence of Hussein's possession of WMDs had yet been found, Levin and other Democrats called for an investigation into prior U.S. intelligence on Iraq. "You have to be able to rely on your intelligence," Levin told an interviewer for the *Detroit Free Press* (October 13, 2003). "You make decisions that are life-and-death decisions based on that intelligence. . . . And if it was stretched, exaggerated, shaped, hyped—either by the intelligence community, presumably to meet the needs of policy makers, or by the policy makers in order to sell a policy to the country, or both, we have to know it for the future." Republicans rejected the establishment of a formal congressional investigation into U.S. intelligence on Iraq.

The Republican-controlled Senate released a report in July 2004 that blamed the CIA for the intelligence failure; it postponed examining the role of the White House until after the 2004 elections. Levin, in response, stated in a press release, "It was the administration, not the CIA, that exaggerated the relations between Saddam Hussein and al-Qaida," as quoted by Douglas Jehl in the *New York Times* (July 9, 2004). Afterward Levin continued to call for an investigation into the possible involvement of the Bush administration in the gathering and dissemination of flawed prewar intelligence. In particular, he questioned the actions of Douglas J. Feith, the undersecretary of defense for policy, whom he accused of misleading Congress.

Since 1997 Levin has served on the Senate Select Committee on Intelligence, which annually authorizes appropriations for U.S. intelligence programs and oversees the Central Intelligence Agency (CIA), the Defense Intelligence Agency (DIA), the National Security Agency (NSA), the National Reconnaissance Office (NRO), and the other federal intelligence organizations. He is a senior member of the Senate Small Business and Entrepreneurship Committee, in connection with which he has introduced policies to help small-business owners, by easing their tax burdens, providing them with loans, and granting financial relief under certain circumstances. The committee approved a three-year reauthorization bill to expand its lending programs, one provision of which, proposed by Levin, provides drought relief to small businesses, including those affected by low water levels of the Great Lakes.

Levin has consistently lobbied for benefits on behalf of his Michigan constituency. He is the co-chair of the Senate Auto Caucus, which discusses policies affecting the U.S. auto industry, which is Michigan's key industry. He has repeatedly defeated clauses in various energy bills requiring auto makers to increase the fuel efficiency of their cars and trucks, most recently in July 2003, when he and Senator Christopher Bond, a Republican from Missouri, successfully argued that lawmakers lacked the expertise to set fuel-efficiency guidelines. He is a member of the Great Lakes Task Force, which, according to his Web site, is "a bipartisan and bicameral organization that works to enhance the economic and environmental health of the Great Lakes." The group has supported cleanup projects and efforts aimed at preventing soil erosion and curbing the invasion and presence of nonnative animals and plants. In July 2003 Levin and other lawmakers introduced a $6 billion plan to fight pollution and other environmental problems affecting the Great Lakes.

Levin is a member of the Michigan and Washington, D.C., bar associations. In 2003 he received a Distinguished Public Service Award from the navy, its highest civilian award. In December 2002, in recognition of his role in orchestrating a bipartisan response to the September 11, 2001 tragedy, he received the Christian A. Herter Award from WorldBoston, formerly the World Affairs Council of Boston.

Levin married Barbara Halpern in 1961. The couple have three daughters—Kate, Laura, and Erica—and three grandchildren. Known for many years for his habit of snacking on chocolate-covered donuts, he later switched to low-fat chocolate-chip cookies as his favorite treat. In his leisure time he enjoys hiking and playing squash.

—P.G.H.

Suggested Reading: Carl Levin Web site; *Detroit Free Press* (on-line) Oct. 13, 2003; *Detroit News* A p8 Oct. 21, 2002, A p7 Nov. 6, 2002; *Forbes* p38+ Nov. 12, 1979, with photo; *New York Times* p19 Nov. 8, 1978, B p16 Apr. 28, 1983; *Time* p30 Nov. 20, 1978

Courtesy of Bank of America

Lewis, Kenneth

Apr. 9, 1947– Banker

Address: Bank of America Corporate Center, 100 North Tryon St., Charlotte, NC 28255

"We want to be best in class and one of the most admired companies in the world," Kenneth D. Lewis, chairman, CEO, and president of Bank of America, told Jacqueline S. Gold for *Institutional Investor* (October 2002). "To do that we have to be totally focused on the consumer, because everything flows from being a customercentric company. We're going to have great service, be overwhelmingly convenient and pay market rates, because we can always make up the difference in productivity so that the shareholder doesn't lose." Lewis, who has worked for the company for 35 years, watched it undergo many mergers and name changes before becoming Bank of America, in 1998; he became its chief executive in April 2001, upon the retirement of his predecessor, Hugh McColl. Bank of America has roughly 27 million retail customers, and the number of its checking accounts has grown at an impressive rate—while there were 193,000 in 2001, there were more than 401,000 by September 2002. Despite a weak econo-

my the company has routinely topped earning estimates since Lewis was named CEO and boasted $45.7 billion in revenues in 2002, second only to Citigroup. One Bank of America employee told *Fortune* (June 10, 2002), "We're finally running on all cylinders. Hugh McColl was a visionary, but Ken Lewis is an operations guy, which is what we need now. It's been a few years since the [BankAmerica/NationsBank] merger, and we are finally putting it all together." In October 2003 Bank of America announced its purchase of Fleet-Boston Financial Corp., then the seventh-largest U.S. bank, for $47 billion, thus creating the third-largest U.S. bank, after Citigroup Inc. and J.P. Morgan Chase.

Kenneth D. Lewis was born on April 9, 1947 in Meridian, Mississippi. At the time his father was in the army, and his mother was a nurse; after they divorced, when Lewis was seven, he moved to Columbus, Georgia, with his mother and older sister. While growing up he held a variety of odd jobs to help the family make ends meet: selling Christmas cards door-to-door, bagging groceries at the A&P, delivering newspapers, and working part-time at a service station, a women's shoe store, and a shipping-and-receiving dock. He earned a bachelor's degree in finance from Georgia State University, in Atlanta, in 1969, working his way through school at a life-insurance company, a bond agency, and United Airlines. He later graduated from the Executive Program at Stanford University, in California.

In 1969 Lewis joined NCNB, a North Carolina regional bank (the predecessor to Bank of America), as a credit analyst, working in Charlotte. After 13 months he was promoted to the national lending division, where he met McColl, then chief of that group. He was a corporate banking officer and Western Area director in the company's U.S. Department before being named manager of NCNB's International Banking Corp., in New York, in 1977; he became senior vice president and manager of the bank's U.S. Department in 1979. About four years later he was named Middle Market Group executive, when that group was created; in that position he expanded and improved service to middle-market companies (those with roughly $50 million to $750 million in market value) in the southeastern U.S. He became president of the company's Florida bank in 1986; in his first year in the position, the bank's profits tripled, to $45 million. From 1988 to 1990 he served as president of the company's recently purchased Texas bank. By keeping costs down and pursuing new commercial accounts, Lewis pushed profits there from practically nothing in 1988 to $165 million (or 37 percent of NCNB's total earnings) in 1989. Lewis was named president of the General Bank in Atlanta, the forerunner of the Consumer and Commercial Banking division of National Bank Corp., as it was then known, in 1991. He held the post until 1994.

Meanwhile, NCNB Corp. had become NationsBank Corp. in 1990, then had another name change, to Bank of America, in April 1998, when

NationsBank bought BankAmerica Corp. for $60 billion. That deal expanded the bank's presence coast-to-coast. Lewis, who was president at the time, ceded that position to David Coulter, CEO of BankAmerica. In his new position as chief operating officer and head of consumer and commercial banking, Lewis had to deal with staff members of BankAmerica who were angry about what they had lost in the merger as well as the fact that the company was under new management and was now based in Charlottett. "I spent about four months full-time in San Francisco, [the headquarters of BankAmerica]," he told Gold. "It was all-consuming. I met with 10,000 associates in these rough town hall meetings. You could feel the bitterness in the air." He was named president as well as chief operating officer of Bank of America in 1999, after Coulter resigned due to his role in a money-losing relationship with the hedge-fund manager D.E. Show & Co. (Like a mutual fund, a hedge fund invests customers' money in other businesses; hedge funds, however, involve fewer legal restrictions, among other differences.) In April 2001 Lewis became chairman, chief executive officer, and president, taking over for Hugh McColl. At that point the bank bore little resemblance to the company Lewis had joined 32 years earlier; it had grown from a small regional bank into a national corporation with $638 billion in assets, 137,000 employees, 32 million retail and small-business customers, relationships with 95 percent of *Fortune* 500 companies, and $300 billion in client funds under management. It also, however, had close to $6 billion in nonperforming assets.

Much has been made of the drastically different business approaches of McColl and Lewis. McColl's primary goal had been growth—he argued that profits would come later; accordingly, he made 60 acquisitions in his two decades at the helm of the company. "McColl was perfecting the banking version of eminent domain. And he succeeded—by guile, by force of personality, by the financial world's equivalent of bomb tossing," Jacqueline S. Gold wrote. "Inside the bank he fashioned a gung ho, charge-the-hill esprit de corps; outside he twisted arms and knocked heads, making deals and enemies with equal abandon." Lewis, on the other hand, has been described as understated, patient, and calm. When he took command of Bank of America, he changed its focus from concerns about its size and scale to results, aggressively trimming costs and decreasing loans. Whereas McColl sometimes angered investors—as when the company's share price dropped precipitously after NationsBank bought the Florida-based Barnett Banks for $15 billion, five times its book value, in 1998—Lewis is seen as a decisive executive who can generate money from a leaner, more focused operation. "Ken's a detail man," the Democratic U.S. senator Zell Miller, who was governor of Georgia during Lewis's tenure in Atlanta, in the early 1990s, said to Gold. "McColl planted far and wide.

Lewis has come along to do the weeding and pruning. He is the perfect person to follow Hugh."

Although he worked with McColl for three decades, Lewis's management style is markedly different from his predecessor's. McColl spent most of the 1990s acquiring new businesses to boost revenues. While he succeeded in creating the largest retail bank in the nation, the bad loans entailed in the process left dissatisfied employees and disgruntled customers in their wake. To change the company's perception among customers, Lewis has worked with consultants for the Walt Disney Co. to train retail personnel to make the banking experience more pleasurable in order to increase customer satisfaction. "The cost of poor quality can be 25 to 30 percent of revenue," he told Gold. "But corrective efforts can increase revenue up to 10 percent a year." In addition, Lewis has required his top managers to use the quality-control process Six Sigma, which is used by big industrial companies. A cost-cutting strategy emphasizing process standardization and optimal performance, Six Sigma also offers revenue-generating strategies including focusing on what customers want and marketing effectively. It uses information and statistical analysis to measure and improve a company's operational performance, by locating and preventing "defects" in manufacturing and service-related processes and prescribing remedies. Due to Six Sigma and its effectiveness in reducing mistakes on credit-card collections and mortgage applications, among other errors, Bank of America cut around $1 billion in expenses.

Under Lewis's leadership, Bank of America has begun offering more competitive rates on checking accounts, and as a result, customer satisfaction has increased. In addition, he has jettisoned underperforming, risky businesses, such as subprime real-estate lending and automobile leasing, to improve credit quality, thereby cutting an additional $1 billion in costs. "We are managing for profitability, not sheer size and league-table rankings," Lewis told Gold. "There is a direct correlation between customer satisfaction and revenue growth." Due to worries about credit risk at a time when the number of corporate defaults on loans was high, he reduced corporate loans from $99 billion in August 2000 to $60 billion in October 2002. The targets of those cuts included Wal-Mart, the world's largest retailer, as well as other accounts that would not hire Bank of America for lucrative investment banking but used it for other services.

Bank of America is distinguished from other large banks, such as Citigroup, J.P. Morgan Chase, and Credit Suisse, in that it has not made an effort at worldwide expansion and gets two-thirds of its revenue from retail transactions, including such services as remittances and car loans, rather than from investment banking and asset management. Lewis hopes that Bank of America will be known for performing small banking transactions more quickly, inexpensively, and soundly than its competitors.

While he had taken pains to convince investors that he was not as merger-minded as his predecessor, on October 27, 2003 Lewis announced that Bank of America was buying FleetBoston Financial Corp., then the seventh-largest U.S. bank, for $47 billion, thus creating the third-largest U.S. bank, after Citigroup Inc. and J.P. Morgan Chase. Bank of America would have become the second-largest U.S. bank were it not for another merger announced in late 2003, between Chase and Bank One. Although the purchase gave Bank of America 1,458 branches in the northeastern U.S., it caused the value of stock shares to fall by 11 percent in two days, from $81.86 to $76.15, the worst two-day drop since Lewis became CEO. Industry observers pronounced the price, 2.78 times FleetBoston's book value, to be too high. The purchase gave Bank of America 5,669 locations and 16,551 automatic teller machines (ATMs), as well as 33 million customers in 29 states. The merged company will have 180,000 workers, operations in 34 countries, and $933 billion in assets. Lewis told investors that $1.1 billion in expense cuts, together with the potential to expand Fleet's consumer business, will make the deal worthwhile. The merger secured for Bank of America almost 10 percent of U.S. banking deposits and more than twice the deposit share of competitors Wells Fargo and Wachovia. Its projected earnings of $10 billion annually would make it the fourth-most-profitable company in the world. While some observers pointed out that New England was the slowest-growing region in the country in terms of population and new accounts, Lewis counters that it is one of the wealthiest markets in the world. "Until very late in the process, I was leaning toward not doing the deal," Lewis told *Fortune* (December 8, 2003). "We had to pay a full price because Fleet had decided to sell and although they preferred to go with us, other banks were pursuing them. What tilted me toward buying Fleet is that we saw opportunities the market hadn't caught onto yet. The economy was improving. Fleet's performance was also improving fast, and that hadn't yet been fully reflected in its share price, which was relatively cheap. . . . The combination of Fleet's improving performance and big cost savings—those things alone will make the merger work. Any cross-selling or other synergies we generate will be gravy."

There is speculation that FleetBoston's longtime presence in Latin America may be phased out with the takeover. Lewis told investors that the bank wants to reduce its "cross-border exposure" by cutting back multicurrency corporate lending in Latin America. A Bank of America spokeswoman said that Lewis's remark referred primarily to FleetBoston operations in Argentina and Brazil, which together have 198 branches. In addition, FleetBoston has approved many large corporate loans in Latin America. Because of economic and political turmoil, Latin American operations have "been a real albatross around the neck of Fleet, at least in the last couple of years," Nancy Bush, managing member of NAB Research LLC (which provides research for the National Association of Broadcasters), told Jon Chesto for the *Boston Herald* (December 3, 2003). "I don't think Ken Lewis is going to give it an opportunity to be an albatross around his neck."

Still, Bank of America, which dominates the American Sunbelt, where Hispanics make up a large portion of the population, has made significant efforts to attract Hispanic customers. "We expect to get no less than 80% of our future growth in retail banking from the Hispanic market," Lewis told *Fortune* (April 14, 2003). As part of this effort, Bank of America is hiring more Spanish-speaking employees and initiating more services friendly to the Hispanic market, such as the low-cost SafeSend method of transferring cash to Mexico and the writing of mortgages secured by the credit of an extended family rather than just one individual. In December 2002 Bank of America bought 25 percent of Grupo Financiero Santander Serfin, Mexico's third-largest bank, for $1.6 billion in an effort to better serve the 36 million Hispanics in the U.S. and boost Bank of America's money-transfer business.

In September 2003 Lewis said that he would hold accountable for their actions employees who had allowed the bank's mutual-fund unit to engage in improper trading with Canary Capital Partners' hedge fund. At the beginning of that month, New York State's attorney general, Eliot Spitzer, had charged that Bank of America had helped Canary earn tens of millions of dollars by engaging in illegal late trading of its mutual funds in exchange for investments that generated millions of dollars in revenue for the bank. Industry regulators said that the actions were spurred by a desire to do business with the family of the billionaire real-estate mogul Leonard Stern, whose son Edward runs Canary. (In 2000 Lewis set a company goal of doubling profits from managed investments, a lucrative area dominated by mutual-fund companies and brokerage firms.) Spitzer made the charge against not only Bank of America but Janus Capital Group, Bank One, and Strong Capital Management; in the case of Bank of America, Spitzer alleged that Theodore Sihpol III, the broker who landed Stern's account, committed securities fraud and grand larceny. Stern and Canary agreed to a $40 million fine to settle the case, but did not admit to wrongdoing. Those developments prompted Bank of America to conduct an internal investigation. "My first reaction was disappointment that somebody could have betrayed our trust," Lewis said on hearing the charges regarding Canary, as quoted by Scott Silvestri in the *Sunday Tribune* (September 7, 2003). "My second was anger." Since he took over as chief executive, Lewis has been quick to fire employees whose conduct he believes will hurt the bank. For example, in January 2002 he terminated three employees who had handled loans to the energy company Enron, which ultimately cost the bank $231 million—after Enron, in what became one of the biggest corporate scandals of recent times, was found to have falsified the state of its finances.

Since he became CEO, Lewis has cut 10,000 jobs at the bank and presided over eight straight quarters of rising profit. Among his targets are 6 to 9 percent annual revenue growth, 10 percent annual growth in earnings per share, and a 20 percent return on equity. Over five years he hopes to increase asset management's revenue share from 7 to 12 or 15 percent while decreasing investment-banking revenue from 25 percent to 20 percent of overall revenues, though with greater profitability. At the same time, he hopes to expand the global corporate and investment bank, which accounted for $9 billion of the company's $35 billion in revenue in 2001.

In 2002 Lewis was recognized as Banker of the Year by *American Banker* and as Top Chief Executive Officer by *U.S. Banker.* "There was plenty of skepticism about Bank of America when Ken Lewis took the helm," David Longobardi, editor in chief of *American Banker*, said on presenting the award, as reported by PR Newswire (December 5, 2002). "But he has been the first in a mega-merged class of banks to show that a bank can be big and be good too." Lewis is a member of the board of directors of Health Management Associates Inc., a publicly owned operator of acute-care hospitals; a director of the Homeownership Education and Counseling Institute; vice chairman and immediate past chairman of the board of trustees of the National Urban League; a member of the board of directors of Lowe's Companies Inc.; a member of the board and past chairman of the Presbyterian Hospital Foundation; a member of the board of the Financial Services Roundtable; a member of the Financial Services Forum; a member of the board and executive committee and past chairman of the United Way of Central Carolinas Inc.; and a member of the Committee to Encourage Corporate Philanthropy.

Lewis was paid $19 million for fiscal year 2001, consisting of $1.33 million in salary, a $5.2 million bonus, $10.8 million for 750,000 10-year stock options, and $150,331 in other compensation; in 2002 he earned a combined salary and bonus of $6.9 million as well as $11.3 million in restricted stock awards. He has been described as modest, soft-spoken, personable, and self-effacing, and devotes most of his energy to business. "His No. 1 object in life is Bank of America," Jim Hynes, the retired chairman of Hynes Inc. in Charlotte, who served with Lewis on the board of the local United Way, told *Fortune* (November 9, 2003). "He is a highly focused, very intense guy." Lewis married during his sophomore year of college; that union ended in divorce in 1978. Two years later he wed again. He and his wife, Donna, live in Charlotte, North Carolina. Their adult son, Shayne (his wife's child, whom he adopted), owns a restaurant in Charlotte.

—K.E.D.

Suggested Reading: CNBC News Transcripts Nov. 3, 2003; *Institutional Investor* p 139+ Oct. 2002, with photo; *Money* p 40+ Jan. 2003

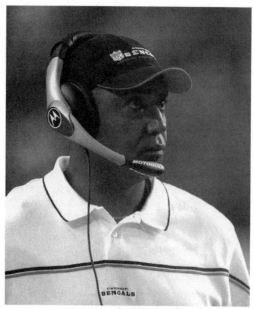

Scott Cunningham/Getty Images

Lewis, Marvin

Sep. 23, 1958– Football coach

Address: Cincinnati Bengals, 1 Paul Brown Stadium, Cincinnati, OH 45202

When the Cincinnati Bengals announced that on January 14, 2003, Marvin Lewis would be joining the franchise as head coach, many observers expressed the view that Lewis's assumption of a professional football team's top post was long overdue. The strength of that sentiment had been growing since 2000, when, under his guidance, the Baltimore Ravens' defensive unit outperformed virtually all others in the history of the National Football League (NFL). Although Lewis masterminded the defense that led to the Ravens' Super Bowl victory in 2001 and helped lead the team's defense to a number-two ranking in the 2001 season—and though he had nine years of NFL coaching under his belt by then, as well as 11 years at various colleges—none of the teams seeking a new head coach in early 2002 offered the position to him. In the *New York Times* (May 2, 2002), a few months after Lewis left the Ravens to work for the Washington Redskins as defensive coordinator, Thomas George wrote, "Men who have accomplished less have leaped past him into head coaching jobs," and then noted, "Lewis will not say that it is all about race but, of course, race matters."

The history of pro football, like that of pro baseball, is stained with racism. As recounted in such sources as the African American Registry, an on-line encyclopedia, the limited integration of pro football that had existed since the early 1900s ended in 1933, when the NFL (organized in 1920) barred African-Americans from the game. The ban was lifted in 1946, but another 16 years passed before every team had signed on at least one black player. From the beginnings of pro football until the 1920s, there was only one black head coach (Frederick "Fritz" Pollard); there were none from 1926 until 1989, when the Oakland Raiders hired Art Shell to serve in that capacity. During the next 14 years, only four other African-Americans attained the same distinction: Dennis Green (Minnesota Vikings, 1992–2001, Arizona Cardinals since January 2004); Ray Rhodes (Philadelphia Eagles, 1995–99, Green Bay Packers, 1999–2000); Tony Dungy (Tampa Bay Buccaneers, 1996–2001, Indianapolis Colts since 2002); and Herman Edwards (New York Jets, since 2001). Currently, in addition to Green, Dungy, Edwards, and Lewis, the ranks of head coaches include one other African-American: Lovie Smith (Chicago Bears, since January 2004). Thus, between 1920 and 2004, only eight of the more than 400 people (or less than 2 percent) who have served as head coaches in the NFL have been African-Americans, in a sport in which, in recent years, more than two-thirds of the players have been blacks.

"We've turned over a new leaf for the Bengals," Mike Brown, the owner of the Bengals, declared during his announcement about his hiring of Lewis, as Jarrett Bell reported for *USA Today* (January 16, 2003, on-line). Brown was not referring to the race of his new head coach, though; rather, he was expressing optimism that Lewis would reverse the fortunes of the team, which had not had a winning season since 1990 and had compiled a win–loss record of 2–14 in 2002. Lewis fulfilled Brown's expectations: during the 2003 season, the Bengals won eight games. Observers have attributed Lewis's accomplishment not only to the changes he made in personnel but, even more, to his effectiveness as a motivator. As the Pro Football Hall of Famer Ozzie Newsome told Paul Attner for the *Sporting News* (December 1, 2003), the Bengals' players "bought into what he wants. He has made them more accountable; he has them hustling to the ball; he has them caring about each other. These aren't the same old Bengals."

The oldest of the three children and only son of Marvin and Vanetta Lewis, Marvin Lewis was born on September 23, 1958 in McDonald, Pennsylvania, a small, predominantly white town near Pittsburgh. His sister Carol Joy—who told Geoff Hobson for the Bengals Web site (July 25, 2003) that she and her siblings always knew that "we were supposed to go to college and succeed"—is a specialist in corporate engineering. His other sister, Andrea Lewis, is a police officer. One of his uncles, Matthew Lewis, a *Washington Post* photographer, won the Pulitzer Prize for feature photography in 1975. Lewis's father worked rotating shifts at a steel mill, as a laborer and then a supervisor, until his retirement, for health reasons, in the mid-1980s. His mother, a high-school valedictorian, earned a nurse-practitioner's license while raising her chil-

dren and then got jobs outside the home. From his parents, Lewis wrote for a *Cincinnati Enquirer* questionnaire (July 4, 2004, on-line), he "learned about hard work and the delegation of time." Even when his father and mother both held jobs, he added, "we always had one parent at home."

Lewis was a model son: according to Geoff Hobson, writing for the Bengals Web site, he "never got in trouble, . . . always did his chores, . . . mowed the acre behind the house every week in the summer even while he worked other jobs." "Always," his father told Hobson, young Marvin had "discipline"—significantly more of it than the average youngster or teenager. He also had many friends, both white and black. According to his sister Carol Joy, being African-American in a mainly white environment never caused him problems. "My brother is one of those people who is running his own race," she said to Hobson. "We always said he pretty much went to the beat of his own drummer. People weren't jealous of him. He could always fit in with anyone anywhere."

At Fort Cherry High School, in McDonald, Lewis has said, he benefitted greatly from the instruction of his football coach, Jim Garry, and the example Garry set. Lewis became an All-Conference quarterback and safety and also earned letters in wrestling and baseball. (He believes that the best high-school athletes, as he told *FanFile Magazine* [2004, on-line], are "well-rounded": they compete in three sports, not one.) Lewis was elected president of the senior class and graduated as its valedictorian. As a teenager he also served as the Sunday-school superintendent at the local Baptist church. He was on the brink of matriculating at Purdue University when, sight unseen, Idaho State University (ISU), in Pocatello, offered Lewis a football scholarship. The offer was prompted by an enthusiastic, serendipitous recommendation in which the McDonald-born John Somsky, a football recruiter for another college, described Lewis to an ISU recruiter as "an outstanding defensive player with good resilient strength, good agility, and very tough-minded," as quoted by Hobson. Happy to relieve his parents of the burden of tuition payments, Lewis enrolled at ISU. He became a linebacker for ISU's football team (named the Bengals), with whom he also played quarterback and free safety. For three consecutive years (1978–80), he earned All–Big Sky Conference honors as a linebacker. He received a bachelor's degree in physical education from the school in 1981 and a master's degree in athletic administration, also from ISU, the next year. Meanwhile, in 1981, he had begun his coaching career, working with ISU's linebackers; the football team finished 12–1 during the first of his four seasons as coach and won the National Collegiate Athletic Association (NCAA) Division 1-A championship that year.

From 1985 to 1986 Lewis coached linebackers at Long Beach State (formally, California State University at Long Beach), and from 1987 to 1989 he performed that job at the University of New Mexico at Albuquerque. For two years beginning in 1990, he coached outside linebackers at the University of Pittsburgh, in Pennsylvania. Lewis took part in the NFL's Minority Coaching Fellowship Program in the summers of 1988 and 1991, interning with the San Francisco 49ers and the Kansas City Chiefs, respectively. In 1992 he got his first job with the National Football League (NFL), as assistant coach with the Pittsburgh Steelers. He helped the Steelers defense capture a top-three ranking in the NFL in each of four successive seasons and guided some of the league's finest linebackers, among them Kevin Greene, Chad Brown, Levon Kirkland, and Greg Lloyd.

For six seasons starting in 1996, Lewis served as defensive coordinator for the Baltimore Ravens, in Maryland. The defensive unit that he guided in 2000 has been ranked among the NFL's finest of all time. During the regular season that year, the Baltimore defense set the NFL record for fewest points allowed in a 16-game campaign (165), 22 fewer points than the previous mark. It also allowed the fewest rushing yards in the NFL that year—970—a league record for a 16-game season, and ranked first in rushing average allowed (2.7); total takeaways (49); fumble recoveries (26); and shutouts (four, the most by an NFL team since 1976). Under Lewis, the Ravens' defense held opponents scoreless in 41 of 64 quarters and allowed no more than one touchdown in 14 of the team's last 18 games (the last four taking place in the postseason). In the 2000–01 postseason the Ravens defeated the Denver Broncos (21–3), the Tennessee Titans (24–10), and the Oakland Raiders (16–3) to advance to Super Bowl XXXV, where they beat the New York Giants, 34–7. In total yardage allowed, Lewis's last three Baltimore defenses (in 1999, 2000, and 2001) each ranked second in the NFL, and they ranked in the top four in seven other categories.

In 2001 Lewis interviewed with the Tampa Bay Buccaneers for the head-coach post. After five hours of talk with the team's owner and president, Malcolm Glazer, according to various sources, he believed that he had landed the job. But, as Thomas George put it, the Buccaneers "pulled a You-Are-Our-Coach, er, excuse us, No-You-Are-Not on Lewis." In late 2001 Lewis turned down an offer to serve as head coach at the University of California. Instead, he signed on as assistant head coach and defensive coordinator for the Washington Redskins, at a salary of $1 million a year (considerably more than he had been earning). He directed the Redskins, whose defensive unit then ranked fifth in the NFL, in 2002.

On January 14, 2003 Lewis signed a five-year, $7.5 million contract to become the ninth head coach of the Cincinnati Bengals. His hiring came after a swelling chorus of protests regarding team owners' repeated failures to even consider him for a head-coaching job, as well as the paucity of black head coaches in all of pro football. It also followed the promulgation of a controversial NFL rule that required every team owner to interview at least one black candidate for every coaching vacancy. That ruling had come after the attorneys Johnnie L. Cochran Jr. and Cyrus Mehri had threatened to sue the NFL for racial discrimination, and after the wide dissemination of Cochran and Mehri's report "Black Coaches in the National Football League: Superior Performance, Inferior Opportunities" (September 30, 2002). In the report, which summarized a study of NFL hiring practices, the attorneys wrote that their experiences in fighting racial discrimination at Texaco, Coca-Cola, and other big corporations had made them "national experts on the effects of glass ceilings and glass walls in denying minority employees a fair chance to compete for positions of leadership." "The parallels between the struggles of African-Americans at these companies and within the NFL coaching ranks are striking," they wrote.

As the Bengals' head coach, in the words of a writer for the *Toronto Star* (January 15, 2003, online), Lewis "start[ed] at the bottom"—a reference not to his title but to the team: in 2002 the Bengals had posted their worst record (2–14) in franchise history. Indeed, the team had been foundering since 1990, earning the nickname "the Bungles"; their cumulative record for the 12 seasons before Lewis came on board was 55–137. During the 2003 off-season, as Dennis Tuttle wrote for the *Sporting News* (March 31, 2003), the players faced "the mile-high obstacle of their past: being a cheap, hapless, sad-sack organization with a losing mentality." Lewis immediately set to work to reverse the players' negativity. "It has been one step at a time in changing the mindset," he told David Elfin for the *Washington Times* (August 7, 2003, on-line). "Habits were the first thing to change—how we do things, how we meet, how we practice, being accountable to each other. I've tried to bring guys to the realization that we don't need to worry about the big picture. If we take care of the little things, they'll take care of the big picture. We're going to hit adversity. How we deal with it will be the test to see how our mindset has changed." In carrying out his strategy, he persuaded the team's owner and president, Mike Brown, to give him the authority to make decisions regarding personnel. Lewis fired from the coaching staff three former Bengal players and the team's longtime strength-and-conditioning coach, Kim Wood, who was unpopular among players. He dismissed veteran players and brought in 21 new ones, earning widespread praise from NFL analysts for quickly signing established NFL free agents; within the first two weeks of the free-agency period, he had signed five likely starters: linebacker Kevin Hardy, defensive linemen John Thornton and Carl Powell, cornerback Tory James, and tight end Reggie Kelly. He also let the Bengals' best defensive player, linebacker Takeo Spikes, leave the team for the Buffalo Bills, noting that he wanted on his team only players who believed in it. He expanded the scouting department and revamped the off-season conditioning program. Lewis also persuaded Brown that developing a better team required a greater expenditure of money. For example, he insisted that players stay in a hotel the night before home games, and he ordered $250,000 worth of improvements for the team's weight room. Brown also agreed to Lewis's unusual request that as head coach, he alone would act as the Bengals' public voice. "By handing over significant authority to Lewis, [Brown] gave him the power and credibility to execute a thorough makeover of the franchise," Paul Attner wrote. "The Bengals always had talent; they just yearned for proper leadership."

Known for his calm demeanor, Lewis "is an incredibly demanding, high-energy perfectionist who is obsessed with athletes following their assignments," according to Attner. As head coach, he has retained his hands-on approach to training and practice. "A lot of head coaches just kind of walk around and supervise," Kevin Hardy told Elfin. "Marvin is doing some actual coaching. Whenever he gets on guys, he's trying to get the most out of you because he knows your potential. He's a great judge of talent. And if Marvin does get on you, he'll come over at the end of the day to make sure that you're not down." The Redskins' defensive end Renaldo Wynn, who played for Lewis in the 2002 season, said that Lewis was a tough coach but one whom players trusted. "Marvin is like taking medicine that tastes bad but is good for you," he told Attner. "He gets on your nerves, but he is going to make you a better player." The team's significant improvement in 2003, when they won eight games and lost eight, provided evidence of the merits of Lewis's philosophy and tactics.

Lewis has participated in charitable events for the Juvenile Diabetes Foundation, the Boys and Girls Clubs, and the United Way in Cincinnati. He was involved with the American Red Cross and Muscular Dystrophy of Baltimore. In 2002 he joined the Washington Redskins Leadership Council's Honorary Committee, assisting in community and youth outreach efforts throughout the D.C. metropolitan area. He and his wife, Peggy, have a daughter, Whitney, and a son, Marcus. The couple established the Marvin Lewis Community Fund in 2003 to work with regional nonprofit organizations; in 2004 the fund gave grants to Boys Hope Girls Hope; the Greater Cincinnati Boys & Girls Clubs; Minorities in Mathematics, Science & Engineering; the National Multiple Sclerosis Society; Youth Inc.; and Success by 6. Lewis was inducted into Idaho State's Hall of Fame in 2001. He received a Queen City Advocate Award from the Greater Cincinnati Convention and Visitors Bureau in 2004.

—K.E.D.

Suggested Reading: AllSports (on-line) Jan. 24, 2003; bengals.theinsiders.com; Cincinnati Bengals Web site; cincinnati.com/bengals; *New York Times* D p3 Jan. 17, 2003; NFL Web site; Pro Sports Daily (on-line); *Sporting News* p18+ Dec. 1, 2003; *Sports Illustrated* p46+ Nov. 24, 2003, with photos; *Washington Times* (on-line) Aug. 7, 2003

Lilly, Kristine

July 22, 1971– Soccer player

Address: c/o U.S. Soccer Federation, 1801 S. Prairie Ave., Chicago, IL 60616

Known as the "Iron Woman" of soccer, Kristine Lilly has played in more international soccer games than any other player, man or woman. While she set the record with her 152d international match, in May 1998, she has now represented the United States in more than 250 matches. Having appeared in 85 percent of the women's national team's games since its inception, she is the team's all-time leader in games and minutes played and is third on the all-time scoring list. A left-footed midfielder who has also played forward, she is known as one of the best technical and tactical players in the sport and has helped lead the U.S. women's national team to two Women's World Cup (WWC) victories, in 1991 and 1999, and a gold medal at both the 1996 and 2004 Olympic Games. "I've always said that U.S. Soccer has got to find a way to clone her," Julie Foudy, captain of the women's national team, said in a story posted on the Illi-

nois Youth Soccer Web site. "She has consistently done everything possible to be one of the best players in the world. Her selflessness is remarkable. She's always the one making the hard run, even if she doesn't get that ball. She has those same qualities on and off the field."

The daughter of Terri and Steve Lilly, Kristine Marie Lilly was born on July 22, 1971 in New York City and grew up with her older brother, Scott, in Wilton, Connecticut, an affluent community about three hours south of Boston. "I was surrounded by guys," Lilly recalled, as quoted on the Illinois Youth Soccer Web site. "And basically whenever we played, I never got treated any differently. I was just one of the boys. I had to be tough. When I fell down, I had to get right up. My brother would always say 'get up, you're fine' and I would. If I ever cried, my brother knew I was really hurt. He was always watching over me, but he let me play hard because he saw that I loved it." From the second through the eighth grades, Lilly played with a boys' traveling soccer team; her teammates did not seem to mind having a girl on the team. In fact, when the organizers of a tournament near Niagara Falls refused to let her play because of her gender, her team withdrew from the competition. She finally

Ben Radford/Getty Images

Kristine Lilly

got to play with a girls' team when she attended Wilton High School, where she led the team to the state title in her freshman, sophomore, and senior years and was team captain during her junior and senior seasons.

Lilly was chosen for the U.S. women's national soccer team in 1987, at the age of 16. She made her first appearance in international competition (known as a cap) against China on August 3, 1987 in Tianjin. The game was only the 16th the U.S. women's team had ever played, and Lilly became the second-youngest player, behind Mia Hamm, in team history. "I can't really remember how I felt," she said, as posted on the Illinois Youth Soccer Web site. "I was nervous, but I wasn't scared. I was just playing. I was so young I didn't know much else except just to play." She scored her first goal on August 13, against China. While continuing to play for the women's national team, Lilly enrolled at the University of North Carolina (UNC) in Chapel Hill. She helped the Tar Heels win four national titles, from 1989 to 1992, and was a four-time First-Team National Soccer Coaches Association of America (NSCAA) All-American, four-time First-Team All-ACC (Atlantic Coast Conference) pick, and four-time First-Team All-South selection. She was named offensive MVP of the National Collegiate Athletic Association (NCAA) championship in 1989 and 1990 and was UNC's athlete of the year as a senior. In 1991 she was a finalist for the Broderick Award, given to the outstanding female athlete among all college sports, and was the second-leading scorer in the nation behind her teammate Mia Hamm, with 15 goals and four assists. That year she won the Hermann Trophy, which honors the top male and female Division I college

soccer players in the U.S. (In 1992 she was a finalist for that award.) She also won the Missouri Athletic Club Player of the Year Award in 1991. In 1993 she graduated with a degree in communications (radio, television, and motion-picture production), having amassed 78 goals and 41 assists during her college career. Her North Carolina jersey number, 15, was retired in 1994. She was named to Soccer America's College Team of the Decade for the 1990s.

During her college years, as a member of the national team (she did not participate in 1989 or 1992), Lilly was on the North soccer team at the Olympic Festival in 1990, helping to win a gold medal, and played on the winning team in the first WWC, in 1991. The Americans beat Germany, 5–2, in the semifinals and defeated Norway, 2–1, to win the title. In 1993 she won the U.S. Soccer organization's Female Athlete of the Year Award, and her team won the Confederation of North, Central American and Caribbean Association Football (CONCACAF) soccer championship. The following year she played for the Tyreso Football Club in Sweden, along with her U.S. national teammates Michelle Akers, Julie Foudy, and Mary Harvey. In 1995 she was the only woman who competed in the Continental Indoor Soccer League (CISL), playing for the Washington Warthogs. (Two other women, Collette Cunningham and Shannon Presley, had played sparingly in the league during the previous season.)

Playing for the U.S. national team, Lilly scored three goals in the 1995 WWC in Sweden, which the U.S. lost to Norway in the semifinals on June 15. "That [loss] proved to be one of our biggest learning experiences . . . ," she told the Ultimate New Zealand Soccer Web site (June 2000). "After that game, we vowed to make sure that we wouldn't allow that to happen in the 1996 Olympics, and as we trained, we remembered how we felt." The team's renewed determination paid off, as they won Olympic gold at the 1996 Atlanta Summer Games, the first Olympics to include women's soccer. Lilly played every minute of the team's five matches and scored the first goal in the championship game, with a crossing shot from the left flank.

In 1997 Lilly started in all of the U.S. team's 18 matches and led the team in minutes played. The following year she set an American record for consecutive games started, with 62. Long known by then as one of the world's best flank midfielders—a position that requires good one-on-one play both defensively and offensively—she spent considerable time at forward that season and notched eight goals and 11 assists, ranking fourth on the team in scoring. In 1998 she was a member of the gold-medal-winning team at the Goodwill Games. On May 21 of that year, in a game in Kobe, Japan, she played her 152d match in international competition, breaking the record for most appearances set by Heidi Stoere, of Norway. During the summer of 1998 she played four matches with the Delaware Genies, of the United Soccer League's women's league, scoring five goals and making two assists.

Lilly played every minute of all six games in the U.S. team's quest for the 1999 WWC, scoring two goals and making one assist. She scored the final goal against Denmark in the 3–0 opening-game victory at Giants Stadium, in New Jersey, and made one of the most memorable plays in team history when she blocked—with her head—a Chinese shot that went past the American goalkeeper, Briana Scurry, preventing a goal that would have given China the game. The two teams were scoreless through two overtimes, which meant that penalty kicks determined the game. Lilly scored the U.S. team's third penalty kick; her teammate Brandi Chastain scored the fifth and final penalty kick, which secured the victory over China, 5–4, and brought the U.S. the World Cup. Lilly was named MVP of the WWC competition.

"The penalty kick goal in the shootout in the World Cup Final was an amazing experience," Lilly said in an interview posted on the My Soccer Web site (October 30, 2002). "I was nervous, but very focused. I couldn't hear the crowd, and there was this one strange moment as I kicked that was very peaceful. I felt confident I would make it." "The thing that I'm most proud of about the World Cup is what our team did or the sport did for America," she told ABC Sports, in an article posted on the ESPN Web site (April 20, 2001). "We had a great victory, we won the World Cup. However, we had a bigger victory in what we did for women's sports. We got soccer out there, but we also got women's sports out. . . . We had the biggest crowd to ever watch a women's sporting event at that game." The year 1999 proved to be special for Lilly not only because of the World Cup victory but also because she scored a team- and career-best 20 goals (becoming only the fourth female player in history to score 20 or more goals in one year), accumulated eight career assists (second on the team), and led the team in minutes played, with 2,397. That year she also reached an important milestone, playing in her 200th game with the U.S. team, in a victory over Canada on June 6.

In 2000 the left-footer played in 34 matches for the U.S. team, starting in 30 of them. She scored six goals and made five assists, including a goal against Nigeria in the Olympic Games. Despite high hopes for a repeat gold-medal Olympic performance, however, the team had to settle for silver when they were defeated in the finals by Norway at the Summer Games in Sydney, Australia. "I am disappointed that we didn't win a gold medal, but I am not disappointed about winning a silver," Lilly wrote in her Olympic diary, as posted on the *Sports Illustrated* Web site (October 5, 2000). "I am proud of myself and my team. I would be lying if I didn't say it hurts. It hurts a lot. . . . I also have learned if you focus too much on what you didn't do and not on what you did do, you will always be unhappy. My team and I accomplished so much this year. . . . Gold medalists we are not, but we are champions in our minds, our fans' minds and our families' minds."

In 2001 Lilly was named captain of the Boston Breakers, a team in the newly formed Women's United Soccer Association (WUSA). Playing every minute of the team's 21 games, she was named the team MVP, was voted to the WUSA First Team, and finished the season as the Breakers' third-leading scorer, with 16 points, three goals, and 10 assists, tying for the most assists in the league. (When determining point totals for statistical purposes in soccer, a goal counts as two points, and an assist counts as one.) In 2002 she tied for fourth in the league in points scored, accumulating 29 with eight goals and 13 assists. By bringing her two-season assist total to 25, Lilly became the all-time assist leader in the young WUSA. In addition, she was named to the WUSA First Team and finished the season with a 10-game point-scoring streak, the longest in league history. In 2003 she played in 19 of the Breakers' 21 games, notching 10 points (scored on three goals and four assists). She was once again named to the league's First Team, becoming the only player in the WUSA to achieve that honor in each of the first three seasons. Due to financial difficulties, the league disbanded after the 2003 season; efforts are being made to revive it.

Spending the bulk of her time with the Breakers, Lilly played in just three matches for the U.S. team in 2001, starting in two. In 2002 she started in 16 national-team matches, notching nine assists, and helped the U.S. qualify for the 2003 WWC by scoring on a volley against Costa Rica at the CONCA-CAF Women's Gold Cup. In the 2003 WWC, hosted by the U.S., Lilly's team made it to the semifinals but was stunned, 0–3, by Germany in a game played in Portland, Oregon. That game marked just the second WWC loss by the U.S. team since the tournament debuted in 1991, the first having come in the 1995 championship game against Norway. The American women managed to defeat Canada, 3–1, for the bronze medal with help from Lilly, who scored in the first period. (Germany defeated Sweden, 2–1, to win the tournament.) During the 19 games she played with the national team in 2003, Lilly managed three goals and three assists and expanded her record for most games played, competing in her 250th on April 26, 2003. On March 3, 2004 the women's national team defeated Costa Rica, 4–0, to qualify for the Summer Olympics competition in Athens, Greece.

In 2003 Lilly joined many athletes in promoting the Defeat the Heat initiative, the first public-safety campaign dedicated to protecting active kids from dehydration and heat illness. In September 2003 she partnered with Stonyfield Farm, an organic-yogurt company, on the Strong Women campaign, speaking at the Strong Women Summit, held in New Paltz, New York, November 14–16, 2003. Also that month she and Mia Hamm participated in a soccer training day, sponsored by Pfizer Inc. and the Groton, Connecticut, Parks and Recreation Department, to raise awareness of bone-marrow diseases. Lilly is on the board of directors of the nonprofit organization EGT Sports (Empowering

Girls Through Sports), whose mission is "to give support, encouragement, and motivation to at-risk young girls from deprived socio-economic environments through the world of sport," as Lilly remarked in her January 6, 2004 journal entry on the Kristine Lilly 13 Web site. The soccer field at her alma mater, Wilton High School, was named Kristine Lilly Field in her honor, and in 2003 the U.S. Youth Soccer National Championships dubbed the Under-15 girls' trophy the Kristine Lilly Cup.

Lilly and her teammates Mia Hamm, Julie Foudy, and Joy Fawcett entered the 2004 Olympic Games in Athens, Greece, with the knowledge that this would very likely be the last time that they would play together. (Hamm, Foudy, and Fawcett had announced that they would retire after the Olympics.) Perhaps as a result of that knowledge, the U.S. women's soccer team overpowered all of their rivals, last among them the team from Brazil, which they vanquished with a score of 2–1 in the deciding game. Lilly, in a 112th-minute game winner, bent a corner kick onto forward Abby Wambach's head for the final goal. This Olympic gold-medal victory cemented the American team's place in sports history as the dominant women's soccer squad of their generation. The last of the Olympic women's soccer contests was the 282d international match in which Lilly played—an all-time record number in both men's and women's soccer. Following the Olympics, the U.S. women's team went on a 10-game "Fan Appreciation Tour," during which Lilly scored her 100th career goal, during a 5–0 victory over New Zealand.

Lilly, who wears the number 13 on the national team, is five feet four inches tall and weighs 125 pounds. She has named Heige Riis of Norway and Sun Wen of China as being among the best players she has faced on the field. "Heige used to play on the flank, and we certainly had our battles—she's such a tremendous player. Sun is a very good, very crafty player whom I really respect," she told the Ultimate New Zealand Soccer Web site. When not playing soccer, Lilly works as a communications specialist. She runs the Kristine Lilly Soccer Academy in Wilton every summer and enjoys bicycling, golfing, reading, listening to music, and watching movies. She has a golden retriever named Scribner and credits her family and teammates for her success. "My family has always been a big influence on my career because they've always been so supportive," she told the Ultimate New Zealand Soccer Web site. "They've allowed me to try everything and basically said, 'This is your world; do what you want.' They've been the backbone, but my team-mates have been my on-field motivation and inspiration, thus enabling me to improve as a player and enjoy myself on the pitch."

—K.E.D.

Suggested Reading: Illinois Youth Soccer Web site May 2, 2003; Kristine Lilly 13 Web site; *Women's Sports & Fitness* p94+ July/Aug. 1998; *The Scribner Encyclopedia of American Lives: Sports Figures*, vol. 2, 2002

Courtesy of the *Chicago Tribune*

Lipinski, Ann Marie

Jan. 1, 1956– Senior vice president and editor of the Chicago Tribune

Address: Chicago Tribune, *435 N. Michigan Ave., Chicago, IL 60611*

Ann Marie Lipinski's rise at the *Chicago Tribune* has been a classic American success story. When she began her career at the newspaper as a summer intern, in 1978, Lipinsky was told not to expect to be rewarded with a permanent position. Not only did she exhibit enough resourcefulness to be hired as a reporter by the end of the summer, but she has since moved through the ranks to become, in February 2001, the first female senior vice president and editor of the newspaper. In that position Lipinski has spearheaded the transformation of the *Chicago Tribune* into a publication that appeals to an unusually broad readership. "It's not that a woman needs to be in charge. But in the journalistic process, there needs to be a diversity of opinion," Lipinski explained during a panel discussion at the Medhill School of Journalism on October 25, 2001, as posted on the school's Web site. "If you have all one kind of person, that's not a good thing. You're not as likely to reflect your community." Founded in 1847, the *ChicagoTribune* is among the nation's oldest newspapers; with a daily circulation of 660,000 Monday through Saturday and over a million on Sunday, it is also among the most widely circulated.

Ann Marie Lipinski was born on January 1, 1956 in Trenton, Michigan, a small community on the Detroit River. In high school she served as the editor of the school newspaper. She enrolled at Michigan State University, but at the last moment she decided instead on the University of Michigan at Ann Arbor, where, as she recalled in an interview with Jennifer Silverberg for *Michigan Today* (Fall 1997, on-line), her love of journalism became the center of her life: "I remember the day my parents drove me to Ann Arbor in 1974. I quickly dumped my stuff in my dorm room at South Quad and I didn't even unpack. I immediately went over to the *Daily*."

The *Michigan Daily,* the University of Michigan's campus newspaper, is published Monday through Friday during the fall and winter terms by university students. Lipinski spent the next four years working at the paper, which has been published for more than a century. Initially she served as the telegraph editor, but she did no editing; her job was to rip pages off the telegraph machine and neatly pile them on the senior editor's desk. She quickly moved into reporting, assigned to the political beat around Ann Arbor. In 1976 she voluntarily traveled to the Democratic Convention in New York City to cover the presidential nomination of former Georgia governor Jimmy Carter. (The *Daily* was unable to fund the trip, so she paid her own way.) She was driven to New York by a *Daily* photographer named Steve Kagan, who was a year ahead of her at the University of Michigan. They stayed at his grandmother's house in Forest Hills, Queens, and rode the subway to the convention each day. Though not an overnight romance, their relationship began to blossom during that trip. They were married in 1981 and are the parents of a daughter, Caroline.

In 1977 Lipinski became the co-editor of the *Michigan Daily*, along with Jim Tobin, who would go on to become a reporter for the *Detroit News*. But Lipinski's journalistic activities were no longer confined to the college paper: in the summer of 1977, she was an intern at the *Miami Herald*, and the next summer she interned at the *Chicago Tribune*, planning to return to the University of Michigan after that internship to complete one more credit and earn her bachelor's degree. When she received her internship at the *Tribune*, the woman who interviewed her told her not to expect a full-time position when the internship ended; the woman even admitted that she disliked hiring college upper-classmen because they always expected a job to be waiting for them after graduation. Confounding her interviewer's expectations, however, the *Tribune* hired Lipinski as a features reporter, and she was unable to return to school. (In 1996 she completed the credit and earned her bachelor's degree from the university.)

After serving for a time as a features reporter, Lipinski joined a three-member investigative team at the *Tribune*. In 1988, when she was still in her early 30s, that team conducted a 10-month investigation into corruption in the Chicago City Council. With her fellow reporters Dean Baquet and William Gaines, she discovered that a number of aldermen (as the council members are called) were us-

ing their political positions for personal gain. The corruption was widespread and varied, ranging from accepting petty perks to demanding kickbacks for zoning decisions and licenses. The series on the corruption, "The Spoils of Power," earned the trio the 1988 Pulitzer Prize for investigative reporting.

In 1989 Lipinski was one of 12 reporters who won Nieman Fellowships at Harvard University, in Cambridge, Massachusetts. The Nieman Fellowships were established in 1938 and are presented to reporters who display journalistic excellence. Lipinski spent the 1989–90 school year at Harvard studying urban affairs, with a concentration on political and economic courses.

After she returned to the *Chicago Tribune*, Lipinski moved into management of the newspaper; in 1991 she was named associate managing editor of news for the metropolitan region. Despite the promotion, about three years later Lipinski told Jeff Borden for *Crain's Chicago Business* (September 26, 1994), "I still think of myself as a reporter. I love being involved with a reporter when they're on a great tale. I try to act the way I wanted editors to act when I was a reporter." As an associate managing editor, Lipinski helped to craft the *Tribune*'s year-long look at the violent deaths of young children in the Chicago area. She reasoned that such incidents deserved to be front-page news and that the entire community should be forced to pay attention. An article in the series appeared on the front page each time a child under the age of 15 was murdered. The death of a seven-year-old boy named Dantrell Davis, on October 13, 1992, had prompted the series. Dantrell had been on his way to school when a sniper's bullet had instantly killed him, in a random act that shocked the city. On the ABC show *Turning Point*, televised on April 13, 1994, Lipinski, according to the show's official transcript, recalled, "That story was a turning point for us and that's the point at which we decided we needed to do something. I mean, what were newspapers for if not to take on a subject like this? We also hoped, frankly, to outrage people."

The *Tribune*'s series "Killing Our Children" offered accounts of the murders of 61 children in the Chicago area over the course of a single year. The stories described everything from acts of random violence, such as the one involving Dantrell Davis, to gang-related deaths, to systematic physical abuse by parents or guardians. In one of the last type, a mentally disturbed woman placed her young son on a chair, placed a rope (affixed to a higher place) around his neck, waved good-bye to him, and kicked the chair out from under him. The courts had removed the boy from a loving foster home just months before to place him in his biological mother's custody, because the first priority of the Illinois Department of Children and Family Services was to reunite children with their natural parents. Partially as a result of the *Tribune* series, sweeping reforms in the system were implemented to emphasize the welfare of the child.

Lipinski's work on the "Killing Our Children" series resulted in her promotion, in January 1995, to managing editor of news for the *Chicago Tribune*. She was the first woman in the history of the newspaper to fill that position. A few months later, in October 1995, she was again promoted, this time to managing editor of the entire publication. In that post she oversaw both the news and features areas of the editorial department. In August 2000 Lipinski became vice president and executive director of the *Tribune*, overseeing all newsroom activity and acting as liaison between the editorial department and other departments at the newspaper. Many industry insiders theorized that Howard Tyner, who had been the paper's editor since 1993, was grooming Lipinski as his successor.

They were proven right in February 2001, when Lipinski became the first female senior vice president and editor of the *Chicago Tribune* in its long history. (Tyner moved up to the position of vice president of editorial services for Tribune Publishing.) Most observers acknowledge that Lipinski has helped to revolutionize the *Chicago Tribune*'s image by focusing on stories of interest to a more diversified readership, and particularly to mothers and other women. "I know I put different stories on page 1—as a woman, and a mother, and a working mother—than my predecessor would have," she said during the panel discussion at the Medhill School of Journalism. One of those stories—about families' plans to keep 2001 Halloween parties low-key in the wake of the terrorist attacks on the United States on September 11 of that year—made the front page, much to the surprise of many of the male staffers at the *Tribune*.

The September 11 attacks had forced newspaper editors all over the country to make difficult decisions. Lipinski considered running graphic front-page pictures of people jumping out of the windows of the burning World Trade Center towers. She decided instead to run the photos inside the paper. "It can't just be a shocking image for the sake of shock. It has to tell a story," she explained in her Medhill School panel discussion. "It told you as much as anything you read about what the conditions were like [inside the towers] and the hellacious choices people had to make." Because the terrorist attacks occurred in the early morning (Chicago is in the Central Time zone, one hour behind Eastern Standard Time), shortly after the newspaper had gone to press, Lipinski decided to print an evening edition for home delivery rather than newsstand sale, because she had overheard other parents talking about keeping out of downtown Chicago that day for fear of further attacks.

Lipinski's decisions as editor of the *Chicago Tribune* made news in September 2002, when she sought the resignation of Bob Greene, one of the paper's longtime syndicated columnists. Greene, a champion of traditional values, frequently wrote about his youth in the Midwest and his strong marriage. He resigned when it became public knowledge that he had had a sexual relationship with a 17-year-old girl during the 1980s, while he was ostensibly happily married. The relationship was revealed by the woman, now an adult, who sent an E-mail message to the newspaper detailing how she had come to the *Tribune* offices to interview Greene as part of a high-school writing assignment. Shortly after the interview Greene had asked her to dinner, and the two began a sexual relationship. Though many fellow journalists felt Greene had gotten a raw deal, since the relationship had occurred many years earlier and the *Tribune*'s rules of conduct for employees did not address situations of the type in which Greene had become involved, Lipinski contended that Greene's resignation was appropriate. "We deeply regret the conduct, its effect on the young woman and the impact the disclosure has on the trust our readers placed in Greene and this newspaper," she wrote in a statement about the matter, as quoted by Peter Johnson in *USA Today* (September 16, 2002).

In May 2003 Lipinski, along with Jim Amoss, the editor of the New Orleans *Times-Picayune*, were named to the Pulitzer Prize board, which oversees annual selections of those journalism awards. In April 2004 the *Chicago Sun-Times* named her the fourth-most-powerful woman in the city, for her stewardship of the *Tribune* as well as the influence she wields as a member of the Pulitzer board and her service with a number of other institutions, including the University of Michigan Journalism Fellows program and the Poynter Institute, a nonprofit journalism school.

In addition to winning the Pulitzer Prize in 1988, Lipinski has received many other awards, most notably the Illinois Associated Press Editors Association Award in 1981, the William H. Jones Investigative Journalism Award in 1987, and the Robert F. Kennedy Journalism Award (for reporting on the problems of the disadvantaged) in 1994. Her husband, Steve Kagan, is a freelance photographer who specializes in photojournalism, commercial photography, and TV and movie production stills.

—C.M.

Suggested Reading: *Chicago Sun-Times* p14 Apr. 21, 2004; *Chicago Tribune* I p8 May 11, 1989, II p1 Jan. 28, 1995, III p3 Oct. 3, 1995, N p1 Aug. 25, 2000; *Crain's Chicago Business* p37 Sep. 26, 1994; Medhill School of Journalism Web site Oct. 25, 2001; *Michigan Today* (on-line) Fall 1997; *Newsweek* p46 Sep. 30, 2002; *USA Today* D p3 Sep. 16, 2002

Gabe Palacio/ImageDirect

Long, William Ivey

1949– Costume designer

Address: c/o Helen Merrill Ltd., 295 Lafayette St., Suite 915, New York, NY 10012

"I love theater and especially costume design because of the psychology of it," William Ivey Long told Susie Eisner Eley for *Dance Teacher* (October 2000, on-line). "I enjoy helping people to leave their own bodies and take on other personas." Since 1976, when he made his professional debut, Long has designed thousands of costumes for the stage (and, occasionally, film and TV), for productions ranging from plays that closed during previews to such blockbuster successes as *Nine, Crazy for You, Contact,* and a revival of *Guys and Dolls.* In 2004 costumes designed by Long adorned performers on Broadway in the hit shows *Little Shop of Horrors, The Boy from Oz, Never Gonna Dance, Hairspray, The Producers,* and *Chicago,* as well as in a revival of *Cabaret* that closed in January of that year after a six-year run. Long's work on any show does not end on opening night; rather, it continues for the entire run. Every day he receives reports about the costumes used in all his current shows (including those on tour); then he and/or his assistants make any necessary repairs, adjustments, or changes. Understudies also need costumes, and whenever there are cast changes, new garments must be constructed. Long guarantees that his costumes have at least a year of wear in them—that is, they are sturdy enough to withstand the rigors of eight performances weekly for 52 weeks—but with careful maintenance most of them last far longer.

In working with dozens of celebrated or little-known playwrights, directors, choreographers, set designers, singers, dancers, actors, and actresses, Long has won affection and respect for his kindness, graciousness, flexibility, and humor as well as his creativity. "He's not married to a concept," Katherine Marshall, the co-owner of a New York City costume shop, told Leslie Talmadge for the *Christian Science Monitor* (August 29, 2003, on-line). "He does what really works well for each individual actor or actress. He'll have a sketch, an idea, a concept, but he's open to anything." The award-winning choreographer and director Susan Stroman, with whom he has often collaborated, told Talmadge that Long "always puts actors and actresses at ease in their fitting. He makes [the actors] feel like they're the most beautiful person [on] earth." Among other honors, Long has earned four Tony Awards, five Drama Desk Awards, four Outer Critics Circle Awards, and one Obie.

One of the three children of William and Mary Long, William Ivey Long was born in North Carolina in about 1949. He has a sister, Laura, and a brother, Robert, who designs theaters and other buildings. Long is a ninth-generation North Carolinian; on his father's side, his family has lived in the state since about 1675. Both of his parents worked behind the scenes in theater and taught drama at the high school and college levels. Until Billy (as he is still known by his family) was about three, his father was the technical director of a theater in Raleigh, North Carolina, and the family lived in a dressing room off stage left. "We didn't have much money, but I had a wonderful upbringing, playing on the stage and in a luxurious civic rose garden that served as my backyard," Long recalled, as reported by Eley. His father later established the theater program at Winthrop University, in Rock Hill, South Carolina, and also worked with the Carolina PlayMakers, the repertory company of the University of North Carolina at Chapel Hill. In the latter young Billy spent much of his free time in the company of Irene Smart Rains, the PlayMakers' costume designer, creating doll-sized clothing out of unneeded bits of fabric. When he was six he put together "an Elizabethan ruff for my dog, who stood very still," as he recalled to Talmadge. "I remember sewing and I remember figuring out, if you sew big stitches, it pleats." During summers the Long family lived in Manteo, North Carolina, where Long's father assisted (in the posts of director, technical director, and property master) with productions of *The Lost Colony*, a drama with music that has been performed outdoors at Fort Raleigh National Historic Site every summer (except one) since 1937; his mother starred as Queen Elizabeth I. At age eight Long, too, was cast in the play, as one of the ill-fated colonists' children. (In 1989 he himself assumed the post of costume designer for *The Lost Colony*, and he has also served as its production designer since 1997.)

Long earned a B.A. degree in French history from the College of William & Mary, in Williamsburg, Virginia, in 1969, then pursued a graduate degree in history at the University of North Carolina. There he renewed his friendships with Rains and the members of the theater troupe, which reawakened his desire for involvement in theater. He told Leslie Talmadge that while working on his doctoral thesis, about the wedding festivals of the Medici family of Florence, Italy, "I realized I wanted to design those Medician wedding festivals. What hubris!" After he left the University of North Carolina, without completing his doctorate, he gained admittance to the Yale School of Drama, in New Haven, Connecticut (where he shared living space with the future actresses Meryl Streep and Sigourney Weaver and became friends with the future playwrights Wendy Wasserstein and Paul Rudnick). He earned a master's of fine arts degree in stage design from Yale in 1975. He then moved into the Chelsea Hotel, in New York City, having landed a job with the fashion designer Charles James, who maintained a studio in the hotel. Known as the first American couturier, James had become famous in the 1940s and 1950s for his glamorous ballgowns and other romantic evening wear. In the *New York Times* (July 30, 2002), the fashion writer Cathy Horyn reported that Long's decision to work with James, who was notoriously malicious, caustic, and insulting, stemmed from his "real reverence for history." As Paul Rudnick told Horyn, James "was a piece of history, and just being in the same room [with him] was enough. William's such a fan of outsize personalities—being one himself—that he just enjoys basking in that extravagance." For some years before he opened his own design studio, Long served as the head of design at the Playwrights Horizons Theater School, a professional training facility associated with New York University's Tisch School of the Arts.

The first show for which Long designed costumes, in early 1976, was the mystery *Me Jack, You Jill,* which never officially opened. Two years later he was chosen to design costumes for a revival of Nikolai Gogol's *The Inspector General,* which closed after two months in the fall of 1978. His next project was Walton Jones's musical *The 1940s Radio Hour* (October 1979–January 1980), an expanded version of a summer cabaret show he had worked on at Yale. That was followed by the short-lived comedy *Passions* (September 23–October 5, 1980) and *Mass Appeal* (November 1981–May 1982).

Long won a Tony Award, a Drama Desk Award, and a Maharam Award for best costumes for his creations for the musical *Nine* (May 1982–February 1984), which premiered under the direction of Tommy Tune. With book by Arthur Kopit and music and lyrics by Maury Yeston, *Nine* was based on the classic Federico Fellini film *8 1/2,* about a director named Guido (portrayed on the stage by Raul Julia), who, desperate for ideas for his next movie after three flops in succession, goes to a spa for inspiration. There, in fantastical sequences, he encounters 21 women from his past and present lives, among them his dead mother, his wife, his lover, his favorite actress, and his producer. Long dressed the women in a series of lavishly decorated costumes, with all 21 wearing gowns of the same color or colors in each scene. In a review of the show for the *Washington Post* (May 14, 1982), Richard L. Coe described the all-black costumes of Guido's "wildly assorted females" in the opening scene as "variations of texture, spangles and feathers assembled with striking ingenuity." Brendan Gill, in the *New Yorker* (May 24, 1982), hailed the costumes as "among the most gorgeous I've ever seen." In addition to the hundreds of sewers who constructed all the apparel, the production required the services of an assistant for each of the 21 actresses, to help with costume changes.

In 1989, after a series of jobs for poorly received stage productions—the one exception being the musical comedy *The Tap Dance Kid* (which closed in August 1985 after 669 performances)—Long debuted as a costumier for a film, with garments seen in the made-for-television movie *Ask Me Again.* His next big success came with Ken Ludwig's farce *Lend Me a Tenor* (March 2, 1989–April 22, 1990), which is set in Cleveland, Ohio, in 1934; he won both Drama Desk and Outer Critics Circles Awards and a Tony nomination for his costumes. *Lend Me a Tenor* marked his first collaboration with the director Jerry Zaks. He later worked with Zaks on John Guare's award-winning tragicomedy *Six Degrees of Separation* (November 1990–January 1992), an examination of contemporary attitudes about race, class, wealth, celebrity, manners, and morals told through the story of a young black man who, pretending to be the son of the actor Sidney Poitier, cons his way into the apartment of a striving white New York couple. Long won an Obie Award for his costumes for Stephen Sondheim's poorly received musical *Assassins,* about people who attempted to kill or succeeded in killing American presidents, from John Wilkes Booth, who murdered Abraham Lincoln in 1865, to John Hinckley Jr., who shot Ronald Reagan in 1981. The show closed in February 1991 after only 73 performances.

Long won Tony, Outer Critics Circle, and Dora Awards (the last given for outstanding Canadian theater productions) for his work for the musical comedy *Crazy for You* (February 1992–January 1996), a huge popular success that won much critical acclaim as well. A major reworking of George and Ira Gershwin's *Girl Crazy* (1930), *Crazy for You* contains nearly two dozen classic and lesser-known Gershwin songs, ranging from "I Got Rhythm" and "Embraceable You" to "Slap That Bass" and "Naughty Baby." Retaining the basics of the plot, Ken Ludwig rewrote the book, about a blue-blooded New Yorker who, in an attempt by his mother to change his infatuation with musical comedy into a love of business, lands in Deadrock, Nevada, where, disguised as a Florenz Ziegfeld–like burlesque producer, he reopens the town's moribund theater. Directed by Mike Ockrent and choreographed by Susan Stroman, *Crazy for You* offered a string of highly inventive dances that triggered memories of Busby Berkeley's spectacular 1930s creations, partly because of the chorus girls' dazzling apparel. In a review of what he called this "lavish revamp" of *Girl Crazy*, Jeremy Gerard wrote for *Variety* (February 24, 1992), "No one dresses Broadway dancers more sexily than William Ivey Long."

Long received a Drama Desk Award for his work on the revival of Frank Loesser's 1950 musical, *Guys and Dolls* (April 1992–January 1995), directed by Jerry Zaks. To match the tone of the production and the brightly colored sets, Long designed flamboyant outfits with mixtures of loud patterns and vivid solids for most of the characters. In contrast, one main character, Nathan Detroit (played by Nathan Lane), wore black, and another, Sky Masterson (Peter Gallagher), wore blue. "Oddly enough, the people who were on the periphery, in order to make someone disappear, I would put them in a bright orange suit," Long told an interviewer for Fashion Finds (on-line). "I know that sounds absolutely insane, but because the shadows were bright orange and bright . . . magenta and stuff, those warm/hot colors were the colors I used for disappearing. And it was the contrasting colors that I used to find the people."

During the next two years, Long designed costumes for three additional Zaks-directed shows. The first, *Face Value*, ran only in previews. The second was Neil Simon's *Laughter on the 23rd Floor* (November 1993–August 1994), a memoir of sorts, set in the early 1950s in the room in which Simon and other comedy writers (among them Mel Brooks, Woody Allen, and Larry Gelbart) came up with the material presented in Sid Caesar's weekly television series *Your Show of Shows*. The third joint Long-Zaks venture was the musical revue *Smokey Joe's Café* (March 1995–January 2000), which celebrated "Love Potion Number 9," "Hound Dog," "Yakety Yak," and other 1950s and 1960s rock-and-roll songs by Jerry Leiber and Mike Stoller. Long also provided costumes for brief revivals, in 1994 and 1995, respectively, of William Inge's 1952 drama, *Picnic*, and Stephen Sondheim's 1970 musical, *Company*. He collaborated with Mike Ockrent and Susan Stroman on the musical-comedy version of the hit 1988 movie *Big*, in which a 12-year-old boy is granted his wish to be a grown-up, only to find that adulthood leaves much to be desired. Long's designs included outfits for the many children who appeared in the show. Despite the hype and abundant publicity that surrounded its opening and the $10.3 million invested in it, *Big* closed after only six months (April–October 1996).

Long's next project, a revival of the John Kander–Fred Ebb–Bob Fosse musical *Chicago* that opened in November 1996, proved to be far more successful than *Big* and even much more popular than its original, 1975 mounting. A jaded view of celebrity in the U.S. and the role of the media in its creation, *Chicago* is set in the so-called Roaring '20s, widely associated with the federal ban against alcohol and the plethora of nightclubs that opened as a result, along with lawlessness, corruption, and gangsterism, the growing popularity of jazz, and flapper dress. Long earned his fourth Tony Award nomination for his designs for the characters, who include Roxie Hart and Velma Kelly, murderesses bent on success as nightclub entertainers; their avaricious, amoral lawyer, Billy Flynn; and newspaper reporters, police officers, prison guards, and incarcerated women who double as the chorus. Long's costumes have also been featured in overseas productions of *Chicago*, in Vienna, Melbourne, Stockholm, and London; the last-named mounting earned him an Olivier Award nomination from the Society of London Theatre. As of February 2004 the Broadway production of *Chicago* was still running.

Long designed the clothes for the musical *Steel Pier* (April–June 1997), which was based on a concept of Stroman's and featured her choreography; the musical *King David* (May 1997); and a revival of the historical musical *1776* (August 1997–June 1998). He was also tapped to create clothes for the revival of another Kander–Ebb musical, *Cabaret*, which opened in March 1998 and ran for close to six years. The costumes for *Cabaret* earned him another Tony nomination as well as nominations for the Drama Desk and Outer Critics Circle Awards.

Two shows for which Long served as costume designer opened in early 1999: a revival of the 1946 Herbert and Dorothy Fields–Irving Berlin musical comedy, *Annie Get Your Gun* (which ran until September 2001), and Frank Wildhorn's original musical *The Civil War* (which closed after a few months). Unlike earlier mountings of *Annie Get Your Gun,* which is about the celebrated markswoman Annie Oakley, the 1999 production was presented as a show within a show. Operating under the conceit that the actors all represented members of Buffalo Bill's Wild West Show, Long created for each performer a so-called unit costume, "which could be adapted for each scene, and which is designed to look as if it came out of a 19th-century theatrical touring trunk," as David Barbour wrote for *Entertainment Design* (July 1999). Many of the costumes were made in part from hand-tooled leather, and, since the members of the Wild West Show included performers of many nationalities, Long hinted at each character's ethnicity in his or her garments.

For *The Civil War,* Long tried to create authentic-looking clothing. "I was very determined that this not be Broadway," he told Barbour. As he recalled to Barbour, he told the director, Jerry Zaks, "We need to make the Mathew Brady photographs [of the Civil War] come alive." In addition to having military uniforms made from a specially woven heavy wool often used for costumes in Civil War reenactments, Long employed "a very limited palette of earth tones," as Barbour wrote. "One of the most striking costumes is worn by actress Beth Leavel, as a mother who loses all her sons in the war," Barbour continued. "She is dressed in a severe wool mourning crepe dress worn over a bone corset taken from an authentic pattern. The dress features a cameo brooch carved in black, with a frame of black gunmetal."

Long next worked on the Zaks-directed, short-lived farce *Epic Proportions* (1999), about the making in the 1930s of an over-the-top biblical film. He designed both 1930s daywear and biblical garments; for the latter, he and his assistants attempted to capture the look of the costumes in such Hollywood spectaculars as *The Sign of the Cross, The 10 Commandments, The Robe, Ben-Hur*, and two versions of *Cleopatra*. "We didn't want the costumes to be funny. We wanted the way they were worn to be funny," Long told David Barbour for *Entertainment Design* (January 2000). Barbour wrote of one character's dress, "Part ancient Egypt, part *Dinner at Eight* [a 1933 Hollywood melodrama] . . . [it] slyly parodies the not-very-accurate costumes of vintage historical films."

After lending his talents to the musical *Swing!* (December 1999–January 2001) and the film *Curtain Call* (1999), Long again worked with Susan Stroman, this time on her highly original so-called dance play, *Contact* (March 1999–September 2002), a collaboration with the writer John Weidman. The play, whose narrative was conveyed through dance and minimal dialogue rather than song, consists of three vignettes, each requiring a different style of clothing. The first, "Swinging," is based on the Jean-Honoré Fragonard painting *The Swing* (1768), in which an aristocratic young woman dressed in a frilly, billowing dress swings exuberantly in a verdant grove, while her lover, barely visible in the shadows, appears to look right up her dress; for that piece, Long re-created the outfits in the painting (and one for a second man), using fabrics imported from London. In the second story, "Did You Move?," the main character, the wife of an abusive mobster, escapes reality in ever-wilder fantasies in which she is a ballerina; Long designed a polyester floral-print dress for her, to fit the setting: a garish 1950s New York City diner. His biggest challenge came in the third section of the show, "Contact," in which a despondent adman abandons thoughts of suicide after dancing with a mysterious woman wearing a canary-yellow dress (played by Deborah Yates) whom he meets at an after-hours club. The first eight dresses he designed proved to be unsatisfactory, some for technical reasons: they tore during the strenuous dance moves, or became wet with perspiration, or were too slippery to enable the male dancers to grip Yates firmly during lifts. Some were inadequate "spiritually," as Long put it, according to the *Broadway in Boston*

Web site: "Spiritually it was that the dress was too short, or the fabric didn't have enough magic to it or the length was too high." He continued, "We started with one that was filmy, floaty and very ethereal and we ended with a totally controlled, form-fitting lady-like womanly dress. One that hides nothing but hides everything." Deborah Yates said, according to the same Web site, that when she put on the ninth dress, "I felt it was perfect. It's feminine. It's strong. It's striking. It's alive. It's elegant." Images of the "girl with the yellow dress," as she came to be known, appeared widely, not only in ads but also on coffee mugs, mousepads, and other items. Long won an American Theatre Wing Hewes Design Award for his *Contact* costumes.

Long earned Tony nominations in 2000 and 2001, respectively, for his designs for two additional Stroman-choreographed and -directed productions: a revival of Meredith Willson's 1957 hit musical, *The Music Man* (April 2000–December 2001), and *The Producers*, the hugely successful musical adaptation of Mel Brooks's 1968 comic film of the same name. *The Producers* is about an over-the-hill impresario who enlists his neurotic accountant in a scheme to bilk investors by mounting what he thinks is a sure-to-fail musical called "Springtime for Hitler"; the show turns out to be a big hit, and the producer and his accountant wind up in jail. Long's challenges included the creation of laughable Nazi uniforms and outfits for a Hitler impersonator who is meant to seem ridiculous. Other characters include a costume designer, whose clothing includes a lavender suit and scarf, and the outrageously inept gay director of "Springtime for Hitler," who at one point appears in a silver beaded dress reminiscent of the Chrysler Building. Long won another Tony for his efforts, as well as a Drama Desk Award and an Outer Critics Circle Award. *The Producers*, which opened in April 2001, was still running in November 2004.

Also still running was the next megahit that benefitted from Long's creativity, the musical *Hairspray*, based on John Waters's 1988 film of that name. The show, which premiered on August 15, 2002 to critical raves, illuminates aspects of the death throes of segregation in 1960s Baltimore through the story of two rival dancers on an *American Bandstand*–style TV show for teens. To gather ideas for the more than 100 costumes needed, Long visited many New York City thrift shops and pored through magazines and clothing catalogues from the late 1950s and early 1960s. "When I do what I call 'previously owned vehicles,' meaning from a film, I ask the director if we are going to be inspired by, or should we not look at, the movie," he told David Caplan for *Women's Wear Daily* (July 17, 2002). With *Hairspray*, "there was a general sense of 'no, we are different from the film, but we want you to have a look at it.' So I purchased the movie and I watched it a total of once and I thought, 'OK, I have committed this to memory. If I watch it twice, I will not be able to be creative.'"

Long won his fourth Tony Award, a Drama Desk Award, and an Outer Critics Circle Award for his designs. Critics who remarked on them included David Denby, who wrote for the *New Yorker* (September 2, 2000), "William Ivey Long's costumes transport the audience to the deepest, gaudiest teen America, in the year 1962," and Orla Swift, who wrote for the Raleigh, North Carolina, *News & Observer* (June 10, 2003), "If costumes were eye candy, Long's would be Jolly Ranchers, tart and boldly colored."

More recently, Long served as costume designer for three musicals that opened on Broadway in the fall of 2003: *Little Shop of Horrors*, based on two films and an Off-Broadway play of the same name, about a man-eating plant who promises the hero wealth and love in exchange for a diet of blood; *The Boy from Oz*, about the Australian entertainer Peter Allen; and *Never Gonna Dance*, inspired by the 1936 Fred Astaire–Ginger Rogers film *Swingtime.* He also designed costumes for *Double Feature,* a full-length, two-act ballet choreographed by Susan Stroman for the New York City Ballet, which opened on January 23, 2004; *Valhalla*, a new comedy by Paul Rudnick, which opened Off-Broadway in early February 2004; an adaptation by Ken Ludwig of the 1932 Ben Hecht–Charles MacArthur comedy, *Twentieth Century*, which ran from March 25 to June 6, 2004; *The Frogs*, an adaptation of a comedy written in 405 B.C. by Aristophanes, which ran from July 22 to October 10, 2004; and *La Cage aux Folles*, a revival scheduled to open on Broadway on December 9, 2004.

In addition to his other honors, Long has received the Leslie Cheek Award for Outstanding Presentation in the Arts from William and Mary College (1990), the Roanoke Island Historical Association's Morrison Award (1992), the UNC-Chapel Hill Playmakers Award (1994), the Medal of Honor in the Arts from Winthrop University, in Rock Hill, South Carolina (2002), and the Legend of Fashion Award from the School of the Art Institute in Chicago (2003). He was named "Person of the Year" by the National Theatre Conference in 2000. In 2001 he became a member of the Order of the Long Leaf Pine, which honors people with an outstanding record of service to North Carolina.

Long, who is gay, owns a brownstone in the Chelsea section of the New York City borough of Manhattan; part of the building houses his design studio. He also owns two old farmhouses, one on his family's property in Seaboard, North Carolina, and the other in western Massachusetts, both of which he has restored. In his leisure time he enjoys reading biographies and history.

—K.E.D.

Suggested Reading: *Christian Science Monitor* Features p13 Aug. 29, 2003; *Los Angeles Times* Sunday Calendar p44 Oct. 26, 2003, with photos; (New York) *Daily News* p46 Oct. 2, 2003, with photos; *New York Times* B p8 July 30, 2002, with photos; *Virginian-Pilot* E p1 July 21, 2003, with photos; *Vogue* p116+ May 1992, with photo; *William and Mary Alumni Magazine* (online) Spring/Summer 2003, with photo

---

Ludacris

Sep. 11, 1977– Rapper

Address: c/o Def Jam Records, 825 Eighth Ave., 19th Fl., New York, NY 10019

Hailing from Atlanta, Georgia, one of a number of southern hip-hop artists to burst onto the music scene in the new millennium, Ludacris is often referred to, along with others, as a "Dirty South" rapper. "Dirty" is particularly apt in the case of Ludacris's songs, which are rife with sexual references and peppered with violent imagery, features that have caused parental advisory warnings to be placed on his albums. "His roar never fades, and his tongue never ceases," Ken Capobianco wrote for the *Boston Globe* (February 27, 2004) about the rapper. "Over the course of three records Ludacris has been one of the loudest—and most prominent—voices in the hip-hop world due to a bravado that just won't quit. He's lewd, rude, never subdued, and mighty proud of it. His vibrant, hot-wired raps have caused a ruckus, and his raucous rants have transformed the former radio DJ into a lightning rod who has generated controversy for his ribald style and persona." Backing up his braggadocio, Ludacris has made three multiplatinum albums, or albums that have sold millions of copies each: *Back for the First Time* (2000), *Word of Mouf* (2001), and *Chicken-N-Beer* (2003). He has also released, sometimes in collaboration with other recording artists, several Top 10 singles—"What's Your Fantasy," "Roll Out (My Business)," and "Stand Up," among them—and earned more than a half-dozen Grammy Award nominations. In *Rolling Stone* (November 13, 2003, on-line), Toure praised him as "one of the most liquid MCs in the game today. He varies his flows with such dexterity and has so much musicality in his tones that his mouth truly seems like an instrument. . . . He's cocksure, witty and just hard enough to be taken seriously, but playful enough to be pop." On the subject of the name Ludacris, the rapper, born Christopher Bridges, told *Ebony* magazine (August 2003), "The name comes from the way I describe my music, and the fact that my first name is Chris. Ludacris means crazy & wild and ridiculous. My music is a little fun in people's lives." For an article posted to the MTV Web site (August 4, 2003), he said to Corey Moss and Joseph Patel that for him,

Jamie Squire/Getty Images

Ludacris

rap is "all about emotion. So you talk about the good times, the bad times." In his music, he added, "you're gonna hear it all, man, things you wouldn't expect."

The rapper was born in Champaign, Illinois, on September 11, 1977. At the time his parents were attending the University of Illinois at Champaign, and he spent several of his earliest years on the school's campus. "I felt like I was a part of the college crowd because they were the kinds of parents that would tug me along with them to certain places," Ludacris told Mark Guarino for the Chicago *Daily Herald* (February 27, 2004). "They would take me to some parties sometimes with them, even house parties . . . because I didn't have a babysitter . . . and I would wake up every morning to music." His parents were fans of such performers as Frankie Beverly, Maze, James Brown, and Michael Jackson.

Ludacris began rapping and composing rhymes at an early age. He recalled to Guarino that he was encouraged by "kids in the fourth grade," who "started giving me feedback on my own music and wanted me to keep rapping." In addition, hip-hop–oriented movies such as *Krush Groove*, *Beat Street*, and *Breakin*, along with the music of the rap legends Run DMC and LL Cool J, inspired him. When he was 12 years old he joined a Chicago-based rap crew called the Loudmouth Hooligans; he gave himself the name Ludacris at around the same time. On the Web site abstracts.net, the rapper is quoted as using words with traditionally negative connotations to describe himself, as rappers often do: "The nickname [Ludacris] is something I made up. I have kind of a split personality—part of me is cool and collected, while the other side is just be-

yond crazy. My lyrics are ludicrous, my live shows are ludicrous—ludicrous like off the chain crazy." (Other examples of the hip-hop world's tradition of transforming connotations include the positive use of the words "ill," "fat," and "nasty.")

When Ludacris was around 13, his family relocated to the Atlanta, Georgia, area. While attending Banneker High School, in College Park, Georgia, Ludacris and his friends often engaged in verbal sparring contests, akin to rapping, during lunch time—often to the exclusion of actual eating. He continued to hone his skill at wordplay while attending Georgia State University, in Atlanta, where he studied music management. During that time, looking to try out his rhymes on audiences, Ludacris often went to open-microphone nights at local clubs, where anyone willing could take the stage and perform.

Ludacris's fortunes took a favorable turn when he landed an internship at the popular Atlanta radio station Hot 97.5, which featured rap and R&B music. He performed his catchy rhymes during the station's promotional spots and was eventually offered a job as a co-host, alongside Poon Daddy, on the station's nighttime segment *Future Flavors*. That development brought Ludacris, who called himself Chris Luva Luva for purposes of the segment, to the attention of Atlanta's hip-hop community. "Once I got the internship up at that radio station things kinda started going real quick . . . ," the rapper recalled for abstracts.net. "I started meeting a lot of people and getting contacts and trying to be in the studio with all kinds of artists and, you know, one thing led to another." He saved enough money from his job at Hot 97.5 to finance the recording of his first album, *Incognegro* (2000), which he released on his own, newly created label, Disturbing Tha Peace Entertainment. The song "What's Your Fantasy" from *Incognegro* became a local radio hit, helping the album to sell 30,000 copies and earning Ludacris attention from major record labels, including Def Jam Records—whose president, Scarface, signed Ludacris to a contract. The top-drawer record producers Timbaland, Jermaine Dupri, and Organized Noize remixed *Incognegro*, which Def Jam released in October 2000 under the title *Back for the First Time*. By December of that same year the album had gone platinum, meaning it had sold at least one million copies. In a review for amazon.com, Kenji Jasper wrote that on *Back for the First Time* Ludacris gives listeners a "variety of contrasting styles and musical feels. . . . No gimmicks. Funny skits. Moving music." By February 2001 the album's track "What's Your Fantasy" had entered the Top 10 of *Billboard* magazine's hip-hop and rap charts. The song "Southern Hospitality" became a hit as well and broke into the Top 40 songs listed on *Billboard*'s charts. Commenting on the immediate success of Ludacris's first album, Ken Capobianco wrote that the rapper's talent was "raw, but you could hear an MC finding his voice. Very little hip-hop had the audacity, immediacy, and nutty charm that Ludacris was bringing." In the summer of 2001, "Loverboy," a remix of Mariah Carey's hit song that Ludacris performed with the female hip-hop star Da Brat, topped *Billboard*'s R&B/Hip-Hop Singles & Tracks chart for two weeks. Also in 2001 Ludacris contributed vocals to Missy Elliott's popular single "One Minute Man." In the fall of that year, the rapper released his second album, *Word of Mouf*, which sold more than a million copies within several months. By year's end both *Back for the First Time* and *Word of Mouf* had achieved triple-platinum status. In a review of *Word of Mouf* for *Entertainment Weekly* (December 7, 2001), Tom Sinclair compared Ludacris to the ribald comedians Redd Foxx and Rudy Ray Moore, writing, "There's some marvelously inventive sexual/sexist wordplay here (most of which, sadly, cannot be reprinted in a family magazine); if you're inured to hip-hop's relentless conflation of sex and thuggery, you'll view [some of the lyrics] as good, dirty fun. If you're not—well, buying this album would simply be ludicrous."

Word of Mouf generated a number of hit singles, including "Roll Out (My Business)," which reached *Billboard*'s Top 10, and "Saturday (Oooh Oooh!)," which climbed into the Top 40. In February 2002 Ludacris was nominated for two Grammy Awards, one for best rap album, for *Back for the First Time*, and the other for best rap/sung collaboration, for the single "Area Codes," which was featured on Def Jam's soundtrack to the movie *Rush Hour 2* (2002) and on which the rapper Nate Dogg also performed.

Along with Papa Roach, Xzibit, and the X-ecutioners, Ludacris was part of the hip-hop superstar Eminem's summer 2002 Anger Management Tour. As Ludacris traveled the country for the tour, the music video for his song "Move" reached the top spot on the MTV video countdown. For the 2002 MTV Video Music Awards, at which Ludacris performed as the opening act, the videos for his singles "Saturday (Oooh Oooh!)" and "Area Codes" were nominated for awards—best rap video and best video from a film, respectively—and the video for Missy Elliott's single "One Minute Man," in which Ludacris appeared (he had also contributed vocals to the song), was nominated for six awards. That same year Ludacris teamed up with his Atlanta-based rap crew, Disturbing Tha Peace, to record the album *Golden Grain*. The group includes Tity Boi, Shawnna, I-20, and Lil' Fate. Jon Caramanica, writing for *Rolling Stone* (October 17, 2002), gave their effort a mixed review, observing that Ludacris's talents as a "commanding, original MC" made his "Disturbing Tha Peace associates . . . sound pale and ordinary next to their leader."

In 2002 the soft-drink company PepsiCo, which had earlier signed Ludacris as a pitchman, quickly terminated its relationship with the rapper after the Fox News commentator Bill O'Reilly, echoing comments by other conservative voices, denounced Ludacris on television. As quoted on the Fox News Web site (August 28, 2002), O'Reilly referred to Ludacris as a purveyor of "antisocial nonsense," a "man who is demeaning just about everybody," and "a man [who] espouses violence, degrading sex, and substance abuse." As an example, O'Reilly pointed to the lyrics of Ludacris's single "Move Bitch," which includes the lines, "I'm DUI, hardly ever caught sober, and you about to get ran the [expletive] over. Grab the peels, cuz' we robbin' tonight. Beat the [expletive] outta security. We startin' a fight." On his *Chicken-N-Beer* album Ludacris responded to his critic with the lyrics, "Shout out to Bill O'Reilly, I'm-a throw you a curve / You mad 'cause I'm a thief and got a way with words / I'm-a start my own beverage / It'll calm your nerves." When the giant beer company Anheuser-Busch signed Ludacris as a spokesperson, in early 2004, O'Reilly, along with others, publicly lambasted the decision and kept up the attack on hip-hop and rap music in general and Ludacris in particular.

Meanwhile, despite such controversy, in early 2003 Ludacris was nominated for an American Music Award for favorite hip-hop/rap album, and he earned two more Grammy Award nominations—for best rap album (*Word of Mouf*) and best male rap solo performance ("Roll Out [My Business]")." The video for the single "Move" was nominated that summer for an MTV Video Music Award for best rap video. Several months later Ludacris released his third album, *Chicken-N-Beer,* which sold more than 400,000 units in its first week in stores and topped *Billboard*'s chart of the Top 200 albums as well as its R&B/hip-hop albums chart. *Chicken-N-Beer* has since achieved multi-platinum status. "I can't say that I don't look at record sales because I do," Ludacris told Ken Capobianco. "You want to be respected artistically, but you also want to be heard, and I want to sell as many records as I can before I'm through. Always taking it higher, never resting on what you've done and always looking at how to make the next song hotter than the [last]. Ask any MC, that's how you sell records."

The album's single "Stand Up" stormed its way to number one, reaching the top spot on *Billboard*'s Rap, Hot R&B/Hip-Hop Singles & Tracks, and Hot R&B/Hip-Hop Airplay charts. In late 2003 "Stand Up" also reached number one on *Billboard*'s Hot 100 Singles Sales and Hot 100 Airplay charts. (Fatboy Slim has produced a remixed version of "Stand Up.") "Splash Waterfalls," another track from *Chicken-N-Beer*, also broke into the Top 10 on *Billboard*'s Hot 100 chart. (Because of its sexually explicit nature, the video for "Splash Waterfalls" has been aired by MTV only between the hours of 10: 00 p.m. and 6: 00 a.m.) In addition to those songs, *Chicken-N-Beer* included the tracks "Black Man's Struggle," "P-Poppin," "Blow It Out," and "Hip Hop Quotables," on which he boasts, "By the time you figure out why your record ain't spinnin', I'm in the strip club smokin' with President Clinton." For the Web site shaking-through.net, which offers commentary on popular culture, Kevin Forest Moreau wrote, "There's no denying that part of [Ludacris's] appeal lies in his audacity. But it's fair to say that he doesn't need to pander so fully to the lowest common denominator, to his own spoiling-for-a-fight id, to the garish extent that he does on his third full-length, *Chicken-N-Beer.* . . . When he strikes the right balance of mischievous charm, rapid-fire wit and genial bravado, Ludacris proves why he's at the top of his game. But *Chicken-N-Beer* too often flashes us threatening glimpses of a less-likable persona behind the avuncular veneer." Writing for *Rolling Stone* (November 13, 2003, on-line), Toure also gave the album a mixed review: "A great style doesn't always equal a great album, and the world's illest flows can't rescue some of these dud beats. . . . *Chicken-N-Beer* is usually entertaining, though."

In early 2004 Ludacris earned more Grammy Award nominations for his work, though once again the rapper went home empty-handed. The nominations were in the categories of best rap performance by a duo or group, for his collaboration with Missy Elliott on the single "Gossip Folks"; best male rap solo performance, for "Stand Up"; and best song written for a motion picture, television, or other visual media, for "Act a Fool," which Ludacris wrote with Keith McMasters and which was featured on the soundtrack to the movie *2 Fast 2 Furious* (2003). (The rapper's music was also featured on the soundtrack to that film's predecessor, *The Fast and the Furious* [2001].) Other movie soundtracks to which Ludacris has contributed include *How High* (2001), *Hollywood Homicide* (2003), *Bad Boys II* (2003), and *Honey* (2003). In addition to lending his musical talents to movies, he has also taken roles in several, including *The Wash* (2001) and *2 Fast 2 Furious*, which grossed more than $125 million at the box office nationwide. He also has a role as a carjacker in the film *Crash*, which co-stars Brendan Fraser, Don Cheadle, Ryan Philippe, Sandra Bullock, and Matt Dillon and is scheduled for release in 2005. On television Ludacris has appeared on the annual MTV Video Music Awards, in 2001, 2002, and 2003; the second annual BET Awards, in 2002; the series *Hard Rock Live*, in 2003; the MTV Movie Awards in 2003; and late-night talk shows such as *The Tonight Show with Jay Leno* and *The Late Late Show with Craig Kilborn*.

Ludacris has collaborated with many other hip-hop and rap artists. He teamed up with Jermaine Dupri on the song "Welcome to Atlanta," on Dupri's album *Instructions*; the single made its way into *Billboard*'s Top 40. He performed with Snoop Dogg and Chingy—the latter a Ludacris protégé whose debut album, *Jackpot*, has sold more than two million copies—on the single "Holidae In." His collaboration with Usher on the song "Yeah" was a tremendous success, as the song went to number one on *Billboard*'s Hot 100 and Hot R&B/Hip-Hop Singles & Tracks charts. Ludacris

also raps on Twista's single "Higher." His contribution to the hip-hop all-star compilation *The Goodlife Album* (2001), the track "Fatty Girl," on which LL Cool J and Keith Murray also performed, was one of the record's hits.

Ludacris continues to head his own record label as well as the rap group of the same name, Disturbing Tha Peace; in February 2004 Disturbing Tha Peace embarked on a nationwide tour. Regarding live performances, Ludacris told Shaheem Reid for the VH1 Web site (February 25, 2004), "You don't want a dull moment. You try to hit [the audience] as much as you can. If you have a certain amount of songs, you might do one or two verses and then switch up. You never really want to tire the crowd out." Concerning opposition to Ludacris and Disturbing Tha Peace's live appearances, by conservative organizations and even white-supremacy groups such as the National Alliance, the rapper told Reid, "Ain't nothing new to us. We've had opposition in a lot of places over the past four years, so [recent incidents] ain't no surprise." Ludacris's next album, *The Red Light District*, was due to be released in December 2004.

The rapper has established the Ludacris Foundation, a nonprofit outreach program dedicated to helping underprivileged youths in the Atlanta area. As part of the contract settlement between Ludacris and Pepsi, the soft-drink company agreed to donate several million dollars to the Ludacris Foundation. Ludacris has described himself as a fan of rock music, in particular the work of the groups Puddle of Mudd, Linkin Park, and Staind. The rapper is depicted as a wrestler in the Entertainment Arts video game *Def Jam Vendetta*.

Ken Capobianco reported that Ludacris has seven different homes around the country. "I have three in Atlanta, two in Miami, one in LA, and one in New York," the rapper told Capobianco with a smile. "Sounds kind of funny, but they all serve a purpose. Those are the towns that I live in most, and I like different kinds of surroundings sometimes."

—C.F.T.

Suggested Reading: *Boston Globe* C p12 Feb. 27, 2004, with photo; (Chicago) *Daily Herald* p5 Feb. 27, 2004, with photo; *Entertainment Weekly* p102 Dec. 7, 2001, with photo; MTV.com; rockonthenet.com; VH1 Web site

Selected Recordings: *Back for the First Time*, 2000; *Word of Mouf*, 2001; *Golden Grain* (with Disturbing Tha Peace); *Chicken-N-Beer*, 2003; *The Red Light District*, 2004

Peter Kramer/Getty Images

Ludwig, Ken

1950– Playwright; lawyer

Address: Steptoe & Johnson, 1330 Connecticut Ave., N.W., Washington, DC 20036-1704

The playwright Ken Ludwig's specialty is farce—in particular, farce that pokes fun at the entertainment world and its denizens. Slapstick and other forms of lowbrow physical humor, groan-inducing puns, mistaken identities, ridiculous mixups, belief-defying coincidences, larger-than-life, stereotypical characters, over-the-top behavior, frenetic action, and other screwball elements abound in such Ludwig plays as *Moon Over Buffalo*, *Twentieth Century*, and *Lend Me a Tenor*, the last of which earned a bevy of prizes. Ludwig is also the author of the book for the immensely successful, multi–award-winning musical *Crazy for You*, which ran for years not only on Broadway but also in theaters in London, England; Toronto, Canada; and Tokyo, Japan. Among his other works are *Sullivan and Gilbert*, *Leading Ladies*, *Shakespeare in Hollywood*, and the book for *The Adventures of Tom Sawyer*. An attorney as well, he has been associated with the prestigious corporate-law firm Steptoe & Johnson since 1976. Ludwig told Liza Mundy in an interview for the *Washington Post* (September 7, 1988), "I write plays because I have an urgent need to write them. I care about the structure, I care about the form, I get a great deal of satisfaction from that. And they're autobiographical in funny little ways. And then, what I hope is that the work will move people, touch them, make them laugh, make them see themselves in ways that touch their lives." He also told Mundy that, to him,

comedy is "serious." "The plays are serious," he said; "they have important things to say about my life, about what I think about life, about how life should be led, about the surprises and adventures that life has to offer." "I suppose I'll go to my grave with critics hounding me, saying, 'He wrote light commercial junk. This was not Art' . . . ," he told William F. Powers for the *Washington Post* (May 28, 1995). "But I suppose a lot of people will say, 'I sure went to the theater and got a lot out of watching his work.'"

Kenneth David Ludwig was born in 1950 in York, Pennsylvania, where he grew up. His older brother, Eugene "Gene" Ludwig, a lawyer, served as the nation's comptroller of the currency during the administration of President Bill Clinton; he currently heads a financial/economic consulting firm, the Promontory Group. Ludwig's father, Jacob, was a dermatologist, and his mother, Louise, a graphic-arts dealer. Before her marriage the Brooklyn-born Louise had been a showgirl and had performed on Broadway; once a year or so, when the Ludwigs visited her parents in New York City, they would attend a show there as well. Ken Ludwig treasures a program signed for him by the actor Cyril Ritchard, whom he met backstage as a six-year-old in 1957, when Ritchard was appearing in Gore Vidal's play *Visit to a Small Planet*. The young Ken also enjoyed listening to the family's large vinyl-record collection of "original cast" albums of musicals.

During his teens Ludwig appeared in productions mounted by students at his school, York Suburban High School. As an undergraduate at Haverford College, in Haverford, Pennsylvania, he majored in both English literature and music theory and composition. He wrote several musicals for the campus drama groups at Haverford and nearby Bryn Mawr College and performed onstage as well. When he told his parents that he wanted to pursue a career in playwriting, they urged him to consider, as a backup, a profession that would provide a steadier source of income. Accepting their advice, he decided to follow in the footsteps of his brother and become an attorney. After he graduated from Haverford, with a B.A. degree, magna cum laude, in 1972, he entered Harvard Law School, in Cambridge, Massachusetts. He took a break to study at Trinity College, a division of Cambridge University, in England. While in Great Britain, he attended several plays a week, in London, Stratford, and elsewhere. He earned an LL.B. (bachelor of laws) degree from Cambridge in 1975. He then returned to Harvard, where he received a J.D. degree in 1976.

That year Ludwig moved to Washington, D.C., renting an apartment in the same complex in which his brother lived. He became a member of the bar and gained employment with the law firm Steptoe & Johnson. There, he broadened his expertise in international law and also became a specialist in publishing law, entertainment law, and intellectual property rights. "I get enormous satisfaction out of the law . . . ," Ludwig told Liza Mundy in 1988, to explain why he continued to practice law after achieving success in the theater. "I come in here, and clients who've become friends have real, specific problems that they need solved. It's very, very satisfying to be able to use skills that I've learned over the years, and to have a specialty, a special area where I really help them." In the meantime, Ludwig continued his playwriting at home. He would wake up at 4:00 a.m., shower and make coffee, and sit down to write by 4:30. Four hours later he would leave for his law office. When he completed a play, he would send it to regional theaters and directors in the hope of having it produced.

In the late 1970s Ludwig's play *Divine Fire*, about the 12th-century lovers Abelard and Heloise, was mounted in a church in Washington; a year later it opened Off-Broadway. Over the next few years, several more of his plays were produced regionally or Off-Broadway, among them *Postmortem*, a murder mystery about the real-life actor William Gillette, who portrayed Sherlock Holmes on stage for decades; and *Joy in Mudville*, a comedy about baseball. During that period Ludwig reduced his hours at Steptoe & Johnson; he would write at home until about midday before going to his job. By the end of 1986, he had become "of counsel" to the firm, meaning that, while representing such clients as authors, publishers, theaters, the estate of a prominent artist, and a cable-TV station, he did so as a consultant rather than as an associate. (As of late October 2004, his name was still on Steptoe & Johnson's on-line list of attorneys.)

The change in Ludwig's law-firm title followed a huge boost to his playwriting career, which occurred after a copy of his farce *Lend Me a Tenor* landed in the hands of the celebrated British theatrical composer and producer Andrew Lloyd Webber. Webber eagerly produced the play, which premiered in March 1986 at the Globe Theatre in London. In *Lend Me a Tenor*, which is set in 1934, Saunders, the buffoonish manager of a Cleveland, Ohio, opera house, must find a spur-of-the-moment replacement for Tito Merelli, a womanizing, supremely egotistical tenor known as Il Stupendo, after the singer becomes incapacitated hours before he was scheduled to perform the title role in Verdi's *Otello*. Other characters include Saunders's nerdy gofer, Max, who steps in for Merelli with the intention of fooling the audience into thinking that *he* is the world-famous tenor; Merelli's long-suffering, fiery wife; a wily, celebrity-worshiping bellhop; and the nymphomaniacal soprano cast as Desdemona. A success with both audiences and critics in London, *Lend Me a Tenor* was nominated for an Olivier Award for best comedy of 1986.

On March 2, 1989 *Lend Me a Tenor* opened at the Royale Theater, in New York City, where it proved to be even more popular and earned much critical acclaim. In an assessment for the *New York Post* (March 3, 1989), Clive Barnes wrote, "The nut-tiness of a farce can be very sweet, and if you are feeling under the weather—or even over the weather, for that matter—and you believe that manic laughter is the best medicine, let me prescribe for you [*Lend Me a Tenor*, a] lovely dose of pure, operatic idiocy. . . . Ludwig is a writer who will descend to any depths for a good laugh . . . but his real skill is a gift for farcical situations." Some critics who enjoyed the play, which Jerry Zaks directed, expressed disappointment that it did not meet their highest standards for successful farce. Among them was John Simon, who wrote for *New York* (March 13, 1989), "The good news about Ken Ludwig's farce . . . is that . . . it is free-flowing, honest-to-goodness, unforced farce; the not so good news is that it is a lot less funny than it ought to be. Mistaken identities, cross-purposes, double entendres of which each party understands only one non-meshing half, doors flying open on mayhem and banging shut on people's noses—all the ingredients are here, knowingly deployed." Similarly, Frank Rich, the reviewer for the *New York Times* (March 3, 1989), wrote, "A farce should be cleverly built, energetically directed and buoyantly acted, but there is one thing it absolutely must be: consistently funny. . . . [*Lend Me a Tenor*] is an impeccable example of how to construct and mount a farce—up to a point. *Lend Me a Tenor* is all things farcical except hilarious. . . . The play looks so much like a prime example of its genre that one is all the more frustrated by the shortage of belly laughs." *Lend Me a Tenor*, which ran on Broadway until April 1990, received seven Tony Award nominations, including that for best play, and won two. It also received four Drama Desk and three Outer Critics Circle awards. The play has been translated into 16 languages and staged in some 25 countries.

Earlier, in 1988, another Ludwig play had premiered, at the St. Lawrence Center, in Toronto. Entitled *Sullivan and Gilbert*, it offers glimpses of both the humor and the pathos in the often hostile relations between the composer Arthur Sullivan and the librettist William S. Gilbert. Universally referred to as Gilbert and Sullivan rather than the reverse, the two created such classic, immensely popular 19th-century operettas as *H.M.S. Pinafore*, *The Pirates of Penzance*, *The Mikado*, and *The Yeoman of the Guard*. They also had bitter feuds, one of which led to a lawsuit in which Sullivan sued Gilbert over the latter's purchase of a carpet for the theater they owned; in their last years they never spoke to each other. Ludwig's play shows the men, along with members of the Savoyards, the company that performed their works, at the final dress rehearsal of a (fictional) revue of their music, which Queen Victoria plans to attend. In a review for *Maclean's* (July 18, 1988), John Bemrose wrote that Ludwig had portrayed Gilbert and Sullivan "at their argumentative best (or worst). . . . The dramatic parts . . . are capable of provoking everything from loud guffaws to sentimental tears. But what gives the show its horn-piping exuberance is the songs, written by the battling masters themselves."

Shortly after *Lend Me a Tenor* opened in New York, the theatrical producer Elizabeth Williams approached Ludwig to write the book for an updated version of *Girl Crazy*, the 1930 musical by George and Ira Gershwin. (According to some sources, representatives of the Gershwin estate made the proposal to him.) The Gershwins' original script dismayed Ludwig. "All those musicals' books of the '20s and '30s were awful, but *Girl Crazy* seemed to me the awfullest of all!" he told Kevin Kelly for the *Boston Globe* (August 3, 1989). "It was dumb, silly beyond silly. And full of ethnic humor that wasn't funny at all. I decided I'd have to rewrite from scratch." *Crazy for You,* as the musical was renamed, contains Gershwin songs from both *Girl Crazy* and other shows, ranging from such classics as "Someone to Watch Over Me," "I Got Rhythm," and "But Not for Me" to such lesser-known songs as "Slap That Bass" and "Naughty Baby." In Ludwig's reworking of the story, an upper-class young man from New York City arrives in Deadrock, Nevada, where, in a plan hatched by his mother, he is supposed to immerse himself in business dealings—specifically, foreclosing on the town's moribund theater—so that a passion for commerce will supplant his love for musical theater. Instead, he fuels his infatuation with show business by pretending to be a producer and reviving the house. Directed by Mike Ockrent (who has also been described as the musical's co-conceiver, along with Ludwig) and choreographed by Susan Stroman, *Crazy for You* premiered on Broadway on February 19, 1992 and was greeted by rave reviews. Among them was that of Jack Kroll, who wrote for *Newsweek* (March 2, 1992), "It took a lot of smarts to create a gloriously mindless musical like *Crazy for You.* That's a salute, not a put-down. The concept . . . is brilliant. . . . Ludwig has taken the [Gershwins'] silly book . . . and mutated it into something so transcendentally absurd that it becomes pure joy." Frank Rich expressed similar sentiments in the *New York Times* (February 20, 1992): "When future historians try to find the exact moment at which Broadway finally rose up to grab the musical back from the British, they just may conclude that the revolution began last night. The shot was fired at the Shubert Theater, where a riotously entertaining show called *Crazy for You* uncorked the American musical's classic blend of music, laughter, dancing, sentiment and showmanship with a freshness and confidence rarely seen during the *Cats* decade"—a reference to Andrew Lloyd Webber's musical *Cats,* which opened in New York in 1982 and ran for 18 years. *Crazy for You* won three Tonys, among them the award for best book of a musical, and was nominated for six others. It ran for almost four years, closing after 1,622 performances.

Ludwig's next play, *Moon Over Buffalo,* opened on Broadway in 1995. It starred Philip Bosco and Carol Burnett (who made her return to Broadway in the production, after an absence of 30 years) as George and Charlotte Hay, a middle-aged, second-

or third-rate acting couple who still long for stardom. The play follows Charlotte and George as they prepare to give a performance at a theater in Buffalo, New York. Over the course of a day, Charlotte discovers that George has gotten a young actress pregnant; he responds to Charlotte's ensuing rage by bingeing on alcohol. Then the couple receives word that the Hollywood director Frank Capra is coming to that evening's performance and is considering casting George in one of his films. Meanwhile, the Hays and all the other members of the cast are divided about which particular play is to be performed that night. *Moon Over Buffalo* received mostly lukewarm reviews (but ran for nine months, thus lasting for a full theater season, longer than 80 percent of the nonmusicals that opened on Broadway in 1995–96). In a representative assessment for the *New York Times* (October 2, 1995), Vincent Canby complained that the work seemed "unfinished." "The awful truth is that *Moon Over Buffalo* has only a couple of real payoffs," he wrote; "mostly it's the spectacle of Ms. Burnett, Mr. Bosco and a cast of energetic farceurs trying desperately to make good on the playwright's I.O.U." Canby also commended Ludwig, however, describing him as "one of those comparatively rare contemporary playwrights who thinks in terms of old-fashioned, knockabout farce. That's something to be cherished and nourished."

With the permission of Ludwig and others, the documentarians D. A. Pennebaker and Chris Hedges had filmed the production of *Moon Over Buffalo*. The resulting movie, called *Moon Over Broadway* (1997), struck Janet Maslin, writing for the *New York Times* (February 18, 1998), as a "tribute to euphemism, spin, flop sweat and culture clash." Eavesdropping on many of those involved with the mounting of *Moon Over Buffalo, Moon Over Broadway* shows some of them bemoaning the paucity of laugh-out-loud jokes in the script, and Ludwig complaining about Burnett's attempts to enliven the dialogue. "This is the pact you make with the devil in the modern theater!" the playwright declares. "You need a star to sell tickets." "*Moon Over Broadway* proves that a life in the theater is not for the faint of heart and that it's a freaking miracle any play makes it to opening night," Andrea Chase wrote for *Movie Magazine International* (April 8, 1998, on-line). Commenting on the many changes in dialogue that are made during rehearsals, Ludwig told Ann Geracimos for the *Washington Times* (August 21, 2003, on-line), "A lot of my work gets done when I get to hear it aloud."

For his next project, Ludwig collaborated with the composer and lyricist Don Schlitz to create a musical version of Mark Twain's *The Adventures of Tom Sawyer*. The show, bearing the same name and directed by Scott Ellis, opened at the Minskoff Theater, in New York City, on April 26, 2001. In general, while reviewers reacted favorably to the acting, the set design, and the costumes, they found the show seriously deficient, because of a childish script and unappealing songs and choreography. Bruce Weber, for example, in the *New York Times* (April 27, 2001), wrote that while the book "does a nifty job of condensing [Twain's] novel, maintaining its episodic character but cleverly joining elements from different scenes to keep the narrative bobbing along," and might appeal to both children and adults, "the tame, middle-of-the-road show . . . feels muddled and torn." Weber left the theater with "the nagging sense that the show never aspires to real creativity, merely to achieve the lowest level of acceptability, to be good enough to engage those new to Broadway but not better than that." Although John Simon, in *New York* (May 7, 2001), noted that "shows have been known to make it on less," *The Adventures of Tom Sawyer* closed after only 21 performances.

The year 2003 saw the premieres of two plays by Ludwig. The first, the high comedy *Shakespeare in Hollywood*, was commissioned by the Royal Shakespeare Company of Great Britain, which, after its completion, declined to produce it. ("Internal political changes" at the company was the reason, its dramaturge, Simon Reade, told William Triplett for the *Washington Post* [August 24, 2003, on-line]). Instead, *Shakespeare in Hollywood* debuted at the Arena Stage, in Washington, D.C., under the direction of Kyle Donnelly. The action takes place on the set of Max Reinhardt's movie version of Shakespeare's *A Midsummer Night's Dream* (1935), one of the few films (and the only one made in the U.S.) by the real-life Reinhardt (1873–1943), a brilliant theatrical director. Chaos ensues after Puck (played by Emily Donahoe) and Oberon (Casey Biggs), two of the characters from Shakespeare's play, magically appear in the form of flesh-and-blood humans, joining fictional creations of Ludwig's as well as the playwright's depictions of such actual people as the gossip columnist Louella Parsons, the producer Jack Warner, the actors Joe E. Brown and James Cagney, the actress Olivia de Havilland (renamed Olivia Darnell in the play, because de Havilland is still alive and Ludwig did not want to offend her), and the notorious film censor Will Hays. The production drew a decidedly mixed response from critics, whose descriptions ranged from "hilarious" (Josh Gottlieb-Miller in *Silver Chips Online*) to "amusing" but "essentially a one-joke act that cries out for more clever material" (Paul Harris in *Variety*) to "isn't as funny as it could have been—settling in at about twenty rungs below the worst of Neil Simon's comedies" (Randy Shulman, who, in the Washington, D.C., on-line publication *MetroWeekly*, blamed poor direction in addition to the script).

Ludwig's second play of 2003, *Twentieth Century*, is an adaptation of the 1934 Howard Hawks film, also called *Twentieth Century*, which was written by Ben Hecht and Charles MacArthur and starred John Barrymore and Carole Lombard. (A musical version, called *On the Twentieth Century*, with book by Cy Coleman and music and lyrics by Adolph Green and Betty Comden, was mounted on Broadway in 1978.) Ludwig reduced the number of characters from 30 to 13 and rewrote about 80 percent of the dialogue for his play, which takes place in 1938 aboard the Twentieth Century, the nation's most famous luxury train. As the streamliner speeds toward New York City, Oscar "O.J." Jaffe, a megalomaniacal theatrical producer who is desperate to avoid bankruptcy and determined to return to the big time, resorts to shameless, farcical attempts to re-sign another passenger—the self-absorbed Lily Garland, born Mildred Plotka, Oscar's one-time lover and protégée, who became a Hollywood star after she left him. *Twentieth Century* debuted at the Signature Theatre, in Arlington, Virginia, in August 2003, with Eric Schaeffer directing and James Barbour and Holly Twyford as Oscar and Lily. It opened on Broadway, at the Roundabout Theatre, the following March, in a production directed by Walter Bobbie, with Alec Baldwin and Anne Heche in the leading roles. This work, too, drew mixed reviews. Tracy Lyon, in *Talkin' Broadway* (on-line), in an assessment of the Signature Theatre production, described it as "a well-paced and witty piece that is hugely entertaining," and John Lahr, reviewing the Broadway mounting for the *New Yorker* (April 5, 2004) noted, "As with all fun-house entertainments, we know from the beginning what the outcome will be; it's the clever maneuvering around the hurdles that makes the ride so thrilling." By contrast, Linda Winer, in *Newsday* (March 26, 2004), labeled the Broadway show as "flat and desperate"—"not the stylish funball that would justify" the contributions of "this first-class creative team."

With his recently completed play *Leading Ladies*, Ludwig made his debut as a director. *Leading Ladies*, which premiered at the Cleveland (Ohio) Play House in September 2004, finds two male actors (Brent Barrett and Christopher Duva in the Cleveland staging) posing as women in order to inherit $1 million apiece. Calling the play "a doozy of a cross-dressing comedy," Tony Brown wrote for the *Cleveland Plain Dealer* (September 13, 2004, on-line), "*Leading Ladies* will never be called great literature, and it wisely never pretends to be anything but belly-laugh bait." Brown judged that Ludwig had acquitted himself admirably as a director, writing, "The author has his play operating with laserlike precision. Much to his credit as a word person, some of the funniest moments are visual, not vocal."

In mid-2003 Ludwig was working on a musical commissioned by (or, according to one source, with the permission of) the daughters of Irving Berlin; tentatively titled "Let Yourself Go!," it will be based on music by Berlin. A screenplay that he wrote for the director Frank Oz and Touchstone Pictures, called "All Shook Up," has not yet been produced.

Ludwig is a founding member of the Shakespeare Theatre of Washington, D.C. He has served on committees that evaluate new plays for the National Endowment for the Arts and the Kennedy

Center American College Theater Festival. In 1995 David L. Roll, then the chairman of Steptoe & Johnson, commenting on Ludwig's persona and his plays, told William F. Powers, "He's a sort of preppy type Harvard guy, and you don't expect to see this kind of abject, complete silliness." Ludwig has been married to Adrienne George since 1976. A journalist turned lawyer, his wife is currently a full-time homemaker. The couple live in Washington, D.C., with their two children, Olivia and Jack, who were 11 and seven, respectively, in mid-April 2004.

—H.T.

Suggested Reading: *Boston Globe* Arts & Film p77+ Mar. 13, 1994, with photos; *Lancaster New Era* H p1+ Sep. 8, 1996, with photos; *Los Angeles Times* F p1+ Jan. 21, 1992, with photos; *Washington Post* F p1+ Sep. 7, 1988, with photos, G p1+ May 28, 1995

Selected Plays: *Divine Fire*, 1979; *Lend Me a Tenor*, 1986; *Sullivan & Gilbert*, 1988; *Crazy for You*, 1992; *Moon Over Buffalo*, 1995; *Adventures of Tom Sawyer*, 2001; *Shakespeare in Hollywood*, 2003; *Twentieth Century*, 2003; *Leading Ladies*, 2004

Courtesy of Warren Cowan & Associates

Madsen, Michael

Sep. 25, 1958– Actor

Address: c/o Warren Cowan & Associates, 8899 Beverly Blvd., Suite 919, Los Angeles, CA 90048

"Michael Madsen is a throwback to a bygone era," J. Rentilly wrote for *Razor* magazine (October 2003), "a 6-foot-2 presence that oozes the devilish charm of Steve McQueen and bleeds the tough guy sensitivity of Humphrey Bogart." Madsen, who has acted in more than 90 movies since his debut on the silver screen, in 1982, is best known for his portrayals of violent sociopaths—most famously, the character called Mr. Blonde, in Quentin Tarantino's cult classic *Reservoir Dogs*, in which he slices off the ear of a bound-and-gagged police officer while dancing to the Stealers Wheel's song

"Stuck in the Middle with You." In an interview with Kristine McKenna for the *Los Angeles Times* (February 6, 1994), Tarantino, too, described Madsen as a "throwback," comparing him to Robert Mitchum, Aldo Ray, Lee Marvin, and other actors who served in the military during World War II. "They'd seen life," Tarantino declared, "and most actors today can't fill their shoes—Harvey Keitel, Sean Penn and [Laurence] Fishburne are the only ones I can think of who have that kind of weight, and Michael has it in spades." In such movies as *The Natural*, *Thelma and Louise*, and *Free Willy*, Madsen—who studied acting briefly with John Malkovich at the renowned Steppenwolf Theatre and was cast in a few dramas there—has demonstrated other facets of his acting skills, particularly his ability to convey kindness, empathy, and other qualities not usually associated with demented criminals. With the exceptions of a few other movies, among them *Donnie Brasco*, *Die Another Day*, *Kill Bill: Vol. 1*, and, most recently, *Kill Bill: Vol. 2*, Madsen has appeared in dozens of sub-par, virtually forgotten films—which accounts in large part for his lack of name recognition among the majority of moviegoers. In an interview with the actor Dennis Hopper for *Razor* magazine (October 2003), Madsen said, "I've lent my name to a couple of pictures that I would rather not have been involved in, but I did so in an effort to keep a roof over my family and bacon and eggs on the table, and I learned my lesson the hard way. A lot of people would seek to put your name on the title and promise a lot of things, but at the end of the day, you're a floating head on a bad poster being shopped all over the world. Those days are behind me now and my once-promising career is showing great signs of resurrection." Madsen also writes poetry and stories and has published several books.

The second of three children, Michael Madsen was born on September 25, 1958 in Chicago, Illinois. His father, Cal Madsen, was a fireman; his mother, Elaine Madsen, is a poet, screenwriter, director, and producer. Michael's younger sister is the actress Virginia Madsen, whose credits include the films *Dune* and *Ghosts of Mississippi*. When Madsen was nine, his parents separated; afterward, his mother eked out a living by holding down two jobs simultaneously. Madsen recalled to McKenna that his mother and her children "never lived in the same place for more than a year." Consequently, young Michael changed schools frequently, often in the middle of the year; repeatedly a newcomer, "I tended to hang out with the outsiders, underdogs and losers," as Madsen told McKenna. "They were more interesting to me and I never fit in with the privileged-people scene, so I wound up getting into trouble." He often engaged in dangerous behavior, such as jumping from roofs, and got into many physical fights. At the same time, his mother instilled in him a love of literature and art, in particular the works of the writers Henry Miller, Jack Kerouac, and Ernest Hemingway and the artist Vincent Van Gogh. His father, meanwhile, told him about "people who were burned alive and run over by trains . . . [and] . . . a very violent aspect of life and maybe that's where I first got a taste for danger," as Madsen told McKenna. Madsen also enjoyed watching television and going to the movies; he liked the actor Humphrey Bogart and two films in particular—*Heaven Knows, Mr. Allison*, starring Robert Mitchum and Deborah Kerr, about a marine corporal and a nun stranded on a Pacific island during World War II, and *Lonely Are the Brave*, a modern-day Western starring Kirk Douglas and Walter Matthau.

After high school Madsen took a series of blue-collar jobs, including gas-station attendant and auto mechanic, and for a while he thought seriously of becoming a police officer. One day in 1980, along with a friend, he attended a performance of John Steinbeck's drama *Of Mice and Men* at the Steppenwolf Theatre, in Chicago; the production starred Steppenwolf's co-founders, Gary Sinise and John Malkovich. Soon afterward he enrolled in an acting class with Malkovich. "I didn't get the idea of studying acting, though. I figured if you can do it, then you do it, and if you can't then you can't," he told McKenna. Within the next couple of years, Madsen appeared in Steppenwolf productions of *Of Mice and Men* and Tennessee Williams's *A Streetcar Named Desire*. In 1983 he won a small role in John Badham's film *WarGames*, starring Matthew Broderick. At around that time he relocated to Los Angeles. For nine months he worked at a gas station; during his off-hours, he told McKenna, "I spent most of my time chasing girls, auditioning for parts, working on my motorcycle and meeting people." Before the year was out, he had landed parts in the television series *St. Elsewhere*. In 1984 he was seen briefly in two other TV series—*Cagney & Lacey* and *Miami Vice*—and in the film *Racing with the Moon*, starring Sean Penn and Nicolas Cage.

Madsen raised his profile considerably in the same year, with his portrayal of Bartholomew "Bump" Bailey in the classic sports-fantasy picture *The Natural*, directed by Barry Levinson and starring Robert Redford. Madsen captured the role through Levinson, whom he had met while working on a television pilot based on Levinson's movie *Diner*. Although in *The Natural* he was on screen significantly longer than he had been in his previous movies, Madsen felt disappointed when he saw the finished film, because two major scenes in which he had acted alongside Redford had been cut. "Nobody had the dignity, honesty or respect to let me know," he asserted to McKenna, "and in the long run that was a good thing because it was a slap in the face that wised me up fast to what this business is really like."

Madsen's next major project was the ABC series *Our Family Honor* (1985–86), which featured Eli Wallach and Ray Liotta; the show, about a Mafia-like family named Danzig, was canceled after 15 episodes. During the following half-dozen years, he appeared in other TV series (*The Hitchhiker* in 1985, *Crime Story* several times in 1986, *Tour of Duty* in 1987, *Jake and the Fatman* in 1987, and *Quantum Leap* in 1989) and in such films as *Blood Red* (1986); *The Killing Time* (1987); *Shadows in the Storm* (1988); *Kill Me Again* (1989); Oliver Stone's *The Doors* (1991), about the rock group led by the self-destructive Jim Morrison; and the hugely popular and controversial *Thelma and Louise* (1991), directed by Ridley Scott from a screenplay by Callie Khouri. In the last-named film, in which Geena Davis and Susan Sarandon portrayed the title characters, Madsen—"bringing shades of Elvis Presley to the role," in the words of Janet Maslin in the *New York Times* (May 24, 1991)—depicted Jimmy, Louise's boyfriend, an immature, footloose musician whose empathy for and devotion to Louise surface in the course of the story. Initially Madsen had been tapped to play the would-be rapist whom Louise guns down, thus setting in motion the cross-country chase in which the two heroines attempt to evade the law. The role of Jimmy interested him more, however, and Scott and Sarandon agreed to the casting change at his request. In *Rolling Stone* (April 18, 1991), Peter Travers described Madsen's portrayal of Jimmy as "subtly detailed," and in the *Washington Post* (May 24, 1991), Rita Kempley mentioned the actor as part of the "brilliant male supporting cast" of the film.

Madsen had some misgivings about playing the psychopathic Vic Vega—also known as Mr. Blonde—in Quentin Tarantino's screenwriting and directorial debut, *Reservoir Dogs* (1992), because Mr. Blonde had relatively few lines, and the scene in which he tortures a police officer seemed too similar to the one in *Kill Me Again* in which Madsen's character beats up a man tied to a chair. Critics, however, applauded Madsen's performance in *Reservoir Dogs*, whose plot centers on the aftermath of a jewel heist gone awry, during which the surviving thieves (played by, among others, Harvey Keitel, Chris Penn, Steve Buscemi, Tim Roth, and Tarantino as well as Madsen, with Lawrence Tierney as the organizer of the crime) come into conflict with one another. "One of the discoveries in the movie is Madsen, who has done a lot of acting over the years . . . but here emerges with the kind of really menacing screen presence only a few actors achieve; he can hold his own with the fearsome Tierney, and reminds me a little of a very mean Robert De Niro," Roger Ebert wrote for the *Chicago Sun-Times* (October 26, 1992). In a review for the *Washington Post* (October 23, 1992), Desson Howe wrote, "Madsen is memorably chilling as Mr. Blonde, whose quiet demeanor belies psychotic impulses." Madsen told an interviewer for *Venice* (March 1997), "Face it, I'm going to be the guy who cut off the cop's ear in *Reservoir Dogs* for the rest of my life. . . . I've done twenty-something films . . . and it's always, 'Hey, there's Mr. Blonde!'"

Madsen's next credits include the films *Almost Blue*, *Trouble Bound*, *Beyond the Law*, and *Straight Talk*, in 1992, and *Money for Nothing, Inside Hedge,* and *A House in the Hills*, all in 1993. Also in 1993 he appeared in the well-received *Free Willy*, directed by Simon Wincer, about a troubled boy named Jesse, who strikes up an unlikely friendship with a killer whale held in captivity at a local animal amusement park. "Michael Madsen, who made a striking impression as the sadist in *Reservoir Dogs,* is utterly winning in a very different role, as Jesse's taciturn but caring foster father," Stephen Farber wrote for *Movieline* (on-line).

In 1994 Madsen was seen in five movies. One was the remake of Sam Peckinpah's 1972 picture *The Getaway* (which, in the original, starred Steve McQueen and Ali MacGraw), for which he worked with Alec Baldwin, Kim Basinger, and James Woods under the direction of Roger Donaldson. Then, teaming up with Kevin Costner, Gene Hackman, and Dennis Quaid, he played Virgil Earp in the Lawrence Kasdan–directed biopic *Wyatt Earp*, about the legendary American frontier lawman. In accepting the role of Virgil, the eldest Earp brother, Madsen had been forced to turn down that of Vincent Vega (Mr. Blonde's brother) in Tarantino's acclaimed hit *Pulp Fiction*, which was shot at the same time. (The role went to John Travolta.) In explaining what led him to do so, he told the *Venice* interviewer, "At that time I was in a place in my life where I wanted to play some good guys"; the prospect of acting in a Western also drew him to *Wyatt Earp.* In preparing for the part, Madsen went so far as to visit Virgil Earp's grave. Despite its respected director and cast, *Wyatt Earp* fared poorly, both critically and at the box office. When the *Venice* interviewer asked Madsen how he felt about passing up the part of Vincent Vega or parts in other movies that proved highly successful, the actor replied, "My regrets are based on other things in life. I don't have a lot of room to regret roles I've chosen to do or not to do because once it's over, it's over. As soon as you walk through one door, another one opens." Also in 1994 Madsen appeared in the little-noticed pictures *Blue Tiger*, which starred Virginia Madsen; *Dead Connection*, in which he had top billing; and *Season of Change.*

Madsen was offered the role of Mickey Knox, the antihero of Oliver Stone's much-debated movie *Natural Born Killers* (1994), only to see it awarded to Woody Harrelson instead; as he explained to the *Venice* interviewer, Warner Brothers, a co-producer of the film, "didn't think I was a big enough star. . . . The studio told Oliver that they would lower the budget if he used me as the lead in the picture and he couldn't make the film for that amount of money." He also observed, "If I had played the guy in *Natural Born Killers*, I probably never could escape playing bad guys," and added, in a reference to the star of Alfred Hitchcock's horror classic *Psycho*, who found himself typecast as a crazy killer, "I would have ended up the Anthony Perkins of the nineties."

In 1995 Madsen rejoined Roger Donaldson to portray a laconic hitman in the science-fiction thriller *Species*, which also featured Ben Kingsley, Forest Whitaker, and Natasha Henstridge. In *Free Willy 2: The Adventure Home* (1995), he reprised the role of the good-hearted father. His next major motion picture was *Mulholland Falls* (1996), directed by Lee Tamahori, with Nick Nolte, Melanie Griffith, Chazz Palminteri, and Chris Penn. Madsen played a no-nonsense member of what Janet Maslin, in the *New York Times* (April 26, 1996), described as an "elegantly brutish foursome"—a team of Los Angeles law-enforcement officers known as the Hat Squad. In 1997 Madsen appeared in 10 films, among which the most noteworthy was *Donnie Brasco*, directed by Mike Newell and co-starring Johnny Depp and Al Pacino in extravagantly praised performances. The screenplay, by Paul Attanasio, is based on a memoir by Joseph D. Pistone, an FBI special agent who, under the assumed name Donnie Brasco, successfully infiltrated the Mafia in the 1970s. Madsen conveyed with chilling verisimilitude a Mafia lieutenant dubbed Sonny Black, having researched the part by studying dozens of real FBI surveillance photos; listening to taped conversations between Pistone (portrayed in the film by Depp) and his Mafia mentor, called Lefty (Pacino's character), and Pistone and the real-life Sonny; and spending time with several actual mobsters, to observe their body language and ways of interacting and to familiarize himself with their lingo. "I got a tremendous amount of information from these guys," he told the *Venice* interviewer. "Everything is very, very subtle, and I think that's the most important thing I picked up on. Everything is said with looks and glances. . . . There's tons of communication, but it's all very silent and very subtle and it's all very, very meaningful. . . . I remembered all that every time we were shooting a scene like that. Also, Joe Pistone was around a lot and I'd look at him and say, 'Joe, what do you think?' and he was my best indicator."

During the next seven years or so, Madsen accepted roles in nearly four-dozen motion pictures, all but a few of which attracted minimal attention. Among them were, in 1997, *The Girl Gets Moe, Catherine's Grove,* and *Rough Draft;* in 1998, *Spe-*

cies II, Fait Accompli, The Thief and the Stripper, and Flat Out; in 1999, The Florentine, Detour, and The Stray; in 2000, Luck of the Draw, The Alternate, The Price of Air, Love.com, The Ghost, Fall, Choke, and Bad Guys; in 2001, Extreme Honor, Pressure Point, Outlaw, and L.A.P.D.: To Protect and to Serve; in 2002, Welcome to America and The Real Deal; and in 2003, My Boss's Daughter, Vampires Anonymous, Hunt for the Devil, and The Distance. When Chaunce Hayden asked him for Steppin' Out (May 28, 2003), "When did your career begin to go south?," Madsen responded, "People don't realize that I did a lot of the pictures that I did because I was trying to pay the mortgage." He also said, "When you make a film, you don't know if that film is going to be any good or not. Also, a lot of things that are promised to you by filmmakers and the way they tell you they're going to tell a story doesn't end up being the way that it is on the finished product. Plus, once you're in the middle of the . . . thing and you know it's going to hell, there's just nothing you can do. It's not like you can throw up your hands and say 'This film is a piece of crap and I'm leaving!'" Two of the actor's 2003 films that fared better were Die Another Day, directed by Lee Tamahori, and Kill Bill: Vol. 1, directed by Quentin Tarantino. In Die Another Day, the 20th film in the James Bond series (which marked the franchise's 40th year), Madsen portrayed Damian Falco, a CIA agent. In Kill Bill: Vol. 1, he portrayed Budd (also known as Sidewinder), one of five members of the Deadly Viper Assassination Squad being hunted by "The Bride" (also called Black Mamba), played by Uma Thurman, a former squad member who vows to avenge the murder of her husband, the attempt on her own life, and the theft of her unborn baby. Budd is one of three of the targeted assassins who survive the mayhem of the first film and reappear in the sequel, Kill Bill: Vol. 2 (2004).

Since the late 1990s Madsen has published several books of raw, autobiographical poetry and/or prose (some of which are out of print): Beers, Blood and Ashes; Eat the Worm; Burning in Paradise; A Blessing of the Hounds; and 46 Down, a Book of Dreams and Other Ramblings. Burning in Paradise (1998) contains an introduction by the actor Dennis Hopper (who worked with Madsen in three films), who told J. Rentilly for Razor that he preferred Madsen's writing to that of the Beat poet and novelist Jack Kerouac, because Madsen's is "raunchier, more poignant. He's got street language. Images I can relate to. He blows my mind with his drifts of gut wrenching riffs." In a brief comment about Burning in Paradise for Rolling Stone (February 4, 1999), Rob Sheffield wrote, "Madsen, the finest tough-guy actor of our time, goes for some literary vengeance unlimited in his volume of verse. . . . Themes: Jack Daniels, cigarettes, bars, cars and what Michael was really thinking on the set of Species. Best opening line: 'Why do some men/Ask for a beating?'" Slated for publication in the near future are two additional books by Mad-

sen: The Blessing of the Hounds (which is also the title of a spoken-word album of Madsen's work, narrated by the author and with a musical score by Nathan Stokes), and 46 Down. "It's a funny thing . . . ," Madsen told Rentilly. "In a way I respect [writing] more than I do film acting."

Madsen has been married three times and divorced twice. His first wife was Georganne LaPierre, the half-sister of the actress and singer Cher. His second wife was the actress Jeannine Bisignano, who bore his first son, Christian. He and his third wife, the former DeAnna Morgan, whom he married in 1996, have four sons. Although he has eschewed the clichés often associated with cinematic celebrity, in 1997, when he talked with Chaunce Hayden (sometime before the birth of his youngest son), he expressed the desire to have a star with his name on it on Hollywood Boulevard. "I think for my boys it would really be nice," he said. "I've long gone past the point of having these things mean anything to my personal ego. But having been a father for a few years, I realize now it's not about me anymore. Anything that happens to me in the future now is for my four boys."

—P.B.M.

Suggested Reading: Los Angeles Times Calendar p3 Feb. 6, 1994, with photo; Michael Madsen Web site; Razor p65 Oct. 2003, with photo; Steppin' Out p30 May 28, 2003, with photo; Venice p41 Mar. 1997, with photo; Washington Post Entertainment Guide (on-line)

Selected Films: WarGames, 1983; Racing with the Moon, 1984; The Natural, 1984; The Doors, 1991; Thelma and Louise, 1991; Fatal Instinct, 1991; Reservoir Dogs, 1992; Free Willy, 1993; The Getaway, 1994; Wyatt Earp, 1994; Species, 1995; Free Willy 2: The Adventure Home, 1995; Mulholland Falls, 1996; The Last Days of Frankie the Fly, 1997; Donnie Brasco, 1997; Species II, 1998; Supreme Sanction, 1999; The Florentine, 1999; Love.com, 2000; Die Another Day, 2003; My Boss's Daughter, 2003; Kill Bill: Vol. 1, 2003; Kill Bill: Vol. 2, 2004

Selected Books: Burning in Paradise, 1998; A Blessing of the Hounds, 2002; 46 Down, a Book of Dreams and Other Ramblings, 2004

Frederick M. Brown/Getty Images

Malina, Joshua

Jan. 17, 1966– Actor

Address: The West Wing, NBC, 3000 W.
Alameda Ave., Burbank, CA 91505

The actor Joshua Malina "fits that proudly nerdish mold, that slightly dorky smart guy who's smart enough to know he's slightly dorky," Rick Kushman wrote for the *Sacramento Bee* (March 2, 2003). Malina is best known for his roles as the television producer Jeremy Goodwin on the critically praised ABC sitcom *Sports Night*, which aired from 1999 to 2000, and as the presidential speechwriter and vice presidential chief of staff Will Bailey on NBC's Emmy Award–winning TV series *The West Wing*. Both series were created by the prolific television and big-screen writer and producer Aaron Sorkin, who is a friend of his. Malina went from a stint on the Broadway stage in the early 1990s to small roles in movies, including *A Few Good Men* (1992), *The American President* (1995), and *Bulworth* (1998), and on such television shows as *Champs* and *Sliders*, before finding critical success with *Sports Night* and a large audience with *The West Wing*. For his work on those programs, he has been nominated for several ensemble Screen Actors Guild awards.

Joshua Malina was born on January 17, 1966 in New Rochelle, New York, the son of Robert Malina, an investment banker. Proud of his Jewish heritage, Malina recalled to Roberta Hershenson for the *New York Times* (November 11, 1990) that his family's gatherings during Jewish holidays were "large, raucous" affairs, during which his relatives sang traditional songs. He participated in community theater from a young age. "I just felt I was an actor," he recalled to Rick Kushman. Knowing early on the path he wanted to follow, he added, "saved me a tremendous amount of angst not having to decide." Malina's cousins Stuart and Joel were high-school friends of Aaron Sorkin, who is five years older than Malina; through that connection, Malina himself eventually formed a friendship with Sorkin. During his high-school years, he performed for several seasons in the Scarsdale, New York, Summer Music Theater. Malina attended Yale University, in New Haven, Connecticut, earning a B.A. degree in theater from the university's prestigious drama school in 1988. After graduating, Malina moved to New York City in search of acting parts. His father, who had co-produced a number of Broadway plays, helped his son to find a few odd jobs, but none of them lasted long.

In 1990 Malina's career was given a boost by a narrowly averted tragedy. Malina and Sorkin were part of the same bowling league; one day the two were competing at the Port Authority Bowling Alley in New York City, when, laughing at a joke while eating a cheeseburger, Sorkin began to choke. As he flailed his arms and knocked bowling balls to the floor, others in their group thought that Sorkin was simply clowning and pretending to be in distress. Malina, however, became alarmed and rushed over to perform the Heimlich maneuver. "Honest to God, I really couldn't breathe," Sorkin recalled to Kushman. "I was well on my way to dying." Malina told Kushman, "I wasn't overly familiar with the Heimlich maneuver. It was not performed with great finesse. Basically, I beat [Sorkin] up from behind. I do remember thinking, 'My friend's going to die in my arms.'" In the end Malina dislodged the piece of food from Sorkin's throat and saved his life. The incident brought the two men closer.

Malina soon earned a role in Sorkin's play *A Few Good Men*, a legal drama focused on crime and punishment in the U.S. military. Malina spent 15 months on Broadway performing in *A Few Good Men*, which was made into the 1992 hit film of the same name, directed by Rob Reiner and starring Jack Nicholson and Tom Cruise, with Malina in a small part. (Bradley Whitford, Malina's future co-star on *The West Wing*, also performed in the Broadway production of *A Few Good Men*.) "I literally had five words," Malina recalled to Kushman regarding his part in the movie, "three of them 'yes,' two of them 'sir,' but if you're going to make a film debut, it's nice making it with Jack Nicholson." By 1992 Malina was living in Los Angeles. He recalled to Kushman that though he was landing small roles in films and on television, "there were times when my parents gave me more than just emotional support."

Following his brief debut in *A Few Good Men*, Malina returned to the big screen with appearances in *In the Line of Fire* (1993), *Malice* (1993), and *Separate Lives* (1995). In the romantic comedy *The American President* (1995), written by Sorkin,

Malina had a small part as the earnest and good-natured assistant of Sydney (Annette Bening), a lobbyist who begins a romance with the widowed U.S. president (Michael Douglas). Next came Malina's turns in the movies *Infinity* (1996), *Clockwatchers* (1997), *Just Friends* (1997), and *My Engagement Party* (1998). In the satire *Bulworth* (1998), directed, co-written, and co-produced by Warren Beatty, Malina played a political aide to the U.S. senator of the title (Beatty)—a weary, jaded politician who, undergoing a change, begins addressing the public in a bluntly honest, at times hip-hop–inflected manner.

On the small screen Malina appeared, once in 1993 and three times during the 1998 season, on the hit HBO series *The Larry Sanders Show*, a parody of the behind-the-scenes workings of late-night talk programs. Starring the comedian Gary Shandling, *The Larry Sanders Show* was regarded by some critics as one of the best programs on television during the 1990s. In 1996 Malina made three appearances on *Tracy Takes On . . .* , which starred the British comic actress Tracy Ullman. In 1998 he played the data technician Tim Messick on one episode of the television miniseries *From the Earth to the Moon*, a dramatic portrayal of the 1969 Apollo space mission.

Malina's first regular role in a TV series came in 1999, on Sorkin's creation *Sports Night*, a fast-paced comedy that took a behind-the-scenes look at a fictitious cable-television sports program. On the show, which aired on ABC, Malina played Jeremy Goodwin, the bespectacled, intellectual, nerdy television producer who carried on a romance with an attractive colleague (Sabrina Lloyd). Writing for *USA Weekend* (October 17, 1999, on-line), Mark Morrison opined that Malina "nearly stops the show even as he steals it. With his horn-rimmed specs and sheepish grin, Jeremy is the Clark Kent of the sports beat, the geek who gets the girl—and Malina fuels him with stage-trained' strength." *Sports Night* was praised by many critics for the quality of its writing. "I'm lucky to play this part," Malina told Morrison, perhaps referring to the writers' sophisticated treatment of the show's characters. "On another sitcom, I'd be the guy who falls off the chair in every episode." Malina, along with the rest of the cast of *Sports Night*, was nominated for a Screen Actors Guild award for outstanding performance by an ensemble in a comedy series in 2000. The sitcom also won an Emmy Award for outstanding cinematography and was nominated for several others, in the same year. Nonetheless, unable to attract a sufficient number of viewers, *Sports Night* went off the air that year, after its third season. Malina next joined the cast of the NBC comedy series *Imagine That*, starring Hank Azaria and Malina as collaborating television-comedy writers. Only six episodes of the comedy were made, and of those only two were aired, in early 2002.

That same year Malina won the part of the presidential speechwriter Will Bailey on Sorkin's television drama *The West Wing*, which began airing in 1999 and centers on the daily concerns and momentous crises facing the fictional Democratic president Josiah "Jed" Bartlet (Martin Sheen) and his staff. The show, whose large cast includes Stockard Channing as the president's wife, John Spencer as the White House chief of staff, Allison Janney as the president's press secretary, and Bradley Whitford as the deputy chief of staff, has won the Emmy Award for outstanding dramatic series, along with a host of other awards, every year since its inception. During *The West Wing*'s first few seasons, Rob Lowe had played the role of the deputy White House communications director, Sam Seaborn; he left the show at the end of the 2002 season after receiving from NBC a development deal for his own program. When Malina read in the trade publication *Variety* that Lowe was planning to leave *The West Wing*, he sent an E-mail message to Sorkin, offering his services as a replacement for Lowe; Sorkin, meanwhile, had already hit upon the idea of Malina's joining the cast. As Will, Malina—like the other members of the cast—delivers intelligent, rapid-fire dialogue related to the inner workings of the White House, from lofty expressions of political philosophy to exchanges during backroom deals. During the 2003–04 season, Malina's character accepted an offer to work for the vice president (played by Gary Cole). In both 2003 and 2004 Malina and the rest of the cast were nominated for a Screen Actors Guild Award for outstanding performance by an ensemble in a dramatic series.

"It's disturbing how much I can trace back to Aaron," Malina told Kushman, referring to Sorkin's help not only in securing his role on *The West Wing* but also in getting him parts in the movies *A Few Good Men* and *The American President*, whose screenplays were written by Sorkin, and *Sports Night*, which Sorkin created. "I have to remind myself how blessed I am, how fortunate I am to have a really good friend who's an incredible creative force," the actor said. Sorkin told Kushman that the relationship has been "mutually beneficial. He's been stellar in everything he's done." Referring to his having filled the spot vacated by the classically handsome Rob Lowe on *The West Wing*, Malina—whom Kushman described as "perfectly decent-looking"—told Kushman, "I think I'm pretty safe saying people aren't going to look at me and think, He's the new hunk. Maybe some people will be picking up the slack, but it ain't gonna be me." Sorkin told Kushman, "What I really have an affinity for is taking guys who would otherwise be thought of as nerdy and making their intelligence and commitment sexy. It's very easy to do that with Josh."

In addition to his other big-screen roles, Malina has appeared in *Kill the Man* (1999), *It's a Shame About Ray* (2000), *It Is What It Is* (2001), *Without Charlie* (2001), and *View from the Top* (2003).

Malina's other television credits—mostly small parts—include *Bob* (a short-lived comedy series starring Bob Newhart), in 1993; the made-for-television movie *Menendez: A Killing in Beverly Hills* (1994); the series *Champs* and *Sliders*, in 1996; the TV movie *How to Marry a Billionaire: A Christmas Tale*, in 2000; *She Spies*, an action/comedy series cenetered on three sexy female ex-convicts, in 2002; and *The Late Late Show with Craig Kilborn*, a talk show, and the television movie *See Jane Date*, both in 2003. In 2004 he appeared in *Nobody's Perfect*, a short film written and directed by Hank Azaria.

Malina enjoys playing chess and is rumored to be a shrewd poker player. Among the actors whose work he admires are Gene Wilder, Charlie Chaplin, Peter O' Toole, and Groucho Marx. Malina and his wife, Melissa, who married in 1996, live in Los Angeles; they have a daughter, Isabel, and a son, Avi. Sorkin told Kushman that Malina is "a guy you want to come to work with every day." Kushman

wrote, "Malina is as egoless as they come in Hollywood. . . . He makes fun of himself for what he is not—hunk, movie star, big name—and downplays what he is—smart, dependable, talented, good guy."

—C.F.T.

Suggested Reading: Internet Movie Database; *Sacramento Bee* Tickets Section p24 Mar. 2, 2003, with photos; *USA Weekend* Oct. 17, 1999

Selected Films: *A Few Good Men*, 1992; *In the Line of Fire*, 1993; *The American President*, 1995; *Bulworth*, 1998; *Kill the Man*, 1999; *View from the Top*, 2003

Selected Television Shows: *Menendez: A Killing in Beverly Hills*, 1994; *From the Earth to the Moon*, 1998; *Sports Night*, 1999–2000; *Imagine That*, 2002; *The West Wing*, 2002– ; *See Jane Date*, 2003

© Parris/Courtesy of George R.R. Martin

Martin, George R. R.

Sep. 20, 1948– Fantasy and science-fiction writer; screenwriter

Address: c/o Devil's Due Publishing, 4619 N. Ravenswood Ave., Chicago, IL 60640-4580

While George R. R. Martin has been known to readers of fantasy and science fiction since he began publishing books, in the 1970s, he did not reach a wider audience until he began the Song of

Ice and Fire series, a yet-to-be-completed sextet of novels whose first three books have reached the *New York Times* and *USA Today* best-seller lists, among others. Martin, who has won many fantasy-genre awards, including six Locus Awards, is noted for injecting gritty realism into a genre often labeled as escapist and characterized by fairy-tale simplicity. Most critics have agreed that the characters in the Song of Ice and Fire series are complex, fully realized human beings who drive the plot as much as they are driven by it. The series has elicited comparisons to J. R. R. Tolkien's *Lord of the Rings* trilogy for its intricate and extensive underlying mythology, which Martin has drawn with uncommon vividness and detail. Already, the first three books in the series—*A Game of Thrones* (1996), *A Clash of Kings* (1999), and *A Storm of Swords* (2000)—fill, in total, 3,000 pages. Martin has attributed their unusual length to his desire to ensure that the details of the stories are "put clearly into the mind's eye" of each reader—"and that takes wordage," as he explained to Roz Kaveney for Amazon.com (Great Britain). The Song of Ice and Fire books have been translated into German, French, Italian, Spanish, Swedish, Dutch, Japanese, Portuguese, Croatian, Russian, Polish, Hungarian, Finnish, and Esperanto.

One of the three children of Raymond Collins Martin, a longshoreman, and Margaret Brady Martin, George Raymond Richard Martin was born on September 20, 1948 in Bayonne, New Jersey. His sisters are Darleen (Martin) Lapinski and Janet (Martin) Patten. Raised in a household in which the only pets allowed were fish and turtles, Martin made the most of the situation: he named his turtles and created adventures for them, set in a toy castle. His first short story, written during his childhood, was titled "Turtle Castle." Martin also honed his craft early on by writing and telling scary stories to his neighborhood playmates. "I would write in block printing in those old black-and-white marbled notebooks," he recalled to Tasha Robinson for SciFi.com. "I would write out these monster stories by hand and sell them to the other kids for a nickel. A nickel was a lot of money in those days; you could get a Milky Way, with two nickels you could get a comic book. So I'd sell the stories and give a dramatic reading of the stories as well, because my audience didn't actually read that well."

Martin attended the Mary Jane Donohue School, a public elementary school, and Marist High, a Catholic college-preparatory institution. While there he became an avid comic-book collector and began submitting his fiction to amateur comic "fanzines." He earned a B.S. degree in journalism and graduated summa cum laude from Northwestern University, in Evanston, Illinois, in 1970, then earned an M.S. in journalism from the same school in 1971. As a conscientious objector, Martin did not fight in the Vietnam War; rather, he completed alternative service through the Volunteers in Service to America (VISTA) program, from 1972 to 1974. From 1973 to 1976 he also directed chess tournaments for the Continental Chess Association, after which he became a journalism instructor at Clarke College, in Dubuque, Iowa, until 1976. He was a writer in residence at the college from 1978 to 1979.

Martin married Gale Burnick in 1975. When the marriage ended, in 1979, he became a full-time writer. In 1974 Martin had won a Hugo Award for his novella *A Song for Lya*. His novel *Dying of the Light*, a romance set on the dying planet of Warlorn, was nominated for the same award in 1977. That year he also published the short-story collection *Songs of Stars and Shadows* and edited *New Voices in Science Fiction: Stories by Campbell Award Nominees*. In 1979 his short story "Sandkings" won the Hugo and Nebula Awards, and his short story "The Way of Cross & Dragon" won the Hugo. In 1981 he published the short-story collection *Sandkings* and collaborated with Lisa Tuttle on the novel *Windhaven*, set in a world of small islands where all communication is conducted through the Flyers, a society of elite hang-glider pilots.

Dubuque had once been a major manufacturer of steamboats, and while Martin was at Clarke College, he became fascinated with them. His novel *Fevre Dream* (1982) is about a steamboat captain who goes into business with a vampire who seeks to teach his fellows to live peacefully among humans. In 1983 Martin published *The Armageddon Rag*, which follows the journalist Sandy Blair as he investigates the ritual murder of an ex-promoter of the defunct rock band Nazgul. Blair, still steeped in the 1960s culture of his youth, discovers an odd plot to resurrect Nazgul, which had dissolved after its lead singer was murdered onstage in the late 1960s. Clarence Peterson, reviewing the book for

the *Chicago Tribune* (January 20, 1985), declared, "Martin . . . has mastered the suspense writer's craft." *The Armageddon Rag* won a Balrog Award for best fantasy novel in 1984. Also in 1983 Martin published the short-story collection *Songs the Dead Men Sing* and co-edited, with the science-fiction writer Isaac Asimov, *The Science Fiction Weight-Loss Book*, a collection of science-fiction short stories that, according to Lois A. Strell in *School Library Journal* (October 1983), "deal with people's obsessions with fat in the present and future." Martin's next book was the short-story collection *Nightflyers* (1985).

In 1986 Martin published *Tuf Voyaging*, a group of tales about the adventures of Haviland Tuf, a humble space traveler who acquires a "seedship" equipped with gene-cloning capabilities that he uses to tackle problems on a host of exotic planets. A reviewer for *Publishers Weekly*, as quoted on Amazon.com, wrote, "These colorful tales mostly skirt the more interesting and prickly issue of Tuf's playing god to fundamentally change the cultures he encounters. Still, the seed-ship is a wonderful idea and Tuf . . . is a droll hero."

Also in 1986 Martin took his first job in television, as story editor for *The Twilight Zone* (1985–87), a new version of the classic series. In 1988 he became a producer for the TV series *Beauty and the Beast*; the following year he was promoted to co-supervising producer. The show, which ran from 1987 to 1990, was a modern-day version of the classic fairy tale. Catherine (Linda Hamilton) is an assistant district attorney in New York City who meets and is transformed by Vincent (Ron Perlman), a creature whose head and face resemble those of a lion and who lives in a secret society of outcasts underneath the city. Martin also worked on various other film and TV projects, including *Doorways*, a pilot he wrote for Columbia Pictures Television, which he also executive produced. His story "Nightflyers" was made into a feature film in 1987, and "Sandkings" was made into a two-hour movie for the TV series *The Outer Limits* in 1995. Most of his efforts, however, were never scheduled for broadcasting.

Martin has said that working in television improved his ear for dialogue and sense of narrative structure but frustrated him, too, because he often felt that his creative vision had been compromised. He began working on the Song of Ice and Fire series partly in reaction to what he saw as the limitations of writing for film and TV. "Television and film were an interesting few years, I learned a lot from it, but it would never replace books as far as I'm concerned," he told Alex von Thorn for the Canadian Web site voyageur.idic.ca. "Certainly, for a writer, books are the ultimate art form. You're everything when you write a book; you're the writer, you're also the director, you're all the actors, the set director, the costume designer, the special effects guy." The idea for the series had come to Martin in 1991, when, for no apparent reason, there came into his mind an image of a litter of wolf pups lying in the snow beside their dead mother. The vividness and power of the image spurred him to write what became chapter one of *A Game of Thrones* (1996), in which young Bran Stark, along with his brother and half-brother, rescue six direwolf pups—one for each of them, their two sisters, and their little brother. (In actuality, the dire wolf has long been extinct.) Their father, the nobleman Ned Stark, is subsequently called away from the family home, Winterfell Castle, to assist his old friend King Robert Baratheon, prompting a reshuffling of power on the continent of Westeros that leads to both open and secret warfare. Martin's fictional world is defined by unpredictable seasons—long summers of plentitude end abruptly in bitter winters that rage for years on end. Much of *A Game of Thrones* follows Ned Stark as he uncovers a plot by the king's wife, Cersei Lannister, and her clan to seize control of the seven kingdoms of Westeros. The book also chronicles the adventures of Daenerys Targaryen, the exiled daughter of a deposed king, who is cast among a wandering tribe of horsemen and may have a link to the world's last remaining dragons. A further subplot involves Ned Stark's illegitimate son, John Snow, who is sent to the north of Westeros, where a 700-foot-tall wall of solid ice borders a forbidding wilderness full of giants and the dreaded, undead "Others."

Martin, who relates his story through alternating chapters told from the points of view of various characters, set out to create an epic tale on a scale similar to that of the *Lord of the Rings* series. Though Martin's series features a huge cast of characters, a wealth of intricate subplots, and a complex history and mythology, much of his creation remains an undercurrent in the fast-moving plot. Martin told Linda Richards for *January Magazine* (January 2001), "I think you have to do the back story in a book like this like an iceberg: most of which would be below the surface. Just enough to show that something huge is there."

A Game of Thrones won nearly universal praise. "Like the best epic fantasy and the best historical fiction, *A Game of Thrones* is about individuals and the effects of vast and small events on their lives," Phyllis Eisenstein wrote for the *Chicago Sun-Times* (August 11, 1996). "Reminiscent of T. H. White's *The Once and Future King*, this novel is an absorbing combination of the mythic, the sweepingly historical, and the intensely personal." A reviewer for *Publishers Weekly*, as quoted on Amazon.com, wrote, "It is fascinating to watch Martin's characters mature and grow, particularly Stark's children, who stand at the center of the book. Martin's trophy case is already stuffed with major prizes, including Hugos, Nebulas, Locus Awards and a Bram Stoker. He's probably going to have to add another shelf, at least."

The second installment in Martin's trilogy is *A Clash of Kings* (1999), wherein the continuing battle between the Starks and Lannisters is told. Also joining the fray are King Robert Baratheon's two brothers, Renly and Stannis, who have as much an-

tipathy toward each other as they do toward the Lannisters. The book also follows Daenerys Targaryen, as she struggles for survival in the exotic reaches of the land, and John Snow, who experiences the coming plague from the north firsthand. A critic for *Kirkus Reviews* (December 1, 1998) wrote that among the many rewards of reading *A Clash of Kings* are "a backdrop of convincing depth and texture; intricate, flawless plotting; fully realized characters; and restrained, inventive magical/occult elements." In the *Santa Fe New Mexican* (May 9, 1999), Terry England argued that, far from being escapist (a label often applied to fantasy), the novel offers valuable commentary on contemporary life, including "our attitudes about women and men, about our love of war, about how [easily] we lie for the simplest of reasons and how easy it is for us to deceive those we profess to love and honor."

In 2000 Martin published *A Storm of Swords*, the third novel in the Song of Ice and Fire series. The war among the Starks, Lannisters, and Baratheons continues to rage, while in the north John Snow finds himself among the barbaric Wildlings as they try to invade the seven kingdoms. His halfbrother Bran is in peril as Winterfell Castle is besieged, and Daenerys Targaryen continues her difficult rise to power as the keeper of the last three surviving dragons. Terry England, writing for the *Santa Fe New Mexican* (December 17, 2000), noted that Martin's series had "vaulted him into the top ranks of science fiction and fantasy publishing" and that the "books do something that happens rarely: Break away from the commonplace." In the Cleveland, Ohio, *Plain Dealer* (December 3, 2000), Julie E. Washington wrote, "Martin creates a gorgeously and intricately textured world, peopled with absolutely believable and fascinating characters."

Many reviewers have agreed that the characters are the strength of Martin's Song of Ice and Fire series, particularly within the genre of fantasy, in which characters often fall into clear categories of good or evil. "I look for ways to make my characters real and to make them human, characters who have good and bad, noble and selfish, well-mixed in their natures . . . ," Martin told Tasha Robinson. "I read too much fiction myself in which you encounter characters who are very stereotyped. They're heroic-hero and dastardly-villain, and they're completely black or completely white. And that's boring, so far as I'm concerned. It's also unreal." Martin's heroes also break the conventions of the fantasy genre in that they are far less glamorous than the norm: Tyrion Lannister is a gnarled, sometimes ruthless dwarf who is also witty and kind; Samwell Tarly is obese and afraid of physical confrontation but displays courage and loyalty in critical situations; and Lady Brienne, a giant coarsefeatured woman uncomfortable with her femininity, is one of the realm's fiercest warriors. As Julie E. Washington noted, Martin further highlights the disparity between the romantic and harsh reality by using a plot line that involves Ned Stark's captive daughter, Sansa, "a dangerously naive girl who believed the songs about fair maidens and brave knights. She learns, in the most brutal ways possible, that life is not a song." Martin told Tasha Robinson, "I think there's a requirement, even in fantasy—it comes from a realm of the imagination and is based on fanciful worlds, but there's still a necessity to tell the truth, to try to reflect some true things about the world we live in. There's an inherent dishonesty to the sort of fantasy that too many people have done, where there's a giant war that rips the world apart, but no one that we know is ever really seriously inconvenienced by this."

In 2001 Martin published *Quartet: Four Tales from the Crossroads*, which includes "Black and White and Red All Over," about a group of journalists who track Jack the Ripper through Victorian Manhattan; "Starport," an unproduced screenplay; *Skin Trade*, a werewolf novella that won the World Fantasy Award; and *Blood of the Dragon*, a precursor to *A Game of Thrones*, which won a Hugo Award. A reviewer for *Kirkus* (May 1, 2001) described *Blood of the Dragon* as being "for fans only." Martin is the editor of the long-running Wild Card series of books, featuring collaborations by various authors. The fourth book in the Song of Ice and Fire series was scheduled for publication in December 2004.

Martin is a member of the Writers' Guild of America and the Science Fiction & Fantasy Writers of America (of which he was south-central regional director from 1977 to 1979 and vice president from 1996 to 1998). He lives in Santa Fe.

—P.G.H.

Suggested Reading: *Daily Oklahoman* D p18 Aug. 15, 2003; *January Magazine* (on-line) Jan. 2001; (Monroe, Louisiana) *News-Star* D p6 Apr. 27, 2003; *Santa Fe New Mexican* D p4 Aug. 25, 1996; SciFi.com; SF Site Web site; voyageur.idic.ca

Selected Books: *A Song for Lya and Other Stories*, 1976; *Dying of the Light*, 1977; *Songs of Stars and Shadows*, 1977; *Sandkings*, 1981; *Windhaven* (with Lisa Tuttle), 1981; *Fevre Dream*, 1982; *The Armageddon Rag*, 1983; *Songs the Dead Men Sing*, 1983; *Nightflyers*, 1985; *Tuf Voyaging*, 1986; *Portraits of His Children*, 1987; *A Game of Thrones*, 1996; *A Clash of Kings*, 1999; *A Storm of Swords*, 2000; *Quartet: Four Tales from the Crossroads*, 2001; *Blood of the Dragon*, 2001; *Skin Trade*, 2001; as editor—*New Voices in Science Fiction: Stories by Campbell Award Nominees*, 1977; as co-editor (with Isaac Asimov)—*The Science Fiction Weight-Loss Book*, 1983

Selected Television Shows: as story editor—*The Twilight Zone*, 1985–87; as producer—*Beauty and the Beast*, 1988–89; as co-supervising producer—*Beauty and the Beast*, 1987–90

Courtesy of Vilma Martinez

Martinez, Vilma

Oct. 17, 1943– Lawyer; social activist

Address: Munger, Tolles & Olson, 355 S. Grand Ave., 35th Fl., Los Angeles, CA 90071-1560

Vilma Martinez—a former president and general counsel of the Mexican American Legal Defense Fund (MALDEF) and currently a potential high-court nominee—grew up in an impoverished, predominantly Mexican-American neighborhood of San Antonio, Texas, where she witnessed firsthand the de facto segregation that seemed designed to make Chicanos a permanent underclass. Symptomatic of this discrimination, Martinez, though she earned near-perfect marks in school, was encouraged by teachers and guidance counselors to attend a vocational institution rather than an academic high school, "because to become a secretary was the highest thing a girl like me could aspire to," as she explained to Grace Lichtenstein for *Quest* (February/March 1980). Refusing to succumb to such low expectations, Martinez gained entry into not only an academic high school but, subsequently, the University of Texas at Austin and Columbia Law School, in New York City, before embarking on her prestigious career at MALDEF and beyond. During her time as MALDEF's president, from 1973 to 1981, Martinez struggled to rectify the injustices suffered by the millions of Latinos living in the United States—injustices she experienced as a child growing up in Texas. Though Martinez has accomplished much since her tenure at MALDEF, her successful stewardship of the civil rights organization remains her principal accomplishment: at MALDEF, as Lichtenstein stated, Martinez "built a bridge from the rural and urban barrios of the Southwest to various enclaves of American wealth and conscience—an achievement that many compare with the early career of César Chávez as leader of the Mexican-American farmworkers."

The eldest of five children, Vilma Martinez was born on October 17, 1943 in San Antonio, Texas, to a Spanish-speaking family of limited means. Describing the segregation that existed in Texas at the time, Martinez remarked, according to a profile posted on the American Bar Association (ABA) Web site, "We [Latinos] weren't allowed to go into some of the parks. When we went to the movies, we had to sit in the back of the theater." Given her gender as well as her ethnic heritage, Martinez found little support for her interest in attending college. When her guidance counselor sent her records to a local trade school, telling her that she would be more comfortable in that environment, Martinez demanded that her transcript be sent to an academic high school, where she was subsequently accepted. The determination she showed in pursuit of her early education became a hallmark of her later career. She has credited her maternal grandmother with instilling this drive in her: "She was forthright," Martinez told Lichtenstein, "she was a coper and a woman of action." Martinez excelled in high school. When she was 15 she volunteered during the summer at the law firm of Alonso Perales, a Latino civil rights attorney; the experience left a lasting impression, and she soon began planning a career as an attorney. Martinez was determined to attend the University of Texas at Austin, but her high-school counselor, as shortsighted as her earlier advisers, refused to help her with the application process. Martinez's father, a carpenter, offered to pay for her education only if she agreed to attend a nearby Roman Catholic college. Again she refused to accede to what others expected of her; she applied to and was accepted at the University of Texas at Austin. "What pushed me," she told Lichtenstein, "was that Mexican-Americans weren't treated on the basis of merit. I was impelled to show them that I could speak English without an accent." To help finance her education, Martinez earned money by cleaning a school science lab and lived frugally in a campus co-op. She completed college in less than three years, graduating with a B.A. degree in 1964. Since her time at Perales's law practice, though many had tried to dissuade her, Martinez had remained intent on becoming an attorney. She wanted to attend the University of Texas law school, but again her gender and race made this an unlikely prospect: "My counselors kept telling me not to get my hopes up," Martinez explained to Lichtenstein. "They finally said, 'Why don't you try those Eastern liberal schools?' So I did." Accepted by Columbia Law School, Martinez headed to New York City. She graduated in 1967.

Martinez initially applied for jobs at several Texas law firms, but was told that many clients were not comfortable with the idea of a female or a Mexican being their legal counsel. So she began her career at the National Association for the Advancement of Colored People (NAACP) Legal Defense Fund, where she worked primarily on cases involving job discrimination and equal employment.

In 1968, a year after Martinez received her law degree and joined the NAACP, MALDEF was founded. The group is often seen as a Chicano parallel to the NAACP; its mission "is to foster sound public policies, laws and programs to safeguard the civil rights of the 40 million Latinos living in the United States and to empower the Latino community to fully participate in our society," its Web site states. Martinez was one of the first women to join MALDEF's board of directors, and she acted as a liaison between MALDEF and the NAACP. MALDEF's mission in promoting Chicano rights, as Martinez later explained to Bill Curry for the *Washington Post* (March 28, 1978), was analogous to the movement in the 1950s and 1960s for African-American civil rights: "The issues are the same. The denial of an equal education opportunity, the denial of jobs, the denial of effective participation in the voting process and police brutality." In 1970 Martinez left the NAACP Legal Defense Fund to become the Equal Employment Opportunity Counsel for the New York State Division of Human Rights. The next year she entered private practice, serving as a litigation associate at the New York firm of Cahill, Gordon and Reindel, though she continued her involvement with MALDEF.

In 1973, not quite 30 years old, Martinez was named president and general counsel of MALDEF. "Getting that job wasn't easy," Martinez stated in a lecture given at Stanford University, as quoted by Marisa Cigarroa in the *Stanford Online Report* (April 29, 1998). Many associates dissuaded her from lobbying for the post, telling her the organization was not ready for a female president—especially one so young—and that the conservative judicial climate created by President Richard Nixon's appointments would make it difficult for MALDEF to achieve any of its goals in the courts. Martinez, as she had in the past, refused to heed these doubters.

When Martinez first took over, the organization had an inexperienced staff and was in difficult financial straits: close to insolvency, MALDEF depended almost entirely on monetary grants from the Ford Foundation. Martinez tirelessly traversed the nation seeking money and increasing support; in so doing she helped transform MALDEF from a disorganized, poorly financed operation into what Lichtenstein described as "a broadly funded enterprise with savvy lawyers, five offices around the country, and a new grass roots organization as well."

In addition to improving MALDEF on an organizational and financial level, Martinez aggressively promoted the group's agenda in the courts. In 1974 she persuaded a United States appeals court to guarantee the right of bilingual education to non–English-speaking students in public schools. In 1975, in what many regard as the organization's—and Martinez's—greatest achievement, MALDEF successfully lobbied Congress to add amendments to the 1965 Voting Rights Act that extended the law's protections to Latinos and required that voting ballots be printed in Spanish as well as English in districts with high concentrations of Latinos. MALDEF also helped delay proposals to punish employers who hired undocumented workers; after these proposals passed, MALDEF strove to lessen their impact on Latinos through legal action and organized studies that demonstrated that the punitive measures had no impact in dissuading employers from hiring undocumented workers, but served rather to promote xenophobia. Under Martinez, MALDEF won lawsuits against the school boards of El Paso and Uvalde, Texas, paving the way for the desegregation of students by ethnicity; the group also defeated the U.S. Border Patrol in court, proving that the organization's height and weight requirements excluded many Latinos. In 1982, Martinez's last year as head of MALDEF, the organization scored another major legal victory when the U.S. Supreme Court ruled (in *Plyer v. Doe*) that undocumented children were entitled to a public education.

Disseminating information about public policy to Latinos was another vital aspect of MALDEF's strategy under Martinez. In 1980, for example, many Latinos were leery of participating in that year's census, fearing that the information might be used by the government as a means of discrimination. However, an undercount of Latinos would diminish their total impact on congressional redistricting and adversely affect their political influence. Consequently, MALDEF teamed up with the Roman Catholic Church to inform Latinos about the census and encourage them to participate.

Describing Martinez's bearing as president of MALDEF, Lichtenstein observed, "[She] at first gives the impression of a mild-mannered, smiling schoolmarm, but one encounter is usually enough to dispel that impression. She is an operator—in the best sense of the word—who brings to her work considerable charm and poise supported by a backbone of steel." Martinez's soft-spoken intensity was often remarked upon by observers; recalling an encounter with her, Carol Lawson wrote for the *New York Times* (May 19, 1978) that Martinez "talked in a bold and blunt manner about how the country's eight million Mexican-Americans [the number has since greatly increased] have been 'oppressed and discriminated against' and had their 'rights trampled upon,' and how 'the country is not honoring its Constitutional commitment to this group of people.' But instead of sounding shrill or even impassioned, her tone was soft and gentle."

Martinez's success at MALDEF raised her profile nationally, and government officials soon began requesting her counsel. President Jimmy Carter named her to his Advisory Board on Ambassadorial Appointments, and in 1976 California governor Jerry Brown selected her to serve on the University of California Board of Regents. U.S. senator Alan Cranston of California then tapped her for the state's Judiciary Selection Committee. "These are all interesting, yet difficult roles," Martinez told Lawson. "I'm chosen because I'm an advocate of Mexican-Americans and women's rights. So I do battle with [diplomats] Averell Harriman and Dean Rusk, trying to convince them that there are qualified Hispanics who could be ambassadors to Europe." In 1976, during Martinez's tenure on the University of California Board of Regents, the board voted on whether to divest the school's portfolio of stock in companies involved in South Africa, a country then in the grip of racial apartheid. Surprisingly to many, Martinez voted in opposition to divestment. She explained to Lawson that her decision was made with the interests of the university in mind: "I thought it would be too costly to sell so much stock, and I wasn't sure that this would be an effective way of remedying the apartheid situation in South Africa."

Martinez continued to serve on the board of regents after leaving MALDEF, in 1982, to become a partner at the Los Angeles law firm Munger, Tolles & Olson. In 1984 she began her term as chairwoman of the board of regents, a post she held until 1986. During Martinez's tenure as chairwoman, the issue of South African divestment reemerged. In June 1985 the board instituted a plan in which a committee reviewed each of the university's stock holdings to ascertain whether the particular companies doing business in South Africa were also helping to promote racial equality in the divided nation. If the companies were not, the panel could recommend that the specific stocks be divested. Not long after this policy was adopted, however, recession and violence erupted in South Africa, and calls for full divestment resurfaced. Nevertheless, Martinez refused to change course, telling David G. Savage for the *Los Angeles Times* (August 28, 1985), "This was a very difficult issue. We gave it careful consideration and a resolution was reached. And I suspect most of us [on the board of regents] will want to give it a chance to work."

Controversy over a job-discrimination lawsuit in Texas engulfed both MALDEF and Martinez in February 1987. Three Latinos, former employees of the H. E. Butt Grocery Co., sued the company for discrimination. MALDEF offered its services on behalf of the plaintiffs, while Martinez, now in private practice, was retained by the grocery-store chain. Subsequently MALDEF's board fired Antonia Hernandez, then the head of MALDEF, for bungling the case. Hernandez's critics claimed that the suit fell apart as a result of her friendship with Martinez, and some felt that Martinez's involvement constituted a conflict of interest. (Legal experts have ruled that Martinez was within her rights to accept the case.) Martinez defended herself in a letter to MALDEF's board, but her missive did little to appease her detractors, who maintained that although she did nothing legally wrong, her judgment in choosing to represent a client taking on MALDEF in court left much to be desired.

The retirement of U.S. Supreme Court justice Harry A. Blackmun, in 1994, led to rampant speculation about his possible replacements. Many felt that President Bill Clinton should nominate a Latino for the position as none had ever before served on the court. Martinez was among those mentioned as a potential candidate, along with Secretary of Transportation Federico Peña and U.S. District Judge José A. Cabranes of Connecticut. (President Clinton eventually tapped Stephen Breyer, a native Californian with a long history of judicial appointments, for the post.) Martinez's name was in the running for another judicial appointment in June 2001, following the death of California Supreme Court justice Stanley Mosk, but she did not get that appointment, either. Most pundits attribute Martinez's failure to receive a high-court nomination to her lack of experience as a judge; most nominees have served in some capacity on the judicial bench in lower courts, something Martinez has yet to do.

Martinez has received numerous accolades for her civic achievements over the years. In 1978 she was honored with Columbia Law School's Medal for Excellence; she later received a Medal for Excellence from Columbia University as well. The University of Texas gave Martinez its Distinguished Alumnus Award, and the American Institute for Public Service bestowed its Jefferson Award on her. In recognition of her contributions to the organization, MALDEF honored Martinez with the Valerie Kantor Award for Extraordinary Achievement. She has also received the John D. Rockefeller III Youth Award from the Rockefeller Foundation, the Maynard Toll Award for Distinguished Public Service from the Legal Aid Foundation of Los Angeles, and the Lex Award from the Mexican American Bar Association. Martinez holds honorary doctorates from Amherst College, in Massachusetts, and the California School of Professional Psychology. In 2003 she and seven other successful women founded the Directors' Council, an executive-search firm whose purpose is to locate qualified women to serve on corporate boards. Martinez is currently a member of the advisory boards of the Asian Pacific American Legal Center of Southern California and of Columbia Law School. She is the chairwoman of the Pacific Council's Study Group on Mexico and serves on the boards of the Los Angeles Philharmonic Association, as well as those of Anheuser-Busch and Sanwa Bank California.

Martinez met her husband, Stuart Singer, a tax lawyer, in a prep course for the New York bar exam. Together they have two children and currently make their home in Los Angeles, where Martinez continues to practice law at Munger, Tolles & Olson, specializing in employment and wrongful-termination litigation in both federal and state courts. Summing up Martinez's legacy, the profile posted on the ABA Web site states, "[Her] steadfast determination to oppose discrimination and injustice presents an inspiring role model to all. Her life reaffirms that hope and perseverance can create exciting and unimagined possibilities."

—P.B.M.

Suggested Reading: American Bar Association Web site, with photo; Columbia Law School Web site, with photo; *Los Angeles Times* p3 Aug. 28, 1985, II p1 Feb. 17, 1987, II p5 Feb. 19, 1987, NT p8 Feb. 9, 1989, with photo, A p1 Apr. 13, 1994; MALDEF Web site; *Metropolitan News-Enterprise* p1 Sep. 19, 2003; *New York Times* A p14 May 19, 1978, with photo; *Quest* p28 Feb./Mar. 1980, with photo; *San Diego Union Tribune* A p3 June 21, 2001; *Stanford Online Report* Apr. 29, 1998; *Washington Post* A p1 Mar. 28, 1978

Massive Attack

Music group

Daddy G
Dec. 18, 1959– Musician

3D
Jan. 21, 1965– Musician

Address: c/o Marc Picken, 12 Pembridge Rd., London W11 3HL, England

Grant "Daddy G" Marshall and Robert "3D" del Naja are the remaining original members of the British music group Massive Attack, which has been widely credited with developing the genre known as "trip-hop." An innovative fusion of hip-hop raps, swirling strings, R&B vocals, and samples (or snippets of other, previously recorded songs), trip-hop became one of the most popular forms of dance music in the 1990s. Sensual, soulful, and dark, Massive Attack's pioneering sound paved the way for such popular and critically acclaimed trip-hop acts as Portishead, Beth Orton, Tricky, and the Sneaker Pimps. Hailing from Bristol, England, a former slave-trading port with a large West Indian population, the members of Massive Attack were influenced by both dub reggae (reggae that uses remixes of other music) and the British punk scene that exploded in the late 1970s. "Massive Attack is quintessentially English music because we take from all the influences that you'd only find in England—punk, reggae, the whole saturation thing," Marshall told Jason Anderson for *Space Age Bachelor* (on-line). "And being a multiracial band in England as well, you're open to different influences." For many, the group's defining

Massive Attack: Daddy G (left) and 3D

musical statement was their first album, *Blue Lines* (1991), which is seen as having given birth to a genre. Writing for *Rolling Stone* (May 16, 1996, on-line), Ernest Hardy called that album "a rich, seamless fusion of musical and cultural references: dub-based U.K. sound systems, classic American pop and soul, and the brash, fearless ingenuity of precocious club kids. The album not only marked a turning point in the British music underground, it also changed the Brit-pop landscape immeasurably." With their third album, *Mezzanine* (1998), Massive Attack further explored this new territory, stressing the link between dub reggae and punk. "Punk and reggae never sounded similar," Marshall was quoted as saying on Artistdirect (on-line), "but they shared a way of thinking. There was an anarchistic feeling about both. Jamaican culture has always been rebellious; it's always been about taking risks." The most recent release by Massive Attack—which until 2000 included founding member Andrew Vowles, also known as Mushroom—is *100th Window* (2003).

Massive Attack traces its roots to the Wild Bunch, a loose-knit group of deejays and vocalists that formed in Bristol in 1983. Including in its ranks Miles Johnson (known as Milo), Nelle Hooper, Grant Marshall (born on December 18, 1959), Robert del Naja (a local graffiti artist also called 3D, born on January 21, 1965), Claude Williams (known as Willie Wee), Adrian Thaws (or Tricky), Shara Nelson, and Andrew Vowles, the group was noted locally for mixing records from a wide range of styles, among them punk, reggae, and R&B. Marshall recalled to Mark Jenkins for the *Washington Post* (September 6, 1998), "When we used to deejay, you wouldn't know what was coming next. It

might be a Public Image record mixed with a hip-hop record, or a Chicago house record mixed with a nursery rhyme, or whatever." This musical eclecticism was influenced by the multicultural Bristol music scene and such groups as Rip Rig & Panic, which fused reggae and jazz funk with punk attitude. The Wild Bunch's performances at the infamous Dug Out club in Bristol quickly became the most popular shows in the area, drawing huge crowds. The Wild Bunch released several local singles and an EP—*Friends and Countrymen* (1987)—before breaking up. Vowles, Marshall, and del Naja continued to work together, forming Massive Attack in 1987. "It just became an apparent thing that we should start making records," Marshall told Jenkins. "'Cause we knew everything about what we wanted. . . . We started making our own acetates to play with the Wild Bunch, and just moved from there, really. We formulated some ideas, and just worked on them when we got the chance." For a time the new group also worked with Nelle Hooper, who would go on to form Soul II Soul and become one of the most popular British dance producers and remixers in the 1990s.

In 1988 Massive Attack released their debut single, "Any Love," with Tony Bryan on vocals. Although the single did not make the U.K. charts, the group sent a copy of the recording to the renowned reggae singer Horace Andy, who, after listening to the music, signed a contract with the group and contributed vocals to a track on their debut album. In addition, the group worked with the singer Shara Nelson, who provided sultry vocals for Massive Attack's second single, "Daydreaming" (1990), which also featured a smooth rap by Tricky. While that single failed to chart, "Unfinished Sympathy"—with its uplifting vocals from Nelson, catchy rhythm, and slow-moving string arrangement—revolutionized the British dance-music world upon its release, in February 1991. Writing for the *All Music Guide* (on-line), John Bush noted that the song "remains, more than a decade after its recording, one of the most elegant, sophisticated works in the history of electronic dance." The single hit number 13 on the British charts, and *Melody Maker* magazine later voted it the best single of 1991. The group's next single, "Safe from Harm," reached number 25 in the U.K. while climbing to number 28 on the *Billboard* Modern Rock Charts in the U.S. Upon its release the influential British music tabloid *NME* named the song as its "single of the week." During this period, when the United States and allied nations were involved in the 1991 Persian Gulf War against Iraq, Massive Attack was forced to change its name briefly to simply Massive, in order to continue receiving airplay from U.K. radio stations worried that the group's original name might suggest insensitivity to the conflict.

After eight months in the studio, Massive Attack released their debut album, *Blue Lines*, in June 1991. The record peaked on the British charts at number 13 and received laudatory reviews. Writing for the *All Music Guide*, John Bush called the record "the first masterpiece of what was only termed trip-hop much later" and praised it as "one of the best dance albums of all time." *Blue Lines* was unprecedented in its fusion of hip-hop, R&B, and dub. Setting both sensual and sinister moods, often on the same song, the album takes on themes of romantic yearning, the desire for world peace, and violence. On the track "Safe from Harm," Nelson croons, "You can free the world, you can free my mind / Just as long as my baby's safe from harm tonight," while also warning, "But if you hurt what's mine, / I'll sure as hell retaliate." Writing for the British magazine *Q* (on-line), Dave Henderson commented that Massive Attack had "come up with storylines that smartly reflect everyday British youth with mentions of Subbuteo, Visa cards and the like. *Blue Lines* is instantly appealing and intensely moving." *NME* gave the record a rare rating of 10 (its highest accolade), while the *Face*, another British magazine, named *Blue Lines* "album of the year." In addition, the album was nominated for a BRIT Award. As a sign of Massive Attack's rapid rise to popularity, in November 1991 the hugely successful rock band U2 asked them to remix their single "Mysterious Ways."

Massive Attack followed their debut album with a 1992 EP that contained three new tracks. Around the same time Shara Nelson told the group that she wanted to focus on her solo career and would be unavailable to work on the band's sophomore effort. Instead of replacing her, the group decided to work with two guest female vocalists: Tracey Thorn, from the group Everything But the Girl, and Nicolette. The group also collaborated again with Horace Andy (on songs including a remake of his 1981 song "Spying Glass") and with Tricky. Regarding the various vocalists with whom the group has worked, Marshall told Jason Anderson, "[Horace Andy] records in Jamaica so there's quite traditional methods he uses to record. But with us, we try to break that down. He's really flexible—that's the reason why he's with us. He's become a quite integral part of what Massive Attack are about— live he's been the main figure. We always seem to change the women singers to give us different textures. Also, I think women get intimidated working with us and off they go. . . . It is quite a male-dominated thing we have going on, so I do believe that women, once they've done their bit, don't want to repeat it." Massive Attack spent most of 1993 in their Bristol studio working on the new album.

The eagerly anticipated recording *Protection* was released in September 1994. Generally smoother and more dub-inflected than the group's debut, *Protection* disappointed many critics in its perceived failure to build on the group's earlier work; a common criticism was that the group had not caught up with the innovations made in the trip-hop genre since *Blue Lines*. Nonetheless, *Protection* managed to reach number four on the U.K. charts, and one critic, writing for *NME* (on-line)

called the record "a sleek triumph of imagination," giving it a rating of eight out of 10. The group released three singles from the album; the dub-heavy title track, the more ethereal "Sly," and the darker "Karmacoma," featuring a rap by Tricky that he would later include on his highly successful and influential debut solo album, *Maxinquaye* (1995). Responding to the album's mixed reception, the group re-released it in February 1995 as *No Protection*, which features dub remixes of the entire album by Mad Professor, who pared down the material to its basic elements and either removed or drastically altered the vocals while adding deep reverb. *No Protection* was far more critically successful than *Protection* and hit number 10 on the British charts. According to *Rolling Stone* (May 16, 1996, on-line), "Mad Professor has taken Massive Attack back to the source—dub—and in the process transformed an indifferent statement into a formidable, deeply rewarding challenge." In 1996 Massive Attack won a BRIT award for "best dance act."

The following year the group launched their own record label, Melankolic, with an album by Horace Andy. They also released "Rising Sun," the first single from their forthcoming third album, in July 1997. The song charted at number 11 in the U.K. The album itself did not appear until 1998; during the process of recording it, tensions within the group were high, and the members were often not even in the same room simultaneously. "Thank God [engineer and co-producer Neil Davidge] was the referee," Marshall told Mark Jenkins, "because we all had different ideas of where we wanted to take this album. We had a lot of personal problems as well, so we decided that the best way to get through was to all go to the studio at separate times. Sometimes there were weeks when we didn't actually see each other at all. Making the record wasn't a very pleasant experience. When I come back to it, it has a lot of pain." Featuring vocals by Horace Andy, the former Cocteau Twins vocalist Liz Fraser, and Sara Jay, Massive Attack's *Mezzanine* was a huge hit upon its release, topping the British charts while debuting at number 60 on the *Billboard* album charts in the United States. With its added live instrumentation, heavier dub grooves, and somewhat abrasive, punk-like guitars, *Mezzanine* represented—in the opinion of many—almost as great an innovation as did *Blue Lines*. A critic for *NME* (on-line) gave it an eight rating and described the band as "the greatest English group of the last ten years." Writing for the *Village Voice* (May 19, 1998), James Hunter declared that on *Mezzanine* the group "intentionally blur the blueprints and the juicy effects of musical slam dunks, achieving the current pinnacle of advanced sonic design. Here is a record actually grounded in architectural concepts applied to the funk, the symphonicism, the dub, even the trip-hop that people associate with Bristol's unique beat magicians. . . . Massive Attack's new music is so blindingly realized it refuses to be heard as hypothesis; the result is post-experimental jams pulled off with plush mentalism by DJ/musician/producers ready for love."

"We wanted to take the album in a new direction, or should I say an old direction?" Marshall told Mark Jenkins. "We thought, Let's go for the things we were into before in the old days, before we became deejays. Things that were more personal to us." "This one has a sense of a journey about it, a feeling of movement," del Naja told Artistdirect (on-line). "And you can listen to it at different levels. If you play it loud, it's quite in-your-face; if you turn it down, it's quite moody. We wanted there to be a lot of depth and scope to it." The album's first single, "Teardrop," charted at number 10 in the U.K. and was named single of the week by the *NME*. "Water is my eye / Most faithful mirror / Fearless on my breath / Teardrop on the fire of a confession," Liz Fraser sang over a dub background. The single was followed by "Angel" and "Inertia Creeps." *Mezzanine* was later shortlisted for the Mercury Music Prize and was chosen as "album of the year" at the *Q* awards. In November 1998 the MTV Europe Awards gave Massive Attack the best video award for "Teardrop." (The band received some negative press with accusations that they behaved rudely in accepting the award.) In January 1999, in the annual *NME* poll, the publication's readers voted to give Massive Attack the Godlike Genius Award for Unique Services to Music.

Vowles made it known in March 2000 that he was leaving Massive Attack, as he was dissatisfied with the musical direction the group was taking, especially the punk influence evident on *Mezzanine*; he planned to pursue a career as a hip-hop producer. The two remaining members said that they would continue the group as a duo. In 2002, however, Marshall announced that he was taking a leave of absence from the group to raise his family. Del Naja decided to continue recording under the name Massive Attack in the interim, recruiting the producer Neil Davidge as a full-time collaborator. In February 2003, with its ranks reduced, Massive Attack released *100th Window*, which included vocals by Horace Andy as well as Sinéad O'Connor. (The title of the album was taken from Charles Jennings and Lori Fena's book *The Hundredth Window: Protecting Your Privacy and Security in the Age of the Internet*.) The album topped the British charts while receiving mixed reviews. "Though del Naja is mostly successful giving the people what they want . . . it unfortunately comes as a sacrifice [of] the very thing that made Massive Attack so crucial to dance music: their never-ending progression to a radically different sound with each release," John Bush wrote in his review for *All Music Guide* (on-line). "For better or worse, *100th Window* has the same crushingly oppressive productions, dark, spiralling bass lines, and pile-driving beats instantly familiar to fans of *Mezzanine*. . . . That's satisfaction enough for those who kept *Mezzanine* near their stereo for years on end,

but a disappointment to those expecting another masterpiece." A critic wrote for *Rolling Stone* (February 20, 2003), "Massive Attack fans won't be startled by anything on *100th Window*, but at nine tracks, this may be the most accessible, freaky, futuristic electronic head-food album on the market." Writing in the *New York Times* (March 16, 2003) after the release of *100th Window*, Jody Rosen noted that while Massive Attack had founded trip-hop, the group's music had since "gotten darker and more abstract. Today, trip-hop is the most toothless of beats-based styles; it's easy listening for hipsters in space-age sneakers. *100th Window* finds trip-hop's progenitor fully broken with the genre it invented, making the bleakest and most beautiful sounds of its career."

In late 2002 del Naja and Damon Albarn, the lead vocalist for the group Blur, who had previously collaborated on the track "One Day at a Time" for the soundtrack to the 2000 film *Ordinary Decent Criminal*, became actively involved in the movement opposing the buildup for a U.S.-led invasion of Iraq. The musicians helped lead a huge protest at Hyde Park, in London, England, in September 2002, and in January 2003 they paid for antiwar ads in *NME*. In an interview with *dotmusic* (February 5, 2003, on-line), del Naja criticized other pop stars for focusing on their careers while ignoring world crises, saying, "I find it amazing that people detach themselves, because regardless of what your band is about, what your music is and how you present yourself to the world as an individual, you are involved. The world's become a smaller place due to communication and due to travel and you get to see things much quicker than you used to and famines and disasters are right there. I don't see how you can remove yourself from that. So as an individual, I'd be getting involved [in the anti-war protests] regardless of the band." In February 2003 del Naja found himself embroiled in another kind of controversy, when he was arrested for purchasing child pornography over the Internet. Del Naja emphatically denied all the charges and, freed on bail, continued with plans for touring. (The charges were later dropped.) Del Naja was a renowned graffiti artist before joining the Wild Bunch and has had his art exhibited on several occasions; Jody Rosen reported that del Naja "likes to paint on a big canvas, in shades of black." He also published a limited-edition art book, entitled *Fitting In*. Grant Marshall performed with Massive Attack on the *100th Window* tour.

—G.O.

Suggested Reading: *All Music Guide* (on-line); Artistdirect (on-line); dotmusic (on-line) Feb. 5, 2003; *New York Times* II p29 Mar. 16, 2003, with photo; *NME* (on-line); *Space Age Bachelor* (on-line); *Washington Post* G p4 Sep. 6, 1998

Selected Recordings: *Blue Lines*, 1991; *Protection*, 1994; *No Protection*, 1995; *Mezzanine*, 1998; *100th Window*, 2003

Donald Miralle/Getty Images

Mayweather, Floyd

Feb. 24, 1977– Boxer

*Address: c/o Top Rank Inc., 3980 Howard
Hughes Pkwy., Suite 580, Las Vegas, NV 89109*

Floyd Mayweather, nicknamed "Pretty Boy," has built a reputation as one of the best boxers of his generation. Mayweather became the first member of the 1996 U.S. Olympic boxing team to earn a professional world title when he won the World Boxing Council (WBC) junior-lightweight championship, in 1998. He went on to capture the lightweight title in 2002, giving it up two years later to compete as a 140-pounder, or junior welterweight; his first foray into that weight class resulted in a victory over DeMarcus Corley in May 2004. Mayweather, undefeated in 32 fights, uses his lightning-fast punches and enormous patience in the ring to dominate his opponents. He has credited much of his success to his versatility. "I can stand there and fight toe to toe; I can box; I can fight offensively or defensively," he told an interviewer for the HBO Boxing Web site. "I can fight whatever style is necessary to win." Often compared to the boxing legend Sugar Ray Leonard for his fighting style and for his reputation as a showman, Mayweather said, as quoted by Tim Dahlberg for the Associated Press (September 10, 1999), "I plan on being in the history books by the time I'm done boxing."

Floyd Mayweather Jr. was born on February 24, 1977 in Grand Rapids, Michigan, into a family of boxers. His father, Floyd Mayweather Sr., retired as a professional boxer in 1990 with a record of 28 wins, six losses, one tie, and 19 knockouts. Floyd Jr.'s uncle Roger Mayweather was a world champion in the junior-lightweight and super-lightweight divisions, while another uncle, Jeff Mayweather, was a world-title contender for several years. When Floyd Jr. was a small child, his father taught him to box, holding up the three-year-old so he could hit the speed bag. "When I was in the crib, I was already throwing punches," he told the interviewer for the HBO Boxing Web site. "Then, as I grew, I started throwing punches at various objects, such as doorknobs." At a young age he decided to make boxing his career. "I was getting in fights all the time anyway," he told Andy Johnston for the *Augusta Chronicle* (July 6, 1996, on-line), "so I figured I'd do it in the ring and make my family proud." As Floyd Mayweather Sr. recalled to Ira Berkow for the *New York Times* (March 24, 1998), he told his son, "You're only young once. You have great ability. You've got a chance to become a rich man, and not have to end up working in someone's factory. Professional boxing is a short career. Be smart; give it everything you have." In amateur fights as a 126-pounder, trained by his uncle Roger, Mayweather compiled a record of 84 wins and six losses. In 1993 and 1994 he won back-to-back national Golden Gloves championships, and he took that title again in 1996. A year earlier he had won the National Police Athletic League championship and been named the United States amateur champion. At around this time he was given the nickname "Pretty Boy." "I got that name not because of my looks," he said for the HBO Boxing Web site, "but because when my fights finished, I never came out cut or bruised. My amateur teammates gave me the name." (His nickname and given name also recall the early-20th-century gangster Pretty Boy Floyd.)

As a competitor at the 1996 U.S. Olympic Games, held in Atlanta, Georgia, Mayweather defeated his first opponent, Bakhtiyar Tileganov of Kazakhstan, in the second round. "I just wanted to tear the guy's head off," Mayweather told Thomas Heath for the *Washington Post* (July 23, 1996). "I went out there and the crowd had me going. The crowd had me pumped." He also noted, "When I went out there, I was so happy. I'm in the Olympics. That's been my dream all my life." He went on to win a decision over Arthur Gevorgyan of Armenia, then to defeat Lorenzi Aragon; the latter fight was the first in 20 years in which an American fighter had bested a Cuban. Mayweather then lost to Serafin Todorov of Bulgaria, in a controversial decision that resulted in a U.S. protest. "Being robbed is part of boxing, both in the amateurs and the pros," Mayweather said, according to the HBO Boxing Web site. "I am just one of many Americans that have been cheated out of a gold medal. . . . Being robbed just made me go into the pro ranks hungrier and more determined." Mayweather was awarded a bronze medal and left the Olympics regarded as a major professional boxing prospect.

Mayweather attributed his success in part to the advice of his father. Although Floyd Mayweather Sr. was in prison during his son's Olympic bouts, because of a 1993 conviction for smuggling cocaine, he was able to coach Floyd Jr. through telephone calls. "When I was in the ring at the Olympics, it was my father's words that I was hearing, not the coaches'," Mayweather told Timothy W. Smith for the *New York Times* (December 18, 1998). "I never listened to what the coaches said. I would call my father and he would give me advice from prison." Because of his father's example, Mayweather vowed never to get involved with drugs. "It hurt me inside when he told me he was going to be locked up," he told Andy Johnston. "It still hurts me. He helps me with everything. I saw my father's downfall. I've learned to stay away from the drug game. It's not a lifelong career. You either wind up dead or in prison."

In his first professional fight, in the 130-pound (or junior-lightweight) class, Mayweather took on Roberto Apodaca in Las Vegas, Nevada, on October 11, 1996, winning with a knockout in the second round. "I like being a pro much better," Mayweather was quoted as saying by Tim Dahlberg for the Associated Press (October 11, 1996). "I feel fighting professionally is easier. . . . You see all the punches much better because there is no headgear. The hooks I hit him with they may have called low blows in the amateurs." In his only other fight that year, Mayweather won a unanimous decision over Reggie Sanders on November 30 in Albuquerque, New Mexico. He dispatched his next five opponents with first- and second-round knockouts. By the end of 1997 Mayweather had compiled a record of 12 wins and no losses. "I know for sure I'm the best fighter in the world," Mayweather said to John Reid for the New Orleans *Times-Picayune* (January 9, 1998). "I got a lot of doubters because I've only fought 12 fights. But I like being in the ring, performing . . . I love being a showman." Mayweather started out the year 1998 with a fifth-round knockout of Hector Arroyo. For Mayweather's fight with Sam Girard, his father, by then out of prison, took over as his manager and trainer; Mayweather knocked Girard out in the second round. After dispatching Miguel Melo, Gustavo Cuello, and Tony Pep, Mayweather faced off against Genaro Hernandez on October 3, 1998 for the WBC junior-lightweight title. In a performance that catapulted the 21-year-old to stardom, Mayweather knocked out the highly regarded Hernandez in the eighth round to win the title. "I never thought I would lose a fight the way I did," Hernandez was quoted as saying on the HBO Boxing Web site. "He was just too quick and good for me. He proved to be the best." As reported by Royce Feour for the *Las Vegas Review-Journal* (October 4, 1998, on-line), Mayweather embraced his father after the fight and said, "I love you dad. I love you dad. This is for you."

For his first defense of the WBC junior-lightweight title, on December 19, 1998, Mayweather faced Angel Manfredy, scoring a knockout in the second round. According to Timothy W. Smith in the *New York Times* (December 20, 1998), Mayweather "stunned Manfredy with a devastating overhand right that crashed on Manfredy's chin. Manfredy's knees buckled and he wobbled into the ropes, where he stayed pinned as Mayweather landed at least 20 unanswered punches, and Referee Frank Santore pondered whether to stop the fight." Mayweather noted that his punches had become more accurate, and that he had received far fewer head butts, since his father had become his manager. "I'm back to using my jab a lot more," he told Smith for the *New York Times* (December 18, 1998). "I've shortened up my punches and I'm moving my head more. I land a higher percentage of punches than any boxer in boxing. I'm landing over 50 percent. That's because I only shoot when I'm in range. That's something my dad has helped me learn." When asked why he took on such touted boxers as Hernandez and Manfredy so early in his career, Mayweather noted, as quoted on the HBO Boxing Web site, "I wanted to give people what they want as soon as possible. I want to keep boxing from becoming like wrestling, where people already know who's going to win. By fighting the best, you create even fights where fans don't know who will be the victor. This creates interest. I also want to create an explosion, and I think I have done that."

After besting Carlos Rios on February 17, 1999 in his hometown of Grand Rapids, Mayweather defeated Justin Juuko on the following May 22 and took on Carlos Gerena on September 11. Although Gerena tried to distract Mayweather by "trash talking," Mayweather beat him in seven rounds. Soon afterward Mayweather rejected a contract with HBO and Top Rank, a Las Vegas–based promotion company, that would have paid him $12.5 million for six fights, calling it a "slave contract." (He later signed a contract with them for $15 million.) His response to the first offer caused a rift between him and Floyd Mayweather Sr., with the result that the fighter threw the older man out of his house and later fired him as his trainer and manager. In his place Mayweather hired James Prince as his manager and started to work with his uncle Roger Mayweather again as his trainer. The change in personnel had no outward effect on Mayweather's prowess. He started 2000 by defeating Coyo Vargas in 12 rounds and followed by scoring a technical knockout (TKO) against Emanuel Burton in nine rounds on October 21, 2000. By the end of that difficult, non-title fight, Mayweather was bleeding from his nose and mouth and had injured his right hand. "I need opponents like Emanuel Burton," Mayweather said, according to Michael Katz in the *Detroit News* (October 22, 2000, on-line). "I need to fight big, strong guys. He was one of my toughest opponents because he was so physically strong." His next fight was against Diego Corrales, who entered the ring with a 33–0 record. Before the bout, Mayweather announced that he was going to beat Corrales "on behalf of all the battered women in the world"—a reference to Corrales's having been charged with beating his wife. Mayweather purchased tickets to the fight for a local women's organization and announced that he wanted to fly Corrales's wife to the bout. With tensions high, the two boxers engaged in several near-scuffles in the days before the event. In the fight, held on January 20, 2001, Mayweather knocked Corrales out in 10 rounds, dominating him throughout and landing 56 percent of his shots. After the fight, as Kevin Iole reported in the *Washington Post* (January 21, 2001), Mayweather told Corrales, "I respect you as a fighter. What I said was only hype to sell some tickets." With that victory, Mayweather's record stood at 25–0.

In his next fight, Mayweather defeated Carlos Hernandez in 12 rounds on May 26, 2001, then won by TKO in nine rounds against Jesus Chavez on November 10, 2001. For his April 20, 2002 bout against Jose Luis Castillo for the WBC lightweight title, Mayweather increased his weight to 135 pounds. In a close and controversial decision, he was awarded a unanimous victory after 12 rounds; *Jet* (May 13, 2002) reported that Mayweather's "stick-and-move style" helped him to win. In a second match against Castillo, on December 7 of the same year, Mayweather won an undisputed victory, "soundly outbox[ing]" his opponent, in the judgment of Richard Hoffer in *Sports Illustrated* (December 16, 2002). On April 19, 2003 Mayweather retained his WBC lightweight title with a unanimous 12-round decision against Victoriano Sosa of the Dominican Republic. He ended the year with a seventh-round TKO of South Africa's Phillip N'Dou on November 1. As reported by a writer for spboxing.com, N'Dou "survived a rough start, came back, and provided a brave effort that enabled Mayweather to display his wares in a true slugfest that had the fans on their feet."

For his first fight of 2004, Mayweather gained weight—and relinquished his WBC lightweight title—to compete in the 140-pound (junior welterweight) class against DeMarcus "Chop Chop" Corley on May 22. According to the Associated Press (May 23, 2004), Mayweather "made the jump in weight class look easy," knocking Curley down twice before winning the 12-round fight. There has been much talk of a possible match between Mayweather and the junior-welterweight champion, Arturo Gatti.

Mayweather lives in Las Vegas, Nevada, where he has formed a rap record label, Filthy Rich Records. In the *Las Vegas Review-Journal* (January 17, 2001), Kevin Iole noted that it is "difficult to pick the real Mayweather from among his many perceived personas." Those personas, he wrote, included the highly gifted athlete; the man whom Mayweather's manager, James Prince, called a "fun-loving, 24-7 bundle of energy"; and a third, less endearing figure. The last-named persona seems to have surfaced in Mayweather's relations with his family and others. He has reportedly fueled the rivalry between his uncle and trainer, Roger Mayweather, and his former trainer, Floyd Mayweather Sr., whom the boxer has said "is jealous of me." (After his professional relationship with his son was severed, Floyd Mayweather Sr. became the trainer of the well-regarded boxer Oscar De La Hoya.) In addition, in 2004 Mayweather was accused of striking the mother of three of his children and, in a separate incident, of kicking a man in a bar scuffle.

For his part, Mayweather told Kevin Iole, "I'm just a regular guy, someone who wants to be a good father and a good friend and who wants to be great at what I do in my job. I'm a guy who loves my kids and who wants them to have the best of everything. And I get such a joy out of them. There is nothing false or dishonest about kids. My kids don't care how much money I have or whether I am a world champion. . . . They just love me for who I am, not for what I have. My kids couldn't care less if I'm in boxing or not. They love me for me." Discussing his lifestyle, he told Chris Cozzone for *Babes of Boxing* (2001, on-line), "I like to drive expensive cars. I like to wear expensive jewelry. . . . But when it's time to work, I'm gonna work. To get those things, you got to work hard. And to keep giving myself gifts and bonuses, I'm gonna keep working hard, to keep getting those things. . . . Eventually, it will wear out when I'm older but right now I'm young. I'm flashy. I'm flamboyant."

—G.O.

Suggested Reading: *Augusta Chronicle* (on-line) July 6, 1996, with photo; HBO.com; *Jet* p54 May 13, 2003; *Las Vegas Review–Journal* (on-line) Jan. 17, 2001, with photo; *New York Times* D p4 Dec. 18, 1998, VIII p6 Dec. 20, 1998; *Washington Post* D J an. 20, 2001

McBride, Martina

July 29, 1966– Country-music singer

Address: P.O. Box 291627, Nashville, TN 37229-1627

Known for her powerhouse vocals and poignant songs, Martina McBride is one of the preeminent female singers on the country-music scene. While her recordings are generally considered contemporary country, she has earned the admiration of traditionalists for her obvious appreciation of the roots of country music. Since the debut of her first recording, in 1992, she has sold almost eight million albums and has seen six of her songs reach the top of the country-music charts. In such songs as "Independence Day," "A Broken Wing," "Cheap Whiskey," and "Concrete Angel," she has ad-

Martina McBride

Courtesy of RCA Label Group

began singing and playing keyboards at local clubs and dances with her father's country-rock band, the Schifters. By the time she reached high school, she was the group's lead singer as well as keyboardist. (Her brother Marty played guitar—he is now a member of her tour band—and her mother worked the soundboard.) She has named Buck Owens, Merle Haggard, Rickie Lee Jones, Aretha Franklin, Lefty Frizzell, K.T. Oslin, George Strait, and Linda Ronstadt among her favorite singers.

After she graduated from high school (in a class of 10), in about 1984, McBride spent one semester in college before dropping out to pursue a career in music. She worked at a local Dairy Queen for a while, then began touring Kansas with various country bands. She moved to Hutchinson and later lived in Wichita, where she gained recognition on the local music scene; in 1990 she settled in Nashville with her husband, John McBride, a sound engineer and production manager, whom she had married in 1988. There she waited tables and made demos while her husband worked for such stars as the singer and bandleader Charlie Daniels and the country musician Ricky Van Shelton. After John McBride became Garth Brooks's production manager, he helped Martina get a job selling T-shirts for the tour, so that they could travel together. At the end of 1991, Martina signed a contract with RCA, and soon afterward she became Brooks's opening act.

McBride's debut album, *The Time Has Come* (1992), spent six months on the country-album Top 50 charts. The title track, released as her first single, remained on the charts for five months; her next two singles, "That's Me" and "Cheap Whiskey," also from *The Time Has Come*, nearly reached the Top 40. With her second album, she made her mark in country music. Released in 1993, *The Way That I Am* contains the singles "My Baby Loves Me the Way That I Am," "Life #9," and "Independence Day," all of which received heavy airplay and helped sales of the album to exceed 500,000 copies. "My Baby Loves Me" rose to number two on the country chart, and "Life #9" to number six. The song and video "Independence Day" deal with a battered wife who takes justice into her own hands; they aroused some controversy and upset some listeners. Nevertheless, the song was a hit and became McBride's signature song.

The title track of McBride's third album, *Wild Angels* (1995), was her first number-one hit. The record also offered the single "Safe in the Arms of Love," which climbed to number four, and a cover version of Delbert McClinton's "Two More Bottles of Wine." McBride's next effort, *Evolution* (1997), became her first Top 10 album on the country chart, selling more than three million copies. The duet she sang with Jim Brickman on it, "Valentine," was a Top 10 country hit and, in addition, crossed over to become her first big single on the adult-contemporary chart, moving to number three. *Evolution* spawned two number-two country hits, "Happy Girl" and "Whatever You Say," and

dressed such social problems as domestic violence, alcohol abuse, and child abuse. In doing so she has distinguished herself from many other country singers and perturbed or even angered some country-music fans as well. McBride, who does not write songs, has maintained that she chooses only material with which she feels comfortable. "I've always had a very strong sense of self, even as a kid," she told Kay West for *Country Music* (August-September 2003). "It was my upbringing, and I am really grateful for that. It has led me through the paths of my career. Looking back, there were a couple of times I was asked to do things I was not real comfortable with or didn't feel suited me, and I just said no, that's not me. It comes down to knowing yourself, and what is right for you, as an artist, as a professional and as a person." By her own account, unlike Faith Hill, Shania Twain, LeAnn Rimes, and various other female country performers, McBride does not aspire to crossover success, although some of her music has appeared on the adult-contemporary and pop charts. "I never feel restricted by [country] music," she told Margo Whitmire for *Billboard* (September 27, 2003). "And I don't necessarily have the desire to be a bigger celebrity than I already am. I love country music, and I love being known as a country music artist."

One of the four children of Daryl and Jeanne Schiff, the singer was born Martina Mariea Schiff on July 29, 1966 in Medicine Lodge, Kansas; she grew up nearby, on the 400-acre family dairy farm, outside Sharon (population 200). She has an older brother, Steve, an older sister, Gina, and younger brother, Marty. Martina became a fan of traditional country music at an early age, and at age seven she

two number-one singles, "A Broken Wing" and "Wrong Again."

In 1998 McBride joined the rock musician Bob Seger to sing "Chances Are," which was included on the soundtrack to the film *Hope Floats*. The song received considerable airplay on pop and adult-contemporary stations. Also that year McBride became the first country star to join the popular annual concert tour Lilith Fair, which featured female singers and female-led bands, and she recorded a collection of holiday songs, *White Christmas*. Her next album, *Emotion* (1999), contains the lead single "I Love You," which hit number one on the country chart and received airplay on adult-contemporary radio as well. The follow-ups, "Love's the Only House," "There You Are," and "It's My Time," were also popular, the first two reaching the Top 10.

In 2001 McBride released *Greatest Hits*, which went double platinum (selling more than two million copies) and became her first album to reach number one on the country chart; it sold well enough to make the pop Top Five as well. *Greatest Hits* contains four new tracks, all of which were released as singles: "Concrete Angel," "Blessed," which hit number one, and "When God-Fearin' Women Get the Blues" and "Where Would You Be," both of which reached the Top 10. "This 18-song CD proves that [McBride] has a solid ear for songs and a high sense of drama when it comes to delivering them . . . ," Robert Baird wrote for *Country Music* (December 2001–January 2002). "'When God-Fearin' Women Get the Blues,' a full-on, Dobro-tinged rocker . . . shows off her ability to adopt an aggressive attitude while letting her phenomenal voice wail. . . . 'Where Would You Be' is the kind of soaring ballad that McBride always nails. 'Concrete Angel' is the weakest new track, though it finds McBride once again focusing on an important social issue—in this case, child abuse. The new song listeners might find most striking is a gorgeous, mid-tempo tune, 'Blessed.' . . . This generous package does a credible job of summing up the highlights of McBride's past and hinting at what the future still holds."

Martina (2003), McBride's first release of all-new music in four years, debuted at number one on the country chart and number seven on *Billboard's* Top 200 chart; the lead single, "This One's For the Girls," became a hit and was nominated for a Grammy Award. Reviewers, however, had reservations about *Martina's* merits. "You'll never hear more beautifully sung sap" was Chris Willman's assessment for *Entertainment Weekly* (October 17, 2003), while Ralph Novak, in *People* (October 13, 2003), wrote, "'She's a Butterfly' and 'Reluctant Daughter'. . . tend to the pedantic, and McBride's penchant for histrionics doesn't make them any more subtle. 'God's Will,' about an impaired boy, is especially on the preachy side. . . . McBride . . . can be restrained and intelligently evocative when she applies herself. Mostly, though, McBride seems to choose and perform material with the prospective video in mind."

In a review of one of her concerts, Jon Pareles wrote for the *New York Times* (December 7, 1999), "Ms. McBride is part of a generation of nominal country singers whose audiences are in the suburbs, and whose strongest musical roots are in 1970's soft rock. Most of her music looks toward the steady-strummed California folk-rock of Sheryl Crow and Tom Petty, with touches of John Mellencamp. She uses her clear voice the way Ms. Crow does, easing down to a breathy, conversational tone before working up to choruses that peal with confidence. Ms. McBride has reserves of lung power; every few songs she would seize a note and hold it until the audience cheered."

McBride won a Country Music Association (CMA) award for video of the year for "Independence Day" in 1994. She was named female vocalist of the year by that organization in 1999, 2002, and 2003. She also received awards as female vocalist of the year from the Academy of Country Music (ACM) in 2002 and 2003. She was honored with the American Music Award for favorite female country artist in 2002 and 2003, the *Billboard* Music Award for country female artist of the year in 2002, and *Country Music Today* (*CMT*) Flameworthy Awards for the "Concrete Angel" and "Blessed" videos. She ranked 25th on *CMT*'s list of the greatest women of country music, and "Independence Day" was ranked ninth on *CMT*'s list of "100 Greatest Songs of Country Music." In September 2003 the Recording Academy (the organization that bestows Grammy Awards) gave McBride its highest honor, the Heroes Award, for her work with various organizations, among them those that strive to end domestic violence. That same month she was also honored with a "Mothers and Shakers" award from *Redbook*, for her inspirational songs as well as her charitable activities. McBride has served as a national spokesperson for the National Network to End Domestic Violence and Domestic Violence Intervention Services; she has spoken with female students at junior-high schools about ways to avoid potentially violent relationships and has established a building fund for Safe Haven Family Shelter in Nashville, to help the shelter expand its facilities. Since 1994 McBride has hosted a charity auction, with proceeds donated to the YWCA; she has also donated items for auctions benefiting St. Jude Children's Research Hospital and the Discovery Fund for Eye Research and has partnered with ChildHelp USA to raise awareness of child abuse.

McBride is a member of the Grand Ole Opry and the board of directors of the Country Music Retirement Center. She and her husband, John McBride, have two daughters: Delaney Katherine, born in December 1994, and Emma Justine, born in March 1998. The family lives in Brentwood, Tennessee, a Nashville suburb. In her leisure time McBride enjoys watching movies, reading, cooking, bowling, and swimming.

—K.E.D.

Suggested Reading: *Billboard* p45 Sep. 27, 2003, with photo; *Country Music* p22+ Aug./Sep. 2003, with photos; *People* p49 Jan. 12, 1998, with photos

Selected Recordings: *The Time Has Come*, 1992; *The Way That I Am*, 1993; *Wild Angels*, 1995; *Evolution*, 1997; *White Christmas*, 1998, *Emotion*, 1999; *Greatest Hits*, 2001; *Martina*, 2003

Courtesy of the Cartoon Network

McCracken, Craig

1971– Creator of The Powerpuff Girls

Address: c/o Powerpuff Girls, *Scholastic World Headquarters, 557 Broadway, New York, NY 10012*

In 1998 television audiences saw the introduction of three very unusual superheroes: Blossom, Bubbles, and Buttercup, the kindergarten-aged protagonists of the Emmy Award–nominated, animated show *The Powerpuff Girls*, on the Cartoon Network cable channel. In their many attempts to "save the world before bedtime" (as the show's voiceover narrator announces), the Powerpuff Girls strike a balance between the girlish and the gruff, the pugnacious and the precious. As is known to fans of the show, Blossom, Bubbles, and Buttercup were created in a lab by Professor Utonium, who combined "sugar, spice, everything nice," and an accidental dose of the powerful Chemical X; each episode of the program begins with a reenactment of the girls' literally explosive origin. In re-

ality, the girls came to life in a slightly less spectacular manner—in the imagination of the animator Craig McCracken.

McCracken was born in Charleroi, Pennsylvania, in 1971 and moved with his family to Whittier, California, at age seven. McCracken's father died when his son was seven, too; afterward, McCracken, his sister, and his brother were raised primarily by their mother and grandmother. As a child in what he has called a family of artists, he was fascinated by cartoons and comics and started drawing by the age of three. Early on, he showed a fondness for stories about superheroes; his favorite animated TV shows included *Batman, The Adventures of Rocky and Bullwinkle, Superman,* and *Underdog.* His mother encouraged his interest by making him a cape, which he donned to become "Super Craig." By age 12 he had decided that he wanted to be a cartoonist, and he began drawing and distributing his own comic books to his friends. McCracken was originally interested in comic books and comic strips; he later changed his focus to animation and filmmaking. After graduating from high school, he enrolled at California Institute of the Arts (CalArts), in Valencia, California, having discovered that the school offered a course in character animation.

At CalArts, animation students' primary goal each year is still to create a short film. McCracken's first film was *No Neck Joe*, about the misadventures of a boy whose affliction is suggested by the title. For his sophomore film project, McCracken wanted to make a superhero cartoon, one that eschewed the cliché of the cape-clad, muscle-bound protagonist. He had difficulty, though, thinking of a character to replace that shopworn model. One day in 1991, while McCracken was struggling to come up with an idea, his mother reminded him that his brother's birthday was approaching. Taking a break from his film project, intending merely to draw a card for his brother, McCracken started doodling and came up with a trio of simple, Pop Art–inspired little girls, similar to the children with huge, sad eyes painted by Margaret and Walter Keane in the 1960s and seen on posters and cards. McCracken was pleased with the resulting birthday card and, later the same day, realized that those cute, big-eyed little girls might be exactly the sort of inventive new superheroes he had been trying to create. He dubbed the trio the "Whoopass Girls," deciding that they were made of sugar, spice, and "a can of whoopass." The three-minute cartoon he built around them, *Whoopass Stew: A Sticky Situation*, was selected for inclusion in the 1994 Festival of Animation.

Shortly thereafter, McCracken left CalArts when a friend recommended him for a job at the animation studio Hanna-Barbera, as art director of the cartoon *2 Stupid Dogs.* (That course of events, he has said, is not unusual; students in McCracken's field often do not stay at CalArts for the full four years.) While at the cable channel Cartoon Network, a division of Hanna-Barbera, McCracken heard about a program of short cartoons that was going to air, and suggested *Whoopass Stew* for inclusion. The studio's executives liked McCracken's concept but, unsurprisingly, felt that the name presented a problem. McCracken explained in an interview with *IGN for Men* (August 20, 1999, on-line), "Somewhere along the line somebody at Cartoon Network said, 'You know, we really can't market a show for kids with the word 'Ass' in it.' So we had to come up with something else." While thinking about new names for the Whoopass Girls, two of McCracken's friends, independently of each other, suggested "Powerpuff," which McCracken liked. In addition, the "can of whoopass" was replaced by the mysterious, science-fictionesque Chemical X, and the show, entitled *The Powerpuff Girls*, premiered on Cartoon Network in 1998.

With a number of helpers working with him, McCracken no longer needed to animate the show himself; he has continued to supervise his team, however, and actively participates in storyboarding and scripting episodes as well. The cartoon is set in the city of Townsville, which is plagued by more than its share of villains, monsters, and disasters of all sorts. One of its citizens, the square-headed, avuncular Professor Utonium, is fed up with all of the unpleasantness surrounding him and takes to his laboratory to create perfect little girls. While mixing a batch of "sugar, spice, and everything nice," he accidentally knocks some potent Chemical X into the concoction, which results in the creation of the three Powerpuff Girls—who fit the professor's ideal and have the added benefit of super powers. The leader of the trio, the pink-clad redhead Blossom, is brainy and occasionally bossy; Buttercup, who has black hair and wears lime green, is a tomboy who loves giving "knuckle sandwiches" to monsters; and Bubbles, a blond who wears light-blue clothes, is the sweetest of the sisters, an animal lover with a penchant for coloring. All three are drawn in a simple, iconic style that McCracken described for *IGN for Men* as "graphic representations of a cute girl, like a symbol." The girls have oversized round heads, enormous, saucer-like eyes, distinctive hairdos (Blossom wears her hair long with a bow, Buttercup has a bob, and Bubbles wears pigtails), belted dresses, white tights, and Mary Jane shoes. Their hands are fingerless, and their noses and ears are not visible. Different episodes pit the Powerpuff Girls against a variety of nemeses; Townsville is not only invaded routinely by nameless monsters, but has resident villains as well, including Mojo Jojo, a maniacal ape with a bulging brain, and Princess Morbucks, a rich, spoiled girl who uses her father's wealth to finance schemes to defeat the Powerpuff Girls, whom she actually wants to join. Among the Powerpuff Girls' allies are Professor Utonium; the bumbling mayor of Townsville; his brilliant and sexy secretary, Ms. Sara Bellum; and the girls' supportive, enthusiastic kindergarten teacher, Ms. Keane.

The enormously popular cartoon, which completed its fifth season in 2003, has been nominated for three Emmy Awards. Most of the episodes have been released on video and/or DVD, and a direct-to-DVD Powerpuff Girls film, *'Twas the Fight Before Christmas*, was released in time for the 2003 holidays. Meanwhile, the Powerpuff Girls had their big-screen debut on July 3, 2002, in *The Powerpuff Girls Movie*, which cost $10 million to make and grossed over $6 million in the first five days of its release. The feature-length film is a prequel to the series, detailing the origins of the Powerpuff Girls and one of their enemies, Mojo Jojo. According to Chuck Koplinski of cinema-scoping.com (2002, on-line), "Much more than a visual overload, *The Powerpuff Girls* is a non-stop barrage of pop culture allusions buoyed by witty puns and a vibrant pallet that has a deceptively minimalist look to it that belies how truly sophisticated it is. [It is] breathlessly entertaining, uncommonly smart." While some critics were less impressed with the picture as a whole, McCracken's animation style and the film's techno-driven soundtrack garnered consistent praise. The Powerpuff Girls have inspired an abundance of merchandise, and their images have been used to sell everything from cereal, bandages, and shower curtains to nail polish, piñatas, and even guitars.

The popularity of *The Powerpuff Girls* has surprised its creator. McCracken told Keith Phipps for the Onion A.V. Club (June 21, 2000, on-line), "I thought I would get a college hit where 20-year-olds would watch it in their dorms when they're stoned. That was it. And it would be real fringe, and maybe rave kids would pick up on it, but I didn't think it would hit as big as it has." While McCracken had relatively low expectations, he had high hopes. He detailed his intentions on Cartoon-Network.com (on-line), explaining that "a big influence on Powerpuff Girls" is the 1960s TV show *Batman*, with Adam West in the title role: "I wanted at some point to make a show like that that could work on two levels where, you know, an adult can watch it and see all the humor in it but a kid can watch it just for pure action and entertainment. And so I thought, well, that would be a really good thing if you could make a show that would work twice in a person's life. You know, they can enjoy it again." McCracken has apparently achieved that goal; popular with children, the show has also attracted a cult following among adults, and in all, approximately 19 million viewers tune in weekly to watch the cartoon. As of late 2004, reruns aired once daily on Cartoon Network.

The cartoon's success with older viewers is due largely to its myriad pop-culture references. McCracken told Keith Phipps that the show contains "a nice little sprinkling of homages to things, as opposed to being direct: 'Here they are, in *Jurassic Park*.' There are a lot of little things like that that people might not pick up on. The mayor's office is actually Commissioner Gordon's office from the *Batman* show. We designed it the same way as kind of a tip of the hat to one of my favorite shows." Similarly, in the episode "Boogie Frights," there is a pointed reference to the film *Star Wars* when Bubbles, pursued by the Boogie Man, must use her laser eye beams to blow up a giant, Death Star–like disco ball that is blocking out the sun. The episode "See Me, Feel Me, Gnomey" is designed as a rock opera in the style of *Tommy,* by the rock group the Who. Another installment represents a tribute of sorts to the Beatles. First broadcast on February 9, 2001, the 37th anniversary of the Beatles' first appearance on the *Ed Sullivan Show,* "Meet the Beat-Alls" overflows with references to the group.

While many adults appreciate such pop-culture references and sly humor, the show appeals to large numbers of children, too. McCracken explained on CartoonNetwork.com that he and the other writers for the show, in order to come up with stories, start "with a foundation of what it's like to grow up and then [apply] the concept of superheroes to that." Thus, even though the Powerpuff Girls are extraordinary in that they have super powers, they have to endure the ordinary trials of childhood. McCracken felt that children would be able to relate to such episodes as "The Mane Event," in which Blossom gets a bad haircut; "Paste Makes Waste," which demonstrates the consequences of teasing; and "Power-Noia," in which the girls must overcome their fears and phobias. Additionally, McCracken has cited the show's treatment of gender as part of its appeal. He explained to Jen Fried for *Bust* (Spring 2002), "We never try to treat girls like, 'Oh, they have to act like little girls.' They're just kids. Five-year-old kids don't really know about gender roles, or sex, or anything. They're just little kids dealing with the same dumb things, whether they're boys or girls. And that's how we've always approached the show. A lot of people respond to it as, 'Oh you really understand little girls.' But I think I just know kids. . . . A lot of shows try to create positive role-model girl figures, but what they end up doing is taking everything that's girly or cool about girls and turning it around by saying, 'OK, well, she hates all that.' Little girls can still like pink and ponies or whatever and there doesn't have to be this new stereotype that ends up more anti-girl."

Despite the fact that boys compose 56 percent of the show's audience, the Powerpuff Girls have frequently been touted as pint-sized feminist icons. Heather Havrilesky of Salon.com (July 2, 2002) considered the issue: "Can a new generation of gender-blind Powerpuffs conquer inequality simply by optimistically refusing to recognize its existence? For many girls today, this approach seems to work. They don't cry out against inequality; they simply take for granted that the world will treat them fairly—and in some cases the world seems to follow suit. 'Of course I should be able to play football, or wrestle,' they tell us nonchalantly, as if suggesting otherwise is downright absurd—and it is, isn't it? A lot of boys seem to agree. (McCracken is one of them.) Power isn't something that many

women feel they should have to struggle for. And for them, dressing sexily or behaving cute is beside the point—those things should enhance their personal power, not diminish it." McCracken has maintained that the infusion of feminism into *The Powerpuff Girls* was done naturally and without much deliberation, since, growing up with his mother, sister, and grandmother, he took for granted the principle of gender equality.

McCracken lives in southern California with the *Powerpuff Girls* writer Lauren Faust and their dog, Lucy. He also works on another Cartoon Network show, *Dexter's Laboratory.* On August 14, 2004 his newest cartoon, *Foster's Home for Imaginary Friends,* premiered on Cartoon Network. McCracken told Jen Fried, "Cartoon Network is a great place to work. They put a lot of trust into their artists." "Unlike those who dream of Peter Pan's never-grow-up idealism, McCracken is living it," Rita Street wrote for *Animation Magazine* (April 2001, on-line). As he told Street, "For me there's really no delineation between what I did as a kid and what I do now."

—K.J.E.

Suggested Reading: *Bust,* with photo; CartoonNetwork.com; *IGN for Men* (on-line) Aug. 20, 1999; Onion A.V. Club (on-line) June 21, 2000; Salon.com July 2, 2002

Selected Television Shows: *The Powerpuff Girls,* 1998– ; *Foster's Home for Imaginary Friends,* 2004–

Selected Films: *The Powerpuff Girls Movie,* 2002

McKeon, Jack

(Mik-KEE-on)

Nov. 23, 1930– Baseball manager

Address: Florida Marlins, Pro Player Stadium, 2267 Dan Marino Blvd., Miami, FL 33056

At 74, Jack McKeon of the Florida Marlins is the oldest manager currently working in professional baseball and the third-oldest in baseball history, after Connie Mack and Casey Stengel (who retired at 88 and 75, respectively). In the 2003 World Series, he also became the oldest manager to lead a team to a world championship, and the Marlins' highly unexpected victory in that series—the first in which McKeon ever participated—marked the first time in his more than 50 years in baseball that any of the five teams with which he has worked won the championship during his tenure. McKeon—who at one time or another has served as player, scout, adviser on personnel matters, assistant general manager, manager, or general manager—began his career in 1949, with a Pittsburgh Pi-

Al Bello/Getty Images

Jack McKeon

rates farm team. For 14 seasons between 1955 and 1972, he managed, and sometimes also played for, a succession of clubs in various minor leagues, posting a 1,145–1,123 win–loss record and earning "manager of the year" honors four times. His résumé in Major League Baseball includes three seasons as manager of the Kansas City Royals (1973–75) and two with the Oakland Athletics (1977 and 1978); 11 seasons as vice president of baseball operations for the San Diego Padres (1980–90), during which he also held the title of general manager for about two-and-a-half seasons; and seven years (1993–2000) with the Cincinnati Reds, half that time as senior adviser for player personnel and the other half as manager. Each of those jobs ended with his dismissal. In May 2003 he came out of retirement to manage the Marlins, who were then in last place in the National League. In a remarkable turnaround a few months later, the Marlins overcame odds estimated at 150 to one to defeat the New York Yankees in six games in the World Series. When, in November 2003, the Baseball Writers' Association of America named him the National League Manager of the Year, McKeon set another record, becoming the first man to assume the job of manager in mid-season to be so honored in the same year. In a bare-bones description of McKeon's managerial skills, the Marlins' pitching coach, Wayne Rosenthal, told John Fay for the *Cincinnati Enquirer* (October 8, 2003, on-line), "He knows when to laugh and have fun, and he knows when to kick butt." McKeon has now completed his second year as the Marlins' manager.

John Aloysius "Jack" McKeon was born on November 23, 1930 in South Amboy, New Jersey, into a family of devout Roman Catholics. According to

different sources, his father, Bill McKeon, worked as a garage mechanic or owned a taxi business. While at St. Mary's High School, the local Catholic school, he served as a starter on the New Jersey high-school state championship basketball squad. After his high-school graduation, in about 1948, he enrolled at the College of the Holy Cross, in Worcester, Massachusetts, on a baseball scholarship. Major League scouts would often come to see him play, and some offered him contracts with their farm teams. McKeon rejected them, because he had promised his father that he would complete his college education. At the school's shrine to the Virgin Mary, however, he would pray that his father would agree to his leaving college to play baseball professionally. During Christmas break in his first or second year, McKeon got his wish, promising his father that he would continue his studies someday. He kept his word, taking courses at Seton Hall University, in South Orange, New Jersey, and later at Elon College, in Elon, North Carolina, where he earned a bachelor's degree in physical education and science in 1963.

In 1949 McKeon was signed as a catcher with the Pittsburgh Pirates organization, at a salary of $215 a month. He played and/or managed minor-league ball with various organizations during the next two decades, except for the year 1951, when he served in the U.S. Air Force; as a 21-year-old player/manager, he led his Sampson, New York, Air Force Base team to the air-force championship. He posted his best offensive numbers in the minor leagues during the 1958 season, when he batted .263 while playing in the Pioneer League in Missoula, Montana. Meanwhile, knowing that such numbers were not good enough for a major-league player, McKeon began to focus on perfecting his managing skills, and at age 24 he landed his first minor-league managing job. For the next 15 years, he would play in or manage 1,994 minor-league games. Initially, he became infamous in the leagues for his antics on the field. Once, as a player in the Carolina Leagues, he ran out a ground ball by passing first, running straight into the outfield, climbing the right-field foul pole, and saluting the crowd. Later, as a Pacific Coast League manager in Vancouver, Canada, he gained a lot of press by wiring two of his pitchers so that he could signal them by means of a walkie-talkie. (The league later banned that practice.) In another, better-known incident, as a minor-league manager in Wilson, North Carolina, he became frustrated while trying to teach a young Cuban player named Juan Vistuer to obey stop signals while running the base pads. "About the only way you could stop him was to tackle him," McKeon recalled to Phil Elderkin for the *Christian Science Monitor* (March 28, 1973). "Finally I told him the next time he disregarded one of my signs, I'd shoot him." Serendipitously, soon afterward he noticed in the window of a local pawnshop an inexpensive pistol that fired blank cartridges. "I bought it. And the next time [Vistuer] ran through my stop sign at third, I hauled out the pistol and pulled the trigger. After that I had no more trouble with Juan."

After spending three seasons (1965, 1966, and 1967) with the Minnesota Twins as a scout, McKeon returned to the minor leagues. He won back-to-back pennants in Omaha, Nebraska, in 1969 and 1970 as the manager of the Kansas City Royals American Association farm team. He secured his first managerial position in the major leagues in October 1972, after the Kansas City Royals fired their manager, Bob Lemon, following the team's fourth-place finish in the National League Western Division. During the 1973 season, under McKeon's tutelage, the Royals won more games than they lost and wound up in second place in the American League West. The team ended the 1974 season in fifth place, having won only 77 of 162 games. After 96 games in the 1975 season, with the team in second place in their division, the Royals' management fired McKeon (and replaced him with Whitey Herzog). Returning to the minor leagues, in 1976 he managed a winter-league team in Puerto Rico as well as an Atlanta Braves' farm team.

In 1977 McKeon was hired to manage the Oakland Athletics, in California. After 53 games the Athletics' owner, Charles Finley, removed him from that position; with Bobby Winkles succeeding him as manager, McKeon became the team's third-base coach. On May 23, 1978 Winkles quit, and Finley asked McKeon to take over again as manager. "I knew [Finley] was gonna offer me the job again . . . ," McKeon recalled to Larry Bortstein for the *Christian Science Monitor* (September 19, 1979). "On my way up to his office I said to myself, 'Why do I need this aggravation?' But by the time he offered me the job there was no way I was gonna turn it down." Under McKeon the Athletics held first place in their division for several weeks of the 1978 season. But as McKeon and the coaches had predicted, the team had insufficient raw talent to maintain that level of playing; at the end of the season, the A's stood in sixth place. McKeon lost his job soon afterward.

After spending the 1979 season as the manager of the Denver Bears, a minor-league team in the American Association, McKeon was hired as the vice president of baseball operations for the San Diego Padres, in California (a front-office position analogous to that of general manager on other teams). In that job, which he began in September 1980, McKeon was responsible for building a championship team from the ground up. He earned the nickname Trader Jack for his willingness to make multi-player trades and his uncanny ability to get the upper hand in most of those deals. During the next decade McKeon made some 45 major trades, his largest and most famous coming in December 1980: an 11-player trade with the St. Louis Cardinals. By April 1981 half of the 32 players on the Padres' spring-training roster had been acquired by McKeon, and the wisdom of his choices began to show: by the All-Star Game break in July 1982, the Padres had compiled the second-best

record in baseball up to that point in the season. By September 1982 they were in contention for the pennant, but the league championship eluded them that year.

Before the start of the 1983 season, McKeon acquired the first baseman Steve Garvey from the Los Angeles Dodgers. With the help of Garvey, the right fielder Tony Gwynn, the shortstop Gary Templeton, and the left fielder Carmelo Martinez, the Padres won the 1984 National League pennant; they then lost the World Series to the Detroit Tigers, four games to one. In the next three seasons, the Padres did not compete in the World Series.

The Padres had won only 16 of the first 46 games of the 1988 season when, on May 28 of that year, the team's owners made the radical move of naming McKeon manager of the team as well as vice president. Among the small number of men in baseball history who have worked simultaneously in the front office and the team dugout, most have not held their dual titles for long. McKeon is among the few exceptions. Under his management, the team won 67 games and lost 48 during the remainder of the 1988 season and finished in third place in their division. That turnaround earned McKeon a new contract that maintained his hold on the two managerial positions for the next three years. Meanwhile, to enable him to give greater attention to managing the dugout, the team's owner, Joan Kroc, lightened some of his front-office duties, though he continued to have a say in the makeup of the team's roster. In 1989 McKeon led the team to second place in its league, with 89 wins and 73 losses—the best Padres record since 1984.

In 1990, after McKeon had managed the team for 80 games (roughly half the season), the Padres' new owners, chaired by Tom Werner, acquiesced to McKeon's request to give up managing but continue as vice president. Soon after San Diego finished the season, in fifth place, the new owners fired McKeon, as part of a shake-up in which even the colors of the team's uniforms were changed. "I think it was a case of the new owners wanting a new identity, like the new uniforms," McKeon said, as quoted by the *Sporting News* (October 1, 1990). "I think [my dismissal] is part of that new identity. I have no problems with that, I am not bitter."

For three and a half years, beginning on January 6, 1993, McKeon served as the Cincinnati Reds' senior adviser for player personnel. On July 25, 1997 he was named manager of the club, succeeding Ray Knight. When McKeon assumed that post, in midseason, the Reds were in fourth place in the National League Central Division, with 43 wins and 56 losses. He proceeded to guide the club to a 33–30 record—the best in its division—for the remainder of 1997. The next year the Reds performed poorly. The year after that they improved dramatically, finishing the season with a record of 96–67 and in a tie with the New York Mets for the wildcard slot in the postseason play-offs. In the one-game contest for the slot, the Reds lost to the Mets.

Nevertheless, McKeon, who had just ended his 50th season in baseball, was honored in several ways: the Associated Press named him Manager of the Year; the Baseball Writers Association of America elected him National League Manager of the Year; he received both the Distinguished Service to Baseball Award and the Manager of the Year Award from the New Jersey Sportswriters Association; and he was inducted into both the New Jersey Sportswriters Hall of Fame and the North Carolina Sports Hall of Fame. In the *Sporting News*'s voting for the Manager of the Year Award, he finished second, behind Bobby Cox of the Atlanta Braves.

Despite his guiding the Reds to another second-place finish in the Central Division in 2000, with a record of 85–77, the club's management announced in October of that year that they would not renew McKeon's contract. McKeon, who was nearing 70, did not expect to receive another offer from a major-league team, so he retired. He spent the next few years at home, his activities in baseball limited to coaching his young grandsons and watching them play. Then, in May 2003, Jeffrey Loria, the owner of the Florida Marlins, feeling unhappy with the team's 16–22 start that season, hired McKeon to replace Jeff Torborg, who had just been fired as the team's manager. McKeon thus became the oldest working manager in professional baseball and the third-oldest in baseball history. Although on May 23 the Marlins' win–loss record dropped to 19–29, McKeon repeatedly advised his players to relax and enjoy themselves. "Winning is fun and fun is winning," he would say, as quoted on MLB.com (November 12, 2003). For some weeks after his arrival, McKeon did not ask the players to become contenders; rather, he told them that he would feel satisfied if each week their percentage of winning games improved. "I told them, 'The only way to get better is to work at it,'" he recalled to John Donovan for *Sports Illustrated* (September 24, 2003, on-line). He also told Donovan, "I like my players to use their imagination. I don't like pushing buttons, like they're robots. I want them to get smarter." According to Donovan, he also wanted the players "to respect their teammates. To be unselfish. To work on how they worked." Moreover, McKeon emphasized to his players early on that he would not base his managerial decisions on any particular player's ego. Thus, when the veteran catcher Ivan "Pudge" Rodriguez fell into in a hitting slump in mid-May, McKeon moved him from the third position in the batting order to sixth; Rodriguez quickly recovered his swing. McKeon also demanded more of his pitchers, especially his starting pitchers Josh Beckett and Brad Penny. In addition, he tried to make the best use of every player's natural abilities; for example, he moved the 20-year-old rookie Miguel Cabrera up in the batting order when he proved he could deliver clutch hits. Overall, McKeon took advantage of every opportunity in a game.

McKeon's approach soon paid off: of the 95 games the Marlins had played by the All-Star break, in mid-July, they had won 49, or over 51 percent. By the end of the regular season, the Marlins had a win–loss record of 91–71, second-best in their division. They then secured the National League wild-card berth in the postseason, becoming the underdogs in the quest for a World Series championship. In the National League Divisional Series, the Marlins faced the Giants, whose player Barry Bonds had become the single-season home-run champion. After losing the first game, 2–0, the Marlins won the next three games in the best-of-five series, stunning the many sportswriters who had predicted that the "overmatched" Marlins would be knocked off in the first round.

In the National League Championship Series, the Marlins faced the Chicago Cubs, the team of the home-run slugger Sammy Sosa. The Cubs were the sentimental favorites of many fans and sportswriters to win the pennant, because the franchise had not won a pennant since 1945 or a World Series since 1908, while the Marlins had won the 1997 World Series. After defeating the Cubs in the first game, in Chicago, the Marlins lost the next three games in the best-of-seven series. They then defeated the Cubs 4–0 in the fifth game and 8–3 in the sixth and clinched the pennant with a 9–6 victory in the seventh game. In contests with two of Chicago's star pitchers—Mark Prior, in Game Six, and Kerry Wood, in Game Seven—the Marlins' Chad Fox and Brad Penny, respectively, were the winning pitchers.

In the World Series the Marlins, whose payroll totaled about $50 million, were pitted against the New York Yankees, whose payroll topped $180 million and who had won four world championships in the previous seven years. In an effort to keep the power-hitting Yankees off-balance, McKeon advised his squad to keep playing the type of "small ball" they had perfected during the regular season—that is, using steal attempts, bunts, singles, and other "small" moves as the means to accumulate runs. As Tom Verducci later wrote for *Sports Illustrated* (October 27, 2003) about the series, "Florida played small ball to such an extreme that the weekend games could have been staged in St. Pat[rick's Cathedral] without knocking over a single votive candle." Game One of the series, played at Yankee Stadium, was a 3–2 win for the Marlins, whose hits—seven singles—included the outfielder Juan Pierre's two-run single in the fifth inning. The Marlins' six hits, again all singles, in Game Two netted them only one run, while the Yankees, thanks in part to Hideki Matsui's three-run homer in the first inning, racked up a total of six. With the series continuing in Miami, the Yankees took the third game, again by a score of 6–1, this time with center fielder Bernie Williams hitting a three-run homer in the ninth inning. Both the Yankees and the Marlins had three runs at the end of the ninth inning of Game Four; a dramatic home run hit by Florida's shortstop Alex Gonzalez, which barely cleared the left-field fence, won that game for the Marlins after three extra innings. The Yankees' loss was the team's first in any extra-inning World Series contest since 1964. Game Five was a 6–4 victory for the Marlins and for Brad Penny, who pitched seven innings and drove in two runs with a single in the second inning. Back in Yankee Stadium, with his team now leading the series, McKeon made the unusual decision to start with pitcher Josh Beckett, although the 23-year-old had had only three days to rest his arm since his work on the pitcher's mound in Game Three. As Tom Verducci wrote for *Sports Illustrated* (November 3, 2003), "Pitching on three days' rest is the baseball equivalent of running with scissors or swimming less than an hour after eating. You just don't do it because . . . well, just because that's the way it has always been." McKeon, however, as Verducci pointed out, "wasn't going to start managing by convention at this point"; McKeon himself said, according to Verducci, "This is the game we want to win. Forget pitch counts, rest, innings pitched and all that. If [Beckett is] pitching good, I'll leave him in there for nine innings." Beckett indeed pitched well, shutting out the Yankees and making the final out, in the bottom of the ninth, by tagging the Yankees' Jorge Posada on the first-base line. The Marlins' 2–0 victory in Game Six marked the first time since 1981 that any team had beaten the Yankees in the World Series in the Yanks' home stadium. "I just needed to get the guys to believe they could have fun coming to the ballpark and go out there and play relaxed baseball," McKeon said after the game, as quoted on CBCSports (October 26, 2003, on-line). "Focus a little better, play a little smarter, work a little harder. That was about the essence of my meeting with them. Pretty soon they started doing all those things and we started winning." Shortly after the Marlins' victory, Jeffrey Loria announced that McKeon would be given a year's extension on his contract, with an option to manage in the 2005 season. In November 2003 McKeon was named National League Manager of the Year by the Baseball Writers' Association of America. The following month *Sporting News* magazine named McKeon, along with the football coach Dick Vermeil, sportsman of the year.

Despite McKeon's sturdy management, the Marlins failed to repeat their success in 2004. During the off-season "Pudge" Rodriguez had left the team to join the Detroit Tigers; afterward the Marlins struggled without success to find a proper replacement for him in the lineup. The Marlins finished the season in third place in the National League East, 13 games out of first place, with a win–loss record of 86–79.

McKeon married the former Carol Isley on October 29, 1954; the couple have two daughters, Kristi and Kori, two sons, Kelly and Kasey, and, as of mid-2003, nine grandchildren. During the off-season McKeon and his wife live in Elon, North Carolina. There, as well as on the road, McKeon attends church daily. He exercises by taking a brisk

walk every morning, and he is seldom without a cigar in his hand. With Tom Friend, he wrote the memoir *Jack of All Trades* (1988), which describes his life until the end of the 1979 baseball season. He is planning to write a sequel.

—C.M.

Suggested Reading: *Christian Science Monitor* p13 Mar. 28, 1973, p10 Sep. 19, 1979; *New York Times* V p3 Feb. 25, 1973; *Sport* p19+ July 1989, with photos; *Sporting News* p29 Apr. 18, 1981, p31 Mar. 26, 1990, p18 July 23, 1990, p18 Oct. 1, 1990, p24 Aug. 4, 1997, p34 Aug. 25, 2003; *Sports Illustrated* p62 Apr. 4, 1983, p55 Apr. 15, 1985, p92 Sep. 26, 1988, p50+ Oct. 27, 2003, with photo; (Toronto) *Globe and Mail* p49 Dec. 7, 1978; *Washington Post* D p1+ July 12, 1982, C p2 July 12, 1990; *Who's Who in America, 2001*

Thomas Dorn/Courtesy of Universal Music

McLaughlin, John

Jan. 4, 1942– Guitarist

Address: c/o Verve Records, 825 Eighth Ave., 23d Fl., New York, NY 10019-8416

While putting together a fusion band in the late 1960s, the jazz legend Miles Davis plucked from obscurity a talented British guitarist named John McLaughlin. Since then McLaughlin has become a widely influential guitarist, known not only for his work with Davis but also for founding the popular Mahavishnu Orchestra and the Indian-influenced band Shakti. Legions of young rock and jazz guitarists have sought to match his speed and fluidity as well as other aspects of his technique, but few have come close to achieving his mastery. McLaughlin is equally adept at electric and acoustic guitar and is fluent in styles ranging from Indian music to jazz to rock to jazz/rock fusion. His latest album, *Thieves and Poets* (2003), offers interpretations of the classic songs of Tin Pan Alley, the area of New York City in which much of the business of popular American music was conducted from the 1890s to the 1950s. In a review of McLaughlin's 1997 recording *The Heart of Things*, Anton Graham wrote for shanghai-ed.com, "There are very few musicians who can survive on the cutting edge of music for decades, admired anew with every album release for their creative freshness, never falling into the golden oldies has-been category. One that makes the grade is guitarist John McLaughlin."

John McLaughlin was born on January 4, 1942 in Yorkshire, England, into a musical family: his mother played the violin, and his three older brothers took turns playing the family guitar. (He also has a younger sister.) According to Jim Jerome in *People* (June 21, 1976), as posted on a Web site of the Cardiff School of Computer Science, his parents separated when he was seven; his mother settled with the children in a coastal village in the far north of England. "I remember very little about my father," McLaughlin told Jerome. At the age of nine, McLaughlin began to learn to play the piano; he gave up the instrument two years later, when the family guitar was passed down to him. During the 1950s he listened to many of the great American jazz, rock, and blues musicians of the era, including Muddy Waters, whose playing McLaughlin tried to imitate. "When I first heard blues music, Muddy Waters, it was amazing to me . . . ," McLaughlin told Bill Stephen for *International Musician and Recording World* (March 1979). "There was such a kind of elegance about it, an urban elegance. I didn't know how to play it, I didn't know anything about it, all I knew was that it was saying something to me which was very important. About feelings and about being." By the age of 15, McLaughlin had discovered Miles Davis and John Coltrane, whose work, as he told Stephen, embodied for him "the music of the future."

During the late 1950s McLaughlin performed with the banjo player Pete Deuchar and his Professors of Ragtime; they concentrated on traditional jazz, then quite popular in England. Eager to play more rock and blues, McLaughlin moved to London in the early 1960s, finding work as a sideman with such musicians as Graham Bond, Brian Auger, and Georgie Fame. All of those men used elements of jazz, rock, and blues in their music—a potent combination of styles that would later influence much of McLaughlin's work. He also played for six months in Germany, with Gunter Hampel's experimental-jazz band.

In 1969 McLaughlin recorded his first album, *Extrapolation,* with John Surman on saxophone, Tony Oxley on drums, and Brian Odgers on bass. Offering an early form of fusion—a style that combines elements of jazz and rock—*Extrapolation* is now considered a fusion classic. That same year McLaughlin traveled to New York City to record with Tony Williams, Miles Davis's former drummer, who had invited him to join his band, Lifetime. While in the recording studio with Lifetime, McLaughlin was summoned by Davis himself; he had heard about McLaughlin from Dave Holland, a studio musician who had worked with the guitarist back in England. McLaughlin played on several of Davis's albums, among them *In a Silent Way* and *Bitches Brew*, both recorded in 1969; the latter included a Davis-composed track titled "John McLaughlin." He also contributed to the Davis albums *Big Fun* (1969), the double LP *Live-Evil* (1970), *On the Corner* (1972), and the legendary *A Tribute to Jack Johnson* (1970)—a two-song jam record that, in the opinion of many critics, fulfilled Davis's boast that he could form the "greatest rock band you ever heard."

While recording with Davis, McLaughlin was also working on his own albums. Some of his notable records of this period include *Where Fortune Smiles* (1970), with John Surman; *My Goal's Beyond* (1970), a solo effort; and *Devotion* (1970), another solo record that is among his most celebrated. Sean Westergaard noted in a review for the *All Music Guide* Web site, "[*Devotion*] is from a pivotal moment in McLaughlin's history. This was just after he left Miles' group, but before Mahavishnu Orchestra started, and the music captures this moment perfectly. McLaughlin's technique had not progressed to 'Mahavishnu' perfection yet, but the music has the in-your-face rock drive of the Mahavishnu Orchestra. . . . McLaughlin is on fire, using fuzzboxes and phasers, over Larry Young's swirling Hammond B-3, with Billy Rich and Buddy Miles as the rock-solid rhythm section. . . . *Devotion* is a complete anomaly in his catalog, as well as one of his finest achievements."

Not long after recording *Devotion*, McLaughlin began to immerse himself in Eastern religion and music, studying with a guru named Sri Chinmoy and emerging with a new spiritual name, Mahavishnu. In an interview with Don Heckman for the *New York Times* (May 14, 1972), McLaughlin said, "When Sri Chinmoy gave me the name Mahavishnu, he explained that it embodied certain qualities, namely compassion, divine strength and justice." In 1971 McLaughlin formed the Mahavishnu Orchestra, with the drummer Billy Cobham, the keyboardist Jan Hammer, the violinist Jerry Goodman, and the bassist Rich Laird. Though often described as a rock band, the group frequently employed elements of jazz, helping to further develop fusion as a musical form. McLaughlin explained to Stephen: "I don't believe one can talk about east-west fusion in music. One can only speak in personal terms—that's people. I feel very much at home in India, with Indian people, culturally speaking." He continued, "The more you understand about [others'] culture and idiosyncrasies, the more at home you feel. For me, that's where fusion takes place. It's not in the music. If you try to make an east-west fusion you're going to be a miserable failure right away."

After recording three highly regarded albums—*The Inner Mountain Flame* (1971), *Birds of Fire* (1972), and the live *Between Nothingness and Eternity* (1973)—the Mahavishnu Orchestra's original lineup disbanded. McLaughlin retreated into the studio to record a spiritual album with Carlos Santana, *McLaughlin & Santana*, in 1973 and emerged with the hopes of resuscitating the Mahavishnu Orchestra. He did so with a new lineup: the violinist Jean-Luc Ponty, the singer and keyboardist Gayle Moran, the bassist Ralphe Armstrong, and the drummer Mike Warden. The band, which underwent additional lineup changes during this short incarnation, broke up in 1975, but not before recording four albums: *Apocalypse* (1974), *Visions of the Emerald Beyond* (1974), *Inner Worlds* (1975), and *In Retrospect* (1976). (In 1984 McLaughlin put together another version of the band and recorded one album, *Mahavishnu*. Most critics contend that the original lineup was better.)

By the mid-1970s McLaughlin was moving away from fusion and toward Indian music. He was also becoming less interested in the electric guitar, preferring to play acoustically. His interests coalesced in the formation of a new band, Shakti, in 1975. Composed of McLaughlin on acoustic guitar, Lakshminarayana Shankar on violin, and Zakir Hussain, T. H. "Vikku" Vinayakram, and Rammad V. Raghavan on traditional percussion instruments, Shakti made an impression on the world-music scene, which was then beginning to develop commercially. In a review for the Toronto *Globe and Mail* (November 11, 1977), Paul McGrath wrote that the band "has brought together as clear a synthesis as can be created of the modal and rhythmic discipline of Indian music with the free-form jazz McLaughlin plays so well." Between 1975 and 1977 the band toured the world and produced three highly regarded albums, *Shakti with John McLaughlin* (1975), *A Handful of Beauty* (1976), and *Natural Elements* (1977). The group disbanded after that, when McLaughlin decided to take on different projects. As he explained to an interviewer for *Down Beat* (April 1982, on-line), "Shakti broke up because I'm a Western musician and harmony is my roots. Shakti's music is non-harmonic and I need, for total satisfaction, harmony."

After disbanding Shakti, McLaughlin returned to his electric-guitar and fusion roots. His album *Electric Guitarist* (1978) was recorded with some of the best-known jazz players of the era, among them Chick Corea, Stanley Clarke, Jack DeJohnette, Tony Williams, and Carlos Santana. In a review for *Rolling Stone* (July 13, 1978), Robert Palmer wrote, "John McLaughlin is still an awesomely powerful electric guitarist, and now that he is playing electric music again, he is playing for keeps."

McLaughlin's desire to record on acoustic as well as electric guitar precipitated a bitter contract dispute with Columbia Records, whose executives thought he should focus on his more commercially successful electric music. After recording the album *Electric Dreams* (1978) with a short-lived group called the One Truth Band, McLaughlin signed a contract with Warner Brothers, which released his mainly acoustic *Belo Horizonte* (1981), recorded in France. That year McLaughlin also completed *Friday Night in San Francisco,* a collaboration with the guitarists Al Di Meola and Paco de Lucia. Recorded primarily live in late 1980, the album was among the first to employ exclusively acoustic-guitar playing in a fusion context. The three musicians followed up that recording with *Passion, Grace and Fire,* in 1982.

During the 1980s McLaughlin continued to experiment with his sound. In addition to recording the solo albums *Adventures in Radioland* (1987) and *Mediterranean Concerto* (1988), he collaborated with the French classical pianist Katia Labeque on *Music Spoken Here* (1985), returned as Miles Davis's sideman on *You're Under Arrest* (1985), and appeared in the jazz film *'Round Midnight* in 1986. In 1988 he formed a jazz trio with the percussionist Trilok Gurtu and a series of bassists. The group toured for four years and recorded two albums, the well-received *Live at the Royal Festival Hall* (1989) and *Que Alegria* (1991).

Following the recording of a tribute album to the pianist Bill Evans, *Time Remembered: John McLaughlin Plays Bill Evans* (1993), McLaughlin again focused on electric guitar and began touring as part of a trio with the drummer Dennis Chambers and the organist Joey DeFrancesco, who had been discovered by Miles Davis shortly before Davis's death, in 1991. They recorded a live album, *Tokyo Live,* which was released in 1993. McLaughlin's next studio album, *After the Rain* (1995), featured DeFrancesco and the drummer Elvin Jones. Also in 1995 McLaughlin recorded with the noted rockers Jeff Beck and Sting on *The Promise.* Other albums of this period include a reunion of his guitar trio on *Paco de Lucia/John McLaughlin/Al Di Meola* (1996); *The Heart of Things* (1997), whose sound recalled the days of the Mahavishnu Orchestra; and *Remember Shakti* (1999), which brought together many of the members of his 1970s band. The reunited members also toured and recorded a live album, *Saturday Night in Bombay: Remember Shakti* (2001).

McLaughlin's first original album in the 21st century, *Thieves and Poets* (2003), made use of the American standard songbook—an entirely unexpected direction for him. With such classics as "Stella by Starlight," "My Romance," and "My Foolish Heart," McLaughlin received some of the best notices of his later career. In a review for the *All Music Guide* Web site (on-line), Alex Henderson wrote, "Yes, 'My Romance,' 'Stella by Starlight,' and 'My Foolish Heart' are warhorses that have been beaten to death over the years—great songs that have been recorded so many times that some jazz enthusiasts feel there should be a moratorium on them in the 21st century. But McLaughlin is such an accomplished, distinctive musician that he's allowed a warhorse or two (or three). Besides, he plays beautifully on these standards, and his lyricism is extremely individualistic. Hearing McLaughlin (who turned 60 in 2002) embracing Tin Pan Alley songs with a classical guitar group is hardly the same as hearing some 19-year-old, knee-jerk Sarah Vaughan wannabe attempting to squeeze the last drops of blood from them. It's the difference between mindlessly going through the motions and saying something personal—and on this memorable CD, McLaughlin's playing is undeniably personal."

McLaughlin has released a number of compilation albums, including *The Best of Mahavishnu Orchestra* (1971), *The Best of McLaughlin* (1991), *The Best of Shakti* (1995), and *The Complete Jack Johnson Sessions* (2003). He is currently working on an interactive instructional DVD for advanced guitar students.

A few months before Jim Jerome interviewed him, in 1976, McLaughlin's second wife had left him. From his first marriage he has one son, Julian, born in the mid-1960s.

—C.M.

Suggested Reading: *All Music Guide* Web site; *Boston Globe* N p7 Nov. 16, 2003; *Down Beat* (on-line) Apr. 1982; *Guitar Player* (on-line) May 1994; *International Musician and Recording World* (on-line) Mar. 1979; *New York Times* II p15 May 14, 1972, II p28 Apr. 1, 1973, II p19 Sep. 20, 1981; *Rolling Stone* p67+ June 3, 1976, p20 July 13, 1978; *Sydney Morning Herald* p11 Nov. 15, 2003; (Toronto, Canada) *Globe and Mail* p16 Nov. 11, 1977

Selected Recordings: with Mahavishnu Orchestra—*The Inner Mountain Flame*, 1971; *Birds of Fire*, 1972; *Between Nothingness and Eternity*, 1973; *Apocalypse*, 1974; *Visions of the Emerald Beyond*, 1974; *Inner Words*, 1975; *In Retrospect*, 1976; *Mahavishnu*, 1984; with Shakti—*Shakti with John McLaughlin*, 1975; *A Handful of Beauty*, 1976; *Natural Elements*, 1977; solo—*Extrapolation*, 1969; *Devotion*, 1970; *McLaughlin & Santana*, 1973; *Electric Dreams*, 1978; *Belo Horizonte*, 1981; *Passion, Grace and Fire*, 1982; *After the Rain*, 1995; *The Heart of Things*, 1997; *Remember Shakti*, 1999; *Thieves and Poets*, 2003

McNabb, Donovan

Nov. 25, 1976– Football player

Address: Philadelphia Eagles, 1 Novacare Way, Philadelphia, PA 19102-5996

At six feet two inches and 240 pounds, the Philadelphia Eagles quarterback Donovan McNabb confounds defenses with a combination of tremendous foot speed, outstanding arm strength, and tenacity. Now in his sixth season in the National Football League (NFL), McNabb has been selected for the Pro Bowl four times and appears poised to be named again in 2005. Among active starting quarterbacks with at least 45 starts, he is tied for third place in winning percentage (.646). On September 27, 2002 the Eagles signed him to a 12-year, $115 million deal, one of the most lucrative in NFL history. Kevin Rogers, McNabb's former offensive coordinator and quarterback coach at Syracuse University, told Gerry Callahan for *Sports Illustrated* (May 17, 1999), "I know what the other quarterbacks can't do, but I'm not sure what Don can't do. He's a dominant player. Is he the prototypical NFL quarterback? No—he's the wave of the future. Teams need a guy who can make things happen when everything breaks down, a guy who can avoid a rush, who can run and who can also throw downfield. Believe me, Don can do it all."

Jamie Squire/Getty Images

Donovan Jamal McNabb was born in Chicago, Illinois, on November 25, 1976 to Sam McNabb, an employee of a Chicago electric company, and Wilma McNabb, a registered nurse. When he was about eight years old, McNabb, along with his parents and his older brother, Sean, moved to Dolton,

Illinois. One of the first African-American families to live in the upscale suburban town, the McNabbs had not long been in the neighborhood when their new home was vandalized. Sam McNabb told John Ed Bradley for *Sports Illustrated* (July 30, 2001), "What we learned from our move to Dolton is that not everyone will be happy for you when you make a success of your life."

An athletic child, McNabb also displayed a talent for making people laugh, particularly with his imitations. (He has been known to entertain his teammates with a very accurate impersonation of Andy Reid, the Eagles head coach.) His mother told Bradley, "We used to think Donovan was going to grow up to be a comedian. It looked like he was going to be another Eddie Murphy." McNabb attended Mount Carmel High School, in Dolton, where he became an All-American and helped to win a state football championship. (He was allowed to play football only after a high-school coach promised his mother that Donovan would not be injured.)

As a freshman at Syracuse University, in Syracuse, New York, McNabb sat on the bench in 1994, but he served as the starting quarterback for the Orangemen from 1995 to 1998, helping the team amass a record of 35–13 and win the Big East conference championship for three straight years beginning in 1996. McNabb, who was also a reserve player on the university's nationally ranked basketball squad, set the school's all-time football records for average total yards per game (221.1), passing-efficiency rating (155.1), yards per attempt (9.1), and total offense in a single season (2,892). He was named all–Big East quarterback four times, Big East offensive player of the year three times, and All-American once. He set Big East career records for touchdown passes (77), touchdowns for which he was responsible (96), passing yards (8,389), total offensive yards (9,950), and total offensive plays (1,403). In 2000 he was named the Big East offensive player of the decade (the 1990s). In his final home game, McNabb helped the Syracuse Orangemen defeat the University of Miami 66–13. (Syracuse was defeated by the University of Florida 31–10 in the Orange Bowl that year.) Paul Pasqualoni, Syracuse's head coach, told Joe Drape for the *New York Times* (November 29, 1998) about McNabb, "He has meant everything to us. . . . He's done so much for this team not only as a football player, but as a person. He could have left for professional football last year, but he came back for the right reason. To have these experiences. To lead a team."

After graduating from Syracuse with a degree in speech communications in 1998, McNabb was drafted by the Philadelphia Eagles as the second overall pick in the 1999 NFL draft. On the day of the draft, which was held in New York City, McNabb was booed by many Eagles fans in attendance, who thought that the Heisman Trophy winner Ricky Williams, a running back from the University of Texas, would have been a better pick than the Syracuse quarterback. "People tried to explain it by saying, 'It wasn't meant against you, it was because they didn't take Ricky Williams,'" McNabb told Thomas George for the *New York Times* (June 22, 2001). "Well, that's like being in a drive-by shooting and saying the bullet was not meant for you, sorry it hit you."

While McNabb, as is common for rookie quarterbacks, did not at first start for the Eagles, he started six of the final seven contests, becoming the first Eagles rookie draft pick to start since John Reaves did so in 1972. In his first NFL start, on November 14, against the Washington Redskins, he led the Eagles to a 35–28 win. He finished the season with a respectable if unexceptional eight passing touchdowns, seven interceptions, and a 49.1 pass-completion percentage. His success as a runner was more remarkable, as he amassed 313 yards on 47 attempts, for an average of 6.6 yards per carry. The Eagles finished the season in last place, with a miserable record of 5–11.

McNabb spent the off-season with the Eagles' veteran receiver Charles Johnson, engaged in an intensive workout program offered by the PerfromancePlus company in the fierce heat of Phoenix, Arizona. "I was a guy coming into my second year who sat out as a rookie for most of the season and I knew I was going to start and I had to improve myself," McNabb explained to Paul Attner for the *Sporting News* (December 18, 2000). "It was really important to get better. They paid a lot of attention to detail, to my drops, to my fundamentals, to my conditioning. I kept the mentality whatever you start you had to finish. So I kept going back. I left there a lot better in everything than when I started." The 2000 NFL season was a major success for McNabb, who finished second in the NFL's Most Valuable Player (MVP) race and was elected to the Pro Bowl as an alternate. McNabb started in all 16 games, completed 58 percent of his passes, threw 21 touchdowns, ran for 629 yards (the most of any quarterback in the NFL), and scored six rushing touchdowns. The Eagles, who were able to reverse their record to 11–5, made the play-offs for the first time since 1996. They defeated the Tampa Bay Buccaneers 21–3 in the wild-card game but were eliminated in the NFC divisional play-off game by the New York Giants, 20–10. Regarding McNabb's performance in 2000, Andy Reid told Paul Attner, "I'm biased, but [McNabb] is the best player out there this season. He has a direct effect on the players around him; he helps them maximize their potential. And isn't that the measure of the MVP—how does he affect his team? I know, because I've been through this before with another, when I was with the Packers. I feel the same with him as I did with Brett [Favre] when he was winning his MVPs."

In 2001 McNabb had another fine season, completing 57.8 percent of his passes and 25 touchdowns and rushing 82 times for 482 yards and two touchdowns. After posting another 11–5 record, the Eagles advanced to the play-offs, first defeating the Tampa Bay Buccaneers, 31–9, in the wild-card game and then knocking off the Chicago Bears, 33–19, in the NFC divisional game. The Eagles then lost, 29–24, to the St. Louis Rams in the NFC championship game. McNabb was elected to another Pro Bowl, this time as a starter.

McNabb started the first 10 games of the 2002 season before fracturing his fibula during a game on November 17, against the Arizona Cardinals. Despite the fracture, McNabb completed the game and threw four subsequent touchdown passes. During his 10 regular-season games, McNabb completed 58.4 percent of his passes, threw 17 touchdowns, and ran the ball 63 times for 460 yards and six touchdowns. After sitting out the last six regular-season games and watching his team post a record of 12–4, McNabb returned for the NFC divisional play-off game against Atlanta Falcons, leading the Eagles to a 20–6 victory and completing 20 of 30 passes for 247 yards and one touchdown. The Eagles were once again stopped just short of the Super Bowl, this time by the Tampa Bay Buccaneers, who beat the Eagles 27–10 and went on to win the championship. McNabb, who completed 26 of 49 passing attempts against the Buccaneers, threw no touchdowns and one interception.

McNabb's sub-par performance in the NFC championship game against the Buccaneers seemed to carry over to the beginning of the 2003 season, as the Eagles dropped their opening two games and went 2–3 over the first five. During this period McNabb threw three times as many interceptions as touchdowns and completed only 42.9 percent of his passes. In a controversial statement on ESPN's *Sunday NFL Countdown* show, the conservative political commentator Rush Limbaugh, who had been hired as a sports analyst by the network, called McNabb overrated and hinted that he had received accolades simply for being a black player in a position that in the NFL is dominated by whites. "The media has been very desirous that a black quarterback do well," Limbaugh said, as quoted on the ESPN Web site (October 7, 2003). "There is a little hope invested in McNabb, and he got a lot of credit for the performance of this team that he didn't deserve. The defense carried this team." After his comments generated a significant backlash, Limbaugh resigned from ESPN. Meanwhile, McNabb proceeded to improve his game drastically, leading the Eagles to seven straight wins, throwing three times as many touchdowns as interceptions, and completing 65.5 percent of his passes. At the end of the 16 regular-season games in 2003, McNabb's quarterback rating (a statistical indicator of a quarterback's overall performance) rose from 51.1 in the first half of the season to 102.9 by the end. As of early November 2004, McNabb had helped to lead his team to a 7–0 start, the first ever for the Eagles. In the team's sixth game, he made four touchdown passes, matching a career high.

In June 2003 McNabb married his longtime college girlfriend, Raquel-Ann Sarah "Roxi" Nurse. He donates his time and money to the American Diabetes Association (his father suffers from the disease) and founded the Donovan McNabb Foundation, which helps fight diabetes and supports children's hospital programs. He was named among the most caring athletes by *USA Weekend* magazine. McNabb, who has endorsement contracts with such companies as Lincoln Financial Services, Sierra Mist, and Nike, said, as quoted on the Philadelphia Eagles Web site, "I play this game to be the best. And the only sure way I know to be the best is to outwork everybody else. Some people take one step toward their dream, accomplish a little something and then feel like that's it. Not me. I'm never satisfied."

—L.A.S.

Suggested Reading: *New York Times* VIII p11 Aug.1 , 1999, IV p1 June 22, 2001, with photo; *Sports Illustrated* p38 May 17, 1999, with photos, p58 July 30, 2001, with photos; *Sporting News* p18 Dec. 18, 2000, p52 June 18, 2001

Aabvaan Barron/Courtesy of Tehreema Mitha

Mitha, Tehreema

[MEETH-a, Tuh-REE-ma]

Nov. 14, 1962– Dancer; choreographer; writer

Address: Tehreema Mitha Dance Company, 8509 Pelham Rd., Bethesda, MD 20817-9520

Tehreema Mitha is the artistic director and founder of the Maryland-based Tehreema Mitha Dance Company, which presents works in the classical southern-Indian dance style called Bharatanatyam, as well as contemporary works in Mitha's unique style. The dancer and choreographer directed a dance troupe in Pakistan before moving to the United States, in 1998. Over the past 14 years, she has created more than 45 dances, based on such diverse themes as chaos theory, the destruction of the environment, marriage, sexuality, including homosexuality, and teenage pregnancy, and she has presented them in Pakistan, the United States, the United Kingdom, China, India, Guatemala, and Germany. She has published many articles as a dance critic and is an active promoter of the performing arts both in the U.S. and in her native Pakistan.

Tehreema Mitha was born in Abbottabad, Pakistan, on November 14, 1962 and was raised in a household with two elder sisters and a younger male cousin. Because her father served in the country's army, her family moved often throughout most of Mitha's childhood. (Her father had also served in the British Indian Army, before the creation of Pakistan, and had fought with the British against the Japanese in World War II; later, he had battled for India's independence from Britain.) At various times Mitha lived in Chittagong, Multan, Abbottabad, and Rawalpindi. In each place, her mother, Indu Mitha, an accomplished Bharatanatyam dancer, taught dance classes, which Mitha joined at an early age. Bharatanatyam may be the oldest of the six forms of classical Indian dance, dating as far back as the fifth century C.E. The technique combines complex footwork with specific hand gestures and theatrical facial expressions and is divided into two distinct types: Nritta, or pure dancing, and Nritya, a narrative told through facial expressions, gestures, and movement. Bharatanatyam developed mainly in southern India and is performed by soloists, who typically dance two-hour routines. Mitha's mother practiced a unique kind of Bharatanatyam, choreographing dances based on themes (as opposed to existing, fixed narratives or pure movement) and setting them to north Indian music.

When Mitha was seven years old, her father was abruptly sent into retirement because of his refusal to participate in political machinations within the army. The government of Prime Minister Zulfikar Ali Bhutto blacklisted him, and for the next 10 years, the Mitha family lived in social and political isolation, and under difficult financial conditions, in Karachi. During their first year there, the young Tehreema began her formal dance training under her mother's instruction. She had become a dedicated practitioner of the art when, in 1977, Pakistan came under the control of an Islamic military dictatorship headed by General Mohammad Zia Ul-Haq, who immediately imposed a rule of martial law. All public dancing was banned, including classical dance performed by women. In 1986 the Goethe Center in Lahore took a risk and hosted Mitha's *Arangatram*, a two-hour solo performance through which a teacher introduces her pupil to so-

ciety as a serious student of dance. Despite the prohibition against dancing in public, Mitha recalled to *Current Biography*, "not only was every seat taken in the audience, there were people standing for the two hours."

Mitha completed a bachelor's degree in philosophy and English literature from Kinnaird College and earned a master's degree in fine arts from the National College of Arts (both schools are in Lahore). She then lived in Kenya for a year before returning to Lahore, where she taught science, geography, history, fine arts, and movement at several private schools and universities. Concurrently, she gave solo dance performances. In 1990 the American Dance Festival, an annual celebration of modern dance held in Durham, North Carolina, invited her to participate in its International Choreographers Workshop. There, she had her first exposure to modern dance and, also for the first time, shared a stage with other dancers. "The impact of dancing and performing with a group of other professionals was tremendous, considering that I had danced in isolation ever since I could remember," she wrote for *Shruti Magazine*. "It also amazed me, too, that in this pioneering country dancers are so marginalized by the largely conservative society and yet they forge ahead, opening new vistas."

Shortly after her participation in the American Dance Festival, Mitha met her future husband, William Barron, in Islamabad, Pakistan's capital, where she embarked on a full-time dance career. In 1992 she married Barron, an American environmental-water engineer, and founded Tehreema Aabvaan Dance Productions. ("Aabvaan" means "protector of water" in Urdu, Mitha's native language; her husband changed his first name to Aabvaan when he married.) Under the auspices of Tehreema Aabvaan Dance Productions, Mitha and her mother taught classes for children and adults. Mitha also gave both solo and ensemble performances. In 1995 she founded the first annual National Dance Festival, with funding from the Norwegian Embassy in Pakistan; the festival toured in Lahore, Karachi, and Rawalpindi, and has continued to this day. Also in 1995 she performed at the United Nations' Non-Governmental Organization (NGO) Forum on Women, in Beijing, China. At first she had difficulty finding classical musicians who were willing to accompany the troupe, as few Pakistanis had ever seen Bharatanatyam performed and apparently had little respect for the form. Over the years, however, that attitude changed, as a growing number of classical artists began composing music with Mitha. In order to expose Pakistanis to classical music, she regularly hosted concerts for classical musicians and vocalists.

In 1998 Mitha and her husband moved to the United States, in part because of the paucity of young Pakistani women available to train for and dedicate themselves to dance careers. (In Pakistan few families would allow their daughters to train, and those young girls who were permitted to do so were usually forced to leave the class or forbidden to perform on stage once they reached marriage-able age.) The following year Mitha settled in Maryland and began to train a group of dancers. In May 2001 the troupe was officially incorporated as the nonprofit Tehreema Mitha Dance Company, which presents both classical and contemporary Indian dances. The company's classical perfor-mances incorporate the Bharatanatyam style but explore contemporary or universal themes rather than traditional mythological themes. One recent work, for example, includes a piece about a woman pregnant with an illegitimate child; another pon-ders the impact of environmental destruction on a mother and daughter. Following her mother's ex-ample, in her classical dances Mitha departs from traditional Bharatanatyam by using northern rath-er than southern Indian music. The company's contemporary pieces retain the classical idiom but make use of a wider range of movement and multi-ple dancers. The themes Mitha explores in her con-temporary dances are typically more radical than those in her classical works. Recent subjects in-clude homosexuality and chaos theory. According to the company's Web site, Mitha is committed to examining themes relevant to the local, national, and global communities; future topics will include "old and new ways of looking at sexuality; the dy-namics of the Stock Market; [the] impact that cross-ing borders has on immigrants and the host coun-try; the road taken by science; human nature; stress and emotions; the body and the soul." "My themes come from within and without me!" Mitha told *Current Biography*. She finds inspiration in histor-ical events and personal experiences. Mitha also told *Current Biography*, "Literature and music

from the [Indian] subcontinent is important, and Sufic philosophy [a generally liberal offshoot of the Muslim religion] interests me greatly."

Critics have responded enthusiastically to Tehreema Mitha Dance Company performances. In a review of a 2002 concert, Claire MacDonald, in the *Washington Post* (November 4, 2002), de-scribed Mitha as a "supple, precise dancer, alive with kinetic energy" and her opening solo dance as "perfect"; MacDonald concluded that the choreog-rapher was "a figure to be watched, with an ambi-tion to be nurtured." Also in the *Washington Post* (October 16, 2001), Lisa Traiger wrote that one of Mitha's contemporary solo pieces "exquisitely melded the ancient with the modern" and stated that Mitha's "torso spoke as soulfully as her hands, the stoop of her shoulders or the twist of her waist signaling internal torment, while the plasticity of her gestures communicated pain."

Mitha has been a staff member of the Joy of Mo-tion Dance Center, in Washington, D.C., since 1999. She has written many articles as a dance crit-ic for the *Dance Insider* and the *Nation*, among oth-er publications. Her work was the subject of the filmmaker Shireen Pasha's documentary *And She Dances On*, which premiered in Pakistan in 1996 and was shown at the 1997 Asian Film Festival, which toured in Europe, Asia, and North America. She and her husband have one son.

—H.T.

Suggested Reading: Tehreema Mitha Dance Company Web site; *Washington Post* C p5 Oct. 16, 2001, C p5 Nov. 4, 2002

Mohammed, W. Deen

Oct. 30, 1933– Islamic scholar; spiritual leader of the American Society of Muslims; social activist

Address: Mosque Cares, Ministry of Imam Wallace Deen Mohammed, P.O. Box 1061, Calumet City, IL 60409

The Islamic scholar Imam W. Deen Mohammed is the spiritual father of the American Society of Muslims, the predominately African-American or-ganization that, with more than two million mem-bers, represents the largest Muslim community in the U.S. (Formerly known as the Bilallian Commu-nity, the World Community of Al-Islam in the West, and the American Muslim Mission, the cur-rent group has sometimes been referred to as the Muslim American Society. "Imam" is an Arabic ti-tle for a Muslim religious leader.) Mohammed's quiet style and inclusive, peaceful vision have won him the respect of religious and political leaders worldwide. In an article posted on the New Africa Intelligentsia Web site, the humanitarian and for-

mer heavyweight boxing champion Muhammad Ali called Imam Mohammed, whom Ali has known since the mid-1960s, a "peaceful warrior, using his wisdom and kindness to fight for the bet-terment of all African Americans as well as Mus-lims."

Mohammed's father, Elijah Mohammed, was for over four decades the leader of the Nation of Islam (NOI), a black separatist religious movement begun in Detroit, Michigan, in 1930. Following the death of his father, in 1975, Mohammed assumed the leadership of the NOI. He subsequently changed the group's name, aligned its beliefs and practices with those of orthodox Sunni Islam, and opened its membership to individuals of all races. (In late 1977 Louis Farrakhan revived the NOI as a separate organization.) In addition to serving as the reli-gious leader of many of America's Muslims, Mo-hammed is the international president of the World Conference on Religion and Peace and a member of the Peace Council and the World Su-preme Council of Mosques. He has met with many world religious and political leaders, including the Dalai Lama and Pope John Paul II.

Courtesy of the Muslim Journal
W. Deen Mohammed

In 2003 Mohammed retired from his post as head of the American Society of Muslims, though he stated that he planned to remain active in the Muslim community and would continue to direct his ministry, the Mosque Cares. "His greatness came from the fact that he brought African American Muslims into a deeper understanding of mainstream Islam," Salam Al-Marayati, executive director of the Muslim Public Affairs Council, a Los Angeles, California–based advocacy group, said, as quoted by Rachel Zoll for the Associated Press (September 1, 2003). "His wealth of Islamic knowledge as well as his experience as an American has really cemented our understanding of what an American Muslim identity should be." Mohammed has written several books and contributes a weekly column to the *Muslim Journal*, the national newspaper of the American Society of Muslims. In addition, he has spread his ministry via a nationally syndicated radio program, *Imam W. Deen Muhammad Speaks*, which in the 1990s could be heard on more than 60 stations across the country. *Ebony* magazine named Mohammed one of the 100 most influential African-Americans in the world in both 2000 and 2001. In 2002 he received the Gandhi King Ikeda Award for Peace and was named one of the most influential people in the city of Chicago by the *Chicago Sun-Times* and the *Chicago Tribune*.

The seventh of the eight children of Elijah and Clara Mohammed, Wallace D. Mohammed was born in Hamtramck, Michigan (some sources say Detroit), on October 30, 1933. (Variations of his name include W. D. Mohammed, Warith Deen Mohammed, Wallace Deen Mohammed, and Wallace Delaney Mohammed. As with his father, many

sources print his last name "Muhammad.") Mohammed's father, who was born Elijah Poole, was the son of a Georgia sharecropper and a Baptist preacher. An unemployed migrant laborer, Elijah Mohammed moved his family to Michigan, where, in the early 1930s, he became a disciple of Wali Farad Mohammed, a mysterious Detroit clothing peddler and self-styled savior who claimed to have come from Mecca, Saudi Arabia—Islam's holiest city. (Farad, known to his followers as Master Farad or Master Fard, was reportedly born Wallace D. Fard.) Farad preached to underclass blacks that the time of white domination (he referred to whites as "devils") was coming to an end, and that African-Americans, the true children of God, should prepare themselves to inherit the new kingdom. Farad told his followers that Islam was their true religion, and Allah their God—though Farad's teachings deviated considerably from those of orthodox Islam. According to an article in *Cornerstone* magazine (Issue 111, 1997), as posted on the Answering Islam Web site, Farad transmitted his ideas not only through preaching, but also through a book, *The Teaching for the Lost-Found Nation of Islam*, as well as through a kind of oath of allegiance known as "The Secret Ritual of the Nation of Islam." Among Farad's (and later Elijah Mohammed's) more outlandish teachings were that blacks were exiled from the moon 66 trillion years ago; that white people were created by a mad black scientist named Yakub; and that a "mother ship," a large undetected aircraft built by black scientists in Japan thousands of years ago, still hovered over the globe, ready to defend the NOI against white America.

Elijah Mohammed became one of Farad's most trusted followers; when Farad mysteriously disappeared in 1934, Elijah Mohammed proclaimed that Farad was God, or Allah, incarnate, and that he himself was Allah's messenger, the last prophet of God on Earth. (Both of these claims represent grave heresies in traditional Islam.) Elijah Mohammed worked to expand the NOI, which then had several thousand members, and continued to stress the group's teachings of racial separatism. According to *Cornerstone*, Elijah Mohammed moved his family to Washington, D.C., in around 1935; they then traveled the country, spreading the NOI message from city to city. Disenfranchised African-Americans were encouraged to transform their lives as black Muslims, to obey strict dietary laws, and to abstain from alcohol, tobacco, drugs, and frivolity. Under Elijah Mohammed the group moved its headquarters from Detroit to Chicago. It continued to expand during the 1950s and 1960s, when many impoverished and imprisoned African-Americans joined the NOI ranks. "Suddenly here were all these clean-cut, well-dressed young men and women—men mostly," Stanley Crouch wrote for the *Village Voice* (October 25, 1985). "You recognized them from the neighborhood. They had been pests or vandals, thieves or gangsters. Now they were back from jail or prison and their hair was cut close, their skin was smooth, they no longer cursed blue streaks, and the intensity in their eyes remade their faces. They were 'in the Nation' and that meant that new men were in front of you, men who greeted each other in Arabic, who were aloof, confident, and intent on living differently than they had." A major factor in the NOI's success during this period was Malcolm X, a brilliant and fiery young minister whose rousing orations regarding black power and the injustice of white supremacy galvanized many African-Americans. In an interview with April Witt for the *Miami Herald* (October 14, 1997), W. D. Mohammed explained Islam's appeal: "African Americans have been disappointed so many times. Islam offers a new life. . . . Africa, during the slave trade to this country, was Islamic in some of its most civilized parts. So Islam is a way to connect with our past and have a comfortable sense of our worth, not just as individuals, but as a people."

According to the *Encyclopedia of American Religion and Politics* (2003), Farad foretold the birth of a favored son to Elijah Mohammed and predicted that the boy, whom he named Wallace Delaney Mohammed, would one day succeed his father as leader of the NOI. Even as a child, however, W. Deen Mohammed was skeptical of Farad and his father's teachings. "I remember I was about 7 years old, and I prayed, Dear Savior, excuse me if I'm not getting it right, but I don't understand," he recalled to Sally MacDonald for the *Seattle Times* (June 14, 1997). "I had common sense, and my common sense told me this was ridiculous, the idea that God is a God that wants one people to dominate others. [Farad] was not God, and I knew he was not God. Elijah Mohammed was not a prophet." Mohammed attended elementary and secondary school at the University of Islam in Chicago; he later studied at Wilson Junior College and Loop College (now Harold Washington College), both in Chicago. Elijah Mohammed hired a tutor from Jerusalem to teach his children Arabic, so that they could read the Koran, Islam's holy book, in the original language. However, reading the Koran only reinforced Mohammed's impression that the NOI's racial theology controverted the basic teachings of Islam. Despite those personal convictions, for many years Mohammed vacillated between acceptance and rejection of the NOI. "I shared something religious with my father. I didn't like his language, but I shared his love of God and his desire to see his people in better circumstances," he recalled to MacDonald. "He was innocent and naive. He was a spiritual man and a social reformer. But he was given a myth that he bought because he didn't know any better. He had only a third-grade education."

Mohammed became a minister in the NOI after completing high school. In 1961 he was drafted by the U.S. Army but refused to serve, and as a result spent the next three years in prison. While in prison he continued his study of mainstream Sunni Islam, and again took note of the considerable differences between it and the ideology promulgated by the NOI. Mohammed came to embrace an inclusive, non-radicalized version of Islam, which ultimately, in 1964, led to his expulsion from the NOI. That same year, Malcolm X was suspended from the organization after tension between him and Elijah Mohammed came to a boil. Like W. Deen Mohammed, Malcolm had come to the conclusion that Elijah was misrepresenting the Islamic faith and was guilty of sexual indiscretions. (In fact, Malcolm X had always felt a strong personal affinity for W. Deen Mohammed. In *The Autobiography of Malcolm X*, the charismatic NOI minister remarked: "I felt that Wallace was Mr. [Elijah] Muhammad's most strongly spiritual son, the son with the most objective outlook. Always, Wallace and I . . . shared an exceptional closeness and trust.") Malcolm X's subsequent assassination, in 1965, served to divide the organization, in large part because NOI members loyal to Elijah Mohammed were suspected of having carried out the murder.

Elijah Mohammed reinstated his son just days after the death of Malcolm X, though later that year he expelled him once again for harboring dissident views. While Mohammed came to reject many of his father's beliefs, he nevertheless felt that the NOI, "with all its extremes, had some good," as he explained to April Witt. "Being self-supporting, being disciplined, believing that we should be constantly refining our own nature—those teachings were very strong." Mohammed was readmitted to the NOI in 1969 but was not allowed to resume his full duties as a minister until 1974.

Soon after Elijah Mohammed's death, in 1975, W. Deen Mohammed was elected supreme minister of the NOI, despite his turbulent relationship with the organization. He immediately set about downplaying the group's idiosyncratic doctrines and practices, and distanced himself from his father's black separatist teachings by welcoming white and other non-African-American Muslims into the group. Also in 1975 he renamed the organization the Bilalian Community, after an Ethiopian Muslim and companion to the Prophet Mohammed, and urged followers to learn Arabic, pray five times a day, and study the teachings of traditional Islam—just as Sunni Muslims around the world do. Mohammed established relationships with other Muslim organizations in the United States and abroad, meeting with the Egyptian president Anwar Sadat in Chicago in 1975 and receiving $16 million from Sheikh Ben Mohammed al-Qasmini of the United Arab Emirates for the purpose of building a mosque (an Islamic place of worship) and a school. Mohammed's Temple #7, the well-known community mosque in the Harlem section of New York City, was renamed Masjid (Arabic for "mosque") Malcolm Shabazz, in honor of Malcolm X, and Mohammed led a group of 400 Muslim African-Americans on a Hajj, or pilgrimage, to Mecca. (The Hajj is one of the five central precepts, or "pillars," of Islam.) In 1977 he changed the name of his organization to the World Community of Al-Islam in the West. He later renamed the group the American Muslim Mission, and still later, the American Society of Muslims.

Not everyone was happy with the direction in which Mohammed was leading his organization. In December 1977 Louis Farrakhan, a charismatic and outspoken minister who professed loyalty to the letter of Elijah Mohammed's teachings, publicly split with the World Community of Al-Islam in the West and reestablished the NOI. Whereas orthodox Sunni Islam avers that Mohammed, who founded the Islamic faith in what is now Saudi Arabia, in the seventh century, was the last of the prophets, Farrakhan, like Elijah Mohammed before him, taught that Elijah Mohammed was the final prophet—a belief that is considered heretical in orthodox Islam. Farrakhan's NOI also continued to teach that whites were "devils" and that African-Americans should establish their own culture and society apart from the white-dominated mainstream. Though the NOI's incendiary teachings gave the organization a certain dynamic appeal among young African-Americans, and despite the fact that the NOI is arguably the better known of the two groups, as of 2003 Farrakhan's NOI had fewer than 200,000 members, while Mohammed's American Society of Muslims had more than two million—more than half of them African-American. (Sources vary widely as to the NOI's total membership—estimates range from 20,000 to 200,000—and Farrakhan does not disclose exact figures. Estimates regarding the total number of Muslims in the United States also vary widely: many sources put the figure at around six or seven million.) Mohammed long considered Farrakhan's NOI misguided; he once called the group a "crippling force" for African-Americans, as quoted by MacDonald. Critics of the American Society of Muslims, on the other hand, argued that that organization focused disproportionately on religion while paying insufficient heed to social issues affecting African-Americans. "The main thing that separates Farrakhan from me," Mohammed told Neil Modie for the *Seattle Post-Intelligencer* (June 23, 1997), "is that his idea of Islam, of the message, is that blacks are the only ones that are worthy of it, that we are not to take others seriously. . . . He's a radical and I'm not." "If [Farrakhan] would accept the religion and respect it," Mohammed told April Witt in 1997, "I would gladly stand for him as a social-reform leader or a leader for economic empowerment in depressed neighborhoods. I would even walk behind him if he would do that."

In 1978, wishing to assume a lower profile and to have fewer organizational ties, Mohammed changed his title from supreme minister to imam, a traditional Islamic designation, and adopted the name Warith Deen Mohammed. He retained his position as the group's spiritual guide. In 1985, dismayed by the resistance of some of the group's leaders to his inclusive teachings, Mohammed dissolved the leadership council he had created in

1978. Most of the mosques that had been a part of the American Muslim Mission remained affiliated with Mohammed's ministry, and most of the organization's members continued to view Mohammed as their spiritual leader. "We shouldn't have so much organization in religion that we depend upon the minister or imam for overseeing our lives," Mohammed told Witt, "telling us when to go out and when to come in, what to wear, how to react. That should come from the word of God, from our own intellect and from the family. That's Islam." "[Mohammed] is shy, it seems, and soft-spoken," Herbert Berg, an associate professor of religion at the University of North Carolina, told Steven G. Vegh for the Norfolk, Virginia, *Virginian-Pilot* (October 10, 2002). "He's not a sound-bite guy. But the effect he has on some of his followers, it's incredibly strong."

In 1993, at the invitation of President Bill Clinton, Mohammed became the first imam to deliver the prayer and invocation on the floor of the United States Senate. That same year he served as the Muslim representative at President Clinton's inaugural interfaith breakfast, which brought together leaders from a variety of religious faiths. In 1995 he was elected a president of the World Conference on Religion and Peace (he later became international president); attended, along with Martin Luther King III and Rosa Parks, the Acts of Kindness Week held in Dallas, Texas; and gave an address titled "How Do We Save Our Youth?" at an event hosted by representatives from *Forbes* magazine in Naples, Florida. In 1996 Mohammed met with Pope John Paul II at the Vatican. (The two leaders, along with the Dalai Lama, the political and spiritual leader of the Tibetan people, met again in 1999, when Mohammed addressed 100,000 people gathered in St. Peter's Square at the Vatican.) In November 1996, as a member of the Peace Council, Mohammed traveled to Chiapas, Mexico, to support the human-rights work of Bishop Samuel Ruiz Garcia by listening to the concerns of Zapatista rebels who were fighting for the autonomy of the region's indigenous peoples. In December, at the invitation of the Palestinian leader Yasir Arafat, Mohammed led a delegation of Muslim Americans to Jerusalem and areas of Palestine. Around that time he also established the Collective Purchasing Conference (CPC), an economic plan to develop poor communities by working toward the establishment of new businesses, affordable housing, and cultural centers. In 1997 President Clinton invited Mohammed to read from the Koran at the Presidential Inauguration Day National Prayer Service. The following year Mohammed participated in the Conference on Religion and Peace held in Auschwitz, Poland.

In the late 1990s Farrakhan began to lead the NOI toward mainstream Islam, and in 2000 Farrakhan and Mohammed publicly embraced, declaring an end to their longstanding dispute. (Farrakhan's battle with and recovery from prostate cancer in 1999 reportedly led him to place greater emphasis on unity and less on racial separatism.) Referring to previous disagreements between himself and Farrakhan, Mohammed said, as quoted by the BBC (February 27, 2000), "Whatever has troubled us in the past, I think we can bury it now and never look back at that grave." Despite the thaw in relations, the NOI and the American Society of Muslims remain mostly separate. In addition, serious differences remain between black Muslims and non-black, immigrant Muslims. (African-Americans constitute roughly 30 percent of all Muslims in the United States, but more than 80 percent of non-immigrant Muslims; many African-Americans have come to the Islamic faith through black nationalist movements such as the NOI.)

In the spring of 2001, Mohammed was a featured speaker at an event, held in South Africa, commemorating 1,400 years of Islamic history on the African continent. Following the September 11, 2001 terrorist attacks on the United States, which led to growing suspicion and resentment of Islam in America, Mohammed continued his efforts to present the peaceful and tolerant version of Islam he had long represented. "Terrorism has no place in Islam, just as it has no place in Christianity or Judaism," he told Stan Swofford and Aulica Rutland for the Greensboro, North Carolina, News & Record (November 2, 2001). Along with Farrakhan and the televangelist Reverend Robert Schuller, Mohammed participated in the October 29, 2001 "Evening of Religious Solidarity," an event meant to foster understanding between Christians and Muslims. That same year he served as a consultant to the actor Mario Van Peebles, who portrayed Malcolm X in the movie Ali (2001). In 2002 Mohammed served as a panel member on the televised program Where Do We Go from Here? Chaos or Community?, a group discussion on the future of the African-American community; opened an office of community relations in Washington, D.C.; and, as international president of the World Council on Religion and Peace, participated in the Conference of Religious Leaders, a meeting held in Nairobi, Kenya, to address the devastation caused in Africa by the HIV/AIDS epidemic. Also in 2002, Mohammed was elected a member of the Martin Luther King Jr. Initial Board of Preachers, and a member of the advisory council for the international Timbuktu Educational Foundation, based in Oakland, California. In 2003 Mohammed and his ministry helped to found Bridges Television, a network focusing on the American Muslim community. Mohammed's ministry has partnered with the Muhammad Ali Community and Economic Development Corporation, an organization dedicated to improving the lives of underprivileged Chicago residents.

After Mohammed retired as official head of the American Society of Muslims, in 2003, he expressed frustration with some of the group's imams. "I have tried over the last 10 or 12 years to encourage them to get more religious education, but I have made no progress," he told Salim Muwakkil for the Chicago Tribune (September 16, 2003). "They want their followers just to obey them, but not question them or right their wrong deeds." Muslim leaders and outside observers have expressed concern that Mohammed's retirement could lead to a leadership crisis within the American Society of Muslims. Nevertheless, many American Muslims continue to regard Mohammed as a spiritual guide, and in September 2004 the Mosque Cares held a convention in Chicago to connect with faithful Muslims.

Mohammed has authored a number of books, including The Teachings of W. D. Muhammad (1976); Prayer and Al-Islam (1982); Religion on the Line (1983); An African American Genesis (1986); Al-Islam Unity and Leadership (1991); Islam's Climate for Business Success (1994); and The Champion We Have in Common: The Dynamic African American Soul (2002). He has appeared on television programs such as Larry King Live, Tony Brown's Journal, and Gil Noble's Like It Is, and has hosted a weekly television program broadcast in the Chicago area, W. Deen Muhammad and Guests. He has lectured at many colleges and universities around the country, among them Morehouse, Yale, Georgetown, Howard, Harvard, Columbia, Fordham, and Duke, as well as at such venues as Radio City Music Hall, Lincoln Center, and the Jacob Javitz Center, all in New York City. In both 1992 and 1993 President Hosni Mubarak of Egypt honored Mohammed with a gold medal in recognition of his religious work in the U.S. In 1994 Mohammed received the Cup of Compassion from the Hartford Seminary, in Hartford, Connecticut. The mayor of Harvey, Illinois, presented Mohammed with a key to that city in 2000. That same year the city of Louisville, Kentucky, honored Mohammed's leadership with a three-day, 25th-anniversary tribute. The mayor of Augusta, Georgia, declared March 13, 2003 "Imam W. Deen Mohammed Day."

Mohammed, a short, balding man with a gray beard, an easy smile, and a booming laugh, lives in Chicago. He has two daughters, Ngina and Laila.
—C.F.T.

Suggested Reading: American Journal of Islamic Social Sciences p245+ vol. 2, 1985; BBC (on-line) Feb. 27, 2000, with photos; Miami Herald C p1 Oct. 14, 1997, with photos; Muslim Journal (on-line); Nation of Islam Web site; New Africa Radio Web site; Peace Council Web site; Seattle Times A p12 June 14, 1997, with photos; Encyclopedia of American Religion and Politics, 2003; Marsh, Clifton E. From Black Muslims to Muslims: The Transition from Separatism to Islam, 1930-1980, 1984

Selected Books: The Teachings of W. D. Muhammad, 1976; Prayer and Al-Islam, 1982; Religion on the Line, 1983; An African American Genesis, 1986; Al-Islam Unity and Leadership, 1991; Islam's Climate for Business Success, 1994;

The Champion We Have in Common: The Dynamic African American Soul, 2002

Jon Kopaloff/Getty Images

Molina, Alfred

May 24, 1953– Actor

Address: c/o William Morris Agency, 151 El Camino Dr., Beverly Hills, CA 90212

Ranked among the most versatile of contemporary actors, the British-born Alfred Molina is also one of the least frequently recognized, perhaps because—like the chameleon, a creature to which he has often been compared—he undergoes actual or apparent physical transformations for many of his roles. "Touch wood, I have been very fortunate that I work and make a living," Molina said to Laura Weinert for *BPI Entertainment News Wire* (October 30, 2002), "and I have the luxury that outside the business, nobody knows who the hell I am." In the more than 60 movies for television and the big screen in which he has appeared, he has portrayed such varied characters as a Russian sailor, a Victorian-era British suitor, an Iranian doctor, an Old West card shark, a Cuban exile, a Guatemalan dissident, a Greek-American lawyer, a French mayor, and the Mexican painter Diego Rivera, in the biopic *Frida* (2002). Although he has often been cast as a villain, Molina has a fine comic sensibility that he has displayed on the stage as well as in film. A classically trained thespian, Molina enjoyed a stint with the Royal Shakespeare Company in the late 1970s, before garnering admiring attention for his role in the first British stage production of *Acci-*

dental Death of an Anarchist (1979), for which he won the Plays and Players London Theatre Critics Award for most promising newcomer. He also delivered award-winning performances in an Off-Broadway mounting of *Molly Sweeney* (1995) and a Broadway production of *Art* (1998), and a Tony Award–nominated turn in a Broadway revival of *Fiddler on the Roof* (2004). "I've never been sure what the word 'career' means," he told Michael Kuchwara for the Associated Press (February 27, 1998). "If it means I want to be at this place by the time I'm 40 or 50, then no, I haven't got a career. I've never planned it. I've got a career in the same way a gypsy has a career. I just go from job to job. Sometimes I've done jobs because it is the only job available. Other times, I've had a choice and I've gone for the ones I like the best. And that's the only criteria I've ever had. I'm a character actor. That's what I've always wanted to be. Character actors tend to have longer careers. Now I've reached the point where I can't do anything else. It's a bit late now. And hopefully I will be working until I drop."

The son of a Spanish father and an Italian mother, the actor Alfred Molina was born on May 24, 1953 in London, England. His father, Esteban Molina, came to England in the late 1930s as a refugee from the Spanish Civil War; his mother, Giovanna, was en route to the United States after World War II, working as an au pair, when she met Esteban in London. The couple married and settled in the Notting Hill Gate section of London, which had a large immigrant population then. Esteban Molina took jobs as a maître d' and waiter; Giovanna Molina worked as a cook and a housekeeper. Alfred Molina spent his childhood immersed in Latin culture; he did not learn to speak English until age six. He has described his parents as loud, expressive, and emotional. "I think I must have reacted against all that volatility," he told Corina Honan for the London *Daily Mail* (July 16, 1994). "My parents were always reminding me of my Latin heritage, with my father wanting me to learn Flamenco guitar and my mother talking to me in Italian. But all the time I was desperate to be English, desperate to assimilate." When he was nine, Molina saw the movie *Spartacus* and told his mother that he wanted to be an actor. In school he was an average student and showed no skill at sports. Driven by his secret passion for acting, he joined his school's drama club, where he enjoyed displaying his talents. He recalled to Michael Kuchwara, "I always knew I could make people laugh. I was the class clown. That was my way of getting in and out of trouble." His parents were not enthusiastic about his love for the dramatic arts. "My father was very disparaging about acting," Molina told Judy Rumbold for the London *Guardian* (January 23, 1992). "He was under the impression that it wasn't quite the sort of thing for a good, upstanding heterosexual man to do."

In 1964, at age 11, Molina began attending the Cardinal Manning Secondary Modern School. His English teacher there, Martyn Corbett, who had once been an actor, helped Molina appreciate the dedication that acting required. The following year Molina's parents divorced; both he and his brother remained with their mother, who was forced to work long hours as a chambermaid and hotel housekeeper to support her family. Molina told Honan that in response to the divorce and its toll on his mother, he became "rather insular." In addition, because he had reached his adult height—six feet three inches—by his early teens, he suffered at the hands of his peers. "I was head and shoulders above the other kids, but a complete physical coward. I used to long to be smaller," he told Honan. "I got picked on and bullied quite badly because I was a bit of a wimp and I learned never to fight back. The few times I did I got the stuffing beaten out of me."

During his early teens Molina developed a love for American culture and film, particularly Westerns. In 1969, at 16, he joined the London-based National Youth Theatre, a small company that enabled teenagers to act in a semiprofessional atmosphere. He remained with the company for three seasons, at the end of which he knew that acting "was absolutely what I wanted to do," as he told Kuchwara. "I had no doubts after that." He next attended the Guildhall School of Music and Drama (GSMD), a London college, where he distinguished himself as a hard worker and what his fellow student Nick Ellsworth described to Rumbold as "a great lolloping joker." While at GSMD Molina became interested in pursuing comedic acting. (Many of his childhood idols had been comedians rather than actors; his heroes included the British comedian Tommy Cooper, whom he described to Zoe Heller for the London Independent [April 7, 1991] as "the greatest clown—in the pure sense—that has ever been.") His goals differed from those of most of his peers. "At the Guildhall it was assumed that all of us would want to go off to [London's Royal] National [Theatre] or some rep theatre," he told Heller. "But I was never a classicist. My soft spot has always been for variety—for tatty, end-of-the-pier acts. When we did Shakespeare, the only things I was enthusiastic about playing were the low, comedy parts—Bottom, or the Fool in Lear."

By the time he left drama school, Molina was determined to become a comedian. He began performing street theater and working as a stand-up comic. His material, he told Heller, was "terrible." "It was before any of the alternative stuff came out," he explained, "so I was still doing mother-in-law jokes and saying things like, 'Take my wife . . . go on, take her.'" In 1975 he joined a theater company that performed for children; at that time it was touring the English countryside with an abridged version of Shakespeare's A Midsummer Night's Dream. He also found work with local repertory companies in Newcastle, Liverpool, Hornchurch, and Leicester. In 1977 Molina became a member of the esteemed Royal Shakespeare Company (RSC) and began appearing in minor roles in RSC productions of plays including Shakespeare's King Lear and Troilus and Cressida, David Edgar's Destiny, Bertolt Brecht's The Days of the Commune, Edward Bond's The Bundle, Barrie Keeffe's Frozen Assets, Howard Baker's That Good Between Us, and Charles Woods's Dingo. "I loved being around those RSC people," he told Heller; "they were all so sexy and posh and they had these mellifluous accents. I was always being told off for gawping at them on stage when I was meant to be playing a centurion. But I knew it wasn't for me. I haven't got the intellectual stamina; I'm more of a modern actor—I think in short sentences." At the end of his first year with the company, the RSC did not renew Molina's contract. Throughout the latter half of the 1970s, Molina supplemented his income from acting—an average of $45 a week, when he had a role—with various jobs, including waiter, chef, mortuary attendant, butler, and litter collector for the railways.

In 1978 Molina won parts in two plays produced in London: Irish Eyes and English Tears, by Nigel Baldwin, at Theatre Upstairs, and Wheelchair Willie, by Alan Brown, at the Royal Court Theatre. His big break came the following year, when he played the lead in Dario Fo's Accidental Death of an Anarchist, a political satire about police corruption in Italy, mounted at London's Half Moon Theatre. "It was an extraordinary play," he told Heller, "and the first time I'd been allowed to go wild on stage—to improvise, throw in gags. . . . It had the added virtue of getting me noticed." For his work in Fo's play, Molina earned the 1979 Plays and Players London Theatre Critics Award for most promising newcomer. On the heels of his theatrical success, Molina made his film debut, in Steven Spielberg's classic Raiders of the Lost Ark (1981). He appeared as Sapito, a villainous South American guide, whose treachery nearly ends the life of Indiana Jones (Harrison Ford) before he himself is killed by tarantulas in the opening sequence. "I couldn't believe my luck on that," Molina told Sandi David for the Daily Oklahoman (May 12, 1995). "I'll always remember that film fondly," he added, "because my daughter was about to be born and we had no money, I was still paying off my college debts and suddenly this job comes along which was offering an extraordinary amount of money [$5,000] for two weeks' work, plus a week in Hawaii. It was like a dream come true."

Molina next appeared in the British television movie Meantime (1981) and, also in Great Britain, the plays Destry Rides Again (1982), Dreyfus (1982), and Viva (1985). In 1985 he accepted a small part in Richard Donner's film Ladyhawke, which was shot in Italy. He earned enough from that job to tide him over during the filming of his next picture, Letter to Brezhnev (1985), Chris Bernard's low-budget romantic farce about a Liverpool woman (played by Tracy Lea) who falls in love with Peter (Peter Firth), a Russian sailor she meets at a dance hall. (The financing for the picture was so minuscule that the actors had to pay their own hotel bills.) Molina was cast as Sergei, another Russian sailor, and, with the exception of two lines in English, spoke all of his dialogue in Russian. Also in 1985 he rejoined the RSC, to play Petruchio in a highly praised stage production of *The Taming of the Shrew*.

After appearing in a small part in the film *Eleni* (1986), Molina tackled the most impressive of his screen roles up to that date: that of Kenneth Halliwell, the real-life lover of the British playwright Joe Orton, in Stephen Frears's harrowing film *Prick Up Your Ears* (1987). In 1967, after a 16-year relationship, Halliwell bludgeoned Orton to death in the men's shared apartment before taking his own life. To portray the obsessed and tormented Halliwell—an unpublished, struggling writer who had been Orton's writing mentor before the younger man rocketed to success—Molina shaved his head (Halliwell had begun losing his hair in his early 20s) and conducted extensive research on Halliwell and Orton's complex relationship. One of the first mainstream British films with an explicitly homosexual theme, *Prick Up Your Ears* received much critical acclaim. Assessments of Molina's performance ranged from dismissive to glowing. Pauline Kael, for example, in the *New Yorker* (May 4, 1987), described the actor as "miscast," while Stanley Kauffmann, in the *New Republic* (April 20, 1987), judged his acting to be "superb." Molina told Marybeth Kerrigan for *Premiere* (March 1988), "A lot of people disliked the performance because [Halliwell] was so ugly. But [he] was difficult, pompous, deeply self-loathing. That's what made him a wonderful character to play."

Molina next appeared in the British made-for-TV film *Virtuoso* (1988), in which he played the concert pianist John Ogden, whose career ended because of mental illness; Jonathan Dent's barely noticed *Revolutionary Witness* (1989); and Les Blair's *The Accountant* (1989), for which he earned a British Academy of Film and Television Award (BAFTA) nomination for best actor for his depiction of an oppressed Jewish accountant. He also had roles in the British television series *Nativity Blues* (1989) and *El Cid* (1989). In addition, he was cast as Charlie Fox, a desperate tinsel-town hustler, in a National Theatre production of David Mamet's *Speed-the-Plow*, for which he earned a nomination for a 1989–90 Olivier Award. In 1991 Molina was tapped to play an Iranian-born, American-ized doctor, Sayyed Bozorg "Moody" Mahmoody, in Brian Gilbert's film *Not Without My Daughter*, based on the true story of Betty Mahmoody. In 1984, weary of anti-Iranian sentiment in the U.S., Moody persuades Betty, his American wife, to accompany him on a two-week visit to Iran with the couple's four-year-old daughter. Once in Iran, Moody becomes inspired by the religious fervor that spread throughout Iran after the Ayatollah Ruholla Khomeini came to power. He announces that the family will remain in Tehran, and Betty becomes a virtual prisoner. While some critics applauded *Not Without My Daughter* for shedding

light on the plight of women in Iran, others considered the movie xenophobic and one-sided; Molina's depiction of Moody's conversion was generally regarded as convincing.

Molina portrayed a ladies' man in Victorian-era England in *American Friends* (1991), which starred Michael Palin, and an emotionally cold British husband who thaws in sunny Italy in Mike Newell's 1920s period piece *Enchanted April* (1992). In the latter year he also played Lawrence Shannon, an alcoholic defrocked minister, in a Royal National Theatre production of Tennessee Williams's *The Night of the Iguana*. Television movies in which he appeared during this period include *The Trials of Oz* (1991), *Hancock* (1991), *Angels* (1992), *Trust Me* (1992), *Typhon's People* (1993), *The Marshal* (1993), and *Requiem Apache* (1994). He played a talkative painter in the 1993 film version of Kafka's *The Trial*, a villain in *White Fang II: Myth of the White Wolf* (1994), a cardsharp in the Western *Maverick* (1994), a Harvard anthropologist in the science-fiction thriller *Species* (1995), and a crass Greek-American lawyer in *Before and After* (1996). He also garnered critical attention as a Cuban political prisoner who comes to the U.S. via the 1980 Mariel boatlift, in Mira Nair's *The Perez Family* (1995).

Molina made his New York City theatrical debut in a 1995 Off-Broadway production of Brian Friel's *Molly Sweeney*. For his portrayal of Sweeney's husband, Frank, a bumbling, sweet-tempered Irishman who delivers many of the play's humorous lines, Molina won a Theater World Award and a nomination for the Drama Desk Award for most outstanding debut performance. For much of the run of *Molly Sweeney*, Molina was also at work on a film, Robert Dornhelm's political thriller *A Further Gesture* (1996), in the role of a Guatemalan exile. "I was playing an Irishman in the evening and a Guatemalan dissident during the day," he told Will Joyner for the *New York Times* (March 3, 1996). "That's the usual for me." In 1998 Molina again impressed New York theater critics, in the role of Yvan in Yasmina Reza's award-winning one-act play, *Art*. (The production, directed by Matthew Warchus and starring Victor Garber and Alan Alda as well as Molina, had had a successful mounting in London before its arrival in New York.) Exploring the complexities of male friendship, *Art* depicts a heated three-way debate sparked by the purchase by Serge (Garber) of a 1970s white-on-white painting. Serge's expensive acquisition infuriates Marc (Alda), Serge's friend of 15 years, an anti-intellectual who considers the painting a threat and a betrayal. Yvan, the most conciliatory and comical of the trio, sees his friendships unravel while he contemplates his impending marriage. The play was a critical success, with all three actors garnering acclaim. In a review for *Entertainment Weekly* (June 5, 1998), Lisa Schwarzbaum wrote, "With a cast of three terrific performers it's tough to honor just one of them, but from the minute Molina bursts on stage with a tour de force monologue, he's a magnetic force field of energy." For his performance in *Art*, Molina received a Drama Desk Award for outstanding featured actor and, along with Garber and Alda, the Outer Critics Circle Special Achievement Award for ensemble performance; he was the only member of the cast nominated for a Tony Award for best actor. He later portrayed Yvan in a Los Angeles production of *Art*, for which he earned a Los Angeles Drama Desk Award.

In the late 1990s Molina made several notable film appearances, in the roles of a gay man whose lover has HIV, in *Nervous Energy* (1995); Levin in Bernard Rose's version of Tolstoy's classic novel *Anna Karenina* (1997); a Russian butcher in the screwball comedy *The Man Who Knew Too Little* (1997); a Depression-era stage actor in Stanley Tucci's directorial debut, *The Imposters* (1998); and Dudley's nemesis, Snidely Whiplash, in the film version of *Dudley Do-Right* (1999). In 1997, in a memorable scene in *Boogie Nights*, Paul Thomas Anderson's complex, compassionate view of people involved in the adult-porn industry, Molina played a crazed, drug-addicted drug dealer clad in nothing but red bikini briefs. Although the role was small, his performance was overwhelmingly applauded by critics. Speaking to Reed Johnson for the *Los Angeles Daily News* (January 19, 1999) of his decision to tackle the part, Molina said, "You know, it's 90 percent luck, 10 percent judgment. Someone said to me, 'That movie, you know, that little 10-minute cameo, will be a defining moment in your career.' And I wish I could say, 'Yes, I knew all that, and that's why I planned it that way.' I wish I could say that, but I can't." For his contribution to *Boogie Nights*, Molina shared a special Screen Actors Guild Award for outstanding performance by an ensemble in a theatrical motion picture. Molina made a cameo appearance as an electronics-store owner in Paul Thomas Anderson's *Magnolia* (1999), which garnered a National Board of Review Award for best ensemble. The actor's film credits also include *Scorpion Spring* (1997), *The Treat* (1998), *Pete's Meteor* (1998), *Texas Rangers* (2001), and the remake for TV of Agatha Christie's *Murder on the Orient Express* (2001). He received acclaim for his depiction of a repressive French mayor, the antagonist of an exotic chocolatier (Juliette Binoche), in Lasse Hallström's *Chocolat* (2000). In *Frida* (2002), Julie Taymor's docudrama about the Mexican artist Frida Kahlo, Molina played the Mexican painter Diego Rivera. Both Molina and Salma Hayek, cast as Kahlo, won rave notices for their acting. As one critic for the *New Republic* (November 18, 2002) observed, "Oddly enough, Hayek's own fine performance depends, as does the whole film, on Alfred Molina's performance as Rivera. He is superb. Large, heavy, swift, he creates a Rivera who sometimes has a touch of the casual about both his genius and his libido, and who is unfailingly serious about one matter: his communism." To portray the hedonistic, womanizing Rivera, Molina gained a great deal of

weight, shaved back his hairline, and wore a bulbous nose. Beyond the physical preparations, he told Weinert that he felt a responsibility to portray Rivera's situation and motivations as honestly as he could, without letting his own attitudes seep in. "The clue seemed to be to find out really what is it about a large man," he explained, "an expansive larger-than-life man who makes no apology for being what he is and how he is. How a big fat guy can, in a sense, delight in that and revel in that, and that it's an essential part of what made him so attractive. So it is clearly not to do with being just a big fat guy. There is something about his attitude, his spirit, and it was really trying to find that joy, his lust for life."

In the short animated film *Ape* (2002), Molina provided the voice of a zookeeper who is devastated when an orangutan under his charge escapes from his cage. The next year he had an uncredited bit part in the movie *My Life Without Me* and a role in the lackluster John Cusack vehicle *Identity*. In *Luther* (2003), Eric Till's historical drama, he was cast as Johann Tetzel, the 15th–16th-century Dominican friar who became embroiled in a notorious argument with Martin Luther over the sale of indulgences and is said to have sparked Luther's split from the Roman Catholic Church. He also appeared in Jim Jarmusch's *Coffee and Cigarettes* (2003), a compilation of 11 seemingly improvised vignettes, starring diverse comics and musicians, that earned both praise and derision. The scene that Molina shared with Steve Coogan was one of only two that consistently drew plaudits. (The other starred Cate Blanchett in two roles.) Molina also starred as a funeral-home director in Nick Hurran's romantic comedy *Plots with a View*; released in England in 2003, the film was scheduled to arrive in the U.S. in late 2004 with the title *Undertaking Betty*.

The year 2004 saw the release of the Spanish-language film *Cronicas*, in which Molina starred with John Leguizamo, and Sam Raimi's *Spider-Man 2*, which raised Molina's visibility considerably. In the latter, the blockbuster sequel to Raimi's 2002 film, Molina played Dr. Otto Octavius, a visionary scientist who, through a botched experiment, becomes Doc Ock, a villain with four massive metal tentacles sprouting from his back. (Computer graphics enhanced the action of the tentacles, which 16 puppeteers controlled.) Most critics preferred the second *Spider-Man* film to its predecessor and praised Molina's performance as the new nemesis of the title character (played by Tobey Maguire), who in ordinary life is named Peter Parker. Andrew Sarris, who disliked what he called the "gimmicky metal appendages," wrote for the *New York Observer* (July 12, 2004), "Fortunately, Mr. Molina is charismatically ambiguous enough to project complex feelings despite his ridiculous encumbrances. His not entirely unsympathetic monster is made to seem humanly redeemable by his recollections of how he'd once inspired Peter Parker, the science student, at Columbia [University]." "Playing villains is always fun, there's no two ways about it," Molina told Anthony Breznican for the *Chicago Tribune* (July 16, 2004). "There's always a lot of freedom and room to be inventive. I could go to my grave playing bad guys. I love it." Molina nicknamed the four extremities Harry, Larry, Moe, and Flo. At the end of one long day of filming, he told Breznican, he spontaneously began singing "If I Were a Rich Man," a song from the musical *Fiddler on the Roof*, which was then in rehearsals. As he sang, the puppeteers controlling the tentacles made the metal arms dance along. That improvised performance appears as one of the extras on the DVD of *Spider-Man 2*.

In recent work on stage, in 2002 co-productions of the Odyssey Theatre and Circus Theatricals, both in Los Angeles, California, Molina played the newly rich businessman Lopakhin in Chekhov's *The Cherry Orchard* and the Duke of Buckingham in Shakespeare's *Richard III*. Since February 2004 Molina has starred in a Broadway revival of *Fiddler on the Roof*, a musical based on stories by the 19th-century Yiddish writer who used the pseudonym Sholom Aleichem. Molina portrays Tevye, an Orthodox Jewish milkman, a character played by Zero Mostel in the original mounting of the musical, which ran on Broadway for more than seven years, beginning in 1964. Many critics considered Molina miscast, in part because he is not Jewish. In an interview with Richard Zoglin for *Time* (March 8, 2004), however, Jerry Bock, who composed the music for *Fiddler* (Sheldon Harnick wrote the lyrics; Joseph Stein wrote the book), pointed out that the musical has been produced around the world, and only a small percentage of the actors cast as Tevye have been Jewish. Zoglin dissented from the prevailing view among critics, who judged the 2004 mounting to be lackluster; he described the production as a "striking Broadway revival that manages to shake off the cobwebs and relocate the emotional core of a show too often typecast as your grandmother's favorite musical. This is a *Fiddler* for everybody." Molina, he continued, "is a younger, more down-to-earth, less clownish Tevye than Zero Mostel." Despite the frequent criticism leveled at the production, it garnered six Tony Award nominations, including a nomination for best actor in a musical for Molina.

Molina is a Circus Theatricals associate artist; he teaches regularly in the company's conservatory. He told Evan Henerson for the *Los Angeles Daily News* (January 15, 2002), "[Circus Theatricals] is my theatrical home in Los Angeles. This is where I work and who I work with. I'm fortunate that I've got the means to make a living in film and television that I can in a way commit a certain amount of time every year to do theater. Hopefully, I'm using that time wisely. I think I am."

Molina has also tried his hand at television series, as the headliner of two CBS comedies: *Ladies Man* (1999), in which he played the only man in a houseful of women, and *Bram and Alice* (2002), in which his character was a wretched, world-famous author who learns that he has an adult daughter. Both sitcoms were canceled after short runs. As of November 2004 Molina was lending his voice to the animated film *Sian Ka'an*, which was still in production, and had been cast in the television film *Where Is the Mango Princess?*

Since 1993 Alfred Molina has made his home in Los Angeles with his wife, the British-born actress and novelist Jill Gascoine, who is 16 years his senior. The two met during the 1982 run of the play *Destry Rides Again,* in which Gascoine was cast as the female lead; Molina described their first encounter to Green as "lust at first sight." Like her husband, Gascoine appears in Circus Theatricals productions. From her first marriage she has two sons, Sean and Adam, the latter of whom is the Odyssey Theatre's technical director. Molina also has a daughter, Rachel, from a previous relationship.
—K.A.D.

Suggested Reading: *Fresh Air* Dec. 21, 2000; (London) *Daily Mail* July 16, 1994, with photo; (London) *Guardian* p22 Jan. 23, 1992; (London) *Independent* p15 Apr. 7, 1991; *Los Angeles Daily News* Jan. 19, 1999, with photo, L p5 Jan. 15, 2002, with photo; *New York Times* C p11 May 15, 1987, with photo, II p11 Mar. 3, 1996, with photo; *Newsday* p17 Jan. 21, 1996, with photo

Selected Plays: *Accidental Death of an Anarchist*, 1979; *Destry Rides Again*, 1982; *Dreyfus*, 1982; *Viva*, 1985; *The Taming of the Shrew*, 1985; *The Night of the Iguana*, 1992; *Molly Sweeney*, 1995; *Art*, 1998; *True West*, 2001; *Richard III*, 2002; *Fiddler on the Roof*, 2004

Selected Films: *Raiders of the Lost Ark*, 1981; *Ladyhawke*, 1985; *Letter to Brezhnev*, 1985; *Prick Up Your Ears*, 1987; *Not Without My Daughter*, 1991; *American Friends*, 1991; *Enchanted April*, 1992; *The Trial*, 1993; *When Pigs Fly*, 1993; *White Fang II: Myth of the White Wolf*, 1994; *Maverick*, 1994; *The Steal*, 1994; *Hideaway*, 1995; *The Perez Family*, 1995; *Species*, 1995; *Nervous Energy*, 1995; *Before and After*, 1996; *Mojave Moon*, 1996; *Anna Karenina*, 1997; *Scorpion Spring*, 1997; *Boogie Nights*, 1997; *The Man Who Knew Too Little*, 1997; *The Imposters*, 1998; *The Treat*, 1998; *Pete's Meteor*, 1998; *Dudley Do-Right*, 1999; *Magnolia*, 1999; *Chocolat*, 2000; *Texas Rangers*, 2001; *Frida*, 2002; *Plots with a View*, 2003; *Identity*, 2003; *Coffee and Cigarettes*, 2004; *Spider-Man 2*, 2004

Selected Television Shows: *Ladies Man*, 1999; *Bram and Alice*, 2002

Kevin Winter/Getty Images

Mortensen, Viggo

(VEE-go)

Oct. 20, 1958– Actor; painter; poet; photographer

Address: c/o Ram Publications, 2525 Michigan Ave., Suite A2, Santa Monica, CA 90404-4031

Like many terms, "Renaissance man" is often applied hastily and inaccurately, but in the case of Viggo Mortensen, the words may be appropriate. Mortensen is a published poet, a photographer and painter who has had his work exhibited in galleries in the United States and abroad, and a spoken-word artist who has released three CDs. He is best known as the actor who portrayed the self-exiled king Aragorn in Peter Jackson's phenomenally successful *Lord of the Rings* film film trilogy, based on the novels by J. R. R. Tolkien. Prior to his work in those movies, he had appeared in close to 40 others, in a career that spans two decades. "I don't separate them," he told Stephanie Snipes for CNN (March 9, 2004, on-line) of his various artistic interests. "Different ways of doing pretty much the same thing, paying attention, being here, being present and noticing what things look like and feel like to you. It's a subjective thing. We sort of go through our days and our lives not really paying attention at all. For me a way that I'm comfortable experiencing life . . . is to do it for the camera, or pen or a paintbrush."

Viggo Peter Mortensen was born on October 20, 1958 in New York City to a Danish-born father, Viggo, and an American mother, Grace. The couple had met in Norway; Mortensen's paternal grandmother came from the Norwegian port city of Trondheim. Mortensen's family moved to South America when he was two, living in Venezuela and Argentina, where his father managed large farms and ranches. Beginning at age seven Viggo attended a boarding school in the mountains of Argentina. When the boy was 11, his parents divorced, and he moved to upstate New York with his mother and two younger brothers; he also spent considerable time in Denmark while growing up. "I didn't have friends when I was little that I know now—there wasn't any sense of continuity like that," he told Alex Kuczynski for *Vanity Fair* (January 2004). "But I got to see a lot of things and learn a lot of things. And I learned to rely on my imagination, and on myself."

Mortensen attended Watertown High School, in a town near Lake Ontario and the Canadian border, where he excelled in his studies and in sports, graduating in 1976. It was in upstate New York that he was introduced to acting, at a repertory theater where he gave his first performance—a monologue inspired by Jack the Ripper. "I never thought it would last," he told Paul Young for *Variety* (October 6-12, 2003) about his involvement with acting. "I just tried it to see what it was like and it just clicked, I guess." He graduated in 1980 from St. Lawrence University, in Canton, New York, with a degree in government and Spanish. From there he moved to Denmark, where he worked at odd jobs while writing fiction and poetry. After returning to New York City (he followed his girlfriend there) in 1982, he studied acting with Warren Robertson for two years while appearing in several Off-Broadway plays. In 1984 he moved to Los Angeles, where his performance in *Bent* at the Coast Playhouse earned him a Dramalogue Critics Award.

Mortensen appeared in the television miniseries *George Washington* in 1984 and made his big-screen debut the following year, as a young Amish farmer in Peter Weir's *Witness,* alongside Harrison Ford and Kelly McGillis. He played Bragg on the soap opera *Search for Tomorrow* in 1985 and appeared in an episode of the popular TV series *Miami Vice* in March 1987. A series of forgettable films followed, including *Salvation!* (1987), *Fresh Horses* (1988), *Prison* (1988), *Leatherface: Texas Chainsaw Massacre III* (1990), *Young Guns II* (1990), *The Reflecting Skin* (1990), *Tripwire* (1990), and the television movie *Once in a Blue Moon* (1990). His profile rose when he was cast as a Vietnam veteran in *The Indian Runner* (1991), Sean Penn's directorial debut. He played a trigger-happy, not very bright ex-convict in the 1993 film *Boiling Point,* which starred Wesley Snipes, and was also seen in *Ruby Cairo* that year. He received good notices for his portrayal of a paraplegic former convict and informant in Brian De Palma's *Carlito's Way* (1993), starring Al Pacino, but his next several projects—*The Young Americans* (1993), the Polish film *Ewangelia wedlug Harry'ego* (The Gospel According to Harry, 1993), *Floundering* (1994), *Desert Lunch* (1994), *The Crew* (1994), *American Yakuza* (1994), and *Black Velvet*

Pantsuit (1995)—failed to capitalize on his budding reputation.

Mortensen's fortunes began to change in 1995, when he played a weapons officer in *Crimson Tide,* starring Denzel Washington and Gene Hackman, and the devil in *The Prophecy,* with Christopher Walken. His next role was in the Spanish production *Gimlet* (1995), and he shared the screen with Brendan Fraser and Ashley Judd in *The Passion of Darkly Noon* (1996). He received good reviews as one of the hostages in *Albino Alligator* (1996). In the adaptation of the Henry James novel *The Portrait of a Lady* (1996) directed by Jane Campion, he played one of the suitors of Isabel Archer (Nicole Kidman), while in *Daylight* (1996) he was a mountain-climbing businessman. He starred in the 1997 television film *Vanishing Point,* as a former racecar driver and Army Ranger trying to elude the police while returning home for the birth of his child.

In what has often been called his breakout role, Mortensen was cast in *G.I. Jane* (1997) as a sadistic military officer—with a penchant for quoting poetry—who trains the first female Navy SEAL candidate (Demi Moore). He appeared in the Spanish production *La Pistola de mi hermano* (My Brother's Gun) in 1997 and the following year was in two movies inspired by Alfred Hitchcock films: a loose adaptation of *Dial M for Murder* titled *A Perfect Murder,* and a shot-for-shot remake of *Psycho.* In the former he played Gwyneth Paltrow's lover, an artist who is later hired by her husband (Michael Douglas) to kill her; in the latter he was the boyfriend of Anne Heche's character, Marion Crane. He played a hippie traveling salesman who woos a dissatisfied housewife (Diane Lane) in upstate New York in 1969 in *A Walk on the Moon* (1999); Lane was so determined that he be hired for the role that she gave up part of her own fee to make it possible. In *28 Days* (2000) Mortensen was seen as a professional baseball pitcher who meets his love interest (Sandra Bullock) while at a rehabilitation clinic.

Mortensen gave his most prominent performances to date when he replaced Stuart Townsend in the role of Aragorn, a self-exiled warrior king, in the *Lord of the Rings* movies—*The Fellowship of the Ring* (2001), *The Two Towers* (2002), and *The Return of the King* (2003)—after filming had begun. All three movies in the trilogy, adaptations of J. R. R. Tolkien's beloved fantasy novels, were shot in the director Peter Jackson's native New Zealand over an 18-month period. Mortensen has said that he might not have taken the role had it not been for his son's intervention. "When they first asked me, the question was, 'Do you want to leave for New Zealand tomorrow?' I knew [the film's cast and crew] had already been there for some months, which wasn't good," he told the Australian publication *Empire* (January 2002), as quoted on the Frostyland Web site. "I knew I wouldn't have time to prepare and I hadn't read the book. There were plenty of reasons not to go. I didn't feel I could do a good job and I didn't want to be away from my

son for that length of time. But my son was familiar with the books, he talked about them with his school friends and he knew about the character of Aragorn. He said, 'Oh, that's pretty cool. You should do that.'" The filming was often grueling. Not only did Mortensen have to learn Elvish, a tongue created by Tolkien for the books—he also had to learn to fight with a sword, for the film's many action sequences. While performing virtually all his own stunts, he had several mishaps, breaking a tooth and two toes while acting in the fight scenes for *The Two Towers.*

"I had no idea what I was getting into," Mortensen told William Arnold for the *Seattle Post-Intelligencer* (February 26, 2004, on-line). "It seemed, for a lot of reasons, a big gamble—a very risky project. And nobody—except maybe Peter [Jackson]—had an idea how successful it would become. It was sure a big surprise to me. But, in retrospect, it shouldn't have been. Because the saga is filled with elements of myth and fable that have universal appeal." Mortensen quickly immersed himself in the role, keeping his sword by his side during his off-hours and often sleeping in his costume. Once, after accidentally killing a rabbit while driving, he roasted the animal over a fire and ate it, as he thought his character would have done; on another occasion Jackson reportedly addressed Mortensen as Aragorn for over half an hour without the actor's realizing it.

The *Lord of the Rings* films were wildly successful and were quickly embraced by critics, fans of the books, and the general public. *The Fellowship of the Ring* earned $860 million worldwide, *The Two Towers* brought in $919 million, and *The Return of the King* became one of only two films to earn $1 billion at the box office worldwide. (The other was *Titanic,* released in 1997.) *The Return of the King* won 11 Oscars, including those for best picture and best director, at the 2004 Academy Awards ceremony.

Mortensen provided the voice for a character in the 2003 animated film *Live Freaky Die Freaky.* It was the following year, with *Hidalgo,* that he first took on the challenge of carrying a movie as the lead actor. That adventure film focuses on Frank Hopkins, a real-life American cowboy. (Although the film is based on Hopkins's autobiography, much of the book is believed to be fictional, so that *Hidalgo* is not billed as a true story.) According to the book, Hopkins witnessed the massacre of 300 unarmed Lakota Indians by the U.S. Cavalry at Wounded Knee, South Dakota, on December 29, 1890. In the film, a guilt-ridden Hopkins—who claimed to be half-white and half-Lakota—turns to drink. Then, while working with Buffalo Bill Cody's Wild West Show, he is approached by a Saudi Arabian sheik who has heard of his long-distance horse-racing skills and is invited to take part in a 3,000-mile race across the Sahara Desert. Hopkins is looked down upon because his horse, Hidalgo, is a mustang, not a pure-bred animal like the horses ridden by his Arabian competitors.

(Mortensen said that the screenplay seized his attention in part because he is a descendant of Buffalo Bill Cody on his mother's side.) *Hidalgo* was shot largely in North and South Dakota, Montana, and Morocco at a cost of $90 million. The film, which co-starred Omar Sharif, performed well in the first few weeks after its release but was not ultimately the commercial smash many had expected. In his review on the ReelViews Web site, James Berardinelli called *Hidalgo* "a sporadically entertaining adventure movie that is hampered by poor pacing, a badly focused screenplay, and cheesy special effects," but added that "in spite of its flaws . . . it nevertheless retains the capacity to engross and inspire." Roger Ebert wrote for the *Chicago Sun-Times* (March 5, 2004, on-line), "Bold, exuberant and swashbuckling, [*Hidalgo*] has the purity and simplicity of something Douglas Fairbanks or Errol Flynn might have bounded through." Mortensen's next film project is *Alatriste* (scheduled for release in 2005), in which he will portray a mercenary in 16th-century Spain. "If I really think about it, there isn't any one movie I would wipe off my slate," the actor told Alex Kuczynski. "Even during the worst experiences, there was somebody I got to know, or something about the place we were in, something memorable. A lesson."

In addition to being an actor, Mortensen is a painter, poet, photographer, and musician. He created the large murals in the artist's studio seen in *A Perfect Murder;* his first photography exhibit was held at the Robert Mann Gallery, in New York, in 2000, and his paintings and photographs have been shown in galleries in Santa Monica, Los Angeles, New York, Denmark, New Zealand, Cuba, and Greece. (Some of his paintings have sold for as much as $5,000.) He has published several volumes of poetry, including *Ten Last Night* and *Coincidence of Memory* (2002). His book *Recent Forgeries* (1998) features his poetry and reproductions of his paintings and photographs, while his photographs in the volume *Miyelo* (2003) document one of the rituals of the Lakota Indian tribe, the ghost dance. He and his longtime business partner, Pilar Perez, co-own Perceval Press, a small publishing company. As a spoken-word performer, Mortensen teamed with the Japanese guitar legend Buckethead on three CDs of experimental rock and jazz— *One Man's Meat, One Less Thing to Worry About,* and *The Other Parade,* all released in 1999—and collaborated with his ex-wife, Exene Cervenka of the punk band X, on music that accompanied one of his art exhibits.

The actor is vocal on the subject of world affairs. With regard to the U.S. military action in Afghanistan, launched in 2001 in response to that year's terrorist attacks on the U.S.; the 2003 invasion of Iraq, carried out for the stated purpose of ridding that country of weapons of mass destruction; and the desire of some to squelch debate about those events, Mortensen told Charlie Rose on his eponymous PBS talk show on December 3, 2002, as quoted on the Artist's Network Web site, "It upsets me

. . . that questioning what's going on right now, what the United States is doing, is considered treasonous really: 'How dare you say that? How un-American of you.' And really, this country is founded on the principle that if the government isn't serving the people you at least have the right to say, 'Wait a minute. What's going on?' And there're no questions really being asked, at large, about what we're doing." Mortensen was offended by some viewers' and critics' interpretations of the *Lord of the Rings* trilogy as a metaphor for the U.S. wars in Afghanistan in Iraq. "I mean, movies are entertainment," he told Kuczynski. "This is a story. It bothered me how some people misapplied the story to the invasion and occupation of Afghanistan and Iraq. It's like the way Hitler misapplied Norse mythology and literature to validate the Third Reich."

Mortensen, who was named one of the world's "50 most beautiful people" by *People* magazine in 2002, speaks English, Spanish, and Danish. He is a fan of the Argentine soccer team San Lorenzo and the New York Mets baseball team. He has many relatives in Denmark and visits the country at least three times a year. Mortensen is known for his modest lifestyle and down-to-earth demeanor; unlike most Hollywood stars, he does not have a personal assistant and does not own a cell phone or a television. Interviewers have noted that he is frequently barefoot. He enjoys horseback riding in his spare time and purchased the horses he rode in the *Lord of the Rings* trilogy and *Hidalgo* after the films were completed. The five-foot 11-inch actor has a scar above his lip, which he says is from a fight he was in at 17. He confesses to a weakness for mate, a South American tea.

Mortensen married Exene Cervenka, a poet and painter, as well as a musician, in 1987, after the couple met while making the film *Salvation!* They divorced in 1997 but continue to collaborate artistically and share custody of their son, Henry, born in 1988. In recent years Mortensen has dated the artist Lola Schnabel, and his name has also been linked to that of the British actress Josie D'Arby. Mortensen, who has been described as introspective, soft-spoken, friendly, and unfailingly polite, has homes in Topanga Canyon, outside Los Angeles, and in Venice, California, as well as a ranch in Idaho.

—K.E.D.

Suggested Reading: *Salon* (on-line) Oct. 24, 2003, with photo; *Seattle Post-Intelligencer* (on-line) Feb. 26, 2004, with photos; *Vanity Fair* p66+ Jan. 2004, with photos; *Variety* p43 Oct. 6–12, 2003

Selected Films: *Witness*, 1985; *Carlito's Way*, 1993; *Crimson Tide*, 1995; *The Prophecy*, 1995; *The Portrait of a Lady*, 1996; *G.I. Jane*, 1997; *A Perfect Murder*, 1998; *Psycho*, 1998; *A Walk on the Moon*, 1999; *28 Days*, 2000; *Lord of the Rings: The Fellowship of the Ring*, 2001; *Lord of the Rings: The Two Towers*, 2002; *Lord of the

Rings: The Return of the King, 2003; *Hidalgo*, 2004

Selected Recordings (with Buckethead): *One Man's Meat*, 1999; *One Less Thing to Worry About*, 1999; *The Other Parade*, 1999

Selected Books: *Recent Forgeries*, 1998; *Miyelo*, 2003

Mark Mainz/Getty Images

Moss, Adam

May 6, 1957– Magazine editor

Address: New York Magazine, *444 Madison Ave., New York, NY 10022-6903*

In the 11 years he worked at the *New York Times*, Adam Moss rose from unconventional new-comer to respected, award-winning leader in his field. Beginning in August 2003 he held the position of assistant managing editor for features, over-seeing the *New York Times Magazine*, the *New York Times Book Review*, and the Culture, Style, Real Estate, Circuits, Travel, and Escapes sections of the newspaper, some of which he created. The former editor of the *New York Times Magazine* and *7 Days*, a short-lived but notable publication, and a onetime deputy editor of *Esquire*, Moss has been credited with adding sparkle and levity to the pre-viously staid *Times*, whose circulation is 1.67 million. Betsy Carter, a former editorial direc-tor of *Esquire*, told Jon Fine for *Advertising Age* (March 12, 2001) that at that magazine Moss had shown "a keen instinct for what was a story and

what needed to be done—the kind of stuff you can't teach people." David Schneiderman, who hired Moss as editor of *7 Days*, said to Frank Bajak for the *Oberlin Alumni Magazine* (Winter 2003–04), "I think Moss is really the editor of his genera-tion." At the *Times* Moss persevered through inter-nal conflicts and potential blows to his credibility to attain what he described to Jon Fine as "the best job in journalism right now." That description not-withstanding, in Feburary 2004 Moss accepted the position of editor of *New York* magazine. Since his arrival he has overseen changes in the design of the publication.

Adam Moss was born on May 6, 1957 in Brook-lyn, New York, and grew up on Long Island. He at-tended Oberlin College, in Oberlin, Ohio, where he majored in both English and government and ed-ited the school's newspaper, the *Oberlin Review*. His first job after he graduated from college, in 1979, was that of a *New York Times* copy boy, which found him running errands—usually, trans-porting articles and other materials among editors and writers. Moss worked there for six months, during which he felt unhappy. He recalled to Frank Bajak, "It was a place where people were very frightened and anxious about authority. . . . Ev-eryone was nervous. There was a lack of confi-dence that bred insecurity and autocracy through-out the organization. I wasn't interested in newspa-pers in the first place, so I split." He moved on to the short-lived *College Papers* and then to *Rolling Stone* before finding work at *Esquire*, where he re-mained for seven years, eventually rising to the po-sitions of managing editor and deputy editor.

In 1987 Moss came up with the idea of creating a weekly magazine for people in mid- to upper Manhattan that would cover New York City poli-tics and social issues; he then read that Leonard Stern, the owner of the *Village Voice*, and David Schneiderman, that paper's editor and publisher, were preparing to start a publication designed for the same readership that Moss had in mind. Moss approached Schneiderman to seek the job of editor of the proposed publication. As he recalled to Al-bert Scardino for the *New York Times* (October 30, 1989), by the time he and Schneiderman "had spent four minutes" together, they were convinced that they would work well together on the project. The spring of 1988 saw the debut of *7 Days*, a week-ly news and entertainment publication; Moss, its 31-year-old founding editor, oversaw an editorial staff of 25. The aim of *7 Days* was to provide cover-age of important events that had taken place in Manhattan during the previous week. Originally published in a tabloid format with a glossy cover, it evolved from a newspaper-magazine hybrid to a more conventional-looking magazine. Moss said to Albert Scardino in 1989, "We are trying to capture what *New York* magazine did in the '60s. It should be very fresh, very exciting, a little bratty." The publication won a National Magazine Award for General Excellence in 1990 as the best magazine among those with circulations of under 100,000.

Nonetheless, after 102 issues, the publication folded in the spring of that same year, hampered by its dependence on local advertising during an economic recession. Recalling the experience of editing *7 Days*, Moss told Frank Bajak, "It was more fun than I'd ever had, an experience of pure joy and little sense . . . a bunch of kids making a virtue out of their amateurism."

After *7 Days* closed, Moss attempted to launch a magazine about the media, to be called "The Industry," while pursuing work as a consultant on the side. In 1991 he met Joe Lelyveld, then managing editor of the *New York Times*, at a dinner party. Lelyveld, eager to restructure the *Times* by adding some new sections and injecting the "gray lady" with some panache, took Moss on as a consultant. According to Michael Wolff in *New York* (January 21, 2002), the *Times* was then being overhauled, "becoming more magazinelike and less newspaperlike, more [baby]-boomer-friendly and less Establishment-pompous. Moss became a guru of this change—an anti-*Times* sort of figure in the middle of the *Times*. A magazine person at a newspaper, an openly gay person in a repressed atmosphere, a mild man among bullies and screamers." Moss's contributions were clearly appreciated by the *Times*'s executives, who offered him a job as editorial director of the *New York Times Magazine*, the color supplement that is included in the Sunday edition of the newspaper and contains features, profiles, and sections on fashion and culture. Tired of his quest for money to start "The Industry" and of having to engage in what he told Frank Bajak were "humiliating turns with bankers," Moss accepted the job in March 1993.

Moss's position replaced the magazine's deputy-editor post, which had been vacant for two months after the previous deputy editor, Jack Rosenthal, was promoted to editor. In his new job Moss collaborated with Rosenthal in all aspects of managing and editing the magazine and helped redesign it as well. In November of the following year, the magazine began running occasional issues devoted to single themes, which included "World War II," "Houses as Art," "Women & Power," and "Love in the 21st Century," and three issues commemorating the magazine's centennial, in 1996. Before Moss began working for the magazine, it had been what Valerie Block, in Crain's *New York Business* (April 21, 2003), called "a hard-news extension of the paper"—a forum in which star *Times* writers could discuss with somewhat less objectivity the same topics covered in the daily newspaper. Moss told Jeff Bercovici for *Media Life Magazine* (January 28, 2003, on-line) that his goal was to "try to make the magazine as innovative and as thrilling to the reader as we can make it and to make it a true complement to the Sunday newspaper without actually duplicating anything in it." Andrew Black, senior vice president of marketing for the advertising firm Laird + Partners, told Valerie Block, "Adam has brought a new dimension to the magazine with great reportage, along with some of the fluffier pieces on style or food. . . . He's made it a more enjoyable Sunday read." In 1998, after five years at the *Times Magazine*, Moss assumed the position of editor, when Rosenthal became editor in chief. Moss was given full responsibility for the magazine's weekly operations and supervisory authority over the magazine staff.

In 2000 the *Columbia Journalism Review* named Moss one of the 10 best magazine editors in America. In March of the following year, Moss was chosen as *Advertising Age*'s Editor of the Year. Jon Fine lauded Moss's leadership of the *Times Magazine*: "A little more than two years after the magazine became [Moss's], it's quietly become one of the best reads in the business. Mr. Moss smartly and subtly remade the title, from its photography to [the] front of the book, all the while navigating the *Times*' internal culture. Under his watch, it's become a showcase for thoughtful, long-form journalism, taking full advantage of the yawn and stretch of Sunday and its lengthened attention span." Moss explained to Fine, "What I'm trying to do is reclaim literary journalism, this form that I loved as a kid growing up. I want to make the case that magazines still matter. . . . If you're a journalist, an editor, trying to do something you hope matters a little bit, [working at the *Times Magazine*] is a gift." In that spirit, Moss attempted to include thought-provoking, myth-exploding articles and essays such as pieces on the club drug Ecstasy, intentionally childless couples, the Christian fundamentalist counterculture, and the aggressive cruelty of some teenage girls toward their peers. After Moss became editor of the publication, it garnered more attention and revenue than it had attracted in years; in 2000, for example, the magazine ran more ad pages than it had printed in any year since 1989. Additionally, under Moss's leadership, the magazine earned a variety of honors, among them two Overseas Press Club Awards, the Livingston Award for international reporting, and selection as Magazine of the Year in 1999 from the Society of Publication Design. Under Moss the *New York Times Magazine* was a two-time finalist for the Pulitzer Prize, and the issue "Talking About Race" was part of the *Times* series that won the Pulitzer for national reporting in 2001. In 2000 Moss was named an associate managing editor of the *Times* in addition to his title as editor of the magazine.

Moss's tenure as editor was not free of controversy. In February 2002 he discovered that a contract writer, Michael Finkel, had taken unacceptable liberties in his article about child slavery on cocoa farms in the Ivory Coast, which appeared in the November 18, 2001 issue of the magazine. In the article Finkel wrote about an African teen, Youssouf Male, who was later revealed to be not a real individual but a composite character created by Finkel. Gabriel Snyder reported in the *New York Observer* (March 4, 2002) that when the deception was uncovered, Moss was "furious." Moss told Snyder, "It was some mix of anger—fury, I would even say. Here is a guy [Finkel] with a tremendous amount of talent, and it was just such a stupid thing to do. And at some level, even though you were furious with him, you couldn't help but feel sorry for him." Despite his sympathy for Finkel, Moss terminated the writer's contract and published an apologetic Editor's Note on February 21. The *New York Times*'s managing editor, Gerald Boyd, dismissed the idea that the incident had damaged Moss's reputation, telling Gabriel Snyder, "To the contrary, I think this reflects very highly on Adam Moss. . . . He did what we expect of any section editor: He spotted the problem, he investigated it, and he put us down the road of fixing it."

On August 5, 2003 Bill Keller, the recently installed executive editor of the Times, named Moss the *Times*'s assistant managing editor for features, a newly created position that involves overseeing the newspaper's Culture and Style sections, the *New York Times Magazine*, the *New York Times Book Review*, and the Travel, Real Estate, Circuits, and Escapes sections. (Circuits deals with the Internet, digital devices, and other aspects of modern technology; Escapes focuses on such topics as weekend getaways and vacation homes.) Moss told Sridhar Pappu for the *New York Observer* (August 11, 2003), "The big reason I took this job was because of Bill [Keller]. I've gotten to know Bill the past couple of years as a writer for the magazine. I've gotten a chance to know him and to become very excited about the way he thinks about the world and the way he thinks about The Times. . . . It's a great team and there's an amazing sense of promise and, I think, of opportunity that everyone feels at this moment." Moss named Gerald Marzorati, the magazine's editorial director, his successor as editor of the magazine. In his new post, Moss told Jerry Walker for *Jack O'Dwyer's Newsletter* (August 13, 2003) that his primary goal was "to make sure we're as good at covering what goes on in people's daily lives and the material they consume as we are in covering Baghdad." As he told Jeff Bercovici, because the magazine is sold only as part of the Sunday Times, he and his staff did not "have to make some of the commercial compromises we would have to make in order to move the thing off the newsstands. . . . We do not have to put a movie star on the cover unless it's someone that we think is actually important and interesting. We do not have to put models on the cover because they're beautiful. We can actually look around and see what's interesting, and we happen to have the kind of readers who, if we're doing our job right, will respond to that. What we have at The New York Times Magazine is The New York Times reader, and that is what makes the magazine so exceptional."

The *Times* reported on February 11, 2004 that Moss had been hired as the new editor of *New York*, replacing Caroline Miller. *New York*, founded in 1968, is a storied publication that has recently faced stiff competition and a decrease in adver-

tising. Moss was courted for the position by the Wall Street financier Bruce Wasserstein, *New York*'s owner; Moss told David Carr for the *Times* (February 12, 2004) that after meeting with Wasserstein and others involved in the hire, he was "persuaded that they had the will and desire to make a great magazine." As Bill Keller told Christine Hauser for the *Times* (February 11, 2004), Moss is, at heart, a "conceiver and inventor of magazines."

—K.J.E.

Suggested Reading: *Advertising Age* S p18 Mar. 12, 2001; *Media Life Magazine* (on-line) Jan. 28, 2003; *New York Magazine* (on-line) Jan. 21, 2002; *New York Observer* p1 Mar. 4, 2002; *Oberlin Alumni Magazine* p20+ Winter 2003–04

Courtesy of Ellicot Talent Group

Murphy, Mark

Mar. 14, 1932– Jazz vocalist

Address: c/o High Note Records, 106 West 71st St., New York, NY 10023

The veteran jazz vocalist Mark Murphy has long been considered one of the hippest denizens of the jazz world. For over four decades he has released a steady stream of successful records—more than 40 to date. The list includes such classic albums as *Rah* (1961), *That's How I Love the Blues* (1962), and *Bop for Kerouac* (1981), as well as the acclaimed recent recordings *Song for the Geese* (1997) and *The Latin Porter* (2000). Tracing his influences back to Nat "King" Cole, Billy Eckstine, and Peggy Lee, he exhibits a rare musical dexterity, moving effortlessly from balladry and standards to hard bop and Brazilian bossa nova. Both icon and iconoclast, he excels at serving up well-known jazz standards, often cleverly reworked to accommodate his distinctive vocal style, which includes both scatting (singing nonsense syllables in emulation of a musical instrument) and vocalese (the art of writing and performing lyrics to an already existing, usually well-known tune originally composed for instruments only). His brand of uncompromising jazz has earned six Grammy Award nominations and won the praises of such esteemed vocalists as Betty Carter, Ella Fitzgerald, and Shirley Horn.

Despite Murphy's significant contribution to jazz, he has remained something of a cult figure, his popularity largely confined to a cadre of jazz enthusiasts. Some attribute this to his less-than-perfect voice—a resonant, at times gravelly, baritone that many fans admit may be an acquired taste. Moreover, his musical innovations and bebop-inspired tendency to sing against the grain of a song tend to make him an artist whom listeners either love or hate. Nevertheless, Murphy retains a sense of humor and an enduring playfulness, which can be detected in many of his songs. In the opening to his version of Antonio Carlos Jobim's "Desifinado," for example, he makes clear his belief that in jazz, personal expression and musical abandon take precedence over technical accuracy. "I wish I had an ear like yours, a voice that would behave," he sings, as quoted by Rob Hancock in a profile for AllAboutJazz.com. "All I have is feeling and a voice God gave."

Mark Howe Murphy was born into a musical family on March 14, 1932 in Syracuse, New York, and raised in nearby Fulton. His mother and father were singers; one of his grandmothers and an aunt played organ at a local church. Murphy joined the church choir, and he began studying piano at the age of seven. As a teenager he played and sang in an older brother's dance band. An uncle sparked his love for jazz, by playing him the recordings of the jazz pianist Art Tatum, well known for his 1933 solo version of "Tiger Rag."

Later, after touring Canada briefly with a jazz trio, Murphy returned to Syracuse. While he was performing there at a local jam session one night, he was discovered by Sammy Davis Jr., who invited him to his show that night and even had Murphy join him on stage. Murphy studied voice and theater at Syracuse University, then, in 1954, moved to New York City, where he appeared with the Gilbert and Sullivan Light Opera Company and performed in amateur contests at the Apollo Theater. He drew enough attention to land a recording deal with Decca Records, and when he was 24 he recorded his debut album, *Meet Mark Murphy* (1956). According to Rob Hancock, the respected jazz producer Orrin Keepnews later commented, "It's remarkable how fully developed as an artist Mark was so early on. He was born with his incredible rhythmic sense."

At about this time Murphy's career got an unexpected boost, owing to his earlier, fortuitous meeting with Davis in Syracuse. One night Murphy happened to see Davis on the *Tonight Show*. Feeling confident, he sent its host, Steve Allen, a letter in which he wrote, according to the National Public Radio series *Billy Taylor's Jazz* (September 16, 1999, on-line), "I just met Sammy and he likes my work." Right after *Meet Mark Murphy*'s release, Allen invited Murphy to appear on the show. Allen became one of the young musician's most influential supporters. According to Mike Joyce in the *Washington Post* (April 1, 1983), Allen once said that anyone interested in jazz singing should have a copy of every Mark Murphy album ever made.

Murphy released another album on Decca, then moved to Los Angeles, California, where he signed a deal with Capitol Records and recorded *This Could Be the Start of Something* (1958). Capitol, for whom he recorded a total of three albums, tried to fashion him as a clean-cut, teen-idol type of pop vocalist, but Murphy shaped the material to his own tastes. He secured the musical accompaniment of prominent West Coast jazz musicians and employed a flavorful vocal style, twisting jazz lines and adding brief scat solos. (Murphy has never had a band of his own; rather, he maintains a large personal registry of musicians and recruits different groups of instrumentalists for each of his gigs.)

When he began recording for the Riverside label, in the early 1960s, Murphy at last became free to pursue the uncompromising style of jazz he was after. He moved back to New York City, and in 1961 he recorded *Rah*, a set of standards and bop vocals, playing alongside the legendary jazz musicians Bill Evans, Clark Terry, Blue Mitchell, and Wynton Kelly. He scored some minor hits with impressive vocal covers of "Milestones" and Annie Ross's "Twisted." In 1962 he made *That's How I Love the Blues*, an album that he later said he considered one of his best. A single from that album, "Fly Me to the Moon," appeared on charts across the nation, and Murphy was soon earning significant critical praise. He was voted "New Star of the Year" in the *Down Beat* magazine readers' poll, and Gene Lees, then editor of *Down Beat*, became a major champion of his music.

The 1960s saw the explosive rise of rock and roll, with the Beatles and other groups overwhelming the American popular-music scene. Jazz musicians found themselves marginalized. Many of the greats relocated to England, where they found a more appreciative audience. Murphy moved to London, where he lived from 1963 to 1972. "It was a bad time for all the boppers," he recalled to Leonard Feather for the *Los Angeles Times* (November 25, 1989). "All the undergrounders had surfaced in the late '50s and early '60s, then we had to scatter again and wait." Murphy made a living as an actor in film, television, and the theater while continuing to give frequent nightclub performances. He issued no albums in the U.S. during his decade overseas; rather, he recorded for such British labels as

Fontana and Immediate. In 1967 he collaborated with the Kenny Clarke–Francy Boland Big Band to record, for the German label Saba, *Midnight Mood*, which earned strong reviews from jazz and vocal critics. He developed a loyal following, and by the time he returned to the U.S., he had become a major name in vocal jazz.

After he signed a deal with Muse Records, Murphy enjoyed a richly prolific period, issuing about one album a year for the next two decades. Many of these recordings, including *Stolen Moments* (1978), *Satisfaction Guaranteed* (1979), the two-volume *Mark Murphy Sings Nat's Choice: The Complete Nat King Cole Songbook* (1983), *Living Room* (1984), and *Beauty and the Beast* (1987), received critical acclaim, earning Murphy a series of Grammy Award nominations. He toured widely, playing with such notable jazz musicians as the Brecker Brothers, David Sanborn, Ritchie Cole, and Eddie Jefferson. While the market for jazz vocalists continued to languish, Murphy endured as one of the very few straight-jazz vocalists (other than such mega-stars as Frank Sinatra and Mel Tormé) to make a living from his music.

One of the highlights of Murphy's Muse days was the release of *Bop for Kerouac* (1981), perhaps his best-known and arguably his best recording. The album evokes the aesthetic of the Beat generation—the literary avant-garde of the 1950s, who were strongly influenced by the bebop jazz musicians of the day. Such songs as "Parker's Mood" and "Ballad of the Sad Young Men" feature Murphy's vocalese adaptations of some of the tunes of the saxophonist Charlie Parker (nicknamed Bird), and readings from *On the Road* and other works by Jack Kerouac accompany many of the selections. "I never saw Bird Charlie Parker until I read Kerouac," Murphy wrote for the liner notes to the album, as quoted by Mike Joyce in the *Washington Post* (February 18, 1982). "I saw Bird through Jack's eyes and phenomenal memory—and clearly." In a recent review of the album for AllAboutJazz.com, Walter Grim declared, "Murphy's performance is nothing less than heart rending. He grabs you in the guts and never lets go. *Bop for Kerouac* is absolute proof why Mark Murphy is one of the most influential jazz singers of the past four decades. . . . If you own just one vocal jazz CD this should be it."

In the late 1980s Murphy recorded two highly acclaimed albums for Milestone Records: *Night Mood* and *September Ballads*. On *Night Mood* (1987) Murphy collaborated with Azymuth, a popular Brazilian electric jazz trio, for a sensual collection of songs by the Brazilian composer Ivan Lins. "The results are engagingly atmospheric," Joe Brown wrote for the *Washington Post* (May 29, 1987). "Murphy has a fine-grained voice and an attractively warm, relaxed delivery. . . . The record is charged with bright sonic colors—the floating calm of 'Nightmood (Lembra)' moves gently into the percussive syllable-play of the bossa nova 'Madalena,' and Murphy's Anglicized lyrics work surprisingly well throughout." The Grammy-nominated *September Ballads* (1988) offered a collection of slower songs by contemporary composers, among them Michael Frank's "When She Is Mine" and Pat Metheny and Lyle Mays's "September Fifteenth."

Murphy revisited his Beat-era nostalgia in *Kerouac—Then and Now* (1989). He described the album to Joe Brown for the *Washington Post* (September 29, 1989) as "a collection of marvelous underground jazz—I suppose you'd call it slightly rap nowadays. I read Kerouac's prose to jazz, which is what they used to do in the old days; I think it's still hanging on in lofts somewhere." The album includes a monologue from Kerouac's novel *Big Sur*, about a wild night in San Francisco, and a passage from *On the Road* in which Kerouac recalled a powerful Chicago jam session featuring the pianist George Shearing. "Unlike the first installment," Mike Joyce wrote for the *Washington Post* (February 16, 1990), "there's no horn present on *Kerouac—Then and Now*, only a neat and often humming rhythm section composed of pianist Bill Mays, bassist John Goldsby and drummer Adam Nussbaum. But then, as Murphy proves so winningly on the medley 'Eddie Jefferson/Take the A Train,' his handsome voice is a horn unto itself, limber and lively as you please."

Murphy's popularity remained strong in the 1990s. He satisfied his already-loyal following with the release of several boxed sets and attracted new listeners by expanding his musical palette, most notably in two recordings he made with the Japanese jazz-dance group UFO, for which he wrote and rapped lyrics. He also benefitted from the inclusion of his acid-jazz version of "Milestones" on the compilation album *Best of BGP* (1990), released by the British label Beat Goes Public.

Murphy received his sixth Grammy nomination for *Song for the Geese* (1997), his first recording for RCA. The album amply demonstrated his flair for scatting, making him one of the few remaining vocalists to employ that vanishing art form; popularized by such jazz legends as Louis Armstrong and Ella Fitzgerald (who is widely quoted as describing Murphy as her "equal" in scat), by the 1990s scat singing had virtually died out. "Singing like a man on a mission, Murphy lets loose with as much scat virtuosity and novel sonic effect as one might hope to hear on a single recording," Howard Reich wrote for the *Chicago Tribune* (November 2, 1997). "Listen to Murphy's vocal flights on 'Baltimore Oriole,' his nimble scat on 'You're Blasé' and his interpretive profundity on the title track, and you are hearing a man who sounds utterly renewed—more than four decades after his recording debut."

On *The Latin Porter* (2000), which featured the trumpeter Tom Harrell as a guest, Murphy offered versions of Cole Porter's standards set to Latin rhythms. "The performances swing with unrelenting force," Don Heckman noted for the *Los Angeles Times* (October 29, 2000). "Ballads such as 'In the Still of the Night' are rendered with Murphy's individualized manipulation of sound, 'I've Got You Under My Skin' emerges differently from the trademark Sinatra version, and Murphy scats hard with both words and syllables on tunes such as 'Get Out of Town' and 'All of You.'" Murphy's most recent album, *Bop for Miles* (2004), was recorded live in Europe in 1990 while the singer was fronting a European quintet.

Murphy continues to tour internationally, performing at festivals and concerts in the U.S., Europe, Australia, and Japan. In 1996, 1997, 2000, and 2001, he won the *Down Beat* Readers Poll for best male jazz singer of the year. "Murphy remains infallibly hip," Rob Hancock wrote for AllAboutJazz.com. "[He is] as cool a name to drop . . . as he was in the 50's and represents that proud strain of individualism in the finest jazz tradition."

—A.I.C.

Suggested Reading: AllAboutJazz.com, with photo; Barnes and Noble Web site; *Chicago Tribune* C p12 Nov. 2, 1997; *Down Beat* p26+

Apr. 1997, with photos; *Los Angeles Times* F p6 Nov. 25, 1989, with photo, p71 Oct. 29, 2000; markmurphy.com; *Billy Taylor's Jazz*, npr.com Sep. 16, 1999, with photo; *Washington Post* C p9 Feb. 18, 1982, p31 Apr. 1, 1983, with photo, N p15 May 29, 1987, N p23 Sep. 29, 1989, with photo, N p22 Feb. 16, 1990; Friedwald, Will. *Jazz Singing: America's Great Voices from Bessie Smith to Bebop and Beyond*, 1996

Selected Recordings: *Meet Mark Murphy*, 1956; *This Could Be the Start of Something*, 1958; *Rah*, 1961; *That's How I Love the Blues*, 1962; *Midnight Mood*, 1967; *Stolen Moments*, 1978; *Satisfaction Guaranteed*, 1979; *Bop for Kerouac*, 1981; *Mark Murphy Sings Nat's Choice: The Complete Nat King Cole Songbook, Volumes 1 & 2*, 1983; *Living Room*, 1984; *Beauty and the Beast*, 1987; *Night Mood*, 1987; *September Ballads*, 1988; *Kerouac—Then and Now*, 1989; *Song for the Geese*, 1997; *The Latin Porter*, 2000; *Bop for Miles*, 2004

Murray, Bill

NOTE: An earlier article about Bill Murray appeared in *Current Biography* in 1985.

Sep. 21, 1950– Actor

Address: c/o Creative Artists Agency, 9830 Wilshire Blvd., Beverly Hills, CA 90212-1825

Bill Murray is one of those rare actors capable of delivering both sublimely comic and achingly poignant performances. His portrayal of the disaffected Hollywood film actor Bob Harris in Sofia Coppola's bittersweet film *Lost in Translation* (2003) led Kenneth Turan to write for the *Los Angeles Times* (September 12, 2003), "Perhaps only Murray had the persona and the skills to capture the exquisite balance between the funny and the forlorn called for by the part. . . . Like Buster Keaton, his deadpan predecessor, Murray has a face that's tragically sad in repose, and the heroic way he copes with civilization's discontents makes you both laugh and shake your head in rueful empathy." Murray's comic gifts came to light in the late 1970s, when he performed on the TV series *Saturday Night Live*. "Reflecting the skepticism of a generation that grew up on television, Murray's humor has always brought wryly heroic dimension to everyday nonconformity," Timothy White wrote for the *New York Times Magazine* (November 20, 1988). "His performances on *Saturday Night Live* were not known for their subtlety, but they ultimately hinged on his forte: discernment. . . . The quintessential Bill Murray portrayal has the actor simultaneously immersed in his role and commenting drolly on it." The actor exploited that

Ray Amati/Getty Images

deadpan, laid-back, cheeky persona to great success in the hit 1980s films *Meatballs*, *Caddyshack*, *Stripes*, and *Ghostbusters*.

For years critics generally dismissed Murray's attempts at pure drama; in particular, most of them thoroughly disparaged his portrayal of a traumatized World War I medic in search of spiritual enlightenment in the 1984 flop *The Razor's Edge*, whose script he co-wrote. Then, in the 1990s, he transformed himself into one of Hollywood's most sought-after serious actors, thanks to his acclaimed performances in such films as *Groundhog Day*, *Rushmore*, *Cradle Will Rock*, and *The Royal Tenenbaums*. His characterization of Polonius in Michael Almereyda's modern-day version of Shakespeare's tragedy *Hamlet* (2000) revealed "the full extent of his spontaneity and grace," as A. O. Scott wrote for the *New York Times* (September 14, 2003). "You can't make Shakespeare up as you go along, but Mr. Murray does just that; he is one of the tiny handful of screen actors who can make Elizabethan stage language sound like natural, human speech. And the result is that the character, and the play, take on a whole new coloration." Murray's gifts, both comic and dramatic, were in full flower in *Lost in Translation*; he received a Golden Globe Award and an Oscar nomination for his work in that movie. In *Lost in Translation*, Jeffrey M. Anderson wrote for the *San Francisco Examiner* (September 12, 2003), Murray "demolished everything he's ever done and leaves it in smoking ruins. He turns in such an accomplished performance of such heartbreaking power that we should just hand him the Oscar right now."

The fifth child and self-described "black sheep" among the nine children of Lucille and Edward Murray, William J. Murray was born on September 21, 1950 in Evanston, Illinois, and raised in Wilmette, a Chicago suburb. His father worked as a lumber salesman until his death, in 1969, from complications of diabetes. According to Murray, humor was a family affair; each of the siblings was a "cutup," all of them vying to amuse their father. Edward Murray, the actor told Timothy Crouse for *Rolling Stone* (August 16, 1984), "was real funny, and he was . . . very tough to make laugh. He was very dry." The Murray household ran on a tight budget; at Christmastime, Murray recalled to Timothy White, he "never asked for toys. Asking for toys was out of the question. . . . It's not that we were denied anything so much as the fact that we knew not to make requests. For Christmas you got essentials: school clothes. Whenever toys surfaced at all, they were pretty much inherited." As youngsters, neither he nor his siblings could afford to buy anything but token presents. "The closest any of us ever came to an allowance was finding change under the couch cushions, so I used to shop each Christmas with a single dollar, getting everybody something that cost a dime," he told White. Murray received his primary education at the St. Joseph School and his secondary education at the boys-only Loyola Academy, both local Catholic parochial schools. He "didn't care for school much," as he told Crouse. "Studying was boring. I was lazy. I'm still lazy. And I had no interest in getting good grades." He was skilled athletically, however, especially in baseball and basketball. Eager to be excused from class for rehearsals, he acted in high-school productions; he played Keefer in *The Caine Mutiny* and was a member of the chorus in *The Music Man*. To help pay his tuition, he caddied for golfers at the upscale Indian Hill Club in nearby Winnetka.

Setting his sights on becoming either a doctor or a baseball player, Murray enrolled as a premed student at the Jesuit-run Regis College in Denver, Colorado. He left school after being arrested for trying to smuggle nine pounds of marijuana through the airport in Chicago; he was found guilty and sentenced to a period of probation. Meanwhile, Murray's older brother Brian Doyle-Murray (who had added "Doyle" to his name to avoid confusion with the British actor Brian Murray) had joined Second City, the Chicago comedy company known for its fresh satirical revues and intense training program in improvisation. Through Brian, Murray met the Second City troupers John Belushi, Harold Ramis, and Joe Flaherty. After what he described as "a lot of watching experience" at the Second City theater, Murray began taking workshops there on a scholarship.

In 1974 Belushi, who had moved to New York City, recruited Flaherty, Ramis, and the two Murray brothers to perform on the *National Lampoon Radio Hour*, which was taped in New York and syndicated nationally. Chevy Chase and Gilda Radner, an alumnus of the Toronto offshoot of Second City, were also on the show. The program spawned a topical cabaret revue called *The National Lampoon Show*, which starred the Murrays, Belushi, Ramis, and Radner and ran at a New York bar-restaurant for 180 performances. Among the many show-business figures who saw the production were the TV producer Lorne Michaels, who was preparing to launch what was first dubbed *Saturday Night* on the NBC network, and the sportscaster Howard Cosell, who was soon to be the host of a new variety show, *Saturday Night Live with Howard Cosell*, on ABC. Cosell recruited the Murray brothers for his series, which premiered on September 20, 1975; Michaels signed Belushi and Radner for his, which began telecasting on October 11, 1975. Among the original Not Ready for Prime Time Players, as the cast of the latter show was known, were Chevy Chase and Dan Aykroyd, another Second City alumnus.

ABC canceled *Saturday Night Live with Howard Cosell* after half a season. Bill Murray spent most of the rest of 1976 in California, contributing comic relief to TV documentaries directed by Michael Shamberg, a so-called alternative media guerrilla. In January 1977, after Chase left *Saturday Night Live*, Lorne Michaels tapped Murray to replace him. Murray slowly worked his way to prominence in the ensemble, which frequently included Steve Martin as a guest performer. Among the comic personae he developed were a ludicrously suave lounge singer; a name-dropping, ostentatiously hip movie critic; and a gossip columnist who takes umbrage at the misbehavior of celebrities. A viewer favorite was his character Todd DiLaMuca, an uncouth adolescent nerd whose idea of fun was to give people "noogies" (knuckle raps on the skull). When he put his arms in a hammerlock around his wretched, nasally congested girlfriend, Lisa (Radner), he uttered not terms of endearment but the rhetorical question "How about a couple noogies?" "Perhaps no one is better than Murray at lampooning the kind of show-biz fatuousness that saturates much of the prime time on NBC and the other two networks as well . . . ," Tom Shales wrote for the *Washington Post* (May 31, 1978). "There is nothing on television at any hour to compare with the breakneck spontaneity and derring-do of *Saturday Night Live*." A year later Frank Rich observed for *Time* (July 16, 1979) that "one of the happier developments" during the show's 1978–79 season was "the unleashing" of Murray. "When he finally seized centerstage, he stopped being a straight man and became a live—or maybe frazzled—wire. Murray is a master of comic insincerity. He speaks in italics and tries to raise the put-down into an art form. His routine resembles Steve Martin's, with a crucial difference. Where Martin is slick and cold, Murray is disheveled and vulnerable. One feels that Murray's manic behavior is a cover for some rather touching neurosis."

In his first motion-picture appearance, as an extra, Murray leaned against a barroom wall in Paul Mazursky's *Next Stop Greenwich Village* (1975). His next, far more substantial role came in *Meatballs* (1979), Ivan Reitman's spoof of life in a summer camp; Murray played Tripper, the head counselor, who, despite his bluff talk and wisecracking, becomes an effective father figure for a troubled camper. Murray accepted the role only after the director agreed to let him make changes in the script. (Much of the dialogue was improvised.) "There was not a second choice," Reitman told Dave Hirshey for the New York *Daily News* (July 15, 1979). "I felt [that Murray] had the perfect image that the part required, an ability to play a semi-loon and at the same time relate to a confused, lonely kid." *Meatballs* became the surprise hit of the summer of 1979, attracting a huge juvenile audience as well as older, hard-core Murray aficionados.

Murray next appeared as the deranged groundskeeper Carl in the golf-course comedy *Caddyshack* (1980); as the counterculture journalist Hunter S. Thompson in *Where the Buffalo Roam* (1980); and in an uncredited and largely improvised supporting role as the roommate of Dustin Hoffman's cross-dressing character in *Tootsie* (1982). In 1981 Reitman and Murray again scored big at the box office with *Stripes*, a frenetic comedy about a hip misfit (Murray) who, after losing his job, girlfriend, and apartment, enlists in the army with his buddy (Harold Ramis), where the two behave with anti-establishment insolence.

In *Ghostbusters* (1984) Murray—for whom one of the parts had been written—and the scriptwriters, Aykroyd and Ramis, co-starred as researchers of the paranormal; discredited as quacks in academe, they turn to serving the "supernatural elimination needs" of New York City. They set up shop as spook-exterminators just in time to confront the first omen of an apocalyptical uprising of the forces of darkness—an ectoplasmic entity that devours

the junk food in the refrigerator of their first client, a pretty penthouse dweller named Dana Barrett (Sigourney Weaver). Murray's character, Peter Venkman, takes more interest in Barrett than in the blob in her refrigerator; throughout the film he comments on the cataclysmic happenings with unimpressed, denigrating wit. Produced and directed by Ivan Reitman, *Ghostbusters* became one of the most popular and financially successful comedies of all time. Murray, David Ansen noted for *Newsweek* (June 11, 1984), "sets the movie's distinctive tone of wacked-out cool. . . . [His] comic genius is that he's always standing one step outside the madness, an invisible microphone in hand, offering a hip running commentary. Essentially he's talking to himself, yet somehow he's able to make smugness endearing." The movie spawned a motion-picture sequel, a TV cartoon show, and a hit song.

Murray made *Ghostbusters* as half of a package deal with Columbia Pictures. The other half, which Columbia reportedly agreed to reluctantly, gave him the opportunity to play his first dramatic role, that of Larry Darrell in *The Razor's Edge*, a remake of a 1946 film classic starring Tyrone Power. Both films were based on W. Somerset Maugham's novel about a young American who, burdened by his battlefield memories, drops out of bourgeois society, rejects Western materialistic values, and embraces Eastern mysticism. The film was directed by John Byrum, who had introduced Murray to the novel and co-wrote the screenplay with him. Most reviewers turned thumbs down at both the film and Murray's characterization. Among them was Michael McWilliams, who wrote for the New York *Daily News* (October 28, 1984), "The problem with Bill Murray's performance . . . stems from a confusion . . . of comedy and drama. In the movie, huge chunks of hackneyed drama are interspersed with Murray doing Murray."

After the film's release Murray spent six months in France with his first wife, whom he had married in 1980, and their son Homer (their second son, Luke, was born during that time), and another six months looking for a good project for himself. He explained to Jay Carr for the *Boston Globe* (November 20, 1988), "People said I was very courageous for making [*The Razor's Edge*]. Sure. So's setting yourself on fire. After that movie, I felt radioactive. . . . The trouble with dramatic movies is you've got to work with someone who knows more than you. A comedy can get away with having a weak structure." He devoted much of the next two years to reworking a script by other writers for *Scrooged*, a contemporary version of Charles Dickens's classic *A Christmas Carol*; Murray played Frank Cross, the miserly president of the International Broadcasting Co., who changes his coldhearted, cruel ways after three ghosts take him on a journey to his past, present, and future. The movie, released in 1988, achieved only moderate success.

Murray's next hit was Frank Oz's *What About Bob?* (1991), a comedy about a needy neurotic who follows his vacationing psychiatrist (played by Richard Dreyfuss) to New Hampshire, where he drives the therapist to distraction. Two years later Murray appeared in Harold Ramis's comedy *Groundhog Day.* He was cast as Phil Connors, a cynical, self-centered TV weatherman, who must cover events connected with Groundhog Day (February 2) for the fifth year in a row in the small town of Punxsutawney, Pennsylvania. He makes no effort to hide his hatred of the assignment and eagerness to get back to his usual workplace; a snowstorm forces him to stay in Punxsutawney another night, however. When he awakens the next morning, he discovers that it is February 2 all over again. He soon realizes that no one but he has already lived through Groundhog Day. The same thing happens the next day, and the next; in reliving Groundhog Day countless times, Phil gradually acquires not only the skills of an expert pianist and ice sculptor, among others, but also decency, kindness, and helpfulness. In a representative review, Hal Hinson, writing for the *Washington Post* (February 12, 1993), described *Groundhog Day* as "brilliantly imaginative," "wildly funny," and "the best American comedy since *Tootsie*," and Murray as "a breed unto himself, a sort of gonzo minimalist. And he's never been funnier as a comedian or more in control as an actor than he is here. It's easily his best movie."

Murray next appeared as a vicious criminal in *Mad Dog and Glory* (1993); as a transsexual in *Ed Wood* (1994); as a malicious bowling champion in Bobby and Peter Farrelly's *Kingpin* (1996); as a motivational speaker in *Larger Than Life* (1996); and as a sleazy lawyer in *Wild Things* (1998). The actor's work in Wes Anderson's critically acclaimed black comedy *Rushmore* (1998) garnered Murray excellent reviews and established him as one of Hollywood's most complex actors. The film is about a barber's son, Max Fischer (Jason Schwartzman), who attends Rushmore Academy, an exclusive prep school, on scholarship. Although his grades are subpar, Max loves the school and participates in everything from the French Club to the Beekeeping Club. Disdainful of adults, Max finds an unlikely friend in the multimillionaire Herman Blume (Murray), a cynical Rushmore graduate who also comes from humble roots. After both Max and Herman fall in love with the same woman (Olivia Williams), a beautiful Rushmore teacher, they engage in an all-out war for her affection. Andrew O'Hehir described *Rushmore* for *Salon* (February 5, 1999, on-line) as "a work of loopy, original comic genius" that had provided Murray with a vehicle for "the finest screen performance of [his] surprisingly varied career." Michael Wilmington wrote for the *Chicago Tribune* (on-line) that Murray "pulls off a deliriously successful comeback. Not that he's really been away, but the old goofball gives us a richly observed, witty characterization that's both one of his best comic and dramatic per-

formances. . . . Here, he uses it to craft a character both believable and hilarious." Murray's performance garnered the New York Film Critics Circle Award and a Golden Globe nomination for best supporting actor.

Between 1998 and 2003 Murray appeared in eight films, among them *Cradle Will Rock* (1999), *Hamlet* (2000), *Charlie's Angels* (2000), and *The Royal Tenenbaums* (2001). He gave what many regard as the performance of his career in the motion picture *Lost in Translation* (2003), which was written, produced, and directed by Sofia Coppola, the daughter of the director Francis Ford Coppola. After she finished working on her debut film, *The Virgin Suicides* (2000), Sofia Coppola wrote a screenplay set in Japan, where she had lived for a while during her early 20s. The story focuses on the unlikely relationship between the unhappily married, depressed Bob Harris, a middle-aged Hollywood movie actor whose career is in decline, and a subdued, 20-something, married American woman, Charlotte, who feels lonely, bereft, and tormented by uncertainty about what to do with her life. Harris is in Tokyo to star in a highly remunerative commercial for a Japanese whiskey; he is exhausted by both jet lag and a midlife crisis and spends large portions of his sleepless nights drinking in the hotel bar. Charlotte has accompanied her husband, a busy fashion photographer, on an assignment and is staying at the same hotel. After she and Harris meet at the bar, they wander Tokyo together, drawn to each other by the estrangement they feel from a foreign culture and the wider world. Coppola wrote the story specifically for Murray, who is notorious for his resistance to reading scripts and reluctance to accept roles. "People said, 'You need to have a backup plan,' and I said, 'I'm not going to make the movie if Bill doesn't do it,'" she told Lynn Hirschberg for the *New York Times Magazine* (August 31, 2003). "Bill has an 800-number, and I left messages. This went on for five months. Stalking Bill became my life's work." She enlisted the help of the screenwriter Mitch Glazer, one of Murray's best friends, and Wes Anderson, who persuaded the actor to meet with Coppola at a restaurant in New York; there, he finally accepted the role.

Lost in Translation was shot entirely in Tokyo in 27 days and cost less than $4 million to make. Coppola gave Murray a lot of creative license, and he improvised in several of the movie's funniest scenes, including a photo shoot in which the Japanese director instructs Harris to imitate James Bond and Frank Sinatra. The resulting film, which also starred Scarlett Johansson (who was still in her teens) as Charlotte, was among the most critically acclaimed movies of the year. Elvis Mitchell, in the *New York Times* (September 12, 2003), described it as "one of the purest and simplest examples ever of a director falling in love with her star's gifts. And never has a director found a figure more deserving of her admiration than Bill Murray." Stephanie Zacharek wrote for *Salon* (September

12, 2003, on-line), "Murray has always been an actor of almost subterranean sensitivity. . . . This is his finest performance. Murray is often funny here—his lines loop around us, their unwitting victims, like licorice whips. But he also shows us a range of feelings that we immediately recognize, among them lovesickness, bewilderment, self-deprecating resignation—such feelings are, after all, universal. But Murray makes them feel new and raw, as if he has locked onto the most universal and most painful truth of all: that even as our bodies age, we're all teenagers inside, susceptible to intensity of emotion and heartbreak that we all think we left behind long ago." Murray won the New York Film Critics, Golden Globe, and BAFTA awards for best actor and was nominated for an Academy Award.

In 2004 Murray lent his voice for the title character of *Garfield: The Movie*, based on the comic strip by Jim Davis, and appeared in *Coffee and Cigarettes*, a series of vignettes directed by Jim Jarmusch. He stars as an oceanographer in Wes Anderson's *The Life Aquatic*, which was scheduled for release toward the end of the year, and will be seen as the patriarch of a Brooklyn family in the throes of disintegration in *The Squid and the Whale*.

Helen Barlow wrote of Murray for the Australian daily the *Age* (January 2, 2004, on-line), "With his pockmarked skin and receding hairline, he is hardly a matinee idol, though what he lacks in looks, he compensates for with his abundance of charm." Murray is married to Jennifer Butler, a costume designer who worked on *Groundhog Day*; the couple have four sons: Jackson, Cooper, Cal, and Lincoln. The actor's 13-year marriage to Margaret "Mickey" Kelley, which produced two sons, ended in divorce. Murray, a passionate baseball fan, owns the Charleston, South Carolina, minor-league team the Riverdogs and co-owns the minor-league team the St. Paul Saints, based in St. Paul, Minnesota.

—H.T.

Suggested Reading: *Boston Globe* Arts & Film p93+ Nov. 20, 1988, with photos; *Film Comment* p5+ Nov./Dec. 1993, with photos; *Interview* p54+ Oct. 2003, with photo; *New York Times* II p1+ Sep. 14, 2003, with photos; *New York Times Magazine* p38+ Nov. 20, 1988, with photos, p18+ Jan. 31, 1999, with photos; *Rolling Stone* p21+ Aug. 16, 1984, with photo, p62+ Oct. 2, 2003, with photo

Selected Television Shows: *Saturday Night Live*, 1977–80

Selected Films: *Meatballs*, 1979; *Caddyshack*, 1980; *Stripes*, 1981; *Tootsie*, 1982; *Ghostbusters*, 1984; *The Razor's Edge*, 1984; *What About Bob?*, 1991; *Groundhog Day*, 1993; *Mad Dog and Glory*, 1993; *Rushmore*, 1998; *The Royal Tenenbaums*, 2001; *Lost in Translation*, 2003; *Coffee and Cigarettes*, 2004

Alex Wong/Getty Images

Napolitano, Janet

(nuh-paul-ih-TAN-oh)

Nov. 29, 1957– Governor of Arizona (Democrat)

Address: Office of the Governor, 1700 W. Washington, Phoenix, AZ 85007

On July 27, 2004 Governor Janet Napolitano of Arizona addressed the delegates at the Democratic National Convention, to voice her support for Senator John Kerry of Massachusetts, who accepted his party's presidential nomination two days later. Napolitano's appearance at the podium during prime time in a lineup that included such longtime Democratic luminaries as Senator Edward M. Kennedy of Massachusetts and such up-and-comers as Barak Obama, Illinois's Democratic nominee for the U.S. Senate, signified more than the party's eagerness to win Arizona's 10 electoral votes in the November presidential election. It also indicated her colleagues' high regard for her, both for her personal characteristics and her professional achievements. Described as highly intelligent, extremely hard-working, open, forthright, courageous, and decisive, Napolitano distinguished herself as an attorney at the Phoenix, Arizona, law firm of Lewis and Roca, where she worked for a decade, beginning in 1984, and became a partner in 1989. During that time she argued many cases before the United States Courts of Appeals for the Ninth and Tenth Circuits; in one of those cases, the Ninth Circuit Court, persuaded by her argument, ruled that the power of federal-government agents to conduct searches does not encompass the right to enter churches in pursuit of alien immigrants who have sought sanctuary. Napolitano also assisted witnesses for the lawyer and educator Anita Hill during the highly controversial and divisive hearings that preceded the U.S. Senate's confirmation of Clarence Thomas as a Supreme Court justice, in 1991.

Napolitano left the private sector in 1993, after President Bill Clinton nominated her to fill the position of United States attorney for the District of Arizona; she joined the ranks of only 92 other U.S. attorneys in the nation. She later won two statewide elections in Arizona—the first in 1998, when she ran for attorney general, the second in 2002, when she sought the governorship—despite its having been a Republican stronghold for decades. A self-described political moderate, Napolitano chose membership in the Democratic Party because it "looks at government as a tool that can be used to create opportunity and improve the quality of justice, rather than as some sort of unwanted imposition," as quoted on *New Democrats Online* (August 1, 2000). Her priorities as governor include making health care available to all Arizonans (she herself is a breast-cancer survivor); ensuring that everyone from preschoolers to graduate students has access to good schools; strengthening the economy of Arizona, which is second only to Nevada as the nation's fastest-growing state; keeping people safe from terrorist attacks; and protecting the natural environment. On the Web site of the University of Virginia School of Law (March 20, 2003), Richard Merrill, a former dean, described Napolitano, an alumna of the school, as "the epitome of what it means to be a public servant as a lawyer."

The first of the three children of Leonard M. Napolitano and the former Jane Winer, Janet Ann Napolitano was born on November 29, 1957 in New York City. She has a younger brother, Leonard Jr., who is a researcher and administrator at Sandia National Laboratories; one photo on her Web site shows her with a younger sister, Nancy. Her father, a professor of anatomy who studied lipids, is dean emeritus of the University of New Mexico College of Medicine. Napolitano and her siblings were raised in Pittsburgh, Pennsylvania, and later in Albuquerque, New Mexico. "I have no complaints about my childhood at all," Napolitano told Amy Silverman for the *Phoenix (Arizona) New Times* (October 22, 1998). "I had a great time." In Albuquerque she attended Comanche Elementary School, Madison Middle School, and Sandia High School. As a junior at Sandia, she participated in New Mexico's Girls State program, an activity, sponsored nationwide by the women's arm of the American Legion, that aims to give girls a taste of leadership in government through role-playing; Napolitano won election to the post of lieutenant governor. She also edited the student newspaper and played the guitar and the clarinet, the latter as a member of the school band. "I was your basic overachieving high school student," she told Kate Nash for the *Albuquerque Tribune* (November 4,

2002, on-line). At her graduation, in 1975, she earned an award as the most accomplished musician in her class.

Napolitano attended Santa Clara University, a Jesuit-run institution in Santa Clara, California, where she majored in political science. She spent one term studying in London, England. During her third year she won a Harry S. Truman Scholarship, awarded to juniors who intend to pursue graduate degrees and careers in public service. In 1979 she earned a B.S. degree summa cum laude from Santa Clara and became the school's first female valedictorian. She also gained membership in the honor societies Phi Beta Kappa and Alpha Sigma Nu (the latter of which is associated with Jesuit colleges and universities). In the same year, thanks to her father's acquaintance with U.S. senator Pete V. Domenici of New Mexico, she secured an internship as an analyst with the Senate Budget Committee. Among other tasks, she helped to project the possible long-term costs to the U.S. government of the so-called Chrysler bailout—the government's lending of $1.5 billion to the auto manufacturer Chrysler in 1979–80, to save the company from bankruptcy.

In 1980 Napolitano entered the University of Virginia (UVA) School of Law, in Charlottesville. While there she held a Hardy Cross Dillard Fellowship, for excellence in legal research and writing. She also won election to the Raven Society, the university's most prestigious honor society, which recognizes service as well as academic excellence. Napolitano received a J.D. degree in 1983. She then moved to Phoenix, Arizona, to work for Judge Mary M. Schroeder in the U.S. Ninth Circuit Court of Appeals. "Everything I had was in a little Honda hatchback and I didn't know a soul," she recalled to Robbie Sherwood for the *Arizona Republic* (August 2, 2002). "But the housing was cheap and the weather was nice." Napolitano became a member of the Arizona bar in 1984.

That year Napolitano left her job with Judge Schroeder after being recruited by the Phoenix law firm of Lewis and Roca, where she specialized in commercial and appellate litigation (the latter referring to cases brought before courts of appeals). In her first year there, she worked with John P. Frank, an esteemed legal scholar who had argued many desegregation cases in the 1950s. Frank, who often worked pro bono, represented Ernesto Miranda in the landmark 1966 Supreme Court case *Miranda vs. Arizona*. Napolitano became a partner in Lewis and Roca in 1989. On her own time during the next year, she traveled in Eastern Europe with a delegation from the American Teacher Federation and advised high-school instructors on ways to teach skills necessary for maintaining a representative democracy.

In 1992 Napolitano served with John P. Frank as co-counsel to Anita F. Hill, a professor of law at the University of Oklahoma, when the U.S. Senate Judiciary Committee questioned Hill regarding charges she had made concerning Clarence Thomas, whom President George H. W. Bush had nominated to succeed the retiring Thurgood Marshall on the U.S. Supreme Court. Through a leak to the press, the committee had learned that before the hearings, Hill had told FBI investigators that during her stint as one of Thomas's staff attorneys at the U.S. Department of Education and the Equal Employment Opportunity Commission in the early 1980s, Thomas had sexually harassed her. The committee, which had closed the hearings after voting 13 to one in favor of sending Thomas's nomination to the full Senate without a recommendation, then reopened them, to question both Hill and Thomas about Hill's accusations. During those special hearings, held on October 11, 12, and 13, 1991 and televised nationally, Frank advised Hill while Napolitano helped to line up and worked with Susan Hoerchner, a California judge, and other witnesses who testified on Hill's behalf. The hearings ended when Thomas, after declaring that he had been subjected to a "high-tech lynching for uppity blacks," announced that he would not submit to any more questioning. On October 15 the Senate confirmed Thomas by a vote of 52–48. The special hearings left Napolitano with feelings of disillusionment and dismay. As she told Amy Silverman, "I'm a very big believer in process, fair process. And I thought the process used by the Senate was terrible. It was terrible for everyone involved. It was terrible for Anita Hill, it was terrible for Clarence Thomas, and I thought the Senate looked very, very bad. It was a real eye-opening experience for me."

In July 1993 Napolitano learned from U.S. senator Dennis DeConcini of Arizona that President Bill Clinton wanted to nominate her for the post of U.S. attorney for the District of Arizona. She admitted to Silverman that when DeConcini phoned her with that news, "I really didn't know what a U.S. attorney did." She soon found out and accepted the nomination, then began working as the acting U.S. attorney. During the hearings the Senate Judiciary Committee held to consider her nomination, in September 1993, several Republican senators contended that she was unfit for the job because she had improperly interrupted Susan Hoerchner during the Clarence Thomas hearings in an attempt to coach Hoerchner. Napolitano vehemently denied that accusation and refused to answer questions about her conversations with Hoerchner, citing attorney–client privilege. On September 30 the Judiciary Committee voted 12–6 to confirm Napolitano, but her Republican detractors blocked the nomination from coming to the floor of the Senate. Several journalists later reported that a Judiciary Committee staff member, not Napolitano, had interrupted Hoerchner. On November 19, 1993, after a vote that ended a Republican filibuster, the Senate confirmed Napolitano by a voice vote.

As a U.S. attorney Napolitano had three primary responsibilities in addition to those of administrator: the prosecution of criminal cases brought by the federal government; the prosecution or defense of civil cases in which the U.S. government was either the plaintiff or the defendant; and the collection of debts owed to the federal government that could not be collected in any other way. Cases involving drug trafficking, gang-related violence on Indian reservations, hate crimes, and white-collar scams made up much of her workload. According to the *Rotarizonian* (October 23, 1998, on-line), under her leadership her office prosecuted more than 6,000 crimes, "more than any other federal prosecutor in Arizona history." Her achievements also included the procurement of $65 million in federal funds to enable Arizona cities to hire additional police officers. In addition, Napolitano helped the FBI set up an office in Kingman, Arizona, and then investigate the activities of Timothy J. McVeigh in Kingman in the months before he bombed the Alfred P. Murrah Federal Building, in Oklahoma City, Oklahoma, on April 19, 1995. (In June 1997 McVeigh was convicted of that crime, which killed 168 people and severely injured many more; he was executed four years later.) During her more than four years as a U.S. attorney, she surmounted a U.S. Postal Service investigator's allegation, made on the ABC-TV program *20/20*, that sympathy for male homosexuals had led her to refuse to issue to postal inspectors a warrant to search the home of a man suspected of involvement in child pornography. Napolitano insisted that she had turned down the inspectors' request because her office lacked sufficient evidence ("probable cause," in legal lingo) and because she believed the man's behavior could have been attributed to his being a victim of entrapment during a federal sting operation. In an undated article in *Insight Magazine* (on-line), Jamie Dettmer paraphrased Napolitano's public-affairs officer as claiming that "under Napolitano, the Arizona U.S. attorney's office has a record second to none in prosecuting child-molestation cases. From July 1993 to July 1995, the office . . . prosecuted 249 cases involving child molestation and sexual contact with minors." In an interview with Peter Loge for the *Phoenix Business Journal* (February 17, 1995), Dennis Garrett, the Phoenix chief of police, said of Napolitano, "I have found her easy to work with, she doesn't dodge issues, and gets as much input as possible."

In November 1997 Napolitano resigned from her job and announced that she would seek the Democratic nomination for attorney general of Arizona. After running unopposed in the Democratic primary, she faced the Republican Tom McGovern, who had served briefly as a special assistant to the state attorney general. With the notable exception of abortion—Napolitano was pro-choice, believed that so-called partial-birth abortions should be legal, and opposed the requirement that parents be notified when minors sought abortions; McGovern opposed those positions—the two candidates agreed on most issues. During their campaigns Napolitano, who is unmarried, rarely veered from remarks about the issues or her professional experience, while McGovern, who has three children, often spoke about his family. On Election Day, November 3, 1998, Napolitano emerged victorious, with 50.4 percent of the vote to McGovern's 47.5 percent. (The Libertarian candidate captured the remainder.) She was the first woman to serve as Arizona's attorney general and also one of the women who, together, occupied all of the state's top five positions. (No other state had ever filled so many of its highest positions with women.) Napolitano (the only Democrat), Governor Jane Dee Hull, Secretary of State Betsey Bayless, Treasurer Carol Springer, and Superintendent of Public Instruction Lisa Graham Keegan were nicknamed the "Fab Five" by the media.

As attorney general Napolitano distinguished herself as an advocate for children, women, senior citizens, and the environment. Her position enabled her "to do good things," as she told the UVA law school interviewer. For example, she said, the damages paid by shoe manufacturers whom she successfully sued for price fixing enabled the state "to keep women's shelters open and add beds." Arizona used the millions of dollars paid by bulk-vitamin producers found guilty of antitrust violations to support nutrition-related programs, "including buying dentures for senior citizens on Medicare, which doesn't cover the expense," as the UVA law school interviewer wrote. Among Napolitano's most significant accomplishments was the reduction of the backlog of unresolved child-abuse cases from 6,000 to fewer than 900. Among other actions, she created an Office for Women as an arm of the attorney general's department. A consumer-fraud lawsuit the state filed against QwestCommunications International, accusing the company of placing unauthorized charges on consumers' bills and engaging in false and misleading advertising, resulted in the firm's refunding of $721,000 to Arizonans. Napolitano also aggressively prosecuted con artists who preyed on the elderly, and she set up a unit to investigate Internet users' exploitation of children and others through an array of enticements and scams. After three police officers died and another was injured in explosions of Ford Crown Victoria sedans, which the Phoenix Police Department used, she exacted an agreement from Ford to install shields around the vehicles' fuel tanks. Napolitano told the UVA interviewer that by the time she left the attorney general's office, she had argued cases in the U.S. Supreme Court, The Hague, in the Netherlands, and "virtually every federal circuit court in the country," as the UVA interviewer put it. Earlier, in 2000, Napolitano had been diagnosed with breast cancer and had undergone a mastectomy.

On January 15, 2002 Napolitano announced her candidacy for the governorship of Arizona; the incumbent, Jane Dee Hull, a Republican, who had served the remainder of Governor Fife Symington's second term after his conviction on charges of bank fraud and who had won election to a full term in 1997, was barred by law from seeking another term. Running against three others in the Demo-

cratic primary, Napolitano secured the nomination with about 57 percent of the total vote. In the general election she faced (in addition to eight minor-party candidates who stood little chance of winning) the Republican Matt Salmon, a former U.S. congressman and former Arizona state senator. In a bitterly fought race that centered on Arizona's looming budget deficit of $1 billion, Salmon branded Napolitano a "tax and spend liberal" while Napolitano derided Salmon's promise not to cut taxes and his assurances that he would "personally" attract a half million new jobs to the state. When the November 5, 2002 ballots were counted, Napolitano's tally came to 566,284 (46.2 percent of the total), only 11,819 more than Salmon's 554,465 (45.2 percent).

Napolitano had campaigned as a so-called "clean candidate": she had abided by the stipulations of Arizona's Clean Elections Act, which voters had approved in 2000. Thus, she had depended entirely on public funds, except for a token amount of "seed money" to cover the expenses of qualifying for those funds. As the law required, she had qualified by gathering a specified number of signatures of registered voters and $5 checks from 4,000 of the same or other voters. Salmon, however, had opted for private contributions; unlike Napolitano, who during the campaign could concentrate entirely on trying to persuade people to vote for her, he had been forced to spend a substantial portion of his time raising money. By Election Day he had collected from private sources less than she had from the state. Some observers have attributed Napolitano's narrow victory to her decision to finance her campaign with public funds.

In an *Online NewsHour* discussion on January 3, 2003, three days before she was sworn in as governor, Napolitano noted that Arizona's financial woes were compounded by population growth: in the previous 10 years, the net number of residents had risen by 42 percent, about three times the rate at which the nation as a whole had grown. In 2002, based on the 2000 census (which reported the state's population to be 5.13 million, up from 3.66 million in 1990), the Arizona delegation in the U.S. House of Representatives had increased from six to eight. "With basically the same revenues we had in 1999, I have 300,000 more people on Medicaid, 100,000 more children in school and 5,000 more inmates in prison," Napolitano said on *Online NewsHour*. She might also have mentioned the greatly expanded needs for many other services as well—police and fire protection, street maintenance, trash collection, and sewage systems, to name a few. As she pointed out in her introduction to her fiscal-year 2005 budget proposal (January 2004, on-line), "Our ability to perform even the most basic governmental functions was seriously as risk." In June 2003, although both the 30-seat state Senate and the 60-seat state House had Republican majorities, and "the process of arriving at a balanced budget was predictably and inevitably contentious," as she put it in her 2005 budget introduction, she and the legislature agreed upon a budget for fiscal year 2004 with which she felt largely satisfied (thanks in part to the governor's right to make line-item vetoes). Although it exceeded the previous year's total by $400 million, it called for no new taxes and no substantive cuts in essential services.

As Napolitano began her second year in office, she expressed confidence that, as she put it in her 2005 budget introduction, "the rebounding economy and sound decision-making in both the Legislative and Executive branches [had] sparked a return to fiscal health." In her January 12, 2004 State of the State Address, she declared that the budget deficit had shrunk by two-thirds. (The Center for Budget Priorities [February 6, 2004, on-line], however, reported the dollar amount of the shortfall to be $1.1 billion.) Also in that address, she announced that through a new process called Efficiency Review, state employees had started to find ways to save millions of dollars, and she predicted that over the next five years, the savings would amount to "more than $843 million." She herself had already saved about $800,000 by closing the Governor's Office for Excellence in Government. "Excellence in government should be the norm," she told New Democrats Online. Among other accomplishments in 2003, she cited the introduction of the CoppeRx Card, which enabled all Arizonans eligible for Medicare to buy prescription drugs at discounts greater than those offered through the far more complicated, newly launched federal program. Also, the state's Child Protective Services department had received additional funds, to hire more people to investigate child abuse and give existing workers what the governor called "long-overdue" pay increases. Money was allocated for the launching of optional all-day kindergartens in hundreds of schools. Napolitano also said that she had overturned lawmakers' proposed funding cuts to KidsCare and KidsCare Parents (programs that provide health care for thousands of children and working adults who lack health insurance), the Homeless Youth Intervention Program, shelters for victims of domestic violence, and services for drug addicts, among other governmental activities. She also made sure that Arizona, unlike many other states, maintained levels of financial support for public community and four-year colleges and universities. In 2003 Arizona became the first state to complete a comprehensive homeland-security plan, and it began setting up a 211 phone system (similar to the 911 system for summoning police or fire fighters) for providing information during emergencies. On another front, in March 2004 Napolitano vetoed a bill that would have imposed a 24-hour waiting period for women seeking abortions and another bill that would have required abortion providers to inform clients about alternatives to abortion and risks associated with abortion.

In the weeks leading up to the 2004 presidential debates between President George W. Bush and Senator John Kerry, Napolitano was one of the Democratic Party luminaries entrusted to negotiate the terms of the debates, which took place in September and October. Others included the high-profile lawyers Vernon Jordan and Robert Barnett and the governor of Michigan, Jennifer M. Granholm.

An avid fan of spectator sports, Napolitano roots for the Diamondbacks and other Arizona teams. She also enjoys whitewater rafting; hiking, especially in the Sandia and Superstition Mountains, in Arizona; and trekking: she has climbed in the Himalayas and scaled Mount Kilimanjaro, in Tanzania. Her favorite leisure activities also include reading, watching movies, and spending time with her relatives.

—H.T.

Suggested Reading: *Albuquerque Tribune Online* Nov. 4, 2002; *Arizona Republic* B p9 Aug. 2, 2002; Associated Press State & Local Wire June 20, 2003; *Business Journal—Phoenix & the Valley of the Sun* p26+ Feb. 17, 1995; Governor Janet Napolitano's Web site; *Inside UVA Online* Apr. 9–22, 2004, with photo; New Democrats Online Dec. 9, 2002, with photo; University of Virginia School of Law Web site

Navratilova, Martina

NOTE: This biography supersedes the article about Martina Navratilova that appeared in *Current Biography* in 1977.

Oct. 10, 1956– Tennis player

Address: Rainbow Endowment, c/o Friends Center, 1501 Cherry St., Philadelphia, PA 19402

Martina Navratilova is known as one of the best tennis players of all time, and her longevity in the sport, her heralding of a new breed of powerful female players, and her openness and outspokenness have endeared her to several generations of fans. Navratilova was a member of the Women's Tennis Association (WTA) tour for an astonishing 22 years before she retired, in 1995; she returned to tennis five years later, having branched out into several other areas, including fiction writing. Her return has proven to be successful—in 2003 she and Leander Paes of India won in mixed doubles at the Australian Open. "As a player, Navratilova was bold and smart, and she dared to do things that others before and since could only imagine," Beth Corbin wrote for the *National NOW Times* (January 1995, on-line) in the year of the athlete's retirement. "She single-handedly reinvented women's tennis, taking the boundaries and limitations of women's tennis and shoving them higher and wider."

Oleg Nikishin/Getty Images
Martina Navratilova

Navratilova, who entered international competition in 1973, won the most consecutive matches (74) of any player and also holds the record for consecutive doubles victories (109). Although in singles competitions she never won a Grand Slam (victories in one calendar year in the four Grand Slam competitions—the Australian Open, the French Open, Wimbledon, and the U.S. Open), she won six titles in a row in Grand Slam competitions in 1983 and 1984 and captured a Grand Slam in doubles with Pam Shriver in the latter year. She is perhaps best known for her victories at Wimbledon, a grass court, where she won six consecutive championships (from 1982 to 1987), holds the record for the most singles titles (nine), and, in a tie with Billy Jean King, has 20 titles overall. Her many other achievements include 58 Grand Slam titles (second only to Margaret Court's 62), a record 167 tournament wins in singles, and 172 wins in doubles. She was the top-ranked player from 1978 to 1979, and from 1982 to 1987 she held the top ranking for all but 22 weeks of a 282-week period.

Navratilova's rivalry with Chris Evert is considered one of the greatest in tennis; for 10 years they battled for the number-one ranking and met in 14 Grand Slam finals, 10 of which Navratilova won. While Navratilova won only four of their first 25 contests, by the time Evert retired, in 1989, Navratilova had edged her out, with 43 wins to Evert's 37. Her training routine—which combined weightlifting, a vegetarian diet, and the use of a personal trainer (she was one of the first tennis players to hire one full-time)—helped to usher in an era of fitter, more-athletic female tennis players. "Martina revolutionized the game by her superb athleticism and aggressiveness, not to mention her outspoken-

ness and her candor," Evert told *Women's Sports and Fitness* magazine upon Navratilova's retirement from singles competition, as reported by Steve Kettmann in Salon.com (April 18, 2000). "She brought athleticism to a whole new level with her training techniques—particularly cross-training, the idea that you could go to the gym or play basketball to get in shape for tennis. . . . And then I always admired her maturity, her wisdom and her ability to transcend the sport. You could ask her about her forehand or about world peace and she always had an answer."

Martina Navratilova was born into a tennis-playing family in Prague, Czechoslovakia, on October 10, 1956. Before World War II one of her grandmothers, Agnes Semanska, was ranked as high as number two in the nation among female tennis players. Soon after her parents separated, when she was very young, her father committed suicide; her mother remarried in 1962. Her stepfather, Miroslav "Mirek" Navratil, an economic adviser in a factory, and her mother, Jana, an office worker, both served as government administrators for the Czechoslovakian Tennis Federation. Her sister and only sibling, Jana, seven years her junior, also played tennis but never turned professional.

Navratilova spent her early childhood in the Krkonose Mountains, where she learned to ski almost as soon as she could walk. When she was five her family moved to Revnice, a suburb of Prague. There, each summer, she watched her parents play in amateur tennis tournaments. "They were at the courts every day and they took me with them," she told Sarah Pileggi for *Sports Illustrated* (February 24, 1975). "I had an old racket that my father cut down [to size] and I hit the ball against a wall. I could do it for hours. They would make me stop and sit me on a chair, but whenever they didn't watch me I would go to the wall again." Recognizing his stepdaughter's innate talent for the game, Mirek Navratil began to coach her, a service he provided until she turned professional.

Inspired by her idols, Margaret Court and Billie Jean King, the eight-year-old Martina signed up to play her first tournament in the 12-and-under age division. Despite protests from officials that she was too small to compete, she made it to the semifinals. By the time she was 14, Navratilova had captured her first national title, in the 14-and-under age division. Over the next two years, she won three national women's championships and the national junior title and became Czechoslovakia's highest-ranking female tennis player. Off the court she swam, skied, and played soccer and ice hockey to strengthen her legs and shoulders. She had little interest in anything other than sports. "I was the third best student in my class but I never studied," she told Pileggi. "By the time I was fifteen and sixteen I didn't have time to study anyway. But I loved geography, and I imagined myself in places like New York and Chicago."

Early in 1973 the United States Lawn Tennis Association (USLTA—later, the USTA, after "Lawn" was dropped from the title), the ruling body of American tennis, announced an eight-week, winter-tournament circuit open to amateur and professional players. To Navratilova's delight, the Czechoslovakian Tennis Federation agreed to let her play the circuit. She thoroughly enjoyed her first visit to the United States and quickly became addicted to pancakes, pizza, and Big Macs; she gained more than 20 pounds in two months. Though she failed to win any tournaments, she did well enough to earn a regular place in tournament draws. Back in Europe she progressed to the doubles finals of the Italian Open, won the Junior Girls Championship at Wimbledon, and stunned Nancy Richey Gunter, an expert clay player, in the third round of the French Open, by winning 6–3, 6–3, before losing in the quarterfinals.

In 1974 Navratilova reached the finals of the Italian and German Opens (she lost both), then returned to the U.S. to join the lucrative Virginia Slims circuit. The left-hander quickly became known for her dynamic serve-and-volley style. (This aggressive strategy involves rushing to the net after each serve, in order to field the return on the fly.) The highlight of her first complete year on the international circuit came on September 22, 1974 in Orlando, Florida, where she defeated Julie Heldman, 7–6, 6–4, for the championship. She also won her first title in a Grand Slam event, in mixed doubles at the French Open. Moreover, her overall performance on the Slims tour, including wins in 13 of 22 matches against some of the toughest competitors in the world, won her rookie-of-the-year honors from *Tennis* magazine.

Despite her success on the court, Navratilova felt dissatisfied with her game when she returned to Revnice for the off-season. While she was undoubtedly the physically strongest woman in tennis, dominating the average opponent with a brute force greater than that of many men, some experienced players succeeded in offsetting her power by waiting for her to make errors or by hitting to her often-ineffective backhand. Determined to become number one in the world, she spent almost two months slimming down, engaging in calisthenics, and hitting backhands to her father. The hard work paid off: after her return to the women's tour, she began to defeat opponents previously beyond her reach—among them, Margaret Court, whom she upset, 6–4, 6–3, in the quarterfinals of the Australian Open in Melbourne in December 1974. Although she lost to Evonne Goolagong in the semifinals, her victory over one of her childhood idols buoyed her confidence. In the quarterfinals of the Virginia Slims tournament in January 1975, Navratilova played one of the best matches of her career, against Evert. When the deciding third set went into a best-of-nine tiebreaker, she quickly gained the advantage. Up 4–2, she returned Evert's dropshot with a slicing forehand volley that just evaded her opponent's outstretched racket. "I watched her

run for the ball," she remembered, as quoted in *World Tennis* (May 1975). "It seemed like it took forever to bounce a second time." She beat Evert and went on to top Virginia Wade in the semifinals and Kerry Melville Reid in the finals. A few weeks later, at the Chicago International Amphitheatre, she trounced Evert for the second time, taking the match 6–4, 6–0.

By the end of 1975, Navratilova had played in the singles finals of seven major tournaments, among them the French and Italian Opens, and, paired with Evert, had taken four doubles championships. (Her second Grand Slam title came in doubles at the French Open.) She also led the Czechoslovakian team to victory over top-seeded Australia in the Federation Cup match, beating Evonne Goolagong, 6–3, 6–4, on May 11, 1975. That victory was the Czechoslovakian team's first in the women's international cup competition since the Federation Cup's inception, in 1963. Navratilova and Evert shared the Silver Ginny, an award given for the most points scored in singles play on the Virginia Slims circuit, in 1975, and *Tennis* magazine singled out Navratilova for the second year in a row, naming her the most improved player.

Throughout 1975 Navratilova had battled with the Czechoslovakian Tennis Federation. The government-controlled organization had objected to her increasingly long stays in the West and complained that she was becoming too "Americanized." After she allegedly snubbed Czech officials during the play-offs at Wimbledon, then overextended her stay at Amelia Island, Florida, for the Family Circle Cup Matches, the displeased federation ordered her home. She eventually complied, but the federation's subsequent attempts to prevent her Americanization by restricting her play within the U.S., clamping down on her commercial endorsements, and refusing to let her sign up for World Team Tennis made her increasingly defiant. "They told me they didn't want me to play in the United States as much," she told Barry Tarshis for *Sport* (March 1976). "They actually wanted me to quit tennis for three months and finish school. I was under tension all the time. It didn't matter to them whether I was number one or number twenty. They wanted tennis to be second in my life. They even gave me trouble when I tried to get permission to play Forest Hills [the U.S. Open]. That's when I realized that I would never have the psychological freedom to play the best tennis as long as I was under their control." On September 6, 1975, following her loss in the semifinals at the U.S. Open, the United States Immigration and Naturalization Service in New York granted Navratilova's request for asylum. At a press conference the following day, she claimed she had no interest in politics and merely sought the freedom to play tennis wherever and whenever she wanted. She emphasized her new independence two weeks later by signing a three-year contract with the Cleveland Nets, of World Team Tennis, for a reported salary of approximately $300,000, and by agreeing to endorse tennis products in return for payment of $100,000.

Navratilova admitted that she was often homesick in the years immediately following her defection and that she often wondered if she had made a good decision. "I didn't want to defect," she told Bud Collins for the *New York Times Magazine* (June 19, 1977). "I miss my family badly. . . . We talk weekly on the phone and, obviously, it is small talk. I worried for awhile that there would be retaliation against them, but there wasn't much. My father will never be promoted, that is clear, but he didn't lose his job. My sister was barred from playing at the leading club in Prague, but she doesn't mind; she plays in Revnice."

Navratilova got off to a good start in 1976, but nagging injuries—including a sprained ankle sustained in a game of touch football, tendonitis in her wrist, and a bruised thumb—affected her play. Other than the Wimbledon doubles championship, shared with Chris Evert, she won no tournaments between January and October. The frustration of that year was most evident at the U.S. Open, when Navratilova, who had been seeded number three, was eliminated in the third round and collapsed in tears. In an interview with Jane Gross for *Newsday* (September 9, 1976), Navratilova's manager, Fred Barman, discussed his client's professional and emotional ups and downs: "Just a year ago, she was in prison. Czechoslovakia is a prison. She's like a young kid going to Disneyland. She wants to do this, she wants to do that. Maybe she's gotten it out of her system now. It's time to get down to brass tacks. This is not just another tennis player. This is another Billie Jean King."

Encouraged by her manager, her coach, and her friends on the Virginia Slims circuit, Navratilova bounced back in 1977, becoming the first female player to earn $100,000 in one year. In the initial round-robin stage of the Slims tournament at Madison Square Garden, in New York City, in March 1977, Navratilova found herself down 1–3 in the first set. She used her powerful serve, smashing forehand ground strokes, and aggressive volleys to win 10 successive games and eliminate Kristien Kemmer Shaw in straight sets, 6–3, 6–1. She went on to win the championship, defeating Betty Stove, 6–0, 6–4, and finished the women's professional circuit in first place. In the quarterfinals at Wimbledon three months later, Navratilova faced Stove again and lost, but she claimed the Wimbledon doubles title and was also the 1977 WTA Tour Championships winner in doubles.

Navratilova's first Grand Slam singles victory came in 1978 at Wimbledon, where she beat Evert for the crown, 2-6, 6-4, 7-5. Later that year she won the doubles crown at the U.S. Open and was the singles winner at the WTA Tour Championships, defeating Goolagong, 7-6, 6-4. She repeated as the Wimbledon singles champ in 1979, defeating Evert in two sets, 6-4, 6-4, and won the doubles event there as well. She also retained the singles title at

the WTA Championships, beating Tracy Austin in three sets, 6–3, 3–6, 6–2. In the following year Navratilova took the doubles crown at both the U.S. Open and the Australian Open and made it to the finals at the WTA Tour Championships, where she was beaten by Austin.

In 1981, nine days after she became a U.S. citizen, Navratilova admitted to a reporter that rumors that she was a lesbian were true. This was a bold step at a time when few athletes had ever admitted to being homosexuals—both because of the attached social stigma and because of the potential loss of endorsement offers. "Outing" herself probably did hurt Navratilova financially, but the fallout from that disclosure did not seem to affect her play. That year she scored a doubles victory at Wimbledon and followed it up, in December, with her first Australian Open singles title, besting Evert, 6–7, 6–4, 7–5. She also won the WTA Tour Championships singles title again, defeating Andrea Jaeger 6–3, 7–6. Navratilova won the singles and doubles titles at the French Open and Wimbledon in 1982 and captured her third Grand Slam doubles title of the year at the Australian Open. (She defeated Jaeger for the French Open singles title, 7–6, 6–1, and Evert at Wimbledon, 6–1, 3–6, 6–2.) At the WTA Tour Championships that year, she lost in the finals to Sylvia Hanika but won the doubles title. She claimed the women's title at three consecutive Grand Slams in 1983, defeating Jaeger (6–0, 6–3) at Wimbledon, Evert (6–1, 6–3) at the U.S. Open, and Kathy Jordan (6–2, 7–6) at the Australian Open. She won the doubles title at all three tournaments as well and regained the WTA Tour Championships singles title, beating Evert, 6–2, 6–0. Overall, her match record that year was 86–1.

Extending her outstanding win–loss record in 1984, Navratilova won 78 matches and lost two. She won the singles trophy at the first three Grand Slam tournaments of the year, beating Evert at the French Open (6–3 6–1), Wimbledon (7–6, 6–2), and the U.S. Open (4–6, 6–4, 6–4). With Pam Shriver, she took the doubles titles at all four Grand Slam events. She faced Evert for a fourth finals, at the WTA Tour Championships, and beat her yet again, 6–3, 7–5, 6–1. In 1985 she won the women's title at Wimbledon for the third straight year, beating Evert in three sets, 4–6, 6–3, 6–2; she defeated her again that year, for her third Australian Open singles crown, 6–2, 4–6, 6–2. She was the doubles champion at both the French Open and the Australian Open and won two mixed-doubles titles, at Wimbledon and the U.S. Open. She beat Helena Sukova, 6–3, 7–5, 6–4, to win the WTA Tour Championships crown.

In 1986 Navratilova won singles titles at Wimbledon and the U.S. Open, defeating Hana Mandlikova 7–6, 6–3 and Sukova 6–3, 6–2, respectively. She claimed the doubles titles at the French Open, Wimbledon, and the U.S. Open and won both the singles title (she defeated Mandlikova, 6–2, 6–0, 3–6, 6–1) and doubles title at the WTA Tour Championships. That year also marked her first return to her native country since her defection, as a member of the U.S. Federation Cup team that eventually defeated Czechoslovakia. Navratilova won six more Grand Slam titles in 1987: in doubles at the Australian Open, doubles at the French Open, singles at Wimbledon (she beat Steffi Graf, 7–5, 6–3), and a rare triple crown at the U.S. Open, winning in singles (against Graf, 7–6, 6–1), doubles, and mixed doubles. Most of Navratilova's titles in 1988 were in doubles competition, as she won the Australian Open, the French Open, the WTA Tour Championships, and the U.S. Open in that event. In the WTA Tour Championships singles competition, she lost to Graf.

Navratilova won her ninth and last Wimbledon singles title in 1990, defeating Zina Garrison, 6–4, 6–1, and breaking the record for most singles victories at Wimbledon. She also earned another victory in doubles in the U.S. Open. Although she did not win any Grand Slam trophies in 1991, she was the WTA Tour Championships doubles winner and made it to the WTA singles final, where she lost to Monica Seles. She again faced Seles in that competition the following year and again was defeated. In 1992 Navratilova won her 158th professional singles title, at the Virginia Slims competition in Chicago, setting a record for the most career singles championships. She won in mixed doubles at Wimbledon in 1993. She retired from singles competition in November 1994, after defeats at the hands of younger players; she had lost in the first round of the French Open earlier that year, smashing her racket in disgust at her performance, but was still ranked in the top five. "It's not like I've really run out of competitive spirit," she told Robin Finn for the *New York Times* (February 16, 1994). "It's more like the body says O.K., I've had enough of this, and then your competitive spirit sort of goes along with it. It's probably a self-preservation mechanism, that moment when you say to yourself, 'I'm too old for this, so it's O.K. to be No. 3 or 4 and not No. 1.'"

Navratilova won another title, in mixed doubles at Wimbledon in 1995, but over the next five years she participated in few tennis matches and no major competitions. "Tennis is no longer the focus of my life," she told Jack Cavanaugh for the *New York Times* (August 27, 1995). "I don't miss it—the nerves, the travel and all of that. So I have no regrets whatsoever, since I think I retired at just the right time: not too early and not too late." Aside from coaching the U.S. Federation Cup team in 1997, Navratilova for the most part stayed away from the tennis court after her retirement. Instead, she took up woodworking, went on a safari in Kenya, mounted a photo exhibition in Prague, earned a pilot's license, and wrote several mystery books with Liz Nickles: *Total Zone* (1994), *Breaking Point* (1996), and *Killer Instinct* (1997).

In May 2000 Navratilova returned to doubles competition, teaming up with Mariaan de Swardt of South Africa in the Madrid Open. They made it to the quarterfinals, where they were defeated by Venus and Serena Williams. During her years away from competition, Navratilova had kept fit by playing hockey, soccer, and basketball; to prepare for her reentry into competitive tennis, she had sprinted, lifted weights, and practiced Pilates. "I can't hit the ball as hard as I used to," she told Saxon Baines for *Sports Illustrated* (June 15, 2000, on-line). "But I know where to hit and in doubles that's half the battle, being in the right position and hitting the ball in the right place." In January 2003 Navratilova paired with Leander Paes to win in mixed doubles at the Australian Open, becoming the first person to win every possible Grand Slam title in the Open Era. (Prior to the designation of the four opens as Grand Slam events, in 1968, Margaret Court also won the singles, doubles, and mixed-doubles titles at each of them: the Australian Open, the French Open, Wimbledon, and the U.S. Open.) Navratilova and Paes also won the mixed-doubles title at Wimbledon that year, which gave Navratilova her 20th Wimbledon trophy, placing her in a tie with Billie Jean King for the record for the most Wimbledon titles ever. At 46, she was also the oldest Wimbledon champion ever.

Navratilova joined Lisa Raymond to enter the 2004 Olympic women's doubles tournament, in which they were seeded third. They achieved an easy 6–0, 6–2 first-round win over Yuliya Beygelzimer and Tetyana Perebiynis of the Ukraine and earned a second-round bye into the quarterfinals when the French team, Mary Pierce and Amelie Mauresmo, were forced to withdraw after Mauresmo developed a skin ailment. Navratilova and Raymond were stopped in a hard-fought 6–4, 4–6, 6–4 match by the fifth-seeded Shinobu Asagoe and Ai Sugiyama of Japan, the eventual fourth-place finishers.

Within days of the closing ceremonies at the Games, Navratilova returned to the U.S. Open to compete in the women's doubles and mixed-doubles categories, teaming with Raymond and Leander Paes, respectively. She and Raymond made the quarterfinals, where they were ousted by the Russians Svetlana Kuznetsova and Elena Likhovtseva, 7–6 (8–6 tie break), 6–7 (5–7), 1–6. She and Paes advanced to the semifinals, where they bowed to the Australians Alicia Molik and Todd Woodbridge, 4–6, 6–3, 7–6 (10–3). Navratilova has said that she plans to retire from doubles competition in 2005.

Among many other honors, Navratilova was named WTA Player of the Year in 1978, 1979, 1982, 1983, 1984, 1985, and 1986, and shared the WTA Tour Doubles Team of the Year title in 1977 (with Betty Stove), in 1978 and 1979 (with Billie Jean King), and every year from 1981 to 1989 (with Pam Shriver). She helped the U.S. win the Federation Cup in 1976, 1979, 1981, 1982, and 1986 and the Wightman Cup, another international women's team tennis competition, in 1983. She served as president of the WTA Tour Players' Association in 1979–80, 1983–84, and 1994–95. Named female athlete of the 1980s by the National Sports Review,

United Press International, and the Associated Press, she was also named to the Associated Press's list of "World's Greatest Athletes of the Century," Sports Illustrated's "Top 100 Athletes of the Century" list, and ESPN's "Top 50 Athletes of the Century" list. In 2000 she was inducted into the International Tennis Hall of Fame. Her autobiography, Martina, co-written with the veteran New York Times sports reporter George Vecsey, was published in 1985. Her first national television endorsement, with the automaker Subaru of America, came in 2000. She has also endorsed Apple Computers, L.A. Eyeworks, and the New York Times and has provided commentary on HBO Sports since 1995.

Had Navratilova withdrawn from competition years before she did, she would still have been remembered as one of the best to play the game; her tenacity in playing a demanding sport until well past the average retirement age has won her additional admiration. "The response that I've gotten from the people has been such that I just didn't want to stop, because people are saying how inspired they were by what I'm still doing out there . . . ," she told Steve Wilstein for the Associated Press (July 9, 2003), as quoted on the Ventura County Star Web site. "Little kids that didn't see me play, didn't even know who I was, now they're like, 'Hey, Martina!' They saw me maybe on Sesame Street, but they didn't see me play. Teenagers getting off the ski lift: 'Hey, Martina, you rock.' And then the middle-aged housewives in the country clubs going absolutely bonkers when they see me, say, 'I can't believe what you're doing. I'm going to get out there and do more.' Older people, too. . . . It runs the gamut, totally. And that's what's amazing, you know, that because I hit a fuzzy yellow tennis ball, that inspires people to do more with life. It just doesn't get any better than that."

Navratilova is also known for her outspokenness—on matters relating to politics and social mores as well as tennis. She is a proponent of equalizing the competition of men and women. (Currently, in most tournaments a man must win three sets to win a match, while a woman need win only two sets.) "We've always been fit and capable . . . and willing to play three out of five, but the powers that be—the tennis establishment—didn't want us to do that," she told Diane Anderson-Minshall for Curve magazine (2002, on-line). "We could have been playing three out of five from day one. . . . It was this old [expletive] established notion that women were frail, fragile, and didn't have the endurance of men, which we know is the opposite, in fact. The longer it goes, the better women do." Navratilova has also lamented the fact that many female athletes gain notoriety for their sexual attractiveness rather than for their athletic skills. "I think it started in the '70s, especially on the women's golf tour," she told Anderson-Minshall. "They tried to sexualize it all. Then it sort of settled down in the late '70s and '80s and the first part of the

nineties. Then in the late '90s it just became this big thing to pose nude and provocatively and all that stuff. . . . I think the women athletes themselves are perpetuating it and not taking themselves seriously, saying, 'Hey, I'm a great athlete, and I have skills and I'm worth watching just because of that. You don't need to sexualize it.' At the same time, I'm not saying hide it. If you're beautiful, flaunt it. But don't sexualize it. I think it can get to be a bit too much."

Navratilova has been active in the environmental, women's, gay-rights, and animal-rights movements. In 1995 she co-founded the Rainbow Card, a credit card to raise funds for the Rainbow Endowment, a nonprofit agency that supports causes important to the gay and lesbian community; so far it has raised more than $1.5 million. She was the keynote speaker at the Millennium March on Washington (in support of equal rights for gays), held in April 2000. The Human Rights Campaign granted her its National Equality Award in 2000 for her work on behalf of gay rights. She is considering running for public office after completing her tennis career. "If [the weight lifter turned film star] Arnold Schwarzenegger can run for governor in California, then who knows? I have the muscles," she told the Associated Press (September 24, 2003), as quoted on the ESPN Web site. "I will be involved [in politics], especially the way things are going right now. The conservative party is too strong."

Navratilova speaks Czech, German, Russian, and English and has won more than $20 million in career prize money. She has cited among her sports heroes the boxer Muhammad Ali, the baseball player Jackie Robinson, and the Olympic sprinter John Carlos. Her favorite television shows include Xena: Warrior Princess, Hercules: The Legendary Journeys, Alias, and Sex and the City. She lives in Aspen, Colorado, and enjoys downhill skiing, snowboarding, scuba diving, ice hockey, and photography. She has had romantic relationships with the writer Rita Mae Brown and with the former Texas beauty queen Judy Nelson.

—K.E.D.

Suggested Reading: Advocate p41+ Jan. 20, 2004, with photos; Curve (on-line) 2002; Lesbian News p26+ Dec. 2002, with photos; Ms. p58+ Feb. 1988, with photos; Salon.com Apr. 18, 2000, with photo; Sports Illustrated p80 Sep. 19, 1994, with photos; Tennis p124+ July 1994, with photos, p36+ Nov. 1994, with photos; Ventura County Star (on-line) July 9, 2003; Navratilova, Martina and George Vecsey. Martina, 1985

Selected Books: Martina (with George Vecsey), 1985; Total Zone (with Liz Nickles), 1994; Breaking Point (with Liz Nickles), 1996; Killer Instinct (with Liz Nickles), 1997

Judy Griesedieck/Time Life Pictures/Getty Images

Nelson, Marilyn Carlson

Aug. 19, 1939– Chairwoman and CEO of Carlson Companies Inc.

Address: Carlson Companies, P.O. Box 59159, Minneapolis, MN 55459

Much has changed in the four decades since Marilyn Carlson Nelson worked briefly in the marketing department of the Gold Bond Stamp Co. in 1964. Gold Bond is now known as Carlson Companies, and what was once a mom-and-pop operation that sold trading stamps to local grocery stores has expanded into a global leader in the travel, hospitality, and marketing industries, with nearly $21 billion in annual sales and 190,000 employees in 140 countries. Among the best-known of the 100 companies that Carlson encompasses are Carlson Wagonlit Travel, Country Inns & Suites, Park Inn Hotels, Park Plaza Hotels & Resorts, Radisson Hotels & Resorts, Regent International Hotels, the restaurant chain T.G.I. Friday's, Radisson Seven Seas Cruises, and Carlson Marketing Group. Leading the charge for Carlson Companies, as it evolves from a mid-20th-century entrepreneur's vision to an enduring 21st-century conglomerate, is its chairwoman and chief executive officer (CEO), Marilyn Carlson Nelson. Nelson assumed the company's helm in 1998, a few years after she rejoined the firm as a full-time employee at the urging of her father. Since then she has turned it into one of the 100 best companies for working mothers, according to *Working Mother* magazine, and transformed herself into one of the 100 most powerful women in the world, according to *Forbes*. Nelson has also followed in her father's philanthropic footsteps,

working energetically for the United Way and the World Childhood Foundation, among other entities. In addition, she has made her firm the first in the U.S. to refuse to conduct business with companies that are known participants in the sexual exploitation of minors.

The older of the two children of Curtis L. Carlson and his wife, the former Arleen Martin, Nelson was born Marilyn Arleen Carlson on August 19, 1939 in Minneapolis, Minnesota. "In a sense, I was born a chauffeur's daughter because I didn't grow up wealthy," she told David Saltman for *Chief Executive* (August/September 2003, on-line). Her birth occurred a little more than a year after her father sold his first set of trading stamps to a Minneapolis grocer. Known as Curt, he had then been working as a Procter & Gamble salesman servicing grocery stores; he had quickly made a name for himself by expanding the company's sales of soap into drugstores. While on his sales beat, he had noticed that a local department store was giving out stamps redeemable for gifts and cash, as a way to build loyalty and encourage return business. Curt, who had earned a bachelor's degree in economics from the University of Minnesota, adapted the department store's idea for the customers he had already cultivated. Using a $55 loan from his landlord, he had formed the Gold Bond Stamp Co. in 1938 and devoted nights and weekends to building it. His goal was to earn, as an independent entrepreneur, $100 a week, almost four times his Procter & Gamble salary. He began his company, Nelson told Ann Merrill for the Minneapolis *Star Tribune* (September 21, 1997), with the impetus provided by "two very powerful formative experiences"— growing up as the child of Swedish immigrants and living through the Great Depression from his mid-teens until his mid-20s. Curt Carlson left Procter & Gamble when Marilyn was an infant. Gold Bond became his passion, and Nelson and her sister, Barbara, came to regard it as virtually a third sibling. "I learned the family business at the breakfast table, at the dinner table, on weekends," Nelson told David Saltman. She also told him, "We gave up dessert when I was in my formative years because we got a little speech about investing and return on investment. If we ate it, it'd be gone. If we put the money in the company, it would grow and we'd get a return." She told Ann Merrill, "The sense of valuing capital, leveraging capital, saving every penny, investing pennies, and recognizing the miracle of compounding was absolutely a driver for us."

Curt Carlson's conservative business methods produced impressive results. In 1953 one of the largest supermarket chains in the nation, Super Valu, began buying Gold Bond stamps, and other chains soon followed suit. In the 1960s, at the peak of the trading-stamp market, of which Gold Bond then controlled about a third, Carlson diversified, first buying Minneapolis's landmark Radisson Hotel and using its brand name to build a nationwide hotel chain, then, in the 1970s, acquiring established hospitality chains, such as T.G.I. Friday's, as well as travel agencies and cruise lines. From 1938 to 1978 Curt Carlson's eye for solid acquisitions and the tight control he maintained over his swelling enterprise produced an average annual rate of growth of 33 percent.

Curt Carlson publicly expressed consternation over not having a male heir, but as he navigated his company, Marilyn Carlson showed signs that she might be as capable as he was. At Edina High School, in a Minneapolis suburb, she was editor of the school paper, a member of the student council, and a popular cheerleader. She briefly considered a career in acting before enrolling at Smith College, in Northampton, Massachusetts, where she majored in international economics and minored in theater. She spent her junior year abroad, studying at the Sorbonne, in Paris, France, and the Institute des Hautes Études Économiques Politiques in Geneva, Switzerland. She graduated with honors from Smith in 1961. Shortly thereafter she married Glen Nelson, who went on to become a surgeon and recently retired as vice chairman of Medtronic Inc., which produced the first implantable pacemaker. She flirted with joining the diplomatic corps before deciding to enter the business world. Early in her marriage she got a job with PaineWebber (then called Paine, Webber, Jackson & Curtis) as a securities analyst; she was the first woman to hold that position in one of the firm's offices in the Midwest (a fact the company apparently did not want to reveal: her supervisor told her to sign all documents as "M. C. Nelson" to hide her gender). Ten months into her tenure she left PaineWebber, having become pregnant with her first child.

Nelson worked full-time for Gold Bond briefly in 1964. Following her departure from the company, during her third pregnancy, she devoted herself not only to motherhood but also to fundraising for local organizations, among them the Minneapolis Symphony and the Minneapolis United Way, and she became a well-liked civic leader. In 1984 she was named the chairwoman of the Minnesota Super Bowl task force, formed to lobby the National Football League (NFL) to bring the championship game to their state in 1992. Nelson relentlessly pursued her task. In one attempt to woo the NFL, she sent life-size chocolate ducks to Tampa, Florida, for a meeting of all the teams' owners. The ducks—the best approximation that she could find of the loon, Minnesota's state bird—arrived with their necks broken. Enlisting the help of a chef at the hotel where she and the owners were staying, she made a paste out of sugar, flour, and water and worked all night to reattach the ducks' heads. To hide the scars, she tied around each duck's neck a ribbon bearing a message from her, and then had a duck placed on each team owner's pillow. The effort paid off: the NFL agreed to hold the 1992 Super Bowl in Minneapolis's Metrodome, and her community's regard for Nelson skyrocketed.

During this period Nelson, who had worked part-time for Gold Bond since the early 1970s, contemplated a run for the U.S. Senate, but her father strongly encouraged her to work for the family firm full-time. "He said: 'If you care about this company, you'll do it,'" Nelson told De'Ann Weimer for *Business Week* (August 17, 1998). She admitted to Weimer that she had felt reluctant to return to a full-time position, and his words had made her "uncomfortable." "I had my own opportunities," she explained to Weimer. "If I was going to be in the company, I needed a role where I was allowed to make an impact." Nelson agreed to her father's request after he named her co-chair of Carlson Holdings, Carlson Companies' parent company, and chair of the audit committee. "My father is tough but he's fair," Nelson said to Khoi Nguyen in 1992. "Above all, he's my father and he's in his advanced years. It's invaluable that I can run across the hall to ask his advice. And later on, I'm sure I will even miss all the times when he comes parading in my office to tell me what to do."

After her promotion Nelson immediately began studying family-owned firms to identify problems prevalent among them. Her research led her to advise her father to bring in outside directors to offer fresh perspectives and stabilize the company during the transition when, at an as yet undetermined date, Curt Carlson would retire. She also discovered a serious lack of internal financial regulation, common in privately held companies because they do not have to disclose profits publicly. In 1993 she helped to recruit Martyn Redgrave from Pepsico to fill the position of chief financial officer (CFO), with responsibility for implementing a stricter accounting system, one more in line with those used by public corporations.

Meanwhile, a year or so before Nelson had rejoined the company full time, Curt Carlson had had to undergo heart surgery and had named as CEO his daughter Barbara's husband, Edwin C. "Skip" Gage, who had worked at the company for about 20 years. After he recovered, Carlson, who was known for watching the bottom line with an eagle eye and managing with an iron fist, clashed with Gage over business philosophies and softening revenues. In 1991 Gage resigned, bought three Carlson marketing companies, and set up the Gage Marketing Group. (He remains a Carlson board member.) Many observers speculated that Carlson would choose Juergen Bartels as Gage's successor. As head of Carlson Hospitality Worldwide, Bartels had made his division Carlson's most profitable business segment during his tenure. However, he grew increasingly intolerant of Carlson's hands-on approach and resigned in 1995 to become chairman and CEO of Westin Hotels.

Beyond the unpleasantness connected with Gage's and Bartels's respective departures, both highlight a larger problem with which Carlson Companies and many other family-owned firms have grappled: the steady loss of top executives who see little chance for advancement. For his part, Carlson settled the issue by grooming Nelson to take over. Also in 1995 he hired a succession consultant, Barbara Hauser, as vice president of financial and tax planning for Carlson Holdings Inc., whose assignments included structuring the company's stock, all of which he owned, so that it could be sold only to the company. Within two years he named Nelson chief operating officer (COO), relinquishing all of Carlson Companies' day-to-day operations to her. In March 1998, at Carlson Companies' 60th anniversary celebration, in Las Vegas, Nevada, Carlson appointed his daughter CEO and president of the firm; he himself retained the title of chairman until his death, in February 1999.

Since she took over the rudder of Carlson Companies, Nelson has changed its corporate culture. "I want to lead with love, not fear," she told De'Ann Weimer. In the conviction that an inspired and dedicated workforce is necessary if the company is to grow and remain strong, she has expanded bonus programs and profit sharing, including "phantom stock," a system of bonuses tied to revenue growth, as well as flextime and child day care—perks that Curt Carlson had resisted. Furthermore, she has increased the representation of women in executive ranks to 40 percent (in 1989 the figure was 8 percent), and she has instituted training programs to encourage workers to prepare themselves for executive positions. Above all, her goal is to lead by example. Drawing upon a skill she developed while working with volunteers whom she did not have the power to hire or fire, she tries to build consensus among her executives so that they feel they have influenced business decisions. Nelson has also spearheaded many projects that have had deep and long-lasting effects on Carlson Companies' organization. As COO she brought the technology infrastructure under her aegis, with the aim of bringing improved technology and increased efficiency to, and integrating, all Carlson units. This enabled the units to track, for instance, a frequent business traveler's preferences.

In the wake of the September 11, 2001 terrorist attacks on the U.S. and the resultant slump in travel and tourism, Nelson reevaluated Carlson's business model and processes and then restructured them to increase efficiency and profitability. Her analyses, which have so far saved tens of millions of dollars in operating and other costs, have continued. Most recently, she has worked with government officials and the media to launch a public-relations campaign to further encourage people to travel. "One out of every seven jobs in America is connected to the travel industry," Nelson observed to David Saltman. "People don't realize that when the travel industry slumps, there's a huge ripple effect in the construction industry, in agriculture, in all sorts of seemingly unrelated businesses."

Recognized as a worldwide business leader, Marilyn Carlson Nelson currently serves on the boards of Exxon Mobile Corp., the Singapore Tourism Council, and the Mayo Clinic Foundation. She is a member of the World Economic Forum and was appointed by President George W. Bush in 2002 to chair the National Women's Business Council, which advises the White House and Congress on public-policy issues that affect female business owners. Among her many honors are the 2000 Woodrow Wilson Award for Corporate Citizenship, her induction into the Sales and Marketing Executives Hall of Fame, and her being named the 1999 *Corporate Reports* Executive of the Year. As her father wished, Nelson is grooming her son, Curtis Nelson, currently Carlson Companies' president and COO, to succeed her. She and her husband also have two daughters, Wendy Nelson, an executive with Carlson Restaurants Worldwide, and Diane Nelson. Their oldest daughter, Juliet, died in a car accident in 1985, a week after leaving for college. "I don't know if I'll be here tomorrow," Marilyn Nelson told David Saltman. "I know that today is a day I have and I've often said that what [Juliet] taught me was that each day should be a day I would sign my name to and that we should live as a kind of artist, because that may be the last day."

—T.J.F.

Suggested Reading: *Business Week* p52+ Aug. 7, 1998, with photos; *Chief Executive* (on-line) Aug./Sep. 2003, with photos; (Minneapolis, Minnesota) *Star Tribune* D p1 Mar. 14, 1997, with photo, D p1 Sep. 21, 1997, with photo, A p1 Mar. 24, 1998, with photos, S p16 Sep. 26, 2003; *Town & Country* p85+ Aug. 1992

Neptunes

Music production team; singer-songwriters

Hugo, Chad
1974– Record producer; singer; songwriter

Williams, Pharrell
Apr. 5, 1973– Record producer; singer; songwriter

Address: Star Trak Entertainment, P.O. Box 1938, Radio City Station, New York, NY 10101-1938

Pharrell Williams and Chad Hugo, the Grammy Award–winning production team known as the Neptunes, began their ascent to the heights of the music world in the late 1990s. Working with the biggest stars in hip-hop, pop, and R&B—Jay-Z, Nelly, Whitney Houston, Prince, Mary J. Blige, Beyoncé Knowles, and Britney Spears, to name only a few—the Neptunes have produced close to 20 platinum singles ("platinum" denoting sales of more than one million units) and are one of the most in-

Scott Gries/Getty Images
The Neptunes: Chad Hugo (left) and Pharrell Williams

demand production teams in the music industry. Among the hit songs the Neptunes have produced, many of which have won or been nominated for awards, are Justin Timberlake's "Rock Your Body," Nelly's "Hot in Herre," and Snoop Dogg's "Beautiful." Terry Sawyer, writing for the Web site popmatters.com, summed up the Neptunes' musical prowess and their wide appeal: "Once the Neptunes have laid their hands on a song, it's indisputably their own. You can recognize a Neptunes track by the way that the song's bones are lifted to the surface and pounded out like a giant's footfalls. The beats are simple, tactile and instantly demand a head nod, an ass shake, and an almost demonic surrender." Sasha Frere-Jones, in the *Village Voice* (February 18, 2003), described the Neptunes as the "first important producers of the 21st century, happy children of the loud, brassy world of digital audio. It's not just how their beats return again and again, deathlessly big like a can-crushing machine. . . . They have come—grind grind—to pump you up. . . . They are the first of a new cognitive class, working without a genre or a map."

In 2003 Hugo and Williams released the compilation album *The Neptunes Present . . . Clones*, which features tracks with an array of top hip-hop performers and made its debut at number one on several of *Billboard* magazine's album charts. *Clones* has since achieved platinum status. Under the name of their alter-ego band N.E.R.D., Hugo and Williams released the albums *In Search Of . . .* (2002) and *Fly or Die* (2004). Referring, respectively, to a hip-hop group that became hugely popular in the early 1990s and a legendary funk/soul group whose heyday was in the 1970s, Hugo told

Tony Ware for the Web site creativeloafing.com (July 17, 2002) that he and Williams started out trying to be "the R&B version of A Tribe Called Quest . . . the new wave Earth, Wind & Fire with turntables and drum machines." The Neptunes are nurturing future recording artists through their own record label, Star Trak Entertainment, which is an imprint of Arista Records. Hugo told Adam Bernard for reactmag.com, "Being a producer you get to kinda provide a backdrop to bring out whatever's in that artist, and you pick up things, like different opinions, it's like goin' to school. Every artist teaching you something in some way, indirectly." As posted on the Web site hip-hop-network.com, Williams told the publication *Rhythm Nation*, "Being a Neptune is all about exploring and discovering and that's no matter what it is that you do—we just happen to be producers . . . whatever it is that you do in your life be prepared to explore and discover, because if you're not, then you're sort of just running across stagnant territory, you're doing a disservice to your soul, your soul is here to learn." In addition to a number of other nominations and honors, in February 2004 the Neptunes won the Grammy Award for producer of the year.

The oldest of three sons, Pharrell Williams was born on April 5, 1973 in Virginia Beach, Virginia, to Pharoah and Carolyn Williams. His father worked as a handyman; his mother was a school-teacher. Williams, an African-American, has recalled that when he was 11 years old, wishing to emulate the then-popular television personality Mr. T, he had his father cut his hair into a mohawk. "Going to school with that haircut taught me a lot of humility," he commented, in answer to a reader's question in *Blender* (April 2004). Williams and Chad Hugo, a Filipino-American who was born in 1974, met while attending separate junior high schools. Their musical interests brought them together: Williams played drums, rhymed, and rapped, and Hugo played saxophone in a special music program, run by their Virginia Beach school system, that focused on improvisational skills. In an interview for *Rhythm Nation* posted on the Web site hip-hop-network.com, Williams recalled that nearly every day he and Hugo "would go over to Chad's house and play [music] equipment [including a cheap Casio keyboard] and just come up with beats and ideas and tracks." The two formed a band, choosing the name Neptunes, after Neptune, the Roman god of the sea, in part because they wanted their music to flow freely and widely over the earth, like water. In addition, Hugo told Scott Poulson-Bryant for *America* magazine, as quoted on startrakmusic.com, he and Williams sought an "alternative name that didn't box us into one style. We didn't want to be typical, we wanted to be like old school bands like Earth, Wind and Fire."

Williams and Hugo were greatly influenced by such standout hip-hop groups of the late 1980s and 1990s as the Native Tongues, De La Soul, the Jungle Brothers, and A Tribe Called Quest, all of whom drew upon a wide variety of musical genres and were known for positive, Afrocentric, socially conscious lyrics highlighted by jazz-inflected beats. Referring to those groups specifically, Hugo told Jim Macnie for the VH1 Web site, "That whole movement's rhyme scheme was different [from most other music of that time]; the loops they sampled were wild. The chords really touched me, man. . . . Hearing those jazz chords . . . I don't want to get technical on you, but [they] hit me hard. They're not your typical A-C-G chords. Sonically, it was crazy." Hugo also told Macnie that in his opinion the most innovative hip-hop albums include A Tribe Called Quest's *The Low End Theory*, Dr. Dre's *The Chronic*, and many of the disks produced by Timbaland. Regarding the music that inspired him early on, Williams told Poulson-Bryant that his favorite parts of Michael Jackson's songs were those in which the keys changed, or the chords flowed toward a bridge. "I didn't know what that was, but it was what got me," he said. As evidenced by the sounds they create, the Neptunes' musical taste is not limited to rap and hip-hop. The men have also named as musical influences such diverse artists or groups as Stevie Wonder, AC/DC, Queen, America, and Steely Dan.

Hugo and Williams both attended Princess Anne High School, in Virginia Beach, and played together in the school band. (Hugo later attended a college, but readily available sources do not reveal which one or how long he studied there.) In 1992, while still secondary-school students, the two friends sold their first song, "Rump Shakur," to the rap duo Wreckx-N-Effects, who performed it. The track sold more than 500,000 copies and thus became Williams and Hugo's first gold single. Although Hugo told Bernard that in Virginia Beach "there is no music scene," the highly regarded producer Teddy Riley worked out of the city. Riley's production studios were located across the street from Williams and Hugo's high school. During a talent show at the school, Riley "discovered" the young beatmasters (who earlier, hoping to land a record deal, had unsuccessfully stalked him) and invited them to work with him. Along with Riley, in 1994 Hugo and Williams helped to produce Blackstreet's debut album and later did the same for the groups S.W.V. and Total. In 1997 Williams and Hugo produced a track on the rapper Mase's successful album *Harlem World* and helped produce rap albums by Jay-Z and MC Lyte.

In 1998 Hugo and Williams ended their apprenticeship with Riley and struck out on their own. They registered a hit with the single "Superthug," by the rapper Noreaga (now known as N.O.R.E.), from his debut solo album, *N.O.R.E.* In "Superthug" Noreaga included the Neptunes' name in his lyrics. "We didn't ask [Noreaga] to do that, that's hot," Hugo told Bernard, while discussing the Neptunes' strong relationship with the rapper. "Ever since then, we sorta took off." Drawing a comparison to the award-winning California-based rapper/producer team of Snoop Dogg and Dr. Dre

and their ability to turn out popular tracks consistently, Noreaga said of the Neptunes, as quoted by Bernard, "It's almost like Snoop and Dre, when I get with the Neptunes, it's a wrap."

The Neptunes' early rap-production successes, many of which were party-themed tracks, included Ol' Dirty Bastard's "Got My Money" (1999), Mystikal's "Shake Ya Ass" (2000), and Jay-Z's "I Want to Love U" (2001). While the duo continued to produce hit songs for some of the biggest names in rap and hip-hop, including L.L. Cool J ("Luv U Better"), Busta Rhymes ("Pass the Courvoisier"), and Nelly ("Hot in Herre"), in 2001 the Neptunes also began producing songs for mainstream pop performers such as 'N Sync ("Girlfriend"). Also that year the pop icon Britney Spears performed her Neptunes-produced hit "I'm a Slave 4U" at the MTV Video Music Awards ceremony, thereby affirming Hugo and Williams's growing prominence within the music industry. In regard to working with artists as different as Busta Rhymes and Britney Spears, Hugo told Ware, "As producers, you have the power to work with anybody every which way. We try to switch sounds with different people. . . . It's our way of being the Wizard of Oz. We run [expletive] from where you can't see us, switching up the styles. Ultimately I'd like it to be where you could turn on any station—rock, R&B, country—and know that the Neptunes did a lot, but not know [specifically] what the Neptunes did."

The Neptunes' artistic process has evolved. When they were younger, Williams and Hugo would listen to certain loops or repeated sections of already-produced songs and then, inspired by what they had heard, turn off the music and mix new sounds of their own. Now Williams and Hugo often listen to samples of songs and try to determine what is missing in them that might have made the tracks better, as Williams said in an interview posted on the VH1 Web site. Hugo concentrates mainly on the backdrop of productions—the beats, samples, and rhythms—while Williams excels at songwriting and possesses a falsetto singing voice that some critics have compared to that of Curtis Mayfield. Hugo told Poulson-Bryant that Williams is a "brilliant songwriter who can take the skeleton of a beat and put a great song on it." When Poulson-Bryant asked him about the Neptunes' collaborations with other musicians, Williams responded, "Artists are like vessels for us [producers] to use . . . I don't put something out if I feel like something is already out there like it. I strive for everything to be different. . . . I want to give [both the artist and the eventual listener] what I think is missing." Hugo told an interviewer for the music Web site rwdmag.com that his favorite piece of studio equipment is the computer: "Everything can be done on the computer, it has sped up the process, with a computer we can knock out 6 songs a day."

In 2001 Williams and Hugo recruited the talents of a high-school friend of theirs, the performer Sheldon Haley, better known as Shay, and along with him created a kind of musical alter-ego for the Neptunes: an alternative hip-hop and rock group called N.E.R.D. (an acronym for "No One Ever Really Dies"). "We weren't really nerds," Hugo told Bernard. "Pharrell got kicked outta band [in high school] a couple times, I got kicked outta my college band for quitting practice, and stole my first equipment. During a [school] pageant I stole a computer because I didn't have one." On the N.E.R.D. Web site, however, the men wrote, "We call ourselves N*E*R*D because we have a different view of life. . . . If you ever listen to a nerd speak about their experiences in high school, they tell an ill ['interesting' or 'cool'] story. They have an ill perspective because of [what] they've been through. . . . I don't mind being called a nerd. We are the people who are proud of being smart, being witty and being clever when everyone else doesn't understand. That's what we do, that's the flag we're raising and waving."

Using electronic samplers and music computer software, the trio recorded tracks in the studio for their first album, In Search Of . . ., which was released in the United Kingdom in 2001. Williams and Hugo, however, feeling dissatisfied with the disk, re-recorded all the songs on In Search Of . . . , this time using live instrumentation, much of it performed by the band Spymob (which has been associated with the Neptunes' Star Trak label). "From the start, we wanted to distinguish what we did [as N.E.R.D.] . . . from what we did as the Neptunes," Hugo told Tony Ware. "People expect the Neptunes to have a drum machine/keyboard sound. We didn't want N.E.R.D. to be the 'Neptunes Project.'" Reviewing In Search Of . . . for Entertainment Weekly (March 15, 2002), David Browne wrote that the album had a "crackling vigor . . . and its melange of genres makes for music unlike anything else around. Tracks like 'Am I High' and 'Things Are Getting Better' pull together jazz-fusion funk, rapping, and slippery soul harmonies into a cogent, kinetic whole." Though Browne qualified his praise, complaining that parts of the album are "ugly, musically and lyrically," he concluded that In Search Of . . . reveals the Neptunes' "real need to stretch out, to see what other musical possibilities are out there. Pop needs to be shaken up, and these extra-loose cannons may be just the ones to do it." Stephen Thomas Erlewine wrote for All Music Guide that despite its flaws In Search Of . . . is a mostly "lively affair" that provides "genuine musical thrills. Although, be forewarned—it's easy to overrate this record simply because it deviates from the norm at a time when nobody deviates from the norm or has deviated from the norm in years. With better lyrics and a little less smirking hipsterism, it could have been the record it was intended to be, but as it stands it's still a pretty terrific listen and one of the most adventurous, intriguing hip-hop albums in a long,

long time." The album's tracks "Lapdance" and "Rock Star" climbed onto Billboard's singles chart. While not as successful commercially as many of the Neptunes' other projects, In Search Of . . . achieved gold status.

By the time In Search Of . . . was released, Williams and Hugo had become as much in demand as producers of rap and hip-hop as Dr. Dre and Timbaland. Also during that period, five Neptunes-produced songs were on Billboard's Hot 100 chart: 'N Sync's "Girlfriend"; Usher's "U Don't Have to Call"; Fabolous's "Young'n (Holla Back)"; Busta Rhymes's "Pass the Courvoisier Part II" (with P. Diddy and Pharrell Williams); and Mystikal's "Bouncin' Back (Bumpin' Me Against the Wall)." Also in 2002 N.E.R.D. went on tour with Spymob.

In the same year the Neptunes signed an agreement that established their own record label, Star Trak Entertainment, and placed it under the wing of the record mogul Antonio Reid at Arista Records. (Reid later resigned from Arista.) Headed by the Neptunes and their manager, Rob Walker, Star Trak produces artists signed to Star Trak or Arista and signs and develops new talent. They have recruited to their label their fellow Virginians Fam-Lay, a rapper, and the rap duo Clipse (Malice and Pusha T). Clipse's album Lord Willin' (2002) debuted in the Top 10 on Billboard's album chart and has sold close to one million copies. In a review of Lord Willin' for Rolling Stone (September 5, 2002), Kathryn McGuire wrote, "[Clipse's] verses roll out with an infectious strut, but it's the beats backing them up, courtesy of hip-hop superproducers . . . the Neptunes, that elevate Malice and Pusha T's cocky gangsterisms to radio-hit heights." Clipse's second album, Hell Hath No Fury, will be released in 2004. Another Star Trak–signed talent, the R&B singer Kelis, has achieved a degree of fame with her highly acclaimed, Neptunes-produced debut album, Kaleidoscope (1999), and the Neptunes-produced song "Milkshake," which was listed in the Top 10 on several Billboard charts in late 2003 and early 2004. Others who record on the Neptunes' Star Trak label are the rock group High Speed Scene and the rapper Rosco P. Coldchain.

In 2003 the Neptunes released The Neptunes Present . . . Clones, which topped Billboard's album chart and sold more than 250,000 units during its first week in stores; it later achieved platinum status. The disk's single "Frontin'," for which Williams sang and Jay-Z rapped, debuted at number one on music charts in August 2003. Featured on Clones are such music stars as Ludacris, Dirt McGirt (the erstwhile Ol' Dirty Bastard), and Snoop Dogg. In Rolling Stone (September 4, 2003), Kelefa Sanneh wrote, "With appearances from most of the big-name rappers and wall-to-wall Neptunes beats, this should be the world's greatest hip-hop compilation—and much of the time it is." Oliver Wang, in LA Weekly (November 21–27, 2003), dubbed the Neptunes "hip-hop's new wave apostles," whose "sonic playfulness has helped them all but make the rest of today's hip-hop, R&B and pop production indistinguishable. . . . So why isn't their new *Clones* album better than it is?" After describing the track "Light Your Ass on Fire" as "all lit up in screaming sirens and jangling guitar hooks," Wang wrote, "But Vanessa Marquez's painfully thin 'Good Girl' isn't even demo good, and N.O.R.E.'s 'Put 'Em Up' seems destined for strip clubs only. . . . The balance of *Clones* still gets a passing grade, but whatever the album boasts in competence it still lacks in adventure." In 2004 the Soul Train Music Awards honored *Clones* as best R&B/soul album by a group, band, or duo.

Fly or Die (2004), the second N.E.R.D. album, quickly jumped to a spot in the Top 10 on *Billboard*'s album chart. For *Fly or Die* Hugo and Williams handled more of the instrumentation while blending aspects of rock, rap, soul, and hip-hop. According to a biography of N.E.R.D. on artistdirect.com, *Fly or Die* reaffirms that the group is "unrelenting in their knack for the absurd." For example, artistdirect.com continued, the video for the album's first single, "She Wants to Move," shows the N.E.R.D. trio in the "derriere" of an imaginary space vessel shaped like a woman's body. David Browne, in *Entertainment Weekly* (April 2, 2004), opined that *Fly or Die* is "craftier and more multilayered" than N.E.R.D.'s first album, and described it as a "set of clever, complex, studio-crafted pop—complete with musicianly, smooth-jazz licks—that doesn't owe allegiance to any one genre." Hugo, Williams, and Shay are not afraid, Browne wrote, "to thrash a melody one minute, caress it with suave harmonies the next, toss in fusion jazz piano, and set it all to beats (with real drums) that truly swing." In a review for Amazon.com, Aidin Vaziri wrote that *Fly or Die* revealed the influence of "Duran Duran's silk-spun new wave classics and the Beatles' strapping psychedelic epics," and praised the album as a "bustling, bumping disc highlighted by rowdy tracks like 'She Wants to Move' and 'Jump.' . . . The nu-metal crunch of the last album gives way to a more suitable '70s vibe, making the band sound like an unholy cross between Sly & The Family Stone and E.L.O.—as filtered through A Tribe Called Quest. That's a good thing." In conjunction with the release of *Fly or Die*, N.E.R.D. appeared as the guest band on *Saturday Night Live* and toured the country for two months.

In the VH1 interview Hugo called the Neptunes' remix of Sade's popular song "By Your Side" their most drastic overhaul of an existing song. In 2002 it was nominated for a Grammy Award. Williams collaborated with Sean "Puffy" Combs, also known as P. Diddy, and Lenny Kravitz to create the song "Lose Your Soul." Among the other big-name artists or groups the Neptunes have worked with or have plans to produce are Alicia Keyes, Nelly Furtado, Counting Crows, No Doubt, Babyface, Lil' Kim, Bow Wow, Janet Jackson, Kid Rock, Toni Braxton, and Moby. Referring to the number and variety of their collaborations, Hugo told Joseph Patel for the MTV Web site, "Sometimes I find myself in the studio doing a song and I don't know who it's for."

In 2002 Hugo, having won praise for such songs as "Cross the Border," "Danger (Been So Long)," and "I Just Wanna Love U (Give it 2 Me)," shared with Dr. Dre the American Society of Composers, Authors and Publishers (ASCAP) award for songwriter of the year. In 2003 both the Neptunes and N.E.R.D. received *Vibe* Award nominations. With another three nominations in his own name, Williams led all performers at that year's *Vibe* Awards. Both Usher and Nelly won Grammy Awards in 2003 for Neptunes-produced songs ("U Don't Have to Call" and "Hot in Herre," respectively). As songwriters, Hugo and Williams were both nominated for Grammy Awards in 2004 for the songs "Beautiful," written with Calvin Broadus (known as Snoop Dogg), and "Excuse Me Miss," written with Shawn Carter (known as Jay-Z). As a singer, Williams (who tied with Jay-Z, Beyoncé, and Outkast as the individuals with the highest total number of nominations—six) also received two nominations for best rap/sung collaboration for the songs "Frontin'" and "Beautiful." Hugo received two individual nominations and three as a member of the Neptunes. The Neptunes earned the 2004 Grammy Award for producer of the year.

Williams told an MTV interviewer that he avoids basking in his own success. "You can't pay attention to that," he said. "That's cancerous. 'Cause then you start believing it and your [expletive] gets weak. You gotta always think, 'There's more to do.' You can't ever look over your shoulder and be like, 'You know what I did?' 'cause you didn't do it—you just did what every other artist did and the people [the fans] embraced it and made it what it was. It was the people."

Because Williams sings the hooks, or repeated themes, on a number of the tracks that the Neptunes have produced, he has appeared in several music videos; his image has appeared significantly more often than Hugo's in magazines and elsewhere. "We do what we do to make music," Hugo, who is married with two children, told an interviewer for rwdmag.com. "I would like to be out there more, but that is not my main thing. Pharrell does what he has to do and it's all good between us. I don't sing hooks; I'm more about production, so I can't expect to be in every video. I also have a family which I'm trying to see as much as possible which is why I'm rarely [in the limelight]. We are two individuals—that's what makes us the Neptunes." Williams told MTV, "I love making music . . . I love playing. The keyboard is my journal."

In 2003 Williams designed a limited-edition athletic shoe for Nike as part of a series the company commissioned from various artists. All proceeds from sales of the shoe will be donated to Goodwill's Good Books Program, which provides free books to children. Williams launched his own clothing line, BBC, or Billionaire Boys Club, in the summer of 2004. In his leisure time, Williams enjoys skateboarding. He and Hugo can be seen moving to their own music in the video for their recent single "She Wants to Move."

—C.F.T.

Suggested Reading: *Blender* p52 Apr. 2004, with photo; *Entertainment Weekly* p44+ Mar. 26, 2004, with photos, p62 Apr. 2, 2004, with photo; MTV Web site; n-e-r-d.com; *New York Times Magazine* p50+ Feb. 8, 2004, with photos; startrakmusic.com; VH1 Web site

Selected Recordings: *In Search Of . . .* , 2002; *The Neptunes Present . . . Clones*, 2003; *Fly or Die*, 2004

Courtesy of Pennsylvania State University

Newsom, Lee Ann

Oct. 26, 1956– Paleoethnobotanist; educator

Address: Pennsylvania State University, Dept. of Anthropology, 316 Carpenter Bldg., University Park, PA 16802

Working in a highly specialized field that is a synthesis of several disciplines, Lee Ann Newsom, a paleoethnobotanist and an associate professor of archaeological anthropology at Pennsylvania State University (commonly known as Penn State), gave perhaps the most concise explanation of what she does: "I am a specialist in a subfield known as 'environmental archaeology.' In my case, this means research based on analysis of ancient plant remains recovered from archaeological and paleon-tological deposits," she told students at Penn State during a commencement address she gave on May 17, 2003, as quoted on the school's Web site. Through that research Newsom seeks to answer questions concerning ancient environments and landscapes and, "where humans are concerned, topics like diet, nutrition, economies, and broader questions such as the origins of agriculture, sustainable land use practices, and more," as she explained in her address. Performing many of her investigations in southeastern North America and the Caribbean, Newsom has analyzed fossilized plants—sometimes no more than bits and fragments of waterlogged remains from archaeological sites—looking for clues to the ways in which prehistoric populations subsisted. In addition, she has spent a great deal of time examining ancient gourds, some more than 30,000 years old—the remnants of some of the earliest domesticated plants in North America. Based on her research, Newsom has put forth new theories regarding ancient populations' methods of cultivating gourds and using them to survive. Newsom is credited with discovering new ways of identifying and cataloguing early plant species. Some of her recent and current projects include examining 40,000-year-old, fossilized feces from mastodons, an ancient species related to the modern elephant; numerous samples from various places in the Caribbean where humans who had migrated from the Amazon region of South America, beginning in the first century B.C., established settlements; and parts of the infamous pirate Blackbeard's flagship *Queen Anne's Revenge*, which wrecked, in 1718, off the coast of what is now North Carolina. Her work constantly reminds Newsom of "the passage of time," she said during her commencement address, and opens a fascinating "window on a particular time, place, people." Newsom has co-edited or co-written several books, including *On the Land and Sea: Native American Uses of Biological Resources in the West Indies* (2003), on which she collaborated with Elizabeth S. Wing. Newsom received a prestigious MacArthur Fellowship in 2002.

Lee Ann Newsom was born on October 26, 1956 in Morocco, while her father worked in intelligence for the U.S. Navy; she grew up in the Jacksonville, Florida, area. "As long as I can remember, since I was at least about seven or eight years of age, I wanted to be an archaeologist. Thus having become one represents the fulfillment of a dream for me," Newsom said in the commencement address to the students at Penn State. In a profile of Newsom and her work that appeared on the Penn State Web site, she recalled for Charles Fergus, "I used to devour *National Geographic* and the Time-Life books on human origins. In the fourth grade, I wrote a report on Neanderthal people. And I've been interested in life sciences from the beginning." After graduating from high school, Newsom trained and worked as a paralegal. She later returned to school to study anthropology. While an undergraduate at the University of Florida, Newsom served as a volunteer at the Florida Museum of Natural History, located on the school's campus. The University of Florida's anthropology department then hired her as a secretary. She recalled that time to Fergus: "I basically typed up archaeologists' resumes. Finally they started giving me artifacts to sort out, and soon I got involved with my first wetsite project." That is, Newsom began searching among the sediments of ancient wet areas, including lakes, ponds, and swamps, for clues about earlier populations. She examined plant remains such as whole gourd squash seeds, hickory nuts, hazelnuts, and pieces of wood. She earned a bachelor's degree, in 1982, a master's degree, in 1986, and a Ph.D. degree, in 1993, all in anthropology, from the University of Florida.

Newsom worked as an associate professor of anthropology and plant biology, and served as curator of the Center for Archaeological Investigations, at Southern Illinois University at Carbondale, before taking her current teaching post, at Penn State, in 2001. Dean Snow, the head of Penn State's anthropology department, told James Young for the *Digital Collegian* (September 25, 2002), an on-line publication run by Penn State students, that Newsom was well liked and respected by both her students and colleagues. "She's one of the most likable people you could ever run into," Snow told Young. At Penn State Newsom has taught a range of courses, including Introduction to Archaeology, Evolution of American Indian Culture, Hunters and Gatherers, Environmental Archaeology, and Wood Anatomy and Variation.

Because there are so few paleoethnobotanists, Newsom and her colleagues often work on several projects simultaneously. She told students during her commencement address that this practice makes her research—which combines biogeographic theory, evolutionary ecology, archaeological fieldwork, and paleoethnobotanical analysis—"hectic" but "very interesting." Among her other projects, Newsom has been examining 12,000-year-old samples from a Paleoindian site—Paleoindians being the first people to cross from northeast Asia to the North American continent over a land bridge during the last Ice Age. The Paleoindians hunted mastodons with spears. Newsom has also been researching samples taken from an 8,000-year-old cemetery found at the bottom of a pond in central Florida, and from a site on the north coast of Haiti, a Taino Indian settlement that marks the spot where Christopher Columbus's famous ship *Santa Maria* ran aground in 1492. Some of the samples from the ancient cemetery in Florida were sealed in sediments inside teepee-style burial structures and so, in some cases, were remarkably well preserved. Seeds found preserved in the stomach of a woman buried in that cemetery allowed Newsom to make reasonable hypotheses regarding the use of medicinal plants at the time. In addition, the presence of gourd remains—some of them more than 30,000 years old—at the ancient cemetery in Florida and other sites in North Ameri-

ca indicate that natives of North America may have begun practicing agriculture earlier than anthropologists previously thought. From the site in Haiti, Newsom and her colleagues have recovered bones and seeds from various European animals and plants, along with the remains of native flora and fauna. Fragments with European provenance may represent La Navidad, the first European settlement in the New World, established by shipwrecked members of one of Columbus's expeditions.

Regarding the people who lived at the settlement in Haiti, Newsom mused aloud to students during her commencement address, "How might it have felt to spend the light of the day cultivating manioc and tropical fruits, or in a dugout canoe fishing for snapper on a beautiful coral reef? . . . And what must it have been like to be a member of a small Caribbean village in Haiti in 1492 and look up to see on the horizon two massive Spanish sailing ships?" In reference to her study of wood remains from Blackbeard's ship, she said, "Or imagine pirates on the *Queen Anne's Revenge* in the spring of 1718, down in the hold of the ship celebrating a successful raid on the port of Charleston, accidentally dropping gold dust onto the floor, where it lodged between the cracks of the ship's timbers until found by archaeologists almost 300 years later." Regarding her expertise at examining old wood samples such as the pieces of timber recovered from the *Queen Anne's Revenge*, Newsom told *Lazine*, a publication of the Penn State College of Liberal Arts, as the article appeared on the Penn State Web site, "I can see wood, see the anatomy. If you tell me a type [of wood], I can visualize it immediately." Newsom expects to be able eventually to tell what kind of wood was used to make the pirate ship, and where the wood might have originated, thus uncovering new information about an intriguing piece of history. Newsom revealed to *Current Biography* that through her knowledge of wood, she has contributed, on an avocational basis, to studies of more than 250 shipwrecks—and that her interest in shipwrecks, ships, and the wood used to build them is fueled by her grandfather's tales of working as a carpenter in the naval shipyards in Belfast, Northern Ireland.

The projects in which Newsom is involved are supported by the National Science Foundation, the National Geographic Society, the Heinz Family Foundation, and the Consejo para la Proteccion del Patrimonio Arqueologico Terrestre de Puerto Rico, among other organizations. Working with Newsom are archaeologists, geologists, soil specialists, and palynologists, among other experts, from Mexico, Europe, the Caribbean, and the U.S.

Along with E. J. Reitz and S. J. Scudder, Newsom co-edited the book *Case Studies in Environmental Archaeology* (1996). She co-wrote, with Elizabeth S. Wing, *On the Land and Sea: Native American Uses of Biological Resources in the West Indies*, which was published by the University of Alabama Press in 2003. Newsom has also written or co-written a number of scientific articles, including "Windover Paleoethnobotany," which appeared in *Windover: Multidisciplinary Investigations of an Archaic Cemetery* (2002), edited by Glen H. Doran, and, with Deborah Pearsall, "Temporal and spatial trends indicated by a survey of Archaic- and Ceramic-Age archaeobotanical data from the Caribbean islands," which was published in *People and Plants in Ancient North America* (2002), edited by Paul E. Minnis.

In her 2003 commencement address at Pennsylvania State University, Newsom spoke of the inspiration young children have gained by observing and even assisting her work first hand, and she told the students in the audience to follow their dreams. Quoting one of her grandfathers, an Irish immigrant to the United States, she exhorted them, "If you can't find a rainbow, paint your own!"

—C.F.T.

Suggested Reading: Pennsylvania State University Web site

Selected Books: as editor—*Case Studies in Environmental Archaeology* (with E. J. Reitz and S. J. Scudder), 1996; as writer—*On the Land and Sea: Native American Uses of Biological Resources in the West Indies* (with Elizabeth S. Wing), 2003

Tony Gerber/Courtesy of the Theatre Communications Group

Nottage, Lynn

(NOT-idge)

Nov. 2, 1964– Playwright

Address: c/o Dramatists Play Service, 440 Park Ave. S., New York, NY 10016

"It is always a struggle as an African-American writer to find a home," the playwright Lynn Nottage commented during an interview for Kentucky Educational Television (KET), posted on the station's Web site. "I mean, there is a reluctance to produce our work because it is unfamiliar. . . . It's an ongoing struggle." Nevertheless, over the course of the past decade, doors to the theater world have opened for Nottage in many places, not only in the U.S. but overseas as well. Her plays, which explore various aspects of African-American experience, have made her "a darling of the nonprofit theater," according to Peter Marks in the *Washington Post* (July 6, 2004). One of the nation's most talented and critically acclaimed young playwrights, Nottage has received fellowships and awards for her writing, which she regards as an exercise in both creativity and political responsibility. "I want people to know that my story, that of the African-American woman, is also the American story," she told the KET interviewer. During a conversation with Vicki Sanders for *Brown Alumni Magazine* (September/October 2003, on-line), she said, "It's my historical mission and desire to rescue characters from obscurity. . . . We have to sing ourselves into existence, and the fact that more and more of us are doing so is a form of advocacy."

Nottage considers herself "an old-fashioned storyteller," as Jan Breslauer wrote for the *Los Angeles Times* (September 8, 1996). "I'm a contemporary playwright in a postmodern world," she told Jason Zinoman for the *New York Times* (June 13, 2004). Although some critics have faulted Nottage for what they see as an occasional failure to establish cohesive story lines or depict fully rounded characters and for a tendency to overwrite, in recent years reviews of Nottage's work have been overwhelmingly positive. In the *New York Times* (April 12, 2004), Margo Jefferson expressed admiration for her "big-hearted plays." Michael Feingold, writing for the *Village Voice* (January 6, 1998), described Nottage as "a playwright of spirit and surprise" and applauded "the vivacity with which she approaches the grimmest subjects."

The elder of two children, Lynn Nottage was born on November 2, 1964 and grew up in the New York City borough of Brooklyn. Her ancestors include natives of the West Indies. Her father, Wallace Nottage, was a psychologist, and her mother, Ruby Nottage, a teacher; her brother is a lawyer. Nottage has credited her parents with instilling in her an early interest in both social activism and the arts. "My parents are avid consumers of art, collectors of African American paintings and have always gone to the theater," she told Jan Breslauer in 1996. "My mother has always been an activist too. As long as I can remember, we were marching in lines." (Ruby Nottage died in 1997.) Nottage has traced her interest in storytelling to her childhood, when she spent many hours listening to female family members and neighbors entertain one another with stories. "I think for me the journey begins downstairs at the kitchen table of my house," she told the KET interviewer. "Down there was a gathering place for so many women. . . . And they all had stories to tell. . . . I think that is where I got all of my inspiration as a writer."

While growing up, Nottage yearned to explore areas of New York City outside Brooklyn. She got the chance to do so when she enrolled at the High School of Music and Art, which was then located in the Harlem section of Manhattan. (Admission to Music and Art, one of the city's four specialized high schools, is competitive. In 1984, when it moved to Lincoln Center, also in Manhattan, the school's name was changed to Fiorello H. LaGuardia High School of Music & Art and Performing Arts.) While in high school Nottage developed an interest in musical theater and wrote plays in her journal. In 1981, along with three other students chosen for the project, she wrote an original musical for the school's young-playwrights' festival.

An excellent student, Nottage was accepted at Brown University, in Providence, Rhode Island. Her high-school guidance counselor discouraged her from attending, however, suggesting that she might feel more comfortable at a state college than at an Ivy League university like Brown, where she would be among only a handful of minority students. Nottage ignored the counselor's advice and enrolled at Brown as a premedical major, with a concentration in marine biology. Before long she became dissatisfied with her course of study and abandoned the sciences in favor of a major in English literature and creative writing. During her senior year she took a course in playwriting with a professor named John Bass, whose ideas made an indelible impression on her. "What [Bass] taught me," Nottage told the KET interviewer, "was the joy of ritual. He taught me that, through playwriting, we could discover our ancestors. We could explore issues. We could find our history."

After she graduated from Brown, in 1986, Nottage enrolled in the playwriting program at the Yale School of Drama, in New Haven, Connecticut. She was reluctant to commit to playwriting as a career, however. As she told Jan Breslauer, "It was absolutely the worst time of my life, and I can say that with no hesitation. . . . I hadn't fully formed the notion of what I wanted to do. I felt playwriting was extremely decadent and useless." In 1989 Nottage received a master of fine arts degree in playwriting from Yale. Back in New York, she took a job as the national press officer for the human-rights organization Amnesty International. For four years

she wrote press releases, op-ed articles, and speeches for the group. While she loved her work, she felt that her artistic abilities were languishing. Determined to reawaken her creativity, she returned to playwriting. She found that thanks to her time away from the theater, she had developed a new perspective on writing and a willingness to experiment. "The plays that I wrote prior to leaving tend to be more serious and didactic," she told Jan Breslauer. "After, I discovered my sense of humor. The plays' subject matter was just as serious, but the strategy was less serious."

In 1992 Nottage wrote a monologue for *A . . . My Name Is Still Alice*, a feminist musical revue. That same year she wrote—in one sitting—a short play for a contest sponsored by the Actors Theatre of Louisville (ATL), in Kentucky. Entitled *Poof!*, the piece "wrote itself," as Nottage recalled during the KET interview, "and it was a joy to rediscover this creativity that was inside of me." *Poof!* is a dramatic comedy about a homemaker named Loureen whose abusive husband, Samuel, spontaneously combusts when she damns him to hell during an argument. When all that remains of him is a pile of ashes, Loureen calls her friend Florence to help her assess the situation. Happy but cautious, she and Florence celebrate Samuel's disappearance. They then plot to use Loureen's powerful voice against Florence's husband, who is also abusive. "That's the essence of the play: women finding the voice to stand up to domestic violence," Rich Copley wrote for the *Lexington (Kentucky) Herald Leader* (October 5, 2003). For *Poof!*, Nottage was a co-winner of the ATL's 1992 Heideman Award. The play premiered in a production at the ATL's 1992–93 Humana Festival. Since then, *Poof!* has been produced in countries all over the world and translated into German and Welsh, among other languages. A 45-minute adaptation of *Poof!* for television, starring Rosie Perez as Loureen and Viola Davis as Florence, aired on PBS in 2003.

"I don't think I made a commitment to being a writer until I finished *Poof!* . . . ," Nottage told the KET interviewer. "I don't think until I put the last punctuation mark on the last sentence in *Poof!* that I decided that this is what I am going to do." From 1992 to 1993 Nottage was a resident artist at Mabou Mines, an avant-garde theater company in New York City. Faced with the difficulty of choosing between her full-time job and her art, she settled upon the latter, quitting Amnesty International and working as a temp to support herself. Around that time she joined Playwrights Horizons, a writers' theater dedicated to supporting contemporary American playwrights, composers, and lyricists. A number of African-American writers had already gravitated to the organization, and Nottage found a nurturing professional community there.

In 1994 Nottage completed a play, called *Por'knockers*, about a revolutionary sect that accidentally kills a group of children while attacking a federal building. An exploration of the tension between political theory and practice,

Por'knockers was mounted at the Vineyard Theater, in New York City, in November 1995. The little attention it attracted among critics was less than favorable. Ben Brantley, in the *New York Times* (November 21, 1995), called it "a short, ambitious and very muddled new play," complaining that as the characters "talk and talk and talk, the emotional tension that is the first requisite of this sort of drama drowns in a bog of words."

In 1995 Nottage received a commission from Second Stage Theatre, in New York City, to write a play for a program aimed at teenage audiences. The result was *Crumbs from the Table of Joy*, a period piece set in the 1950s, whose title comes from a poem by Langston Hughes. Written for a multi-generational audience of teenagers and adults, the play received its world premiere in May 1995 at Second Stage. A "charming coming-of-age fable," according to Kyle Lawson in the *Arizona Republic* (November 5, 2000), *Crumbs from the Table of Joy* is about a teenager named Ernestine, whose widowed father, Godfrey, uproots her and her younger sister from their home in Pensacola, Florida, and transplants them to a predominantly white neighborhood in Brooklyn. Trouble ensues when Lily, Godfrey's sister-in-law, a brassy, free-thinking, hard-drinking feminist and Communist, arrives unannounced from Harlem and moves in, having promised her late sister that she would take care of the girls.

Nottage based the plot of *Crumbs from the Table of Joy* on the experiences of her godsister, who, like Ernestine, moved from Florida to Brooklyn shortly after her mother's death, lived with a feisty aunt, and later had a white, German stepmother. Nevertheless, Nottage told the KET interviewer that she regarded the play as "an allegory about the civil rights movement, about the women's rights movement." Some critics expressed admiration for what Ken Keuffel, in the *Winston-Salem (North Carolina) Journal* (February 24, 2002), called "Nottage's poetic and often funny script." Another enthusiastic assessment came from Karen D'Souza, who, in the *San Jose (California) Mercury News* (June 24, 2000), described the play as a "mesmerizing reverie on race, family and class" and praised its "sheer theatrical firepower." Other reviewers were less favorably impressed. In the *Philadelphia Inquirer* (February 11, 2000), Clifford A. Riley criticized the play as "slight and imperfect at best," declaring, "Crumbs, indeed." In the *Los Angeles Times* (September 23, 1996), Laurie Winer wrote, "Innocent of boring the audience . . . [Nottage] is guilty of being pleased with the sound of her own sentences." Still, Winer added that Nottage "[showed] promise, both as a prose writer and a playwright." Similarly, Greg Evans, in *Variety* (June 26, 1995–July 9, 1995), noted that "the play contains some exquisite passages that, although never really coalescing, make Nottage a playwright to watch." Despite mixed reviews, *Crumbs from the Table of Joy* was nominated for an NAACP award and a Black Theatre Alliance award, and quickly became "one of the most performed plays on the regional theater circuit," according to Anne Marie Walsh in the *San Diego Union-Tribune* (February 12, 2001).

Nottage's 1996 play, *Mud, River, Stone*, focuses on a middle-class, African-American couple who, while vacationing in Mozambique, find themselves stranded in an old colonial hotel with a taciturn black bellhop and a white African businessman. When a monsoon hits the area, a Nigerian aid worker and a Belgian anthropologist check in. Taking advantage of the circumstances, the bellhop, a demobilized soldier, takes the five others hostage and demands, in return for their freedom, grain for his village and a wool blanket for his mother. The play, which was inspired by a 1994 *New York Times* article about demobilized soldiers in Mozambique, ends on a pessimistic note, suggesting a "grim view . . . of Africa's future," according to Michael Feingold. During the KET interview, Nottage described *Mud, River, Stone* as a way of "dealing with my own romanticized notion" of Africa. "The play is really about my search for some sort of understanding of this place—where I have this genetic and emotional connection, but also this great distance," she explained.

Mud, River, Stone was mounted in the fall of 1996 at the Studio Arena Theatre of Buffalo, in New York State, and had its official world premiere in April 1997, in a production by the Acting Company at Montclair State University, in New Jersey. For that play, Nottage was named a finalist for the Susan Smith Blackburn Prize (which each year honors a woman who has written "a work of outstanding quality for the English-speaking theatre," according to the Smith Blackburn Prize Web site). Michael Feingold praised the script, declaring, "Each of Nottage's characters is a rich bundle of ideas and issues, as well as a sharp but sympathetic psychological portrait." In contrast, Peter Marks, in the *New York Times* (December 16, 1997), criticized the play as overly didactic: "Ms. Nottage is more concerned here with issuing position papers than with plot development. Her characters are not so much living, breathing people as walking, talking points of view."

In October 1997 the world premiere of Nottage's next play, *Las Meninas,* was mounted at the Stuart Theatre at Brown University. *Las Meninas* is about an illicit romance that is said to have taken place in 1661 between Queen Marie-Thérèse, the wife of Louis XIV of France, and her African servant, Nabo, a dwarf from Dahomey, in West Africa. The alleged liaison produced a child named Louise Marie, who was sent to live in a convent, where she eventually became a nun. Nottage spent nearly eight years engaged in research for the play, whose title is that of a famous painting by the great 17th-century Spanish artist Diego Velázquez. (The painting depicts a different royal family and various servants, including a dwarf.) "What fascinated me about this story," Nottage told the KET interviewer, "is that these people [Nabo and Louise Marie] were part of the historic record, but over the

course of the next 100 years they were very carefully erased. . . . I find that so many people from the
African Diaspora find themselves marginalized by
history. Completely erased from history. And part
of my mission as a writer is to sort of resurrect
some of these figures." Like its predecessors, *Las
Meninas* received mixed reviews. Steven Winn,
writing for the *San Francisco Chronicle* (March 25,
2002), found the play to be peppered with "flashes
of passion, energy and cheeky wit" but "more static
artifact than flowing drama." Dennis Harvey, in
Variety (April 1–7, 2002), wrote that while the play
"doesn't penetrate deeply into the hidden chapters
of Euro-African colonization, . . . it does provide
an entertaining two hours' historical exotica." Other reviews were more positive. The play earned for
Nottage both an AT&T OnStage Award and a
Rockefeller grant.

Nottage collaborated with her husband, the independent filmmaker Tony Gerber, to write the
script for Gerber's feature film *Side Streets* (1998).
The movie, which includes scenes set in each of
the five boroughs of New York City, consists of a
series of intertwined tales featuring people from
diverse ethic and racial backgrounds. Emanating
from Merchant Ivory Productions, *Side Streets* was
an official selection at the Venice and Sundance
Film Festivals. In 1999–2000 Nottage had a year-
long residency at Freedom Theatre, in Philadelphia, Pennsylvania, supported by a grant from the
National Endowment for the Arts and the Theatre
Communications Group. Her children's musical, *A
Walk through Time*, was mounted by Freedom
Theatre in 2000. In 2002 Nottage contributed a skit
to *Snapshot*, a collaborative project by the ATL
that offered works by 17 playwrights. Nottage's
skit, *Becoming American*, was a comedy about an
instructor of telephone-support personnel, who
teaches his Ghanaian recruits how to sound
American for the brief duration of a telephone call.

Nottage's full-length play *Intimate Apparel* debuted at Center Stage, in Baltimore, Maryland, in
2003. In preparing to write the play, which takes
place in 1905, Nottage spent about a year and a half
perusing items in the collections of the New York
Public Library, poring over African-American society pages and classified ads from the early 1900s.
The protagonist of *Intimate Apparel* is a successful, 35-year-old black seamstress named Esther,
whose character is based on Nottage's great-
grandmother Ethel Boyce Armstrong. Esther lives
in a Manhattan boardinghouse and sews intimate
apparel for prostitutes and wealthy socialites. Suppressing her romantic feelings for an Orthodox
Jewish fabric merchant named Mr. Marks, she falls
in love with George, a West Indian who is working
on the construction of the Panama Canal, with
whom she exchanges letters. Esther is illiterate, so
she enlists the help of her clients to keep up her
end of the epistolary courtship, which results in
George's coming to New York to marry her. The
match quickly turns sour, however: unemployed,
George squanders Esther's savings on prostitutes

and half-baked investments, and Esther leaves him
to begin anew. "It is to playwright Nottage's credit," Frederick M. Winship wrote in a review for
United Press International (May 1, 2004), "that she
does not give us an explicit ending to Esther's
quest for happiness, leaving the audience to relish
its own ideas of what lies in store for her." *Intimate
Apparel* was received warmly by other critics as
well. In 2003 Nottage became the first African-
American woman since Lorraine Hansberry to win
the New York Drama Critics Circle Award for best
play. (Hansberry was honored for *A Raisin in the
Sun* in 1959.) Nottage's other awards for *Intimate
Apparel* included the Outer Critics Circle Award
for outstanding Off-Broadway play, the John Gass-
ner Award, an AT&T OnStage Award, the $10,000
Francesca Primus Prize, and the $15,000 American
Theatre Critics Association's Steinberg New Play
Award. In addition, Nottage's script was included
in the collection *The Best Plays of 2003–2004*, edited by Jeffrey Eric Jenkins.

Simultaneously with her work on the script for
Intimate Apparel, Nottage wrote a companion
piece, *Fabulation, or the Re-Education of Undine*,
which treats similar themes but takes place nearly
a century later. In comparing the two plays, Nottage told Jason Zinoman, "*Intimate Apparel* is a
lyrical meditation on one woman's loneliness and
desire. . . . *Fabulation* is a very fast-paced play, of
the MTV generation." *Fabulation* is about a successful black publicist, Undine, who has spent
years erasing her past. Born Sharona Watkins and
raised in a low-income neighborhood, she has
changed her name to that of the heroine of an Edith
Wharton novel (*The Custom of the Country*) and
told her friends that her parents died in a fire long
ago. After her husband, who is Hispanic, absconds
with all their money, leaving her penniless and
pregnant, Undine is forced to return to her family's
home in a Brooklyn housing project. She is caught
buying drugs for her grandmother, a heroin addict,
and ordered to join a drug-therapy group, entering
a world that she has spent her life trying to avoid.
Surrounded by welfare mothers and drug addicts,
pitted against New York's social-services system in
her quest for financial assistance and employment,
Undine must come to terms with her past as she
makes plans for her future and that of her unborn
child.

Previews for *Fabulation* began on June 3, 2004
at Playwrights Horizons' Peter Jay Sharp Theater;
the play received its world premiere on June 13.
Thanks to the success of *Intimate Apparel*, which
earned Nottage the respect of Playwrights Horizons' subscribers and other theatergoers, the show
sold out before it opened. While some critics found
fault with the script—Peter Marks called it "a bit
unwieldy," Ben Brantley mentioned "overextended monologues," and Frederick M. Winship, writing for United Press International (July 18, 2004),
detected "an occasional lack of focus"—
Fabulation received mostly enthusiastic reviews,
even from some of the complainers. "Nottage may

have at last found her true voice, and it is one laced with sardonic wit," Peter Marks wrote. Ben Brantley praised the play's "syncopated breeziness" and labeled *Fabulation* "one of the livelier comedies available at the moment."

In 2004 Nottage earned a PEN/Laura Pels Foundation Award for Drama, which included a $5,000 prize. The judges praised her "gorgeously written, richly conceived plays," declaring that "Nottage has serious respect for her craft; her plays eschew the cheap and flashy; they're built to last," according to an article in *BackStage* (May 7, 2004).

Lynn Nottage met her husband, Tony Gerber, at Brown University when both were students there. Gerber is descended from Eastern European Jews. (Unbeknownst to them at the time, his father and Nottage's mother grew up within the same square mile of the Crown Heights section of Brooklyn.) The couple live with their daughter, Ruby Aiyo (born on October 2, 1997), in Brooklyn, on the top two floors of the same house in which Nottage spent her childhood; her father, who is retired, lives downstairs. Nottage is a visiting lecturer on playwriting at the Yale School of Drama and a member of New Dramatists and the Artists' Advisory Committee of the New York Foundation for the Arts. She is currently working on a play about social tensions between dark-skinned and light-skinned African-American women in 1950s New York and has expressed interest in writing a modern adaptation of Bertolt Brecht's 1941 play, *Mother Courage and Her Children.*

—L.W.

Suggested Reading: *Brooklyn Rail* (on-line) June 2004; *Brown Alumni Magazine* (on-line) Sep./Oct. 2003; *Cleveland Jewish News* (on-line) Aug. 1, 2003; Kentucky Educational Television Web site; *Los Angeles Times* Sep. 8, 1996, Apr. 13, 2003; *Orlando (Florida) Sentinel* Apr. 11, 2004

Selected Plays: *Poof!*, 1992; *Por'knockers*, 1994; *Crumbs from the Table of Joy*, 1995; *Mud, River, Stone*, 1996; *Las Meninas*, 1997; *Intimate Apparel*, 2003; *Fabulation, or the Re-Education of Undine*, 2004

Okrent, Daniel

(OH-krint)

Apr. 2, 1948– Public editor of the New York Times

Address: New York Times, *229 W. 43d St., New York, NY 10036*

In late 2003, in the aftermath of scandals involving reporters at the nation's most prominent newspaper, the *New York Times*, the management of the 152-year-old publication created the position of public editor, for the purpose of safeguarding the paper's integrity and helping to repair the damage to its reputation. According to Jacques Steinberg's report in the *Times* (October 27, 2003), Bill Keller, the paper's executive editor, wrote in an internal E-mail message that he wanted the public editor to be "someone smart, curious, rigorous, fair-minded and independent" who had the "reporting skills to figure out how decisions get made at the paper, the judgment to reach conclusions about whether and where we go astray, and the writing skills to explain all of this to our readers." Daniel Okrent, Keller declared, "fits the bill." The choice was unusual, in that those chosen for equivalent positions (often called ombudsmen) at other newspapers are most often picked from within those papers' ranks, while Okrent—with the exception of his stint in the 1960s as a college-campus reporter for the *Times*—had never been a newspaperman. As Okrent said to Brooke Gladstone in an interview for the WNYC radio program *On the Media* (October

Courtesy of Daniel Okrent

31, on-line), "There are things that you take for granted if you're part of a culture, whether it's the newsroom culture of the *Times* or the news culture generally, that can give you a hermetic feeling. So coming from outside, yet being a journalist and knowing how to ask questions, I think I may be able to find out things and have a perspective that would be more parallel to the readers' perspective."

Okrent's background is in book and magazine publishing. He rose to the position of editor in chief of the book firm Harcourt Brace Jovanovich in the 1970s, then worked in important posts at *Time* and *Life* beginning in the following decade. In addition, he is the author or editor of a number of books, most of them about baseball. *The Ultimate Baseball Book* (1979), which he edited with Harris Lewine, has appeared in several editions. His volume *Nine Innings* (1985) is an account of a single game, and with Steve Wulf he wrote *Baseball Anecdotes* (1989). Okrent's *Great Fortune: The Epic of Rockefeller Center* (2003) gives a historical view of the section of New York that became Rockefeller Center, and features portraits of such notable figures as the architect Raymond Hood, the Mexican muralist Diego Rivera, and John D. Rockefeller Jr., whose creative financing made the landmark office and entertainment complex possible. With regard to his current position, Okrent told Brooke Gladstone, "I'm entering this being hopeful about people operating with good will. If they don't, there's nothing I can do about that. Certainly I don't want to damage anybody or any institution carelessly. But they have asked me to be honest. They have asked me to offer my opinion, and I feel compelled to do it."

Daniel Okrent was born April 2, 1948 in Detroit, Michigan, to the former Gizella Adler, a social worker, and Harry Okrent, an attorney. In the December 7, 2003 article in which he introduced himself to readers of the *New York Times* as public editor, Okrent wrote that he is a Democrat "by upbringing." (He added that he remains one, by "habit.") As he recalled in a lecture he delivered at Columbia University, as quoted in *Digital Journalist* (on-line), reading the newspaper was an important part of his family life during his boyhood. "I remember what it was like when I was a child, and my father brought home the newspaper after work," he said. "My mother would take what we called in those distant, benighted days the women's section—recipes, fashion news, the advice columns. My older brother, who was readying himself for a business career—he took the stock market pages. I reached for sports, the news of the athletic wonders committed daily by my heroes. My father had the general news section, and we'd each disappear into our own engagements with the wider world, regrouping in time for dinner and a shared conversation about what we had encountered in the daily paper." Okrent attended Cass Technical High School, in Detroit, where his extracurricular activities included theater; he played Harvey Johnson in the school's production of *Bye Bye Birdie*. He took up journalism as a student at the University of Michigan. During that time, the politically turbulent 1960s—which Okrent called "that hyperventilated era"—he was a "not-very-good" campus correspondent for the *New York Times*, as he wrote self-deprecatingly in his December 7, 2003 article: "I was . . . a little on the lazy side, rarely willing to make the third or fourth phone call to confirm the accuracy of what I'd been told on the first one. Instead I expended my energies . . . as a shamelessly partisan and embarrassingly inaccurate reporter for my college newspaper. . . . I got fairer, and better, as I got older."

After graduating with a B.A. degree, in 1969, Okrent moved to New York City, where he went to work in the editorial department of the book-publishing house Alfred A. Knopf. From 1973 to 1976 he was editorial director of a division of Viking Press, and during 1976 and 1977 he served as editor in chief of Harcourt Brace Jovanovich. Okrent then moved on to the magazine world, acting as publishing consultant for *Texas Monthly* until 1983, when he became the founding editor of *New England Monthly*. That publication garnered two National Magazine Awards for General Excellence. While serving as its editor, he also wrote a column for *Esquire*. In 1991 he moved to *Life*, where he had become managing editor by 1996, the year he took on the duties of editor of new media at Time Inc., the parent company of *Life*. His title there later changed to editor at large. During that period he wrote many articles for *Time* on topics that ranged from baseball to jazz to the computer giant Microsoft. (In 2001 *Life* closed.) Okrent was named a fellow in new media at the Columbia University School of Journalism, in New York, in 1999.

Concurrent with his career as a magazine editor, Okrent began writing and editing books of his own, mainly about baseball. He told *Contemporary Authors*, "I began to write by accident—I had always loved baseball, and devoted rather more time to it than was reasonable for a grown man. Editor friends, bemused by my passion, threw a little money at me to share it with a magazine public. Soon, I had talked myself into believing their entreaties were wise, and my first book was the result." He added, "I still don't consider myself a writer. . . . I have been an editor for too many years to believe that one is a writer simply by claiming to be one." In 1979, with Harris Lewine, Okrent compiled *The Ultimate Baseball Book*, a collection of essays about the sport by such distinguished writers as Tom Wicker, Red Smith, and Robert Creamer; the book has since appeared in several revised editions. In 1985 he published *Nine Innings: The Anatomy of a Baseball Game*, a detailed examination of a single 1982 contest between the Milwaukee Brewers and the Baltimore Orioles. His 1989 book *The Way We Were: New England Then, New England Now* contains photographs of the region taken between 1944 and 1951 and accompanied by Okrent's text. Okrent continued to cover his favorite sport in *Baseball Anecdotes* (1989), written with Steve Wulf. Christopher Lehmann-Haupt, reviewing the book in the *New York Times* (April 3, 1989), praised the authors for ignoring a number of "twice-told tales" and finding "fresh ways of handling those chestnuts they do include." Meanwhile, in 1980, Okrent had helped to invent rotisserie baseball. The name came from the New York restaurant where Okrent and a group of other, like-minded baseball fans gathered to simulate the owning and managing of baseball teams, choosing players from the real teams in the American and National Leagues based on the players' actual batting, pitching, and fielding records. Rotisserie baseball has since become a popular American pastime.

Okrent's 2003 book *Great Fortune: The Epic of Rockefeller Center* chronicled the building of a New York City complex derided at first and later recognized as an architectural masterpiece. Rockefeller Center currently houses the performance venue Radio City Music Hall and a number of shops and serves as the headquarters of General Electric and the NBC television network, among other concerns. The *Economist* (November 8, 2003) called the book an "obsessively detailed yet readable story about the transformation of 12 acres of speakeasies and flophouses in midtown Manhattan into a soaring city-within-a-city."

The year 2003 saw two scandals at the *New York Times*, one involving fabricated reports and plagiarism on the part of the journalist Jayson Blair, the other caused by the correspondent Rick Bragg's failure to acknowledge information provided by a freelancer for one of Bragg's articles. In July a new executive editor, Bill Keller, was appointed to replace Howell Raines. Keller, in turn, hired Okrent in October 2003 as the *Times*'s public editor. Okrent's mandate at the *New York Times* is to explain the newspaper's coverage to the public, to engage in discussion with readers, and to write columns detailing faults he himself might have found as a reader of news reports or opinion columns. According to Harry Berkowitz in New York *Newsday* (October 28, 2003), Okrent said that he won that position partly because he was an outsider, both to the *New York Times* and the newspaper business as a whole, having spent his career in magazine and book publishing. His being an outsider means that "I can ask stupid questions," Okrent said, according to Berkowitz. "Presumably, there's no conventional wisdom that I automatically buy into because I have a history in the place." He wrote in his inaugural column in the *Times* (December 7, 2003) that he was "the first person charged with publicly evaluating, criticizing and otherwise commenting on the paper's integrity." Okrent's tenure is scheduled to expire on May 29, 2005. ("If I were running for re-election," he wrote, "you'd have every reason to doubt my independence.") Okrent told an interviewer for *Newsweek* (December 29, 2003–January 5, 2004, on-line) that in the two days following the publication of his first column as public editor, he received 1,300 E-mail messages from readers.

In his next column (December 21, 2003), Okrent discussed the decision by *Times* editors to assign to a former reporter for the paper a story about the painkiller addiction of the radio personality Rush Limbaugh. The reporter, Barry Meier, had written earlier about the recreational use of the drug OxyContin and its having gone from being a drug for cancer patients to being a commodity on the underground market. Okrent found Meier's reporting on OxyContin to be "generally accurate and fair, even if the way some of the pieces were played . . . sometimes seemed the work of an especially ferocious terrier that had gotten its teeth into someone's ankle." The manufacturer of OxyContin, Purdue Pharma, on the other hand, complained about Meier's articles, which they called "sensationalized and skewed." Meier later left the *Times* to write a book (favorably reviewed in the paper) that was highly critical of the drug. In the fall of 2002, when Limbaugh revealed his addiction, Meier approached a *Times* editor about writing an article for the paper that would consider painkillers in the light of Limbaugh's experience and would mention OxyContin "only peripherally." The editor said yes, and the article ran; though Purdue Pharma representatives ultimately concluded that the article was fair, when approached for comment in connection with it, they complained that Meier's authorship of both the *Times* piece and his book amounted to a conflict of interest. This case, Okrent declared, did not have the importance of the occasion in 1963 on which the *Times* kept David Halberstam on as a Vietnam War correspondent after President John F. Kennedy asked for him to be reassigned. "A newspaper shouldn't take a reporter off a running story because of complaints from subjects if it doesn't find the complaints valid," Okrent concluded. "But neither should a newspaper automatically defend the principle when it is neither material nor mission-critical. Meier had not been covering Purdue Pharma or OxyContin for 18 months, and the paper and its readers could have been well served on the Limbaugh piece by one of the reporters currently on the beat. Certainly the paper's reputation could have been served by removing even the slightest hint of conflict. Assistant managing editor [Allan] Siegal acknowledges that giving Meier the go-ahead—which Meier properly sought under the *Times*'s own rules and procedures—was 'probably a mistake.'"

Okrent later arrived at a different conclusion with regard to a somewhat similar matter. Okrent disagreed with the *Times* editor Jill Abramson about the paper's coverage of Richard Clarke's testimony before the panel investigating inadequacies in U.S. antiterrorism efforts prior to the attacks of September 11, 2001, and its coverage of the almost-simultaneous appearance of Clarke's book on the same subject. Abramson's rationale for not giving front-page coverage to Clarke's book was that the *Times* should not promote books. "I disagree," Okrent wrote for the *Times*'s on-line message board. He maintained that if a news item is "consequential, it shouldn't matter where it comes from; whether or not you're promoting a book is less important than whether you're serving your readers."

Perhaps the most important piece by Okrent as public editor of the *Times* was his contribution to the newspaper's mea culpa involving its coverage of Iraq's supposed possession of weapons of mass destruction. Over a year after President George W. Bush declared victory in the 2003 war that was to rid Iraq of those weapons, they had still not been found; Okrent faulted the *Times* for accepting at face value much of the Bush administration's argument that Iraq possessed such weapons. Okrent's column titled "Weapons of Mass Destruction? or Mass Distraction?" (May 30, 2004) came a few days after the apology printed on the newspaper's editorial page. "Some of the *Times*'s coverage in the months leading up to the invasion of Iraq was credulous; much of it was inappropriately italicized by lavish front-page display and heavy-breathing headlines; and several fine articles . . . that provided perspective or challenged information in the faulty stories were played as quietly as a lullaby. . . . The *Times*'s flawed journalism continued in the weeks after the war began, when writers might have broken free from the cloaked government sources who had insinuated themselves and their agendas into the prewar coverage," Okrent wrote.

Okrent has even challenged the traditional designation of the *New York Times* as the "newspaper of record." On April 25, 2004 he quoted Bill Borders, a senior editor at the paper, as saying, "Long ago, the *Times* used to feel an obligation to print lots of things that we knew no one much would read—the new members of the Peruvian cabinet, for example—just to get them on the record. Fortunately those days are over." Okrent wrote, "With very few exceptions, the longer you've been [on the *Times* staff], or the higher you've risen in the organization, the less likely you are to believe *The Times* is, or should be, the paper of record."

Okrent displayed his impish sense of humor when he told of his brief appearance in Woody Allen's 2000 film *Sweet and Lowdown.* "You know me," he wrote in *Entertainment Weekly* (January 7, 2000). "I'm the guy with the goatee who captures the screen moments into . . . . Woody Allen's latest film." He went on to relate the story of his being chosen to appear in the movie: "Allen had some narrative problems with his picaresque tale of the . . . fictional 1930s jazz guitarist Emmet Ray. . . . The picture had wrapped, but he needed some talking heads to goose the story along by reminiscing about Emmet, as if he were a real historical figure. I can talk; I have a head; I'm a friend of . . . one of Allen's casting directors; I was hired."

Okrent lives on the Upper West Side of Manhattan with his wife, Rebecca Kathryn Lazear, a landscape designer and writer. They have a son and a daughter. In his *Entertainment Weekly* article, he noted that his friends referred to his wife as "LSB, or Long-Suffering Becky." In his first column as public editor of the *Times*, Okrent wrote about himself: "I'm a registered Democrat, but notably to the right of my fellow Democrats on Manhattan's Upper West Side. . . . I'm an absolutist on free trade and free speech, and a supporter of gay rights and abortion rights who thinks that the late Cardinal John O'Connor was a great man. I believe it's

unbecoming for the well off to whine about high taxes, and inconsistent for those who advocate human rights to oppose all American military action. I'd rather spend my weekends exterminating rats in the tunnels below Penn Station than read a book by either Bill O'Reilly or Michael Moore. I go to a lot of concerts. I hardly ever go to the movies. I've hated the Yankees since I was 6."

—C.T.

Suggested Reading: *Economist* p82 Nov. 8, 2003; *New York Times* C p21 Apr. 3, 1989, D p8 Feb. 8, 1993, B p2 Dec. 2, 1999, A p19 Oct. 27, 2003, 4 p2 Dec. 7, 2003; *Newsday* D p28 Oct. 19, 2003, A p57 Oct. 28, 2003

Selected Books: *The Ultimate Baseball Book* (with Harris Lewine), 1979; *Nine Innings*, 1985; *Baseball Anecdotes* (with Steve Wulf), 1989; *Great Fortune: The Epic of Rockefeller Center*, 2003

Getty Images

O'Malley, Sean Patrick

June 29, 1944– Archbishop of Boston

Address: Chancery, 2121 Commonwealth Ave., Boston, MA 02135-3193

On September 7, 2003 Sean Patrick O'Malley, the archbishop of Boston, reached a landmark settlement with 550 people who claimed to have been sexually abused by priests. The settlement was a crucial step in helping the U.S. Catholic Church confront what many regard as the worst scandal in its history. The archdiocese of Boston had been rocked in 2002, when it was revealed that the city's archbishop, Cardinal Bernard Law, had covered up for priests accused of sexually abusing children by moving them to new parishes and failing to report the accusations to the proper authorities. Under intense criticism from both clergy and laity, Cardinal Law resigned in disgrace in December 2002. (He remained a cardinal, thus retaining the right to assume another church post as well as vote in a papal election.) O'Malley was appointed six months later to lead the country's fourth-largest diocese out of the crisis and begin the process of rebuilding the laity's confidence in the Church.

O'Malley began handling abuse cases during the 1990s, when he served as archbishop of the Fall River, Massachusetts, diocese, where, in the biggest abuse scandal of the decade, a priest was accused of molesting more than 100 children. While there he implemented a zero-tolerance policy toward priests accused of sexual abuse, established abuse-education classes, and reached settlements with most of the victims. O'Malley did the same with the Palm Beach, Florida, diocese, where he served as archbishop from 2002 until his appointment in Boston. Many saw his installation in Boston as a sign that the Vatican had finally begun to take the crisis seriously. "It's really a watershed moment for a diocese to receive a new bishop," Reverend James A. Field, the pastor of the Parish of the Incarnation of Our Lord and Savior Jesus Christ, in Melrose, Massachusetts, told Michael Paulson for the Boston Globe (July 30, 2003). "The installation is a way of symbolizing that a new day has begun and that we have a new shepherd."

The Catholic Church in the U.S. is at a turning point in its history. In addition to the abuse crisis, the Church faces the closing of numerous schools and parishes due to declining numbers of students and parishioners, a shrinking pool of young priests, and low funds. Further, the ethnic makeup of the Church is changing in the U.S., as most new parishioners are immigrants who come from predominately Catholic countries. According to Monica Rhor in the Boston Globe (July 3, 2003), whites make up only half of all Catholic teenagers in America; within a few years, Latinos will make up the majority of Roman Catholics in the country. Many experts therefore believe that the future of the Catholic Church rests on the shoulders of immigrants. O'Malley, who holds a doctorate from the Catholic University of America, in Washington, D.C., and speaks six languages, has spent most of his career ministering to immigrant populations in the D.C. area, as well as in the U.S. Virgin Islands. Mario J. Paredes, one of O'Malley's coworkers at Centro Catolico Hispano, told Monica Rhor, "Rome made his appointment with all sorts of messages and meanings. He is being sent to a church that is no longer Irish, no longer the old boys. It is a church that is heavily Hispanic, heavily Portuguese, diverse, multicultural, and multilingual."

O'Malley's work with immigrants is part of his ministry as a Capuchin-Franciscan Friar. The Capuchin religious order is dedicated to following the teachings of the 13th-century Catholic mystic St. Francis of Assisi, an ascetic whose life was said to be characterized by humility, poverty, devotion, and joy. Members of the order live together in a community and take vows of poverty, chastity, and obedience; in addition to contemplation and prayer, they perform duties in accordance with the teachings of the New Testament. O'Malley was professed in the order at the age of 21 and ordained as a priest at 26. As a Capuchin, he wears sandals and a simple brown frock with a pointed hood, an outfit he wore even at his installation ceremony in Boston in 2003. He also insists on living in humble settings and refused to move into the archbishop's mansion, preferring instead a small apartment in an unfashionable section of the city. His views on Catholic life are orthodox; staunchly against abortion, he participates in the Church's annual rally in Washington, D.C. Above all else, O'Malley, who prefers to be called "Archbishop Sean," is known for his love of and commitment to the poor, his joyful demeanor, and his absolute devotion to others. As quoted by Linda Kulman, Jeff Glasser, Angela Marek, and Nancy L. Bentrup in U.S. News & World Report (July 14, 2003), Mary Ann Glendon, a member of the Pontifical Council for the Laity and a professor at the Harvard Law School, remarked after O'Malley's first press conference as archbishop, "[He] spoke words of great simplicity and power. This is really a case of what you see is what you get. The man radiates a certain kind of Franciscan personality that is going to be very, very good for wounded Boston."

The younger of the two sons of Theodore and Mary Louise O'Malley, Sean Patrick O'Malley was born on June 29, 1944 in Lakewood, Ohio, and raised in Herman, Pennsylvania. His family was devoutly Catholic and often participated in religious retreats. It was after one such occasion that O'Malley had a formative encounter with a friar: returning home from a visit to a Franciscan retreat in Pennsylvania, the 10-year-old and his father met a mendicant dressed in a tattered robe and wearing a rosary around his neck. Afterward Theodore O'Malley commented to his son, "You know, that's the happiest man in the world," as Sean O'Malley recalled to Eric Convey for the Boston Herald (July 28, 2003). The encounter left a deep impression on O'Malley, who had already expressed a profound interest in matters of faith. He began to seriously consider entering the religious life and, two years later, enrolled at St. Fidelis Seminary, in Herman (other sources say Butler), Pennsylvania. A boarding school for teenagers wishing to enter the Capuchin order, St. Fidelis required its students to undergo rigorous training in the foreign languages: six years of Latin, four years of German, two of Spanish, two of Greek, and one of Hebrew. While other students spent much of their time playing sports, O'Malley preferred to participate in the school's theatrical productions and help out in the kitchen, where German nuns prepared meals for students and their teachers. "He's always been very unusual, really," Jack Healey, a human-rights worker and fellow student at St. Fidelis, told Convey. "Most of us were ballplayers hoping to be priests one day. Sean was a little priest the whole way through . . . he was a little Franciscan the whole way through. He was the real thing from day one."

O'Malley was professed in the Capuchin order in 1965 and ordained as a priest in 1970. After graduating from St. Fidelis, he continued his studies at Capuchin College, in Washington, D.C. At the Catholic University of America, O'Malley earned a master's degree in religious education and a doctorate in Spanish and Portuguese literature. Between 1969 and 1973 he taught at Catholic University and planned to eventually pursue missionary work oversees. That plan changed in 1973, when the archbishop of D.C. asked the Capuchins to help minister to the city's growing Latino population. O'Malley subsequently founded Centro Catolico Hispano, which provided immigrants and others with legal advice, employment referrals, English-as-a-Second-Language (ESL) and GED classes, and medical and dental services. He also confronted foreign ambassadors serving in D.C. about the way they treated domestic help, transported medical supplies to Central American countries, doled out food and medicine to those in need, opened a Spanish-language bookstore, and founded the first Spanish newspaper in the area. This work, coupled with O'Malley's Sunday Masses in English, Spanish, Portuguese, and French, cemented his connection to immigrant communities, a connection that would become the hallmark of his career.

O'Malley's commitment to immigrants was particularly manifest in his work at the Kenesaw, a dilapidated apartment building located in Adams Morgan, then one of the most impoverished neighborhoods in the nation's capital. For decades the building's owner, the Antioch Law School, had refused to provide tenants with even the most basic services, such as heat, hot water, and pest control. Nevertheless, the school continued to collect rent from tenants. In addition, drug dealers worked out of several of the apartments, and prostitutes routinely brought customers to unoccupied rooms there. In 1977 Antioch, which was in financial trouble and hoped to renovate and sell the building, served the tenants with eviction notices. When he heard about the plight of the tenants, O'Malley himself moved into the Kenesaw, taking two rooms—one in which he slept on the floor and one that he turned into a chapel. "It was a dangerous place to live, believe me," the lawyer and Kenesaw community activist Silverio Coy told Alan Cooperman and Pamela Ferdinand for the *Washington Post* (July 2, 3002). "He wanted to make a statement that not only was he going to help these people, he was going to share their needs and anxieties every single day." O'Malley helped the tenants renovate the building and fight the eviction. Refusing to pay rent to Antioch, the tenants repaired, cleaned, and painted the Kenesaw. They also took turns using a baseball bat to patrol the area for rats and drug dealers. Eventually, O'Malley helped the tenants organize themselves into a cooperative, which allowed them to secure enough funding from public agencies and banks to buy the building themselves. "A lot of good people lived there, but they didn't coordinate anything before Father O'Malley came," Coy said. "He transformed their lives."

O'Malley's work in the Washington, D.C., diocese prompted his installation as an Episcopal vicar for the Hispanic, Portuguese, and Haitian communities, and as executive director of the archdiocesan Office of Social Ministry in 1978. Six years later the Vatican granted his wish to serve in a foreign mission by appointing him coadjutor bishop of St. Thomas, U.S. Virgin Islands; a year later he was made full bishop. While there he built shelters for the homeless, established an AIDS hospice, and helped islanders rebuild after Hurricane Hugo, in 1989. One parishioner, Charlene Kehoe, said that attending a midnight Mass held by O'Malley inspired her to return to the Catholic Church after an absence of several decades. "I would never have come back to the church except for him," she told Thomas Farragher for the *Boston Globe* (July 27, 2003). "I thought I had found something better than the church. It wasn't until [the midnight Mass] that I saw that, aha, the church can be really spiritual—to really have truth within it. He has the ability to connect emotionally with people and to really hear them—to let them say their piece and to figure out what the next step would be with a deep spiritual understanding."

The U.S. Catholic Church was first confronted with a major sexual scandal in 1985, when a Louisiana priest, Gilbert Gauthe, was sentenced to 20 years in prison for molesting children. In 1992 Reverend James Porter of the Fall River diocese was accused of sexually abusing dozens of boys in five different states during the 1960s and 1970s. (He later pled guilty to 28 counts of abuse and was sentenced to 18 to 20 years in prison.) The Vatican subsequently sent O'Malley there to serve as bishop of the diocese and to help the largely Latino and Portuguese population heal. He helped settle 101 cases that had been brought against the diocese, instructing the church's lawyers that "it was the right thing to do." The bishop then initiated a zero-tolerance policy against sexual abuse (a policy that included running background checks on all clergy and church personnel) and provided sexual-abuse training to priests and lay volunteers alike. In addition, O'Malley set up the diocese's first Latino parish, Nuestro Senora de Guadalupe.

Ten years later, in 2002, the Vatican called on O'Malley to restore order to another diocese in crisis. This time he was sent to Palm Beach, Florida, where two consecutive bishops had left after sex-abuse scandals. Bishop J. Keith Symons had resigned in 1998, after admitting that he had molested five boys in three parishes; his replacement, Reverend Anthony J. O'Connell, resigned four years later, after admitting that he had repeatedly molested an underage student at a Missouri seminary where he had served as rector. As bishop, O'Malley promised to report all allegations of abuse to the proper authorities and to remove all guilty priests from service. He also issued a public apology to the victims and appointed a sheriff and a rabbi to an independent review board that had earlier been formed to handle sex-abuse accusations.

O'Malley's work in Palm Beach was stopped short, however, when the Vatican called on him to take over the archdiocese of Boston, the city that was at the center of the Church's sex-abuse crisis. After the Massachusetts priest John Geoghan was convicted, in January 2002, of molesting a 10-year-old boy, Cardinal Bernard Law, who was then archbishop of Boston, insisted that, while the case was an isolated incident, he would act decisively on all future charges of pedophilia brought against priests. Soon thereafter, documents were released showing that over the years Geoghan had been accused of molesting boys at several different parishes—yet instead of removing him from office, Cardinal Law had repeatedly reassigned him. Upon further investigation, a pattern of deception began to emerge: Law had regularly failed to report sex-abuse allegations to the proper authorities, had moved accused priests to new parishes (where many continued to molest children), and had either ignored or paid off victims. Amid calls for his resignation from both lay people and clergy, Cardinal Law stepped down as archbishop of Boston on December 13, 2002.

On July 1, 2003, Pope John Paul II appointed O'Malley to the position. The Capuchin priest was characteristically humble upon hearing the news, remarking, as quoted on CNN (July 2, 2003, on-line), "I feel acutely aware of my own deficiencies in the face of the task at hand, and I ask for everyone's prayers and collaboration as I embark on this ministry." During his installation ceremony, a sober affair devoid of the usual pomp and finery, O'Malley asked for forgiveness from those who had suffered sexual abuse at the hands of Catholic priests: "The whole Catholic community is ashamed and anguished because of the pain and damage inflicted on so many young people and because of our inability or unwillingness to deal with the crime of sexual abuse of minors," he said, as quoted on the CBS News Web site (July 31, 2003). "To those victims and to their families, we beg forgiveness and assure them that the Catholic church is working to create a safe environment for young people."

O'Malley's first act as archbishop was to replace the church's lead council working on the hundreds of civil lawsuits facing the Boston diocese, sending a signal to the city's Catholics that settling the cases was his top priority. O'Malley chose Thomas Hannigan, the attorney who had helped him settle abuse claims in Fall River, to replace Wilson Rogers Jr., who had been criticized for using hardball tactics against the plaintiffs. Within nine days of being installed, O'Malley offered a $55 million settlement to be divided among the victims, nearly twice the amount any diocese or archdiocese had paid at one time to settle claims of abuse. Although the settlement was rejected, both lawyers and victims were impressed by O'Malley's speedy offer, particularly considering that Cardinal Law and his lawyers had stalled negotiations for 18 months. "Any negotiation has to start in a certain place, and this is a good place," Roderick MacLeish Jr., a lawyer representing 260 victims, told Ralph Ranalli and Stephen Kurkjian for the *Boston Globe* (August 9, 2003, on-line). "We believe that there is a lot of good faith being shown by the archdiocese. There are still a lot of obstacles, but we are finally having a worthwhile and constructive dialogue." Negotiations continued, with O'Malley personally attending the bargaining sessions. He also met with many of the victims in private.

On September 7, 2003, barely a month after O'Malley became archbishop, the Boston archdiocese reached a settlement with 550 people who claimed to have been sexually abused by members of the church. The victims received an $85 million compensation package to be divided among them according to the severity and duration of the abuse, the largest amount ever in a clergy sexual-abuse case. The settlement also stipulated that victims would be included on all boards governing abuse, that the church would offer the victims mental-health counseling regardless of whether they accepted the settlement or not, and that the details of all such counseling would be kept confidential. Many credit O'Malley with persuading the victims to accept the offer. In addition to changing lawyers and participating in the negotiating sessions, he won over many of the bitter victims through his attention, his patience, and his sensitivity. Many have said that they came to believe he truly cared about them. One example of O'Malley's personal attention to the victims was his response to the mental breakdown of a 25-year-old man who claimed he had been raped by a priest when he was five. After the breakdown, in September 2003, O'Malley immediately met with the man's parents and promised to do whatever was necessary to help their son, including paying for a residential treatment. A year earlier, Cardinal Law had sent a letter to the family in response to their lawsuit, suggesting that the parents' negligence had allowed the rape to occur. "It was a major change," the father told Kevin Cullen for the *Boston Globe* (September 10, 2003). "They reached out to my son at a time of need, no questions asked. This guy [O'Malley] has done everything he can since he got here to change the way things were done before, and he should get credit when he does the right thing." "Sean O'Malley has always struck people here as someone who puts people first, and there's no doubt in my mind that he will do so," Fall River's mayor, Edward M. Lambert, told Alan Cooperman and Pamela Ferdinand. "I don't think it's the safe choice for the church. But I certainly think it's the right one."

In his position as archbishop, O'Malley has weighed in on some of the more controversial moral issues of the day, and he has been critical of elected officials over such matters. For example, according to LifeSiteNews.com (January 23, 2004, on-line), O'Malley said regarding Catholic politicians, "These politicians should know that if they're not voting correctly on these life issues [such as abortion] that they shouldn't dare come to communion." As quoted by the *Catholic Online* (March 12, 2004), he addressed the issue of marriage and homosexuality. Referring to proposals brought before the Massachusetts State Legislature, which sought to link the definition of marriage as a union between one man and one woman with a law giving same-sex civil unions the same protection under the law as marriage, O'Malley said, "We support the Marriage Affirmation and Protection Amendment as it has been presented, without the introduction of civil unions language. The amendment seeks to protect a social institution that is essential to our society. A debate about social benefits given to other individuals in our law is a separate issue. . . . The amendment reaffirming marriage as the union between one man and one woman must be approved on its own merits. . . . Linking the two [proposals] coerces people in a way that is unfair." As quoted in the *Washington Times* (October 4, 2004), while speaking at the annual Red Mass at the Cathedral of St. Matthew the Apostle, in Washington, D.C., O'Malley said, "Too often when politicians agree with the Church's position on a given issue, they say the Church is prophetic and should be listened to, but if the Church's position does not coincide with theirs, then they scream separation of church and state."

O'Malley is an active member of the United States Catholic Conference of Catholic Bishops. He is the chairman of the conference's Committee on Consecrated Life and serves on the Committee on Shrines and the Catholic Campaign for Human Development.

—H.T.

Suggested Reading: *Boston Globe* (on-line) July 27, 2003; *Boston Herald* p1+ July 28, 2003, with photos; *Providence Journal-Bulletin* A p1+ May 5, 2000, with photos; *U.S. News & World Report* p36+ July 14, 2003, with photos; *Washington Post* A p3+ July 2, 2003

O'Neal, Jermaine

Oct. 13, 1978– Basketball player

Address: Conseco Fieldhouse, One Conseco Court, 125 S. Pennsylvania St., Indianapolis, IN 46204

Pronounced by Chris Ballard in *Sports Illustrated* (January 21, 2002) to be "the most complete big man in the Eastern Conference," the Indiana Pacers' young star center, Jermaine O'Neal, has traveled a difficult road to become one of the most dominant players in the National Basketball Association (NBA). In 1996, at the age of 18 years and one month, O'Neal became the youngest player ever to compete on an NBA court; he endured several dismal seasons with the Portland Trail Blazers before moving to the Pacers and emerging as a star. At six feet 11 inches, O'Neal has the height to compete with other NBA centers but also possesses a rare quickness and athleticism for such a big man. "O'Neal . . . is a classic post player," Ballard wrote in *Sports Illustrated* (February 9, 2004), "who prefers the ball on the right [side of the court] where he can take one dribble and drop in a soft jumphook with either hand, lean back for a fadeaway, or pump fake and spin baseline to the basket, a move so quick and slippery that it brings to mind the light feet of [the legendary center] Hakeem Olajuwon." O'Neal is a precious commodity in that he

Courtesy of NBA Photos

is a seasoned veteran at only 26 years of age. A three-time All-Star, now in his ninth season as a pro, he is the acknowledged leader of the Pacers.

Jermaine O'Neal was born in Columbia, South Carolina, on October 13, 1978. His father, Clifford Lee O'Neal, became estranged from Jermaine's mother, Angela Kennedy, while she was pregnant with the boy. Kennedy worked two jobs, as a hotel maid during the day and as a night clerk at a Wachovia bank, in order to support Jermaine and his older brother, Cliff Jr. By the time he had reached high school, O'Neal had begun getting into trouble—fighting, being suspended from school, selling drugs, and "making other trouble he won't even discuss today," as Will Allison put it in *Indianapolis Monthly* (January 2002). The first sport he played upon entering Eau Claire High School in the fall of 1992 was football, as a quarterback and defensive back with the junior-varsity team. One day, on his way to practice, he flagged down the school's basketball coach, George Glymph (pronounced "glimp"). As Glymph recalled to Will Allison, "Jermaine says, 'Hey coach, I'm going to be your star.' And I said, 'What do you mean?' He said, 'I'm going to be your star basketball player.' I said, 'You're a very arrogant little sucker. We'll see about that.'"

"Growing up, O'Neal was as gangly and wobbly as a newborn deer," Ballard reported in his February 9, 2004 article. Between September 1992 and January 1993, O'Neal sprouted from six feet four inches to six feet nine inches, which helped him keep his promise to Glymph and become a star basketball player at Eau Claire (despite the fact that his growth spurt initially left him "so uncoordinated that he couldn't dunk," as Ballard wrote in 2004). With his greater height he became a formidable shot blocker as well as a potent scorer, and the Eau Claire basketball team went on to win the state championships in each of O'Neal's first three seasons. Glymph not only helped O'Neal improve as a player but became a father figure for the young athlete. "He really cared about me," O'Neal told Allison. "He called me all the time on the weekend. He came and took me to breakfast just to see how I was doing. He always made sure I was feeling okay. That meant a lot to me." He also said that before he met Glymph, "I thought street life was the best life for me to help my family. Coach Glymph helped me realize there's a better way to do for your family and be happy at the same time." (Glymph recalled to Allison that he and O'Neal's teammates "got the arrogance out" of the boy.) Despite Glymph's mentoring, however, O'Neal found himself in trouble in November of his senior year, when he was caught in bed with his 16-year-old girlfriend by the girl's father, who pressed charges. Because his girlfriend was younger than the legal age of consent, O'Neal was forced to do jail time and enter a counseling program.

Planning to attend a four-year college, O'Neal, after several tries, was unable to score high enough on the SAT test to compensate for his 2.35 grade-point average, forcing him to consider junior college instead. His grades had little bearing on his eligibility for the NBA, however, and upon returning

to his high-school team, in 1996, O'Neal did much to whet the appetites of pro scouts. That year he was voted Player of the Year in South Carolina, named Mr. Basketball and first team all-state by the Associated Press, and voted to the *USA Today* All-USA Basketball Team. During his high-school career O'Neal averaged 5.2 blocks, 22.4 points, and 12.6 rebounds per game and hit more than 68 percent of his shot attempts. He scored a total of 1,372 points, hauled in 833 rebounds, and set school records for blocks in a game (16), season (170), and career (397).

Against the wishes of his mother and Glymph, O'Neal made himself eligible for the 1996 NBA draft. "The decision wasn't something I just came up with right before the draft," he told Conrad Brunner for the *Indianapolis Star* (October 29, 2000). "I had thought about it for four months. My mother worked hard all of her life to take care of me and my brother and I just knew I had a chance to take care of my mother and learn from the best in the world. I knew this was going to be my four years of college." (Just after O'Neal announced his eligibility, his father introduced himself to the athlete, but O'Neal rebuffed his approaches.) The Portland Trail Blazers chose O'Neal as the 17th overall pick and signed him to a three-year, $2.85 million contract. "The sight of 17-year-old Jermaine O'Neal at his introductory Portland Trail Blazers news conference . . . caused beat writers in attendance to snap the tips off their pencils in shock," Sam Silverstein wrote in *Sport* (July 1, 1999). "Into the room strode a man's body—6 feet, 10 inches in all—that tapered toward a child's face and the skinniest pair of shoulders this side of [the sitcom *Happy Days*'s teen character] Richie Cunningham. For a long moment you could have heard a pin drop. Then the cameras finally began to click." (Silverstein reported that O'Neal later "[grew] an inch and added 35 pounds of muscle, mostly around his neck and those shoulders.")

O'Neal moved to Portland, bringing with him his brother and his cousin Quante Nash. Despite their support, O'Neal's first year in the pros proved very difficult. He missed the first 17 games of the season after sustaining a knee injury during the preseason. The Trail Blazers already had a strong roster of big and tall players to fill in the center and power-forward positions—including Arvydas Sabonis, Brian Grant, and Rasheed Wallace—which meant that O'Neal saw little playing time. In the 1996–97 season he appeared in only 45 games and averaged just 4.1 points and 10.2 minutes of playing time per game. Prior to the 1997–98 season, Glymph, who was hired by the Trail Blazers as director of player development, reunited with his young prodigy. That season, however, O'Neal showed little improvement: in 60 games he averaged 4.5 points and 13.5 minutes played. Glymph was forced to return home before the 1998–99 season to undergo open-heart surgery; O'Neal, who during the off-season had had "Year of the Resurrection" tattooed on his arm, performed even worse that year than in his first two: during the abbreviated season, which began late due to a players' strike, he played in 36 games and averaged 2.5 points and 8.6 minutes per contest.

Despite O'Neal's minimal impact on the team's play during his first three seasons, in August 1999 the Trail Blazers signed him to a four-year, $24 million contract. That fall O'Neal's girlfriend, Lamesha Roper, gave birth to their daughter, Asjia. O'Neal began the 1999–2000 season full of hope and enthusiasm, but his fourth year proved to be a disappointment as well. Unable to win the respect of the Trail Blazers' head coach, Mike Dunleavy, he played in 70 games but started only eight, averaging three points and 12.3 minutes per game. Feeling stifled in Portland, O'Neal made it known that he wanted to be traded. In August 2000 he was overjoyed to learn that the Indiana Pacers were interested in signing him. "I knew this was my chance," he told Brunner, "and I told my mother, 'I'm not going to mess this up. I'm going to prove everybody wrong. I'm going to show everybody I can score, I can shoot with either hand, I can defend, I can block shots, I can do all the things everybody said I couldn't do.'"

The trade was at first unpopular with Pacers fans, who were sad to see the well-liked veteran Dale Davis dealt to the Trail Blazers for the unproven and relatively unknown O'Neal. After the trade, Dunleavy, who had been more than willing to part with O'Neal, publicly commented, as quoted by Rick Bonnell in the *Charlotte Observer* (December 7, 2000), "Honestly, I don't think [O'Neal] was as talented as the guys who were playing in front of him." The statement angered O'Neal and solidified his determination to prove his detractors wrong. During the 2000–01 season, in which he started 80 games, his points-per-game average soared to 12.9, and he became a defensive force, blocking 228 shots (tying with Shawn Bradley for the most in the league) for an average of 2.81 per game (second in the league). He also vastly improved his rebounding, averaging 9.8 per game, and led the Eastern Conference with 40 double-doubles (games in which he notched double digits in two of four categories—points, rebounds, assists, or steals). The Pacers made it to the play-offs as the eighth and last seed in the Eastern Conference but fell in the first round to the Philadelphia 76ers.

After his impressive play during the 2000–01 season, O'Neal received much adulation, but he insisted that he could do better. "Everybody said last year was a great year for me, but it was an average year," he said, as quoted by Mark Montieth in the *Indianapolis Star* (October 28, 2001). "I know what I'm capable of doing." O'Neal backed up his words in the 2001–02 season, capturing the NBA's Most Improved Player Award. He averaged 19 points, 10.5 rebounds, and 2.31 blocks per game (all team highs) as the Pacers once again squeezed into the play-offs as the eighth seed. In the first round they challenged the top-ranked New Jersey Nets but lost in overtime in the decisive fifth game. O'Neal

earned his first trip to the All-Star Game and was selected for the Third-Team All-NBA squad and the team representing the U.S. in the 2002 World Basketball Championship, in Indianapolis.

O'Neal continued to play at a very high level during the 2002–03 season. He averaged 20.8 points, 10.3 rebounds, and 2.31 blocks per game, becoming one of three players in the NBA—and the only one in the Eastern Conference—to average more than 20 points and 10 rebounds. He was twice voted the Eastern Conference Player of the Month, in January and April 2003, and was once again voted an All-Star (this time as a starter) and an All-NBA Third-Team player. He was also chosen for the U.S. Olympic team for 2004. The Pacers fared better than in the two previous regular seasons, posting a 48–34 win–loss record to capture the third seed in the Eastern Conference, but, despite O'Neal's best efforts (he led the team with an average of 22.8 points and 17.5 rebounds in the series), they once again lost in the first round of the play-offs, this time to the sixth-ranked Boston Celtics.

In July 2003 O'Neal signed a seven-year, $120 million contract with the Pacers, making him the highest-paid player in the team's history. At a July 16 news conference announcing the deal—and during which Indianapolis, Indiana, mayor Bart Peterson proclaimed "Jermaine O'Neal Day" in the city—O'Neal thanked the team's owners and fans and said, as quoted in *Sports Illustrated* (July 16, 2003, on-line), "Hopefully, I can bring you an NBA championship, be an All-Star every year and win an Olympic gold medal for you next year." (He then burst into tears.) In the 2003-04 regular season O'Neal averaged 20.1 points, 2.55 blocks, and 10 rebounds per game. He was again voted to start in the All-Star Game, in which he scored 16 points and hauled in nine rebounds, and graduated to the All-NBA Second Team, after having been named to the Third Team the previous two years. The Pacers as a team also excelled, compiling a formidable 61–21 record, the best in the NBA that season. In the first round of the play-offs, the Pacers easily dispatched the Boston Celtics, sweeping the best-of-seven series in four straight games. O'Neal scored 24 and 22 points in games one and two, respectively; after getting a sinus infection, he scored 14 and 18 points in games three and four. In May the Pacers defeated the Miami Heat in six games to advance to the Eastern Conference finals; O'Neal was the team's top scorer in the series.

The Pacers fell to the Detroit Pistons in six games in the Eastern Conference finals. (Detroit went on to capture the NBA title.) O'Neal scored 21 points and grabbed 14 rebounds in the first game; in the third game, he scored 24 points and gained nine rebounds. A knee injury suffered during the fourth game did not keep O'Neal from scoring 20 points and compiling 10 rebounds. In the play-off games, O'Neal averaged 19.2 points and 9.1 rebounds. After the season ended O'Neal's injury kept him from competing with the U.S. national team at the 2004 Summer Olympics. Heading into the 2004–05 season, O'Neal was sidelined during the preseason because of a strained ligament in his left foot.

In January 2004 O'Neal won the NBA Community Assist Award for his holiday charity activities. He lives in Indianapolis, as do his brother, mother, daughter, and girlfriend, to whom he is engaged. Chris Ballard wrote about O'Neal in 2004, "Though fiercely driven, he's logical and meticulous, the type of guy who irons his jeans. He treats the game as a job, one he must work at to succeed." Ballard also reported that the athlete "adores jerk chicken wings the way most people adore their children,"

and that O'Neal was so fond of the wings as they were prepared at an Indianapolis restaurant that he hired the cook to work for him.

The Los Angeles Lakers' star center, Shaquille O'Neal, told Ballard of Jermaine O'Neal in 2002, "He's playing hard, making strong, aggressive moves. He'll be the dominant big man one day—after I leave."

—P.G.H.

Suggested Reading: *Indianapolis Monthly* p80+ Jan. 2002; *Indianapolis Star* P p9 Oct. 29, 2000, P p8 Oct. 28, 2001; *Sport* p50+ July 1, 1999; *Sports Illustrated* p46+ Jan. 21, 2002

OutKast

Rap duo

Andre 3000
May 27, 1975– Rapper; songwriter

Big Boi
Feb. 1, 1975– Rapper; songwriter

Address: c/o LaFace Records, 3350 Peachtree Rd. N.E., Suite 1500, Atlanta, GA 30326

During the Democratic presidential campaign in 2003 and 2004, two of the nominees courting young voters posed as fans of the ultra-cool hip-hop group OutKast: Howard Dean, the former governor of Vermont, sought to impress potential supporters with his rendition of the duo's 2001 hit "Ms. Jackson," while General Wesley K. Clark publicly mentioned a rumored OutKast split and demonstrated his hip-hop knowledge by quoting the line "I can shake it like a Polaroid picture!" from the OutKast song "Hey Ya!" Since the release of their first album, *Southernplayalisticadillacmuzik* (1994), when they were still in high school, Out-Kast's members—Big Boi (Antwan Patton) and Andre 3000 (Andre Benjamin, also called Dre)—have dazzled the music-buying public and professional critics. Their first album and each of their next five have sold more than a million copies each, thus reaching platinum or even multi-platinum status; their most recent recording, *Speakerboxxx/The Love Below* (2003), sold more than eight million copies in the U.S. in less than six months. What makes these numbers especially remarkable is that OutKast is far from the typical pop group: Andre and Big Boi have achieved success not by adhering to musical conventions but by breaking them, forging a genre-busting brand of hip-hop that celebrates eccentricity and, in the words of the hip-hop superstar LL Cool J, makes fans feel that "it's okay to be yourself and give[s] them a feeling of being free," as quoted by Chris Campion in the London *Observer* (February 22, 2004).

OutKast is the product of a strange musical alchemy, as its masterminds, though old friends, could scarcely be more different. The lanky Andre is the mercurial artist, always searching for different forms of personal expression and attracting attention with his flashy ensembles, which incorporate such seemingly disparate elements as billowing ascots, hot-pink silk shirts, plaid or sequined pants, and feather boas. Big Boi, widely considered the practical glue behind the duo, exudes a tough, no-nonsense persona and favors more typical hip-hop attire: diamond-encrusted jewelry, Phat Farm sweat suits, and sports jerseys, to name a few favorite items. But Big Boi and Andre share an important trait: eclectic taste in music. "I consider me and Dre to be funkateers, man," Big Boi told Campion. "Growing up, we listened to everything and I think that gives us the ability to make a free-flowing type of music. It doesn't matter whether it's country, reggae or rock and roll." "We wanted to revive [music]," Andre told Rob Brunner for *Entertainment Weekly* (November 10, 2000), "kind of like church: a hip-hop Holy Ghost. We're in the age of keeping it real, but what we're trying to do is to keep it surreal. Real has gotten really boring."

The only child of Lawrence Walker, a collections agent, and Sharon Benjamin-Hodo, a real-estate agent, Andre Lauren Benjamin was born on May 27, 1975 in Atlanta, Georgia. Andre was raised by his mother, with whom he moved frequently in southwestern Atlanta until, at the age of 15, he went to live with his father. Andre's partner, Antwan Andre Patton, was born on February 1, 1975 in Savannah, Georgia, the oldest of the five children of Rowena Patton, a retail supervisor, and Tony Kearse, a marine-corps sergeant. The rappers met as students at Tri-Cities High, a performing-arts school in suburban Atlanta, when they ran into each other at a mall. Their shared fashion sense drew them together. "We were preps," Big Boi told a reporter for *People* (February 16, 2004). "We wore loafers, argyle socks and V-neck sweaters with T-shirts. We were new to the school and we didn't know anybody." Andre and Big Boi also shared a love of rap, and they decided to try to

Frederick M. Brown/Getty Images

Big Boi (left) and Andre 3000 of OutKast

make some of their own. "We were in my living room one day watching videos," Big Boi recalled to Rob Brunner, "and we was like, 'Man, we can do that [expletive].' From that day forward we formed a group." At that time, Big Boi has said, he aimed to become either a child psychologist or a football player; Andre was interested in architecture but disliked math.

Initially calling themselves 2 Shades Deep, Andre and Big Boi soon met Rico Wade, who worked in a beauty-supply shop and headed the Organized Noize rap-production group. Wade impressed the duo with his originality and helped them conceive a sound that was quintessentially southern— emphasizing laid-back beats and southern drawls—rather than being an imitation of the two dominant rap styles of the time, West Coast and East Coast. The three began hanging out in Wade's basement at all hours, writing rhymes, toying with beats, and experimenting with their sound. In 1993 they landed an audition with the president of La-Face Records, Antonio "L.A." Reid (who is currently the chairman of the Island Def Jam Music Group). "They were a little shy, a little nervous," Reid told Brunner. "They were good, but they weren't ready yet. So they auditioned again. I told them, 'You're much closer, but still not yet.' Then I got home and thought, Am I out of my mind? These guys are incredible."

Changing their name to OutKast, Big Boi and Andre released their first single, "Players' Ball," on the album *LaFace Family Christmas* (1993). The bouncy rap number was somewhat out of place among the Christmas songs, performed by such R&B artists as TLC and Usher, but it nevertheless found its way onto radio and television (the video

for the song was directed by Sean "Puffy" Combs, now known as P. Diddy) and reached the top position on the *Billboard* Hot Rap Singles chart. By then, having become consumed with making music, both Big Boi and Andre considered dropping out of high school. Andre did so but later returned, completing his high-school education in 1996. Big Boi, who had reportedly maintained a 3.68 grade-point average, decided to continue working toward his diploma. He graduated from high school in 1994.

Meanwhile, OutKast's first album, *Southern-playalisticadillacmuzik*, was released in 1994; within a year, it had gone platinum. The title seemed to be a play on the rapid-fire utterances of Andre and Big Boi, who somehow sounded laid-back and casual despite the speed of their vocals. Though the young rappers' lyrics tended to reflect the hip-hop "playa" cliché, presenting them as perennial ladies' men and hard partyers, musically the album was groundbreaking, and its blending of funky beats, catchy vocal hooks, aspects of 1970s soul music, and live instrumentation became a prototype for southern rap. At the *Source* rap awards in 1995, OutKast was named best new rap group.

In 1996 OutKast issued *ATLiens*, whose title refers to their Atlantan roots, which the duo felt made them aliens in the East Coast/West Coast world of rap. The album revealed more of the rappers' idiosyncrasies and signaled their movement from safer, laid-back grooves toward choppier, propulsive rhythms. The production was more experimental as well, much of it drenched in spacey reverb and peppered with dub-reggae flavors as well as even more live instrumentation. In their lyrics,

OutKast turned away from the "playa" themes of their first album to focus on more serious topics, such as black identity and, on "Decatur Psalm," the poverty and violence that pervade many African-American communities and the inadequate education provided in many of their schools. "When you're 17 and 18," Andre told Cheo Hodari Coker for the *Los Angeles Times* (December 22, 1996), "you think you can smoke and drink all day and sleep around. You feel invincible. Then there comes a time where you have to [rise] up and do something else with yourself. On our first album, we were determined to smoke herb until the world ended. Now, I've stopped smoking and drinking, and I'm trying to live up to my abilities, and take life much more seriously." The song "Elevators (Me and You)" topped the *Billboard* Hot Rap Singles and Hot R&B Singles Sales charts and made it to the Top 40, while *ATLiens* shot to number one on the *Billboard* Top R&B Albums chart and went double platinum. In the *Washington Post* (October 11, 1996), Richard Harrington, echoing the sentiments of many reviewers, called it "proof (if any were needed) that hip-hop innovation isn't just an East-West thang."

With *Aquemini* (1998), OutKast continued in the vein of their previous effort, splicing together laid-back grooves with more futuristic sounds and showing further interest in social issues. The album also features guest performances by the funk guru George Clinton as well as the hip-hop vocalists Cee-Lo, Witchdoctor, Raekwon, and Erykah Badu, among others. Critics hailed the recording as OutKast's most fully realized up to that time and one of the best of the 1990s. "*Aquemini* fulfills all its ambitions, covering more than enough territory to qualify it as a virtuosic masterpiece, and a landmark hip-hop album," Steve Huey wrote for the All Music Guide Web site. A reviewer for *Source*, as excerpted on Amazon.com, gushed, "It possesses an uncanny blend of sonic beauty, poignant lyricism and spirituality that compels without commanding. The record offers a rich blend of potent beats—tight snares, booming kicks and cool rimshots—and a diverse tapestry of various musical textures." Within a couple of months, *Aquemini* went platinum (and later, double platinum).

In January 1999 "Rosa Parks," one of the tracks on *Aquemini*, was nominated for a Grammy Award for best rap performance by a duo or group. (It did not win.) A few months later the real Rosa Parks sued OutKast. Parks, the legendary civil rights figure whose refusal to give up her seat to a white man on a segregated public bus in Montgomery, Alabama, in 1955 was crucial in the emerging civil rights movement, claimed that her name had been used without her permission and exploited for financial gain. She also declared that the song defamed her, because, although her name is not in the lyrics, the title and veiled references to her automatically linked her to the profanity and sexual vulgarities in the words. OutKast claimed that the song was about the rap industry; the words in the

repeating hook, or chorus, as quoted on the Lyrics A-Z Universe Web site, are "Ah ha, hush that fuss / Everybody move to the back of the bus / Do you wanna bump and slump with us / We the type of people make the club get crunk [intoxicated]." U.S. district judge Barbara Hackett dismissed the suit in 1999; in 2003 it was reinstated by the U.S. Court of Appeals for the Sixth Circuit, in Cincinnati, Ohio. That year the U.S. Supreme Court, which had been asked to intervene in the case, declined to do so, thus returning it to a lower federal court. A decision has yet to be reached.

In 2000 Big Boi and Andre unveiled *Stankonia*, a meandering, 24-track album that gave free rein to their experimental impulses and—somewhat paradoxically—made them pop superstars. Created largely from a series of improvisational sessions, *Stankonia* is an album of extremes. It contains some of OutKast's most head-bobbing songs—such as "B.O.B." and "Gasoline Dreams"—as well as some of their most abstract and offbeat pieces. "In rap there's nothing new under the sun," Andre told a reporter for *Newsweek* (October 30, 2000). "But I think it's the way you say it and how you approach it. People are afraid to step out. There's a formula to making music now, and no one really has the courage to do their own thing." OutKast's courageousness paid off for them, as *Stankonia* became a huge commercial and critical success. In *Entertainment Weekly* (November 3, 2000), Ken Tucker praised OutKast for being "endlessly good-humored and imaginative even when dealing with the most grim and mind-deadening facets of ghetto life," and he asserted that the album "reeks of artful ambition rendered with impeccable skill." Hua Hsu, in a review for Amazon.com (which included *Stankonia* on its list of best albums of 2000), wrote, "At a time when the hip-hop 'album' seems to be sadly declining in significance, Atlanta's finest deliver a classic package of space-case imagery, curbside poetry, and delicious experimental funk. . . . While *Stankonia* certainly isn't an 'easy' album, its ambition and vision easily rank it among hip-hop's greatest in some time." *Stankonia* went quadruple platinum, peaked at number two on the *Billboard* album chart, and won a Grammy Award for best rap album. The hit song "Ms. Jackson," a farcical apology to a girlfriend's mother, topped the *Billboard* Hot 100, the R&B/Hip-Hop Singles Sales chart, and the Hot Rap Singles chart, and made it into *Billboard*'s Top 40.

Late in 2001 OutKast released the hits collection *Big Boi & Dre Present OutKast*, which also presented three new songs; one of those, "The Whole World," won a Grammy Award for best rap performance by a duo or group. The album went platinum and peaked at number 18 on the *Billboard* album chart. Around this time, following extensive touring in support of *Stankonia*, Andre began to show signs of burnout. "It got to a point where I would be onstage going through the motions while performing every night," he told Joe Silva for *Remix* (August 1, 2003). "I was totally distant from what I was doing. It was like I was watching myself. There was no passion in it at all." After the tour Andre began to focus on playing guitar, resolving to become proficient in time to play one onstage for the next tour. Soon the guitar became a new songwriting tool for him, helping to spur his creativity. (He has also taken saxophone lessons.) With a wealth of new material, Andre wanted to release a solo album, but both his manager and Big Boi were against it. One argument they offered was that fans would be eagerly anticipating a new release by OutKast following the group's Grammy Award for *Stankonia*, and a solo album would detract from that momentum. Andre was not deterred and even asserted that he would give the music away for free if need be. In response, Big Boi undertook and soon completed his own solo project. "[Big Boi's] was scheduled to come out in February, and mine was scheduled to come out this summer [in 2003]," Andre told Silva. "But I said that it's so close of a release, why don't we just put them together? And to him, that was really the best thing that I could have said because no one really wants to go out there and do it by themselves."

The result, which appeared after several postponed release dates, was the two-disk album *Speakerboxxx/The Love Below* (2003), which is essentially a joint packaging of two not-quite-solo projects. (Andre co-wrote four tracks on Big Boi's *Speakerboxxx*; Big Boi co-wrote and guest rapped once on *The Love Below*.) Anchored in heavy beats, Big Boi's contribution is the more traditional, but as Stephen Thomas Erlewine wrote for the All Music Guide Web site, "it's clear that Boi is ignoring boundaries. . . . [His tracks are] grounded firmly within hip-hop, but the beats bend against the grain and the arrangements are overflowing with ideas and thrilling, unpredictable juxtapositions, such as how 'Bowtie' swings like big-band jazz filtered through George Clinton, how 'The Way You Move' offsets its hard-driving verses with seductive choruses, or how 'The Rooster' cheerfully rides a threatening minor-key mariachi groove, salted by slippery horns and loose-limbed wah-wah guitars." On *The Love Below* Andre did more singing—mainly in a Prince-like high falsetto—than rapping. His songs could as easily be classified as funk or soul as labeled hip-hop, and he even incorporated a liberal sprinkling of lounge music. Experimentation—and what some critics saw as self-indulgence—is rampant, as evidenced by the accelerated drum-and-bass rendition of Richard Rodgers and Oscar Hammerstein's "My Favorite Things" and odd numbers such as "God (Interlude)."

With the number-one singles "I Like the Way You Move" (Big Boi) and "Hey Ya!" (Andre), *Speakerboxxx/The Love Below* was a smashing success. It reached the top positions on the *Billboard* 200 album chart and the *Billboard* R&B/Hip-Hop Albums chart. Critical reaction was generally positive, although some reviewers felt that, taken separately, the OutKast duo amounted to less than the sum of their parts. "*Speakerboxxx* is solid but ultimately [only] decent," Baz Dreisinger wrote for Salon.com. "*The Love Below* often bears the mark of an artist who's been trapped in the studio too long. Like an ivory-tower academic, Andre occasionally forgets that an audience hopes to understand what he's getting at." On the other hand, Will Hermes, writing for *Entertainment Weekly* (September 19, 2003), asserted that the two disks, "if released separately, would each be a candidate for Hip-Hop Record of the Year. Packaged together, they make a twofer whose ambition flies so far beyond that of anyone doing rap right now (or pop, or rock, or R&B), awards shows may need to create a special category for it." In December 2003 *Rolling Stone* named "Hey Ya!" the best single and video of the year, *Speakerboxxx/The Love Below* the best album of the year, and OutKast the artist of the year and best hip-hop artist. *Rolling Stone* readers agreed, picking "Hey Ya!" as the best single and best video and OutKast as the best hip-hop artist. In February 2004 OutKast won three Grammy Awards, for album of the year, best rap album, and best urban/alternative performance ("Hey Ya!").

Andre has a son named Seven Sirius from a now-ended relationship with the R&B artist Erykah Badu. In *Time* (September 29, 2003), Josh Tyrangiel suggested that Andre might be in the process of toning down his famously ostentatious appearance and also noted that the rapper had expressed interest in enrolling at Oxford University. At the Grammy ceremonies in 2004, however, Andre showed up in one of his most flamboyant costumes, wearing a leaf-green, fringed outfit made of buckskin-like material to perform, along with a group of similarly clad female dancers, a rendition of "Hey Ya!" The performance angered many Native American groups, including the National Congress of American Indians and the National Indian Gaming Association, who accused Andre and, by association, the Grammy Academy, of making a mockery of American Indian ceremonies. Andre, who lives in Los Angeles and has taken acting classes at the University of Southern California (USC), appeared as the character Silk Brown in the film *Hollywood Homicide* (2003) and will appear in *Be Cool*, the sequel to *Get Shorty* (1995), scheduled for release in 2004. He also plans to play one of his idols, Jimi Hendrix, in a biopic to be directed by the Hughes Brothers.

Big Boi, who is single, has referred to himself as a "soccer dad," according to *People* (February 16, 2004); he lives in Fayetteville, Georgia, with his three children—a daughter, Jordan, and sons Bamboo and Cross, who were eight, four, and three, respectively, in early 2004. He is an avid pit-bull breeder and owns the lucrative Pitfall Kennels, known for breeding "rare blue pits," which have grayish-blue coats and light-blue eyes. Other OutKast-related businesses include Aquemini Records, an OutKast clothing line, and several Atlanta apartment complexes. Rumors about an impending OutKast breakup have been circulating since before the release of *Speakerboxxx/The Love Below*, but Andre (who has repeatedly expressed discontent with making music) and Big Boi have insisted that the group will be together for years to come. Their next album, Andre told Chris Campion, will be a soundtrack for an HBO movie that is "a period piece not an OutKast biography."

—P.G.H.

Suggested Reading: All Music Guide Web site; *Entertainment Weekly* p81 Nov. 3, 2000, p36+ Nov. 10, 2000, with photos, p83+ Sep. 19, 2003; *Los Angeles Times* Calendar p78 Dec. 22, 1996; *Newsweek* p88 Oct. 30, 2000; *People* p87 Feb. 16, 2004; *Remix* p8+ Aug. 1, 2003

Selected Recordings: *Southernplayalisticadillacmuzik*, 1994; *ATLiens*, 1996; *Aquemini*, 1998; *Stankonia*, 2000; *Big Boi & Dre Present Outkast*, 2001; *Speakerboxxx/The Love Below*, 2003

Courtesy of TBA Entertainment

Patty, Sandi

July 12, 1957– Christian singer

Address: TBA Entertainment Corp., 3000 10th Ave. S., Nashville, TN 37203

Sandi Patty has sold more than 11 million records over the course of the last two decades and sung at the inaugural galas of three U.S. presidents: George H. W. Bush (in 1989), Bill Clinton (1997), and George W. Bush (2001). The recipient of five Grammy Awards, four *Billboard* Awards, and 39 Dove Awards (given by the Gospel Music Associa-

tion), she is one of the most honored female vocalists in the history of contemporary Christian music. The singer, who has also been known professionally as Sandi Patti (the latter spelling appears on several of her albums), is sometimes called the "First Lady of Inspirational Music" or simply the "Voice" by the gospel-music press. Thanks in part to her frequent appearances on the *Tonight Show* and various other television programs, Patty has become popular with mainstream audiences, in addition to her devoted Christian-music fans. By her own account, she feels a special responsibility when performing for non-Christian listeners. "Someone like Johnny Carson [then host of the *Tonight Show*] is very aware that I am a Christian artist," Patty told Holly G. Miller for the *Saturday Evening Post* (December 1986). "So it becomes more than my name at stake when I encounter him. It's the name of Christianity, and as we know, so many things have given that a negative connotation. It's a challenge to present who I am in the light of being a Christian and to leave a positive feeling with people. I only have one shot to do it, or maybe a couple."

Sandi Patty was born on July 12, 1957 in Oklahoma City, Oklahoma. (Some sources list July 14 as her birthdate.) Her mother, Carolyn Patty, was a church pianist; her father, Ron Patty, was a minister who used music to spread the Christian Gospel. After Sandi Patty made her musical debut, at the age of two, when she sang "Jesus Loves Me" at a Church of God service, she, her parents, and her two brothers began touring small churches around the country as the Ron Patty Family. "I really wasn't a rotten kid," Patty said to Susan Reed for *People* (December 2, 1985). "I had a messy room, but I got along with my parents and I enjoyed school. Saying you were 'born again' has taken on a negative idea for the general public, but I knew that one day I would have to make a personal commitment to Jesus Christ. It was my eighth birthday and I decided that was as good a time as any. It was very special, a personal and public commitment."

When she was growing up, Patty never intended to become a professional singer; she wanted instead to be a music teacher. She spent two years studying music at San Diego State University, in California, before transferring to Anderson University, a Church of God college in Anderson, Indiana. To help pay her tuition, Patty sang on commercials for Juicy Fruit chewing gum, a fast-food chain, and the Ohio State Fair. At Anderson she met John Helvering, whom she married shortly before she graduated.

Meanwhile, impressed by her talent, Helvering persuaded Patty to record an album, which she produced herself; her last name was mistakenly spelled "Patti" on the album cover, and rather than go through the expense of changing it, she allowed it to remain. The couple planned to sell the disk after church concerts to earn extra income. Patty recalled to Charles W. Phillips for the *Saturday Evening Post* (May 1983), "John was a business major in college, and I was getting my teaching credentials. A week before our wedding, a record company executive called and said he had heard my custom album and wanted to talk with me. I told him I was getting married on Friday and didn't want to think about anything else for a couple of months. He understood and waited about eight weeks before he called back and set up a meeting. Everything started to mushroom from that point on. We hadn't planned on a music career, but it felt right."

In 1979 Patty signed a contract with the independent Christian label Benson Records; that same year she released the album *Sandi's Song*. She then went on a series of musical ministry tours, including several with the acclaimed Christian music group the Bill Gaither Trio, winning a growing number of loyal fans in the process. Patty next recorded *Love Overflowing* (1981) and *Lift Up the Lord* (1982). In 1982, at the 13th Annual Dove Awards, she was named "artist of the year" and "female vocalist of the year" by the Gospel Music Association. She retained the title "female vocalist of the year" for an unprecedented 10 years in a row and also garnered the title "artist of the year" several more times during that decade. In addition, she was named *Billboard*'s "inspirational artist of the year" each year from 1986 through 1989.

In 1983 Patty won her first Grammy, for best gospel performance by a duo or group, for the song "More Than Wonderful," a duet she had recorded with Larnelle Harris. Over the next decade she won four more Grammys—one in 1985, for a duet with Harris titled "I've Just Seen Jesus"; two in 1986, for "They Say," a duet with Deniece Williams, and the solo effort "Morning Like This"; and one in 1990, for the album *Another Time, Another Place*.

During the 1980s and early 1990s, Patty released several albums, including five that went gold (meaning sales of at least half a million copies): *The Gift Goes On* (1983), *Songs from the Heart* (1984), *Make His Praise Glorious* (1988), *The Finest Moments* (1989), and *Another Time, Another Place* (1990). Three of her recordings from this period achieved platinum status (sales of at least a million copies): *More Than Wonderful* (1983), *Hymns Just for You* (1985), and *Morning Like This* (1986). By the mid-1980s, thanks to her prolific touring and recording, most fans of Christian music were familiar with Patty's work, but she remained largely unknown to mainstream audiences. That changed on July 6, 1986, when her rendition of the "Star-Spangled Banner" was televised at the end of ABC's *Liberty Weekend* programming, aired in honor of the centennial and rededication of the Statue of Liberty. Patty had recorded the song as a track on *They Come to America* (1986), the official album of the Statue of Liberty–Ellis Island Foundation, and A&M Records, the company that distributed the album, had sent a copy to ABC Television executives. Because the decision to play the track over the closing montage of the broadcast was made at the last minute, ABC officials were unable to alert Patty that her song was

airing. "It was the strangest feeling to be watching the celebration at home with my family and suddenly to hear myself singing on television," she told Miller. "I had no idea that was going to happen. I was shocked, but pleasantly shocked."

Following the broadcast, ABC was flooded with more than 1,000 calls asking the identity of the singer. George H. W. Bush, then vice president, subsequently asked Patty to the White House for tea, and Johnny Carson asked her to make the first of four visits to the *Tonight Show*. As her popularity with non-Christian audiences grew, she made numerous other public appearances, including performances at the Fiesta Bowl and Disneyland.

Throughout her career Patty had presented herself as wholesome, family-oriented, and devoted to her ministry. Thus, it shocked many of her fans when, in 1992, she filed for divorce from John Helvering. Then, at a press conference held in 1993, Patty revealed that she had been sexually abused as a child by a family friend. In 1995, at another press conference, Patty admitted that she had been unfaithful while married to Helvering. Later that year she married Don Peslis, a backup singer with whom she had conducted an affair. With the news of the infidelity spreading through the Christian-music world, several radio stations refused to play her records. "I got a variety of letters," she told Wayne Bledsoe in an interview for the *Knoxville (Tennessee) News-Sentinel* (November 10, 2002). "I got people saying 'Hey, we love you. Whatever you're going through, take your time and do what you need to do, but come back.' And I got letters from people who were very hurt and angry and very confused, and I totally understand that. . . . I was able to write them back and say, 'You know what? I understand. I've let God down and some friends and fans down' and I had to do some healing and reconciliation." The controversy prompted Patty to stop touring for a while.

She continued to record, however; in 1996 Patty made three highly successful albums: *O Holy Night, An American Songbook,* and *It's Christmas.* The following year she sang the "Star Spangled Banner" at President Bill Clinton's inaugural gala, the second of three such galas at which she has performed. In 1998 she recorded *Artist of My Soul* and *Libertad Me Das* (You Set Me Free), which won a Dove Award as best Spanish-language album of the year. That year, buoyed by support from Peslis and her fans, she began touring again.

Patty continues to record regularly. Her recent releases include *Together: Sandi Patty and Kathy Troccoli* (1999), *These Days* (2000), *For God and Country* (2001), *All the Best Live* (2001), *Take Hold of Christ* (2003), which was nominated for a 2004 Dove Award for "inspirational album of the year," and *Hymns of Faith . . . Songs of Inspiration* (2004). She has also begun to branch out from the world of Christian inspirational music by performing with regional and national symphony orchestras. During those performances she sings selections from Disney soundtracks and Broadway shows, as well as patriotic and big-band tunes.

Patty and Peslis have eight children—four from Patty's previous marriage, three from Peslis's, and one the couple adopted after their marriage. They live in Anderson, Indiana. Speaking about how she and her husband juggle parenthood and demanding careers, Patty told Alyssa Roggie for the Lancaster, Pennsylvania, *Intelligencer Journal* (April 21, 2000), "It keeps us insanely busy. But you know what, it's what we signed up for. We love the business, and we love the kids. We just have to take one day at a time and enjoy the chaos."

—H.T.

Suggested Reading: *Chicago Tribune* C p6 Sep. 25, 1986, with photo; *Knoxville (Tennessee) News Sentinel* G p1 Nov. 10, 2002, with photo;

People p193 Dec. 2, 1985, with photo; *Saturday Evening Post* p16+ May 1983, with photo, p64+ Dec. 1986, with photo, p44+ Jan. 1989, with photo

Selected Recordings: *Sandi's Song*, 1979; *Love Overflowing*, 1981; *Lift Up the Lord*, 1982; *The Gift Goes On*, 1983; *Songs from the Heart*, 1984; *Make His Praise Glorious*, 1988; *The Finest Moments*, 1989; *Another Time, Another Place*, 1990; *It's Christmas*, 1996; *These Days*, 2000; *For God and Country*, 2001; *Take Hold of Christ*, 2003; *Hymns of Faith . . . Songs of Inspiration*, 2004

Evan Agostini/Getty Images

Pekar, Harvey

Oct. 8, 1939– Comic-book writer

Address: 3061 E. Overlook Rd., Cleveland, OH 44118-2437

"Sad-sack," "pessimistic," "cynical," "whiny," and "schlubby" are not adjectives typically applied to celebrities. Yet all of these terms are frequently used to describe Harvey Pekar. In fact, Pekar's celebrity status is directly related to his lack of glamour, his quotidian lifestyle, and his general attitude of gloom. A downbeat Cleveland, Ohio, native with a receding hairline and a voice said to evoke thoughts of sandpaper, he is the creator of the 27-year-old alternative comic-book series

American Splendor, which, with its detailed descriptions of the trials of everyday life, has attained cult status. With the release, in 2003, of a film based on the series and bearing the same name, Pekar's creation has also gained widespread recognition.

The older of the two sons of Jewish immigrants from Poland, Harvey L. Pekar was born in Cleveland on October 8, 1939. His father, a Talmudic scholar, supported the family as a grocer. Pekar and his brother, who is about six years his junior, did not become close until 1990, when Pekar was diagnosed with cancer. According to the October 7, 2003 entry in his Web site log, Pekar was "extroverted to the point of obnoxiousness" as a child and liked to engage in sports; his brother, by contrast, was quiet and unathletic. The one interest they enjoyed in common was music: Pekar loved jazz, and his brother studied the trumpet. One of Pekar's most vivid (and often cited) memories of his childhood involves Halloween: one year, instead of wearing a superhero costume or some other traditional outfit to go trick-or-treating in his neighborhood, the young Harvey dressed in his everyday clothes—and wound up without candy. The incident provides evidence that even early in life, he maintained a fatalistic, unvarnished sense of self that he refused to sugarcoat or compromise for anyone's benefit, including his own.

In the early 1960s, while Pekar was working as a filing clerk at a Veterans Administration hospital in Cleveland and as a freelance music and book reviewer, he met the legendary alternative-comics artist R. Crumb. The two shared a passion for collecting jazz records and became friends. In lamenting to Crumb that there were no comics about ordinary people, Pekar realized that he could write one himself. In a recent comic that appeared briefly on the Web site of the *New York Times* (August 11, 2003), the character based on Pekar recollected the moment of that revelation. "Comics for adults," the character thinks. "Why not? I have access to every word that Shakespeare used. And there's so much that could be done in comics that hasn't been done. I have a chance to be an innovator."

Since Pekar's drawing abilities had never progressed beyond the rendering of stick figures, Crumb provided the illustrations for the comic. The first issue of *American Splendor,* a collection of short comics in which Pekar is the main character, was published in 1976. Most of the stories deal with minor, everyday grievances and irritations; Pekar's annoyance with chatty women who hold up supermarket lines, his interactions with his co-workers, his ordeals with lost keys, and his dating debacles have all provided fodder for his *American Splendor* comics.

Although he lost money on the first issue of *American Splendor*, the comic found a small cult following, and Pekar continued to produce it approximately once a year. While Crumb's illustrations are the ones most readily identifiable with Pekar's comics, a variety of artists later executed the drawings; they have included Frank Stark, Jim Woodring, Joe Zabel, Gerry Shamray, Chester Brown, Spain Rodriguez, Greg Budgett, Drew Friedman, and Gary Dumm. Pekar told Sacha Molitorisz for the *Sydney Morning Herald* (September 5, 2003), "At that time I was single and I was spending thousands of dollars on rare records, so I thought I'd put out a comic. And so I lost money on that instead." As he explained in a cartoon that appeared fleetingly in *Entertainment Weekly* (August 15, 2003, on-line), he enjoyed writing *American Splendor* and rationalized, "So what if I lose a couple thousand a year? At least I'll finally be doin' somethin' creative." That creativity earned Pekar the 1987 American Book Award for *American Splendor.*

Among those who appreciated Pekar's work was a Delaware writer, teacher, and activist named Joyce Brabner. In the early 1980s she contacted Pekar about one of his comics, and the two began corresponding. On their first date, Brabner became so upset that she vomited. As she explained in an interview with George M. Thomas for the *Akron Beacon Journal* (August 15, 2003, on-line), "I was irritated because I realized that I met my soulmate. . . . I was disturbed at what I was realizing and I didn't just throw up—I backed up the toilet—and that's when I saw my [future] husband, with his pants rolled up, mopping up the floor and offering me all sorts of herbal teas he'd bought simply because we'd discussed that over the phone, and that's all I needed to know about the kind of husband he would be." On their second date, Pekar and Brabner bought engagement rings; on their third, they got married.

In 1990 the couple faced a major challenge when Pekar was diagnosed with non-Hodgkins lymphoma, a form of cancer. He underwent chemotherapy and radiation therapy, and the disease later went into remission. Following his ordeal, Pekar and Brabner co-wrote *Our Cancer Year,* a full-length graphic novel, the longest installment yet of the *American Splendor* series. According to George M.

Thomas, writing the story jointly "was an opportunity for the couple to experience catharsis together." The book, illustrated by Frank Stack, deals not only with Pekar's illness but also with the politics of that period, and includes Pekar's opinions on the United States–led Persian Gulf War of 1991. Pekar's motivation for writing *Our Cancer Year* was consistent with the impetus for the whole series, as he explained in an interview conducted by Jim Ottaviani and Steve Lieber for *Slate* (on-line): "Well, I write about my life, choosing incidents that I think will be, for one reason or another, significant to people. Often because they may have experienced the same things, and often because few or no people have written about them before. I hope that in reading them people can identify with the character and in some cases take comfort from what I write or know that maybe they're not the only person in the world that's had this experience, so they shouldn't feel so weird about it or something." In January 2002 Pekar suffered a recurrence of lymphoma. He received treatment again, and the disease again went into remission.

As far back as 1980, a film version of *American Splendor* had been suggested. The first person to approach Pekar was the then-fledgling director Jonathan Demme, but neither he nor other filmmakers after him could finance the proposed film. Then, in 1999, Ted Hope, of the New York City–based company Good Machine, a producer of independent films, persuaded the cable channel HBO to provide financing for the project. Written and directed by Shari Springer Berman and Robert Pulcini, a husband-and-wife team, the film *American Splendor* premiered in 2003. An unusual blend of documentary and traditional, narrative filmmaking, *American Splendor* includes some unconventional techniques. Pekar, for example, narrates the film and periodically appears on-screen and in documentary footage, while there is also a character named Pekar, portrayed by the actor Paul Giamatti. In addition, in one scene, Giamatti-as-Pekar watches Donal Logue play Pekar in a stage production. Meanwhile, animated and illustrated versions of Pekar occasionally appear. Brabner appears as herself and is also played by the actress Hope Davis and—in the play-within-the-film—Molly Shannon, known for her work on the long-running television sketch-comedy series *Saturday Night Live.*

Both viewers and the notoriously cantankerous Pekar liked the film. Pekar told Sacha Molitorisz, "It got the mood right, even if in some cases there were changes made as far as the actual details of my life." *American Splendor* garnered awards at the 2003 Sundance, Cannes, Edinburgh, and Montreal film festivals. In one of the uniformly positive reviews, Peter Brunette wrote for *indieWIRE.com* (August 11, 2003), "This is a movie that demonstrates some real filmmaking prowess. Even better, and even more rarely, some deep thought as well." Pekar's graphic novel *Our Movie Year,* an account of the making of the film, was due to be published in December 2004.

In 2001, after 30 years of service, Pekar retired from the Veterans' Administration. Despite the longevity of the *American Splendor* series and the barrage of media attention it has attracted since the release of the film, Pekar has never profited much from it financially. In a conversation with Andrew D. Arnold for Time.comix.com (August 8, 2003), he admitted, "I'm really kind of scared of what the future holds for me. I've got to put my kid through school. I got this small pension from the federal government and I gotta supplement that with other income, hopefully from freelance writing. And I'm just wondering if this movie is going to be enough to do it—to gain me that attention to get that income." In his cartoon for *Entertainment Weekly*, Pekar speculated that, following the success of the film, he might "become a beloved man of the people. . . . Of course I don't think I have it made by any means. I'm too insecure, obsessive, and paranoid for that."

In addition to his role in *American Splendor*, Pekar has appeared as himself in the films *Comic Book Confidential* (1988),*Vinyl* (2000), *I, Curmudgeon* (2004), and *All That You Love Will Be Carried Away* (2004), and in the television series *Festival Pass with Chris Gore* (2002). He was a guest on the NBC program *Late Night with David Letterman* eight times between 1986 and 1988. His association with Letterman ended after an on-air diatribe in which Pekar denounced NBC's affiliation with General Electric, one of the show's sponsors, railing about the company's antitrust violations and the health problems suffered by people who lived near General Electric power plants. (In the early 1990s, when the Letterman show was still on NBC, Pekar returned as a guest twice more.) His freelance work as a storyteller and commentator for radio station WKSU, which he began in 1999, has earned him two awards. His reviews have been published in the *Boston Herald*, *Jazz Times*, the *Austin Chronicle*, and *Down Beat* magazine, among other journals.

Pekar was divorced twice before he married Brabner; in 2003 the couple celebrated their 20th wedding anniversary. In 1998 Pekar and Brabner became the legal guardians of a 10–year-old girl named Danielle, who has since appeared as a character in Pekar's comics. (The movie *American Splendor* portrayed Danielle as the daughter of Frank Stack [called Fred in the film], but she is not.) Pekar, Brabner, and Danielle all have their own Web logs on HarveyPekar.com.

—K.J.E.

Suggested Reading: *Chicago Tribune* V p17E June 26, 1986, with photo, XIV p7 Nov. 20, 1994; *Film Threat* (on-line) Aug. 15, 2003; Harvey Pekar's Web site; metroactive.com; *Sacramento Bee* (on-line); *Slate* (on-line); *Time* (on-line) Aug. 8, 2003; *Washington Post* C p1+ Nov. 2, 1987, with photos

Selected Books: *American Splendor*, 1976; *The New American Splendor Anthology*, 1991; *Our Cancer Year*, 1994; *Harvey Pekar's American Splendor: Unsung Hero: The Story of Robert McNeill*, 2003; *Our Movie Year*, 2004

Selected Films: appearing as himself—*Comic Book Confidential*, 1988; *Vinyl*, 2000; *American Splendor*, 2003; *I, Curmudgeon*, 2004; *All That You Love Will Be Carried Away*, 2004

Selected Television Shows: *Festival Pass with Chris Gore*, 2002

Robert Laberge/Getty Images

Phelps, Michael

June 30, 1985– Swimmer

Address: c/o Octagon, 2 Union St., Suite 300, Portland, ME 04101

In a career that began only four years ago, the swimming sensation Michael Phelps has proven to be a world-beater. The list of his achievements is a dizzying parade of firsts and other stunning performances, and as a result he has brought new excitement and attention to a sport generally eclipsed in the U.S. by several others, among them baseball, basketball, and football. In the months leading up to the 2004 Olympic Games, in Athens, Greece, Phelps became one of America's most talked-about athletes and one of its brightest hopes for winning gold medals. Some swimming enthusiasts and other observers expressed the belief that he had a chance to tie or break the American swimming legend Mark Spitz's record of seven gold medals at a single Olympic Games, set in 1972 in Munich, Germany. In response to these projections, the swimwear company Speedo, which had already signed Phelps to an endorsement deal through 2009 reportedly worth $2 million to $9 million, promised to pay the swimmer another $1 million if he could match Spitz's memorable Olympic performance. Ultimately, Phelps fell short of this goal, which a number of experts (including the head coach of the 2004 U.S. men's Olympic swim team, Eddie Reese) had deemed unrealistic. However, he left Athens with an impressive total of six gold and two bronze medals, becoming the first athlete since 1980, and the first American ever, to win eight medals in a single Olympics. He also tied Mark Spitz's record for individual gold medals, capturing four. Calling Phelps "swimming's wonder boy," Michael E. Ruane wrote for the *Washington Post* (April 18, 2004) that Phelps is not just a remarkable teenage talent but the "most dominant swimmer in the world." His coach has likened Phelps to a musical virtuoso, and the Canadian writer and swimming expert Cecil Colwin has compared him to the late Russian ballet legend Rudolf Nureyev.

Phelps's ascent began in 2000, when he became, at 15 years of age, the youngest male in more than 60 years to qualify for any U.S. Olympic team. The following year he became the youngest male in modern history to break a world record and one of the youngest American male athletes ever to turn professional. At the 2003 World Championships, in Barcelona, Spain, Phelps became the first swimmer in history to set five individual world records at one international meet. At the U.S. Olympic trials in July 2004, he emerged as the first U.S. swimmer ever to qualify for the right to compete in six individual events at the Olympic Games. Overall, he is a five-time swimming world champion and a winner of 20 U.S. national championship titles. He has held 13 swimming world records and 18 American records. As of mid-November 2004, he was the current world-record holder in the 200-meter butterfly (1: 53.93—one minute, 53 and 93 one-hundredths of a second), 200-meter individual medley (1: 55.94), and 400-meter individual medley (4.08.26), and the American-record holder in four different events: the 200-meter butterfly, the 200- and 400-meter individual medleys, and the 200-meter freestyle. In addition, the hard-training and never-satisfied Phelps has set more than 40 national age-group records in seven different swimming events. Regarding the enormous buzz that Phelps has generated, the American swimmer Lenny Krayzelburg, who won two gold medals at the 2000 Olympics, in Sydney, Australia, told Diane Pucin for the *Los Angeles Times* (May 24, 2004), "I know this sounds a little crazy, but I am not thinking of Michael in terms of being one of the greatest swimmers ever. I am thinking of him as one of the greatest athletes ever. . . . What he is doing is amazing. . . . When you have someone like Michael come along in a sport which doesn't get all

the attention it can only be good." Among other honors, Phelps was named swimmer of the year by U.S.A. Swimming in 2001 and 2003. In the latter year he also won the prestigious James E. Sullivan Award.

The only boy among Fred and Debbie Phelps's three children, Michael Phelps was born near Baltimore, Maryland, on June 30, 1985. His parents separated when the children were young; they are now divorced. Phelps and his sisters grew up with their mother. A big, strong man, Phelps's father had been an athlete in his youth; he retired from the Maryland State police in 2004, after more than 25 years of service. He and his son are estranged and are said to see each other only rarely. Phelps's mother is a former Baltimore County middle-school teacher who was twice named Maryland teacher of the year; more recently she worked as a public-school administrator. Phelps has said that he owes much of his success to her.

Michael E. Ruane wrote that Phelps and his sisters, Hilary and Whitney, had been raised "by the side of the swimming pool," and he described the Phelpses as a "talented, driven, if somewhat fractured, swimming family." As that suggests, all three children began swimming at a very young age. Hilary, the older sister, had a special knack for swimming the butterfly but did not stick with the sport for very long. Having shown even greater swimming potential than her sister, Whitney began winning medals at competitive races but was crushed when, as a 15-year-old, she failed to qualify for the 1996 U.S. Olympic swim team. Afterward she stopped swimming altogether. Hilary and Whitney Phelps reportedly follow their brother's career with great enthusiasm.

As a child Phelps accompanied his sisters to the Loyola High School swimming pool, in Towson, Maryland, and to the Meadowbrook Aquatic and Fitness Center, in Baltimore, which houses the North Baltimore Aquatic Club (NBAC)—one of the premier competitive swimming clubs in the country. The NBAC has helped to train and develop numerous world-record holders as well as 10 Olympic athletes who, together, have won five gold medals. After learning the basic swimming strokes, Phelps joined the NBAC. When he was 11 years old, he drew inspiration from watching on television the American swimmers Tom Malchow and Tom Dolan win medals at the 1996 Olympics. That same year Bob Bowman, the NBAC coach, took Phelps's parents aside at the pool and told them that their son was an "extraordinarily gifted swimmer who had a fabulous future ahead of him," as paraphrased by Ruane. Bowman has been Phelps's trainer and coach ever since. "On most days, he's easy to coach," Bowman told Frank Litsky for the *New York Times* (February 11, 2004), "but maybe once every six weeks or six months he isn't. I think fatigue causes it. When he was young, fatigue was caused by a growth spurt. He'd be difficult for a week or two. Then I'd look and he's two inches taller. He's still growing." Describing the swimmer's physique, Litsky wrote, "The 6-foot-4 1/2 Phelps has an ideal build for a swimmer: wide shoulders, big chest, narrow waist and big feet (size 14)."

There are four strokes in competitive swimming: butterfly, backstroke, breaststroke, and freestyle. The butterfly, a difficult stroke but one of Phelps's strongest (the event in which he qualified for the 2000 Olympics and later broke his first world record), is sometimes described as a "dolphin-like" or undulating motion. For the butterfly, swimmers propel themselves facedown through the water by lifting their arms above the surface, stretching them forward while rotating them at the shoulder, bringing them together below the surface, and pulling them back through the water to their hips; simultaneously, they move their hips up and down and kick. For the backstroke—which is unique, in that one faces the sky, or the roof of the pool, while performing it—swimmers stretch their arms behind their heads, parallel with their torsos, then pull them back through the water in a strong circular motion toward their hips. The breaststroke involves simultaneously kicking in a frog-like fashion and moving one's arms through the water in a circular motion, similar to that of the backstroke, except that one is facedown in the water. Freestyle (sometimes called the crawl), perhaps the best known of the four strokes, is often the first that children and adolescents learn. In freestyle the body is facedown; the legs scissor-kick up and down; the arms are thrown straight forward above the water, one at a time, then pulled back through it; and the head is turned to the side to take a breath after every other stroke.

Whereas many swimming races involve the use of just one stroke for the entire distance, an individual medley requires the swimmer to execute each of the four strokes, in the above order, for one-fourth of the total race distance. (Medley relays, which are performed by teams consisting of four swimmers each, require a different sequence of the four strokes.) During an individual medley a swimmer starts by using the butterfly, and then—after completing the number of laps that constitute one-fourth of the race's total distance—switches to the backstroke, after making a turn in the pool. (Turning in races, or pushing off from the wall of the pool and heading back in the other direction, requires a special technique whose execution is a crucial part of competitive swimming.) The swimmer then completes the required laps in the remaining two strokes.

To increase their speed in the water, at some point every year, most professional swimmers shave their entire bodies, as even small amounts of hair on one's arms or legs, for example, can create frictional drag in the water, thereby slowing a swimmer down. As little as one-tenth or one one-hundredth of a second can decide a swimming race. As he told usolympicteam.com, Phelps shaves his body roughly twice a year; he recommends shaving the day before a meet.

Competitive swimming is famous for the rigorous practice it requires, and Phelps and Bowman are known for their hard training regimens and their perfectionism. Michael E. Ruane wrote that Phelps trains at the Meadowbrook Aquatic and Fitness Center "seven days a week, almost 365 days a year." During practices Bowman walks the pool deck above Phelps, blowing a whistle and shouting encouragement at his star pupil as he courses through the water. On some days Bowman has Phelps swim laps with sneakers on to weigh him down and make him work harder in the water. "The physical part is all Bob," Phelps explained to Ruane, regarding the close relationship between athlete and coach. "I just swim. It's something that he's taught me to do. . . . If he says 'Your left hand is coming higher than your right,' then I try to fix it, then just keep on swimming." (Bowman was named one of five finalists for the United States Olympic Committee's 2003 national coach of the year award; for his work with Phelps, U.S.A. Swimming named Bowman coach of the year in both 2001 and 2003.) Kevin Clements, a fellow swimmer for the NBAC team and an Olympic hopeful who has trained with Phelps, told Frank Litsky for the New York Times (February 16, 2004) that Phelps "likes to train. He's never satisfied. Outside the pool, he's a normal guy to hang out with. He likes to tease and fool around with other [swimmers]. . . . But he's mature in ways, too. He kind of makes training fun." Concurrently with his training and competing in major swimming meets, Phelps attended Towson High School, on the outskirts of Baltimore. (Towson High School did not have a swim team.) Despite his grueling schedule, Phelps graduated from the school in 2003.

In 1999 Phelps made the U.S. National B Team, whose members are alternates; he has been a National A Team member every year since then. (Phelps has been named a National Team All-Star every year since 2001.) In 2000 Phelps fulfilled a dream, qualifying for the U.S. Olympic swimming team by placing second in the 200-meter butterfly event at the U.S. Olympic Trials. He then competed in the 2000 Olympic Games in Sydney, Australia, just four years after watching the likes of Malchow and Dolan achieve Olympic swimming glory. At the Sydney Games Phelps placed fifth in the 200-meter butterfly; his time set an American age-group record. At the 2000 U.S. Spring Nationals Phelps placed third in that same event. According to the Web site of the Fédération Internationale de Natation, Phelps, who had not yet reached his full potential, was ranked in the top 50 swimmers worldwide in two categories in 2000: the 200-meter butterfly (seventh) and 400-meter individual medley (44th). By the following year Phelps was ranked first worldwide in the 200-meter butterfly; fourth in both the 200- and 400-meter individual medleys; 13th in the 100-meter butterfly; and 19th in the 200-meter backstroke. Phelps's rankings were boosted in large part by his first truly dominant performance as a world-class swimmer: at the

2001 Phillips 66 U.S. National Championships, also known as the Spring Nationals, he set his first world record, winning the 200-meter butterfly in 1 minute, 54.92 seconds. Only 15 years old, Phelps had become the youngest male world-record holder in modern history. He showed further signs of greatness that same year, winning the 200-meter butterfly at the Pan Pacific Championships and two events at the U.S. Summer Nationals. In addition, Phelps lowered his own world record in the 200-meter butterfly (1.54.58) while swimming to victory in that event at the 2001 World Championships. That win brought him his first international medal.

That same year, Phelps, then 16 years old, became the youngest male swimmer ever to turn professional, accepting the sponsorship offered by various companies. He has since earned millions of dollars in endorsement deals. In the *Washington Post* (June 1, 2004), Michael E. Ruane wrote, "Twenty-five years after the Olympic movement allowed professional athletes to compete in the games, Phelps has become the epitome of the modern American corporate Olympian." (Under the direction of Peter Ueberroth, then head of the U.S. Olympic Organizing Committee, the 1984 Olympic Games, in Los Angeles, California, marked the world's first privately funded Olympics.) Many corporations lend Olympic athletes financial support in the hope that their association with a high-profile figure on the world's most prominent athletic stage will help them sell more products. "Everybody is now desperately trying to reach Generation Y," Phelps's agent, Peter Carlisle, who works for the sports-marketing firm Octagon, explained to Eric Fisher for the *Washington Times* (June 10, 2004), "and guys like [Phelps] are Generation Y. Everybody is after that star who's young, bright, hip and personable, and Michael arrives completely pre-packaged for that." The money received from sponsors and endorsements is often what enables athletes to support themselves while they train. Phelps has also signed lucrative endorsement deals with the credit-card company Visa; Argent, a California-based mortgage company; Omega, the Swiss watch firm; AT&T Wireless; and Power Bar, a food company.

At the 2002 Phillips 66 National Swimming Championships, also known as the Summer Nationals, Phelps won four events. His time in the 400-meter individual medley (4: 11.09) set a world record. (He broke his own record in August 2004, in Athens, with a time of 4: 08.26.) In winning the 200-meter individual medley and 100-meter butterfly, Phelps set American records. He also touched the wall first in the 200-meter butterfly, recording the third-fastest time in history. At the 2002 Pan Pacific Championships, Phelps won the 200-meter individual medley (1: 59.70) and the 400-meter individual medley (4: 12.48), and swam to victory with his team—which set a new world record (3: 33.48)—in the four-man 400-meter medley relay. In addition, he won a silver medal in the 200-meter butterfly (1: 55.41).

In 2003 Phelps set the swimming world alight. At the 2003 U.S. Spring National Championships, he captured three titles, winning the 200-meter freestyle, the 200-meter backstroke, and the 100-meter butterfly, thus becoming the first man ever to win titles in three different strokes at one national championship. In an outstanding performance, Phelps then captured six medals, including four gold, and set five world records at the 2003 World Championships, held in Barcelona, Spain. He thereby became the first swimmer in history to set five world records at one international meet, and the first male swimmer to break two world records in separate events on the same day. Referring to Phelps's ability to remember his times in record-breaking performances, and to break world records continually, Ruane called him a "keen swimming mathematician" and a "human calculator." ("That's all the sport is," Phelps told Ruane. "A bunch of numbers.") In Barcelona Phelps lowered his world record in the 200-meter butterfly—his signature stroke—to 1.53.93. He was also victorious in the 200- and 400-meter individual medleys, swimming both events in world-record time, and Phelps's team of American swimmers won gold in the 400-meter medley relay. For his record-shattering performance, Phelps was named swimmer of the meet. A few weeks later, at the 2003 Summer Nationals, held in College Park, Maryland, Phelps turned in another stellar performance, becoming the first man ever to win five national titles at a single meet. (Two women, Tracy Caulkins, in 1978, and Natalie Coughlin, in 2002, have accomplished the feat.) He finished first in the 100-, 200-, and 400-meter freestyle races and in the 200-meter backstroke; his times in the latter two races set American records. Phelps's winning time in the 200-meter individual medley, 1 minute 5.94 seconds, set a new world record—and helped Phelps win a bet with his coach, Bob Bowman, who as the loser of the bet had to shave his head, much to Phelps's amusement. The occasion marked the fourth time in the first six months of 2003 that Phelps had set a new world record in the 200-meter individual medley. Phelps was given the Kiphuth Award for the best performance at the Summer Nationals, for the third year in a row. (The award is named in honor of the former longtime Yale University swimming coach Bob Kiphuth.) In all, Phelps recorded more than 45 first-place finishes in 2003, while losing just two races the entire year. In recognition of his accomplishments that year, he was named the U.S.A. Swimming male athlete of the year and one of the top-100 stories of 2003 by ESPN, and he was listed among the Associated Press's top 10 male athletes of the year.

At the Conoco Phillips National Championships in Orlando, Florida, in February 2004, Phelps won five national titles at a single meet for the second time in his career, after becoming the first man to do so six months earlier at the 2003 Summer Nationals. Far outpacing his competition, he won one race with nine meters of distance between him and the second-place finisher; in two other events that he won, the distance was five meters. Despite those convincing victories, after the meet Phelps and Bowman agreed that the swimmer's form during the competition was not always correct, and that much practice was needed. "Things could have gone better, but I'm fairly pleased," Phelps told Frank Litsky. "I'm trying to improve my turns a little bit. We started to work on my start, but Bob [Bowman] said it was getting worse so we stopped." After the championships, in regard to his star pupil, Bowman told Litsky, "Some things have to be improved. Some practice habits have to be corrected. But I'm really splitting hairs. He needs fine-tuning more than adjustments. Over all, I'm very happy." Phelps was named the meet's best performer and picked up his fourth Kiphuth Award.

At the Santa Clara International Invitational in May 2004, held at the George Haines International Swim Center in Santa Clara, California, Phelps did something rare for him: he failed to win two events in which he competed. In both the 100- and 200-meter backstroke events, Phelps finished behind Aaron Peirsol, a world-record holder and back-stroke specialist. On the positive side, Phelps defeated fellow American and world-record holder Ian Crocker in the 100-meter butterfly. (Crocker had beaten Phelps in that same event at the 2003 World Championships; stung by the defeat, Phelps had subsequently hung a picture of Crocker in his house, to fuel his competitive drive.) "I love to race the best people in the world and the fastest people in the world," Phelps told Ann Tatko for the *Contra Costa Times*, a California newspaper (May 23, 2004), referring to the stiff competition he faced at the Santa Clara Invitational. "It definitely makes things fun and keeps things interesting." Some observers of American swimming deem Peirsol and Crocker (both students at the University of Texas at Austin and, like Phelps, members of the U.S. national team), along with the breast-stroke specialist Brendan Hansen, to be as talented as Phelps. Still, while each of those swimmers is a specialist who trains and competes in just one stroke, Phelps is a rare talent who excels in a variety of strokes and events.

At the end of 2003, Phelps was ranked first in the world in the three events in which he holds the world record and second in the 100-meter butter-fly, 200-meter freestyle, and 200-meter backstroke. He was ranked third in the world in the 400-meter freestyle. In early June 2004 the Australian swimmer Ian Thorpe, who has been acknowledged as one of the best swimmers in the world since 1998, broke Phelps's world record in the 200-meter free-style.

One of the most important meets of Phelps's career, the 2004 U.S. Olympic Trials, took place from July 7 to 14 in Long Beach, California. Phelps made a strong start at the trials, winning the 400-meter individual medley by breaking his own world record in that event. Competing in a total of 17 races during the trials, Phelps became the first American swimmer ever to qualify for six individual events at the Olympics. He won four of those events and placed second behind Aaron Peirsol and Ian Crocker in the 200-meter backstroke and 100-meter butterfly, respectively. (Both Peirsol and Crocker set world records in beating Phelps.) Having chosen not to compete in the 200-meter backstroke, Phelps is expected to race in five individual events (the 100- and 200-meter butterfly, the 200- and 400-meter individual medleys, and the 200-freestyle) and up to three team relays in Athens. At the awards ceremony concluding the trials, in a poignant moment before 10,000 fans, Mark Spitz joined Phelps on the podium, presented the young man with a medal, and raised Phelps's right arm high in the air. Describing the scene, a reporter for the Associated Press (July 14, 2004) wrote, "The message was clear: Phelps was Spitz's heir apparent and had his support." As evidenced by the competition given Phelps by his American teammates, the 2004 U.S. men's swimming team was a very strong one. Some observers believed that the team was the best the U.S. had had since the 1976 Olympics, held in Montreal, Canada, where the U.S. men's team won 27 swimming medals, among them 12 gold. (At the 2000 Olympics the U.S. men and women swimmers won a total of 33 medals.)

The pre-Olympics media attention on Phelps was intense. "Right now, Michael has to be self-ish," Peter Carlisle told Paul McMullen for the *Baltimore Sun* (June 11, 2004). "We've turned down about 10 endorsement offers. . . . We've had to turn down media. . . . there's just not [enough] time. You try to do the best you can to accommodate everyone, but every 15 minutes [of Phelps's time] is accounted for."

Phelps has made a number of television appearances, both in commercials and on programs such as the *Today Show*. In the spring of 2004, he appeared in commercials that aired during the Kentucky Derby and the Preakness, two of the three most important annual events in horseracing and among the most prominent contests in all of sports. Phelps also appeared on the NBC network in television promotions for the 2004 Olympic Games. In a Visa television commercial that began airing in June 2004, through special effects Phelps could be seen swimming from Athens to the Statue of Liberty, in New York City's harbor, where he turned around for a return lap as though he were in a swimming pool. According to Ruane, a picture of Phelps appeared on the cover of a Visa brochure that was mailed to 57 million Visa customers in early 2004. In March 2004 he was featured on the cover of *ESPN* magazine.

Phelps began the 2004 Olympics with a record-breaking achievement. In his first contest at the Games, the 400-meter individual medley, he won a gold medal and set a world record for the event (4:08.26); Erik Vendt, another American, claimed second place. Although Phelps's winning performance seemed to bode well for his goal of matching Mark Spitz's seven Olympic gold medals, he failed to win either of his next two events, claiming the bronze in both the 400-meter freestyle relay and the 200-meter freestyle race. The latter event has never been Phelps's strongest, but he swam his best time ever and set an American record (1: 45.32). The two bronze finishes meant he had lost his chance to repeat Spitz's 1972 performance. Phelps claimed gold medals in all five of his remaining events: the 200-meter butterfly (1: 54.04); the 800-meter freestyle relay (7: 07.33); the 200-meter individual medley (1: 57.14); the 100-meter butterfly (0: 51.25); and the 400-meter medley relay (3: 31: 54). For the final heat of the medley relay, in a decision widely touted by sports critics as an exemplary display of sportsmanship, Phelps chose to relinquish his place in the butterfly leg of the race to his teammate Ian Crocker, thereby giving Crocker a chance to take home a gold medal.

Phelps has already begun training for the 2008 Olympic Games, which will be held in Beijing, China. He recently enrolled as a freshman at the University of Michigan, where he will train with the elite swim program Club Wolverine and where Bob Bowman has signed on as head swim coach.

Phelps is a national spokesman for Boys & Girls Clubs of America and an honorary board member of the Boys & Girls Club of Harford County, Maryland, and Pathfinders for Autism. In addition, Phelps has served as a volunteer at the Child Life Center at Johns Hopkins University. In addition to his other awards, in 2003 Phelps was honored by the Amateur Athletic Union with the James E. Sullivan Award. He became the first swimmer since Janet Evans, in 1989, and just the 10th swimmer ever, to win the award. (Though the Sullivan Award has traditionally been given to the best amateur athlete in the country, in recent years the list of candidates has grown to include young professional athletes and athletes of any age who are relatively new to their sports' professional ranks.) In 2004 Phelps was nominated for two ESPY Awards and was named the American–International athlete of the year.

By all accounts an outgoing and likable young man, Phelps lives with his mother in a Tudor townhouse in Rodgers Forge, near Baltimore. In the house is a case full of the trophies and medallions he has won. In addition to swimming Phelps enjoys such sports as lacrosse, football, and soccer. He is a big fan of rap music, the *Austin Powers* movies, starring Mike Myers, and the work of the late comic actor Chris Farley. When he began earning money from endorsements, Phelps bought a Cadillac Escalade for himself and a silver Mercedes-Benz for his mother. Phelps's mother grudgingly allowed her son to get a tattoo of the interwoven Olympic rings, the well-known symbol of the Games, on his right hip; it is usually covered by Phelps's swimsuit. Hardworking and rarely at rest, Phelps told Joseph White for an Associated Press article (August 11, 2003), "I guess I'm kind of antsy

when I spend too much time out of the water."

—C.F.T.

Suggested Reading: Associated Press Aug. 11, 2003; ESPN Web site; Fédération Internationale de Natation Web site; *Los Angeles Times* D p1 May 24, 2004, with photos; Michaelphelps.com; *New York Times* D p4 Feb. 11, 2004, D p10 Feb. 16, 2004, with photos, D p1 Aug. 21, 2004, with photos; *New York Times Magazine* p20+ Aug. 8, 2004; North Baltimore Aquatic Club Web site; usolympicteam.com; usaswimming.org; *Washington Post* E p1 Apr. 18, 2004, A p1 June 1, 2004, with photos

Courtesy of Tribune Publications

Pitts, Leonard Jr.

Oct. 11, 1957– Newspaper columnist; nonfiction writer

Address: Miami Herald, 1 Herald Plaza, Miami, FL 33132

"I try to intrigue one reader, which is me," the syndicated newspaper columnist Leonard Pitts Jr. told Gregg Fields for the *Miami Herald* (April 6, 2004). Pitts, however, has been intriguing scores of readers since his column debuted, in 1994, in the *Miami Herald*; the twice-weekly column currently appears in more than 200 newspapers throughout the country. Pitts writes about pop culture, social issues, and family life, among other topics. "My interests tend to gravitate to things I see in my own proverbial backyard," he told Dave Astor for *Editor & Publisher* (April 5, 2004, on-line).

Pitts gained considerable attention for a column published the day after the September 11, 2001 terrorist attacks on New York City and Washington, D.C. The piece testified to the resolve and fortitude of the American people and was widely circulated on the Internet after its publication; Pitts received almost 30,000 responses from readers touched by his words. When Pitts won a Pulitzer Prize for commentary, in 2004, many observers thought the honor long overdue.

Leonard Pitts Jr. was born on October 11, 1957 in Orange, California, and was raised in a housing project near downtown Los Angeles. His father, who had served in the military, was an abusive alcoholic; he was frequently absent, and money was always in short supply for the family.

When Pitts was just five years old, he began writing stories, which were generally "about a boy who was secretly a superhero, with super strength and the ability to fly," as he wrote in a column for the *Miami Herald* (April 9, 2004, on-line). His mother, who died of breast cancer 16 years before Pitts won his Pulitzer, greatly encouraged him; she bought him a toy typewriter when he was eight and helped him buy a real typewriter on the layaway plan when he was 14. "She was not a learned woman, never finished high school. But then, it's hard to be learned when you grow up black in Depression-era Mississippi," he wrote in the column. "Still, not being learned is not the same as not being smart. [She] was a voracious consumer of books and newspapers, a woman filled with a thirst to know." He concluded, "Idealistic young scribes who insist their work is for them alone will disagree, but a writer without readers is like a person shouting in an empty room. And I'm humbled to think how much I owe to all the people who've kept me from shouting into that silence all these years. It is a line that stretches from you who are reading this right now all the way back to a woman in the projects trying to get dinner on, but still finding time to hear stories about a boy who can fly."

In 1973 Pitts entered the University of Southern California, in Los Angeles, at the age of 15, through a special honors program; four years later he graduated summa cum laude, with a degree in English. He began writing about pop music in 1976, as a stringer and later editor of *Soul*, a now-defunct black newspaper in the Los Angeles area. His work subsequently appeared in such publications as *Musician, Spin, Right On!, TV Guide, Reader's Digest*, the *Los Angeles Herald-Examiner, Oui, Billboard, Essence*, and *Parenting*. He also wrote several books on entertainment figures, including *Reach Out: The Diana Ross Story* (1983), *Papa Joe's Boys: The Jacksons Story* (1983), and *The Glamour Girls of Hollywood* (1984).

Pitts was also making his mark in radio during the 1980s. He wrote for the news stations KFWB and KNX, in Los Angeles, and he was the co-creator and editor of *Radioscope*, an entertainment program aimed at black audiences. He served as producer of the award-winning radio documentary

Who We Are, about the history of black Americas, which aired in 1988, and has also written and produced many other radio programs on topics ranging from the appeal of the pop singer Madonna to the life of the civil rights leader Martin Luther King Jr. He won several awards for his radio work, including two from the World Institute for Black Communications.

In 1991 Pitts joined the *Miami Herald* as a pop-music critic. The following year, while attending a U2 concert, he was knocked down by a swarm of teenagers. The experience helped Pitts, then in his mid-30s, to realize that he did not enjoy writing about pop music anymore, and he began searching for other subjects. In 1994 the editors of the *Miami Herald* agreed to let him write a column on subjects of broader interest. "I didn't have to pretend to take Britney Spears seriously [any more]," he joked to Fields. His column is now syndicated by Tribune Media Services and appears in more than 200 newspapers, including the *Chicago Tribune*, the *Atlanta Journal-Constitution*, the *Dallas Morning News*, the Milwaukee *Journal Sentinel*, and the New Orleans *Times-Picayune*.

Pitts, remembering his own youth and the encouragement given to him by his mother, often writes about the importance of literacy. In his September 20, 2000 column (as posted on the *Detroit Free Press* Web site), he decried the efforts of some parents and church members to ban J. K. Rowling's popular Harry Potter novels from libraries. (Harry and the other characters in the series attend Hogwarts School of Witchcraft and Wizardry, leading critics to charge that the books promote an unwholesome agenda.) "I don't deny that parents have a right to regulate the literature their children are exposed to," he wrote. "What irks me is when they try to regulate the literature my children are exposed to. And what bugs me even more is when librarians and other guardians of intellectual freedom cave in to some small group for whom fantasy is forbidden. . . . The fact is, the last thing any of us need to do is discourage a child from reading. It inspires me that J.K. Rowling, Harry's creator, is treated like a rock star wherever she goes. I like that her work has made reading cool again. Because people who can't read can't participate fully in the nation's life."

On September 11, 2001 Pitts was preparing to write an article on Andrea Yates, a Texas woman suffering from severe mental illness and religious delusions who had killed her own children. When hijacked planes hit the World Trade Center and the Pentagon and crashed into a field in Pennsylvania, he instead wrote a column addressed to the perpetrators. "The only words that seem to fit, must be addressed to the unknown author of this suffering," he wrote in his column, which appeared the next day under the headline "We'll go forward from this moment." As posted on the Web site of the *Miami Herald*, he continued, "You monster. You beast. You unspeakable bastard. What lesson did you hope to teach us by your coward's attack on our World Trade Center, our Pentagon, us? What was it you hoped we would learn? Whatever it was, please know that you failed. Did you want us to respect your cause? You just damned your cause. Did you want to make us fear? You just steeled our resolve. Did you want to tear us apart? You just brought us together." He concluded, "You don't know what you just started. But you're about to learn." The column was forwarded repeatedly via E-mail and posted on many Internet sites. House Democratic leader Richard Gephardt paraphrased Pitts's words in a radio broadcast soon afterward, and Regis Philbin read the column on the television show *Live with Regis and Kelly*. Pitts received more then 30,000 E-mail messages from people around the world. "I've heard from Hungary, New Zealand, France, Great Britain, and Canada," he told Joan Fleischman for the *Miami Herald* (September 23, 2001). "It's gone crazy. [I've] never seen anything like it—in my life. You know those Internet urban legends? That's what I feel like." For his columns relating to the terrorist attacks, Pitts was named the 2001 columnist of the year by *Editor & Publisher* and received the President's Award from the National Association of Black Journalists. He was also honored with a Sunshine State Award for best Florida journalism and a Green Eyeshade Award from the Society of Professional Journalists. (He had previously won several other Green Eyeshade Awards.)

Pitts has spoken out against the erosion in civil liberties that has taken place since the 2001 terrorist attacks. He took umbrage when a deputy with the U.S. Marshals, who provide security for U.S. Supreme Court justices, confiscated and erased the contents of a digital recorder and a cassette tape belonging to two reporters, who had used the devices to record an address Supreme Court justice Antonin Scalia delivered at a high school in Hattiesburg, Mississippi. (While Scalia does not generally allow recordings to be made of his speeches, no announcement to this effect was made prior to his talk, which was open to the public.) Although Scalia wrote a letter of apology and promised to allow future speeches to be recorded, Pitts wrote in his column of April 18, 2004, as posted on the *Seattle Times* Web site, "Still, the transgression was so profound, so antithetical to the letter and spirit of the Constitution, that it's hard to let it go at that." He continued, "You might write it off as an isolated example of a judge's bad judgment, except that there is a context here, isn't there? It's a context that finds the government's powers of surveillance expanded, Americans of Arab heritage detained indefinitely without access to counsel, [Attorney General] John Ashcroft legally empowered to poke into our reading habits. Now there's this: government officials seizing what amounts to a reporter's notes. There can be few things more intimidating or less likely to instill confidence in government's respect for constitutional guarantees."

Pitts frequently addresses race relations in his writing. "Some well-meaning people think it would be best if we could somehow factor race—race alone, of all the things I am—out of the picture," he wrote in a column that was posted on the PBS Pioneer Living Web site in 2002. "Their mantra: Let us be colorblind. If all they meant by that was 'equality,' I'd have no disagreement with them. But for them, the term seems to mean something considerably more radical. For them, colorblind means making oneself literally blind to color. . . . Given that each of us is a combination of many characteristics, why is it necessary to make such an ostentatious show of not seeing one: race?" He continued, "Decent people should seek balance instead—to make race neither smaller than it is nor larger. Because race is neither a defining facet, nor a demeaning facet, of individual identity. It's a facet, period. Unfortunately, much of what passes for racial dialogue in this country is the chatter of two extremes: the Afrocentric-to-the-point-of-paranoia one that says race matters always, and the 'colorblind' one that says it matters never. That's a false dichotomy. Race matters when it matters, and it doesn't when it doesn't."

In a column posted on the Affirmative Action and Diversity Project Web site and dated April 7, 2003, Pitts defended affirmative-action programs for racial minorities. (The column was sparked by a U.S. Supreme Court case testing the legality of affirmative-action policies at the University of Michigan law school.) "Although affirmative action was defended before the court as a means of achieving diversity, it's important to remember that this was never its most important function. Rather, it was born as a means of repairing damage America spent 3 1/2 centuries inflicting." Pitts does not feel, however, that affirmative action is the only answer to the ills that plague the black community. "Truth is, much of what ails black folk is within the power of black folk to fix. We need to bring fathers back into our families. We need to prioritize education above entertainment. We need to shut off the television sometimes and read. We need to support black business. We need to bling-bling less and save-save more," he wrote for the *Miami Herald* (March 29, 2004, on-line).

Pitts describes himself as a moderate; while he clearly outlines his position, he is typically respectful of those who disagree with him. His columns often call for increased tolerance and urge readers to empathize with others and find common ground. In his April 12, 2004 column, for example, he criticized radio hosts for the extremism and rigidity of their views. He named the conservative Rush Limbaugh in his criticism of such bias but pointed out that liberal commentators were taking on some of the same characteristics. "While you can hardly blame them for that, you still have to wonder if, in the long run, the quality of public discourse is really improved just because somebody is hollering at us from the other direction for a change," he wrote, as posted on the *Miami Herald*

Web site. "Noise is still noise, whatever its origin. Meantime, it feels like the middle ground is shrinking faster than the Amazonian rainforest. That's distressing for those of us who live there. More to the point, those of us who remain unconvinced that either ideology enjoys a monopoly on right— or wrong." He concluded, "Some people live in a world of stark either or, this or that. Bound by ideology, they lack the flexibility, imagination and intellectual agility to reason their way through life's contradictions and complexities. . . . But what gives me optimism is my conviction that most of us are not rigid ideologues. Most of us are reachable by reason. Most of us willingly work to figure out what the right thing is."

Perhaps because Pitts refuses to be labeled either conservative or liberal, his opinions sometimes surprise even longtime readers, which he views as a positive attribute. "The best that anyone can tell me about my column is that it is unpredictable; that they can't figure out what I'll say on any given subject," he told Hector Hernandez for the *Miami Herald* (March 4, 2001).

In addition to writing his column, in 1999 Pitts published the book *Becoming Dad: Black Men and the Journey to Fatherhood.* "[This] is a moving portrait of pain, suffering, and guilt as Pitts recounts a number of stories in which black fathers simply are not there for their kids," Anthony O. Edmonds wrote for *Library Journal* (June 1, 1999). "Although he offers no easy solutions, he does use the Million Man March of 1995 as a hopeful symbol that black men can learn to take more responsibility for their lives and those of their children. Although repeti-tious in places, this is a very well written and provocative work."

Pitts is a fellow of the Society of Professional Journalists. He has won numerous awards from the American Society of Newspaper Editors, the Scripps Howard Foundation, the National Society of Newspaper Columnists, and the Simon Wiesenthal Center. He is a three-time recipient of the National Headliners Award, given by the Press Club of Atlantic City. Pitts was a finalist for a Pulitzer Prize in 1992 and won the award, for commentary, in 2004.

Pitts was a Scripps Howard Visiting Professional at the School of Journalism and Communications at Hampton University, in Hampton, Virginia, for the spring semester of 2004; he taught one course in opinion writing and criticism and a second in popular-culture journalism. He is an avid reader of comic books and a die-hard fan of the Los Angeles Lakers basketball team. He and his wife, Marilyn, have five children and live in Bowie, Maryland, a suburb of Washington, D.C.

—K.E.D.

Suggested Reading: *Editor & Publisher* (on-line) Apr. 5, 2004, with photo; *Miami Herald* (on-line) Sep. 12, 2001, Mar. 29, 2004, Apr. 9, 2004

Selected Books: *Papa Joe's Boys: The Jacksons Story*, 1983; *Reach Out: The Diana Ross Story*, 1983; *The Glamour Girls of Hollywood*, 1984; *Becoming Dad: Black Men and the Journey to Fatherhood*, 1999

Potter, Myrtle S.

Sep. 28, 1958– President of commercial operations at Genentech

Address: Genentech, Inc., One DNA Way, South San Francisco, CA 94080-4990

In the early 1990s, as a mid-level executive with the pharmaceutical giant Merck & Co., Myrtle S. Potter was put in charge of marketing a medication designed to treat heartburn and stomach ulcers: Prilosec, which up until then had had mediocre sales. To the amazement of her superiors, she soon helped turn Prilosec into not only the world's best-selling drug of its type, but also one of the best-selling prescription drugs ever. With her next employer, the drug company Bristol-Myers Squibb, Potter rose to hold the title of president of the firm's U.S. Cardiovascular/Metabolics business unit. Under her leadership, that division grew faster than any of the company's others, despite intense competition from other drug makers, and its sales and profits increased steadily. In 2000 Potter accepted an invitation to become chief operating officer and executive vice president of commercial operations at the biotechnology firm Genentech, which, nearly two decades earlier, had turned her away when she tried to get work there as a sales representative. During the next four years, she directed the successful launch of six new medications, and, thanks in large part to her efforts, the company's revenues from sales doubled. In March 2004 she was promoted to president of commercial operations at Genentech, with responsibility for overseeing commercial development and marketing, among other areas. Potter is known for her exceptional ability to lead and inspire members of her marketing teams by fostering mutual respect and open communication; she has strived to learn from people at all rungs of the corporate ladder and to serve as both a mentor and a role model to her fellow workers. "Teaching never stops," she told Robin Madell for *Pharmaceutical Executive* (April 2000). "One of my goals is to just keep my mentoring circle as wide as I possibly can handle with my schedule. And I greatly value the mentoring I receive on an ongoing basis. You can touch people in very small ways without ever realizing the im-

Jamie Tanaka

Myrtle S. Potter

pact you're having, and it's something I've always tried to stay conscious of." In 2002 Potter was ranked 18th on *Fortune* magazine's list of the "50 Most Powerful Black Executives in America," and *Time* magazine named her among "15 Young Global Business Influentials" who demonstrated exceptional promise. In 2003 she was ranked 29th on *Fortune*'s list of the "Top 50 Most Powerful Women In Business."

A daughter of Albert Stephens and Allene Baker Stephens, Potter was born Myrtle Stephens on September 28, 1958 in Las Cruces, New Mexico. Her father, a military veteran, ran his own business; even when he had little money to spare, Potter told Robin Madell, his neighbors knew that he would help them financially to whatever extent he could. Her mother was a social worker; for a time she served on the New Mexico Governor's Commission on the Status of Women. "My mother was a wonderful example for us and a tremendous influence at a time when many African-American women certainly didn't have the kind of career that she had mapped out," Potter told Madell. "She truly was a visionary, both for her own life and for what she wanted to see in us." When Madell interviewed her, in 2000, several of Potter's five siblings held senior managerial positions in such prominent companies as Time Warner and Excell Agent Services. Growing up in modest circumstances, Potter often had to share the family's limited resources with her brothers and sisters, an experience, as she told Madell, that taught her the meaning of teamwork: "We really did learn what it meant to give to one another, to look out for one another, to be thinking of things outside ourselves."

When Potter was around 14, her father's business began to prosper, and the family moved to a more affluent, mostly white community in Las Cruces. There, Potter was exposed to overt racism for the fist time. "It was really incredible," she recalled to Noel M. Tichy, a professor at the University of Michigan Business School, for his book *The Cycle of Leadership: How Great Leaders Teach Their Companies to Win* (2002), as quoted by Robin Grugal in *Investor's Business Daily* (December 26, 2002). "Neighbors wouldn't speak to us. Things were thrown at the front of our house. But I clearly remember what my parents said to me about that. . . . 'They're just ignorant. It has nothing to do with you.' There was no hate. There was no anger. [The message] was [to] just simply ignore them."

Potter performed exceptionally well in high school and also participated in many extracurricular activities, including serving in the student government and cheerleading. As she approached college, she told her father that she wanted to study law at the University of Chicago. Her father did not have enough money to pay for tuition, however, so he made a deal with her: if she aced her courses in her first semester at a local college, he would agree to her attending the college of her choice, even if it meant remortgaging their house. Potter succeeded in earning A's in all her courses and, at the beginning of the next academic period, began studying law at the University of Chicago. By her third year there, she had lost her interest in becoming an attorney. A part-time job at the university hospital had sparked her interest in medicine, but she had no desire to become a doctor or nurse. After she worked as a marketing intern at IBM (1979–80), she seized on the idea of combining her interest in medicine with her business acumen. Soon after she received a B.A. degree, in 1980, she landed a position with the multi-product–company Procter & Gamble, as a salesperson in a new division that specialized in items for patient care. "The girl from New Mexico who had never really driven in snow before was suddenly in charge of a territory covering three-quarters of the state of Wisconsin and the upper peninsula of Michigan," she recalled to Madell. She also told Madell that she encountered subtle prejudice connected not only with her race but also with her sex and her upbringing in a small-town environment—obstacles that she regarded as "layer[s]" that "people worked through over time." "I viewed it as, 'This is me. Over time, you will come to know and respect me for who I am.'" In 1981–82 she held the title of district sales training manager.

In 1982, after she interviewed unsuccessfully for a sales-representative job with Genentech, Merck & Co. (then called Merck Sharp & Dohme) hired Potter for an equivalent position. She came on board at an exciting time; as she told Madell, "The talent pool, the support, the teamwork, and the camaraderie were unique and very special." Potter proceeded to gain a series of increasingly responsible posts: marketing analyst, training and planning manager, field meeting services manager, district sales manager, and product manager. In 1993 Merck promoted her to vice president of the firm's Northeast Business Group, part of the Human Health Division. Not long afterward she was given the assignment of reviving the sales of two products, Plendil and Prilosec, both of which Merck had licensed from the Swedish drug company Astra. Under an agreement between Merck and Astra, if sales of Prilosec reached a specified level by a given date (known as the "trigger"), the two firms would jointly launch a new U.S.–based drug company. Because of Prilosec's lackluster sales, most Merck executives regarded Potter's task as futile and assumed that such a collaboration would never come to pass. "I don't believe they put me in charge of that marketing team because they thought, 'Myrtle Potter is so brilliant; she'll come up with these strategies, turn these brands around, and we'll hit the trigger and form this $4 billion company.' I believe they were thinking, 'We'll probably miss the trigger. Here's an opportunity for one of our folks who started with us in the sales organization to come in and learn marketing in a relatively low-risk environment, and if we hit the trigger along the way, that's a beautiful thing.'" Potter not only hit the trigger four months ahead of schedule, but also saw Prilosec become a best-selling drug. In addition, working with a legal team, she helped protect the brand with a series of patents, thus discouraging competition from manufacturers of generic drugs.

Her achievement earned Potter the Merck Chairman's Award. She was also placed on the planning team for the launch of Astra Merck, which in 1999 merged with Zeneca (a maker of pharmaceuticals and agrichemicals) to form AstraZeneca. After the patent on Prilosec expired, AstraZeneca obtained approval from the U.S. Food and Drug Administration (FDA) to market a similar drug, called Nexium. According to an AstraZeneca press release dated February 21, 2001 (on-line), launches of Nexium in Europe, led by Potter, were "among the best in the pharmaceutical industry's history." Potter has called her oversight of the Astra Merck venture a turning point in her career: "It was the first time that I had a CEO view of an enterprise," she said, as quoted in *Business Dateline* (April 18, 2003). According to Gardiner Harris in the *Wall Street Journal* (June 6, 2002), as reported on the consumer-protection Web site Span Coalition, the ways in which AstraZeneca marketed Prilosec and Nexium have become models for drug companies seeking to maximize profits. The widespread use of Potter's tactics has led to a decrease in the availability of generic drugs and an overall increase in drug prices. According to Harris, "The Prilosec pattern, repeated across the pharmaceutical industry, goes a long way to explain why the nation's prescription-drug bill is rising an estimated 17 percent a year even as general inflation is quiescent. Just a few dozen high-priced branded drugs are driving this increase. As the drugs near the end of their market exclusivity, the maker typically brings out a new branded drug for the same condition, then launches a huge promotional campaign to convert users to the new one. And as in the Prilosec case, the new drug often is little better, or even little different, owing to growing difficulties drug-company labs face in finding novel drugs."

Potter left AstraZeneca in April 1996, when the U.S. Pharmaceutical Group of Bristol-Myers Squibb (BMS) hired her to fill a newly created position: vice president of strategy and economics. In that post she oversaw various game plans connected with managed-care contracts and primary-care business. In February 1997 Bristol-Myers Squibb promoted Potter to group vice president of the firm's Worldwide Medicines Group. She soon assembled a new marketing team; made up of people from the company's clinical-development, marketing, and sales divisions, it formulated a new, more comprehensive marketing plan. In March 1998 Potter was named senior vice president of sales in Bristol-Myers Squibb's 3,000-person U.S. Cardiovascular/Metabolics business unit. Among the medications she helped to promote were Pravachol (designed to lower high cholesterol) and Glucophage (for the control of blood-sugar levels in those with type 2 diabetes), both of which became hugely popular. Potter earned her next promotion after about eight months, becoming president of her unit in November 1998. While with Bristol-Myers Squibb, Potter earned the company's Leadership Development Award.

In 2000 Genentech lured Potter away from Bristol-Myers Squibb with the offer of the titles of chief operating officer and executive vice president of commercial operations and a $1 million bonus. Genentech, which calls itself "the founder of the biotechnology industry," was established in 1976; it is among the oldest and most productive biotechnology companies in the world. Its current chairman and CEO is Arthur D. Levinson. Traditional biotechnology, in which living organisms are used to make or change chemical compounds, has existed for thousands of years; examples include the use of yeast to make bread and bacterial cultures to make yogurt and cheese. With regard to the work of Genentech, modern biotechnology can be defined as "the application of scientific knowledge to transfer beneficial genetic traits from one species to another." It involves the manipulation, or recombining, of protein molecules that constitute DNA (deoxyribonucleic acid, the basis of heredity, which exists within the nuclei of cells) to form recombinant DNA. Within a few years of its founding, Genentech's researchers showed that it was possible to splice recombinant DNA into fast-growing bacteria, which then produced proteins helpful to humans. The first substance produced in that way, in 1978, was recombinant human insulin, used to treat diabetes; the second, created in 1979, was recombinant human growth hormone. Currently second in sales among biotechnology companies, after Amgen Inc., Genentech has achieved success largely by focusing on "targeted therapies," which are fabricated to treat "relatively small subsets of patients," as David Stipp wrote for *Fortune* (June 9, 2003). Owned in large part by the Swedish company Roche Holding Ltd., Genentech manufactures drugs for treating cancer (Herceptin, Rituxan, Avastin); heart disease (Activase, TNKase); cystic fibrosis (Pulmozyme); growth abnormalities (Nutropin); psoriasis (Raptiva); and asthma (Xolair). It has been listed on *Fortune's* list of "100 Best Companies to Work For in America" for five consecutive years; in 2001 and 2002 it was named one of *Red Herring* magazine's "Red Herring 100," the 100 companies deemed most likely to change the world. A year before Potter's arrival, the company had agreed to pay $50 million to settle federal criminal charges, after pleading guilty to marketing human growth hormone for unapproved uses from 1985 to 1994. (It is legal for doctors to prescribe FDA-approved drugs for conditions not described in the makers' applications for approval, but *marketing* the drugs for such uses is *not* legal.)

In her new positions Potter worked in the areas of marketing, managed care, commercial development, and dedicated support (the last referring to those employees whose sole jobs are to help customers who call with problems or questions). By 2002 she had helped the company's output rise to an average of three new products per year and planned to add to that number. "This company is about to enter the greatest phase of commercialization in its history," she told a reporter for *Med Ad News* (May 1, 2002). Potter reorganized Genentech's commercialization department, creating specialized sales groups for each of the company's drugs; thus, separate groups handled sales of Rituxan, Avastin, and Herceptin, all of which are prescribed to treat cancer. Potter told *Med Ad News*, "We know it's a little different than what most organizations do, particularly within the pharmaceutical industry, but the nature of our selling effort is at such a high scientific level that we believe that there's greater value in our leverage. They probably are the most scientifically sophisticated group of salespeople that I have ever seen." In early 2004 Potter was promoted to president of commercial operations. She also serves on Genentech's executive committee and, with Susan D. Hellmann, Genentech's president of Product Development, as co-chair of its Product Portfolio Committee.

"I've always had incredible physical stamina," Potter told Robin Madell. "I'm up very early and I'm up very late at night." Potter serves on the boards of directors of Amazon Inc. and the California Healthcare Institute; she is president-elect of the latter. Her honors include the Healthcare Business Women's Association's "Woman of the Year" Award, in 2000, and the National Woman of Distinction Award from the Girl Scouts of the USA and the beacon Award of the Girl Scouts of San Francisco Bay Area, both in 2004. Potter is married to James G. Potter, a graduate of the University of Chicago and Harvard Law School, who is currently senior vice president, general counsel, and secretary at Del Monte Foods. She and her husband share homemaking and child-raising duties, she told Madell. The couple's son, Jamison, and daughter, Lauren, are teenagers. When Jamison was three, Potter was told that he had a developmental disability and, as quoted by Grugal, would never "be able even to place an order at McDonald's." Thanks to her strenuous efforts and those of her husband and various experts, he now reportedly excels in academics and music. Despite her busy schedule, Potter makes time to participate fully in her children's lives; she attends many of their activities and does not hesitate to take family phone calls at work, even during meetings. She encourages the same dedication to family among those she supervises, although, as she told Madell, "until employees see someone on the executive team leaving to go to a soccer match or tend a family situation, they're not going to do it no matter what you say."

—P.G.H.

Suggested Reading: Genentech Web site; *Investor's Business Daily* A p3 Dec. 26, 2002; *New York Times* III p1 Oct. 1, 2000; *Pharmaceutical Executive* p48+ Apr. 2000; PR Newswire (on-line) Mar. 9, 2004; *Time* (on-line) Nov. 22, 2002

Powell, Kevin

Apr. 24, 1966– Journalist; nonfiction writer; commentator

Address: c/o Random House Inc., 280 Park Ave., New York, NY 10017

Kevin Powell achieved celebrity of sorts when he appeared on the first season of MTV's *The Real World*, in 1992. One of the earliest reality shows, *The Real World* aired glimpses of the interactions among seven people, previously strangers, chosen to live together for several months in an apartment in New York City. In the series' weekly installments, Powell, who is black, often appeared angry and quick to argue with his housemates. Since then, Powell, a journalist and political and social activist, has criticized reality television as one of many factors contributing to a lack of political and social engagement among Americans, particularly young people and African-Americans. "People are paralyzed by fear, do not question the information they are being spoonfed, and think they do not have the right to speak out if something around war or the war on terrorism seems a bit off," he told Ichiban Son, in an article posted on the *CyberKrib* Web site. "Thus, if a people have been lulled to sleep by cable or digital TV, by the internet, by friv-

Courtesy of Random House

Kevin Powell

olous magazines and very dumb reality TV shows, why would anyone ask the critical questions, why would anyone care to think, deeply, anyhow? But I have faith because I do think young people possess the brilliance and outspoken independence to make a difference in this world, the way young people did back in the 1960s when they led the Civil Rights and anti-Vietnam War movements right here in America. But it is going to take a spark, something tangible, to get folks moving again." With the aim of providing such a spark, Powell has spoken to and worked with young people throughout the United States. He has also disseminated his views and calls for action in articles published in *Rolling Stone*, *Essence*, *Vibe*, and other national periodicals and three books, including, most recently, *Who's Gonna Take the Weight?: Manhood, Race, and Power* (2003). According to the writer, educator, and clergyman Michael Eric Dyson, Powell is "one of America's most brilliant young cultural critics."

Kevin Powell was born in Jersey City, New Jersey, on April 24, 1966. He was raised by his mother, Shirley Mae Powell, a factory worker and home-health aide; the two shared a one-bedroom tenement apartment in a poor neighborhood with his aunt Kathy and cousin Anthony. According to Powell, his mother was verbally abusive and behaved in an overbearing manner toward him, as ways of keeping him out of trouble and trying to ensure that he would not turn out to be like his father, who had abandoned the family. His mother introduced him to reading and the library when he was very young; his love of learning, he has said, has been key to his success. "Without question, my mother had the most profound effect on me as a

child," he told Ichiban Son. "She, a working-class Black woman from the American South, raised me in incredible poverty, with a limited education, limited skills, and limited resources, and without the help of my father, who turned his back on her basically from the time I was born. It was my mother who instilled in me a love of knowledge, of reading, of seeing possibilities not readily in front of us. And my mother taught me how to make something out of nothing, how to make things happen with very little money."

Powell studied English and political science at Rutgers University in Camden, New Jersey, where he became a political and social activist; he took part in anti-apartheid protests (which sought to end the brutal repression of people of color in South Africa), helped to conduct voter-registration drives, worked on welfare-related issues in New York City, assisted with Jesse Jackson's 1988 presidential campaign, and helped run a summer camp for troubled youth in North Carolina. Also in the 1980s he began his career in journalism; within a few years he was freelancing for publications including the *Black American*, *San Francisco Weekly*, *Rolling Stone*, *Interview*, *YSB*, *Emerge*, the *City Sun*, *Black Enterprise*, *LA Weekly*, and the *Amsterdam News*.

In 1988 the university expelled Powell after he threatened a female student with a knife during an argument. According to Powell, he flashed the weapon to prove that he was serious but never intended to hurt the woman. After leaving Rutgers, he took a job at Newark Head Start, referring people, primarily single mothers, to social-service agencies that might help them. He later became an English instructor at New York University's Saturday high-school program.

From February to May 1992, during the first season of the MTV series *The Real World*, Powell appeared as one of seven previous strangers sharing a four-bedroom apartment in New York City's Soho neighborhood. The only African-American male in the group, he sometimes engaged in what a writer for *Horizon Magazine* (on-line) described as "angry, racially charged confrontations" with his roommates. "When I did *The Real World* I still had some lingering stereotypes of my own about people who were different than me. You bring some of your own defensiveness with you," he told the *Horizon Magazine* writer. "It just so happened that situation was taped for national and international television."

After his stint with *The Real World* ended, Powell wrote and hosted the award-winning MTV special *Straight from the Hood*. The documentary concerned the lives of Los Angeles youth before and after the 1992 riots that erupted in that California city after a mostly white jury acquitted four white Los Angeles police officers accused of using excessive force against a black man, Rodney King. Powell also landed a high-profile job at the hip-hop magazine *Vibe*, writing the cover story for its first issue, in 1992. Founded and owned by the African-

American entertainment mogul Quincy Jones, *Vibe* focused overwhelmingly on the music of urban minorities and other subjects of interest to blacks and Hispanics. In 1996, after years of working at *Vibe* as a senior editor and writing exclusively for that publication, Powell was fired; the precipitating event, which followed occasional run-ins with his supervisors, was an extended outburst in which he decried the failure of management to hire more minority editors.

Powell felt despair after his dismissal, but he came to view his termination as beneficial to him. "It was meant for me to get fired from *Vibe*," he explained to Katti Gray for *Newsday* (September 10, 2003). "I had to learn some lessons. I had to grow, do some serious self-analysis. It pushed me toward my purpose." After Powell had lived without a paycheck for some time, a gay quilter named William Cummings invited him to share his home in Manhattan. Cummings refused to judge Powell for his homophobic attitudes; rather, he became something of a father figure to Powell and prompted him to rethink his opinions about homosexuality. During that period Powell also stopped drinking heavily and quit smoking.

Powell's first book, a volume of poetry titled *Recognize*, was published in 1995. His second book, *Keepin' It Real: Post-MTV Reflections on Race, Sex, and Politics* (1998), is a collection of his critical and personal essays. He co-edited, with Ras Baraka (a son of the poet and dramatist Amiri Baraka), the anthology *In the Tradition: An Anthology of Young Black Writers* (1993); he also edited the anthology *Step into a World: a Global Anthology of the New Black Literature* (2000). Powell wrote the text that accompanies Ernie Paniccioli's photographs in *Who Shot Ya? Three Decades of HipHop Photography* (2002). He met Paniccioli, a noted photographer of rap-related subjects, while serving as guest curator of the Brooklyn Museum of Art exhibit *Hip-Hop Nation: Roots, Rhymes, and Rage*, in 2000. Powell was also a major contributor, along with editors of *Vibe*, to the book *Tupac Shakur* (1998).

Powell's book *Who's Gonna Take the Weight?: Manhood, Race, and Power* (2003) contains three previously published essays. In the first, "The Breakdown," Powell examined the suicidal feelings he experienced after *Vibe* ousted him and discussed such subjects as integration, multiculturalism, celebrity, and success. In "Confessions of a Recovering Misogynist," the second essay, Powell described his sexist views and how he has tried to overcome them; he also looked critically at the popular concept of manhood in the U.S., which he believes is often based on domination and violence. In the last essay, "What Is a Man?," he focused on the murdered rapper Tupac Shakur, black leadership, the gains and losses of the civil rights movement, and relations between the races. In a review of *Who's Gonna Take the Weight?* for the *San Francisco Chronicle* (August 17, 2003), Joshunda Sanders wrote that the book "establishes [Powell] as a prolific and sincere representative of the hip-hop generation, if not the most acute. . . . The standout of the collection, 'Confessions of a Recovering Misogynist,' revisits a recurring theme for Powell—his relationship with his mother. . . . Here, Powell navigates the mores of hip-hop culture, patriarchy and sexism with profundity—a rare feat for hip-hop journalists." Sanders found the last essay to be "the most erratic" in the collection. "Not only does 'What Is a Man?' not answer its own question, but it also creates a visceral connection between Powell and Tupac Shakur that at times seems overwrought."

In all three essays, Powell criticized rap and hip-hop music for shifting its focus from celebrating good times to an obsession with heavy drinking, illegal drugs, sex, violent encounters, and the objectifying of women. He admitted that he took many years to come to terms with his own blind spot about discrimination against women and their oppression. "We had a women's college called Douglass College [at Rutgers]," he told Tavis Smiley during an installment of the *Tavis Smiley Show*, on National Public Radio (September 25, 2003). "I was one of the many men who called himself a leader or an activist who never bothered to go over to Douglass College to take a single . . . women's studies class. You know, my activism was strictly male-centered, and so when I thought about activism, I thought of men as the leaders only, and as a result, I became like a lot of us . . . who call ourselves leaders, totally oblivious to gender oppression. And my thing now all these years later is that you can't just be opposed to oppression that's convenient to you. You've got to be opposed to all forms of oppression."

Powell had often written about Tupac Shakur before the rapper died, on September 13, 1996, six days after he was shot by unidentified assailants, and has remained fascinated by him and his continuing popularity. "Tupac Shakur has become this iconic figure in the way that Elvis [Presley has] for the rock 'n' roll community or Marilyn Monroe or James Dean or Dr. [Martin Luther] King or Malcolm [X] . . . and I've been struck particularly [by] how a lot [of] men of color have gravitated towards him," Powell told Smiley, discussing the "What Is a Man?" essay. "It says a couple of things to me. One is a serious void in black male leadership in this country. . . . The other part of it was to really begin to de-construct what has happened with black manhood over the last 30 years. . . . A lot of us are in a state of arrested development and we don't want to deal with that. It's like a lot of us have not even grown from where our fathers were a generation ago. In some cases, we've even deteriorated as far as I'm concerned when you look at the images that are being put out there now by black men." In his essay, Powell argued that while black female writers including Toni Morrison, Alice Walker, Toni Cade Bambara, and bell hooks have struggled with race, gender, and class issues in their books from the 1960s to the present, very few black male writers have done so.

Powell has often risked the ire of both African-Americans and the hip-hop community by criticizing them harshly. He has condemned the profanity, images of violence, and hatred of women found in hip-hop and rap lyrics, as well as the excessive materialism, stereotypical beliefs, self-hatred, and apathy toward political involvement that they convey. For instance, he has faulted rap record labels for choosing names such as Murder Inc., and thereby perpetuating negative stereotyping of blacks. He has also criticized African-American leaders for focusing on issues of little importance to the community as a whole and ignoring those that are of greater import. "I'm tired of black leaders that are only out for self," he said at the Fourth Annual Youth and College Leadership Summit held in Baltimore, Maryland, in November 2002, as reported by Jayson Rodriguez for the All Hip Hop Web site (November 11, 2002). "They go and protest [the film] Barbershop, but none of them show up at Jam Master Jay's funeral. [The rapper, a member of Run DMC, was shot and killed in his recording studio in October 2002.] None of them address molestation, education or AIDS."

In an article in the August 2003 issue of Essence, Powell criticized African-Americans for supporting black celebrities accused of or convicted of crimes. As an example, he cited the case of the R&B singer R. Kelly, who was charged with 21 counts of child pornography, including having sex with a 14-year-old girl. Despite those allegations, Kelly's album Chocolate Factory hit number one on the Billboard charts, and a rally in support of him was held in Chicago. "Do we remain silent because White racism is alive and well [and] we fear we may add to the troubles of Black celebrities by weighing in on their sins? Are we subconsciously saying it's okay for us to be abused, molested and lied to because we don't expect more for ourselves and our race? . . . Rather than challenging R. Kelly to seek help, we're sending a message that the charges against him shouldn't be taken seriously, and that his life should return to normal. But R. Kelly will never be 'normal' or healthy as long as he thinks haters are at the root of his problem. And neither will we, as long as we don't demand more of ourselves and of the people we call our heroes."

Powell has also faulted the U.S. government for what he perceives as an unwillingness to deal with racial issues in a meaningful way. In an article in Horizon Magazine, Powell criticized President Bill Clinton's apology for the suffering of slaves in the United States. "Symbolism, in the form of memorials, holidays, and the renaming of streets, has been used, habitually, to downplay the centuries of wrong done to African Americans. . . . For me and my kin and several blacks I've spoken to, a slavery apology means nothing if this nation isn't willing, for once, and without the make-up and the fanfare, to go to the mirror and look itself in the eyes." Powell also spoke out against the repeal of civil liberties and the public's unwillingness to tolerate dissent after the terrorist attacks on the World Trade Center and the Pentagon on September 11, 2001. "People in this country should not allow the tragedy of September 11th to become the tragedy of an era of silence and blind acceptance based on fear and ignorance," he told Charlie Braxton in an interview published on the Davey D Web site (March 24, 2002). "To me, to be patriotic means to fight for democracy in its purest form. Or what Patrick Henry said during the Revolutionary War period: Give me liberty or give me death. Liberty, the way I define it, is supposed to be about truth. And liberty, to me, means I have the right and freedom to say what I want whenever I choose, particularly if it is about the issue of democracy."

A popular speaker, Powell frequently lectures on such topics as racism, sexism, American popular culture, American and African-American history, contemporary literature, multiculturalism, and the history of hip-hop. He continues to write about hip-hop culture, sexual issues, politics, and black literature for publications including Essence, Rolling Stone, Ms., Newsweek, the Washington Post, Code, and the BET Web site. Since 1996 he has held about 100 informal meetings with young people in prisons, churches, community centers, schools, colleges, and literary conferences in various parts of the country. He asks them to discuss the problems they and their communities face, and hopes he can help them and other teenagers find potential solutions to such problems and envision their role in applying those solutions.

In 1995 Powell and his longtime friend Darwin Beauvais, a Philadelphia attorney, set up the non-profit organization Get Up on It, which ran a multi-media political-awareness campaign to encourage activism among youths. In 1999 Powell and April Silver, a friend whom he had met in his student-activist days, launched "Hiphop Speaks," a college speaking tour and quarterly community forum in New York City, which stressed the history and elements of hip-hop (for example, DJs, MCs, graffiti writing, and dance) and the political and social responsibilities of the art form. Powell was also chairperson of the initiative, which was dissolved in June 2003.

In the summer of 2001, Powell was arrested for assaulting the journalist Knox Robinson, who he believed had misquoted him in an article for Code magazine. Although Robinson pressed charges, Powell did not receive jail time. He replaced Robinson's glasses, which he had broken, and later apologized to him.

While Powell has focused much of his energy on getting African-Americans involved in political and social actions, he has said that he realizes that to achieve real change, people must come together across barriers that have grown up around racial, gender, and religious differences. "For me, it's about building something specifically for the black community, but I also want to be a bridge builder because I think we've got to have progressive people of different backgrounds—black, white, Latino, Asian, Native American," he told Tavis Smiley.

"We've got to work together with some coalitions and get beyond these divisions of race and gender and class, and sexual orientation and stuff like this. . . . You look at Malcolm X at the end of his life where he turned the corner and was talking in broader terms, . . . you look at the fact that Dr. King's last act was the attempt to create a Poor People's campaign. He didn't say poor black people. He said poor people because he understood that it was poor blacks and poor whites who were being sent to fight poor yellow people"—a reference to the Vietnam War.

A self-confessed workaholic, Powell has undergone 15 years of psychotherapy. He has cited James Baldwin and bell hooks as his literary heroes. Powell lives in the New York City borough of Brooklyn. He recently announced that he plans to run for Congress in 2006.

—K.E.D.

Suggested Reading: *All Hip Hop* Web site Nov. 11, 2002; *CyberKrib* Web site, with photos; *Horizon Magazine* (on-line); *Newsday* B p8 Sep. 10, 2003, with photos; *Tavis Smiley Show* Sep. 25, 2003

Selected Books: *Recognize*, 1995; *Keepin' It Real: Post-MTV Reflections on Race, Sex, and Politics*, 1998; *Who Shot Ya? Three Decades of HipHop Photography* (with Ernie Paniccioli), 2002; *Who's Gonna Take the Weight?: Manhood, Race, and Power*, 2003; as editor—*In the Tradition: an Anthology of Young Black Writers* (with Ras Baraka), 1993; as editor—*Step into a World: a Global Anthology of the New Black Literature*, 2000

Robert Laberge/Getty Images

Pujols, Albert

Jan. 16, 1980– Baseball player

Address: St. Louis Cardinals, Busch Stadium, 250 Stadium Plaza, St. Louis, MO 63102

At 24 years of age, Albert Pujols has proven to be one of the finest hitters in Major League Baseball. In his first three seasons, the St. Louis Cardinals first baseman amassed a career .334 batting average, 114 home runs, and 381 RBIs, statistics that correspond to those of the baseball greats Joe DiMaggio and Ted Williams early in their careers. In

the 2004 season he added to those terrific numbers, batting .331, with 46 home runs and 123 RBIs. Many sportswriters have called Pujols a natural, a description that does not completely do him justice, suggesting as it does that his talent takes the place of hard work. Since he joined the majors, in 2001, Pujols has adhered year-round to a demanding training schedule. He studies videos of his at-bats and of the pitchers he will face, and he continues to work on his swing by spending a great deal of time in batting cages. The Cardinals' manager, Tony La Russa, has in interviews called Pujols the best player he has ever managed—no small praise, considering that he has managed such outstanding hitters as José Canseco and Mark McGwire. La Russa believes that Pujols's approach to the game sets him apart from other players. "Albert is so professional in his approach, whether it's the winter, the spring, or the summer," La Russa remarked in an interview with Michael Northrop for *Sports Illustrated for Kids* (June 2004).

The youngest of 12 children, Jose Alberto Pujols was born on January 16, 1980 in the Dominican Republic and grew up in the Dominican capital, Santo Domingo, in a poor area. (He has been referred to as Albert at least since his name began appearing in the media.) At an early age he developed a love of baseball. As a teenager he was invited to baseball camps sponsored by major-league teams, who were always on the lookout for raw talent they could sign to their farm systems. Though Pujols did not initially make the cut, he decided not to give up on his dream of playing professional baseball. When he was 16 he, along with his father, Bienvenido, moved to the United States. They stayed in New York City for a month before settling permanently in Independence, Missouri, where a number of Pujols's aunts and uncles had found employment as school-bus drivers. In Independence Pujols enrolled as a sophomore at Fort Osage High School and took daily, one-on-one lessons in English. He also joined the school's baseball team. Because of the language barrier, he had trouble at first in understanding the game's rules; despite that, he twice earned all-state honors in baseball, primarily due to his unusual hitting ability. (He smashed one home run—at rival Liberty High School—across center field, over the 402-foot fence, and into an air-conditioning unit atop a nearby two-story building.)

After graduating from high school, in 1998, Pujols earned a baseball scholarship to Maple Woods Community College, in Kansas City, Missouri, where he continued to impress his coaches and teammates with his innate skills and his dedication. After playing a season with the Maple Woods team, Pujols was signed by the St. Louis Cardinals scout Dave Karaff. Shortly thereafter he left school to join the Cardinals farm system. Most of his only minor-league season was spent with the Peoria Chiefs, where he batted .314 with 19 home runs and 96 runs batted in (RBIs). The Cardinals' manager, La Russa, had planned for Pujols to spend more time playing minor-league ball, this time with the Memphis Redbirds, following spring training in early 2001. But after the starting outfielder Bobby Bonilla injured his hamstring, La Russa called the eager young minor leaguer up to play Bonilla's left-field position on Opening Day. During his first Major League series, against the Arizona Diamondbacks, Pujols got seven hits, including his first big-league home run, and drove in an impressive eight runs. Following that stellar debut, Pujols's place on the Cardinals was secure for the season.

Unlike many minor leaguers, who come to the Major Leagues, play well for a couple of games, and subsequently falter, Pujols has made good on his early promise. During the 2001 season he played in 161 of 162 games, which proved to La Russa and Cardinal fans alike that he was a true workhorse. He also showed his extreme versatility in the field, playing first base, third base, shortstop, and the outfield at various times over the course of the season. (Pujols's favorite position was third base; he has since become the Cardinals' starting first baseman, because the team needed a solid fielder in that position.) Most importantly, in those 161 games he hit 37 home runs and drove in 130 runs while posting an impressive .329 batting average, becoming the first rookie to bat over .320 with more than 35 homers since Hal Trosky of the 1934 Cleveland Indians. His 130 RBIs set a National League rookie record, as did his total bases (360) and extra-base hits (88). His home-run tally was just one shy of the record held by Frank Robinson of the Cincinnati Reds, who hit 38 in his rookie year, 1956.

During the 2001 season the Cardinals' lineup was racked with injuries. Among those who either could not play up to par or spent long periods on the disabled list were Jim Edmonds, J.D. Drew, and Mark McGwire, St. Louis's legendary power hitter. Pujols, already showing promise as a hitter early in

the season, quickly made up for the lack of run production and took over McGwire's power-hitting number-four spot in the batting order in June. Pujols also helped St. Louis to clinch the National League Central Division championship over the Houston Astros at the end of the season. The Cardinals went on to compete in the first round of the play-offs, the Division Series, in which they were swept by the Arizona Diamondbacks three games to two in that best-of-five series. (The Diamondbacks went on to win the 2001 World Series against the New York Yankees.)

Just a day after McGwire retired from baseball, Pujols, McGwire's natural successor, was named National League Rookie of the Year. Ken Gumick of *MLB.com* quoted Pujols as saying, shortly after he won the award, "If you work hard every day you always reach your goal. Tony [La Russa] put trust in me and gave me the opportunity to prove myself and make the team. This is an exciting day for me. I never thought about Rookie of the Year. I'm just glad and blessed to be here and thinking of having a great year."

Pujols's second season in the Major Leagues proved to be as impressive as his rookie season, if not more so. By the end of the 2002 regular season, he had racked up a batting average of .314 with 34 home runs and 127 RBIs–becoming the first player in the majors to have a .300-plus average with more than 30 homers and 100 RBIs in each of his first two seasons. For some time during the season, many sportswriters and fans felt that he had a chance to win baseball's elusive Triple Crown—to become the player who records the highest batting average with the greatest home-run and RBI production. Though Pujols was unable to finish first in all three categories (the last man to do that was Carl Yastrzemski of the Boston Red Sox in 1967), he was a contender for the Most Valuable Player award, coming in second only to the San Francisco Giants slugger and single-season home-run champion, Barry Bonds. After finishing 13 games ahead of the Houston Astros, the Cardinals clinched the National League Central Division and headed into the play-offs to face the Diamondbacks in the 2002 Division Series. Avenging the previous season's loss, the Cardinals bested the defending World Series champions in a three-game sweep. They were defeated in the National League Championship Series, however, by the Giants, led by Bonds.

At the end of the 2003 season, Pujols emerged as the first major-league player in history to have batted over .300 with more than 30 home runs and 100 RBIs over his first three seasons of play. Moreover, as had been the case for the 2002 season, he was in pursuit of the Triple Crown for the majority of the season. Though he did not achieve that goal, he won the 2003 National League batting title with an incredible .359 average, beating Todd Helton of the Colorado Rockies by .00022. Over the course of the season he hit 43 home runs (tying Ralph Kiner's record, set during the 1946, 1947, and 1948 seasons, of 114 home runs for the first three seasons of Major League play) and batted in 124 runs. He also topped both leagues that year by hitting 51 doubles, and as in the previous year, he came in second in the National League Most Valuable Player voting behind Barry Bonds.

Following his spectacular season, Pujols negotiated a new contract with the Cardinals' management. Pujols, who had made over $900,000 during the 2003 season, would have been eligible for free agency after 2006. The Cardinals, not wanting to lose one of their few home-grown stars of recent years, offered Pujols a seven-year contract worth $100 million, with an option for an eighth year and an additional $11 million. He would also become the club's starting first baseman, following the trade of Tino Martinez to the Tampa Bay Devil Rays. Despite tough negotiations—Pujols was reportedly firm about signing a long-term contract—both sides were pleased with the results. Pujols vowed to continue to play ball aggressively. "The money will mean something in a small way with my family, but it won't change the way I play baseball," he remarked following the negotiations, as quoted on *ESPN.com* (February 20, 2004).

In addition to the salary guaranteed by his long-term contract, Pujols will earn $100,000 for his first national endorsement deal, with the nutritional-supplement maker MuscleTech. His image was also used on the cover of EA Sports' *MVP Baseball 2004* video game. Other endorsement contracts are forthcoming, according to Kimberly Woods, marketing director of the agency Beverly Hills Sports Council, which represents Pujols. "There are plenty of opportunities out there, but Albert is particular about what he attaches his name to," Woods explained to a reporter for the *St. Louis Business Journal* (December 12, 2003). "The fact that he's been in the league for only three years and already has a national campaign, that's pretty few and far between."

At the beginning of the 2004 season, Pujols found himself being compared to baseball greats Ted Williams and Joe DiMaggio. The numbers he had posted over the course of his first three seasons, in the opinion of many sportswriters, put him in the company of the two men who have been called arguably the greatest all-around baseball players of all time. His batting average over three season is .334—between those of DiMaggio (.331) and Williams (.356). He also fell between the two men in RBIs, with 381 for Pujols, 378 for Williams, and 442 for DiMaggio. With 114 home runs, Pujols hit more homers in three years than either man (DiMaggio had 107; Williams 91). As Peter Gammons noted in his article for *ESPN.com* (March 8, 2004): "In many ways, Pujols is a throwback to those Hall of Famers who starred in the 1930s because he is a contact, line-drive hitter. In the last two seasons [2002-03], he's hit 77 homers, but, unlike most of his slugging contemporaries, has walked 14 more times than he's struck out."

Pujols ended the 2004 season with a .331 batting average, 46 home runs, and 123 RBIs. His clutch power hitting, along with those of his teammates Jim Edmonds and Scott Rolen, helped the Cardinals clinch the National League Central Division championship. The team won 105 games in the regular season—more than any other in Major League Baseball—and most sportswriters regarded them to be an odds-on favorite to win the World Series. In the postseason the Cardinals beat the Los Angeles Dodgers in four games in the best-of-five division series and went on to face the Houston Astros in a gripping National League Championship Series. Although the teams had finished 13 games apart in the regular season, they battled throughout those contests, with the Cardinals ultimately triumphing in seven games. Pujols batted an outstanding .500, with four homers and nine RBIs, and helped to bring the Cardinals their first National League pennant since 1987.

In the World Series the Cardinals faced the Boston Red Sox, who had overcome a three-games-to-none deficit in the American League Championship Series to beat the New York Yankees for the pennant. Since the Red Sox had not won a World Series since 1918, the team was the sentimental favorite of many fans and sportswriters, many of whom believed that St. Louis, with its power-hitting trio of Pujols, Edmonds, and Rolen, would deny Boston a world championship. That prediction proved to be incorrect: the Red Sox vanquished the Cards in four straight games. Pujols batted a solid .333 in the series, with five hits in 15 at bats, but failed to earn any home runs or RBIs.

Pujols has told interviewers that he attributes his success as a batter and fielder to his training and conditioning. During the off-season he uses weight machines and dumbbells to strengthen his arms and allow him more control of the bat. During the season he always comes to batting practice early and continues up until 15 minutes before every game, going through batting drills taught to him by Alex Rodriguez of the New York Yankees. "They help me out, especially when I'm jumping at the ball," he explained to Daniel G. Habib for *Sports Illustrated* (June 30, 2003). "They just remind me to stay back, use my hands and stay inside the ball." Pujols's intensive practice has allowed him to refine his swing to such an extent that he is able to cover the entire plate—hitting balls largely where he wants, off just about any pitcher. As his former teammate Tino Martinez said about Pujols for the same *Sports Illustrated* article: "Lefthander, righthander, soft thrower, power guy, fastballs away, fastballs in—he doesn't have any holes. It's a long season, with a lot of at bats, and it's hard to stay focused and not give any away, yet I can count on one hand the number of at bats he's given away."

Pujols also credits his wife, Deidre, whom he met in his senior year of high school, with helping him to stay focused. On a shelf in his locker is a present from his wife, a ceramic baseball with an inscription from the biblical Book of Ecclesiastes:

"Whatever your hand finds to do, do it with all your might." Married since January 1, 2000, the couple have two children, Alberto Jr. and Isabella, Deidre's daughter from a previous relationship.

Pujols understands that he is a role model, not only to his fellow Dominicans and other Latin Americans but to all American children. He tries to live up to that responsibility, primarily by eschewing the decadent lifestyle embraced by so many other professional athletes. As he noted in his interview with Peter Gammons: "Whenever I walk out of this game I want to be one of the best players, but at the same time I want my fans to remember me as one of the best persons to ever get along with the fans."

—C.M.

Suggested Reading: *ESPN.com*; *MLB.com*; *New York Times* D p3 Sep. 29, 2003, D p4 Feb. 19, 2004; *Sports Illustrated* p48+ Apr. 16, 2001, p44+ Oct. 1, 2001, p32 June 30, 2003p59 Sep. 1, 2003; *Sports Illustrated for Kids* p21 Dec. 2003, p22 June 2004; *St. Louis Business Journal* p5 Dec. 12, 2003

Courtesy of Ballet Hispanico

Ramirez, Tina

Nov. 7, 1933(?)– Founder and artistic director of Ballet Hispanico

Address: Ballet Hispanico, 167 W. 89th St., New York, NY 10024

For Tina Ramirez, the founder of the dance company and school Ballet Hispanico, dance "is not only an artform but a source of self-esteem, cultural awareness, and social mobility," as *Dance Teacher* (February 2003, on-line) noted. Trained in classical ballet as well as Spanish dance, the Latin American–born Ramirez performed professionally for more than 15 years, beginning when she was 14, before assuming the directorship of a small, existing dance studio in New York City in 1963. When she formed Ballet Hispanico, seven years later, she hoped not only to continue to offer Hispanic youngsters rigorous training in modern and Latin dance forms and ballet but also to give a select number of talented young dancers (including non-Hispanics) the chance to perform in public as members of an established troupe. She resolved, moreover, to use the school and troupe to help build confidence among budding dancers and provide them with tools to become high-functioning adults, and to awaken her students to the richness of their heritages. Ramirez also wanted to show people of other ethnicities and nationalities "who Hispanics are," as she explained to Jennifer Dunning for the *New York Times* (November 28, 1994). "Our culture. Why we move the way we do. Our music. There is so much that unites us, like language and love of home and family. Yet there's so much variety within the given." By the early 1990s almost two million people on three continents had attended performances by Ballet Hispanico. In 1973, with the goal of "teach[ing] children that there is another world beyond theirs and that dancing is a part of life," as she told an interviewer for the National Education Association (on-line), and also introducing them to Hispanic culture, she created an educational-outreach arm of Ballet Hispanico, called Primeros Pasos ("first steps"); the program now reaches some 25,000 schoolchildren a year nationwide.

By general agreement, Ballet Hispanico is "recognized worldwide as the foremost dance interpreter of Hispanic culture in the United States," as the Skidmore College magazine *Scope* (Summer 2003, on-line) put it; a writer for the *Buenos Aires (Argentina) Herald* (July 1, 1993) declared that it is "hands down the leading Hispanic-American dance company in North America," and added, "To miss one of their performances is to miss a great treasure in the dance world." In the *Boston Globe* (February 7, 1998), Elijah Wood described the troupe as "a sort of Latino counterpart to [the African-American company] Alvin Ailey: a group that draws on and celebrates an ethnic tradition, but is not limited by it." Anna Kisselgoff, in the *New York Times* (October 31, 1991), wrote that its "polished group of performers exud[e] the sheer joy of dancing. . . . One attends Ballet Hispanico to share the kinesthetic excitement of its dancers in all their energy and exuberant sophistication." After noting that the dancers' agility and passion had earned them a standing ovation at a 2003 concert, the *Scope* reporter wrote, "Whether individually or in groups, the dancers' explosive split-jumps, scissor kicks, acrobatic leaps, and ultra-high lifts give the impression of human fireworks. Yet they move with a rubber-like grace—precise, but never stiff as they glissade, linger midair, and spin and sweep into something like ice dancers' death spirals. There's no denying that the dazzle factor is huge."

Since 1970 Ramirez has commissioned for her company more than 70 new works by 45 choreographers (set, with very rare exceptions, to music by Hispanic composers), among them Talley Beatty, Graciela Daniele, Geoffrey Holder, Ralph Lemon, Vicente Nebrada, Ann Reinking, and David Rousséve; she herself has choreographed four dances and co-developed another. Ballet Hispanico has performed at major dance festivals in the U.S. and abroad and at such well-known venues as the John F. Kennedy Center and Ford's Theater, in Washington, D.C.; Carnegie Hall, the Joyce Theater, and the Delacorte Theatre, in New York City; and the Annenberg Center, in Philadelphia, Pennsylvania. "A hot pride burns in Ramirez's dancers, both men and women, as they cross a stage," Chuck Graham wrote for the *Tucson (Arizona) Citizen* (March 18, 1991). "It is always there, in the carriage of their shoulders, the confident way they take each step. It is a pride that has jumped the Atlantic Ocean and spanned the centuries. Their art is not a matter of style, but of heat. Every serious dancer and lover of dance needs to see Ballet Hispanico. Ramirez is creating a new dance form, not ethnic nor modern nor classical, that can not be seen in any other company."

Tina Ramirez's date of birth appears to be a closely guarded secret. She was probably born in the early to mid-1930s; according to *Contemporary Hispanic Biography*, the day was November 7. Her father, José Ramirez, was a Mexican matador known as Gaonita; her mother was a native of Puerto Rico. In "true theatrical tradition," as Ramirez put it in an interview for *Scope*, her birth took place in a hotel room in Caracas, Venezuela, a stop on the so-called bullfight circuit. She has at least one sibling—a sister, Coco Ramirez, a dancer who appeared in a 1965 Broadway production of *Hello, Dolly!*, among other shows. In the 1950s the sisters performed for a while as the duo Tina and Coco Ramirez. By her own account, Tina Ramirez's interest in dance began in her early childhood, when her father would "put me on his feet and teach me to dance," as she told Jennifer Dunning. She told Valerie Gladstone for the *New York Times* (November 21, 1999), "From my father I learned to appreciate grace, since the bullfight is a dance." She has recalled that as a youngster, she would run alongside her father while he practiced maneuvers out-of-doors. "I remember him clapping and stomping with a fury," she told Ashley Fantz for the *Memphis (Tennessee) Flyer* (April 3, 2000, on-line). "I loved watching him move. I would go home and [stand] up on my tippy-toes barefoot and just walk around like that. I could do that without toe-shoes until I was 16." When Ramirez was six, according

to Dolores Tropiano in azcentral.com (February 18, 2004), her parents divorced; her mother moved to the East Harlem neighborhood of New York City, where Ramirez's maternal grandmother took care of the children while their mother was at work. Ramirez told Tropiano that she "always wanted to be in show business"; her mother, however, whose father was a schoolteacher, considered dancing only a hobby and urged her daughter to set her sights on teaching. Ramirez—who told Valerie Gladstone that she "learned respect for education" from her mother—convinced her mother of her seriousness about dance, and within the next half-dozen years, she took lessons with several preeminent dance teachers: Lola Bravo, who has been called "New York's grande dame of Spanish dance"; the great Russian-born ballerina Alexandra Danilova, who had worked with the master choreographers Sergei Diaghilev and George Balanchine; and the Polish-American Anna Sokolow, who had been trained by the pioneering modern-dance choreographer Martha Graham.

Ramirez's professional life began when she was a young teenager. In her earliest jobs, as Edmund Newton reported for the *New York Post* (November 17, 1975), she danced in clubs and stage shows. In the latter half of the 1940s, she joined the Federico Rey Dance Company. (Rey, who had studied Spanish dance, was a costume designer as well as a dancer; he later turned to designing for the theater full-time under his real name, Freddy Wittop.) On tour with Rey's company, Ramirez performed in venues in the U.S., Canada, and Cuba. "It was a great period, there was plenty of work," she told Newton. The archives of the Jacob's Pillow Dance Festival and school, in Massachusetts, contain a film, made in 1948 and 1949, in which Rey and Ramirez perform Basque dances together and separately. In the mid-1950s Ramirez danced in Spain with a popular flamenco singer and dancer named Enrique Vargas (known as El Príncipe Gitano), who had invited her to join his company after he noticed her dancing at a street fair in Madrid. In other work during this period, she appeared in the chorus of the original Broadway production of the musical *Kismet*, which ran from December 1953 to April 1955, and danced with three others (among them her sister) in the roles of "children" in a 1959 revival of the 1946 musical *Lute Song*. She was also seen in a television version of the musical *Man of La Mancha*.

In 1963, at the invitation of Lola Bravo, who had decided to retire, Ramirez became the director of what had been Bravo's dance school, set up in a Manhattan apartment building. Bravo had been seeking "a woman to continue in her tradition of teaching children," as Ramirez recalled to Iris Dorbian for *Dance Teacher* (February 2003, on-line). The offer came at an opportune moment for Ramirez: dancing had become increasingly difficult for her, because she had been suffering from the lingering effects of an old back injury, and, in addition, she had begun to feel unfulfilled as a dancer. "I wanted to do more positive things in my life—that's what I was thinking at the time," she explained to Dorbian. "I had been performing for a very long time. . . . I thought, 'Is that all there is to life?'" Under Ramirez's guidance, enrollment at the school doubled within months, and the landlord told her that he would no longer rent the space to her. "There were just too many people going in and out—you know, these are Latin people so they are bringing their brothers, sisters, cousins, uncles," Ramirez told Ashley Fantz. (The school subsequently moved twice more. It now operates in a Ballet Hispanico–owned facility on the Upper West Side of Manhattan.)

In 1967 Ramirez launched Operation High Hopes, a dance program for inner-city children; dubbed the Tina Ramirez Dancers, her pupils performed in local neighborhoods, using a flatbed truck as a stage. Three years later Ramirez founded her own company of professional dancers, with "five girls and two understudies," as she recalled to Anna Kisselgoff for the New York Times (August 20, 1976). At first she called the troupe the New York City Hispanic-American Dance Company. "But that sounded like a museum," as she said to Kisselgoff; soon afterward she changed the name to Ballet Hispanico of New York. (On its Web site, the name appears as simply Ballet Hispanico.) "From the beginning," she told Jacqueline Maar for the University of California–Los Angeles Daily Bruin (March 2, 2000, on-line), "I wanted to present a forum where Hispanic dancers could do contemporary work using the techniques that they have, like Spanish dance, classical ballet, Caribbean and South American forms." As an integral part of the curriculum at the Ballet Hispanico School of Dance (whose enrollment is currently about 600), she also wanted to teach her students about their cultures. "Hispanic children living in New York were losing their identity," she told Jennifer Dunning. "They don't know who they are, even now. They say proudly, 'Oh, I'm Dominican,' but they can't point to their country on a map. They don't know Spanish comes from Spain. I think it's very bad for children—any child—not to know. It defines you." Ramirez also aimed to educate non-Latino audiences about Hispanic dance; as she remarked to Kenneth LaFave, as quoted on the New York Dancewear Co. Web site (2004), "People think wrongly that Latin dancing is one kind of thing. The different dances actually have different characteristics." (In the Los Angeles Times, Jan Breslauer [March 30, 1995] wrote that Ballet Hispanico is "the antidote for anyone who thinks Spanish dance is all clacking castanets and combustible cha-cha-chas.") And not least, Ramirez wanted to disabuse non-Latinos of negative or stereotypical ideas about Hispanics. At one of her troupe's performances, at a school in Albany, New York, as she recalled to David Dudley for AARP Magazine (March/April 2004, on-line), students booed when the dancers revealed their ancestries or countries of origin. "I remember thinking, Boo

all you like. In the end you'll be applauding"—which is precisely what happened. After another performance, at a school in Wisconsin, a fourth-grader from the audience said to Ramirez, "I wish I was Puerto Rican." "That's the power of education—the power to touch," she declared to Dudley. "Above all else," she told the Scope interviewer, "Ballet Hispanico celebrates the power of dance to unite people everywhere through joy, emotion, and passion in everything we do."

Ramirez has been described as tiny and as having seemingly limitless energy. Among other honors, she has earned, in New York City, the Mayor's Award of Honor for Arts and Culture in 1983 and the Mayor's Ethnic New Yorker Award in 1986. She received the New York State Governor's Arts Award in 1987 and, in 1988, the Manhattan Borough President's Award. She received citations of honor at the 1992 Capezio Dance Awards and the 1995 "Bessies" (New York Dance and Performance Awards) ceremonies. She was presented with a Hispanic Heritage Award in 1999, in recognition of her achievements in the field of education, and the Dance Magazine Award in 2002. In 2004 AARP Magazine named her a "cultural trailblazer" and one of 10 "people of the year." She has served on the New York City Advisory Commission for Cultural Affairs, the New York State Council on the Arts, and the Association of Hispanic Arts.

—K.J.E.

Suggested Reading: azcentral.com Feb. 18, 2004; Ballet Hispanico Web site; csufresno.edu; dance-teacher.com Feb. 2003; Memphis (Tennessee) Flyer (on-line) Apr. 3, 2000; National Education Association Web site; New York Post p41 Nov. 17, 1975; New York Times D p20+ Oct. 14, 1979, C p13 Nov. 28, 1994, II p40 Nov. 21, 1999; Skidmore College Scope (on-line) Summer 2003

Ramos, Jorge

(RAY-mohss, HOR-hay)

1958– Newscaster and journalist

Address: Univision, 9405 N.W. 41st St., Miami, FL 33178

According to Louis Aguilar in the Denver Post (November 11, 2002), the broadcast journalist Jorge Ramos is "the Spanish-language equivalent of Tom Brokaw, Oprah Winfrey and Horatio Alger wrapped in one." Calling himself "the voice of those who have none," the Mexican-born Ramos is the co-anchor for Noticiero Univision (Univision Newscast), which airs nightly on the Los Angeles–based Univision television network, and the host of the network's weekly news-magazine program Aqui y Ahora (Here and Now). Since he joined Univision, in 1985, Ramos has reported from the field

J. Emilio Flores/Getty Images

Jorge Ramos

on five wars, traveled to more than 60 countries in pursuit of stories, interviewed six U.S. presidents, and traded pointed barbs with the Cuban dictator Fidel Castro and the controversial Venezuelan president Hugo Chavez, among many other public figures. He conducted the first televised interview with George W. Bush following Bush's acceptance of the Republican Party's nomination for the presidency in 2000, and spoke with the Democratic presidential aspirant John Kerry in a highly publicized interview on the Mexican holiday Cinco de Mayo on May 5, 2004. Ramos has become both famous and influential among Latinos in the U.S. and has developed a reputation as one of the foremost journalists in Latin America—a judgment reinforced by his receipt in 2001 of the prestigious Maria Moors Cabot prize from Columbia University's School of Journalism (a rare feat for a television journalist) and by the sizable viewership of his evening news program. Indeed, the nightly ratings for *Noticiero Univision*, which Ramos has co-anchored, with María Elena Salinas, for 17 years, surpass those of ABC, CBS, and NBC in some major markets—specifically, Houston, Los Angeles, and Miami—and are competitive in many others; moreover, as Ramos explained to Eliot Tiegel for *Television Week* (June 23, 2003), "We're seeing an incremental increase in our audience on a year-to-year basis, which is the opposite of what's happening with the English-language networks, which see decreasing viewership." Ricardo Brown, a radio personality and the news director of the national network Radio Unica, described Ramos's appeal to Lydia Martin for the Hispanic Online Web site (January/February 2001): "People perceive him not only as a solid, honest, hardworking journalist, but

as a warm, kind human being who identifies with the reality here. All the success he's had is due to the same work ethic and desire to better your life that Hispanics here have. That's his magic."

In addition to his work for Univision, which has earned him and the network a total of seven Emmy Awards, Ramos has written six books, pens a weekly column that is syndicated to three dozen newspapers, and offers daily commentary on many Latino radio stations. Although he has retained his Mexican citizenship, he has often pointed out that his evolution from a penniless newcomer to the United States to an interviewer of presidents and world-renowned journalist is an example of the fulfillment of the American dream. Consequently, he believes that he has a twofold responsibility to the public. The first is "to inform the community and the Hispanic community on what's important for us and what's going on on a daily basis," as he said to Sandy Mazza for the Greensboro, North Carolina, *News & Record* (October 24, 2003); the second is to convey "a very simple message: If I made it, you can make it." In a conversation with Matthew Estevez for *Latin Trade* (January 2002), he said, "I believe the most important social responsibility for a journalist is to stop the abuse of power. If we don't ask the questions, nobody will."

The eldest of four brothers and one sister, Jorge Ramos was born in 1958 in Mexico City. "My father was an architect," Ramos told Mike McDaniel for the *Houston Chronicle* (October 16, 2002), "at a time [when] Mexico was not building a lot, so I grew up never knowing if we were going to have the means to [make it] the following month." As a boy Ramos attended Catholic parochial schools and was active in sports; indeed, as a 10-year-old, during the 1968 Olympic Games, held in Mexico City, he watched Kenyan marathoners run past his grandfather's house, and afterward he aspired to become an Olympic athlete himself. An injury to his spinal cord that he suffered as a teenager ended that dream. "So many years, so much hard work and so many pains, all in vain," he wrote in *No Borders*, according to Veronica Villafane in the *San Jose Mercury News* (October 24, 2002).

Ramos attended the Universidad Iberoamericana, in Mexico City, where he found another outlet for his youthful exuberance: journalism. After he graduated, in about 1980, he embarked on his career as a reporter, working in a series of jobs, with newspapers, a radio station, and a television station. He soon found the pervasive government-imposed censorship stifling. The first article he wrote for a newspaper was censored, Ramos told Sandy Mazza, "because it criticized the [Mexican] president"—José López Portillo, who served from 1976 to 1982. In 1983, after a segment he had edited for a Mexican television program was bowdlerized for a similar reason, Ramos resigned his position, sold his car, and moved to Los Angeles, California. "If I had remained in Mexico, I would probably have been a poor, censored, frustrated journalist, or maybe a psychologist or university professor speaking out eternally and pathetically against those who censored me. . . . I wanted a life, more independent and free, less structured, open to the world," Ramos wrote in *No Borders*, as quoted by Villafane.

With a student visa, Ramos enrolled at the University of California at Los Angeles (UCLA), where he took courses in journalism (without earning a degree). To support himself, he waited tables, earning $15 a day. One-third of his wages paid for a room in a run-down motel in which he lived during his first year in the United States. With another $5, he bought Rice-a-Roni—his dietary mainstay—which he prepared on a portable burner (the motel kitchen was off-limits to residents). He used the last $5 "to get to know the United States," as he recalled on his Web site. In 1984 he took a job as a reporter at KMEX-TV in Los Angeles. The next year he was hired by the U.S.-based Spanish International Network, later renamed Univision. Quickly climbing the corporate ladder, in 1986 he was tapped to host Univision's morning news program *Mundo Latino*, relocating to Miami, Florida, to take up his new duties. A few months after he debuted on *Mundo Latino*, in November 1986, the 28-year-old Ramos was named co-anchor, with María Elena Salinas, of Univision's nightly news broadcast, *Noticiero Univision*, a post he has held ever since. In the following years Univision extended its reach as a news source, setting up bureaus in New York City, Washington, D.C., Chicago, San Antonio, San Francisco, and Los Angeles as well as in Miami, and overseas in Mexico, Peru, Colombia, and El Salvador; in addition, the network employed freelance reporters in Brazil, Argentina, Ecuador, Nicaragua, Guatemala, Venezuela, and Colombia. *Noticiero Univision* is now broadcast in 13 Latin American countries as well as the United States, where, in many big markets, its ratings are competitive with or surpass those of the major networks. Thus, in terms of viewers, Ramos is as successful as Dan Rather, Tom Brokaw, and Peter Jennings. Within the Hispanic community, according to a report by the research group Hispanic Trends, in 2000 Ramos ranked third on a list of the most admired Latinos in the United States, behind the actor Edward James Olmos and Henry Cisneros, a former Secretary of Housing and Urban Development. Over the years Ramos has interviewed the Cuban dictator Fidel Castro (whom he pointedly snubbed, refusing to allow Castro to place a hand on his shoulder), Hugo Chavez, the leftist president of Venezuela, and other public figures accustomed to a censored and sycophantic press. "I do not believe in objectivity," Ramos told Matthew Estevez. "I believe in giving each one what they deserve." His tough questioning cemented his status as a serious and fearless journalist, further adding to his already considerable popularity.

In a column for *Segunda Juventud* (July 2003), a Spanish-English publication of the American Association of Retired Persons (AARP), Ramos listed the 10 events or situations he has witnessed as a journalist that he felt were of the most significance in his career. One was the strengthening of democracy in Mexico following the election of Vicente Fox Quesada as president, in July 2000. Ramos had difficulty remaining outwardly objective about Fox's election, which heralded an end to generations of de facto one-party rule in Mexico. As he recalled to Martin, on December 1, 2000, the day of Fox's inauguration, he felt "torn between being a journalist and being a Mexican." According to Martin, "Ramos managed to cover all the hoopla and all the politics with his usual stiff upper lip. But when Univision's evening news was over and Ramos signed off, he took to the streets of Mexico City, one more jubilant face in the crowd." "For the first time in 17 years," Ramos recalled, "I sang the Mexican National Anthem. I got goose bumps. Then I felt tears coming. I really had to celebrate."

Ramos also reported on the September 11, 2001 terrorist attacks on the World Trade Center and their immediate aftermath. With all planes grounded, he traveled from Miami to New York City by car, driving for 24 hours straight. What he beheld at Ground Zero, the site of the disaster, "was worse than any of the five wars I have covered," as he wrote for *Segunda Juventud*. "I could not believe what I saw. It wasn't until a few days later that I was able to cry. For several days, I blocked myself emotionally to be able to do my job as a journalist. I have never seen anything like it."

Another event on Ramos's list is the bombing of Afghanistan by the U.S., which began in the fall of 2001 in an attempt to destroy the ruling Taliban, which had sheltered Osama bin Laden and other members of Al Qaeda, the terrorist group responsible for the September 11 strikes. Although Univision executives felt hesitant to send anyone to cover events there, given the danger and uncertainty of the situation, Ramos refused to be dissuaded; he went there on his vacation, paying his own way. Within Afghanistan he traveled with a group of guerrillas (opponents of the Taliban), who were "supposed to take care of me," as he recalled to Russ Mitchell for CBS's *The Early Show* (October 11, 2002). One day, one of the men "told me that he was a follower of Osama bin Laden. He started playing with his rifle and aiming it . . . at my face. At one point I told him, 'You take care of me, I'll take care of you.' At the end of the trip . . . I gave him $15. I think those $15 truly saved my life."

The other stories that Ramos listed in his article for *Segunda Juventud* are the fall of the Berlin Wall, in 1989; the transfer of Hong Kong from British to Chinese rule, in 1997; Pope John Paul II's trip to Cuba, in 1998; the drug war in Colombia, which has continued for nearly two decades; the botched coup in Venezuela, in 2001; the U.S.-led war in Iraq launched in March 2003; and the ongoing controversy regarding the illegal crossings of undocumented workers over the Mexican–U.S. border, some of which have ended in tragedy (as in cases of Mexicans who died of suffocation in locked truck trailers).

Ramos has written six books, the first of which, *Detrás de la máscara* (Behind the Mask, 1997), offers his impressions of people he has interviewed. "I was tired of telling stories in two minutes," Ramos explained to Adriana Lopez for *Publishers Weekly* (October 14, 2002). "Books were a place to express my opinion on what I [was] seeing— something you're unable to do in television." In addition, Ramos informed Mazza, the events he had covered "leave an emotional scar. I cannot tell those emotional experiences on TV, and that's why it's important to write because books compensate for the lack of time and emotion on TV."

Ramos's next book, *Lo que vi : experiencas de un periodista alrededor del mundo* (What I Saw: Experiences of a Reporter Around the World, 1999), sold 50,000 copies, 2,000 more than its predecessor. The book that followed, *La otra cara de América: historias de los inmigrantes latinoamericanos que están cambiando a Estados Unidos* (2000), was translated into English in 2002 with the title *The Other Face of America: Chronicles of the Immigrants Shaping Our Future;* in it Ramos attempted to show that in terms of their aspirations for themselves and their descendants, and various other characteristics, recent immigrants from Latin America differ little from immigrants from elsewhere who arrived in the U.S. in decades past. *The Other Face of America* met with a mixed critical response. In the *Washington Post* (February 18, 2002), Mary Beth Sheridan wrote, "The 47 short chapters . . . read like extended sound bites. Ramos has dumped not only his notebook but his mailbag and apparently anything he found in his pockets into a book that's a mishmash of pro-immigration arguments and impressions, unleavened by serious analysis or reporting." Sam Quinones, a reviewer for the *Los Angeles Times* (January 13, 2002), agreed, complaining that the book was "the prose equivalent of television news. Every page shows that the reporter hasn't spent the time to make his characters come alive and understand their contradictions." By contrast, Fabiola Santiago, writing for the *Miami Herald* (February 7, 2002), described the contents of the work as "readable, straight-forward people stories mixed with acute observations and analysis of U.S. policy." Ramos next wrote *A la caza del león* (In the House of the Lion, 2001), a collection of interviews with, among others, candidates in the Mexican and U.S. presidential elections of 2000, Venezuelan president Hugo Chavez, and former Mexican president Carlos Salinas.

The year 2002 saw the publication of Ramos's memoir *Atravesando fronteras: un periodista en busca de su lugar en el mundo,* translated in the same year as *No Borders: A Journalist's Search for Home.* In writing the book, Ramos told McDaniel, he had three audiences in mind: "The first was my children. . . . I wanted to let them know who their father is and what I went through in the 44 years of my life." The second was composed of Spanish-speaking Americans who watched his news program every night yet knew little about him; in the third were English-speaking Americans who needed to know "that immigrants are here to work and make this a better country and that we are not criminals and that we are not terrorists," as he told McDaniel. In *No Borders* Ramos revealed that, like countless other immigrants, he did not feel at home in his adopted country, in his native land, or anywhere else. Shannon Brady Marin, who reviewed *No Borders* for the *New York Times Book Review* (March 16, 2003), felt that "the most successful portions of the book . . . are the personal narrative and reportorial reminiscences." Jeanne Jackle, writing for the *San Antonio Express-News* (November 7, 2002), characterized *No Borders* as "an unusually intimate autobiography. . . . Ramos shares sweet and bittersweet moments from his childhood and adolescence; difficulties he encountered when breaking into journalism in this country; and perhaps best of all, fun little memories and quirks that can't help but bring a smile." Juliet Wittman was less enthusiastic, commenting for the *Washington Post* (February 2, 2003), "Although Ramos tells us he was moved to write this book because it is impossible to do justice to complex issues on a television newscast, there's a casual conversational tone to the writing that skirts depth." Ramos's latest book is *La Ola Latino* (*The Latino Wave: How Hispanics Will Elect the Next President*, 2004). In a review for the *Los Angeles Times* (July 2, 2004), Anthony Day avowed, "All Americans ought to read this book—or at least know what it says. It is about the future of the United States."

Ramos has earned five Suncoast Regional Emmy Awards, in the categories "reporting spot news" (for his story "Kuwait: The Price of Victory," in 1991), "individual achievement" (for the special program "A Divided Nation," in 1992), both "talent" and "public affairs segment/community issues" (for "Chiapas," in 1995), and "talent" (for "Subcomandante Marcos," in 1996), and he anchored two news stories for which *Noticiero Univision* and Univision News won national Emmys, both in 1998. His other honors include the 2001 Maria Moors Cabot Prize, from the Columbia University Graduate School of Journalism, for "distinguished journalistic contributions to inter-American understanding"; the 2003 David Brinkley Award, from Barry University, in Miami, for excellence in communication; and the 2004 AAP Honors, from the Association of American Publishers. At Barry University's award ceremony, according to the school's Web site, Ramos advised aspiring journalists to prepare themselves for their careers by studying history, sociology, philosophy, psychology, and ethics. He also quipped, "I am very proud of my Spanish accent. Especially because I cannot get rid of it."

Ramos and his wife, Lisa, a Cuban-American, live with their son, Nicolas, in southern Florida. Ramos also has a teenage daughter, Paola, who lives in Madrid, Spain, with her mother. In his spare time he enjoys playing soccer as a member of Univision's company team.

—P.B.M.

Suggested Reading: Greensboro, North Carolina) *News & Record* D p1 Oct. 24, 2003; *Hispanic Online* Jan.–Feb. 2002, with photo; *Houston Chronicle* p1 Oct. 16, 2002, with photo; Jorge Ramos Web site; *Latin Trade* Jan. 2002; *Latina* p76 Nov. 1, 2002; *Publishers Weekly* p20 Oct. 14, 2002; *San Jose Mercury News* Oct. 24, 2002; *Television Week* p23 June 23, 2003; *Washington Post* T p10 Feb. 2, 2003

Selected Books: *Detrás de la máscara* (Behind the Mask), 1997; *Lo que vi: experiencas de un periodista alrededor del mundo* (What I Saw: Experiences of a Reporter Around the World), 1999; *La otra cara de América: historias de los inmigrantes latinoamericanos que están cambiando a Estados Unidos*, 2000 (*The Other Face of America: Chronicles of the Immigrants Shaping Our Future*, 2002); *A la caza del león* (In the House of the Lion), 2001; *Atravesando fronteras: un periodista en busca de su lugar en el mundo* (*No Borders: A Journalist's Search for Home*), 2002; *La Ola Latino* (*The Latino Wave: How Hispanics Will Elect the Next President*), 2004

Todd Warshaw/Allsport/Getty Images

Rampone, Christie

(ram-PONE)

June 24, 1975– Soccer player

Address: c/o U.S. Soccer Federation, 1801 S. Prairie Ave., Chicago, IL 60616

Still widely known by her maiden name, Christie Pearce, the women's soccer player Christie Rampone is among the superstars of her sport. As a member of the U.S. women's soccer team since 1997, Rampone has been hailed for her remarkable speed, agility, flexibility, and endurance. She has played in more than 100 international competitions with the U.S. Women's National Team, as it is known formally, including Women's World Cup

matches in 1999 and 2003 and the 2000 and 2004 Olympic Games. In high school and college, she shone in basketball and field hockey as well as soccer, and on the soccer field, she has performed outstandingly in three positions: forward, midfield, and defense. Referring to her alma mater Monmouth University, in New Jersey, many sources have noted that she is the only player on the national team to graduate from a "small soccer school." She is also said to be the finest athlete ever produced by Ocean County, New Jersey (whose population exceeds half a million), where she has lived since infancy. Rampone is a co-founder of the Women's United Soccer Association, which came into being in 2001 and ended operations (but did not cease to exist) in 2003; with that league, she is a member of the New York Power. In 2001 she suffered a serious knee injury and underwent surgery; through intensive rehabilitation, she regained enough skill and strength to rejoin the national team in 2002 but not enough to regain her position as an international competitor. Thanks to her determination and rigorous conditioning regimen, she achieved that goal the following year, when she made her 100th appearance in world soccer in a game against the Brazilian women's team. Indeed, by that time, according to April Heinrichs, the coach of the U.S. Women's National Team, Rampone had become an even better player than she had been before her injury. "She no longer relies on natural athletic ability," Heinrich said, as quoted on NBCOlympics.com (July 2004). "She has become a student of the game."

Christie Rampone was born Christie Patricia Pearce on June 24, 1975 in Fort Lauderdale, Florida, to Bob and Sandy Pearce. (Some sources list her given name as Christine or identify her as Christie Pearce-Rampone. The Women's Soccer World Web site and some other sources have erroneously reported her birthday to be May 24.) Her father teaches eighth grade at a public middle school; her mother is a librarian. She and her siblings—her older sister, Wendi, and younger brother, Jeff—grew up in Point Pleasant, New Jersey, a town of about 20,000 on the Atlantic coast. Rampone attended Point Pleasant Boro High School, where she was an All-State athlete in soccer, basketball, and field hockey; she was the first person to lead the Shore Conference (which consists of 44 high schools from New Jersey's Ocean and Monmouth Counties) in scoring in all three sports. In 1993, when she was a senior, the New Jersey Nets basketball team named her New Jersey Female Athlete of the Year. After she graduated from high school, Rampone entered Monmouth University, in West Long Branch, New Jersey, where she majored in special education. She served as both a point guard and a shooting guard on the Monmouth Hawks, the women's basketball team, which she co-captained in her senior year; she became famous on the court for her speed, passing skills, and tenacity as a one-on-one defender. As a member of the women's soccer team (1993–96), also called the Hawks, she started all 80 games of her college career; she became the school's all-time leading scorer (79 career goals, 54 assists, 212 career points) and record holder for goals (19), assists (15), and points (53) in a season (in 1995, when she finished eighth in the nation). In 1995 and 1996 she was named Northeast Conference Player of the Year. Nevertheless, according to NBCOlympics.com, in college "basketball was her primary sport. . . . She considered soccer something she did for fun." As an undergraduate she earned all-league honors in field hockey as well as in basketball and soccer. In her senior year she played in two school lacrosse games, too. While student-teaching in a middle school, she coached soccer and basketball there as a volunteer. Rampone graduated from Monmouth with a bachelor's degree in special education in 1997; she later earned a teaching certificate.

A year or so earlier, Tony DiCicco, who was then the coach of the women's national soccer team, had visited Monmouth at the suggestion of Rampone's college soccer coach, Ken Van Shaak, to watch Rampone on the playing field; he observed her during part of a game against Central Connecticut State. Rampone struck him as, in his words, an "incredible athlete"; he remembered thinking, as he told Michael Lewis for Scholastic News (2003, on-line), "If I can turn her into a soccer player, maybe we have something special." "She was a forward for [the Hawks] and a big scorer," he said to Lewis. "I was looking for defenders with speed and comfort with the ball." When, in December 1996, she received a fax inviting her to train with the U.S. women's national soccer team, "she thought it was a joke," as NBCOlympics.com reported. Rampone began training under DiCicco in San Diego, California, in January 1997. She debuted on the U.S. Women's National Team at age 21, in a match against Australia on February 28 of the same year, which the U.S. won, 4–0; she made her first goal with the team on May 2, in a game against South Korea, which ended with a score of 7–0. Rampone played right midfield in all three games at the U.S. Women's Cup in 1997, in which the U.S. defeated Canada (4–0), Australia (9–1), and Italy (2–0); in the contest with Australia, she scored the 100th goal in the history of the competition, which was launched in 1994.

In 1998 Rampone started 14 of her 19 matches and was a member of the gold-medal team at that year's Goodwill Games. "She's probably one of the most athletic people on this team," the veteran player Carla Overbeck, who had taken maternity leave that season, told Gary Davidson for Soccer Times (June 30, 1999, on-line). "She's very quick, she's fast. She's very good in the air. She's tough. Very rarely does some attacker get in behind her because of her speed 'cause she reads the game so well. When she comes into a game defensively, she gives our attack a spark just because of that attacking mentality she has." Tony DiCicco told Davidson, "For sure, she is one of the two or three fastest. . . . She has a 29-inch vertical [leap]. She's come so far in really a short time." DiCicco also said of Rampone, "She's one of the nicest people on the team. She's unassuming, she's caring, she's always got a smile. She's very coachable. She's a joy to coach." In the summer of 1998, she played in several matches with the New Jersey Stallions of the W-League.

The following year Rampone participated as a U.S. Women's National Team substitute during the final 17 minutes of a match against North Korea in the Federation Internationale de Football Association (FIFA) Women's World Cup. Speaking of that game, she told Gary Davidson, "It was amazing. . . . It was just such adrenalin. I was like in my own little world, my own little focus. It was like I didn't hear anything once I got on the field, and I just kind of relaxed and just said, 'I worked six months for this. I'm going to go out and have fun.' And I totally enjoyed every minute I was out there. On the bench, you are always aware of the crowd and making sure they're getting into the game and seeing what they're doing, but once I got into the game, I wasn't aware of the crowd at all." The U.S. team won the World Cup tournament, which attracted far more attention than any previous women's soccer event. An unprecedented 660,000 spectators attended the 32 games, which were played in large stadiums for the first time and were broadcast live on national TV, with an estimated 40 million viewers tuning in.

In 2000 Rampone participated in 32 matches and started in 30, among them the five games in which the U.S. women's soccer team competed at the Sydney Olympics; she remained in each of the five for their entirety. The U.S. team, which entered those Games as the defending champion, won the silver medal that year; in the final contest, Norway scored three goals to the Americans' two. In 2001 Rampone played with the U.S. national team in only four games. That year saw the launching of the Women's United Soccer Association (WUSA), created in the belief that the FIFA Women's World Cup had marked the beginning of a promising new era in women's soccer. The founders of the WUSA included John Hendricks, the founder and CEO of the Discovery Channel, who was the primary investor, and 20 female soccer players, among them Rampone, Mia Hamm, Julie Foudy, Michelle Akers, Brandi Chastain, Joy Fawcett, and Kristine Lilly; Tony DiCicco was named WUSA's commissioner. Rampone became a defender and midfielder with the New York Power, one of the eight teams set up within the league. (The others were the Atlanta Beat, the Boston Breakers, the Carolina Courage, the Philadelphia Charge, the San Diego Spirit, the San Jose Cyber-Rays, and the Washington Freedom.) Her teammates included Shannon Boxx, who, like Rampone, played with the 2004 U.S. women's Olympic team.

In a game against the Carolina Courage on August 2, 2001, Rampone—who had started in all 18 New York Power games in which she had played—tore the anterior cruciate ligament (ACL) in her right knee. The injury, which forced her to miss the two final regular-season games and the play-off, against the Bay Area (now San Jose) CyberRays, required surgery. Rampone began rehabilitation immediately after the operation, which was performed in late August, so that she would be able not only to rejoin her team as soon as possible but also to dance at her wedding, to Chris Rampone, on November 9, 2001. "I'm doing a lot of exercises to strengthen my hip so I don't have a swing in my walk," she said, as quoted in a WUSA press release (2001, on-line) that is no longer on the Web. She continued with her rehab regimen during her honeymoon and afterward. During the last week of November, she and the Washington Freedom's goalkeeper Siri Mullinix hosted what was dubbed the CP3 Soccer Clinic at an indoor facility at the Meadowlands in New Jersey. "I just wanted to be able to come back and give something to the kids and let them know that it's attainable and reachable coming out of Jersey," Rampone said, as quoted on the WUSA press release. "There is so much opportunity out there for them at such a young age and with the professional league underway and doing well, there's just a great future for them."

In 2002 Rampone returned to the Power; she played in 19 games, starting in all of them. She was often in pain, however, because tendonitis had developed in her surgically repaired knee; the problem led to her failure to make the national-team rosters for the Nike Cup or the Gold Cup. Rampone lamented to Matthew James Weeks for USA Today (February 13, 2003) that 2002 "just was not a great year for me. . . . And it was so disappointing to not see my name on that [U.S.] roster after so many years of being on it. But that really lit the fire for me to make it this year." Meanwhile, she had been training with the soccer coach Mike Lyons, who had worked with her when she was in high school. To regain her speed and agility, she used strength bands on both legs and practiced distance running, among other exercises. She also strived to recover her ability to "cut on a dime," or pivot, as she put

it in an interview with Howard Bass for the Asbury Park Press (November 6, 2002, on-line), a New Jersey newspaper.

Her hard work paid off: by January 2003 Rampone had returned to active play. She played in two of the U.S. team's three games in the Four Nations Tournament in China, which also included clubs from the host nation, Norway, and Germany. A few weeks later April Heinrichs, the coach of the U.S. National Team, told Weeks that Rampone deserved an award for "most improved player." "She has absolutely excelled the last couple of months," Heinrichs said. "It's just been wonderful to have her back in our camp." Later that year Rampone told Michael Lewis for Scholastic News that her forced sabbatical from soccer after her injury "really made me realize how much I enjoyed it and how much I missed it. Just playing it every day and loving it I got my confidence back. I was playing better. I'm really confident right now." Heinrichs told Lewis that Rampone had become a "smarter player." "She is playing the best soccer of her career," she said. Rampone played with the U.S. team in the 2003 Women's World Cup, held in October of that year. After emerging victorious over Sweden, Nigeria, and North Korea in the first round of that competition, and over Norway in the quarterfinals, the U.S. team lost to Germany in the semifinals and then won a game against Canada, 3–1, to finish in third place. Rampone played in all four matches but scored no goals.

In 2004, along with 17 other female U.S. soccer players (among them such "living legends" as Hamm, Chastain, Foudy, Fawcett, and Lilly), Rampone participated (but scored no goals) in the Summer Olympic Games, held in Greece. The U.S. team won the gold medal in those Games, after a tie with the Australian team and victories in contests against the teams from the host country, Japan, Germany, and Brazil. (The U.S. defeated Brazil twice, the second time in the final match of the Games, on August 26, which the Americans won 2–1 in overtime.) To rejoice in their triumph along with their fans, the players planned to launch a 10-game "Fan Celebration Tour" on September 25 in Rochester, New York.

Earlier, on September 15, 2003, the WUSA had announced that it would cease operating immediately, for financial reasons; the outpouring of fan and other support that had been expected had not materialized. The league's efforts to stanch the flow of red ink, among them the lowering of the founding players' salaries (with their approval) by $20,000, to $60,000, had proved fruitless. (Other two-year WUSA veterans were earning $31,500—a pittance in the world of professional sports.) "In retrospect the WUSA could not have picked a more difficult time to launch its inaugural season," John Philip Wyllie wrote for Soccer Digest (June/July 2003, on-line), referring to the nation's dismal economic climate. "The league has succeeded in providing entertaining, world-class women's professional soccer, but that achievement has not been matched on the balance sheet." WUSA did not end its existence, however; John Hendricks and others associated with it formed what was dubbed a reorganization committee, in hopes of reviving it. In June 2004 the league hosted weekend "soccer festivals" at sites in California and Minnesota, at which WUSA teams played demonstration games. "The WUSA Soccer Festivals are a terrific opportunity for soccer fans to witness the world's best female players right before the Athens Summer Olympic Games," Tony DiCicco remarked, as quoted on a WUSA press release (March 1, 2004, on-line).

Along with her personal trainer, Mike Lyons, Rampone has held soccer workshops for children and teenagers in New Jersey. She herself trained with workshop attendees in July 2004, in preparation for the Olympic Games. She has also worked with a fitness trainer, Mike Greenblatt, with whom she concentrated on increasing her speed and endurance. While with the U.S. team in China in 2003 and Costa Rica in February 2004, Rampone wrote long, humorous "postcards" for the U.S. Soccer Web site, in which she described her impressions of those countries. In one she admitted that she missed her "boys," as she referred to them—her husband, Chris Rampone, who works as a baseball coach at Montclair State University, and the couple's dog, a black Labrador named Tiger, with whom the couple live, in Point Pleasant. Christie Rampone is a skilled seamstress; in high school she made her own prom dress, and she took her sewing machine with her to the 2000 Olympics, so that she could help her teammates when their uniforms needed mending.

—K.J.E.

Suggested Reading: NBCOlympics.com; *Scholastic News* (on-line) 2003; *Soccer Times* (on-line) June 30, 1999; *USA Today* (on-line) Feb. 13, 2003; *WUSA* (on-line)

Jon Kopaloff/Getty Images

Reilly, John C.

May 24, 1965– Actor

Address: c/o United Talent Agency, 9560 Wilshire Blvd., Fifth Fl., Beverly Hills, CA, 90212

Until a couple of years ago, movie audiences might have been hard-pressed to put a name to John C. Reilly's face. Although the multifaceted character actor had appeared in nearly 30 films since 1989, he had managed to remain under the radar of the media, thanks largely to his choice of small supporting roles. Reilly's anonymity disappeared in 2002, when he appeared in three movies nominated for that year's Academy Award for best picture: Stephen Daldry's *The Hours*, in which he played a dull but doting husband; Martin Scorsese's *Gangs of New York*, which found him in the role of a corrupt policeman; and Rob Marshall's *Chicago*, in which his performance as the passive husband of a would-be showgirl earned him an Oscar nomination for best supporting actor. When the *Toronto Star* (January 3, 2003) asked Reilly about his secret to getting cast in three exceptional films at one time, the actor replied, "I don't have a secret. I aim for versatility and adaptability, because that's something a director's always looking for. My job is to bring their vision to life. Someone who has a very rigid way of working isn't as attractive to some directors. I just go with the flow." In his most recent film, Reilly can be seen as a con artist in *Criminal* (2004).

The fifth of six children, John Christopher Reilly was born on May 24, 1965 in Chicago, Illinois. His father ran a linen-supply business. Reilly grew up in a rough neighborhood, in the Irish section of the city's Marquette Park area. As a child he often got into fights at school and in his neighborhood; indeed, as Steve Daly reported in *Entertainment Weekly* (November 15, 2002), Reilly "brought home report cards with one box invariably checked: *lacks self-control.*" What "really did save" him, as the actor told Daly, was that at age eight he was invited by a friend to attend a drama class. He took to acting instantly. After that, in his neighborhood, as he recalled to Mary Rochlin for the *Los Angeles Times* (January 26, 2003), "it was like, 'Hey! It's the great actor kid!' They were just kind of amused by me. It was like, 'We probably should be picking on you but you have two huge older brothers, so we're not going to.' . . . It wasn't exactly a neighborhood for an aesthete." Reilly performed at the all-boys Catholic high school he attended, as well as at local all-girls schools. While he loved acting, he "wasn't one of those kids saying, 'I'm gonna be a movie star, I'm gonna be a world-class actor,'" as he told Renee Graham for the *Boston Globe* (October 13, 2002). "I come from a background where the thinking was you do what you do for fun, but you have to have a job that makes money."

After high school Reilly attended DePaul University's Goodman School of Drama, in Chicago, where he received a B.F.A. degree in 1987. He subsequently landed a job performing Shakespeare for high-school students with the renowned Steppenwolf Theater Company. That experience convinced him that he wanted to pursue acting as a full-time career. An audition tape landed him a walk-on role in Brian De Palma's gritty military drama *Casualties of War* (1989), a film starring Sean Penn and Michael J. Fox. De Palma was so impressed with the diligence with which Reilly approached his one-line role that he promoted him to the movie's fourth-largest part, as the soldier Hatcher, who commits rape. Art Linson, the producer of *Casualties of War*, told Steve Daly, "When the good ones walk in, you can tell. John understood that the smallest thing you do is all you *need* to do if it's got truth to it." The actor later appeared in two more films with Penn: *We're No Angels* (1989) and *State of Grace* (1990).

In the early and middle 1990s, Reilly appeared in nearly a dozen films, including *Days of Thunder* (1990), *Shadows and Fog* (1992), *Hoffa* (1992), *What's Eating Gilbert Grape* (1993), *The River Wild* (1994), and *Georgia* (1995). In 1997 he collaborated for the first time with the writer/director Paul Thomas Anderson, in the latter's debut film, *Hard Eight* (also known as *Sydney*). The movie also marked the first time that Reilly played a lead film role. Anderson and Reilly had become acquainted at the Sundance New Filmmakers Workshop, in Utah, where fledgling filmmakers met with and had the opportunity to cast young professional actors. Reilly was Anderson's first pick from the pool of performers, and the two quickly became close friends. "I went through some heavy emotional things right around then and he was right there for it," Reilly told Bob Strauss for the London *Guardian Unlimited* (March 11, 2000, on-line). "It's almost like he was writing for me before he knew me, like he had an instinctive feeling for a lot of the issues in my life. Just one of the things you feel like, it was destined to happen. We were right on the same wavelength right away." The film noir *Hard Eight* is about the relationship between a professional gambler, Sydney (Philip Baker Hall), and his protégé, John (Reilly). The movie also featured Gwyneth Paltrow as a waitress/con artist with whom Reilly's character falls in love. In the *Boston Globe* (March 14, 1997), Jay Carr described Reilly's performance as "impressively subtle," and Michael Wilmington wrote for the *Chicago Tri-*

bune (February 28, 1997), "Reilly, with his bulldog face, mumbling speech and shambling manner, easily catches neophyte John's looseness of spirit."

Reilly appeared in two more of Anderson's films: *Boogie Nights* (1997) and *Magnolia* (1999). The former, which starred Mark Wahlberg as the porn star Dirk Diggler, drew a portrait of the 1970s pornographic-film industry and was widely regarded as one of the best films of 1997. Reilly played Reed Rothchild, Diggler's fellow porn star and brotherly sidekick. In *Magnolia*, which followed the intersecting lives of nine alienated characters over the course of 24 hours in Los Angeles, Reilly appeared as Jim Kurring, a compassionate but incompetent police officer whose desire to help others is so great that he falls in love with a drug addict (Melora Walters). Charles Taylor opined in *Salon* (December 17, 1999, on-line) that Reilly "pulls off the nearly impossible feat of making a character's decency funny without making him seem like a fool." Peter Travers of *Rolling Stone* (on-line) wrote, "Reilly is the heart of the film; you don't just feel him ache to make a human connection, you ache with him."

After the success of *Boogie Nights*, Reilly appeared in several critical and popular flops: *The Thin Red Line* (1998), *Never Been Kissed* (1999), and *For Love of the Game* (1999). In the hit summer movie *The Perfect Storm* (2000), which starred George Clooney and Mark Wahlberg, he played a fisherman whose wife leaves him because he spends so much time away at sea. That same year Reilly also starred in the critically acclaimed revival of the Sam Shepard play *True West*, at the Circle in the Square Theater in New York City. That unsettling comedy explores the symbiotic relationship between two seemingly opposite brothers: Lee, a petty thief, and Austin, an Ivy League–educated writer; in the course of competing to sell their respective screenplays to the same producer, the two realize they are not as different as they thought. Reilly and his co-star, Philip Seymour Hoffman, who has appeared in a number of Paul Thomas Anderson's films, alternated in the lead roles of Lee and Austin. Both Reilly and Hoffman received nearly universal praise for their performances; Ben Brantley enthused in the *New York Times* (March 10, 2000), "If you've followed Mr. Hoffman's and Mr. Reilly's work on film, you probably have your own ideas of who was meant for which part. Forget it. Whichever way you've sliced it, you're right. To see both versions of the current *True West* . . . is to enrich deeply your experience of just what good actors can do with the limited instruments known as the human body and voice." Both actors received Tony Award nominations for best actor.

After appearing in *The Anniversary Party* (2001), Jennifer Jason Leigh and Alan Cumming's scathing look at love and friendship in the Hollywood acting community, Reilly was seen opposite Jennifer Aniston in the critically acclaimed independent comedy-drama *The Good Girl* (2002).

Reilly played Phil, the husband of Teeny, the title character; a housepainter, Phil spends his free time using recreational drugs and watching television with his friend Bubba (Tim Blake Nelson). Phil's neglect of his wife furthers Teeny's feelings of unfulfillment, which eventually prompt her to become romantically involved with a teenage clerk (Jake Gyllenhaal) in the discount store where she works. Michael H. Kleinschrodt observed in the New Orleans *Times-Picayune* (August 23, 2002) that Reilly and Nelson "wring an incredible amount of pathos out of their roles, creating fully realized characters out of what could have been seen as stock redneck types."

At the end of 2002, Reilly's already familiar face became even more well known to audiences when he appeared in the high-profile movies *Gangs of New York*, *The Hours*, and *Chicago*, all of which were nominated for Oscars for best picture. In *Gangs of New York*, Martin Scorsese's epic drama about gang warfare in lower Manhattan during the 1860s, the actor played a corrupt policeman called Happy Jack. Because the role, though relatively small, required him to spend several months filming in Rome, Italy, Reilly had considered turning it down. His friend Anderson talked him into taking the part. "It was this massive script, but there didn't seem to be a lot to my part," Reilly explained to Steve Daly. "So I was a little torn. . . . Am I really gonna go to Italy for all these months? I called Paul and he was like, 'Are you [expletive] crazy? . . . It doesn't matter about the role. If [Scorsese] says to come, you just *go*.'" *Gangs of New York* became one of the most successful movies of the year, garnering 10 Academy Award nominations. In *The Hours*, which received nine Oscar nominations, Reilly played Dan Brown, the devoted but clueless husband of Laura Brown (Julianne Moore), a depressed housewife who finds solace by reading Virginia Woolf's novel *Mrs. Dalloway*. The film intersperses scenes from Laura and Dan's lives in the 1950s with scenes from two separate but related story lines, one featuring Meryl Streep as a contemporary New York book editor, the other centering on Nicole Kidman as Woolf.

The 1926 play *Chicago*, by Maurine Dallas Watkins, inspired movies in 1927 and 1942 and Broadway musicals in 1975 and 1996 before Rob Marshall directed the 2002 film version. Its story is that of an aspiring showgirl, Roxie Hart (played in the Marshall film by Renée Zellweger), who goes on trial for murdering her lover. Taking cues from her lawyer (Richard Gere) and fellow showgirl Velma Kelly (Catherine Zeta-Jones), Hart takes advantage of the media's obsession with the trial and becomes a celebrity. In Marshall's *Chicago*, Reilly played Hart's sweet but overly passive husband, Amos, whose amiability is easily exploited by his unfaithful wife and her lawyer. The part required Reilly to sing and dance, notably in the number "Mr. Cellophane," in which his character laments his nonentity status: "Cellophane, Mister Cellophane / Shoulda been my name . . . / 'Cause you can look

right through me / Walk right by me / And never know I'm there." "I think Rob [Marshall] really wanted me in this movie," Reilly told Ernio Hernandez for *Playbill* (December 24, 2002, on-line). "The feeling I got was he was hoping I could sing and he was hoping I could dance, but what he really wanted me for was the acting. That was his big thing; he knew he could get the numbers right because that's his background." *Chicago* opened in December 2002 to outstanding reviews and went on to garner 12 Academy Award nominations. Critics described Reilly's character as the moral center of the movie and called "Mr. Cellophane" one of the film's best musical numbers. "Reilly is a revelation as Roxie Hart's husband," Michael Sragow wrote for the *Baltimore Sun* (December 27, 2002, on-line). "In ['Mr. Cellophane'] Amos Hart acknowledges his own invisibility, and Reilly delivers a note of genuine heartbreak through the glitz." The actor received Golden Globe, Academy Award, and Chicago Film Critics Award nominations for best supporting actor for his work in the film.

In 2002 Reilly returned to the stage to originate the title role in the musical *Marty*, which opened on October 18 at the Huntington Theater in Boston, Massachusetts. The musical, based on the 1953 television drama and 1955 Oscar-winning movie of the same name, is about a lonely butcher from the Bronx who is looking for love. Reilly's performance was highly praised by critics; Ed Siegel wrote for the *Boston Globe* (November 1, 2002) that the actor "has never turned such an ordinary person as Marty into such an extraordinary character," and called his acting "so compelling that his Marty immediately wins your heart—before breaking and mending it. Everything about his character is thoroughly believable—from the low self-esteem to the high hopes for finding the right woman."

Reilly next appeared in the comedy *Anger Management* (2003), which starred Adam Sandler and Jack Nicholson, and in the independent film *Piggie* (2003), directed by Alison Bagnall. His credits for 2004 include *Criminal*, which opened in theaters in September. In *Criminal*, which Stephen Holden of the *New York Times* (September 10, 2004, on-line) called a "clever and diverting caper film," Reilly played Richard, a con artist involved in a counterfeit scheme. Reilly has roles in the films *The Aviator* and *Dark Water*, which were scheduled for release in late 2004. The actor has maintained that he prefers playing smaller, offbeat roles, typically described as "character parts," to playing the lead. "You have to do things that you believe in," he said in an interview for CBS's *The Early Show* (January 21, 2003, on-line). "You got to do things that are going to make you grow or expand your work somehow. You also have to have time to learn about life. I think if you just go from job to job to job, you are not really absorbing life. You are not reflecting. Everything is a reflection of a reflection. I value my down time in that way. It teaches me about life, which is what you need to be an actor."

Reilly and his wife, the independent-film producer Alison Dickey (who produced *Piggie*), live in the Silver Lake district of Los Angeles, California, with their two sons.

—H.T.

Suggested Reading: *Boston Globe* N p1+ Oct. 13, 2002, with photos; *Chicago Tribune* C p11+ June 8, 1997, with photos; *Entertainment Weekly* p76+ Nov. 15, 2002, with photos; *Los Angeles Times* 5 p6+ Jan. 26, 2003, with photos; *Orlando Sentinel* E p1+ Jan. 18, 2003, with photos; *Toronto Star* D p3 Jan. 3, 2003, with photo

Selected Films: *Casualties of War*, 1989; *We're No Angels*, 1989; *State of Grace*, 1990; *Shadows and Fog*, 1992; *Hoffa*, 1992; *What's Eating Gilbert Grape?*, 1993; *River Wild*, 1994; *Georgia*, 1995; *Hard Eight*, 1997; *Boogie Nights*, 1997; *The Thin Red Line*, 1998; *Magnolia*, 1999; *The Perfect Storm*, 2000; *The Anniversary Party*, 2001; *The Good Girl*, 2002; *Gangs of New York*, 2002; *The Hours*, 2002; *Chicago*, 2002; *Anger Management*, 2003; *Piggie*, 2003; *Criminal*, 2004

Reinhardt, Uwe E.

(RINE-hart, OO-vah)

Sep. 24, 1937– Economist; educator

Address: 351 Wallace Hall, Woodrow Wilson School, Princeton University, Princeton, NJ 18544-1013

"Economics is anything but a dismal science when Uwe E. Reinhardt takes the rostrum," Stephen Murata wrote for *Medical Economics* (August 11, 1997). The German-born Reinhardt is the James Madison Professor of Political Economy and professor of economics and public affairs at the Woodrow Wilson School of Public and International Affairs of Princeton University, in Princeton, New Jersey. Those ponderous titles belie his reputation as a compelling, witty, and refreshingly forthright speaker and instructor. In his lectures and writings, Reinhardt focuses primarily on the policies and economics of the U.S. health-care system; in doing so he has often criticized both the public, which he sees as having an overdeveloped sense of entitlement, and the government—suggesting in an interview with Mark Holoweiko for *Medical Economics* (November 2, 1992) that the United States "ought to emulate" parts of the health systems of Canada and Germany. "In particular," he said, "we ought to make health insurance universal and foolproof, so that even if a person is negligent, demented, and homeless, there's a fail-safe system that catches him. Then, no matter who the patient is, every doctor should get paid. There's no uncompensated care in Canada and Germany."

Reinhardt laments the fact that health benefits are so often tied to employment, making many a worker and his or her family entirely dependent upon a particular job for their health care. He has also dismissed the idea that health costs paid by corporations have rendered the U.S. noncompetitive in the business world, thus challenging the suggestion that spending on health care directly compromises competitiveness and profitability. Still, according to *PR Newswire* (January 18, 1990), Reinhardt warned, "Every dollar wastefully or needlessly spent by employers on health care impoverishes at least one of the firm's stakeholders, and, almost always, it is employees who pay the bulk of that price." In the two-tiered system he envisions, every American would receive a health-insurance voucher from either a public or a private source. Employers would give their workers vouchers, and the unemployed would collect from the public trough. A voucher would then entitle the bearer to select from several health maintenance organizations (HMOs) or could be given to a private insurance company in exchange for a policy. In his interview with Mark Holoweiko, Reinhardt displayed some of his trademark plainspokenness: "I believe that the American elite, which we might say is the wealthiest 15 percent of the population, basically wants a two-tiered health system that gives them something better than everyone else. But the conservative congressmen who represent them cannot admit that in public. It's politically incorrect. Can you imagine one of them getting up in the Senate and saying: 'Yes, I want something better for the elite than for other Americans. Let's give the rest something, but keep the fee-for-service system intact for the upper crust'? Therefore, for these conservative politicians, the best policy is to do nothing. They can say, 'We are egalitarians. We want to ensure the best health care for everyone. We just don't quite know how to do it.' Then they don't have to reveal their ethics. The minute a congressman drafts legislation, people like me can analyze it and tell you what social ethics are at work. To my mind, that's holding up a legislative solution. We have this image that we are egalitarian, yet we really are not. I don't know why we should be. Nobody else is."

Uwe E. Reinhardt was born on September 24, 1937 in Germany, which was then ruled by the Nazi dictator Adolf Hitler and would soon precipitate World War II. According to an article he wrote for the *New York Times* (March 22, 2003, on-line), as a small boy Reinhardt lived "near one of the most ferocious battle grounds of the European war theater—the notorious Hurtgen forest, where American and German soldiers fought one another in hand-to-hand combat for more than four months in the fall of 1944." Reinhardt later immigrated to the U.S., where he became a citizen; he received his bachelor of commerce degree from the University of Saskatchewan, in Canada, in 1964, when he was also awarded the governor general's gold medal as most distinguished graduate of his class. In

Courtesy of Uwe E. Reinhardt

Uwe E. Reinhardt

1970 he earned his Ph.D. degree in economics from Yale University, in New Haven, Connecticut; his doctoral dissertation, "Physician Productivity and Demand for Health Manpower," was later published as a book. Meanwhile, in 1968, he had begun teaching at Princeton University, rising from his initial position as assistant professor of economics to his current title. At Princeton he has taught courses in both micro- and macroeconomics; accounting for commercial, private, nonprofit, and governmental enterprises; financial management for commercial and nonprofit enterprises; and health economics and policy. His classes are marked by the pointed wit and irreverent slides Reinhardt incorporates into his lectures.

During the more than 30 years Reinhardt has spent researching and commenting on the economics of health, he has come to the conclusion that, although Americans spend more money on health care than do citizens of any other nation, they are among the people least satisfied with their system. The problem, Reinhardt suggested to Mark Holoweiko for *Medical Economics* (February 17, 1992), began in the early 1980s, when, under the administration of President Ronald Reagan, the health-care industry "was totally deregulated, with the idea that entrepreneurship would bring out the best in American health care." Reinhardt cited as one of the plan's major failings the fact that "most health-care dollars are spent on patients who are very sick, very frightened," and are not inclined to make economically sound choices. "They're not consumers who, before a lifethreatening operation, go to the Yellow Pages to pick a cheap anesthesiologist." He further clarified this opinion in an interview with *PR Newswire* (June 8, 1993). "People

[think] healthcare is a commodity," Reinhardt said, "but healthcare is unique. When illness strikes, people switch from being consumers to being patients." In the early and mid-1990s, Reinhardt approved of President Bill Clinton's ultimately unsuccessful proposal (formulated under the direction of Hillary Rodham Clinton) to create compulsory universal coverage, but was pessimistic that Clinton's plans would come to fruition. In addition, he objected to the forced equity of the single-tiered Clinton reform plan, which Reinhardt considered impractical and falsely egalitarian. Similarly, Reinhardt told Sharon Worcester for *Family Practice News* (December 15, 2001) of his dismay with the emerging system, which has left the uninsured with virtually no health care but allowed wealthier patients to create "designer health care." In the *Milwaukee Journal Sentinel* (February 1, 2003, on-line), Reinhardt derided Americans' unrealistic expectations about health care and their unwillingness to pay any of the costs themselves: "What Americans want is really quite simple: all the health care they or their doctors can imagine, virtually free, without added taxes for health care and without higher out-of-pocket costs for their 'employer-provided' health insurance. That's all. Call it part of the American dream."

In addition to the economics of health care, Reinhardt has written articles and essays on other topics, such as the recent U.S.-led war in Iraq, fought for the ostensible purpose of ridding that nation of so-called weapons of mass destruction. That subject holds particular significance for Reinhardt, as one of his children is a Marine officer who has been fighting in Iraq. In an article he wrote for the *Daily Princetonian* (February 13, 2003, on-line), Reinhardt questioned what was called the "moral clarity" of the preemptive strike on Iraq, stating, "My argument was not with the war itself, on whose merit honorable people can disagree honorably. My argument was with the chronic hypocrisy among seasoned adults. Why can't the erstwhile 'realists' of the 1980s who now orchestrate this war frankly admit that it is fought chiefly for U.S. control over arguably the most precious piece of real estate in the Middle East? What has happened to honest-to-goodness, old-fashioned, time-hallowed 'Realpolitik'?" In a more personal piece for the *New York Times* (March 22, 2003, on-line), he expressed his sympathy for both Americans and Iraqis, soldiers and civilians alike, and recalled his own experiences growing up in Germany during World War II. "Because we lived so near the Battle of the Bulge and the advancing allied forces," he wrote, "our village was strafed and bombed routinely. One such attack came as my friends and I were playing outside. We ran as the planes approached, taking shelter in the cavernous basement of the convent. There we spied a row of stretchers. On each was a body covered entirely by a blanket. Possibly to overcome our own terror, we dared one another to pull back a blanket on one of the stretchers, to see what a dead man looked like.

Someone did. We fell silent instantly as we beheld the serene, waxen face of a very young soldier who could not have been older than 16 or 17. . . . More than 50 years later, I can still see his face clearly. The shock of it recurs whenever I hear the chirpy anchors on the morning programs (not to mention the hawkish talking heads) prattle on about innocent civilians, as if the number of fallen enemy soldiers did not count. What does 'innocent' mean in the context of war?"

Reinhardt's wit and irreverence make him a sought-after public speaker, even on topics unrelated to either economics or health care. For example, when he was selected as the faculty speaker for Class Day at the Princeton commencement of 1995, he delivered a lengthy but amusing speech, entitled "Like, Entering the Real World 'N Stuff, with Particular Emphasis on 'N Stuff," after a suggestion of one of his children. In his remarks of May 29, 1995 (which are posted on the Princeton Web site), Reinhardt quantified education as "30 Courses + 2 Junior Papers + 1 Senior Thesis" and categorized the students of the graduating class as "geeks," "policy wonks," "Tigers," and "party animals." True to form, Reinhardt punctuated his speech with slides.

Reinhardt has served on a variety of governmental commissions and committees, such as the National Council on Health Care Technology of what was then the U.S. Department of Health, Education and Welfare, from 1979 to 1982, and the Special Medical Advisory Group of the Veterans Administration, from 1981 to 1985. He served three consecutive terms, from 1986 to 1995, as a Commissioner on the Physician Payment Review Commission (PPRC, now called the Medicare Payment Advisory Commission, or MedPAC), which was established by Congress in 1986 to provide advice on issues relating to the payment of doctors. He currently serves on the Institute of Medicine of the National Academy of Sciences' Board on Health Care Services, is a member of the Council on the Economic Impact of Health Reform (a privately funded coalition of health experts designed to examine the economic impact of changing health-care delivery and cost control), and is on the board of advisers for the National Institute of Health-Care Management, a Washington group established to study issues in managed care. From 1987 to 1990 Reinhardt was a member of the National Leadership Commission on Healthcare; he continues to serve on the successor to that organization, the National Leadership Coalition on Healthcare, which is co-chaired by former presidents Jimmy Carter and Gerald Ford. Since 1997 he has served on the board of trustees of the Duke University Health System, and as of 2001 Reinhardt also served on the board of trustees of Duke University. In March 2002 the managed health-care company the Amerigroup Corp. appointed Reinhardt to fill a vacant seat on the company's board of directors. Amerigroup's chairman, Jeffrey L. McWaters, announced on the corporation's Web site (March 11, 2002, on-line), "Dr. Reinhardt is an exceptional leader and is unique in that he has extensive experience in managed health care, the uninsured, economics and medicine. His diverse background will be an invaluable addition to the board of directors as we work with the current administration and states to expand managed care to low income families and the uninsured."

Reinhardt has received honorary doctorate degrees from the Medical College of Pennsylvania, the Mount Sinai School of Medicine, the City University of New York, and the College of Optometry of the State University of New York. In 1998 the Columbia University School of Nursing honored him with the Second Century Award for Excellence in Health Care, and in 2000 he was elected to serve as a senior associate of the Judge Institute for Management of Cambridge University, in Cambridge, England.

Reinhardt is or has been a member of various editorial boards, which include those of the *Journal of Health Economics*, the *Milbank Memorial Bank Quarterly*, *Health Affairs*, the *New England Journal of Medicine*, and the *Journal of the American Medical Association*. His articles have been published in a variety of journals, magazines, and newspapers, and he has authored, co-authored, or co-edited books in both English and German, among them *Accountable Health Care: Is It Compatible with Social Solidarity?* (1998); *Technology, Bureaucracy, and Healing in America: A Postmodern Paradigm* (1988), co-authored with Roger J. Bulger; and *Strategic Choices for a Changing Health Care System* (1996), which he co-edited with Stuart H. Altman.

Reinhardt is the father of three children.

—K.J.E.

Suggested Reading: *Federation of American Hospitals* (on-line); Harry Walker Agency Web site; *Medical Economics* p126 Nov. 2, 1992, p72 Dec. 26, 1995; *Journal of the American Medical Association* p1332+ Sep. 9, 1992; *New York Times* (on-line) Mar. 22, 2003

Selected Books: *Accountable Health Care: Is It Compatible with Social Solidarity?*, 1998; as co-author—*Technology, Bureaucracy, and Healing in America: A Postmodern Paradigm* (with Roger J. Bulger), 1988; as co-editor—*Improving Health Policy and Management: Nine Critical Research Issues for the 1990s* (with Stephen M. Shortell), 1992; *Strategic Choices for a Changing Health Care System* (with Stuart H. Altman), 1996; *The Future U.S. Healthcare System: Who Will Care for the Poor and Uninsured?* (with Stuart H. Altman and Alexandra E. Shields), 1998

Peter Kramer/Getty Images

Reinking, Ann

(RINE-king)

Nov. 10, 1949– Dancer; choreographer; actress; educator

Address: c/o Lee Gross Associates, 119 W. 57th St., Suite 1215, New York, NY 10019

The legendary choreographer Bob Fosse considered Ann Reinking "one of the finest dancers in the jazz-modern idiom." That is how he described her to George Perry for the London *Sunday Times Magazine* (May 8, 1983), after he had worked with Reinking for more than 10 years. "What's always interested me besides her good looks and her beautiful legs is the joy she brings to dancing and performing, which she transmits to an audience," Fosse told Perry. "She's worked hard at dancing, singing and everything else and she's become very accomplished. There may be a lot of accomplished people, but they don't have her special joy, that feeling that she likes what she does." The names of Fosse and Reinking are closely linked: after they met, in 1972, when she joined the chorus of the musical *Pippin*, she became his muse, his protegée, and, for about six years, his live-in companion. Under his direction, in such Broadway hits as *Chicago* and *Dancin'* and in his semi-autobiographical film *All That Jazz*, she developed into the quintessential Fosse dancer. Fosse's distinctive style "suits me very well," she told Ann Guarino for the New York *Daily News* (January 1, 1979). "It looks good on me. [Fosse] cultivates what you have and doesn't try to squelch your personality or style."

Reinking, who has identified herself as a "musical performer," studied classical ballet as an adolescent and teenager; her training in dance for musical theater began on the job in 1968, at Radio City Music Hall. Her stage credits include roles in *Fiddler on the Roof, Cabaret, Goodtime Charley, Sweet Charity, The Unsinkable Molly Brown, Bye Bye Birdie*, and *Fosse*, the last of which won the Tony Award for best musical in 1999. *Fosse* is one of more than two dozen works that Reinking has choreographed; also among them are original ballets, created for such companies as the Connecticut Ballet Theatre and Ballet Hispanico. Reinking has danced for television shows and commercials and appeared on the silver screen in *Movie Movie, Annie,* and *Micki and Maude* as well as *All That Jazz.* Passionately dedicated to the survival of American musical theater and the legacy of Fosse and other masters of choreography, for many years she has taught aspiring dancers in master classes throughout the U.S. "I enjoy teaching . . . ," she told Carol Krucoff for the *Washington Post* (May 6, 1983). "I learn from teaching. Having to break things down and explain them makes me a better dancer." Since 1991 she has served as the artistic director of the Broadway Theatre Project, in Tampa, Florida, a three-week summer program that she founded to enable young people to gain exposure to the ideas and techniques of dance professionals like herself. Her many honors include the 1992 Dance Educators of America Award, the 1997 Drama Desk, Outer Critics Circle, and Tony Awards for choreography for a revival of *Chicago,* the 1998 Dance Library of Israel Award, the 1999 Drama League Award for distinguished achievement in musical theater, the 2000 *Dance Magazine* Award for choreography, the 2000 Olivier Award for best theater choreography, for *Fosse,* and the 2002 Rolex Dance Award for outstanding contributions to dance.

The third of seven children, Ann H. Reinking was born in Seattle, Washington, on November 10, 1949. She has five brothers and one sister. Her father, Walter Floyd Reinking, was a hydraulic engineer; her mother, Frances (Harrison) Reinking, was a homemaker. Although she described her family to Joanna Ney for *Cue* (January 5, 1979) as "upper middle class," she told Ellen Levene for *Newsday* (December 2, 1984) that on occasion, the Reinkings went through hard times financially. "We weren't in the ghetto," she said to Levene, "but we were always having to be careful." From her parents, she told Carol Krucoff, she learned "the basics of being practical and looking out for myself"—strengths that have helped her keep her spirits up during low points in her professional and personal lives. At eight she underwent a tonsilectomy that left her once clear voice somewhat husky.

Reinking grew up in Seattle and Bellevue, a nearby suburb. Watching another girl in her sixth-grade class perform the role of the Sugar Plum Fairy from the ballet *The Nutcracker* in a school production triggered her desire to dance professionally. After her mother turned down her request for ballet classes, citing their prohibitive cost, young Ann approached one of her aunts, a former singer, and performed for her a dance, which she had taught herself, from the ballet *Swan Lake*; impressed, the aunt, along with Reinking's grandfather, agreed to pay for one year's lessons for her. She began her training locally at age 11. "My earliest mentors were my first ballet teachers," she told Sid Smith for the *Chicago Tribune* (March 11, 2004). "They were a married couple who'd been with Diaghilev's Ballets Russes de Monte Carlo." At Ann's request, her parents installed a barre in her bedroom, which enabled her to practice ballet steps at home.

Reinking attended Bellevue High School, where she met William Whitener, another student who, like her, loved to dance. (He is now the artistic director of the Kansas City Ballet.) "We would get dressed up, have a hamburger and walk in to somebody else's prom to dance," Reinking told Damien Jacques for the *Milwaukee Journal Sentinel* (January 6, 2002); sometimes, all the other young couples would stop dancing to watch them. For three summers (1964–66) during her teens, Reinking studied at the San Francisco Ballet School, in California, with a Ford Foundation scholarship. In 1967, again on scholarship, she attended the Joffrey School of Ballet, in New York. The school's founder, Robert Joffrey, struck by her outgoing personality and love for acting and singing as well as dancing, encouraged her to explore types of dance in addition to ballet.

With Joffrey's suggestion in mind, in 1968 Reinking moved to New York City, with $500 in savings from waitressing jobs. She booked a room at a YWCA and, following the advice of one of her former teachers, auditioned successfully for the Radio City Music Hall's corps de ballet (which is distinct from the famed Rockettes). As she explained to Joanna Ney, "I was a giggly, pranksterish type of girl with bad self-control, and my teacher thought the Music Hall would be a safe place to learn the ropes and what being a professional meant." Reinking performed at Radio City for several months.

Within the next year Reinking had landed a job—and membership in Actors' Equity—with a company that mounted a touring production of the musical *Fiddler on the Roof.* Also in 1969 she made her Broadway debut, in the role of a performer in the seedy Kit Kat Klub in John Kander and Fred Ebb's musical *Cabaret.* In 1970 she appeared in another hit musical, *Coco,* starring Katharine Hepburn, about the comeback at age 70 of the real-life Paris fashion designer Coco Chanel. "My part was *two* inches big," Reinking recalled to George Perry. "I used to come off the stage and cry because I was no good, I so lacked confidence. And then Katharine Hepburn told me that I *could act.* I figured that if she could say that then she had to be right." Also in 1970 Reinking married Larry Small, a singer; their seven-month union ended in divorce.

Reinking's first big break came in 1972, when she was chosen for the chorus of *Pippin*, about a son of the medieval king Charlemagne. With book by Roger O. Hirson and music and lyrics by Stephen Schwartz, *Pippin* was choreographed and directed by Bob Fosse and starred Ben Vereen and John Rubinstein. Thanks to Fosse's penchant for building upon individuals' gifts, each dancer played a prominent role in *Pippin*; thus, despite being part of an ensemble, Reinking stood out. The show became hugely popular, running for 1,944 performances (October 23, 1972–June 12, 1977). *Pippin* marked the beginning of Reinking's personal as well as professional relationship with Fosse. The two became romantically involved and lived together for several years.

On the strength of her work in *Pippin*, Reinking was next cast in the World War II–themed *Over Here!* The musical, which opened on March 6, 1974 and closed on January 4, 1975, starred Maxene and Patty Andrews, of the once immensely successful singing trio the Andrews Sisters; Treat Williams; Marilu Henner; and a then-unknown John Travolta. Reinking's performance earned her the Theater World, Outer Critics Circle, and Clarence Derwent Awards. It also led to her being cast in her first leading role: that of Joan of Arc in the musical *Goodtime Charlie* (1975; sometimes spelled *Goodtime Charley*), a comic take on the story of King Charles VII of France (portrayed by Joel Grey) and the 15th-century farmer's daughter who led French army troops against the British and was burned at the stake for heresy. The opening of *Goodtime Charlie* was postponed for two months, until March 1975, while Reinking recovered from a back injury she had sustained while dancing the jitterbug in *Over Here! Goodtime Charlie* closed three months after its premiere, when Reinking contracted the flu and Grey accepted a leading role in a Hollywood film. Despite the brevity of its run, *Goodtime Charlie* received seven Tony Award nominations, among them "best actor" nods for both Reinking and Grey.

In 1976 Reinking replaced Donna McKechnie in the celebrated role of Cassie in Michael Bennett's *A Chorus Line.* A broadway blockbuster, *A Chorus Line* presented the stories of fictional dancers auditioning for the chorus of a fictional upcoming musical. It revolutionized the structure of theatrical musicals and became one of the most beloved, and longest-running, musicals of all time. A year later Reinking replaced Gwen Verdon in *Chicago,* Kander and Ebb's musical about an aspiring chorus dancer named Roxie Hart, who murders her lover and then exploits her crime to gain celebrity. The press made much of the fact that Verdon, who was still legally Fosse's wife, helped Reinking, his lover, to prepare for the role.

Reinking next appeared as the lead in *Dancin'*, an all-dance revue that Fosse choreographed in various styles—jazz, modern, ballet, and tap. The first show of its kind, *Dancin'* celebrated pure dance, unembellished by plot, dialogue, or original music. Critics responded negatively to *Dancin'*; nevertheless, it ran for 1,774 performances after its debut, on March 27, 1978, and gave rise to a new genre, the dance musical. It also marked the emergence of Reinking as a major stage performer. Jennifer Dunning, in the *New York Times* (April 2, 1978), noted that with *Dancin'*, Reinking had "joined the ranks of Broadway's brightest stars. With her long legs, mane of silky, flying hair and feline intensity, Reinking is a standout in some very fast company."

Earlier, Reinking had told Bernard Carragher for the New York *Daily News* (August 8, 1976), "I don't want to give up the theater but I'd like to get into films [because] you can do your best work there. I'd also like to do films for a purely selfish advantage, because once you do a film it's always there. After I get through doing *A Chorus Line*, what is there left but a playbill." Reinking made her screen debut in the role of Troubles Moran, a nightclub singer, in *Movie Movie* (1978), Stanley Donen's spoof of 1930s-era double bills at movie theaters.

In 1979 Reinking appeared in Fosse's semi-autobiographical, musical film *All That Jazz*. That picture is about Joe Gideon, a successful Broadway choreographer and director whose compulsive work habits, pill popping, cigarette smoking, and womanizing are beginning to take their toll. Burdened also by the demands of his ex-wife (portrayed by Audrey Paris), daughter (Erzsebet Foldi), and girlfriend, Kate (Reinking), he suffers a heart attack during rehearsals for a new musical. While in the hospital Joe imagines his death, depicted on the screen in a fantastic dance sequence featuring Reinking, Paris, Foldi, and Ben Vereen. Reinking's other big-screen roles include those of Grace Farrell, the assistant to Daddy Warbucks (Albert Finney), in the musical *Annie* (1982), and of a workaholic lawyer married to a bigamist (Dudley Moore) in Blake Edwards's comedy *Micki and Maude* (1984).

During the next years of the 1980s, Reinking's star power began to wane. She performed in several Off-Broadway one-woman shows, none of which pleased critics. Reinking appeared on Broadway only once during the 1980s, in 1986–87, when she succeeded Debbie Allen in the role of Charity Hope Valentine, in a revival of Fosse's *Sweet Charity*. Years before, she had ended her live-in relationship with Fosse and had married and divorced her second husband, Herbert A. Allen, a businessman. She was married to her third husband, James M. Stuart, a businessman and educator, when, in September 1987, Fosse suffered a fatal heart attack. "If there is a heaven, I think Bob can look down and be satisfied. He really did have an exponential effect on the next generation of choreographers and dancers," Reinking told Michael Kuchwara for the Texas newspaper the *Amarillo Globe-News* (July 2, 2000, on-line).

In 1990 Reinking toured nationally with the actor, singer, dancer, and choreographer Tommy Tune in a revival of *Bye Bye Birdie*. Also that year, after having suffered several miscarriages, she gave birth to a son, her only child. By that time she had turned her creative energies increasingly to choreography and, to a lesser degree, teaching. She had constructed her first work, a series of dances for a musical called *Eleanor*, about First Lady Eleanor Roosevelt, for the Williamstown Theater Festival, in Massachusetts, in 1986. She told Michael Kuchwara that she had never considered choreographing until the Williamstown Theater's artistic director, Nikos Psacharopoulos, persuaded her to try her hand at it. Much to her surprise she discovered that creating dances came easily to her. "Somehow I had learned a craft throughout the years," she told Kuchwara, "and when Nikos said, 'Do this,' I did 17 numbers in one week." Later, she created dances for Robert Fall's mounting of Richard Rodgers and Lorenz Hart's musical *Pal Joey*, in 1988, at Chicago's Goodman Theatre; *Simple Gifts*, with music by Aaron Copland, for the Connecticut Ballet, and *Nilsson/Schmilsson*, set to music by the pop singer/songwriter Harry Nilsson, for the Spectrum Dance Theater, in Seattle, both in 1990; and Bertolt Brecht's *The Threepenny Opera,* for the Williamstown Theater Festival, in 1992. In 1996–97 she created *Ritmo y Ruido* (Rhythm and Noise) for Ballet Hispanico, a company based in New York City. According to Dottie Ashley in the Charleston, South Carolina, *Post and Courier* (April 11, 2004, on-line), in *Ritmo y Ruido* Reinking "meshed her torso-undulating, head-popping, hip-swiveling theatrical style with Latin folklorico" and chose music containing "a pastiche of hip-hop and Afro-Cuban rhythms."

In 1996 the director Walter Bobbie recruited Reinking to reinterpret the dances in *Chicago* for a four-performance revival at City Center in New York. For this project, Reinking wanted her work to serve as an homage to Fosse that would reflect the magnitude of his genius. She retained Fosse's original choreography only for the finale, "Hot Honey Rag." "Her *Chicago* is a good deal softer [than Fosse's]," Herbert Allen, echoing the views of many others, told Nancy Hass for the *New York Times* (November 10, 1996). "The show is more lyrical now. It's funnier and less sleazy. There was a good deal of darkness to his vision; there is a lightness to hers. There's heat there, but there's a great deal of illumination, too." While Reinking was in the process of reinterpreting Fosse's work, Bobbie proposed that she take on the role of Roxie. Then in her mid-40s and semi-retired as a performer, she at first refused. "I just didn't think I would be able to make the transition back," she explained to Hass. "So much would be riding on it, and . . . I'd had a kid and everything." In time she relented, after Bobbie assured her that he understood that, as she put it to Hass, "I might get hurt, or lose my voice or something, that it was a big risk."

The revival, staged in May 1996 and co-starring Bebe Neuwirth as Velma Kelly, dazzled critics, some of whom had earlier questioned the wisdom of mounting it at all, not only because a mere two decades had elapsed since its debut but also because trying to present a Fosse musical in the absence of Fosse seemed futile. "From the moment the show's superb, scantily clad corps de ballet saunters onto the stage—wrists and pelvises cocked in the signature Fosse style—you feel reassured," Ben Brantley wrote for the *New York Times* (May 4, 1996). "Yes, there will be dancing and not just as a bonus grace note; the choreography is again the very motor of the show." Brantley also praised Reinking's performance: "The years have mellowed her Minnie Mouse voice into a sensual smokiness and refined her comic timing. Her deceptively casual dancing both exudes ripe sexuality and winks at it. And her show-stopping performance of 'Roxie,' with a cadre of chorus boys, is really a blissed-out, erotic duet between a star and her audience."

The revival generated such enthusiasm that the production was moved to the Richard Rodgers Theater in November 1996 and became the biggest attraction on Broadway. In a glowing review for the *New Republic* (January 6–13, 1997), Robert Brustein, the founding director of the American Repertory Theatre, in Boston, reported that after the show, he felt "exhilarated, not only curiously moved by the high quality of the professionalism but also filled with unaccustomed feelings of hope—about the future of the American musical, about the future of the American theater, even a little bit about the future of the nation." He also wrote that Reinking had "brilliantly recreated the Fosse-style choreography—the spider walk, the tipped derby, the hiked shoulder, the bent knees, the arched back. . . . Aside from the fact that Reinking gives a wonderfully comic performance—her hoarse whiskey voice oozes sentiment, then breaks it with a callow aside—her somewhat ravaged features make for a truly poignant connection with her rival, the dynamic young Neuwirth." In *Newsweek* (November 25, 1996), Marc Peyser described the revival as "smashing" and wrote, "It's Reinking's choreography that steals the show. She's taken Fosse's . . . vocabulary of angled limbs, pulsating pelvises and writhing bodies and refashioned them into a string of hormonal showstoppers." Reinking won her first Tony Award for her choreography for *Chicago*; the production also won five other Tonys. A back injury that she suffered in March 1997 forced her to miss some performances before her departure from the show, the following June.

In 1999, in a joint venture that also involved Gwen Verdon, Fosse's daughter, Nicole Fosse, the country musician Chet Atkins, and the lyricist and theatrical director Richard Maltby Jr., among others, Reinking served as co-creator, co-director, and co-choreographer of *Fosse: A Celebration in Song and Dance*. The "hardest part" of her job, she told Patricia O'Haire for the New York *Daily News* (January 12, 1999), was choosing what to include in the show. "A lot had to do with the cast itself, finding numbers that would fit them, make them fly, yet flow into each other. The second-hardest was to make it look like entertainment. We didn't want a retrospective, we didn't want it to look like a memorial service." *Fosse* received mixed reviews. Its admirers included Clives Barnes, who wrote for *Dance Magazine* (May 1999), "*Fosse* proves a pungent celebration of showbiz dancing and a remarkable living memorial to the special talents of one of Broadway's master hoofers. . . . The show's elements—both in its material and its performance—are perfectly fused into a single entity: the absolute, distilled magic of Fosse, with all that odd, alienating and alienated difference that made him a cut apart, and in many ways a cut above, his Broadway contemporaries." Ben Brantley, in the *New York Times* (January 15, 1999), by contrast, complained that the dances did not project "a sense of character": "In a Fosse show you were almost always aware of every person onstage as an individual. . . . [In *Fosse*] there are only a few instances in which an infectious rush in the joy of performing gets past the footlights." *Fosse* ran on Broadway from January 14, 1999 to August 25, 2001 and won the 1999 Tony Award for best musical. (Critics noted that its competitors in that category were lackluster or worse.)

Reinking's recent works include *Slices* (2002), a dance created for Ballet Hispanico, which is based in New York City; *Suite Kander* (1999), which honors John Kander and was commissioned by the Missouri State Ballet; and *Within You and Without You: A Tribute to George Harrison* (2002), commissioned by American Ballet Theatre. *Within You and Without You* is made up of four dances, conceived individually by Reinking and three other choreographers, each of whom used the music and lyrics of the former Beatle, who had died earlier that year. She also choreographed *The Look of Love: The Songs of Burt Bacharach and Hal David* (2003), which was directed by Scott Ellis, and the Roger Rees–directed *Here Lies Jenny* (2004), starring Bebe Neuwirth as the unlucky heroine, both of which premiered on Broadway.

Reinking's first three marriages ended in divorce. Since 1994 she has been married to Peter Talbert, a 1970s tennis champion (and son of tennis Hall of Famer Bill Talbert), who has written two tennis-related books. Reinking's son, Christopher, is a teenager. In her leisure time she enjoys hiking, skiing, swimming, and horseback riding.

—H.T.

Suggested Reading: *Cue* p25+ Jan. 5, 1979, with photos; *Dance Magazine* p84+ Mar. 1987, with photo; *Harper's Bazaar* p38+ Aug. 1990, with photo; (London) *Sunday Times Magazine* p24+ May 8, 1983, with photos; *New York Times* II p1+ Apr. 2, 1978, with photos, II p5+ Nov. 10, 1996, with photos, B p9+ Oct. 11, 1997, with photo, II p12 Dec. 1, 2002, with photos; Washington Academy of Performing Arts Web site; *Washington Post* B p1+ June 16, 1980, with photo, V p1+ May 6, 1983, with photos

Selected Shows: as dancer—*Fiddler on the Roof*, 1969; *Cabaret*, 1969; *Coco*, 1970; *Pippin*, 1972; *Over Here!*, 1974, *Goodtime Charlie*, 1975; *A Chorus Line*, 1976; *Sweet Charity*, 1986; *Bye Bye Birdie*, 1990; as choreographer: *Eleanor*, 1986; *Pal Joey*, 1988; *The Threepenny Opera*, 1992; *Chicago*, 1996; *The Look of Love: The Songs of Burt Bacharach and Hal David*, 2003; *Here Lies Jenny*, 2004; as co-creator, co-director, and co-choreographer: *Fosse: A Celebration in Song and Dance*, 1999

Selected Dances: as choreographer—*Simple Gifts*, 1990; *Nilsson/Schmilsson*, 1990; *Ritmo y Ruido* (Rhythm and Noise), 1996–97

Selected Films: as actress—*Movie Movie*, 1978; *All That Jazz*, 1979; *Annie*, 1982; *Micki and Maude*, 1984

Clive Brunskill/Getty Images

Roddick, Andy

Aug. 30, 1982– Tennis player

Address: c/o ATP International Headquarters, 201 ATP Blvd., Ponte Vedra Beach, FL 32082

When the 21-year-old Andy Roddick won the 2003 U.S. Open Tennis Championship, he confirmed what sports insiders had been saying for years: that Roddick was the "future of American tennis." A six-foot two-inch, right-handed player with one of the best serves in the game, Roddick began competing as a junior when he was in his early teens; by the time he turned professional, in 2000,

he was ranked as the number-one junior tennis player in the world. In 2001, his first full season as a pro, he climbed into the top-20 rankings. Over the next several years he won numerous Association of Tennis Professional (ATP) titles, as well as two heavily publicized matches against the legendary player Pete Sampras. When Roddick won his first Grand Slam title, at the U.S. Open on September 7, 2003, fans and reporters alike welcomed him as tennis's new star. "I can't imagine my name and U.S. Open champion going together," he said in a postgame interview posted on the U.S. Open Web site. "It's more than I could ever dream of."

The youngest of three sons, Andrew Stephen Roddick was born on August 30, 1982 in Omaha, Nebraska. His father, Jerry, was a businessman, and his mother, Blanche, was a teacher. The Roddicks were a sports-oriented family: his brother Lawrence was a member of the U.S. Senior National Team in diving, and his brother John was an All-American tennis player at the University of Georgia. Andy first picked up a tennis racket when he was four years old, the same year that the family moved to Austin, Texas. Six years later they moved to Boca Raton, Florida, so that John could benefit from better tennis coaching. It was Andy's game, however, that began attracting the attention of the tennis world. As he entered his teens, he began playing in junior tournaments, and by the age of 16, he was winning nearly every competition he entered.

In 1999 Jerry and Blanche Roddick hired the French coach Tarik Benhabiles, who had helped Cedric Pioline and Nicolas Escude become top-20 players, to work on Andy's game. As a senior at Boca Raton Preparatory School, Roddick spent his mornings at school; then he would meet Benhabiles at the Roddick home, where the two would practice on the backyard court until dark. The teenager's work paid off in January 2000, when he defeated Mario Ancic from Croatia to win the Australian Open Junior Championship, thereby becoming the first American since Butch Buchholtz in 1959 to win that title. The victory encouraged Roddick to turn professional, and in March 2000 he made his pro debut at the Citrix Championships (sponsored by the computer-technology firm) in Delray Beach, Florida, where he lost to Italy's Laurence Tieleman in the first round. Roddick's first major event as a pro was the Ericsson Open in Key Biscayne, Florida. (This tournament is sometimes called the "fifth Grand Slam event.") He won his first-round match against Spain's Fernando Vicente before being knocked out of contention by the American star Andre Agassi in the second. In August Roddick participated in the main draw at the U.S. Open, where he lost to Albert Costa in the first round. In total he played nine tournaments as a professional in 2000 and ended the season ranked at number 160 in the world.

Until his 18th birthday, in August of the 2000 season, Roddick continued to play junior tournaments as well as professional ones, winning both the Sugar Bowl Classic and the U.S. Open Junior Championship. He finished the year ranked as the number-one junior tennis player in the world. Roddick's status as tennis's rising star was confirmed in April, when the U.S. Davis Cup captain, Patrick McEnroe, invited him to join the American tennis team as a practice partner, thus giving him the opportunity to spar against Agassi and Sampras.

The following season pressure on Roddick began to increase, as tennis observers labeled him the next great American player. That year McEnroe named him a full member of the Davis Cup Team, on which he joined Todd Martin, Jan-Michael Gambill, and Justin Gimelstob in facing off against Switzerland's Roger Federer, Michel Kratochvil, George Bastl, and Lorenzo Manta in the first round. Although Roddick won his match against Bastl, 6–3, 6–4, Federer beat Gambill 7–5, knocking the U.S. team out of competition. In March Roddick qualified as a wild-card draw for the Ericsson Open in Miami, Florida, where, to the amazement of everyone, he beat Pete Sampras, who is often called the greatest tennis player of all time, in straight sets, 7–6 (2), 6–3, during the third round. Roddick's serves were consistently clocked at more than 130 miles per hour. "The way he played today, the future of American tennis is looking very good," Sampras said in a press conference following the game, as quoted by Charlie Nobles in the New York Times (March 26, 2001). "He possesses a big cannon. He's serving consistently in the 130s and making them. That's pretty tough to play against." The win marked Roddick's first against a top-10 player. He was eventually beaten by the Australian Lleyton Hewitt in the quarterfinals, having become the youngest player ever to advance that far in the Ericsson Open. The two victories put him on the ATP's top-100 list.

In April Roddick won two more ATP tour events: the Verizon Tennis Challenge, in Atlanta, Georgia, and the U.S. Men's Clay Court, in Houston, Texas. As a result, his ranking soared to number 21. Less than a month later, a pulled hamstring forced him to withdraw from the third round of the French Open, in which he had again been battling Hewitt. After losing to Goran Ivanisevic, 6–7(5), 5–7, 6–3, 3–6, at Wimbledon, in England, Roddick won his third professional title of the year at the Legg-Mason Classic, in Washington, D.C. The win nudged him to number 18 in the rankings, making him the first American teenager to reach the top 20 since Michael Chang in the early 1990s. A month later, in his second outing at the U.S. Open, Roddick progressed as far as the quarterfinals, in which he was defeated yet again by Hewitt, who won 6–7(5), 6–3, 6–4, 3–6, 6–4 and went on to win the tournament. The match was not without controversy; in the 10th game of the fifth set, Roddick became enraged at a call the umpire had made. Slamming his racket onto the ground, he called the official a "moron." After receiving a verbal-abuse warning, a tearful Roddick told the press, "You fight so hard for something and then you feel that someone takes it away from you. It's just infuriating; I don't even remember what happened after that call," as quoted by Selena Roberts in the New York Times (September 7, 2001). Nevertheless, Roddick finished the year ranked as the number-14 tennis player in the world, up from number 158 at the start of the season.

Roddick captured his first title of the 2002 season at an ATP tournament in Memphis, Tennessee, defeating James Blake 6–4, 3–6, 7–5 in a thrilling three-set match. In spite of a strong beginning, he won only one other title that season, beating Sampras in straight sets at Houston. Roddick made a poor showing in the first three Grand Slam events of the year, being eliminated in the second round of the Australian Open, the first of the French Open, and the third of Wimbledon. He redeemed himself at the U.S. Open, however, by advancing to the quarterfinals for the second year in a row. For the third time in Roddick's career, he was matched against Sampras; in this instance the 13-time Grand Slam champion routed Roddick in straight sets (6–3, 6–2, 6–4), and went on to win the U.S. Open.

Roddick began the 2003 season with an impressive run to the semifinals of the Australian Open, where Rainer (sometimes spelled "Rainier" in the press) Schuettler defeated him 7–5, 2–6, 6–3, 6–3. His quarterfinal match there against Younes El Aynaoui is now widely regarded as one of the most exciting matches of the season, a grueling five-hour battle that Roddick won in the fifth set, which alone lasted more than two hours. The match set the record for the longest men's single match at the Australian Open since 1971, when tiebreakers were introduced for Grand Slam events. After a devastating first-round loss to Sargis Sargsian at the French Open, Roddick fired Benhabiles and hired Andre Agassi's former coach, Brad Gilbert. Roddick saw results immediately; he won his first tournament—the Queen's Club in England—under Gilbert's tutelage. After an impressive semifinal showing at Wimbledon, he went on to win three of the next four ATP events. One of the favorites going into the U.S. Open in late August, Roddick faced stiff competition from Federer, Hewitt, and Agassi. In five stellar rounds of play, Roddick advanced to the semifinals by trouncing his competitors without losing a single set. He then faced the Argentinean David Nalbandian in the semifinals. The match started slowly, with Nalbandian returning each of Roddick's searing 140-mph serves. Roddick served 18 aces in the first set and still lost it to Nalbandian. (In tennis parlance, an ace is a serve that is untouched by the other player, usually because its power and swiftness make it unreturnable.) He unleashed four more aces in the second set but lost yet again. Roddick rallied in the third set, however, and won the match 6–7 (4), 3–6, 7–6 (7), 6–1, 6–3. During the match he served a career-high 38 aces. A day later, on Sunday, September 7, Roddick won his first Grand Slam event, when he beat top-ranked Juan Carlos Ferrero, the French

Open champion from Spain, in straight sets, 6–3, 7–5 (2), 6–3. Roddick played brilliantly, serving 23 aces and winning 89 percent of his service games. After belting three aces in a row down the mid-court to win the match, Roddick fell to the ground in tears. He then climbed through the crowd to hug his family, friends, and coach. When asked during the postgame interview, as posted on the U.S. Open Web site, if he had been worried about not living up to the expectations that had followed him into the Open, he replied, "No . . . I don't play for others. I don't play for what people might say or what people will say. I play for myself. I play for the people that I love and that share in the joy that I get out of it. But, you know, you can't be scared of what's gonna be written about you or what's gonna be said. . . . Bottom line is I'm a pretty good player and I just won a Grand Slam."

In 2004 Roddick won the Queen's Club tournament for the second time in a row, defeating Sebastien Grosjean with a 7–6 (4), 6–4 victory in the final. He then qualified for the first time for the Wimbledon finals, after beating Mario Ancic of Croatia, 6–4, 4–6, 7–5, 7–5 in a nearly three-hour-long semifinal match that, because of rain delays, was spread over the course of two days. Roddick lost in the finals to the defending champion, Roger Federer, 4–6, 7–5, 7–6, 6–4; afterward, Roddick called Federer, who had by then won six of the pair's seven matches, "just too good." He told Ossian Shine for the *Scotsman* (July 5, 2004, on-line), "I was throwing the kitchen sink at [Federer], but he went to the bathroom and got his tub. I am going to have to start winning some of these matches if we are going to call it a rivalry." When the pair faced off in the finals of the Tennis Masters Canada tournament, a month later, Federer again beat Roddick, 7–5, 6–3. "I'd like to congratulate Roger," Roddick said, as quoted in the *New York Times* (August 2, 2004). "You're certainly becoming very annoying," he joked.

At the 2004 Olympic Games, in Athens, Greece, Roddick was eliminated after the third round. Although the Olympics are often not considered as important in tennis as Grand Slam events (only five of the top 20 men's players opted to compete in the 2004 Olympics), Roddick told Christopher Clarey and Liz Robbins for the *New York Times* (August 30, 2004) that the loss was difficult for him. "I think with each player it's personal how big [a deal] it is. Some guys really don't care. I cared a lot. [The Olympics is] not the biggest thing in our sport, but it's the biggest thing in sports." Roddick followed his disappointing Olympic performance with another letdown, at the quarterfinals of the 2004 U.S. Open, when he lost to Joachim Johansson of Sweden, 6–4, 6–4, 3–6, 2–6, 6–4. "I'll recover, I'll be fine," he told Jason Brown for the U.S. Open Web site (September 9, 2004, on-line). "If I didn't feel bad, something would be wrong. Losses like this make me hungrier. So hopefully, I'll come back with something good." His failure to retain his title notwithstanding, he set a U.S. Open record

for measured speed of a served ball: 152 miles per hour.

Roddick lives in Boca Raton, Florida, with his pet rabbit, Stifler. He is an avid fan of the Cornhuskers, the University of Nebraska's football team. Roddick made headlines in 2004 for his heroism during a fire at the Grand Hotel Parco dei Principi, in Rome, Italy, that broke out on the morning of May 1 of that year. He herded nearly a dozen fellow guests into his suite and onto his balcony, out of harm's way. He also helped others—among them the Dutch tennis player Sjeng Schalken and his wife—reach the balcony, by catching them as they jumped from the floor above his. Roddick used his mobile phone to contact his mother during the ordeal; she later told Karen Crouse for the *San Diego Tribune* (May 2, 2004, on-line) that when firefighters arrived at the scene, Roddick called out to them, "Hey. You guys with the ladder. If you come over here, I'll buy you pizza!"

—H.T.

Suggested Reading: andyroddick.com; *New York Times* D p8+ Mar. 26, 2001; usopen.org

---

Romenesko, Jim

Sep. 16, 1953– Journalist

Address: Poynter Institute, 801 Third St. S., St. Petersburg, FL 33701

The journalist Jim Romenesko was among the Internet users who introduced Web logs, known as blogs (sites that list links to other sites or that serve as on-line personal diaries to be read by Web surfers). Blogs, which sprang up in the 1990s, disseminate information in an amazingly rapid way. Drawn to bizarre news stories since his days as a police reporter for the *Milwaukee Journal*, in 1998 Romenesko set up a Web site called the Obscure Store and Reading Room, for which he writes summaries of and posts links to strange or shocking stories that he finds daily in on-line newspapers and magazines. That project led to his establishment of another Web site, mediagossip.com, on which he posted links to gossip and news concerning newspaper and magazine publishing, television, and other media-related fields. Mediagossip.com quickly became a "must-read" for media professionals nationwide, among them some of the most influential. Romenesko currently runs a slightly altered, though still influential, version of mediagossip.com under the auspices of the Poynter Institute, a nonprofit journalism school located in St. Petersburg, Florida. (Once known as medianews.org, Romenesko's new site is located at poynter.org.) "My No. 1 reason for doing this is enjoyment and entertainment," he told Kimberly

Courtesy of Jim Romenesko

Jim Romenesko

Marselas for *American Journalism Review* (September 1999). With medianews.org, Greg Mitchell wrote for *Editor & Publisher* (November 25, 2002), "Romenesko gained no small measure of fame (at least in [the publishing] world), and a familiar cry was heard across the land: 'Have you seen Romenesko today?' Here at [*Editor & Publisher*] we are proud of our Web site, which last month hit new highs in unique users and page views, but getting a link on Romenesko always guarantees additional (though sometimes hysterical) feedback." In 2000 Romenesko was included on *Forbes* magazine's list of the "Power 100," the 100 most-powerful people working in the media.

One of 10 children, James P. Romenesko was born on September 16, 1953 in Walworth, Wisconsin, a town close to the northern border of Illinois. His father, Merlin, was the town's school superintendent, and his mother a homemaker. When Simon Dumenco, writing for *New York* (May 8, 2000), asked him about the occupations of his siblings, Romenesko replied, "Well, let's see, one brother is a CFO for a company in Chicago. Um, most of 'em are accountants, actually. And one owns a hardware store." Four of his five sisters are schoolteachers; the fifth is in marketing. From early on Romenesko had an interest in news and journalism. He recalled to Dumenco that each week the Walworth Public Library received the Sunday *New York Times* on the following Wednesday, and he was "always the only person who touched it or read it."

Romenesko graduated in about 1975 from Marquette University, in Milwaukee, Wisconsin, where he had studied journalism. He then began working for the *Milwaukee Journal.* "Graduating

and getting hired was like the greatest thing in the world," Romenesko recalled to Dumenco. "I mean, I just remember springing out of bed in the morning, anxious to go to work." Romenesko served as the *Journal's* suburban reporter during the day and its police reporter at night. His night job showed him a "side of life that I never saw when I grew up," as he told Dumenco. "In Walworth, . . . probably the most riveting thing was a truck went the wrong way around the village square—and this is the truth. The picture [of the truck] was in the paper. . . . Then you're thrown into a situation where, you know, people are stabbed 55 times and you get to go to the morgue and look at the Polaroid snapshots." In a conversation with Jacquelyn Mitchard for the Madison, Wisconsin, *Capital Times* (June 30, 1981), as quoted on obscurestore.com, Romenesko said that the first morgue report he ever saw literally nauseated him: he vomited after reading its first half. He gradually lost his squeamishness, and in his final months with the *Milwaukee Journal,* in 1981, self-published dozens of coroner's reports (with the names of the dead deleted) in a 150-page book called *Death Log.* The book contains sections on such causes of death as "autoerotic mishaps" and misadventures involving pork chops, and offers "uncensored logs . . . of some of the most grisly and sorry finales as ever were," as Jacquelyn Mitchard wrote. "They're the details that never make the newspaper reports, the grim facts masked by the word 'unexpectedly' in obituaries. . . . The cackle of police-beat humor . . . runs throughout the book." In early 2004 used copies of *Death Log,* which is out of print, were being offered for sale on the Internet at prices ranging up to nearly $265.

After he left the *Milwaukee Journal,* Romenesko worked from 1982 to 1995 as an editor at *Milwaukee Magazine.* There, he wrote a column called "Pressroom Confidential," which offered his insider's take on Milwaukee newsroom and television-station politics. Romenesko described "Pressroom Confidential" to James Poniewozik for Salon.com (June 10, 1999) as the "best-read column" in the magazine according to reader surveys; it won national awards in three consecutive years. From 1996 to 1999 Romenesko served as a new-media and Internet reporter for the St. Paul, Minnesota, *Pioneer Press.*

Earlier, from 1989 to 1999, Romenesko published a print newsletter called *Obscure Publications,* which covered the world of fan magazines, known as fanzines. The newsletter often discussed legal issues facing small, underground publishing ventures and featured strange news reports that appeared either in print or on the Web. In early 1998, as an offshoot of *Obscure Publications,* Romenesko set up the Web site Obscure Store and Reading Room (obscurestore.com), which every day contains brief summaries of and links to weird, ludicrous, or sordid news stories. Romenesko wakes at around 6 a.m. daily to search for such accounts in scores of newspapers and periodicals found on the

Web; he then posts his selections on his site, along with short summaries and links to the original sources. On July 18, 2003, for example, Romenesko's own headlines for the links listed on obscurestore.com included "[Department of Motor Vehicles] refuses to give driver's license to man with upside-down signature," a story from the news section of delawareonline.com; "Boy, 6, drives car 30 miles in search of his mother," from the Austin, Texas, *American-Statesman* Web site; and "Judge green-lights inmate's goal to become a woman—on taxpayers' dime," from the *Newsday* Web site. In the "store" part of the site, Romenesko offers for sale copies of old and obscure magazines—for example, *Angry Thoreauan, Jersey Beat*, and *Temp Slave*.

In May 1999, having come across and featured many stories related to the media (accounts of celebrities in the publishing world, editors, television broadcasters, media tycoons, and gossip columnists, for example), Romenesko set up a Web site dedicated exclusively to news stories about the media. On mediagossip.com, as he called it, he posted a roundup of what he considered each day's top media news stories, in addition to links to a variety of publications and commentaries about the media. Mediagossip.com was an immediate hit. Almost from its inception, the site had several thousand daily readers. "The not-so-secret reason for Romenesko's success is the media's incredible self-absorption," Dan Kennedy wrote in an article posted on bostonphoenix.com (September 9–16, 1999). "I confess to having been immediately hooked after I saw that he'd included me in his list of media columnists."

In 1999 the Poynter Institute, a Florida-based nonprofit journalism school, hired Romenesko to maintain a media news site. Romenesko's new Web page, found at poynter.org, was averaging more than 14,000 page views per day in 2000, according to Lori Robertson in *American Journalism Review* (September 2000).

According to Simon Dumenco, Romenesko often receives E-mail messages from "journalists plugging their own stories, journalists passing along industry gossip, journalists complaining about other journalists." Dumenco wrote, "Romenesko's site has become the place for journalists to see and be seen—sort of like a virtual Michael's or Elaine's," referring to two New York City restaurants popular with media professionals. The influence of Romenesko's site can be measured by the number of powerful and well-known people in media who have relied on it as a source of news or a forum in which to publicize their views. When Peggy Noonan, a former speechwriter for President Ronald Reagan, wanted to respond to reviewers who had criticized her book *The Case Against Hillary Clinton*, she aired her remarks on Romenesko's poynter.org Web site. Noonan told Dumenco, "A friend of mine at *Entertainment Weekly* told me [that Romenesko's is] the first site she goes to in the morning, and that's true of most of the people she works with. So now I visit regularly. I like it that [Romenesko] worries about journalistic standards. The way I see it, the site is a public service." "Getting picked up by [Romenesko] is the new bragging right among gossips," Tom Prince, the executive editor of *Allure*, told Dumenco. The *Washington Post* and CNN media commentator Howard Kurtz, who also reads Romenesko's Web pages daily, told Dumenco, "I think the clever and sometimes sardonic way that Romenesko packages and presents his daily media download has a lot to do with the site's charm."

Romenesko has taught courses in fanzine publishing and history at the Milwaukee Institute of Art and Design and in feature writing for newspapers at the University of Wisconsin, in Milwaukee.

When Simon Dumenco talked with him in 2000, Romenesko was living in and working by himself out of a 500-square-foot, one-room condominium in Evanston, Illinois. He told Dumenco that he often drank 10 to 12 cups of coffee a day. Dumenco, a co-worker of Romenesko's in the late 1980s, described him as "look[ing] about the same as he's always looked, which is to say slightly worn around the edges—thin build with the hint of a gut, thinning sandy-blond hair—and at 46, he's got the same terrifically endearing perma-grin on his face. Not the *I-know-something-you-don't-know* smirk of a media insider but an open, honest near smile that suggests he manages to find things pretty consistently amusing."

—C.F.T.

Suggested Reading: *American Journalism Review* p15 Sep. 1999, p28+ Sep. 2000; *Folio* p33+ Dec. 2002, with photo; *New York* p32+ May 8, 2000, with photo; obscurestore.com; poynter.org

---

Rose, Jalen

Jan. 30, 1973– Basketball player

Address: Toronto Raptors, Air Canada Centre, 40 Bay St., Toronto, Ontario M5J 2X2, Canada

At six feet eight inches, the basketball player Jalen Rose is agile enough to play the guard positions but large and strong enough to fill in at forward as well. His facility in a range of positions has earned him the nickname "the Natural," but it has not made his road through the National Basketball Association (NBA) any smoother. Rose was a member of the University of Michigan's "Fab Five," the school's famous group of freshman basketball stars who, in 1992, were embraced by the media like no other college team before them, but who, following an investigation into the team's having accepted illegal loans, fell from grace. After being drafted by the Denver Nuggets in 1994, Rose was traded in 1996 to the Indiana Pacers and for a period was

Courtesy of the Toronto Raptors

Jalen Rose

der to gain psychological advantage over opponents. One day, Rose was playing basketball and talking trash at St. Cecilia's gym in Detroit when he was pulled aside by Sam Washington, a basketball counselor, who showed Rose a game film of his father. "You've got that in you, so don't be messing around," Washington told Rose, according to Hank Hersch in *Sports Illustrated* (December 20, 1996). "When you're on the floor, give it your all."

Rose attended Detroit's Southwestern High School, where, alongside the current NBA players Voshon Lenard and Howard Eisley, he helped the basketball team to win the High School National Championship in 1991. As a senior Rose was named a *Parade Magazine* All-American and a *USA Today* Third-Team All-American and was invited to the McDonald's All-American Team. Accepting a scholarship from the University of Michigan, he soon found himself a part of the Michigan Wolverines' famous "Fab Five" freshman group, which, in addition to himself, consisted of Chris Webber (one of Rose's childhood friends), Juwan Howard, Ray Jackson, and Jimmy King. Hailed by many as the greatest freshman class of all time, they instantly gained celebrity status, identifiable by their black socks, baggy shorts, and bravado. Rose, in particular, gained a reputation for what many thought an arrogant attitude. "Understand that the group of kids at Michigan was really the first in college to have that stage," Perry Watson, Rose's high-school coach and mentor, told Sean Deveney for the *Sporting News* (April 3, 2000). "They were constantly microphoned, always on TV. Jalen just gave them what they wanted."

While Chris Webber was considered the team's most talented player, Rose was its leader. With his help, the Wolverine's compiled an impressive record of 56 wins and 14 losses and appeared in back-to-back National Collegiate Athletic Association (NCAA) championship games, in 1992 and 1993, both of which they lost. After Webber's departure for the NBA, following his sophomore season, Rose escalated his play and became the Wolverines' foremost star, leading them in 1994 to the NCAA Final Four, where they lost to the eventual tournament champions, the University of Arkansas Razorbacks, in a hard-fought 76–68 contest. "If ever we've bashed a player, this is the one . . . ," Gene Wojciechowski wrote in the *Sporting News* (March 21, 1994), following Michigan's tournament run. in previous seasons, he recalled, "too often Rose would forget to play defense, or dazzle you with a magical pass, but then make two silly turnovers. His shot selection seemed to be based on whim, not logic or instinct. This season has been different. Rose has combined his wonderful flair with a sense of maturity and responsibility. With Webber gone and the Wolverines' bench suspect, Rose has played nearly every position and played them well. He has often said he deserved more respect as a player. This year he earned it."

coached by the NBA legend Larry Bird. During the 2001–02 season Rose was again traded, this time to the struggling Chicago Bulls, with whom he stayed for a season and a half, before being traded to the Toronto Raptors in 2003. While Rose has occasionally been branded as arrogant, Rick Carlisle, the Pacers' head coach and the NBA's 2001–02 coach of the year, told Chris Broussard for the *New York Times* (June 13, 2000), "The one thing about him is that he's a joyous kid. He's an upbeat, positive thinker. Not many people know this, but when he was sitting on the bench in Indiana and in Denver, he was spending a lot of time by himself in some deserted gym just working on his game, dreaming about being on this sort of stage." Rose was named the Chicago Bulls' most valuable player in 2003 and won the NBA's Most Improved Player Award in 2000.

Jalen Rose was born in Detroit, Michigan, on January 30, 1973, the youngest son of Jeanne Rose, a single mother of four, and Jimmy Walker, the number-one pick in the 1967 NBA draft. Walker, who played for the Detroit Pistons and was married to another woman, abandoned Jeanne Rose before the birth of their son. Rose remains estranged from his father. "I'm sure Jalen is apprehensive about meeting me. And I understand that . . . ," Walker told Mitch Albom for his book *Fab Five* (1993), as excerpted in the *Sporting News* (December 6, 1993). "We didn't communicate right, and now Jalen has gone 20 years without meeting his father." Growing up in a rough section of Detroit, Jalen Rose often carried around his father's basketball card; being the son of Jimmy Walker allowed Rose to play with older, tougher kids. In so doing he learned how to "talk trash," or use taunts in or-

Rose, who finished his college career averaging 17.5 points and 4.7 rebounds per game, is one of only two players in Michigan history to compile at least 1,500 points (1,788), 400 rebounds (477), 300 assists (401), and 100 steals (119). A Naismith and Wooden Award finalist, he received All–Big Ten First Team honors, *Basketball Times* First Team All-American honors, the *Sporting News* First Team All-American honors, and an Associated Press All-American Honorable Mention in his freshman season. However, many of his college accomplishments were officially nullified in 2002, when, after a long investigation, the University of Michigan expunged the records and NCAA appearances of the "Fab Five" following the revelation that members of that class had illegally received loans from a team booster named Ed Martin. Martin, a retired auto worker who was in regular contact with the Wolverines' head coach, Steve Fisher, and was a fixture at team gatherings, admitted to lending a total of $616,000 to four Michigan players: Webber, Robert Traylor, Maurice Taylor, and Louis Bullock. Among the penalties the university voluntarily imposed on itself was the forfeiting of all games won while the four players were on the team, including the 1992 and 1993 Final Four appearances, the whole 1992–93 season, and every season from fall 1995 through spring 1999. The university also repaid the NCAA some $450,000 that it had received for postseason play while those players were on the team and put its basketball program on probation for two years.

Drafted by the Denver Nuggets as the 13th overall pick in the 1994 NBA Draft, Rose had a very successful rookie season as a point guard, setting a Nuggets rookie record for assists (389) and being named to the NBA All-Rookie Second Team. In his second season Rose was ranked 17th in the NBA in assists per game (6.2) but was nevertheless replaced as a starter just four games into a season that also saw the team go through three head coaches. Rose refused to let these setbacks affect his faith in himself. "I know what people say about me: He can't do this, he isn't that," he told Hersch. "In my own mind, I look at myself as being a point guard who is able to do other things because of my size. . . . I want to get my opportunities to pass. Or to make plays. Or see that the plays are made. Or push it when we need to run. Or stop the bleeding when we need the bleeding stopped. And I'm used to being able to make those kind of decisions."

Before the start of the 1996–97 season, Rose was traded to the Indiana Pacers, along with Reggie Williams, for Mark Jackson, Ricky Pierce, and a first-round draft pick. Rose, who developed a tumultuous relationship with the Pacers' head coach, Larry Brown, saw his playing time dip to less than 20 minutes per game. "[Brown] didn't hit it off with me from Day 1," Rose recalled to Broussard. "So what I did, as opposed to just crying out to the public, I just kept working on my game. I stayed away from the world, pretty much. I cut off my phone. I didn't want to hear nobody's opinion

of what was going on. I didn't want nobody to come and watch me play that year. It was kind of like I was in jail that season, so I just did my time." On May 8, 1997 Larry Brown was replaced by Larry Bird, a player whom Rose had grown up disliking because he was his idol Magic Johnson's chief rival but whose extremely successful NBA career he nonetheless respected. "[Bird's] been there before, so you've got to listen," Rose told Deveney. "You think you have a good game, think you're having a good year. Then you see him walk in and you think, 'You ain't done anything.'" Bird, while acknowledging some of Rose's shortcomings, saw his potential and gradually increased his playing time. "[Rose's] concentration is key," Bird told Broussard. "If he could concentrate through practices and games, I think his game would improve 15, 20 percent. And that would put him over the top. Some days in practice, he's just not there. He won't work on his game as hard as I would like him to. One of Jalen's problems is he doesn't think anybody can guard him. But they can. But I have great respect for the kid. I like him. That's why I play him."

After giving Rose more and more time on the court during the 1998–99 season, Bird made Rose a starter in the 1999–2000 season—a move which many believed was responsible for the Pacers' first trip to the finals, that year. During that series, Rose started as a shooting guard and led his team in scoring average (23), but the Pacers fell to the Los Angeles Lakers in six games. A starter in all 80 games he played that season, Rose averaged a then–career best of 18.2 points per game and was named the NBA's most improved player. He was also named NBA player of the week in March 2000, posting per-game averages of 26.8 points, 7.5 rebounds, and 4.5 assists.

Larry Bird retired following the 2000 finals, but Rose continued to play well under the Pacers' new coach, Isiah Thomas. During the 2000–01 season he started in all 72 games in which he played and averaged 20.5 points per game. During the 2001–02 season Rose played 53 games for Indiana, averaging 18.5 points per game, but he had a hard time fitting into Thomas's offensive schemes and, on February 19, 2002, was traded to the Chicago Bulls, along with Travis Best and Norman Richardson, for Ron Artest, Kevin Ollie, and Ron Mercer. The trade represented a step down for Rose, because the Chicago Bulls had been descending precipitously since Michael Jordan's departure from the team after the 1998–99 season. However, Rose finished the 2001–02 season averaging a much-improved 23.8 points per game with the Bulls and was able to spread the wealth to his teammates as well. "Now we have a guy who's looking for us," the Bulls' Eddy Curry told a reporter for *Sports Illustrated* (March 11, 2002). "After running the same screen-and-roll plays all season without getting the ball, you begin to think you're not open. But Jalen always finds you."

In his first full season with the Bulls, in 2002–03, Rose averaged a team- and career-high 22.1 points, becoming the first Chicago Bull since Michael Jordan to finish in the NBA's top 15 in scoring average. He also averaged 4.8 assists and 4.3 rebounds per game and hit 40 percent of his two-point shots, 37 percent of his three-pointers, and 85 percent of his free throws. Over the course of 82 games, he played a career-high 3,351 minutes (among the NBA's top 10) and averaged 40.9 minutes per game (seventh-most in the NBA). He scored more than 30 points on 14 occasions and posted seven double-doubles (reaching double digits in two categories, such as points and assists), including his first career triple-double, a 21-point, 14-rebound, 11-assist showing in a victory over the play-off–bound Phoenix Suns on February 24, 2003. Sixteen games into the 2003–04 season, Rose was again traded, this time to the Toronto Raptors. Although he missed several weeks of play after fracturing a bone in his left hand during a February 10, 2004 game against the Golden State Warriors, Rose finished the 2003–04 season with an average of 15.5 points, 4.2 assists, and four rebounds per game.

Rose had a small part in the highly successful film *Barbershop* (2002), which starred Ice Cube, Cedric the Entertainer, and the rap star Eve. In addition, Rose has appeared in music videos for the rap stars Ludacris, Sean "P. Diddy" Combs, Nelly, and Style. He is a regular participant in the Make-A-Wish Foundation (which grants the wishes of children with life-threatening medical conditions) and, while with Chicago, created the Jalen Rose Chicago Children's Foundation to provide financial support for single-parent families and support nonprofit organizations that assist children in their education goals. "I'll do what I have to [to] win," Rose told Deveney. "I can play point guard, I can play forward. You want me to play center? You want me to be the scorekeeper? If it helps us win, I'll do it."

—L.A.S.

Suggested Reading: *New York Times* IV p2 June 13, 2000, with photo; *Sporting News* p44 Dec. 6, 1993; *Sports Illustrated* p20 Apr. 6, 1992, with photo, p28 Dec. 20, 1993, p44 Dec. 20, 1996, with photos

Selected Films: as actor—*Barbershop*, 2002

Ross, Gary

Nov. 3, 1956– Screenwriter; filmmaker; producer

Address: c/o Creative Artists Agency, 9830 Wilshire Blvd., Beverly Hills, CA 90212

The screenwriter, director, and producer Gary Ross has had a hand in creating several memorable, award-winning movies. His screenplay for the comedy *Big*, which was co-written with Anne Spielberg and told the story of a young boy's magical, physical overnight transformation into an adult, was made into one of the most successful movies of 1988; helped to usher its lead actor, Tom Hanks, to major stardom; and earned Ross an Academy Award nomination. His screenplay for the movie *Dave* (1993) also earned an Academy Award nomination and garnered critical plaudits. In 1998 Ross wrote, directed, and co-produced the critically acclaimed film *Pleasantville*, a fantasy in which two children are transported to a black-and-white world resembling a 1950s television show. Five years later Ross cemented his reputation as one Hollywood's most creative and talented writers and directors, when he adapted for the big screen Lauren Hillenbrand's best-selling book, *Seabiscuit*, about the unlikely champion racehorse that galvanized Americans in the 1930s. *Seabiscuit*, which stars Tobey Maguire, Jeff Bridges, and Chris Cooper, received seven Academy Award nominations in 2004 and grossed more than $120 million at the box office. Concerning his ca-

Carlo Allegri/Getty Images

reer as a writer and director for the big screen, Ross, whose work has often included elements of fantasy, mused to Jamie Allen for CNN (October 12, 1998, on-line), "I get to dream for a living. It's kinda cool." The politically active Ross, who served as a speechwriter for President Bill Clinton, was presented with the American Civil Liberties Union's (ACLU) Bill of Rights Award in 2000.

Gary Ross was born in Los Angeles, California, on November 3, 1956 and grew up in the Los Angeles suburb of Studio City. His father, Arthur Ross, is an acclaimed screenwriter whose credits include *Creature from the Black Lagoon, Brubaker,* and *The Great Race.* Amid the widespread fear of Communist infiltration that infected the movie business along with American politics during the 1940s and 1950s, Arthur Ross was blacklisted—shut out of projects and shunned—because of suspicions about his political affiliations. Paraphrasing Gary Ross's words, Jamie Allen wrote that Arthur Ross was "a liberal, but far from being a Communist." Gary Ross's mother, Gail Ross, was a speech pathologist. His older sister, Stephanie, is a civil rights lawyer.

While attending high school in California, Ross began trying his hand at writing novels. He continued to write as a student at the University of Pennsylvania, which he attended for three years before dropping out to pursue what he thought was the true writer's life. Referring to the adventuresome writer Ernest Hemingway, Ross recalled to Bernard Weinraub for the *New York Times* (May 11, 1993), "I went down to South Carolina to work on a fishing boat because I thought that's what you had to do to be a writer. It's a cliché. Embarrassing. It was an ersatz bad Hemingway trip." While at the University of Pennsylvania, Ross, who was interested in politics, spent summers working as an intern at the U.S. Capitol, in Washington, D.C.

After his misadventure in South Carolina, Ross studied acting with the legendary teacher Stella Adler, but his interests still lay with writing. He obtained an advance from a publishing company for a novel-in-progress and spent the money before he completed the book. An appearance on the television game show *Tic Tac Dough* netted Ross $50,000 in winnings, which he used to support himself while he finished his novel. When Paramount Pictures hired Ross to write a treatment for a film, he met the producer Leonard Goldberg, who assigned him to write a script. That screenplay went unproduced, as did two others Ross subsequently wrote.

Big was the first of Ross's screenplays to be made into a movie. It centers on an adolescent boy, Josh (played by David Moscow), who after making a wish is magically turned into a 30-year-old man (Tom Hanks). As innocent and childlike within as he is adult-looking without, Josh must navigate the grown-up world, where he finds a job with a toy company and begins a romance with a woman. One of the blockbuster hits of 1988, *Big* grossed more than $100 million at the box office and brought Academy Award nominations for Ross, who also co-produced *Big;* his writing partner, Anne Spielberg, sister of the legendary director Steven Spielberg; and Hanks. Ross and Spielberg also received a nomination for a Writers Guild of America Award for their screenplay. Writing for

the *Washington Post* (June 3, 1988), Hal Hinson commented, "It would have been easy for the screen writers to score points against their grown-up characters by portraying them as soulless monsters who've lost contact with the kid inside them. (The film's message, simply put, is, 'Hold on to that kid.') But the movie resists the temptation to turn Josh's fantasy into a nightmare." The movie, he wrote, would send viewers "out of the theater with a lighter step."

After *Big,* Ross busied himself by rewriting and polishing the scripts of several movies, including *Short Time* (1990), *Beethoven* (1992), *Little Big League* (1994), and *The Flintstones* (1994). Meanwhile, he kept up his interest and activities in Democratic politics. In the late 1980s he wrote speeches for then–Massachusetts governor Michael Dukakis, who won the 1988 Democratic presidential nomination but lost the general election. According to some sources, including Alan Citron and Kathryn Harris in the *Los Angeles Times* (March 1, 1994), Ross later wrote speeches for President Clinton. He also attended the Democratic National Convention in 1980 as a delegate representing Edward M. "Ted" Kennedy, a U.S. senator from Massachusetts, who unsuccessfully sought the Democratic presidential nomination that year. Ross's political sensibilities found expression in the screenplay he penned for the film *Dave* (1993), whose decent, ordinary title character (Kevin Kline), a dead ringer for the U.S. president (also played by Kline), is recruited to stand in for the commander-in-chief at minor public events. When the real president suffers a stroke, the good-natured Dave must continue to play the part. The comedy was directed by Ivan Reitman and co-starred Sigourney Weaver as the First Lady; Ross himself appeared briefly in *Dave* as a policeman. According to Weinraub, President Clinton watched a special screening of *Dave* at the White House.

To some degree *Dave* presented Ross's vision of an ideal, uncynical political world. "The trouble is Hollywood often treats Washington cynically," Ross commented to Weinraub, explaining why he wanted to express something different with *Dave.* "A political film works if it's also an idealistic film. That's why films set in Washington succeeded in the 1930's. . . . People want to feel renewed about their politics. . . . The worst thing I hear about *Dave* is that it's too sweet. I'll take that criticism. Or some people say it's blindly optimistic. I'll take that, too. I'm not naive about politics. But if this movie serves as a reminder that politics ought to be, like Dave, uncynical, then I'm really happy." In his review of the film for *Rolling Stone* (June 10, 1993, on-line), Peter Travers called it "a winner" and added, "*Dave* is a prankish sparkler that lets screenwriter Gary Ross . . . get in his [political] licks." Roger Ebert, in the *Chicago Sun-Times* (May 7, 1993), called *Dave* "wonderful lighthearted entertainment." In addition to critical plaudits, the movie brought in more than $60 million at the box office. For his original screenplay for *Dave*, Ross received his second Academy Award nomination and was honored by the Writers Guild with its Paul Selvin Award, which is given to a screenplay that, as quoted on filmbug.com, "embodies the spirit of the constitutional and civil rights and liberties which are indispensable to the survival of free writers everywhere."

In addition to his other movie work in the 1990s, Ross received writing credits for the scripts for *Mr. Baseball* (1992), which focuses on a fading American baseball star (Tom Selleck) who struggles to adapt to playing for a Japanese team, and *Lassie* (1994), based on the earlier movies and TV series about a brave and loyal dog. Ross also appeared in *The Misery Brothers* (1995) and served as a producer for the romantic comedy *Trial and Error* (1997).

Ross's directorial debut came with the film *Pleasantville* (1998), which he also wrote and produced. The movie tells the story of two teenagers (played by Tobey Maguire and Reese Witherspoon) from a dysfunctional, modern-day family who, thanks to a television repairman (Don Knotts), are transported to a town that has the look and feel of a 1950s black-and-white television show. As the two teens teach the sitcom-like people about everything from love to racism, each black-and-white character, discovering his or her individuality, literally becomes colorful. Those on-screen transformations made *Pleasantville* an extremely difficult movie to shoot. It was filmed in technicolor; when necessary, the color was digitally removed to create black-and-white frames. In total *Pleasantville* required approximately four times the amount of special-effects work lavished on the average action film.

Also starring William H. Macy and Joan Allen, *Pleasantville* debuted at the fifth annual Austin (Texas) Film Festival and Heart of Film Screenwriters Conference. According to Jamie Allen, the festival audience gave *Pleasantville* a standing ovation. Speaking of the movie's black-and-white world, a metaphor for tidy, overly simple views of life, Ross told Jamie Allen that "pleasant" does not always equal "good." "You can drain the life and nuances and complexity out of things by homogenizing them to make everything harmoniously dull, flat, conflict-free, strife-free. In a complex and troubling world, who wouldn't want to simplify? Everybody does. Everybody wants to simplify and put up a picket fence. The tougher thing is to give yourself that kick to be alive and to be fully engaged and stay alive. I guess if the movie has a message, it's that it's worth that price, as difficult or strife-ridden as it may be. . . . I grew up with that memory and understanding that you can appear to be in a very safe, progressive, open environment but still be pretty close to that kind of repression"—a reference to his father's experiences in Hollywood. Ross revealed to Allen that the perspective he brought to *Pleasantville* is "due very much to the way [his father] looked at the world."

Roger Ebert, in the *Chicago Sun-Times* (October 23, 1998), judged *Pleasantville* to be "one of the year's best and most original films." Echoing that praise, Janet Maslin in the *New York Times* (October 23, 1998) labeled Ross's movie an "ingenious fantasy." *Pleasantville* was nominated for three Academy Awards—none of them for Ross, who did, however, win a Golden Satellite Award for best screenplay and was nominated for another award, in the best-director category. Despite a largely positive critical response, *Pleasantville* grossed only a modest $40 million at the box office.

Ross's next big project, the movie *Seabiscuit*, is linked to one of his passions: horse racing. As he recalled to John Horn for the *Los Angeles Times* (July 23, 2003), on his 13th birthday, as a "rite of passage," his parents took him to the famed Santa Anita Racetrack in southern California to watch thoroughbreds race. Fascinated by horse racing and the world of betting that surrounded it, Ross visited the racetrack throughout high school; later, in the late 1980s, he and his wife regularly attended horse races. In addition, according to Horn, Ross owns a partial share of the horse Atswhatimtalknbout, who finished fourth in the 2003 Kentucky Derby. After reading the best-selling nonfiction book *Seabiscuit: An American Legend* (2001), by Lauren Hillenbrand, Ross decided to turn that story—about the racehorse that inspired millions of Depression-era Americans by becoming an unlikely champion—into a movie. Ross directed and produced the film and wrote the screenplay; Tobey Maguire played the jockey Johnny "Red" Pollard, who was too large for his profession and blind in one eye but nonetheless rode Seabiscuit to glory; Chris Cooper filled the role of Tom Smith, the horse's taciturn trainer; and Jeff Bridges, the part of Seabiscuit's owner, Charles Howard, who was scarred by the death of his young son and the dissolution of his first marriage. *Seabiscuit* was a resounding success, both critically and popularly. The movie earned seven Academy Award nominations, including one for Ross for best screenplay based on previously published material, and another for Ross and fellow co-producers Kathleen Kennedy and Frank Marshall; it also pulled in more than $120 million in box-office receipts.

Ross has served as the president of the Los Angeles Public Library Commission, a post in which he set up mentoring programs for inner-city children and expanded library services for teenagers. For those efforts he was given the 1999 Light of Learning Award by the Los Angeles Public Library. The following year he gave the keynote address at a conference of the American Library Association.

Ross is married to Allison Thomas, who served as a White House intern during the presidency of Jimmy Carter, working with Carter's assistant for public liaison; she later established her own public-relations firm and helped her husband to produce both *Pleasantville* and *Seabiscuit*. The couple have twin children, Claudia and Jack.

—C.F.T.

Suggested Reading: CNN (on-line) Oct. 12, 1998; *Los Angeles Times* D p4 Mar. 1, 1994, with photo, V p1 July 23, 2003, with photo; *New York Times* C p13 May 11, 1993, with photo

Selected Films: as screenwriter—*Big*, 1988; *Dave*, 1993; as screenwriter, director, and producer—*Pleasantville*, 1998; *Seabiscuit*, 2003

Courtesy of the Hearst Corp.

Rubenstein, Atoosa

Jan. 20, 1972– Editor in chief of Seventeen; *founding editor of* CosmoGIRL!

Address: Seventeen, *1440 Broadway, 13th Fl., New York, NY 10018*

Atoosa Rubenstein made headlines in 1999, when she became the founding editor of *CosmoGIRL!* magazine—and the youngest editor in chief in Hearst Magazines' long history. Rubenstein climbed another rung on the publishing ladder in 2003, when she was named the editor in chief of *Seventeen*, one of the most popular teen publications on the market. Particularly loved by young readers for her sisterly, spunky advice columns, Rubenstein is often described as among the most ambitious and talented figures in magazine publishing.

Atoosa Rubenstein was born in Iran on January 20, 1972 to parents who practiced the Muslim faith. The family moved to the United States when Rubenstein was three years old, initially settling near John F. Kennedy Airport, in the New York City borough of Queens. Their first home routinely hosted members of their extended family, providing a warm and culturally rich environment for Rubenstein and her siblings. The family later relocated to Malverne, a quiet neighborhood in Nassau County, on Long Island, New York. Rubenstein told Taylor K. Vecsey for the *East Hampton Star* (September 11, 2003, on-line) that, at night, theirs was "the kind of street you could sleep in the middle of."

Rubenstein's upbringing was strict; she was not allowed to date boys, participate in sleepovers, tweeze her eyebrows, dye her hair, or shave her legs. When her mother mandated that she be home by nine o'clock, even on the night of her prom, she opted to skip the event. Rubenstein's problems were not limited to the cultural restrictions her parents placed on her; she complained to Lorrie Cohen for the *Tucson Citizen* (August 10, 2002), "Boys didn't like me at all. And, I was bright but [dyslexic], so I had the worst grades. But our experiences are what we grow from and we need to figure out, 'OK, here's how to grow from them instead of letting them get you down.'" At one point Rubenstein began cutting herself, a form of self-abuse practiced most often by girls from middle-class backgrounds. (Psychologists now believe that the practice is more widespread than previously thought and indicates a lack of self-esteem.) "So many girls are pained for so many reasons that they don't feel they can talk about it," Rubenstein told Vecsey, explaining how the experience informed her later work. "I know when I was cutting myself in college, I had no idea what I was doing. I thought it was very weird. *CosmoGIRL!* says to those girls, 'You are not alone.'"

Rubenstein attended Barnard College, a women's school affiliated with Columbia University, in New York City. Although she studied political science, Rubenstein told Carolina Vester for the *Student Press Review* (August 6, 2003, on-line), "I was always reading magazines under my desk in class, which is probably not a great thing to do. So one day I thought, 'Someone must work at these magazines. Why can't it be me?'" After that epiphany, Rubenstein applied for a public-relations internship at the company that owned the now-defunct *Sassy*, where, after much lobbying on her part, she was hired for $15 a day. Any misgivings on the part of Rubenstein's employers quickly disappeared: "I did my job as if it were the most important thing in the world, and no task was too small," she told Vester. "I would practically follow the people from *Sassy* into the bathroom, just so that they would notice me and know that I was there." Her efforts paid off, and Rubenstein was awarded an unpaid internship in the beauty and fashion department of the magazine. (To earn money, she took assorted retail jobs.) When she added another internship, this one in the editorial department of *American Health* magazine, Rubenstein quit her sorority and began taking night classes to accommodate her hectic schedule.

Despite her obvious drive and dedication, Rubenstein's parents were less than enthusiastic about the direction her career was taking. "During [the] process of becoming a journalist, I got little support from my family," she told Vester. "My mother always wanted me to become an attorney, and my family had high expectations of me, especially since I had to compete with the fact that my sister was a doctor and my brother a university professor." However, Rubenstein persisted in her choice of career. When she graduated from Barnard, in 1993, she had two job offers: one from *Cosmopolitan*, for a position as a fashion assistant, and one from *Seventeen*, for a job as a beauty assistant. She accepted the offer from *Cosmopolitan*, then under the leadership of the renowned editor Helen Gurley Brown. Within five years, Rubenstein had moved up to the position of senior fashion editor.

In 1998, when Cathleen Black, the president of Hearst Magazines, decided that it was time to develop a new teen publication, Rubenstein created a prototype within 48 hours of being asked to do so. Rubenstein explained to Vester that "I just took a look at what I thought was missing in teen magazines. . . . There needed to be a modern magazine where girls are portrayed as the smart generation they are becoming." The prototype was so well received that Black immediately asked Rubenstein to run the project. Rubenstein thus became the editor in chief of her own magazine, dubbed *CosmoGIRL!*. Then 26, she was the youngest person to have her name slated to appear at the top of the masthead of any Hearst publication. (She is not the youngest woman ever to helm a glossy, however; Jane Pratt began editing *Sassy* for an Australian media conglomerate in 1987, at the age of 24.)

The first issue of *CosmoGIRL!* appeared in August 1999, with the goal of creating what Rubenstein, in an interview with Janelle Brown for *Salon* (September 10, 2001, on-line), called the "kind of world we wanted to live in but couldn't seem to find. . . . The real version of our daydream. A place where we're all accepted. All beautiful. All nice to each other. All friends. Strong, full of guts and passion." Under Rubenstein's leadership, *CosmoGIRL!* espoused a youthful brand of feminism. "The essence of our mag is about giving girls power and empowering them when it comes to their lives," she told Brown. "Even makeup—it may seem the antithesis, but the fact is girls are into makeup. Instead of throwing products at them and saying buy buy buy, we are saying, 'Here is how you put different looks on.'"

Rubenstein's advice columns, published in the monthly *CosmoGIRL!*, as well as in assorted newspapers around the country, earned her legions of teenage fans—as well as criticism from conservatives unhappy with the frank advice she dispensed on such topics as sex and birth control. "We're not a bunch of heathens trying to corrupt girls," Rubenstein told Catherine Donaldson-Evans for *Fox News* (June 5, 2003, on-line), explaining that the magazine was meant to provide a forum about the issues relevant to its readers. "We are that big sister on their team, encouraging them."

On a typical day, Rubenstein arrived at the offices of *CosmoGIRL!* at seven o'clock in the morning, spent 12 hours there, and continued to answer E-mail messages and letters from readers even after she got home. Although a staff member helped her with her research, Rubenstein asserted that she read all 500 to 1,000 daily items of correspondence herself. Her hard work won immediate results; the magazine was recognized as *AdWeek*'s start-up of the year for 1999 and as one of the five best magazines of 2000 by *Ad Age Magazine*. By February 2003 *CosmoGIRL!* had grown from its initial base of 500,000 to 1.25 million readers.

In June 2003 Hearst purchased *Seventeen* magazine, first published in 1944, from Primedia Inc. for $180 million—and Rubenstein made the switch from *CosmoGIRL!* to a position as the editor in chief of her company's new acquistion. She explained the move to Megan Greenwell for the *Columbia Spectator* (October 15, 2003, on-line): "It was a wonderful opportunity that was presented to me. *Seventeen* [with more than 2 million readers] is the biggest brand in the market, and a brand that I have admired for a long time, from my time as a reader to the time that I started this magazine [*CosmoGIRL!*], that was a bit of an underdog in the market, and so we always thought, 'Wow, if we could ever be as big as *Seventeen*.' [*CosmoGIRL!*] has now been very successful, but *Seventeen* is still the power brand, and it's a wonderful opportunity to be able to lead that brand."

Rubenstein has repeatedly explained that the two publications target different audiences. "The psychographic of the *Seventeen* reader is less future-driven [and more concerned with the here and now] than the *Cosmo* girl, who is so focused on one day running for President, but in high school is a little bit quirky, a little bit of an oddball. The *Seventeen* reader is not so focused on changing the world—not because she won't, but because her focus is on ruling the school," she told Megan Greenwell. "I think every girl has a piece of both girls inside of her, but they tend to want to primarily be one way or the other."

Although some critics have complained that publications like *CosmoGIRL!* and *Seventeen* set unrealistic beauty standards, push unnecessary products, and bombard readers with sexual imagery, Rubenstein disagrees. She explained to Megan Greenwell, "Some people say 'You're telling girls they're not good enough.' Well, we never tell people they're not good enough. Girls like to play with makeup and fashion. There's no big political statement in that; there's nothing wrong with wanting to experiment, and I think to bastardize that would be a misrepresentation of what's going on."

Rubenstein and her husband, Ari, an equity trader, lived full-time in New York City until recently, when they bought a home in East Hampton, on Long Island. (The move was said to be prompted by an incident involving a bird and a ruined

$3,000 jacket.) She now divides her time between the two residences. Many journalists have commented not only on her ambition and determination but also on her height (she is five feet 11 inches tall), her striking black hair (it was deemed newsworthy that she had it straightened before joining *Seventeen*), and her sense of style (she has reportedly had accidents attributable to wearing very high heels). Rubenstein has been featured on *Crain's New York Business*'s "40 Under 40" list and *Folio*'s "30 Under 30." While at the helm of *CosmoGIRL!*, she founded Project 2024, a campaign designed to put a woman in the White House by the year 2024. She supports the White House Project, which seeks to increase the number of female political leaders.

—K.J.E.

Suggested Reading: *Columbia Spectator* (on-line) Oct. 15, 2003; *East Hampton Star* (on-line) Sep. 11, 2003; *Salon* (on-line) Sep. 10, 2001; *Student Press Review* (on-line) Aug. 6, 2003; *Tucson Citizen* D p1 Aug. 10, 2002

Rus, Daniela

(ROOS)

1963(?)– Computer scientist; roboticist

Address: MIT Laboratory for Computer Science, 200 Technology Sq., Bldg. NE43, Cambridge, MA 02139

Imagine a robot roaming the surface of a remote planet. It moves along smoothly until it encounters an obstacle over which it cannot glide. The small machine then whirs and clicks as it changes shape to form a climbing device capable of mounting the object blocking its path. Later, it transforms itself again, to squeeze through a tight space between boulders. Suddenly part of the machine begins to malfunction; the robot detaches it, replaces it with another part, and continues on its way. While this scenario may seem to be exclusively in the realm of science fiction, the ability to build such robots is within reach, according to Daniela Rus, an associate professor in the Department of Electrical Engineering and Computer Science at the Massachusetts Institute of Technology (MIT). Rus believes that such self-reconfiguring robots, which are able to change shape on their own, are the next step in the rapidly expanding field of robotics. (By 2005 the number of robots in use, which is growing at a rate of 7.5 percent annually, is expected to exceed 960,000, according to a United Nations Economic Commission survey.) "An assembly line robot will not make a good Mars rover," Rus told *Wired* (October 7, 2002, on-line). "A robot designed for a single purpose may perform a task well, but it will perform poorly on a different task, in a different envi-

ronment. For tasks in hard-to-reach areas like space or the ocean, where it is impossible to say ahead of time what the robot will have to do and when it will have to do it, it is better to use robots that can change shape because that gives the robots versatility." Along with colleagues and students, Rus, who until recently was director of the Dartmouth Robotics Laboratory and co-director of the Dartmouth Transportable Agents Laboratory, at Dartmouth College, in Hanover, New Hampshire, has been developing robots that can adapt to their environments. Her other research interests include developing sensor networks (decentralized devices that have communication capabilities and limited sensing capabilities), mobile agents (computer programs that can interrupt execution, move to different places, and start computation from where they left off), and new methods of accessing and organizing information.

Daniela Rus was born in Cluj-Napoca, in the Transylvanian region of Romania, in about 1963. She immigrated to the United States with her parents, Teodor and Elena Rus, in 1982, partly to escape the political situation in Romania. (Like many other East European nations, Romania came under the control of the Soviet Union after World War II. The rule of the dictator Nicolae Ceausescu was marked by human-rights violations, government corruption, an extremely low standard of living for all but a few, and isolation from the West.) The Rus family settled in Iowa City, Iowa, where Teodor Rus still teaches computer science at the University of Iowa; Elena Rus, a physicist who built a career in research in the U.S., is now retired. Daniela Rus earned a B.S. degree with honors in computer science and math at the University of Iowa in 1985; her minor was astronomy. Robotics began gaining attention as she was completing her undergraduate studies; a lecture given at the University of Iowa by John Hopcroft of Cornell University led her to pursue it as a career. Hopcroft "was very persuasive and talked about the grand challenges of computer science and the great promise of computer science . . . and one of the greatest challenges of the time was robotics," Rus told *Current Biography*. She attended graduate school at Cornell, in Ithaca, New York, receiving both her master of science and her Ph.D. degrees in computer science, in 1990 and 1992, respectively. In addition to Hopcroft, who was her doctoral-thesis adviser, she has named Bruce Donald (then an associate professor of computer science at Cornell and now the Joan P. and Edward J. Foley Jr. Professor at Dartmouth) as one of her mentors. She was a research associate at the university from the fall of 1992 to the summer of 1994.

Rus joined the faculty of Dartmouth College in 1994, teaching computer science. In the same year she founded the Dartmouth Robotics Laboratory, of which she was the director, and in 1995 she co-founded and became co-director of the Dartmouth Transportable Agents Laboratory. She has been a strong advocate for undergraduate research at the

Daniela Rus

school and worked on research projects with more than 50 students. She has also done work at Dartmouth's Center for Mobile Computing and has been involved in the school's D'Agents project, a collaboration with George Cybenko and David Kotz to study mobile agents and their applications.

Rus is perhaps best known for her work on self-reconfiguring robots, machines that can adapt to various environments by changing shape without human control. "The modules [independent parts of the robots] organize and then reorganize," Rus told Anne Eisenberg for the *New York Times* (February 28, 2002). "If they come to a cave, for instance, they might form themselves in a slinky, snakelike line to get inside, then broaden out once they were within." A robot composed of these modules could also form legs to walk over rough terrain and then reconfigure itself again to climb stairs. Rus is particularly interested in creating robots that can repair themselves when necessary, as well as machines that can self-replicate. "In order to solve these problems, you really need to think hard about engineering and design questions," she told *Current Biography*. "What would such a robot look like? What kind of capabilities would it have to have on board? But that's not enough. Once you put those hardware capabilities in, the questions of planning and control (which allow the robot system to autonomously accomplish the shape or the replication operation) are really challenging algorithmic questions."

For Rus the primary impetus behind her work is the challenge of building something new and innovative. "My main research motivation is, 'Can you do it?'" she told *Current Biography*. "Can you get a new and improved and better kind of robot? Can

you move away from the traditional paradigm of a fixed-architecture robot that is useful for a fixed set of tasks, but if it has to do anything different it gets stuck? That naturally begs the question why." She added, "Besides just the intellectual challenge of just being able to do it and the coolness factor . . . you can think of a lot of uses." Exploration of space and oceans, in particular, is a natural candidate to benefit from such technology, because in those environments no one can predict what the robots will encounter. Rus also believes such robots would be useful for inspecting large structures, such as bridges, and in construction, for which they could possibly be used as scaffolding. (Self-reconfiguring robots could be employed in instances in which traditional human-built scaffolding is not feasible because of dangerous conditions, such as a collapsed mine; once the space has been made safe, humans would be allowed to enter.) Architects could also use the robots as "digital clay" to model projects three-dimensionally before they are built, and if produced on a tiny scale, the robots could be used for medical purposes. Rus even speculated that they could be marketed as toys, while others suggest that such robots could be quite useful for military objectives, such as performing reconnaissance missions. "You can imagine making everything around you out of these modules that are smart and adaptive and customized," Rus told *Current Biography*. "You could put a bag in a backpack, go to the top of a mountain and if you want to rest you could just get the modules to assemble themselves into a chair. This is the promise that is making it all so exciting for us, in addition to the very interesting technical science and engineering problems." There are currently three types of reconfiguring robots: chain, lattice, and mobile-reconfiguration models. (In a lattice-based robot, the modules are arranged in a lattice formation, while in a chain robot, the modules form linear structures that can move in space. Lattice and chain robots are static; the structures they form do not move once completed, while a mobile robot can keep moving after changing shape.) Rus and other researchers at the Dartmouth Robotics Laboratory have built a lattice robot called a crystal robot, which can change from a dog-shaped to a couch-shaped object.

With her research group, Rus has built modular robots that mirror the flexibility of living cells. Each module has a cube-shaped unit, or atom, with its own battery and sensors, as well as computation and communication capabilities. The atoms are able to expand from two to four inches wide and attach to and detach from one another; each atom can move independently and has a tiny motor and rotating connections to change positions. When atoms lock together, the robot can move like an inchworm or arrange its atoms into other shapes, depending on the task at hand—which can involve movement, grasping, or sensing. Rus hopes to build robots that each have thousands of miniature atoms made of microelectromechanical devices, each scarcely bigger than the biological cells they would mimic. "The key challenges are how to design a basic unit that is small yet capable enough," she told *Wired.*

Rus has also worked on distributed robot systems, or collections of individual robots that work cooperatively to accomplish tasks as a unit. In these systems an individual robot "doesn't do very much by itself, but together with a lot of other modules it can do a whole lot," she told *Current Biography.* "This is in contrast with the centralized robot system, where you have one robot, one brain, a single point of failure, and if something goes wrong, that's it. . . . With a distributed robot, you have parallelism and you have tolerance; if one member of the team fails, that doesn't matter because the rest of the team can compensate and keep going." With her colleague Bruce Donald, she worked on a project in which teams of independent robots cooperated to rearrange furniture, first by pushing the items and then by using ropes as tools to move objects.

Rus has developed what have proven to be functional algorithms for coordinating subunit interactions. "An algorithm is kind of like a recipe for a delicious chocolate cake," she said to *Current Biography.* "It gives you the steps that you need to follow in order to accomplish the task. And so when a robot has to go from point A to point B, the robot has to perceive its environment and take that information and make decisions about every step it has to carry out in the physical world. . . . You can think of an algorithm as a sequence of commands that have to be followed in order for the task to be accomplished."

Information access is another of Rus's research interests. "I became interested in information access as I was finishing my Ph.D. thesis, before the Web explosion," she revealed to *Current Biography.* "It was clear that information was going to dominate us, so I started thinking about paradigms that would make information processing easier." She explained that to process information it is necessary to locate both the data and the program needed to process it. There are two ways to access data: downloading it to the program searching for it, or downloading the program to where the information is located. The Internet relies on the first method. "But that usually implies that lots of bits fly over networks, and sometimes uselessly, because maybe you take a quick look at the data and decide that it's no good," Rus told *Current Biography.* "So I was thinking maybe a more efficient way of doing that is to send the program to where the data is located, because the program is small as compared to the data." She was involved in a lengthy research project involving mobile agents, small computer programs able to travel over networks and the Internet to perform pre-determined tasks. She compares mobile agents to applets, programs that can be downloaded once. A mobile agent, while working similarly, has its own control and volition. It can be transferred to a machine and

begin operating, then move to a different location and begin running from the point at which it was interrupted. "The mobile agent is more like a program with a brain," Rus told *Current Biography.* While such programs can be compared to computer viruses in the way they can move from computer to computer, their purposes and their effects on computers are vastly different. Unlike a virus, which attempts to spread to as many programs as possible, a mobile agent minimizes transfers. Rus's research on mobile agents was conducted with the mobile-agent research group at Dartmouth, which included her colleagues David Kotz and George Cybenko in addition to several students.

Rus's attention is now on the broader mobile-computing paradigm, which would encompass the building of a wireless world and make it possible to use a network without having the Internet as infrastructure. "In systems like this [mobile computing], how do you guarantee message delivery, how do you route messages effectively so as to not kill the batteries on these machines by talking too much . . . and what can you do with these devices?" she asked rhetorically during her interview with *Current Biography.* Such a system, she went on to explain, might involve small computers the size of such personal digital assistants as Palm Pilots and could use an alternative to the Internet to connect electric devices. "These computers can talk to each other but range is really small," she said. Because the system is mobile, "you don't have established routes the way we do in the Internet world."

Mobile computing could be useful in coping with disasters including earthquakes, fires, and hurricanes. "When such a disaster occurs, all your infrastructure is taken down," Rus said to *Current Biography.* "People are sent in there and they have to assess damage, they have to identify where the victims are, they have to figure out who needs medical attention and direct medics and doctors to those people, but they don't have an infrastructure to rely on." Rescuers would be able to use mobile computing to perform all of those tasks before entering the site. Mobile sensor networks would occupy the space and establish a communications network; they could also monitor the space looking for specific items. For example, in a fire, the system could keep temperature maps and locate people. "This is very hard to do at the moment, because without an infrastructure you have no idea what's in there," she told *Current Biography.* Such technology could also be used in remote sites that do not have existing infrastructures.

"What I'm interested in is how to provide a communication infrastructure that guarantees message delivery if you have these simple communication and sensing devices," Rus told *Current Biography,* "and how to actually deploy such systems and get them to control their own movement so as to be most effective at relaying the information that's needed for us to be proactive, anticipating the needs of the user and the network." The end result would be a distributed information repository, which, she suggests, could also be used to operate surveillance and security systems or to track people or objects.

Rus has also researched ways to combine mobile-agent technology with self-reconfiguring robots. "You can build smarts into that computation—you can make it intelligent," she told Gail Balfour for *ComputerWorld Canada* (September 11, 1998). "It removes the human from the loop for some of the low-level kinds of operations." Rus's future projects include more work on self-reconfiguring machines. She has recently collaborated with other Dartmouth researchers to develop a system for regulating the movements of cows with the aid of robotic controls and low-level electric shocks. One possible project would involve networked robots, or robots working together from respective positions on the ground, in the air, and underwater. She would also like to determine how small such robots could be.

Rus has co-written the two-volume *The Systems Methodology for Software* (1994 and 1995) with her father, Teodor Rus, and has contributed chapters to 22 books. She has published articles in several professional journals, including *World Scientific*, *Computing Surveys*, and the *International Journal of Robotics Research* (*IJRR*), and has been guest editor of *Autonomous Robots* and the *International Journal of Robotics Research*. In addition, she edited (with Sanjiv Singh) *Experimental Robotics VII* and (with Bruce Randall Donald and Kevin M. Lynch) *Algorithmic and Computational Robotics: New Directions*, both published in 2001. She organized the National Science Foundation Workshop on Self-reconfiguring Robots at Johns Hopkins University in January 1999 and was the general co-chair of both the WAFR 2000 (Workshop on Algorithmic Foundations of Robotics) at Dartmouth in March 2000 and the International Symposium on Experimental Robotics in Waikiki Beach, Hawaii, in December 2000. Rus is a member of the Institute of Electrical and Electronics Engineers (IEEE) and the Association of Computing Machines. She has received grants from the MacArthur Foundation (the "genius" grant), the National Science Foundation, Sandia National Labs, the Honda Corporation, NASA, the Alfred P. Sloan Foundation, the Air Force Office of Scientific Research, and the Air Force Intelligence Agency, as well as the Office of Naval Research and the Defense Advanced Projects Agency. A member of the Phi Beta Kappa Society, she was listed in *Who's Who Among America's Teachers* in 1998. Her honors include the National Science Foundation Career Award (1996). In 2003 she joined MIT as an associate professor in the Department of Electrical Engineering and Computer Science. Upon her appointment, John Guttag, head of the department, called her "an incredibly creative and energetic researcher and dedicated educator," according to the Tech Talk page on the MIT Web site (May 14, 2003). "She brings a sense of excitement and fun to everything she does."

In September 2004 Rus and several other researchers at the Dartmouth Robotics Lab published a paper in the *IJRR* detailing their most recent work, which includes their development of "the first control methods that guarantee [that] self-reconfigurable robots won't fall apart as they change shape or move across a surface," as reported in *M2 Presswire* (September 16, 2004). As Rus told *M2 Presswire*, "These latest papers show it is possible to develop self-reconfiguration capabilities in a way that has analytical guarantees."

Rus and her husband, Javed A. Aslam, who teaches in the College of Computer and Information Science at Northeastern University in Boston, Massachusetts, have two young daughters. "Between my work and the family I have my hands quite full, but I believe that it's important to always find a little time for yourself, because that's how you grow as a person," Rus told *Current Biography*. In her free time she enjoys reading, hiking, scuba diving, painting, and cooking. She and her family live in the Boston area.

—K.E.D.

Suggested Reading: Dartmouth College Web site, News & Events Sep. 25, 2002; *New York Times* G p5 Feb. 28, 2002; *TechTalk* (on-line) May 14, 2003, with photo; *Wired* (on-line) Oct. 7, 2002

Selected Books: *The Systems Methodology for Software* (with Teodor Rus), 1994 and 1995; as co-editor—*Experimental Robotics VII* (with Sanjiv Singh), 2001; *Algorithmic and Computational Robotics: New Directions* (with Bruce Randall Donald and Kevin M. Lynch), 2001

Russell, Kurt

Mar. 17, 1951– Actor

Address: c/o Creative Artists Agency, 9830 Wilshire Blvd., Beverly Hills, CA 90212

Over the course of four decades, from his work as a child actor to his performance as an uncompromising hockey coach in the movie *Miracle* (2004), Kurt Russell has become a familiar screen presence to several generations of viewers. After starring in lightweight Walt Disney film comedies in the 1960s and 1970s, Russell moved on to play gruff figures in action-oriented movies, including *Escape from New York* and *Tombstone*, comedic parts, in such movies as *Overboard*, and characters in highly regarded dramatic films, among them *Silkwood* and *Backdraft*. Away from the cameras, Russell has earned a reputation as an anomaly among movie actors. Amid the so-called political correctness of Hollywood, he is a member of the National Rifle Association and an avid hunter, and

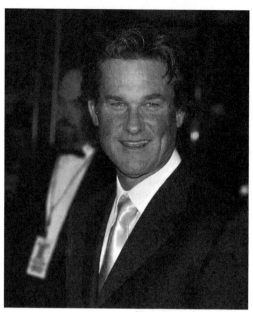

Kevin Winter/Getty Images

Kurt Russell

while many film stars approach their work with an almost clergy-like seriousness and devotion, Russell said to Roderick Mann for the *Los Angeles Times* (July 6, 1986), "To go on about acting as an art is ridiculous. If it is an art, then it's a very low form." Mann observed, "Spend half an hour with [the actors] Al Pacino and Robert De Niro and you walk away convinced that only those touched by the Muse have a chance, that there's something semi-mystical about their craft. Spend the same amount of time around Kurt Russell and you feel sure you could have a crack at it yourself, given some encouragement."

Kurt Vogel Russell was born on March 17, 1951 in Springfield, Massachusetts. His father, Neil "Bing" Russell, was a professional baseball player turned actor, best known for playing the sheriff on the long-running TV Western drama *Bonanza* and for bit parts in Western films. Russell's mother, Louise "Lou" Crain, was a former dancing teacher and beauty-contest winner. The Russell family, which included Kurt's younger sisters, Jody and Jami, his older sister, Jill, and his brother, Doug, moved to California when Kurt was four years old. Sports were popular in the family; by the time Kurt was eight years old, according to the *Christian Science Monitor* (December 16, 1966), he had become the world champion quarter-midget race-car driver. Playing baseball, a passion that Bing Russell shared with his sons, was more important to Kurt during his boyhood than acting. Although, since the age of nine, he had appeared on television periodically in such shows as *Our Man Higgins*, he developed a real interest in acting only when it coincided with his interest in baseball: having heard that the baseball stars Mickey Mantle and Roger

Maris were slated to appear in a film called *Safe at Home!* (1962), Kurt asked his father's agent, a family friend, to set up an audition for him. While he did not get the part, the experience led him to audition for other projects, which resulted in his winning the title role in the television series *The Travels of Jaimie McPheeters* (1963-64) and a spate of guest roles on shows including *The Virginian* (in 1964), *Gilligan's Island* (in 1965), and *Lost in Space* (in 1966). Russell's film debut was in 1963, when, in *It Happened at the World's Fair*, he played the (uncredited) part of a boy who kicks the singer Elvis Presley in the shins. The film *Follow Me, Boys!* (1966) represented the start of Russell's association with the Walt Disney Co. Russell came to know Disney himself, who, as he told Jerry Parker, was "a lot like a grandfather to me." Russell signed a 10-year contract with the Disney Co. and appeared in numerous family films, with titles such as *The Horse in the Gray Flannel Suit* (1968), *The Computer Wore Tennis Shoes* (1969), *The Barefoot Executive* (1971), and *Superdad* (1974). While Russell's roles in those movies were seldom challenging—he usually played a good but misunderstood teenager—he considered his tenure with Disney to be good training for his future. "I liked doing Disney pictures," he explained to Dan Yakir for *USA Weekend* (July 11, 1986). "When people congratulate me as if I had overcome some immense barrier, it's funny because I'm proud of that period in my life."

Despite his success in Disney films, Russell still preferred semiprofessional baseball to acting; in fact, his contract stipulated that he could leave film sets at 3: 30 P.M. on days when he was scheduled to play baseball. When he got older Russell played on several minor-league teams, such as the Walla Walla Islanders, the El Paso Sun Kings, and the Portland Mavericks, a team owned by his father. His baseball career was cut short when, during a game in 1973, a rogue ball hit him in the shoulder, tearing his rotator cuff. His doctor told him that he would no longer be able to play; Russell nonetheless showed up the following year for spring training, only to give out after three days. It was then that he gave serious thought to acting as a career. "Knowing that I was going to have to make my living at something other than baseball, I decided for the first time to diversify myself as an actor, to be a little more serious about the whole thing. Not a whole lot more serious, but a little," he told Larry Kart for the *Chicago Tribune* (July 26, 1981).

To that end, Russell performed in several television movies, among them *The Deadly Tower* (1975), in which he earned rave notices for his performance as the mass murderer Charles Joseph Whitman. His career got a major boost in 1979, when he was selected to play Elvis Presley for the TV movie *Elvis*. Russell, who shared few physical traits with the late Presley, compensated for that disadvantage by studying footage of Presley and talking to the singer's friends and aides. Russell's performance garnered praise from audiences and critics, who found that he had managed to capture the attitude and spirit of the music legend. While making *Elvis*, Russell forged two important relationships: he became close friends with the movie's director, John Carpenter, and married the actress Season Hubley, who co-starred as Priscilla Presley, the singer's wife. With Hubley Russell had a son, Boston Oliver Grant, in 1980. The couple later divorced.

Russell followed his performance as Presley with his turn as a sleazy salesman in *Used Cars* (1980). He next collaborated with Carpenter on *Escape from New York* (1981), in which Russell played one of his best-known characters to date—the antihero Snake Plissken, a hardened veteran of World War III. Scowling and squinting out of his one eye, Snake stalks through a future version of Manhattan, which has in effect become a maximum-security prison, trying to liberate the president of the United States, who has been taken hostage. Snake, while hardly a likable character, held an appeal for the actor, as he told Guy Trebay for the *Village Voice* (July 8, 1981): "There are things about [Snake] . . . that all of us have felt. His anguishes, desires, fears. But when he walks down the street, he's in *control*, an island, totally alone. I like that." *Escape from New York* quickly achieved cult status, as did, to a lesser extent, Russell's next film with Carpenter, *The Thing* (1982), a remake of Howard Hawks's 1951 science-fiction film *The Thing from Another World*. (Between work on *Escape from New York* and *The Thing*, Russell provided the voice of the titular hound dog in Disney's 1981 animated *The Fox and the Hound*.)

For his next film Russell played a character very different from Snake Plissken. In *Silkwood* (1983), which was based on the true story of Karen Silkwood (played by Meryl Streep), a worker at a nuclear power plant, Russell was seen as the sensitive, supportive boyfriend of the title character. In 1984 Russell appeared in the World War II romantic drama *Swing Shift*, which, although widely panned, was significant in that it marked the beginning of Russell's relationship with the actress Goldie Hawn. The two had a son, Wyatt, born in 1986.

None of Russell's projects over the next few years managed to appeal to both reviewers and ordinary moviegoers. He played a reporter in *The Mean Season* (1985), receiving mixed reviews despite his intense preparation for the role, which involved accompanying real-life reporters on assignments. The following year he co-starred with Robin Williams in the sports comedy *The Best of Times* and also appeared in John Carpenter's action comedy *Big Trouble in Little China*. Although this collaboration with Carpenter was not quite as critically successful as *Escape from New York*, it, too, performed well at the box office and has since attained cult recognition. He co-starred with Goldie Hawn in the poorly received 1987 comedy *Overboard*. Next he starred in *Tequila Sunrise* (1988), in which he played a detective who is

charged with investigating his friend, a former drug dealer (Mel Gibson). A critical success, *Tequila Sunrise* was a disappointment at the box office, whereas Russell's next film, *Winter People* (1989), was an all-around flop. The same year Russell paired with Sylvester Stallone to make *Tango & Cash*, a buddy-cop movie that performed well in theaters but received dismal reviews.

Backdraft (1991), on the other hand, was a hit with both critics and audiences. In it, Russell played a fireman, Stephen "Bull" McCaffrey, who is committed to his job, devoted to the memory of his late father (also a firefighter), and too hard on his younger brother, a firefighter-in-training (played by William Baldwin). Russell performed his own stunt work, which involved fighting actual fires; professional stuntmen and computer graphics were kept to a minimum in the production. Russell recalled to Lawrence Grobel for *Entertainment Weekly* (June 14, 1991): "All of us were getting burned every day. . . . Your hair would burn. You'd put this gel on to keep your skin from burning, but it also attracted these little bits of ash which stuck to your face. Billy [Baldwin] got set on fire twice. I got set on fire three times." For the same article, the movie's director, Ron Howard, expressed his admiration for Russell's performance and stunt work. "What Kurt did during those fires scared the crap out of me," he said. "All the fire fighters [professionals who were on the set to supervise] really admired Kurt. In the movie he epitomizes the most aggressive fire fighter, and particularly in Chicago, where they pride themselves on an old-fashioned, physical, almost cowboy-like approach to the job. They were thrilled with the way Kurt took to it." Russell called the film "the best thing I've ever done."

After the success of *Backdraft, Unlawful Entry* (1992), a rote thriller, was a disappointment, as was *Captain Ron*, made the same year. *Tombstone* (1993), Russell's next effort, fared better. A retelling of the story of the Western gunfighters Doc Holliday (Val Kilmer) and Wyatt Earp (Russell), it outperformed the 1994 film version of the legend, which was entitled *Wyatt Earp* and starred Kevin Costner. Russell had a tiny, uncredited voice-over part in the 1994 film *Forrest Gump*, starring Tom Hanks, in which Russell, once again, found himself linked to Elvis Presley—when he provided the voice for an actual film clip of the singer (to which digital effects were added).

Russell made headlines in 1993 when it was revealed that he would receive $7 million for his upcoming role in *Stargate*, a science-fiction adventure film. In it Russell played Jack O'Neil, a bitter, uncommunicative army colonel who leads a reconnaissance mission through a "stargate," or a portal to another world. Though critical reception was tepid, the movie was a box-office hit and spawned several sequels (none of which featured Russell). The success of *Stargate*, coupled with that of his next picture, the action adventure *Executive Decision* (1996), allowed him to command a salary of

$10 million for his follow-up film, *Escape from L.A.* Another collaboration between Russell and director John Carpenter, the film—the sequel to *Escape from New York*—found Russell reprising his role as the snarling Snake Plissken. The film received mixed reviews and was a box-office flop. Russell next starred in *Breakdown* (1997), a well-received thriller, and the far less successful *Soldier* (1998).

In 2001 Russell teamed up with Kevin Costner for *3000 Miles to Graceland*, in which Russell's character, an ex-convict, joins a gang led by his old friend (Costner) with the intention of robbing a Las Vegas casino. With the heist scheduled to take place during International Elvis Week, the gang members disguise themselves in Presley attire. Still another Elvis—Elvis Mitchell, of the *New York Times* (February 23, 2001)—complained that the movie "feels longer than Presley's career and as irrelevant as he was by the end," citing Russell's Presley imitations as "the few crumbs of fun that he and the audience get" from the film. Also in 2001, Russell had a small part in *Vanilla Sky*, a remake of the 1997 Spanish film *Abre los Ojos*. In the following year Russell had roles in *Interstate 60*, a little-known but well-received movie, and in *Dark Blue*, in which he played a corrupt police officer.

Most recently Russell tackled the role of Herb Brooks, the notoriously uncompromising coach of the U.S. Olympic hockey team, in *Miracle* (2004). *Miracle* showed how Brooks whipped the team into shape and helped them to accomplish what had been thought to be impossible: beating the well-trained Soviet team at the 1980 Winter Olympics, in Lake Placid, New York, and winning the gold medal. In preparing for the role, Russell spent time with the real Herb Brooks, who died in a car accident before the movie was completed. Jack O'Callahan, a defenseman on the 1980 U.S. hockey team, told Helene Elliott for the *Los Angeles Times* (February 8, 2004), "In most movies you see Kurt Russell, he's Kurt Russell. But this wasn't like watching an actor. . . . This was actually like watching Herb Brooks, and . . . I give a lot of credit to Kurt for getting to know Herbie and really picking up little things about him." Russell considered *Miracle* one of his best movies and also appreciated that it brought him closer to his son Wyatt, a goalie for the Richmond Sockeyes in the Pacific International Junior Hockey League.

When not acting in films, Russell enjoys watching Wyatt's games, piloting his two airplanes, driving boats, racing cars, and hunting. According to Russell, although Goldie Hawn does not hunt, she cooks what he catches. He is a member of the National Rifle Association but declined to be their spokesman; in the late 1980s he caused a flap when he sponsored a celebrity hunt to benefit the homeless. Although many animal-rights groups and liberal celebrities reacted with rage, Russell ignored their criticism, saying to Tom Green for *USA Today* (July 13, 1992), "How many of those actors have fed 16,000 homeless people?"

Russell and Hawn, who have never married, have been a couple since Valentine's Day 1983. Together they raised Hawn's two children from her marriage to Bill Hudson, Oliver and Kate Hudson; Russell's son Boston, who also spent time with his mother, Season Hubley; and Russell and Hawn's son, Wyatt. Hawn and Russell own a number of houses; they most recently purchased a home in Vancouver so that they could stay close to Wyatt while he pursues his hockey career. When their children were young, Russell and Hawn tried to ensure that at least one parent was at home at all times; Russell explained to Jeffrey Wells for the New York *Daily News* (October 23, 2004) that he found it "easier to work around Goldie's schedule than for her to work around mine. Men get more material and opportunities in the picture business than women [do]." Russell told Dan Yakir in 1986, "I don't believe in the notion of 'quality time.' I believe in the quantity of time spent with [children]. The more you're around, the better and the more secure they feel." Kate Hudson, herself an actress, and her husband, Chris Robinson of the rock band the Black Crowes, named their son Ryder Russell Robinson in honor of Kurt. Russell told Tom Green about Hawn, "Goldie's a blast. I just have a great time with her. I'm with her every day and I don't feel like I get to spend enough time with her." The actor's upcoming projects are the films "Sky High," scheduled for release in 2005, and "Dreamer," slated for 2006.

—K.J.E.

Suggested Reading: *Chicago Tribune* VI p17 July 26, 1981, with photos, p7 July 11-13, 1986, with photo; *Entertainment Weekly* p18+ June 14, 1991, with photos, p44+ Feb. 13, 2004, with photo; *GQ* p126+ June 1991, with photos; Internet Movie Database Web site; *New York Times* II p21+ Mar. 24, 1996, with photo; *USA Today* July 13, 1992, with photo; *Village Voice* p51 July 8, 1981

Selected Films: *The Horse in the Gray Flannel Suit*, 1968; *The Deadly Tower*, 1975; *Elvis*, 1979; *Escape from New York*, 1981; *Silkwood*, 1983; *Tequila Sunrise*, 1988; *Backdraft*, 1991; *Tombstone*, 1993; *Executive Decision*, 1996; *3000 Miles to Graceland*, 2001; *Vanilla Sky*, 2001; *Miracle*, 2004

quins, elaborate beadwork, or embroidery, and featuring plunging necklines and thigh-high slits. "Saab has a limited repertoire, but what he does, he does well," an unsigned article in *WWD* (January 23, 2004) declared. In the on-line edition of *Stars* magazine (2002), Claire High wrote, "His couture gowns capture the romance and opulence of a bygone era—with a modern, sexy twist." Saab himself told High, "What I mainly do is use the warmth of the Orient and add it to the European style." The designer has showrooms in Paris, France; Milan, Italy; and Beirut, Lebanon, in the last of which his staff of 100 fabricates his haute-couture collections. In addition to those designs, since 1998 he has offered a line of ready-to-wear clothing, also for evening events, which sells in select stores in a dozen countries. "I want to turn every woman into a butterfly," Saab told Hal Rubenstein for *In Style* (January 2003), "to make her every movement appear buoyed by a passing breeze, as if at any moment she could fly away."

Elie Saab was born on July 4, 1964 in Beirut to a wood merchant and his wife. Early on he felt drawn to art and fashion. As he recalled to Claire High, "I started designing when I was little, using any kind of fabric I could possibly find at that time—dressing my sisters and [other] members of the family." By age 16 he knew he wanted to pursue a career in fashion design. "I was interested in glamour and was just born to do it," he told Eilidh MacAskill for the London *Sunday Express* (April 1, 2001). His mother and father disapproved of his vocational plans; as he explained to MacAskill, "They just didn't understand. They still don't like the fact I work in fashion. In my country, especially then, being a fashion designer was not that prestigious." Their displeasure did not dissuade him, though. In 1982, without any formal training, the 18-year-old Saab opened an atelier in Beirut and launched his own company. Damage to his workshop by shells dropped by one of the Lebanese factions involved in the long-running war (or from outsiders who had gotten involved in the fighting, among them Sudanese, Israeli, and U.S. soldiers) interrupted his business but did not discourage him. Later in 1982 Saab presented his first collection of women's evening wear and bridal gowns, in one of the showrooms cum theaters at the Casino du Liban, an upscale entertainment facility located in the seaside resort town of Maameltein, north of Beirut. The show was a smashing success; it attracted the attention of a bevy of Middle Eastern princesses and other members of social elites, who sought Saab's lavish dresses for weddings or other special events.

The popularity of Saab's gowns grew throughout the 1980s. By the 1990s the designer had moved his boutique to a larger space in Beirut and had begun to hold private fashion shows in Paris and Switzerland. He garnered more notice when, in 1997, he became the first non-Italian designer to present his haute-couture collection, by invitation, during *Alta Moda* (High Fashion) Week in Rome.

Jean-Pierre Muller/AFP/Getty Images

Saab, Elie

(sahb, EL-ee)

July 4, 1964– Fashion designer

Address: c/o MHA Media, 5709 Melrose Ave., Los Angeles, CA 90038-3807

The presentation of the Academy Award for best actress to Halle Berry, on March 24, 2002, for her performance in *Monster's Ball* marked a milestone not only in the history of the Oscars (it was the first time that an African-American woman had won in that category) but also in the career of Elie Saab, who designed the gown Berry wore to the ceremony. The gown's five and a half minutes of international exposure via television brought Saab incalculably more attention than he had received in the two decades since he had launched his career, at age 18, in his native Lebanon. "This is huge for me," he told Cheryl Lu-Lien Tan for the *Baltimore Sun* (March 28, 2002) a few days later. "The phones have been ringing off the hook. . . . I feel extremely happy and proud." Notwithstanding his lack of widespread name recognition outside the Middle East before the 2002 Academy Awards ceremony—and even since then, in comparison with such giants of the fashion world as, say, Coco Chanel or Christian Dior—Saab has enjoyed notable success virtually from the start, despite the complex, semi–civil war that raged in Lebanon for some 15 years, beginning in 1975, and devastated Beirut and other parts of the country. His specialty is formal women's attire, including wedding gowns, many of them made of chiffon, lace, tulle, or other diaphanous fabrics, decorated with se-

Participating in that show was "quite exciting but challenging as well . . . ," he told Claire High. "Thank God it all went very well at that time and the success encouraged me to go back and do more and more." In 1998 Saab introduced his pret-a-porter (ready-to-wear) collection in Milan. Manufactured in Italy, those clothes are currently sold at Bergdorf Goodman and Neiman Marcus stores in the U.S. and in a dozen other countries: Greece, Spain, Monaco, Great Britain, Suadi Arabia, Kuwait, and Egypt, as well as France, Italy, Switzerland, and Lebanon. When asked if he would considering relocating his company's headquarters to a location outside Lebanon, Saab told Eilidh MacAskill, "I'm so proud of my country I will never ever leave. . . . I want to prove that Lebanon is no different from anywhere else." He explained to Hal Rubenstein, "Of course, you sacrifice certain clients if they can't see you as easily as they would like, even though I do travel a lot. I prefer to be in my country because I have a staff that understands how I want to make clothes, and because I am more inspired by my clients here, Asian women, who are often less afraid of sensual clothes than Americans are. They more naturally gravitate toward elegance."

The prices for Saab's lavish, intricately decorated couture apparel start at about $10,000 per gown. Besides being out of reach financially for most women, Saab's gowns are designed for people with slim, well-toned bodies; as a writer for Agence France-Press put it, as quoted on-line at ClariNet (January 22, 2003), they "are certainly not for those without a personal trainer." The designer, who has been dubbed the Lebanese Versace (a reference to the late, eminent Italian-born designer Gianni Versace), encourages wearers to apply a minimum of makeup, keep their hairstyles simple, and complement their gowns with jewelry, shoes, and bags designed by his younger sister, Mona Saab. He told Claire High that his sister "started making a few designs and I admired her talent and her love for details, so I decided to work with her on one collection and have been doing it since then." His devotees include Queen Rania of Jordan, who wore a gown of his design to the 1999 coronation of her husband, King Abdullah, and such actresses as Catherine Deneuve, Penelope Cruz, Bo Derek, Victoria Principal, Bridget Fonda, Calista Flockheart, Patricia Arquette, Mena Suvari, and Halle Berry. Berry's stylist, Phillip Bloch, was, in his words, "blown away" by one dress he saw on the runway during Saab's fall 2001 haute-couture show in Paris; as he recalled to Cheryl Lu-Lien Tan, "I just thought, 'This is an amazing dress. Somebody needs to wear it to an amazing event.'" During that time Bloch had looked at hundreds of gowns while searching for one for Berry to wear to the 2002 Academy Awards ceremony. The one that caught his eye at Saab's show had a sleeveless, embroidered tulle bodice that ended at a slant below the waist, a high, rounded neckline, a voluminous taffeta skirt, and a zipper in the back. For Berry, Bloch asked Saab to create two alternate versions, each with a side zipper, more embroidery on the top (for a less risqué look), and a somewhat more fitted skirt. The color Bloch and Berry chose for the fabrics has been described variously as garnet, claret, burgundy, and merlot (the last three being the names of wines). Bloch and Berry also worked with the jeweler Harry Winston to create custom accessories—two rings, a bracelet, and a pair of earrings. Saab's first sight of Berry in the dress, on television on the night of the awards ceremony, "thrilled" him, as he told Alev Aktar for the New York *Daily News* (March 28, 2002). Saab also noted to Cheryl Lu-Lien Tan that Berry "could breathe and move freely in the dress, which only added to her beauty and charm." Thanks to the publicity generated by the televised proceedings on Oscar night, Saab became an instant celebrity. Bloch commented to Aktar, "It's so nice to launch a designer's career. . . . This will change his life."

Saab outfitted Berry in a gold-colored gown for the 2003 Oscars ceremony, in which she presented an award. He also designed the gowns worn by the actresses Rachel Griffiths, Jill Hennessey, and Anne Hathaway at the 2003 Golden Globe Awards presentations, and the dress worn by Debra Messing when she won the award for outstanding actress in a comedy series at the 2003 Emmy Awards ceremony. That same year, Saab collaborated with the Canadian-based company MAC (Make-up Art Cosmetics Ltd.) to create a limited-edition collection of makeup based on the golden, brown, and beige tones in his spring-summer couture collection. Also in 2003 the BMW X5 Elie Saab Limited Edition was unveiled; Saab chose black and white for the car's interior. That spring, by invitation, he became a member of the couture industry's trade association, the Chambre Syndicale de la Haute Couture.

In early 2004 Saab presented a collection in London, England, for the first time. The show took place at the annual charity dinner of the British Lebanese Association, at the London Natural History Museum. Among the designs was a cream satin wedding gown whose bodice was decorated with 2,000 carats' worth of emeralds and 400 carats' worth of diamonds. The gown, worth an estimated $2 million, had been bought earlier by a princess from Qatar.

Saab lives with his wife, Claudine, and their three children in Beirut.

—K.J.E.

Suggested Reading: *Baltimore Sun* E p1 Mar. 28, 2002; Elie Saab Web site; *In Style* p46 Jan. 2003; (London) *Sunday Express* p70 Apr. 1, 2001; (New York) *Daily News* ; stars.com

James Keivom/Liaison

Sanger, Stephen

Apr. 10, 1946– Chairman and CEO of General Mills Inc.

Address: General Mills Inc., One General Mills Blvd., Minneapolis, MN 55426

As the chief executive officer (CEO) and chairman of General Mills Inc., Stephen W. Sanger presides over the fifth-largest food-manufacturing company in the world. In his 20 years at General Mills, Sanger has risen through the ranks, earning recognition for his superior marketing skills and novel ideas. Once primarily known for its cereals—Cheerios, Wheaties, and Lucky Charms, among others—and Yoplait yogurt, General Mills is now associated also with products made by Pillsbury, which the company acquired in 2001. The fun-loving Sanger—who has been known to inject humor into corporate presentations—has attempted to revamp the company's image, by incorporating natural foods into its offerings, for example. He has also encouraged innovation and the use of new technologies and has earned praise for promoting employee diversity, instituting an unusual number of family-friendly policies and benefits, and sponsoring programs to benefit inner-city residents of Minneapolis, Minnesota, where General Mills is based.

Stephen Sanger was born on April 10, 1946 in Cincinnati, Ohio. As a high-school student, he spent several summers working at the firm of his father, who was a real-estate attorney, and in a local probate court. In the latter job he questioned "people who wanted to commit other people to mental institutions," as he recalled to Joel Hoekstra

for *DePauw Magazine* (Spring 2002, on-line). "If you thought your husband or wife or kid was seriously mentally ill and you wanted them picked up and institutionalized, you came to the court, and I would take the information and type it up." That experience led him to reconsider his plan to pursue a career in law; by his own account, it also helped him to get high marks in his college psychology course.

Sanger attended DePauw University, in Greencastle, Indiana, where for a while he served as president of the student union. Charged with securing entertainment for campus events, he booked such major acts as the Temptations, the Four Tops, and Smokey Robinson and the Miracles. Selling tickets to their concerts was easy, but with lesser-known bands he had to resort to promotion. That experience led to Sanger's interest in marketing. "The whole notion of having a product, marketing it, and getting people interested in it really was fun," he told Hoekstra. After he earned a B.A. degree, in 1968, Sanger attended the University of Michigan at Ann Arbor, where he received an M.B.A. in 1970. He then returned to Cincinnati, where he worked in sales and marketing for Procter and Gamble until 1973.

In 1974 Sanger relocated to Minneapolis, to take a position in the consumer-foods division of General Mills. While progressing through a series of positions in the consumer-foods field, Sanger made some small but very successful changes. In 1975, after he introduced blue, diamond-shaped marshmallows to the already popular Lucky Charms, sales of the cereal jumped 31 percent. His addition of purple horseshoes, in 1983, resulted in a 25 percent increase in sales. (Both were permanent gains.) In 1988 Sanger added new flavors to the Cheerios lineup, one of which, honey nut, has for some years been the company's second-best-selling cereal, behind only the original Cheerios. In time he was named General Mills' executive vice president. He was elected to the board of directors in 1992 and shortly thereafter, along with Mark H. Willes and Joe R. Lee, became one of three vice chairmen, each of whom was a potential candidate for the presidency of General Mills. Although, at 47, Sanger was the youngest of the three by five or six years, in October 1993 he was chosen over the others, largely because of his marketing expertise. One of Sanger's priorities as president was to cut cereal prices by 30 to 70 cents a box rather than increasing prices and then offering discount coupons, as other cereal makers were doing. Sanger explained to John Holusha for the *New York Times* (April 5, 1994), "There is tremendous cost associated with printing, distributing, handling and redeeming coupons. Because of this inefficiency, the 50 cents that the consumer saves by clipping a coupon can cost manufacturers as much as 75 cents. It just doesn't make sense."

On May 28, 1995 Sanger became chairman and CEO of General Mills, succeeding H. Brewster Atwater Jr., who explained to Julie Forster for *Busi-*

ness Week (March 26, 2001) that Sanger had long been earmarked for success: "Steve was identified as someone with great potential. . . . He had interesting ideas about how to develop new products and get new business." As CEO, Sanger has encouraged the implementation of time- and cost-saving measures, regardless of how unconventional they may be. His interest in sports led to one such improvement: Sanger sent technicians to observe NASCAR pit crews and apply their observations to the problem of shifting assembly-line machinery from one function to another. Following the introduction of modifications, the switches, which had taken up to five hours, in some cases took only 20 minutes.

Perhaps Sanger's most notable action as CEO thus far is his negotiating the $10.5 billion acquisition of Pillsbury from the British firm Diageo PLC, a process he began in July 2000 and completed in November 2001. The merger, one of the largest ever in the food industry, nearly doubled the size of General Mills, making it the world's fifth-largest food company. Pillsbury's performance has improved, but it has not yet met General Mills' standards. Meanwhile, Sanger established the Health Ventures division, which packages organically grown foods (fruits, vegetables, and dairy products) under the brand names Cascadian Farm, Muir Glen, and 8th Continent. (A joint venture between General Mills and DuPont, the 8th Continent label is currently on a single product: "soymilk," which is derived from soybeans.) In September 2004, in response to consumer demands for more healthful breakfast foods, General Mills announced that the company would increase from 60 percent to 100 percent the number of its ready-to-eat cereal brands made with whole grains. (Whole grains, used to make such cereals as Cheerios, Wheaties, and Total, contain their entire complement of germ and bran; they thus provide significantly more folic acid, fiber, magnesium, vitamin E, and other nutrients than processed, or refined, grains, such as those used to produce Trix, Cocoa Puffs, Lucky Charms, and white bread.)

As CEO Sanger has sought to use the Internet to cut the company's costs, particularly in the areas of transportation, market research, and procurement. He has also emphasized the need for diversity among General Mills employees, not merely for reasons connected with politics or even ethics. As Sanger explained in a speech at the 9th Annual Multi-Cultural Forum on March 6, 1997, as posted on the Center for Ethical Business Cultures Web site, "Perhaps the biggest reason we so aggressively pursue a diverse mix of backgrounds and viewpoints in our workforce, in our marketing and among our suppliers . . . is that diverse viewpoints produce innovation. I am absolutely convinced that a team of people encompassing different life experiences and different points of view will consistently 'out-innovate' a very homogeneous team. And innovation is the force that drives our business." Although General Mills is located in

Minnesota, where over 91 percent of the population is white, more than 12 percent of the company's workers are members of minority groups; 18 percent of its corporate officers are female. The spring 2003 issue of *Business Ethics* magazine ranked General Mills at the top of its list of "100 best corporate citizens," primarily for its service to the Minneapolis community and its efforts on behalf of women and minorities. One example that illustrates both, according to a DePauw University news release (on-line), was the creation of 150 jobs in inner-city Minneapolis funded by $2 million from General Mills. The October 2002 issue of *Working Mother* magazine named General Mills among the 10 U.S. companies that try hardest to meet the needs of working mothers, by providing such benefits as company-based child care, fitness centers, and prescription-filling and medical services. General Mills was also included on *Fortune's* January 12, 2004 "100 Best Companies to Work For" list.

In February 2004 General Mills received a Wells Notice from the staff of the U.S. Securities and Exchange Commission (SEC), following the commission's launch of an inquiry into the company's sales practices and related accounting. The notice indicates the intention of the commission to bring a civil action against General Mills—including its CEO and chief financial officer—but gives the company a chance to respond before a formal suit is launched. "General Mills believes its sales practices and related accounting comply with all applicable rules and regulations," the company contended in response to the notice, as posted on the General Mills Web site. "General Mills said it is continuing to cooperate with the SEC in its investigation." As of early November 2004, neither General Mills nor the SEC had publicly reported any action regarding that matter.

When Sanger took over the post of CEO from his somewhat conservative predecessor, he immediately retired the General Mills dress code, which called for dark suits and white shirts, and allowed employees to leave work at noon on Fridays during the summer. He has earned a reputation at General Mills not only for his innovations, but for being somewhat eccentric and playful. Once, for example, before a presentation of a new, larger muffin, Sanger swapped the labels on the new and old versions. On another occasion, at a meeting, Sanger reportedly recited song lyrics and interrupted the proceedings to look up lines he had forgotten. "It's corny, but sweet," a *Business Week* (January 8, 2001) reporter wrote, adding that Duane Benson, who at that time headed the Minnesota Business Partnership, described Sanger as "like a Doris Day of guys." An avid college basketball fan, Sanger arranges his schedule so as not to miss NCAA Final Four tournaments.

Sanger is a board member of Catalyst, a nonprofit organization that promotes the advancement of women in business; the National Campaign to Prevent Teen Pregnancy; and the Minnesota Business

Partnership. He is a director of the Target Corp. and chairman of the boards of the Grocery Manufacturers of America and the Guthrie Theater. Sanger is also a member of the Business Council, the Conference Board, the Committee for Economic Development, and the Board of Advisors of the Retail Food Industry Center. In May 2002 the Food Marketing Institute presented him with its 2002 William H. Albers Industry Relations Award for exemplary industry leadership and community service. *Working Mother* named him its 2002 "family champion," for "making moms' needs a priority."

Sanger and his wife, Karen, a lawyer, have one son and one daughter. General Mills' family-friendly policies may possibly be traced to Sanger's experiences as a parent. Bonnie Miller Rubin reported in *Working Mother* (October 2002), as quoted on the *Working Mother* Media Web site, that shortly after becoming CEO of General Mills,

Sanger took his family with him to New York City when he was to speak before a group of Wall Street analysts; minutes before his presentation, his daughter accidentally locked herself in the hotel bathroom. "I was in a suit on my knees talking to a two-year-old through a keyhole—a very comical scene that took my mind off the presentation for the five minutes until we got her out," Sanger recalled. Rubin reported that the experience was "a defining moment in parenthood" for Sanger and quoted him as saying, "It was a momentary panic. It's funny how your priorities shift when you have children."

—K.J.E.

Suggested Reading: *Business Week* p67 Jan. 8, 2001, p75 Mar. 26, 2001; *DePauw Magazine* (online) Spring 2002; General Mills Web site; *Supermarket News* p64 July 21, 2003

Linda A. Cicero, Stanford News Service.

Sapolsky, Robert

Apr. 6, 1957– Neurobiologist; writer; educator

Address: c/o Steven Barclay Agency, 12 Western Ave., Petaluma, CA 94952

"I joined the baboon troop during my twenty-first year. I had never planned to become a savanna baboon when I grew up; instead, I had always assumed I would become a mountain gorilla." Those are the opening words of Robert Sapolsky's acclaimed book *A Primate's Memoir: A Neuroscientist's Unconventional Life among the Baboons*

(2001). In *A Primate's Memoir* Sapolsky, a professor of biological and neurological sciences at Stanford University, in Stanford, California, described his more than 20 years of experiences in studying a group of baboons, a primate species closely related to Homo sapiens, in the Serengeti region of Kenya, in East Africa, as part of his longtime examination of stress and stress-related disease. In addition to serving as a research associate at the Institute of Primate Research in Nairobi, Kenya, Sapolsky heads a research laboratory at Stanford, where he focuses on stress-related hormones and how they may damage neurons in the brain; he also seeks ways of strengthening the brain against such damage through the use of gene therapy. He and other researchers at the laboratory were among the first to demonstrate that sustained stress can damage the hippocampus, a region of the brain that controls memory and learning. "Specifically in the area I look at, which is why do some individuals have more stress-related diseases than others, baboons are perfect; they are great models for a Westernized stress lifestyle," Sapolsky told *Current Biography*, explaining that most of the stress they experience stems from interactions among themselves, as is true with humans. "[Baboons are] among the easiest [primates] to observe, and one of the few that I could have done my physiology studies on," he said in an interview posted on the Web site BookBrowse.com. "They live in these big social groups out in the open; you're not craning your neck to watch someone up in the trees, or trying to shoot him with a blowgun dart. They're not endangered, there's a lot known about their physiology. . . . The social groups remain reasonably intact year after year, and [individual baboons] are easy to recognize." In addition, unlike humans, baboons present few variables to complicate research on stress. As Sapolsky explained to *Current Biography*, "Wild baboons don't smoke; they don't drink;

they don't take drugs; they all get exercise; they don't lie on questionnaires."

In addition to *A Primate's Memoir*, Sapolsky is the author of *Stress, the Aging Brain, and the Mechanisms of Neuron Death* (1992); *Why Zebras Don't Get Ulcers: An Updated Guide to Stress, Stress-Related Diseases and Coping* (1994); and *The Trouble with Testosterone: And Other Essays on the Biology of the Human Predicament* (1997), the last two of which were finalists for the *Los Angeles Times* Book Award. As quoted on the Web site of the Steven Barclay Agency, which represents Sapolsky in his activities as a lecturer, the neurologist and writer Oliver Sacks has called Sapolsky "one of the best scientist-writers of our time." Nearly echoing that pronouncement, Rob Nixon, in the *New York Times Book Review* (April 1, 2001), declared that Sapolsky is "one of the finest natural history writers around." At universities and other institutions around the United States, Sapolsky has lectured on a wide range of topics, among them stress-related issues and the biology of individuality, religious beliefs, memory, schizophrenia, depression, and aggression. His honors include the National Science Foundation Presidential Young Investigator Award and a MacArthur Fellowship.

Robert M. Sapolsky was born to Thomas and Nelle Sapolsky, both Russian-Jewish immigrants, on April 6, 1957 in the New York City borough of Brooklyn. His father was an architect; before his death, in 1994, from complications of a neurological disease, he worked on renovations of the landmark New York City restaurants Luchow's and Lundy's, among other projects. "For an architect's son, I am remarkably uninformed in my architectural tastes," Sapolsky told Patricia Leigh Brown for the *New York Times* (April 19, 2001). "I suppose my ideal would be some huge, open atrium-like space with lots of tiny claustrophobic burrows leading off it." (Brown wrote that Sapolsky's workroom in his home, in the Bay Area of California, is indeed a "tiny claustrophobic burrow" off the bedroom and accessible only by a ladder.) Sapolsky grew up in the Bensonhurst section of Brooklyn, which he described to Brown as a "true tribal enclave." (The majority of the residents during those years were middle-class Italian-Americans.) As a boy Sapolsky spent many hours at the American Museum of Natural History, in Manhattan; he was particularly fascinated by the primates in the museum's dioramas of African flora and fauna, which led him to dream of living with mountain gorillas. By age 12 Sapolsky was "your basic misanthropic egghead," as he told Brown. He read the books of such primatologists as Irven DeVore, Harry Harlow, and Stuart and Jeanne Altmann and sent them fan letters. While attending John Dewey High School in the Coney Island section of Brooklyn, Sapolsky assiduously studied Swahili, a language native to East Africa, in a self-paced course. (He discovered later, as he recalled in *A Primate's Memoir*, that the Swahili he had learned during that time was not the same as the Swahili spoken in Kenya.) Sapolsky yearned to escape Brooklyn. "Bensonhurst was not the place to be a short scholarly Jewish kid with no proclivity toward athletics or gang violence," he quipped to Brown.

While Sapolsky attended Harvard University, in Cambridge, Massachusetts, in the mid- to late 1970s, his interest in primates began to coalesce with a budding interest in neurobiology, and he decided to study the relationship between stress and the social hierarchies found in primates, as a possible way to discover something about humans. He graduated summa cum laude from Harvard in 1978, with a bachelor's degree in biological anthropology. He conducted his graduate work at Rockefeller University, in New York City, specializing in neuroendocrinology (a branch of the life sciences that concerns the physiological interactions between the central nervous system and the endocrine system, the latter of which produces the hormones that regulate metabolism, growth, and sexual development). While pursuing his doctorate, which he earned in 1984, Sapolsky worked in a Rockefeller University laboratory under the guidance of Bruce S. McEwen, the "father of hormone-brain interaction research," as Sapolsky identified him in his comments to *Current Biography*. Their research, funded by the federal government and various foundations, focused on the effects of stress on the nervous system. In 1985 Sapolsky took a job as a researcher at the laboratory of Wylie Vale, at the Salk Institute for Biological Studies, in La Jolla, California; Vale is renowned for the co-discovery of corticotropin releasing factor (CRF), which figures prominently in the body's response to stress. (The Salk Institute was founded in the 1960s by Jonas Salk, who created the first successful vaccine against polio.) In 1987 Sapolsky was named an assistant professor of neuroscience at Stanford University; he then rose through the academic ranks, being promoted in 1995 to full professor in Stanford's Neuroscience Program and its Program in Molecular and Genetic Medicine. Currently, he is the John A. and Cynthia Fry Gunn Professor of Biological Sciences and a professor of neurology and neurological sciences.

In the laboratory he heads at Stanford, Sapolsky and his colleagues showed that during periods of intense stress, glucocorticoids (a class of steroid hormones secreted by the adrenal gland) can damage neurons in the hippocampus, a region in the brain involved in learning and memory. "We have no primates in the lab," Sapolsky told Katie Bacon for the *Atlantic* (April 25, 2001) when asked what his laboratory experimentation entailed. "We almost never have a whole rat in there. Most of what we do is single neurons growing in dishes. . . . We are trying to understand at a molecular level how a neuron dies after a [person suffers a] stroke, a seizure, Alzheimer's, brain aging, and what these stress hormones do to make it worse." Most recently Sapolsky's laboratory has focused mainly on gene therapy—primarily, employing gene-transfer techniques to implant genes into the hippocampus in order to render the brain more resistant to neurological disease. When Katie Bacon asked Sapolsky if humans had the capacity to change their behaviors so as to avoid the possibly deleterious influences of social stress, Sapolsky replied, "That's what stress management is about, that's what psychotherapy is about, finding religion, or finding your loved one or your hobby—any of those, they give you more outlets, more of a sense of control, more of a sense of predictability, of social support."

Earlier, in 1978, after his graduation from Harvard, Sapolsky had spent more than a year in the small section of the Serengeti Plains that lies in Kenya, as part of his research on stress and its physiological effects. In the Serengeti Sapolsky studied a troop of 60 baboons, whom he came to know as individuals; he gave them names from the Old Testament—Obadiah, Saul, Aaron, and Bathsheba, for example. Baboons are "big aggressive animals that could shred someone fairly easily," Sapolsky told *Current Biography*. The species he studies (there are five baboon species in total) range from about 70 to 100 pounds and have, in his words, "gigantic sharp canines that they use for fighting" and "considerably more limb strength than a human. They're formidable animals." With the exception of several years in the early 1990s and the year 2003 (because of political unrest in Kenya), Sapolsky has returned to Africa annually to study the same troop of baboons; during his field trips he leads a spartan existence, living in a camp of tents and thatched mud-and-dung huts with no electricity, running water, telephone, or radio and minimal access to the outside world.

Sapolsky explained to *Current Biography* several of the advantages to studying stress in baboons rather than humans, though his goal is to help humankind: "It is much easier to take biological measures on a baboon, and it's easier to trace their physiology over the span of their whole lifetime"— roughly 20 years, on average. Furthermore, because baboons usually avoid predators and spend only three hours a day gathering food, they have up to nine waking hours daily to interact with one another and "stir up social stress among themselves," as Brown wrote. One of the drawbacks to studying baboons, Sapolsky revealed on BookBrowse.com, is that they are "so damned smart" that they often succeed in playing tricks on him.

"In the lab I was studying why an excess of stress hormones had adverse consequences for health . . . while with the baboons, I wanted to understand what social factors predicated who secreted more or less of those stress hormones," Sapolsky explained on BookBrowse.com. To that end he looked closely at the relations among a baboon's rank within its social group, its behavior and personality, and any stress-related diseases it might have. To take measurements of heart rate, blood pressure, adrenaline levels, etc., and draw blood samples, Sapolsky had to tranquilize his subjects using a blowgun; he then lugged their anesthetized bodies to his research area. He discovered that baboons of lower rank in the troop's stable social hierarchy had higher testosterone levels, spent more time fighting over status, experienced more stressful situations, and were more prone to stress-related illness than the dominant baboons. He also found that the elusive factor of personality played a significant role in how individual baboons handled stress.

One of the behaviors that most endeared the baboons to Sapolsky indicated that they viewed him as an "incredibly low-ranking primate," as he explained to *Current Biography*. When a male baboon is about to be attacked by a baboon of a higher rank, it will try, through gestures, to enlist the help of other males in its defense. "Every now and then you'll get some baboon who is just about to get trounced, and he tries to get this guy or that guy to join this coalition, and nobody is interested, and . . . as a desperate last measure, he'll turn to me and see if I want to join. I'm clearly way down on the ladder; they've got to try everybody else out there before they even think of resorting to me." Among other personal lessons that he learned from his animal subjects, Sapolsky told Brown, was how to survive the "dominance hierarchies" present in the academic world.

During the early years of his baboon study, Sapolsky would spend three months out of each year in Africa. Although his field work has become shorter in duration with the passing years, it has become larger in scale, in his view. "These days," he said on BookBrowse.com, "I study things like differences in 'cultures' between troops of baboons, how the cultures are propagated, the consequences of the differing cultures for the health of individuals." The last surviving male among the original members of Sapolsky's first study troop died in around 1994. Sapolsky now observes descendants of those baboons. As he told BookBrowse.com, although he believes that his laboratory work is "more useful" than his field work, he is happier in Africa. "When I'm there, 95% of the time I can relax in a way that I never can here. And the other 5%, I am stressed because of some horrific, [defecate]-in-your-pants piece of reality that evaporates all the neuroses and angst for weeks afterward, which is heavenly."

In his first book, *Stress, the Aging Brain, and the Mechanisms of Neuron Death*, published in 1992, Sapolsky delved into the ways in which stress and stress-related hormones can imperil the brain. According to a brief review found on the Massachusetts Institute of Technology Web site, the book is "accessible and engagingly written." His next book, *Why Zebras Don't Get Ulcers: An Updated Guide to Stress, Stress-Related Diseases and Coping* (1994), established Sapolsky as one of the finest natural-history writers in the country. Its title refers to the automatic responses of zebras in the wild to the scent or sight of lions: physiologically, the response is the production of stress-related hormones, and behaviorally, it is flight—the zebras run away from lions. "For most of the beasts on this planet, stressful situations include about three minutes of screaming terror, after which the threat is over or you are over," Sapolsky said in a talk at the Thought Leader Forum held in Santa Fe, New Mexico, in September 2002, a transcript of which appeared on the Sente Corp. Web site. The physiological responses of human beings (who, as Sapolsky is fond of saying, are simply an advanced species of primate) to stress are similar to those of zebras, and they serve humans well in cases of imminent physical danger; but for people not caught up in wars or other external threats, the sources of nearly all stress are thoughts and emotions, and flight is rarely possible or appropriate. "We humans turn on the exact same stress-response [by] thinking about 30-year mortgages, and the catch is that this response did not evolve to be turned on chronically. . . . If we turn on the stress-response chronically, we are going to get sick," he said during his talk. In *Why Zebras Don't Get Ulcers*, Sapolsky discussed such phenomena as the connections between stress, on the one hand, and, on the other, heart disease, memory loss, depression, ulcers, and colitis, and why our nervous systems trigger the emptying of our bladders when we are extremely frightened. In the *Washington Post* (September 20, 1994), Natalie Davis Spingam wrote that *Why Zebras Don't Get Ulcers*, which includes cartoons by Gary Larson, provides an "unusual opportunity" to learn from a researcher who has an impressive level of experience both in the laboratory and in the wild.

Sapolsky's next book-length offering was *The Trouble with Testosterone: And Other Essays on the Biology of the Human Predicament*. Drawing on the findings of psychiatry, animal behavioral science, neurobiology, and evolutionary biology, among other disciplines, Sapolsky explained why counting one's steps or breaths might be reassuring in times of stress; why drivers slow down when passing the scenes of accidents; and why some people are more likely than others to seek excitement. In the title essay Sapolsky examined the link between the hormone testosterone and aggressive behavior. He also offered readers what Laura P. Bonetta, in *Nature* (August 1997), called a "fascinating tour of neuropsychiatric oddities, including Tourette's syndrome ['hiccups of the id'], obsessive-compulsive disorder and schizophrenia." Bonetta wrote that the book "makes for very interesting and enjoyable reading. . . . Sapolsky clearly loves science and imparts that enthusiasm to the reader."

Sapolsky drew from letters, journals, and diaries he wrote during his yearly sojourns among the baboons for his book *A Primate's Memoir* (2001). In addition to recounting his fascinating and often humorous experiences with the primates, Sapolsky described scams and tricks played by corrupt local officials; the many cross-cultural misunderstandings that arose between him and his African hosts; his dealings with the neighboring Maasai tribe; the lamentable state of the Kenyan park system; and his journey to Lake Victoria, the source of the Nile River. He also wrote about Dian Fossey, the American woman who studied mountain gorillas in East Africa. In the *New York Times Book Review*, Rob Nixon wrote of *A Primate's Memoir*, "The book's life flows largely from the youthful Sapolsky's penchant for throwing himself at the world and weighing the consequences later. Case in point: what specific aspect of his fancy education can help him escape a cave that he finds himself sharing with a large, drugged baboon and an impala (half-eaten, but alive enough to keep kicking him in the head)? His strategy also has to accommodate the baboon troop that's massing at the cave's entrance and hollering for impala blood. . . . But the adventures that Sapolsky recreates in *A Primate's Memoir* are undergirded by a serious scientific intent: a study of male stress." In his conclusion Nixon wrote that after finishing the book, one would be "a lot more knowledgeable about plenty of baboon-related matters. But mostly one has already begun to miss the company of this sometimes cranky but always impassioned, learned and winningly irreverent man." On Bookreporter.com, Roz Shea called *A Primate's Memoir* "witty, poignant and enlightening. . . . For readers fascinated by the human condition, *A Primate's Memoir* is nearly un-put-down-able." *A Primate's Memoir* won the 2001 Bay Area Book Reviewers Award for nonfiction.

Sapolsky sits on the editorial boards of several journals, among them the *Journal of Neuroscience, Psychoneuroendocrinology, and Stress*, and he was a contributing editor of the *Sciences* before it ceased publication. His articles have appeared in many periodicals, including the *New Yorker, Discover, Scientific American*, and *Harper's*.

In addition to his other honors, Sapolsky has won the Young Investigator of the Year Award from the Society for Neuroscience, the Biological Psychiatry Society, and the International Society for Psychoneuro-Endocrinology; an Alfred P. Sloan Fellowship; the Klingenstein Fellowship in Neuroscience; Stanford University's Bing Award for Teaching Excellence; and an award for outstanding teaching from the Associated Students of Stanford University.

Sapolsky's wife, Lisa, a neuropsychologist, accompanied Sapolsky on his trips to Kenya from 1988 until the mid-1990s. The couple live in San Francisco with their two young children, Benjamin and Rachel, who were given the names of Sapolsky's favorite male and female baboons in Kenya. Sapolsky told *Current Biography*, "Once the kids get a bit older we're going to start heading out [to Africa] as a family."

—C.F.T.

Suggested Reading: *Atlantic* (on-line) Apr. 25, 2001; BookBrowse.com; *New York Times* F p1 Apr. 19, 2001, with photos; *New York Times*

Book Review p14 Apr. 1, 2001; Serengeti.org; Steven Barclay Agency Web site; *Washington Post* Z p18 Sep. 20, 1994; Sapolsky, Robert M. *A Primate's Memoir: A Neuroscientist's Unconventional Life among the Baboons*, 2001

Selected Books: *Stress, the Aging Brain, and the Mechanisms of Neuron Death*, 1992; *Why Zebras Don't Get Ulcers: An Updated Guide to Stress, Stress-Related Diseases and Coping*, 1994; *The Trouble with Testosterone: And Other Essays on the Biology of the Human Predicament*, 1997; *A Primate's Memoir: A Neuroscientist's Unconventional Life among the Baboons*, 2001

Courtesy of the office of Jan Schakowsky

Schakowsky, Jan

May 26, 1944– U.S. representative from Illinois (Democrat)

Address: 515 Cannon House Office Bldg., Washington, DC 20515

Jan Schakowsky, a Democratic U.S. representative who has served Chicago, Illinois, and its suburbs for the past five years, is known as one of the most progressive voices on Capitol Hill. A citizens' advocate and grassroots organizer before her election to the Illinois General Assembly and, later, the U.S. House of Representatives, Schakowsky has long sought universal health care, increased funding for public education, and the protection of the rights of women and senior citizens. A vocal critic of President George W. Bush's administration, she has spoken out against both its domestic and inter-

national policies. "I'm scared of this administration," she told Eric Martin for the *Daily Northwestern* (April 29, 2003). "Their vision of the world and the role the United States should play and the heavy hand in shaping the rest of the world really does frighten me." Her victories in Congress include the passage of bills created to increase federal assistance for abused women and children, protect the rights of battered immigrant women, reform election laws to guarantee that registered voters are not turned away at the polls, expand low-income housing opportunities, and assist small business owners and farmers. "Schakowsky is articulate, outspoken with a disarming wit and unabashed in her support of a progressive political agenda," Lynn Sweet wrote for the *Chicago Sun-Times* (January 9, 2003), and John Nichols, writing for the *Nation* (January 26, 2004), called her "a savvy liberal who knows not only how to be right on the issues but also how to win elections."

The congresswoman was born Janice D. Danoff in Chicago on May 26, 1944 to Irwin and Tillie (Cosnow) Danoff. She received a B.S. degree in elementary education from the University of Illinois in 1965, and soon afterward she married and began raising a family. Her first experience in running a campaign came in 1969, when she led the fight to put dates indicating freshness on products sold in supermarkets. Along with five other women living outside Chicago, Schakowsky, then the mother of two young children, formed the group National Consumer Union. Its members questioned stock clerks and store managers to decode the meaning of the bar codes on products, which were the only indication of how long they had been sitting on store shelves. From their basements, the women of the National Consumer Union printed and sold 25,000 "code books," gaining publicity—including a spot on the *Huntley-Brinkley Report*, a nationally broadcast news program—and eventually succeeding in getting so-called freshness dates put on many food items that have limited shelf lives. "That experience with our little group of women was so incredibly empowering that it changed my life," she told Peter Brand for the *Hill* (May 14, 2003). "And my view of myself was changed from being an ordinary housewife to an ordinary housewife that could really make a difference."

When her children were older, Schakowsky began working for Illinois Public Action, the state's largest public-interest organization, which fought for tougher measures to protect the public from toxic industrial chemicals, among other goals; she was the group's program director from 1976 to 1985. She served as executive director of the Illinois State Council of Senior Citizens from 1985 to 1990, leading campaigns for lower-cost prescription drugs and tax relief for seniors as well as financial support for spouses of nursing-home residents.

Schakowsky was elected to the Illinois State Assembly in 1989 and served for eight years, representing the state's 18th District. A Democratic floor leader and secretary of the Conference of Women

Legislators, she also chaired the Labor and Commerce Committee and served on the Human Service Appropriations, Health Care, and Electric Deregulation Committees. As a state representative she sponsored bills to strengthen the Hate Crimes Act, which targets crimes motivated by the victims' race, gender, nationality, or sexual persuasion; to increase support for public libraries, daycare centers, and home-delivered meals for seniors; and to allow parents leave from work for school conferences. She also introduced the first bill in the nation aimed at guaranteeing homeless people the right to vote.

In November 1998, with 74.6 percent of the vote, she was elected to represent Illinois's Ninth District in the U.S. House of Representatives, replacing the outgoing Democrat Sidney Yates, who had served 24 terms. The Ninth District, a Democratic stronghold, includes several neighborhoods in northwest Chicago as well as the suburbs of Evanston, Skokie, Des Plaines, Park Ridge, Golf, Morton Grove, Glenview, Lincolnwood, and Niles. Schakowsky currently serves on the Energy and Commerce Committee and on the subcommittees for Oversight and Investigations, Environment and Hazardous Materials, Commerce, Trade, and Consumer Protection, on which she is the ranking member. In past years she sat on the Banking and Financial Services Committee, the Government Efficiency Committee, and the Financial Management Committee, for which she was the top Democrat on the Government Reform Subcommittee. She is chief deputy whip of the House Democratic Leadership team and a member of the Congressional Human Rights Caucus. She lists her top priority as providing universal health care for Americans; her other causes include economic and social justice, the prevention and punishment of violence against women, stricter gun-control measures, and a national investment in public education and housing.

In November 2000, in cooperation with Fannie Mae, a government-backed organization that promotes home ownership, Schakowsky announced the Anti-Predatory Lending Act, which she authored to help home owners refinance bad loans, save their home equity, and prevent foreclosure. She has also introduced the Financial Consumers' Bill of Rights Act, a comprehensive bill to put an end to automatic teller machine (ATM) surcharges and excessive bank fees and to provide effective privacy protection for customers.

Schakowsky has voted for funding for alternative sentencing options for criminals and against tougher prosecution and sentencing of juveniles. She opposes the death penalty; supports more extensive DNA testing in criminal cases, including mandatory DNA testing in all cases involving federal executions; and advocates stricter sentences for hate crimes. Schakowsky voted against funding military border patrols to battle drugs and terrorism, while coming out in favor of allowing needle-exchange programs in Washington, D.C., and legal-izing the medical use of marijuana. In the area of education, she voted to require states to test students, supported the effort to reduce class sizes to 18 students for first, second, and third grades, and argued for increased funding for teacher training. She supported the White House–sponsored Leave No Child Behind Act, which provided funds for teacher training, smaller classes, school construction, and after-school programs, but has said that the law will be ineffectual since the budget for the program is $7 billion short. In 2003 she voted with the minority against the national energy policy supported by President Bush and Vice President Richard B. Cheney, which provided tax breaks to companies to promote energy research and development; the plan, she maintained, endangers the environment. She voted to raise Corporate Average Fuel Economy (CAFE) standards, aimed at energy conservation; to provide incentives for the development of alternative fuels; and to prohibit oil drilling and development in the Arctic National Wildlife Reserve. She also wants to regulate wholesale electricity and gas prices.

In the international arena, Schakowsky voted to uphold the ban on U.S. citizens' traveling to Cuba until that country's political prisoners are released, to give $156 million to the International Monetary Fund (IMF) for Third World debt reduction, and to provide food and medical aid to Africa. She voted against permanent normal trade relations with China, in light of that nation's human-rights abuses and labor practices, and against withholding $244 million in back payments owed to the U.N. by the U.S. A strong defender of civil liberties, she has been particularly vocal about the need to protect the rights of U.S. citizens since the September 11, 2001 terrorist attacks on the United States, which, she maintains, resulted in legislation curbing these liberties. "I feel many civil liberties have become the casualty of 9/11," she told Nicole Adamson for the *Northwestern Chronicle* (November 1, 2002, on-line). "The Attorney General and the President through executive orders have been all too willing to sacrifice civil liberties. Particularly at times of stress we need to be very careful that we don't limit constitutional rights." She has criticized the detention of prisoners without due process at U.S. facilities in Guantanamo Bay, Cuba, and has voted against a constitutional amendment prohibiting desecration of the American flag.

Schakowsky has sponsored the Women's Caucus policy agenda, which includes legislation aimed at curbing violence against women and children, reducing child abuse and neglect, reauthorizing the Violence Against Women Act of 1999, providing housing assistance to victims of domestic violence, and protecting female prisoners from sexual assault by prison employees. The congresswoman voted against banning so-called partial-birth abortion, human cloning, and the funding of family-planning programs as part of U.S. aid to foreign countries. She also voted against the funding of health-care providers who do not supply information on abortion; fought for affordable prescription drugs for senior citizens and people with disabilities, as well as quality home, hospice, and nursing care for seniors; and supported financial assistance for child care and child health and housing initiatives.

Prior to the 2003 U.S. invasion of Iraq, undertaken for the stated purpose of ridding that nation of weapons of mass destruction, Schakowsky was one of 126 House Democrats to vote against legislation giving President George W. Bush authority to use military force there; she contended that the U.S. should have worked harder to gain international support for the war. The measure passed both the House and Senate, allowing Bush to launch an attack against Iraq on March 19, 2003. "It is in the United States' interest to have strong international bodies in order to isolate rogue nations and rogue states," Schakowsky said in an appearance on *Crossfire* on CNN (March 12, 2003, on-line). "And just to say, 'It's my way or the highway,' or 'If the United Nations won't rubber-stamp what we believe is right, then good-bye, Charlie,' that is ridiculous. . . . The United States itself is becoming isolated, and unless we decide we're going to be the policemen everywhere and go in guns blazing . . . then I think we need to be helping to strengthen the United Nations." She said that while the president was not obligated to seek the U.N.'s permission to go to war if U.S. security was at stake, Iraq did not present an imminent threat to America. She later co-sponsored a resolution calling for an independent commission to investigate the intelligence used to justify the preemptive attack against Iraq, where, as of early November 2004, no weapons of mass destruction had been found.

In October 2003 Schakowsky voted against giving an additional $87 billion for the occupation of Iraq, pointing out that Congress had authorized $63 billion for the Iraq war and occupation in April 2003 and arguing that additional money would not further the security of U.S. troops. She said that the initial funding would have been enough to support operations in Iraq if the Bush administration had not given a significant portion of it to companies that were supposedly rebuilding Iraq but have allegedly been involved in war profiteering. While Schakowsky did not support the war initially, she said that the U.S. now has an obligation to maintain a presence in Iraq until the Middle Eastern country is stabilized. "Let's do what is right in terms of internationalizing the effort in Iraq, to bring real peace and democracy there, to, in a reasonable time bring our troops home. . . . Right now, this administration is unwisely spending the money, giving it away, war profiteering is going on," she told Neil Cavuto for Fox News, in an interview available on CEOWire (October 10, 2003, on-line).

Schakowsky hopes the United States will play a constructive role in ending violence in another conflict in the Middle East, that between Israelis and Palestinians. The congresswoman, who is Jewish, told Eric Martin that she is a Zionist who supports a two-state solution to the conflict, with Palestinians given a homeland and with security guaranteed for Israel. She said that important prerequisites for achieving peace in the region are an end to violence and terrorism on the part of Palestinians and an end to the expansion of Israeli settlements.

In addition to opposing President Bush's policy in Iraq, Schakowsky has denounced his tax policy as being unfairly advantageous to the rich at a time when basic social needs are not being met. "I'm very concerned with reordering priorities," she told Nicole Adamson. "It seems to be the priority of President Bush and the Republican leadership to give tax breaks to the people who need it least. We need to address unmet needs such as health care, drug benefits for the elderly, education, and the need for affordable housing. This is a big issue in our community with the elderly and families who need a roof over their heads. Also we need to make social security truly secure. It's these bread and butter, kitchen table issues that affect most Americans. Also pensions security needs to be addressed. There is a need for genuine homeland security where we protect our ports, chemical plants, and nuclear power plants. There are people trying to hurt and kill us and we have not done a good job in addressing some glaring problems. Right now all this is taking a [backseat] to tax cuts for the rich."

While many liberal voters and political leaders in the U.S. have backed the Green Party, often complaining that the Democratic Party has moved too far to the political center, Schakowsky believes that the Democratic Party is progressives' best hope for enacting change. "My view is that our future isn't in the Green Party but the Democrats can't dismiss their arguments and positions," she told the Web site BuzzFlash (February 2001). While she lauded the Green Party's position on environmental and trade issues, she expressed anger that the third-party presidential candidacy of the consumer advocate Ralph Nader had drawn votes away from the Democratic nominee Al Gore in the hotly contested 2000 election. (After the U.S. Supreme Court called a halt to vote recounts in Florida, Gore—who had won the popular but not the electoral vote—conceded the election to the Republican George W. Bush.) "I'm mad at Ralph," she told BuzzFlash. "I think of myself [as] someone who is an organizer and wants to build a progressive majority. I don't hold Al Gore and the Democrats blameless. But . . . the indisputable fact is that without the Nader votes, Gore would be President." During the 2004 presidential campaign, Schakowsky initially backed the former Vermont governor Howard Dean, who dropped out of the race in February.

In a speech at Northwestern University, in Evanston, Illinois, Schakowsky said that politicians need aggressive strategies to combat low voter turnout. "People don't vote, even those who care, because they believe they can't influence the outcome of public policy issues," she said, as reported by Jennifer Leopoldt for the *Daily Northwestern* (May 20, 2002). "Politicians themselves contribute to the lack of public involvement by misreading what people want." She said that while many believe that large financial contributions have more influence on political policy than does lobbying, "people power still trumps money power every day of the week." At the same time, she believes Americans must make a greater effort to influence public policy and that the wealth of information available on the World Wide Web can help them do so. She told BuzzFlash, "In my thirty years of organizing, the common things I would hear at meetings and gatherings are 'I don't know what's going on' and 'I don't know who to write to.'" With the Internet, she said, "all that info is a click away. . . . There's no excuse anymore for people not to be completely wired, literally, into what is going on."

Although she is considered to be one of the most progressive members of the House of Representatives, Schakowsky has forged alliances with conservative members of Congress. "My colleagues, in general . . . are pretty rigid," Dan Burton, a Republican from Indiana who has worked with her on children's issues and open-government initiatives, told Brand. "I think [Schakowsky] is someone that realizes you have to work together."

Schakowsky has amply demonstrated her skill as a fund-raiser for her party, having raised, or contributed from her campaign funds, a total of $1.2 million for the Democratic Congressional Campaign Committee, with additional funds going to candidates for statewide races. She has said that the secret to raising money is dedication; when she ran for Congress in 1998 and faced two Democrats in the primary race, she called almost every female law partner in Chicago, asking for support and mentioning that Illinois's House delegation had no women. "Twenty-five hours a week I would sit on the phone," she told Brand. "It's not like I'm well connected. There's no rocket science here—it's just about doing it." As the chair of Women LEAD, a fund-raising subsidiary of the Democratic Congressional Campaign Committee that targets female donors and contributes money to female candidates, she raised approximately $25 million during the 2000 election cycle. One of her strategies as head of Women LEAD is to recruit more minority women as candidates and to seek the help of Hispanic, African-American, and Asian-American women in selecting them.

In 2000, in her race against Republican challenger Dennis Driscoll, Schakowsky was reelected with 76.4 percent of the vote; she spent about $1 million on her campaign, while Driscoll spent $60,000. She received 70.2 percent of the votes cast in the 2002 election, spending $864,500 to beat her Republican opponent, Nicholas Duric, and the Libertarian candidate, Stephanie Sailor. Although there was speculation that Schakowsky would run

for the Senate against Republican incumbent Peter Fitzgerald in 2004, she ultimately decided against it, and backed Barack Obama, a lawyer and senator in the Illinois General Assembly, in the race. Schakowsky defeated her opponent in the 2004 congressional race, the Republican Kurt Eckhardt, with 75.4 percent of the vote.

Schakowsky was named Rookie of the Year by the Illinois Environmental Council in 1991 and Outstanding Legislator by the Interfaith Council for the Homeless in 1993. She has been named Legislator of the Year by many organizations, including the Community Action Association (1991), the Champaign County Health Care Association (1992), the Illinois Nurses Association (1992), the Coalition of Citizens with Disabilities (1993), the Illinois Council of Senior Citizens (1993), and the Illinois Association of Community Mental Health Agencies (1994). She is a member of the American Civil Liberties Union, the National Organization for Women, the National Council of Jewish Women, the Illinois Pro-Choice Alliance, the Midwest Governing Council of the Jewish Congress, the Labor Union UNITE!, the Evanston Mental Health Association, the Evanston Historical Society, Evanston Friends of the Library, and the Rogers Park Historical Society. She is also on the advisory council of the board of directors of Palliative Care Center of the North Shore. The congresswoman married Harvey E. Schakowsky in 1965; the couple divorced in 1980 after having a son, Ian, and a daughter, Mary. From her 1980 marriage to Robert Creamer, she has a stepdaughter, Lauren. She has four grandchildren. She and her husband live in Evanston, Illinois. In her spare time she enjoys traveling, horseback riding, and reading.

—K.E.D.

Suggested Reading: BuzzFlash (on-line) Feb. 2001; *Hill* p10 May 14, 2003; Jan Schakowsky congressional Web site; *Northwestern Chronicle* (on-line) Nov. 1, 2002

Schwarzenegger, Arnold

NOTE: Earlier articles about Arnold Schwarzenegger appeared in *Current Biography* in 1979 and 1991.

July 30, 1947– Governor of California (Republican); actor

Address: State Capitol Building, Sacramento, CA 95814

The election of Arnold Schwarzenegger as governor of California, on October 7, 2003, marked the second career change for the man who immigrated to the United States from his native Austria in 1968. The former world-champion bodybuilder

Courtesy of the office of Arnold Schwarzenegger
Arnold Schwarzenegger

had become one of the most popular actors in the world, starring in 10 films in the 1980s—including *Conan the Barbarian*, *The Terminator*, *Commando*, and *Predator*—that took in a combined total of more than $1 billion worldwide at the box office. With those action-oriented movies, the physically imposing actor with the heavily accented English created a persona that transcended heroism or villainy: that of the indestructible warrior. John Milius, who directed *Conan the Barbarian*, described him to Bill Zehme for *Rolling Stone* (August 22, 1991) as embodying "the Superior Man. Arnold is the Nietzschean man. There's something wonderfully primeval about him, harking back to the real basic foundational stuff: steel and strength and will." In a conversation with David Friedman for *New York Newsday* (June 30, 1991), James Cameron, the director of *The Terminator* and its first sequel, praised Schwarzenegger's ability to project "an amazing combination of physicality, warmth, menace, humor, and intelligence."

While his film career began to wane with a string of box-office disappointments in the late 1990s, Schwarzenegger's enduring popularity undoubtedly contributed to his taking the reins of the most populous state in the U.S. and the sixth-largest economy in the world—as did the unflagging toil and self-confidence, charisma, and media savvy that enabled him to emerge from an obscure Alpine village to become the most famous of all musclemen. Schwarzenegger's election was the culmination of the campaign to recall Democratic governor Gray Davis, the recipient of much of the blame for California's economic woes; although many derided Schwarzenegger's run for the governorship as an ego trip on a grand scale by a man with no politi-

cal experience, he was able to capture over 48 percent of the vote in a crowded field. And as governor he has silenced many of his detractors. Facing a huge financial shortfall in the state budget, Schwarzenegger won approval for measures aimed at reducing it, ending "years of paralysis in the California Legislature," as a writer put it in the *New York Times* (May 4, 2004). That writer for the paper's editorial page, which had been critical of the former bodybuilder's candidacy, acknowledged Schwarzenegger's 64 percent approval rating in his state and concluded, "The accidental governor . . . is starting to seem almost inevitable."

Arnold Alois Schwarzenegger, whose surname means "black plowman," was born on July 30, 1947 in Graz, Austria, the younger son of Gustav Schwarzenegger and Aurelia (Jadrny) Schwarzenegger. His father was the police chief in Thal, a nearby village where Arnold and his brother, Meinhard, grew up in postwar austerity. The family did not have indoor plumbing, a telephone, or a refrigerator until Arnold was 14, and he credits this environment for his desire to succeed. "Today in America," he commented in an interview with Richard Corliss for *Time* (December 24, 1990), "I see kids comfortable, getting everything they want. . . . And I realize that stability will never create the hunger it takes to go beyond the limits where others have been. For that, you have to be a little off. Something has to happen in your childhood that you say, 'I am going to make up for this.'"

Among the factors that he has cited as possible contributors to his overwhelming drive are his having had to compete for his father's attention with Meinhard, who became a champion boxer before his death in a car accident at the age of 23, and his rigorously disciplined upbringing. His days began with chores at 6:00 a.m. "Every morning at our house," he wrote for *Newsweek* (May 21, 1990), "we had squats and situps fifteen minutes before breakfast. My father used to say, 'First you have to earn your breakfast.'" On Sunday afternoons the boys would attend the theater or go to a museum, after which they were expected to write 10-page essays on their excursions. In an interview with Nancy Collins for *Rolling Stone* (January 17, 1985), Schwarzenegger described his relationship with his father as "very solid, with a tremendous amount of discipline but also a lot of respect—respect enough to know the difference between father and child. There was a real wall. . . . I always felt I could go to him with my problems, but I always knew that punishments could come up any minute if I screwed up. . . . But I loved my father; he was very affectionate." His mother supervised the boys' daily routine and kept the house immaculate. "The household was a full-time occupation," he told Collins. "I have one of the best mothers anybody could have."

After seeing his first movie, when he was 11, Schwarzenegger became fascinated with America and began to feel that he was meant for something big. Suddenly, he "despised being in a little country . . . ," as he wrote for *Men's Fitness* (August 1991): "I did not want anything about my life to be little. What I wanted was to be part of the big cause, the big dreamers, the big skyscrapers, the big money, the big action. Everything in the United States was so big. That's what I enjoy about this country."

Figuring that bodybuilding could gain him entrance into the United States, Schwarzenegger became serious about physical culture in his early teens, when he began to lift weights in order to train for the local soccer team. In a futile attempt to deflect their son from his newfound obsession, his parents forbade him to spend more than three nights a week in the local gym, but he circumvented their intentions by working out in an unheated room of the house. "When I was fifteen I had a clear vision of myself being onstage winning the Mr. Universe contest, and I was driven by that thought," he recalled in his interview with Nancy Collins. "It was a very spiritual thing in a way, because I had such faith in the route, the path, that it was never a question, in my mind, that I would make it."

After graduating from secondary school, in 1965, Schwarzenegger joined the Austrian army, which served meat every day, instead of once a week, as his mother had done at home. "The meat made my body respond tremendously," he told Collins, "because all of a sudden it got all this protein." After only one month in military service, he won the Junior Mr. Europe title in Stuttgart, Germany. Having gone AWOL (absent without leave) to compete, he spent a year in the brig. Although he grew strong enough to bench-press 500 pounds, he eventually abandoned the potentially injurious power lifts in favor of developing all the muscles of his body in perfect proportion. Schwarzenegger trained for five hours a day during his bodybuilding career. In an interview with Joan Goodman for *Playboy* (January 1988), he said, "I was taught that pain and suffering were not obstacles you should even think about. You just go through them." His stoic attitude paid off in 1967, when, at the age of 20, he became the youngest man ever to win a Mr. Universe title. The year before he had been named Mr. Europe, Best-Built Man of Europe, and winner of the International Powerlifting Championship.

In 1968 Schwarzenegger fulfilled another dream when he arrived in the United States to compete in a Mr. Universe contest in Miami Beach, Florida. Shocked by placing second—a rare loss—he resolved to win the next time. At the invitation of Joe Weider, the publisher of *Muscle and Fitness*, *Flex*, *Shape*, and other bodybuilding magazines, he went to Los Angeles to write articles (in German) for Weider's publications and to trade training tips. In 1970 he scored an unprecedented triple by winning the Mr. World, Mr. Universe, and Mr. Olympia titles. By 1975, when he retired from bodybuilding, the "Austrian Oak" had won the Mr. Olympia title six consecutive times and the Mr. Universe title five times.

Following his retirement from bodybuilding, Schwarzenegger lost no time in taking advantage of other opportunities. With a fellow bodybuilder, Franco Columbu, he founded a bricklaying business called Pumping Bricks. Then, with money saved and borrowed, he started a mail-order business in fitness books and cassettes and bought an apartment building, the first in a series of lucrative real-estate investments. He began attending college part-time in 1973, and in 1980 he received a bachelor's degree in business and international economics from the University of Wisconsin, in Superior, accumulating the necessary credits mostly by correspondence. Along the way he took English lessons, developed a rehabilitation-through-weight-training program at California prisons, and became the national weight-training coach for the Special Olympics in 1977.

Those accomplishments, however, were not enough to satisfy Schwarzenegger. As he said to Corliss, "I wanted to go again for discomfort, to create the old hunger, to get into acting. Because I knew it was going to happen." In fact, Schwarzenegger had started acting in the early 1970s and had appeared, under the pseudonym Arnold Strong, in *Hercules Goes to New York* (1970), a low-budget affair made for Italian television. Using the same name, he obtained a bit part in Robert Altman's *The Long Goodbye* (1973). After several television appearances, Schwarzenegger landed his first important—albeit small—role in film in 1976, in *Stay Hungry*. As the leader of a contingent of bodybuilders in that comedy-melodrama based on Charles Gaines's novel, Schwarzenegger won a Golden Globe Award as best new actor.

While competing in a Mr. America contest in New York City, Schwarzenegger had been recruited as the subject of a documentary book and film on bodybuilding. Written by Charles Gaines with photographs by George Butler, the book *Pumping Iron* became a surprise best-seller in 1974. Butler also produced a living-art exhibit at the Whitney Museum of American Art in New York City, for which Schwarzenegger and other bodybuilders posed alongside slides of sculptures by Michelangelo and Auguste Rodin in order to promote the idea of body sculpting with weights as an art and to lend respectability to the pastime, which then had a shady reputation.

The documentary film *Pumping Iron* (1977), directed by George Butler and Robert Fiore, brought Schwarzenegger into the limelight. Nik Cohn, in his review for *New York* (January 24, 1977), wrote that the bodybuilder "lights up the film like neon every time he comes on-screen. . . . His physical power is balanced by great humor [and] prodigious charm." Schwarzenegger's next two film appearances did nothing for his career. He played a cowboy in the Western comedy *The Villain* (1979), with Kirk Douglas, and starred opposite Loni Anderson in the made-for-television movie *The Jayne Mansfield Story* (1980). In 1980 he emerged from retirement as a bodybuilder to win the Mr. Olympia contest for an unprecedented seventh time, making him winner of more professional-bodybuilding contests than any other competitor in the world.

The 1982 action film *Conan the Barbarian* proved to be the ideal vehicle to capitalize on Schwarzenegger's prime assets. As a sword-and-sorcery fantasy-adventure figure derived from the *Weird Tales* magazine character created by Robert E. Howard in 1932, Schwarzenegger performed almost all of his own stunts during six months of filming in Spain. The sequel, *Conan the Destroyer* (1983), which co-starred Grace Jones, contained less gore and more tongue-in-cheek humor than the original. While critics savaged both films (and Schwarzenegger's performances), the first *Conan* grossed $100 million worldwide, and the second earned $80 million.

James Cameron's *The Terminator* (1984), in which Schwarzenegger played a villainous cyborg (a hybrid of human and mechanical components) whose mission is to murder Sarah Connor (Linda Hamilton) before she gives birth to a future messiah, made him a star. As Owen Gleiberman explained in *Entertainment Weekly* (July 12, 1991), "By casting Arnold the robot actor as a futuristic killing machine, this unbelievably canny thriller unshackled Schwarzenegger's appeal in two ways: it merged his hulking gladiatorial presence with the gaudy, bloody nihilism of contemporary action flicks, effectively turning him into a postpunk Dirty Harry; and, more than that (for this was the movie's genius), it transformed his lugubrious one-dimensionality into a comic attribute." Though he was told that his acting ability was not enough to overcome the limitations imposed by his massive build and thick accent, Schwarzenegger did not appear concerned with such criticism. "As far as I'm concerned, I will, in a few years, be where the top people are now—whether it's [Clint] Eastwood, [Sylvester] Stallone, or [Robert] Redford—anyone who makes the top salary," he told Collins in 1985. "I feel absolutely convinced that's where I will be." *The Terminator* was a huge success, with a $100 million box-office take.

In *Commando* (1985), Latin American guerrillas kidnap the young daughter of a retired army colonel (Schwarzenegger), who takes revenge. *Commando*, which also grossed $100 million, was followed by *Raw Deal* (1986), in which Schwarzenegger played a retired FBI agent who infiltrates the Chicago Mafia. In *Raw Deal*, Pauline Kael wrote for the *New Yorker* (June 30, 1986), "Schwarzenegger seems happy to laugh at himself; he's like a granite teddy bear." *Predator* (1987) featured Schwarzenegger loping through Central American jungles on a hostage-rescue mission and had earned $107 million by December 1987. *The Running Man* (1987), based on a novel by Richard Bachman, a pseudonym for Stephen King, had Schwarzenegger dispense with one gladiator after another in a deadly television game show hosted by Richard Dawson; that film made $10.5 million in its first

week. In *Red Heat* (1988) Schwarzenegger returned to Chicago as a Soviet cop teamed with James Belushi in hot pursuit of a vicious Russian drug dealer. In Ivan Reitman's *Twins* (1988), Schwarzenegger took his career in a new—and lucrative—direction, by essaying a comedic role as the twin brother of the rotund, diminutive Danny DeVito. "Beneath all those deltoids and pectorals," Mike McGrady wrote in his review for *New York Newsday* (December 9, 1988), "there has always been a lighthearted, fun-loving fellow trying to come out." By mid-1991 *Twins* had taken in more than $120 million. Returning to the science-fiction genre in the commercially successful *Total Recall* (1990), based on Philip K. Dick's short story "We Can Remember It for You Wholesale," Schwarzenegger played a construction worker whose memory has been tampered with by evil alien forces. The mellower Schwarzenegger of *Twins* reemerged in Ivan Reitman's *Kindergarten Cop* (1990).

Schwarzenegger's cyborg returned in James Cameron's *Terminator 2: Judgment Day* (1991). As a model T-800 killer whose mission, this time, is to protect the 10-year-old boy who will grow up to be the leader of a human revolt against the ruling computers of the 21st century, Schwarzenegger played "a kinder, gentler terminator," locked in mortal combat with a superior T-1000 cyborg. Released just before the long Fourth of July weekend, *Terminator 2* had grossed nearly $200 million by November 1991.

Schwarzenegger directed a 25-minute episode of the Home Box Office cable-television series *Tales from the Crypt*, called "The Switch," in 1990. He directed the television movie *Christmas in Connecticut* in 1992 and had a small, uncredited cameo in the picture as well. He returned to the big screen with *The Last Action Hero* (1993), an action film with comedic overtones that featured him as a film hero whose exploits cross over into the real world. While that movie was poorly received by critics and lost money at the box office, he scored another hit with James Cameron's action comedy *True Lies* (1994), in which he played a secret agent whose wife (Jamie Lee Curtis) thinks he is a computer salesman. In *Junior*, also released in 1994, Schwarzenegger starred as a scientist who becomes pregnant through a biotechnological experiment; the comedy co-starred the English actress Emma Thompson and reteamed Schwarzenegger with DeVito and Reitman. Though the movie's box-office performance was modest compared with those of most Schwarzenegger films and got a mixed appraisal from critics, it earned the actor a Golden Globe nomination for best actor for a musical or comedy. In the action film *Eraser* (1996), Schwarzenegger was a government agent who "erases" the pasts of federal witnesses. He followed that film with *Jingle All the Way* (1996), in which he portrayed a father desperately seeking the Christmas season's most popular toy for his child; that comedy was a commercial disappointment and critical bomb. He played the villainous Mr. Freeze in *Bat-*

man & Robin (1997), which grossed over $100 million in the U.S. and an additional $130 million worldwide despite being panned by film reviewers.

The commercial failure of Schwarzenegger's next two films seemed to indicate that his star power had diminished. End of Days (1999) was lambasted by critics and did not recoup its expenses in its U.S. release. Although The 6th Day (2000) borrowed heavily from the plot of one of his earlier hits, Total Recall, and received some positive notices, it fared even worse than End of Days financially. Schwarzenegger played a firefighter whose wife and child are killed in a terrorist bombing, and who sets off for Colombia to find the perpetrator, in Collateral Damage (2002). In 2003, after a dozen years, he made another outing as a cyborg, in Terminator 3: Rise of the Machines, a role for which he reportedly earned $30 million. He plays Prince Hapi in a new movie version of Jules Verne's classic adventure novel Around the World in 80 Days, which stars Jackie Chan as Passepartout reached theaters in June 2004.

It had been known since the 1990s that Schwarzenegger was interested in someday seeking public office. Earlier, he had begun taking an active role in Republican politics, using his celebrity to support the party's candidates. As a Republican, Schwarzenegger is something of an oddity in liberal Hollywood; it might even be said that he is an anomaly in his own family, since, in wedding the television journalist Maria Shriver in 1986, he married into the most prominent Democratic dynasty in the country. (Shriver's mother, Eunice Kennedy Shriver, is a sister of U.S. senatorEdward M. Kennedy of Massachusetts; the late U.S. senator and attorney general Robert F. Kennedy; and John F. Kennedy, the 35th president of the United States.) Having left a Socialist country whose government exercised considerable control of day-to-day life, Schwarzenegger has said that the Republican Party was the natural choice for him. In an October 29, 2002 interview with Chris Matthews of MSNBC, held at Chapman University, in Orange, California, he said, as quoted on the Wikipedia Web site, "When I came over here in 1968 with the presidential elections coming up in November . . . I heard a lot of the press conferences from both of the candidates [Hubert H.] Humphrey and [Richard] Nixon, and Humphrey was talking about more government is the solution, protectionism, and everything he said about government involvement sounded to me more like Austrian socialism. Then when [I] heard Nixon talk about it, he said open up the borders, the consumers should be represented there ultimately and strengthen the military and get the government off our backs. I said to myself, what is this guy's party affiliation? I didn't know anything at that point. So I asked my friend, what is Nixon? He's a Republican. And I said, I am a Republican."

A naturalized American citizen since 1983, Schwarzenegger described himself to Christina Valhouli for Salon (January 29, 2001, on-line) as "socially liberal and fiscally conservative." He supports abortion rights and greater civil rights for gays; at the same time, he feels that two-parent households are important. "I believe that every good idea that was ever done in the world came from a grass-roots organization, or from one person," he told Valhouli. "They did something and it mushroomed and grew, and eventually the government heard about it and it was enacted. It has to start on a level where the cities take care of themselves; it can't start at the federal government and trickle down." He has expressed admiration for the presidency of the Republican Ronald Reagan, who spent eight years in the White House (1981–89), but was critical of his fellow Republicans for their behavior during the impeachment trial of the Democratic president Bill Clinton—which followed charges that Clinton had lied under oath about his extramarital affair with Monica Lewinsky. The first President Bush appointed Schwarzenegger chairman of the President's Council on Physical Fitness and Sports in January 1990; he served in that post until 1993, traveling across the country to promote physical fitness to children. Later he was chairman of California governor Pete Wilson's Council on Physical Fitness and Sports. Many Republicans hoped he would run for governor of California in 2002, but he declined. Schwarzenegger's first political success came that year, however, with the passage of Proposition 49, which he created and put on the state ballot through the initiative, or petition, process. Nearly 57 percent of voters approved the measure, officially known as the "After School Education and Safety Program Act of 2002," which provided after-school care for children through state grants. When the federal government cut $400 million from after-school programs in 2002, Schwarzenegger worked with legislators in an attempt to reverse the cuts.

Calls to oust Davis began in the spring of 2003, primarily due to the state's massive budget shortfall, which at that time was estimated to be about $20 billion. (Later estimates put the figure at around $38 billion.) A petition supporting a special election, to determine whether to recall him from office, collected a more-than-sufficient 1.6 million signatures. (California is one of 18 states with provisions for recalling state officials. The recall of a governor had never before come to a vote in California.) Rumors that the movie star would campaign to replace Davis, should he be recalled, began swirling that summer, and on the Tonight Show on August 6, Schwarzenegger announced his candidacy for governor. Other candidates in the crowded race, which became something of a national spectacle, were the former child actor Gary Coleman, best known for playing Arnold Drummond in the 1980s sitcom Diff'rent Strokes; Larry Flynt, the publisher of Hustler magazine; the comedians Gallagher and D.L. Hughley;

Angelyne, a model, and the socialite turned columnist Arianna Huffington. (The California secretary of state recorded over 350 official notices of candidacy.) Because of Schwarzenegger's status as a film star, his decision to seek the governorship immediately attracted the attention of both the national and international media. He capitalized on the attention by peppering his speeches with lines from his movies and references to his bodybuilding career—promising to "pump up" Sacramento, the state capital, telling Davis "Hasta la vista" (Spanish for "goodbye," and an allusion to a famous line from *Terminator 2*, "Hasta la vista, baby"), and calling Davis and California's lieutenant governor, Cruz Bustamante, also a candidate, "the twin Terminators of Sacramento."

Schwarzenegger announced that his first act, if he were elected, would be to order an audit of the state budget, to identify wasteful spending. Citing security concerns, he also promised to rescind driver's licenses given to undocumented illegal aliens and to strengthen the patrolling of the border between Mexico and California, so that no one could enter the state illegally. Permitting such entry "sends the wrong message to other people that are filing officially for immigration, to get their green cards and their visas here and all that stuff," he told Bill O'Reilly on the TV program *O'Reilly Factor* (September 10, 2003, on-line). He said that he supported U.S. senator John McCain's idea for visas or working permits for undocumented aliens, however.

The candidate campaigned hard to battle criticism that he had little grasp of the state's economic troubles. He also faced many charges about his past, including allegations that he had groped or otherwise made unwanted sexual advances toward women on movie sets and in other settings; that he had used illegal drugs and participated in orgies during his bodybuilding days; and that he had once expressed admiration for the Nazi dictator Adolf Hitler. He issued a public apology to women who had been offended by his past behavior, saying, "I have done things that at the time I thought . . . playful but now I recognize that I have offended people. And those people that I have offended, I want to say to them I am deeply sorry about that and I apologize," as quoted in a story by Linda Douglass on the ABC News Web site (October 2, 2003). He also vigorously denied having Nazi sympathies, pointing to his contributions to several Jewish groups. (ABC News obtained a copy of a proposal for an unpublished book containing quotes from a 1975 interview with Schwarzenegger, conducted during the filming of *Pumping Iron*. Asked to name his heroes, the bodybuilder said, "I admired Hitler, for instance, because he came from being a little man with almost no formal education, up to power. I admire him for being such a good public speaker and for what he did with it," according to Douglass. Schwarzenegger later said that he did not remember making the comments and that he despised everything for which Hitler and the Nazi Party stood.) Schwarzenegger was also questioned about his commitment to the environment; while he claimed to be concerned about environmental issues, it was revealed that he drove a Humvee, an extremely fuel-inefficient army-style vehicle that gets only 14 miles per gallon of gasoline.

In a special election on October 7, 2003, California voters were given the option of recalling Davis, with 55.4 percent choosing to do so, and presented with a choice of candidates to replace him; voters could choose a candidate (the list did not include Davis) even if they voted against the recall. With 48.6 percent of the vote, Schwarzenegger beat out the other challengers, including Bustamante, a Democrat, who came in second, receiving 32 percent of ballots cast. (Davis thus became the second governor in U.S. history to be recalled from office; the first was a governor of North Dakota, in 1921.) While some observers attributed the election results to a combination of Schwarzenegger's charisma and pure celebrity worship on the part of Californians, others pointed to deep discontent with the status quo, represented by Davis.

Schwarzenegger was sworn in on November 17, 2003. In his first few hours in office, he fulfilled a campaign promise to repeal a 200 percent increase in vehicle-license fees that had been put in place by Davis's administration, and the next day he proposed a three-point plan to address the state's financial crisis. The plan called for issuing $15 billion in bonds, asking voters to pass a constitutional amendment to limit state spending, and overhauling California's expensive system for workers' compensation. The governor also called a special session of the state legislature to implement budget cuts and declared that he would forego receiving the governor's salary of $175,000 to assist in balancing the budget. (The governor, who has invested his earnings in real estate, has amassed a personal fortune estimated at $100 million.) Both Proposition 57, the plan for the $15 billion in bonds, and Proposition 58, the proposed constitutional amendment, passed in the March 2, 2004 primary election, leaving Schwarzenegger hopeful that California could get its finances in order without his having to raise taxes, which he has promised not to do. In April the legislature approved his overhaul of the workers' compensation system. "I'm trying to teach them slowly here that we should just get rid of these words 'we can't' or 'I can't,'" Schwarzenegger said, as quoted in the *New York Times* (April 17, 2004). "Everything is possible." In a *Times* article dated May 14, 2004, in discussing the $102.8 billion budget Schwarzenegger had just submitted to the state legislature, John M. Broder reported that the governor had "already negotiated central elements of the new spending plan with some of the state's most powerful interests—teachers unions, public colleges and universities, local government leaders. . . . The budget deals are part of a pattern the governor has followed since he was inaugurated. . . . Instead of slowly rolling bills uphill through the Legislature, Mr. Schwarzenegger has gone directly to the voters and interest groups and struck a separate peace. The deals have left some legislators spluttering. But they cannot undo them without angering important constituents and contributors."

In the first few months of 2004, after President George W. Bush expressed support for a constitutional amendment banning gay marriage, and legislators in several states worked either to defend or outlaw such unions, California became involved in the national debate on the issue. Schwarzenegger said that the flurry of marriages of same-sex couples performed in San Francisco in late February and March 2004, after the city's leaders issued marriage licenses to gays, were illegal under a state law defining marriage as a union between one woman and one man; the law had been approved by voters as a ballot measure. "I believe in domestic partnership," Schwarzenegger told Jay Leno on the *Tonight Show*, as reported by Steve Gorman for Reuters (March 1, 2004), in an article available on the Find Law Web site. "If the people change their minds and they want to overrule that, that's fine with me. But right now, that's the law, and I think every mayor and everyone should abide by the law." He added, however, that he did not support President Bush's call for a constitutional amendment, as he believes the matter should be settled on a state-by-state basis.

On November 2, 2004 Californians approved the Schwarzenegger-backed Proposition 71, which called for $3 billion to be spent by the state on human embryonic stem-cell research. Embryonic stem cells are more useful than those from adult tissue for research into the treatment of disease; their use has been highly controversial, however, since they are generated by the creation of test-tube embryos, which die when stem cells are removed—a practice vehemently opposed by antiabortionists. While some in California argued that the state could not afford the measure, supporters of Proposition 71 argued that its passage could put California at the forefront of an enormous new industry.

Schwarzenegger has named New York governor George Pataki, U.S. senator Orrin Hatch of Utah, and George W. Bush, all Republicans, as politicians he admires. Speaking of Bush, he told Valhouli in 2001, "[Bush] was a different type of human being once—a rowdy guy who had his problems and stuff—and he got his act together. . . . To me, it's extraordinary and admirable that he got his act together, studied the issues, came up with a philosophy of compassionate conservatism and really went with it full speed ahead." He added that he also admired many Democrats, among them his father-in-law, R. Sargent Shriver, who helped to establish the Peace Corps and Head Start, and his mother-in-law, Eunice Kennedy Shriver, who founded the Special Olympics.

On August 31, 2004 Schwarzenegger spoke at the Republican National Convention, in New York City, where President Bush accepted his party's nomination for a second term. In speaking before a nationwide audience in support of Republican values, he praised the United States, comparing it favorably with the Austria of his childhood, which had been partly under Soviet occupation. He told listeners, as quoted in the New York Times (September 1, 2004), "My fellow Americans, this is an amazing moment for me. To think that a once-scrawny boy from Austria could grow up to become governor of California and stand in Madison Square Garden to speak on behalf of the president of the United States . . . is an immigrant's dream. It is the American dream."

The California governor's business holdings include his own film-production company, Oak Productions, and choice west-side property in Los Angeles. He was a partner in the restaurant chain Planet Hollywood before selling his shares in 2000. He is the author of *Arnold: The Education of a Bodybuilder* (1977), *Arnold's Bodyshaping for Women* (1979), *Arnold's Bodybuilding for Men* (1981), and the 700-page *Arnold's Encyclopedia of Modern Bodybuilding* (1985). In 1993 he collaborated with Charles Gaines on three fitness guides for children.

Schwarzenegger underwent cosmetic surgery in the 1980s to alter his jutting jaw line, and in April 1997 he had an operation to correct a congenital heart-valve defect. In January 2003 he had surgery to repair a torn rotator cuff he had suffered on the set of *Terminator 3*. Schwarzenegger stands six feet two inches tall and weighs 220 pounds, about 20 pounds less than at the height of his bodybuilding career. He and Maria Shriver have four children: Katherine Eunice, born in December 1989; Christina Maria Aurelia, born in July 1991; Patrick Arnold, born in September 1993; and Christopher Sargent, born in September 1997.

—K.E.D.

Suggested Reading: BBC News (on-line) Oct. 8, 2003, with photos; *Biography* p26+ May 2000, with photos; *Interview* p85 July 1991, with photos; *New York Times* A p8 Apr. 17, 2004, A p28 May 4, 2004, A p16 May 14, 2004; *Rolling Stone* p12 Jan. 17, 1985, with photos, p38+ Aug. 22, 1991, with photos; *Salon* (on-line) Jan. 29, 2001; *Time* p52+ Dec. 24, 1990, with photos

Selected Films: *Stay Hungry*, 1976; *Pumping Iron*, 1977; *Conan the Barbarian*, 1982; *Conan the Destroyer*, 1983; *The Terminator*, 1984; *Commando*, 1985; *Raw Deal*, 1986; *Predator*, 1987; *The Running Man*, 1987; *Red Heat*, 1988; *Twins*, 1988; *Total Recall*, 1990; *Kindergarten Cop*, 1990; *Terminator 2: Judgment Day*, 1991; *The Last Action Hero*, 1993; *True Lies*, 1994; *Junior*, 1995; *Eraser*, 1996; *Jingle All the Way*, 1996; *Batman & Robin*, 1997; *End of Days*, 1999; *The 6th Day*, 2000; *Collateral Damage*, 2002; *Terminator 2: Rise of the Machines*, 2003

Selected Books: *Arnold: The Education of a Bodybuilder*, 1977; *Arnold's Bodyshaping for Women*, 1979; *Arnold's Bodybuilding for Men*, 1981; *Arnold's Encyclopedia of Modern Bodybuilding*, 1985; *Arnold's Fitness for Kids Ages Birth–5*, 1993; *Arnold's Fitness for Kids Ages 6-10*, 1993; *Arnold's Fitness for Kids Ages 11-14*, 1993

Max B. Miller/Fotos International/Getty Images

Scott, Tony

July 21, 1944– Film director

Address: RSA USA, 270 Lafayette St., Suite 203, New York, NY 10012

When the British-born Tony Scott made his debut as a Hollywood director, in 1983, with the cult horror classic *The Hunger*, his older brother Ridley Scott had already made a name for himself as the director of the films *The Duellists*, *Alien*, and *Blade Runner*. Although to this day he is said to be less well known than his brother, Tony Scott has become one of the silver screen's most bankable directors; according to the Web site The Numbers in early October 2004, a dozen of his films have, together, grossed upwards of $867 million (some $90 million more than his brother's). Scott was a self-acknowledged "hired gun" when he directed such motion pictures as *Top Gun*, *Beverly Hills Cop II*, *The Last Boy Scout*, *Crimson Tide*, and *Enemy of the State*, which established his technical proficiency, expertise at guiding action sequences, virtuosic handling of cinematography, and "exuberant sense of tempo," in the words of a writer for

the Web site Rope of Silicon, which offers movie news and reviews. In *Daily Variety* (August 6, 1996, on-line), the screenwriter Michael Dare described Scott as "a master of the visceral" with a "penchant for creating miraculous fantasy babes"—among them the flight instructor played by Kelly McGillis in *Top Gun*, the doctor portrayed by Nicole Kidman in *Days of Thunder*, and the whore with a heart of gold depicted by Patricia Arquette in *True Romance*. With *True Romance*, which was released in 1993, Scott "totally hit his stride . . . ," Dare declared. "In his quest to perfectly integrate plot and action, it turns out that all he really needed was a script by Quentin Tarantino. Scott took Tarantino's backwards and sideways script, straightened it out, and gave it a miraculously happy ending." During the past three decades, in partnership with his brother, Scott has directed and produced thousands of commercials, most of them for television; some of them have earned him the most prestigious honors of the advertising world.

The youngest of three sons, Anthony Scott was born on July 21, 1944 in northeastern England, six and a half years after his brother Ridley. His oldest brother, Frank, and his father died within weeks of each other, in 1980. His place of birth was Stockton-on-Tees (according to the Internet Movie Database, on-line) or Newcastle-on-Tyne (*Who's Who in America 2001*). *Who's Who* and similar reference works do not include the names of his parents. The name of his mother, Elizabeth Jean Scott, appeared in a dedication to her at the end of Scott's film *Spy Game* (2001), which was released shortly after her death.

Scott developed a love of film while watching Saturday matinees at the local movie house. At 16 he played the title role in his brother's first motion picture, *Boy and Bicycle*. (Also known as *Boy and a Bicycle* [1965], it can be seen as an appendage to a DVD of Ridley Scott's film *The Duellist*.) Scott earned a bachelor's degree in fine arts at Sunderland College of Art, near Newcastle, in about 1965 and then studied at the Leeds College of Art, a drive of about two hours south, with the intention of pursuing a career as a painter. While there, when he was 21, he received £700 from the British Film Institute to make a short film about the American Civil War. "It was a fortune then; the responsibility nearly killed me," he recalled to Marion Collins for the *New York Daily News* (May 17, 1987). The half-hour movie, *One of the Missing*, which is based on a short story by Ambrose Bierce, is dated 1971 but was completed earlier. Scott later made a one-hour student film, called *Loving Memory* (1969), which, according to a profile of him on Rope of Silicon, used "an original script financed by [the actor] Albert Finney." Later that year he left the Leeds College of Art. In 1972 he received an M.F.A. degree from the Royal College of Art, in London.

Earlier, in Los Angeles, California, Tony and Ridley Scott formed an advertising production company—Ridley Scott Associates (also referred to variously as Ridley Scott & Associates and as RSA)—which specializes in the creation of what the RSA Web site calls "groundbreaking" commercials for television. The brothers soon became two of Great Britain's top directors of TV ads. Since RSA's founding the Scotts have opened offices in New York City and London, too, and have worked on thousands of ad campaigns, for such high-profile companies as Philip Morris, Coca-Cola, and American Express. Tony Scott told Kevin Lally for *Film Journal International* (2004, on-line) that he and his brother enjoy "a healthy rivalry, a sibling rivalry." "I tend to work on the people side, Ridley works on the business side, but it's a good combination," he added. "We never share directing notes, but we're always looking at what each other is doing."

Scott's first Hollywood film, *The Hunger* (1983), was produced by Richard Shepard, who had earlier co-produced *The Fugitive Kind* and *Breakfast at Tiffany's*. Set in the 1980s, *The Hunger* starred Catherine Deneuve as the immortal, centuries-old Miriam, and David Bowie as John, whom Miriam had turned into a fellow vampire when she took him as her lover 200 years earlier. Miriam, it transpires, has not given John eternal life. Horrified to discover one day that he is growing visibly older by the minute, John unsuccessfully seeks a cure from Sarah (Susan Sarandon), a scientist who is studying the aging process. Miriam promptly seduces Sarah, who nevertheless foils the vampire's long-term plans for her. *The Hunger* failed to attract viewers (though it later became a cult classic) and did not please most critics.

"Hollywood hated *The Hunger*," Scott once said, according to Michael Dare. "They said it was arty and indulgent, which it was. . . . It took me two years to get another movie." That movie was *Top Gun* (1986), which the producer Jerry Bruckheimer chose Scott to direct on the strength on some of Scott's television commercials. In *Top Gun*, which became the biggest hit of the year, Tom Cruise portrayed the cocky Maverick, an ace pilot training at the U.S. Navy's elite Fighter Weapons School, who is determined to graduate first in his class. Many reviewers praised Scott's handling of action scenes and aerial shots, such as those showing F-14 Tomcat jets streaking across the sky. Stanley Kauffmann, for example, in the *New Republic* (June 9, 1986), wrote that "the exciting air action is as clear and complex as in any film" he had ever seen; Roger Ebert, in the *Chicago Sun-Times* (May 16, 1986, on-line), wrote, "The remarkable achievement in *Top Gun* is that it presents seven or eight aerial encounters that are so well choreographed that we can actually follow them most of the time, and the movie gives us a good second-hand sense of what it might be like to be in a dog-fight."

The success of *Top Gun* led its producers, Don Simpson and Jerry Bruckheimer, to offer Scott the director's chair for *Beverly Hills Cop II* (1987) after Martin Brest, who had directed the highly popular

original, declined to take the job. In the first film, a streetwise Detroit police officer named Axel Foley (played by Eddie Murphy) has to travel to Beverly Hills, California, to solve a mystery while eluding the Beverly Hills police. In the sequel, Foley must team up with the same Beverly Hills officers in another case. The *New York Times* (May 20, 1987) critic Janet Maslin noted, "The new film has at least some of its predecessor's appeal. But it can't match the first film's novelty, or recapture the excitement of watching a great comic character like Axel Foley as he first came to life." Despite such criticism, *Beverly Hills Cop II* became a major hit, earning more than $300 million worldwide.

With the success of *Beverly Hills Cop II*, Scott found himself very much in demand as a potential director of big-budget films. His next film, however, was the low-cost thriller *Revenge* (1990), with Anthony Quinn, Kevin Costner, and Madeleine Stowe, which received dismal reviews and attracted relatively few moviegoers. Decidedly more profitable was *Days of Thunder* (1990), starring Tom Cruise as a stock-car driver trying to make a comeback after a devastating accident. Though many critics derided it as being "*Top Gun* on the racetrack," the film grossed $165 million worldwide. Scott's action-adventure buddy movie *The Last Boy Scout* (1991), a moderate box-office success, is about a washed-up private investigator (Bruce Willis) and a star athlete (Damon Wayans) who, in the course of trying to solve a murder, uncover corruption in professional football. The film received thumbs-down critical notices but generated nearly $60 million in profits in the U.S. alone.

When Scott received the script for *True Romance* (1993) from the independent director and screenwriter Quentin Tarantino—known for his crisp, hip dialogue and ultraviolent plots—he jumped at the opportunity to direct it. "I've always worked as a hired gun," Scott remarked to an *Entertainment Weekly* (August 27, 1993) reporter. "This is the first time I've had creative control, though I was very loyal to the script because it just sucks you in and doesn't allow you to draw a breath." In *True Romance* Christian Slater and Patricia Arquette played an unusual couple: Clarence, a clerk in a store that sells comic books, has wooed and won Alabama, a prostitute. After killing her pimp (Gary Oldman) and stealing his million-dollar stash of cocaine, the newlyweds flee to the West Coast with the pimp's bosses in hot pursuit. As they try to sell the cocaine, they become embroiled in a battle among gangsters, undercover cops, and the FBI. In the *Chicago Sun-Times* (September 10, 1993), Roger Ebert declared, "*True Romance*, which feels at times like a fire sale down at the cliché factory, is made with such energy, such high spirits, such an enchanting goofiness, that it's impossible to resist. Check your brains at the door."

Scott's next film, the critically acclaimed *Crimson Tide* (1995), adapted from a novel by Richard P. Henrick, focused on two navy nuclear-submarine officers competing in a test of wills. Captain Ramsey (Gene Hackman) is the tough-as-nails commander, schooled in the traditions of the U.S. Navy; Lieutenant Commander Hunter (Denzel Washington), his new second-in-command, is a younger man whose ideas about protocol clash with Ramsey's. After Ramsey receives a message stating that right-wing Russian rebels have seized control of some missile silos, he orders his ship, the USS *Alabama*, on full war alert. The sub will have to launch a preemptive strike if it becomes apparent that the rebels intend to strike the U.S. with nuclear weapons. Suddenly, the *Alabama* is attacked and its communications apparatus knocked out, but not before the arrival of part of a second message, whose meaning Ramsey and Hunter interpret differently. Since the captain of a submarine and his executive officer must agree on any orders given, a stalemate ensues, during which the crew splits into two camps, one loyal to Ramsey and the other to Hunter. All the while, the fate of the world hangs in the balance. In a review for the *Chicago Tribune* (May 12, 1995), Roger Ebert called the film "an uncommonly intelligent dramatization about the choices, dangers and duties of nuclear warfare. . . . What's unique about *Crimson Tide* is that it doesn't offer clear-cut choices between good and evil. Hackman may be violating procedures, but perhaps he has good reasons. Washington, fearing to unleash war, may leave his country unprotected. . . . This is the rare kind of war movie that not only thrills people while they're watching it, but invites them to leave the theater actually discussing the issues."

In 1996 Scott directed another thriller, *The Fan*. In that film, which received mediocre to dismissive reviews and middling box-office revenues, Robert De Niro portrayed an unemployed knife salesman who becomes the obsessed fan of a baseball player (Wesley Snipes). Scott followed that with another thriller, *Enemy of the State* (1998), with Will Smith as Robert Dean, a labor lawyer who unknowingly possesses evidence that renegade intelligent agents murdered a congressman, because he opposed a bill designed to make governmental electronic surveillance easier to implement. The same agents then use such surveillance in an effort to frame Dean for the killing. Gene Hackman played a former intelligence agent who comes to Dean's aid. Many critics compared the film to Francis Ford Coppola's *The Conversation* (1974), which offered Hackman's earlier portrayal of a professional eavesdropper.

Scott returned to the world of government-intelligence intrigue in *Spy Game* (2001), set in 1991 and featuring Robert Redford and Brad Pitt as Nathan Muir and Tom Bishop, a pair of Central Intelligence Agency (CIA) operatives. Muir is about to retire when he learns that Bishop, his protégé, has been captured by the Chinese and that the CIA has decided to sacrifice Bishop in exchange for better relations with China. As he works behind the scenes to free Bishop, Muir recalls recruiting and training the younger man and sharing adventures with him over the years. In a review for *Newsweek* (November 25, 2001), David Ansen wrote, "Scott is working in the flashy-gritty style of his *Enemy of the State*. Dense and gripping, *Spy Game* gives good surface: its evocation of ravaged Beirut is ominously atmospheric. But the 'realistic' look invites us to take this thriller more seriously than it deserves."

Scott's most recent film is the revenge thriller *Man on Fire* (2004), starring Denzel Washington as John Creasy, a former covert-operations officer now assigned to the job of bodyguard to an American family in Mexico City. When the family's young daughter (played by Dakota Fanning) is kidnapped, Creasy uses all means at his disposal to get her back. Though the film received very negative reviews—Lisa Schwartzbaum in *Entertainment Weekly* (April 30, 2004) sneered: "Finding heft or coherence within all the lugubrious agitation is a lost cause worthy of St. Jude"—it was a commercial success. Scott's next film, "Emma's War," based on a book by the *Atlanta Journal-Constitution* journalist Deborah Scroggins, will star Nicole Kidman as a real-life British aid worker in the Sudan who married a Sudanese warlord. A project Scott has long expressed an eagerness to develop is a film about Pancho Villa and Tom Mix. "It's a true story, a huge epic—it's *Lawrence of Arabia* and *The Wild Bunch*," he declared to Kevin Lally.

In 1995 Tony and Ridley Scott formed Scott Free Productions, a film and television production company. Among other features for the silver screen, the firm has co-produced the Ridley Scott–directed *White Squall* (1996), *G.I. Jane* (1997), *Matchstick Men* (2003), *Gladiator* (2000), *Black Hawk Down* (2001), and *Hannibal* (2001). For television, Scott Free has co-produced *The Hunger* (1997), for Showtime; *RKO 281* (1999), for HBO, and *The Gathering Storm* (2002), for HBO and the BBC, among other films or series.

Tony and Ridley Scott own the Mill (also called Mill Films), a state-of-the-art visual-effects studio with locations in London and New York, which in 2000 was producing some 1,500 ads annually. In 1995 they paid a reported £12 million to acquire the historic Shepperton Studios, in London, where in the past decades some 600 motion pictures have been made. They also acquired Pinewood Studios, in London, which, like Shepperton, provides stages and other sites for shooting films, as well as postproduction and other services.

Tony Scott has been married and divorced twice.

—C.M.

Suggested Reading: *Chicago Sun-Times* (on-line) Sep. 10, 1993, May 12, 1995; *Entertainment Weekly* p22 Aug. 27, 1993, p55+ Nov. 30, 2001, with photo, p139 Apr. 30, 2004; *International Who's Who*, 2002; *Internet Movie Database* (on-line); (New York) *Daily News* p5 May 17, 1987, with photo; (New York) *Newsday* II p8 June 26, 1990, with photo; *New York Times* II p17 May 1, 1983, (on-line) May 16, 1986, C p28 May 20, 1987, C p8 Feb. 16, 1990; *Newsweek* p75 Nov. 26, 2001; *Variety* p4 Feb. 13, 1995; *Washington Post* (on-line) Dec. 13, 1991, Sep. 10, 1993, May 12, 1995, Aug. 16, 1996

Selected Films: *The Hunger*, 1983; *Top Gun*, 1986; *Beverly Hills Cop II*, 1987; *Revenge*, 1990; *Days of Thunder*, 1990; *The Last Boy Scout*, 1991; *True Romance*, 1993; *Crimson Tide*, 1995; *The Fan*, 1996; *Enemy of the State*, 1998; *Spy Game*, 2001; *Man on Fire*, 2004

Courtesy of the office of Kathleen Sebelius

Sebelius, Kathleen

(seh-BEEL-ee-us)

May 15, 1948– Governor of Kansas (Democrat)

Address: Office of the Governor, Capitol, 300 S.W. 10th Ave., Suite 212S, Topeka, KS 66612-1590

A Democrat in a state in which registered Republicans outnumber registered Democrats by more than three to two, Kathleen Sebelius captured the governorship of Kansas in 2002. Sebelius—daughter of a former Democratic governor of Ohio who had represented Ohio in Congress, and daughter-in-law of a former Republican congressman from Kansas—began her political career in 1986, when she won a seat in the Kansas House of Representatives. In 1994 she became the first wom-

an—and the first Democrat—to be elected to the office of Kansas state insurance commissioner. In February 2002, toward the end of her second term as insurance commissioner, she gained national attention when she rejected the proposed sale of Blue Cross and Blue Shield of Kansas to the Anthem Insurance Co. of Indiana, after an analysis showed that the merger would lead to large increases in customers' insurance premiums. The decision added to Sebelius's already considerable popularity among Kansans, and two weeks later she announced her candidacy for governor. A coalition of Democrats and moderate Republicans helped Sebelius defeat her socially conservative Republican opponent in the election for governor in November 2002. Nearly two years into her term, the words of an opinion column in the *Southwest Daily Times* (January 12, 2002, on-line), written before her run for governor, still ring true: "Sebelius personifies a New Kansas Democrat—a moderate, prairie-style [Bill] Clinton. . . . She is only one member of what could prove a remarkable generation of Kansas Democrats. While they probably won't break the GOP's 140-year hold on Kansas, these Democrats could become a dynamic force for change in the state."

The second of the four children of John "Jack" Gilligan and Mary Katherine "Katie" Gilligan, Sebelius was born Kathleen Gilligan on May 15, 1948 in Cincinnati, Ohio. She has two brothers and a younger sister. The Gilligans descended from Irish Catholics who immigrated to Cincinnati in the 1860s and became active in the community. John Gilligan, a literature professor, left academia for politics; a Democrat, he served six terms in the Cincinnati City Council before winning a seat in the U.S. House of Representatives in 1964—becoming the first Democrat from his congressional district in more than six decades. A foe of the Vietnam War and a strong proponent of the civil rights movement, Gilligan was reelected in 1966. In his race for the U.S. Senate, in 1968, he met defeat. Two years later he captured the governorship; his bid for reelection, in 1974, failed.

While growing up the Gilligan children worked on their father's campaigns and saw firsthand his commitment to public service. "We always talked politics at home," Sebelius told the *Topeka Capital-Journal* (July 28, 2002). "We talked about issues, we talked about problems. . . . I think we grew up with the notion . . . that we owed the community something." "The downside," Sebelius continued, was that her father "was gone a lot. He was busy a lot. And he won some elections and he lost some elections, so I knew personally how difficult that was, how painful that was to have people angry and upset at him." Sebelius's mother, a high-school teacher, gave her husband honest and often critical political advice. "She was incredibly supportive and proud of what my dad did and really gave that sense to all of us of how important it was to be involved in public life," Sebelius told the *Topeka Capital-Journal* reporter.

From grammar school through college, Sebelius attended all-female Roman-Catholic institutions. Being educated with girls only "did two things for me," she told Susan Fahlgren Rothschild for the *Topeka Capital-Journal* (October 19, 2003). "Not only did it let me play sports . . . but also I was in an environment where I was never told, overtly or covertly, girls couldn't do everything." Sebelius played basketball, tennis, golf, and field hockey, among other sports. She also volunteered at a nursing home, a camp for physically disabled youngsters, and at a hospital, as a Candy Striper. After graduating from high school, in 1966, she enrolled at Trinity College in Washington, D.C. As an undergraduate she competed on Trinity's basketball, tennis, and field-hockey teams and tutored local schoolchildren. Sebelius also became involved in campus politics and the burgeoning feminist movement. She earned a B.A. degree in political science from Trinity in 1970.

In 1971 Sebelius got a job as the director of planning for the Center for Community Justice, in Washington, D.C. In 1973 she met Keith Gary Sebelius (known as Gary), a Georgetown University law student, whose father, Keith Sebelius, a Republican, represented a Kansas district in the U.S. House of Representatives from 1969 to 1981. (He died in 1982.) The couple married on December 31, 1974 and moved to Topeka, where Gary Sebelius began practicing law. When Kathleen Sebelius applied for a position as a juvenile probation officer for Shawnee County (in which Topeka is the only big city), she was told that the county government did not hire women. She ruled out suing for sexual discrimination after making "a conscious decision that that probably wasn't the best way to introduce myself in a new community," as she recalled to Rothschild. "Yeah, maybe I could prevail legally, but maybe it might brand me for the rest of my life here. I've always sort of struggled with that decision, wondering how many more people were denied that [opportunity, for whom] I could have opened that door." In 1974 Sebelius became a special assistant with the Kansas Department of Corrections, a post that she held for about four years. Concurrently, she worked toward a master's degree in public administration at the University of Kansas, which she earned in 1977. The next year Sebelius was hired as the executive director of the Kansas Trial Lawyers Association, a job that involved interaction with state legislators. In 1981 she gave birth to her first child, Edward (called Ned). Eager to take the baby with her to the office until he reached six months of age, she instituted a "bring your child to work" program at the association. Her second child, John, who was born in 1984, also came with her to her office for the first six months of his life.

In 1986 Sebelius defeated the Republican Peggy M. Boggs to win election to the Kansas House of Representatives from Potwin, the section of Topeka in which she lived; she won reelection in 1988, 1990, and 1992. The lawmakers worked only four months out of the year, with summers off, and held their sessions in Topeka; thus, not only could Sebelius go home every evening after work (as legislators from elsewhere in the state could not), she could even go to her sons' school when she had a break during the day, to read stories to their classes, for example. "In many ways, it was a great part-time job" for a woman with young children, as she told Rothschild. As a Kansas state legislator, Sebelius championed many traditionally Democratic causes, such as abortion rights, and argued against the death penalty. She opposed a highway bill that raised taxes on gas and a measure that limited the amount of money patients could receive as a result of medical-malpractice lawsuits. A strong proponent of education, in 1992 Sebelius backed the imposition of increases in the state sales and income taxes to provide funds for schools and, simultaneously, the lowering of property taxes. Sebelius also gained a reputation for her commitment to children and pregnant women: she conducted hearings that resulted in more state-funded programs for youngsters, sponsored a bill that established Kansas's Office of Children and Families, and worked to increase funding for the neonatal and pediatric-care programs of the state Department of Health and Environment. Though some Republicans dismissed her as a typical liberal, Sebelius won respect from colleagues on both sides of the aisle.

In 1994 Sebelius made her first bid for statewide office: that of insurance commissioner, head of the Kansas Insurance Department, which regulates the companies and agents that sell automobile, life, health, long-term care, homeowner's, renter's, and other types of insurance in the state. She criticized the department for poor performance and her opponent, the incumbent commissioner, Ron Todd, a Republican, for his ties to the insurance industry; with many others, she also raised questions about the propriety (though not the legality) of Todd's earlier receipt of $95,000 in workers' compensation and, along with his commissioner's salary, a state pension. As evidence of her own independence, she—unlike her opponent—refused to accept campaign donations from insurers. Because neither a woman nor a Democrat had ever won election as insurance commissioner, and because males dominate the insurance industry, Sebelius faced a great deal of skepticism as to her qualifications for the job and her ability to handle it. "I think there's always that sort of test [for women]," she told Rothschild: "You have to jump higher; you have to run faster. There are a lot of [potential women candidates] who just aren't willing . . . to put up with it. 'Why should I have to prove myself?' But I've always liked the challenge and the opportunities presented by whatever job it was. [Each job] seemed worth the extra mile." On Election Day Sebelius handily defeated Todd.

Sebelius was sworn in as insurance commissioner in early 1995. Bringing a technocrat's sensibility to an agency long identified with political patronage and ineffectiveness, she streamlined and modernized its operations while increasing its responsiveness to consumers and working to protect their interests. In one example of her successful initiatives, she ordered a comprehensive review of the department's operations; one result was that fully half of the department's enormous number of regulations were discarded as unnecessary. She continued her efforts after easily defeating her Republican challenger (Bryan Riley, a securities-firm economist) to win reelection in 1998. In August 2000 the Democratic Leadership Council, an organization of moderate Democratic officeholders, named her one of the party's 100 rising stars. Later that year she became president of the National Association of Insurance Commissions.

In January 2001 Sebelius conducted highly publicized hearings into whether the state should permit the $370 million acquisition of Blue Cross Blue Shield of Kansas by Anthem Insurance. An independent panel of experts concluded that the sale would cause insurance premiums for big companies, small businesses (including physicians' practices), and families in Kansas to rise much faster than they would otherwise. In February 2002 Sebelius disallowed the move, thus becoming what the organization Community Catalyst described in its on-line publication (February 12, 2002) as "the first industry regulator in the nation to reject a move by an out-of-state for-profit conglomerate to buy the state's Blue Cross and Blue Shield Plan, an independent, nonprofit plan that has served [Kansas] for generations." Most Kansans applauded her decision, and her popularity grew. Later, a state judge overturned Sebelius's ruling; in 2003 the Kansas Supreme Court reinstated it.

Meanwhile, on February 25, 2002 Sebelius officially announced her candidacy for the Kansas governorship, to succeed the popular incumbent, the Republican Bill Graves, who, because of state-mandated term limits, could not run again. She pledged to "fight for everyday Kansans," as Chris Grenz quoted her as saying in the Topeka Capital-Journal (February 26, 2002). "Putting the people first—that's what it's all about. . . . As governor, I will use my principles and experience, my common sense and my faith to always put the people of Kansas before anything else." Sebelius ran unopposed in the Democratic primary. In the general election she ran against State Treasurer Tim Shallenburger, a conservative Republican. During the campaign she promised to work to improve public education (by means of higher taxes, if necessary), reduce health-care costs, and make the state government more efficient and more ethical. Crossing party lines, she picked as the candidate for lieutenant governor the Republican John Moore, an aviation executive, who subsequently joined the Democratic Party in order to get his name on the ballot.

Shallenburger and Sebelius differed on several key issues. He opposed legalized gambling while she supported it, provided that the communities affected also approved it. He opposed abortion; she supported abortion rights. He supported and she opposed a law that would have allowed Kansans to carry concealed firearms with a permit. In a series of debates, Shallenburger sought, disparagingly, to label Sebelius a liberal, while she accused him of lacking a real commitment to public education. Sebelius earned support from some moderate Republicans who judged Shallenburger to be too conservative, and she remained ahead in opinion polls until the last weeks of the campaign, when the gap narrowed considerably. Nevertheless, on November 5, 2002 she was elected governor of Kansas by a comfortable margin, garnering 53 percent of the vote to Shallenburger's 45 percent. (Third-party candidates won the remaining votes.) Her victory marked the first time a Democrat had won an open governorship (so-called because no candidate sought reelection) in Kansas since 1936 and the first time anywhere in the U.S. that a former governor's daughter had been elected a governor in her own right.

After the election (but before she was sworn into office), with the state facing a projected $255 million budget deficit despite the large spending cuts Governor Graves had recently made, Sebelius formed five so-called Budget Efficiency Savings Teams (BESTs) to identify sources of waste and inefficiency within the government. The BESTs operated in secret; Sebelius's refusal to permit members of the press to view the proceedings led various media organizations to sue for access, but it was denied. Meanwhile, Sebelius had appointed a bipartisan cabinet, retaining some of her predecessor's appointees and filling a few other high-profile positions with Republicans.

On January 15, 2003, two days after her inauguration and one month ahead of schedule, Sebelius unveiled a tentative budget (one that balanced, as the state constitution required). It protected funding for essential social services and education and salary increases for state employees. While it did not call for boosts in taxes, it included increased fees for state services and cuts in funding to local governments and to the state's 10-year, $13.5 billion highway plan. The response to Sebelius's proposals was uniformly positive. The budget process was not over, however, in part because of shortfalls in tax collections. On March 25 Sebelius released a $405 million revenue plan with three components: a legalized-gambling provision, an initiative to speed the collection of property taxes, and the sale of $175 million in state bonds. On April 3 the Republican-controlled House passed a budget similar to the one Sebelius had proposed in January but discarded much of her plan to cover the revenue shortfall. Consequently, a $254 million budget deficit remained. "Voting against pieces of the revenue package when there have been no other proposals or solutions offered is a disservice to the people of Kansas," Sebelius declared, as quoted by Chris Moon in the Topeka Capital-Journal (April 4, 2003). The plan the Republicans offered, in late April, to reduce the budget shortfall relied on delays in both some school funding and tax refunds totaling $60 million. When the House and Senate passed the proposed spending plan, in early May, Sebelius vowed to veto the refund-delay provision. Soon afterward she and Republican lawmakers reached an agreement whereby the state would postpone paying about $50 million in tax refunds; if tax collections continued to lag, Sebelius could institute speedier property-tax collections. As the session drew to a close, Sebelius and the legislature agreed to a $146 million tax adjustment that postponed a scheduled reduction in the 5.3 percent state sales tax until July 1, 2006.

In October 2003 the BESTs announced cost-cutting initiatives to save the state over $76.3 million per year. For example, they estimated that by sending state workers E-mail rather than Postal Service messages regarding the automatic deposits of their paychecks, Kansas could save $500,000 per year. Republicans claimed that the $76.3 million figure was exaggerated, with most of the supposed savings coming from the collection of overdue taxes under an amnesty plan instituted by Sebelius. Later that month the governor formed the Office of Health Planning and Finance, with the goal of maximizing the state's health-care buying power. In November she announced the sale of 739 state-owned vehicles and a two-year moratorium on the state's purchases of new automobiles, for a net savings of over $8.5 million.

On December 2, 2003 District Judge Terry Bullock of Shawnee County ruled that the state was not funding its public schools adequately; he ordered Kansas policy makers to come up with a solution to the problem by July 1, 2004. Estimates made after the ruling suggested that to meet its obligations to schoolchildren, the legislature had to allocate another $1 billion to education. Meanwhile, many experts expected another large budget shortfall in 2004.

In her State of the State speech on January 12, 2004, Sebelius proposed a $300 million increase in education funding over three years, to be paid for in various ways. The state's sales tax would rise from 5.3 percent to 5.7 percent over three years, the so-called mill levy for education (a mill being a tax of $1 for every $1,000 worth of property) would increase by one mill on July 1, 2005 and again by one mill two years later, and a 5 percent surcharge would be added to personal income taxes. The state Senate rejected both Sebelius's suggestions and a compromise approved by the House, and the 2004 legislative session concluded without an education bill. The state's appeal of Judge Bullock's ruling may be heard this fall. Earlier, on January 30, Sebelius unveiled her legalized-gambling initiative. "For too long, Kansans have been taking their gaming dollars to Missouri, Iowa and elsewhere because we have too few options her at home," she said, according to Ric Anderson in the *Topeka Capital-Journal* (January 31, 2004). "It's time to keep these dollars in Kansas and put them

to work for us." Sebelius suggested that a maximum of five state-owned casinos be constructed, with their managers, private firms, giving at least 18 percent of their revenues to the state. Other aspects of the plan included the installation of as many as 2,500 digital gambling machines at Kansas racetracks, from which the state would receive 45 percent of the proceeds. Republicans in the legislature immediately expressed their opposition to Sebelius's plan; the state Senate rejected it in late April. (The legislature is expected to revisit the issue in the 2005 session.) Also in April Sebelius vetoed legislation that would have permitted qualified owners to carry concealed handguns. In May she signed a bill specifying that regarding the amount of tuition to be paid for attendance at public colleges or universities in Kansas, illegal immigrants living in the state must be treated like other residents, provided that they are "actively seeking legal immigration status or plan to do so when eligible," as John Hanna reported for the Associated Press (May 4, 2004, on-line).

Sebelius's husband—the self-named "First Dude" of Kansas—became a federal magistrate judge on June 11, 2003. The couple's sons both attended public schools through high school. The older son, Ned, graduated from Georgetown University and plans to attend law school; in 2004 he worked on John Kerry's presidential campaign. The younger son, John, attends the Rhode Island School of Design. Sebelius is a member of the National Governors Association Committee on Education, Early Childhood, and Workforce and co-chairs the association's Long-Term Care Task Force; she serves as the policy chair of the Democratic Governors' Association. She is a longtime parishioner of Assumption Catholic Church in Topeka. In her leisure time she enjoys jogging, skiing, scuba diving, playing tennis and golf, cooking, entertaining, and reading historical novels. She is also a music enthusiast, with a particular fondness for the Dixie Chicks and Marcia Ball. In September 2003 she appeared onstage at the Topeka City Theatre & Academy in the role of Ambassador Magee in Woody Allen's comedy *Don't Drink the Water.*
— P.B.M.

Suggested Reading: *Best's Review* p30 June 2000; *Business Insurance* p2 Jan. 15, 2001, with photo; *Governing* p27 Nov. 2001, with photo; Kansas Governor's Office Web site; National Governors' Association Web site; *Topeka Capital-Journal* Nov. 16, 1998, Feb. 25, 2002, Feb. 26, 2002, with photo, July 28, 2002, with photos

Ted Thai/Getty Images

Simpson, Lorna

Aug. 13, 1960– Photographer and video artist

Address: c/o Sean Kelly Gallery, 43 Mercer St., New York, NY 10013

The work of the African-American photographer and videographer Lorna Simpson is among the most widely exhibited in the contemporary American art scene. Simpson gained recognition in the 1980s with photographic installations that deconstructed stereotypical notions of race, gender, and sexuality, building a body of work that Alexandra Schwartz described in *New Art Examiner* (May/June 2001) as a "searing commentary on the complex and elusive ways in which identity is constructed." In 1990 Simpson became the first African-American woman to exhibit in the prestigious Venice Biennale and to have a solo exhibition in the *Projects* series at the Museum of Modern Art (MoMA) in New York City. She began her career in the field of documentary photography, but as she increasingly questioned the assumed objectivity of the photographer, her work became more conceptual, challenging viewers to question their own positions in relation to the subject of each photograph. Her signature work, which largely consists of portraits of African-American women accompanied by text, is rife with ambiguities; the artist has said that she wants the audience to connect the dots for themselves. "One needs wisdom, patience, intellect, and wit to decode Simpson," according to a writer for *Contemporary Women Artists* (1999), "but once that is accomplished (though the multiple layers of dialogue are not easy to fathom), her work is sheer joy."

Lorna Simpson was born in New York City, in the Crown Heights neighborhood of the borough of Brooklyn, on August 13, 1960. She grew up in the borough of Queens. Raised during the civil rights movement, she developed an early interest in social justice while reading the works of African-American writers such as Langston Hughes. Her parents provided her with a rich cultural background, taking her to museums and enrolling her in art lessons. "I always had an interest in art and my parents provided an arena to practice it," she told Abigail Foerstner for the *Chicago Tribune* (November 20, 1992).

After graduating from the renowned High School of Art and Design, Simpson attended the School of Visual Arts in New York, where she initially studied painting and later switched to documentary photography. Discouraged by the dearth of African-American role models in the white-dominated world of contemporary art, during her college years she successfully sought an internship at the Studio Museum in Harlem, an institution that focuses on artists of African descent. Simpson explained to Ronica Sanders Smucker in an interview for *Hurricane Alice* (1995) that her work has been more influenced by such artists as David Hammons and Adrian Piper than by contemporary photographers. Piper and Hammons, who have both exhibited at the Studio Museum, are known for creating installations that utilize a wide range of mediums as means of examining the issue of race in America.

After earning her B.F.A. degree, in 1982, Simpson traveled through Europe and Africa with her camera at her side, then returned to the U.S. to pursue her M.F.A. degree in visual arts at the University of California, San Diego. She graduated in 1985; that year also saw her first solo exhibition, at the Alternative Gallery in San Diego, and her receipt of an Arts Management Fellowship from the National Endowment for the Arts. She returned to New York after graduation and was selected for P.S.1's National Studio Program, which provided her with rent-free studio space for a year.

In the course of her graduate studies, Simpson had begun to question the traditional role of documentary photography, challenging the assumed objectivity of the photographer; as a result her work adopted a conceptual bent. "I started to concentrate more upon how the viewer looks at photographic images," Simpson explained for the Web site of the Chicago Museum of Contemporary Art. "I took elements from my own documentary work and abstracted particular qualities, putting them into very stark environments—meaning, perhaps, the way a person stands or a particular gesture—but leaving the photographic subject blank or not permitting the photographic subject's face to appear. That way, all the information or clues that point to a particular individual were eliminated from the image. From there, I would insert my own text or my own specific reading of the image to give the viewer something they might not interpret or surmise, due to their 'educated' way of looking at images, and reading them for their emotional, psychological, and/or sociological values."

It was also during her graduate studies that Simpson began to develop the theme that would underpin much of her work: what she consider to be the anonymity, or invisibility, of black women in American society. As Ariella Budick reported in *Newsday* (October 20, 2002), the exhibition catalog for Simpson's 2002 show *31,* at the Whitney Museum of American Art, in New York, describes how Simpson "felt like a member of a category rather than an individual," in Budick's words, while attending graduate school. Simpson's classmates often mistook her for one of her two black friends in the program—one of whom was the artist Carrie Mae Weems—despite their strikingly different body shapes and sizes. "Our presence was as interchangeable as it was invisible," she recalled.

Those confrontations with racial stereotypes, and the move to a more conceptual approach to her art, served as the catalysts for Simpson's signature work: portraits of individual women, their backs to the camera or their faces cropped off, often accompanied by laconic text engraved on plastic plaques. The style is typified by *The Waterbearer* (1986). In that photograph, shot from behind, a black woman with disheveled hair, wearing a white shift, pours water from a plastic jug held in one hand and a metal decanter held in the other. The inscription beneath reads: "She saw him disappear by the river They asked her to tell what happened Only to discount her memory." In her essay on the piece for *ArtForum* (September 1993), bell hooks wrote that the seeming innocence of the woman in the photo is belied by the threat evinced in the accompanying text. "It invites us to consider the production of history as a cultural text—a narrative uncovering repressed or forgotten memory," she wrote.

The text describing Simpson's photographs—often referencing party games, proverbs, fragments of conversation, or clichés, such as "black as coal"—are designed to create tension between what is seen in the photos and implied by the words. Simpson told Ronica Sanders Smucker that her text is influenced by the ability of such African-American novelists as Ishmael Reed, Alice Walker and Toni Morrison to reflect the psychology of their characters through dialogue. Simpson's work can be viewed as a series of open-ended conversations; there is an intentional ambiguity in her work, and she has often said that she prefers the viewer to fill in the blanks. "Words proximate to images in each of Simpson's combines are not narratives but non sequiturs and platitudes," Arlene Raven wrote in the *Village Voice* (July 26, 1988). "Together with the photographs, though, they hint at stories and energetically engage spectators to fill in the vast blank spaces with assumptions of knowledge and belief. However those spaces may be filled in the mind's eye, race, gender, and age rest as stereotypes because they are the only human qualities Simpson makes known. Thus she

lays open the inadequacies of generic clichés as the sole terms of representation."

In the late 1980s and early 1990s, Simpson's work appeared in solo exhibitions and group shows at major art institutions and galleries throughout the United States and abroad. In 1987 she became one of the few African-American artists ever to have exhibited at *Documenta*, an exhibition of the work of international contemporary artists held in Kassel, Germany. (She returned to exhibit there in 2002.) Ashyia Henderson wrote in *Contemporary Black Biography* (2002), "Every museum and gallery, it seemed, wanted a piece of the Lorna Simpson phenomenon, and in retrospect it was easy to see why: Simpson joined together a number of new artistic ideas in a synthesis that was multi-layered, entirely her own, and uniquely African-American."

Around 1990 Simpson began examining the role of hair as a social and political marker. *Wigs* (1994), a portfolio of 21 lithographs, featured a variety of wigs, from silky blond to short Afro style. According to the description on the Web site of MoMA, where it is part of the permanent collection, "Text panels interspersed among the wigs record Simpson's wide-ranging commentary on their use by women, entertainers, and transvestites. The wig's potential as an instrument for conformity, metamorphosis, and concealment is thereby underscored." Clothing is also heavily imbued with meaning in Simpson's work; Simpson has often dressed her models in white shifts, chosen for the sense of anonymity they reinforce. Challenging traditional gender roles, Simpson also plays with cross-dressing in her portraits, as in *She* (1992), which finds the female subject dressed in a man's suit and seated in a masculine pose.

Having cemented her reputation by the mid-1990s, Simpson told Joy Duckett Cain in an interview for *Essence* (May 1995) that she was ready to "break the formula that I developed for myself." People, she said, "hold certain expectations about my work, but outside expectations can be paralyzing. I always feel more confident when I've listened to my own intuition." She avoided portraiture entirely for her 1995 show, *Figuring Absence*, at New York's Sean Kelly Gallery, offering a series of black-and-white photographs of a bleak urban landscape, the human presence alluded to only in the accompanying text.

Simpson began mixing film with printed photographs in her installations with *Interior/Exterior, Full/Empty* (1997), filmed in Ohio during her residency at the Wexner Museum. The work comprised seven short films, projected concurrently on multiple walls, running in 20-minute cycles; the main image was that of lovers meeting in a park, while the rest were interior shots. The characters in each scene, disconnected from each other by their different locales, were caught in moments of everyday life: two old women gossip, a woman makes arrangements over the phone to meet her lover, two old men stare silently out a window. "I see *Interior/Exterior, Full/Empty* as a way of looking at the physical space the viewer occupies and the way one's attention, one's voyeurism, is pulled," Simpson explained to Siri Engberg and Sarah Cook in an interview posted on the Walker Art Center Web site.

While many critics note that the subject of race in Simpson's work has receded into the background somewhat since the mid-1990s, her concern with the relative invisibility of black women is still evident in works such as *31* (2002). Shown at the Whitney Museum of American Art concurrently with her still-photograph installation *Cameos and Appearances, 31* captured the minutiae of the daily life of an African-American woman—footage of her at home, at work, and on the subway ride in between—projected on 31 screens simultaneously. Grace Glueck, an art critic for the *New York Times* (November 1, 2002), wrote that the work "expresses the anomie and aloneness of one whose presence is not registered." In an essay in Kellie Jones's book *Lorna Simpson* (2002), published by Phaidon Press as part of the Contemporary Artist Series, Chrissie Iles, the Whitney Museum's curator of film and video, wrote that "the collective social invisibility of the black female was given another narrative form when Simpson began to work in film."

Simpson currently serves on the faculty at the International Center for Photography, in New York, and her works continue to be shown throughout the United States and abroad; they are included in the permanent collections of many prestigious institutions, including New York's Metropolitan Museum of Art, the Whitney Museum of American Art, the San Francisco Museum of Modern Art, the Corcoran Gallery of Art, and the Art Institute of Chicago. She is the recipient of the Louis Comfort Tiffany Award and was a finalist for the Hugo Boss Prize in 1998.

Simpson lives in a brownstone in Brooklyn with the photographer Jim Casebere, whom she met while serving on a panel for the National Endowment for the Arts. The couple have a daughter, Zora Simpson Casebere.

—J.C.

Suggested Reading: *Art Monthly* p29+ May 2003; *Hurricane Alice* p10+ Dec. 31, 1995; Museum of Modern Art Web site; *Village Voice* p91 July 26, 1988

Spiropulu, Maria

(spir-uh-POO-loo)

1969– Particle physicist

Address: P.O. Box 500, MS 318, Batavia, IL 60510

"We are very close to a new reality," the physicist Maria Spiropulu told Peter Gorner for the *Chicago Tribune* (February 18, 2002). "We imagine space and time as static entities and we solve equations as a function of space and time. But we're learning that at the very large scale—the cosmos—and at the very teeny scale of particles, space and time are dynamic, constantly changing. What is happening at those scales we can't explain. So we have to wonder: Do these scales hold some extra dimensions?" Spiropulu's research focuses on that question; by making particles collide and then observing the results, she hopes to discover the existence of dimensions outside both three-dimensional space and time. A former fellow at the Enrico Fermi Institute at the University of Chicago, Spiropulu currently works at CERN, the world's largest particle-physics laboratory, in Geneva, Switzerland. She is a member of a new generation of physicists who are challenging the traditional ways of understanding the material world. "Physics is not my job; it is my life," she told Dennis Overbye for the *New York Times* (September 30, 2003). "The world is what you measure."

Jeff Sciortino/Jeff Sciortino Photography

Maria Spiropulu was born in the fall of 1969 in Greece and raised in Kleisoura, a village of roughly 1,000 residents located in the northern mountains of Greece. Her younger brother, Markos, a world rowing champion at the age of 14, is currently a yachting instructor and professional skipper in Athens. Spiropulu's father was a businessman; her mother was a teacher of fashion design. As a child Spiropulu had a passion for reading and a taste for music and theater. She was also fascinated by the way things work and loved to take objects apart and put them back together. Early on she began conducting scientific experiments; in one, carried out when she was seven, she made a pair of Styrofoam wings and fastened them to the arms of one cousin after another, each of whom jumped from the top of a garden wall at her command. When the would-be aerialists landed on their faces, she told them to flap harder the next time they jumped.

Spiropulu excelled not only in the sciences and mathematics but also in philosophy, history, and literature. Her teachers encouraged her to consider studying philology and law. By the time she was 14, though, she knew she wanted to specialize in physics. In high school she developed an interest in particle physics. As an undergraduate at Aristotle University of Thessaloniki, in Greece, she found herself, in her own words, in a state of "creative confusion." Among other subjects, she studied material science, surface physics, and dosimetry, defined as "a system of therapeutics which uses few remedies, mostly alkaloids, and gives them in doses fixed by certain rules." After she graduated from the university, with a bachelor's degree in physics, in 1993, she borrowed $500 from her father and moved to Geneva, Switzerland. There, she got a summer job as a technical assistant at CERN (the acronym for Conseil European pour la Recherché Nucleaire, or European Laboratory for Particle Physics), the world's leading institution devoted to the study of fundamental particles.

During that summer she resolved to build a career in particle physics, and she set her sights on investigating proton-antiproton collisions at the Fermi National Accelerator Laboratory (Fermilab), in Batvia, Illinois. Fermilab is the home of the Tevatron, a circular structure in which particles are accelerated to an enormously high speed: only a tiny fraction of a second slower than the speed of light, which travels at 186,000 miles per second, or 669.6 billion miles per hour. With a circumference of 6.5 kilometers, or slightly over four miles, the Tevatron is the world's largest particle accelerator. Connected with the Tevatron are two so-called detector complexes—the Collider Detector Facility and the D0 Detector Facility, each of which is three stories tall; the detectors determine the presence of all the elementary particles and fragments of particles produced in particle collisions.

At the end of that summer, Spiropulu enrolled at Harvard University, in Cambridge, Massachusetts, as a graduate student in particle physics. During much of the next half-dozen years, she served an apprenticeship at Fermilab investigating particle collisions. To facilitate her project, she developed a mathematical-analysis tool that searched the accelerator's data for evidence of supersymmetry.

According to the theory of supersymmetry, all known particles have associated "shadow partners." The nature of the shadow partner depends upon the type of particle with which it is associated: if the particle is of the type categorized as a boson, which transmits a force, its shadow partner (also called a partner particle or superpartner) will be of the type categorized as a fermion, which makes up matter; conversely, the counterpart of a particle of the fermion type will be a particle of the boson type. Among fermions, the superpartner of an electron is called a selectron; the superpartner of a muon is a smuon; that of a quark, a squark, and so on. (The name of a fermion's superpartner is generated by adding "s" to the name of the particle.) Among bosons, the superpartner of a photon is a photino; that of a gluon, a gluino; that of a Higgs, a Higgsino, and so on. (The name of a boson's superpartner is formed by substituting "ino" for "on" or simply adding "ino.") In addition, the particle/superparticle connection involves the highly theoretical concept of spin, which in particle physics is defined as the intrinsic angular momentum of a particle (and has nothing to do with anything actually spinning). According to the theory of supersymmetry, the spins of a particle and its associated superparticle differ by half a unit. Thus, the spin of a Higgs is zero, and the spin of a Higgsino is one-half; the spin of an electron is one-half, and the spin of a selectron, zero. Spiropulu searched for evidence of gluinos and squarks, the superpartners of gluons and quarks, respectively. The fact that she did not find them did not detract from her research, because, as the doctoral judges determined, her methods and calculations were correct. "Everybody is entitled to their own opinion, but they're not entitled to their own facts," she remarked to Dennis Overbye. "The data is the data." Spiropulu earned her Ph.D. in 2000; her dissertation bears the title "A Blind Search for Supersymmetry in p pbar Collisions at 1.8 TeV Using the Missing Energy plus Multijet Channel." In the same year she became an Enrico Fermi Fellow at the Enrico Fermi Institute at the University of Chicago. Concurrently, she continued to study particle collisions at Fermilab.

At the 2002 annual convention of the American Association for the Advancement of Science, held in Boston, Massachusetts, Spiropulu presented a paper on experiments that had led her to believe that a new understanding of reality would emerge by 2005. "Reality, to us, is a world where events happen over time within a three-dimensional space, but the way we think about things is about to completely change," she predicted at the convention, as quoted by Peter Gorner in the *Chicago Tribune* (February 18, 2002). According to traditional physics, humans exist in four dimensions: one time direction and three spacial dimensions (left-right, forward-backward, and up-down; a line is one-dimensional, a square is two-dimensional, and a cube is three-dimensional). In recent years, physicists have become increasingly interested in superstring theory, which aims to shed light on such phenomena as gravity and the quantum nature of light, which traditional physics cannot explain. String theory attempts to unravel the mysteries of space, time, matter, and energy by positing the existence of tightly bundled, vibrating "strings" of incredible tininess (about a millionth of a billionth of a billionth of a billionth of a centimeter). The theory makes mathematical sense only if there are 10 dimensions rather than four. In order to explain the fact that humans experience only four dimensions, string theorists suggest that the extra dimensions are rolled up into tiny balls less than a trillionth the size of elementary particles. The existence of extra dimensions might also help explain why gravity is so weak compared with the other three forces of nature: electromagnetism, the strong nuclear force, and the weak nuclear force (the latter two of which act only within the nucleus of the atom); if other dimensions exist, then gravity appears weak because it must be transmitted through those dimensions.

In order to discover whether extra dimensions really exist, Spiropulu and her colleagues at Fermilab conduct experiments in high-energy particle collision. Using the Tevatron, they force protons and their antimatter mirror particles, antiprotons, to collide with one another. (Antimatter mirror particles are different from shadow partners.) Theoretically, these collisions should produce gravitons, a hypothetical particle of force that carries gravity. (Physicists have not yet detected gravitons; they believe they exist because particles associated with the other three forces have been detected.) According to traditional physics, gravitons are massless and undetectable. The forced particle collisions in Spiropulu's experiments produce less energy than mathematically predicted, thus suggesting that some of the particles might have been absorbed into extra dimensions. "We do have things that give us the right to think we are seeing a little hint of new physics," she told Dennis Overbye. "It's an educated hope. It's not wishful thinking."

Spiropulu is currently conducting her research at CERN. A strikingly attractive woman, she has green eyes and black hair that she often streaks with blue and orange dyes. She enjoys dancing the tango, kickboxing, and playing the drums. While working toward her Ph.D., she served as a drummer for Fermilab's resident band, Drug Sniffing Dogs.

—H.T.

Suggested Reading: *Chicago Tribune* Metro p4+ Feb. 18, 2002, Tempo p1+ July 11, 2002, with photos; *New York Times* F p1+ June 20, 2000, with photos, F p1+ Sep. 30, 2003, with photos

Stanton, Andrew

1966(?)– Animator; filmmaker

Address: Pixar Studios, 1200 Park Ave., Emeryville, CA 94608

Andrew Stanton is the creative force behind *Finding Nemo*, the biggest film hit of 2003 and the latest in the Pixar Studios' series of critically acclaimed and commercially successful computer-animated films. Stanton—who had long sought to tell an entertaining story of undersea life in a realistically rendered, computer-generated environment—spent more than a decade developing *Finding Nemo*. In the meantime, he served as co-writer and story artist on Pixar's other highly successful computer-animated movies, *Toy Story* (1995), *Toy Story 2* (1999), *Monsters, Inc.* (2001), and *A Bug's Life* (1998), of which he was co-director. Together, Pixar's films have earned nearly $2 billion.

Andrew Stanton was born in around 1966 and grew up in Rockport, Massachusetts. As a child he developed a fascination with fish during his routine visits to his dentist, who had a small aquarium in his office. Stanton studied animation at the California Institute of the Arts, in Valencia, graduating in 1987. He has recalled that he enjoyed all aspects of the animation process and found it difficult to decide which area to pursue. As it turned out, he

Courtesy of Pixar Inc.

was hired by the upstart Pixar Animation Studios in 1990 (some sources say 1989). Early in his career he had worked on *Mighty Mouse, the New Adventures*, a TV series that was distributed in the U.S.

by Paramount Television and Viacom; aired on Saturday mornings for one season, that series, along with Stanton's five-minute film *A Story* (1987), caught the attention of John Lasseter, Pixar's artistic director. Pixar had been formed in 1984 by Lasseter, who had left his position at the Walt Disney Co. to join George Lucas's computer-special-effects studio. In 1986 Lucas's studio was purchased by Steve Jobs, formerly of Apple Computers, and christened Pixar. Stanton became only the second animator—and ninth employee overall—hired by Pixar.

In the late 1980s the company was making short films and television commercials to display and promote the possibilities of computer animation. After Stanton had worked on a number of such projects, his talents as a writer and illustrator came into full blossom when Pixar began to develop its first feature-length computer-animated film, *Toy Story*, which would debut in theaters in 1995. Stanton contributed not only to the design of the characters in *Toy Story* but also to the film's plot line, thereby earning a co-writing credit. *Toy Story*, which features the voices of Tim Allen and Tom Hanks and follows a pair of action figures as they lead a legion of other toys on a series of misadventures (when no people are watching), made history not only as the first fully computer-animated feature film, but also as the highest-grossing film of 1995, earning more than $192 million in the United States alone. The movie—which, like all of Pixar's subsequent films, was distributed by Walt Disney—went on to gross more than $358 million worldwide. *Toy Story*'s director, John Lasseter, was presented with an award for Special Achievement at the 1996 Academy Awards ceremony, and the film earned several Oscars in technical categories. (With *Toy Story* a resounding success, Pixar gave an initial public offering of stock that same year and raised $140 million.) Many reviewers noted that *Toy Story*'s success was due in part to its appeal for people of all ages.

The Pixar team next began to develop another original feature-length film, *A Bug's Life*, about an oddball ant who searches for soldiers to save his colony from grasshoppers and winds up recruiting bugs who are actually incompetent circus performers. "Original stories are the hardest things to do," Stanton told Steve Daly for *Entertainment Weekly* (July 18, 2003) in a conversation about *Finding Nemo*. "At least, my writer's pride would like to think that. . . . They're more satisfying when you're done." For *A Bug's Life*, Stanton shared directing duties with Lasseter, as well as writing the script and serving as story artist. Typically, a director of an animated movie works with a team to develop the film's plot structure. Then the team hand-draws story reels, which are scanned into a computer and edited. Next, the script is fine-tuned as the animators, guided by the director, develop the appearances of the characters and the settings. At that point the director supervises the hiring of actors to record the dialogue. A rough draft of the film is then edited to accommodate those recordings. One sequence, called a tent-pole sequence, is fully animated, for use as a template that shows how the rest of the film should look. The animators then complete the illustrations. During that time a score and sound effects are added, and then a final version of the whole film is produced.

Released on Thanksgiving weekend in 1998, *A Bug's Life* went on to shatter all previous box-office records for that holiday weekend and ultimately earned $163 million at the U.S. box office alone. It became an international hit as well, topping $362 million in worldwide ticket sales. Like its predecessor, it earned two Academy Awards for technical achievement.

Part of Pixar's success has been the staff's willingness to lavish care on its films, letting them develop slowly and thus allowing each finished product to shine as a distinctly original work—rather than seem as if it had come off an assembly line. "To paraphrase that old wine commercial, we will release no movie before its time," Stanton remarked in an interview with Jeff Vice, movie critic for the *Deseret News* (June 1, 2003). "It's got to be aged properly." As work was being completed on *A Bug's Life*, Stanton and others were writing and developing *Toy Story 2*, which they had initially planned as a direct-to-video project. Shortly before the film was due to be released, they completely rewrote and reedited the film because, as Stanton has noted in interviews, "it sucked." When the reworked sequel—about the continuing adventures of the sentient toys—was shown to test audiences, it proved to be so popular that Pixar decided to release it theatrically. The result was another smash hit: the film earned $245 million domestically and $483 million internationally and broke box-office records in the United States, Great Britain, and Japan. The film also earned a host of awards and nominations, including a Golden Globe nomination for best picture.

With *Monsters, Inc.* (2001), Pete Docter took over the director's job while Stanton served as the film's executive producer and contributing screenwriter. The premise of the film—that monsters' actual, salaried jobs are to scare young children—grew out of Docter's own childhood fears that monsters were lurking in his closet and under his bed. *Monsters, Inc.* became the highest-grossing animated film that year, as well as the second-highest-grossing animated film in history. (It generated more than $100 million in ticket sales in just nine days.) After its release on DVD, in September 2002, it became the top-selling DVD of the year.

While Pixar was racking up hit after hit, Stanton was mulling over a film of his own, about his childhood fascination: fish. In 1992, while walking with his one-year-old son, Ben, through Marine World in San Francisco, he stopped to study an exhibit of a coral reef. He realized that computer animation had the potential to replicate everything he was seeing in that exhibit. For the time being, however, he kept his idea to himself, as no one knew if large numbers of people would be willing to sit through a computer-animated film. (Stanton's visit to Marine World took place three years before *Toy Story*'s release.) When *Toy Story* proved to be a success, he decided that computer animation might indeed bring an underwater world to life for a large audience. Yet he still needed a story. "A movie has to be about something," Stanton told Barry Koltnow for an article published in the Fort Lauderdale, Florida, *Sun-Sentinel* (June 3, 2003). "It has to be deeper than a situation. I needed a story, and I waited for something to happen that would give me that missing piece of the puzzle. There was no rush; I had plenty of work to do while I waited."

A few years later, during a walk through a neighborhood park with his son, Stanton was struck with an idea. Having put in long hours while working on *A Bug's Life,* he wanted to have some "quality time" with his son; but as the two walked through the park, "I kind of tarnished the experience because the whole time I was barking at him: 'Don't touch that! . . . Get away from there! . . . Be careful!'" Stanton recalled in an interview with Chuck Barney for the *Contra Costa Times* (May 25, 2003). "Suddenly, I became aware of what I was doing, and of how a parent can sometimes be consumed by his own protective instincts. I became obsessed with this premise that fear can deny a good father from being one."

With a story idea now clear in his mind, Stanton went to Lasseter and made an hour-long pitch for a funny, touching film about a father-and-son pair of fish. During the pitch, Stanton showed drawings he had made to give an idea of the look of the film (so-called concept drawings) and discussed his thoughts on the use of computer graphics in depicting life under the sea. Lasseter was quickly persuaded. Over the next four years, Stanton and his team immersed themselves—literally and figuratively—in the study of undersea life. They installed a fish tank in the studio and filled it with the types of fish that would be seen in the movie. They also spent hours watching videos of underwater expeditions, researched the physics of water, traveled to Hawaii for further study, and even became certified scuba divers. The staff's overarching goal was to make sure that their computer-generated water world looked real, so that audiences would feel that they were watching something really taking place under water.

In *Finding Nemo* (2003), Albert Brooks provided the voice for Marlin, a neurotic clown fish whose only child, Nemo ("voiced" by Alexander Gould, who turned nine in May 2003), is kidnaped by an Australian dentist and given to his bratty niece. In order to get his son back, Marlin enlists the aid of fish and other sea creatures, including a forgetful fish named Dory, whose voice is that of Ellen Degeneres. (Stanton contributed his own vocal talents to the role of Crush, a 152-year-old "surfer-dude" turtle.) Released on May 30, 2003, the film grossed $70.2 million in its opening weekend, shattering box-office records for an animated feature film. As of the July 4 weekend, the film had surpassed other summer blockbuster films, such as *The Hulk* and *The Matrix: Reloaded,* to become the top-grossing film of 2003, with more than $275 million in ticket sales. The film also received across-the-board praise from critics and moviegoers. In *Time* (May 26, 2003) a reviewer proclaimed: "*Nemo*, with its ravishing underwater fantasia, manages to trump the design glamour of earlier Pixar films. The dramatic set pieces—Marlin and Dory eluding jellyfish stings, Nemo's claustrophobic panic in a plastic bag—are realized with assured energy and balanced by a dozen deft comic performances, notably those of DeGeneres and Stanton himself as the lead sea turtle." David Ansen, in a review for *Newsweek* (June 2, 2003), was equally enthusiastic: "The Pixar animators have outdone themselves in creating their luminous underwater world where everything is in constant motion. Much of the movie is like a hallucinatory scuba dive, but it's equally eyepopping above the surface and within the superreal confines of the dentist's tank, where Nemo and his fellow prisoners plot their high-risk escape. . . . A visual marvel, every frame packed to the gills with clever details, *Finding Nemo* is the best big-studio release so far this year."

Despite *Finding Nemo's* phenomenal success, Stanton remains humble about his accomplishment. "No Pixar movie really belongs to one person—or a few people, for that matter," he told Jeff Vice. "We're so proud of everything we produce that everybody tries to get their fingers in the pie—and not just so they can receive part of the credit, either"—instead, he suggested, they simply desire the opportunity to participate in such projects.

Andrew Stanton lives in the San Francisco Bay area with his wife and two children. He is currently at work on two upcoming Pixar productions, "The Incredibles," due in the fall of 2004, and "Cars," scheduled for release in 2005. Stanton told Mary Kalin-Casey for Reel.com (on-line), "I remember when I was in college, somebody asked me what I wanted to do—you couldn't really start out as a director, and I don't think I ever really thought that high and mighty about wanting to be one—but I remember saying 'I like doing it all, and I can't decide.' And I feel very fortunate that that's pretty much how it's turned out in my real, professional life. I get to do it all, and I still can't decide. And fortunately, I'm not really forced to."

—C.M.

Suggested Reading: *Boston Herald* p25 June 7, 2003; *Contra Costa News* F p4 May 25, 2003; *Deseret News* W p1 May 30, 2003, E p10 June 1, 2003; *Entertainment Weekly* p36 July 18, 2003; (Fort Lauderdale, Florida) *Sun-Sentinel* E p1 June 3, 2003; Internet Movie Database (on-line); *Kansas City Star* p8 May 30, 2003; *Newsweek* p44 June 2, 2003; Pixar Studios Web site; Reel.com; *Time* p60+ May 26, 2003

Selected Films: as animator and co-writer—*Toy Story*, 1995; *Toy Story 2*, 1999; as writer, co-director, and animator—*A Bug's Life*, 1998; as co-writer and executive producer—*Monsters, Inc.*, 2001; as co-writer and director—*Finding Nemo*, 2003

Courtesy of the office of Michael Steele

Steele, Michael S.

Oct. 19, 1958– Lieutenant governor of Maryland (Republican)

Address: The Statehouse, 100 State Circle, Annapolis, MD 21401

On November 5, 2002 the Maryland Republican Party activist Michael S. Steele made history as the first African-American elected to serve as the state's lieutenant governor—or in any statewide Maryland office. A lawyer raised in a Democratic neighborhood in Washington, D.C., Steele became a member of the Republican Party while in college. His loyalty to the GOP since that time has been steadfast. In 1994 he assumed the post of chairman of the Republican Central Committee for Prince George's County, becoming the first African-American to do so, and in 2000 he was elected chairman of the Maryland State Republican Party, again making history, as the first African-American to serve as a state Republican Party chairman anywhere in the U.S. In 1998 Steele ran unsuccessfully for Maryland state comptroller. Abandoning his lucrative career as a corporate securities attorney, in 1999 he started his own consulting company, the Steele Group. While the firm never turned a profit

and Steele struggled with his personal finances, he nonetheless dedicated himself to his duties as party chairman and to making the party more attractive to Marylanders, in part by distinguishing its positions more clearly from those of the Democrats. At times he adopted positions contrary to those of his fellow Republicans. In early July 2002 he accepted the offer of then–Republican gubernatorial candidate Robert L. Ehrlich to join the GOP's ticket. "Over the last three years, I've put my family through hell," Steele told Lori Montgomery for the *Washington Post* (July 2, 2002). "But I have the conviction of belief that we're really doing something important here to try to turn this party around. The rewards, whatever they are, will come."

Michael S. Steele was born on October 19, 1958 on Andrews Air Force Base, in Prince George's County, Maryland. His biological parents gave him up for adoption through a Catholic charity, and he became the legal son of Maebell and William Steele, who had migrated to Washington, D.C., in the early 1940s from the South. Maebell Steele worked for 45 years at a laundry in the Petworth neighborhood of northwest Washington, earning the minimum wage; William Steele was a gardener. (According to several accounts, for a time he worked at John F. Kennedy's Georgetown home, when Kennedy was a U.S. senator.) In 1962 William Steele died of alcoholism-related liver disease at age 36, leaving his wife to raise their son on her own. While she had to work long hours to support him and herself, she refused to go on welfare. "I never wanted the government to raise my child," she once told the boy, as quoted by Steve Vogel in the *Washington Post* (October 31, 2002). In 1966 she married John Turner, a truck driver with the U.S. Department of Defense, with whom she had one daughter, Monica Turner. (Steele's half-sister, a pediatrician, married the boxer Mike Tyson; the couple divorced in 2003.) Throughout Steele's childhood, his mother remained a dominant figure in his life, instilling in him a strong work ethic and strict Roman Catholic values. As he recalled to Tim Craig for the *Baltimore Sun* (October 27, 2002), "It was your typical African American household. . . . The women are very, very strong." From an early age, Steele demonstrated some of the skills that would later enhance his career as a politician, such as his knack for connecting with individuals. "He was always jolly and talkative," John Turner recalled to Montgomery. "He would talk to everybody and anybody. We kept the belt kind of tight but gave him his freedom."

Throughout his childhood Steele served as an altar boy in the local Catholic church. He attended Catholic parochial schools—St. Gabriel's Elementary School and Archbishop Carroll High School. At the latter he was known as a serious student whose favorite subject was British history. Though he was never an outstanding athlete, despite his six-foot four-inch frame, Steele played soccer; he also participated in school plays. "He was Mr. Charisma," Jim Mumford, the principal of Archbishop Carroll and one of Steele's former teachers, told Craig. "He was very popular, very respected, and it was clear he had intellectual gifts." After completing high school, Steele enrolled at Johns Hopkins University, where he majored in international relations on a partial scholarship. Although his mother had urged him to attend Georgetown University, a Jesuit institution in Washington, D.C., she worked extra hours to help him pay the balance of his Johns Hopkins tuition and other expenses. "When it came to education, [my family] sacrificed," Steele told David Nitkin and Howard Libit for the *Baltimore Sun* (July 2, 2002). While studying at Johns Hopkins, Steele became involved in student politics; in his senior year he won election as president of his class. He considers that experience among the most important in his education. "I really kind of fine-tuned the art of politics," he told Vogel. "Student government associations are state parties in miniature. You've got to build coalitions, work with diverse constituencies, learn how to hold your own." During that period Steele also found himself leaning toward the Republican Party; he had been inspired by Ronald Reagan's 1980 presidential campaign, particularly its emphasis on smaller government. (He and his stepfather, a confirmed Democrat, debated passionately about politics at the dinner table.) "I know for a lot of blacks, they hear Ronald Reagan and they say, 'Oh, my God,'" he told Craig. "But if you listened to the man he made a lot of sense, he talked about the core values my mother and grandmother talked about. For me, the [Republican] party was a very, very comfortable fit."

Steele graduated from Johns Hopkins University in 1981 with a B.A. degree in international relations. While he considered pursuing the field of law or medicine, he also harbored strong feelings about entering a different type of life: that of a Catholic priest. Toward that end, he entered the Augustinian Friars Seminary at Villanova University, in Villanova, Pennsylvania, and studied religion and philosophy for a year. The following year he accepted an invitation to become a novitiate and live as an Augustinian monk in Lawrence, Massachusetts. As the time approached for him to take the vows of poverty, chastity, and obedience and thus formally enter the religious community, Steele felt himself getting increasingly less sure about his chosen path. After much thought, he told Vogel, he "decided God was calling me to come back to the world." As he said to Craig, "It came down to 'Am I called to serve the people of God as a priest or in a business suit?'"

In 1983 Steele returned to Washington, D.C., and took a job as a paralegal at the law offices of Hunton & Williams. He also began dating Andrea Derritt, a friend whom he had known at Johns Hopkins; the couple married in 1985. Soon afterward he gained admittance to the Georgetown University Law School, where he began attending night classes; he earned a J.D. degree in 1991. He was then hired as an associate at the Washington, D.C.–based international law firm Cleary, Gottlieb, Steen & Hamilton, where he worked from 1991 to 1997. Most of Steele's assignments during that period dealt with financial transactions of Wall Street underwriters. He also worked in the firm's office in Tokyo, Japan, specializing in the area of product-liability litigation, and in its office in London, England, representing clients during initial public offerings of stock on the London Stock Exchange. In 1997 Steele left Cleary, because he had concluded that he was not on track to become a partner in the firm. Having been what he described to Montgomery as a "middle-of-the-road law student," he said that he had never expected to rise through the company's upper ranks. "I just wanted to prove I could get there," he explained. He took a position as in-house counsel for the real-estate development firm Mills Corp., located in Arlington, Virginia. (Steele, who was admitted to the Pennsylvania bar one year after earning his J.D. degree, was never admitted to the bars of Virginia, Maryland, or the District of Columbia; however, such memberships were not required for the positions he held at Cleary or the Mills Corp.)

Throughout the 1990s Steele became increasingly active in Republican politics. He had attended his first party event, the Prince George's County Republican Party Lincoln Day dinner, in 1988, shortly after moving from Washington to Largo, Maryland. As he recalled to Craig, "I got to the event, and I was all psyched to be there. I was thinking, 'Wow. Maryland, they've got a state party, they have a county party. They have an organization.'" Steele's enthusiasm was quickly deflated when he found himself ignored, if not ostracized, by everyone at the dinner except the keynote speaker, Elizabeth Dole, who was then U.S. secretary of transportation. "I was not welcome at all," he noted. "I was an outsider, a new face." While many of Steele's relatives and friends argued that his experience proved that a black man would not be welcomed by the Republican Party, Steele nevertheless vowed to continue to devote much of his time and efforts to local Republican politics. "A lot of people said they would have just walked away," he said to Craig, "but I had a different conclusion. I knew the only way to change the Republican Party was to get involved and turn this party around to make it more warm and welcoming."

Steele honored his pledge, continuing his grassroots involvement with the local party. In 1994 he won a seat on the Prince George's County Republican Central Committee. Within months he had been named its chairman, marking the first time that an African-American held the position. Steele worked hard to elevate his party's prominence within the community. At that time in Prince George's County, registered Democrats outnumbered registered Republicans six to one; the percentage of registered Republicans had declined in recent years. In one notable achievement in 1996, Steele led a successful referendum campaign against a ballot initiative supported by County Executive Wayne K. Curry, a Democrat, which would have resulted in a repeal of the county's cap on property taxes. Despite the influence of Curry, who is African-American, over 60 percent of the voters who cast their ballots rejected the measure. In 1998 Steele was recruited by the Republican candidate for governor, Ellen R. Sauerbrey, to run on the GOP ticket for state comptroller, the chief fiscal officer for the state. Still relatively unknown, Steele assured Michael Dresser for the *Baltimore Sun* (July 15, 1998) that he provided voters with "a choice between the old style of machine politics and a new style of leadership." After a campaign that he described to Craig as "freeing," he finished third in the Republican Party's September primary.

That taste of the political life inspired Steele to leave his job at the Mills Corp. after 18 months and to start his own business, the Steele Group, a legal consulting firm. Because he had never passed Maryland's bar, Steele was unable to charge clients standard legal fees; in addition, many of his clients never paid him anything. His company never turned a profit, and Steele was forced to drain his retirement savings to keep afloat financially. According to court records in Prince George's County, two banks filed foreclosure proceedings against Steele and his wife after the couple failed to make payments on their home mortgage and a separate home equity loan in 2001. (Steele resolved both problems and kept his home.) "It was a tough juggle," he told Craig, "but I survived through it."

In December 2000, after campaigning nearly one year for the position, Steele was elected chairman of the Maryland State Republican Party. The unpaid position, while a boon to his political career, caused even more financial strain for Steele and his family. Despite those hardships, he threw himself into the task of reinvigorating Maryland's Republican Party, which had not succeeded in electing a Republican governor since Spiro T. Agnew's election in 1966. Steele was credited with helping to give the Republican Party a new face and thus broadening its appeal to black voters and other minorities, who have traditionally supported Democrats; he also helped to boost fund-raising in preparation for the 2002 gubernatorial campaign. He was the first Maryland Republican Party chairman to serve on the Republican National Committee's board of directors.

Steele supported some positions that leaders of his party opposed. For example, he advocated affirmative action—favorable treatment based on race or gender in situations in which individuals were deemed disadvantaged because of their race or sex—and restoring voting rights to some felons. He also tried to transform Maryland's GOP into what he described to Daniel LeDuc for the *Washington Post* (July 2, 2002) as "a true opposition party." One of his most aggressive attacks against the state Democrats came in the summer of 2002, when Steele led his party's efforts to challenge a redistricting plan set forth by Democratic governor Par-

ris N. Glendening. (In Maryland, district lines are redrawn every 10 years to reflect shifts in population.) The governor's plan potentially would have facilitated Democrats' gaining seats in the state House of Delegates (which, with the state Senate, makes up Maryland's General Assembly). In response, Steele filed a petition in the Maryland Court of Appeals, the state's highest court, accusing state Senate president Thomas V. Mike Miller Jr. and three other state senators of having improperly contacted judges to discuss the legislative redistricting while more than a dozen lawsuits regarding the plan were pending. He filed similar complaints with the State Ethics Commission and the General Assembly's Joint Committee on Legislative Ethics. In June 2002 the Court of Appeals rejected Glendening's redistricting plan. Steele's efforts prompted state investigations into the lawmakers' conduct; the General Assembly's ethics committee later reprimanded Miller for his actions, saying that he had "abused his position" as Senate president, as quoted by Howard Libit in the *Baltimore Sun* (August 17, 2002). Paul D. Ellington, the executive director of the state Republican Party in 2002–03 (and currently Steele's chief of staff), told Craig that Steele was "probably the most active [Maryland Republican Party] chairman we have ever had."

On July 1, 2002 Robert L. Ehrlich, a U.S. congressman from Maryland and Republican candidate for governor, announced his choice of Steele as his running mate in the upcoming election. Ehrlich's Democratic opponent was Kathleen Kennedy Townsend, who was then the state's lieutenant governor (and whose father was the late U.S. senator and attorney general Robert F. Kennedy). Steele became the second African-American to run for the lieutenant governor's post in Maryland. In making his choice of Steele public, Ehrlich said, as quoted by Nitkin and Libit, "Today is born the opportunity ticket in the state of Maryland. It's history standing before you today. Working together, Republicans, Democrats, Independents, black, white—it doesn't matter. The old lines are gone. This is a new era. It's a new generation." While Ehrlich and Steele shared similar views on many issues, they differed on others. For example, Steele staunchly opposed abortion, while Ehrlich favored abortion rights in many cases; Ehrlich supported the death penalty, whereas Steele firmly opposed it and endorsed Governor Glendening's moratorium on executions. Nevertheless, Steele maintained that such differences would have little impact on his ability to serve Ehrlich effectively. "It's part of my religious upbringing," he told Daniel LeDuc. "I will follow the next governor. I will argue my beliefs when asked." The Ehrlich–Steele platform called for balancing the state's budget, improving education, combating crime, reforming the juvenile justice system, expanding health-care opportunities for Marylanders, cleaning up Chesapeake Bay, and initiating a "new era of governance" in the state's capital.

Midway through the campaign, when, as required, Steele filed financial disclosure reports with the State Ethics Commission, his personal monetary troubles became an issue. Although he was running on a ticket emphasizing fiscal responsibility, Steele had debts in excess of $35,000 and a $25,000 unpaid loan from his 1998 campaign for state comptroller. Steele defended his situation, telling Montgomery for the *Washington Post* (July 4, 2002), "At least my report reflects a blue-collar man, an entrepreneur out there trying to start a business in Maryland. . . . I don't have trusts that are going to cover me. I don't have that luxury." In part to help diffuse Steele's financial strain, Maryland's GOP in August hired the candidate as a consultant, for which he was to be paid $5,000 per month for the remaining six months of 2002. Democrats assailed the deal, claiming that Steele was being paid to serve as a candidate, but he insisted that, as he told Craig Whitlock for the *Washington Post* (August 28, 2002), "There's nothing illegal or unethical or immoral about it." Under the terms of the contract to which he and Republican Party officials agreed, his tasks included raising money for the party, advising candidates, and creating a long-term plan for the state Republican Party—many of the same duties that he had undertaken as state party chairman.

On November 5, 2002, despite the fact that registered Democrats outnumbered Republicans statewide by nearly two to one and Maryland had not had a Republican governor in more than 30 years, Ehrlich and Steele won the election. "Welcome to history," Ehrlich announced in his acceptance speech, as quoted by S. A. Miller and Vaishali Honawar in the *Washington Times* (November 6, 2002). "There's walking history here, and his name is Michael Steele." Soon after, Ehrlich announced that Steele would lead his transition team and would play an active role as lieutenant governor, focusing on economic development and education. "I have to be prepared to hit the ground running," Steele told Steve Vogel for the *Washington Post* (November 7, 2002). Ehrlich and Steele were sworn into office on January 15, 2003.

According to his biography on the Maryland state government Web site, Steele's priorities include "reforming the state's Minority Business Enterprise [MBE] program, improving the quality of Maryland's public education system, expanding economic development in the state and fostering cooperation between government and faith-based organizations to help those in need." Within two months of his inauguration, Steele told Todd Beacon for the *Baltimore Sun* (March 10, 2003, online) that bureaucratic obstacles, lack of accountability, and inaccurate or misleading record-keeping had thwarted the MBE program. "It's not enough just to create these businesses, and give them access to credit and capital, but it's also our responsibility to make sure that the incentives are there for them to invest back in the neighborhood," he told Beacon. "We want to take the boards off those boarded-up buildings and homes and businesses in Baltimore and allow businesses to come in to create jobs for young people and to create a sense of community identity that's tied to the life and the quality of life in that community." The Governor's Commission on Minority Business Enterprise Reform, established in June 2003 and headed by Steele, presented its findings to Ehrlich six months later. On February 27, 2004 the governor announced that, based on the commission's report, he was proposing legislation that would require the government to award at least 10 percent of state contracts to minority-owned businesses and would require all contractors, when making bids, to identify the minority subcontractors they intended to hire. Among other measures, the governor also proposed reforms of the bidding process and the formation of a mentoring program whereby small and minority businesses would learn from successful larger enterprises.

In April 2004 the Maryland legislature approved a spending plan designed to decrease the state's $1 billion budget deficit and raise enough money to pay for the recently adopted Thornton Commission plan, which called for an increase of $1.3 billion in spending on education annually. The legislature rejected the plan supported by Governor Ehrlich and Lieutenant Governor Steele to increase revenues to the state by legalizing 10,500 slot machines (also known as one-armed bandits) at three Maryland racetracks and at a fourth that was scheduled for construction. Instead, the lawmakers opted to raise fees, such as the tax on cigarettes. Greater-than-anticipated revenue from Maryland's income and other taxes in the current fiscal year have also helped to shrink the deficit.

On another front, Steele, with the approval of the governor, launched a study of capital punishment in Maryland, in an effort to determine why a disproportionate number of the inmates on death row were black people (eight out of a total of 12) or people convicted in Baltimore County (nine of the 12) and why, statistically, the killer of a white person is far more likely to be sentenced to death than someone who kills a member of racial minority. (Each of the 12 people on death row murdered a white person.) "Clearly, there's a linkage to race, and clearly there's a linkage to jurisdiction," Steele said at a press conference, according to Sarah Koenig and Stephanie Hanes in the *Baltimore Sun* (January 28, 2003, on-line). A moratorium on capital punishment imposed by Parris Glendening during his tenure as governor is still in force in Maryland. Steele's extensive public service includes his chairmanship of the Maryland State Minority Outreach Task Force (1995–97) and his work as a member of the NAACP (National Association for the Advancement of Colored People) Blue Ribbon Panel on Election Reform (2001). He hosted an hour-long radio program, *Lunchtime with Maryland's GOP*, on the local Baltimore radio station WOLB-AM for a while and has appeared on such television programs as *Politically Incorrect with*

Bill Maher, Metro Talk, the *Joe Madison Show*, *Capitol Sunday*, and *BET Tonight*. On September 1, 2004 he spoke at the Republican National Convention, in New York City, in support of President George W. Bush's reelection bid.

Steele lives in Largo, Maryland, with his wife, Andrea, and two sons, Michael II and Drew. He is an active member of St. Mary's Catholic Church in Landover Hills, Maryland, and in 1998 was honored by his church community as "man of the year."

—K.A.D.

Suggested Reading: *Baltimore Sun* A p1+ July 15, 1998, with photo, A p1+ July 2, 2002, with photo, B p1 Oct. 27, 2002, with photo; (Maryland) Office of the Governor Web site; Maryland State Archives Web site; *Washington Post* A p1 July 2, 2002, B p8 July 2, 2002, B p2 July 4, 2002, B p5 Aug. 28, 2002, B p1 Oct. 31, 2002; *Washington Times* B p1 Nov. 6, 2002

Courtesy of World Wide Technologies

Steward, David L.

July 2, 1951– Founder and chairman of World Wide Technology Inc.

Address: World Wide Technology Inc., 60 Weldon Pkwy., St. Louis, MO 63043

David L. Steward is the founder, chairman of the board, and former chief executive officer of World Wide Technology Inc. (WWT), a leading electronic procurement and logistics company in the information-technology (IT) and telecommunications industry—as well as the largest African-American–owned business in the country. A "well-connected, gregarious entrepreneur," according to Derek T. Dingle in *Black Enterprise* (June 1998), Steward is also the chairman of Telco-buy.com, an Internet marketplace that specializes in providing technology products and services to the telecommunications industry. Over the past 20 years, Steward has transformed what began as a small entrepreneurial venture into a billion-dollar business with offices all over the United States. A devout Christian, he has attributed his financial success to a combination of business savvy and professional ethics, citing the Bible as a main source of inspiration and guidance. During an interview for the LifeChasers Web site in early 2003, he explained, "Employees watch and mimic those values that they see exhibited to them by their leaders. I try to set the tone for our company to be a giving and serving culture. . . . I want that attitude to permeate our whole organization." WWT employees have cited state-of-the-art office facilities and generous benefits packages as evidence of Steward's commitment to worker satisfaction. In *Black Enterprise* (June 30, 1999), Tariq K. Muhammad wrote, "Profit-making aside, it's obvious that Steward pays as much attention to his employees' needs as his customers'."

Born in Chicago, Illinois, on July 2, 1951, David L. Steward grew up in Clinton, Missouri. His father was a mechanic. His mother always told Steward and his brothers and sisters, as he recalled for an article in the business section of the *New York Times* (October 31, 2001), "You can do anything you want." The only African-American male in his class, Steward graduated from Clinton Senior High School in 1969. He studied management at Central Missouri State University, in Warrensburg, earning a bachelor's degree in 1973. Like his grandfather, a Pullman porter, and several of his siblings, Steward began his professional career at a railroad company, working in sales and marketing for the Missouri Pacific Railroad. He has noted parallels between his early experiences as a railroad employee and his later experiences as the head of WWT, telling Derek T. Dingle, "I traded in one transportation system for another. . . . But now I am responsible for moving information." He later held a sales and marketing position at Wagner Electric Corp. and a management job at Federal Express Corp., where he was a top salesman.

Unsatisfied with the extent of his achievements at Federal Express, Steward decided to strike out on his own. "I didn't want to wake up at 70 or 80 and wonder why I didn't do more," he wrote in his *New York Times* article. He embarked on his first entrepreneurial venture, a company called Transport Business Specialists (TBS), in 1984. Having learned that railroad companies were losing hundreds of thousands of dollars through inadequate billing procedures, Steward launched TBS to audit shipping rates and rectify inefficiencies among rail and trucking companies carrying commercial freight. In 1987 Union Pacific Railroad contracted TBS to audit three years' worth of freight bills, a massive project that led Steward to expand the scope of his business. "The only way to handle that amount of information," he told Tariq K. Muhammad, "was through a local area network to link all their operations, so we built the biggest one in St. Louis at the time." Realizing that he could further boost the efficiency of his clients' operations through the development of such local area networks (LANs), Steward founded a second company, Transportation Administrative Services (TAS), which built on TBS's computerized auditing system to create an even larger and more complex system of network applications. Encouraged by that venture's successful integration of technology and business practice, Steward broadened and diversified his commercial interests. In 1990, together with James Kavanaugh, a former sales and technology specialist at Future Electronics, a technology distributor based in Montreal, Canada, Steward launched WWT, an Internet-based marketplace dedicated to the buying and selling of IT products and services, including computer hardware and software. Kavanaugh did not own any part of the company at that point.

WWT began humbly, with a staff of four and 4,000 square feet of office space. Steward leveraged $250,000 in seed money from his other companies to fund the venture, which was conceived as a means of distributing technology products and services to the federal government and installing IT systems at corporations as well as government agencies. At first Kavanaugh managed WWT's day-to-day operations while Steward divided his time among his three businesses; eventually Steward shut down TBS and TAS in order to focus his energies on WWT. The four founding members of the company (readily available sources do not name the other two) developed an initial customer base by cold-calling potential clients listed in the local telephone directory. Steward used his corporate contacts to secure WWT's first contract—an agreement to provide computer equipment and technical support to Southwestern Bell Telephone Co., which remains one of WWT's largest customers. Another early customer was McDonnell Douglas (now Boeing Defense and Space Group). Before long WWT had established professional relationships with other large companies, in the automotive, retail, and telecommunications industries, as well as with government agencies. The firm, which Steward has described as "a one-stop shop," as quoted by Matthew S. Scott in *Black Enterprise* (June 2001), currently maintains strategic partnerships with many industry leaders, among them Alcatel, Cisco Systems, Fujitsu, IBM, Lucent Technologies, Netscape Communications, Oracle, Sun Microsystems, and Tellabs.

In 1992 WWT reported revenues of $8 million. Concurrently, by 1993, the company had amassed about $3.5 million in debt, due in part to misappropriation of funds by some of Steward's colleagues.

"It was a difficult time on many levels," Steward said during the LifeChasers interview. "They were people I had known and trusted for years. Looking back, I believe God allowed it to happen to prepare me for the success that came later and is ahead." Determined to get back on track, Steward and Kavanaugh discussed ways in which they might be able to improve WWT's operations. They decided to create "a more team-oriented approach to developing the company," as Kavanaugh told Tariq K. Muhammad, and to focus more on customer service. Steward promised Kavanaugh ownership of at least 15 percent of the company if they could turn WWT around and make it profitable.

In 1993 WWT expanded its services to include the integration of telecommunications networks and company-wide consulting and imaging. (The last-named service is a process in which companies served by WWT streamline their paperwork by transforming paper documents into electronic images that can then be filed away in computers.) The addition of these services enabled the company to secure several lucrative government contracts, which brought in $30 million over 18 months in 1993 and 1994 and generated 71 percent of gross revenues in 1998. WWT secured additional contracts with telecommunications companies. Two years after Steward and Kavanaugh began implementing their new business plan, WWT emerged from debt. The company has been debt-free ever since. In 1994, when revenues totaled $17 million, Steward honored his pledge to Kavanaugh, making him his only equity partner, with a 15 percent ownership stake.

Between 1990 and 1997 WWT's staff grew to more than 150. The company's 1997 gross sales topped $135 million, a 1,325 percent increase over 1992 sales. In 1997 WWT was selected from a field of 25 bidders to become one of three minority-owned companies to sign a $150 million, five-year contract with Southwestern Bell and Lucent Technologies. According to the terms of the agreement, Lucent Technologies was contracted to sell electronic component materials to WWT and the other two selected companies, who then tested, assembled and configured the materials for use in Southwestern Bell's telecommunications network. Also in 1997 WWT implemented an Oracle enterprise resource planning (ERP) system, which linked all of WWT's internal operations and cut down on redundancy and misinformation by allowing employees to enter data into a central database. The Oracle ERP system served as the basis for WWT's Internet-based customer-service operations, which Tariq K. Muhammad described as "WWT's signature" and "one of the company's most innovative offerings," by making inventory and shipping information readily available to employees, vendors, and customers. That year, Steward was honored with the federal Small Business Administration's (SBA) Minority Small Business Person of the Year award for Missouri, Iowa, Kansas, and Nebraska, an annual distinction limited to 10 businesspeople.

In 1998 WWT earned revenues of nearly $203 million, prompting *Black Enterprise* magazine to rank it 11th on its list of leading African-American–owned industrial and service companies. That same year Steward was named Technology Entrepreneur of the Year by Ernst & Young, ranked as 14th-best entrepreneur in the U.S. by *Success* magazine, and named the 33d annual Small Business Person of the Year by the St. Louis Regional Chamber and Growth Association (RCGA) and the SBA.

The following year WWT more than doubled its sales, with revenues of about $413 million. Federal business generated 50 percent of the total, telecommunications 35 percent, and commercial business 15 percent. WWT was named *Black Enterprise*'s company of the year for 1999, having ascended to number six in the magazine's rankings of African-American–owned industrial and service businesses. Furthermore, Steward was named Missouri's Small Business Person of the Year by the SBA.

Also in 1999, with $25 million invested by two Boston-based venture-capital firms, WWT created Telcobuy.com, a spin-off company that started as the telecommunications division of WWT. Steward and other WWT executives teamed up with telecommunications and IT providers to establish a business-to-business service offering telecommunications and IT products over the Internet, with Telcobuy.com receiving a small percentage of each transaction. The new company specialized in helping customers build and deploy IT infrastructure, virtual private-network (VPN) security, universal dial access, wireless LAN services, and logistics, technical, and electronic-business (e-business) consulting. While Steward remained chairman of WWT and became a majority owner and board member of Telcobuy, Kavanaugh stepped down as president and chief operating officer of WWT to become Telcobuy's chief executive officer. Telcobuy's gross revenues for 1999 were about $250 million, up from about $50 million in 1998. In 2000 Telcobuy filed to make an initial public stock offering of up to $100 million, but withdrew the offering that December, citing unfavorable market conditions for Internet stocks. The company's sales and gross revenue soared that year, but Telcobuy did not record a profit.

In addition to Telcobuy, WWT has launched two other e-business portals: Fedbuy.com, which is aimed at government buyers of computer equipment, and Ugsource.com, which targets computer-aided design engineers. In combination the three e-marketplaces generated 75 percent of WWT's 1999 revenues, thanks largely to the increasing popularity of Web-based commerce. The *St. Louis Business Journal* (February 14, 2000) noted that the kind of e-commerce to which Telcobuy is dedicated, "between businesses rather than between retailers and consumers, is the fastest-growing part of the Internet." According to Steward, as quoted in *Black Enterprise* (June 30, 2000), "The utilization of the Web has allowed us to grow the business, bring value to customers and supplier relationships and drive down the cost of business. . . . The e-marketplaces have changed the way we do business with our partners and clients. The availability of information is much broader and deeper than ever before."

In 2000 WWT had revenues of $802 million, nearly double the company's 1999 earnings. That year, to keep up with growth, WWT hired 156 new workers, bringing the company's total staff to 516. *Black Enterprise* magazine named WWT America's most successful black-owned company, marking the first time that a technology company had ascended to the top of that list. Also in 2000 WWT was honored by *Federal Computer Week* and *Washington Technology* as the top minority technology contractor in America.

In 2001 WWT's revenues climbed to $924 million, and the company was again rated the most successful African-American–owned business in the U.S. by *Black Enterprise.* Telcobuy.com ranked fourth, with revenues of over $600 million, and that same year the *St. Louis Business Journal* awarded Telcobuy first place in the business-to-business category of its annual e-business awards.

In 2002 WWT's revenues dropped to $716 million and the business relinquished its position as *Black Enterprise*'s number-one African-American–owned company, slipping to seventh in the rankings. However, Telcobuy, with 2002 revenues of $604 million, ranked second on the magazine's list of industrial and service companies. That same year WWT launched SDE Business Partnering (renamed World Wide Technology—Automotive in January 2004), a spin-off company focused on serving the automotive industry. In May 2002 Steward was featured in *Ebony* as one of the 100 most influential black people in the U.S.

In 2003 WWT revenues climbed to $1.1 billion, making it only the second black-owned company in history to record annual earnings of over a billion dollars. That year WWT and Telcobuy.com merged to become the World Wide Technology Holding Co. Inc. (WWT Holding).

In 2004, with Robert L. Shook, Steward published *Doing Business by the Good Book: 52 Lessons on Success Straight from the Bible.* In it he outlined 52 ways in which he has applied biblical principles to business; he also described his professional experiences in terms of his religious faith. "I believe in applying biblical principles to all my life—principles like sowing and reaping and blessing and giving to others and seeing it return to you," Steward commented during the Life-Chasers interview. "It's not just about what is good business. It's about what is good for the broader scope of my life. My whole life is God's business." Also in 2004 Blackmoney.com named Steward one of the 50 most important African-Americans in the field of technology. In June 2004, as it had in 2000 and 2001, *Black Enterprise* hailed WWT as the largest black-owned business in the U.S. According to Derek T. Dingle, as quoted in the *St. Louis*

Business Journal (May 13, 2004), WWT Holding's "strategy to recombine its World Wide Technology and Telcobuy.com units as well as aggressively pursue government and corporate contracts paid off handsomely." Currently, WWT and Telcobuy.com are the nation's leading electronic-procurement and logistics companies in the information-technology and telecommunications industries.

David Steward has served on many boards in the St. Louis metropolitan area, including those of the St. Louis RCGA, the Missouri Technology Corp., the Centene Corp., Webster University, the Harris-Stowe State College African-American Business Leadership Council, Barnes-Jewish Hospital, First Banks Inc., St. Louis Science Center, United Way of Greater St. Louis, and the Greater St. Louis Area Council of Boy Scouts of America. In September 2000 he became the first African-American to be elected to membership in Civic Progress of St. Lou-

is, an organization of chief executives from leading St. Louis–area businesses. In 2003 the National Minority Supplier Development Council honored him for his long-term achievements in minority business development.

Steward lives in St. Louis with his wife, Thelma Steward, a registered nurse, and their children. In 2000 the couple co-chaired the United Way's African-American Leadership Giving Initiative, a fund-raising effort aimed at wealthy and middle-class black Americans.

—L.W.

Suggested Reading: *Black Enterprise* p146+ June 1998, p118+ June 30, 1999; *New York Times* C p6 Oct. 31, 2001

Selected Books: *Doing Business by the Good Book: 52 Lessons on Success Straight from The Bible*, 2004

Matthew Peyton/Getty Images

Stewart, Jon

Nov. 28, 1962– Comedian; host of the Daily Show

Address: Daily Show, *513 W. 54th St., New York, NY 10019*

In September 2003, when U.S. senator John Edwards of North Carolina made the on-air announcement of his candidacy for the Democratic presidential nomination, he did so not on a news program on ABC, CBS, NBC, or Fox News, but on

a cable-TV comedy show. Far from puzzling voters or frustrating the candidate's campaign staff, the announcement on the *Daily Show*, which airs on the Comedy Central channel, lent Edwards an air of hipness among the coveted demographic of viewers under 35. Edwards's choice of venue spoke volumes about the *Daily Show*'s status as a cultural touchstone, and much of the credit for the program's influence on the public belongs to Jon Stewart. Before he took over hosting duties, in 1999, the humor of the faux newsmagazine often targeted entertainment celebrities or focused on light or bizarre news stories. Stewart oversaw the revamping of the show's focus, which is now on politics, current events, and the news media, and during his tenure the *Daily Show*'s ratings—like its reputation among critics—have risen dramatically.

"Deftly parodying a medium that regularly borders on self-parody is a formidable challenge, which hasn't prevented Comedy Central's *The Daily Show with Jon Stewart* from becoming a welcome alternative to the unintentionally amusing TV news that runs against it," Brian Lowry wrote for the *Los Angeles Times* (May 26, 2003). He added, "Stewart's program remains one of the few truly clever half-hours on television." In an article for *Newsweek* (December 29, 2003–January 5, 2004, on-line), Marc Peyser and Sarah Childress wrote, "The program . . . is becoming the coolest pit stop on television. And it does it the hard way. Unlike late-night talk shows that traffic in Hollywood interviews and stupid pet tricks, the *Daily Show* is a fearless social satire." Prior to his success with the *Daily Show,* Stewart worked in television as a comic actor and comedy writer and appeared in a half-dozen films. He also authored the best-selling humorous volume *Naked Pictures of Famous People.*

The comedian was born Jonathan Stewart Leibowitz in New York City on November 28, 1962 to Donald and Marian Leibowitz. He grew up in Lawrence, New Jersey. His father was a physicist, while his mother worked as an educational consultant and special-education teacher. Stewart has recalled that belonging to one of the few Jewish families in the middle-class town made him a target for anti-Semitic slurs and bullying; on one occasion, when he was in seventh grade, he was punched out at a bus stop. His parents divorced when he was 12 (some sources say 10). He harbored deep resentment of his father, who later remarried and had more children, and remains distant from him. (Donald Leibowitz has reportedly never seen his son perform.) Stewart graduated from Lawrence High School in 1980 and earned a B.A. degree in psychology from William and Mary College, in Williamsburg, Virginia, in 1984. He has described his years in Williamsburg as unhappy; he was a member of Pi Kappa Alpha fraternity for six months before quitting because he disliked the hazing rituals and forced camaraderie. He did, however, enjoy playing on the soccer team, which continues to give out an award called the "Leibo"—named for Stewart—to the team clown.

After graduation Stewart returned to New Jersey, where he held a series of odd jobs, such as putting on puppet shows about the handicapped for public-school children and working at a pet store. His older brother, Larry, fired him from the latter job after he jumped into a beanbag chair in the store and crashed into some aquariums, causing over $10,000 in damage. "I was a little lost from the age of eighteen to twenty-four," he told Tad Friend for the New Yorker (February 11, 2002). "I had my midlife crisis early. In 1986, I was living in Hamilton, New Jersey, working for the state and bartending and playing on a landscape company's softball team. I started thinking, This is it for the next seventy years? So I told my mom I was going to New York to do comedy." On his second night as a standup comic at the Bitter End, a New York club, he dropped his last name—both because the emcee had trouble pronouncing it and because Stewart associated the name with the resentment he still felt over having been taunted during his childhood. "It was grueling and hilarious," he told Bruce Fretts for Entertainment Weekly (October 31, 2003) of his standup years. "I remember walking home at three in the morning going, If it doesn't get any better than this, it's still better than I ever thought it'd be."

Stewart's first break came when he served as the opening act for a Sheena Easton concert in Las Vegas, Nevada. His performance caught the attention of executives at Comedy Central, who hired him to host the television series Short Attention Span Theater for the cable station in 1989. He was also a writer and occasional performer for the short-lived Comedy Central sketch-comedy series The Sweet Life, which aired the same year. He wrote for Caroline's Comedy Hour in the early 1990s, and in 1992 he hosted You Wrote It, You Watch It, writing most of the skits for the latter show, which ran on MTV. In addition, he appeared on HBO's Young Comedians Special. As Stewart became better known, there were rumors that he would replace various departing late-night talk-show hosts; he was mentioned as a possible successor to David Letterman on Late Night, when Letterman moved to CBS, but the job went to Conan O'Brien.

Stewart had his own half-hour program on MTV, the Jon Stewart Show, in 1993. Although MTV soon dropped the show, Paramount picked it up, expanding it into a one-hour talk show featuring celebrity guests from the worlds of music, entertainment, sports, and fashion and airing the program in syndication from September 1994 through June 1995. Despite its short run, the Jon Stewart Show gained its host a great deal of attention; among his antics on the program were sitting on the lap of the actor William Shatner and playing ping-pong with the tennis star Gabriella Sabatini. In the mid-1990s Stewart participated in Comedy Central's national "Stand Up for Sanity" comedy tour and also did some acting, including several appearances as himself on The Larry Sanders Show—the premise being that he was trying to take over the fictional talk show from its eponymous host (played by Garry Shandling). Stewart also served as a creative consultant on the series. His one-hour HBO comedy special, Jon Stewart: Unleavened, which aired in September 1996, was nominated for a CableAce Award. He has had guest spots on the television series The Nanny (1997), NewsRadio (1997), and Spin City (1999) and was host of the Sesame Street special Elmopalooza in 1998. The films in which he appeared during those years include Mixed Nuts (1994), Wishful Thinking (1997), Half Baked (1998), the TV film Since You've Been Gone (1998), The Faculty (1998), and Playing by Heart (1998).

Stewart's book Naked Pictures of Famous People (1998) made the best-seller list of the New York Times. The book skewers public figures ranging from Martha Stewart to Adolf Hitler and includes an imagined correspondence between Princess Diana and Mother Teresa. The 18 pieces in Naked Pictures of Famous People are "on a par with Woody Allen's Without Feathers and Steve Martin's Cruel Shoes," Bruce Fretts wrote in a review for Entertainment Weekly (October 2, 1998), giving the book an "A-" rating. Fretts called the book "brutally witty" and concluded, "Naked Pictures reveals a basic truth that's too often forgotten by the shock-for-shock's-sake satirists of the South Park era: You've got to be smart to be a smart-ass."

Stewart took over hosting duties on the Daily Show, which airs on Comedy Central, on January 11, 1999, after Craig Kilborn left the program to host the Late Late Show on CBS. (Stewart had often filled in for Tom Snyder, the previous host of the Late Late Show, and it had been rumored that he might take over that job when Snyder left.) Stewart's contract includes a $1.5 million salary, which is quite high for cable television (although low compared with the salaries of network television late-night hosts), as well as time off to pursue acting jobs. In addition, his name was added to the program's title, which is now officially the *Daily Show with Jon Stewart*. The program airs Monday through Thursday nights at 11 p.m., Eastern Standard Time, opposite several network news programs. The *Daily Show* was described as "a welcome antidote to the rise in self-important TV newsmagazines, blustering pundits and celebrity-worship programming" by Paul Brownfield, writing in the *Los Angeles Times* (December 25, 1998). Under Stewart, the show concentrates less on appearance-based humor and more on significant current events. While the administration of President George W. Bush is a frequent target of jokes, the media, particularly local and cable news, is the primary object of ridicule. Celebrities from the entertainment world are still among the guests and provide fodder for jokes, though several observers have noted that the show is at its weakest when tweaking show business.

The September 11, 2001 terrorist attacks on the World Trade Center and the Pentagon shook Stewart and signaled a further shift in the show's focus. Stewart, who lives in downtown Manhattan, where the attacks occurred, told Tad Friend, "I felt sick, I didn't want to eat. I felt like I imagine a person feels when he's depressed." The staff of the *Daily Show* met two days later at its offices in the Hell's Kitchen neighborhood of Manhattan. The show resumed on September 20, with Stewart giving a nine-minute monologue on his feelings about the disaster. "They said to get back to work," he began, as quoted by Friend. "And there were no jobs available for a man in the fetal position, which I gladly would have taken." He concluded by noting, "The view from my apartment was the World Trade Center. Now it's gone. . . . But you know what the view is now? The Statue of Liberty. You can't beat that." While the show was noticeably timid for several weeks about attacking America's political leadership, it was soon getting laughs by mocking the paranoid tone of the press. Many critics have said that the show hit its stride after September 11, targeting a media that was often hyperbolic, fear-mongering, and blindly patriotic. "It's as though there's only two positions you can have—you're either for the war or against the troops," Stewart complained to David Folkenflik for the *Baltimore Sun* (April 22, 2003). Stewart stands in contrast to many other late-night television hosts, who have softened their attacks on political figures since the start of the Bush administration's war on terror. Many of his guests are political commentators, politicians, and journalists, who are usually treated seriously, although Stewart does not hesitate to make jokes at their expense. While the show is often said to promote a liberal viewpoint and to be anti-Republican, Stewart has also been merciless with regard to the Democratic Party; for example, in the

early stages of the 2004 campaign, the show called its coverage of the Democratic contenders "The Race from the White House," claiming that none of the candidates could succeed in ousting Bush.

Stewart has said that many in the media are "too easy" on politicians. "They've forgotten that their relationship with politics is an adversarial one," he said in a presentation at Harvard University's Kennedy School of Government, as reported by Katie Krey on the school's Web site (December 16, 2002). He also maintains that politicians are adept at manipulating news professionals, who have "never caught up. They've let everyone down, and that's a shame." In an interview with Peter Jennings for ABC News (December 12, 2001, on-line), he said, "I can't tell you how many times we'll run into government officials or people in the press who say, 'Yeah, you tell it like it is, I'd love to be able to say that.' Geez . . . maybe *you* should. . . . Maybe you should say it all the time." Despite his no-holds-barred approach to interacting with political figures, many of them have clamored to appear on his show. Former U.S. senator Bob Dole was Stewart's co-host for the program's coverage of the 2000 presidential election and its aftermath, called "Indecision 2000." Former secretary of state Madeleine Albright, former vice president Al Gore, and the 2004 presidential contenders Wesley Clark and Howard Dean have also appeared on the show, and the Democratic National Committee invited the *Daily Show* to cover its convention. Many Democrats have appeared on the program, among them the party's 2004 presidential candidate, John Kerry, feeding the perception that the *Daily Show* has a liberal bias—an argument Stewart denies. "The point of view of this show is we're passionately opposed to bulls– – –," he told Bruce Fretts. "Is that liberal or conservative?"

The fact that public figures flock to appear on the program is less surprising when one considers that the *Daily Show* is among the prime sources of news for people under 35. Stewart denies that his "fake news show" has much of an influence on the way people think. "Our politics are fueled by the comedy," Stewart told Peyser and Childress. "We're not a power base in any way. Our show is so reactionary, it's hard to imagine us stimulating the debate." That comment notwithstanding, the *Daily Show* reaches sought-after demographic groups in greater numbers than its competitors, be they the actual newscasts it runs against (and parodies) or other late-night talk shows. The median age of *Daily Show* viewers is 33, compared to a median age in the 40s for the *Tonight Show* with Jay Leno and the *Late Show* with David Letterman. In addition, Stewart is extremely popular with college students.

Part of what sets Stewart apart from his late-night brethren is the manner in which he delivers his barbs. The *Daily Show*'s humor is much more aggressive than that of its competitors; Stewart and his "correspondents"—who claim to report on current events from around the globe but in reality never leave the studio—are known for their ability to make interviewees squirm by asking uncomfortable questions. They typically do so in a spirit of goodwill, however, making potentially discomforting situations humorous instead. "Oftentimes, people who say satiric or unpleasant things are labeled as curmudgeons," Ben Karlin, the show's co-executive producer and head writer, told Peyser and Childress. "Jon has a very rare gift for being able to deliver material that has bite, but not in a mean or nasty way." Peter Jennings of ABC News told Fretts, "Stewart is an essential character in the national political landscape. There's nothing mean about him. And in a society where there's so much mean talk, someone who punctures the balloons with grace and elegance and humor is just a blessing."

Stewart says that his comedy represents the views of the majority of the populace, which is by turns angered and bewildered by the extremism of both the political far right and the far left. "My comedy is not the comedy of the neurotic," he told Friend. "It comes from the center. But it comes from feeling displaced from society because you're in the center. We're the group of fairness, common sense, and moderation. We're clearly the disenfranchised center because we're not in charge." He has said that his show reflects, and perhaps heightens, the public's cynicism about politics—but does not create it. He has dismissed claims that the Daily Show has an influence on public attitudes and does not believe that comedians can effect social change through such means.

The Daily Show increased its audience by 15 percent from 2002 to 2003. Its new viewers were mostly those aged 18 to 34, who had not shown much interest in the topical humor that was the show's main focus before Stewart took over. The program currently attracts an audience of about one million, large for late-night cable standards and sufficient to beat offerings in its time slot from CNN, MSNBC, and Fox News, at least among young adults. (The Daily Show averaged 350,000 viewers when Kilborn was host.) Since the spring of 2003, the program has broadcast a weekly edition on CNN International, available in 200 countries. The show earned a prestigious Peabody Award for its coverage of the 2000 presidential election and won an Emmy Award for writing in 2001. In 2003 it received two more Emmys, for writing and for Outstanding Variety, Music or Comedy Series. Stewart's current contract extends through the November 2004 elections. Because of his popularity there is much talk that he could eventually replace the host of a network late-night television show, although it is doubtful that he would have as much freedom at a network as he has at Comedy Central.

To mark the 2004 presidential-election season, Stewart and his fellow writers on the Daily Show wrote The Daily Show with Jon Stewart Presents America (The Book): A Citizen's Guide to Democracy Inaction (2004). This satiric look at American government is a take-off on high-school social-studies textbooks; its chapters have such titles as "The Founding Fathers: Young, Gifted, and White" and "The Media: Can it Be Stopped?" Among its textbook-like features are end-of-chapter discussion questions, which prompt readers to consider topics such as "Why do you think the Framers made the Constitution so soul-crushingly boring?" In her review of the book for the New York Times (September 16, 2004), Janet Maslin wrote, "A little of it is silly. ('If the president were the longest recorded flight by a chicken, he would be 13 seconds.') A little, like a picture that claims to show the Supreme Court justices naked, is just plain unforgivable. But the rest is the devil's own comedic handiwork, a side-splitting guide to the abuses and absurdities built into our political processes and institutions." Two weeks prior to the presidential election, the book ranked number one in sales on Amazon.com and on the New York Times nonfiction best-seller list.

The five-foot seven-inch Stewart has been described as self-effacing. He "looks like a college kid," Tad Friend wrote in 2002, "except that his hair is now a distinguished gray. He is conventionally handsome, and yet his face is all nose and recessed, worried-looking brown eyes." Stewart, who is head writer and executive producer of the Daily Show, continues to appear in films. In the last few years he has been seen in Big Daddy (1999), Committed (2000), The Office Party (2000), Jay and Silent Bob Strike Back (2001), and Death to Smoochy (2002); he also provided a voice for the animated video The Adventures of Tom Thumb and Thumbelina (2002). He hosted the 2001 and 2002 Grammy Awards show, and in 2003 he was part of a team of 11 comedians who co-hosted the Emmy Awards program.

The comedian was named one of the "50 most beautiful people in the world" by People magazine in 1999, World News Tonight's person of the week in December 2003, and one of the "People Who Mattered" in 2003 by Time magazine. He has written pieces for the New Yorker, Esquire, and George. When not at work Stewart spends much of his time at home, doing crossword puzzles or watching SportsCenter. He married the veterinary technician Tracy McShane in 2000. They live in Manhattan with their cat and two dogs.

—K.E.D.

Suggested Reading: Entertainment Weekly p30+ Oct. 31, 2003, with photos; New Yorker p28+ Feb. 11, 2002; Newsweek p70+ Dec. 29, 2003–Jan. 5, 2004, with photo

Selected Books: Naked Pictures of Famous People, 1998; The Daily Show with Jon Stewart Presents America (The Book): A Citizen's Guide to Democracy Inaction, 2004

Selected Television Shows: *Short Attention Span Theater*, 1989; *You Wrote It, You Watch It*, 1992; *The Jon Stewart Show*, 1993–95; *The Daily Show*, 1999–

Barry Wetcher, courtesy of American Ballet Theatre

Stiefel, Ethan

(STEE-fel)

1973– Dancer

Address: American Ballet Theatre, 890 Broadway, New York, NY 10003

Described in 1999 by Harris Green of *Dance Magazine* as "the finest young American classical dancer in forty years," Ethan Stiefel is among the ballet world's few male superstars. Stiefel began taking ballet lessons at age eight and made his professional debut eight years later, in 1989, with New York City Ballet (NYCB). After three years with NYCB, he danced for one year with the Zurich Ballet and then returned to the New York company for another three years. Since 1997 he has held the title of principal dancer with American Ballet Theatre (ABT), also based in New York City. Writing for *Newsday* (October 17, 1999) when Stiefel was 26, Susan Reiter hailed him as "one of the most elegant and technically astonishing American ballet dancers of his generation, a rare home-grown talent amid ABT's imposing, highly international male roster. His performances," Reiter continued, "blend virtuosic feats with a disarming, personable stage presence that communicates the sheer joy of dancing." Stiefel's repertoire includes such roles

in classical ballet as Albrecht in *Giselle*, Siegfried in *Swan Lake*, Romeo in *Romeo and Juliet*, the pirate in *Le Corsaire*, and Basil in *Don Quixote*; in addition, he has had principal roles in many contemporary ballets, in such George Balanchine works as *The Four Temperaments*, *Apollo*, *Symphony in Three Movements*, *Symphony in C*, and *Stars and Stripes*; such Jerome Robbins ballets as *Dances at a Gathering*, *West Side Story Suite*, *The Goldberg Variations*, *2+3 Part Inventions*, *The Cage*, and *Quiet City*; and in Twyla Tharp's *Push Comes to Shove*, *The Brahms-Haydn Variations*, and *Known by Heart*. In 2000 he appeared in a leading role in the ballet movie *Center Stage*. He has danced with such companies as the Royal Ballet, in England, the Munich Ballet, in Germany, and the Kirov Ballet, in Russia, and has performed in many countries overseas. The dancer and choreographer Kevin McKenzie, who has served as ABT's artistic director since 1992, told Kristin Hohenadel for the *Los Angeles Times* (January 31, 1999) that what distinguishes Stiefel from most other dancers is his "uncanny ability to keep a very individual voice while absorbing a style that he's never done before. And hence something completely unique comes out of it. It doesn't hurt that he's got a tremendous facility and that he's smart and musical. It's as if there were no technical barriers there." In a "Critic's Pick" item for *Time* (September 3, 2001), Stiefel was described as "the greatest American-born male ballet dancer since Edward Villella" and as having performed in a "dazzlingly wide range of works . . . with a casual virtuosity and unmannered grace worthy of Fred Astaire."

Ethan Stiefel was born in early 1973 in Tyrone, Pennsylvania, to Mima and Alan Stiefel. His sister, Erin Stiefel, who is one year older, is also a dancer; she was a member of the Zurich Ballet until 1998, when a knee injury forced her to resign from the company. Stiefel's father graduated from Yale University Divinity School and, at the time of Ethan's birth, worked as a minister. In about 1975, feeling the need to earn more money, among other reasons, he left the ministry and took a job as a state trooper in Texas. After living in Houston for two years, the Stiefels moved again, this time to Portage, Wisconsin, where Alan Stiefel became an employee of the federal correctional system—a position that was to require several additional relocations during the next decade. Alan Stiefel accepted transfers only to places within driving distances of dance schools; through the years he and his wife chauffeured the children to and from the schools, with trips ranging from 45 minutes to two hours each way.

An exceedingly energetic youngster, Ethan Stiefel would "play football and baseball in the house, and break the furniture," as he told Finis Jhung for DanceArt.com. in mid-2002. When he was six his mother enrolled him and his sister in a gymnastics class; two years later he and Erin began taking ballet lessons at the Monona Academy of Dance in Madison, Wisconsin. Speaking of his early classes, he explained to Harris Green for

Dance Magazine (December 1995), "Our parents couldn't take us two places at once, so I followed. And I couldn't just sit around watching so I got into my little shorts and socks and gave it a shot." As the only boy among the 20 girls in the dance class, he recalled to Finis Jhung, "I enjoyed being active and jumping around, but I didn't have an instant connection, like 'this is going to be my lifelong pursuit.'" In his first public appearance, about a half-year after his first lesson, he performed a Mexican hat dance. When Stiefel was about 12, his family settled in Milwaukee, Wisconsin, and he began studying with the former American Ballet Theatre principal dancers Ted Kivitt and Paul Sutherland at the Milwaukee Ballet School. As children, both Ethan and Erin performed in a mounting of the traditional Christmastime ballet The Nutcracker in Chicago, a commute of four hours from their home.

Speaking with the dancer Jock Soto for the publication ASAP (April 2000, on-line), Stiefel recalled that his family owned a large video collection of 1940s and '50s movie musicals starring such singer/dancers as Fred Astaire and Gene Kelly. "I was surrounded by all of that," he said. "My mom and my sister were nuts for them, watching them over and over. . . . And at that time I was like, 'Turn them off! Put Indiana Jones on!'" In time, Astaire's and Kelly's films became his favorite dance movies, too. Stiefel also enjoyed dirt-biking, playing peewee football, and long-distance running.

Stiefel's talent in dance was obvious when he was very young. According to a profile of him posted on the Web page of the Atlanta Ballet, his "natural gifts" included flexibility; highly arched feet; turnout—his ability, when facing forward, to rotate his legs so that his left knee and foot pointed directly to the left of his body, and his right knee and foot directly to the right; and elevation—his ability to jump or leap to unusual heights. Sutherland recalled to Green, "I had Ethan taking classes with the adults, using a girl his age for partnering, and I gave him exercises to strengthen his back. I remember I showed Ethan what a double tour [a double turn in the air] looked like, and the kid said, You mean this? And he did it!" In an interview for Ballet Review (Fall 2001), Stiefel told the veteran ballet critic Francis Mason that Sutherland "basically introduced me to male technique in ballet. He had me doing handstand pushups and back exercises. . . . He really opened me up to male technique, partnering. He stressed partnering a lot. He had a trick: walking around chairs and spinning them while maintaining the balance and the spin. You had to find the balance point, to be able to feel the balance. He said something once that has always stayed with me: 'The sign of a good partner is that he moves very little. If a partner's feet are always shuffling and moving that means he is not in the right place.'"

The Stiefel family next moved to Selinsgrove, Pennsylvania. Ethan and Erin attended Marcia Dale Weary's Central Pennsylvania Youth Ballet in Harrisburg, Pennsylvania, an hour and 15 minutes from their home. In the summer of 1987, Stiefel and his sister took classes at the School of American Ballet, in New York City, one of the premier ballet schools in the world and the official training facility of New York City Ballet. At the end of the summer program, the school offered both teenagers scholarships to study there full-time in the fall. Eager to give their son and daughter the opportunity to do so, Alan Stiefel secured a job transfer to a correctional center in Manhattan; Mima Stiefel found work at the same place, as an accounting technician. The family moved yet again, this time to Somerset, New Jersey, and embarked on a grueling daily schedule. "It was a horror story . . . ," Stiefel recalled to the longtime dance writer Anna Kisselgoff for the New York Times (February 6, 1994). "We'd all wake up at 4: 30 a.m., drive in and stay in my dad's office. So there we were, sleeping on chairs from 6 to 7: 30 a.m., and the criminals are dusting around us." Stiefel and his sister attended classes at the Professional Children's School until 10 a.m. and then studied at the ballet school until between 2: 00 and 4: 00 p.m. "Then it was back to my dad's office, and the drive through the Holland Tunnel," he told Kisselgoff. "It was eat, homework and sleep, because you had to get up and do it the next day."

During the summer of 1988, Stiefel studied at Mikhail Baryshnikov's short-lived School of Classical Ballet. "Baryshnikov was an inspiring teacher," he has said, as quoted on the Atlanta Ballet Web site. Stiefel told Kristin Hohenadel that Baryshnikov had "keys to simplify everything. I think that was a really important thing for me to learn—that, you know, it's not all that complicated. I'm not saying it's not difficult, but it's not all that complicated." In 1989 Stiefel won the silver medal at the prestigious Prix de Lausanne, an international ballet competition held in Switzerland for young, preprofessional dancers. He hoped to work with Baryshnikov at American Ballet Theatre, where the older dancer was then artistic director, but Baryshnikov left ABT that year. Instead, Stiefel accepted the invitation of Peter Martins, NYCB's ballet master, to join that company's corps de ballet. Within a few weeks of his coming on board, the 16-year-old Stiefel performed a solo role in the "Tea" section (also known as the "Chinese Dance") of Tchaikovsky's Nutcracker. Jennifer Dunning, in the New York Times (December 12, 1989), described his performance as a "standout debut," noting that Stiefel had "brought a kind of detail to the role one doesn't expect, dancing it with a tapering turnout and supple footwork, as well as a clarity and an ease associated with more purely classical dancing, but he never violated the essential character-dance nature of the solo." Also when Stiefel was 16, Martins, who created Les Gentilhommes, cast the young dancer in that ballet, "which put me alongside the best dancers in the company," as Stiefel recalled to Finis Jhung. "That was a big challenge, and I think it proved that I could hold my own." Speaking of that period, Jhung told Stiefel, "I . . . remember seeing you do *Tchaikovsky Pas de Deux*, and throwing double-double tours, where no one else had. I was very impressed with your thrill of the risk. We weren't used to seeing male dancers with the complete splits and sharply arched feet, and the speed, and the turns, and the jumps. The audience went wild. Your attack and fearlessness won the hearts of everyone watching and insured you a devoted band of followers, both audience and critics alike."

In 1991, while still a dancer in the corps of NYCB, Stiefel won an "Emerging Artist" grant from the Princess Grace Foundation–USA. During the following year he pulled a muscle in his hip, an injury that, in a conversation with Harris Green, he attributed to the overly strenuous demands of two works that he had danced back-to-back in NYCB's first Diamond Project, a four-day festival. While Stiefel was recuperating, Bernd Bienert, the artistic director of the Zurich Ballet (which Erin Stiefel had joined), offered him a place in that company. Stiefel welcomed the chance for a change, because he had been growing increasingly dissatisfied with his circumstances at NYCB. As he told Anna Kisselgoff in 1994, "They ran me ragged there. Physically and mentally, I needed to chill out." His decision to leave a renowned troupe and an apparently assured future astonished his friends and others in the field of ballet. But to him, as he told Kristen Hohenadel, "it just seemed like the right thing to do—and it was possible to do it." He added that going to Zurich "gave me the confidence to know that whatever the situation was, whether I made a right decision or a wrong decision, I could still kind of just go with it and make it work for myself." Soon after his arrival in Zurich, Stiefel danced in a new version of *The Nutcracker*, staged by Bienert specifically for him, and his image appeared on T-shirts sold in conjunction with the performance.

In 1994, after a year in Zurich, Stiefel returned to NYCB. "Artistically," he told Finis Jhung, "I wanted to continue the progress I had made before I went to Europe. I felt that Zurich had given me a lot, but . . . I felt I had reached the capacity it had to offer. . . . I had kept close contact with City Ballet and Peter Martins, so it was understood that I would be returning to City Ballet." After one year—during which, he told Jhung, "I hardly danced. . . . I needed to understand that one doesn't leave and return without repercussions"—Martins promoted him to principal dancer. While with the company he performed in such works as *Harlequinade*, *The Four Temperaments*, *Apollo*, *Stars and Stripes*, *Symphony in C*, *Chaconne*, *A Midsummer Night's Dream*, *Dances at a Gathering*, *West Side Story Suite*, *The Goldberg Variations*, and *The Cage*. He also appeared in new works by Peter Martins (among them *Mozart Piano Concerto*, *Ash*, *Tchaikovsky Pas de Quatre*, and *Fearful Symmetries*) and by David Allan, William Forsythe, Kevin O'Day, Robert LaFosse, and Richard Tanner. In addition, Stiefel worked extensively

with Jerome Robbins. "What he gave me was the ability to dance even abstract ballets with a deep sense of meaning and purpose," he told Jhung.

After seeing him at a concert at the New York State Theater, a delighted Jennifer Dunning wrote for the *New York Times* (June 28, 1994), "Ethan Stiefel is clearly one of the most promising and accomplished of the New York City Ballet's rising stars. But Mr. Stiefel astonished even his most fervent admirers with his first performances as Oberon in George Balanchine's *Midsummer Night's Dream*. . . . Mr. Stiefel had an authority surprising in a 21-year-old performer. His technical skills are prodigious. Jumps, turns and especially his beats were so clearly and perfectly shaped you could have photographed him at almost any moment and had a textbook illustration of the step. . . . It was clear that Mr. Stiefel had put considerable thought into the character and its choreography. Mr. Stiefel danced with something of the bigness and propulsive force of the Soviet male dancers who thrilled dancegoers in an earlier era. There were times when one wished for more softness and dynamic variation, as well as a little less conscious focusing on the look of the performance. But those are skills that tend to develop with time and experience in gifted dancers, and that is a category to which Mr. Stiefel obviously belongs." In a review for the *New York Times* (January 5, 1995) of a NYCB concert that took place a few months later, Anna Kisselgoff was similarly enthusiastic: "Happiness is Ethan Stiefel . . . in George Balanchine's *Stars and Stripes*. . . . Mr. Stiefel reminded us why we go to the ballet at all. Steps and structures, with the latter especially vital to Balanchine, came together through the talent of an exceptionally gifted dancer. As the parade-ground Romeo in Balanchine's tribute to Sousa, Mr. Stiefel begins his solo with a soaring beat in the air; he remains suspended longer than expected in this sharply placed cabriole. Later, he keeps the same pure form as he rebounds into the flexed-foot entrechats and coiled jumps that make up the choreography's kinetic jokes. At the end of the variation, Mr. Stiefel throws in a scissored air-turn to the knee, Russian bravura streamlined into American bravado. To watch Mr. Stiefel here is to feel a smile spread across one's face, from the sheer pleasure of his dancing."

In spite of his successes, in 1996 Stiefel again left NYCB in favor of the Zurich Ballet. As he explained to Susan Reiter, "I could either stay with City Ballet and continue with the way things were, which was fine, or else, make a tough decision and say, 'OK, I might have to leave a place . . . I've grown up in and loved to try and see how far I can go with doing other stuff.' The essence of it is my drive to explore so many different facets of dance." By contrast, he told Jhung that since he had found himself "wait[ing] in line behind others" to be cast in certain major Balanchine roles, he decided to take "the opportunity to use that time to experiment with other repertoire." In addition, he said,

Martins had rejected his request to be allowed to dance as a guest with other companies. Then, in 1997, Stiefel accepted Kevin McKenzie's invitation to join American Ballet Theatre as a principal dancer. There, "I felt very comfortable very soon," he recalled to Jhung. He immediately began to dance leading roles in such classics as *Swan Lake*, *The Sleeping Beauty*, *Giselle*, *La Bayadère*, *La Fille Mal Gardée*, *Don Quixote*, and *Romeo and Juliet*. In such full-length works, he noted to Jhung, "you have to pace yourself, in that you have 3 hours to maintain, not just 30 minutes. You can't give everything you've got in the first act, beause you've two more to go." He also devoted much attention to character development; as he told Jhung, "I discovered that when I was fully immersed playing a character, then the technical aspects of the dancing came naturally and felt easier to do." His repertoire also included many contemporary works, including *Push Comes to Shove*, *Fancy Free*, *Dim Lustre*, *Variations for Four*, *Drink to Me Only with Thine Eyes*, *Billy the Kid*, and *Sinfonietta*. In 1998 Stiefel was nominated for the Benois de la Danse Award (the so-called ballet Oscar, established by the International Choreography Association in 1991) as "one of the rising stars of ballet." In 1999 the Princess Grace Foundation presented Stiefel with its highest honor, the Statue Award.

Also in 1999 the PBS television series *Great Performances/Dance in America* aired an ABT production of Marius Petipa's *Le Corsaire*, in which Stiefel danced the part of Conrad the pirate; that presentation of *Le Corsaire*, a ballet that includes one of the most famous pas de deux in the genre, won the 2000 Emmy Award for outstanding classical/dance program. Along with the dancers Jose Manuel Carreño, Angel Corella, and Vladimir Malakhov, Stiefel was featured in the documentary *Born to Be Wild: The Leading Men of American Ballet Theatre* (2003), also on the Great Performances series; in addition to being interviewed, he performed in a new work by Mark Morris, called *Non Troppo*. On April 21, 2004, in another installment in the series, he appeared as Oberon in Frederick Ashton's ballet *The Dream*, choreographed to music composed by Felix Mendelssohn for Shakespeare's *A Midsummer Night's Dream*.

In 2000 Stiefel appeared in the movie *Center Stage*, directed by Nicholas Hytner, about a group of young, aspiring ballet dancers. Stiefel played Cooper Nielsen, an impetuous dancer and budding choreographer who has an affair with another young dancer (portrayed by Amanda Schull). Whereas with ABT he rehearses for six or seven hours daily, the shooting of *Center Stage* called for 12-hour days, a schedule that exhausted him. With few exceptions, critics dismissed the film as clichéd fluff but praised the dance scenes, choreographed by Susan Stroman and Christopher Wheeldon.

In the summer of 2001, Stiefel organized Stiefel and Stars, a touring ensemble of ABT dancers; they performed for the first time at that year's Vail International Dance Festival, in Colorado. Most recently, in August 2004, Stiefel and Stars gave a performance at the Martha's Vineyard Performing Arts Center, in Oak Bluffs, Massachusetts, to benefit the Martha's Vineyard Hospital. In February 2004, with ABT, Stiefel appeared in Nacho Duato's *Without Words*, set to music for cello and piano by Franz Schubert. Subsequently he performed in *Raymonda*, *Tchaikovsky Pas de Deux*, *Don Quixote*, *La Bayadère*, *Swan Lake*, and *Romeo and Juliet*.

Since age 17 Stiefel has spent much of his leisure time riding his Harley motorcycles. "I enjoy riding because I feel it amplifies so many of one's senses," he told Jhung. "You're constantly feeling your balance, feeling the wind, and seeing things not filtered through a car window. . . . Although I love New York, I realize that I need to get away, from time to time, and get back to my roots, so to speak." For some years Stiefel has lived with his girlfriend, Gillian Murphy, who is also an ABT principal dancer. In a note for *Dance Magazine* (September 2003) about the Youth America Grand Prix, held in April 2003, Hanna Rubin wrote, "For most contestants, athleticism trumped artistry. It was left to . . . Gillian Murphy and Ethan Stiefel, who performed a pas de deux from *Le Corsaire*, to remind viewers of artistry's elusive magic."

—H.T.

Suggested Reading: American Ballet Theatre Web site; *Ballet Review* p31+ Fall 2001, with photo, p12+ Winter 2001, with photos; *Dance Magazine* p60+ Dec. 1995, with photo, p54+ Nov. 1999; *Los Angeles Times* p3+ Jan. 31, 1999, with photos; DanceArt.com, 2002; *New York Times* II p21 Feb. 6, 1994, with photo; *Newsday* D p18+ Oct. 17, 1999, with photo

---

Thain, John A.

1955– CEO of the New York Stock Exchange

Address: New York Stock Exchange, 11 Wall St., New York, NY 10005

In January 2004, after a tumultuous year of scandal and investigations at the New York Stock Exchange (NYSE), the largest and most prestigious stock exchange in the world, John A. Thain assumed the post of the NYSE's chief executive officer (CEO). Prior to his appointment, Thain had spent two dozen years with the preeminent global investment-banking and securities firm Goldman Sachs, working his way up from finance associate to chief operating officer and president. In contrast to his predecessor at the NYSE, the gregarious Richard Grasso, Thain—a financial wizard who specializes in cutting costs and managing capital— is typically described as a precise and dispassion-

Stephen Chernin/Getty Images

John A. Thain

ate technocrat, qualities that, most agree, are now sorely needed at the helm of the exchange.

Thain's move to the NYSE came at a crucial time in the history of the 211-year-old exchange. Many critics have argued that the NYSE's operation—a floor-trading system in which brokers buy and sell stock for investors—is antiquated and should be replaced with an electronic system. Moreover, in 2003 the NYSE was rocked by two corporate scandals that severely undermined investor confidence. In April the exchange revealed that it was under investigation for allowing specialists, who manage the buying and selling of specific stocks, to use inside knowledge to gain profits for themselves at the expense of investors; four months later came the disclosure that Grasso, the NYSE's chairman and CEO, had accumulated $140 million in deferred compensation and retirement savings, payable in one lump sum of cash, along with millions of dollars in additional earnings in 2002 and 2003. His remuneration stood in stark contrast to those of other executives at the NYSE, who have received most of their yearly, million-dollar-plus compensation in the form of stocks, which means that their fortunes rise and fall with those of the stock exchange; Grasso, by contrast, continued to receive millions of dollars even when the market was performing poorly. The disclosure prompted calls for his resignation; on September 17 he stepped down and was replaced by an interim CEO and chairman, John Reed.

Thain's main jobs are to restore investor confidence in the NYSE and to quiet those critics who complain that the exchange is out of date. "I was looking for someone to be a guiding force in our evolutionary pathway," Reed told Landon Thomas

Jr. for the *New York Times* (December 19, 2003) in praising Thain, "someone with knowledge of the markets, who understands the role of technology and is a person of great integrity." "Thain brings youth, intelligence, energy and a deep understanding of technology and markets," Roy Smith, a professor of finance at New York University and a former Goldman Sachs partner, told Thor Valdmanis for *USA Today* (December 19, 2003). "They couldn't have picked a better person."

The son of Alan L. Thain, a physician, and his wife, Sophey, John A. Thain was born in Antioch, Illinois, in 1955. According to the Warren-Newport Area Community Information Home Page, on the Web, his great-great-great-grandfather John Thain immigrated to Illinois from Scotland in 1845. John A. Thain graduated from the Massachusetts Institute of Technology, in Cambridge, Massachusetts, with a bachelor's degree in electrical engineering in 1977 and earned a master's degree in business administration from Harvard University, also in Cambridge, in 1979. He then realized his ambition of landing a job with Goldman Sachs: he was hired as an associate in the finance department. He spent the early part of his career in investment banking and mortgage securities, helping to develop the firm's division of mortgage-backed fixed income, defined as "fixed-rate investments that represent an ownership interest in a pool of many mortgages."

In 1994 Thain was handpicked by Jon S. Corzine, then Goldman Sachs's chairman and CEO, to fill the posts of chief financial officer and head of operations, technology, and finance. One of Thain's main interests in those positions was exploring the intersection of technology and finance. "John has been centrally involved in many of the firm's most important decisions about information technology and electronic trading platforms," Lucas van Praag, a managing director at the firm, told Landon Thomas Jr. "He has a deep interest in how things work." Thain also helped the firm to make the transition from a private partnership to a publicly traded company in 1999. Between 1995 and 1997 he served as co–chief executive officer for European operations; during this period he was also named a managing director. In 1999 Corzine stepped down from his position as co-CEO (the title also held by Henry M. Paulson Jr. since mid-1998); it was rumored that Goldman's five-man executive committee, which included Thain, had ousted him because of the company's heavy trading losses in the fall of 1998 and a delay in its much-anticipated initial public offering. Thain was subsequently promoted to the position of co-president and co–chief operating officer (COO), along with the firm's top investment banker, John Thornton—the idea being to combine Thain's financial skills, particularly his ability to keep costs down and use capital wisely, with the flamboyant Thornton's talent for cultivating relationships with high-profile clients. In July 2003 Thain became Goldman Sachs's sole COO and president, after

Thornton announced his retirement. Thain thus emerged as the heir apparent to Goldman's CEO, Henry M. Paulson Jr., who was expected to retire within five years.

In a presentation at the Merrill Lynch Banking and Financial Services Investor Conference in November 2003, Thain made it clear that he believed some NYSE stocks should be traded electronically rather than through specialists, because electronic trades can be executed faster. His remarks came as a shock to his colleagues at Goldman Sachs, which owns Spear, Leeds and Kellogg, the second-largest specialist firm on the NYSE.

On December 17, 2003, in the wake of the controversy surrounding Grasso and the trading specialists, the Securities and Exchange Commission (SEC) voted unanimously to restructure the NYSE by splitting the roles of chief executive officer and chairman and by creating an independent board of directors, a separate board of executives made up of industry insiders, and an autonomous regulatory apparatus. A day later the exchange announced its choice of Thain to replace John Reed as chief executive of the board. (Reed will serve as chairman at least until the annual meeting of shareholders in 2005.) Thain agreed to accept a compensation package of $4 million per year, substantially less than his earnings at Goldman Sachs ($6.3 million in 2002 and $10.5 million the year before). Some critics argued that the exchange needed someone from outside the industry, rather than an investment banker, to lead it out of the recent crisis; others praised the NYSE's choice of the serious-minded Thain. Leon E. Panetta, a former congressman and White House chief of staff who served on the NYSE board's governance committee, commented to Landon Thomas Jr., "John Thain is not a bell ringer, but the stock exchange doesn't need a bell ringer now"—a reference to Grasso, who often brought in celebrities and other luminaries to ring the exchange's opening bell. "You need a technocrat now—someone to restore trust with investors, as well as someone who understands how the markets operate." Others saw Thain's appointment as a sign that the exchange was willing to introduce electronic trading on the floor. "John Reed sent a very strong message to the NYSE membership and to the public by choosing someone who is such an advocate of technology," Jodi Burns, an analyst with Celent Communications, told Isabelle Clary for the *Securities Industry News* (December 22, 2003). "Now, what we have with Thain is someone who recognizes there is a need for the specialists, but there is also an opportunity to increase the level of electronic trading on the floor."

On February 5, 2004 the NYSE board of directors approved a plan to expand electronic trading at the exchange by eliminating two rules regarding those trades. The first rule limited electronic orders to 1,099 shares; the second stipulated a 30-second waiting period between electronic trades by any one investor. "Our goal is to continue offering investors the best price as well as the most com-

pelling array of order-execution choices," Thain said at a news conference called to announce the new rules, as quoted on the New York Stock Exchange Web site (February 5, 2003). He added, "Our commitment to create the best price for investors remains paramount. Today's initiative complements market-structure rules that ensure investors in NYSE-listed stocks receive best-price trade executions. We will work to keep those rules in place."

Thain and his wife, the former Carmen M. Ribera, have four children. His wife is the president of the board of trustees of the Rye Country Day School, a college-preparatory academy. The couple have homes in Rye, in Westchester County, New York, and Vail, Colorado, where Thain enjoys skiing. In January 2004 the Carmen and John Thain Labor and Delivery Unit at the Sloane Hospital for Women was dedicated at the Morgan Stanley Children's Hospital of New York-Presbyterian Hospital, in Manhattan.

—H.T.

Suggested Reading: *Economist* p64 Jan. 10, 2004, with photo; *Investor's Business Daily* A p3+ Jan. 16, 2004; *Los Angeles Times* C p1 Dec. 19, 2003, with photo; *New York Times* A p1+ Dec. 19, 2003, with photo; *Wall Street Journal* Eastern Edition C p1+ Dec. 19, 2003

Theron, Charlize

(char-LEEZ)

Aug. 7, 1975– Actress

Address: c/o United Talent Agency, 9560 Wilshire Blvd., Suite 500, Beverly Hills, CA 90212

Though the South African–born actress Charlize Theron had won critical praise for her work in such films as *The Devil's Advocate* (1997), *The Cider House Rules* (1999), and *The Italian Job* (2003), until recently she was known more for her beauty than for her performing skills. Said to embody the old-style dazzle of such golden-era movie stars as Lana Turner and Carole Lombard, Theron seemed "genetically engineered for Hollywood stardom," as Kathy Passero noted for *Biography* (November 2002). Doubly powerful, therefore, was Theron's decidedly unglamorous, Academy Award–winning turn as the real-life prostitute and serial killer Aileen Wuornos in the movie *Monster* (2003)—the performance that cemented Theron's standing as one of the most formidable actresses of the silver screen. As quoted by the Web site Women24.com, Theron, who is often described as "down to earth," told Ruda Landman for *Carte Blanche* that in her view many actors have been distracted by the trappings of fame and "gotten so

Mark Mainz/Getty Images

Charlize Theron

caught up in the celebrity world that we've forgotten that actors are supposed to transform and tell stories."

An only child, Charlize Theron was born in Benoni, South Africa, on August 7, 1975. Her father, Charles, was of French descent; her mother, Gerda, is of German lineage. As a child Theron was exposed to the cultures and languages of the more than 26 ethnic groups represented by the employees of her parents' road-construction business. The family lived on a farm, where Theron grew up surrounded by sheep, goats, ostriches, and dozens of dogs. She told Kathy Passero, "When you're growing up on a farm and you don't have siblings to play with, you have to keep yourself busy, so you get creative. I spent my childhood pretending—pretending I had friends, pretending the dogs could speak, pretending my St. Bernard was a zebra." Theron described her mother to Passero as "one of the strongest, most fearless women I know." Sometimes, Theron recalled, a road-related emergency would require her mother to drive to a site in the middle of the night, with Charlize in tow, "rolled up in a blanket in the backseat, fast asleep."

Despite the fact that her mother sometimes worked 18-hour days, as Theron recalled to Passero, she always put her daughter first: "There was time for anything I wanted to do. I was in ballet classes, music classes, taken to museums." At the same time, Gerda Theron taught her daughter to be self-reliant. If she got herself into trouble, Theron recalled to Emma Brockes for the London *Guardian* (April 2, 2004, on-line), she knew that she would have to "sort it out myself. There is no running-to-mum to fix it. At one point, somebody stole my ruler and she [told me], 'Well then steal it back!' She always said, you have to take care of things yourself."

Theron began studying dance at the age of four (other sources say five or six). Her love of movies can be traced to a drive-in theater, 45 minutes from the Theron farm, where Gerda Theron took her daughter once a week. Later the family bought a VCR. "We watched everything," Theron recalled to Passero. "There was such a tiny selection [of videotapes] at the store in town that we couldn't be choosers. I grew up on Goldie Hawn and Tom Hanks movies like *Overboard* and *Splash*." It was *Splash*, which starred Daryl Hannah (as a mermaid) and Tom Hanks, that first inspired her interest in acting. "I was in love with Tom Hanks instantly," she told Dan Jewel for *People* (October 14, 1996). "I hated Daryl Hannah. I was sitting there saying, 'I could have done that part so much better. That should have been me!'" When she was 13 years old, Theron enrolled in a boarding school in Johannesburg, South Africa, where she danced for eight hours a day and dreamed of becoming a world-class ballerina. In Johannesburg she became aware for the first time of the political and social reality of her country's system of racial apartheid. "I'm the first person to admit I've never been to a township," she told Dana Kennedy for the *New York Times* (November 15, 1998). "I didn't hear the word apartheid until I went to school in Johannesburg. I didn't have racist parents. I never witnessed anything bad."

There was, however, turmoil in the Theron household. Charlize Theron's father, a heavy drinker, was frequently abusive toward his wife and sometimes disappeared for days at a time. When Theron was 15 she watched as her mother fatally shot her father, who had attacked Gerda Theron in a drunken rage. (The incident was judged by the local court to be an act of self-defense.) Theron described the matter to Brockes as "very, very sad . . . I wish they'd divorced years and years before, because I think he would have been a happy man. I think my mum would've been a happy woman. But . . . they were miserable." Theron remains very close to her mother; the actress told Passero, "I can share everything with her. . . . I feel extremely lucky. She's quite fearless, and that gave me a certain fearlessness growing up."

About a year after Charles Theron's death, Gerda Theron entered her daughter in a local modeling contest; Charlize won the contest and the prize—a modeling contract in Europe. She moved to Milan, Italy, where she learned to walk runways at fashion shows and posed for print layouts. "I went because I wanted to go on the adventure, not because I wanted to be a model," Theron told Passero. The world of modeling quickly grew stale for her. "Dancing requires such discipline, and modeling doesn't have any of that. All I had to care about was what I ate and how small my waist was. There was no creative satisfaction. After a while, my head became empty," the actress recalled to Passero. On the other hand, as she told Jamie Diamond for *Mademoiselle* (December 1998), modeling "gave me a business sense at a young age. If I wanted to have an apartment and clothes, I had to have a job."

At 18 years of age, Theron moved to New York City, where she began studying at the prestigious Joffrey Ballet School and continued to model in order to support herself. She has recalled stealing bread from restaurants on occasion during that financially lean period. A knee injury sustained during a dance class quickly ended her dreams of a ballet career. She realized at that point, as she recalled to Passero, that what most interested her was "telling stories, being onstage and pretending"; if she could no longer do so through dancing in productions of narrative ballets such as *Swan Lake* and *The Nutcracker*, she decided, then she would have to find a new medium. "The idea of acting slipped out of either [my mother's] mouth or mine . . . I had never thought of [acting] seriously, but suddenly it made a lot of sense."

Seeking a career as an actress, in the early 1990s Theron moved to Los Angeles, California. With little money, knowing virtually no one in the city, she lived in a cheap motel called the Farmer's Daughter. To perfect her English (Theron's first language is Afrikaans) she recited what she heard on television, which she kept on all the time, so as to be constantly surrounded by the sound of the language. During that time she made a brief, uncredited appearance in the 1995 film *Children of the Corn II*. The story of Theron's big break, which came shortly afterward, might have been conceived by a Hollywood screenwriter. As many sources have reported, one day Theron went to a bank to cash the last of the checks from her modeling work in New York; when the teller refused to cash her check, Theron became enraged, stomping her feet and yelling. In the bank at the time was the talent agent John Crosby, who, impressed by Theron's dramatic display, gave the young woman his business card.

With Crosby's help, Theron soon landed her first movie role, that of the sexy hit woman Helga Svelgen in *2 Days in the Valley* (1996), which also starred James Spader, Danny Aiello, Jeff Daniels, Eric Stoltz, and Marsha Mason. Theron recalled to Passero that seeing herself on screen for the first time was "very frightening." Only 21 years old when the film was released, Theron thought that "nothing [she] did was good enough," and she also feared that her work in *2 Days in the Valley* would lead to her being typecast as a femme fatale. Indeed, casting directors and producers soon offered Theron roles similar to that of Helga. The actress told Passero, "I knew I had to prove I was versatile, so I said 'no,' which meant I didn't work for almost a year."

Theron's childhood idol Tom Hanks gave her a small but memorable role as a woman who leaves her boyfriend, a rock-and-roll drummer, for her dentist in the movie *That Thing You Do!* (1996),

which Hanks wrote and directed. Next, in the thriller *The Devil's Advocate* (1997), Theron played the wife of an ambitious lawyer (Keanu Reeves) who enters into a partnership with Satan incarnate (Al Pacino). That film received mixed reviews. Among those who praised it was Mick LaSalle, who in the *San Francisco Chronicle* (October 17, 1997) singled out Theron's performance: "These days most 30-year-old actresses seem 22, but Theron is the opposite, a 22-year-old with a mature aura." *The Devil's Advocate* performed fairly well at the box office, taking in more than $60 million. Theron next appeared on the big screen as a sexually charged supermodel in Woody Allen's film *Celebrity* (1998). Again, while the film as a whole earned mixed reviews, Theron received praise; reviewing *Celebrity* for *Rolling Stone* (November 28, 1998), Peter Travers called Theron a "knockout who can toss her curves or curve a comic line with stunning dexterity."

In 1999 Theron co-starred in *The Astronaut's Wife*, a science-fiction thriller about an astronaut (Johnny Depp) who returns from space a changed man; his wife (Theron), after conceiving a child with him, begins to suspect that what is growing inside her is not of this world. The movie was a critical and commercial disappointment. That same year Theron co-starred with Tobey Maguire, Michael Caine, and Delroy Lindo, among others, in *The Cider House Rules* (1999), which John Irving adapted for the big screen from his novel of the same name. Theron played Candy Kendall, the young daughter of a lobster fisherman and the lover of the protagonist, Homer Wells (Maguire), an orphanage resident unofficially trained as a doctor. In lauding the movie and the actors' performances, Stephanie Zacharek opined for the on-line publication *Salon* (January 25, 2000) that Theron's turn as Candy, "with her apple cheeks and tousled blond curls, is the perfect picture of toughed-up innocence and fragility." In addition to earning critical praise, *The Cider House Rules* was nominated for more than a half-dozen Academy Awards, including one for best picture.

Now much in demand as an actress, Theron appeared in four movies in 2000. In the *The Legend of Bagger Vance*, a drama directed by Robert Redford, she played the girlfriend of a golfer (Matt Damon) who attempts to recapture his former athletic prowess—and his faith in the world—with the help of a caddy (Will Smith). The movie did not fare well at the box office and received mostly negative critical reviews, but once more, a number of critics complimented Theron, who was nominated for a Blockbuster Entertainment Award for her performance. According to most accounts she was underused as the wife of the alcoholic, tortured U.S. Navy master chief Billy Sunday (Robert De Niro) in *Men of Honor*.

According to the Internet Movie Database, Theron turned down the lead female role in *Pearl Harbor* (2001), choosing instead to star alongside Keanu Reeves in the romance *Sweet November*

(2001). A remake of the same-titled film made in 1968, it tells the story of a young woman (Theron) who, aware that she is dying of an incurable disease, attempts to teach a different man each month how to derive more enjoyment from life. The movie was widely panned. The following year Theron co-starred with Kevin Bacon, Courtney Love, and the Irish actor Stuart Townsend in the thriller *Trapped,* in the role of a woman whose daughter is kidnapped. The movie was unsuccessful both critically and commercially. On a positive note, her co-star Kevin Bacon complimented Theron as an actress, telling Passero, "Every scene [in *Trapped*] is filled with unrelenting panic and anguish and uproar, but she wasn't afraid to do anything to get the scene right—to do take after take of really painful stuff. There are plenty of beautiful girls out there, but in Hollywood being beautiful only gets you so far. Charlize has chops. She works very hard to make the scene, the character, and the picture work." Also in 2002 Theron co-starred with Patrick Swayze, Billy Bob Thornton, and Natasha Richardson in the little-seen romantic comedy *Waking Up in Reno,* a movie about two southern couples on their way to Reno, Nevada, to attend a monster-truck show. Theron's next big-screen role was that of a safecracker in *The Italian Job* (2003), a remake of a 1969 movie of the same name, which starred Michael Caine. *The Italian Job* is the story of a group of thieves (Mark Wahlberg, Seth Green, Jason Statham, Edward Norton, Mos Def, and Donald Sutherland) who steal $35 million in gold bars from a palazzo in Venice, Italy. When one of the members betrays the group and takes the gold for himself, the others, along with Theron's character, attempt to get the booty back. Reviews of *The Italian Job* were mixed, but the movie was a commercial success, grossing over $100 million in box-office receipts.

Theron's next movie role proved to be the most challenging, and rewarding, of her career to date. At the urging of Patty Jenkins, who wrote the screenplay and directed the film, Theron agreed to portray the real-life prostitute turned serial killer Aileen Wuornos in the critically acclaimed *Monster* (2003). (Theron herself helped to produce it.) The movie co-starred Christina Ricci as Selby Wall, a character based on the teenage girl who became Wuornos's lover and eventually testified against her in the case that led to Wuornos's execution by the state of Florida in 2002. What attracted Theron to the role was that Wuornos, as depicted in Jenkins's screenplay, had suffered much but had also killed mercilessly, and thus evoked both sympathy and revulsion. Theron told Rob Blackwater for the Web site splicedonline.com, "This was the first time, I think, in my entire career, when by the second-to-last page, I still didn't know how I felt about the character"; that ambiguity appealed to the actress. Among other ways of trying to understand the real Wuornos, Theron watched the documentary *Aileen: Life and Death of a Serial Killer,* by Nick Broomfield and Joan Churchill, and read intimate letters that Wuornos had written to friends over a span of 12 years. Theron also transformed herself physically, gaining 30 pounds and, with the help of makeup artists, making herself appear plain and worn on screen. In a tribute to the effectiveness of the actress's transformation, Roger Ebert wrote for the *Chicago Sun-Times* (January 9, 2004), "I confess that I walked into the screening [of the movie] not knowing who the star was, and that I did not recognize Charlize Theron until I read her name in the closing credits. . . . Watching the film, I had no sense of makeup technique; I was simply watching one of the most real people I had ever seen on the screen." Ebert called *Monster* "the best film of the year" and Theron's performance "so focused and intense that it becomes a fact of life. Observe the way Theron controls her eyes in the film; there is not a flicker of inattention, as she urgently communicates what she is feeling and thinking. There's the uncanny sensation that Theron has forgotten the camera and the script and is directly channeling her ideas about Aileen Wuornos. She has made herself the instrument of this character." One scene in *Monster* required Theron to simulate being raped, beaten, and tortured, as Wuornos was, before killing her attacker. Theron told Emma Brockes that she would not have been able to perform the role just a few years earlier. "It would have ruined my life. It took me a couple of years to get to a place where I could teach myself to do that kind of material."

Made for just $5 million, a pittance by Hollywood standards, *Monster* took in more than $30 million at the box office. For her performance Theron won a number of honors, including a Golden Globe Award, a Broadcast Film Critics Association Award, a National Society of Film Critics Award, a Screen Actors Guild Award, and an Academy Award for best actress. After winning the Oscar Theron traveled to her native South Africa, where she was a guest of honor of the Nelson Mandela Foundation. Mandela, the former antiapartheid activist and former South African president, announced on that occasion that Theron had "put South Africa on the map." In reaction, Theron burst into tears. (Theron and Djimon Hounsou, who received an Oscar nomination for best supporting actor for *In America,* are the only African-born actors to be shortlisted for an Academy Award.)

In 2004 Theron appeared in two movies: the romantic drama *Head in the Clouds,* which co-starred Stuart Townsend and Penelope Cruz, and the made-for-television film *The Life and Death of Peter Sellers. Head in the Clouds* was panned in the press and bombed at the box office. Echoing several other critics who compared Theron's role in her latest movie unfavorably to her outstanding work in *Monster,* Peter Travers wrote for *Rolling Stone* (September 16, 2004) that in *Head in the Clouds* Theron "dives back into diet, hair and makeup to portray glam party girl Gilda Besse in a World War II melodrama of epic silliness and supreme vapidity." Theron will also appear in the action picture "Aeon Flux" and the drama "Class Action," which is based on the true story of female iron miners who became the plaintiffs in the first major successful sexual-harrassment case in the United States; both films are scheduled for release in 2005. Other movies in which she has appeared include *Mighty Joe Young* (1998) and *The Curse of the Jade Scorpion* (2001). Theron hosted the award-winning late-night sketch-comedy show *Saturday Night Live* in 2000 and served as a narrator of the television series *When I Was a Girl* (2001).

The visually striking Theron is five feet 10 inches tall; she has long legs, broad shoulders, and blond hair. She has often changed her appearance—in particular the color and style of her hair—and has consistently dazzled her fans and the celebrity media with the eye-catching, elegant dresses she has worn to the annual Academy Awards ceremony and other highly publicized events. According to Jill Gerston in *Biography* (January 2001), Theron once told a reporter, "I think old-time glamour will never go away, and I'm glad about that." The actress appeared in the May 1999 issue of *Playboy* magazine, and the following year *People* included Theron on its list of the "50 Most Beautiful People."

Despite her fame, Theron tries to maintain a semblance of a private life. She confessed to Passero, "It's very strange to walk out of a restaurant and have all these photographers snap away or to have people interested in what's in my garbage. Sometimes it feels like a huge invasion in your life, and that sucks." The actress told Daniel Robert Epstein

for ugo.com that she makes "clear decisions on what part of my life becomes public and what part doesn't. . . . I have a great time talking about my work as an actress. But I have no desire to be on 50 [magazine] covers and television. I get sick of myself after a while."

Theron's favorite charities and causes involve animals. She lives—with several dogs—in Hollywood Hills, on property that she described for Passero as a "little green haven for myself, a smaller version of a farm." She dated Stephan Jenkins, the lead singer of the band Third Eye Blind, from about 1998 to 2001. Since 2002 she has been romantically linked to the Irish actor Stuart Townsend, her co-star in *Trapped* and *Head in the Clouds*. Theron enjoys riding around Los Angeles on her Harley Davidson motorcycle.

—C.F.T.

Suggested Reading: *Biography* p42+ Jan. 2001, with photos, p48+ Nov. 2002, with photos, p34 Mar. 2003, with photos; Internet Movie Database; (London) *Guardian* Apr. 2, 2004, with photo; slicedonline.com

Selected Films: *2 Days in the Valley*, 1996; *That Thing You Do!*, 1996; *The Devil's Advocate*, 1997; *Trial and Error*, 1997; *Celebrity*, 1998; *Mighty Joe Young*, 1998; *The Astronaut's Wife*, 1999; *The Cider House Rules*, 1999; *Reindeer Games*, 2000; *The Yards*, 2000; *The Curse of the Jade Scorpion*, 2001; *15 Minutes*, 2001; *Waking Up In Reno*, 2002; *Trapped*, 2002; *The Italian Job*, 2003; *Monster*, 2003

Thompson, Lonnie

July 1, 1948– Glaciologist

Address: Ohio State University, 108 Scott Hall, 1090 Carmack Rd., Columbus, OH 43210

"I believe ice is our best archive of the history of the Earth's climate," the glaciologist Lonnie Thompson said during a 2001 interview with *CNN Presents*. "Understanding how the climate system works and has worked in the natural system is absolutely essential for any prediction of what's going to happen to the climate in the future." Glacial ice, found atop mountain ranges and at the North and South Poles, reveals changes in the climate that have occurred over thousands of years; scientists study the ice in order to understand the impact of human industry on the climate. Thompson focuses on ice taken from the highest elevations of Earth's tropical regions, including the Andes, in South America; the Himalayas, in Asia; and Mount Kilimanjaro, in Tanzania. Over the last 30 years, he has led more than 40 expeditions on five conti-

nents, climbing to altitudes as high 20,000 feet and staying there for as long as six weeks in fiercely cold and windy conditions. "I've never sought extreme adventure. It scares me," he told Kevin Krajick for *Science* (October 18, 2002). "I only want the data." Thanks to his work at Ohio State University's Byrd Polar Research Center, scientists now know that temperature and precipitation in tropical zones have fluctuated more than previously thought, and that the tropics were colder during the last Ice Age than was once believed.

Thompson's findings have provided the clearest evidence yet to support the theory of global warming, which holds that Earth's atmosphere is getting warmer as a result of human industrial activity. At the 2001 meeting of the American Association for the Advancement of Science, in San Francisco, California, Thompson announced that 80 percent of the ice on Mount Kilimanjaro, the highest peak in Africa, had melted since 1912, which he had discovered by mapping the ice cap and comparing it with similar measurements taken before World War I; one-third of the ice loss had occurred since 1989. The ice atop Mount Quelccaya, in the Peruvi-

Courtesy of Ohio State University

Lonnie Thompson

an Andes, was also melting at an alarming rate, Thompson informed his colleagues, predicting that at the current rate, all of the ice located in tropical regions would vanish within two decades. Not only does this mean the loss of an important record of the planet's natural history, he warned, but it also presents a dire threat to local economies and to Earth's ecology in general. "The work [Thompson] and his colleagues have accomplished has serious implications for every person on the planet," Brad Moore, the vice president of research at Ohio State University (OSU), explained in an interview for the school's Office of Research Web site. "His dedication to this research—especially in the face of many colleagues' claims that such work could never be done—and his personal courage in obtaining these climate records is an inspiration to scientists everywhere." In 2002 OSU named Thompson a Distinguished University Professor.

The second of three children, Lonnie Thompson was born on July 1, 1948 in Huntington, West Virginia. He was raised on a small farm in nearby Gassaway. Neither of his parents attended school beyond the eighth grade—though his mother continued her education later—and his father, an electrician by trade, struggled to make ends meet. Thompson has credited his rugged upbringing on a country farm with laying the groundwork for the physical endurance that has served him well on expeditions. As a child he evinced an early interest in the climate, setting up weather instruments in the barn and making bets with his friends about the chance of rain. Winning a scholarship to Marshall University, in Huntington, West Virginia, Thompson studied geology; in 1970 he became the first member of his family to earn a college degree.

Thompson began graduate work at Ohio State University, originally intending to earn a Ph.D. in coal geology. But a part-time job analyzing the first ice cores retrieved from Antarctica changed his mind and the focus of his studies. As part of a research project for Ohio State's Institute of Polar Studies, he dissected the layers of the ice cores and discovered evidence of nuclear tests conducted by the Soviet Union during the 1960s, as well as of a volcanic eruption that occurred in Indonesia in 1815. He became intrigued with the idea of using dust, pollen, and geochemical shifts found in the ice to understand global climate patterns. Each layer of ice that is part of a core represents a different period of time; the layer's thickness shows how much precipitation occurred during that period, and the oxygen isotopes reveal the temperature. "The beauty of ice . . . is that it's a physical parameter," he explained to CNN. "It's not biological. It records what's going on in the . . . Earth's system. But it is layered just like a tree; only it'll go back thousands and thousands of years." In order to understand the impact of human industrial activity on climate, scientists have traditionally studied ice from the polar regions, which contain approximately 98 percent of the world's glaciers. Thompson, on the other hand, decided to focus on the ice found in the highest altitudes of the tropics. "When you look at the Earth, 50 percent of the surface of this planet lies between 30 [degrees] north [latitude] and 30 south in the tropics," he told CNN. "This is where the energy comes in to drive the climate system."

After receiving a Ph.D. in geology, in 1976, Thompson became a professor at Ohio State University. Three years earlier he had organized his first ice-drilling expedition to the Andes. In 1974 he embarked on his first exploration of the Quelccaya Mountain ice cap in southern Peru's Cordillera Oriental range. He had wanted to drill for ice cores, but could not get funding for the expedition because the mountain was considered too dangerous for humans to scale. In 1979 he persuaded the National Science Foundation to fly a drill and generator to the top of Quelccaya with a helicopter, but the project was scrapped because of extreme winds near the mountain. Thompson subsequently asked Bruce Koci, an engineer at the University of Nebraska, to design a lighter drill that ran on solar energy and could be dismantled for easy transportation.

Thompson returned to Quelccaya in 1983 and succeeded in obtaining a sample from the ice cap. His team spent 10 weeks on the mountain extracting from a depth of 160 meters two cores that contained a record of the local climate going back to 470 CE. Studies on dust trapped in the ice and on oxygen-isotope levels revealed that there had been a series of marked swings in precipitation—from wet to dry—and temperature that mirrored the rise and fall of nearby ancient civilizations over the last 1,500 years. The results startled scientists, many of whom believed that tropical climates had barely fluctuated throughout the history of the planet.

Thompson's evidence was not enough to change the scientists' overall view of tropical climates, so he set about excavating ice cores from some of the world's highest tropical elevations, including Kilimanjaro, the Andes, and the Himalayas. Each of these expeditions involved hauling several tons of equipment to high elevations, using yaks or relying on the local workforce. (Because the drill is powered by the sun, however, the teams did not need to carry up fuel and generators for it.) Thompson also needed to acquire the permission of numerous local organizations and governments in order to scale each mountain; in the case of the 2000 Kilimanjaro expedition, he had to obtain 25 different permits. In addition to the logistical and bureaucratic difficulties of an expedition, physical hardship accompanies every trip. Thompson and his crews work in sub-zero temperatures, windstorms, and thin air for weeks at a time. (His team set a record for spending the longest period of time at the highest elevation: three weeks on the 23,622-foot Dasuopu Glacier in Tibet. On another expedition the team passed 53 days at an elevation of 19,837 feet.) Thompson has taken great personal risks on each expedition; once, a gust of wind hurled his tent toward a 3,000-meter drop over a cliff, and he saved his life with a well-planted ice pick. His physical ailments have ranged from cold-damaged extremities to chest infections. He has ignored a heart defect doctors diagnosed in his 30s, and he has waged a constant battle with chronic asthma, which becomes worse at higher elevations. In 1997, on an expedition to Tibet, a 26-year-old Ohio State graduate student, Shawn Wight, died after contracting altitude sickness. (Wight's parents sued Ohio State for $21 million in damages, claiming that the safety precautions were inadequate. The case was dismissed three years later, and Thompson was excused from culpability.)

Thompson has excavated ice cores from some of the tropics' highest elevations, including the Dunde and Guliya ice caps in China, Mount Huascarían in Peru, Mount Sajama in Bolivia, and Dasuopu Glacier and the Puruograngri ice cap in Tibet. The oldest cores he has excavated reach back 70,000 years and confirm the occurrence of numerous ice ages. These caps prove that the tropics were much colder 20,000 years ago than they are today, again countering the prevailing theory that tropical climates have barely changed over time.

In 2000 Thompson spent a month on Mount Kilimanjaro, camping at 19,300 feet and retrieving six ice cores. Studies of these cores revealed that the glaciers began to form over 11,000 years ago, when the climate was warmer and wetter, and that three catastrophic droughts had occurred—8,300, 5,200, and 4,000 years ago. "Whatever happened to cause these dramatic climate changes in the past, could certainly happen again," he said in an interview posted on NASA's Earth Observatory Web site. "But today, 70 percent of the world's population lives in the tropics. They would be dramatically affected by events of this magnitude. We have to find out what causes them to happen." Thompson also discovered that, just like the glaciers of Peru and Tibet, the ice on top of Mount Kilimanjaro has been melting at an astonishing speed, and will be gone by 2020 or even earlier. Thompson attributed the loss to global warming: as Earth's atmosphere heats up as a result of an increase in carbon dioxide and other gases, the glaciers are melting and thus retreating. When the ice melts, Thompson argued, the record of Earth's climate contained in the glaciers will be wiped out. Kilimanjaro's ice cap, in particular, is melting very rapidly; the mountain is covered by 80 percent less ice today than it was in 1912, with a third of that loss occurring in the last 15 years.

Since his watershed 2001 announcement at the American Association for the Advancement of Science gathering, Thompson has developed a plan for drilling at 13 tropical peaks in an attempt to preserve as much ice as he can before it all disappears. He plans to bring it back to his laboratory at Ohio State, where he will keep it in a freezer for future research. His recent drill sites include, in 2002, Mount Bona-Churchill, in Alaska, and in 2003, Mount Coropuna, in Peru. In addition, in the latter year he again drilled in the Quelccaya ice cap.

Thompson is a fellow of the American Geophysical Union, an honor awarded to only one percent of the scientists in the field. He is the recipient of the Distinguished Scholar Award, Ohio State University's highest honor, the $150,000 Heineken Prize from the Royal Netherlands Academy of Arts and Sciences, and the Swedish Vega Award. His research is conducted under the auspices of Ohio State University's Byrd Polar Research Center.

Thompson, who was named one of America's top scientists by CNN and *Time* in 2001, conducts some of his research with his wife and colleague, Ellen Mosley-Thompson, a climatologist who studies ice cores from the polar regions; Mosley-Thompson earned her Ph.D. from Ohio State in 1979. The couple, who met at Marshall University, have a grown daughter, Regina E. Thompson. The husband-and-wife team were awarded the Common Wealth Award from PNC Bank. "If there's a message that I would send to other young scientists coming along, [it] is to study nature, not books," Thompson told CNN. "It's the real world that we ultimately have to understand and let the records tell you what actually took place."

—H.T.

Suggested Reading: BBC (on-line) Oct. 18, 2002; CNN (on-line); *Science* p518 Oct. 18, 2002, with photos; *Time* p42 Aug. 20, 2001, with photos

Jacques-Jean Tiziou, courtesy of jjtiziou.net

Tridish, Pete

(TREE-dish)

Nov. 17, 1969– Co-founder and technical director of the Prometheus Radio Project

Address: Prometheus Radio Project, P.O. Box 42158, Philadelphia, PA 19101

Pete Tridish is the co-founder and leader of the Prometheus Radio Project, a nonprofit organization whose motto is "freeing the airwaves from corporate control" and whose mission is to fight media consolidation by providing legal, technical, and organizational support to low-power, community-based FM radio stations. Tridish, whose real name is Dylan Wrynn, has been fighting against the monopolization of radio since 1996, the year he helped to establish and operate the pirate radio station Radio Mutiny in Philadelphia, Pennsylvania. The Federal Communications Commission (FCC) shut the station down in 1998, having banned such low-power stations 20 years earlier with the rationale that the signals of low-power community-based stations would interfere with the broadcasts of a national radio network and large commercial radio outlets. After agitating for the rights of noncommercial groups, such as nonprofit organizations, community collectives, and schools, to set up small radio stations, in the late 1990s Tridish worked with the FCC to establish rules that once again legalized the existence of and granted licenses to low-power FM radio stations. Since that time Tridish and his Prometheus Project colleagues have been successful in helping to establish several small, community radio stations in ru-

ral areas around the United States. Tridish told Laurie Kelliher for the *Columbia Journalism Review*, as posted on the publication's Web site, that a large part of community radio's mission is to "broaden and deepen the listening experiences of its audience. . . . [People] want to hear Britney Spears because that's what they've heard. That doesn't mean they wouldn't appreciate music from Kenya. It's really a question of what people are exposed to and what their options are. It really is important for there to be a place on the dial that in some ways is less successful, that presents programs that are not going to be as popular—but is a place where you can go when your ear grows past the bubble-pop of our culture. I think those are the sort of green spaces—the common public spaces—that we need to be thinking about as a culture. They have an effect that goes beyond the audience numbers." Along with a number of other concerned parties, in 2003 he and his Prometheus colleagues persuaded a federal court to temporarily block the FCC from easing restrictions designed to prevent large media companies from monopolizing the airwaves. The Prometheus Radio Project's work has been recognized and supported by the Open Society Institute and the Ford, List, and MacArthur Foundations.

Pete Tridish was born Dylan Wrynn on November 17, 1969 in the New York City borough of Brooklyn. His father, Stephen Wrynn, sporadically held jobs as a maintenance worker, keeping in good repair the heating, ventilating, and air-conditioning systems in various New York City office buildings. After his father's death, Tridish's mother, Phyllis Wrynn, a public-school teacher, married Mitch Friedlin, who worked as a roadie for blues musicians, then in a hardware store. Tridish has a half-brother and a stepsister, neither of whom was present while he was growing up. His mother and stepfather currently operate a small picture-framing business out of their home.

For 10 years during the 1980s and 1990s, Tridish worked intermittently as a carpenter and, to a lesser extent, in various other trades, among them masonry, plumbing, and electrical wiring. Some of his jobs involved solar heating; he told *Current Biography* that his original goal after finishing his schooling was to become a solar-heating contractor or a housing-rights organizer. He received a B.A. degree from Antioch College, in Yellow Springs, Ohio, in 1992; his self-designed major was called "appropriate technology."

After college, social activism became the focus of Tridish's life. "I was working with activists in various movements," Tridish recalled to Kelliher, "and we all thought that our voices had been marginalized in the campaigns we were working on. I had been involved ever since high school in campaigns, from the nuclear freeze to the anti-apartheid movement, and had always found that the stumbling block to getting exposure for our issues had to do with corporate control of the media. We felt that to make a difference in the way people thought about these issues we'd have to try to change the way the airwaves are regulated." In 1996 Tridish co-founded Radio Mutiny, a pirate radio station (91.3 FM) that broadcast from secret locations in Philadelphia, Pennsylvania. (It was referred to as a "pirate" station because it was operating without a license and so in violation of FCC regulations.) "None of us had been on the radio and none of us knew much about radio," Tridish told Kelliher. "For about seven or eight months, we tried to build a transmitter and finally, after blowing it up a couple times, got it going early in 1997." As a way to hide his identity and avoid the heavy fines that operating a pirate radio station would incur, that same year he assumed the name that he goes by, which sounds like "petri dish"—a small glass or plastic container for growing bacteria for research. (Other members of Radio Mutiny became Millie Watt, from "milliwatt," Anna Tennah, as in "antenna," Noah Vale, as in "no avail," and Bertha Venus, as in "birth of Venus.")

Radio Mutiny offered an eclectic mix of programming, which included reggae, poetry, dramas, plus a segment called the "Condom Lady," which offered safe-sex tips, and "Incarceration Nation," a regular report on the U.S. penal system. After broadcasting for less than a year, Radio Mutiny received a knock on the door. "FCC, open up," the visitors said, according to Tridish, as quoted in the *Indianapolis Star* (September 15, 2003, on-line). He continued, "The girl who went to the door said, 'Yeah, right,' because there were always people coming to the door and making jokes. But then she looked out, she saw some guy she didn't know and a couple of cops. She told them she wouldn't open the door unless they had a warrant, so they went away." Soon afterward Tridish and his Radio Mutiny partners demonstrated in front of the site where Benjamin Franklin's printing press once stood, in downtown Philadelphia, and challenged the FCC to arrest them. They held a large banner that read, "1763, Benjamin Franklin challenges the Stamp Act and refuses to pay taxes to King George. 1996, Radio Mutiny defies the FCC for Freedom of Speech." During a similar demonstration held at the building where the Liberty Bell is displayed, also in Philadelphia, Tridish and his Radio Mutiny colleagues again broadcast from their transmitter, which they had carried with them, in open defiance of the FCC rules prohibiting low-power community broadcasting. In 1998 the FCC returned to the group's broadcast location with a court order, broke down Radio Mutiny's door, and confiscated the transmitter, thus shutting down the station for good. Nevertheless, Radio Mutiny's members continued to agitate for freedom of the airwaves. In 1998 Tridish organized a 25-city Radio Mutiny tour, during which he was the principal speaker for the group, which spoke out against commercial monopolization of radio and FCC restrictions. He also served as an organizer for the initial microradio conferences—meetings of advocates of low-power FM radio stations—on the East Coast; the

first was held in Philadelphia in April 1998, and the second, during which fellow radio pirates broadcast directly into the FCC's main offices, was held in Washington, D.C., the following October.

After the demise of Radio Mutiny, in about 1998, Tridish helped to found the nonprofit Prometheus Radio Project (named for the character in Greek mythology who steals fire from the gods and gives it to man), setting up offices in the basement of Calvary United Methodist Church in Philadelphia. In addition to Tridish, members of the Prometheus Project include Anthony Mazza, Jaclyn Ford, Levi Roman, and Hannah Sassaman. The Prometheus Radio Project has been a leading advocate for community groups that want to establish low-power FM stations, mostly in rural areas underserved by commercial broadcasters. (The push for the legalization of low-power community-based radio stations is sometimes referred to as the microbroadcasting movement.) "Prometheus staff members started their voyages on the oceans of aether as pirates to protest media concentration and demand access to the airwaves," the group's Web site explains. "With the possibility of legal low-power radio stations on the horizons they turned in their hooks and patches to help foster the free radio movement." Tridish explained to Kelliher that his objective in forming the Prometheus Project was to "take the FCC at its word—that they really did care about community radio—and try to get them to pass a proposal that would actually be good for community broadcasters around the country." (A typical commercial radio station has a 50,000-watt signal that can reach listeners within a radius of hundreds of miles; the signals of low-power stations, which by federal law may not exceed 100 watts, seldom extend beyond 10 miles.)

In the late 1990s, spearheaded by the likes of Tridish and his colleagues, the microbroadcasting movement expanded, "using exponential growth, mass media exposure, and stubborn noncompliance with FCC 'cease and desist broadcasting letters,'" as Kate Duncan wrote for *Z Magazine* (July/August 1998). "Pirates also adhere to the safety-in-numbers rule, helping establish and keep other stations on the air." The FCC expressed its willingness to discuss the possibility of legalizing low-power FM stations, though commission members often contended that interference from such stations would disrupt preexisting licensed programming. The commission began to reconsider its position on community radio and began discussing ideas with leaders of the microbroadcasting movement, among them Tridish. As quoted by Duncan, then–FCC chairman William Kennard stated that proponents of noncommercial low-power FM radio stations "have a legitimate issue in that there are, in some communities, no outlets for expression on the airwaves, and I believe that is a function, in part, of the massive consolidation that we are seeing in the broadcast industry."

In 1999 Tridish led the Prometheus Radio Project on a 20-city tour around the U.S. to bring attention to the group's crusade. He began working closely with the FCC on proposals for establishing the legality of community radio stations. "There was a long period of time when many of [my fellow radio pirates] called me a sell-out for working so closely with the FCC," Tridish recalled to Kelliher. He actively participated in the FCC rulemaking process that led, in 2000, to the adoption of regulations sanctioning low-power FM (LPFM) stations and offering radio licenses to select nonprofit groups, community organizations, and schools, among other interested parties.

Despite the FCC's issuance of licenses to small community stations beginning that year, Tridish was not satisfied, "because low-power FM has done nothing for the big cities," as he told Kelliher. Indeed, returning to the familiar objection that low-power stations would create unwanted interference, large broadcasting entities (including the National Association of Broadcasters, a powerful trade association representing the interests of established radio and television broadcasters) persuaded Congress to pass a bill that overrode the FCC's changes and limited new licensing to low-power stations in, for the most part, small towns or rural areas. Low-power stations in urban areas were all but banned. Therefore, according to Eils Lotozo in the *Philadelphia Inquirer* (March 7, 2002), the FCC rejected nearly 80 percent of the thousands of license requests that had poured in after the new regulations were announced in 2000. "That was very unusual," Tridish told Lotozo. "We were kind of blindsided. Congress doesn't know a watt from a volt, and it has never overruled the FCC on a technical issue." He told Kelliher, "To this day Philadelphia, where I come from, doesn't have a low-power radio station. It's kind of ironic that I haven't been able to bring to Philadelphia the dreams and successes we had as pirates back in 1998. . . . I think the FCC put together low-power FM as a patch to its rules so it could maintain authority over the airwaves because, frankly, it had badly misallocated the airwaves in the past."

In 2001, to examine the common claim that LPFM stations create detrimental interference, the FCC, at Congress's command, hired the Mitre Corp., a federally funded research and development center, to conduct independent LPFM field tests. The FCC's report to Congress on the findings of the Mitre study (dated February 19, 2004 and posted on the official FCC Web site) concluded that interference from LPFM stations was very minimal and that no significant interference from an LPFM station existed beyond a radius of a few hundred meters around the LPFM station's transmitter site—meaning that the FCC's relegation of LPFM stations to areas outside urban centers or locations with preexisting full-service FM stations is unnecessary. The FCC report, which counseled Congress to "re-address this issue and modify the statute" that relegates LPFM stations to areas outside major

urban centers, signaled a victory for Tridish and his colleagues. Tridish told *Current Biography* that U.S. senator John McCain, an Arizona Republican, for one, has expressed his desire to introduce legislation that would further empower the LPFM or microbroadcasting movement.

Despite having had to contend with financial and technical difficulties, the Prometheus Radio Project has helped to establish and construct a number of small, community-based, independent radio stations around the U.S., including, in 2002, KOCZ-FM in Opelousas, Louisiana, which plays zydeco music, offers local news, and is owned by a civil rights group; WRYR-FM in Arundel County, Maryland; and KRBS in Oroville, California. Prometheus members, and others of like mind, say that these start-up stations, while somewhat unpolished and limited, are much-needed outposts standing against the rapid consolidation occurring in the radio industry, a trend that is making it increasingly difficult for people with viewpoints that differ from those of the mainstream media to have their voices heard.

In the summer of 2003, the Republican-dominated FCC passed new regulations that, if implemented, would have allowed individual companies to own as many as three television stations and eight radio stations in the same market and to own television stations serving up to 45 percent of the nation's viewers. (The FCC regulations previously allowed up to 35 percent.) After the commission passed the new regulations, members of Congress received from constituents hundreds of thousands of letters, E-mail messages, and phone calls questioning or objecting to the new rules, as reported by Suzanne Charlé in an article on the Ford Foundation Web site. In July this strong public response led the House of Representatives to stop funds required by the FCC to carry out the rule changes.

The administration of President George W. Bush has argued that new FCC regulations easing rules on media ownership are necessary to help broadcasters compete in a market altered by the dominance of television and the advent of the Internet. The FCC and representatives of major television networks assert that, in the face of rapidly advancing digital technology, the proposed FCC changes would actually promote competition and preserve diversity in the nation's media. Among other concerned groups and individuals who do not agree with those opinions, Prometheus members have argued that the FCC changes threaten diversity, competition, and the public nature of the airwaves. As an example of media consolidation, the company Clear Channel owns more than 1,200 radio stations around the United States. "[Big media companies] need to be curtailed in how far they can spread their arms over the countryside," Hannah Sassaman, a Prometheus staff member, told David B. Caruso, an Associated Press reporter quoted in the *Indianapolis Star*. "It will change the way broadcasting sounds in America if it is all centralized out of the big cities." Among those who do not agree with Prometheus's grievances is the National Association of Broadcasters' senior vice president, Dennis Wharton, who told Caruso, "We don't buy into their claim that radio has somehow lost its local flavor. The reality is that today most successful stations are highly committed to serving their local audiences."

In about August 2003 Tridish and his associates filed a little-noticed suit against the FCC stating that the commission's changes furthered the monopolization of media and undermined the diverse and public nature of the airwaves. (The Prometheus Project was the "lead plaintiff" or "plaintiff of record," as Tridish told *Current Biography*; later, other media-justice groups, as well as organizations pushing for consumer rights and other causes, joined the suit on Prometheus's side.) In September a Third Circuit federal court in Philadelphia ruled in favor of the Prometheus Group's complaint, granting an emergency stay that temporarily barred the FCC from implementing the new rules. Soon afterward, the U.S. Senate, employing a rarely used legislative device called the Congressional Review Act (CRA), voted to repeal the new FCC regulations. Echoing the sentiments of Tridish and his colleagues, as quoted in an Associated Press article posted on the Virginia Press Association Web site, Democratic U.S. senator Patty Murray of Washington State said, "We have to ensure that the marketplace of ideas is not dominated by a few conglomerates at the expense of our citizens and our democracy." While pleased with those results, Tridish remains skeptical: "I'm always cautious about getting too excited about court victories," he told Caruso. "Eventually, the weight of the system always seems to wind up catching up with you."

Despite considerable bipartisan opposition, in January 2004 Congress passed, and President Bush signed into law, the Omnibus Appropriations Bill, which contains a provision setting at 39 percent the maximum allowable percentage of U.S. television households reached by outlets under the ownership of a single company. Critics deplored the decision to raise the cap from the previous 35 percent and said the easing of the restriction was a White House–tailored concession to the media companies Viacom (which owns CBS) and NewsCorp (which owns Fox), both of which already owned outlets that reached between 35 and 39 percent of all television households: thus, before the Omnibus Bill passage, both companies had actually been operating in violation of the law.

In early February 2004 Prometheus's case against the FCC was heard in the United States Third District Court of Appeals, in Philadelphia. Though the Omnibus Bill passed in January rendered moot Prometheus's fight against raising the broadcast-ownership cap, the judge who reviewed the case examined all other current FCC regulations concerning issues of media consolidation: for example, broadcast cross-ownership (a television station's current right to own a newspaper, for example); the diversity index (which deals with what percentage of a station or stations an individual party owns); and the definition of radio markets. On June 24, 2004 the court ruled that the FCC's recent attempts to loosen media-ownership regulations were unjustified. According to a press release on the Prometheus Web site, "The court determined that the FCC relied on 'irrational assumptions and inconsistencies' in determining the new cross-ownership caps, and ordered them to make a new decision that takes seriously their duty to regulate media to preserve the public interest." Although the ruling was a major triumph for Prometheus and other independent radio stations seeking media diversity, Tridish has emphasized the importance of sustaining activist efforts on behalf of LPFM radio in order to ensure that the verdict is upheld by the U.S. government. "Our next step," he told Katherine Stapp during an interview for the Inter Press Service (June 29, 2004), "will be a campaign to get the president to respect this decision, and persuade the administration not to appeal it."

The most recent victory for the LPFM movement occurred on July 22, 2004, when the U.S. Senate Commerce Committee voted to approve legislation authorizing low-powered radio stations to broadcast in areas previously deemed off-limits due to "potential interference" with major stations. The bill, which received bipartisan support from John McCain and Patrick Leahy, a Vermont Democrat, has the potential to increase substantially the number of low-power community radio stations broadcasting in the United States.

On the Prometheus Radio Project Web site, the group states that they are "looking for potential stations and potential volunteers." Prometheus is accepting proposals from groups "in cities throughout the northeast region [of the U.S.] to be subjected to our 'Special Treatment.' If selected, the lucky group (and lucky city!) will receive a special visit or two from Prometheus Radio People, complete with workshops, technical info, obnoxious advice, a good bit of nere-do-welling, and perhaps a little bit of something that might help your group establish a community radio station." Prometheus offers a mentorship program that helps to link those aspiring to start community radio stations with already-established licensed stations in the same area. Two or three times a year, Prometheus members tour different sections of the country, visiting anywhere from five to 20 groups in each region. In addition to its work in the U.S., Prometheus has taken its message abroad, helping to establish community stations in Colombia and Nepal. In early March 2004 Tridish traveled to Guatemala to conduct for local groups a standard Prometheus Project workshop on how to set up a small noncommercial community radio station.

Tridish has lectured widely around the U.S., everywhere from small coffee shops to the Cato Institute, and has been interviewed by National Public Radio, CNN, and the Freedom Forum as well as the

Philadelphia Inquirer, the *Chicago Tribune*, the *Nation*, the *Los Angeles Times*, the *Washington Post*, and *Broadcasting and Cable*, among other publications. He told Bruce Schimmel for the *Philadelphia City Paper* (July 17–23, 2003, on-line) that his office, in the basement of the United Methodist Church in West Philadelphia, is filled with posters from radio stations, props from political demonstrations, bullhorns, bits of electrical wire, and hulks of half-built transmitters. "Yeah, I'm a geek, and I have a lot of geek pride." At the end of an E-mail response to *Current Biography*, in the place where his name would have gone, Tridish wrote, "pe'tri dish: a squat, cylindrical, transparent article of laboratory glassware, useful in observing resistant strains of culture in aetherial media."

—C.F.T.

Suggested Reading: Associated Press Sep. 15, 2003; *Columbia Journalism Review* (on-line); *Mother Jones* p24+ Mar. 1, 2004; *Philadelphia Inquirer* Mar. 13, 2002; Prometheus Radio Project Web site

---

Tritt, Travis

Feb. 9, 1963– Country musician

Address: c/o William Morris Agency, 151 El Camino Dr., Beverly Hills, CA 90212

"I refuse to be muzzled," the country musician Travis Tritt told Kate Meyers for *Entertainment Weekly* (June 10, 1994). "I was brought up in a family where above everything else, you tell the truth. If you don't want to know how things are, don't ask me." During the early years of his career, Tritt made waves in the country-music world because of his outspokenness and his refusal to conform to the stylistic and musical conventions of country music. Eschewing the traditional cowboy hat worn by most performers in the genre, Tritt kept his hair long and favored leather clothing over mainstream country garb. He refused to live in Nashville (the accepted center of the country-music scene), employed a Hollywood agent, and vocally criticized his industry for embracing what he saw as a formulaic sound. ("I think the Nashville community is starting to realize that the cookie-cutter mentality is, in the end, not productive," he told an interviewer for the Country Stars Web site. "It may produce a tremendous amount of revenue for a certain period of time, but it has no longevity.") Musically, Tritt separated himself from the pack by incorporating rock into his sound. His first album, *Country Club* (1990), featured the song "Put Some Drive in Your Country," which acknowledged his love of the classic country sound embodied by such performers as Roy Acuff and George Jones but also re-

called the excitement he felt upon discovering such "outlaw" country artists as Waylon Jennings and Hank Williams Jr., who were also influenced by rock music. Despite his image as a rebel and outsider, Tritt quickly rose to fame and eventually came to be accepted by the country-music establishment. He has sold some 20 million albums, recorded three number-one hits on the country-music charts, and won two Grammy Awards. He has also collaborated with older, more traditional artists and appeared at the Grand Ole Opry. "For years, I've heard people talk about the outlaw image, [calling me] a rough-around-the-edges country rocker," he told Angela King for *Billboard* (September 14, 2002). "Then [*Down the Road I Go* (2000)] came out, and they are calling me a traditionalist. People like to try and put a label on things, put you in a box. I hate those boxes. It limits you if you're trying to do different things and experiment with music."

Travis Tritt was born in Marietta, Georgia, outside Atlanta, on February 9, 1963 to James Tritt, a bus driver and former farmer, and Gwen Tritt, a bookkeeper. Along with his younger sister, Sheilah, he grew up on a 40-acre property. The Tritt family was prominent in Marietta, having once owned much of northeastern Cobb County; several roads, neighborhoods, and an elementary school bear the Tritt name. Travis's love of music began in childhood; he sang gospel in a youth choir at First Assembly Church of God and taught himself to play guitar at age eight. He began to write songs at 14 (around the time his parents divorced) and played in bluegrass, rock, and country bands as a teenager. Known in school for his Elvis Presley impersonation, he was similarly influenced by such bluegrass performers as Merle and Doc Watson, as well as by Johnny Cash, Willie Nelson, George Jones, Merle Haggard, and the southern rock band Lynyrd Skynyrd. He embarked on his musical career despite his parents' reservations and struggled through the early 1980s while holding a variety of jobs. While he was working at an air-conditioning company, its president, a guitarist who had abandoned his goal of being a professional musician, urged Tritt to pursue his dream; in 1984 the young man quit to do just that. "I didn't want to wind up sitting on a porch when I'm old and wondering if I could have done it," he told Cynthia Sanz and Gail Wescott for *People* (June 1, 1992).

Tritt, who had recorded his first demo in 1982, cut several more songs over the next few years while also touring the honky-tonk circuit. After signing a major-label deal in 1989, he released his first Top 10 single, "Country Club"; an album of the same name followed, in 1990. His second album, *It's All About to Change* (1991), went multiplatinum. Among its hits was the number-one "Here's a Quarter (Call Someone Who Cares)," which he wrote while going through his second divorce, and the ballad "Anymore." *T-R-O-U-B-L-E*, his follow-up album, released in 1992, did not sell

Travis Tritt

Fredrick M. Brown/Getty Images

use of traditional instrumentation, including fiddle and Dobro. "The whole album talks about growing up," he said in an interview posted on the Country Stars Web Site. "Every young guy I've ever known in my life, practically, wanted to get away. And a lot of them end up going out and sowing their wild oats, and they end up coming back to the very thing they tried to get away from. I think that this album is probably a very good representation of that journey."

Tritt described his next album, *No More Looking Over My Shoulder* (1998), as "definitely a sample of what's been going on in my life, being married recently and having a brand new baby," as he told Ron Tank for the CNN Web site (October 16, 1998). "The music is still out on the edge, but it's a little bit different message than it had in the past. It's reflective of how happy I am as a husband and father." Tritt's penchant for mixing rock influences into his music was still on display—the album included two cover songs by rockers, one by Bruce Springsteen, the other by Jude Cole—but the slick production associated with Nashville's star artists was also evident. The disk did not enjoy as much commercial success as had most of his others.

In 1999, dissatisfied with what he viewed as a lack of publicity, Tritt left his label, Warner Brothers. "The last album that I did for Warner Brothers got no promotion, no backing," he told King. "It was almost like the label said, 'Tritt's records sell themselves; we have other fish to fry.'" After taking a two-year hiatus from touring and recording (during which he did not listen to country radio), Tritt signed a contract with Columbia Records in 2000 and released *Down the Road I Go*. The album scored four hit singles, including "It's a Great Day to Be Alive" and the ballad "Best of Intentions." For the first time in Tritt's recording career, a bluegrass influence could be discerned in his work; Tritt played banjo (a traditional bluegrass instrument) on several of the album's tracks. In a review of one of his live performances, Jeffrey Lee Puckett, writing for the (Louisville) *Courier-Journal* (November 16, 2002, on-line), characterized changes in Tritt's sound since his early days with Warner Brothers Records: "When Tritt was filling arenas his shows often seemed more like warmed-over Lynyrd Skynyrd than traditional country. . . . [Now] his approach is a bit more mellow and grounded more strongly in the past; fiddles and pedal steel are part of the sound, not tacked on for the sake of appearances." Though *Down the Road I Go* sold well, reviews were mixed. "After taking 18 months off . . . Tritt emerges sounding strangely like Kenny Rogers, right down to the hokey catch in the voice and the melodramatic story song, in this case an ill-advised tribute to a couple of sadistic thugs, 'Modern Day Bonnie and Clyde,'" a *People* (November 13, 2000) critic wrote. "Tritt's slightly gravelly voice has always resembled Rogers's, of course. But that hardly obliges him to emulate the schmaltzier, least admirable aspects of the Gambler's style. Happily, Tritt sounds

as well as his first two and did not receive as much critical acclaim. "Tritt's third album is so moany-whiny and self-pitying that he counteracts the affection and admiration he earlier won," Ralph Novak wrote for *People* (October 26, 1992). "Consider the titles: 'Looking Out for Number One,' 'I Wish I Could Go Back Home,' 'Leave My Girl Alone.' Not even the clever, jaunty title tune can relieve the oppressive tone." The album went gold nevertheless, on the strength of the number-one single "Can I Trust You with My Heart." Tritt's next album, *Ten Feet Tall and Bulletproof* (1994), went platinum, partly due to the hit "Foolish Pride." Another notable song on the album was "Old Outlaws Like Us," which featured performances by the country legends Waylon Jennings and Hank Williams Jr. Tritt has said that he composed the song late at night while thinking about his musical influences. "From the humorous macho self-ridicule of the title cut to the sensitivity of 'Foolish Pride,' from the Tritt-Waylon Jennings-Hank Williams Jr. teaming on 'Old Outlaws Like Us' to the sizzling rage of Marty Stuart's 'Hard Times and Misery,' this is a package that underscores the wide diversity of Tritt's artistry," Jack Hurst wrote of the album for the *Chicago Tribune* (May 8, 1994).

A scant five years after his first major-label release, Tritt came out with *Greatest Hits: From the Beginning* (1995). Featuring the number-one single "The Whiskey Ain't Workin'"—which Tritt and his fellow country musician Marty Stuart had been singing together on their "No Hats" tour—the album went platinum. In 1996 Tritt released *The Restless Kind*, which was considered a departure for him because of its stripped-down sound and

more like himself on the trenchant 'Southbound Train' . . . and 'Just Too Tired to Fight It.'"

In 2002 Tritt issued *Strong Enough*. Featuring his writing or co-writing on nine of the 12 tracks, the album had strong commercial appeal. "*Strong Enough* is Tritt doing what he does best, flexing his vocal muscles on up-tempo cuts . . . and running on pure emotion on the ballads . . . ," Todd Sterling wrote for the Country Review Web site. "Travis Tritt may be on his eighth studio album, but he still sounds like he's having the time of his life. . . . There's enough fiddle and Dobro to please the older crowd, plenty of ballads to prick the hearts of the sensitive, and a handful of country rockers to keep the rowdies up until the wee hours playing air guitar and tabletop drums. Who said country music was dead? It isn't here." In *People* (October 21, 2002), Ralph Novak called Tritt "the George Jones of his generation, a throwback to elemental country music," and gave the album an "A" rating.

Also in 2002 Rhino Records released two compilations of Tritt's work, *The Rockin' Side* and *The Lovin' Side*, the first containing his rock-influenced numbers and the latter his romantic ballads. "Put simply, Tritt is a double threat and one hell of a Southern rock singer when he wants to be," Michael Paoletta wrote of *The Rockin' Side* for *Billboard* (February 16, 2002). Paoletta also gave high marks to the companion collection of ballads: "Tritt's dead-on delivery of such neo-classics as 'Between an Old Memory and Me' are whiskey-tinged, [Vern] Gosdin-esque perfection, delivering a mixture of regret, self-pity, and resignation that is the sole property of country music at its best." A reviewer for *Country Music* (June/July 2002) was not as pleased with the division of Tritt's songs along stylistic lines, pointing out, "Tritt's music always worked best when alternating his sensitivity with his swagger." Describing *The Lovin' Side*, the reviewer wrote, "The ballads collection features several memorable cuts . . . but even the best of Tritt's sensitive stuff pales in comparison to rockers like the hayseed-meets-hellion 'Ten Feet Tall and Bulletproof.'"

Rhino Records released another collection of Tritt's songs, *The Essentials*, in 2003. In March of that year, Tritt publicly criticized Natalie Maines, a singer in the country group the Dixie Chicks, after she told a London audience, "We're ashamed the president of the United States is from Texas," as quoted on the *CBS News* Web site (March 15, 2003). Tritt said that it was cowardly of Maines to attack President George W. Bush while she was overseas and dared her to make the same remark in the Houston Astrodome. In response to Maines's comment, many country radio stations stopped playing Dixie Chicks songs and some fans boycotted the group; Tritt urged them on, telling people to "hit 'em in the pocketbook," as quoted on the Boston Channel Web site (March 18, 2003). "I feel it is one of our God-given rights as Americans to speak our minds freely and honestly. The First Amend-

ment is one of the things that makes our country great. However, in such a fragile time in the world, with that privilege comes the need to be responsible and mindful of the repercussions." Tritt, who often visits military bases to meet soldiers and has performed at a rally in support of American troops, said that the morale of servicemen and -women could be damaged if they heard negative comments about U.S. military policy.

Tritt assembled a large cast of guest musicians for his 2004 studio release, *My Honky Tonk History*. Again, the result is a rocking blend of country, blue. The fourth, especially noteworthy of the album's 12 tracks, "What You Say," features a duet between Tritt and the roots rocker John Mellencamp, set off by the twang of a banjo played by Béla Fleck. In *All Music Guide* (on-line), the reviewer Thom Jurek wrote of the album, "In all, *My Honky Tonk History* is a solid, sure-voiced outing from an enduring and committed artist."

Tritt has received many awards and honors. In 1991 he won the Horizon Award from the Country Music Association (CMA) and the TNN Music City News Song of the Year Award. In 1992 he was inducted into the Grand Ole Opry cast, was given the Vocal Event of the Year Award by the CMA, was named a star of tomorrow by TNN Music City News, and won a Grammy for best vocal collaboration for his duet with Marty Stuart, "The Whiskey Ain't Workin'." In 1993 he won the Vocal Event of the Year Award from the CMA once again and captured an award for vocal collaboration of the year from the TNN Music City News. In 1998 he received his second Grammy Award, for best country collaboration with vocals, with Earl Scruggs, Emmylou Harris, Joe Diffie, Marty Stuart, Merle Haggard, Pam Tillis, Patty Loveless, Randy Travis, and Ricky Skaggs for the song "Same Old Train." He was presented with a Public Service Award from the Department of Veteran Affairs in 2003 for his support of veterans. Tritt, who portrayed a disabled Vietnam veteran in three of his music videos and was a spokesman for Disabled American Veterans from 1994 to 1996, received the Veterans Administration's Secretary's Award in 1993 and the Hall of Fame Award from the Veterans of Foreign Wars in 2001.

Tritt has participated with other country stars in a series of radiothons to benefit St. Jude Children's Research Hospital, in Memphis, Tennessee. In August 2002 he donated $25,000 to the Sipesville, Pennsylvania, Volunteer Fire Company, which led the rescue of nine miners trapped underground for three days in late July of that year. The state of Georgia renamed a three-mile stretch of route 92 "Travis Tritt Highway" in 2001, and a Winchester gun, dubbed the Travis Tritt Tribute Rifle, has been created in his honor.

Tritt has appeared in several movies and television shows. His big-screen film cameos include *The Cowboy Way* (1994), *Sgt. Bilko* (1996), *Fire Down Below* (1997), and *Blues Brothers 2000* (1998); on TV he had parts in the films *Rio Diablo*

(1993), which co-starred the singers Kenny Rogers and Naomi Judd; *Christmas in My Hometown* (1996), in which he played a sheriff; and *Outlaw Justice* (1999), in which he worked with Rogers again. Among the TV shows in which he has appeared are *Tales from the Crypt* (1995), *The Jeff Foxworthy Show* (1995), *Dr. Quinn, Medicine Woman* (1996), *Diagnosis Murder* (1999), *Touched by an Angel* (1999), and *Arli$$* (1999). He also hosted the weekly television program *Country Countdown with Travis Tritt* on VH1 in the 1990s. His autobiography, *Ten Feet Tall and Bulletproof*, co-written with Michael Bane, was published in 1994.

Tritt, who admits to being "the ultimate control freak," was divorced twice before finding success in his music career. His first marriage, to his college sweetheart, ended after two years; his second lasted four years. (He has admitted that his heavy drinking contributed to the failure of that marriage and has since curbed such excesses.) On April 12, 1997 he married the model Theresa Nelson. The couple live on a 75-acre farm in Hiram, Georgia, outside Atlanta, with their three children—a daughter, Tyler Reese, born in 1998; a son, Tristan James, born in 1999; and a second son, Tarian Na-

thaniel, born in 2003. Tritt enjoys riding horses and Harley-Davidson motorcycles in his free time. "I like to do a little bit of a lot of different things," he told M.B. Roberts for *Country Music* (June/July 2002). "That's the way my music has always been. There's certain days when I feel like doing nothing but rock. Some days, it's straight-ahead country. Some days, bluegrass or the blues. I like being able to do all those different things."

—K.E.D.

Suggested Reading: *Country Music* p74 Oct./Nov. 2001, with photos; Country Stars Web site; *People* p25 Oct. 26, 1992; Travis Tritt Web site; Tritt, Travis and Michael Bane. *Ten Feet Tall and Bulletproof*, 1994

Selected Recordings: *Country Club*, 1990; *It's All About To Change*, 1991; *A Travis Tritt Christmas*, 1992; *T-R-O-U-B-L-E*, 1992; *Ten Feet Tall and Bulletproof*, 1994; *Greatest Hits: From The Beginning*, 1995; *The Restless Kind*, 1996; *No More Looking Over My Shoulder*, 1998; *Down the Road I Go*, 2000; *Strong Enough*, 2002; *The Essentials*, 2003; *My Honky Tonk History*, 2004

Troutt Powell, Eve

June 30, 1961– Historian; writer; educator

Address: 00338 LeConte Hall, Dept. of History, University of Georgia, Athens, GA 30602-1602

Eve Troutt Powell, an associate professor of history at the University of Georgia, was one of the 24 people (12 men and 12 women) to win a MacArthur Foundation Fellowship, a $500,000, "no strings attached" grant, in 2003. The foundation recognized Troutt Powell for her unique studies of the Middle East, particularly Sudan and Egypt. A former newspaperwoman, Troutt Powell is the author of two unconventional books: *The African Diaspora in the Mediterranean Lands of Islam* (2002, co-written with John O. Hunwick) and *A Different Shade of Colonialism: Egypt, Great Britain, and the Mastery of the Sudan, 1865-1925* (2003), both of which examine the issue of slavery in the Middle East—a topic about which few others have written. Through her works, Troutt Powell has attempted to convey her love for the Middle East and to dispel many misconceptions about that part of the world, without shying away from aspects of Middle Eastern culture, among them slavery, racial stereotyping, and colonialism, that many Westerners would condemn. She has presented compelling portraits of countries that became "colonized colonizers," and, drawing upon materials ranging from literary texts to songs and cartoons, she has scrutinized and exposed the historical imperialistic tendencies of those nations.

Courtesy of the MacArthur Foundation

Troutt Powell was born Eve Marie Troutt on June 30, 1961 in Detroit, Michigan, and grew up in the Washington Heights section of Manhattan, in New York City. Her father, a management consultant, was Jewish; he died when Troutt Powell was 14. Her mother, an African-American who was raised in a coal-mining area of Kentucky, earned four master's degrees while raising her three children and became a psychotherapist. She encouraged her children to strive academically, and Troutt Powell regards her as her first role model. By the age of 10, Troutt Powell was already demonstrating a special fondness for history and a particular interest in the Tudor period of Great Britain, which extended from the late 15th century to the early 17th century and encompassed the reign of King Henry VIII. At age 18 she gained admission to Harvard University, in Cambridge, Massachusetts, where she earned a bachelor's degree in history and literature magna cum laude in 1983.

Feeling a desire to see the ancient temples of Egypt, Troutt Powell then traveled to that nation as an intern with American University in Cairo. Although she had no knowledge of Arabic, Egypt's official language, and arrived unable to read so much as a street sign, she was captivated by the cultures of both ancient and modern Egypt. As she told *Current Biography*, she loved Egypt in part because "it has so much rhythm and soul. It's so rich and diverse." According to Phil Williams in a profile of Troutt Powell for the University of Georgia Web site (October 5, 2003), "Before she arrived back home in New York City, she knew that her future was the past, and that past was written in Arabic."

Troutt Powell told Kelly Simmons for the *Atlanta Journal-Constitution* (October 5, 2003, on-line) that her travels have had an enormous impact on her: "I came back on a crusade to change the way Americans think about the Middle East." Following her return to the U.S., with the intention of continuing her education in the future, she worked as a news clerk and reporter trainee at the *New York Times*. There, as she told Ross Markman for the *Athens Banner-Herald* (October 7, 2003, on-line), a Georgia newspaper, she felt determined to persuade people responsible for gathering, reporting, or editing the news to cover the Middle East more fairly and less stereotypically. "Americans have a tremendous misunderstanding of the vast diversity of this incredible area, the Middle East . . . ," she lamented to Williams. "We seem to be stuck in these images of fanatics, terrorists, and belly dancers when there's so much to know about the art, economy, politics, and culture of this region." Before her visit to Egypt she had planned to study French history in graduate school; having reconsidered her academic direction, she instead focused on the Middle East. She earned both a master's degree and a doctoral degree from Harvard, the former in Middle Eastern studies in 1988 and the latter in history and Middle Eastern studies in 1995. Also in 1995 she joined the faculty of the University of Georgia at Athens as an assistant professor; currently, she holds the title Lilly Teaching Fellow at the school. In 1999 she was a fellow at the Institute for Advanced Study in Princeton, New Jersey. During the 1990s she made periodic trips to the Middle East, living in Egypt intermittently for about three and a half years—including all of 1992—while she conducted research for her doctoral dissertation. By the time she had completed her studies, Troutt Powell had become fluent in written and spoken Arabic. "It's not as hard a language as people try to make it," she explained to Williams. "It's easy to learn. And it opened up the world of Cairo to me."

In addition to presenting a variety of scholastic papers on Middle Eastern culture at conferences and conducting research supported by several grants, Troutt Powell has written two books: *The African Diaspora in the Mediterranean Lands of Islam* (2002), on which she collaborated with John O. Hunwick of Northwestern University, and *A Different Shade of Colonialism: Egypt, Great Britain, and the Mastery of the Sudan, 1865-1925* (2003). *The African Diaspora* is unusual in that, in discussing the selling of African slaves, it focuses not on the trans-Atlantic slave trade—the subject of many other books—but on the forced migration of Africans to Islamic areas of the Mediterranean between the ninth and early 20th centuries. "For every gallon of ink that has been spilt on the trans-Atlantic slave trade and its consequences, only one very small drop has been spent on the study of the forced migration of black Africans into the Mediterranean world of Islam," the Web site of the book's publisher, Markus Wiener, pointed out. According to *Publishers Weekly*, as quoted on the Barnes & Noble Web site, *The African Diaspora* was the first definitive history of this often-ignored slave trade; it "offers scholars and students insight into the relationships between the brutal culture of slavery and the rich traditions of the Islamic world."

In *A Different Shade of Colonialism*, Troutt Powell discussed the national identity of Egypt when it was a British colony. She then detailed the way in which the formerly British-colonized Egypt became the colonizer of Sudan in 1820 and 1821, thus finding previously unexplored parallels between Britain and Egypt in terms of the racial stereotyping and slavery in which both nations engaged. In the *International Journal of African Historical Studies* (2003), Robert L. Tignor described the work as "an engaging and provocative book in Middle Eastern history, one of the best to appear in some time. . . . Richly grounded in source materials, and it is also historiographically sophisticated." Similarly, Heather J. Sharkey wrote for the *Middle East Journal* (Autumn 2003), "Scholars and students of modern Egyptian history will find *Different Shade of Colonialism* to be a fascinating and thought-provoking study. For a start, it is methodologically creative in marshaling literary texts for the study of Egyptian social and cultural history. . . . Powell's exposure of Egyptian attitudes towards Sudanese peoples does provide valuable material for understanding Sudanese-Egyptian relations in the 20th century."

In 2003, in recognition of Troutt Powell's achievements in literature and the field of Middle Eastern studies, the John D. and Catherine T. MacArthur Foundation awarded her a $500,000 fellowship. Candidates for the MacArthur Fellowship (often referred to as the "genius grant") are nominated and chosen without their knowledge; they may not apply for the fellowships and are not interviewed during the selection process. Fellows are chosen as much for the potential they demonstrate as for the originality and value of their past works. Ross Markman quoted the program's associate director, Mark Fitzsimmons, as saying, "This is not a prize for past efforts. . . . We're betting on their future." Unlike most grants, the MacArthur Fellowship is given without guidelines for its use; as Fitzsimmons explained, "If, for example, [recipients are] using [the grant] to take care of an elderly parent, and that frees up time for them to work, it's just as valuable." Troutt Powell is the first University of Georgia faculty member and only the fourth individual living in Georgia to receive a Mac-Arthur Fellowship since the program's inception, in 1981. At the time she received the telephone call informing her that she had won the award—her first indication that she had even been considered for it—she was writing a proposal for a $5,000 grant. Recalling her response to the news, she told Ross Markman, "After I tried to find my husband, I ran to the bathroom. And then I went back to the grant I was writing. . . . Then I realized . . . I didn't have to write that grant proposal anymore." Troutt Powell plans to apply the $500,000 toward researching and writing a book about former Suda-

nese slaves, including St. Josephine Bakhita, who, after being kidnapped and sold into slavery at age nine, was canonized by Pope John Paul II in 2000 in recognition of her service to the poor. Troutt Powell intends to continue teaching; her students have consistently given her excellent marks on faculty evaluations. "I am really really grateful and astounded and also thrilled that my field is being represented here," Troutt Powell said to Phil Williams. "The United States' relationship to the Middle East and how we are dealing with it has never been worse. I hope my work contributes in some way to understanding this vital part of the world."

Trout Powell married Timothy Powell, an associate professor of English at the University of Georgia, in 1986; they met during her first trip to Cairo. The couple have two sons, Jibreel and Gideon.

—K.J.E.

Suggested Reading: *Athens Banner-Herald* (online) Oct. 7, 2003; *Atlanta Journal Constitution* D p1 Oct. 5, 2003; MacArthur Foundation Web site; University of Georgia–Athens Web site

Selected Books: *The African Diaspora in the Mediterranean Lands of Islam* (with John Hunwick), 2002; *A Different Shade of Colonialism: Egypt, Great Britain, and the Mastery of the Sudan 1865-1925*, 2003

Tull, Tanya

Mar. 22, 1943– Social activist

Address: Beyond Shelter Inc., 520 S. Virgil Ave., Suite 200, Los Angeles, CA 90020

As Tanya Tull and Ruth Schwartz reported in an opinion column in the *Los Angeles Times* (March 6, 2004), on any given night in Los Angeles, California, alone, more than 8,000 children in homeless families struggle to find places to sleep. According to the National Coalition for the Homeless, as of mid-2003 more than 14 million families in the United States had critical housing needs and were at risk of becoming homeless. Tull has dedicated her professional life to the eradication of those problems, and her innovative solutions for alleviating them in Los Angeles and elsewhere around the U.S. have won national and international attention. Tull is the president and chief executive officer (CEO) of Beyond Shelter, an award-winning, Los Angeles–based nonprofit organization that she founded in 1988. Much of Beyond Shelter's focus is on helping homeless families to find permanent housing and then providing social services for six months to one year, to help those families rebuild their lives; in Los Angeles more than 3,000 families have benefitted from those services. The organization's programs have served as blueprints for new

Courtesy of Tanya Tull

ways of attacking the societal scourge of family homelessness and poverty on a national level. For example, beginning in 1999 the organization's methods were praised, documented, and disseminated by the Pew Partnership for Civic Change as part of the latter's national initiative known as Wanted: Solutions for America. In 2004 Beyond Shelter employed more than 60 people and operated on a budget of $3.4 million. Through Beyond Shelter Tull has developed six permanent, affordable, multi-unit housing projects for low-income persons or homeless families in Los Angeles County, with six additional new housing projects in development. Over the years she has raised millions of dollars in grants and donations to fund her humanitarian work.

The older of two children, Tanya Tull was born on March 22, 1943 in San Francisco, California. Her father, Sam Cherry, was a painting contractor who later owned and operated a bookstore and art gallery in San Bernardino, California; her mother, Clare Cherry, was a noted early-childhood educator and the author of several books on teaching children. Tull's brother, who goes by the name of Neeli Cherkovski, is a poet and the author of biographies of the writers Lawrence Ferlinghetti and Charles Bukowski, among other books. Tull's parents were first-generation American Jews whose parents had fled persecution in the Ukraine and immigrated to the U.S. as teenagers. In San Francisco Sam and Clare Cherry "were involved in the Bohemian world of artists and writers for a few years," as Tull informed Current Biography. "My parents were extremely liberal, offbeat and non-judgmental, with friends from all walks of life and ethnicities." Her father's older brother, Herman Cherry, was a New York–based artist, a leading abstract expressionist closely associated with such figures as Jackson Pollock and Willem de Kooning. That artistic world "provided a background for my life, albeit from a distance," Tull told Current Biography. After Tull's birth, her family moved to Los Angeles. As a child she was an avid reader; she has also done abstract painting.

Tull graduated with a B.A. degree in arts and humanities from Scripps College, in Claremont, California, in 1964. She then spent a year working on a kibbutz in Israel. In 1967 she moved with her husband, a Moroccan-born Israeli artist, and their baby boy to Los Angeles. Tull and her husband were unable to find employment, and the young family was forced to rely on welfare for three months. Told by a social worker who had visited her family about a job opportunity at the Los Angeles County Department of Public Social Services, Tull applied and was hired for on-the-job training as a social worker. Within weeks, in 1967, she had begun her career in social work, handling the cases of 60 families in need in South Central Los Angeles. "Our [family's] nightmare was over," Tull said in a speech she gave upon accepting the National Citizen Activist Award from the Gleitsman Foundation, in 1996, as quoted in a Beyond Shelter press release. She added, however, that she has "never forgotten how I felt—the helplessness, bewilderment, and feelings of despair. . . . If things could go so wrong for me, then how much more

wrong can they go for those who did not have the opportunities and education that I had? My life work eventually was directed by those feelings."

Dispirited by what she saw as government malfeasance and insensitivity, in 1970 Tull left her job at the Department of Public Social Services. The next year she earned a life-teaching credential from the School of Education at the University of California, Los Angeles (UCLA); she then taught elementary school for a short while, spending most of the rest of the decade raising her growing family. (Her first marriage had ended in 1968; in 1971 she had remarried and had two more children.) In 1980, as she recalled in her speech at the Gleitsman Foundation award ceremony, she was moved to action by an article in the Los Angeles Times describing the hundreds of poor children living among rats and garbage in the transient hotels of Los Angeles's Skid Row. "Within a week, a woman possessed, I was walking the streets of Skid Row," she said. Within two months, despite her lack of experience in the field, she had founded Para Los Ninos, Spanish for "For the Children." Armed with a letter of support from Mayor Tom Bradley, with whom she had met, she began seeking grants for the organization from foundations and corporations. Focused primarily on the immigrant community in downtown Los Angeles, Para Los Ninos runs child-care and family-support programs. Tull served first as executive director and then as president of the organization until 1996.

While maintaining that post, Tull also cofounded, in 1983, and served as co-director of L.A. Family Housing Corp., a nonprofit agency that operates emergency shelters and transitional housing and develops permanent housing for the homeless. From 1986 to 1988 she was executive director of the organization. In 1988 Tull founded two more nonprofit organizations, A Community of Friends and Beyond Shelter. The former develops permanent housing for the mentally ill throughout Los Angeles County. The latter organization, Beyond Shelter, has been the chief focus of Tull's work ever since.

According to both the U.S. Department of Health and Human Services and the U.S. Interagency Council on Homelessness, an estimated two to three million people find themselves homeless at some point each year. A study conducted by the National Alliance to End Homelessness has found that families with children are the fastest-growing group among the homeless. Because of poor credit and histories of being evicted from housing, many homeless people have a very difficult time finding places to live. Further, those families who have recently been placed in housing are still at a high risk of becoming homeless again. In their Los Angeles Times article, Tull and Ruth Schwartz, executive director of the Shelter Partnership in Los Angeles, wrote that in Los Angeles the "majority of families that become homeless are headed by single mothers, surviving on incomes as low as $600 per month for a family of four if the parent is unemployed to about $900 per month if the parent is working." The authors wrote that homeless families are "generally 'invisible' to the public," but that "their numbers are growing."

Beyond Shelter's chief program is Housing First, through which Tull helps homeless families move from emergency shelters to permanent, affordable housing in residential neighborhoods throughout Los Angeles County. Much of the program's methodology arises from Tull's and Beyond Shelter's conviction that homeless families, once housed, can begin to regain self-confidence and control over their lives, and, furthermore, are much more likely to benefit from the other social services provided by groups such as Beyond Shelter and mainstream programs. Therefore, placing homeless families in housing as quickly as possible is Beyond Shelter's primary goal. The program's methods are described on the organization's Web site: homeless families are referred to Housing First by more than three dozen agencies throughout Los Angeles County. After being enrolled in the Housing First program, a family is assigned a case manager, who, working through Beyond Shelter's Housing Resources Department, moves the family into affordable rental housing in a neighborhood of the family's choice. Next, the case manager helps to introduce the family members to their neighborhood—educating them as to the shops, local transportation, and community services available in the area—and helps to enroll the family's children in schools. The Beyond Shelter Web site states that even six months to a year after a family has been moved into new housing, the case manager "provides individualized, supportive social services to help each family move toward improved social and economic well-being." The success of Housing First has attracted both national and international attention. The program, funded through donations and grants, was chosen by the U.S. Department of Housing and Urban Development to represent the United States as one of "25 U.S. Best Practices" at the United Nations Conference on Human Settlements, Habitat II, which was held in Istanbul, Turkey, in 1996. There, it was chosen as one of the "100 International Best Practices" by the U.N. Center on Human Settlements for dissemination worldwide.

Other major programs of Beyond Shelter include the Rental Assistance Department, which helps to run the Emergency Housing Assistance Program and the various Rent to Prevent Eviction Programs for Los Angeles County—all of which are dedicated to aiding homeless families and elderly or disabled individuals in obtaining and maintaining permanent housing. The Employment Services Department helps families to obtain and maintain employment by offering access to job listings, the use of computers so that the unemployed can search for work, tutorials in typing and other basic skills, and other job-placement and job-retention support. A Beyond Shelter case manager and employment counselor work together on a client's be-

half, a method that was developed and conducted by Beyond Shelter for the U.S. Department of Labor as a Welfare-to-Work Demonstration Project.

The Beyond Shelter Housing Development Corp. develops, manages, and operates affordable housing in low-income neighborhoods, primarily in Central and South Central Los Angeles, and is currently developing neighborhood resource centers within, or adjacent to, many of its new housing projects. In addition, for the past 10 years Tull and Beyond Shelter have led a neighborhood revitalization project in South Central Los Angeles. With the agency's programs in Los Angeles serving as a laboratory for systemic changes, Tull is focusing her efforts on promoting Beyond Shelter's key initiatives—helping homeless people to secure and maintain housing—on a national scale. Beyondshelter.org reports that the program's methods are being taught to other organizations across the country with the help of Beyond Shelter's Institute for Research, Training and Technical Assistance and the National Alliance to End Homelessness.

Tull has spoken at many national forums and institutions around the country. She is a member of the advisory committees of the Washington, D.C.–based National Alliance to End Homelessness and the Housing Plus Services Committee of the National Low Income Housing Coalition. She is also a member of the Right to Housing Working Group at the National Law Center on Homelessness and Housing, and she sits on the board of directors of the National Housing Conference. In addition, she is an adjunct professor for research at the University of Southern California School of Social Work.

Tull and her organization have often been recognized for their tireless efforts to help those less fortunate. She received the Jefferson Award from the National Institute of Public Service in 1982 and the Ralph Bunche Peace Award during the "Year of the Homeless" from the United Nations Organization, Pacific Chapter, in 1987. Tull was named one of *Newsweek*'s "One Hundred Heroes of Our Time" in 1986. Two years later she received the Founders Award from the National Association of Fundraising Executives. In addition, Beyond Shelter was given the Community Service Excellence Award by the Federal Interagency Council on the Homeless in 1992. That same year Whittier College, in California, awarded Tull an honorary doctorate in social sciences. Tull and Beyond Shelter were honored with the Nonprofit Sector Achievement Award by the National Alliance to End Homelessness in 1996. She was named an "Unsung Hero" in 2000 at the 85th anniversary celebration of the California Community Foundation. In 2002 Tull was selected as one of *Los Angeles Business Journal*'s "Women Who Make a Difference" and received the Community Service Award from the Mexican American Legal Defense and Educational Fund.

From her first marriage Tull has a son, Dani, an artist; she has two daughters, Deborah, a social activist, and Rebecca, a special-projects associate with Beyond Shelter, from her second marriage. In

1985 Tull's second husband died of cancer. She informed *Current Biography* that on December 5, 2004 she would marry B. J. Markel and become stepmother to his 14-year-old son. In her speech at the Gleitsman Foundation award ceremony, Tull stated that when she feels "tired and overwhelmed" by her work and all the suffering and hardship she sees in the course of it, she needs only think of "the single mother with three young children living in her car during a cold Fall in Los Angeles, holding down a job . . . and bringing [her children] home to the car each night because, after taxes, she could not buy food, pay for the car and child care, and still maintain a roof over their heads. And ultimately I accept the fact that, of everything there might be to do in my life today, nothing could be more important than what I have chosen to do." Tull told *Current Biography*, with regard to the artistic aspirations she had in her youth, "I finally found peace in the work that I do, which represents the integration of the right and left sides of my brain! I apply the creative process to social problems in a way that completely fulfills my multiple interests and skills, i.e. deep thinking, problem-solving, integrating existing information in new ways, writing, creating. . . . In this work daily, I get to use words and my mind to both write and speak out about issues/problems/-causes/solutions in a way that shares information with others, helps them to view things differently and to understand, and helps to promote systemic change on a national scale. . . . Sometimes I get to apply my artistic side to the affordable housing that I build. . . . My dream in the future is to write more . . . I actually have a lot more I want to say."

—C.F.T.

Suggested Reading: Beyond Shelter Web site; *Los Angeles Times* B p21 Mar. 6, 2003; pew-partnership.org; U.S. Department of Health and Human Services Web site; U.S. Interagency Council on Homelessness Web site

---

Jeff Haynes/AFP/Getty Images

Vinatieri, Adam

(vin-uh-tee-AIR-ee)

Dec. 28, 1972– Football player

Address: New England Patriots, One Patriot Place, Foxborough, MA 02035

Most young sports fans and athletes dream of winning a championship by sinking a basket or scoring a goal in the final seconds of a deciding game. Thoughts of such glory drive athletes through long years of physical toil. The New England Patriots' placekicker Adam Vinatieri has fulfilled such a dream not once but twice, kicking last-second field goals in two Super Bowls, in 2002 and 2004, to win the National Football League (NFL) championship for his team. Though Vinatieri, at around five feet nine inches and 190 pounds, is one of the smaller players in the NFL and often the smallest on the field of play, his strong and accurate kicking has made him an NFL giant killer and kingmaker. He is one of only two NFL kickers ever to record at least 100 points in six consecutive seasons, and his career 80.6 percent accuracy on field-goal kicks is 10th-best in NFL history among kickers who have made more than 100 field goals. Greg Boeck, in *USA Today* (February 2, 2004), called Vinatieri a "cold-blooded kicker for the ages," and the kicker's teammate Ty Law, referring to Vinatieri's seeming immunity to the pressure of crucial moments, told Boeck, "He's ice cold. . . . He lives for those type situations."

A placekicker's job entails field-goal kicks, which are normally attempted 15 to 60 yards from the goalposts; kickoffs at the starts of games and second halves and after touchdowns by his team; and one-point conversions, often called extra points, which are kicked after his team's touchdowns. Placekickers also double sometimes as punters. (Whereas placekickers kick the ball from its stationary position on the ground, punters—who do not score points—drop the ball from their hand, and kick it as it is falling.) Some football observers and fans give little credit to placekickers, who appear on the field only for a select number of plays during games and rarely engage in any of the bruising physical contact that defines the sport. In addition, kickers sometimes receive scorn due to the seeming absurdity that games contested by 300-pound men are often decided by small players who trot in from the sidelines in clean uniforms to kick the ball. Perhaps because of his resounding success, Vinatieri has escaped such derision; indeed, he has been praised by his coaches and teammates for his toughness and athleticism. As quoted in an article found on the Canadian Web site TSN.ca, the Patriots' head coach, Bill Belichick, called Vinatieri "more of a football player than he is a kicker." According to the same article, the Patriots' special-teams coach, Larry Izzo, described Vinatieri as a "great athlete" and a "tremendous competitor" who can run quickly and make tackles when necessary.

The second of Paul and Judy Vinatieri's four children, Adam Vinatieri was born in Yankton, South Dakota, on December 28, 1972. He has three siblings: Chad, Christine, and Beau, who, like his older brother Adam, was a placekicker in college (Black Hills State University, in South Dakota). Their father works for an insurance company. When Adam Vinatieri was five years old, his parents moved the family to Rapid City, South Dakota. As a child Vinatieri had trouble reading and was enrolled in classes for children with learning disabilities. During his adolescence he spent his summers working on the South Dakota farm owned by his grandfather and uncle. At Rapid City Central High School, Vinatieri, an avid athlete, was a member of the football, soccer, track, and wrestling teams. In 1991 he earned first-team all-state honors in football. After graduating from high school, Vinatieri enrolled in the United States Military Academy, but he lasted only two weeks there. He then enrolled in South Dakota State University, where he continued to excel on the football field. He served as the school football team's placekicker for four years and as the team's punter for three (1992-94), earning first-team all-conference honors each season. By the end of his four years at South Dakota State, Vinatieri held the record as the school's all-time leading scorer in football, having tallied 185 points with his right foot.

After graduating in 1995 with a degree in health and physical education, Vinatieri spent the latter part of that year training for professional football. Having gone to a relatively small and obscure university, however, he was unknown to most NFL scouts and team officials. Since no NFL team showed interest initially in drafting him, Vinatieri tried out for a spot as a placekicker and punter with the Amsterdam Admirals of the World League. He played one season with the Admirals, recording nine field goals on 10 attempts. His luck changed in 1996, when, hoping to add depth to their team's kicking, the Patriots signed Vinatieri as an undrafted free agent.

Vinatieri immediately proved his worth to the Patriots. In his first season, 1996, he set a team rookie record by recording 120 points (27 field goals and 39 extra points). His scoring total was also the highest on the team, which that year finished the regular season with an 11–5 record and won the American Football Conference (AFC) championship before losing to the Green Bay Packers in Super Bowl XXXI. The following season Vinatieri again helped the Patriots to qualify for the play-offs by recording 115 points on field goals and conversions. In the 1998 season Vinatieri, succeeding on 80 percent of his attempts, kicked a career-high 31 field goals. Over the next three seasons, 1999–2001, he was consistently excellent, averaging roughly 25 field goals per season while succeeding on an average of 80 percent of his attempts.

The Patriots finished the 2001 regular season with an 11–5 record. In their divisional play-off game against the Oakland Raiders, in January 2002, New England's star quarterback, Tom Brady, rallied the Patriots for a final drive that put the team in position to attempt a game-tying field goal in the closing seconds. Vinatieri then marched onto the field and, despite a snow storm and strong winds, calmly kicked the ball 45 yards through the goalposts to send the game into overtime. That kick, which catapulted Vinatieri to NFL stardom, is considered by many to have been more difficult—and therefore more remarkable—than those he has made to win Super Bowls. The inspired Patriots won the game against the Raiders in overtime, 16–13, on another field goal by Vinatieri, this one from 23 yards away. In that memorable contest, as described by the Web site puresportsart.com, "greatness, controversy, karma, and mother nature collided like never before."

After defeating the Pittsburgh Steelers, the Patriots advanced to the Super Bowl for the third time in franchise history. The championship game, Super Bowl XXXVI, was hard fought: the Patriots took an early lead, but the talented St. Louis Rams tied the score at 17 late in the fourth quarter. Tom Brady then drove the team far enough down the field to put the goalposts within Vinatieri's range. With seven seconds left on the game clock, Vinatieri sent his teammates, coaches, and fans into a frenzy by kicking a 48-yard field goal to win the game, 20–17. To celebrate the first NFL championship title in the Patriots' history, the state of Massachusetts held a victory parade for the team on the streets of Boston, in early February 2002, during which the players were hailed as heroes by more than one million fans.

The team stumbled the following year and failed to make the play-offs. Despite the Patriots' struggles, Vinatieri had a phenomenal year, making 27 of his 30 field-goal tries, including the longest of his career, 57 yards, in a game against the Chicago Bears. Under Brady's leadership, the Patriots returned to top form in the 2003 season, posting a league-best 14–2 record. (Vinatieri was successful on 74 percent of his field-goal attempts that year, which was, for him, a career low.) The Patriots racked up 14 victories in a row, including two play-off wins against the Tennessee Titans and Indianapolis Colts, respectively, to reach the Super Bowl for the second time in three years. Super

Bowl XXXVIII, which pitted the Patriots against the Carolina Panthers, was held at Reliant Stadium, in Houston, Texas. More than 70,000 fans were in attendance at the game and millions more watched it on television.

In the first quarter Vinatieri uncharacteristically missed a 31-yard field-goal attempt, kicking too far to the right, then had another blocked in the second quarter. Referring to his failure to take advantage of those scoring opportunities, Vinatieri told Tim Polzer for the Web site superbowl.com, "Honestly, you just have to get those out of the back of your head and move forward. You can't think about that too terribly much and hope that you have an opportunity at the end of the game to make a difference." When the game was on the line, tied at 29 points apiece, and it was up to Vinatieri to decide the outcome, his teammates apparently had no doubt that their placekicker would bring them victory. Referring after the game to Vinatieri's two missed field-goal attempts, the Patriots' defensive end Richard Seymour told Joseph Duarte for the *Houston Chronicle* (February 2, 2004), "Never mind what happened in the past. With the game on the line, he's the best pressure kicker in the league."

Before Vinatieri could go onto the field to attempt the goal, the Panthers had called a time-out—a common tactic, meant to rattle an opposing kicker by giving him more time to think about the pressure he faces. Nonetheless, with fewer than 10 seconds remaining on the clock, Vinatieri kicked the 41-yard field goal straight through the uprights to lift the Patriots to a 32–29 victory—and to their team's second Super Bowl championship in three years. The wide receiver Ricky Proehl had been a member of the Rams when they lost to the Patriots, thanks to Vinatieri's kick, in 2002; in the 2003 season he played for the Panthers, and so had the misfortune to watch again as a Vinatieri kick sent his team to defeat. "It was like déjà vu all over again," Proehl told Duarte. "It was like living a nightmare all over again." Regarding the winning kick, Vinatieri told Andrew Fraser for BBC News (February 2, 2004, on-line), "I was just very happy that I looked up and saw [the football] going down the middle. With the pressure on, it's never easy. You try to block all the external things out and kick it." The occasion marked the 16th time in Vinatieri's career that he had kicked a winning field goal in the final minute of the fourth quarter or overtime of a game. Some observers commented on the fact that the retractable roof of Reliant Stadium was closed during the Super Bowl contest, and that Vinatieri has been successful on 32 of 36 field-goal attempts in his career when kicking in a closed stadium. Vinatieri has said that he tries to approach his field-goal attempts in the crucial moments of important games as if they were no different from those he attempts in practice. He is one of three players in the Patriots' franchise history to record more than 600 points.

The Patriots continued their winning ways at the start of the 2004 season, overcoming their competitors in their first six games. At that point their 18 straight wins in regular-season games set a league record, breaking that of the 1933–34 Chicago Bears. (Taking into account the play-offs, the Patriots won 21 consecutive games.) Their winning streak ended on October 31, 2004, when they lost to the Pittsburgh Steelers, 34–20. Vinatieri had by then completed a total of 14 out of 15 attempted kicks in the season.

Vinatieri has appeared on television on the *Late Show with David Letterman* and *Late Night with Conan O'Brien*. He has been active in his community and has often donated money and time to charities, including the Rhode Island Coalition Against Domestic Violence, the Fellowship of Christian Athletes, Athletes in Action, D.A.R.E., and the Governor's Highway Safety Bureau. In addition, he is the spokesperson for the Blue Cross & Blue Shield of Rhode Island's Teen Anti-smoking Contest. He is an active partner in the on-line magazine findRI.com, which provides information on the state of Rhode Island, where Vinatieri lives with his wife, Valerie.

Vinatieri is a first cousin of the legendary motorcycle daredevil Evel Knievel. (Riding motorcycles is one of Vinatieri's own hobbies; another is hunting.) His great-great-grandfather, Felix Vinatieri, a musician and composer, served as the bandmaster for General George Custer, who earned a reputation in the Union Army during the American Civil War and is best remembered for his ill-fated campaign, in 1876, against Native Americans in the Battle of Little Bighorn.

—C.F.T.

Suggested Reading: Adam Vinatieri Web site; National Football League Web site; New England Patriots Web site; *New York Times* VIII p15 Feb. 10, 2002, with photo; *USA Today* (on-line) Feb. 2, 2004, with photo

---

Wallace, Ben

Sep. 10, 1974– Basketball player

Address: Detroit Pistons, Palace of Auburn Hills, 2 Championship Dr., Auburn Hills, MI 48326

Standing six feet nine inches, Ben Wallace, center for the Detroit Pistons, is the shortest person ever to lead the National Basketball Association (NBA) in blocked shots, and he led the league in rebounds in the 2001–02 and 2002–03 seasons; his tenacity has twice brought him defensive-player-of-the-year honors, and he has garnered comparisons to such defensive greats as Bill Russell and Dennis Rodman. Wallace, who was never drafted by an NBA team, has been instrumental in helping

Courtesy of the NBA

Ben Wallace

the Pistons to grow from a lackluster unit into the 2004 NBA champions. After playing basketball at a small community college in Ohio and at Virginia Union University, Wallace was drafted as the 15th overall pick by the Oklahoma City Cavalry of the Continental Basketball Association (CBA). Opting instead to try out for the Boston Celtics of the NBA, Wallace failed to make the team's roster and was then passed over by an Italian team as well. Making it at last to the NBA, he joined the Washington Wizards' roster during the 1996–97 year, remaining with the team until the 1999–2000 season, when he started in 81 games for the Orlando Magic. After being traded at the end of that year to the Pistons, Wallace became the team's defensive anchor. Since 2002, under Wallace's leadership, Detroit has claimed three Central Division titles in a row—and the 2003–04 NBA championship. Short for his position and hardly an offensive threat (his career scoring average is 6.1 points per game), in 2003 Wallace nonetheless became the first non-drafted player ever to be voted as a starter at the All-Star Game. He told Roscoe Nance for *USA Today* (January 6, 2003), "I feel like I'm going to get every rebound. If I don't get the ball, I feel I'm going to get my hand on it. If I can't get my hand on it, I'm going to be as close as I possibly can get to it. I'm definitely going to attack the boards when the shot goes up."

The 10th of 11 children, and the youngest of eight brothers, Ben Wallace was born to working-class parents on September 10, 1974 in rural White Hall, Alabama. Wallace explained to Brian C. Hedger for *Hoophype* (April 21, 2002, on-line) that his incredible rebounding skills stem from his having played basketball with his older brothers, who

were bigger than him: "I'm the smallest one. In order to be out there and play with 'em I had to rebound the loose balls and all the other grunt work on the court. I've just been doing it ever since." During the summer between his sophomore and junior years of high school, Wallace earned money by giving three-dollar haircuts to his family and friends. That allowed him to attend a nearby basketball camp in York, Alabama, hosted by Charles Oakley, then a formidable defensive presence in the NBA. Oakley became Wallace's mentor at the camp. Speaking with Daniel G. Habib for *Sports Illustrated* (October 29, 2001), Wallace recalled engaging in a one-on-one drill with Oakley, which both taught him a lesson and demonstrated his persistence: "I wasn't really taking the camp seriously, and [Oakley] wanted to show me how serious basketball really was. So he beat on me a little bit, and I beat on him a little bit, but I think he was most surprised that I didn't back down. When he hit me underneath the boards, I just kept coming."

In high school Wallace ran track and earned all-state honors in baseball and football in addition to playing basketball; he decided to focus on the latter sport after a growth spurt in his senior year. Even so, colleges were more interested in Wallace as a football player than as a basketball player, which led to several offers of football scholarships—as well as to some confusion. As he told William C. Rhoden for the *New York Times* (May 11, 2002), he agreed to go to one school, then asked the coaches if they were "going to let me go both ways. . . . They were like yeah. When I signed and got there, they said they meant offense-defense; I meant football and basketball." As Wallace recalled, one football coach said to him, "Football and basketball? We're not giving a guy a full scholarship in football to play basketball." Football aside, Wallace's grades were not good enough for him to attend a four-year college, but Charles Oakley arranged for him to enroll at Cuyahoga Community College, in Cleveland, Ohio. In the fall of 1992, after packing for the warm climate he was used to, Wallace left for the school; as Sean Deveney wrote for the *Sporting News* (April 15, 2002), "The story would not be too good to be true unless it was snowing in Cleveland when Wallace arrived. It was." Wallace told Deveney, "It was definitely a shock to me. I wanted to go home. But Charles went out of his way to be there for me. Whenever I needed to talk on the phone, he was there. I went to his mom's house in Cleveland for home-cooked meals. He gave me a job in his car wash. He committed to me, and he stuck to his word." After two years Wallace transferred to Oakley's alma mater, Virginia Union University, in Richmond, where he majored in criminal justice. He was named a Division II All-American in 1996, when he helped Virginia Union compile a record of 28–3 and make it to the Division II Final Four. Wallace garnered statistical averages of 12.5 points per game, 10.5 rebounds per game, and 3.68 blocked shots per game that season; his averages for his overall career at the school were 13.4 points per game and 10 rebounds per game. Referring to his later accomplishments in the NBA, Dave Robbins, the head coach at Virginia Union, told Sean Deveney, "Even when he was here, I did not see this coming. I thought he needed to hone his offense in a lesser league first. What I did not know is that they don't care about your offense if your defense is that good."

That assessment notwithstanding, after college Wallace was passed over by the NBA and by a team in an Italian league before making his way onto the Washington Wizards squad as a backup player. In 34 games during the 1996–97 season, Wallace averaged 1.7 rebounds in 5.8 minutes of play. In the following year, over 67 games, his averages increased to 16.8 minutes of play and 4.8 rebounds per game. Wallace's defensive play began to make a strong impression around the league that year. In the 1998–99 season Wallace played in 46 games, averaging 26.8 minutes on the court and 8.3 rebounds per game; in one contest, a 97–86 win over the Cleveland Cavaliers on April 29, 1999, he posted a career-high 20 points while shooting nine-of-nine from the field and grabbing 10 rebounds.

On August 11, 1999 Wallace was traded, along with Tim Legler, Terry Davis, and Jeff McInnis, to the Orlando Magic for Isaac Austin. It was with the Magic that Wallace became a well-known defensive threat. He started in all 81 games in which he played, averaging 8.21 rebounds per contest. He had trouble, however, making free-throw shots, telling Steve Wyche for the *Washington Post* (March 24,1999), "Everybody says that should be the easiest shot in the game. On the same token, once you go to [the free-throw] line you're by yourself. You got no help from your teammates. The refs can't give you a call. I think it's a matter of being put in that situation so many times you find yourself in a comfort zone. Once you get in a comfort zone and you know you're going to make that shot, things change for you."

Along with Chucky Atkins, Wallace was traded again, on August 3, 2000—this time to the Detroit Pistons in exchange for the superstar Grant Hill. Wallace's first season with the struggling Pistons proved to be memorable. After signing a six-year, $30 million contract with the team, Wallace proceeded to lead the league in rebounds that year, with 1,052; he also became the first Piston to lead the league simultaneously in rebounds, steals (107), and blocks (186). In 60 of the games in which he played that season, Wallace made more than 10 rebounds; he was second in the league for average rebounds per game (13.2) and ranked 10th in the NBA for blocks per game (2.33). He grabbed a career-high 28 rebounds against the Toronto Raptors on April 17, 2001. During the 2001–02 season Wallace joined NBA legends Hakeem Olajuwon, Bill Walton, and Kareem Abdul-Jabbar as the only players ever to have led the league in blocks (138) and rebounds (1,039) in the same season. Thanks in large part to Wallace's contribution, the Pistons compiled an impressive 50–32 record and cap-

tured the Central Division title of the Eastern Conference. (They were then eliminated in the conference semifinals by the Boston Celtics.) Wallace was named NBA defensive player of the year, honored with a spot on the NBA All-Defensive First Team, and named to the All-NBA Third Team. Also that year, at the 2002 World Championships, Wallace was part of the U.S. Team, which finished in sixth place.

In a game against the Miami Heat on November 20, 2002, Wallace tied his personal record for blocked shots (10). Also during the 2002–03 season, he led the NBA in rebounds (15.4 per game, with a career-high total of 1,126), including offensive rebounds (293), while helping the Pistons set an NBA record for most games in overtime without a loss (eight). Wallace was named to the All-NBA Second team and again was chosen as the NBA defensive player of the year; through his leadership on defense, the Pistons allowed an average of only 87.7 points per game—a league low—to be scored against them that year. One day after his mother's funeral, Wallace became the first non-drafted player to start an All-Star Game. He then led the Pistons to another Central Division title, with a record, again, of 50–32. The team compiled the best record in the Eastern Conference and then, in the first round of the play-offs, became only the seventh team in NBA history to overcome a three-games-to-one deficit, by beating the Orlando Magic—after Wallace pulled down 21 rebounds in the fifth game. After dispatching the Philadelphia 76ers in the conference semifinals, the Pistons advanced to the Eastern Conference Finals, where they lost to the New Jersey Nets in a four-game sweep. Wallace's per-game averages during the play-offs were impressive: 8.9 points, 16.3 rebounds, 2.47 steals, and 3.06 blocks. During Detroit's championship season in 2003–04, Wallace averaged 9.5 points per game with 12.4 rebounds; he also registered 3.04 blocks per game. In recognition of his strong performance, Wallace was named to the 2004 All-NBA Second Team and the All-Defensive Team. In the play-offs, against the Los Angeles Lakers, he averaged 10.3 points per game, with 14.3 rebounds and 56 total blocks, while the Pistons claimed the NBA title, winning four of the five games.

Ben Wallace and his wife, Chanda, have two sons. Wallace enjoys fishing as well as building and racing remote-control cars. Occasionally his hair has generated as much interest among reporters as his play; at various times on the court, he has sported cornrows or a large Afro, the latter of which, as William C. Rhoden noted, "adds four inches to his 6-foot-9 frame, making him a sort of 7-footer." As Sean Deveney reported, Wallace "has learned from the generosity of [Charles] Oakley" and helped secure spots on the Virginia Union team for two of his nephews, Brian Underwood and Hugh Taylor. Wallace also gives a scholarship to the school annually. As for being named to All-NBA Teams despite his not being an overwhelming offensive threat, Wallace told Perry A. Farrell and Helen St. James for the *Detroit Free Press* (May 7, 2003, on-line), upon making the All-NBA Second Team in 2003, "I think it's a great compliment to me as a person and as a player. It says that the league is allowing people to be themselves and recognize players for the things they do. Scoring in this league for so long has been what everybody has recognized, but now we have a new generation of guys coming in. We have so many great scorers that some people have to do other things, and that's what I've tried to do. To come out and play the way I play, not scoring a lot of points, and people still recognize me as one of the best in the league, is an honor."

—L.A.S.

Suggested Reading: *Detroit Free Press* (on-line) Feb. 25, 2003, Apr. 30, 2003, May 7, 2003; *Sports Illustrated* p103 Mar. 9, 1998, with photo, p180 Oct. 30, 2000, p150 Oct. 29, 2001; *Sporting News* p12 Apr. 15, 2002

Thomas J. Gibbons/Getty Images

Waters, Alice

Apr. 28, 1944– Executive chef and owner of Chez Panisse Restaurant

Address: Chez Panisse, 1517 Shattuck Ave., Berkeley CA 94709

"Is there an emerging American cuisine? Well, it's difficult to say," the chef and restaurateur Alice Waters told Dean Riddle for *Waitrose.com* (November 1998). "We live in such a large country. But I do feel something is unfolding. Cuisine, however,

is a word I hardly ever use, and I don't really care for the word chef, either. To me, the words imply that your work is done, and I believe cooking to be a work in progress." Since she founded Chez Panisse, in Berkeley, California, over three decades ago, Waters has revolutionized restaurant cooking and how people think about food in the U.S. "More than any other single figure, Miss Waters has been instrumental in developing the exciting and imaginative style that has been labeled New American cuisine," Marian Burros wrote for the *New York Times* (September 26, 1984). "Its trademarks . . . are an adventurous, often improvised use of the finest American ingredients and an exquisitely simple and straightforward approach to their preparation." Before Waters's arrival on the culinary scene, prepackaged, chemical-laden convenience foods such as frozen dinners constituted a large part of the American diet, and gourmet dining was virtually synonymous with French cuisine. The menu Waters offered in her restaurant helped to change matters. Chez Panisse—widely recognized as one of the best restaurants in the world—serves a different, simply prepared, five-course, fixed-price meal daily; the ingredients depend on the availability of fresh ingredients sold by local farmers and other providers. Thanks largely to Waters and Chez Panisse, American cuisine is now as respected as French cuisine and is a fixture of fine dining establishments everywhere. Moreover, Americans are more likely than ever before to purchase and prepare locally grown fruits and vegetables. As the on-line magazine *California Monthly* noted, "Anyone who has been to a local farmer's market, bought organic produce, or eaten a café-baked pizzetta has been touched by Waters' gentle, discriminating hand."

Waters wants Chez Panisse to do more than bring people pleasure; she hopes it is helping to initiate a social revolution. She believes that people who eat food grown or produced by local farmers, instead of processed and packaged foods, will be more apt to take care of one another and the environment. Waters is a staunch proponent of the Slow Food Movement, whose founders deplore the fast-food industry's effects on cultures and environments. The movement stresses the importance of eating as a family-centered act and of sustainable agriculture, which, according to the Web site of the Alliance for Sustainable Agriculture, means "ecologically sound, economically viable, socially just and humane" agricultural practices. Waters has set up a number of school-based community-garden projects, with the goal of showing youngsters the rewards of eating home-grown fruits and vegetables. "We need to wake up and pay attention and educate ourselves about what we are eating and what the consequences are," she said to *AgBiotech Buzz* (July 29, 2002), an on-line newspaper funded by the Pew Initiative on Food and Biotechnology. "I call it a rather delicious revolution. It isn't hard to do. This isn't like a diet. This is the ultimate diet. You eat delicious things and it makes you feel better and it changes how you relate to people. You become part of a community."

The second of the four daughters born to Pat Waters, an accountant and business-psychology consultant, and Margaret Waters, a social worker, Alice Waters was born in Chatham, New Jersey, on April 28, 1944. During World War II her mother and father, responding to an appeal from the federal government, grew a so-called victory garden, as did millions of other people, as a way of decreasing the country's dependence on imported products. After the war ended her parents continued to maintain their garden. Waters told *California Monthly* that her mother always served healthful, nutritious meals, but she "really wasn't a very good cook. We never had anything especially fancy; . . . but we always had dinner together, at the table, at the same time, and we always had to sit there and do that every night." At the New Hampshire lake where the family spent summers, the neighboring families would gather for huge picnics featuring seasonal New England food: blueberries, clams, corn on the cob, tomatoes. When Waters's parents entertained at home in New Jersey, young Alice insisted on playing hostess by setting the table and making flower arrangements and name tags. Pat Waters recalled to Linda Witt for the *New York Times* (May 11, 1986), "Two things emerged rapidly in Alice's personality. She was a great socializer. If she wanted a party, she had a party. Even if she had to ask the boy and then go over and get his suit pressed for him, if she wanted to go to a school dance, you could bet she'd find a boy. And that's the second thing—she was determined. If Alice wanted to do something . . . Well, Margaret and I finally figured out the only way to handle the situation was to say to ourselves, 'Okay now, how do we help her?'" As a child, according to Dean Riddle, Waters once won a costume contest outfitted as the "Queen of the Garden."

After leaving New Jersey and living for several years in Chicago, Illinois, the Waters family settled in Van Nuys, California, in 1962. The following year Waters and several of her friends enrolled at the University of California at Santa Barbara. To their dismay, they found that campus life revolved around sororities, fraternities, and beach games rather than academics. They also discovered that their burgeoning left-wing political consciousness put them at odds with many of their fellow students. In the spring of 1964, they transferred to the University of California at Berkeley; the following fall the Free Speech Movement swept the campus. The movement began when student activists staged a two-day protest sparked when school administrators declared off-limits to political activities parts of the campus traditionally used for such purposes. "We came at the right moment," Waters told Witt. "It was a great time. The Free Speech Movement immediately focused one's energies. It was impossible to be left out of the rage at what was happening here on campus and in society." Waters subsequently became involved with local politics,

working for the journalist and peace activist Robert Scheer during his unsuccessful campaign for a seat in Congress.

When she was 19 Waters spent a year in France. "I lived at the bottom of a market street"—a street on which farmers sold their produce—"and took it all in by osmosis, and I hung out in a lot of great French kitchens," she told Dean Riddle. Referring to the nearly ubiquitous farmers' markets in France, she recalled to *AgBiotech Buzz*, "People wouldn't think of having food several days old. There was a kind of life to everything I ate, a kind of beauty about it. I just had never experienced those tastes." A dinner she ate in a small inn in the Brittany region made an especially strong impression on Waters. The chef, a woman, served cured ham with melon from her garden, trout caught a few hours earlier from a nearby stream, and small tarts made with fresh raspberries. "It was a wonderful experience for [Alice]," Pat Waters recalled to Linda Witt. "When everyone gave the chef a standing ovation, she said, 'Ah that's it. A way to entertain my friends and have a wonderful time.'"

After she graduated from Berkeley, in 1967, with a bachelor's degree in French cultural studies, Waters spent a year in London, England, studying the Montessori method of early-childhood education. Back in Berkeley she got a job as a teacher in a Montessori school and moved in with the illustrator David Lance Goines, who would later design and illustrate two Chez Panisse cookbooks. In her leisure time she prepared meals for friends, following the recipes in Elizabeth David's classic book *French Country Cooking*. The home she and Goines shared soon became a place to meet and eat for people seen by themselves or others as political radicals. Goines told Leslie Crawford for Salon.com (November 16, 1999), "Alice wanted to have her friends to dinner every night. The only way to do that was to open a restaurant." In addition, as Eleanor Bertino, one of Waters's college roommates, told Witt, Waters and her friends saw themselves as "part of a community, part of a greater world. Alice's first fantasies about a restaurant came out of that. It would have one fixed price. Friends cooking. It would be a replacement for the family. This was 1968 or 1969. We didn't see ourselves getting married or having children. We saw ourselves in this greater community of peers."

In 1971 Waters and several friends opened a small restaurant on Shattuck Street near the Berkeley campus; they funded their venture with a $10,000 loan from Waters's father, who had agreed to mortgage the family house to help them. The restaurant was designed to resemble the sorts of bistros that Waters had seen in the province of Provence, in southern France. She named it after a character (an elderly sail maker) in the films *Marius, Fanny*, and *César* (known as the Marseilles Trilogy), which the French writer Marcel Pagnol adapted from his own plays. At that time many fine restaurants in the U.S., inspired by their counterparts in France, served rich, heavily sauced dishes made with imported products. American cuisine—macaroni-and-cheese and meatloaf, for example—was widely ridiculed by chefs and gourmands. Familiar with the abundant resources of the area surrounding her restaurant, Waters decided to serve the same simple meal for all patrons on any particular day, using the freshest food available from local markets. "The food began with very much a French country overtone, simple and uncomplicated," Goines told Crawford. "You served a fresh fish and left it alone. You didn't tart it up with all sorts of sauces. This basic philosophy matured over the years into Alice's search for pure fresh ingredients."

Her first few years as a restaurateur proved exceedingly difficult for Waters. Her workload was exhausting: in addition to taking care of the administrative aspects of the business, she cooked almost every night. As Tom Luddy, a film producer with Francis Ford Coppola's Zoetrope Studios who became romantically involved with Waters, recalled to Witt, "Many, many times I'd pick her up from the restaurant after an 18- or 20-hour day, walk her to the door, put the key in the lock, and she'd faint. She'd just pass out, and I'd have to carry her in and I'd put her to bed. The next morning at 7 she would come awake like a shot, saying, 'I have to call about the chickens.' I'd literally have to hold her down and tell her to 'slowly count to ten. Then you can use the phone.'" In the beginning the restaurant lost money, in part because organic ingredients are far costlier than others, and the food required more extensive preparation than meals served elsewhere. (Apparently, the prices Waters charged were not high enough to cover her costs.) As word spread about the culinary revolution being waged at the California eatery and its extraordinary menu, "foodies" began to flock to eat there, along with superstars and power brokers from many fields. At the same time glowing reviews of Chez Panisse started to appear in the media. Through the years the restaurant continued to draw high praise. In 1992 the James Beard Foundation (named for one of the nation's most celebrated cooks) chose Chez Panisse as the best restaurant in the U.S.; in 2001 Gourmet magazine honored it with the same encomium.

Chez Panisse has spawned dozens of imitators, many protégés, and eight cookbooks, most of them co-written by Waters: Chez Panisse Pasta, Pizza and Calzone (1984), Fanny at Chez Panisse (1992), Chez Panisse Vegetables (1996), Chez Panisse Cooking (1996), Chez Panisse Desserts (1996), Chez Panisse Café Cookbook (1999), Chez Panisse Menu Cookbook (1999), and Chez Panisse Fruit (2002). Currently, the restaurant has two facilities: a formal dining room upstairs and a more casual eatery, called the Café at Chez Panisse, downstairs. Chez Panisse takes reservations up to one month in advance. A Tuesday night dinner menu at Chez Panisse might include Monterey Bay squid and cherry tomato pasta with garlic and savory, grilled leg of James Ranch lamb with chanterelles, chard

alla parmigiana, fresh shell beans, and mulberry ice cream and pear sherbet with Warren pears. Prices for a three-course meal typically range from $50 to $75.

One of Waters's chief contributions to American eating habits has been her emphasis on using only locally grown, seasonal produce that has not been treated with hormones or other chemicals. She has influenced not only the menus of the nation's restaurants but also which foods the public purchases and where. In her books and interviews, Waters has urged people to shop at their local farmers' markets and abstain from buying food that has been genetically modified. "I like to buy my food from people who have integrity and honesty about what they are doing, people who care about nourishment and that's their primary purpose," she told AgBiotech. "They take care of the land for the future and think about consequences for the next generation." On the subject of genetically modified food, she said, "I'm not coming from any scientific view. I've just listened to all my friends, some of them very informed and some less informed. They all agree we don't know enough yet to proceed. It seems to be the big companies trying to make food available all year long to make money from it, like making genetically modified tomatoes. I'm very happy eating tomatoes three months out of the year. I don't want them all year long." Some 75 farmers, ranchers, fishermen, cheese makers, vintners, and florists in the Berkeley area provide Chez Panisse with produce, poultry, fish, meat, cheese, wine, and flowers. Waters employs a "forager," who scours local markets and farms for the best ingredients.

Waters's work at Chez Panisse can be seen as a continuation of the radical politics she espoused as a college student. She believes that by working and shopping near their homes, people create and nourish healthy communities. As she explained in an interview for Seasonal Chef (on-line), communities come together "when the person growing the food is connected with the person who is eating it. A result of those connections is a sense of caring about somebody else's welfare. That's how you build up those bonds which ultimately lead you to a sense of a group made up of people who care about one another." In Waters's view, eating is a political act. As such, it may benefit farmers who practice sustainable agriculture and those who distribute their products; or it may support large corporations that care more about profit margins than public health. "Good healthy eating is simply not compatible with processed food," she told California Monthly. "When you eat together, and eat a meal you cook yourselves, such meals honor the materials from which they are made; they honor the art by which they are done; they honor the people who make them, and those who share them. I believe food is a medium for us all to do more meaningful work in our own lives. And, more than that, I believe we have an ethical obligation to do this work, for the sake of humanity—better lives for each other and for the generations who come after us."

In 1996 Waters established the Chez Panisse Foundation, which, according to its Web site, is committed to "transforming public education by using food traditions and rituals to teach, nurture, and empower young people." The foundation donates money to nonprofit organizations that promote sustainable agriculture. One of its main recipients is the Edible Schoolyard at Berkeley's Martin Luther King Jr. Middle School. Students in the project plant vegetables and fruits on a half-acre of school property and then harvest, cook, and serve them for lunch. In 2003 Waters initiated a pilot program at Yale University, in New Haven, Connecticut, called the sustainable food project, whereby one of the school's 12 dining halls serves food prepared from locally grown products. "The essence of it is to integrate food into the curriculum at Yale," Waters told Marc Santora for the *New York Times* (August 16, 2003). "When one out of every three kids is likely to be obese, I think the importance of what we eat is hitting home in a shocking way." (According to the Web site of the U.S. surgeon general's office, "In 1999, 13% of children aged 6 to 11 years and 14% of adolescents aged 12 to 19 years in the United States were overweight. This prevalence has nearly tripled for adolescents in the past 2 decades.") The foundation is also involved with two programs at the San Francisco County Jail: the Horticulture Project and the Garden Project, which provide job training to inmates as well as marketable produce.

Waters's many honors include the James Beard Special Achievement Award, the Restaurant and Business Leadership Award from *Restaurants and Institutions* magazine, the Excellence in Education Award given by U.S. senator Barbara Boxer of California, the Rachel Carson Environmental Award from the National Nutritional Foods Association, and the Lifetime Achievement Award from *Bon Appetit* magazine; *Cuisine et Vins du France* magazine named her one of the world's top 10 chefs in 1986, and the James Beard Foundation, the best chef in America in 1992. She is a visiting dean at the French Culinary Institute, in New York City; an honorary trustee of the American Center for Food, Wine and the Arts, in Napa, California; and a board member of the San Francisco Ferry Plaza Farmers Market. In 2004 Dartmouth College, in Hanover, New Hampshire, awarded her an honorary doctor of arts degree. In a signal honor, in light of its location, in 1998 the Louvre, in Paris, France, invited Waters to open a restaurant in the museum. After she realized that museum officials wanted simply an eatery and had no interest in her suggestions of making it a place to educate the public about food as well, Waters withdrew from the project.

Waters is married to Stephen Singer, an olive-oil and wine merchant and painter. The couple have a daughter, Fanny, born in 1983 and named for one of the characters in the Marseilles Trilogy. Fanny at age eight, the supposed narrator of the first part

of *Fanny at Chez Panisse: A Child's Restaurant with 46 Recipes,* introduces readers to some of the people who work at the restaurant, provision it, or patronize it. Waters and her family live in what Crawford described as an "unassuming, slightly ramshackle house" in Berkeley, near Chez Panisse. According to Crawford, Waters "lives her own life with as little pretension and as much simplicity as she demands of her food."

—H.T.

Suggested Reading: *AgBioTech Buzz* (on-line) July 29, 2002; *California Monthly* (on-line) Dec. 1999; *Chicago Tribune* C p10+ May 11, 1986, with photos; Salon.com Nov. 16, 1999

Selected Books: *Chez Panisse Pasta, Pizza, and Calzone,* 1984; *Fanny at Chez Panisse,* 1992; *Chez Panisse Vegetables,* 1996; *Chez Panisse Desserts,* 1996; *Chez Panisse Menu Cookbook,* 1999; *Chez Panisse Fruit,* 2002

Stephen Dunn/Getty Images

Wells, David

May 20, 1963– Baseball player

Address: San Diego Padres Baseball Partnership, P.O. Box 2000, San Diego, CA 92112-2000

Weighing 250 pounds, give or take 20, David Wells, a left-handed pitcher with the San Diego Padres, looks more like a beer-guzzling fan than a professional athlete. Nevertheless, in the last 17 years, Wells has enjoyed a successful career in Major League Baseball as a pitcher with seven teams, most notably the New York Yankees, the Toronto Blue Jays, and the Detroit Tigers. Nicknamed "Boomer," Wells has frequently brushed off criticism about his weight by pointing to the achievement of two other rotund baseball players: the pitcher Mickey Lolich, who racked up 217 victories (1963–79) and won three games for the Tigers in the 1968 World Series, and Babe Ruth, who pitched for the Boston Red Sox before he was traded to the Yankees, after the 1919 season. As one of baseball's most colorful characters, Wells is famous for his partying to excess, drinking great quantities of beer, speaking his mind (often profanely), and having many run-ins with baseball owners, executives, managers, umpires, and fans as well as other players. Wells enjoyed two of his best years with the Yankees, in 1997 and 1998, pitching a perfect game and then helping the team win the World Series in the latter year. He was shaken when, a few months after the team became the world champions, the Yankees traded him to the Blue Jays for Roger Clemens, one of the best pitchers in baseball. In 2002 Wells returned for his second tour of duty in New York, signing a lucrative contract with the Yankees. He lived up to his reputation during the 2002 and 2003 regular seasons but performed poorly in the postseasons. After the Florida Marlins defeated the Yankees in the 2003 World Series, he left New York and signed a one-year contract with the San Diego Padres. "More than anybody I know, I love this game," he told Jeff Pearlman for *Sports Illustrated* (July 10, 2000). "I take a lot of pride in what I do and what we do as a team. People make a big deal out of success. I feel like you're supposed to succeed. It's what you're paid for."

David Lee Wells was born on May 20, 1963 in Torrance, California. His parents never married; he was raised by his mother in a tough area of San Diego, California. While growing up he assumed that his father, David Pritt, was dead. (When he was 22 he learned that Pritt was alive and working for a railroad in West Virginia. Wells tracked him down and established a relationship with him.) Wells's mother, Eugenia, supported him and his four siblings—who had different fathers—by working at various factory jobs and collecting welfare payments. For a time Eugenia, nicknamed "Attitude Annie," dated a biker from the Hell's Angels motorcycle gang. "She didn't take no [expletive]," Wells told Michael P. Geffner for *Details* (October 1998). "If *anybody* messed with us, she'd haul off and deck ya. I saw her hit some pretty big men—guys bigger than me. She didn't do all the right things in life, but she's still my mom and I respect her. She was a rebel—she did everything she wanted to do." Wells and his friends often found trouble, sometimes of their own making. One day, while walking past a house, they heard a man beating a woman. Wells yelled, "Leave her alone," as quoted by Buster Olney in the *New York Times* (March 15, 1998). Someone in the house responded by firing a gun at the boys, hitting a sign behind

them. On another occasion Wells and a friend blew up an abandoned car in an empty lot by igniting its gasoline tank. "We made sure nobody was around—nobody got hurt," Wells told Olney. "I was crazy, but my friend, he was a maniac."

Wells began playing baseball as a pitcher in the local Little League. Hell's Angels bikers often showed up at his games and rewarded him with money for playing well. "I could pull in $100 a game, and nobody dared to screw around with me," Wells told Frank Lidz for *Sports Illustrated* (September 8, 1997). "Try, and I'd say, 'I'll get my mom's boyfriend on you.'" A passionate fan of professional baseball, Wells divided his loyalties between the Padres and the Yankees. He also idolized Babe Ruth, one of the Yankees' greatest players. "I did all my reports in school on Babe Ruth," he told a writer for the Gannett News Service, as quoted in the *Ottawa Sun* (July 9, 2000). "I learned everything—when he was born, when he died, what he did and all that stuff." Wells was a mediocre student. "I wasn't a brain," he admitted to Geffner. "When I beared down, I got better grades. But I never wanted to bear down."

Wells attended Point Loma High School, in San Diego, where he played basketball and baseball. (Don Larsen, who pitched a perfect game for the Yankees in the 1956 World Series, was an alumnus of the school.) Wells became the team's star pitcher, pitching a perfect game in his senior year. In 1982 the Toronto Blue Jays drafted Wells. After his graduation that year, he played for the Medicine Hat Tigers (a Toronto farm team) in the Pioneer League, in Canada. As a starting pitcher he compiled a record of 4–3 with a 5.13 earned-run average (ERA). In 1983 Wells pitched for Toronto's Class A affiliate in Kinston, North Carolina, amassing a 6–5 record with a 3.73 ERA. The next year he divided his playing time between Kinston and the Blue Jays' Class AA affiliate in Knoxville, Tennessee. Wells struggled in Kinston that year, winning only one game and losing six. In Knoxville, however, he pitched well, putting together a 3–2 record with an impressive 2.59 ERA before an elbow injury sidelined him. Wells spent the entire 1985 season on the disabled list, after surgery that repaired a torn ligament in his pitching elbow. When he returned, in the following year, he had stints with each of Toronto's four minor-league teams. At the end of the season, he underwent arthroscopic shoulder surgery.

In 1987 Wells began the season with Toronto's Class AAA affiliate in Syracuse, New York. In late June the Blue Jays called him up to the majors. He made his major-league debut on June 30, 1987, starting a game against the Yankees. In two starts, he pitched poorly and lost both games, then was sent back to the minors. "When I went back down, I was all frustrated," he told Neil MacCarl for the *Sporting News* (July 30, 1990). "I talked to Dave LaRoche, who was our pitching coach [at Syracuse], and I asked him about pitching relief. He said they had been waiting for me to say something." Wells returned to the Blue Jays when the major-league rosters were expanded in September. In 16 appearances as a relief pitcher, he performed well, compiling a 4–1 record with one save and an impressive 1.50 ERA. (His overall record with the Blue Jays in 1987 was 4–3 with a 3.99 ERA.) Over the next two seasons, the Blue Jays used Wells in long relief and as a setup man for Tom Henke, the team's hard-throwing closer. In 1989 the Oakland Athletics defeated the Blue Jays in the American League Championship Series (in which Wells appeared in only one game). During the 1990 season injuries temporarily sidelined two of the Blue Jays' starting pitchers, Jimmy Key and John Cerutti. This created an opportunity for Wells, whom Cito Gaston, the Blue Jays' manager, inserted into the starting rotation. Wells found immediate success as a starter; his record, which included appearances as a long reliever, was 11–6 with a 3.14 ERA. In his 28 starts and 12 relief appearances in 1991, Wells's record was 15–10, and his ERA climbed to 3.72.

During his years with the Blue Jays, Wells often clashed with the team's front office. The Blue Jays thought Wells, whose weight neared 270 pounds, would pitch more effectively if he were in better shape, and executives constantly pressured him to lose weight. They also expressed their anger about Wells's excessive beer drinking, quick temper, sharp tongue, and habit of blasting his heavy-metal CDs in the locker room. Wells refused to change his ways. "We did everything we could to control Boomer," Gord Ash, then the Blue Jays' assistant general manager, told Pearlman. "We learned the hard way: The worst way to control him is to try and control him." During the fifth inning of a game on August 9, 1991, Mike Greenwell of the Boston Red Sox came up to bat against Wells with runners on base. Gaston signaled Wells to throw a change-up, a slow pitch thrown in the same manner as a fastball and meant to fool the batter. Wells, who has a weak change-up and is more effective at throwing fastballs, curves, and sliders, did not cooperate at first; in the end he gave in to Gaston's order (which had to be repeated several times), and Greenwell reached base with a single. Gaston then went to the pitcher's mound to relieve Wells. Instead of handing him the ball, Wells threw it into left field and told Gaston, as quoted by Lidz, "If you want it, go get it," then stormed off the mound. Gaston later took Wells to task for behaving unprofessionally. In the postseason the Blue Jays lost the American League pennant to the Minnesota Twins; Wells made four relief appearances in the series, striking out nine batters and giving up two runs in seven and two-thirds innings.

After posting solid numbers in 1990 and 1991, Wells hoped the Blue Jays would make him a full-time starter in 1992. Instead, Gaston kept Wells in the bullpen and used him as a starter infrequently. Wells had one of the worst seasons of his career, going 7–9 with a 5.40 ERA. The Blue Jays, however, went on to win their first World Series, defeating the Atlanta Braves. (Wells pitched briefly in four games.)

Before the start of the 1993 season, the Blue Jays released Wells. The Detroit Tigers, under Sparky Anderson's management, signed him. Wells has credited Anderson, who won three World Series championships—with the Cincinnati Reds in 1975 and 1976 and the Tigers in 1984—with turning his career around. Anderson made him a full-time starter and persuaded him to change his attitude. "Sparky believed in me," Wells explained to Geffner. "He turned me into a human being. He got into my head and got me to stop running away from all my problems. I was always quick to say something . . . throwing my opinion out there and not listening to anybody. Sparky made me listen." In his first season in a Tigers' uniform, Wells's record was 11–9. He missed two additional months of the strike-shortened 1994 season while on the disabled list and finished 5–7 in 16 starts. In 1995 Wells got off to an excellent start with the Tigers. Still, on July 31, 1995, the Tigers traded him to the Reds for two pitchers, C. J. Nitkowski and Dave Tuttle, and an infielder, Mark Lewis. In a game against the Philadelphia Phillies on September 23, Wells blew a no-hitter in the seventh inning. Wells later claimed that two defensive changes made by Davey Johnson, the Reds' manager, had disrupted his rhythm, and after leaving the mound Wells cursed out and then head-butted Johnson (but was not punished). In the first round of the postseason, the Reds swept the Los Angeles Dodgers. Wells pitched well, winning the third game. In the National League Championship Series, the Atlanta Braves swept the Reds. Although he gave up only three runs in six innings, Wells took the loss in the third game.

On December 26, 1995 the Reds traded Wells to the Baltimore Orioles for two outfielders, Curtis Goodwin and Trovin Valdez. He had a disappointing season in 1996, posting an 11–14 record with a 5.14 ERA. In the first round of the postseason, in which the Orioles defeated the Cleveland Indians in five games, Wells started two of the games and got one win. The Orioles then battled the Yankees in the American League Championship Series. Wells's previous success in pitching against the Yankees, especially at Yankee Stadium, had earned him a reputation as a "Yankee killer"; after the Orioles lost the first game (thanks, in part, to a young fan who caught a fly ball that was ruled a home run for the Yankees), Wells evened the series with a victory for the Orioles. The Yankees won the next three games, eliminating the Orioles from the postseason, and went on to win the 1996 World Series.

After that season, when Wells's contract expired and he entered the free-agent market, the Yankees were among the teams that expressed an interest in signing him. In a meeting he had with George Steinbrenner, the Yankees' legendary owner, "we talked about everything but baseball," as Wells told Lidz. "It was more of a personality check. George wanted to see if I was a sane person or the crazy son of a bitch he'd heard about." In December

1996 the Yankees signed Wells to a three-year contract worth $13.5 million. Wells jokingly requested that Steinbrenner let him wear Babe Ruth's number, 3, which had been retired. In the end he settled for 33, telling Lidz, "This way, I can be the Babe twice over."

The Yankees' newest pitcher immediately sparked controversy. In January 1997 Wells and a friend were involved in a fight with two men outside a bar in San Diego. Wells suspected the two men of stealing his car keys and claimed that one of them punched him after Wells and his friend confronted them. Wells broke his pitching hand during the fight and was unable to pitch for most of spring training. (The San Diego police did not file assault charges against Wells.)

Wells's hand healed by the time the 1997 season began. He got off to an excellent start, winning many games and becoming a favorite with the fans. Pitching in the first inning of a game on June 29, 1997, he wore a cap that had belonged to Babe Ruth—until Joe Torre, the Yankees' manager, noticing that Wells's cap was different from the other players', ordered him to replace it. (Wells, who collects baseball memorabilia, had bought the cap from a dealer for about $35,000.) Wells pitched his best game of the season against the Athletics on July 30, 1997, striking out a career-high 16 batters and giving up only three hits. He entered a slump late in the season, losing five games in a row. Fans at Yankee Stadium began booing him. On August 30, after Wells was taken out of a game against the Montreal Expos, he had a confrontation with Steinbrenner in the Yankees' clubhouse. According to Geffner's account, Wells complained about a fan who had caught a fly ball that was ruled a home run for the Expos and suggested that there should be more security at the stadium. Steinbrenner responded, as quoted by Geffner, "Never mind about the . . . security, you just worry about pitching. You'd better start winning some games, because you're not the pitcher I thought you were." After the two exchanged more angry words, Wells threatened to punch out Steinbrenner if he did not leave the clubhouse. Though Steinbrenner refused to back down, he and Wells did not come to blows. Wells later expressed regret over the incident. He finished the 1997 season with 16 wins, 10 losses, and a 4.21 ERA. In the postseason the Cleveland Indians eliminated the Yankees in the first round. Although some observers thought Wells would not pitch in the postseason, he did so in game three, giving up only one run in nine innings for the win.

Wells improved in 1998, going 18–4 with a 3.49 ERA and leading the American League in shutouts, with five. On May 17 he threw a perfect game against the Minnesota Twins. "To pitch a perfect game wearing pinstripes at Yankee Stadium, it's unbelievable," he told L. Jon Wertheim for *Sports Illustrated* (May 25, 1998). "Growing up a Yankee fan, to come out here and make history, it really is a dream come true." After defeating the Texas Rangers in the first round of the postseason, the

Yankees faced the Cleveland Indians in the American League Championship Series. Wells won the first game; the series was tied when Wells was scheduled to start in the fifth game, at Jacobs Field in Cleveland. While warming up before the game, he was angered when several fans made remarks about his mother, who had died in 1997. Wells channeled his rage into his performance on the mound, pitching well in eight innings. As he walked to the dugout, he tipped his cap to the Cleveland fans. The Yankees' bullpen saved the game for him, and the team clinched the pennant the next day. Wells was named the series' Most Valuable Player (MVP). On October 15 Michael White, the mayor of Cleveland, publicly apologized to Wells for the fans' behavior. The Yankees went on to sweep the Padres in the World Series, in which Wells won the game he pitched.

On February 18, 1999 the baseball world was surprised when the Yankees traded Wells, Graeme Lloyd, a relief pitcher, and Homer Bush, a second baseman, to the Blue Jays for Roger Clemens, the veteran pitcher who had previously won five Cy Young Awards. The Yankees were initially unwilling to part with Wells, one of their best pitchers in 1998, but agreed to do so when the Blue Jays offered them Clemens, who was expected to leave Toronto upon becoming a free agent. The trade stunned Wells. "He didn't take it very well at all," the Yankees' pitcher David Cone, one of Wells's best friends, told Lawrence Rocca for *Newsday* (February 20, 1999). "He is very depressed. He truly loved playing for the Yankees and he truly loved everything surrounding the Yankees." The trade divided many Yankee fans. While some were saddened at the departure of Wells, others welcomed the Yankees' acquisition of one of the best pitchers in baseball.

Playing under Toronto's manager, Jim Fregosi, Wells found success with the Blue Jays, who had become a mediocre team in the late 1990s. In 1999 Wells boasted a 17–10 record and led the American League in the number of innings pitched, with 231 and two-thirds. At the same time, his ERA rose to 4.82. In 2000 he had one of his best seasons ever, chalking up a career-high 20 victories, which led the American League and represented over one-fourth of the Blue Jays' total wins for the season. Wells's ERA dropped to 4.11, and he struck out 166 batters and walked only 31.

Despite having two winning seasons with the Blue Jays, Wells grew disillusioned with playing in Toronto. In the *New York Post* (January 4, 2001), Andrew Marchand quoted him as making derogatory comments about the Blue Jays' fans and management. Wells, who claimed that the Blue Jays were not trying to win, asked to be traded to the New York Mets; several weeks later the Blue Jays traded him to the Chicago White Sox. Wells missed half of the 2001 season after undergoing surgery on his lower back. Limited to 16 games, he finished the year 5–7, then became a free agent. Despite questions about his age and health, several teams pursued the 38-year-old left-hander, including the Yankees and the Arizona Diamondbacks, who had defeated the Yankees in the 2001 World Series. According to Buster Olney in the *New York Times* (January 11, 2002), Wells agreed to sign a contract with the Diamondbacks but backed out of the deal after George Steinbrenner made him a better offer. The Yankees signed Wells to a two-year contract that included a no-trade clause. "David Wells is a winner and he belongs in pinstripes," Steinbrenner said, as quoted by Olney. "People may say we're going out on a limb, but we'll see. We're betting on the Boomer." For his part, Wells was happy that he would again be playing in the city he loved.

Wells bounced back in 2002, leading the Yankees' injury-plagued starting rotation with 19 wins. He pitched 206 and a third innings and had a 3.75 ERA, his best total in four seasons. In the first round of the postseason, the Anaheim Angels exploited the Yankees' weakened pitching and fielding to win the series, three games to one. Wells was the losing pitcher in the final game, giving up 10 hits and eight runs in four and two-thirds innings. "We pitchers just didn't do our job," he told the press after the game, as quoted by Helene Elliott in the *Los Angeles Times* (October 6, 2002). "That's the bottom line. They outpitched us and outplayed us. We didn't expect it, because we all had good vibes coming into this series, but the better team won." The Angels went on to win the World Series, defeating the San Francisco Giants in seven games.

On September 7, 2002 Wells got into a fight in a Manhattan diner. According to an account in *Newsday* (September 8, 2002), while he and a friend were eating breakfast at about 5: 50 a.m., a bartender named Rocco Graziosa walked into the diner and began taunting him. Graziosa angered Wells by insulting his late mother and then jokingly threatening him with a butter knife. After the pitcher stood up to confront him, Graziosa punched him, knocking out two of his front teeth and cutting his forehead. Using his cellphone, Wells then summoned the police, who arrested Graziosa and charged him with assault, harassment, and the criminal possession of a weapon. At his well-publicized trial in November 2002, Graziosa claimed that he had defended himself against Wells, whom he alleged had been drunk. A six-member jury found Graziosa guilty of assault, and he was subsequently sentenced to 45 days in jail. In September 2003 Wells filed a civil suit against Graziosa; the case has not yet gone to trial.

More controversy surrounded Wells when, in February 2003, the media disclosed some of the contents of his forthcoming autobiography, *Perfect I'm Not!: Boomer on Beer, Brawls, Backaches and Baseball*, which he co-wrote with Chris Kreski. In those excerpts Wells revealed that he had been half-drunk when he pitched his perfect game against the Twins in 1998. He also criticized his teammates Roger Clemens and Mike Mussina (both starting pitchers), alleged that 25 to 40 percent of baseball players use steroids, and claimed that many use amphetamines. One photograph in the book showed Wells sitting naked in a field of sheep. Wells's statements outraged the Yankee management and led them to consider trading him. After a discussion with Yankee representatives, Wells issued a public apology for tarnishing the team's image and agreed to pay a $100,000 fine, which was distributed to three charities. In the version of the book that reached bookstores, in March 2003, the allegations of steroid and amphetamine use among players were milder.

During the 2003 season Wells tried to put the controversy behind him and focus on pitching. Although he was plagued by back problems, he finished with a 15–7 record. In the first round of the postseason, the Yankees defeated the Twins. Wells clinched the series for the Yankees with an easy victory in the final game. The Yankees then battled the Boston Red Sox in a memorable series for the American League Pennant. In the fifth game Wells pitched well, giving up only four hits and one run in seven innings for the win. In the seventh and final game, the Red Sox soon led 4–0, forcing the starter Roger Clemens to leave in the fourth inning. Jason Giambi, the Yankees' power-hitting first baseman, narrowed the Boston lead with two solo home runs. Wells pitched the eighth inning in relief and gave up a solo home run to David Ortiz. In the bottom of the eighth inning, the Yankees staged a remarkable comeback, scoring three runs against Pedro Martinez, the ace of the Red Sox rotation and a three-time winner of the Cy Young Award, to tie the game. The star Yankee pitcher Mariano Rivera replaced Wells on the mound and pitched three scoreless innings. In the bottom of the 11th inning, Aaron Boone, the Yankees' third baseman, sent Tim Wakefield's first pitch into the outfield seats for a home run, bringing a thrilling game to a dramatic end and clinching the pennant for the Yankees.

In the World Series the Yankees were considered the favorites against the Florida Marlins. Wells was the losing pitcher in the first game, in which the Marlins edged out a 3–2 win. With the series even at two games apiece, Wells took the mound for game five. Severe back spasms forced him to leave the game after one inning. His replacement, Jose Contreras, gave up four runs and was charged with the loss. (The day before, Wells had boasted that he could pitch effectively even at his relatively advanced age even without adhering to a rigorous exercise and conditioning program.) In game six Josh Beckett, pitching a complete game, shut out the Yankees and clinched the World Series for the Marlins.

After the season the Yankees declined to exercise their option on Wells, and he became a free agent. In December 2003 he underwent surgery to repair a herniated disk in his spine. Although the Yankees expressed an interest in re-signing him, Wells signed a one-year contract with the San Diego Padres. Although he missed several starts because of a hand injury, Wells pitched well for San

Diego in 2004. Starting 31 games and pitching 195.2 total innings, he compiled a record of 12 wins and eight losses with 101 strikeouts and only 20 walks. His 3.73 ERA was among the best in the league. A free agent following that season, as of November 2004 Wells had yet to sign a contract for 2005.

According to Jeff Pearlman, "Wells is a fat guy who is content being fat." The pitcher's first marriage ended in divorce. He and his second wife, Nina, live in Clearwater, Florida. He is the father of two sons: Brandon, from his first marriage, and Lars, from his second.

—D.C.

Suggested Reading: *Details* p135+ Oct. 10, 1998, with photos; *New York Post* p76 Jan. 4, 2001, with photo; *New York Times* VIII p9 Mar. 15, 1998, with photos, D p3 Jan. 11, 2002, with photo; New York Yankees Web site; *Newsday* A p47 Feb. 20, 1999; *Ottawa Sun* Sports p32 July 9, 2000; *Sporting News* p9 July 30, 1990, with photo; *Sports Illustrated* p70+ Sep. 8, 1997, with photos, p52+ May 25, 1998, with photos, p42+ July 10, 2000, with photos

Time Life Pictures/Getty Images

Wheeldon, Christopher

Mar. 22, 1973– Choreographer

Address: New York City Ballet, New York State Theater, 20 Lincoln Center, New York, NY 10023

"Classical ballet is fairly limiting, and it's enormously challenging to find fresh ways of presenting it," Christopher Wheeldon told Jennie James for *Time Europe* (June 11, 2001). The British-born Wheeldon had not yet turned 30 when he began to be hailed as one of the world's most talented young classical choreographers. A former dancer with the Royal Ballet in London and the New York City Ballet, he has served as the latter's resident choreographer for the past three years. Since he began creating dances, during his student days, he has choreographed two dozen works for eight companies, among them the San Francisco Ballet and the Bos-

ton Ballet as well as the London and New York City troupes. "Ballet has to move forward, yes, but it doesn't have to lose its magic and romanticism and lyricism," Wheeldon told Terry Teachout for *Time* (May 31, 1999). According to many ballet aficionados, Wheeldon has succeeded in infusing his dances with those qualities and many more. "No ballet choreographer of his generation can match his imaginative use of the classical vocabulary," the veteran dance critic Anna Kisselgoff declared in the *New York Times* (May 1, 2000). Another dance expert, Joan Acocella, wrote for the *New Yorker* (June 30, 2003), "Wheeldon is a natural as a ballet-maker. He knows how to fill the stage with an ensemble, and have the dancers surge and pulse and make you wonder what's coming next. He knows how to give steps meaning . . . [and] even when he's working without a narrative his tone is still human, engaging. In consequence, the dancers . . . look happy in his work. They glow, they grow." Containing elements of both abstraction and narrative, Wheeldon's dances reflect the influence of such British ballet masters as Frederick Ashton and Kenneth MacMillan, particularly with regard to sets, costumes, and dramatic flair. In terms of musicality, mastery of space, and distinctive use of ballet steps, his works also display the powerful influence of George Balanchine, the founder of the New York City Ballet. Indeed, Wheeldon has been compared to the great Balanchine, widely considered the most important choreographer of the 20th century—a comparison that he regards somewhat dubiously. "I think I've managed to find the confidence in myself to know that it's not always going to be bunches of flowers and chocolates boxes," Wheeldon told Ismene Brown in an interview for the London *Daily Telegraph* (July 26, 2003). "There's a lot of attention, but I take this stuff about the next Balanchine with such a grain of salt. It's just that I happen to be here at a time where there aren't many [other classical choreographers] around."

The son of an engineer and a physical therapist, Christopher Wheeldon was born on March 22, 1973 in Yeovil, a small town in Somerset County, England. At the age of seven, he saw a Royal Ballet production of Frederick Ashton's comic ballet *La Fille mal Gardée* and asked his parents to enroll him in dance classes. The following year he began training at the East Coker Ballet School, in a village near Yeovil. Not long afterward the Wheeldon family moved to Guildford, about 30 miles from London. Acting on the advice of his East Coker dance teacher, young Christopher auditioned successfully for the Royal Ballet School, an arm of the Royal Ballet that aims to prepare future members of that and other major ballet corps for careers in classical dance. Even as a youngster Wheeldon was interested in choreography; at age eight he produced his first piece, a prequel to the ballet *Swan Lake* that featured three little girls hatching from swans' eggs. As he grew he continued to create dances, entering the school's junior and senior choreography competitions. In 1990, the year he graduated, Wheeldon received the Royal Ballet School's Ursula Moreton Award for Choreography for *Boxes*, a piece about the homeless set to music by the British composer Benjamin Britten.

The next year, as a dancer, Wheeldon won the Gold Medal at the Prix de Lausanne, in Switzerland, a prestigious international ballet competition for preprofessionals. Also in 1991, at the invitation of the Royal Ballet's artistic director, Anthony Dowell, Wheeldon joined that company's corps de ballet (which can be likened to the chorus in musical theater). Wheeldon soon caught the eye of the Royal Ballet's principal choreographer and former artistic director Kenneth MacMillan, who specialized in creating tragic story ballets, such as *Manon*, *Anastasia*, and *Romeo and Juliet*. Until his death, in 1992, MacMillan encouraged Wheeldon as a dancer and as a choreographer. Wheeldon told Jane Albert for the *Australian* (August 23, 2002), "[MacMillan] said: 'You have to take all the opportunities you can and just practise, and you'll get better because you've got talent.' It was an enormous compliment. I think it was the point where I thought, 'Maybe I can do this on a higher level.'"

In 1993 an injury forced Wheeldon to stop dancing temporarily. After he had healed sufficiently, he took a trip to Manhattan, where he enrolled in several classes as a guest with the New York City Ballet. Founded in 1948 by Balanchine and the impresario Lincoln Kirstein, the New York City Ballet is one of the premier classical-ballet companies in the world, with a repertoire heavily devoted to Balanchine's abstract, neoclassical works. "Ever since I danced in [Balanchine's 1967 work] *Valse Fantastique* for a Royal Ballet school graduation performance, I'd had a passion for Balanchine's choreography," Wheeldon told Hilary Ostlere for the *New York Times* (May 26, 1996). "I was keen to see how City Ballet's dancers trained and performed. . . . Taking classes, I felt, would help me grasp their way of doing things." Jenifer Ringer, a principal dancer with City Ballet, recalled to Iris Fanger for the *New York Times* (September 24, 2000), "All of a sudden this new boy was here. He looked 12. He was so open and friendly. And then

he started dancing, and we were amazed at what a beautiful dancer he was. Any time there was a five-minute break, if he had any energy, he would get up and do some choreography. He'd bring a girl over and say, 'Try this.'" After Wheeldon had attended classes for two days, City Ballet's artistic director, Peter Martins, invited him to become a member of the corps; he joined soon afterward. In 1998 Wheeldon was promoted to the rank of soloist. During his tenure as a dancer with City Ballet, he appeared in Balanchine's *Chaconne, Donizetti Variations, The Four Temperaments, A Midsummer Night's Dream, The Nutcracker*, and *Scotch Symphony*, and Jerome Robbins's *The Concert, Dances at a Gathering*, and *The Goldberg Variations*. He also originated roles in Robbins's *West Side Story Suite* (1995) and *Brandenburg* (1995), Peter Martins's *Symphonic Dances* (1994), *Reliquary for Igor Stravinsky* (1996), and *Swan Lake* (1999), and Richard Tanner's *Episodes & Sarcasms* (1994).

According to Joseph Carman in the *Advocate* (March 19, 2002), the dancer regarded his move to New York as "the opportunity of starting a fresh life, to really be myself." As Carman wrote, "That meant coming out as a gay man." Wheeldon told Carman, "I [had] felt like such a coward. It was my mother who finally said, 'We know you're gay, we still love you for it, so get over it!'"

Virtually from the moment he joined the company, Wheeldon made it known to Martins that he wanted to choreograph as well as dance. After Martins viewed videotapes of several works Wheeldon had created while at the Royal Ballet, he asked the younger man to create a piece for the workshop performance of the School of American Ballet (the dance school of City Ballet). Wheeldon also continued to choreograph pieces for the Royal Ballet and several regional companies in the U.S. As Wheeldon told Anna Kisselgoff for the *New York Times* (May 23, 2003), "Peter started me off gently, and I am grateful for that. I thought I was ready to choreograph for the big stage and the company, not just workshops with students. But he was giving me a chance to develop while I was going off and making my mistakes at the Royal Opera House and in other companies." Wheeldon quickly drew critical attention for his inventive use of the classical vocabulary. In 1996 he received the Mae L. Wien Award from the School of American Ballet for choreography, and in 1997 he won the Martin E. Segal Award from Lincoln Center for most promising newcomer in choreography. His work during this period included *Slavonic Dances* (1997), *Scènes de Ballet* (1999), and *Mercurial Manoeuvres* (2000) for the New York City Ballet, *Firebird* (1999) for the Boston Ballet, and *Sea Pictures* (2000) for the San Francisco Ballet.

In 2000 Wheeldon, then 27, retired from the New York City Ballet in order to become a full-time choreographer. He did so because he realized that if he wanted to attain his long-held goal of becoming a principal dancer, he would have to devote more time to improving his technique, which would leave no time for choreography. At that point Martins created a job for him—that of the company's artist-in-residence. Wheeldon's first piece in his new post was *Polyphonia* (2001). Set to music by the 20th-century composer György Ligeti, the ballet intertwines a series of dances performed by four couples, who assume sculptural, angular postures. Abstract yet intensely emotional, *Polyphonia* was hailed by critics as Wheeldon's most important work to date. In the *New York Times* (January 6, 2001), Anna Kisselgoff described the dance as "astonishingly fresh" and a "major ballet." "The work was so rich in originality that it would seem impossible to take in every inventive detail in an initial viewing," Jennie Schulman declared in *Backstage* (January 26, 2001). "Several visits would seem essential, as well as pleasurable." Clive Barnes, too, praised the work, writing for *Dance Magazine* (May 2001), "There is not a step in *Polyphonia* that doesn't progress naturally from the step before it. The dance—prickly, angular—moves with the force of nature like the wind." A mounting of *Polyphonia* by the New York City Ballet at the Sadler's Wells Theatre, in London, won the 2003 Olivier Award for best new dance production.

In an article for the *New Criterion* (March 2002), Laura Jacobs wrote that Wheeldon's absence from the stage was "a loss" for dance aficionados. "His presence onstage was 110 percent," she explained. "To see him as the happy lover in *A Midsummer Night's Dream*, picking imaginary flowers oh so preciously (like an eager decorator matching swatches), was to glimpse the John Gielguds and Benny Hills in every Englishman's background. Still," she added, "Wheeldon brings his 110 percent to his own ballets. It's clear he adores the art."

In May 2001 Martins changed Wheeldon's title to resident choreographer (a position, like that of artist-in-residence, designed expressly for him). Since then, Wheeldon has choreographed five works for City Ballet: *Variations Serieuses* (2001), which "revealed once again his flair for bringing out the personalities of his dancers as well as dressing the stage imaginatively," as Lynn Garafola wrote for *Dance Magazine* (October 2001), and whose set, by Ian Falconer, "puts the audience in the wings, stage left," in Laura Jacobs's words; *Morphoses* (2002), a complex piece performed to music by Ligeti; *Carousel* (2002), a 10-minute romance set to tunes from the famous, same-titled Richard Rodgers–Oscar Hammerstein musical; *Carnival of the Animals* (2003), a humorous, family-oriented ballet, with the much-loved 1886 score by Camille Saint-Saëns and a new narrative written by John Lithgow, about a little boy from the Upper West Side of Manhattan who becomes trapped overnight in the American Museum of Natural History; and *Liturgy* (2003), an intricate pas de deux set to music by the Estonian-born composer Arvo Pärt. Wheeldon also choreographed *Continuum* (2002), for the San Francisco Ballet; *A Midsummer Night's Dream* (2002), for the Colorado Ballet; *Corybantic Ecstasies* (1999) and *The Four Seasons* (2000), for the Boston Ballet; and *There Where She Loves* (2000; Wheeldon later changed the title to *There Where She Loved*) and *Tryst* (2002), for the Royal Ballet. In the Italy-based periodical *Ballet 2000*, the British critic Clement Crisp wrote, as quoted by Joseph Carman in *Dance Magazine* (May 2003, on-line), "*Tryst* . . . is a splendid acquisition [for the Royal Ballet], and proof that the classic language can still say new and stimulating things."

In a conversation with Carman, Wheeldon said that he seeks dancers "who can create in their mind an atmosphere or an environment for themselves. Musically I like someone who isn't predictable, who finds a way to shape the phrase of the movement and brings some sort of dramatic flair to what they do." His favorite dancers include Jock Soto, Alexandra Ansanelli, Jenifer Ringer, and Wendy Whelan. The particular dancers with whom he works, he told Jennie James, are central to the creative process, in the sense that in each of his works, as James put it, he tries "to let both his choreography and [the dancers'] abilities shine through." Noting that he had constructed *Polyphonia* in that sort of collaboration with Wendy Whelan, he told James, "It was incredible. Her physical attributes contributed to the personality of the ballet." According to Terry Teachout, Wheeldon is "a sucker for tutus, toe shoes and moonlit pas de deux." "I don't have much angst in me," Wheeldon told Teachout. "I love to be romantic."

In 2002 Wheeldon choreographed the dance numbers for a Broadway musical, *Sweet Smell of Success*, for which Craig Carnelia wrote the lyrics, Marvin Hamlisch the music, and John Guare the book (based on a gritty 1957 nonmusical film starring Burt Lancaster and Tony Curtis). Nicholas Hytner directed the show, about a powerful gossip columnist (portrayed by John Lithgow) who uses an ambitious, sleazy press agent (Brian D'Arcy James) to spy on his half-sister (Kelli O'Hara) and carry out other despicable jobs for him. Wheeldon's choreography as well as the musical as a whole received negative reviews; the play closed after three months. Wheeldon found that choreographing for a Broadway stage production was far more difficult than what he had done in the past for ballet troupes. "In a ballet company you are left to work completely on your own," he explained to Judith Mackrell for the London *Guardian* (August 15, 2001). "The first time the dancers ever get in front of an audience is the opening night. In a Broadway show, the director and even the producers have the right to say, 'Oh, this jump would look better over there,' even though they have no idea what they're talking about." Wheeldon conceded that working with theater producers and directors forced him "to step back and question whether a sequence means anything or is just an attractive bit of dance," as he put it to Mackrell. Earlier, the choreographer had created a small piece for Hytner's poorly received dance movie, *Center Stage* (2000).

At the 2003 Edinburgh International Festival, held in Scotland, the San Francisco Ballet performed a full evening of Wheeldon's ballets. The program included *There Where She Loved, Continuum*, and the world premiere of a dance commissioned by the festival: *Rush*, set to Bohuslav Martinu's jubilant *Sinfonietta La Jolla*. In an assessment of the concert for the Scotland *Sunday Herald* (September 7, 2003, on-line), Ellie Carr wrote, "In *There Where She Loved* . . . we see the softer side of Wheeldon's early choreographic output. . . . A Chopin mazurka tinkles: love is young and fresh. But Chopin is soon replaced by the raw torch songs of Kurt Weill. Wheeldon shifts gear too, leavening soft, yielding pas de deux and lilting phrasing with surprising, animalistic moves. A wretched ballerina clings to her lover's back; another is dragged across the floor. This is Wheeldon's romantic side. But it is far from precious. His dancers are not the gay young things of more fey choreographers, but real men and women, who as the title suggests, have loved, in the red-blooded sense." In his enthusiastic review of the concert for the British magazine *Ballet* (September 2003, on-line), Bruce Marriott described Wheeldon's choreography in *Continuum* as "stunningly confident." "In fact my first note, scrawled in the dark, says 'masterwork,'" Marriott wrote. "The choreography is precise, mathematical even as the women are folded (origami comes to mind), lifted and deposited as if manikins. . . . The stillness and calm of the action merely sharpens all your senses. But despite the mechanics there is still human spirit here and naturally rippling movement spills out at times. . . . *Continuum* . . . struck me dumb." According to Marriott, *Rush* was "less consequential" than the first two dances, but with movements that were "all joyful action for the 16 dancers involved," it offered "the most balletic dancing . . . of the evening." Ellie Carr reported that *Rush*, "as its title suggests, is over too soon. This joyous world premiere . . . sweeps in on a wave of fizzy leaps, soaring lifts and pas de deux that explode like firecrackers. No sooner have our eyes caught up with the dazzling pace than this body-rush of a ballet has gone."

In 2004, as part of the New York City Ballet's centennial celebration of George Balanchine's birth, Wheeldon choreographed a new ballet, *Shambards*. The score for that work, by James MacMillan, was inspired partly by the Edward Muir poem "Scotland 1941," which offers "a scathing look at Scottish culture," as Anna Kisselgoff put it in the *New York Times* (May 10, 2004); that theme infuses *Shambards* as a whole. Kisselgoff called the work a "fascinating if exasperating ballet" in which "the overall story may be murky" but in which "there is the usual amount of stunning technical detail that fills a Wheeldon ballet." In June, a month after the premiere of *Shambards*, the Wheeldon-choreographed full-length version of *Swan Lake* premiered at the Academy of Music in Philadelphia, Pennsylvania, to celebrate the Penn-

sylvania Ballet's 40th anniversary. "Wheeldon's production may have lost some of the romanticism of traditional versions and the emotion may not be quite so high, but this is a version where the story is at least plausible and makes sense," David Mead wrote for *Ballet* magazine (July/August 2004, on-line). "Perhaps most importantly he has given the ballet a freshness and vitality that, for some of us at least, it so badly needed." The U.S. premiere of *VIII*, which Wheeldon had choreographed for the Hamburg Ballet in 2001, took place at the City Center in New York in late October 2004. That ballet focuses on King Henry VIII of England and several of his six wives. "Reduced to an *All About Eve* storyline with one rival succeeding another, *VIII* rarely illuminates an oft-told tale," Kisselgoff wrote for the *New York Times* (October 25, 2004). "Yet there are set pieces of choreography . . . that have Mr. Wheeldon's customary sure touch."

Terry Teachout described Wheeldon as "engaging" and as having "a big bright smile." The choreographer lives on the Upper West Side of Manhattan.

—H.T.

Suggested Reading: CBS News Transcripts Apr. 14, 2002; *Dance Magazine* p50+ Nov. 1996, with photo, p26+ May 2003; *New York Times* E p1+ May 10, 2001, with photos, E p1+ May 23, 2003, with photos; *New Yorker* p98+ June 4, 2001

Selected Dances: *Slavonic Dances*, 1997; *Scènes de Ballet*, 1999; *Firebird*, 1999; *Corybantic Ecstases*, 1999; *Mercurial Manoeuvres*, 2000; *Sea Pictures*, 2000; *The Four Seasons*, 2000; *There Where She Loved*, 2000; *Polyphonia*, 2001; *Variations Serieuses*, 2001; *Tryst*, 2002; *Morphoses*, 2002; *Carousel*, 2002; *Continuum*, 2002; *A Midsummer Night's Dream*, 2002; *Carnival of the Animals*, 2003; *Liturgy*, 2003; *Shambards*, 2004; *VIII*, 2004; *Swan Lake*, 2004

Selected Musicals: *Sweet Smell of Success*, 2002

Selected Films: *Center Stage*, 2000

Williams, Armstrong

Feb. 5, 1959– Radio and television talk-show host; columnist; businessman

Address: 201 Massachusetts Ave., N.E., Suite C-3, Washington, DC 20002-4957

A staunch advocate of Christian and conservative values, Armstrong Williams has been called "one of the most recognized conservative voices in America." Williams, who is African-American, has disseminated his views through his nationally syndicated radio and television shows (the former named him one of the 100 most important radio talk-show hosts in the country.

Armstrong Williams was born in Marion, South Carolina, on February 5, 1959. His father had four children with his first wife, who died in childbirth; with his second wife, Williams's mother, he had six more children. Williams grew up on the family's tobacco farm with his nine siblings and half-siblings. In a column paying tribute to his mother on Mother's Day in 1996, Williams wrote, as quoted on the Web site of the Thomas Road Baptist Church (whose senior pastor is Jerry Falwell), "My mother . . . raised eight sons. And because of her lessons, each of us has found his place in the world. . . . I am who I am because of my mother. Because of her example and strong moral compass, I have never used one word of profane language, I have never smoked any kind of cigarette or exposed myself to any illegal drugs, and I have never tasted any kind of alcoholic beverage, beer or wine, in my 37 years of living." While growing up Williams helped his father on the farm. In a 2001 column about his father, a Republican, published shortly before that year's Father's Day, Williams wrote, as posted on townhall.com, "Certainly it made [my father] proud that I chose to embrace the values that he taught me: personal responsibility, economic independence, thrift, a strong work ethic, an essential optimism that things will work out for the best."

Williams displayed an early gift for public speaking, winning an orating contest at his high school in 1976. He graduated from South Carolina State University, in Orangeburg, in 1981. That same year he moved to Washington, D.C., where he served as an aide to the late Senator Strom Thurmond, a South Carolina Republican, whom Williams, while still in high school, had boldly approached during the senator's public appearance at a Marion restaurant. Impressed by the young man's confidence, Thurmond offered Williams an internship. (Thurmond, who died in 2003, was known early in his career for his segregationist views; he ran for president in 1948 on a segregationist platform as the candidate of the States Rights' Democratic Party. Later in his long career in politics, Thurmond reached out to African-Americans, hiring blacks to his staff and nominating black candidates for government positions. Following his death it came to light that at the age of 22, Thurmond had fathered a child with Carrie Butler, a 16-year-old African-American housekeeper employed by his parents.)

From 1982 to 1986 Williams served as an assistant to Clarence Thomas, who at that time was the chairman of the U.S. Equal Employment Opportunity Commission (EEOC) and is now a U.S. Supreme Court associate justice. Williams's other experiences in public service during the 1980s included stints as a legislative assistant to two Republicans who represented South Carolina in Congress—Caroll A. Campbell, who later became governor of the state, and Floyd D. Spence—and as a

Courtesy of Armstrong Williams

Armstrong Williams

since 1992 and the latter since almost as long ago), on which he conducts interviews with newsmakers and discusses current events—and in newspapers around the country. Among his core concerns are the reform of welfare and affirmative-action programs, the restoration of morality in our society, and what he calls "right living." His radio program is broadcast to dozens of markets by the National Radio Network. His television show, called *The Right Side with Armstrong Williams*, is carried by a number of television outlets, many of them featuring Christian and family-oriented programming.

Williams is a syndicated columnist for Tribune Media Services, through which his articles are distributed to more than 75 newspapers across the country, and a guest columnist for *USA Today* and *Reader's Digest*. In addition, his often highly opinionated articles have appeared in the *Washington Times*, the *Detroit Free Press*, the *Boston Globe*, and his hometown paper, the *Marion Star-Mullins Enterprise*, in South Carolina. Williams's book, *Beyond Blame: How We Can Succeed by Breaking the Dependency Barrier* (1995), encourages readers, especially young African-American men, to develop strong families and communities, take personal responsibility for their actions and circumstances, and embrace spiritual values. Williams's official Web site states that he has taken "countless provocative stances, buoyed by conservative ideals and a little swagger" and that his mission has always been to "provide intelligent and value-oriented commentary on American culture and politics." In 1996 *Vanity Fair* voted Williams into its hall of fame as one of the most influential radio voices in America, and in 2003 *Savoy* magazine

presidential appointee in the U.S. Department of Agriculture. Williams then entered the field of public relations, as a vice president of governmental and international affairs with B&C Associates, based in High Point, North Carolina, which describes itself on the company Web site as the "oldest and most widely respected African American owned public relations and crisis management group in the United States." In that capacity Williams managed such individual and corporate clients as the acclaimed poet Maya Angelou, the Sara Lee Corp., Kinney Shoes, Shoney Inc. (a restaurant chain), and the Oprah Winfrey Charitable Giving Foundation.

The course of Williams's career changed suddenly in 1991, during the Senate Judiciary Committee's confirmation hearings on Clarence Thomas's nomination to the Supreme Court. Thomas's confirmation had hit a snag when Anita Hill, a University of Oklahoma law professor, testified that he had sexually harassed her when she worked as his assistant at the EEOC in the early 1980s. In defense of Thomas, Williams published a number of articles that were reprinted in newspapers around the country, bringing him national attention. In the following year Williams launched his first radio show, *The Right Side with Armstrong Williams*, on WOL-AM (1450 AM) in Washington, D.C., a station owned by the radio mogul Cathy Hughes. The show was simulcast to station WOLB-AM (1010 AM) in Baltimore, Maryland, and aired weekly. It soon attracted growing numbers of listeners and was given a daily time slot. The often confrontational Williams was known for presenting to his predominately black audience what he believed were the perspectives of white Americans and offering observations concerning stereotypes that African-Americans harbor about whites. "We frequently say that members of the white majority think about African Americans in stereotypes," Williams told Jeffrey Yorke for the *Washington Post* (February 1, 1994). "We may overlook that black people also stereotype white people. It works both ways." He welcomed as guests on his program such well-known and sometimes controversial figures as David Duke, the former Ku Klux Klansman and onetime Louisiana gubernatorial candidate; Vice President Dan Quayle; U.S. Senator Bob Dole; the television interviewer Larry King; Maya Angelou; the television producer Norman Lear; the presidential candidate Steve Forbes; the televangelist Robert Schuller; and the conservative politician and commentator Pat Buchanan. In 1995 *The Right Side* achieved national distribution when the program was syndicated by the Talk America Radio Network, airing from noon to 2 p.m. five days a week. Williams's radio commentary is now broadcast daily in dozens of markets around the United States via the National Radio Network (formerly the Langer Broadcasting Network), a fast-growing radio syndication company based in Framingham, Massachusetts. Once every two weeks Williams also contributes a two-minute segment to

the National Public Radio (NPR) program *Marketplace*, which offers economic, financial, and business news (or news about other fields of endeavor that affect, or are affected by, the marketplace) and is heard by millions of listeners each week.

On his nationally syndicated television show, *The Right Side with Armstrong Williams*, Williams conducts interviews with guests and leads discussions of news events, often concentrating on issues of race and religion in politics and culture. The show was carried in the 1990s on the now-defunct National Empowerment Television (also known as America's Voice), a cable-TV network that specialized in conservative programming. *The Right Side* is now carried by a number of television outlets, including the Christian Television Network; DCTV, in Washington, D.C.; the Liberty Broadcasting Television Network, which is affiliated with the Thomas Road Baptist Church and Jerry Falwell Ministries; WBTW-TV in South Carolina; WTCN WB 15 in Florida; Arlington Community Television, in Arlington, Virginia; and the Sky Angel Network, among others. Williams's latest television venture, a program called *On Point with Armstrong Williams*, began airing in early 2004 on the African-American–oriented cable network TV One, which is the product of a partnership between Comcast and the urban radio network Radio One. Like *The Right Side*, *On Point* features interviews with newsmakers and discussions of current events. A segment from early March 2004 featured Williams's interview with President George W. Bush's national security adviser, Condoleeza Rice. Williams has also appeared on a number of TV programs besides his own, including the *Oprah Winfrey Show*, *CNBC Crossfire*, *Firing Line with William Buckley*, *America's Black Forum*, the *Today Show*, the Black Entertainment Television (BET) *Nightly News*, BET's *Lead Story*, and *CNN Showdown*.

Williams's first published article, titled "A Pledge of Values," appeared in the *Marion Star-Mullins Enterprise* in about 1988. He has written one book, *Beyond Blame: How We Can Succeed by Breaking the Dependency Barrier* (1995), based on a series of letters that he wrote to a young black man named Brad, who was raised in a two-parent, middle-class home and is described as a drug dealer and murderer. In the letters Williams explored the plight of young African-American males and the ideas of the American political right and advocated adopting Christian values, working hard, and assuming personal responsibility for their actions as the best ways for young blacks to succeed. In 1996 the book was reprinted with the title *Letters to a Young Victim: Hope and Healing in America's Inner Cities*. That year the Los Angeles Times Syndicate began distributing Williams's articles in more than 30 U.S. newspapers. Since 2002, when Tribune Media Services bought that syndicate, Williams's column has been carried by more than 75 U.S. and overseas newspapers, including the *New York Amsterdam News*, the *Washington Afro-*

American, the *Washington Times*, *USA Today*, and the *Los Angeles Times*. Williams's subjects have included spousal abuse, racial profiling by police, racial and ethnic attitudes among America's Hispanic population, and ESPN's firing of Rush Limbaugh in 2003, after he made what were widely seen as racist comments about the Philadelphia Eagles quarterback Donovan McNabb. The topics of Williams's columns from early 2004 have included the Vietnam War record of U.S. senator John Kerry of Massachusetts, a Democratic presidential hopeful; gay marriage; and the plight of the Palestinian people.

In 2003 Williams helped organize several meetings between prominent conservative African-Americans and leaders of the national Republican Party. The aim of the meetings, he told Ralph Z. Hallow for the *Washington Times* (January 13, 2003), was to create a "Republican Party unified behind a push—unlike anything yet attempted—to recruit conservative black candidates for office from all over our country." Williams has often been criticized for encouraging African-Americans to join the Republican Party. "Many black people cannot understand why African Americans such as Williams . . . stand behind a party that embraces members who stood in the way of civil rights and voting rights legislation, school busing, laws against racial profiling and hate crimes, and a holiday in remembrance of the Rev. Martin Luther King Jr.," Darryl Fears wrote for the *Washington Post* (January 5, 2003). (Fears reported that according to the Joint Center for Political and Economic Studies, only 50 of the 9,040 black elected officials in the U.S. are registered Republicans, while more than 3,700 of that same group have declared themselves Democrats.) Calling him a "Talking Android," a reference to a black robot used by whites seeking to curtail black culture in Ishmael Reed's novel *Mumbo Jumbo*, staff writers for *Africana* (June 30, 2003, on-line) presented Williams, along with Clarence Thomas, Ward Connerly (a black anti–affirmative-action activist), and Thomas Sowell (an economist who is often described as a black conservative), as a powerful African-American who shows "uncritical loyalty" to the American political right and works diligently "against the interests of black culture." Williams has, however, urged the GOP to do more to improve the lives of African-Americans. According to Stanley Crouch in the New York *Daily News* (June 23, 2003), Williams was instrumental in persuading congressional Republicans to pass a bill that led to the refurbishment of the building in Washington, D.C. that was once the home of the black leader and abolitionist Frederick Douglass. In their attack on Williams, the *Africana* writers further charged that Williams "brings together all the familiar black conservative/freelance moralist tropes—his hardworking father, who turned down all scholarship offers because he proudly wanted to pay for his own son's schooling; the insufferability of black Harvard students wallowing in self-perceived victimhood; the continuing need, nonetheless, to help the 'truly needy.'"

Williams told Amy Bernstein for *U.S. News & World Report* (December 26/January 2, 1994) that his critics were often bothered by the fact that he refused to "blame whites for what's wrong with blacks." He expanded on that idea in an article he wrote for the *Washington Post* (August 20, 1995): "While some people suppose that as a black man I must be hostile toward 'white' mainstream society, some also think that being a conservative makes me a toady to 'the power' or a mindless defender of the 'status quo.' Sometimes the misconceptions compound one another. People think that as a black American I must be angry; liberals think I must lack compassion, while conservatives think I must resent the abuse I take from liberals and other blacks. None of it is true. I'm not angry, heartless or resentful—toward mainstream America or toward other black Americans."

Williams co-founded the Graham Williams Group, an international public-relations firm, with Stedman Graham, who is widely known as Oprah Winfrey's boyfriend. The company's clients include the real-estate corporation Century 21, Terry Giles (of Giles Enterprises), and Maya Angelou. Williams is also a former partner in Premier Limousine, Garden Grove Toyota, and Onyx Travel. In 2002 he established the Right Side Productions, which is responsible for syndicating and distributing his daily television show on cable outlets across the country. In partnership with the National Radio Network, the Right Side Productions also syndicates Williams's biweekly commentaries to radio stations around the nation. He has hosted on-line chat programs for the Heritage Foundation (on the organization's Town Hall Web site) and America Online (NetNoir.com). He sits on the boards of the Childhelp USA charity and the *Washington Afro-American* newspaper and is a member of Phi Beta Sigma fraternity. Williams is single.

—C.F.T.

Suggested Reading: Africana.com; Armstrong Williams Web site; townhall.com; *Washington Post* C p7 Feb. 1, 1994, A p5 Jan. 5, 2003

Selected Books: *Beyond Blame: How We Can Succeed by Breaking the Dependency Barrier*, 1995

Selected Radio Shows: *The Right Side with Armstrong Williams*, 1991– ; *On Point with Armstrong Williams*, 2004–

Selected Television Shows: *The Right Side with Armstrong Williams*, mid-1990s–

Courtesy of Deborah Willis

Willis, Deborah

Feb. 5, 1948– Photographer; writer; curator

Address: Tisch School of the Arts, Photography and Imaging, New York University, 721 Broadway, 8th Fl., New York, NY 10003

As an award-winning art photographer, writer, educator, one of the country's leading historians of African-American photography, and one of its chief curators of images relating to African-American culture, Deborah Willis has honored and helped to preserve the rich history of black life in the United States. She is a professor of photography and imaging at New York University's (NYU) Tisch School of the Arts and a curator of exhibitions at the Center for African-American History and Culture at the Smithsonian Institution in Washington, D.C. When asked what, in her role as a curator, she looks for in photographs, Willis told C. Gerald Fraser for the *New York Times* (August 6, 1989), "My approach is how photographs talk back to me. That's how I've looked at photographs throughout my life: if it talks back to me, if I respond to it visually and emotionally." Among the many books of photography that Willis has published are *Reflections in Black: A History of Black Photographers, 1840 to the Present* (2000), and, with Carla Williams, *The Black Female Body: A Photographic History* (2002). *Reflections in Black* is considered to be one of the first comprehensive histories of black photographers in America. An excerpt of Willis's writing from that book, as it appears on the George Mason University Web site, sums up much of her work: "It is my hope that by making the achievements of this rich and vital tra-

dition [of African-American photography] available to a new generation of photographers, these new photographers will be inspired to continue the lineage of artistic and documentary achievement and to challenge the rigid conceptions of race and gender that persist in our culture." Willis's photography is a permanent part of the collections of the Benton Museum of Art, at the University of Connecticut; the Center for Creative Photography, in Arizona; the University of Alabama; and the Los Angeles County Museum of Art. In addition to her professorship at NYU, Willis has served as a teacher, academic consultant, featured lecturer, or visiting artist at many other universities and art institutions in the United States, including the Rhode Island School of Design, Princeton University, and the International Center of Photography. She has received many honors, including the Anonymous Was a Woman Foundation Award, in 1996; a MacArthur Foundation Fellowship, in 2000; and a Lifetime Achievement in Photography Award from Exposure Group, in 2002.

One of the three daughters of Thomas M. and Ruth E. Willis, Deborah Willis was born on February 5, 1948. After serving in the U.S. Army, Willis's father became a policeman and a grocery-store owner, while her mother worked as a beautician. Willis's sisters are Yvonne Brooks and Leslie Willis Lowery. Willis told *Current Biography* that her father's amateur interest in photography helped to inspire her own. She was further drawn to photography after reading as a child the book *The Sweet Flypaper of Life* (1955), which contained text by the celebrated black poet Langston Hughes and photographs by Roy DeCarava, and offered intimate images of African-Americans in the Harlem section of New York City.

Willis attended Temple University, in Philadelphia, Pennsylvania, from 1967 to 1972. (She did not earn a degree there.) She received a B.F.A. degree in photography from the Philadelphia College of Art in 1975, and in 1980 she earned a master of fine arts degree in photography from Pratt Institute, in Brooklyn, New York. Continuing her education, she next earned a master's degree in art history, with a concentration in museum studies, from the City University of New York (CUNY) in 1986, and later, in 2003, Willis completed work toward her Ph.D. degree in cultural studies from George Mason University, in Fairfax, Virginia.

Earlier, after having earned her master's degree from Pratt, in 1980 Willis joined the New York Public Library's Schomburg Center for Research in Black Culture as a curator of the center's photographs and prints. The Schomburg Center, located in Harlem, is a national research library dedicated to preserving and providing access to resources documenting the experience of people of African descent all over the world. According to its official Web site, the Schomburg Center contains more than five million items, including newspapers, prints, books, films, audiotapes, and recorded music. Later, Willis became director of the center's photographs and prints division, which holds hundreds of thousands of images, including the work of such distinguished African-American photographers as Gordon Parks and Chester Higgins Jr. Willis's duties at the Schomburg Center included organizing original exhibitions and building the center's collection. (A curator customarily selects the theme or focus of an exhibit, the individual pieces of art that will be shown, and the sequence or pattern in which the pieces are displayed.) Among the exhibitions Willis curated at the Schomburg Center were *Black Dance in Photographs* (1982); *Scenes from the 20th Century Stage: Black Theatre in Photographs* (1983); and *Black Images in Film: A Photographic Exhibition* (1984). Willis remained at the Schomburg Center for more than a decade, until 1992.

That same year Willis became an exhibitions curator at the Center for African-American History and Culture at the Smithsonian Institution, in Washington, D.C. The Smithsonian Institution is one of the world's largest museum complexes and research organizations and one of the oldest and most respected institutions of knowledge and culture in the United States. It comprises 17 different museums and is affiliated with more than 100 other museums, in addition to nine research centers whose work spans everything from marine science to space exploration. The institution has more than two million members and hosts tens of millions of visitors to its facilities every year. Willis later assumed the post of associate director for research and collections at the Smithsonian's Center for African-American History and Culture. The original exhibitions she organized there included *Imagining Families: Images and Voices* (1994–95); *Reflections on Rights* (1995–1996); *Visual Journal: Photography in Harlem in the 30's and 40's* (1996); and *In Search of Balance: The Artist/Scholar* (1997). Willis left the Smithsonian in 2000.

In addition to her work for the Schomburg Center and the Smithsonian, Willis has curated many other photographic exhibitions around the United States, among them *Black Photographers: 1840–1940*, at the University of Vermont's Fleming Museum, in 1986; *HerStory/HerSpace/HerMoments: 7 Women Photographers*, at the Rotunda Gallery in Brooklyn, New York, in 1987; *HerStory: Black Women Photographers*, as part of the Houston Fotofest at the Firehouse Gallery, in Houston, Texas, in 1988; *Black Photographers Bear Witness: 100 Years of Social Protest*, at the Williams College Museum of Art, in Massachusetts, in 1989; and *Photobiographers*, at the Atlanta Gallery of Photography, in Georgia, in 1992.

In the late 1980s, concurrently with her work as a curator, Willis began exhibiting her own photography at galleries and other venues across the United States. Her work has been part of many exhibitions, including *Reflections of Self: Women Photographers*, at Fordham University, in New York City, in 1986; *Occupation and Resistance,* at the Alternative Museum, in New York City, in 1990;

Deborah Willis/Christian Walker, at the Jane Jackson Gallery, in Atlanta, Georgia, in 1992; *Prisoners of War: In My Native Land and On Foreign Soil*, at the New School Gallery, in New York City, in 1992; *Personal Narrative: Women Photographers of Color*, at Southeastern Center for Contemporary Art, in Winston-Salem, North Carolina, in 1993; *Searching for Memories: Black Women and the 1895 Atlanta Exposition*, which was a collaborative installation by Willis, Carla Williams, and Clarissa Sligh, for the 1995 Atlanta Arts Festival; *Eye of the Beholder: Photographs from the Avon Collection*, at the International Center of Photography, in New York City, in 1997; *Memorable Histories and Historic Memories*, at Bowdoin College's Museum of Art, in Maine, in 1998; *Re/Righting History: Counternarratives by Contemporary African-American Artists*, at the Katonah Museum of Art, in Katonah, New York, in 1999; *Embracing Eatonville*, at Light Works, in Syracuse, New York, in 2003-04, which, along with Willis's photographs, included the work of Carrie Ann Weems, Dawoud Bey, and Lonnie Graham, and was a survey of Eatonville, Florida, the oldest incorporated black town in the United States; and *Through the Gates: Brown v. Board of Education*, at the California African American Museum, in Los Angeles, in 2004. Willis told *Current Biography* about her photographs, "My interest in photography focuses on family images and stories that are developed about community, strength, and beauty. I have for the last 20 years made photographs that tell visual stories and am interested in documenting the family unit. I focus on gesture and placement, gatherings and individual portraits. I believe . . . focusing the camera on a single subject or a group portrait offers the viewer an opportunity to imagine the space around the subject."

Willis has edited or co-edited a number of books. Among those are *An Illustrated Biobibliography of Black Photographers, 1940–1988* (1989) and *Lorna Simpson* (1992), which looks at the work of the eponymous, contemporary African-American photographer and artist. In the photographic survey *J.P. Ball: Daguerrean and Studio Photographer* (1993), Willis presented more than 200 photographs taken by James Presley Ball (1825–1904), an African-American, who was regarded as one of the best American photographers of his day. As quoted on amazon.com, a *Book News, Inc.* review found the volume "thrilling" as it "not only brings to light an important chapter in African-American history, but . . . brings long-overdue recognition to Ball." For *Picturing Us: African American Identity in Photography* (1994), Willis invited 18 African-American writers, critics, and filmmakers to choose one photograph each that held particular meaning for them and to write about the photograph's significance. Among the contributors were Angela Davis, Adele Alexander, and bell hooks. The images ranged from family portraits to a photograph of a lynching. *Picturing Us* won the International Center of Photography's

1995 Infinity Award for writing on photography. Willis then served as photo editor for the book *Million Man March* (1995), with text by Michael H. Cottman. The book depicted in words and pictures the massive public gathering of African-American men in Washington, D.C., that year, which was organized by the Nation of Islam leader Louis Farrakhan and attended by many prominent African-Americans, who called for, among other things, unity and strength in the country's black communities. The following year Willis co-edited, along with Jane Lusaka, *Visual Journal: Harlem and D.C. in the Thirties and Forties,* and edited *The Family of Black America,* which contains text written by Michael H. Cottman. (Because of earlier marriages, for the books she has been involved in creating, Willis has in some cases been credited as Deborah Willis-Thomas, Willis-Ryan, or Willis-Braithwaite.)

For her book *Reflections in Black: A History of Black Photographers, 1840 to the Present,* Willis culled nearly 600 images that, in the words of Rhonda Stewart for *Emerge* magazine (May 2000), amount to a "breathtaking collection that gives a panoramic and awe-inspiring look at Black life." The book has been called the first comprehensive history of African-American photography. Willis has cited the special importance of the work of African-American photographers from the period between 1840 and the American Civil War (1861–65). (Willis notes that blacks began producing photographs in 1840, the year after Louis J. M. Daguerre invented what is known as the daguerreotype, a method by which the likeness of a person could be captured on iodized paper.) Slavery existed during that time, and most images of blacks—produced by whites—showed them with "exaggerated features" and in "demeaning situations," as Willis wrote in the excerpt from *Reflections in Black* that appeared on the George Mason University Web site. "Concerned about how black people were portrayed in a world of rank racist imagery," Willis wrote, "black photographers were especially sensitive to negative depictions of black Americans during the mid-1800's." Their pictures were of ordinary black men and women, both free and enslaved; newly arrived immigrants to the U.S.; and slave owners and their families, among others. In the book Willis reprinted the work of such early African-American photographic pioneers as James Presley Ball and Augustus Washington, both of whom used the craft to promote their stand against slavery; James VanDerZee, who most famously captured images of the artistic renaissance among African-Americans in Harlem in the early 20th century and who became the first African-American photographer in that century to achieve commercial success and fame; Gordon Parks, who worked as a photographer for *Life* magazine; and Monet Sleet Jr., the first black man to win the prestigious Pulitzer Prize for photography. Also featured in *Reflections in Black* is the work of photojournalists who recorded events related to the civil rights and black-power movements. There are photographs of athletes, such as the boxing champion Muhammad Ali and an all-female basketball team, and music legends such as Dinah Washington and John Coltrane. Rhonda Stewart found that *Reflections in Black* "illuminates brilliantly" the complex interior lives of blacks in America. The book's publication was timed to complement the opening of a traveling exhibit of the same name, in Washington, D.C. (Along with Thomas Allen Harris, Willis is co-producing a four-part documentary titled *Reflections in Black*, which is due to be completed in 2005.)

Willis's next book project, entitled *The Black Female Body: A Photographic History* (2002), was inspired by the story of Sarah Baartman (also known as Saartje or Saartjie Baartman), a black woman from South Africa who came to be called the Hottentot Venus. In the early 19th century, Baartman was taken to Europe and crudely displayed in public at museums and fashionable parties, among other places, as a sexual and physical curiosity due to her large, protruding buttocks and genitalia. Willis explained to Ana Acosta Larkin for the Smithsonian Institution's Web site that "stereotypical caricatures of Baartman portrayed her as entertainment while also sexualizing her image." To create the book, Willis enlisted the help of Carla Williams, a friend and fellow photographer. (Willis and Williams's book, "They Called Her Venus: The Life of Sarah Baartman," is scheduled for publication in 2005.) Together they examined Western culture's fascination with the bodies of black women and the different ways in which those women have been portrayed over the years, through pictures ranging from 19th-century shots of African women in tribal dress and slaves working in fields to photographs of modern-day female bodybuilders. Searching in art museums, private collections, books, and archives in Europe and the United States, Willis and Williams selected for their book nearly 200 images of black women from three different centuries. As Willis told Larkin, the earlier photographs revealed how black women were "simultaneously lusted after and despised." In contrast, other photographs of black women often "robbed black women of their femininity and portrayed them more as genderless workers," especially during the slavery era, Larkin wrote. The African-American men who began working as photographers in the 19th century rendered more respectful, elegant images of black women, often with their families. The more contemporary images in *The Black Female Body* include a nude pregnant woman; a black woman admiring the body of a friend in a tight dress, and an African woman with untreated hair walking by a Revlon advertisement showing a black model with straightened hair. Among the photographers whose work is featured in the book are Edward Weston, Lorna Simpson, and Carrie Mae Weems. The book also contains shots by Willis herself.

In a review that appeared on the Temple University Web site, Henry Louis Gates Jr., a well-known intellectual and Harvard University professor, called *The Black Female Body* an "astonishing collection of previously unfamiliar images" and wrote that the book "compels us to re-imagine much of what we thought we knew about African and African American history and culture." Shauna Frischkorn wrote for *Library Journal*, as quoted on amazon.com, that Willis and Williams's book "provides a fascinating view into a long-neglected and even taboo subject."

The Black Female Body won several awards, including a National Gold Ink Award, which honors achievements in print media, in 2002. It was also named an outstanding academic title by *Choice* magazine, which reviews books and other media for academic libraries, and chosen as a finalist for the Ben Franklin Award by the Publishers Marketing Association. At about the time of its publication, a companion exhibit to *The Black Female Body* opened at the Smithsonian Institution's Arts and Industries Building before traveling to other venues around the country. The year 2003 saw the publication of Willis's photography book *Black: A Celebration of Culture*, which contains more than 500 photographs, hand-picked by Willis, and shows slices of 20th-century African-American life in its great variety. Included along with shots of ordinary people at parties or at church are photographs of the athletes Jesse Owens and Barry Bonds, the singer Ella Fitzgerald, and the movie star Halle Berry.

In addition to her other written work, Willis has contributed essays or chapters to several books, among them *Harlem Renaissance: The Art of Black America* (1987); *VanDerZee: Photographer, 1886–1983* (1993); *Africana: The Encyclopedia of the African and African American Experience* (1999); *One Shot: The Photographs of Charles "Teenie" Harris* (2002); *A Small Nation of People: W.E.B. Dubois and African-American Portraits of Progress* (2003); and *Small Towns, Black Lives: African-American Communities in Southern New Jersey* (2003).

Among the other artistic media she has used to express herself, Willis has also created quilts, a craft that as a young girl she had first seen practiced by her aunt Cora. Willis has made and exhibited what she calls "photo quilts," printing photographs on linen that she then sews onto the fabric of the quilts. On the Web site of the Bernice Steinbaum Gallery, where her work has been shown, Willis described her photo quilts as "visual diaries" that tell stories about "who we are and who and what our ancestors have been to us and the larger society."

Willis's teaching experience is vast. Prior to her current professorship, at NYU, she held academic appointments in photography and African-American culture and art at CUNY, from 1989 to 1990; the Maryland Institute College of Art, in 1995 and 2000; Duke University and the University of North Carolina, from 2000 to 2001; and Princeton University, in 2003. Willis has also served as an academic consultant at Ohio State University, Howard University, the New York School of Visual Arts, and the Southeast Museum of Photography, among a dozen other institutions of higher learning. She has lent her talents as a consultant to many museums, including the Studio Museum in Harlem, the Birmingham Civil Rights Museum, the Corcoran Gallery of Art, the Whitney Museum of Art, and the California College of Arts and Crafts. She has also consulted on several films and television documentaries, among them the PBS documentary *American Photography* (1999).

Willis has been a visiting artist or critic in residence at a number of universities, artists' colonies, and art institutions, among them Columbia University and Light Works, both in New York City; the University of Colorado; and Maryland Art Place, in Baltimore. As a panelist or reviewer, she has assisted the National Endowment for the Arts; the National Endowment for the Humanities; the Jewish Museum in New York City; the Ohio Arts Council; the W. Eugene Smith Memorial Fund; and the Kentucky State Council for the Arts, among many other institutions. She has lectured widely at schools and art institutions around the United States. Willis has been a professionally affiliated member of the American Studies Association; the American Association of Museums; Women's Caucus for the Arts; the Society for Photographic Education; and the College Art Association, among other groups.

In addition to her other awards, Willis has been honored with the Manhattan Borough President's Award for Excellence in the Arts (1986); the Pratt Institute Alumni Achievement Award in Education (1993); the Alumni of the Year Award from the University of the Arts, in Philadelphia, Pennsylvania (1995); Women of Color Research Grant from the Ford Foundation (1999 to 2001); the Studio Museum in Harlem Award for Achievement in Scholarship (2001); and the 2001 Missouri Honor Medal from the University of Missouri School of Journalism. In 2001 she was also awarded a Townsend Harris Medal by the City University of New York, and in 2003 she was awarded an honorary doctorate by the Maryland Institute. Also in 2003 she received a grant from the National Endowment for the Humanities.

Willis has a son, Hank Sloane Willis Thomas, who is a photographer and art historian. She is married to Winston Kennedy, a printmaker and a professor of art at Howard University.

—C.F.T.

Suggested Reading: Bernice Steinbaum Gallery Web site; *Emerge* p68 May 2000; George Mason University Web site; *New York Times* II p49 Aug. 6, 1989, with photo; New York University Web site; Smithsonian Institution Web site

Selected Books: *An Illustrated Bio-bibliography of Black Photographers, 1940-1988,* 1989; *Lorna Simpson,* 1992; *J.P. Ball, Daguerrean and Studio Photographer,* 1993; *Picturing Us: African American Identity in Photography,* 1994; *Million Man March* (text by Michael H. Cottman), 1995; *Visual Journal: Harlem and D.C. in the Thirties and Forties* (co-edited by Jane Lusaka), 1996; *Family of Black America (*with text by Michael H. Cottman and research by Linda Tarrant-Reid), 1996; *Reflections in Black: A History of Black Photographers, 1840 to the Present,* 2000; *The Black Female Body: A Photographic History,* 2002

Henri Leutwyler/Courtesy of the White House Project

Wilson, Marie C.

Sep. 6, 1940– Co-founder and president of the White House Project; former president of the Ms. Foundation for Women

Address: The White House Project, 110 Wall St., 2d Fl., New York, NY 10005

"In a democracy, a group with over half your population deserves to be represented at the highest levels," the women's advocate Marie C. Wilson wrote in response to a *Des Moines Business Record* (October 5, 1998) questionnaire. "In over 20 countries, there has been a woman prime minister or president. We're the leading democracy, so others wonder why we haven't had a woman leader." Since the 1970s, when she directed women's programs at a midwestern college, Wilson has worked to achieve gender equity in all spheres of society.

For two decades, from early 1985 to mid-2004, she led the Ms. Foundation for Women, which describes itself as the country's "only national multi-issue women's fund." "The mission [that its founders] put in place has basically held: to make sure women have the resources to influence their own lives and the world around them," Wilson told *AAUW Outlook* (Fall/Winter 2002, on-line), a publication of the American Association of University Women. According to the Ms. Foundation's Web site, "Through its leadership, expertise and financial support, the Foundation champions an equitable society by effecting change in public consciousness, law, philanthropy and social policy." Under Wilson's direction the foundation provided training, technical assistance, and millions of dollars in grants to grassroots organizations striving to improve the health and safety of women and girls; enable women to gain economic self-sufficiency; and help women gain the skills, and develop the desire and confidence, to hold leadership positions in the public and private sectors of American society. It did so through such groundbreaking programs as the Institute for Women's Economic EmPOWERment (an annual event launched in 1986); the Reproductive Rights Coalition and Organizing Fund (set up in 1989); the Collaborative Fund for Women's Economic Development (1990); Take Our Daughters to Work Day (1993), now called Take Our Daughters and Sons to Work Day; the Collaborative Fund for Healthy Girls/Healthy Women, the Women and AIDS Fund, and the Democracy Funding Circle (all 1996), the last of which, according to the foundation's Web site, aims "to combat the growing influence of conservatism" by supporting "organizations working toward a progressive vision of democracy"; and the Collaborative Fund for Youth-Led Social Change (2002).

Wilson stepped down from the presidency of the Ms. Foundation for Women to concentrate on her work with the White House Project, a national, nonpartisan organization that she co-founded in 1997. The White House Project seeks to increase the number of female political leaders; one of the group's principal goals is the election of a female U.S. president or vice president. A poll conducted four years ago indicated that "79 percent of the public feel that women's leadership in America is not truly going to be accepted until women hold one of these high offices . . . ," as Wilson told an interviewer for the *Women's Review of Books* (July 2000). "So one of the most important things that we can do is to intensify our efforts to educate people about possible women candidates." As of June 30, 2004, according to the Inter-Parliamentary Union (on-line), women made up 14.8 percent of the delegates in the U.S. House of Representatives; thus, in terms of the percentage of women serving in their countries' lower or single legislative body, the U.S. ranked 58th (along with Andorra) among the world's nations, behind Rwanda and Sweden (which ranked first and second, respectively, with

48.8 and 45.3 percent) and such countries as Cuba (36.0 percent), Bulgaria (26.2), China (20.2), and Peru (18.3). Keenly aware of that fact, Wilson and her colleagues have encouraged American women to run for office at all levels of government and have tried to create an environment in which their election will become a reality. Wilson believes that the day a woman will occupy the White House is not far off. "This is our time," she told Lynda Richardson for the *New York Times* (February 17, 2004). "I think by 2008, we're going to see several women in the race." She added, "And that's the point, to get enough women running so they are seen and they're evaluated on their agenda, not just gender."

The daughter of a typesetter and a dental hygienist, Marie C. Wilson was born on September 6, 1940 in Georgia and raised in Atlanta, the state capital. She has recalled that once, when she was a child, a bus driver dragged her, weeping, from the back of the bus, where she had been sitting next to her black babysitter, to the front section, reserved for whites. Her memory of that incident contributed to her later involvement, in the early 1960s, in the civil rights movement. Earlier, in high school, she was a cheerleader and, one year, homecoming queen. In about 1963 she earned a bachelor's degree in philosophy from Vanderbilt University, in Nashville, Tennessee. Some years later, when she was a full-time homemaker with four children, she and her husband adopted a baby boy who, they later learned, suffered from cerebral palsy. "I worked with the school system to help him get what he needed," she told Judith Stone for *O, the Oprah Magazine* (March 2004). "I lobbied for affordable childcare. Then I realized, *Oh, my God, politics is about me!*" Wilson's husband was a minister of music (a person who plans services and oversees the choir and various other congregational activities in a place of worship), and she and their children accompanied him each time he got a job with a different church, in Delaware, Pennsylvania, and Iowa. In Des Moines, Iowa, Wilson earned a master's degree in education from Drake University in 1980. Subsequently, she was appointed director of women's programs at Drake; in that position she assisted in career-development efforts and instituted such workplace innovations as flextime and job sharing. In 1983 she became the first woman to be elected as an at-large member of the Des Moines City Council.

In the mid-1980s a representative of the Ms. Foundation for Women "came to Des Moines and asked a group of us what was happening for women in Iowa," as Wilson recalled for *AAUW Outlook*. "Right then I swore I would work for that organization. No one had ever asked us what was happening for women in Iowa. No one had ever told women in local communities that we mattered." In 1985 Wilson was named president of the foundation, which was organized in 1972 as a conduit for transferring some of the profits generated by *Ms. Magazine* to the grassroots women's movement. (*Ms.*,

launched earlier that year by Gloria Steinem, Patricia Carbine, Letty Cottin Pogrebin, and Marlo Thomas, was an instant popular, though not financial, success. The foundation has raised funds independently of the magazine since 1974.) When Wilson arrived, the foundation had four staff members and an annual budget of $500,000; currently, it has 40 employees, a budget of over $10 million, and an endowment fund of over $20 million.

Under Wilson's leadership, the Collaborative Fund for Women's Economic Development, a preeminent model of collaborative grant-making by individual, family, and institutional donors, began operating in 1990. Since 1991 that fund has committed over $10 million to support local programs that create jobs for low-income women. The Ms. Foundation's most recent venture of this sort is the Collaborative Fund for Youth-Led Social Change, which supports programs that develop new ways for adolescent and teenage boys and girls to work together and explore nontraditional gender roles, among other activities. In addition to the Ms. Foundation, the 19 donors or sponsors of that fund include the Diana, Princess of Wales Memorial Fund (U.S.); the Women's Foundation of Colorado; the Girl's Best Friend Foundation, in Chicago, Illinois; and Polly Howells, a Brooklyn, New York–based psychotherapist. The 12 grantees include the Appalachian Women's Leadership Project, in Hamlin, West Virginia; Asian Immigrant Women Advocates, in Oakland, California; Sista II Sista, in Brooklyn, New York; and Sisters in Action for Power, in Portland, Oregon.

In 1993, along with Gloria Steinem, Wilson created Take Our Daughters to Work Day, a public-education campaign that, according to the Ms. Foundation's Web site, "focused on making girls visible, valued, and heard." The event was also designed to expose girls to the variety of careers open to them and to foster dialogue about women's changing roles in the workplace. In 2003 the project was renamed Take Our Daughters and Sons to Work Day. "The new program," the foundation's Web site states, "encourages both girls and boys to share their expectations for the future and think about how they can participate fully in family, work, and community"; it also "challenges workplaces to consider policies that will help their female and male employees better integrate these multiple demands." Wilson also regarded the event as a way to decrease, with time, the reluctance of many men to take advantage of family-leave benefits; studies have shown that men who take family leave assume more responsibilities at home than men who do not. In recent years an estimated 15 million adults have brought one or more children to their jobs on Take Our Daughters and Sons to Work Day; about 30 percent of U.S. businesses take part.

One of Wilson's top concerns is obtaining paid family leave, in which, when member of their families need special care, employees can take up to six weeks of leave while earning 50 to 60 percent of their salaries (after first using their vacation time), in arrangements similar to those that provide disability benefits. "Studies show when employees can take some time away from work to handle crises, they're happier and more productive," Wilson told Geoff Williams for *Entrepreneur* (May 1, 2003). "This isn't full paid leave, so employees aren't going to make this decision lightly. But it's a safety net, and if it's not there, [employers are] going to pay full price for a lot of lost productivity." In a commentary for the Spokane, Washington, *Spokesman-Review* (October 27, 2003, on-line), Wilson noted, "Of the industrialized nations, only Australia and the United States do not provide paid family leave." While the federal Family Medical Leave Act, passed in 1993, allows workers to take off six weeks without pay, millions of people cannot afford to forgo their salaries for so long. In addition, many employees do not take needed leave for fear of being labeled disloyal or worse by their employers. "One of the best things about paid family leave is that it could help change the corporate culture," Wilson told Williams. "By letting your employees know you support paid family leave, you can send the message to your employees that their family lives and personal growth matter to you. Ultimately, that's going to make your company stronger and attract more qualified people."

In 1997, along with Laura Liswood, who then taught at the Kennedy School of Government at Harvard University, Wilson launched the White House Project (WHP), a national, nonpartisan organization dedicated to fostering the entry of women into leadership positions, among them the U.S. presidency. In July 2004 the WHP's home page noted that of the 12,000 people who have served in the U.S. Congress since its inception, only 215 have been women. Wilson is endeavoring to increase the number of women at all levels of government. "We make up 52 percent of the population but only 14 percent of Congress," she told Stone in 2004. "And men are 86 percent of elected officials under the age of 35—from whose ranks come half of our presidents, governors, and members of Congress." She contends that women bring valuable assets to public service that are rare in men. "Research shows that women legislators look at issues more broadly, are more open, and bring more people into the [legislative] process," she told Stone. "If leading by consensus-building weren't devalued because it's something women do, it would already have transformed the world."

The WHP is focusing on three major projects. The first is a study called "Framing Gender on the Campaign Trail," which examines how the media's treatment of female and male candidates for public office differs. In the second, called "Six to Sixty," WHP is attempting to educate and train females ages six to 60 for activities or careers in politics. The third project involves analyzing barriers to and opportunities for women's leadership in public life and defining what is meant by the phrase "qualified woman." Wilson has observed that the

expectations regarding female candidates are much higher than those for males. "When we did focus groups I could hardly believe the stress on perfection, the feeling that 'whoever does this has to be the perfect person' . . . ," she told the *Women's Review of Books.* "If the first woman to be, say, president has to represent this perfect standard, she will not be able to bring her whole self into the process; most likely, she'll be a woman who fits a more masculine model. We want a woman who can be her whole self, all her masculine self, all her feminine self, her whole self. That will not happen if she's forced into being the first token [female president]. She'll have to meet standards that are really about gender. . . . That's why we have to keep pushing numbers, so we get beyond gender. Because this project—electing a woman to the White House—is about having a democracy and moving beyond gender." The White House Project recently teamed up with V-Day, an organization founded by the playwright Eve Ensler with the goal of eradicating violence against women, on Women Elect the Future, a national effort to mobilize women to vote and to develop leadership skills. According to various polls, a far greater percentage of the public than ever before professes willingness to vote for qualified female candidates. Indeed, many people perceive women as having special expertise and even "more credibility," in Wilson's words, on issues connected with family, health care, education, and the workplace, and view women as generally more trustworthy than men. "For better or worse, the growing dissatisfaction with politicians has really been pushing people to think differently about leadership," she told the *Des Moines Business Record.* "Our polls show that people think women provide more integrity in leadership."

Wilson has maintained that popular culture should not be ignored as a means of changing perceptions about gender and power. The film *Air Force One,* for example, in which the actress Glenn Close played the U.S. vice president, may have led many people to consider the idea of a woman in a powerful position, according to Wilson. In 2000, at Wilson's suggestion, the giant toy manufacturer Mattel introduced a President Barbie doll. (Wilson had learned that in 1994, according to Mattel, American girls ages three to 10 owned an average of eight Barbie dolls each.) President Barbie is available as a Caucasian, an African-American, and a Latina (but not an Asian or a Native American). "I almost lost my feminist credentials for suggesting the doll," Wilson told Stone—referring to Barbie as a target of feminists who criticize the doll as an example of a highly unrealistic female body image, a symbol of materialism, and the epitome of an unhealthy emphasis on fashion and appearance. "But to make change, you've got to go where the people are. And more and more girls think they're going to grow up to be president and call a joint session of Congress because their dolls can." (Other feminists have noted with approval that Barbie holds a job outside the home and is self-supporting.) Included with every President Barbie is the WHP's Girls' Action Agenda for children and parents and a Girls' Bill of Rights, prepared by Girls Inc. (which, its Web site states, is a nonprofit organization "dedicated to inspiring all girls to be strong, smart, and bold").

After a WHP study found that between January 1, 2000 and June 30, 2001, only 11 percent of guests on the five major Sunday-morning television news shows were women, WHP created a database of the names of female experts in various fields, in the so-called Visibility Project. With Elizabeth Debold and Idelisse Malavé, Wilson wrote *Mother Daughter Revolution: from Betrayal to Power* (1993), which, as Catherine Hunter wrote for *Herizons* (Summer 1994), "places the problematic relationship between mothers and daughters in its wider political context." Her second book, written solo, is *Closing the Leadership Gap: Why Women Can and Must Help Run the World* (2004). She co-wrote the preface to *Girls Seen and Heard: 52 Life Lessons for Our Daughters* (1999), by Sondra Forsyth and Ms. Foundation staff members. Wilson and her successor as president of the Ms. Foundation, Sara K. Gould, wrote the preface to *Kitchen Table Entrepreneurs: How Eleven Women Escaped Poverty and Became Their Own Bosses* (2002), in which Martha Shirk and Anna S. Wadia wrote about 11 women who received grants from the Ms. Foundation to start their own businesses. Wilson also wrote the forewords to *Woman: A Celebration to Benefit the Ms. Foundation for Women* (2002), a compendium of essays and photographs of and by women, and to *If Women Ruled the World* (2004), another compilation of essays by women, edited by Sheila Ellison.

Wilson has received the Robert W. Scrivner Award for Creative Grantmaking, the Leadership for Equity and Diversity (LEAD) Award from Women & Philanthropy, and an honorary doctorate of public service from Drake University. In 2004 the Ms. Foundation established the Marie C. Wilson Leadership Fund in her honor. She is a sought-after speaker at local, state, national, and international events; her topics include a variety of women's, philanthropic, and political issues. Wilson served as an official U.S. delegate to the United Nations' Fourth World Conference on Women, held in Beijing, China, in 1995. Although the Ms. Foundation and the White House Project are nonpartisan, she has identified herself as a Democrat.

Wilson, who is divorced, has five children and several grandchildren. She and her partner of 15 years, Nancy A. Lee, a *New York Times* vice president for business development, live in New York City.

—K.E.D.

Suggested Reading: ms.foundation.org; *New York Times* B p2 Feb. 17, 2004, with photo; *O, the Oprah Magazine* p72 Mar. 2004, with photo; White House Project Web site; *Women's Review of Books* p14+ July 2000, with photo

Selected Books: *Mother Daughter Revolution: from Betrayal to Power* (with Elizabeth Debold and Idelisse Malavé), 1993; *Closing the Leadership Gap: Why Women Can and Must Help Run the World*, 2004

Witherspoon, Reese

Mar. 22, 1976– Actress

Address: c/o Stev Dontanville, William Morris Agency, 151 El Camino Dr., Beverly Hills, CA 90212

Reese Witherspoon, recognized as one of the most unconventional young actresses currently working in film, is also one of the few actresses of her generation to earn the respect of Hollywood executives and critics alike. The former appreciate her for her ability to carry a movie nearly single-handedly, as illustrated by the phenomenal box-office success of the surprise-hit comedy *Legally Blonde* (2001), in which she played the lead, Elle Woods. The latter have remarked upon her unique combination of innocence, wit, toughness, spiritedness, and determination, and have praised her performances in such independent films as *Man in the Moon* (1991) and *Election* (1999). "It's the tough side of Witherspoon that grounds her performances," Peter Travers wrote for *Rolling Stone*

(October 17, 2002). "She's unafraid to squint and screw up her pretty face until she resembles a pissed-off Pekingese. Her lack of vanity helps put the crunch in her comedy. . . . Witherspoon has the class, the sass and the full-out talent to sustain a major career. . . . She's one of that select group who [are] worth watching in anything."

Laura Jean Witherspoon was born on March 22, 1976 in New Orleans, Louisiana. (Some sources report her given name as Laura Jean Reese.) Her ancestor John Witherspoon, a Scottish immigrant to America, signed the Declaration of Independence and became president of what is now Princeton University. Her father, also named John Witherspoon, is an ear, nose, and throat surgeon with the U.S. Air Force; her mother, Betty (Reese) Witherspoon, is a professor of pediatric nursing. Witherspoon spent her earliest years in Wiesbaden, Germany, where her father served a four-year tour of duty. When she was five years old, the family, which includes her older brother, John, settled in Nashville, Tennessee. "I had a very definitive Southern upbringing . . . ," she told Scarlet Cheng for the *Los Angeles Times* (April 11, 1999). "It bred

Stuart Franklin/Getty Images

Reese Witherspoon

in me such a sense of family and tradition. . . . It helped me establish a sense of normalcy in life that I hope will stay with me for the long haul." Witherspoon attended Harpeth Hall, a prestigious all-girls college-preparatory school in Nashville. She has described her English teacher in her junior year of high school as particularly inspiring; the teacher helped Witherspoon develop a "passion for reading and studying material that was so helpful for me [as an actor]," as she told Andy Jones in an interview for *TNT Rough Cut* (May 17, 1999, online).

Witherspoon got her first acting job when she was seven, appearing in a TV commercial for a local flower store owned by a family friend. When she was 14 she auditioned for a part as an extra in the film *The Man in the Moon* (1991). Impressed by her abilities, the director of the movie, Robert Mulligan (whose credits include *To Kill a Mockingbird*), offered her the central role—that of Dani Trant, a young tomboy who falls in love for the first time. (Sam Waterston and Tess Harper played her parents in the film, which is set in 1950s Louisiana.) Critics praised the actress's work; in a representative review, John Hartl wrote for the *Seattle Times* (October 4, 1991), "Witherspoon is especially fine," bringing "an independent, precocious quality to Dani's scenes that's never trying or exaggerated."

More roles came Witherspoon's way; she often worked 14-hour days in TV and cinema in productions that highlighted her image of virginal, wide-eyed innocence. On television, she appeared in the films *Wildflower* (1991) and *Desperate Choices: To Save My Child* (1992) and the CBS miniseries *Return to Lonesome Dove* (1993). On the big screen

she had a small role as a 12-year-old hippie in the Danny DeVito film *Jack the Bear* (1993) and a starring role in the Disney film *A Far Off Place* (1993). In the latter she played Nonnie Parker, a child raised in Africa whose parents are murdered by elephant poachers. To prepare for the role, Witherspoon studied with the Matabele, an African tribe, and learned the basics of what is commonly called the "click" language.

Back at her high school, Witherspoon downplayed her Hollywood career. "I just wanted to seem normal. . . . I was just constantly trying to acclimate and trying to be like everybody else," she told Andy Jones. She joined the cheerleading team, had a debutante ball, and went to her senior prom with her father. By her own account, attending an all-girls school benefited her. "An all-girls school helps you develop solid female friendships, makes you secure in your femininity and with other women," she told Nina Malkin for *Sassy* (May 1996). "That makes you secure in your relationships with men, because you realize, 'Hey, I don't need this relationship.'"

In 1994 Witherspoon enrolled at Stanford University, in Palo Alto, California, where she concentrated in English literature. She also contemplated following in her parents' footsteps and studying medicine. Meanwhile, she continued to make movies. In her freshman year she played the survivor of a hostage crisis in the poorly received satire *S.F.W.* (1994). In the psychological thriller *Fear* (1996), she portrayed 16-year-old Nicole Walker, who is tormented by an ex-boyfriend (played by Mark Wahlberg). That same year Witherspoon appeared in *Freeway*, an independent film loosely based on the classic fairy tale "Little Red Riding Hood." Witherspoon portrayed Vanessa Lutz, a teenager whose parents are jailed. While heading to her grandmother's for shelter, she encounters a child psychologist (Kiefer Sutherland) who encourages her to confide in him; he turns out to be a serial rapist and killer who intends to make her his next victim. For her portrayal, she was named best actress at the Catalonian International Film Festival, in Spain. During filming, Witherspoon's mother visited the set and was reportedly shocked by the skimpy outfits Witherspoon had to wear for the role, in which she did not project the sweet image she had developed in her previous roles. "Being cast as the good girl was fairly inescapable for the first four years of my professional life," she told Susan Stark for the *Detroit News* (May 1, 1999). "*Freeway* changed the industry perceptions—and my own perceptions—of who I am as an actor. . . . From then on, my agenda was, 'Whatever is most different from the last thing I played.'"

Also during her first year of college, the director and screenwriter Robert Benton telephoned Witherspoon to offer her a role in the film *Twilight*, featuring Paul Newman, Susan Sarandon, and Gene Hackman. The opportunity led her to quit school. "It was Psych 101 or working with Paul Newman," she recalled to Amy Longsdorf for the

Allentown, Pennsylvania, *Morning Call* (July 7, 2001). "It wasn't a hard decision. I was, like, 'Pack me up. See you kids later.'" In *Twilight*, released in 1998, Witherspoon played the prodigal daughter of a dying movie star. In one scene she argues in the nude with Newman's character. "I was frightened to death at first, and then I got to the set and I thought, I'm not embarrassed about my body," she told Michele Shapiro for *Glamour* (November 1998).

Witherspoon starred in the straight-to-video teen comedy *Overnight Delivery* (1998) before appearing opposite Tobey Maguire in Gary Ross's *Pleasantville* (1998), in which she played a hip teenager who is magically transported with her brother from the 1990s to the world of a 1950s television sitcom. Witherspoon's next film, Alexander Payne's *Election* (1999), earned the actress rave reviews and established her as one of Hollywood's most talented actresses. She earned a Golden Globe nomination for best actress for her performance as Tracy Flick, a high-school overachiever whose campaign to become school president both irritates and titillates one of her teachers (Matthew Broderick), who, as the student-government faculty adviser, tries to ensure that she will lose the election.

Earlier, at her 21st birthday party, in 1997, Witherspoon had met the actor Ryan Phillippe, and the two had become romantically involved. On March 2, 1999 they announced their engagement and revealed that Witherspoon was pregnant. Shortly afterward, moviegoers saw them together in *Cruel Intentions* (1999), an adaptation (the fourth for the silver screen) of *Les Liaisons Dangereuses,* Choderlos de Laclos's 1782 novel about betrayal and sexual intrigue among French aristocrats. In the film, set in a New York City high school, Witherspoon was cast as Annette Hargrove, an idealistic teenager who wants to preserve her virginity until she meets the right man. She becomes the target of a teenage Lothario (played by Phillippe) who has bet his equally amoral half-sister (Sarah Michelle Gellar) that he can seduce Annette. Despite mixed reviews, the film was a commercial success, earning four times its modest $11 million production cost. In Mike Barker's neo-noir film *Best Laid Plans* (1999), Witherspoon took on the part of Lissa, the girlfriend of a factory worker named Nick (Alessandro Nivola). After Nick finds himself owing thousands of dollars to a drug lord, the couple try to pay off the debt by blackmailing one of Nick's college buddies. In Mary Harron's *American Psycho* (2000), adapted from a highly controversial novel by Bret Easton Ellis, Witherspoon portrayed a socialite engaged to a yuppie (Christian Bale) with a penchant for murder. Also in 2000 she appeared in the widely panned Adam Sandler vehicle *Little Nicky*, in the role of the title character's mother, an angel named Holly.

Witherspoon achieved superstar status in 2001 with the comedy *Legally Blonde*, directed by Robert Luketic. The actress played Elle Woods, a perky Beverly Hills sorority girl whose sole ambition in life is to marry her seemingly perfect boyfriend (Matthew Davis). On the night Elle expects him to propose marriage, he breaks up with her, explaining that he is headed to Harvard Law School with the hope of becoming a senator by the time he reaches 30, a goal that dictates that his wife have more substance than Elle. Outraged, Elle decides to attend Harvard Law School herself, and—thanks to a personal essay in the form of a video of herself, which captivates the men on the admissions committee—gains entrance to the school. There, she soon lands a coveted internship with one of the school's top law professors. Witherspoon's portrayal of Elle won rave reviews from critics. In the *Los Angeles Times* (July 13, 2001), Kenneth Turan described her as an actress "willing to throw herself completely into the part to excellent effect. . . . Elle's determination is at the heart of her irrepressible character. Faultlessly played by Witherspoon, Elle is all bounce all the time, so filled with positive energy that the actress reported it was actually tiring to play the part." Stephanie Zacharek, in an assessment for *Salon.com* (July 13, 2001), wrote, "[Witherspoon's] sophisticated-pixie brilliance practically makes the movie, and her easy, confident, curvaceous carriage doesn't hurt either—she's the thinking guy's cupcake, maybe because her mind is just as supple as her curves." *Legally Blonde* became the surprise hit of the summer, debuting at number one at the box office; it ultimately earned $95 million (some $77 million more than it cost to make). "Before it opened, my agent called to say, 'I want to let you know, however the movie does, I still love you,' . . . ," Witherspoon told Rebecca Ascher-Walsh for *Entertainment Weekly* (August 17, 2001). "The next day he was hyperventilating." The actress's performance garnered her a second Golden Globe nomination.

After she appeared in Oliver Parker's adaptation of the Oscar Wilde novel *The Importance of Being Earnest* (2002), Hollywood tested Witherspoon's bankability by giving her another film to carry: *Sweet Home Alabama* (2002). The actress was cast as Melanie Smooter, who, after abandoning her husband, flees to New York City, where she changes her surname to Carmichael and becomes a chic New York fashion designer. After she reluctantly returns to her humble roots, in Pigeon Creek, Alabama, she discovers that underneath her carefully crafted urban patina, she is still an old-fashioned country girl. The film pulled in "the biggest box-office ever for a September opening," according to James Bowman in the *American Spectator* (November/December 2002) and earned a box-office total of $100 million, thus solidifying Witherspoon's status as one of the few actresses of her generation who can carry movies virtually on the strength of their names alone.

Legally Blonde 2: Red, White and Blonde, directed by Charles Herman-Wurmfeld, opened on July 2, 2003, with Witherspoon reprising the role of Elle Woods (and serving as executive producer as well). Elle has graduated from Harvard and headed to

Washington, D.C., where—after discovering that the mother of her pet Chihuahua is being used to test cosmetics—she lobbies for the passage of a bill that would ban animal testing. While the film received mixed reviews, Witherspoon was singled out for her sparkling performance.

Much of the success of the *Legally Blonde* movies can be attributed to the lure of Elle Woods, one of only a handful of empowered young, smart, female—and feminine—characters to appear on the silver screen in recent years. "The response I got from young women was enormous, although a lot of people couldn't really articulate why they liked it," Witherspoon told Ivor Davis for the *Ventura County [California] Star* (July 2, 2003). "But they knew it was great. Older women say, 'I love the fact that she's girly and feminine, but she's also very accomplished and driven,' and that's just like me. I don't want to just be serious and be the head of a corporation. I want to get my nails done too and look pretty, and, also, I like the idea that there's a film made entirely without any sort of angst about [the heroine's] love life."

Most recently, Witherspoon appeared in a film version of the classic William Thackeray novel *Vanity Fair*, in which she portrayed the main character, Becky Sharp, a fiercely determined young woman from the lower class who uses her wit and charm to rise socially in 19th-century London, England. The film, which was directed by Mira Nair and was much anticipated, received mixed reviews. Many critics objected to Witherspoon's characterization of Becky as a charming, plucky protofeminist rather than the conniving social climber of Thackeray's story. The actress is currently filming *Walk the Line*, a movie about the country-music legend Johnny Cash, in which she has been cast as Cash's wife, June Carter Cash. She is also slated to appear in the upcoming films *Whiteout, If Only It Were True, Sports Widow*, and *Rapunzel Unbraided*, none of which had begun production as of October 2004.

In 2000 Witherspoon co-founded, with the producer Jennifer Simpson, a new production company, called Type A Films. She did so because, as she explained to Lynn Smith for *Newsday* (October 8, 2002), "there aren't that many great scripts out there. Only I know what I'm capable of, and I see it myself in my own mind. So, I'm feeling frustrated, going, 'Why isn't there that kind of role?' I just realized at a certain point I had to create it." Type A Films' projects include *Legally Blonde 2* and *Sports Widow*.

Witherspoon and Philippe have two children: a daughter, Ava, born in September 1999, and a son, Deacon, born in October 2003. The couple's household includes Cheech, Witherspoon's Chihuahua. —H.T.

Suggested Reading: (Allentown, Pennsylvania) *Morning Call* A p35+ July 7, 2001; *Biography Today* p147+ Apr. 2003, with photo; *Cosmopolitan* p170+ July 1, 2001; *Glamour* p81

Nov. 1998, with photo; *Los Angeles Times* Apr. 11, 1999, with photo; *New York Times* II p71 Sep. 13, 1998, with photo; *Newsday* B p2+ Oct. 8, 2002, with photo; *Sassy* May 1996, with photos; *Seventeen* p101 May 1996, with photo, p217+ Sep. 1997, with photo; *Vanity Fair* p172+ June 2002, with photo; *Vogue* p244+ June 2003, with photo

Selected Films: *The Man in the Moon*, 1991; *Wildflower*, 1991; *A Far Off Place*, 1993; *Jack the Bear*, 1993; *Return to Lonesome Dove*, 1993; *S.F.W.*, 1994; *Freeway*, 1996; *Pleasantville*, 1998; *Twilight*, 1998; *Election*, 1999; *Best Laid Plans*, 1999; *American Psycho*, 2000; *Little Nicky*, 2000; *Legally Blonde*, 2001; *The Importance of Being Earnest*, 2002; *Sweet Home Alabama*, 2002; *Legally Blonde 2: Red, White, and Blonde*, 2003; *Vanity Fair*, 2004

Brian Bahr/Getty Images

Woodson, Rod

Mar. 10, 1965– Football player

Address: c/o Network Associates Coliseum, 7000 Coliseum Way, Oakland, CA 94621

Dubbed "one of the great leaders in all of sports" by the *Sporting News* (January 20, 2003), the Oakland Raiders free safety Rod Woodson is also widely considered to be one of the foremost defensive players in National Football League (NFL) history. Plagued by a debilitating knee injury, Woodson was waived by the Raiders after failing a preseason physical in the summer of 2004; consequently, his

NFL career is likely at an end. His seemingly unceremonious retirement, however, does not detract from his impressive legacy. Since the Pittsburgh Steelers drafted him, in 1987, Woodson has appeared in an astonishing 11 Pro Bowls, earned the NFL's defensive-player-of-the-year honors for 1993, was ranked the NFL's 30th best player of all time by *Pro Football Weekly*, and was named to the NFL's 75th Anniversary Team in 1994 as well as the All-NFL Team of the 1990s. He has appeared in three Super Bowls and was a member of the Super Bowl XXXV champion Baltimore Ravens. Woodson holds the record for most interceptions—71—among active players (pending his official retirement) and is third on the all-time list. He likewise set the career mark for most interceptions returned for touchdowns (12) and for the most yards on interception returns (1,483). During his 10 years with the Pittsburgh Steelers, Woodson established several team records that endure to this day: in numbers of punt returns (256), punt return yards (2,362), kickoff returns (22), kickoff return yards (4,894), and interceptions returned for touchdowns (five). Those achievements are all the more notable given the difficulties that Woodson has had to surmount, among them a childhood stained by racial prejudice and, in 1995, an injury that nearly ended his career.

Roderick Kevin Woodson was born on March 10, 1965 in Fort Wayne, Indiana, the youngest of three brothers. His father, James Woodson, was African-American; his mother, the former Linda Jo Doerflein, is white. The Woodsons lived in a predominantly black neighborhood in Fort Wayne during a turbulent time for racial relations in the U.S., and their mixed-race status brought out hostility in their neighbors, black and white alike. The Ku Klux Klan harassed the family, and the local Black Muslims took a particular dislike to Linda Jo Woodson, often threatening her and, once, even physically assaulting her. The family refused to let those difficulties get the better of them. Woodson recalled to Jill Lieber for *Sports Illustrated* (September 7, 1992), "I was taught to never back down. . . . When you're mixed, you have three options: stay in the middle, pick a side or stand on your own. My parents let me know I didn't have to pick a side, because I always had a friend in my family. I learned to stand up for myself and to never be afraid." Woodson's mother and father took an active role in the lives of their children, with Linda Jo Woodson serving as a Boy Scout troop leader and often volunteering at her sons' schools. James Woodson, who was employed during the day at the International Harvester factory, took his boys with him when he worked his evening job—cleaning several local theaters. The strength, self-esteem, and familial loyalty that were instilled in the young Woodson by his parents proved essential in helping him navigate a youth that was continually marred by racial bigotry: "The whites would call me mulatto, nigger, zebra and half breed. . . . The blacks would call me yellow boy, white boy or mixed breed. I dated both black and white girls, and when I was with the white girls, I'd hear, 'Can you believe she's with that nigger?' I never knew who my true friends were, so I had to stick with my own. The only people I knew who were mixed, like me, were my brothers, and that made us a very close and protective family. No threats could intimidate our family," Woodson told Lieber.

Sports became a much-needed outlet for Woodson and his brothers, keeping them away from the social ills that plagued their neighborhood and distracting them from race-related hardship. Woodson initially took up football simply to be with his siblings: "All we did was play sports all day. There's nothing good in the streets for a young kid," he told John Rolfe for *Sports Illustrated for Kids* (September 1995). He played organized football in the Police Athletic League and then for the team at R. Nelson Snider High School; there, he also ran track and played basketball. Despite his talent on the field, as a sophomore Woodson nearly left the football team, explaining to Rolfe, "The coaches were yelling at me and I said, 'My dad doesn't yell at me this much. I don't need that stuff.'" Woodson's track-and-field coach talked the youth into remaining on the team, however. Because of his versatility, Woodson never specialized in one position on the gridiron; rather, coaches would move him from one position to another, depending on where he was needed. Named a Parade and Blue Chip All American as a cornerback and halfback, Woodson graduated from R. Nelson Snider in 1983 and headed to Purdue University, in Indiana, on a football scholarship.

As in high school, Woodson was not assigned to one position at Purdue, but played all over the field, on both offense and defense, in his 44 consecutive starts. He mostly played safety during his first two and a half years before moving to cornerback, but he also lined up, at various times, as a wide receiver, kickoff and punt returner, and running back. His statistics at Purdue were exceptional: he broke 13 Purdue records, registering the most interceptions (11), the most interceptions returned for a touchdown (three), the most solo tackles (320), and the most kickoff return yards (1,535), to name a few categories in which he distinguished himself. In 1984 he registered 136 tackles and made 19 in that year's Peach Bowl alone. As a junior he grabbed a career-best five interceptions, broke up 13 passes, and was named an All-American for the first time; as a senior he led the Big Ten Conference with 108 tackles as a defensive back, was honored as a First Team All-American, and was runner-up for the Jim Thorpe Trophy. Woodson's final game at Purdue, in 1986, was representative of his performance throughout his collegiate career and highlighted the exceptional athleticism and versatility he would bring to the NFL: playing cornerback and—for the first time—tailback in addition to returning kicks, Woodson caught three passes for a total of 67 yards, forced a fumble, made 10 tackles, and returned two kickoffs and three punts for a combined 76 yards in Purdue's 17–15 victory over Indiana. Woodson's statistics, however, do not tell the whole story. As he was one of the foremost cover backs in the college game, opposing offenses simply did not throw to the men he was covering; his dominance forced opposing teams to change their offensive game plans completely.

Woodson also ran for the Purdue track-and-field team with great success. A two-time All-American, he captured the Big Ten indoor championship in the 55-meter hurdles each of his four years and won the 60-meter-dash title twice. He also was a two-time Indiana champion in both low and high hurdles and set the Indiana low-hurdle record with a time of 36.04 seconds in 1984. He qualified for the National Collegiate Athletic Association (NCAA) Championships as well as the Olympic trials in the 110-meter hurdles. Commenting on Woodson's drive and determination, Mike Poehlein, Purdue's track coach, recalled to Jill Lieber, "In practice, blood was always streaming down his legs. He had scars all over his knees. Most hurdlers would call for medical attention, but Rod wouldn't stop until practice was over. If you could strap a heart monitor on him before an athletic performance, you'd find that his pulse doesn't go up." Woodson's potential as a track athlete was hard to overstate, as John Rolfe wrote: "With further training, he could have become one of the Top 10 hurdlers in the world. He might have reached the Olympics."

Prior to graduating from Purdue in 1988 with a B.S. degree in criminal justice, Woodson entered the 1987 NFL draft. The Pittsburgh Steelers selected him in the first round, as the 10th pick overall. Because he and the Steelers did not reach agreement on a contract until October 28, he missed the first eight games of the season. Once Woodson signed, the Steelers decided to use him as a cornerback. He initially had some doubts as to whether he would make it as a professional cornerback: "I was a nervous wreck . . . I'd relied too long on my speed and physical talents, and I didn't understand the game," he told Lieber. But the Steelers' assistant coaches Tony Dungy (now head coach of the Indianapolis Colts) and Rod Rust showed him the ropes, instructing him on how to anticipate the moves of the opposing offense in general and receivers in particular. At first, Woodson recalled to the *Sporting News* (September 28, 1998), "I didn't know how to study film. . . . A coach would ask me what I saw and I would say, 'Well, ah, well, ah—what should I have seen? . . . But [defensive coach] Rod Rust taught me how to watch film. . . . He told me that offenses can only run so much stuff from so many different personnel packages and eventually they all run the same patterns. All we do when we study is to complicate things. Once I started seeing things as being more simple, my film study got better. You start thinking that way—simple—and you say, 'Oh wow, is that all they are doing?' It clicked in." At six feet and 200 pounds,

Woodson was not the usual tall, slim, fleet-footed cornerback; rather, he combined the speed of a track star with the powerful and compact stature of a running back. In his first campaign with Pittsburgh, Woodson played as a kick returner and cornerback in the final eight games of the season; he was credited with four fumble recoveries, one interception, and 20 tackles. He ran his first career NFL interception 45 yards for his first touchdown; and, as a kick returner, Woodson fielded 16 punts for an average run back of 8.4 yards, and made 13 kickoffs for an average of 22.3 yards.

Woodson started all 16 games for the Steelers in 1988, most of them at the right cornerback position. He was credited with four interceptions, 18 pass defenses, a forced fumble, and 88 tackles. He excelled as a kick returner, with an average punt return of 8.5 yards and an average kickoff return of 23 yards, the sixth-highest average in the NFL. On October 9 he also ran a kickoff 92 yards for a touchdown against Arizona. He was named the Steelers' co-MVP with his teammate David Little. In 1989 Woodson established himself as one of the top defensive players in the game, despite missing some time due to injury. Starting in 14 of his 15 games, he caught three interceptions, defensed 18 passes, forced four fumbles, recovered three fumbles, and recorded 80 tackles. In addition, he won the NFL's kickoff-return title after averaging 27.3 yards per reception and sprinting for an 84-yard touchdown return against San Diego on November 19; he averaged 7.1 yards per punt return. The second-year cornerback excelled for the Steelers in the postseason, making eight tackles and, in a game against the Houston Oilers on New Year's Eve, engineering a turnover that set up Pittsburgh's game-winning field goal in overtime. After that season the NFL invited him to the Pro Bowl—pro football's all-star game—as a kick returner, and the Associated Press (AP) and Pro Football Writers of America selected him for the All-NFL team and the All-Pro First Team.

The Steelers' 1990 season saw Woodson capture his second team-MVP award to become only the fifth player in the franchise's history to do so. He also successfully defensed 16 passes, forced one fumble, made five interceptions, and netted 66 total tackles. He continued his success as a kick returner, averaging 21.8 yards per kickoff and 10.5 yards per punt. Again he was named a First-Team All-Pro and selected for the All-NFL team. Woodson returned to the Pro Bowl, this time as a starting cornerback. United Press International (UPI) also named him to the All–American Football Conference (All–AFC) team as a kick returner and cornerback. In the 1991 season Woodson returned 44 kickoffs for a total of 880 yards, a Steelers' record, and led the AFC with an 11.4-yard punt-return average. He also registered 71 tackles, picked off three interceptions, defensed a team-high 16 passes, recorded one sack, and forced one fumble while recovering two. For the third consecutive year, Woodson was selected for the Pro Bowl.

In May 1992 Woodson's father died while recuperating from brain surgery. The resulting stress in the family led to a physical fight between Woodson and his older brother Jamie. The police were called and arrested the brothers on misdemeanor charges that included battery involving a police officer. Despite those developments, a partially torn calf muscle suffered in the preseason, and a shift from the right cornerback spot to left cornerback, the 1992 season was a tremendously successful one for Woodson: he had six quarterback sacks, 17 passes defensed, four interceptions, four forced fumbles, one fumble recovery, and 85 solo tackles out of 100 total. He continued his high output as a kick returner, registering 18.8 yards per kickoff reception and leading the AFC with 11.4 yards per punt return. In the Steelers' September 6 opener against the Oilers, Woodson made two interceptions. A week later, in a remarkable performance against the New York Jets, he blocked a field-goal attempt, sacked the quarterback, forced a fumble, and registered six tackles. In a September 27 game against the Green Bay Packers, however, Woodson was beaten twice by the receiver he was assigned to cover, resulting in two Packer touchdowns; he also misplayed a punt return. But he soon regained his all-star form, sacking the quarterback twice in an October 19 matchup with the Cincinnati Bengals. On November 1 he knocked Houston quarterback Warren Moon out of the game in the process of racking up an eight-tackle, one-sack performance. A concussion suffered in the second quarter of Pittsburgh's January 9, 1993 play-off game with the Buffalo Bills ended Woodson's season, in which he was voted to his fourth Pro Bowl. Several months after the season concluded, in March 1993, a jury acquitted Woodson of the charges stemming from his May arrest.

After signing a contract extension early in the 1993 season, Woodson further established himself as one of the premier players in the NFL, intercepting eight passes, making 95 tackles, sacking the quarterback twice, and defending 30 passes. He similarly maintained his high standard as a kick returner, with an 8.2-yard punt-return average and a 19.6-yard kickoff-return average. In the opening game of the season, a September 5 showdown with the San Francisco 49ers, he intercepted two passes, blocked a field goal, and made eight tackles. Over the following weeks Woodson extended his dominance, registering seven interceptions in the first six games of the season, with two against the Atlanta Falcons on September 27 and two against the New Orleans Saints on October 17, a game in which he ran one interception back 62 yards for a touchdown. With all these interceptions, quarterbacks learned to avoid throwing to any receiver covered by Woodson. He also showcased his versatility, running a reverse as a wide receiver in the matchup with the Falcons. In a November 14 game against the Cincinnati Bengals, he made headlines by attempting to attack the Cincinnati wide receiver Carl Pickens. Woodson said afterward that Pick-

ens had yelled "jungle fever" at him, a reference to his interracial parentage as well as his marriage to a white woman. Despite that unpleasantness, Woodson maintained his dominance on the field for the rest of the season. In two games—one against the Miami Dolphins on December 12 and the other against the Houston Oilers on December 19—he made 26 tackles. In a play-off game with the Kansas City Chiefs on January 8, 1994, he defended one pass and notched six tackles. At the end of the season, the AP and *College and Pro Football Newsweekly* named Woodson the NFL defensive player of the year; the NFL Players' Association selected Woodson as the AFC's defensive back of the year; UPI named him AFC defensive player of the year; and he was again tapped for the All-NFL First Team, named Pittsburgh's MVP, and sent to the Pro Bowl. More telling than the awards were the raves Woodson received from his football peers: San Diego Chargers general manager Bobby Beathard told Paul Attner for the *Sporting News* (November 29, 1993), "He's one of those fantastic athletes that everyone would like on their team. He can cover and he can tackle and he can blitz and he has so much speed and quickness and size." Bernie Kosar, a quarterback with the Dallas Cowboys, said, "He's probably one of the most talented athletes in the league."

With four interceptions, three sacks, four forced fumbles, 20 passes defensed, 83 tackles, and two touchdowns in 1994, Woodson earned yet another trip to the Pro Bowl, voted in as a starting cornerback. Perhaps more noteworthy was Woodson's selection to the NFL's 48-man 75th anniversary team; he was one of only five active players so honored. In addition to his defense, he continued to demonstrate his effectiveness as a kick returner. On October 16 he recorded 13 tackles in a contest with the Cincinnati Bengals. Then, in a November 14 game with the Buffalo Bills, he returned an interception for a touchdown and recorded nine tackles, a quarterback sack, and a forced fumble; for his performance in this game, Woodson was named the AFC's defensive player of the week. The Steelers advanced far into the play-offs, taking on the San Diego Chargers for the AFC championship on January 15, 1995; Woodson performed well in a losing effort, nabbing an interception and notching six tackles. More awards and accolades were presented to him at the season's conclusion: he was again chosen the AFC's defensive back of the year by the NFL Players' Association, and he was declared an All-Pro by the AP, *Football Digest*, and the *Sporting News*.

In the 1995 season opener, against the Detroit Lions on September 3, Woodson tore the anterior cruciate ligament in his right knee as he tackled Lions running back Barry Sanders. Though the severity of his injury meant, for all intents and purposes, that his season was over, Woodson rehabilitated his knee with great intensity in hopes of making a return to the team. As he recovered, the Steelers advanced through the postseason, winning the

AFC championship and heading to Super Bowl XXX, in which they faced the Dallas Cowboys, on January 28, 1996. In the third quarter, Woodson was sent in to cover the Cowboys' great wide receiver Michael Irvin and successfully defended a pass. Woodson's inspirational return, however, was not enough to overcome a superior Cowboys team, and the Steelers' season ended in defeat.

Though his statistical performance—a team-leading six interceptions, 67 tackles, one sack, and 19 passes defensed—remained among the best in the sport in 1996, and he once again received a number of awards (including Pro Bowl honors and the Ed Block Courage Award from his teammates), Woodson performed poorly in that year's postseason and could not shake the impression that his best games were behind him. His knee injury, his age (32), and his high salary made the Steelers leery of keeping him at the cornerback position after the season. For a while contract negotiations continued fruitlessly. Then, after Woodson turned down a contract offer from the Steelers on draft day (April 19) in 1997, the team selected a college cornerback to replace him, effectively bringing to an end his decade-long tenure in Pittsburgh. Woodson told Gerry Dulac for the *Sporting News* (May 12, 1997), "I feel that I wasn't the major factor as a corner with the Steelers. I was the fourth choice. They gave Willie [Williams] and Deon [Figures] and Cris Dishman offers first, and when they all turned them down, they came to Rod Woodson. I think my integrity means way more to me than playing for the Pittsburgh Steelers." Two weeks later, in *Sports Illustrated* (May 26, 1997), Michael Silver quoted Woodson as saying, "I had a good thing going in Pittsburgh, and I would have loved to have stayed, but leaving is not going to break me. I want to be appreciated and treated with dignity. People don't realize that being in a place where the management and coaches think I can still play is a lot more important to me than being with the Steelers."

Despite his impressive record, other franchises did not show much interest in Woodson. Ultimately he was forced to hold a workout (akin to an audition) for several teams at Purdue before accepting an offer from the San Francisco 49ers. During the 1997 season, playing for the first time for an NFL team other than the Steelers, he registered 48 tackles, three interceptions, and 20 passes defensed in 14 starts for the 49ers. He recorded the three interceptions in one game, a September 14 contest with the New Orleans Saints, in which he also forced a fumble, recovered a fumble, and notched three tackles, a performance that earned him NFC defensive-player-of-the-week honors. The 49ers advanced to the NFC championship game that year, losing to the Green Bay Packers. Woodson's season was considered a disappointment, however, as he racked up a significant number of penalties and otherwise had difficulty adjusting to San Francisco's defensive schemes. After the season, the 49ers let Woodson go.

For the 1998 campaign Woodson joined the Baltimore Ravens, with whom he regained much of his pre-injury form, starting all 16 games and notching 88 tackles, six interceptions (two of which he ran back for touchdowns), and 16 passes defensed. He made two interceptions in a game against the New York Jets, on September 13, returning one for a touchdown, and was named AFC defensive player of the week. He moved to free safety from the cornerback position at the start of his second season with Baltimore. In 1999 he went to the Pro Bowl for the eighth time, thus becoming the first player to have made the Pro Bowl at three different positions. He caught seven interceptions—almost matching his career high of eight—returning them for 195 yards and two touchdowns. He also was credited with 66 tackles and 18 passes defensed.

An essential component of the Baltimore Ravens world-championship team, Woodson snatched four interceptions, forced a fumble, recovered four fumbles, defensed 10 passes, and piled up 77 tackles—67 of them solo—during the 2000 season. He was named AFC defensive player of the week after recording an interception, a fumble recovery, and eight tackles against the Cleveland Browns on October 1. Woodson saved his best performance for the play-offs, accounting for 24 tackles throughout the Ravens' run, the second-highest total on the team, and taking credit for two batted passes. In Super Bowl XXXV, which found the Ravens pitted against the Giants, he contributed to Baltimore's victory with six tackles. At season's end he was named to an unprecedented ninth Pro Bowl.

During the 2001 campaign Woodson earned his 10th Pro Bowl berth, with three interceptions, 12 passes defensed, and 76 total tackles. He reached several milestones during the season, setting the NFL record with his 10th touchdown on an interception return and recording his 60th career interception. In a Ravens' play-off showdown with the Pittsburgh Steelers, he recorded 10 tackles.

Woodson's career with the Ravens came to an end following the 2001 season. He then moved on to the Oakland Raiders for the 2002 campaign. Notching eight interceptions to match his career high, recording 92 tackles, 16 passes defensed, and running back two interceptions for touchdowns, he was a major contributor to Oakland's march to Super Bowl XXXVII, helping to nurture a young defensive backfield and developing into one of the team's primary leaders. In a game against the Denver Broncos on November 11, Woodson returned an interception 92 yards for a touchdown, the second-longest such return in Raiders history. He played well in the postseason, contributing seven tackles in a January 12 matchup with the Jets; seven tackles and a pass defensed against the Tennessee Titans on January 19; and an eight-tackle, one-pass-defensed performance in a losing effort against the Tampa Bay Buccaneers in the Super Bowl on January 26. At season's end he was named to the AP's All-Pro team and to *Football Weekly's*

All-NFL and All-AFC teams. Though the start of the 2003 season was disappointing for the Raiders, he recorded 38 tackles through eight games and recorded a pass defensed and an interception.

In August 2003 Woodson injured ligaments in his left knee while practicing in the Raiders' training camp. On September 9, after playing in Oakland's first, losing game of the season, he underwent arthroscopic surgery. Although his knee was not fully rehabilitated, he returned to the field two weeks later and played in the Raiders' next nine games, contributing two interceptions for 18 yards as well as a total of 51 tackles, including 42 solo. (The Raiders ended the year with a disappointing record of four wins and 12 losses.) The condition of Woodson's knee worsened as the season progressed; in November he took himself out of the Raiders' lineup and opted for an experimental procedure in which doctors replaced his damaged knee ligaments with tendons from donors. In the summer of 2004, after he underwent a physical, the Raiders concluded that he was no longer fit to play and took him off their roster. Facing the possible conclusion of his NFL career, Woodson displayed

a positive attitude; as he told reporters, as quoted by Greg Bell in the *Sacramento Bee* (July 28, 2004), "If the knee heals, I'll play one more year. If not, I've had 17 great seasons in the NFL." Woodson plans to retire from the NFL officially in 2005. He is currently serving as an analyst for the NFL Network.

Woodson met his wife, Nicki, in 1989; they married in 1991. The couple have three daughters and two sons and make their home in Wexford, Pennsylvania. Woodson is involved in numerous charities and is a member of the board of directors of the Leukemia Society. He owns a sports-oriented restaurant, Woodson's All-Star Grille, located in downtown Pittsburgh.

—P.B.M.

Suggested Reading: ESPN Web site , with photo; NFL Web site, with photo; Oakland Raiders Web site, with photo; *Sporting News* p10 Nov. 29, 1993, with photo, p30 Sep. 28, 1998; *Sports Illustrated* p58 Sep. 7, 1992, with photo, p70 May 26, 1997, with photo; *Sports Illustrated for Kids* p36 Sep. 1995, with photo

Wright, Will

Jan. 20, 1960– Computer-game designer

Address: c/o Electronic Arts, 209 Redwood Shores Pkwy., Redwood, CA 94065

Called a "pioneer of simulation" by Stephen Miller in the *New York Times* (December 11, 1994), Will Wright is the creator of *The Sims* (short for "simulations"), the top-selling personal-computer (PC) game franchise of all time. More than 20 million copies of the games in *The Sims* series—which Wright began in 1989, with the release of *SimCity*, and which now includes *SimCity 3000 Unlimited, The Sims, The Sims Online,* and *The Sims 2,* among other variations—have been sold worldwide, their contents translated into more than a dozen languages. In *SimCity* players take on the role of city planner and mayor, building and managing towns and urban areas. In *The Sims*, which Wright introduced in 2000, players create and control the lives of simulated characters who can be either re-creations of the players themselves, possessing the same general qualities and appearances as their creators, or entirely different personas. By selecting from menus of actions and interactions, a player chooses a character's personality traits, skin color, and clothes, then guides the simulated character through the common events of everyday suburban life, finding the character a job and food, decorating his or her house, and having him or her make friends and form a family, for example. The goal is for a player to keep his or her simulated characters healthy and happy. Wright

Courtesy of Electronic Arts/Maxis

has often referred to his game as a "dollhouse for adults." "The game's genius lies in exactly what should have made it a flop: its mundanity," Lev Grossman wrote for *Time* magazine (November 25, 2002). Having sold more than eight million copies, *The Sims* is the best-selling individual PC game of all time.

"When I was a kid, I spent a lot of time building models," Wright recalled to Mike Snider for *USA Today* (December 16, 2002). "One of my first attractions on the computer was simulations, a different type of modeling. For me the computer can be used to help you understand your environment, so, just naturally, I've wanted to model parts of the real world." "What I like about *The Sims* is that after playing it for a while, you realize how much of your actual life is a real-time strategy game," Wright said, as quoted by *Time Digital* (October 4, 1999). *The Sims* series has been hailed in many corners as a welcome alternative to the glut of computer games characterized by unrelenting violence. David Walsh, the president and founder of the National Institute of Media and the Family, recalled to Mike Snider for *USA Today* (August 2, 2001), "The first *Sim* game [my family and I] had was *SimCity*, and I just remember sitting in the living room being so impressed about my son and a group of friends arguing that 'If we develop that part of town, this is what's going to happen.' That's when I became a fan. . . . Games like these engage the mind in sophisticated ways." In 1999 *Entertainment Weekly* named Wright one of the 100 most creative people in entertainment, and *Time Digital* placed Wright among its "Digital 50," a list of the most important people shaping technology today. In 2002 Wright was inducted into the Academy of Interactive Arts and Sciences Hall of Fame.

Will Wright was born in Atlanta, Georgia, on January 20, 1960. His father was a chemical engineer, and his mother a community-theater actress. While growing up in Georgia, Wright often played chess, the Chinese game Go, and "elaborate historical war games," as he told Mike Snider (August 2, 2000). He was also fond of playing with model ships and airplanes and showed a strong interest in robotics. "I was very interested in the idea of animating inanimate objects," Wright recalled to Snider. "At some point I bought my first computer and attached my robot to control it. Once I got my hands on my first PC, I became totally enamored with it." Studying architecture, mechanical engineering, aviation, and computer science, Wright attended three different colleges—Louisiana State University, Louisiana Technical University, and the New School for Social Research (now called the New School University), in New York City—but did not earn a degree.

Beginning in 1981 Wright worked as a programmer for Broderbund, a PC game maker based in Novato, California. While helping to create a war game, Wright was asked to design islands for the game's warplanes to destroy, a task that required programming skills as well as imagination. Interested in urban planning, Wright found himself more absorbed by the process of creating the islands' infrastructures—complete with refineries and other buildings, streets, and ports—than by the game as a whole. The experience led him to begin designing, in the mid-1980s, a game in which players would build their own cities. In 1989, by which time he was no longer with Broderbund, Wright introduced *SimCity*, which instantly became a bestseller. Each *SimCity* player acts as an urban planner, building a city by adding to a blank screen residential areas, streets, police and fire departments, and stores, among other structures and concerns. As the city grows the computer program calculates such variables as land values, environmental changes, and crime statistics; the game is designed so that, among other possibilities, the population grows restless if the quality of life in the created city declines. Each action a player takes creates an effect, and great care is required of the player to keep the city functioning smoothly. "The model is very sophisticated, yet understandable," Dr. James A. Segedy, a teacher at the College of Architecture and Planning at Ball State University, in Muncie, Indiana, told Julie Lew for the *New York Times* (June 15, 1989) regarding *SimCity*. (Wright's game has been used at various schools, including Louisiana State University, to teach urban planning.) According to the Web site of the Academy of Interactive Arts and Sciences, *SimCity* has won 24 domestic and international awards.

In 1987 Wright and Jeff Braun had co-founded Maxis, an Orinda, California–based computer-software company. Responding to the success of *SimCity*, Wright, acting as chief designer for Maxis, designed an ongoing series of simulation games, including *SimEarth* (1991), in which players control the atmosphere, biosphere, and civilizations of random planets. (*SimEarth* was inspired by the scientist James Lovelock's Gaia hypothesis, in which Earth is seen as a self-regulating system.) In 1992 Wright introduced *SimAnt*, in which the player is the leader of a black-ant colony that must compete with red ants for food and territory while avoiding the perils of lawn mowers and other hazards. (*SimAnt* was co-created by Justin McCormick.) Other simulation games Wright created while with Maxis are *SimLife*, *SimTower*, *SimHealth*, and *SimCity 3000 Unlimited*, the last of which sold more than a million copies in 1999 alone, according to *Time Digital*. Electronic Arts (EA), the world's leading independent developer and publisher of interactive entertainment software, bought Maxis in 1997. EA has published all of the titles in the *Sims* series since that time.

In 2000 Wright released *The Sims*, a game that allows players to create and control the lives of simulated characters, directing them through the details of ordinary life, finding them homes and jobs, and having them make friends, build families, and even get married. Players must meet the characters' physical needs as well, making sure they eat regularly and go to the bathroom, for example. (The simulated characters can even make love, albeit discreetly.) A player's character interacts with other computer-controlled characters inhabiting the same suburban world. Writing for the *New York Times* (November 24, 2002), David Brooks described *The Sims* as "suburban conquest in its rawest form. You've got to get the kids scrubbed and fed by the time the school bus comes around in the morning. You have to select the right coffee table to go with your love seat. You have to remember to turn off the TV if you want to take a nap, because the noise will keep you up. There's no winning and losing in *The Sims*. No points, no end. In the game, as in life, you just keep doing the dishes until you die."

Though the game does not set specific goals for a player, one objective is to find happiness for the simulated characters, just as people search for happiness in real life. Whereas video games have traditionally used numerical scores as specific goals and incentives for players, *The Sims* gives players a "rich environment with goals embedded in it," Wright told Janelle Brown for the *New York Times* (October 24, 2002). "I'm interested in rewarding imagination: letting [players] leverage creativity to build an interesting external artifact of their imagination." "What you end up with is something of a reflection of yourself," Wright explained to Snider. "We don't tell players they have to get rich or get married. You look at your own values and say to yourself, 'What to me is winning?'" The game is rated "T for teens," meaning that it is considered appropriate only for individuals aged 13 and older, due to its "mature sexual themes, comic mischief and mild animated violence," as quoted by Snider (August 2, 2001). Wright told Snider that die-hard computer-game fans "tried *The Sims* for a while, said 'that's cute,' and went on to something else. But if they hadn't played it, then their spouses or girlfriends wouldn't have seen it. Those are the ones who became amazing fans and are spreading it." (According to Snider's August 2, 2001 piece, of the millions of people who have played *The Sims*, 35 percent are female, an unusually high figure and a testament to the game's broad appeal.)

Strategy titles, or "God games," as the industry sometimes refers to such products as *The Sims*, are the most popular computer games in the United States. Mike Snider reported (August 2, 2001) that one out of every four of the 30 million PC games sold in the first half of 2001 were strategy titles, whereas action games accounted for only 11 percent and adventure games 5 percent of those same sales. There are hundreds of Web sites created by *Sims* players who have designed everything from home furnishings to fashion accessories that can be downloaded and imported by other players into *The Sims*, adding more realistic detail to the game.

The Sims Online, in which players' characters interact with simulated characters created and controlled by other PC users, was released in late 2002. (Playing the game on the Internet requires special software and a small monthly payment.) In *The Sims Online* players are permitted to create three simulation characters; thousands of players, at different locations, can have their simulations interact with one another within the game at the same time. When *Sims Online* players chat with each other over the Internet, their comments appear in little balloons or thought bubbles above their characters' heads. The on-line world contains cafés, banks, bed-and-breakfasts, pizzerias, houses, and condominiums, among other simulated elements. Characters earn money—by cooking pizzas or running telemarketing operations, for example—and socialize, and though violence is possible and characters can die, most players have created fairly normal characters who are friendly and cooperative. Each player is given a piece of real estate to develop as he or she chooses. Geoff Keighley, in *Entertainment Weekly* (December 6, 2002), reported that one player had created a "Sim/university"; days later, another player had put up a sorority house across the street. The world of *The Sims Online*, David Brooks wrote, gives one the impression of "some mass creative process" at work, "like the writing of a joint novel with millions of collaborative and competitive authors." Lev Grossman wrote that the release of *The Sims Online* signaled the "birth of Simulation Nation. . . . To a greater extent than the original game, *The Sims Online* has built-in group activities to encourage people to get together and socialize. . . . You can see the outlines of a fantasy America emerging, one that's touchingly utopian and crassly commercial at the same time."

Since the mid-1990s games played on personal computers have lost market share to console video games, which are played on entertainment systems such as *Playstation*, Microsoft's *Xbox*, and Nintendo's *GameCube*. (A version of *The Sims* that can be played on the *Playstation 2* console system was released in 2003.) Mike Snider reported in *USA Today* (December 15, 2002, on-line) that in 2002, console video games outsold PC games by a ratio of four to one, and that 2002 marked the first year in which sales of PC games had actually fallen. Many observers of the electronic-game industry predicted that *The Sims Online* had the potential to reinvigorate the PC game market. Calling *The Sims Online* the first multiplayer game "that isn't focused around standard fantasy and sci-fi monster killing," Jeff Green, editor in chief of *Computer Gaming World*, told Mike Snider (December 15, 2002), "It has the potential to appeal to people who have never played any kind of computer game before."

Wright has created software add-ons, or "expansion packs," that allow players to expand *The Sims*. For example, *The Sims: Vacation* allows players to take their characters on vacation; *The Sims Unleashed* lets players acquire dogs or cats as pets and learn to garden; and *The Sims: Hot Date* gives players the chance to have their simulations meet prospective mates. Those three expansion packs, along with the original *Sims* game, were among the 10 top-selling PC games in 2002. Other recent additions to *The Sims* series include *The Sims House Party*, *The Sims Livin' Large*, *The Sims Superstar*, *The Sims Bustin' Out*, and *The Sims Makin' Magic*.

In September 2004 EA published *The Sims 2*, a much-anticipated sequel to *The Sims*. Developed by a 140-person team over the course of four years,

The Sims 2 shares the original game's focus on guiding characters through the mundane trials and tribulations of everyday life, but it also differs from the The Sims in several major ways. Not only are the graphics of the new game much more sophisticated and realistic than those of the earlier version, but, more importantly, the characters have been endowed with a quality that they all but lacked in The Sims: psychological depth. The key to the artificial intelligence of the new characters lies in the addition of long-term goals to the basic data profile of each Sim, as well as in accumulations of "memories" that affect how individual characters act in specific situations. "The emotional range is much wider," Wright told Dean Takahashi for the Detroit Free Press (September 16, 2004). "The player can build a much more elaborate narrative."

Wright has participated in the Robot Wars, an event held regularly in San Francisco, California, in which inventors enter their homemade, remote-controlled, artificial-intelligence machines into battle against one another. He has also appeared with his robot creations on the television program BattleBots, on which contestants pit their robotic inventions against each other in a kind of gladiatorial sport. (Battlebots aired on the Comedy Central cable channel from 2000 to 2003.) Entertainment Weekly (October 12, 2002) reported that Wright's robot entry, named Misty the WonderBot, advanced to the final rounds of the competition in 2001.

As quoted on the Academy of Interactive Arts and Sciences Web site, on the occasion of Wright's induction into the academy's Hall of Fame, the academy president, Paul Provenzano, credited Wright with "creating gaming experiences that are constructive, socially responsible, truly original and totally entertaining," and he stated that Wright's games "have introduced people of all ages to the interactive art form, redefining the popular perception of the audience for games."

Wright is married to Joell Jones. The couple's daughter, Cassidy, has on occasion competed in the Robot Wars with her father. Wright is said to enjoy snorkeling in the tropics.

—C.F.T.

Suggested Reading: Biography Today p170+ Apr. 2004, with photo; Electronic Arts Web site; Entertainment Weekly p62 Oct. 12, 2002, with photo, p38+ Dec. 6, 2002; Esquire p146+ Dec. 2002, with photo; Forbes p346+ Dec. 23, 2002, with photo; ID p78+ Nov. 2001; New York Times III p8 Dec. 11, 1994, with photo; Newsweek p48 Oct. 24, 1994, with photo, p53+ Nov. 25, 2002, with photo; thesims.ea.com; Time p78+ Nov. 25, 2002, with photos; Time Digital p50 Oct. 4, 1999, with photo; Wall Street Journal Eastern Edition B p1+ July 9, 1999; Wired p176+ Nov. 2002, with photo

---

Wright, Winky

Nov. 26, 1971– Boxer

Address: c/o International Boxing Federation, 516 Main St., 2d Fl., East Orange, NJ 07018

Though his nickname may evoke the image of someone coy, there is very little that is indirect or coquettish about Ronald "Winky" Wright's fighting style, and the only thing the once-unheralded boxer has flirted with of late, at least publicly, is boxing glory. In March 2004 Wright became the first undisputed light-middleweight or junior-middleweight (154 pounds) boxing champion in 29 years, when he defeated "Sugar" Shane Mosley at Mandalay Bay Resort & Casino in Las Vegas, Nevada. (Prior to Wright, the last undisputed light-middleweight champion was the Japanese boxer Koichi Wajima, who achieved that status in 1975.) In winning, Wright laid claim to the light-middleweight titles of all three major boxing federations: the World Boxing Council (WBC), World Boxing Association (WBA), and International Boxing Federation (IBF). "I deserved it. It's been a long time," he said, according to Jet magazine (April 5, 2004), referring to the more than 10 bruising years he has spent pursuing success in the ring.

Wright is a southpaw, meaning that his dominant hand is his left, and his fighting stance is distinguished by his tendency to keep his legs far apart, which leaves him looking like a "guy trying to straddle a wide ditch" or "someone trying to step over a deep puddle as they hurry across the street in a rain storm," as Rick Folstad described it in an article for the International Brotherhood of Prizefighters Web site. Alluding to, among others, the once-dominant heavyweight fighter Mike Tyson, whose skills have been eclipsed in the public's mind by his outrageous behavior—including bizarre prefight threats against his opponents—Folstad wrote that Wright is not a "heavy hitter or a dancer or a cheap-shot artist. He doesn't call you names or threaten to eat your cat. He's just a tough, awkward guy to fight, one who never gets careless and who doesn't let himself get into a situation he can't get out of. He's not pretty, but he doesn't try to be. He's just good. And now he's got one of the hotter names in the fight game." As of November 2004 Wright's overall record was 48–3, with 25 knockouts.

An only child, Ronald Lamont Wright was born in Washington, D.C., on November 26, 1971. He grew up with his uncle Byron Dorsey, who is roughly the same age as Wright. Wright's grandmother, who helped to raise the future boxer, gave him the nickname Winky. Athletically inclined

Jed Jacobsohn/Getty Images

Winky Wright

from an early age, Wright played baseball both at school and with his friends, learning a number of different positions, including shortstop, pitcher, second base, and catcher. In his early teenage years, he moved with members of his family to St. Petersburg, Florida. There, when he was 16, he began training as a boxer at the local St. Pete Boxing Club after a friend told him about the establishment. Wright immediately took to the sport, which soon became the center of his life. Pernell Whitaker and Sugar Ray Leonard became his boxing heroes. According to Tim Smith, writing for the New York *Daily News* (March 12, 2004, on-line), Wright won six international amateur boxing competitions before he turned professional, in 1990, the same year he graduated from Gibbs High School, in St. Petersburg.

Wright initially fought almost exclusively in Florida, beating such opponents as Glenn Major, Edison Martinez, and Persephone Van Reenen on his way to a 16–0 record. Next, because there was little money in boxing in Florida, he began fighting in Europe—primarily in France—as well as elsewhere in the United States. In Levallois, France, during 1993 and 1994, Wright defeated Gilberto Barreto, Tony McCrimmion, and Orlando Orozco, by either knockout or technical knockout (TKO), which occurs when a referee declares one boxer unable to fight any longer. After having won 25 fights—albeit against sometimes dubious competition—Wright lost his first professional bout in the summer of 1994 by unanimous decision, when he faced the Argentine boxer Julio César Vasquez, then the WBA light-middleweight title holder, in Saint-Jean-de-Luz, France. As reported by Scoop Malinowski on boxinginsider.com (March 15,

2004), Wright felt that the decision was unfair, as the referee judged as knockdowns several instances in which Wright claimed he merely slipped, and ruled several of Wright's knockdowns of Vasquez to be slips by the Argentine fighter. (According to the Internet Boxing Records Archive, Wright was knocked down four times in the fight.) Wright bounced back in early 1995, defeating the North American Boxing Federation (NABF) light-middleweight champion Tony Marshall, in the process claiming the first title of his career. After twice defending the title that he had wrested from Marshall, Wright became the World Boxing Organization (WBO) light-middleweight champion, besting Bronco McKart in a 1996 12-round split decision (meaning that one of the three fight judges determined McKart to be the winner). Wright then successfully defended his WBO title in three fights in England, winning the last of the three against a previously undefeated boxer, Adrian Dodson, by TKO.

Wright suffered his second loss as a professional, and lost his WBO title, when he battled the undefeated Namibian boxer Harry Simon, nicknamed "the African Tyson," at the Carousel Casino in Hammanskraal, South Africa, in 1998. (Simon has not fought since he was injured in a car accident in 2003.) The following year Wright failed to capture the IBF light-middleweight crown when he lost to Fernando Vargas in a very close match (indeed, a number of observers felt that Wright was the winner). Since his defeat by Vargas, however, Wright has not lost a fight. He claimed the then-vacant IBF light-middleweight title by besting Robert Frazier in October 2001, then successfully defended it over the next several years against Jason Pipillion, Bronco McKart (whom Wright has beaten three times), Juan Carlos Candelo, and Angel Hernandez.

Having compiled an impressive record of 46 wins and just three losses in over a decade of fighting, Wright had proven himself to be one of the best middleweight boxers in the country. He was still relatively unheralded in the boxing world, however, due in part to his unspectacular fighting style, and was even lesser known among sports fans in general. Because it can affect everything from sponsor participation to television viewer ratings, a fighter's public profile has much to do with determining both who decides to fight him and the amount of money he is offered to fight. Therefore, despite his record and his status as the reigning IBF light-middleweight champion, Wright had not received offers to fight the very best of the middleweight boxers, Oscar De La Hoya and Felix Trinidad among them. That situation changed when the popular WBC and WBA champion Shane Mosley, who then had a record of 39–2, with 35 knockouts, offered Wright the chance to box him. "When they first told me about this fight, I thought it was a joke," Wright told Tim Smith before the title bout. "I didn't think it was real until I saw the contract. I signed it and sent it back in an hour. . . . This is a fight for history. Once I win this fight, the money will be there."

To prepare for the fight with Mosley, Wright decided to train in Houston, Texas, rather than in his hometown of St. Petersburg, as he had done in the past, reasoning that in Houston there would be fewer distractions. Before the fight, Dan Birmingham, Wright's trainer since the fighter's amateur days, told Smith, "He has trained twice as hard away from home. For the first time in years you're going to see a stronger, more improved Winky Wright." The title fight was broadcast live on HBO from Las Vegas on March 13, 2004, and was attended by such celebrities as the actors Sylvester Stallone and James Caan and the baseball star Barry Bonds, who is a good friend of Wright's. The match proved to be a relatively easy victory for Wright, who dominated the action from the first minute to the last, winning a unanimous 12-round decision. While claiming that he felt less than his best during the fight, due to dehydration and muscle fatigue, Mosley praised Wright's abilities. Wright, for his part, said, as quoted by *Jet*, "I always thought I was better [than Mosley]. Shane has speed, but I was better all around." Backing up Wright's claim were the statistics for punches landed: Wright had connected 250 times, Mosley just 166. Mosley earned more than $2 million for the bout, while Wright took home $750,000, the biggest payday of his career. The victory gave Wright the light-middleweight title belts of the WBC and WBA—both of which Mosley had held going into the match—along with his IBF belt.

Wright has been praised by boxing insiders and journalists as a "class act." After the match between Wright and Mosley, Brad Cooney wrote for the Web site boxingscene.com (March 20, 2004) that the postfight remarks by both boxers "proved what kind of guys they are. Both humble, and classy . . . both representing the sport of boxing with dignity." Following the bout, more than one fight-game observer commented that other top boxers, such as Oscar De La Hoya, had apparently avoided scheduling fights with Wright for fear of losing. Wright's contract with the boxer Roy Jones's Square Ring agency, signed in 2002, expired after the fight against Mosley, meaning that Wright is now a free agent. The contract for the championship fight gave Mosley the option, in the case of his defeat, of a rematch against Wright. Mosley chose to exercise that option, and the two boxers faced off again on November 20, 2004 at Mandalay Bay Resort and Casino, in Las Vegas. Again, Wright defeated Mosley.

Wright has said that he hopes to fight just a few more times, against the best fighters in—or close to—his weight class, including Felix Trinidad, Bernard Hopkins, and Oscar De La Hoya, then retire from boxing. He told the Web site sportz-newz.com, "I'm the type of fighter that [wants] to fight for the people. I just want to fight, and when it's over, people will say that he fought and beat the best and should be considered one of the best."

Wright has invested his money in several businesses. He is the owner of a record company, Pound for Pound Records, and a real-estate firm. He hopes to use government grants to build low-income housing in St. Petersburg, where he is a popular local figure and lives with his daughter, Raven, his son, Roemello, and his partner, Tammye Ryan. Wright is a golf and bowling enthusiast.

—C.F.T.

Suggested Reading: boxinginsider.com; Internet Boxing Records Archive; International Brotherhood of Prizefighters Web site; New York *Daily News* (on-line) Mar. 12, 2004; *St. Petersburg Times* (on-line) Mar. 16, 2004, with photo; World Boxing Council Web site

Frazer Harrison/Getty Images

Wylde, Zakk

Jan. 14, 1967– Rock musician

Address: c/o Spitfire Records Inc., 22 W. 38 St., 7th Fl., New York, NY 10018

"Zakk Wylde live. It's an unforgettable experience. An endless hurricane of sweat-soaked blonde hair whipping around as fast and furious as the ear-bleeding [decibel] riffs this muscular Thor-turned-guitar hero churns and burns on his ready and willing audience. . . . Pure, raw, unapologetic heavy metal thunder. Indeed, Zakk Wylde may not have invented rock and roll . . . but, he's doing his damndest to save it." That is how a reviewer for the Web site monstercable.com described Wylde, the hard-driving guitarist for Ozzy Osbourne's band.

Wylde is also the leader of his own band, Black Label Society, whose music he has characterized as "alcohol-fueled brewtality [sic] for the next millennium." Wylde came out of obscurity in 1987, when Osbourne named the 20-year-old his lead guitarist. Playing guitar for and writing songs with Osbourne from 1988 to 1994, Wylde contributed to several hugely successful heavy-metal albums, including the multiplatinum *No More Tears* (1991) and the Grammy-nominated, multiplatinum *Ozzmosis* (1995), before leaving to form his own band and pursue a solo career. One of the premier heavy-metal guitarists working today, Wylde—who reunited with Osbourne in 2001—has contributed to the latter's continuing success and the popularity of the annual Ozzfest heavy-metal tours. In both 2003 and 2004, Wylde was voted most valuable player in *Guitar World* magazine's annual readers' poll. Although he is known best as a guitarist, Wylde has also impressed critics and fans with his skill at playing other instruments as well as with his songwriting. He is also known for his plain, candid speech, which tends to be rich in expletives, his disdain for soft music, the bull's-eye designs on his guitars, and his love of beer.

Zakk Wylde was born in Jersey City, New Jersey, on January 14, 1967. (According to various sources, his name at birth was Jeff Wiedlandt; an article posted on the Web site blacklabelsociety.net reported that he called himself Zakari Wyland when he was a teenager playing with the band Zyris, and, after joining Osbourne's band, changed his name legally to Zachary Phillip Wylde—the "Zachary" inspired by the character Dr. Zachary Smith from the TV show *Lost in Space*.) He took piano lessons as a youngster and again in his early teens, only to quit each time after a few lessons. Some sources state that he played the bass clarinet in school. While in his early teens, he began learning the guitar; by 17 he had formed his first band, Stone Henge, and played with others, performing regularly in bars near the New Jersey shore. Wylde became known for his speed and soulful sounds on the electric guitar. One night, after a gig in a bar, a patron suggested that Wylde audition for Ozzy Osbourne's band. (Osbourne has been a heavy-metal and rock icon since his days as a singer and songwriter for the seminal British band Black Sabbath, whose fame and popularity date from the 1970s. With the sinister, gothic imagery of his lyrics and his sometimes extreme stage antics, Osbourne was derided by some as a Satanist. He has enjoyed enormous success, however, and is considered one of the most important figures in the heavy-metal, hard-rock genre.) Wylde recorded himself playing guitar and sent the tape to Osbourne, who then invited him to audition. Osbourne liked Wylde's playing style and look and in 1987 hired him to replace Jake E. Lee as the band's lead guitarist. "It was like a dream come true," Wylde said to R. Scott Bolton in an interview posted to the Web site Roughedge.com. "I was a huge [Black] Sabbath fan and we all loved Ozzy when he started his solo ca-

reer." (In another version of events, which Wylde has occasionally confirmed, Wylde met Osbourne while selling him drugs.)

As Osbourne's stage and studio guitarist and co-songwriter, Wylde contributed to a series of albums that were critical and popular successes, among them the multiplatinum *No Rest for the Wicked* (1988); *Just Say Ozzy* (1990), a live album recorded during one of the band's national tours; *No More Tears* (1991); *Live and Loud* (1993), a double album that won a Grammy Award for best live performance for the song "I Don't Want to Change the World"; and the Grammy-nominated *Ozzmosis* (1995), which despite mixed reviews sold three million copies within a year of its release. ("Platinum" indicates that an album has sold at least a million copies.) In a review of *No Rest for the Wicked* that appeared on the Web site artistdirect.com, Steve Huey wrote, "Things start to improve here, as Zakk Wylde replaces Jake E. Lee on guitar and Ozzy comes up with his best set since 1983. Again, it's not quite up to the level of excellence his Blizzard of Ozz band achieved, but Osbourne sounds somewhat rejuvenated, and Wylde is a more consistently interesting guitarist than Lee." Popular songs from the album are "Miracle Man," "Crazy Babies," and "Breaking All the Rules." Regarding *No More Tears*, a *CMJ New Music* review posted on the Web site cdnow.com stated, "[The title song] boasts a sowing[-destruction,] armies-on-the-march rhythm, a haunting chorus and some killer slide work from Zakk Wylde, who doesn't put a finger wrong on the entire album: his tasteful but ferocious mixture of rootsy and futuristic licks marks him as one of the best guitarists of the genre." Wylde co-wrote the above-mentioned title track; it is considered one of the album's better songs.

Wanting to return to his southern-rock roots, Wylde left Osbourne in 1994 and formed the band Pride and Glory with himself as lead guitarist and front man. Pride and Glory's self-titled debut album melded blues and rock in the style of the Allman Brothers and Lynyrd Skynyrd. A writer for metal-reviews.com commented, "As the album progresses you'll notice the skillful integration of banjos, harmonicas, and other non-rock standard noise makers into the songs. Nice gruff vocals—which are also performed by [Wylde]." At about the same time, Axl Rose invited Wylde to join his legendary hard-rock band Guns N' Roses, whose members were thinking about attempting a comeback. (Wylde and the Guns N' Roses guitarist Slash had been mutual fans.) The collaboration never came to fruition. In 1996 Wylde released a solo album, *Book of Shadows*, for which he played electric guitar, acoustic guitar, harmonica, piano, keyboards, and bass. In a review of *Book of Shadows* on the Satan Stole My Teddybear Web site, Rog Billerey-Mosier wrote, "Paradoxically, what makes [Wylde] interesting is not his guitar playing, which is good but rather unimpressive. . . . He is passable as a singer, and one must give him credit for working on his vocals after his first album. . . . But what is interesting is the quality and range of songwriting on this album. The songs are very introspective, often slow and melancholy, and incorporate Wylde's conflicting influences very successfully: country blues, rock, metal and soulful [balladry], among others." In a dissenting opinion, Geoffrey Himes wrote for the *Washington Post* (August 16, 1996), "Wylde's fatal weakness . . . is his tendency to write shameless, humorless, grammarless lyrics along the lines of 'Without you woman by my side / I'm contemplating suicide torn from all my pride' . . ."

In 1998 Wylde, who earlier had disbanded Pride and Glory, formed Black Label Society. "We're out to destroy bands like Third Eye Blind and Blink-182," Wylde told Richard Bienstock for the *Guitar World* Web site, when asked about Black Label Society's mission. "Since the whole grunge thing died it's like nobody plays guitar anymore unless it's these [expletive] pop songs. It makes you think. Haven't these bands ever heard of Sabbath or Zeppelin or anything that rocks?" The group's debut album, *Sonic Brew*, was released first in Japan and then, in early 1999, in the United States. On the band's second album, *Stronger Than Death* (2000), Wylde played guitar, bass, and piano, handled all of the vocals, and served as the album's producer; the only other performer was the drummer Philth Ondich. Both *Sonic Brew* and *Stronger Than Death* earned praise from heavy-metal fans and critics. Bienstock, for example, wrote, "The album brings together all of the guitarist's musical characteristics—squealing harmonics that have been Wylde's trademark since his years with Ozzy Osbourne, the bluesy, drawling vocal style he developed while fronting the southern-rock band Pride and Glory, the lighter, more melodic aspects explored on his 1996 solo album, *Book of Shadows*—and wraps them up in pummeling, Pantera-esque guitar riffs." (Pantera is a popular heavy-metal group known for its furious, searing music.) The next offering from Black Label Society was *Alcohol Fueled Brewtality Live + Five* (2001), which was given an "explicit" rating. His next album, *1919 Eternal* (2002), a tribute to Wylde's father, Jerome, who was born in 1919, earned positive critical reviews. Referring to his father and others of the World War II generation, Wylde told a writer for the Spitfire Records Web site, "You can beat those suckers down, but they'll always get back up again. It's a mindset, and it's about strength and determination, merciless forever, man. It's the same with [Black Label Society]. . . . You gotta keep on marching. That's why we've got the song 'Berserkers' on there; it sums up this band's whole mentality." In a review of the album that appears on the Web site mfnrocks.com, Bryan Shaw called Wylde "one of America's last true guitar heroes of note" and wrote that on *1919 Eternal* "Wylde continues to showcase his incredible musicianship by handling virtually all the instruments himself." In an interview posted on the Web site monstercable.com, the guitarist stated,

"As a musician I like doing different things. I don't like just doing one thing. I don't sit around all day just practicing scales. Black Label is just another extension of the stuff I like, ya know. I'll listen to like Neil Young when I'm kicking back, but when I want to lift weights and get rowdy as hell, I'll put on Pantera. At the end of the day I'm a musician. Period. I don't care about any of that rock star b.s."

Black Label Society's album *The Blessed Hellride* (2003) further cemented Wylde's status as one of the heroes of heavy-metal music. The album debuted at number 50 on *Billboard* magazine's Top 100 albums chart and was voted the best heavy-metal album of the year in *Guitar World*'s readers' poll. Reviewing *The Blessed Hellride* for amazon.com, Dominic Wills praised the music's intensity and Wylde's "crushing riffs and head-spinning solos," especially on the tracks "Blackened Waters," "Suffering Overdue," and "Stillborn," a song that laments lost love and features vocals by Osbourne. The DVD *Black Label Society: Boozed, Bruised & Broken-Boned*, released in 2003, includes footage of a Black Label Society concert held in Detroit, Michigan; a clip from a guitar-instruction video that Wylde has released; and the video, directed by Rob Zombie, for the track "Stillborn." Wylde and Black Label Society's fifth studio album, and sixth overall, *Hangover Music Volume VI*, was released in the spring of 2004. While the album features a number of guest musicians, Wylde wrote all of its songs, in addition to singing and playing guitar, bass, and piano. *Hangover Music* offers an interpretation of Procol Harum's hit song "Whiter Shade of Pale" (1967) and the song "Layne," a tribute to the late singer Layne Staley, the front man for the band Alice in Chains. On his personal Web site, Wylde described *Hangover Music* as "darker and heavier than some of our previous cds."

Earlier, Wylde had toured with Black Label Society as part of Ozzfest 2001, a hard-rock and heavy-metal tour of the U.S. and other countries by Ozzy Osbourne's band and many others. Performed annually since 1996, the Ozzfest tour has featured such bands as Pantera, System of a Down, Marilyn Manson, Megadeath, Motorhead, Slayer, and a reunited Black Sabbath. Wylde, having been asked by Osbourne to return to play with his band, laid down guitar tracks on Osbourne's album *Down to Earth* (2001); the record received fairly positive reviews. Unlike the earlier Osbourne albums on which the two men collaborated, *Down to Earth* did not contain any songs written by Wylde. "I love being in Black Label, but I'll always be around Ozzy, too," the guitarist told a writer for the Spitfire Records Web site. "Ozzy knows all he has to do is call and I'll be there." At Ozzfest 2002 Wylde played two sets in every show—one with Black Label Society and another with Osbourne's group. The demands of the two performances over the course of the tour left Wylde mentally and physically exhausted; his condition led to the cancellation of the final two weeks of the European leg of the tour. Either as the lead guitarist for Osbourne's band or with Black Label Society, Wylde was also an integral part of the Ozzfest tours in 2003 and 2004.

Wylde has named as his major influences the guitarists Jimmy Page, of Led Zeppelin; Randy Rhoads, a member of Osbourne's band who died in a plane crash in 1982; and Al DiMeola. His favorite acts include Van Halen, Neil Young, Black Sabbath, Led Zeppelin, and Pantera. He has played live or in the studio with Mike Inez, Randy Castillo, John Sinclair, Derek Sherinian, James LoMenzo, and the Allman Brothers, among others. Wylde's friends include several professional wrestlers; in 2001 he composed entrance music for the popular Stone Cold Steve Austin of the World Wrestling Federation. In addition to writing and performing much of the music on the soundtrack to the movie *Rock Star* (2001), starring Mark Wahlberg and Jennifer Aniston, Wylde appears in the film as the ferocious guitarist Ghode. He has also appeared on

television on *Saturday Night Live*, *Mad TV*, and the popular cable show *The Osbournes*, which stars Ozzy Osbourne and members of his family.

Wylde is married and has three children, two sons and a daughter, whose godfather is Osbourne.

Wylde told R. Scott Bolton, "Somebody was asking me, 'Is that all there is to your life? Beer, music, and that's it?' And I was like, 'Oh, dear God, I hope so.'"

—C.F.T.

Suggested Reading: blacklabelsociety.net; electricbasement.com; metal-reviews.com; monstercable.com; ozzfest.com; roughedge.com; xtrememusician.com; zakkwylde.com

Selected Recordings: *No Rest for the Wicked*, 1988; *No More Tears*, 1991; *Live and Loud*, 1993; *Pride and Glory*, 1994; *Ozzmosis*, 1995; *Book of Shadows*, 1996; *Stronger Than Death*, 2000; *1919 Eternal*, 2002

David Brauchli/Getty Images

Yagudin, Alexei

Mar. 18, 1980– Figure skater

Address: c/o International Skating Center of Connecticut, P.O. Box 577, Simsbury, CT 06071

The 24-year-old Alexei Yagudin has come closer to perfection in figure-skating competitions than any other man in history. The Russian-born Yagudin won the World Figure Skating Championships in 1998, 1999, and 2000. Two years later he

took first-place honors at the Winter Olympic Games, the World and European Figure Skating Championships, and the International Skating Union's Grand Prix of Figure Skating Championships, becoming the first figure skater to win all four events in one year. His marks at both the 2002 Olympics and the 2002 World Championships were the highest ever achieved in those competitions, and in the latter he was the second-youngest and first Russian man ever to win first place. "Yagudin is such a great all-around exponent of his craft," the 1980 Olympic men's figure-skating champion Robin Cousins told a reporter for the *Chicago Tribune* (February 11, 1998). "His jumps are textbook, his spins are textbook, his footwork is textbook. He is the best-rounded skater out there. The way he does a triple axel, fly isn't the word for it. It is more like soar. Even someone who has never seen figure skating before would know in watching Yagudin that this was something special." Outstanding early in his career for his powerful, seemingly effortless execution of flawless jumps, Yagudin gradually became an artist as well, communicating emotion in every gesture. At the 2002 Olympics he earned four perfect scores for artistry—a record at the figure-skating event. "I don't feel like I am the greatest in this world," Yagudin said to Ed Will for the *Denver Post* (January 20, 2003). "For example, I don't see any perfect skaters, the same as there are no perfect people in the world. In the past four years, I have been dominating and won four world championships. It is great, but still I know there is a lot I have to work on." In October 2003 Yagudin announced his retirement from competitive skating. He is a member of the 2004 Smucker's Stars on Ice tour and plans to coach other skaters.

YAGUDIN

An only child, Yagudin was born with the given names Aleksei Konstantinovich on March 18, 1980 in Leningrad (now called St. Petersburg), Russia, in what was then the Soviet Union. His parents divorced in 1991, after his father, Konstantin Yagudin, abandoned the family and moved to Germany; Yagudin has reportedly had no contact with him since then. Yagudin grew up in a tiny communal apartment with his mother, Zoya, and maternal grandmother. He began skating when he was four, after his mother, a recreational ice skater, saw an ad in the local paper for tryouts, presumably for a government-run program. According to some sources, Alexei was a sickly child, and his doctor had advised his mother to introduce him to skating as a way of strengthening him. His first coach, Alexander Mayorov, recognized his talent immediately, and starting at the age of about five, Yagudin was assigned to a grueling practice schedule, skating twice a day for 90 minutes at each session. His mother helped him stay focused and disciplined. "My mom was like father and mother," Yagudin told E. M. Swift for *Sports Illustrated* (February 12, 2002). "If I didn't do a jump in practice, she used to take away the cable TV. I used to watch an American soap opera called *Santa Barbara,* so this was the worst threat she could make." When Yagudin was 10, Mayorov moved to Sweden, and the boy began working at the Yubileiny Sport Club with St. Petersburg's most sought-after trainer, Alexei Mishin. By that year, some of his Internet fan sites have reported, he had mastered the triple jump and incorporated two of them in his programs.

In figure-skating competitions, all individuals and pairs must present both a short program and a long program (the latter is also called the free skate). For the short program, skaters must perform a combination of eight specified jumps, spins, and footwork sequences; for the long, skaters may choose whatever steps or moves they prefer. In both programs, skaters are judged on both technical merit and artistry of presentation; thus a skater receives two scores for the short program and two scores for the long. Until the 2003–04 season, skaters began each program with two perfect scores—a 6.0 for technical merit and a 6.0 for presentation—from which the judges deducted points. For the short program, points were deducted for every flaw in execution; for the long, they were deducted if errors interfered with the flow of the skating or reduced the program's difficulty. At the highest competitive levels, scores typically ranged from about 5.2 to 5.9. Each judge used the two scores for a given program to come up with a preference ranking for each skater; all the judges' rankings were then combined to give each skater an overall placement for that program, with the top being first place. To determine the final scores, the placements of the skaters in the short and the long programs were combined. During the 2003–04 season, the International Skating Union began a transition to a new, computer-based system designed to make scoring more objective. Judges now score each technical element and also, on a scale of one to 10, each skater's artistry in five presentation categories (skating skills, transitions, performance, choreography, and musical interpretation). After each athlete's highest and lowest scores are discarded, the remaining scores are averaged; the skater with the highest average is the first-place winner.

Yagudin began competing internationally in 1994. That year he finished fourth at the World Junior Figure Skating Championships. In 1996 he won the gold medal in the same competition. He competed in the Olympics for the first time in 1998, in Nagano, Japan, finishing fifth. He came in first in 11 other competitions in which he participated that year, among them the European and the World Championships. At the European Championships, at which the Russians Evgeni Plushenko and Alexander Abt came in second and third, respectively, Yagudin skated a nearly flawless program; his jumps—including a quadruple and seven triples—were the cleanest and the highest in the competition. At the World Championships Yagudin finished first in the short program; although his long program had errors, he won the title, his closest competitors having faltered during their long programs.

After his stellar performance at the World Championships, Yagudin stopped training with Mishin, because the coach was unwilling to drop one of Yagudin's rivals, the Russian skater Evgeni Plushenko, and other students and devote himself exclusively to Yagudin. "Mishin had so many good students that he couldn't work with just me," Yagudin told E. M. Swift. "I like it when I can't escape the coach's eyes." The figure skater then moved to New Jersey, without his mother, to work with the coach Tatiana Tarasova, who, before coming to the U.S., had helped the Russian figure skater Ilia Kulik win the gold medal at the 1998 Nagano Olympics. "All my life changed in a few months," Yagudin told Swift. "I knew very little English. I was alone. And I was young." Tarasova, an expert in ice dancing and ice theater who had stopped skating because of an injury, encouraged Yagudin to develop his artistry and helped him become a balletic performer as well as a powerful athlete. In 2000 Yagudin began training with Tarasova at the Connecticut International Skating Center, in Simsbury.

During this period Yagudin's behavior away from the rink began to interfere with his skating, and reports began to circulate that he was drinking to excess. In the summer of 1999, he was ousted from the Champions on Ice tour because of an alcohol-related incident. Nevertheless, he won the World Championships in 1999 and 2000 and continued to dominate men's figure skating. In 2001 Evgeni Plushenko defeated an overweight, out-of-shape Yagudin in five out of seven competitions, including the World Championships, the Russian Nationals, the European Championships, and the Grand Prix finals. Stunned by his failures to win the top spots, in mid-2001 Yagudin quit drinking and undertook an extremely rigorous regimen of dieting and exercise. He moved into Tarasova's home in Newington, Connecticut, to ensure that he would remain disciplined, and in a few weeks, he lost more than 20 pounds. "I became [a] perfect person," he told E. M. Swift. "I had a couple of glasses of wine the whole summer. No parties. Every night asleep by 11. It was like a sickness for me to lose weight. I was on the scale 100 times a day. I understand now about girls with anorexia." Yagudin felt emotionally and physically prepared as the 2001–02 season opened, with the Goodwill Games in Brisbane, Australia, in August. He was not able to land any of his jumps, however, and finished a distant third to the first-place and second-place winners, Plushenko and the American Michael Weiss, respectively. Yagudin later said that the event marked a turning point in his professional life. "I'd done everything, and this is how I end up, third place," he told Swift. "So I decided I'm going to be the same Alexei I was five years ago. I'm going to have fun, to eat normal, to party, to go to discos if I want. Not to be crazy, but to have fun."

That approach to skating succeeded: Yagudin beat Plushenko to win the gold in the 2001 Grand Prix and the European Championships. For his long program at the Winter Olympic Games in February 2002, in Salt Lake City, Utah, Yagudin skated to music from the 1998 movie *The Man in the Iron Mask* and landed two quadruple jumps. When he finished his program, he fell to his knees and kissed the ice, then joyfully jumped into the air. The judges responded with corresponding enthusiasm: a record four of the nine judges gave him scores of 6.0 in the free-skate competition, with the remaining five awarding him 5.9s. He thus won the gold medal with a program deemed closer to perfection than any in Olympic history. (Among his chief rivals, Plushenko fell on a quadruple jump in his short program and the American skater Scott Eldredge failed to land a triple axel.) Just over a month later, offering a routine identical to the one he had skated at the Olympics, Yagudin made history again, when he received six perfect scores in the short program at the World Championships. One of those scores was for required elements, marking the first time a man had received a perfect mark in that category at that competition. Yagudin went on to win the World Championships title for the fourth time in five years. "It feels great to get my title back," he told Salvatore Zanca in an interview for the Associated Press (March 21, 2002). "I had this title for three years in a row and then, unfortunately, I lost it last year. It was pretty hard to get the fourth one, and I kind of lost it. This time, I am very happy I decided to come to this championship."

A hip injury forced Yagudin to withdraw from all competitions during the 2002–03 season. In May 2003 he underwent hip surgery, with the hope of returning to the ice within a few months. The following August he was charged with driving while intoxicated and was subsequently placed in an alcohol education program. Two months later he announced through his agent that he was ending his career as a competitive skater and would devote himself to skating with the Smucker's Stars on Ice tour and helping Tarasova coach her students. He gave a farewell performance in a ceremony held at the conclusion of Skate Canada, in Mississauga, on November 2, 2003.

The five-foot eight-inch, 155-pound Yagudin lives in Newington, Connecticut.

—H.T.

Suggested Reading: *Boston Globe* D p1 Feb. 15, 2002, with photos; *Denver Post* F p1 Jan. 20, 2003, with photos; *Hartford [Connecticut] Courant* E p6 Feb. 17, 2002, with photo; *Sports Illustrated* p16+ Feb. 12, 2002, with photos

Frederick M. Brown/Getty Images

Zellweger, Renée

Apr. 25, 1969– Actress

Address: c/o Creative Artists Agency, 9830 Wilshire Blvd., Beverly Hills, CA 90212-1825

Renée Zellweger had appeared in a dozen movies for television and the big screen before she gained widespread notice, in 1996, when she beat out several far better-known actresses to star opposite Tom Cruise in the highly popular film *Jerry Maguire*. After that breakthrough performance, for which she was nominated for a Screen Actors' Guild Award for best supporting actress, she captured leading roles in such 1998–2000 box-office successes as *One True Thing*, *Nurse Betty*, and *Me, Myself & Irene*. In an assessment of her work for *Vogue* (September 1998), Bob Ickes referred to her "homespun allure" and the "intensity and vulnerability" that she brought to the screen. The announcement that she had been cast as the title character in *Bridget Jones's Diary*, the screen adaptation of Helen Fielding's best-selling novel, led many of the book's enthusiasts (especially those in Great Britain) to complain that an American, and certainly a Texan, was a poor choice for the role of Bridget, a never-married, insecure, overweight Londoner in her early 30s. Zellweger proved them wrong, earning many critical plaudits and an Oscar nomination for her depiction. A year later, despite the lack of singing or dancing credits on her résumé, the actress won the part of the aspiring singer Roxy Hart in the film version of the Broadway musical *Chicago*, and once again she rose to the challenge. While some viewers ranked her dancing skills below those of her co-stars, she received generally good reviews and a second Oscar nomination. In one of her most recent projects, Zellweger was praised for her portrayal of the earthy, scrappy country woman Ruby Thewes in *Cold Mountain*, which the director Anthony Minghella and the writer Charles Frazier adapted from Frazier's award-winning 1997 novel.

Renée Kathleen Zellweger was born on April 25, 1969 in Houston, Texas. Her father, Emil Zellweger, a Swiss-born engineer, and her mother, Kjellfried, a Norwegian-born nurse and midwife, met in Denmark and moved to Houston shortly after they married. There, her father worked in the oil-refining business. When Zellweger was nine, the family moved about 30 miles from Houston to Katy, a small town that had neither a movie theater nor connections to cable television. "Texas is pretty . . . Texan, but I was exposed to different things than my friends," Zellweger told Chris Mundy for *Redbook* (March 1998). "It may be true that we're not educated enough about what's out there besides what's on this continent, but that was definitely not a problem in my house. The mail was always going to strange places." With her parents and her brother, Drew (who is two years her senior and is now a marketing executive), she frequently traveled overseas to visit relatives.

In high school Zellweger participated in a variety of activities, including track, basketball, cheerleading, and theater. She has said that she was more of a tomboy than a drama queen and that she never seemed to fit in with any particular group of students. "On weekends, I was by myself most of the time," she told Mundy. The actress also said that she and her brother often felt misunderstood by their parents, whose European backgrounds and experiences were very different from their children's lives.

After her graduation from high school, in 1987, Zellweger entered the University of Texas at Austin. With the goal of becoming a journalist, she chose English as her major. "I went all over the place, from Puritanism to British [literature] to the Victorians to Hawthorne to Faulkner to—name it," she told Jason Cohen for *Texas Monthly* (September 1997). After enrolling in a drama class as an elective and appearing in a play by Henrik Ibsen, Zellweger sought work as an actress in television commercials and films. Before long she became so successful that she quit her waitressing job and paid for the remainder of her education with the money she earned in TV ads for beer and fast-food restaurants. Sometimes she traveled as far as Dallas (about 180 miles away) for auditions and shoots. She graduated from the University of Texas in 1990, after just three years, with a bachelor's degree in English. Rather than move to Los Angeles, where the U.S. film industry is based, she elected to remain in Texas and seek parts in productions being filmed in her home state.

After Zellweger appeared in an April 1991 episode of the television sitcom *Married . . . with Children*, two TV projects followed: the film *A Taste for Killing* (1992) and the fact-based miniseries *Murder in the Heartland* (1993). She had uncredited walk-on parts in two films released in 1993, *My Boyfriend's Back* and *Dazed and Confused*. In the latter she worked with a classmate from the University of Texas—Matthew McConaughey, who later, in the mid-1990s, starred in such successful films as *A Time to Kill* and *Lone Star*. The two worked together again in 1994, when they were cast as leads in the low-budget *Return of the Texas Chainsaw Massacre*. That movie was re-released in 1997 (after both Zellweger and McConaughey had become box-office attractions), with the title *Texas Chainsaw Massacre: The Next Generation*. Although neither the film nor the actors' performances earned praise, Janet Maslin of the *New York Times* (August 29, 1997) noted, "Should anyone have the patience to look closely, the two leading players do show signs of what would soon make them famous. Ms. Zellweger, sweet and sprightly and a natural-born ditz, may be the only actress who could point a gun bravely at a killer, then simply shriek, and drop it, and scamper away." Zellweger also appeared in *8 Seconds* (1994), a drama based on the life of the bull-riding world champion Lane Frost.

After another walk-on role, in the film *Reality Bites* (1994), which starred Winona Ryder, Zellweger moved to Los Angeles, where she rented a garage apartment and took a job busing tables at a restaurant. She soon landed her first leading part, in *Love and a .45* (1994), which she has described as a "white-trash road film." She followed up with appearances in the made-for-TV movie *Shake Rattle and Rock* and the feature film *Empire Records* (1995), which Cohen described as "an alternative rock soundtrack disguised as a full-length feature film." In her talk with Cohen, Zellweger referred to all the characters whom she had portrayed until then as examples of "Generation X whatever."

Zellweger had a small part in the little-noticed drama *The Low Life*, in 1995. During the next year she began to attract attention, with her portrayal of Novalyne Price in the director Dan Ireland's film *The Whole Wide World*. The movie tells the true story of a west Texas schoolteacher and her relationship with the creator of the pulp-fiction character Conan the Barbarian, Robert E. Howard (played by Vincent D'Onofrio), who committed suicide in 1936. Coincidentally, an old friend of Zellweger's, Sims Ellison, a heavy-metal singer for a popular group in Austin, had recently committed suicide. Speaking of *The Whole Wide World*, Zellweger said to Cohen, "I love that story. It was the kind of film that moves me. And a story about a woman who has this incredible friendship and love with this man who is her inspiration, and then she loses him. . . . I could not believe the parallels. I kind of had to do it."

The call to audition for the part of Dorothy Boyd in *Jerry Maguire* came to Zellweger not, as has been reported, because of her performance in *The Whole Wide World*, which was highly praised at the 1996 Sundance Film Festival, but because of her work in the far less critically and commercially successful *Empire Records*. Cameron Crowe, the director of *Jerry Maguire*, recalled to Mundy that an *Empire Records* casting director had told him, "Look, [Zellweger] is not right for your movie. She is too young, but you should meet her because she's gonna be a star." Crowe told Mundy that he had often heard the same thing about people who, in his view, had insufficient talent, but that in Zellweger's case it was true. "She came in and brought a really fresh thing to it," he said. "She left the room and I thought, 'Totally, she's gonna be a star.'" Her callback was less successful, however, because Zellweger was preoccupied about her dog's ill health. Crowe told Mundy, "I just saw her slip away as somebody that was going to be a bit part in the movie." But her next two readings, during which she interacted with the film's star, Tom Cruise, put her back in the running. While in her hotel room during the Sundance Film Festival, Zellweger got the phone call from Crowe offering her the part. "I just began screaming and dancing around the room," she told Bernard Weinraub for the *New York Times* (January 31, 1996).

In light of reports that such well-known actresses as Winona Ryder, Bridget Fonda, Marisa Tomei, and Mira Sorvino had also wanted the role of Jerry Maguire's humble, admiring office assistant cum love interest, Zellweger had a suspicion that financial considerations had dictated her being selected. "I was the one where they said, 'If we hire that girl, we'll save money,'" she said to Cohen. Crowe, however, told Weinraub that what determined his choice of the lesser-known actress was Zellweger's "freshness" and the confidence with which she carried herself. "Even well-known actresses crumble a little bit when they come into a room with Tom Cruise . . . ," Crowe said. "More than anybody, Renée came in with an enormous sense of

herself." Zellweger told Weinraub, "You kind of forget you're supposed to be intimidated by someone like Tom Cruise. Before I met him, I thought I'd get sick and faint. But as soon as we began, I went off on my merry way." Janet Maslin of the *New York Times* (December 13, 1996) called Zellweger "an inspired choice to play opposite a dreamboat of Mr. Cruise's stature. Her fetching ordinariness, which happens to be quite extraordinary, brings him down to earth in ways no movie queen could manage." *Jerry Maguire*, which earned $270 million at the box office, was nominated for the Academy Award for best picture of 1996. For her work in *The Whole Wide World* and *Jerry Maguire*, Zellweger received the National Board of Review's Best Breakthrough Performer Award for that year.

After the release of *Jerry Maguire*, Zellweger received offers for parts in a wide array of films. By her own account, she is more interested in choosing good roles than in becoming a bona fide movie star. "When the mystery is gone from a person, you can't really believe them in a lot of different roles," she told Cohen. "I don't want to be all over the place." Zellweger's next three projects were *Deceiver* (1997), a mystery in which she played a prostitute, opposite Tim Roth; *A Price Above Rubies* (1998), in which she portrayed a troubled Hasidic homemaker in New York City who breaks several taboos of Orthodox Judaism in a quest for self-fulfillment; and *One True Thing* (1998), in which she was cast as a woman who struggles with caring for her terminally ill mother and dealing with her father, whom she idolizes despite his remoteness. "It is the craftsmanship that elevates *One True Thing* above the level of a soaper. . . ," Roger Ebert wrote for the *Chicago Sun-Times* (November 1998, on-line). "Renée Zellweger . . . is able to create a place for herself and work inside it, not acting so much as fiercely possessing her character."

In 1999 Zellweger played Chris O'Donnell's long-suffering girlfriend in the critically panned comedy *The Bachelor*. The following year she earned her first Golden Globe nomination, for her portrayal of the title character of the dark comedy *Nurse Betty*, which co-starred Morgan Freeman, Chris Rock, and Greg Kinnear. Betty is an unappreciated wife who, after witnessing the murder of her husband, comes to believe that the characters of her favorite soap opera are real; she then embarks on a quest to meet them in Los Angeles, unaware that she is being followed by her husband's killers. "Nothing would work here without Renée Zellweger, who manages to blur superbly the line between outer performance and interior life without a drop of sentimentality," the film critic Joan Ellis wrote in a review posted on her eponymous Web site. "She projects the innocence and honesty essential to Betty's character. Drawn into illusion at the drop of a hat, or a well-chosen soundtrack song, Betty is believable and original." Zellweger scored again with *Me, Myself & Irene* (2000), a comedy written and directed by Bobby and Peter Farrelly and starring Jim Carrey as a state trooper with a split personality. (Zellweger became romantically involved with Carrey and was briefly engaged to him.)

Zellweger's competitors for the part of the title character in *Bridget Jones's Diary* (2001), Sharon Maguire's directorial debut, reportedly included the British actresses Kate Winslet and Helena Bonham Carter. To prepare for the role of Bridget, who agonizes over her weight, inability to stop smoking or drinking, and single status, Zellweger worked as an assistant at a London publishing house (as does the character), gained 20 pounds, and trained with a dialogue coach to perfect a British accent. Her performance won over both critics and ordinary moviegoers and earned her an Oscar nomination. "Zellweger was a controversial choice for the role (any American would have been), but she turns out to have been the perfect one . . . ," Stephanie Zacharek wrote for Salon.com (April 13, 2001). "Zellweger walks the line between being pouty and eternally optimistic without ever turning it into a routine." In a review for the *New Yorker* (April 16, 2001), Anthony Lane wrote, "Zellweger was an inspired choice for the title role. . . . The actress has the precise degree of emotional quiver that the role requires." *Bridget Jones's Diary* grossed $281 million worldwide and boosted Zellweger's salary per picture to between $3 million and $5 million. Zellweger next appeared in *White Oleander* (2002), in a supporting role, that of the foster mother of a teenage girl whose mother (Michelle Pfeiffer) is in prison for murder.

Zellweger gained her second Oscar nomination and a British Academy of Film and Television Arts (BAFTA) award nomination, and won both Screen Actors Guild and Golden Globe Awards, for her performance as Roxy Hart in the musical motion picture *Chicago* (2002). Imprisoned for killing her lover and dreaming of becoming a vaudeville star, the duplicitous Roxy projects an image of innocence and wholesomeness. Zellweger was initially reluctant to take the role, having had no training in dancing or singing, but *Chicago*'s director, Rob Marshall, felt sure that she was the right choice. For 10 months before shooting began, she took dance and voice lessons. "This was an extraordinary experience; to learn a new medium of expression is unbelievable," she told an interviewer for CBS's *The Early Show* (January 14, 2003, on-line). "Singing makes me feel very vulnerable. Because I had to open that up, say 'Here's my heart. What do you think?' . . . It was scary." While reviewers and audiences were enthusiastic about the film, several critics commented that Zellweger's dancing skills were not of the caliber normally expected in musicals. In a review for the *New York Times* (December 27, 2002, on-line), Elvis Mitchell wrote that her "float-like-a-butterfly voice doesn't triumph over her my-left-foot dance skills," but he went on to say, "Ms. Zellweger's performance is alternately subtle and reptile; she can still win the

day. Who would have expected Ms. Zellweger . . . to come through in a musical?" Roger Ebert, writing for the *Chicago Sun-Times* (December 27, 2002, on-line), had another view: "Zellweger is not a born hoofer, but then again Roxie Hart isn't supposed to be a star; the whole point is that she isn't, and what Zellweger invaluably contributes to the role is Roxie's dreamy infatuation with herself, and her quickly growing mastery of publicity." *Chicago* garnered over $100 million at the box office.

Zellweger next appeared in *Down with Love* (2003), a romantic comedy set in the 1960s. Co-starring Ewan McGregor, the film struck many viewers as a paean to the Doris Day–Rock Hudson comedies of that era. In *Cold Mountain* (2003) Zellweger co-starred with Jude Law, who played a wounded Confederate soldier returning to his home during the Civil War, and Nicole Kidman, as the woman he loves. In a brief review for *People* (December 22, 2003), Leah Rozen wrote, "A spunky Zellweger is both forceful and funny as a can-do handywoman." A. O. Scott, a film critic for the *New York Times* (December 25, 2003), wrote, "Ms. Zellweger, wild-haired and ornery, clomps through the scenery like a migrant from Li'l Abner's Dogpatch. Her earthiness warms up *Cold Mountain* considerably, and her scenes with Ms. Kidman have a loose, improvisatory rhythm missing from much of the movie. They work together like a seasoned comedy team, and Mr. Minghella makes the most of their differences in temperament and appearance."

Zellweger appeared in late 2004 in a Bridget Jones sequel, called *Bridget Jones: The Edge of Reason*, and has signed on for the films *Cinderella Man* and *Piece of My Heart*, which were due for release in 2005. She will also produce *Piece of My Heart*, in which she stars as the singer Janis Joplin. She lent her voice to a 2001 episode of the animated television series *King of the Hill* and to the animated DreamWorks' film *Shark Tale* (2004).

Actors and directors have described Zellweger as intelligent, hard-working, and unpretentious. "What you see is exactly what you get with Renée," Laurence Mark, a co-producer of *Jerry Maguire*, told Marjorie Rosen for *Biography* (June 2000). "One of the things the camera responds to is her openness. She's amazingly free about herself, and the camera picks that up. Offscreen, too, she never seems to have hidden agendas." Of her hectic life as an actress, Zellweger told Mundy, "There are so many things I miss, a lot of things I sacrifice. This has to mean something more than being applauded, because there are Thanksgivings you spend alone and birthdays you miss. It's not the glam life it seems to be." Zellweger has said that her closest friend is her dog, Dylan (also called Woof), a collie–golden retriever mix who travels with her and sometimes accompanies her on movie sets. Marjorie Rosen reported that Zellweger "keeps a basketball in the trunk of her car just in case she can find a pick up game." The actress has advocated actively for increased funding for breast-cancer research and has participated in the Revlon Run/Walk for Women, which raises money for research involving all female-related cancers. (She lost a friend to breast cancer, and her publicist has also battled the disease.)

Zellweger owns a $6.8 million house in Bel Air, near Los Angeles; recently, she told interviewers that she plans to move to New York City. *Biography* included her as one of its "Knockouts of 1999." *People* listed her among the 50 most beautiful people in the world in 2001 and among the 10 best dressed in 2003.

—K.E.D.

Suggested Reading: *Biography* p86+ June 2000, with photos; *Good Housekeeping* p152+ June 2003, with photo; *InStyle* p422+ May 2003, with photo; *Interview* p64+ June 2003, with photo; *New York Times* C p11 Jan. 31, 1996, with photo, C p12 Aug. 29, 1997; *Premiere* p56+ Nov. 2003, with photo; *Redbook* p86+ Mar. 1998, with photos; *Texas Monthly* p112+ Sep. 1997, with photos; *Vogue* p269+ Dec. 2003, with photo

Selected Films: *Dazed and Confused*, 1993; *Reality Bites*, 1994; *8 Seconds*, 1994; *Return of the Texas Chainsaw Massacre*, 1994; *Love and a .45*, 1994; *Empire Records*, 1995; *The Low Life*, 1995; *The Whole Wide World*, 1996; *Jerry Maguire*, 1996; *Deceiver*, 1997; *A Price Above Rubies*, 1998; *One True Thing*, 1998, *The Bachelor*, 1999; *Nurse Betty*, 2000; *Me, Myself & Irene*, 2000; *Bridget Jones's Diary*, 2001; *White Oleander*, 2002; *Chicago*, 2002; *Down with Love*, 2003; *Cold Mountain*, 2003; *Bridget Jones: The Edge of Reason*, 2004

Harry How/Getty Images

Zito, Barry

May 13, 1978– Baseball player

Address: Oakland Athletics Network Associates Coliseum, 7000 Coliseum Way, Oakland, CA 94621

Barry Zito of the Oakland Athletics stands out among the dominant left-handed pitchers in Major League Baseball. As a southpaw with great control of his pitches, Zito has befuddled batters throughout his five seasons in the majors. In 2003 he was one of three left-handed hurlers—the other two were Jamie Moyer of the Seattle Mariners and Dar-

rell May of the Kansas City Royals—to pitch more than 200 innings, win 10 or more games, and register an earned-run average (ERA) under 4.00. What distinguishes Zito even in that company has only partly to do with baseball. In talking with the press, he often gives the impression of being as focused on surfing, playing the guitar, or writing songs as he is on pitching, and he has shown what is at the very least an eccentric streak: he once devoted an interview with ESPN to the subject of his stuffed-animal collection, and he has claimed to hold discussions on the mound with his left arm ("whenever I need someone to talk to," as he explained to a writer for *Sports Illustrated* [January 15, 2001]). Such behavior, however, has not gotten in the way of his pitching performance. Zito, who began his major-league career in 2000, with the Athletics, has amazed fans, baseball experts, and other players alike with his feats on the mound, so much so that in 2002 he won the coveted Cy Young Award. Zito told John Schlegel for the Major League Baseball (MLB) Web site, "You should always try to be the best you can be. It's not like I shoot for the Cy Young. That's not my goal. My goal is to be the best I can be. . . . I have big aspirations for what I want to do in this game and what I want to achieve in what's hopefully a long career."

Barry William Zito was born on May 13, 1978 in Las Vegas, Nevada, to Roberta and Joe Zito, a show-business couple who met and married while working with the famed singer and pianist Nat King Cole in the 1960s; Joe Zito conducted and provided arrangements for Cole's band, while Roberta performed in Cole's group of backup vocalists, the Merry Young Souls. Barry Zito has two sisters, Sally and Bonnie, who are, respectively, nine and 13 years older than their brother. As quoted on Jock-Bio.com, Zito has said that he "had three 'moms'" while growing up. Because of the inconsistent nature of employment in the Zitos' line of work, the family often found itself in tough financial straits.

According to various sources, when Barry Zito was seven years of age, a teacher had the children in his class draw pictures representing what they wanted to do when they grew up; Zito's drawing showed him as a pitcher, with a caption that read, "Make a Million Dollars." His mother recalled for the 2001 *Sports Illustrated* article that even as a toddler, Zito showed potential as a pitcher: "[Barry] had a funny knack for throwing a ball wherever he wanted it—through a hole, or in a corner," she said. Although he knew little about baseball, Joe Zito recognized his son's promise. He began reading books on pitching strategy and discussing the subject with young Barry, and he even built a pitcher's mound in the family's backyard, where the father and son practiced for two hours every day. By this time the family had moved to San Diego, California, where, in spite of the Zitos' uncertain financial state, Barry's father hired Randy Jones—a former Cy Young Award winner—to give the boy private pitching lessons for $50 an hour. Barry Zito recalled the experience for John Schlegel: "I didn't know so much at the age of 12 or 13 what a Cy Young was, but I knew it was a great honor. I knew it was the highest honor a pitcher could get, and I knew he'd won it. It was sitting there in his living room, and every day I'd just kind of look at it and marvel at it. . . . When I'd do something incorrectly, he'd spit a big wad of tobacco on my shoes, my brand new Nike high-tops that I could barely afford. He's spitting tobacco juice on them, saying, 'Do it right, Lefty. Do it right.'"

Zito became the star pitcher at Grossmont High School before transferring, for his senior year, to University High, a private school. He earned all-league honors there, with an 8–4 record , a 2.92 ERA, and 105 strikeouts in just 85 innings. During those years, "Unlike most of his teammates," as the writer of the 2001 *Sports Illustrated* article reported, Zito "spent his off-field time not as the stereotypical cocky athlete, but as a long-haired, oft-ostracized member of the slacker skateboarding clique." That behavior was perhaps an early sign of what the *Sports Illustrated* writer called Zito's "goofy confidence, an all-knowing-yet-unassuming aura." Zito's mother recalled for the article, "He would wear his hair the way he wanted to, and he would dress how he wanted to. He'd want to get a certain style of clothing, and the first thing I'd say was, 'Are you sure it's what the kids are wearing?' He'd say, 'Mom, it's what I'm wearing.'"

While Zito was able to throw a "wicked" curveball, in Schlegel's words, and had a greater understanding of the game in general than most people his age, the velocity of his pitches topped out at about 85 miles per hour (mph), which was not fast enough to interest many colleges or professional baseball scouts. Zito was, however, picked in the 59th round of the 1996 MLB draft by the Seattle Mariners. Craig Weissmann, then a scout for the Mariners, saw vast potential in Zito. He told *Sports Illustrated* in 2001, "He threw way too far across

his body, and that killed his velocity. But there was something special about the kid." For several weeks Weissmann worked closely with the young pitcher, and soon Zito's pitches were clocking in at over 90 mph. On the strength of that improvement and the scout's positive assessment of Zito's potential, the Mariners offered to sign Zito for $90,000, an unusually high figure for such a late draft pick. Zito, displaying his singular independence of mind, turned the offer down. His father told *Sports Illustrated* in 2001, "I'll never forget us sitting there with Craig. At one point Craig turned to Barry and said, 'The offer is very good. What's the problem?' And my son—who was picked in the 59th round but knew he was going to be great—looked up and said, 'I think I should be a first-rounder.'" In the summer of 1996, Zito began working with Rick Peterson, a pitching coach with the Toronto Blue Jays organization. He developed a close relationship with Peterson, who helped to strengthen the young pitcher's mental approach to the game.

In 1997 Zito began attending the University of California at Santa Barbara. That year he struck out 123 batters in 85 1/3 innings for the school. (During the same period he took up surfing, becoming a devotee of the sport, despite one episode in which he "almost died," and which "wasn't so cool," as he told *Sports Illustrated*.) At Santa Barbara Zito was named a freshman All-American. Then, so that he would be eligible for the MLB draft in his sophomore year, he transferred to Pierce Junior College, in Los Angeles, California. On that school's team Zito earned All-State and All-Conference honors while accumulating a 9–2 record with 132 strikeouts in 103 innings. With this performance, Zito gained national prominence and was selected by the Texas Rangers in the third round of the 1998 MLB draft. Instead of turning professional and accepting the Rangers' offer of $300,000, however, he decided to transfer to the University of Southern California (USC). At USC Zito garnered First-Team All-American honors after notching a record of 12–3 with 154 strikeouts in 113 innings of work. Zito was then drafted as the third overall pick in the 1999 draft by the Oakland Athletics. He joined the team, receiving a $1.59 million signing bonus, and was assigned to Oakland's Class-A squad in Visalia, California.

In eight games as a starter, Zito compiled a record of 3–0 with a 2.45 ERA. His mother, meanwhile, had developed cirrhosis of the liver and fell desperately ill that spring; Zito regularly made six-hour drives to visit his mother at Cedar Sinai Hospital, in Los Angeles, until she underwent a liver transplant and recovered. He recalled that experience for the 2001 *Sports Illustrated* profile: "What do you think about for six hours? I guess I accepted my mother would probably die. I thought about my family–what we would be like without my mom. Mainly, I knew I had to be strong." Zito was then promoted to Oakland's Class-AA team in Midland, Texas, and garnered a 2–1 record. Moving up again, to a Class-AAA team in Vancouver, British Columbia, Zito played an important part in the Canadian Pacific Coast League AAA World Series championship, allowing only four earned runs in two postseason starts. He began the 2000 season at Oakland's major-league spring-training camp. The team's executives decided to send him to the Athletics' new AAA affiliate in Sacramento, California, however, to gain more experience. There, Zito started in 18 games and went 8–5 with a 3.19 ERA.

On July 22, 2000 Zito was called up to the majors. His first game as a big-league starter was against the California Angels; his performance went well until the fifth inning, when the Angels were able to load the bases with their best hitters coming up to bat. In an eye-popping display, Zito proceeded to strike out Mo Vaughn, Tim Salmon, and Garret Anderson, the heart of the Angels' batting order. Vaughn, an All-Star, said after the game, as quoted by Sean Deveny in the *Sporting News* (April 2, 2001), "You expect to score in that situation. That kid has good stuff, and he showed a lot of poise out there." Zito's rookie-season record was 7–4 with a 2.72 ERA, with other teams' batters averaging a meager .195 against him. During that season's tight pennant race between the Athletics and the Mariners, Zito's record in the pivotal month of September was 5–1, which included a shutout of Tampa Bay. During the play-offs the Athletics were down two games to one against the New York Yankees when Zito started the crucial game four in front of a hostile crowd at Yankee Stadium; in six innings he allowed only one run on seven hits, and the Athletics won the game, 11–1. They then lost the deciding fifth game. Bernie Williams, the Yankees' All-Star center fielder, described the effectiveness of Zito's pitches to Harvey Araton for the *New York Times* (April 26, 2002): "Everything looks the same. The curveball is so slow compared to the fastball. You don't pull the trigger because you think it's going to be a ball, and it ends up a strike."

During the 2001 season, after Zito allowed 25 runs in his first 26 innings of pitching, for a record—after 22 starts—of 6–7 with an ERA over 5.00, his father moved in with him. For four straight days in July, the two did little other than talk about pitching and read from Ernest Holmes's *Creative Mind and Success*, a book about positive thinking. The result was remarkable: for the remainder of the season, Zito became the best pitcher in baseball, with a record of 11–1 and a 1.32 ERA. His overall record for the season was 17–8 with a 3.49 ERA. He recorded 205 strikeouts, becoming the first left-handed Oakland Athletics pitcher since the 1975 Cy Young Award winner, Vida Blue, to reach that mark. Again, Zito faced the Yankees in the play-offs and pitched very well, giving up only two hits; unfortunately for him and the Athletics, one of the hits was a game-deciding home run by Jorge Posada. After two more games, the Athletics were eliminated from the play-offs.

A week before his 24th birthday, just after the start of the 2002 season, Zito signed a four-year, $9.8 million contract with the Athletics. Also that year he won the American League Cy Young Award, given by the Baseball Writers' Association of America, after accumulating a record of 23–5 with a 2.75 ERA; he ranked fifth in the AL for innings pitched (229.1) and fourth in the league for lowest opposing batters' average (.218). Besides being the youngest winner of the Cy Young Award in 16 years, Zito was also awarded the *Sporting News* American League pitcher of the year honors and the Players' Choice award for American League pitcher of the year, an honor bestowed by his peers. His 23 wins were the most by a left-handed pitcher in the American League since Frank Viola in 1988. (While about 10 percent of people in the U.S. are left-handed, 29 percent of pitchers are lefties, according to *Sports Illustrated* [March 23, 2004, online]. In general balls pitched by southpaws to right-handed batters are more difficult to hit than those thrown by right-handed pitchers.) On September 14, 2002 Zito took a no-hitter into the eighth inning against the Mariners, but ultimately had to settle for a two-hit shutout. In 2003 the Athletics advanced as far as the American League Division Series, which they lost in five games to the Boston Red Sox; the game- and series-clinching home run was hit by Manny Ramirez off a fastball from Zito. The pitcher ended the regular season with 14 wins, 12 losses, and a 3.30 ERA.

Zito struggled during the first half of the 2004 season, winning four games and losing seven. As in previous years, he improved after the All-Star Game, held in July, winning seven games and losing four. Many observers concluded that Zito could have won 10 games in the second half of the season if the Athletics bullpen had not squandered the leads he had achieved for them. At the end of the season, Zito posted 11 wins and 11 loses, with a 4.48 ERA—the highest of his career.

Zito's avocational pursuits include practicing yoga and studying Eastern religions. Several years ago he took up the guitar, and he recently began writing songs; his progress has been such that he performs with the Sally Zito Project, a professional band headed by his sister. On the subject of his various interests, he said to Jack Curry for the *New York Times* (February 24, 2003), "I refuse to be molded into some stereotypical ballplayer that has no interests, really, no life, no depth, no intelligence. The fact that I'm weird in the game, I think I'm more normal because I'm a normal person that has hobbies and things I like to do and it's not hunting and golf. So people get all excited and make a fuss because it's not the things a normal ballplayer might do." The Athletics' general manager, Billy Beane, told Joe Lapointe for the *New York Times* (October 4, 2002) about Zito, "He's . . . a bit of a Renaissance man. He's very open-minded, very eager to learn. And that's why he's a great baseball player as well. He has mentally and physically prepared to pitch in the major leagues his entire life. Things don't happen by accident with Barry. He's very methodical and very disciplined and very focused. He's always sort of searching for a better way to make a wheel." Beane told *Sports Illustrated* in 2001, "Barry isn't flaky. He's eccentric. He's a kaleidoscope. He takes the Zen approach to things."

—L.A.S.

Suggested Reading: Major League Baseball Web site; *New York Times* IV p1 Apr. 22, 2002, IV p2 Oct. 4, 2002, IV p2 Nov.8, 2002; *Sporting News* p12 Apr. 2, 2001; *Sports Illustrated* p94 Jan. 15, 2001

Courtesy of M.L. Falcone

Zukerman, Eugenia

(ZOOK-er-man)

Sep. 25, 1944– Flutist; writer; television journalist

Address: c/o M. L. Falcone, 155 W. 68th St., Suite 1114, New York, NY 10023-5817

Torn as a young adult between choosing a career in music or pursuing one in writing, Eugenia Zukerman did both. Zukerman is a renowned flutist and the author of four books—two novels, a collection of reminiscences by accomplished women, and an account of her ordeal in fighting a life-threatening lung disease. Since 1980 she has also worked as a journalist for the CBS-TV show *Sunday Morning*, and since 1998 as the assistant art director of the Bravo! Vail Valley Music Festival, in

Colorado. According to Zukerman, her varied vocations have two important elements in common: "structure and form," as she wrote for the Hong Kong Philharmonic Orchestra Web site. "When I look at a piece of music, I look at it in an intellectual way . . . ," she explained. "When I'm writing, I think that writing has to be musical to be good. Journalism is about listening. . . . Music is about listening. . . . I use all of the skills I've learned."

The second of the three children of Shirley Cohen Rich and Stanley Rich, Zukerman was born Eugenia Rich on September 25, 1944 in Cambridge, Massachusetts; she grew up in Hartford, Connecticut. Her older sister, now Julie Ingelfinger, is a pediatric nephrologist; her younger sister, Laurie Rich Alban, is a media consultant and writer. Zukerman has credited her mother—a modern dancer and the first woman accepted into the graduate engineering program at the City College of New York—with encouraging her and her two sisters to be guided by the knowledge that life is filled with possibilities. Her father was a nuclear physicist who taught at the Massachusetts Institute of Technology; a prolific inventor and entrepreneur, he developed a scanning sonar device used in submarines during World War II. Zukerman's parents both loved music, and her father played the piano. When Eugenia was 10 years old, the Hartford Symphony Orchestra performed at her grade school. The orchestra's flutist caught her attention immediately. "It was one of the huge moments in my life," she told Richard Duckett for the Worcester, Massachusetts, *Telegram & Gazette* (January 10, 2002). "I just ran home and said I have to do this." She soon began taking flute lessons. During her senior year at William Hall High School, in West Hartford, she began studying with Julius Baker, the principal flutist of the New York Philharmonic.

After she graduated from high school, Zukerman enrolled at Barnard College, in New York City, where she majored in English and struggled to decide which of her passions, writing or music, she would pursue as a career. "Academics told me you will never be a writer if you play the flute. And the musicologists were saying you have to choose something," she told Linda Lehrer for the *Chicago Tribune* (February 13, 1994). Julius Baker, however, encouraged her to study both music and writing; she could get a job in an orchestra to support herself while writing a novel, he told her. After her sophomore year at Barnard, she transferred to the Juilliard School of Music, also in New York City. At Juilliard, where she earned a bachelor's degree, she became friendly with the violinist and violist Pinchas Zukerman, who won the highly prestigious Leventritt Competition in 1967. The two married in 1968. Eugenia Zukerman spent the next several years accompanying her husband on his concert tours. The couple's two daughters, Arianna and Natalia, were born in 1972 and 1975, respectively.

Earlier, on March 9, 1971, shortly after she won a Young Concert Artists competition, Eugenia Zukerman made her solo concert debut, at New York City's Town Hall. Since then she has performed as a soloist with more than 100 orchestras and other musical ensembles, among them the Royal Philharmonic Orchestra (London); the National Symphony Orchestra (Washington, D.C.); the Los Angeles Philharmonic; the Minnesota Orchestra; the Moscow, Prague, Stuttgart, Slovakian, Israel, Denver, and English Chamber Orchestras; the Shanghai Quartet (China); and the Chamber Music Society of Lincoln Center (New York City). She has also collaborated with many other soloists, among them the cellist Yo-Yo Ma and the pianist Emanuel Ax, and, in a recital, with the actress Claire Bloom. In addition, she has performed at many music festivals, including the Aspen festival, in Colorado; Mostly Mozart (New York City); OKMozart (near Tulsa, Oklahoma); Ravinia (near Chicago, Illinois); Tanglewood (Lenox, Massachusetts); Edinburgh (Scotland); South Bank (London); Spoleto (Italy); Schleswig-Holstein (Germany); Gstaad (Switzerland); and Angel Fire (New Mexico).

Zukerman has recorded more than 20 albums, among them *Music for a Sunday Morning* (1995) and *ChinaSong* (2002, both with the Shanghai Quartet), *Incantation* (1996), *Mozart: Flute Concertos, Clarinet Concerto* (1996, with the English Chamber Orchestra), *Aria* (1997, with the oboist Allan Vogel and the pianist Dennis Helmrich), and *Lowell Liebermann: Symphony No. 2, Concerto for Flute & Orchestra* (2000, with the Dallas Symphony Orchestra). She has also contributed to various albums, among them *CBS Masterworks Dinner Classics: Sunday Brunch, Volume II* (1991, with the English Chamber Orchestra), *For the Friends of Alec Wilder* (1994, with the Manhattan Chamber Orchestra), *The Essential Classics Collection* (1997), *Engineer's Choice II* (1997), *Music of Alan Hovhaness* (2000), and many compilations of music for children, among them *Heigh-ho! Mozart: Favorite Disney Tunes in the Style of Great Classical Composers* (1995), *Bibbidi! Bobbidi! Bach: More Favorite Disney Tunes* (1996), *Baby Needs Mozart* (1998), *Baby Needs Baroque* (1998), *Baby Needs Bach* (1999), *Baby Needs More Mozart* (1999), and *Baby Needs Music* (2002).

In a review of *Time Pieces* (1991), for which Zukerman and the harpsichordist Anthony Newman played works by Haydn, Mozart, Hemmel, and Kuhlau, Joseph McLellan wrote for the *Washington Post* (March 17, 1991), "*Time Pieces* is a meeting of minds between two strong musical personalities who do not know how to play a phrase routinely." After attending a performance of Christopher Rouse's Flute Concerto by Zukerman and the Colorado Symphony Orchestra, Kyle MacMillan wrote for the *Denver Post* (May 20, 2001), as quoted on Zukerman's Web site, "Zukerman was quite simply superb throughout. The flutist capably handled all of the many technical challenges, from the twists and jolts of the fourth movement to

the minute phrasings necessary in the first, and she did it with a warm, inviting and enveloping tone. But what was more important was the result: a subtle, sensitive and expressive interpretation that revealed the heart and soul of this deeply moving music and made it achingly and movingly vivid." Martha Erwin, reviewing a concert by Zukerman and the harpist Yolanda Kondonassis for the *Richmond [Virginia] Times Dispatch* (October 3, 2002), was impressed by the pair's rendering of Hovhaness's "The Garden of Adonis" and Persichetti's Serenade No. 10. Of the former, Erwin wrote, "Zukerman's flute, sounding a trifle more breathy than usual for this veteran, weaved skillfully through the difficult intervals and echoed the composer's fondness for the music of India and Japan by minimizing the vibrato." Commenting on the latter piece, she wrote, "The scherzando, typically a high-energy movement, pushed the flutist into the extremes of high and low range. Both performers were up to these challenges, and the final movement—marked vivo—was fast, furious, and expressive. . . . The flutist needs the diaphragm of a long-distance swimmer, and Zukerman sustains long melodic lines with never a gasp."

Zukerman spent three and a half years, during breaks in her performance schedule, writing her first novel, *Deceptive Cadence* (1981). The story is about a Hungarian pianist who disappears before a major concert. In a review for the *New York Times* (December 28, 1980), Alan Cheuse described *Deceptive Cadence* as an "admirable and entertaining first novel" and "a pleasure to read." Zukerman's second novel, *Taking the Heat* (1991), focuses on a flutist who leaves her husband to play chamber music near Auschwitz, Poland, the site of an infamous World War II concentration camp. Joseph McLellan wrote that *Taking the Heat* is "a superbly crafted story of suburban family life, adultery, guilt and retribution, peopled with vividly realized characters and weaving music . . . deftly into its fabric." Jack Sullivan, who assessed *Taking the Heat* for the *Washington Post* (March 22, 1991), praised Zukerman's dramatic depiction, in "vivid fictional scenarios," of the "intimate, authoritatively sketched details of a musician's life—the womanizing conductor, the guerrilla warfare of competitive players, the incredible adrenaline level required for a successful performance." Sullivan complained, however, that Zukerman's "characters often exist not as people but as didactic mouthpieces. . . . Other musician-writers, from E.T.A. Hoffman to Anthony Burgess, have found ways to fuse musical prose with musical form. Here one simply wants to put down this oddly unmusical book and put on one of the author's wonderful recordings."

For her nonfiction book *In My Mother's Closet: An Invitation to Remember* (2003), Zukerman interviewed 42 women, among them her mother and daughters; the actresses Carrie Fisher, Claire Bloom, and Mary-Louise Parker; the singers Judy Collins and Renee Fleming; Joy Behar of the ABC daytime talk show *The View*; and the writer Erica Jong. Colette Bancroft, in a review for the *St. Petersburg [Florida] Times* (May 10, 2003), found the book to be "an affecting and sometimes surprising look at the infinite variety of ways that mothers can be role models for their daughters. From thrifty homemakers who sewed their own clothes . . . to a movie star whose massive closet includes the 'Shrine of the Wigs,' their closets tell their stories."

In her third career, as a television journalist, Zukerman has served since 1980 as the arts correspondent for the CBS show *Sunday Morning*, reporting on theater, music, the visual arts, and film by interviewing noteworthy professionals in those fields. (She had neither seen the program nor had any experience in television journalism before Shad Northshield, one of *Sunday Morning*'s cocreators, recruited her.) She told Linda Lehrer that the program "brings people into live performance in a way I don't think any other [network news] show does." Zukerman was nominated for an Emmy Award for her piece on the violinist Itzhak Perlman (whom she has known personally for many years) and received the New York Foundation for the Arts' Champions of the Arts award for her work on *Sunday Morning*. In addition, she has written articles for *Vogue*, the *New York Times*, the *Washington Post*, and *Esquire* and has sold screenplays to three major Hollywood studios.

In 1995 Zukerman was diagnosed with eosinophilic pneumonitis, a rare, occasionally fatal lung disease. Prednisone, the drug she took to combat her illness (which is now in remission), led to side effects—bone loss, mood swings, and panic attacks—that to her seemed almost as difficult to bear as the symptoms of the disease. *Coping with Prednisone* (1997), which she wrote with her sister Julie Ingelfinger, describes her experiences during her illness and with the drug. "With her sister . . . Zukerman has written an empathetic, easy-to-understand, and factually accurate guide that offers suggestions, recipes, and exercises for relieving the drug's unpleasantness," Margaret Norden wrote in a review for *Library Journal* (July 1, 1997). "I feel lucky to be alive but I feel urgently that I have things to do," Zukerman told Richard Duckett.

Zukerman, who currently gives from 40 to 60 concerts a year, has been the artistic director of the six-week Bravo! Vail Valley Music Festival, in Colorado, since 1998. Since her arrival the Dallas Symphony Orchestra, the Rochester Philharmonic, and the Colorado Symphony, among other groups, have served as orchestras in residence. The violinists Pamela Frank and Nadja Salerno-Sonnenberg, the pianists Andre Watts and Garrick Ohlsson, the Shanghai Quartet, and the ensemble eighth blackbird have performed at the festival in recent years. During her travels Zukerman often visits schools to talk about music and a life in music, hoping to inspire young students to pursue careers in the arts. "I'm a real champion of outreach programs, being a musician [myself] because of an outreach pro-

gram," she told Lehrer. "I remember the feeling of that day, hearing the sound of the flute—which was completely magical—and being transformed. And you have to say to yourself if that happened to me it can happen to other children. I want to make that possible for them."

Zukerman also hopes to change how children and others perceive classical music. "People look at classical music as a dinosaur," she told Lehrer. "Well, dinosaurs became extinct because they failed to adapt to a change in climate. I think it is possible to adapt to a change in the climate in America without compromising the arts." Zukerman believes that because American society has become so visually oriented, she and her colleagues must find new ways to draw audiences and make them want to return. In her own concerts, she often talks about the pieces on her program. "As a flute player, lots of the music I play is not well known. So I find myself . . . giving historical context to the music, and information about the composer," she told Elizabeth Murfee for the *Carnegie Hall Stagebill* (October 1993). "There has been a change in the way concerts are presented today. The concert hall is no longer a 'temple of art' with the audience playing the role of worshiping acolytes. The atmosphere is friendlier, more relaxed. You can see it in the clothing of the audience and even the performers. Talking to the audience is an outgrowth of this."

Zukerman's marriage to Pinchas Zukerman ended in divorce in 1983. In 1988 she married the film writer and director David Seltzer, whose screenwriting credits include *The Omen* and *My Giant*. The couple have homes in Venice, California, and New York City. Zukerman's older daughter, Arianna Zukerman, is a professional soprano who performs regularly with her mother. Her younger daughter, Natalia Zukerman, is a professional guitarist and singer-songwriter. In her free time Eugenia Zukerman enjoys the outdoors, especially hiking on mountain trails. "I feel, as [do] many women my age, that I want to age gracefully," she told Lehrer. "I want to be one of those great old ladies. I want to have young friends, to be able to be supportive of my kids and other kids and play the flute until I can't breathe anymore."

—K.E.D.

Suggested Reading: *Chicago Tribune* VI p8 Feb. 13, 1994, with photo; *New York Times* XIV p11 Oct. 18, 1998, with photo; *People* p213 Sep. 15, 1997, with photo; (Worcester, Massachusetts) *Telegram & Gazette* C p1 Jan. 10, 2002, with photo

Selected Recordings: *Time Pieces*, 1991; *CBS Masterworks Dinner Classics: Sunday Brunch, Volume II*, 1991; *For the Friends of Alec Wilder*, 1994; *Music for a Sunday Morning*, 1995; *Heigh-ho! Mozart: Favorite Disney Tunes in the Style of Great Classical Composers*, 1995; *Bibbidi! Bobbidi! Bach: More Favorite Disney Tunes*,

1996; *Incantation*, 1996; *Mozart: Flute Concertos, Clarinet Concerto*, 1996; *Aria*, 1997; *The Essential Classics Collection*, 1997; *Engineer's Choice II*, 1997; *Baby Needs Mozart*, 1998; *Baby Needs Baroque*, 1998; *Baby Needs Bach*, 1999; *Baby Needs More Mozart*, 1999; *Music of Alan Hovhaness*, 2000; *Lowell Liebermann, Symphony No. 2, Concerto for Flute & Orchestra*, 2000; *ChinaSong*, 2002; *Baby Needs Music*, 2002

Selected Television Shows: *Sunday Morning*, 1980–

Selected Books: fiction—*Deceptive Cadence*, 1981; *Taking the Heat*, 1991; nonfiction—*Coping with Prednisone*, 1997; *In My Mother's Closet: An Invitation to Remember*, 2003

Obituaries

Written by Kieran Dugan

ABELSON, PHILIP H. Apr. 27, 1913–Aug. 1, 2004 Scientist; a wide-ranging researcher and administrator of research in physical chemistry; held a B.S. degree in chemistry, an M.S. degree in physics, and a doctorate in nuclear physics; with Edwin M. McMillan of the Lawrence Radiation Laboratory at the University of California, Berkeley, discovered the radioactive element neptunium, which became chemical element 93 in the periodic table in 1940; with John I. Hoover at the Naval Research Laboratory in Washington, D.C., during World War II, developed the liquid thermal diffusion process for the separation of uranium isotopes, which greatly reduced the time needed to produce the atomic bomb; prepared the first blueprints for a nuclear-powered submarine; meanwhile, had joined the staff of the Carnegie Institution of Washington (D.C.) in 1939; at that institution in the years from 1946 to 1953, directed research in which radioactive isotopes were used to trace the chemical processes of life in microorganisms; was president of the institution from 1971 to 1978; edited the journal *Science*, published weekly by the American Association for the Advancement of Science, from 1962 to 1982; died in Bethesda, Maryland. See *Current Biography* (October) 1965.

Obituary *New York Times* p34 Aug. 8, 2004

ADAMS, BROCK Jan. 13, 1927–Sep. 10, 2004 U.S. congressman; senator; government official; a liberal Democrat who served as secretary of transportation for two years in the Cabinet of President Jimmy Carter; ended his brilliant, long career under a cloud of scandal; was born in Georgia and grew up in Iowa, Oregon, and Washington State; after service in the U.S. Navy, earned a B.A. degree in economics at the University of Washington and a J.D. degree at Harvard Law School; subsequently, worked with Seattle, Washington, law firms, including one that he cofounded; in 1960, managed John F. Kennedy's presidential campaign in western Washington State; when Kennedy took office, in 1961, was appointed U.S. attorney for the western district of Washington State; in 1964, was elected to the U.S. House of Representatives from Washington's Seventh Congressional District; was reelected in 1966, 1968, 1970, and 1972; in Congress, supported President Lyndon B. Johnson's Great Society programs while turning against Johnson's policy in Vietnam; played a leading role in the creation of the House Budget Committee, whose first chairman he became; drafted successful home-rule legislation for the District of Columbia; emerged as a congressional expert on transportation matters; was a chief sponsor of the Airport and Airways Development Act of 1970 and the Rail Passenger Service Act of 1970, which established Amtrak; was also principally responsible for the Regional Rail Reorganization Act of 1973 and a 1975 extension of that act; resigned from the House to accept appointment as President Carter's secretary of transportation, effective January 1977; in that position, sought to transform a national "every-industry-for-itself transportation system" into an "interlocking network," as he put it; with the aim of reducing the use of energy, vigorously pursued initiatives in mass transit and greater automobile fuel efficiency; also endorsed such non–mass-transit projects as the Westway project replacing Manhattan's then decrepit West Side Highway and the construction of six-lane highways in the District of Columbia as well as New York City; led the effort that resulted in mandatory installation of air bags in private automobiles; disagreed with the Carter administration on some issues; urged the administration to pursue its stated aim of transit deregulation with caution, especially in the airline industry; proposed improved screening for potential hijackers at airports; was credited with opening the U.S. Coast Guard to female cadets; in 1979, approved the federal bailout of the Chrysler Corp.; later in the same year, resigned from the Cabinet; practiced law in the District of Columbia until 1986, when he was elected to the U.S. Senate; in the Senate, was a leader of the liberal opposition to much of the legislative agenda of Republican presidents Ronald Reagan and George H. W. Bush; voted against aid to the Contras in Nicaragua and the military in El Salvador; was instrumental in forcing President George H. W. Bush to seek "explicit authorization" from Congress for U.S. entry into the Gulf War; championed women's health programs, abortion rights, and increased funding for AIDS and cancer research; worked to protect old-growth forests against depredation by logging companies; opposed creation of a nuclear-waste depository at the Hanford (Washington) Nuclear Reservation; following the Exxon Valdez oil spill in Alaska, introduced and pushed to passage a legislative amendment requiring double hulls on oil cargo ships; began to labor under a cloud of scandal in 1987, when Kari Tupper, a young Senate committee aide who was the daughter of old friends of his, filed charges of sexual aggression against him; decided not to seek reelection to the Senate in March 1992, shortly after the *Seattle Times* revealed that it had sworn statements from seven women in addition to Tupper—all Democrats and all former employees or political associates of his—who, while preferring anonymity, affirmed that they would if necessary testify in court that he had committed against them acts of sexual misconduct ranging from inappropriate touching to outright rape (in some cases after he had allegedly drugged them); died at his home in Stevensville, Maryland; was survived by his wife, Mary Elizabeth Adams, four children, and seven grandchildren. See *Current Biography* (July) 1977.

Obituary *New York Times* B p8 Sep. 11, 2004

ALIYEV, HEYDAR May 10, 1923(?)–Dec. 12, 2003
President (1993–2003) of the predominantly Muslim
Republic of Azerbaijan, which was part of the Union
of Soviet Socialist Republics from 1922 to 1991,
when it became an independent nation upon the dissolution of the USSR; was a nominally democratic
authoritarian whose foreign policy was friendly to
the West; succeeded in attracting multinational companies to invest heavily in the exploration and development of his country's vast oil and gas reserves;
promoted the billion-dollar project to build an oil
pipeline from Baku, Azerbaijan's capital, to Ceyhan
in Turkey via the republic of Georgia; siding with the
U.S. and Britain in the war against international terrorism, in August 2003 contributed 150 Azeri soldiers to the coalition forces in the war in Iraq; domestically, making the most of a losing situation, kept violence in Azerbaijan's rebellious enclave of Na-
gorno-Karabakh (populated predominantly by Christian ethnic Armenians) to a minimum by enforcing
a ceasefire in the hostilities there; beginning in the
1940s, rose through the ranks of the Soviet secret po-
lice/military counterintelligence system; in 1969,
was elevated to the position of first secretary of the
Communist Party in Azerbaijan by Leonid I. Brezhnev, the general secretary of the Soviet Communist
Party; following the death of Brezhnev, in 1982, became a full member of the Soviet Politburo at the invitation of Brezhnev's successor, Yuri Andropov,
former head of the KGB, the Soviet secret po-
lice/intelligence agency; after the death of Andropov
(in 1984) and of his successor, Konstantin Ch-
ernenko (in 1985), fell from grace in the era of per-
estroika (restructuring) and glasnost (openness) introduced by the reformist Soviet Communist Party
secretary general and Soviet president Mikhail
Gorbachev; in 1987, was forced to resign his membership in the Politburo; in 1990, was elected a deputy in the Azerbaijani legislature; in 1991, was appointed chairman of the Supreme Majlis (Council) of
the semiautonomous state of Nakhchivan, his native
region; in mid-June 1993, joined the Azeri government of President Abulfez Echibey with the title of
deputy chairman of the Supreme Council of Azerbaijan; within two weeks, on June 30, 1993, when Echibey was forced into exile by Surat Huseynov, the
prime minister and commander of a private militia,
became acting president and chairman of the Supreme Council of Azerbaijan as part of a deal with
Huseynov (who would hold the office of prime minister until he himself would flee the country after an
unsuccessful coup attempt by his supporters in
1994); claimed popular endorsement of his presidency with 98.8 percent of the vote in an election
fraught with irregularities in October 1993; in another questionable election, received 77 percent of the
vote in 1998; remained president until October 2003,
when his son, Ilham Aliyev, was elected to succeed
him; died in a clinic in Cleveland, Ohio, where he
was being treated for congestive heart failure. See
Current Biography (September) 1999.

Obituary *New York Times* A p17 Dec. 13, 2003

ANDERSON, ROY Dec. 15, 1920–Oct. 18, 2003
Chairman emeritus and former chief executive officer of the Lockheed Corp., which merged with the

Martin Marietta Corp. to form the Lockheed Martin
Corp. in 1996; in the late 1970s and early 1980s, stea-
died a Lockheed Corp. weakened by mismanagement and shaken by near-fatal financial and ethical
crises, returned it to a solid position among aerospace companies and credit standing with investors,
and steered it on its way back to the top of the de-
fense-contractor industry; earned a B.A. degree in
economics at Stanford University and an M.B.A. degree at the Stanford School of Business; served in the
U.S. Navy in World War II and the Korean War; began his corporate career in positions with the Westinghouse Electric Corp. and the Ampex Instrumentation Products Co., successively, in the early 1950s;
joined the Lockheed Aircraft Corp., as it was then
known, as a staff accountant with the corporation's
subsidiary Lockheed Missile & Space Co. in 1956;
advanced to the posts of assistant director of financial operations and director of financial and management controls in the subsidiary's space-systems division; in 1965, transferred to the Lockheed-Georgia
Co., where he was director of finance until his appointment as treasurer of the Lockheed Aircraft
Corp. in 1968; became vice president and controller
of the corporation in 1969 and senior vice president
for finance and a member of the board of directors in
1971; four years later, was promoted to vice chairman of the board and chief financial and administrative officer; in 1977, made his first appearance as
board chairman and chief executive officer at a
stockholders' meeting at which the corporation's
name was changed to Lockheed Corp. and also at
which the stockholders were informed, for the ninth
year in a row, that they would receive no dividends
(a condition imposed by the 24 banks to which Lockheed was in debt); took the helm of a corporation that
had been weakened by such financial factors as cost
overruns on the C-5A Galaxy military transport
plane and the L-1011 TriStar commercial jetliner
and by a bribery scandal (the disclosure that Lockheed had been making under-the-counter payoffs to-
talling $38,000,000 to government officials in more
than a dozen foreign countries); immediately instituted new ethical standards in Lockheed's business
practices; stopped production of the L-1011 and took
Lockheed out of competition in the commercial-
jetliner field; concentrated on the corporation's
forte, defense contracts, including those for navy
submarine-launched missile and air-force transport,
antisubmarine, and cargo planes; expanded its missiles and space subsidiary in prescient anticipation
of demands by the administration of President Ronald Reagan for military applications of space technology; succeeded in retiring a loan guarantee Lockheed had been driven to negotiate with the federal
government in order to avoid bankruptcy; made it
possible for Lockheed to obtain credit in the private
sector once again and to report sustained growth in
profits; resumed the payment of dividends to stockholders; retired as CEO in 1985 and as a member of
the board of directors in 1990; died at his home in
greater Los Angeles, California. See *Current Biography* (August) 1983.

Obituary *New York Times* C p15 Oct. 23, 2003

BATES, ALAN Feb. 17, 1934–Dec. 27, 2003 British actor; on stage and screen, immersed himself self-effacingly in a wide range of challenging and often offbeat contemporary and classical roles—"an unforgettable gallery of husbands, fathers, lovers, brothers, friends, heroes and villains, each unique, each alive with the Bates blend of humor, passion, intelligence," as Karen Rappaport observed for the Alan Bates Archive (December 28, 2003, on-line); began his rise to stardom on stage, with his creation in 1956 of the supporting role of Cliff Lewis in the original production of John Osborne's landmark anti-Establishment drama *Look Back in Anger*; made his motion-picture debut as a homebody son of the extroverted has-been vaudevillian Archie Rice (Laurence Olivier) in *The Entertainer* (1960); was subsequently cast as the fugitive murderer mistaken for Jesus Christ redux by a group of children in *Whistle Down the Wind* (1961), the honest bridegroom (opposite June Ritchie) in *A Kind of Loving* (1962), the deranged Mick (a role he had created on the stage) in *The Caretaker* (1964), the social-climbing James Brewster in *Nothing but the Best* (1964), the introverted English intellectual in *Zorba the Greek* (1964), a Scottish soldier in France in *King of Hearts* (1966), and Gabriel Oak in *Far from the Madding Crowd* (1967); received his only Academy Award nomination for his performance as Yakov Bok, the Jewish handyman unjustly imprisoned in Czarist Russia, in *The Fixer* (1968); was cast as the farmer clandestinely in love with an aristocrat (Julie Christie) in *The Go-Between* (1971), which won the Palm d'Or at Cannes; with the exception of the madcap scamp Jos in the seriocomic character drama *Georgy Girl* (1966), was in his screen portrayals "subtle, gentle, watchful, deadpan, and more comic than many people guessed until Butley came along," as the film historian David Thomson has observed; created the role of Ben Butley (a university literature instructor beset with psychological and emotional problems and, in Thomson's words, "teeming with jaundiced eloquence, carrying all before him in tirades of despairing superiority") in the original West End production of Simon Gray's outlandish play *Butley*, directed by Harold Pinter, in 1971; won the Tony Award for best actor for his performance in that role on Broadway during the 1972–73 season; reprised the role in the filmed version of *Butley*, directed by Harold Pinter and released by the American Film Theater in 1974; after studying on a scholarship at the Royal Academy of Dramatic Arts in London and doing two years of National Service as a signalman in the Royal Air Force, made his professional debut as the juvenile lead in *You and Your Wife* with the Midland Theatre Company in Coventry in 1955; joined the English Stage Company at the Royal Court Theatre in London in April 1956; following the sensational success of the company's staging of *Look Back in Anger* in London's West End in 1956, traveled with the production to Moscow in July 1957 and to Broadway the following October; at the Edinburgh Festival in September 1958, was cast as Edmund Tyrone (the younger son, a self-portrait of the author) in Eugene O'Neill's *A Long Day's Journey into Night*, which moved to the Globe Theatre in London the following month; received the Clarence Derwent Award for the best interpretation of a non-

featured role in the 1958–59 West End season; on Broadway during the 1964–65 season, created the title role of the alcoholic, lady-charming Richard Ford in Jean Kerr's *Poor Richard*; in the West End in August 1965, co-starred (as Adam) with Diane Cilento in the brief run of Arnold Wesker's *The Four Seasons*; later starred in London in David Storey's *In Celebration* (1969), *Life Class* (1974), and *Stages* (1992), *Down Cemetery Road*, readings from the poetry of Philip Larkin (1984), the one-man show *Alan Bates: A Muse of Fire* (1988), Thomas Bernhard's *The Showman* (1993), and Simon Gray's *Otherwise Engaged* (1975), *Stage Struck* (1979), *Melon* (1987), and *Life Support* (1997); in 2002, returned to Broadway as Vassily Semyonitch Kuzovkin in a revival of Ivan Turgenev's *Fortune's Fool*, for which he won his second Tony Award, for outstanding actor in a play; on the screen, accrued a total of approximately 50 credits, including a role involving a nude wrestling scene in *Women in Love* (1970), as the father of a severely retarded 10-year-old daughter in *A Day in the Life of Joe Egg* (1972), a writer in midlife crisis in *Story of a Love Story* (1973), the callous manager of a self-destructive female American rock singer in *The Rose* (1979), a closeted middle-aged homosexual in *We Think the World of You* (1988), and the stellar barrister Tom Connolly in *Evelyn* (2002); had numerous credits on television, including leading roles in the made-for-TV movie *The Trespasser* (1981) and the miniseries *The Mayor of Casterbridge* (1978) and the role of Saint Patrick's father in the Fox Family Channel original film *Saint Patrick, The Irish Legend* (2000); in the made-for-TV true-story film *An Englishman Abroad* (1983), gave a masterly performance as the British traitor Guy Burgess living sadly in exile in Moscow; in addition to numerous theatrical roles in classical drama (by such masters as Ibsen, Chekhov, and Strindberg as well as Shakespeare), was cast as Claudius to Mel Gibson's Hamlet in the film *Hamlet* (1990); was appointed a CBE (Commander of the British Empire) in 1995 and knighted in 2003; by his late wife, Victoria Ward, had two sons, the actor Ben Bates and the late Tristan Bates (namesake of the Tristan Bates Theatre at the Actors Centre, Covent Garden, London); died in London, England. See *Current Biography* (March) 1969.

Obituary *New York Times* B p6 Dec. 29, 2003

BECKMAN, ARNOLD O. Apr. 10, 1900–May 18, 2004 Scientist; inventor; entrepreneur; philanthropist; chairman emeritus, the Beckman Coulter Corp., a global leader in the development and manufacture of laboratory systems that have automated—and thus simplified, accelerated, and made more accurate—formerly laborious methods of chemical, biological, and biotechnical analysis, most famously in the fields of life science and clinical diagnosis; held 14 patents for equipment greatly facilitating scientific investigations, some of which have transformed medical research and the practice of clinical medicine; as a young man, worked in electronic technology for two years with Western Electric/Bell Laboratories (1924–26); earned undergraduate and graduate degrees in chemistry at the University of Illinois and a Ph.D. in photochemistry at the California Institute of Technology; taught at Caltech from 1928 to 1939;

in the mid-1930s, invented the pH meter, a device for measuring relative acidity and alkalinity, now an indispensible tool in analytical chemistry and medicine; in 1935, founded National Technical Laboratories (later renamed Beckman Instruments Inc.) and began producing the pH meter for general sale; went on to introduce the DU spectrophotometer, an ultraviolet instrument for determining the chemical composition of a substance through analysis of its light absorption spectrum, a microammeter and quartz-fiber dosimeter used in the development of the first atomic bombs, the Helipot helical potentiometer for radar systems (and later applicable to other electronics, including games), an oxygen monitor for submarines and high-flying aircraft (and later applicable to incubators for premature infants), an ultracentrifuge for breaking down compounds and measuring molecular structures, an apparatus for recording air-polluting gases in the atmosphere, a protein sequencer for separating and identifying amino acids, and a NASA rock smasher, among other scientific instruments; resigned from the presidency of Beckman Instruments in 1965 but remained chairman of the board; was deeply involved in negotiating the temporary merger of the company with the SmithKline Corp. in 1982; became chairman emeritus in 1988, nine years before the company's acquisition of the Coulter Corp., best known for its application of technology to health care, chiefly the study of blood cells; with his wife, in 1977 established the Arnold and Mabel Beckman Foundation, dedicated to supporting scientific research in the fields of chemistry and the life sciences; dispensed hundreds of millions of dollars in grants, scholarships, and funding of five research facilities, including the Beckman Institute at the University of Illinois at Urbana-Champaign and facilities at Caltech and Stanford University; died in San Diego, California. See *Current Biography* (January) 2002.

Obituary *New York Times* A p25 May 20, 2004

BERLITZ, CHARLES Nov. 23, 1913–Dec. 18, 2003 Linguist; author; explorer of geographical and archaeological myths, seemingly paranormal events, and other such mysteries; wrote books on the "lost continent" of Atlantis, Noah's "lost ark," the Bermuda Triangle (an area of the Atlantic Ocean in which, some people believe, ships and planes have inexplicably disappeared), the so-called Roswell Incident (the alleged crash and recovery—by the U.S. Air Force—of an extraterrestrial vehicle and its alien occupants near Roswell, New Mexico in July 1947), and the so-called Philadelphia Experiment (an alleged secret Navy wartime project to render a material object—namely, a warship—invisible, an experiment that, in his account, succeeded only too well, with dire consequences for the ship's crew); as a scion of the founding Berlitz Languages Schools family, was involved in the publishing of Berlitz language texts until the Berlitz organization was bought by the Crowell Collier & Macmillan publishing firm in the mid-1960s; as the only child of Charles and Millicent (Berlitz) Frambach, was born Charles Frambach; changed his name to Frambach-Berlitz at the request of his maternal grandfather, Maximilian D. Berlitz, who had founded the first Berlitz language school in

Providence, Rhode Island, in 1878; dropped the hyphen when he became a counter-intelligence officer with the U.S. Army during World War II; ultimately, dropped "Frambach" altogether; growing up in a multilingual household, spoke four languages by age three; later mastered at least 27 more languages; while majoring in literature and languages at Yale University (where he received his B.A. degree in 1936), taught at the Berlitz school in New York City; later directed several of the Berlitz schools; as a vice president of the Berlitz Schools of Languages (then numbering some 30 in the U.S., with 350 more, under independent ownership, abroad), beginning in 1946, was in charge of the New York–based Berlitz Publications Inc.; in that position, was editor in chief of 47 textbooks, tourist phrase books, and pocket dictionaries, which together sold a total or more than 28,000,000 copies; with Robert Strumpen-Darrie, was credited with the authorship of the *Berlitz World-Wide Phrase Book* (1962); also directed a research bureau, a translation service, and phonograph-record and tape language courses; helped set up language courses for American companies with employees working abroad; published *The Mystery of Atlantis* in 1969 and *Atlantis, the Eighth Continent* in 1984; in collaboration with J. Manson Valentine, wrote *The Bermuda Triangle* (1974), which sold 10 million copies, and its sequel, *Without a Trace* (1977), which included additional testimony of people claiming to have had experiences relating to the alleged Triangle phenomenon; also in collaboration with Valentine, wrote *Doomsday, 1999 A.D.* (1981), an end-of-the-world forecast; collaborated with William L. Moore in the writing of *The Philadelphia Experiment: Project Invisibility* (1979) and *The Roswell Incident* (1988); published *Native Tongues*, an anecdotal etymological excursion through various languages, in 1982; revised Rick and Barbara Carrier's *Dive: The Complete Book of Skin Diving* (1973); revised and updated C. O. Sylvester Mawson's *Dictionary of Foreign Terms* (1979); died in Tamarac, Florida. See *Current Biography* (February) 1957.

Obituary *New York Times* A p17 Dec. 31, 2003

BILLER, MOE Nov. 5, 1915–Sep. 5, 2003 President emeritus, American Postal Workers Union (APWU); an old-fashioned labor leader with a heavy-handed and sometimes abrasive executive style; with his aggressive bargaining, helped to win for postal workers their right to collective bargaining and to a substantial raise in their pay scales and benefits; in 1937, went to work as a substitute clerk at the Knickerbocker postal station in lower Manhattan; almost immediately, became involved in the activities of Local 10 of the old Manhattan-Bronx Postal Union, the forerunner of the New York metropolitan area APWU; rose through the ranks to win election to the presidency of the Manhattan-Bronx Postal Union in 1959; first gained national attention in March 1970, when he led a strike (instigated by the National Association of Letter Carriers) that began in New York City and spread to 30 other cities and involved 200,000 workers across the U.S.; following the reorganization of the U.S. Post Office into the quasi-private U.S. Postal Service and the consolidation of postal workers into the APWU in 1971, became the northeast regional coordinator of the APWU; was elected president of the APWU in 1980 and retained that position until his retirement in 2001; died at his home in Manhattan. See *Current Biography* (June) 1987.

Obituary *New York Times* B p16 Sep. 6, 2003

BOORSTIN, DANIEL J. Oct. 1, 1914–Feb. 28, 2004 Historian; Librarian of Congress emeritus; best-selling and prize-winning author; a polymathic "amateur historian," as he called himself, who, in his words, not having been "trained in the ruts" of the professional historian, naturally "stay[ed] out of them," writing about what "interest[ed him], like packaging, for instance, or broadcasting"; wrote more than a score of books tracing the convergence of strands of social and cultural history, which were translated into some 30 languages and sold millions of copies worldwide; is best known for his trilogies *The Americans* (1958–73) and an intellectual world history consisting of *The Discoverers* (1983), *The Creators* (1992), and *The Seekers* (1995); in *The Image: Or, What Happened to the American Dream* (1961), was prescient in deploring how mass-media technology, in conjunction with corporate and government power and the public-relations industry, was transforming the "language of ideals" into the "language of images"; in that work, was the first to give a name to the "pseudo event," staged to make news, and the first to define the celebrity as a person famous for being famous; predicted our current obsession with celebrity and technology-powered "evanescent" show business in all its manifestations; in one of the essays in his collection *The Decline of Radicalism: Reflections on America Today* (1963), pointed out that "the designer label [on merchandise] is the application of the concept of celebrity to a consumption community"; was firm in his belief that the book remains the "greatest technical advance" in history and is "the antidote to the image" and "the refuge from the flood of trivia"; was descended from immigrant Russian Jews; as an undergraduate in history and English literature at Harvard University, was Phi Beta Kappa and won the Bowdoin Prize for his senior honors essay on Edward Gibbon's *The Decline and Fall of the Roman Empire*, one of the models for his own writing of history; in philosophy, was influenced by William James's pragmatism; subsequently studied law at Oxford University (as a Rhodes scholar) and at the Yale University Law School, where he obtained his doctorate in juridical science; joined a Communist Party cell in 1938 but resigned in disillusionment the following year; was admitted to the Inner Temple bar in London in 1937 and to the Massachusetts state bar in 1942; in the early 1940s, taught American history and literature at Harvard University and history at Swarthmore College; in 1944, joined the faculty of the University of Chicago, where he remained for 25 years, becoming Preston and Sterling Morton Distinguished Service Professor of American History; earned much of the leftist bias against him by his cooperation with the U.S. House of Representatives Un-American Activities Committee in 1953 and by his lashing out against the rampant, sometimes violent, student radicalism of the late 1960s; left the University of Chicago to become director of the National Museum of History and Technology of the Smithsonian Institution in Washington, D.C., in 1969; four years later, moved on to the duties of senior historian of the Smithsonian; when nominated for Librarian of Congress, in 1975, was opposed (unsuccessfully) by the American Library Association, because he was not a professional librarian, and by the Congressional Black Caucus, because of his objection to unmandated implementations (such as minority preferences and quotas) of the Civil Rights Act of 1964 and the related presidential order of 1965, resulting in what he viewed as an undermining of standards; also said that "we Americans are congenitally multicultural" and that "Afrocentrism is a fraud and a denial of our humanist heritage"; after resigning from his post at the Library of Congress, in 1987, was editor at large for Doubleday books; published, among other books, *The Mysterious Science of the Law: An Essay on Blackstone's Commentaries* (1941), *The Genius of American Politics* (1953), *The Lost World of Thomas Jefferson* (1960), collections of essays, including *Hidden History* (1987) and *Cleopatra's Nose: Essays on the Unexpected* (1994), and *The Daniel J. Boorstin Reader* (1995), edited by his wife, Ruth Frankel Boorstin; co-wrote *The Landmark History of the American People* (1987) and the high-school textbook *A History of the United States* (1968); among other awards, won the Pulitzer Prize, for *The Democratic Experience* (1973), the third volume in *The Americans* trilogy; edited the 30-volume *Chicago History of American Civilization*; died in Washington, D.C. See *Current Biography* (January) 1984.

Obituary *New York Times* B p7 Mar. 1, 2004

BRANDO, MARLON Apr. 3, 1924–July 1, 2004 Actor; a neurotic and irreverent rebel with revolutionary talent; with his disdain for calcified convention and his genius for spontaneous and intense naturalistic character invention (a genius often frivolously squandered late in his career), was arguably the most influential American male actor of the 20th century; during his early, brief stint on the stage, electrified Broadway in the late 1940s with his earthy, sexually charged creation of the brutish Stanley Kowalski in the original production of Tennessee Williams's *A Streetcar Named Desire*, directed by Elia Kazan; during a subsequent film career spanning half a century, was nominated for eight Academy Awards, beginning with one for his 1951 screen re-creation of Stanley Kowalski, the "animal id" of which introduced a "new kind of leading man" to the screen, "miles away from the pomaded perfection of the classical Hollywood type," as Dave Kehr observed in *Entertainment Weekly* (July 16, 2004); won two Academy Awards for best actor—the first for his portrayal of Terry Malloy, the simple, heroic longshoreman (and failed boxer) who breaks the code of silence on the New York/New Jersey docks and sparks a rank-and-file rebellion against waterfront labor-union racketeers in Elia Kazan's *On the Waterfront* (1954); the second was for his celebrated interpretation of the Mafia family patriarch Don Vito Corleone in Francis Ford Coppola's film version of Mario Puzo's novel

The Godfather (1972), a comeback achievement for Brando following a string of box-office flops; in keeping with his penchant for speaking out on moral and political issues, refused to accept the second Academy Award in protest of Hollywood's treatment of Native Americans; is regarded as "the unpredictable and truly existential actor of our time" by the young actor Leonardo DiCaprio, who was quoted by Tom Gliatto et al. in People (July 19, 2004): "It is a rite of passage of every young actor to study Marlon Brando's performances in films. At first his films were charged with a sense of brilliant defiance. This eventually changed, mostly through a maniacal restlessness, and he created a series of unpremeditated characters"; in Manhattan beginning in 1943, studied acting—regarded by him as an art of "pretension"—under Erwin Piscator, who recognized his virtually infallible "inner rhythm," and Stella Adler, the preeminent American teacher of the Stanislavian "method," not based on external technique but drawn from the actor's inner resources, including his internalization of his observances of the actions of others; in the spring of 1944, made his professional stage debut in a bit part in Stanley Kauffmann's Bobino; according to Kauffmann, writing in the New Republic (August 2, 2004), even then had a reputation for being "difficult": "Apparently he had in him what Poe called 'the imp of the perverse.' Precisely because [he] was so gifted . . . , he was offhand about acting, bothering to be serious about it only when he actually was performing"; played the adolescent Nels in I Remember Mama on Broadway for two years beginning in October 1944; subsequently, performed on the New York stage in Truckline Cafe, A Flag Is Born, and a revival of George Bernard Shaw's Candida (as Marchbanks); created the role of Stanley Kowalski in the 1947–48 Broadway season; left the cast of A Streetcar Named Desire in the middle of the second year of the play's run; began his movie career in The Men (1950), a pseudo-documentary about hospitalized paraplegic war veterans in which he portrayed with convincing bitterness and anger a wheelchair-bound vet paralyzed from the waist down; was nominated for Oscars for that role, for the title role in Viva Zapata! (1952), and for the role of Marc Antony in Julius Caesar (1953); established a mythic screen presence as Johnny, the leather-jacketed leader of a gang of rampaging motorcyclists in The Wild One (1953); was miscast as Napoleon Bonaparte in Desiree (1954) and Sky Masterson in the musical Gus and Dolls (1955); received his fifth best-actor Oscar nomination as the southern-bred air-force officer involved in an interracial romance in Japan in Sayonara (1957); was cast as a sympathetic Nazi officer disillusioned with the Hitler regime in The Young Lions (1958); directed himself in the quirky Western cult classic One-Eyed Jacks (1961); was cast as Fletcher Christian in Mutiny on the Bounty (1961), as the title character in The Ugly American (1963), as the rich American diplomat entangled in a shipboard romance with a Russian stowaway in A Countess from Hong Kong (1967), and as the latently homosexual Major Pendleton in Reflections in a Golden Eye (1967); drew his seventh nomination for the best-actor Academy Award for his daring performance in his most personal character creation, in large measure a self-

portrait, that of the sad, sexually obsessed, and suicidal middle-aged architect Paul in Last Tango in Paris (1973); after recuperating from that emotionally exhausting performance, returned to the screen as a hired gunman hunting down a horse thief in the savage, silly Western The Missouri Breaks (1976), a tour de force in flippancy; as was widely publicized, was paid millions of dollars for his small roles as Superman's father on the planet Krypton in Superman (1978), the crazed Colonel Kurtz in Apocalypse Now (1979), and Torquemada in Christopher Columbus (1992); was nominated for a supporting-actor Oscar (his final nomination) for his performance as an anti-apartheid South African lawyer in A Dry White Season (1989); gently parodied his Godfather role in the comedy The Freshman (1990); as he aged, became obese and unpredictably eccentric in his performances; plummeted to the nadir of his bizarre late-career bent as the eponymous mad scientist in The Island of Dr. Moreau (1996); made more than 40 motion pictures, including The Teahouse of the August Moon (1956), The Fugitive Kind (1959), Bedtime Story (1964), Morituri (1965), The Chase (1966), The Appaloosa (1966), Candy (1968), The Night of the Following Day (1968), Burn! (1970), The Nightcomers (1972), The Formula (1980), Don Juan de Marco (1995), The Brave (1997), Free Money (1999), and The Score (2001); by a number of women, including three wives, had at least 11 children, including a son Christian and a daughter Cheyenne; was emotionally shattered when Christian in 1991 was convicted of voluntary manslaughter for the fatal shooting of Cheyenne's boyfriend Dag Drollet and again when Cheyenne committed suicide in 1995; when he was 70, decided "to tell the story of my life as best I can, so that my children can separate the truth from the myths that others have created about me"—myths based, he said, on hearsay, often sensationalistic or prurient; with the help of Robert Lindsey, wrote Brando: Songs My Mother Taught Me (1994); lived on and off for many years in Tetiaroa, the sanctuary comprising a string of 13 coral islets that he owned in Tahiti; died in Los Angeles, California. See Current Biography (March) 1974.

Obituary New York Times A p1+ July 3, 2004

BREATHITT, EDWARD T. Nov. 26, 1924–Oct. 14, 2003 Governor of Kentucky (1963–67); a liberal Democrat; joined the law firm of Trimble, Soyars & Breathitt in Hopkinsville, Kentucky, in 1950; was elected to three terms in the Kentucky state legislature during the 1950s; subsequently, as state personnel commissioner, introduced a merit system for state civil-service employees; in November 1963, was elected governor on a platform of prohibiting racial discrimination in public accommodations; in his inaugural speech, on December 10, 1963, made racial harmony a theme, calling on Kentuckians to be "first in their determination to cast away hate, bigotry, and prejudice"; led the promotion of a civil rights law, the first such in the South, enacted in Kentucky in 1966, that went further than federal law at that time in prohibiting racial discrimination in hiring; also successfully promoted improvements in parks, social services, and the establishment of a state vocational-training program and the Kentucky Educational Television Network; after leaving state government, was the Southern Railway System's general counsel and chief lobbyist in Washington, D.C., for 20 years; died in Lexington, Kentucky. See *Current Biography* (July) 1964.

Obituary *New York Times* A p27 Oct. 16, 2003

BRONSON, CHARLES Nov. 3, 1921–Aug. 30, 2003 Motion-picture actor; with his craggy poker face, brawny physique, and rough-hewn and laconic manner, brought to action movies an intractable monolithic presence as powerful in implicit menace as in overt violence; reminded the director John Huston of "a hand grenade with the pin pulled"; was dubbed a "monstre sacré" in France and "Il Bruto" in Italy; unlike some of his cartoonish imitators, often harbored a core of sentimental human concern in his tough-guy characterizations; after being cast in a series of supporting parts, often gangsters and other villains, rose through meatier character roles to such starring portrayals as that of the New York City architect turned urban vigilante in the *Death Wish* feature films; was born Charles Buchinsky to Russian-Lithuanian immigrant parents in the Scooptown neighborhood of the coal-mining town of Ehrenfeld, Pennsylvania; went to work in the mines when he was 16; after military service in World War II, joined Play and Players, an amateur theater troupe in Philadelphia, as a scenery painter; was soon given bit parts in the troupe's productions; in 1949, began taking instruction in speech at the Pasadena (California) Playhouse; was credited as Charles Buchinski in his screen debut, in the bit part of Wacscylewski, a prize-fighting sailor, in *You're in the Navy Now* (1951) and in several subsequent minor parts and as Charles Buchinsky in such supporting roles as Jocko in *House of Wax* (1953), Pinto in *Riding Shotgun* (1954), and Pittsburgh in *Vera Cruz* (1954); was first billed as Charles Bronson in a co-starring role in *Drum Beat* (1954); in that film, set in the era of the Modoc Indian wars in southern Oregon, impressed critics in the role of Kintpuash, a.k.a. Captain Jack, the Modoc chief who rejects the peaceful overtures of a former federal Indian fighter (Alan Ladd); began to attract significant international attention in the title role, that of the Depression-era gangster George Kelly, in Roger Corman's low-budget biopic *Machine-Gun Kelly* (1958); was featured as one of the hired gunslingers in *The Magnificent Seven* (1960), as Flight Lt. Danny Willinski, the "Tunnel King," in *The Great Escape* (1963), and as one of the criminals turned combat soldiers in the World War II hit *The Dirty Dozen* (1967); did not achieve a succès fou until he went to Europe and co-starred with Alain Delon in the British-French production *Adieu, L'Ami* (1968); maintained his huge new international popularity with his starring roles in some half-dozen subsequent films made in France, Italy, or Spain, including the "spaghetti" Western *C'era una volta il West* (1968, *Once Upon a Time in the West*, 1969), the thriller *Le Passager de la pluie* (1969, *Rider on the Rain*, 1970), and those released in English as *Someone Behind the Door* (1971) and *Chato's Land* (1971); scored his first popular success in the U.S. as the Mafia turncoat Joseph Valachi in the fact-based *The Valachi Papers* (1972); in *The Mechanic* (1972),

starred as a professional assassin under contract to the Mafia; in *Death Wish* (1974), created the character Paul Kersey, who dedicates himself to stalking and exterminating New York City street criminals after the murder of his wife and the brutal rape (and reduction to a vegetative state) of his daughter; reprised that role in four *Death Wish* sequels (1981–93); starred as the itinerant prizefighter in *Hard Times* (1975), the bush aviator carrying out a prison escape in *Breakout* (1975), the two-fisted undercover lawman seeking gun runners in the top-notch Western *Breakheart Pass* (1976), the legendary bank robber unable to live up to his own legend in the quirky Western satire *From Noon Til Three* (1976), the Soviet agent in the Cold War thriller *Telefon* (1977), and the police officer hunting down a pimp specializing in child prostitutes in *Kinjite: Forbidden Subjects* (1989); on network television in the 1950s and 1960s, had numerous guest roles in such dramatic series as *Playhouse 90*, *Have Gun Will Travel*, *Alfred Hitchcock Presents*, and *Rawhide*; starred as the adventurous photographer Mike Kovac in the ABC weekly dramatic series *Man with a Camera* (1958–60) and as Commissioner Paul Fein in the made-for-TV films *Family of Cops* (1995) and its two sequels (1997, 1999); was married to the second of his three wives, the actress Jill Ireland (who had principal roles in a number of his films), from 1969 until her death, in 1990; died in Los Angeles, California. See *Current Biography* (March) 1975.

Obituary *New York Times* B p7 Sep. 1, 2003

BROWN, CHARLES L. Aug. 23, 1921–Nov. 12, 2003 Former chairman and chief operating officer of the American Telephone and Telegraph Co. (AT&T), which, with its Bell System, functioned through much of its history as a legally sanctioned, government-regulated monopoly dedicated to universal American phone service; presided over the historic dismantling of the Bell System, which, with some few exceptions, had for decades been the sole provider of phone service across the U.S; first worked for AT&T during the summers of 1939 and 1941, doing construction for its Long Lines department in Cleveland, Ohio; after graduating from the University of Virginia with a degree in electrical engineering in 1943, served with the U.S. Navy in World War II, in the Pacific theater; joined the AT&T Long Lines department in Hartford, Connecticut, as an equipment-maintenance worker in 1948; over the next 15 years, rose through a succession of managerial positions with AT&T; with the Bell System's Illinois Bell Telephone Co., became vice president and general manager in 1963, a director in 1965, and president in 1969; five years later, moved to New York City as executive vice president and chief financial officer of AT&T; in 1976, was promoted to vice chairman of the board of directors; was elected president and chief operating officer of AT&T in 1977; assumed the chairmanship of the board of AT&T in 1979; as chair of what was then the world's largest corporation, had to deal with the U.S. Justice Department's long-running antitrust suit against AT&T; in 1982, made what he termed the "wretchedy difficult" decision to settle the litigation by agreeing to divest the Bell System of its local phone operations while retaining

AT&T's long-distance operations as well as its equipment-manufacturing operations (which would be divested in 1996); signed off on a consent decree that took effect in January 1984, breaking the "Ma Bell" into seven "Baby Bells," later consolidated into the four known today as BellSouth Corp., Qwest Communications International, SBC Corp., and Verizon Communications Inc.; later said of the "traumatic" divestiture that "it was not necessary" and that "if you try to fix something that doesn't need fixing, you don't know what's going to happen, especially when it's done in a hurry"; after overseeing the divestiture, managed the beginning of the largest corporate reorganization in history, the transition from monopoly to competitive force; launched AT&T's ventures into business units and partnerships in Europe and Asia; took mandatory retirement at age 65, in 1986; died in Richmond, Virginia. See *Current Biography* (September) 1981.

Obituary *New York Times* B p9 Nov. 13, 2003

BUNIM, MARY-ELLIS July 9, 1946–Jan. 29, 2004 Television producer; a much-imitated pioneer in the development of television's genre of unscripted "reality" drama, a cross between soap opera and documentary that she aptly described as "voyeuristic TV"; in partnership with Jonathan Murray, created and produced, for broadcast on network and cable television and for syndication, a number of reality series, the first and most successful of which was *The Real World*, in its 15th season on the MTV cable network in 2004–05; in the mid-1960s, when she was studying at Fordham University, was hired by the CBS network as an assistant on the daytime show *Search for Tomorrow*; with that long-running soap opera, was soon promoted to booth promotion director and later became associate producer and executive producer (1976–81); at CBS, also produced the soap *As the World Turns* (1981–84); subsequently, produced the NBC soap *Santa Barbara* (1984–86); with Jonathan Murray, founded Bunim/Murray Productions in 1988; inspired in part by the 12-part 1973 PBS documentary *An American Family* (an ostensibly uncensored look at the day-to-day existence of the Louds, a Santa Barbara, California, family), conceived with Murray the idea of a series that would, in her words, be "the true story of seven strangers, picked to live in a house and have their lives taped, to find out what happens when people stop being polite and start getting real"; on MTV in 1992, launched *The Real World*, consisting of 13 half-hour episodes (edited down from hundreds of hours of tape) of the spied-on lives of seven young people brought together in a Lower Manhattan loft; in subsequent seasons, focused on new groups in new cities, including San Francisco, Las Vegas, and London; in *Road Rules*, a road-trip variation on the same format (which first aired on MTV in 1995), placed young adults in a Winebago recreational vehicle and documented their odysseys across North America and other continents; for the NBC network in 1996, produced *Class Reunion*, which threw classmates from a 10-year high-school reunion into close proximity for several days; from tryouts to first tour, documented the making of the band O-Town by the pop-music impresario Lou Perlman in *Making*

the *Band*, launched on the ABC network in 2000 and circulated to MTV two years later; on the Fox network in 2001, produced *Love Cruise*, a matchmaking and elimination game set on a Caribbean cruise ship in which 16 young singles competed to be the final male and female standing after 15 days of voting; for Fox in the 2003–04 season, created *The Simple Life*, a seven-episode reality sitcom (a recycling of the sitcom *Green Acres*), in which two pampered young city women (Paris Hilton and Nicole Richie) were transplanted onto an Arkansas farm; in the melodramatic reality series *Starting Over* (syndicated by NBC Enterprises beginning in September 2003), focused on six troubled women living together and seeking to change their lives with the help of life coaches; also with Jonathan Murray, produced the motion picture *The Real Cancun* (2003), a visual recording of the uninhibited partying of 16 American college students during a spring break in Mexico, and the fictional made-for-television film *The Real World Movie: The Last Season* (2002), in which a psychotic fan kidnaps the cast of *The Real World*; died in Los Angeles. See *Current Biography* (May) 2002.

Obituary *New York Times* C p13 Feb. 3, 2004

CARNEY, ART Nov. 4, 1919–Nov. 8, 2003 Actor; a nimble character actor honored for dramatic portrayals on radio, television, stage, and screen but best, and most fondly, remembered as half of one of the legendary comic duos in show-business history: Ed Norton, the goofy, happy-go-lucky foil to Jackie Gleason's hot-tempered, blustery Ralph Kramden in the classic TV sitcom *The Honeymooners*, first televised in the 1950s and 1960s and popular in syndicated reruns (especially of the 39 episodes filmed before live audiences with a system called Electronicam in the 1955–56 TV season); possessed natural-born vocal and physical flexibility and a gift for mimicry; won five Emmy Awards as Norton, a sixth for an Art Carney special on NBC in 1960, and a seventh for his supporting role in the CBS made-for-TV movie *Terrible Joe Moran*, in 1984; on Broadway in 1965, created the role of the obsessive fussbudget Felix Unger in the comedy *The Odd Couple*, co-starring Walter Matthau as the cheerful slob Oscar Madison; in 1969, was nominated for a Tony Award on Broadway for his role in *Lovers* (1968); won the Academy Award for best actor for his performance in the wistful and picaresque film *Harry and Tonto* (1974), as a retired schoolteacher who embarks on a cross-country journey with his cat after he is evicted from his apartment; began his career doing impersonations and novelty songs on the road with the Horace Heidt Orchestra (1936–41); on radio, was an announcer and master of ceremonies on *Heidt's Pot O' Gold* musical quiz program; after leaving the Heidt band, performed in vaudeville and nightclubs; beginning with bit parts in late 1942, found increasing employment on radio, with vocal assignments in dramas on *Columbia Workshop*, *Daytime Showcase*, and other series and, on the CBS program *Report to the Nation*, imitations of the voices of Franklin Delano Roosevelt, Winston Churchill, and other Allied leaders; contributed voices to the comedian Fred Allen's show; drafted into the U.S. Army in World War II, was sent to France in July 1944; wounded in the right leg by friendly shrapnel, was left with a permanent limp; after the war, returned to CBS radio and roles on such series as *Suspense* and *Danger*; in June 1948, became second banana (as, at first, the daffy doorman Charlie and, later, the waiter Newton) on *The Morey Amsterdam Show*, a CBS comedy/variety program set in a fictional nightclub; moved with that show to the CBS TV network in December 1948 and then to the DuMont network (also spelled Dumont), April 1949–October 1950; during the golden age of TV drama, had roles in productions on dramatic anthologies, including *Studio One*, *Playhouse 90*, and *Kraft Theatre*, as well as other series, including *The Twilight Zone*; gave an award-winning performance in the children's musical *Art Carney Meets Peter and the Wolf* on the ABC network in 1958; on NBC, was a regular on Henry Morgan's comedy-variety show in 1951; meanwhile, at DuMont in 1950, had become Jackie Gleason's sidekick on the weekly comedy/variety hour *Cavalcade of Stars*; in the show's skit "The Honeymooners," set in a Brooklyn tenement, created the character Ed Norton, a "subterranean sanitation expert" (read "sewer worker"), the extroverted neighbor and pal of Gleason's irascible bus driver Ralph Kramden; in 1952, moved to CBS with *The Jackie Gleason Show* and its sketches, including "The Honeymooners," which was spun off into the half-hour sitcom *The Honeymooners*, the replacement for *The Jackie Gleason Show* during the 1955–56 season; in 1956–57, returned with Gleason to *The Jackie Gleason Show*; between 1966 and 1970, was reunited with him in a new *Jackie Gleason Show* that showcased "The Honeymooners"; gave guest performances on sitcoms and other series; starred as the police chief in the crime show *Lanigan's Rabbi* on ABC in 1976 and '77; acted in made-for-TV movies, among them *Death Scream* (1975), *Izzy and Moe* (1985), and *Where Pigeons Go to Die* (1990); made his Broadway debut in *The Rope Dancers* (1957–58); created the role of Frank Michaelson in the comedy *Take Her, She's Mine* on Broadway in 1961; later accrued stage credits in *Flora*, *The Prisoner of Second Avenue* (as a replacement) and *The Red Menace* (as the voice of Franklin Roosevelt); co-starred as an aging private eye in the feature film *The Late Show* (1979); among many other big-screen roles, appeared in *W.W. and the Dixie Dancekings* (1975), *House Calls* (1978), and *Going in Style* (1979); received an American Comedy Award for lifetime achievement in 1990; was inducted into the Academy of Television Arts and Sciences Hall of Fame in 2003; maintained a home in Westbrook, Connecticut, since 1975; died in a nursing and rehabilitation center in Chester, Connecticut. See *Current Biography* (April) 1958.

Obituary *New York Times* C p13 Nov. 12, 2003

CARTIER-BRESSON, HENRI Aug. 22, 1908–Aug. 3, 2004 French photographer; fine artist; a documentary realist described by Val Williams in the *London Independent* as "a visual poet of the real world"; helped to define photojournalism, although he did not think of himself as a journalist; in the introduction to his 1952 collection of photographs *Images à la Sauvette* ("Pictures on the Run"), published in the

U.S. as *The Decisive Moment*, wrote: "To me, photography is the simultaneous recognition, in a fraction of a second, of the significance of an event as well as of a precise organization of forms which give that event its proper expression"; told Alan Riding for the *New York Times*: "For me, photography is instant drawing. My real obsession is drawing"; elsewhere said: "To photograph is to hold one's breath"; with his vintage Model-G Leica camera, and using only that camera's standard lens, traveled the world capturing on film the faces and figures of ordinary people in "decisive" instants, often in the context of extraordinary events, including the coronation of King George VI of Great Britain in 1937, the Spanish Civil War, Mahatma Gandhi's funeral, China in transition, the Cuban missile crisis in 1962, and the student protests in Paris in 1968; was famous for never cropping any of his photographs; was originally attracted to drawing and painting; as a student artist in Paris in the late 1920s, was greatly influenced by the Cubists (including Georges Braque, who introduced him to Zen Buddhism), and especially the Surrealists, from whom he learned his practice of "wandering," taking seemingly aimless "walks of discovery" (at first through the streets of Paris) in search of serendipity; began experimenting with photography (which he thought of as "a quick way of drawing intuitively") using a Brownie box camera; in Marseilles in 1931, bought his first Leica and "prowled the streets all day, . . . ready to pounce, determined to 'trap' life—to preserve life in the act of living," as he recalled; with his camera, proceeded to travel the world; after spending a year on the Ivory Coast of Africa and traveling throughout Europe, lived for a year in Mexico and visited the U.S.; back in France in the mid-1930s, became an apprentice to the filmmaker Jean Renoir; in 1937, directed his own first motion picture, *Return to Life*, a documentary about medical aid to the Popular Front loyalists in the Spanish Civil War; subsequently, worked alongside the photographers Frank Capa and David Seymour on the French Communist newspaper *Ce Soir*; as a corporal in the French army's film and photographic corps during World War II, was incarcerated in a German prisoner-of-war camp from 1940 to 1943, when he escaped; organized an underground photographic team for the purpose of documenting the German occupation of France; went on to photograph the Allied invasion of France and the subsequent German retreat; for the U.S. Office of War Information, directed *The Return* (1945), a profoundly moving documentary film about the repatriation of French prisoners of war and deportees; in 1947, with Frank Capa, David Seymour, and others, founded Magnum, a photographic agency owned and managed by the photographers themselves; in 1948, left France for the Far East; traveled in India, China, and Indonesia for three years; visited the Soviet Union in the mid-1950s and Cuba in the early 1960s, when he also revisited Mexico; over the years, contributed individual photos as well as photo spreads and essays to such magazines as *Paris-Match*, *Life*, and *Popular Photography*; did portraiture of a wide range of public figures, from Henri Matisse and Albert Camus to Mahatma Gandhi and Marilyn Monroe; for West German television, made a documentary film on Bavaria in 1962; for the CBS network in the U.S., made the documentaries *Impressions of California* (1969) and *Southern Exposure* (1971); in the last decades of his life, returned to his first loves, painting and, especially, figural and landscape drawing; collected his photographs in numerous books, including the retrospectives *The World of Henri Cartier-Bresson* (1968) and *Henri Cartier-Bresson: The Man, the Image & the World* (2003); also published *Line by Line: The Drawings of Henri Cartier-Bresson* (1989) and *Tête à Tête: Portraits by Henri Cartier-Bresson* (1998); died at his home in Lisle-sur-la-Sorgue, France; was survived by his second wife, the photographer Martine Franck, and an adopted daughter, Mélanie. See *Current Biography* (May) 1976 and *Current Biography International Yearbook 2003*.

Obituary *New York Times* A p1+ Aug. 5, 2004

CASH, JOHNNY Feb. 26, 1932–Sep. 12, 2003 Singer; guitarist; composer; a craggy, larger-than-life presence in country music for half a century; one of Nashville's original self-described "outlaws"; a pioneer in bridging the gap between country and pop, including rock music; as "The Man in Black" (the title of one of his signature songs), performed in black clothes, including a tail coat and striped morning pants, a Lincolnesque costume suggestive of a frontier preacher/undertaker; in that grim persona (one authentically rooted in real-life adversity), projected a spiritual and emotional gravitas expressly suited to his brooding songs—which gave stoic voice to the working poor, the downtrodden, the marginalized, the forgotten outcasts, including the imprisoned—as well as his melancholy romantic ballads and guilt-ridden and fatalistic confessional pieces and gospel songs; created his songs without notation, because he could not read music; sang them in a booming, gravelly bass-baritone voice, almost a monotone, to his own choked guitar accompaniment, usually with bass-guitar backup; shared only with Elvis Presley the distinction of induction into both the Country Music and the Rock and Roll Halls of Fame; grew up in Arkansas in a hardscrabble cotton-farming family, recalled in the song "Daddy Sang Bass," written for him by Carl Perkins; upon his discharge from the U.S. Air Force, in 1954, settled in Memphis, Tennessee, with his first wife, Vivian Liberto, with whom he had four daughters, including Rosanne Cash, a singer, songwriter, and short-story writer; in Memphis, began playing rockabilly with the group Johnny Cash and the Tennessee Two; with that group, successfully auditioned for Sam Phillips's Sun Records, in Memphis; in 1955, released a single comprising his songs "Hey, Porter" and "Cry, Cry, Cry," which sold more than 100,000 copies in the South alone; soon afterward, scored nationally with his "Folsom Prison Blues" (with "So Doggoned Lonesome"on the flip side); inserted paper in the sound hole beneath the strings of his guitar to effect a slappy bass sound when, in 1956, he recorded his signature song "I Walk the Line," which sold more than two million copies; reached number one on the country charts with his next single, "There You Go"; recorded "Ballad of a Teenage Queen"/"Big River" in 1957; at Sun Records, recorded his first album, *Johnny Cash and His Hot and Blue Guitar*; while with Sun, wrote "You're My Baby" for Roy Orbison and

"Get Rhythm" for Elvis Presley; in 1958, left Sun and began his 28-year association with Columbia Records; also in 1958, began appearing regularly on Grand Ole Opry, the national country-music radio show originating in Nashville, Tennessee; at the same time, was touring constantly throughout the U.S. and Canada; in 1959, recorded his first album-chart entry, *The Fabulous Johnny Cash*, and the single "Don't Take Your Guns to Town," which sold more than 500,000 copies; in the early and middle 1960s, recorded a string of concept albums, including *Ride This Train* (1960), *Blood, Sweat, and Tears* (1963), and *Bitter Tears: Ballads of the American Indians* (1964); on tour in 1968, performed to a full house in New York's Carnegie Hall and set a new attendance record at London's Palladium; realized one of the greatest hits in his repertoire with "Ring of Fire," written by June Carter (with Merle Kilgore) when she fell in love with Cash; in 1968, following his divorce from Liberto, in 1967, married June Carter, a member of one of country music's legendary dynasties; the following year, recorded *Hello, I'm Johnny Cash*, whose title was his trademark salutation; co-starred in the Western film *A Gunfight* (1972) and played many dramatic roles on television; as host of *The Johnny Cash Show* (ABC, 1969–71; CBS, 1976), an hour-long weekly musical/variety program, was supported by the Carter family, among other regulars; with June Carter Cash, performed and recorded many duets, including two Grammy Award winners, "Jackson" and a cover of Tim Hardin's "If I Were a Carpenter"; for her, wrote "Meet Me in Heaven," a statement of the durability of their love; had his greatest sales with his prison albums, *Johnny Cash at Folsom Prison* (recorded in 1968) and *Live at San Quentin* (produced in 1969); from the latter, had the hit single "A Boy Named Sue," a humorous ditty by Shel Silverstein; recorded *The Man in Black* in 1971; for many years, struggled with an addiction to drugs, chiefly amphetamines; beginning in 1985, toured and recorded as a member of the "supergroup" the Highwaymen, with Willie Nelson, Waylon Jennings, and Kris Kristofferson; in 1986, moved to Mercury Records, which released his album *Boom Chicka Boom* (1989); five years later, signed with American Records; accompanied only by his acoustic guitar, mixed some of his own compositions with covers of folk/pop songs by Tom Waits and others on *American Recordings* (1994), which won a Grammy Award in the contemporary folk album category; on *Unchained* (1996), covered a range of genres from vintage country to alternative rock; covered songs by Tom Petty and Neil Diamond, among others, on *American III: Solitary Man*; in 1999, won the Grammy Legend Award; on *The Man Comes Around* (2002), included songs by, among others, Tom Petty, Elvis Costello, and John Carter Cash (his son by June Carter Cash), who wrote the title song as well as "Give My Love to Rose," for which Johnny Cash won his 11th Grammy, in the best country male vocalist category; won other awards for another cut on the album, Trent Reznor's "Hurt"; according to his Web site, recorded a total of more than 1,500 songs on some 500 albums, including the three CDs in the boxed set *Love God Murder* (Sony/Legacy, 2000), a career compilation, and the five (including *My Mother's Hymn Book*) in the boxed set *Unearthed*

(American/Lost Highway, 2003); collaborated on recordings with Bob Dylan and with Bono and his U2 rock band, among others; had two stepdaughters, Carlene Carter and Rosey Nix Adams, from June Carter Cash's two previous marriages; lived in Hendersonville, Tennessee; died in Nashville, four months after the death of June Carter Cash and six weeks before the death of Rosey Nix Adams. See *Current Biography* (September) 1969.

Obituary *New York Times* A p1+ Sep. 13, 2003

CHARLES, RAY Sep. 23, 1930–June 10, 2004 Singer; pianist; composer; recording artist; a major crossover force in 20th-century popular music; combined the fervor of black gospel with the artistry of improvisational jazz and the passion of the blues; carried his soul-felt sound into every musical genre he chose, including R&B, barrelhouse, country and western, rock and roll, pop, and show tunes; began reaching a wide general audience with one of his own compositions, "I Got a Woman" (1955); went on to create numerous Ray Charles "classics," including his unique transformation of the anthem "America the Beautiful" (1972); won 12 Grammy Awards, including one each for his recordings of "Busted" (1963),"Crying Time" (1966), and "A Song for You" (1993), two for his version of Hoagy Carmichael's "Georgia on My Mind" (1960), others for his covers of "Let the Good Times Roll" (1960), "Hit the Road Jack" (1961), "I Can't Stop Loving You" (1962), and "Living for the City" (1975), another for "I'll Be Good to You" (1990), a duet with Chaka Khan, and a lifetime achievement Grammy (1987); through the 1950s, concentrated on his own compositions; thereafter applied his raspy, rough-edged, often raucous delivery chiefly to interpretations of songs written by others; for decades, toured nationally and internationally with his own bands and with his female backup singers, the Raelettes; when he entered show business, shortened his birth name—Ray Charles Robinson—so as to avoid confusion with the boxer Sugar Ray Robinson; was born out of wedlock in Albany, Georgia; grew up in poverty in Greenville, Florida; was blind from the age of seven; learned to play several instruments and to compose and arrange music in Braille during eight years at the St. Augustine (Florida) School for Deaf and Blind Children; began to perform professionally in black honky-tonks and small clubs in Florida; subsequently, formed a combo with Gossady McGee in Seattle and went on the road with the blues band of Lowell Fulsom as pianist, singer, and arranger; in Los Angeles, formed his own first trio, with which he proceeded to tour what was then known as the "chitlin' circuit"; meanwhile, had begun recording on the black Downbeat and Swingtime labels; with his 1951 single "Kissa Me Baby," had a hit on the "race records" (as rhythm and blues was then known) charts and caught the attention of Ahmet M. Ertegun at Manhattan-based Atlantic Records; until then, had been overly influenced by the urbane piano and singing styles of Charles Brown and, especially, Nat King Cole; at Atlantic Records, moved into his own spirited delivery, gradually at first and fully in the late 1950s in such recordings of his own composition as "Drown in My Own Tears," "Hallelujah, I

Love Her So," "The Nighttime Is the Right Time," and his signature song "What'd I Say?"; later recorded for and/or had his albums and singles released by ABC Records, Columbia Records, Warner Brothers Records, and his own labels, Tangerine and Crossover; included in his large output of albums a number of collaborations with a who's who of blues, jazz, country, rock, and pop artists; with David Ritz, wrote an autobiography, *Brother Ray* (1978); was the subject of a film biography, *Ray* (2004), not yet released at the time of his death; was divorced twice and had many affairs; was the father of nine children (or as many as 12, according to various sources, among them four by his two wives); died at his home in Beverly Hills, California. See *Current Biography* (June 1992).

Obituary *New York Times* A p1+ June 11, 2004

CHIANG MEI-LING Mar. 5, 1898–Oct. 23, 2003 The grande dame of Nationalist Chinese politics; the widow of Generalissimo Chiang Kai-shek, president of the Republic of China on the Chinese mainland and later in exile on the island of Taiwan; was born Mei-ling Soong in Shanghai, China, the younger sister of Ai-ling Soong (Madame H. H. Kung) and Qingling Soong (Madame Sun Yat-sen); with her siblings, including her brother T. V. Soong (who served as finance minister in Chiang Kai-shek's governments), was raised in a Westernized, Christian household, presided over by her father, Charles Jones Soong, a wealthy and influential entrepreneur; in 1908, when she was 10, was sent to the U.S. to study at the Wesleyan College for Women, in Macon, Georgia; after five years there, entered Wellesley College in Wellesley, Massachusetts, where she majored in English literature; after graduating from Wellesley, in 1917, returned to China speaking better English than Chinese (in which language she had to undergo accelerated tutoring); met Chiang Kai-shek in 1922, when he was the military aide to the philosopher/statesman Sun Yat-sen (1867–1925), leader of the Nationalist Party revolution (dedicated to democratic parliamentary government and social reform) that had overthrown China's last emperor, in 1911; married Chiang Kai-shek in 1927, shortly after he had succeeded Sun Yat-sen as leader of the Kuomintang (the official name of the Nationalist Party) and two years before he became president of the Republic of China; as first lady of the republic, instituted the New Life Movement, aimed at ridding China of primitive superstitions, modernizing it in such areas as hygiene and sanitation, and promoting the social virtues of courtesty, service, honesty, and honor; was a close partner to her husband in his governmental decision-making, including his handling of shifting alliances with Chinese warlords; ran the government's propaganda operations; more important, was the Kuomintang's diplomat at large, personifying an attractive "free China" in the world arena; began lobbying in the U.S. for support of the Kuomintang in the 1930s; in 1943, barnstormed the U.S., giving electrifying speeches (including one before a joint session of the U.S. Congress); succeeded in garnering hundreds of millions of dollars in aid for the Chinese Nationalists in their war with the Japanese; during that war, was instrumental in building up the Nationalist air force and hiring Claire Chennault to form and lead the group of mercenary aviators known as the Flying Tigers; after World War II, again traveled to the U.S. to seek support for the Nationalist forces in their civil war with Mao Zedong's Communist army; when Chiang Kai-shek was forced to concede victory to the Communists, in January 1949, retreated with him—along with two million Kuomintang supporters—to the island of Taiwan; helped Chiang Kai-shek establish Taiwan as the seat of the Republic of China (recognized by the U.S. until 1978, when Washington switched recognition to the People's Republic of China on the mainland); moved to the U.S. in 1975, after Chiang Kai-shek died and was succeeded in the presidency of the Taiwan government by his son from a previous marriage, Chiang Ching-kuo, with whom Madame Chiang had a less than congenial relationship; maintained two residences, an apartment in Manhattan and a mansion on Long Island; died in Manhattan. See *Current Biography* (May) 1940.

Obituary *New York Times* A p15 Oct. 25, 2003

CHILD, JULIA Aug. 15, 1912–Aug. 13, 2004 Master chef and teacher of cookery; a television personality with a comic sense of theater; as the spirited and jolly "French Chef," entertainingly demystified French home cooking for U.S. public television audiences; was introduced to gastronomy by her husband, Paul Child, a cosmopolite whom she met when both were working for the Office of Strategic Services, the predecessor of the Central Intelligence Agency, during World War II; moved to France with her husband in 1948, when he was assigned to the American Embassy in Paris by the U.S. Information Agency; in Paris, studied at the Cordon Bleu, the world-renowned cooking school, and under the master chef Max Bugnard; at the invitation of Simone Beck, became a member of Le Cercle des Gourmettes, where she met Louisette Bertholle; with the two French women, started a cooking school, L'École des Trois Gourmandes, and wrote the acclaimed best-seller *Mastering the Art of French Cooking* (1961); after several changes of residence (when her husband was posted to Marseilles, Bonn, and Oslo), returned to the U.S.; following her husband's retirement, in 1961, bought with him a house in Cambridge, Massachusetts; also maintained homes in Santa Barbara, California, and in Grasse, in southern France; after three pilot programs, launched the half-hour *The French Chef* on Boston station WGBH-TV in February 1963; within four years, was being seen weekly on more than 100 National Education Television affiliates; later moved to the PBS network; did 119 programs in black and white between 1963 and 1966 and 90 in color between 1970 and 1973; later hosted such series as *Julia Child & Company, Dinner at Julia's, Baking with Julia*, and *In Julia's Kitchen with Master Chefs*; with the bakery chef Jacques Pepin, presented the series *Julia and Jacques*; wrote or co-wrote 17 books, including the second volume of *Mastering the Art of French Cooking* (1970), *The French Chef Cookbook* (1968), and *Julia's Kitchen Wisdom* (2000); lived full-time in Santa Barbara after the death of her husband; died in Santa Barbara. See *Current Biography* (February) 1967.

Obituary *New York Times* A p1+ Aug. 14, 2004

CONABLE, BARBER B. Nov. 2, 1922–Nov. 30, 2003 U.S. Congressman (1965–85); president of the International Bank for Reconstruction and Development, commonly known as the World Bank (1986–91), which lends billions of dollars annually to developing countries; in domestic politics, was a Republican who regarded himself as a conservative in the tradition of Edmund Burke; according to the Washington journalists Bob Woodward and Carl Bernstein, "was regarded by his colleagues as almost puritanical in his standards of personal and political conduct, a man of unquestioned integrity"; in his fund-raising as a congressional candidate, refused to accept more than $50 from any political action comittee (PAC) or private donor and any honorarium of more than $500; successfully directed the World Bank (where the president is traditionally American because the U.S. is its major lender) through a tumultuous period of defaults and reorganization; held degrees in medieval history and law from Cornell University; served with the U.S. Marines in World War II (in combat in the Pacific) and in the Korean War; practiced law in Buffalo and Batavia, New York; after serving in the New York State Senate for two years, was elected in November 1964 to a two-year term in the U.S. House of Representatives from New York's 37th Congressional District (which would subsequently be reapportioned into, first, the 35th and then the 30th), a largely rural, conservative constituency in western New York; went on to win reelection nine times; was chairman of the House Republican Policy Committee (1973–76) and a member of the powerful House Ways and Means Committee (1967–85); was the ranking minority Ways and Means member during his last eight years in Congress; also sat on the Joint Ethics, Budget, Taxation, and Economic committees; supported the American war in Vietnam, major defense spending, prayer in public schools, and campaign-finance reform; opposed establishment of a consumer-protecton agency and funding for public television; because of his support for the Equal Rights Amendment and federal assistance for family planning and his moderate stance on other "cultural" issues, was denied the endorsement of the small New York Conservative Party, which often shifted its support behind Republican candidates; within the Ways and Means Committee, was the prime mover for passage in 1972 of the State and Local Fiscal Assistance Act, a revenue-sharing bill originally opposed by Republican as well as Democratic leaders; during the 1970s, devoted much of his energy to supporting measures for tax reduction and amelioration, including greater depreciation allowances for businesses; following Ronald Reagan's assumption of the presidency, in 1981, helped guide through Congress the legislative agenda of the Reagan administration, including the Economic Recovery Act of 1981; as a member of the Social Security Advisory Commission formed by Reagan, warned of a possible future "generational war," a rebellion of young payroll-tax payers against a system likely to run out of funds before their retirement; chose not to run for reelection to Congress in 1984; after a year in retirement, was named by Reagan to head the World Bank; took the bank's helm at a time when it was over-bureaucratized and when much of the Third World was in a debt crisis and being abandoned by the commercial banks; proceeded to restructure the bank, to move into the banking breach, and to reverse the international debt relationship; made the bank more market-oriented; turned its lending increasingly away from such projects as sports arenas and palaces and office buildings for ruling elites and in the direction of the bank's original mission, the promotion of global economic development and relief of poverty; with his clout on Capitol Hill, was able to lobby Congress to join other lending nations in nearly doubling the bank's available capital, to a total of $171 billion; sat on a number of corporate boards and public panels, including a U.S. Securities and Exchange Commission advisory committee; with his wife, maintained a permanent home in Alexander, New York; died at their winter home in Sarasota, Florida. See *Current Biography* (July) 1984.

Obituary *New York Times* B p8 Dec. 2, 2003

COOKE, ALISTAIR Nov. 20, 1908–Mar. 30, 2004 British-born, New York–based journalist; broadcaster; interpreted the American experience to audiences on both sides of the Atlantic with urbanity and wit for 66 years; was, as Leonard Miall observed in the London *Independent*, "a graceful essayist of the air"; having "perfected his broadcasting technique in the heyday of the scripted talk," was, in Miall's words, a master of "the art of colloquial writing and informal delivery that concealed the art of reading"; at Cambridge University, studied English and co-founded the campus Mummers drama troupe; began writing theater criticism as an undergraduate; on a Commonwealth Fund fellowship (1932–34), traveled in the U.S. and studied at the Yale School of Drama and Harvard University; back in England, was film critic with the British Broadcasting Co. (1934–37); during that period, also began delivering radio reports on topical events, some of which were relayed to the National Broadcasting Co. in the U.S.; in 1937, took up permanent residence in the U.S.; became an American citizen in 1941; began commenting on U.S. affairs for the BBC in 1938; initiated his weekly BBC radio program *Letter from America* in 1946; meanwhile, had been contributing to several major British newspapers; for the *Manchester* (now London) *Guardian*, was U.N. correspondent (1945–48) and chief American correspondent (1948–72); from 1952 to 1961, was master of ceremonies of the weekly program *Omnibus*, one of the most respected cultural series in the history of American network TV, a popular high-brow magazine of the arts offering classical and contemporary drama, musicals, and documentaries; in the 1950s and 1960s, was M.C. of *International Zone*, an informational series produced by United Nations Television; traveled 100,000 miles to historical U.S. sites as host and narrator of the BBC-produced, NBC-imported 13-episode TV documentary series *America: A Personal History of the United States* (1972–73), which won four Emmy Awards; on public TV, was the first and longest-serving host (1971–92) of *Masterpiece Theatre*, an anthology of serialized British TV dramas, including original miniseries and series adapted from literary works; continued his weekly *Letter from America* radio broadcasts until February 20, 2004, when he delivered his 2,869th dispatch for the BBC; published a score of books, including *Around the World in Fifty Years: A Political Travelogue* (1966), *Alistair Cooke's America* (1973), *The American in England* (1975), the collection of biographies *Six Men* (1977), *The Americans* (1979), *America Observed* (1988), *The Vintage Mencken* (1990), and *Memories of the Great & the Good* (1999); in 1973, was named an honorary Knight Commander, Order of the British Empire; died at his home in Manhattan. See *Current Biography* (May) 1974.

Obituary *New York Times* C p12 Mar. 31, 2004

CORELLI, FRANCO Apr. 8, 1921–Oct. 29, 2003 Italian opera singer; "the Apollo of bel canto"; was ranked by the Austrian conductor Herbert von Karajan as "the most viscerally thrilling and handsome" *tenore di forza* (tenor who can sing both lyrically and powerfully) of the post–World War II era; possessed a strong and vibrant tenor voice with trumpet-like timbre, brilliant tone, and a ringing and extraordinarily sustained middle and upper registers; breaking from the mold of tenorial obesity, graced the lyric stage with a strapping macho presence in response to which, as the obituary writer for the *Economist* observed, "for once, the raptures of a Mimi or a Violetta made sense"; belying that presence, suffered from career-long stage fright, which he overcame, performance by performance, with the hectoring assistance of his wife and manager, the singer Loretta Di Lelio; aside from three counterproductive months at the Pesaro (Italy) Conservatory, was self-taught, chiefly by listening to recordings of such great tenors as Enrico Caruso, Beniamino Gigli, and Giacomo Lauri-Volpi; in May 1951, won the singing competition at Maggi Musicale in Florence, Italy; on that occasion, was discovered by Maestro San Paoli, the director of the Teatro dell'Opera di Roma (Rome Opera House); at San Paoli's urging, entered another competition, in Spoleto, Italy, from which he again emerged the winner; made his professional debut as Don José in *Carmen* at Spoleto's Teatro Nuovo in August 1951; began performing at Rome's Teatro dell'Opera in 1952; soon, was invited to sing in opera houses and theaters in cities throughout Italy, including Naples, Venice, Bologna, San Remo, and Parma; sang Licinio in *La Vestale* in his debut at La Scala, in Milan; made several television films, in the first of which, in 1956, he sang the role of Mario Cavaradossi in *Tosca* and gained international stardom; in 1957, launched his international career with performances in Lisbon, Portugal, and Madrid, Spain; later performed in Paris, France, and Vienna, Austria, among other European cities; made his Covent Garden debut in London in June 1957 and his debut at the Metropolitan Opera in New York City in January 1961; during 15 years, on and off, with the Met, gave 365 performances and sang 19 roles, including those of Radames in *Aida*, Manrico in *Il Trovatore*, Calaf in *Turandot*, Enzo in *La Gioconda*, Maurizio in *Adriana Lecouvreur*, Rodolfo in *La Bohème*, and the title roles in *Ernani* and *Werther*; mastered a total repertoire of some 30 roles, including Don Alvaro in *La Forza del Destino*, Gabriele Adorno in *Simon Boccanegra*, Canio in *Pagliacci*, the False Dimitri in *Boris Godunov*, Pollione in *Norma*, Poliuto and Raoul in *Gli Ugonotti*, Pierre Bezukhov in

Guerra e Pace, and the leading tenor roles in *Andrea Chénier, Cavalleria Rusticana, Fanciulla del West,* and *Aida;* away from the Met, appeared in most of the major opera venues of the world during the 1960s; often performed with Maria Callas, Leontyne Price, Birgit Nilsson, Eileen Farrell, and Renata Tebaldi; made international concert tours with Renata Tebaldi in the early 1970s; recorded a copious discography; after his retirement from the musical stage, in 1976, taught singing in New York City and Milan; also modeled men's evening clothes; in Ancona, Italy, his birthplace, founded Concorso Lirico Internazionale Franco Corelli, an annual singing competition; died in Milan. See *Current Biography* (February) 1964.

Obituary *New York Times* C p14 Oct. 30, 2003

COX, ARCHIBALD May 17, 1912–May 29, 2004 Harvard University professor of law, emeritus; former solicitor general of the U.S.; drew national attention as special prosecutor in the Watergate scandal, which culminated in Richard M. Nixon's resignation from the presidency of the U.S. on August 9, 1974; was admitted to the Massachusetts bar in 1937; in Washington, D.C., during World War II, held several minor federal legal posts, including one in the Department of Justice and another in the Department of Labor; became a lecturer at Harvard Law School, his alma mater, in 1945; was raised to the rank of professor in 1946; specialized in the teaching of constitutional law; remained on the school's faculty for three decades, taking time out occasionally to fill a government position or to arbitrate a wage dispute; in December 1960, was nominated for the Justice Department position of solicitor general by incoming Democratic president John F. Kennedy; was sworn in as solicitor general in January 1961, when Kennedy took office; as solicitor general, argued government cases before the U.S. Supreme Court through 1965, during the administration of President Lyndon B. Johnson; returned to the national scene in the midst of the scandal over the burglarizing of the Democratic National Committee's headquarters in the Watergate office complex in Washington on June 17, 1972 by Republican "plumbers" and over the Nixon White House's cover-up of its connection to the burglary; when a Democratic-controlled Senate Judiciary Committee forced Nixon to allow Attorney General Elliott Richardson to appoint a special prosecutor to look into the Watergate matter, was chosen by Richardson (a former student of his) serve in that position, in May 1973; the following October, reached a showdown with Nixon, who refused to surrender to him tape recordings of Oval Office conversations and who ordered Richardson to fire him; Richardson refused, as did his deputy, William Ruckelshaus; on October 20, 1973, in what became known as the "Saturday Night Massacre" (an event that included the resignations of Richardson and Ruckelshaus), was fired by acting attorney general Robert H. Bork; wrote or co-wrote such books as *Law and the National Labor Policy* (1960), *Civil Rights, the Constitution, and the Courts* (1967), *The Role of the Supreme Court in American Government* (1976), *Freedom of Expression* (1981), and *The Court and the Constitution* (1987); between the late 1940s and early 1990s,

edited or co-edited a series of editions of *Cases and Materials on Labor Law;* died in Brooksville, Maine. See *Current Biography* (June) 1961.

Obituary *New York Times* B p7 May 31, 2004

CRAIN, JEANNE May 25, 1925–Dec. 14, 2003 Motion-picture actress; during World War II, with her well-scrubbed youthful beauty as a new contract player under Hollywood's old studio system, was Twentieth Century Fox's patented girl "back home" and "next door," a wholesome ingenue status that Fox was reluctant to allow her to grow out of; in one of the serious deviations from type that the studio permitted her, was cast as Patricia "Pinky" Johnson, the "Negro" woman passing for white in *Pinky* (1949), a portrayal for which she was nominated for the Academy Award for best actress; began her career as a teenage model and beauty-contest winner (Miss Long Beach, California, 1941, Camera Girl of the Year, 1942); made her film debut in an uncredited one-line appearance, lounging beside a swimming pool in a bathing suit, in Busby Berkeley's choreographed musical *The Gang's All Here* (1943); made an average of two pictures a year at Fox; in her first principal role, played Char, the tomboyish equestrienne in the horse-racing saga *Home in Indiana* (1944); in her first leading role, was cast as Maggie Preston, the adolescent heiress who learns to rough it as the child bride of a G.I., in *In the Meantime, Darling* (1944); was one of the four army wives in *Winged Victory* (1944); achieved stardom in *State Fair* (1945), the only musical ever written expressly for the screen by Richard Rodgers and Oscar Hammerstein; as the love-struck Iowa farm girl Margie Frake in that picture, lip-synched such songs as "It's a Grand Night for Singing" and "It Might as Well Be Spring" (all dubbed by Luanne Hogan, who would go on to dub Crain's singing in subsequent screen musicals); played Ruth Berent, the sweet foster sister of the mean Gene Tierney character in the suspense drama *Leave Her to Heaven* (1945); "sang" Jerome Kern songs as Julia Rodgers, the sister and love rival of the Linda Darnell character in *Centenial Summer* (1946); in the title role in *Margie* (1946), set in 1928, was a schoolgirl with a crush on her French teacher; in *You Were Meant for Me* (1948), a romantic musical comedy set in the 1920s, was cast as Peggy Mayhew, a young small-town woman who elopes with a famous band leader (Dan Dailey); played the title role in *Apartment for Peggy* (1948), about a young couple settling on a college campus; was cast as the insecure and shy Deborah Bishop in *Letter to Three Wives* (1949) and *Lady Windermere in the Fan* (1949); was cast as Ann Gilbreth, the eldest daughter, in *Cheaper by the Dozen* (1950) and its sequel, *Belles on Their Toes* (1952); starred as Liz Erickson in *Take Care of My Little Girl* (1951), an indictment of the college sorority system; co-starred with Cary Grant in the offbeat comedy *People Will Talk* (1951) and with Farley Granger in "The Gift of the Magi," a touching story within *O. Henry's Full House* (1952); sought and was denied the roles that went to Anne Baxter in *All About Eve* (1950), Susan Hayward in *With a Song in My Heart* (1952), and Jean Simmons in *The Robe* (1953); after leaving Twentieth Century Fox, took on new challenges, including the gutsy female leads in the Westerns *City of Bad Men* (1953), *Man without a Star* (1955), *The Fastest Gun Alive* (1956), and *Guns of the Timberland* (1960) and such sophisticated roles as one of the two love interests of the nightclub singer/comedian Joe E. Lewis (Frank Sinatra) in *The Joker Is Wild* (1957); in Italy in the early 1960s, was cast as one of Pontius Pilate's lovers in *Ponzio Pilato* and the Queen of the Nile in *Neferti-ti, regina del Nilo*; made a total of approximately 60 pictures; was survived by two sons and three daughters; died at her home in Santa Barbara, California. See *Current Biography* (November) 1951.

Obituary *New York Times* B p10 Dec. 16, 2003

CRICK, FRANCIS June 8, 1916–July 28, 2004 British theoretical biologist; Nobel laureate; the co-discoverer, with James D. Watson, of the double helix structure of deoxyribonucleic acid, or DNA, the micromolecular heredity component within chromosomes, in which is encoded the genetic instructions for the specific development of each and every cellular form of life and of some viruses; with the Watson-Crick hypothesis, as it came to be called, virtually created the science now known as molecular biology and gave new direction to genetics studies in general and in particular to a host of endeavors in medicine, forensics, and other fields; followed up his work on DNA with groundbreaking insights into the role of ribonucleic acid, or RNA, in the transmission of genetic information; after earning a B.S. degree in physics at University College, London, worked at designing mines with the British Admiralty during World War II; after the war, decided to study "the chemical physics of biology"; entered the doctoral program at Cambridge University, where he was drawn to the Cavendish Laboratory, a leading center for the study of proteins by X-ray crystallography analysis; in his research into DNA there, was joined in 1951 by the young American biologist James D. Watson; building on the work of others, including that of Maurice H. F. Wilkins, Rosalind Franklin, and Linus Pauling, arrived with Watson in February 1953 at the revolutionary model of DNA's structure, one that consists of two strands of polynucleotides with complementarily paired hydrogen bases (by hydrogen bonding, the two strands come together and entwine like vines to form a double helix); announced their discovery in the British scientific journal *Nature* in April 1953; at the end of the announcement, remarked, "It has not escaped our notice that the specific pairing we have postulated immediately suggests a possible copying mechanism for the genetic material"; in elaborating on that remark in their next paper, published in *Nature* five weeks later, explained how the specific base pairing could provide the mechanism for genetic information duplication: each double helix contains the information twice, once in each strand, and separated, each strand can serve as a template for a new double helix; drew support for the model from subsequent work by other biochemists; during 1953, received his doctorate from Cambridge for work unrelated to his DNA research; in the following years, concentrated his efforts on cracking the genetic code, which he once described as "the dictionary between the four-letter language of nucleic acid and the twenty-letter

language of proteins"; soon came to the conclusion that RNA, a single-stranded nucleic acid transcribed from DNA, was crucial to the process of directing various amino acids to join in the formation of growing protein in accordance with the genetic code; in informal collaboration with Watson, George Gamow, and Sydney Brenner, contributed to the development of the hypotheses explaining the roles of "transfer RNA" and "messenger RNA" in translating the genetic message from the language of nucleic acids into that of proteins and carrying it from the DNA to the ribosomes; together with James D. Watson and Maurice H. F. Wilkins, received the 1962 Nobel Prize in medicine or physiology; in his later years at Cambridge, worked on morphogenesis with Peter Lawrence; remained at Cambridge through 1976, eventually becoming co-director, with Sidney Bremmer, of the Cell Biology Division of the Medical Research Council Laboratory there; in 1977, quit that position with the intention of devoting himself to brain research; moved to the U.S. to become a research professor at the Salk Institute for Biological Studies in San Diego, California; did dream research; collaborated with Christopher Kock in studying the biological nature of consciousness; published the books *Life Itself: Its Origin and Nature* (1981), in which he argued that life on Earth may have been seeded by microorganisms ("direct panspermia") sent from a higher extraterrestrial civilization, and *The Astonishing Hypothesis: The Scientific Search for the Soul* (1994); died in San Diego. See *Current Biography* (March) 1983.

Obituary *New York Times* A p1+ July 30, 2004

DE JONG, DOLA Oct. 10, 1911–Nov. 19, 2003 Dutch-born author; wrote novels, including mysteries and thrillers, and some juvenilia; also worked as a literary agent and editor; wrote in Dutch and English; was also fluent in Flemish, French, German, and Afrikaans; was born into a Jewish family in Arnhem, the Netherlands; as a young woman, pursued two careers, those of journalist and ballet dancer; reviewed plays and films for the Amsterdam newspaper *De Telegraff*; danced with the Royal Dutch Ballet; anticipating Nazi Germany's invasion of her country, fled the Netherlands in 1940; left behind a father, stepmother, and brother who did not share her fears and who perished under the Nazi occupation; following a sojourn in Morocco, immigrated to the U.S. in 1941; for young children, wrote the nonsense book *Nikkernik, Nakkernak, and Nokkernok* (1942) and *Sand for the Sandman* (1944); for older children, wrote *The Level Land* (1943), a novel about a Dutch family, the Van Oordts, before and during World War II; returned to her native land for a visit during the summer of 1946; carried the Van Oordt family saga into the postwar period in *Return to the Level Land* (1947); meanwhile, had written her first adult book, *En de akker is de wereld* (translated into English as *And the Field is the World*); for that tragic tale of juvenile European Jewish refugees in Morocco during World War II, won the City of Amsterdam Literary Prize in 1947; in 1954, published *De thuiswacht*, translated into English as *The Tree and the Vine* (1961); in that adult novel, told the story of two young female Jewish friends and roommates in the Netherlands in the late 1930s: Erica, a lesbian, and Bea (the narrator, recounting from memory), a heterosexual who, in retrospect, questions the stability of sexual identity; for her mystery novel *The House on Charlton Street*, was runner-up for the Edgar Allan Poe Award in 1963; the following year, won the Poe Award for *The Whirligig of Time*; became a naturalized American citizen in 1947; graduated from Empire State College in New York City when she was 72; subsequently, taught creative writing at the college for several years; was married twice; was survived by a son and a granddaughter; died at her home in Laguna Woods, Los Angeles County, California. See *Current Biography* (Yearbook) 1947.

Obituary *New York Times* B p8 Nov. 26, 2003

DE SAPIO, CARMINE Dec. 10, 1908–July 27, 2004 Democratic Party politician; the last of the bosses of Tammany Hall, the New York City political machine that acquired a reputation for autocracy and corruption during its long, on-and-off hegemony; as a teenager, joined the Huron Democratic Club, Tammany's base in Manhattan's First Assembly District, West, centered in Greenwich Village; became district leader in 1943 and head of the New York County Democratic organization in 1949; was, in his words, "proud of the tradition, the heritage, the record of Tammany Hall" and sought to rehabilitate it by changing it into a modern political organization "geared to the times and interested in 'political service'"; named the first Puerto Rican district leader, Anthony Mendez; backed Hulan Jack, the first black Manhattan borough president; was instrumental in the appointment of Judge Harold A. Stevens to the Court of General Sessions, the highest judicial post to be held by an African-American in New York State up to that time; supported fair employment practices and rent control and advocated the lowering of the voting age to 18; was seen as the king maker behind the election of Robert F. Wagner to the mayoralty of New York City in 1953 and of W. Averill Harriman to the governorship of New York State in 1954; by dissuading Franklin D. Roosevelt Jr. from running for governor in 1954, earned the enmity of Roosevelt's mother, Eleanor; served as secretary of state in Harriman's administration; began his fall from public grace in 1957, when he raised editorial eyebrows by leaving $11,200 in hundred-dollar bills behind in a taxicab and then denying that the money was his; in the mayoral election of 1961, when Robert F. Wagner (who had defected from Tammany) was running for a third term, backed Arthur Levitt, who lost to Wagner by a large margin; in the First Assembly District, West, lost his position as Democratic Party leader to a reformist candidate endorsed by Eleanor Roosevelt in 1961; failed to regain the district leadership in the elections of 1963 and 1965; was indicted on perjury charges twice, in 1969 and 1976; served a prison term following his conviction in the first case; died in Greenwich Village. See *Current Biography* (September) 1955.

Obituary *New York Times* C p12 July 28, 2004

DELLINGER, DAVID Aug. 22, 1915–May 25, 2004 Radical pacifist; while independent of any political grouping, joined on moral grounds with Marxists and anarchists in resisting a capitalist system perceived by them as a cause of racism and economic injustice as well as war; in the course of a long life committed to nonviolent activism, escaped the national spotlight until his emergence as the elder member of the notorious Chicago Seven, the group of New Left agitators convicted of inciting disruptive anti–Vietnam war demonstrations in the streets of Chicago on the occasion of the Democratic National Convention there in 1968; was born into a New England conservative Republican family with deep Yankee roots; began developing a nonviolent egalitarian perspective as an undergraduate at Yale University, where he was involved in a union-organizing protest; after earning a B.A. degree in economics at Yale in 1936, studied for a year (1936–37) on a fellowship at New College, Oxford University; abortively aspiring to the Christian ministry, took courses at the Yale Divinity School (1937–38) and Union Theological Seminary in New York City (1939–40); for refusing to register for military conscription in 1940, was sentenced to a year and a day in federal prison; after refusing to report for a preliminary physical examination for wartime military service in 1943, served another two years in prison; in Glen Gardner, New Jersey, with the backing of such towering Old Left peace activists as A. J. Muste and Dorothy Day, cofounded a cooperative community that farmed and ran a radical publishing enterprise; at Glen Gardner, founded and edited for two decades *Liberation*, a monthly magazine concerned with issues ranging from war and disarmament to political and social justice, including civil rights and prisoners' rights (a publication not to be confused with more recent periodicals with the title *Liberation*, including one promoting a Buddhist prison outreach project and another devoted exclusively to animal rights and environmentalism); was a coordinator of the October 1965 Fifth Avenue Peace Parade, the first major anti–Vietnam War demonstration in New York City; became chairman of the National Mobilization Committee to End the War in Vietnam, which sponsored a massive antiwar rally in Washington, D.C., in October 1967; subsequently, co-chaired the New Mobilization Committee to End the War in Vietnam, which staged huge demonstrations in Washington (in October and November 1969) and sit-ins at draft boards, induction centers, ROTC buildings on college campuses, and other venues; on another front, helped to organize the antiwar demonstrations at the Democratic National Convention in Chicago in August 1968, which erupted beyond his control, into a violent confrontation between Chicago police and demonstrators; with seven others—Tom Hayden, Rennie Davis, Abbie Hoffman, Jerry Rubin, John Froines, Lee Weiner, and Bobby Seale (whose case was later separated from those of the others)—was indicted on charges of criminal conspiracy to commit violence and of crossing state lines to incite to riot; at the conclusion of their raucous trial in February 1970, was (with four of his co-defendants) found guilty of incitement to riot and of contempt of court but acquitted of the conspiracy charge; was the most severely punished of the group, the recipient of a five-year prison term and a $5,000 fine; saw all the convictions overturned on appeal; meanwhile, had become an unofficial liaison with the government of North

Vietnam; met with Ho Chi Minh in Hanoi in the fall of 1966 and with North Vietnamese officials engaged in the peace talks in Paris in June 1968 and July 1969; as co-chairman of the Committee of Liaison with the Families of Servicemen detained in North Vietnam, played a major role in the release of American prisoners of war by the North Vietnamese; escorted three American POWs home from North Vietnam in August 1969 and another three in September 1972; published six books, including the essay collection *Revolutionary Nonviolence* (1970) and the volumes *More Power Than We Know: The People's Movement Toward Democracy* (1975) and *From Yale to Jail: The Life Story of a Moral Dissenter* (1993); during the 1970s, moved with his family to Peacham, Vermont; taught in the adult education program at Vermont College in Burlington, Vermont; in 2001, at age 85, participated in a demonstration against the North American Free Trade Agreement in Quebec City, Canada; died in Montpelier, Vermont. See *Current Biography* (August) 1976.

Obituary *New York Times* B p9 May 27, 2004

DUGAN, ALAN Feb. 12, 1923–Sep. 3, 2003 Poet; a writer of unsentimental, vigorously original verse, whose mission was, in his words, "to walk into the daily accident"; while distancing himself from the intense anti-formalism of the Beat poets, was, like them, influenced by the stylistic freedom, plain language, and quotidian themes of William Carlos Williams; on the other hand, worked from a lifelong Marxist perspective, feeling himself to be "a unique rebel within the [capitalist] system," in which there are "plenty of cracks and niches . . . where a shrewd amoralist can survive"; resorted, as Thomas Mc-Clanahan wrote for *Dictionary of Literary Biography*, to "many ironic poses" that made it "difficult to get close to a poet like Dugan"; following two years at Queens College in New York City, served as a U.S. Army Air Force mechanic in the Pacific during World War II; after the war, studied at Olivet College, in Michigan, and at Mexico City University, in Mexico, where he earned a B.A. degree in history in 1949; for a dozen years while writing poetry (some of which was published first in *Poetry* magazine and then in the *New Yorker, Accent*, and the *Saturday Review*), worked at a series of jobs, including running a greeting-card production company with his wife, the painter and printmaker Judith Shahn Dugan (daughter of the artist Ben Shahn); later, contributed poems to *Partisan Review* and the *American Scholar*; in 1961, published his first book, *Poems*, which had (in manuscript) won the Yale Younger Poets Prize and went on win the National Book Award, the Pulitzer Prize, and the Prix de Rome; spent the years 1961 through 1964 on scholastic fellowships in Rome and Paris; in 1965–66, was a visiting lecturer in poetry at Connecticut College; later, traveled in Mexico and Central America on a Rockefeller Foundation grant and a Guggenheim fellowship; published *Poems 2* (1963), *Poems 3* (1967), *Collected Poems* (1969), and *Poems 4* (1974); included *Poems 5* as a section of his *New and Collected Poems, 1961–1983* (1984); published *Poems 6* (1989) and *Poems Seven: New and Complete Poetry* (2001); with his wife, lived in a rent-controlled apartment in New York City's Greenwich Village until the 1990s, when their rent rose to a free-market level; at that point, moved permanently to their summer house in Truro, Massachusetts, on Cape Cod; did stints as poet-in-residence at Sarah Lawrence College and the University of Colorado at Boulder; conducted a poetry workshop at the Truro Center for the Arts; was associated with the Fine Arts Work Center in Provincetown, Massachusetts, since 1969; died in Hyannis, Massachusetts. See *Current Biography* (November) 1990. — K.D.

Obituary *New York Times* C p11 Sep. 5, 2003

DUNLOP, JOHN T. July 5, 1914–Oct. 2, 2003 Economist; industrial-relations expert; Lamont University Professor, emeritus, Harvard University; outside academia, had extraordinary success as a mediator and arbitrator of management-labor disputes; concentrated on building consensus among all parties, including government executives when they were involved; earned the trust of both business and union leaders; put his expertise at the service of 11 U.S. presidents, beginning with Franklin Delano Roosevelt and including Gerald R. Ford, in whose Cabinet he was secretary of labor (March 1975–January 1976); earned his Ph.D. degree in economics at the University of California at Berkeley in 1939; meanwhile, had joined the faculty of Harvard University in 1938; became a full professor at Harvard in 1950; at the university, was chairman of the Department of Economics from 1961 to 1966 and dean of the faculty of arts and sciences from 1970 to 1973; over a period of six decades, shuttled constantly between Cambridge, Massachusetts, and Washington, D.C.; was research director with the National War Labor Board from 1943 to 1945; later served as a consultant to the Office of Economic Stabilization and the Council of Economic Advisers and a member of the National Labor Relations Board and the Equal Employment Opportunity Commission, among other federal and state economic panels; from 1948 to 1957, chaired the National Joint Board for the Settlement of Disputes in the Building and Construction Industry; was a public member of the Wage Stabilization Board from 1950 to 1952 and a member of the Federal Railroad Commission from 1960 to 1962; during the administration of President Richard M. Nixon, directed the Cost of Living Council, concerned with wage and price controls (1973–74); under President Ford, was a member of the president's Labor-Management Committee and Economic Policy Board as well as secretary of labor; resigned as secretary of labor when Ford vetoed a bill that would have expanded picketing rights for construction trade unions, as he had promised the unionists; was on President Ronald Reagan's National Productivity Advisory Committee from 1981 to 1984 and President George H. W. Bush's Social Security advisory council from 1989 to 1991; under President Bill Clinton, chaired the Commission on the Future of Worker-Management Relations, popularly known as the Dunlop Commission, from 1993 to 1995; according to Thomas Kochran, who served with him on the Dunlop Commission, "had an unparalleled ability to move across the worlds of academic theory, policy-making, and mediation"; as a mediator and arbitrator, was instrumental in resolving disputes in the building and construction, railroad, textile and apparel, and other industries as well as disputes involving state and local government unions; worked out a three-way agreement among migrant agricultural workers, small farmers, and the Campbell Soup Co. that was renewed several times; successfully arbitrated a wage dispute between the *New York Times* and the Newspaper Guild in 1950; in the late 1950s and early 1960s, served as arbitrator under collective-bargaining agreements between the International Ladies' Garment Workers' Union and its St. Louis Joint Board and affiliated locals and other Associated Garment Industries of St. Louis; established the analytic framework for the field with *Industrial Relations Systems* (1958), a standard reference work; with Derek C. Bok, wrote *Labor and the American Community* (1970); with three academic colleagues, conducted a six-year research project culminating in a major book on the textile, apparel, and retail sectors, *A Stitch in Time: Lean Retailing and the Transformation of Manufacturing* (1999); wrote, co-wrote, or edited a total of some dozen books on wages and prices, union management, collective bargaining, negotiation and consensus building, technological change and automation, business and public policy, and labor in the 20th century; remained active at Harvard University after taking emeritus status in 1985; died in Boston, Massachusetts. See *Current Biography* (April) 1951.

Obituary *New York Times* A p14 Oct. 4, 2003

DUNNE, JOHN GREGORY May 25, 1932–Dec. 30, 2003 Novelist; essayist; journalist; screenwriter; a correspondent imbedded in celebritydom who revealed that glitzy world's underbelly with dark humor and "perfect pitch for the brash and cynical Hollywood argot," as Valerie Takahama of the Knight/Ridder News Service observed (November 2, 1994); was praised by Richard Schickel in *Time* (January 12, 2004) for novels that are "true expressions of a complicated, cranky, lovable man whose hatred of hypocrisy was legendary" and for his books and articles anatomizing the movie game with "unsurpassed . . . dry wit" and "understated truthfulness" and "without the malevolence and condescension many writers bring to their true tales of movie work"; as a student at an elite Catholic boarding school in Rhode Island, was stymied by a stammer, which drove him to seek excellence in the written word; after graduating from Princeton University and serving in the army, was a staff writer with *Time* for five years; regularly contributed nonfiction to the *Saturday Evening Post* for many years; published his first book, *Delano: The Story of the California Grape Strike* in 1967; two years later, published *The Studio*, a behind-the-scenes report on movie-making at Twentieth Century Fox; realized that his "mother lode" was his tortured Irish Catholic sensibility when he was writing his first novel, *Vegas: a Memoir of a Dark Season* (1974), a quasi-autobiography set in "a netherworld of losers"; with his keen eye and ear for the colloquial and his mordant sense of humor, established himself as a distinctive voice in fiction with the best-seller *True Confessions* (1977), a raunchy novel in the guise of a hardboiled detective

story, an elliptical moral tale about the complex psychological and emotional relationship between the Irish-American Spellacy brothers: Monsignor Des, chancellor of the Archdiocese of Los Angeles, and Tom, a self-hating Los Angeles homicide detective investigating a notorious sex murder; in that novel, conveyed the inbred sense of universal "original sin" and "fallen human nature" shared by Irish Catholics of all social classes; intensified his personification of that sensibility in the protagonist of his second novel, *Dutch Shea, Jr.* (1981), an externally cheerful and witty criminal lawyer who, oppressed by the sleazy world with which he deals and obsessed with lost honor, finds himself in a vortex of suicidal depression; crammed his fourth novel, *The Red, White, and Blue* (1987), with a wickedly manic and droll proliferation of grotesque characters and incidents on all social levels, from an execution in a California gas chamber and an irreverent Christmas pageant to an affair the president of the U.S. had with the late sister of the narrator, Jack Broderick, a billionaire's son and social buzzard who plays at earning his livelihood as a columnist for his father's newspaper and as a screenwriter; made Broderick the narrator of his satirical novel *Playland* (1994), about Blue Tyler, a child movie star of the 1940s who ends up decades later as a derelict bag lady in Detroit; before his death, completed a final novel, *Nothing Lost* (2004); with his wife, Joan Didion, co-wrote the screenplays for *Panic in Needle Park* (1971) and the film adaptation of Didion's novel *Play It as It Lays* (1972), both of which were co-produced by Dunne's older brother Dominick; with Didion, worked on the early drafts of the screenplay for the 1976 remake of *A Star Is Born* (1976); again with Didion, co-wrote the screenplays for the film adaptation of *True Confessions* (1981) and for *Up Close and Personal* (1996); in the latter project, spent eight years writing 27 drafts of the script, an experience he recounted in *Monster: Living Off the Big Screen* (1997), a devilishly funny documentation of the tortuous process of consensus filmmaking in Hollywood; wrote the memoir *Harp* (1990); reviewed books for the *New York Review of Books* from 1979 until the eve of his death; published two collections of his essays: *Quintana & Friends* (1978), the title referring to Quintana Roo, the daughter he and his wife adopted, and *Crooning* (1990); wrote several scripts for television, including the teleplay *Broken Trust* (1995); with his wife, lived in Los Angeles from 1964 to 1988, when they moved back to New York City; died in their Manhattan apartment. See *Current Biography* (June) 1983.

Obituary *New York Times* B p9 Jan. 1, 2004

FERRÉ, LUIS A. Feb. 17, 1904–Oct. 21, 2003 Former governor of Puerto Rico, a self-governing commonwealth of the U.S.; leader of the movement for Puerto Rican statehood; philanthropist; classical pianist; was born into a wealthy industrial family in Ponce, Puerto Rico; was sent by his family to the U.S. to attend high school in Morristown, New Jersey, and the Massachusetts Institute of Technology, in Cambridge, where he earned a B.S. degree in mechanical engineering and an M.S. degree in electrical engineering; also studied piano at the New England Conservatory of Music; after he returned to Puerto Rico, took charge of organization and labor relations in the family company, Ferré Industries, a small foundry that grew into a major supplier of cement in Miami, Florida, as well as Puerto Rico and also the operator of paper, clay, and glass plants; in 1952, running on the Statehood Republican ticket, was elected to Puerto Rico's legislative assembly; led the opposition to Governor Luis Muñoz Marín and his pro-commonwealth Popular Democratic Party until Muñoz retired, in 1964; co-founded the pro-statehood New Progressive Party in 1967; was governor from 1969 until 1973; served as president of Puerto Rico's Senate from 1977 to 1980; outside politics, founded the Ponce Public Library in 1937; at about the same time, bought Ponce's then moribund newspaper, *El Dia*; when he became governor, turned the paper over to his son, Antonio, who moved it to San Juan, where it became *El Nuevo Dia*, Puerto Rico's largest daily; with paintings from his own collection, opened the Ponce Museum of Art in 1959; donated hundreds of thousands of dollars to educational institutions, including the University of Miami and the Pontifical Catholic University of Ponce, which was founded largely through his beneficence; died in San Juan, Puerto Rico. See *Current Biography* (March) 1970. — K.D.

Obituary *New York Times* A p21 Oct. 22, 2003

FONG, HIRAM L. Oct. 1, 1907–Aug. 18, 2004 Republican U.S. senator from Hawaii (1959–77); lawyer; businessman; self-made millionaire; the first person of Chinese descent to serve in the U.S. Congress; worked his way through the University of Hawaii and Harvard Law School; during World War II, served as judge advocate in an air force fighter command; in Honolulu, founded Fong, Miho, Choy & Robinson, an intentionally multiracial law firm; earned his fortune through investments in real estate, shopping centers, finance, insurance, and a banana plantation; was president of Grand Pacific Life Insurance Co. and several financial corporations; before his election to the U.S. Congress in 1959, when Hawaii became a state, served in Hawaii's House of Representatives for 14 years; died in Honolulu, Hawaii. See *Current Biography* (February) 1960.

Obituary *New York Times* C p13 Aug. 19, 2004

GADES, ANTONIO Nov. 16, 1936–July 20, 2004 Spanish dancer; choreographer; choreographed and performed a unique theatrical style of balletic flamenco, preserved for posterity in several motion pictures, most notably a narrative trio made in collaboration with the filmmaker Carlos Sauro in the 1980s: *Bodas de sangre* ("Blood Wedding"), *Carmen,* and *El Amor Brujo* ("Enchanted Love"); born Antonio Esteve Ródenas; came up through the ranks of Spanish dance repertory with the Pilar López company (1952–61); in the early 1960s, worked in choreography and ballet in Italy, at the Rome Opera, at La Scala in Milan, and at the Festival of the Two Worlds in Spoleto; in 1963, drew wide international attention in his film debut, acting and dancing the role of Mojigondo in *Los Tarantos;* that same year, founded the Antonio Gades Spanish Dance Company; dancing with that troupe, electrified spectators at the Spanish Pavilion at the New York World's Fair in

1964; later toured England, continental Europe, South America, and Japan; in 1972, returned to the U.S. with his company; in 1976, was named charter director of the National Ballet of Spain; held that post until 1980, when he founded the Ballet Antonio Gades; with that group, performed in New York City in 1985; nine years later, choreographed his last major work, *Fuenteovejuna*, which was filmed; meanwhile, in 1975, danced for the first time in Fidel Castro's Cuba, which he adopted as his second country; subsequently, performed on stage several times—including once at the Metropolitan Opera—with Alicia Alonso, the director and prima ballerina of the Ballet Nacional de Cuba; did choreography for that company; joined the Cuban Communist Party and became a "compadre" of General Raúl Castro, Fidel Castro's brother and the head of the Cuban armed forces; traveled to Cuba regularly, occasionally for protracted visits; in November 2003, went there by sea, crossing the Atlantic Ocean in his sailboat; early in June 2004, received the Order of José Martí, the Castro government's highest decoration; in a letter subsequently sent to Raul Castro, said that "the only thing [he was] sorry about is not having done enough for the revolution"; on July 21, 2004, the day following his death in Madrid, was cremated; in accordance with his wishes, his ashes were delivered by his second wife, Eugenia Eriz, and his daughters Maria, Tamara, and Celia to Raul Castro for burial alongside "martyrs of the revolution" in a mausoleum in Cuba. See *Current Biography* (February) 1973.

Obituary *New York Times* C p13 July 22, 2004

GIBSON, ALTHEA Aug. 25, 1927–Sep. 28, 2003 Tennis champion; sports pioneer who broke the color barrier in professional tennis; in the late 1950s, won five Grand Slam singles titles and participated in the winning of three Wimbledon doubles titles; was born into a family of African-American sharecroppers on a cotton farm in South Carolina and was raised on welfare in the Harlem section of New York City, where she began playing tennis in the city's parks-department competitions; in 1942, was introduced to Manhattan's interracial Cosmopolitan Tennis Club by Buddy Walker, a bandleader who was also a Police Athletic League play-street supervisor; at the club, was coached by the one-armed tennis pro Fred Johnson; when she was 15, won the New York State girls' championship sponsored by the all-black American Tennis Association, which had been organized by black players excluded at that time from the U.S. Lawn Tennis Association; four years later, won the American Tennis Association's women's championship; successfully defended that championship for nine years; meanwhile, had found a sponsor in Sugar Ray Robinson, the prize fighter, and mentors in two southern physicians, Hubert A. Eaton and R. Walter Johnson, who were devoted to integrating mainstream tennis; attended Florida Agricultural and Mechanical University on a tennis and basketball scholarship; in the wake of a guest editorial in the July 1950 issue of *American Lawn Tennis* in which the tennis champion Alice Marble challenged the "de facto color line" in tennis, became the first African-American to compete in the National Grass Court Championships (the precursor of the U.S.

Open) at Forest Hills, Queens, New York, in 1950, and in the All-England Championships at Wimbledon; won the French Open in 1956; won the Wimbledon doubles with Angela Buxton in 1956, with Darlene Hard in 1957, and with Maria Bueno in 1958; on July 6, 1957, won the Wimbledon singles title in a 6–3, 6–2 victory over Hard; was honored with a ticker-tape parade in New York City and the Medallion of the City after that success; on July 21, 1957, defeated Hard in the U.S. National Clay Court Championships; on September 8, 1957, won the U.S. women's singles title at Forest Hills by defeating Louise Brough, 6–3, 6–2; reprised her Wimbledon and Forest Hills triumphs in 1958; was named Female Athlete of the Year by the Associated Press in 1957 and 1958; for financial reasons—her championships brought her no prize money—relinquished her amateur status in 1959, when there was no professional women's tennis circuit; toured with the Harlem Globetrotters, spelling that basketball team's games with exhibition tennis matches; competing with Karol Fageros in a series of 119 exhibition tennis matches in 1960, won 114 of the contests; subsequently, turned her hand to golf; competed on the Ladies Professional Golf Association tour during the 1960s and 1970s; in 1975, was appointed New Jersey State Commissioner of Athletics, a post she held for a decade; served on the New Jersey State Athletics Control Board until 1988 and the New Jersey Governor's Council on Physical Fitness until 1992; published the autobiography *I Always Wanted to Be Somebody* (1958), edited by Ed Fitzgerald; co-wrote, with, among others, her friend Fran Gray, who established the Althea Gibson Foundation, *Born to Win: The Althea Gibson Story*, scheduled for publication in 2004; lived to see the African-American sisters Venus and Serena Williams rise to the top ranks of women's tennis; died in East Orange, New Jersey. See *Current Biography* (October) 1957.

Obituary *New York Times* B p8 Sep. 29, 2003

GOLD, THOMAS May 22, 1920–June 22, 2004 Austrian-born astrophysicist; professor emeritus of astronomy and electrical engineering, Cornell University; a daring contrarian among astrophysicists; was co-author of the controversial "steady-state" cosmological theory, a concept radically at odds with the widely accepted "Big Bang" explanation of the origin of the universe; also disputed the conventional wisdom regarding the generation of petrochemicals, rejecting the "fossil fuel" explanation and arguing that natural gas and oil are not products of fossilization but are hydrocarbons of nonbiological origin, formed along with the planet Earth itself by solar-system processes and embedded deep within the planet; is credited with realizing that pulsars are radio emissions from spinning neutron stars, a view now generally accepted; was educated at a secondary school in Switzerland and at Cambridge University, in England; during World War II, worked on radar research and development for the British Admiralty; after the war, became a fellow and demonstrator in physics at Cambridge University's Cavendish laboratory; with his close associates at the laboratory, Hermann Bondi and Fred Hoyle, began working out the steady-state theory in 1948; five years later,

formally presented that theory, which proposes the universe to be a continuous creation, without beginning or end; in 1952, left Cambridge to become chief assistant to the astronomer royal at the Royal Greenwich Laboratory; in 1953, formulated a hypothesis (later confirmed) regarding the traveling speed of interplanetary shock waves, thus shedding light on the hazards of space travel; in 1957, moved to the U.S. to accept a professorship in astronomy at Harvard University; participated in installing in the radio telescope at Harvard a maser (the acronym for "microwave amplification by stimulated emission of radiation"), a crystal amplifier extending the telescope's range 10-fold; in 1959, joined the faculty of Cornell University as director of Cornell's new Center for Radiophysics and Space Research, a position he held until 1981; also chaired the Department of Astronomy at Cornell; served as a consultant to NASA during the *Apollo* lunar expeditions during the 1960s; correctly predicted that the first astronauts to land on the moon would find its surface to be pulverized, a sea of dust or powder (although not as deep as he had predicted); in the 1980s, argued for unmanned space flights in preference to manned flights, pointing out that "failures of unmanned launches (and there will be some) will cost money, but will not risk human lives, nor the prestige of the United States"; became professor emeritus at Cornell in 1986; during the 1980s, persuaded the Swedish government to engage in a $40 million project calculated to prove his theory that oil is not a fossil fuel; regarded as proof of his theory the 80 barrels of oil produced by Swedish engineers drilling approximately four miles down at a site near Siljan Lake—a result dismissed by his critics as inconclusive at best; wrote the books *Power from Earth: Deep Earth Gas—Energy for the Future* (1987) and *The Deep Hot Biosphere: The Myth of Fossil Fuel* (1999); co-edited several books, including *The Nature of Time* (1967); died in Ithaca, New York. See *Current Biography* (June) 1966.

Obituary *New York Times* A p21 June 24, 2004

GOLDSMITH, JERRY Feb. 10, 1929–July 21, 2004 Prolific composer of motion-picture and television music; a classically trained musician who, in a career spanning half a century and work on more than 200 productions, ranged from a traditional symphonic style through a variety of modernist experiments; among his film scores, echoed Aaron Copland in his first credit, *Lonely Are the Brave* (1962), went atonal in *Freud* (1962) and electronic in *Runaway* (1985), was brassily martial in *Patton* (1970), pushed the symphonic envelope in *Planet of the Apes* (1968), and was jazz-oriented in *Chinatown* (1974) and sensually seductive in *Basic Instinct* (1992); leaned to the operatic in his compositions for three *Star Wars* films and one *Star Wars* TV series; was nominated for 18 Academy Awards, including one for best song for "Avi Satani" in the film *The Omen* (1976); won his only Oscar for the overall score of *The Omen*; for his work in television, won five Emmy Awards, including one for the main title theme for the 1995 *Star Trek: Voyager* series; was born in Los Angeles to musical parents, who hired private tutors to educate him; as a child and young adult, studied piano with Jakob Gimpel, theory and counterpoint with Mario Castelnuovo-Tedesco, and cinematic composition with Miklós Rózsa; as a young man, joined the music department of the Columbia Broadcasting System as a clerk-typist; soon, was writing scores for such CBS radio programs as *Romance* and *CBS Radio Workshop* as well as for two early live-TV dramas, on the CBS showcases *Studio One* and *Playhouse 90*; during the 1950s, wrote music for a number of CBS TV series, including *Wagon Train* and *Perry Mason*; especially enjoyed composing for *The Twilight Zone*, where he was allowed, he said, to "try anything, any experiment . . . , just to see what different combinations of sounds would be like"; made his motion-picture debut with the uncredited score for *Don't Bother to Knock* (1952); was first credited on the silver screen for the score of *Black Patch* (1957); in 1960, was hired by the renowned film composer Alfred Newman to score live TV drama at Revue Studios, which soon merged with Universal Pictures and gave him his full entrée to motion pictures; during the 1960s, scored an average of six films a year, among them *Lilies of the Field* (1963), *Seven Days in May* (1964), *Von Ryan's Express* (1965), *A Patch of Blue* (1965), *The Sand Pebbles* (1966), and *The Blue Max* (1966); during the 1970s, composed the music for such films as *Wild Rovers* (1971), *Papillon* (1973), *The Wind and the Lion* (1975), *Twilight's Last Gleaming* (1977), *Coma* (1978), and *Alien* (1979); in addition to his work on the *Star Trek: Voyager* TV series, scored three *Star Trek* films, beginning with *Star Trek: The Motion Picture* (1979); scored the films *Gremlins* (1984), *Gremlins 2* (1990), *Medicine Man* (1992), *L.A. Confidential* (1997), and *Small Soldiers* (1998); also wrote orchestral music and conducted symphonic orchestras, including the Royal Philharmonic, in the performance of his works and those of others; was survived by his second wife, Carol, a singer, and a number of progeny, including his son Joel, a motion-picture and TV composer, and his daughter Ellen, who sang on *Wild Rovers*. See *Current Biography* (May) 2001. — K.D.

Obituary *New York Times* A p21 July 23, 2004

GOLDSTINE, HERMAN HEINE Sep. 13, 1913–June 16, 2004 Mathematician; computer pioneer; after earning a doctorate at the University of Chicago, taught there and at the University of Michigan; as a ballistics officer with the U.S. Army during World War II, participated in the development of ENIAC (the acronym for "electronic numerical integrator and computer"), a first-generation computer weighing 30 tons; after the war, joined the Institute for Advanced Study in Princeton, New Jersey, as assistant director of the institute's electronic-computer project; at the institute, developed methods for handling the partial differential and integral equations of mathematical physics in high-speed automatic computation; contributed to the development of ED-VAC (electronic discrete variable automatic computer), the second-generation computer designed by John von Neumann; in 1958, joined the computer-manufacturing company IBM as director of its mathematical sciences department; later directed development of data processing at IBM; after retiring, in

1969, remained an IBM consultant; wrote, among other books, *The Computer from Pascal to von Neumann* (1972), *Full Moons from 1001 B.C. to A.D. 1851* (1973), and *A History of the Calculus of Variations from the 17th through the 19th Century* (1980); died at his home in Bryn Mawr, Pennsylvania. See *Current Biography* (November) 1952.

Obituary *New York Times* A p14 June 27, 2004

GOLUB, LEON Jan. 23, 1922-Aug. 8. 2004 Artist; a painter who thought of himself as a reporter of the "real," "the dark side of things," "the state we are in right now" in a world whose "nature . . . is unending, fatalistic aggression"; inspired by his archive of thousands of news photo clippings of military and paramilitary violence and other scenes of inhumanity from around the world, applied acrylic to canvas and then abraded it, to create figural paintings with a flayed and pitted effect; pursued his figurative work undaunted (albeit with one brief period of self-doubt) in the shadow of abstract expressionism and a succession of other trends in the international art world for three decades before he earned wide recognition with the emergence of a New York school of neo-expressionism in the early 1980s; was a founding member of the artists' section of the antiwar group Refuse and Resist and, in June 2002, one of the first prominent signers of "Not in Our Name," a "statement of conscience" calling "on the people of the U.S. to resist the [government] policies and overall political direction that have emerged since September 11, 2001 and which pose grave dangers to the people of the world"; after majoring in art history at the University of Chicago and serving with the U.S. Army in World War II, went on to earn two degrees in art at the Chicago Art Institute; joined with other institute students who were war veterans in producing works described as marked by "a violent and desiccated expressionism and a surreal fancy both obsessive and disturbed"; rejecting most of the art of the postmedieval Western tradition, drew inspiration from classical Greek, Roman, and Etruscan art and that of other early cultures as well as such modern influences as German expressionism; painted in oil before turning to acrylic; became identified with Chicago's school of "monster" artists, whose dramatic images of the human condition were at odds with the ascendent abstractionism of the time, in which reference to human figures or real objects was vaguely allusive at best; was comparable to the British painter Francis Bacon in his dedication to depiction of the human figure and to the French painter Jean Dubuffet in his brutal expressionism; showed a Hellenistic influence in such paintings as *Damaged Man* (1955) and *Fallen Warrior* (1960); with his wife, the artist Nancy Spero, lived and worked in Paris from 1959 to 1964; during that period, became imbued with the spirit of Roman Republican sculpture and the French Revolutionary art of Jacques-Louis David; after his return to the U.S., settled in Greenwich Village in New York City; joined the Artists' and Writers' Protest Against the War in Vietnam and created a series of enormous, angry Vietnam canvases; continued in that vein in his *Napalm Gates* series (1970–71), in which the paint suggests severely burnt skin, and his *Assassins* series (1972–73); having previously survived the hegemony first of abstract expressionism and then of pop art, found himself in the mid-1970s in a no-man's land between prevailing minimalist and conceptualist orthodoxies; suffering a crisis of confidence, destroyed some of his paintings and temporarily retreated into portraiture; in the late 1970s, working from photographs, painted approximately 100 portraits (one-and-a-half times life size) of world leaders, including Mao Zedong, Ho Chi Minh, Augusto Pinochet, Richard M. Nixon, Henry Kissinger, and Fidel Castro; in the 1980s and 1990s, following the latter-day surge in his career, painted large canvases (mostly 10 by 12 feet), with such titles as *Mercenaries, Interrogation, Riot,* and *White Squad;* in a large number of those paintings, explored themes of domestic American thuggery; saw a career retrospective of his work, titled *Leon Golub: Echoes of the Real,* mounted in Dublin, Ireland, in 2000 and remounted in reduced form at the Brooklyn Museum of Art in 2001; taught at the School of Visual Arts in Manhattan and at Rutgers University; died in Manhattan. See *Current Biography* (August) 1984.

Obituary *New York Times* C p14 Aug. 12, 2004

GORSUCH, ANNE Apr. 21, 1942–July 18, 2004 U.S. Environmental Protection Agency administrator during the first administration of President Ronald Reagan; a conservative Republican; held degrees in political science and law from the University of Colorado; early in her career, was assistant district attorney of Jefferson County, Colorado, deputy district attorney of the city of Denver, a hearing officer for two Colorado state regulatory agencies, and corporate counsel for Mountain Bell Telephone; before her appointment to the EPA, served two terms in the Colorado House of Representatives; in February 1981, was named EPA administrator by President Reagan, who understood that she was in agreement with his goals of more disciplined government spending, minimal regulatory burdens on business and industry, and the return of more governmental responsibilities to the states; was confirmed by the U.S. Senate three months later; as administrator, was widely accused by many environmentalists and other critics of "dismantling" the EPA in the name of governmental reform; in particular, clashed with a House of Representatives subcommittee investigating what it considered mismanagement of the EPA's Superfund for the cleanup of the nation's hazardous waste sites; when the subcommittee demanded that she turn over Superfund records, she refused on grounds of executive privilege, in accordance with orders from the White House and advice from the Department of Justice; when cited for contempt of Congress, was left in the lurch by the Reagan administration and the Justice Department, which failed to come to her defense; resigned on March 9, 1983; returned to the private practice of law; died in Aurora, Colorado. See *Current Biography* (September) 1982.

Obituary *New York Times* C p13 July 22, 2004

GRAY, SPALDING June 5, 1941–Jan. 10, 2004 Writer; stage, screen, and television actor; performance artist; storyteller; realized his distinctive talent in autobiographical monologues—quirky, free-associative solo performances in which he saw himself as "a collage artist, cutting and pasting memories from [his] life": in those performances, interwove episodes of personal experience, often traumatic and anxiety-ridden, with the wider troubled history of his time, bringing antic therapeutic wit to the darkness in both; reworked "his own life as a tragi-comic road movie" in which he starred "as a perpetual innocent abroad, revealing elemental truths in spite of himself," as Simon Prosser observed in the London *Daily Telegraph;* wrote and performed a score of confessional monologues, including the Obie-winning *Swimming to Cambodia* (the text of which was published in 1985 and which became his most celebrated performance after it was filmed under the direction of Jonathan Demme in 1987) and six monologues whose texts were published in paperback under the title *Sex and Death to the Age 14* in 1986; grew up in a deceptively respectable Rhode Island WASP household characterized by him as "filled with all manner of lies and every kind of neurosis"; would rebel against his background, including the Christian Science religion introduced to him and his two brothers by their mother, a woman he remembered as "cracking up" mentally and emotionally and whose suicide in 1967 would spark the longest of his chronic bouts of depression; remembered himself as a "shy, backward" child, impeded in schoolwork by undiagnosed dyslexia; after studying theater at Emerson College in Boston, Massachusetts, acted in summer stock on Cape Cod and in regional theater; in 1967, moved to New York City to venture into experimental theater; in 1970, joined Richard Schnechner's Performance Group at the Performing Garage (also referred to as Performance Garage) in Lower Manhattan; there, created the leading role of Hoss in Sam Shepard's *Tooth of Crime* (1973–75); meanwhile, was growing increasingly "dissatisfied with having to . . . mimic make-believe emotions" in fictional roles; with Elizabeth LeCompte, founded the Wooster Group at the Performing Garage in 1977; with that group in the late 1970s, produced and starred in his trilogy of plays *Three Places in Rhode Island,* a harrowing recounting of childhood experiences that was directed by LeCompte; appended to the trilogy an epilogue, *Point Judith;* presented his first monologue, *Sex and Death to the Age 14,* at the Performing Garage in 1979; subsequently, developed the monologues *Booze, Cats,* and *College Girls* (in which he detailed his misadventures with all three) and *India (and After)* (an account of his tour of India with a Wooster Group production and of his nervous breakdown during that tour); early on, established his practice of delivering his monologues while sitting behind a small desk, referring to handwritten notes and punctuating his delivery with well-timed sips from a glass of water; in a solo tour of Europe in 1980, introduced *Interviewing the Audience;* later took that kaleidoscopic improvisational piece on tour across the U.S.; in 1981, interviewed carnival and sideshow people at the Tennessee State Fair, an experience that resulted in the monologue *In Search of the Monkey Girl* and the book of the same name (1982), with photographs by Randal Levenson; was cast as the American ambassador's aide in the feature film *The Killing Fields* (1984), about the U.S. bombing of Cambodia in 1975 and the bloodbath launched by the Khmer Rouge in Phnom Penh within the same year; in coming to grips with the subject of that movie, realized that he was dealing "with a larger psychosis than [his] own neurosis"; explored that realization in *Swimming to Cambodia*, the success of which paved the way for his move uptown for the premiere at Lincoln Center of *Terrors of Pleasure*, a monologue (inspired in part by his purchase of a decrepit, problem-fraught cabin in the Catskills) that was made into a television movie, broadcast on HBO in 1988; spoke about nervous collapse and writer's block in his next monologue, *Monster in a Box*, which was made into a documentary film (1992); told about his efforts to deal with a serious eye problem in the monologue *Gray's Anatomy* (text published in 1994; videorecorded for BBC television in 1997); using skiing as a metaphor, and combining sadness with humor, dealt with drug use, sex, mortality, agoraphobia, infidelity, and the transition from his first marriage (to Renée Shafransky) to his second (to Kathleen Russo) in *It's a Slippery Slope* (1996), the text of which was published in 1997; in the upbeat monologue *Morning, Noon, and Night* (published in 1999), focused on a day in the life of his new family; in breaks from his monologues, played on Broadway as the Stage Manager in a revival of *Our Town* in 1988 and as a political candidate in a revival of *The Best Man* in 2000; had roles in more than 30 feature films, including *True Stories* (1986), *Beaches* (1988), *Straight Talk* (1992), *King of the Hill* (1993), *The Paper* (1994), *Beyond Rangoon* (1995), *Diabolique* (1996), and *Kate and Leopold* (2001); on television, had the recurring role of Dr. Jack Miller in the situation comedy *The Nanny*; wrote an autobiographically based novel, *Impossible Vacation* (1992); during a vacation in Ireland in June 2001, was in an automobile accident that left him with a broken hip, a fractured skull, and a torn sciatic nerve and plunged him into a despondency reflected in the darkness of his final monologues, *Life Interrupted* and *Blind Spot*; attempted suicide at least twice; maintained residences in North Haven, Long Island, and Manhattan; went missing after telephoning home from the Staten Island ferry terminal in Lower Manhattan on January 10, 2004; was confirmed deceased on March 8, 2002, the day after his body was recovered from New York City's East River; was survived by his wife, Kathleen, two sons, and a stepdaughter; had suggested his own epitaph: "An American Original: Troubled, Inner-Directed, and Cannot Type." See *Current Biography* (September) 1986.

Obituary *New York Times* A p1+ Mar. 9, 2004

GUNN, THOM Aug. 29, 1929–Apr. 25, 2004 British-born poet best known for his poetic reflections on his adopted milieu, the California counterculture, its denizens, and his offbeat experiences there, including his experiments with drugs; had a special affinity for muscular male heroism, especially in the outlaw and the outsider; ventured into nonmetrical verse forms but was rooted and most at home in the traditional meter and rhyme absorbed in his early reading of the likes of John Donne and Ben Jonson; earned a B.A. degree (1953) at Trinity College, Cambridge University, England, and an M.A. (1958) at Stanford University, in Stanford, California; at the beginning of his career, was briefly and only very loosely identified with the Movement, a group of English writers that included Philip Larkin and Kingsley Amis; in 1954, published his first collection, *Fighting Terms* (1954), which included his first efforts at making his perceptions of heroism credible; in 1957, published his second collection, *The Sense of Movement* (1957), which showed in part the influence of Yvor Winters, his mentor at Stanford, and exhibited his own deepening commitment to what he called the "the pose," his viewing himself "as an actor trying to play a part," a stance providing "rich material for poetry"; in person, as Clive Wilmer wrote in his obituary of Gunn for the London *Independent*, "cultivated a piratical appearance—an earring and tattoos long before they were fashionable, motorcycling jackets and boots, outrageous T-shirts, and so on"; in "On the Move," the best known of the 30 poems in *The Sense of Movement*, pictured a motorcycle gang coming up the road, "the Boys / Until the distance throws them forth, their hum / Bulges to thunder held by calf and thigh"; also included in that collection poems about soldiers and various hustlers and, as Wilmer noted, "a famous poem on Elvis Presley, a celebration of the American city, and explorations of sexual irregularity"; began to experiment with departures from traditional meter in the poems in *My Sad Captains and Other Poems* (1961), the first half of which was written in iambic meter and the second in syllabic stanzas, his bridge to free verse; in the poems (including "Misanthropos") in his fourth collection, *Touch* (1967), balanced the cerebral and the sensual in pursuing such themes as rebirth; was inspired by his experience with the hallucinogen LSD in writing the metamorphosis-themed poems in *Moly* (1971); for the first time, explicitly acknowledged his homosexuality, until then implicit in his work, in the poetry collected in *Jack Straw's Castle* (1976); made homosexuality and male friendship major elements in *The Passages of Joy* (1982); beginning in the late 1980s, wrote, in a stoical Elizabethan style, a sequence of elegies for friends felled by AIDS, which were among the poems collected in *The Man with Night Sweats* (1992); as he aged, confessed to a "weakness [for] shocking people"; followed up *Collected Poems* (1993) with *Boss Cupid* (2000), which included a poem (written, like Dante's *Inferno*, in terza rima) about a homosexual orgy in a San Francisco bathhouse and the sequence "Troubadour," consisting of lyric poems sympathetically presenting the perspective of the homosexual Wisconsin serial killer, necrophile, and cannibal Jeffrey Dahmer; in the English Department at the University of California at Berkeley, was successively lecturer and associate professor (1958–66), visiting lecturer (1975–79), and senior lecturer (1990–99); died at his home in San Francisco, California; was survived by Mike Kitay, his companion of 52 years. See *Current Biography* (November) 1988.

Obituary *New York Times* A p19 Apr. 28, 2004

HAGEN, UTA June 12, 1919–Jan. 24, 2004 German-born actress; esteemed acting teacher; one of the great leading ladies of the New York stage; made her professional debut as Ophelia, opposite Eva Le Gallienne's Hamlet, in a summer-stock production of *Hamlet* in 1937; made her Broadway debut as Nina in Alfred Lunt and Lynn Fontanne's 1938 revival of *The Sea Gull*; was Desdemona to Paul Robeson's Moor of Venice in a production of *Othello* (1943–44) that established a Broadway record for a Shakespearean run (295 performances); after touring as Blanche DuBois nationally (1948–49), replaced Jessica Tandy in the original Broadway production of *A Streetcar Named Desire* (1949); won two Tony Awards for best actress in a Broadway play, for her creations of Georgie in *The Country Girl* (1950–51) and Martha in *Who's Afraid of Virginia Woolf?* (1962–63); accrued a total of 16 Broadway credits, including starring roles in *The Happiest Days* (1939), *Key Largo* (1939–40), *Vickie* (1942), *Saint Joan* (1951), *In Any Language* (1952), and *Island of Goats* (1955); received a third Tony, for lifetime achievement, in 1999; was one of the recipients of a 2002 National Medal of the Arts, presented in 2003; especially liked interpreting roles in *The Cherry Orchard* and other works by Chekhov, because of her appreciation for a playwright with, in her words, "the wit and sense of humor" to see "the most tragic event without . . . sentimentality," to see "in any life experience something ludicrous"; was cast on television in such plays as *Macbeth* and *Out of the Dust* and on the motion-picture screen in *The Other* (1972), *The Boys from Brazil* (1978), and *Reversal of Fortune* (1990); when she was seven, was brought by her parents from Göttingen, Germany, to Madison, Wisconsin, where her father had founded and become head of the Department of Art History at the University of Wisconsin; acquired an early enthusiasm for theater from both her father and her mother, who was an occasional opera singer; after graduating from the University of Wisconsin High School, studied for one term at the Royal Academy of Dramatic Art in London and for one semester at the University of Wisconsin; in summer stock in 1938, co-starred in *The Latitude of Love* with José Ferrer, who became her first husband (in December 1938) and frequent stage partner over the following several years; with Ferrer, had a daughter, Leticia; in addition to her stage relationship with Paul Robeson in *Othello*, formed an intimate offstage liaison with the great African-American actor, singer, and civil rights activist (as well as outspoken radical leftist) that was controversial in the context of the culture of the time and accented her reputation as a self-described political "progressive"; in the political inquisition waged on the government level by the House Un-American Activities Committee and Senator Joseph McCarthy (in conjunction with such private-sector forces as the publication *Red Channels* and the compliance of some motion-picture and television producers), was named on the "Hollywood blacklist"; in the prime of her career, in 1951, when she was beginning to get big offers from the studios and networks, suddenly found herself non grata; "never got another television [offer], never got another film offer," as she recalled in an interview with Terry Gross on National Public Radio (November 4, 1998), referring to the approximately 10 years that she remained blacklisted; was "graylisted," as she put it, for an additional two decades; was "frightened" by the blacklisting, but, on the bright side, felt that it "kept me pure," preventing her from "being

tempted by movies and stuff that I would have been sorry [for] afterwards"; reached what she considered a turning point in her career when, in 1947, she worked under the stage director/teacher Harold Clurman, who relieved her of the "externally theatrical" baggage, the "Broadway tricks," she had acquired; when acting under Clurman's direction in *The Whole World Over* in 1947, met Herbert Berghof, a replacement in the cast, who had founded the Herbert Berghof Studio, a school for actors, two years before in Manhattan; after divorcing José Ferrer, in 1948, married Berghof, in 1951; became a teacher at the Herbert Berghof Studio and headed it after Berghof's death, in 1990; in the interim, while blacklisted in the 1950s, performed Off-Broadway or in summer theaters, as Natalia Petrovna in *A Month in the Country*, all of the female roles in *The Affairs of Anatol*, and Argia in *The Queen and the Rebels*; after a decade-long absence from the stage, in the 1995–96 Off-Broadway season was cast in the title role in the hit American premiere of *Mrs. Klein*, a play based on the private-life sorrows of Melanie Klein (1882–1960), the controversial Austrian-born psychoanalyst who pioneered child analysis and play therapy in Great Britain; regarding *Mrs. Klein*, told Mark Steyn for the *New York Times* (October 22, 1995), "The play is loaded with . . . loss, which isn't very hard for me to particularize"; Off-Broadway in 1998, played Ruth Steiner, a reclusive writer/teacher betrayed by a young female writing protégée in *Collected Stories*; in her last stage performance, starred in Richard Alfieri's *Six Dance Lessons in Six Weeks* in Los Angeles in 2001; published two books on acting, *Respect for Acting* (1973), written with Haskel Frankel, and *A Challenge for the Actor* (1991), and an autobiography, *Sources* (1983); said that she thought of her roles as "not acting, [but] living"; as an actress, sought "the spontaneity that comes without planning"; explained to Terry Gross, "When you are creating a role you are selecting from various aspects of your life and putting it together to create that new character"; at the Herbert Berghof Studio, taught two generations of actors (including the likes of Anne Meara, Jerry Stiller, Jack Lemmon, Lily Tomlin, Stockard Channing, Whoopie Goldberg, and Matthew Broderick) to eschew formal acting and "imitation of nature" and to "bring onstage" not an actor or actress but "a real human being with selected reality"; died in her home on Washington Square, in the Greenwich Village section of Manhattan. See *Current Biography* (October) 1963.

Obituary *New York Times* A p31 Jan. 15, 2004

HARDIN, GARRETT Apr. 21, 1915–Sep. 14, 2003 Ecologist; author; emeritus professor of biology and environmental studies at the University of California, Santa Barbara; was lettered in zoology as well as biology; at Stanford University (1942–46), conducted laboratory research on algae as an antibiotic and large-scale food source; withdrew from that work in 1946 because he had come to believe that its encouragement of overpopulaton outbalanced the potential production of food; in 1946, joined what is now the University of California at Santa Barbara, where he became a full professor of biology in 1957 and, in addition, professor of human ecology in 1963; in 1949, published *Biology: Its Human Implications*, which became a widely used college textbook; explained his views on genetics and evolution in *Nature and Man's Fate* (1959); in 1968, published his best-known work, the essay "The Tragedy of the Commons," in which he argued that the human race must sacrifice some of its freedoms in order to control population and pollution; enlarged on the ideas in that essay in the book *Exploring New Ethics for Survival: The Voyage of the Spaceship Beagle* (1972); also wrote, among other books, *Birth Control* (1970), *The Limits of Altruism: An Ecologist's View of Survival* (1977), *Living Within Limits: Ecology, Economy, and Population Taboos* (1993), and *The Immigration Dilemma: Avoiding the Tragedy of the Commons* (1995); published some 130 essays and reviews in professional journals; during the 1960s, lectured throughout the U.S. in favor of the legalization of abortion on demand, contributing to the climate of opinion resulting in the U.S. Supreme Court's decision in Roe v. Wade, in 1973; with his wife, Jane, was a member of End-of-Life Choices (originally, the Hemlock Society); with Jane, committed suicide in their home in Santa Barbara, according to one of their sons. See *Current Biography* (September) 1974.

Obituary *New York Times* C p15 Oct. 28, 2003

HARGROVE, MARION Oct. 13, 1919–Aug. 23, 2003 Writer; best known as the author of the phenomenal World War II nonfiction best-seller *See Here, Private Hargrove*; with the *Charlotte News*, a North Carolina newspaper, was features and obituary editor and re-write man from 1939 to 1941; following his induction into the U.S. Army at Fort Bragg, North Carolina, in July 1941, published humorous vignettes of his misadventures in basic training in the column "In the Army Now" in the *Charlotte News*; brought the vignettes together in *See Here, Private Hargrove* (1942), which included a foreword by the playwright Maxwell Anderson, reached the rank of sixth among best-sellers in American publishing history up to that time, and became the basis of two motion pictures, *See Here, Private Hargrove* (1944) and *What Next, Private Hargrove?*, in both of which Robert Walker played the author; in May 1942, became a staff writer for the army newspaper *Yank* in New York; in March 1943, was sent to China as a *Yank* correspondent; subsequently edited the China-Burma-India edition of *Yank*; in May 1944, returned to New York as *Yank*'s feature editor; was the newspaper's correspondent in the Philippines from August to October 1945, when he was discharged from the army with the rank of sergeant; wrote two novels, *Something's Got to Give* (1947), about radio broadcasters, and *The Girl He Left Behind: Or, All Quiet on the Third Platoon* (1956), about a peacetime army recruit, played by Tab Hunter in the movie version, released by Warner Brothers in 1956; with that film, began a long association with Warner Brothers; for Warners' television division, wrote the script for the TV film *Girl on the Run* (1957), which served as the pilot for the series *77 Sunset Strip*; wrote episodes of the television series *Maverick* (1957-62), *Destry* (1964), *I Spy* (1965-68), and *The Waltons* (1972-81); co-wrote the screenplay for the Warner feature film *Cash McCall* (1960); wrote the screenplays for the

Warner screen comedy *Boys' Night Out* (1962) and the studio's screen adaptation of the musical *The Music Man* (1962); died in Long Beach, California. See *Current Biography* (June) 1946.

Obituary *New York Times* B p9 Aug. 28, 2003

HEILBRUN, CAROLYN G. Jan. 13, 1926–Oct. 9, 2003 Feminist scholar; revisionist literary critic; polemicist; university professor; writer of mysteries; in her work, distinguished between sex and gender, calling the latter a cultural form or social construct; deconstructed traditional notions of male and female gender; encouraged her readers to escape from "the prison of gender," to question "the marriage script," and to realize, in Diane Sherlock's paraphrase, that "the stories that we tell define who we are"; dedicated her life to the cause of changing "the possible expectations for girls and the possibilities for women"; in addition to her nonfiction, wrote the Kate Fensler series of mystery stories under the pen name Amanda Cross; majored in English and philosophy at Wellesley College; received a Ph.D. degree in English literature at Columbia University in 1959; in an interview with Diane Sherlock for the *Radcliffe Review* (Winter 1998), recalled, "In graduate school, we all practiced New Criticism; you never mentioned the author [only the work]; you spoke only from Olympus. . . . You absolutely never talked about yourself"; after teaching at Brooklyn College for a year, joined Columbia's Department of English and Comparative Literature as an instructor in 1960; became an associate professor in 1967 and a full professor in 1972; was named Avalon Foundation Professor of Humanities in 1985; the following year, became the first director of Columbia's Institute for Research on Women and Gender; in 1961, published her first book, *The Garnett Family*, an expansion of her doctoral dissertation; in that work, revealed the beginning of her continuing fascination with the Bloomsbury group of English writers and intellectuals; published *Christopher Isherwood* in 1970; thought "that all of American literature was pretty horrible about women," as she told Diane Sherlock, but kept her silence until James Dickey's novel *Deliverance* was published, in 1970, prompting her to write the scathing article "The Masculine Wilderness of the American Novel," published in the *Saturday Review of Literature*; with that revolutionary piece, "infuriated everyone at Columbia, who never forgave [her] for it"; did not know she "was being brave," because she perhaps "wouldn't have done it" if she "had known what the result would have been"; was propelled to the forefront of the academic feminist movement by her book *Toward a Recognition of Androgyny: Aspects of Male and Female in Literature* (1973), in which she applied a feminist lens to the examination of world literature, from the Bible and the Greek classics through Shakespeare and Jane Austen to Virginia Woolf (perceived by Heilbrun as close to the androgynous ideal) and other moderns; wrote autobiographically for the first time in the introduction to her book *Reinventing Womanhood* (1979); in *Writing a Woman's Life* (1988), focused on autobiographical and biographical traditions; in the introduction to that book, argued that "men have always had narrative stories such as the quest motif and warrior examplar" while "well into the twentieth century it continued to be impossible for women to admit into their autobiographical narratives the claim of achievement, the admission of ambition, the recognition that accomplishment was neither luck nor the efforts or generosity of others"; went on to offer George Sand, Willa Cather, and Dorothy L. Sayers as examples of women breaking the traditional mold and to say that "only in the last third of the twentieth century have women [including the poets Denise Levertov, Anne Sexton, and Sylvia Plath] broken through to a realization of the narratives that have been controlling their lives"; in the essays collected in *Hamlet's Mother and Other Women* (1990), analyzed the representation of women in literature and the perceptions and misperceptions of that representation by critics; in that collection, defined a feminist as one who "questions the gender arrangements in society and culture and works to change them"; in 1995, published the biography *The Education of a Woman: The Life of Gloria Steinem;* included "A Unique Person," her essay on her friend May Sarton, the poet, in the collection of essays *The Last Gift of Time: Life Beyond Sixty* (1995); in another of the essays, wrote that she would decide each day whether to keep on living; in 1999, published *Women's Lives: The View from the Threshold,* a collection of lectures delivered at the University of Toronto two years before; in 2002, published the memoir *When Men Were the Only Models We Had: My Teachers Barzun, Fadiman, and Trilling;* co-wrote or edited other books on the politics of gender and related subects; served as president of the Modern Language Association in 1984 and, for years after that, as one of its three trustees; under the pen name Amanda Cross, introduced her fictional creation Kate Fensler, a feminist Manhattan university professor who moonlights as an amateur detective, in the mystery novel *The Last Analysis* (1964); went on to publish 13 more Kate Fensler novels (the last, *The Edge of Doom,* in 2002), sophisticated, intricately plotted whodunits rich in literary allusion; in addition, wrote short stories with Fensler as protagonist, nine of which are in *The Collected Stories of Amanda Cross* (1997); was the subject of Susan Kress's book *Carolyn Heilbrun: Feminist in a Tenured Position* (1997); feeling marginalized at Columbia University, took early retirement in 1992; died in her Manhattan apartment, apparenty by suicide—"She wanted to control her destiny, and she felt her life was a journey that had concluded," her son, Robert, explained, according to the *New York Times* (October 11, 2003); was survived by her husband, James Heilbrun, an economist and the co-author of *The Economics of Art and Culture,* and three children. See *Current Biography* (January) 1993.

Obituary *New York Times* A p13 Oct. 11, 2003

HERRING, PENDLETON Oct. 27, 1903–Aug. 17, 2004 British electrical engineer; inventor; shared the 1979 Nobel Prize for Physiology or Medicine for his work in developing computerized axial tomography, or CAT scanning, the application of computer techniques rather than, say, conventional X-rays to show parts of the insides of human body, which revolutionized medical diagnosis by making possible accurate three-dimensional representations of internal body parts; growing up on his father's farm in Nottinghamshire, England, "played around with farm machinery," as he recalled, "and . . . started to reason why things might work"; after graduating from a local grammar school, studied radio communications at City and Guilds College, London; with the Royal Air Force during World War II, was trained in radio mechanics and became an RAF instructor in radar; later, earned a diploma at Faraday House Engineering College, London; held no university degree; in 1951, joined the electronics-research staff of the conglomerate EMI Inc. (now Thorn EMI), where he worked for several years on radar and missiles guidance systems before concentrating on computer design; 1n 1958 and 1959, was the engineer in charge of the team that built EMI-DEC 1100, the first British all-transistor computer, which, while solid-state, was still very large; in the early 1960s, when the development of miniature integrated circuits was opening the way for the minicomputer, contributed to that development by designing a system capable, in his words, of "driving the transistor with a magnetic core"; also conducted research on "thin film," one of the approaches to large-capacity memory storage; in 1967, while working at EMI's central research laboratories on pattern-recognition studies, was struck with the idea that if a computer could recognize printed characters, it could also be used in connection with X-rays to create "picture reconstruction" of internal biological structure, organs, and tissue; working without publicity, completed the prototype of the CAT scanner in 1971, when the invention (then limited chiefly to scanning of the human head) was used for the first time on a human being, a woman with a suspected brain lesion who was a patient of the nuerosurgeon James Ambrose at Morley's Hospital in Wimbledon, Greater London; publicly discussed his invention for the first time in April 1972, when EMI announced that it was beginning production of the first commercial model, the EMI-CT 1000; in the December 1973 issue of the *British Journal of Radiology,* published the paper "Computerized Transverse Axial Scannng (Tomography)," in which he explained how the EMI-CT 1000 collated sequences of two-dimensional, cross-sectional scans to construct high-resolution three-dimensional representations of internal organs and tissues; estimated that the EMI-CT 1000 was a hundred times more efficient than conventional X-ray technology in processing information gathered; in succeeding years, conducted research to improve CAT technology and extend it to whole-body scanning; also contributed to another technique, magnetic resonance imaging (MRI); shared the 1979 Nobel Prize for Physiology or Medicine with the South African–born American medical physicist Alan McLeod Comack, who, independently of Hounsfield, had published mathematical calculations related to the development of computer-assisted tomography; was head of the medical-systems section at AMI from 1972 to1976, when he became chief staff scientist; was senior staff scientist from 1977 to 1985 and thereafter a consultant to AMI laboratories until his retirement, in 1986; was knighted in 1981; never married; died in Kingston upon Thames, Surrey, England. See *Current Biography* (March) 1980.

Obituary *New York Times* A p13 Aug. 21, 2004

HICKS, LOUISE DAY Oct. 16, 1916–Oct. 21, 2003 Former Democratic congresswoman; lawyer; political activist; in the 1960s and 1970s, led the opposition to the busing of schoolchildren out of their neighborhoods in Boston, Massachusetts; according to the London *Guardian* (October 29, 2003), "She always denied being a bigot, but was at the very least an opportunist for championing the prejudice of Irish-American Boston and its seething hatred of blacks"; after graduating from Wheelock College, in Boston, taught at a primary school in Brookline, Massachusetts, clerked in the law office of her father, William J. Day, a South Boston lawyer and judge, and married John Hicks, a design engineer; after earning a J.D. degree at Boston University, in 1955, established the law firm of Hicks and Day with her older brother John; was elected to the first of three two-year terms on the Boston School Committee in 1961; became its chair in her second term; staunchly fought imposition of busing as a means of alleviating de facto racial segregation in the Boston school system; did not back down when, in 1965, the state legislature enacted a law denying state financing to any school district refusing to desegregate; described the legislators as "suburban" politicians using urban schoolchildren as "scapegoats" for their own failure "to solve the housing, economic, and social problems" of minorities; once said, as quoted in the *Boston Globe* (October 22, 2003), "A large part of my vote probably does come from bigoted people. But, after all, I can hardly go around telling them, 'Don't vote for me if you're bigoted.' The important thing is that I'm not bigoted. To me, that word means all the dreadful Southern segregationist, Jim Crow business that's always shocked and revolted me"; ran unsuccessfully for mayor of Boston in 1967; was elected to the Boston City Council in 1969; in 1971, again lost in a mayoralty election; retained her Boston City Council seat while representing Massachusetts' Ninth Congressional District in Washington (1971–73); lost her bid for reelection to Congress; back in Boston, became the City Council chair; when phased busing was imposed on the Boston school system by order of U.S. district judge W. Arthur Garrity Jr. in 1974, attacked Garrity as a patrician whose decision "discriminates against the poor"; was reelected to the City Council in 1975; failed to win reelection in 1977; was later appointed to fill a vacancy on the council (1979–80); died at her home in South Boston. See *Current Biography* (March) 1974.

Obituary *New York Times* C p15 Oct. 23, 2003

HILL, HERBERT Jan. 24, 1924–Aug. 15, 2004 Civil rights activist; university professor; a white man who directed labor relations at the National Association for the Advancement of Colored People for a quarter-century and later helped establish the black studies program at the University of Wisconsin, Madison; after completing his studies at New York University and the New School for Social Research (Now the New School University) and working as an organizer for a steel-workers' union, became an NAACP staffer in the late 1940s; became the association's labor secretary in 1951; in that position, at first tried to work closely with organized labor toward the goal of eliminating racial discrimination in employ-

ment; assumed an adversarial stance after finding, in his words, that "many labor unions have become narrow, restrictive, protective associations, and the American working class is predominantly racist"; in January 1959, sent a memorandum to George Meany, the president of the American Federation of Labor–Congress of Industrial Organizations, charging that the AFL-CIO violated its own constitutional pledge in failing to eliminate racial discrimination and segregation in many of its affiliated unions; later that year, told an interviewer: "The real corruption of the American labor movement is not the fast-buck boys or the racketeers who have worked their way in. The real corruption is moral. It's when unions say they're against discrimination and then go right on keeping Negroes out of membership and out of jobs"; in the 1960s, went on to attack not only trades and crafts unions—including the building-trades unions—with broad patterns of bias against minorities but even some that claimed to have relatively clean records, such as the International Ladies' Garment Workers Union; also targeted complicit industrial and other entities, from Hollywood studios and construction contractors to such corporations as General Motors, Lockheed Aircraft, Shell Oil, and General Electric; during the 1960s and 1970s, with NAACP lawyers, filed scores of legal injunctions and hundreds of complaints with the National Labor Relations Board and the federal Equal Employment Opportunity Commission against employers, employment agencies, and unions; in addition, sometimes led direct-action campaigns; during the 1970s, concentrated much effort into litigation against the willy-nilly discrimination against minorities resulting from seniority systems; was furious when, in 1977, the U.S. Supreme Court ruled that intentionality must be proved before the courts could declare such systems illegal; in August 1977, left the NAACP staff; was a professor of industrial relations and Afro-American studies at the University of Wisconsin, Madison from 1977 to 1997; wrote *The AFL-CIO and the Black Worker* (1982); with Jack Greenberg, wrote *Citizen's Guide to Desegregation: A Study of Social and Legal Change in American Life* (1955); edited, among other books, the anthology *Anger and Beyond: The Negro Writer in the United States* (1966); died in Madison, Wisconsin. See *Current Biography* (September) 1970.

Obituary *New York Times* A p13 Aug. 21, 2004

HOUNSFIELD, GODFREY Aug. 28, 1919–Aug. 12, 2004 British electrical engineer; inventor; shared the 1979 Nobel Prize for Physiology or Medicine for his work in developing computerized axial tomography, or CAT scanning, the application of computer techniques to the process of producing images of internal parts of the human body, which revolutionized medical diagnosis by making possible accurate three-dimensional representations of those body parts; growing up on his father's farm in Nottinghamshire, "played around with farm machinery," as he recalled, "and . . . started to reason why things might work"; after graduating from a local grammar school, studied radio communications at City and Guilds College, London; with the Royal Air Force during World War II, was trained in radio mechanics and became an RAF instructor in radar; later, earned a diploma at Faraday House Engineering College, London; held no university degree; in 1951, joined the electronics-research staff of the conglomerate EMI Inc. (now Thorn EMI), where he worked for several years on radar and missile guidance systems before concentrating on computer design; 1n 1958 and 1959, was the engineer in charge of the team that built EMI-DEC 1100, the first British all-transistor computer, which, while solid-state, was still very large; in the early 1960s, when the development of miniature integrated circuits was opening the way for the minicomputer, contributed to that development by designing a system capable, in his words, of "driving the transistor with a magnetic core"; also conducted research on "thin film," one of the approaches to large-capacity memory storage; in 1967, while working at EMI's central research laboratories on pattern-recognition studies, was struck with the idea that if a computer could recognize printed characters, it could also be used in connection with X-rays to create "picture reconstruction" of internal biological structures, organs, and tissues; working without publicity, completed the prototype of the CAT scanner in 1971, when the invention (then limited chiefly to scanning the human head) was used for the first time on a human being, a woman with a suspected brain lesion who was a patient of the neurosurgeon James Ambrose at Morley's Hospital in Wimbledon, Greater London; publicly discussed his invention for the first time in April 1972, when EMI announced that it was beginning production of the first commercial model, the EMI-CT 1000; in the December 1973 issue of the *British Journal of Radiology*, published the paper "Computerized Transverse Axial Scannng (Tomography)," in which he explained how the EMI-CT 1000 collated sequences of two-dimensional cross-sectional scans to construct high-resolution three-dimensional representations of internal biological organs and tissues; estimated that the EMI-CT 1000 was a hundred times more efficient than conventional X-ray technology in processing information gathered; in succeeding years, conducted research to improve CAT technology and extend it to whole-body scanning; also contributed to magnetic resonance imaging (MRI); shared the 1979 Nobel Prize for Physiology or Medicine with the South African–born American medical physicist Alan McLeod Comack, who, independently of Hounsfield, had published mathematical calculations related to the development of computer-assisted tomography; was head of the medical-systems section at AMI from 1972 to 1976, when he became chief staff scientist; was senior staff scientist from 1977 to 1985 and thereafter a consultant to AMI laboratories until his retirement, in 1986; was knighted in 1981; never married; died in Kingston upon Thames, Surrey, England. See *Current Biography* (March) 1980.

Obituary *New York Times* A p21 Aug. 20, 2004

ISTOMIN, EUGENE Nov. 26, 1925–Oct. 10, 2003 Pianist; one of the first great classical pianists born in the U.S.; a publicity-shy virtuoso with, in his words, "a natural inclination toward the intellectual and toward the deeper aspects of playing"; had "a unique commitment to both the standard solo repertory and to chamber music," as Robert Jacobson observed in his book *Reverberations*; was the last surviving member of the famed trio that included the violinist Isaac Stern and the cellist Leonard Rose; was born to two professional singers who had emigrated from Russia; when he was six, accompanied his mother in a recital at the Brooklyn Academy of Music, the occasion of his being discovered by the pianist and conductor Alexander Siloti; after studying under Siloti's daughter Kyriena, studied at the Mannes College of Music, in Manhattan (1935–38) and at the Curtis Institute, in Philadelphia (1939–42), where his piano teacher was Rudolf Serkin; through the influence of the composer Harold Brown, became a devotee of the recordings and concerts of the pianist Artur Schnabel; in 1943, performed the Chopin Piano Concerto in F minor with the Philadelphia Orchestra and the Brahms Piano Concerto no. 2 in B Flat Major with the New York Philharmonic; following his first New York City recital, at Town Hall in April 1944, toured the U.S. with Adolph Busch and his Chamber Players for a number of months; was often a soloist with the New York Philharmonic in the late 1940s; with Alexander Schneider in 1949, performed all of Beethoven's sonatas for violin and piano in Chicago, New York, and Cambridge, Massachusetts; with Schneider in the summer of 1950, traveled to Prades, France, to participate in a series of Bach bicentennial concerts conducted by the cellist Pablo Casals, which set the precedent for the annual Prades Festival; repeatedly turned to Prades in the summer; with Casals and Schneider, made recordings of Beethoven and Schubert chamber works; with Casals, privately and publicly, played most of the standard piano chamber repertory; maintained his close relationship to Casals until Casals's death, in 1963—and even beyond, in a sense, through his marriage to Casals's widow, Marta; with her, established festivals in Casals's memory in Puerto Rico and Mexico; in 1956, made the first of the world tours that would ultimately comprise some 4,000 concerts on six continents; in 1961, began touring with Isaac Stern and Leonard Rose; concertized and recorded with that trio for 23 years, playing chamber pieces by Beethoven, Mozart, Mendelssohn, Schubert, Ravel, Brahms, and others until Rose's death, in 1984; with the trio, won a Grammy Award in 1971; in addition to his chamber-music recordings, recorded concertos by Mozart, Chopin, Brahms, Tchaikovsky, and Rachmaninoff; performed under the batons of such orchestra conductors as Bruno Walter, Fritz Reiner, Georg Szell, Leopold Stokowski, and Leonard Bernstein; included in his repertory compositions written for him by Henri Dutilleux, Roger Sessions, and Ned Rorem; with the baritone Donald Gramm, made a recording of some of Rorem's songs; beginning in 1988, took two of his pianos (and a technician to maintain them) with him on his tours of the U.S.; taught at the Manhattan School of Music (where Marta Casals Istomin has served as president since 1992) and took part in Professional Training Workshops at Carnegie Hall; died at his home in Washington, D.C. See *Current Biography* (October) 1977.

Obituary *New York Times* A p13 Oct. 11, 2003

IZETBEGOVIC, ALIJA Aug. 8, 1925–Oct. 19, 2003 Bosnian Muslim leader; former president of Bosnia and Herzegovina, in the former Yugoslavia; lawyer; during the Communist regime of Josip Broz Tito and his successors in Yugoslavia in the decades following World War II, was imprisoned twice, for a total of nine years, for defying the government's religious restraints and disseminating "Islamic propaganda"; published the journal *Mujahid* (The Warrior), which was considered subversive; tried to define the "place of Islam in the general spectrum of ideas" in his book *Islam between East and West* (1980); was better known, or more notorious, for *The Islamic Declaration of Alija Izetbegovic* (1970), which Serbs exhibited during the 1990s Bosnian war as alleged evidence that Islamic fundamentalism was poised to inundate the Balkans and Western Europe as well; alsowrote *Izetbegovic of Bosnia-Herzegovina: Notes from Prison, 1983–1988* (2002); in 1990, when the Communist Party abdicated its rule of Yugoslavia, led a group of Bosnian Muslims in forming the Party of Democratic Action, which dominated the first non-Communist elections in Bosnia, where Muslims made up about half the population, with ethnic Serbs and Croats making up the other half; assumed the presidency in a coalition government, with an ethnic Croat as prime minister and an ethnic Serb as speaker of Parliament; after Yugoslavia began to disintegrate, with the secession of the republics of Croatia and Slovenia in 1991, decided that life in a Yugoslavia ruled by the Serb Slobodan Milosevic would be intolerable for Bosnia's Muslims; on February 29 and March 1, 1992, offered the voters of Bosnia and Herzegovina a pro-independence referendum, boycotted by Bosnia's ethnic Serbs, that was overwhelmingly approved by the Bosnians who voted; proclaimed Bosnia and Herzegovina an independent republic on March 3, 1992; with the establishment of his independent government in Sarajevo, Bosnia's capital, in April 1992, sparked violent rebellion by ethnic Serbs, who were joined by ethnic Croats and armed by Serbia—the start of a protracted war in which at least 200,000 people died, many by "ethnic cleansing," and a million became homeless; on his side, welcomed the enlistment of Islamic warriors from such nations as Iran, Saudi Arabia, and Libya; under U.S. auspices, made peace with the Croats in March 1994; then concentrated on his fight with the Serbs, in which he was aided by U.S.-led NATO air strikes beginning in August 1995; at Wright-Patterson Air Force Base, in Ohio, in November 1995, joined the Serbian president, Slobodan Milosevic, and the Croatian president, Franjo Tudjman, in initialing an agreement to end the war; in Paris the next month, signed the agreement, which preserved the "state" of Bosnia-Herzegovina while dividing it into a Serb Republic and a Muslim-Croatian Federation; thereafter, presided over the bifurcated state alongside two co-presidents, a Serb and a Croat; resigned from the uneasy triumvirate in 2000; died in Sarajevo. See *Current Biography* (August) 1993. — K.D.

Obituary *New York Times* A p15 Oct. 20, 2003

JULIANA QUEEN OF THE NETHERLANDS Apr. 30, 1909–Mar. 20, 2004 A popular monarch, known as Princess Juliana before and after her reign (1947–1980); christened Juliana Luise Emma Maria Wilhelmina; as the young Princess Juliana, formed her country's National Crisis Committee during the great economic depression of the 1930s; for many years, headed the Netherlands Red Cross; in exile in Canada during World War II, was active in war charities; ruled as regent from September 1947 until September 1948, when she was inaugurated as Queen of the Netherlands upon the abdication of her mother, Queen Wilhelmina; proceeded to preside over her country's recovery from World War II and the Nazi occupation and the final dissolution of the Dutch colonial empire; with her simplicity and accessibility, earned the affection of the Dutch people and brought the royal family closer to them; is fondly remembered for her devotion to such causes as the relief of the destitute and European displaced persons in the postwar years and especially for her actions on the occasion of the disastrous flood in the southern Netherlands in February 1953, in which some 2,000 people died; during the flood, traveled the stricken provinces by boat, plane, and helicopter, participating in the rescue work; established a fund for the victims; lobbied for the renovation of old dikes and the construction of new ones; in November 1953, stood on one of new dikes to celebrate with her people the final damming-out of the North Sea waters that had caused the flood; was touched by some controversies, the first in 1953, when, in her desperation to find a cure for the near-total blindness of her youngest daughter, Marijke Christina (called Christina), she fell under the sway of the faith-healer Greet Hofmans, to the widely reported annoyance of her husband, Prince Consort Bernhard; in the mid-1960s, was embarrassed by her daughters Irene and Beatrix, the former of whom flouted the Calvinist tradition of the House of Orange by converting to Roman Catholicism and then married, without government approval, a claimant to the Spanish throne who was also a leader in Spain of the right-wing Carlist Party, and the latter of whom married a German aristocrat and diplomat, Claus von Amsberg, who had been a member of the Hitler Youth and had served in the German armed forces during World War II; was most disgraced in 1976, when her husband was forced to resign various positions, including that of commander of the Dutch armed forces, after he was found guilty of soliciting and accepting kickbacks connected with the Netherlands' purchases of aircraft from the Lockheed Corp.; abdicated in April 1980, making way for the ascension to the throne of the eldest of her four daughters, Beatrix; died in Soestdijk Palace in the municipality of Baarn, the Netherlands. See *Current Biography* (January) 1955.

Obituary *New York Times* A p33 Mar. 21, 2004

KASE, TOSHIKAZU Jan. 12, 1903–May 21, 2004 Japanese diplomat; was a son of a vice president of Chuo University in Tokyo; after studying for the foreign service in Japan and earning an M.A. degree at Harvard University (in 1928), was successively a Japanese attaché in Washington, D.C., and to the League of Nations in Geneva, Switzerland, and a vice consul in Bangkok, Siam (now Thailand); was a secretary in the information bureau of the foreign ministry in Tokyo from 1934 to 1937 and a secretary in the Japanese Embassy in London from 1937 to 1940, when he was made secretary to the foreign minister in Tokyo; in 1941, helped to draft the document in which the Japanese government presented an ultimatum to the U.S. government coinciding with the Japanese military attack on Pearl Harbor; at the end of World War II, drafted the English version of the Japanese document accepting the terms of the Potsdam Declaration, which defined the terms for Japan's surrender; was on the deck of the battleship *USS Missouri* in Tokyo Bay when the Japanese surrendered unconditionally to the U.S., on September 2, 1945; was reinstated in his former position at the foreign ministry in 1946; held that position until 1948; returned to government as the chief adviser to Foreign Minister Mamoru Shigemitsu in 1954; the following year, became Japan's first ambassador to the United Nations; subsequently, was ambassador to Yugoslavia and Bulgaria (simultaneously); after retiring from government, in 1960, concentrated on lecturing and writing a newspaper column; in 1995, as chairman of the conservative National Committee for the 50th Anniversary of the end of World War II, opposed a Japanese apology for World War II atrocities, arguing in part that Japan's actions had helped break the grip of Western colonialism in Asia; wrote several volumes of autobiography/contemporary history, including that translated under the title *Journey to the Missouri* (1950), published in England as *Eclipse of the Rising Sun* (1951); lived in Kamakura, a coastal town southwest of Tokyo. See *Current Biography* (April) 1957.

Obituary *New York Times* B p10 June 2, 2004

KAZAN, ELIA Sep. 7, 1909–Sep. 28, 2003 Stage and screen director; one of Broadway and Hollywood's most honored, albeit controversial and divisive, directors; typically, dealt with American themes with both social concern and mastery of naturalistic melodrama; on Broadway, was most renowned for his original productions of plays by Arthur Miller and Tennessee Williams; received best-director Tony Awards for Miller's *All My Sons* (1947) and *Death of a Salesman* (1949) and Archibald MacLeish's *J.B.* (1959); with seven of his films, drew 20 Academy Awards, including two best-director Oscars—one for *Gentleman's Agreement* (1947), a daring (for its time) indictment of subtle but rampant anti-Semitism in the post–World War II U.S., and *On the Waterfront* (1954), a powerful drama about a simple, anguished stevedore who, breaking the code of silence on the New York/New Jersey docks, sparks a rank-and-file rebellion against waterfront labor-union racketeers; intended *On the Waterfront* to "exemplify the way self-appointed tyrants can be defeated by right-thinking people in a vital democracy"; elicited from Marlon Brando in the role of Terry Malloy, the heroic longshoreman, an intense performance that stands as one of the screen's most striking examples of natural, "method" acting; also contributed seminally to the acting development of James Dean, Warren Beatty, Natalie Wood, Lee Remick, and Andy Griffith, among others; was born to Anatolian Greek parents in what is now Istanbul, Turkey; immigrated to the U.S. with his parents when he was four; after earning a B.A. degree in En-

glish at Williams College, studied briefly at the Yale University Drama School; in the 1930s, was influenced by communism and other political and cultural movements that found fertile ground in the great economic depression of that era; in 1933, moved to New York City and joined the Group Theater, a radical leftist experimental troupe that specialized in the Stanislavski method of acting; with the Group Theater, served an apprenticeship in assistant stage managing and bit-part acting until 1935, when he was cast as the "proletarian thunderbolt" taxi driver Agate Keller in the group's most famous original production, Clifford Odets's agitprop play *Waiting for Lefty*; during the last several years of the group's existence, played Kewpie in Odets's *Paradise Lost* (1935) and the gangster Eddie Fuselli in Odets's *Golden Boy*, among other roles; was cast in two films directed by Anatole Litvak, *City of Conquest* (1940) and *Blues in the Night* (1941); meanwhile, had begun directing at the Group Theater in 1935; on Broadway, directed the comedy *Cafe Crown* in 1942; later in the same year, achieved acclaim on Broadway as director of *The Skin of Our Teeth*; over the following four years, directed, among other Broadway productions, the musicals *One Touch of Venus* and *Sing Out, Sweet Land*; in 1947, began his collaboration with Arthur Miller and Tennessee Williams with his direction of Williams's *A Streetcar Named Desire* and Miller's *All My Sons*; in 1951, directed the acclaimed screen adaptation of *A Streetcar Named Desire*; in 1948, assisted Lee Strasberg and other Group Theater alumni in founding the Actors Studio, a less political "method" troupe/school than its predecessor; joined the American Committee for Cultural Freedom, a liberal anti-communist organization founded in 1951; in the most controversial act of his career, in 1952 cooperated with the House Un-American Activities Committee in its investigation of communist infiltration into the entertainment industry (chiefly, its Hollywood sector); admitted that he had been a member of the Communist Party from 1934 to 1936, and supplied the committee with the names of others in the Group Theater who had been party members; on Broadway during the 1950s, directed Tennessee Williams's *Camino Real* (1952), *Cat on a Hot Tin Roof* (1955), and *Sweet Bird of Youth* (1959), George Tabori's *Flight into Egypt* (1952), Robert Anderson's *Tea and Sympathy* (1953), and William Inge's *Dark at the Top of the Stairs* (1957); left the Actors Studio and Broadway to devote himself to other tasks, including co-supervision of the founding of the Lincoln Center Repertory Company; in the mid-1960s, directed five dramas under that company's banner, including the original production of Arthur Miller's *After the Fall*; meanwhile, had been directing films on and off for three decades; following a brief venture into documentary filmmaking, scored a popular and critical success with his first feature film, *A Tree Grows in Brooklyn* (1945); secured his position in Hollywood with *Boomerang* (1947); felt that his first truly cinematic picture, more than a filmed play, was the thriller *Panic in the Streets* (1950); in *East of Eden* (1955), used Cinemascope imaginatively; directed and, with Tennessee Williams, co-wrote the screenplay for *Baby Doll* (1956); explored youthful sex, insanity, and adult hypocrisy in *Splendor in the Grass*

(1961); in 1963, made *America, America*, the screen adaptation of his same-titled 1962 novel; in 1969, adapted for the screen *The Arrangement*, his 1967 novel about a married middle-aged executive who becomes an adulterous philanderer; wrote the novels *The Assassins* (1972), *The Understudy* (1974), and *The Anatolian* (1982); in 1976, directed his last film, *The Last Tycoon*; in 1988, published the autobiography *Elia Kazan: A Life*; received an Academy Award for lifetime achievement in 1999; died at home in Manhattan. See *Current Biography* (October) 1972.

Obituary *New York Times* p1+ Sep. 29, 2003

KEESHAN, BOB June 27, 1927–Jan. 23, 2004 Television actor and producer; a gentle, avuncular pioneer in children's television; preceded by years even the late Fred Rogers (of public television's *Mr. Rogers' Neighborhood*) in offering a low-keyed alternative to the fast-paced animation, slapstick, and occasional violence of much of the TV programming for children; was the creator and host of *Captain Kangaroo*, commercial television's longest-running program for preschoolers and kindergarteners, which was broadcast on weekdays for 29 years on the CBS network and subsequently for six years on PBS and received six Emmy Awards and three Peabody Awards; like Fred Rogers, addressed himself not to a studio audience but directly to the child watching at home; without patronization, tried to prepare that child "to be good to other people and to consider other people"; before and after serving in the U.S. Marine Corps (1945–46), worked as a page at the National Broadcasting Co.'s studios in Manhattan; on the NBC television network's children's show *Howdy Doody*, appeared as Clarabell the clown (1948–52); while working on *Howdy Doody* (a show that, in his words, he "never understood" and was "completely beyond" him), realized that the typical television offering for children was a shoddy and overly violent offering and began to think about producing a show that would respect the intelligence, sensibility, curiosity, and potential good taste of the average child; began to put some of his ideas into practice at ABC-TV, the ABC network's flagship station in New York City, as the host of the local shows *Time for Fun* (1953–55) and *Tinker's Workshop* (1954–55); left ABC-TV to produce (originally in collaboration with Jack Miller) *Captain Kangaroo* for the CBS network, where the hour-long show premiered in the morning prime-time slot on October 3, 1955; on that program, portrayed the Captain of Treasure House, a domain strewn with items calculated to delight and inform children and arouse their wonder and imaginations; in that portrayal, was assisted by Mr. Green Jeans (Hugh "Lumpy" Brannum), a simple farmer who acted as Treasure House's expert on natural history and custodian of the cats, dogs, and other animals introduced, and, behind the scenes, the puppeteer Cosmo "Gus" Allegretti; succeeded in presenting a show that "felt like an impromptu walk through a child's ideal playground" but "was actually smartly scripted," as Peggy Charren (founder of Action for Children's Television) observed, and which was, as its pre–*Sesame Street* Peabody citation read, "the only children's program on network television . . .

which puts the welfare of the children ahead of that of the sponsor; which instructs children in safety, in ethics, in health, without interrupting the serious business of entertaining them at the same time"; briefly starred in the Saturday morning children's show *Mr. Mayor* (1964–65); with others, lobbied for the federal Children's Television Act (implemented in 1990), which requires broadcasters to run three hours of programming beneficial to children weekly; co-founded Corporate Family Solutions, an organization providing day-care programs to businesses; believed that "play is the the work of children," that "it's very serious stuff," and "if it's properly structured in a developmental program, children can blossom"; wrote several books, including *Growing Up Happy* (1989), which was in part an autobiography, and *Good Morning, Captain: 50 Wonderful Years with Bob Keeshan, TV's Captain Kangaroo* (1996); introduced children to a variety of music on his television show and on recordings on the Columbia and Golden Records labels; lived in Hartford, Vermont; died in a hospital in Windsor, Vermont. See *Current Biography* (May) 1965.

Obituary *New York Times* A p13, Jan. 24, 2004

KELMAN, CHARLES May 23, 1930–June 1, 2004 Physician; surgeon; an inventive ophthalmologist whose landmark innovations beginning with the surgical instrument known as the cryostylet were at first fiercely resisted by the ophthalmological establishment; with his invention of the phacoemulsification and aspiration procedure, made possible the transformation of the once dreaded cataract operation into a relatively routine outpatient procedure; as a child growing up in New York City, was originally drawn to music; by age nine, had mastered the clarinet and the saxophone; without abandoning his interest in music, entered the medical profession at the insistence of his father; after completing the premed program at Tufts University, obtained his M.D. degree at the medical school of the University of Geneva in Switzerland (1956) and subsequently interned and did postgraduate work and residency in ophthalmology in New York City and Philadelphia; in 1962, became intrigued by the possibility of applying to ophthalmology the cryogenic technique pioneered by the New York neurosurgeon Irving S. Cooper, who was using steel rods supercooled by liquid nitrogen in treating tumors and Parkinson's disease; in 1963, succeeded in refining Cooper's probe into the cryostylet, a cryoprobe small enough for use in removing cataracts (an achievement already realized, he soon learned, by an eye surgeon in Poland); in addition to reducing the size of the probe, obtained the necessary low temperature (40 degrees below zero Fahrenheit) with ordinary water rather than the expensive liquid nitrogen; with the cryostylet, improved the success rate of cataract surgery, an operation that still required a hospital stay of several days followed by four to six weeks of convalescence; under grants from the John A. Hartford Foundation, went on to seek ways of breaking up a cataract and removing it through a needle puncture; later recalled, "I had seen patients who after cataract surgery had to lie in bed for ten days immobile. A lot of them never recovered. I decided I had to use my inventing talents to develop something important"; when having his teeth cleaned by his dentist one day, was inspired with the idea of adapting the ultrasonic dental drill to cataract surgery; developed an ultrasonic ophthalmic needle for the phacoemulsion and aspiration procedure that he first used in a cataract operation in 1967; in the early 1980s, perfected two "Kelman lenses," artificial intraoccular lens (IOL) implants, one for the anterior chamber of the eye and the other for the posterior chamber; became chief of ophthalmology at the Lydia E. Hall Hospital in Freeport, New York, where he performed between 800 and 1,000 cataract operations a year; also maintained an office with a staff of 18—including four ophthalmologists and two optometrists—occupying an entire floor of the Empire State Building in New York City; on and off over the years, kept a public hand in music, performing in such venues as the Concord Hotel in the Catskills and the Fontainebleu in Miami Beach and headlining a Carnegie Hall benefit for Ichilov Hospital in Israel; also on the bill at Carnegie Hall were, among other musical luminaries, the opera singer Jan Peerce and the jazz vibraphonist Lionel Hampton, both of whom had been patients of his; wrote the memoir *Through My Eyes: The Story of a Surgeon Who Dared to Take on the World* (1985); died in Boca Raton, Florida. See *Current Biography* (June) 1984.

KERR, CLARK May 17, 1911–Dec. 1, 2003 Educator; a visionary, seminal planner in American higher education; professor emeritus of economics and industrial relations, University of California at Berkeley; president emeritus, University of California; was the father of California's Master Plan for Higher Education, which has influenced public higher-education planning across the U.S. and to a significant extent internationally; after earning a B.A. degree at Swarthmore College and an M.A. degree at Stanford University, studied at the London School of Economics and the Graduate Institute of International Relations in Geneva, Switzerland, as a traveling American Friends Service Committee fellow during the 1935–36 academic year; subsequently, was an instructor at Antioch College and a teaching assistant at the University of California–Berkeley; after submitting a dissertation entitled "Productive Enterprises of the Unemployed," earned his Ph.D. degree in economics at Berkeley in 1939; taught labor economics at Stanford University in 1939–40 and at the University of Washington in Seattle from 1940 to 1945; outside academia, was for two decades, beginning in 1942, a private and federal mediator and arbitrator in scores of labor-management disputes, chiefly on the West Coast, including some involving longshoremen's, warehouse workers', and packinghouse workers' unions; in 1945, returned to Berkeley as a professor and, in addition, as the first director of Berkeley's Institute of Industrial Relations; under the imprint of the institute, published pamphlets on such subjects as collective bargaining, pension plans, and wage-and-hour policies; also headed Berkeley's faculty committee on tenure; in that position, defended faculty members who refused to sign a Cold War–era patriotic loyalty oath (although he himself signed the oath); in 1952, became Berkeley's first chancellor; in 1955, anticipating the coming of

age of the post–World War II generation, commonly known as the "baby boomers," coined the phrase "tidal wave of students"; in 1957, began work on a long-range higher-education development plan with two factors in mind: the imminent "tidal wave" and the increasing amounts of federal research money pouring into universities after World War II; in 1958, was appointed president of the University of California's statewide, multi-campus system by the university's 26-member Board of Regents; in 1960, began to implement the Master Plan for Higher Education, a cost-containing plan for balancing high standards of teaching and research with a universal admissions policy, promising that all who sought a higher education could, tuition free, find a place in one or another of three tiers: the University of California, comprising general or comprehensive/selective research campuses accepting the top 12.5 percent of high-school graduates, the California State University, comprising campuses accepting the remainder of the top third, and two-year vocational schools (community colleges), open to all; restructured the system's specialized schools into comprehensive universities alongside the crown jewel of the University of California system, Berkeley; added three new campuses (San Diego, Irvine, and Santa Cruz) to those in the top tier, which now number nine and are scheduled soon to number 10; following the eruption of the turbulent student "free speech" movement on the Berkeley campus in 1964, was caught in a crossfire from "an absolute movement with absolute values on the left and an absolute reaction and counterrevolution on the right," as Neil J. Smelser, university professor emeritus at Berkeley, has observed; in January 1967, following the election to the governorship of California of Ronald Reagan (who had promised to "clean up the mess at Berkeley"), was dismissed by the Board of Regents; did not survive as president because, in Professor Smelser's words, he was the victim "of a wider polarization in the large society in which he became . . . the major scapegoat of vilification by both left and right"; after his dismissal, was chairman and executive director of the Carnegie Commission on Higher Education (1967–73) and chairman and staff director of the Carnegie Council on Policy Studies in Higher Education (1974–79); published many books on labor economics, education, and related sociopolitical subjects, including *Unions and Union Leaders of Their Own Choosing* (1957), *Marshall, Marx and Modern Times: The Multi-Dimensional Society* (1969), *The Future of Industrial Societies* (1983), and *The Great Transformation in Higher Education* (1991), and, written with others, *Troubled Times for America: Higher Education in the 1990s and Beyond* (1994) and *Higher Education Cannot Escape History: Issues for the Twenty-first Century* (1994); in 1963, delivered three Godkin Lectures at Harvard University, the basis of his best-known book, *The Uses of the University* (1963), a groundbreaking work that has become a classic, now in its fifth edition (2001, with a new chapter on challenges facing higher education); in that partly cautionary work, argued that the American research university had become a "fractionalized" "multiversity," a subsidized "instrument of national purpose" providing "service stations of society" and training professionals for a "military-industrial complex";

also co-edited several books; wrote the memoir *The Gold and the Blue*, covering the period 1949 to 1967 and published in two volumes, the first subtitled *Academic Triumphs* (2002) and the second *The Years of Turmoil* (2003), both with forewords by Neil Smelser; died in El Cerrito, California. See *Current Biography* (April) 1961. — K.D.

Obituary *New York Times* B p7 Dec. 2, 2003

KING, ALAN Dec. 26, 1927–May 9, 2004 Comedian; actor; as a monologist, evolved early in his career from a callow borscht-belt vaudevillian with chutzpah to a swaggering "crabgrass" (his term) humorist venting the frustrations of an average married suburban male stymied by traffic jams on the Long Island Expressway, household and homeowners' problems, and difficult dealings with insurance companies, the telephone company, airlines, and other "nonservice" institutions, as he called them; later, broadened his comedic brush to include wider social and political jibes; was born Irwin Alan Kniberg to Russian-Jewish immigrant parents in Brooklyn, New York City; grew up there and on Manhattan's Lower East Side; while still a teenager, began his apprenticeship as a stand-up comic in occasional low-paying gigs in burlesque houses and small Catskill Mountains resorts; subsequently, performed regularly in a weekly showcase for new talent at a Manhattan nightclub and joined the Paramount Theater vaudeville troupe, one of the last of its kind; in the early 1950s, toured with variety acts built around performances by Lena Horne, Patti Page, and other pop singers; beginning in 1956, toured the U.S. and Great Britain with the singer Judy Garland; by the early 1960s, was appearing on network television as a panelist on quiz shows and a guest on variety shows; over a period of some 10 years, made dozens of appearances on *The Ed Sullivan Show*; for decades, was a frequent guest on *The Tonight Show Starring Johnny Carson* and sometimes substituted as host of that show; among many other television credits, was co-host of the Academy Awards presentations in 1971 and host ("the Abbot") of the New York Friars Club Roast of Hugh M. Hefner in 2001; had his own HBO special in 1987; in motion pictures, was cast in nearly 30 character roles, including those of rabbis in *Bye Bye Braverman* (1968) and *Enemies, A Love Story* (1989) and underworld types in *Night and the City* (1992) and *Casino* (1995); accrued several stage credits, including the role of Samuel Goldwyn in the Off-Broadway play *Mr. Goldwyn* (2002); produced a number of stage, screen, and TV projects; was much in demand as a toastmaster and after-dinner speaker; in collaboration with professional writers, put together four collections of humor, including *Anybody Who Owns His Own House Deserves It* (1962): wrote the autobiography *Name Dropping: The Life and Lies of Alan King* (1996) and the book *Matzo Balls for Breakfast and Other Memories of Growing Up Jewish*, scheduled for publication in 2005; founded the Alan King Tennis Classic in Las Vegas, Nevada, and the Alan King Diagnostic Clinic in Jerusalem, Israel; was a fund-raiser for the Nassau Center for Emotionally Disturbed Children on Long Island, New York; established a chair in dramatic arts at Brandeis University, in Waltham, Massachu-setts; lived in Kings Point, New York; died in Manhattan. See *Current Biography* (June) 1970.

Obituary *New York Times* B p7 May 10, 2004

KITTIKACHORN, THANOM Aug. 11, 1911–June 16, 2004 Thai military and political leader; former prime minister of Thailand; a staunch anti-Communist who supported U.S. policy in Southeast Asia, including the Vietnam War; an advocate of democracy whose rule was tainted with allegations of corruption, nepotism, and violations of human rights; as a career officer in the Royal Thai Army, rose to the rank of field marshal; following a military coup led by his mentor, Field Marshal Sarit Thanarat, in 1957, served as figurehead prime minister for nine months and defense minister for six years; following the death of Sarit, in 1963, ruled Thailand as a member of a triumvirate known as the "Three Tyrants"— which included his son, Colonel Naron Kittikachorn, and the son's father-in-law, Field Marshal Praphas Charusathien—until forced into exile by a bloody student-led rebellion in 1973; after returning to Thailand in 1976, was ordained a Buddhist monk; died in Bangkok, Thailand. See *Current Biography* (December) 1969.

Obituary *New York Times* B p8 June 18, 2004

KLEIBER, CARLOS July 3, 1930–July 13, 2004 Conductor; a reclusive perfectionist who conducted sparingly but, when he did, thrilled audiences with passionate, incandescent performances; was regarded by the singers Placido Domingo and Luciano Pavarotti, respectively, as "the consummate conductor" and "a musical genius beyond words"; built his impressive reputation on an unusually small repertoire of operas—including *Wozzeck, Der Rosenkavalier, Otello, Carmen, La Bohème*, and *Elektra*—and an even smaller symphonic repertoire; was the son of an Austrian father and an American mother; was born in Berlin, Germany, where his father, the conductor Erich Kleiber, was the general music director of the State Opera before resigning that position in 1934, after the Nazis began banning the performance of modernist musical works; immigrated with his family to Argentina; began to study music in Buenos Aires, although his father discouraged his pursuit of a musical career; returned to the study of music after briefly studying chemistry at the Technische Hochschule in Zurich, Switzerland; when he was 23, obtained a conducting position at the Theater am Gartnerplatz in Munich, Germany; subsequently, conducted at the Deutsche Oper am Rhein in Dusseldorf and Duisberg, Germany (1956–4), the Zurich Opera (1964–66), the Wurttemberg State Theatre in Stuttgart, Germany (1966–68), the Bavarian State Opera in Munich (1968–73), and the Vienna State Opera (1973); thereafter, held no permanent conducting positions, preferring to make guest appearances only; guest-conducted often in Munich, at the Beyreuth Festival, at La Scala in Milan, and at the Royal Opera House in Covent Garden, London; regularly conducted the New Year's concert of the Vienna Philharmonic Orchestra; made his American conducting debut in San Francisco in 1977; did two stints with the Chicago Symphony Orchestra, in 1978 and 1980; conducted 19 performances in two stints with the Metropolitan Opera in New York City, in 1988 and 1990; during the last years of his life, emerged from seclusion to conduct the Bavarian State Orchestra in 1995 and the Bavarian Radio Symphony Orchestra in 1999; lived for many years in Zurich and in Munich; had a few of his sessions conducting Beethoven, Brahms, and Schubert symphonies made available on recordings, as were his Vienna Philharmonic New Year's concerts and four operas: *Die Fledermaus, La Traviata, Der Freischütz,* and *Tristan und Isolde*; was predeceased by seven months by his wife, a Slovenian-born dancer; was buried beside her in Konjsica, Slovenia. See *Current Biography* (July) 1991.

Obituary *New York Times* B p9 July 20, 2004

KÜBLER-ROSS, ELISABETH July 8, 1926–Aug. 24, 2004 Swiss-born psychiatrist; thanatologist; the preeminent pioneer in the death-awareness and hospice movements; out of her experience with terminally ill patients, wrote the landmark book *On Death and Dying: What the Dying Have to Teach Doctors, Nurses, Clergy, and Their Own Families* (1969), which broke a taboo on such discussion; subsequently, turned to spiritualistic research; edited the prose and verse collection *Death: The Final Stage of Growth* (1975); collaborated with the photographer Mel Warshaw on *To Live Until We Say Goodbye* (1979), essentially a collection of statements by and portraits of dying patients; published her autobiography, *The Wheel of Life: A Memoir of Living and Dying*, in 1997; as a teenager during World War II, was a volunteer hospital aide at the Kantonsspital in Zurich, Switzerland; when peace came, hitchhiked through nine war-ravaged European countries, helping to set up typhoid and first-aid stations; decided to become a psychiatrist to help people deal with death when she was assisting in the care of survivors of the Nazi concentration camp in Majdanek, Poland; after obtaining her M.D. degree at the University of Zurich in 1957, married the American neuropathologist Emanuel Robert Ross, a fellow graduate of the University of Zurich medical school; moved to the U.S. with her husband in 1958; following internship and residencies in hospitals on Long Island and in New York City, was a fellow (1962–63) and instructor (1963–65) in psychiatry at the University of Colorado School of Medicine in Denver; in treating schizophrenics in Denver, achieved some success using a technique she would later use in her work with the dying: asking patients what they thought would be most helpful to them; when she was assistant professor of psychiatry at the University of Chicago Medical School (1965–70), began to organize seminars and workshops in which dying patients were the "teachers," talking about their thoughts and feelings with varied groups of professionals, including physicians, chaplains, theology students, and social workers; from those sessions, distilled five stages typically experienced in dying: denial, anger, bargaining, depression, and acceptance; left the University of Chicago when it declined to offer her tenure; served as medical director of the Family Services and Mental Health Center of South Cook County in Chicago Heights, Illinois, from 1970 to 1973; meanwhile, profoundly affected by the "near-death"

experiences described by patients after their revival from clinical death, arrived at a firm belief in the spirit world and began seeking "hard data" confirming the existence of an afterlife; in the mid-1970s, was much in demand on the lecture circuit not only on the subject of dying but also on that of life after death, or "life after life," as she put it; in 1976, began an unfortunate (as she would later acknowledge) association with the spiritualist "healers" Jay Barham and his wife Marti and their San Diego–based Church of the Facet of Divinity; in 1977, bought 42 acres of land near a ranch owned by the Barhams in the mountain foothills north of Escondido, California, where she established a teaching and healing center called Shanti Nilaya (Sanskrit words meaning "Home of Peace"), envisioned by her as the first of a worldwide network of retreats affirming "survival of the spirit after death in the form a living entity"; participated with the Barhams in gatherings at which they, as mediums, or "channelers," claimed to materialize "spirit guides" into human form; found her own reputation undermined when scandal struck in 1979, in the form of charges that Jay Barham, masquerading as various "spirit entities," had sexually seduced a number of females, including, allegedly, an underage girl; in 1984, moved to a 300-acre farm in Head Waters, Virginia, in the Shenandoah Valley, where she raised pet llamas and set up the Elizabeth Kübler-Ross Center; when she initiated a program of caring for babies and children with AIDS at the center, was vilified as "the AIDS lady" by some neighbors, who launched a series of break-ins and other acts of harassment against her center, culminating, apparently, in arson; after her home was destroyed in a suspicious fire in 1994, moved to Scottsdale, Arizona, where her son, Kenneth, a photographer, was living; died in Scottsdale; divorced in 1979; was survived by her son, a daughter, a sister, and two granddaughters. See *Current Biography* (June) 1980.

Obituary *New York Times* B p8 Aug. 26, 2004

LASSAW, IBRAM May 4, 1913–Dec. 30, 2003 Artist; abstract sculptor; one of the lesser known but most durable of the first wave of New York School artists; applied the tools and techniques of the metallurgist, the coppersmith, the welder, and the solderer to the creation of colorful free-form metal structures, from small metal jewelry and such moderate-sized pieces as *Milky Way* and *Moons of Saturn* to *Pillar of Fire*, a 28-foot bronze sculpture adorning the façade of Congregation Beth El in Springfield, Massachusetts, a work described by Janay Jadine Wong in *Art Journal* (December 22, 1994) as a "fluid and dynamic . . . design [that] thrusts upward, tree-like, with the multiple 'branches' seeming to shimmer and waver as light flickers across their surfaces"; was born in Egypt to Russian-Jewish émigré parents; in 1921, came to the U.S. with his parents, who settled in Brooklyn, New York; as a teenager, frequented the Brooklyn Museum, studied art at the Brooklyn Children's Museum, and read extensively in art history and aesthetics; was formatively influenced by Laszlo Moholy-Nagy's recounting of tactile experiments at the Bauhaus that suggested new sculptural materials and processes, by Buckminster Fuller's connecting architectural design with such natural systems as plants, trees, and the human body, and by the work of Joan Miro and Wassily Kandinsky, among other artists; was enrolled at the Beaux-Arts Institute of Design in Manhattan for a year (1930–31); also studied under Dorothea Denslow at the Clay Club in Manhattan; during the Depression of the 1930s, worked on various Federal Arts Project assignments; after trying his hand at Constructivist drawings, began experimenting with open-form sculpture in the early 1930s; at first, worked with clay and plaster, both of which proved to be too fragile for open-form; then tried liquid latex and rejected it, partly because of its smell; then, was influenced by the work of the Spanish artist Julio González, a pioneer in metal sculpture; in 1936, bought a forge and hammered out his first metal sculptures, which he considered too two-dimensional; subsequently, constructed sculptures from old motor parts, steel rods, plaster-coated wire, various wooden shapes (including shadow boxes), and even organic material; was a founder of American Abstract Artists, whose 1941 exhibition in New York City included his steel-and-plastic sculpture titled *Intersecting Rectangles*; during a stint in the U.S. Army during World War II, learned to weld; back in civilian life, applied his newly learned welding skill to his art; in Manhattan's Greenwich Village in 1949, began meeting with other artists (including such abstract-expressionist painters as Franz Kline and Willem de Kooning) in a group they called the Club; in 1950, began using an oxyacetylene torch to melt and fuse metals; with his rod-and-wire pieces *Milky Way* (1950) and *The Hyades* (1951), set a new direction for himself; pursuing that direction, encrusted the wires and rods in his architectonic structures with drops of melted metal or plastic; achieved striking variations in color and brilliant flame-like effects by applying to the drops various alloys and such chemicals as nitric acid, potassium nitrate, and lead acetate; also incorporated in his works, according to his own cataloging, "red copper, rusted iron, corroded green bronzes, bright gold, lead, chromium, silver and all colors of mineral and gem stones"; in 1951, had his first solo exhibition, at the Kootz Gallery in Manhattan, and began to sell his work to Nelson A. Rockefeller and other wealthy private collectors; in 1952, made his first sale of sculpture to a museum, the Whitney Museum of American Art; later became represented in the permanent collections of other major museums, including the Museum of Modern Art and the Solomon R. Guggenheim Museum, both in New York City; during the 1950s and 1960s, created more than 15 sculptures on commission for five synagogues and temples, including Temple Beth El in Providence, Rhode Island, and the Temple of Aaron Congregation in St. Paul, Minnesota; told Janay Jadine Wong that he did not consider such work "synagogue art"; did not compromise his freedom and integrity as an abstract artist because, as he explained (regarding *Pillar of Fire*), he "made the model first, and then I thought, what am I going to call it to make it fit in with the synagogue"; among other commissions, created *The Clouds of Magellan*, a suspended wire sculpture occupying a seven-by-three-by-nine-foot space in Philip Johnson's home near New Canaan, Connecticut; in the 1950s, settled with his wife, Ernestine, in the Spring section of East

Hampton, New York, where he worked in a studio behind their home; died at home. See *Current Biography* (January) 1957.

Obituary *New York Times* B p7 Jan. 2, 2004

LAUDER, ESTÉE July 1, 1906(?)–Apr. 24, 2004 Cosmetician; business executive; founder of the beauty enterprise now known as Estée Lauder Companies Inc., a leading manufacturer and marketer of upscale skin-care, makeup, fragrance, and hair-care products sold internationally under 19 brand names, including Estée Lauder, Clinique, Origins, Prescriptives, and Aramis (men's toiletries); was born into an Hungarian Jewish family in the borough of Queens, New York City; was formatively inspired by an uncle, John Schott, a chemist who brewed skin creams and lotions for women in his home laboratory; as a teenager, helped Schott sell his preparations; in developing her own business, refined Schott's treatments and concocted others of her own; thought of herself as "selling jars of hope"; initially attracted a clientele by demonstrating her wares in beauty salons in the New York metropolitan area and in Miami Beach, Florida; opened concessions in some of the salons; incorporated her flagship company, Estée Lauder Inc., in 1946; with a large order from Saks Fifth Avenue in Manhattan two years later, gained entrée to prestigious department stores across the U.S.; by the early 1950s, had counters (viewed by her as "spas") in branches of such stores as Marshall Field, I. Magnin, Neiman Marcus, and Bonwit Teller; later opened a counter in Bloomingdale's Manhattan store; in addition to her corporate headquarters, in Manhattan, oversaw laboratories and manufacturing facilities in Melville, New York; employed more than 20,000 persons; was assisted in running her cosmetics enterprise in the early decades by her businessman husband, Joseph H. Lauder, who died in 1983; in 1973, turned the presidency of Estée Lauder Inc. over to her older son, Leonard, who proceeded to acquire for the company its own retail outlets, to expand Estée Lauder Inc. into Estée Lauder Companies Inc., and to take the enterprise public in 1995, when its sales were reported to be $5 billion; with her husband, founded the Lauder Foundation, a medical and educational philanthropy; published the autobiography *Estée: A Success Story* (1985); died at her home on the Upper East Side of Manhattan; was survived by her son Leonard, now chairman of Estée Lauder Companies Inc., her younger son, Ronald, chairman of Clinique, and her grandson William Lauder, who became president and chief executive officer of Estée Lauder Companies Inc. on July 1, 2004. See *Current Biography* (July) 1986.

Obituary *New York Times* B p1+ Apr. 26, 2004

LEWIS, DAVID S. JR. July 6, 1917–Dec. 15, 2003 Former chairman, chief executive officer, and president of the General Dynamics Corp.; was a major force in the defense and aerospace industries for more than three decades; after receiving a B.S. degree in aeronautical engineering at the Georgia Institute of Technology, was employed as an aerodynamicist with the Glenn L. Martin Co. from 1939 to 1946; with Glenn L. Martin during World War II, worked on performance and flight testing of many new aircraft, including the B-26 Marauder; in 1946, joined the McDonnell Aircraft Corp. as chief of aerodynamics; as such, managed the development of the navy jet plane F2H Banshee and the air force strategic interceptor F-101 Voodoo; in 1956, headed a regrouping of diverse McDonnell engineering units into a single fast-track development team, which within two years produced the F-4 Phantom II jet-fighter plane, of which a total of more than 5,000 were ultimately sold to the U.S. Navy and Air Force and to foreign air forces; was also active in the development of McDonnell's Space Division, which produced the pioneering spacecraft *Mercury* and *Gemini* for NASA; rose through the ranks to become president and CEO of McDonnell Aircraft in 1962; led McDonnell into a merger with the Douglas Aircraft Corp., resulting in 1967 in the creation of the McDonnell-Douglas Corp.; became chairman of the new corporation's Douglas Division, a position in which he was responsible for the timely production of the DC-8 and DC-9 aircraft; in addition, successfully promoted the sale of the DC-10 airbus to American Airlines and others; attracted by the challenge of reviving the financially ailing General Dynamics Corp., accepted an offer to chair and serve as CEO of that company in October 1970; became president six months later; among other changes, centralized decision making, improved procurement procedures and tooling, introduced stricter inventory controls, made profitable acquisitions in the commercial field, and developed a better balance between the company's commercial interests and its defense interests (including the Trident submarine, the M1 Abrams tank, and the F-16 Falcon, the new standard fighter plane of the U.S. Air Force and four allied NATO air forces); guided General Dynamics from a $6.9 million loss in 1970 to a profit of $381.7 million in 1984; resigned in 1985, when the business conduct of General Dynamics was subjected to a U.S. Department of Justice investigation, which was dropped in 1987; died at the Bishop Gadsden Retirement Community in Charleston, South Carolina. See *Current Bography* (August) 1975.

Obituary *New York Times* B p9 Dec. 18, 2003

LÓPEZ PORTILLO, JOSÉ June 16, 1920–Feb. 17, 2004 President of Mexico (1976–82); a member of the Partido Revolucionario Institucional (Institutional Revolutionary Party, PRI), the party that ruled Mexico for 71 years (1929–2000); an expert on economic and political theory who could not handle power; began his presidency with high expectations, promising "to defend the peso like a dog"; proceeded to worsen PRI's reputation for brazen graft, nepotism, and venality; by squandering the windfall from newly tapped petroleum reserves in the Gulf of Mexico through profligate spending, the diversion of public moneys to personal purposes, and reckless borrowing abroad, plunged the peso into the depths of devaluation (70 pesos to the dollar, down from 20) and left Mexico with the world's second-largest foreign debt; studied law at the National Autonomous University of Mexico, where Luís Echeverría Álvarez was a classmate; subsequently, earned a degree in political science at the University of Chile with a thesis that was published in 1946 with the title *Va-*

loración de lo estatal (An Appraisal of the State); practiced law for several years; during the 1950s, taught law, political science, and public administration at the National Autonomous University of Mexico; in 1959, entered Mexican government service in a technical position in the Ministry of National Patrimony ("patrimony" referring to the nation's heritage); ascended governmental ranks to become minister of finance and public credit following the election of Luís Echeverría Álvarez to the presidency, in 1970; as Echeverría's successor in the presidency (limited by law to one six-year term), carried forward Echeverría's "dirty war" on radical leftist guerrillas (resulting in the disappearance of approximately 800 people, referred to as the "disappeared"); like Echeverría, ostensibly promoted a mixed economy while pursuing a program of bureaucratic central planning, deficit spending, redistribution of wealth, and state capitalism; increased the number of state-owned businesses, mostly money-losers, run by party members, from 750 to 1,100; diverted public moneys to personal projects, including a multi-mansioned estate for himself and another for his mistress, Rosa Luz Alegria (whom he appointed secretary of tourism); recklessly borrowing against anticipated petroleum revenues, built up a foreign debt that was passing the $70 billion mark in August 1982; at that point, announced that Mexico was not able to service the interest payments on the debt; blamed the default and the debt crisis on Mexico's private banking system, which he nationalized; after leaving office, divorced his first wife, Carmen; reviled at home, lived in Spain and other European countries for a few years with his mistress, Rosa; later married the retired actress Sasha Montenegro; wrote a scholarly work on modern political theory, *Génesis y téoria general del estado moderna* (1958), and another on the concept and scope of the novel, *La novela, su concepto y su alcance* (1962); subsequently, wrote two novels, *Quetzalcoatl* and *Don Q* (1969); later wrote and illustrated (with 103 drawings) a book on the Spanish conquest of Mexico translated into English as *They Are Coming* (1992); died in Mexico City. See *Current Biography* (June) 1972.

Obituary *New York Times* B p9 Feb. 19, 2004

LOUDON, DOROTHY Sep. 17, 1933–Nov. 15, 2003 Actress; comedienne; singer; honed her craft in cabaret; on Broadway, won a Tony Award for her portrayal in 1977 of the mean-spirited orphanage director Aggie Hannigan in the smash-hit musical *Annie*, produced by Mike Nichols; in that role, according to the critic Jack Kroll, raised "mugging to a high art," mugging "with her face, her voice, her body . . . with her very mind"; among numerous other stage roles, starred as Dorothy Otley in the original Broadway cast of the backstage farce *Noises Off*, which began a 15-month run at the Brooks Atkinson Theatre in December 1983; was perhaps best known to the general public for her television appearances, especially as Carol Burnett's successor as a regular on *The Garry Moore Show* (1962–64); after her first appearance on that variety program, was described by the *New York Post* television columnist Bob Williams as having "a sweet and saucy flair for humor, a versatile vocal style, . . . and a fine fast-draw, slow-take sense of sketch comedy"; learned a repertory of some 1,500 songs from her mother, who played the piano in the sheet-music department of Filene's department store in Boston, Massachusetts; took dancing and piano lessons as a child; at Stevens High School in Claremont, New Hampshire, appeared in student theatrical productions; studied at Syracuse University on a drama scholarship for several semesters; subsequently, studied at the American Academy of Dramatic Arts in New York City; in the early 1950s, began singing torch songs and pop standards in Manhattan lounges and supper clubs; also recorded covers of song hits for RCA Records and appeared occasionally on radio and television; in 1954, successfully auditioned for Julius Monk, the enterprising owner of the chic supper club Ruban Bleu in Manhattan, who recognized her talent for comedy and persuaded her to put together an act satirizing the "chanteuse" style; with her new show, caricaturing such popular song stylists as Ella Fitzgerald, Anita O'Day, and Chris Connor, scored such a succès fou with patrons of the Ruban Bleu that she became a regular there; in the following years, in engagements at the Ruban Bleu, the Blue Angel, Mister Kelly's, and other top nightclubs across the U.S., polished and revised her repertory, adding such items as a devastating takeoff of Shirley Temple and other songs lampooning American show business and theatre, including "I've Got Those Tennessee Williams Southern Decadence Blues"; by the early 1960s, was one of the leading comediennes on the cabaret circuit; found an even wider audience with her recordings, such as *Dorothy Loudon at the Blue Angel* (1960), and her numerous appearances on television; performed in several television musical specials, including *Those Ragtime Years* (1960) and *Music of the Thirties* (1961); made guest appearances on the TV variety shows of Ed Sullivan, Perry Como, and others; made her stage debut in a revue in Philadelphia in 1957; played the Chaplinesque chimney sweep turned sexpot in the skit "Passionella" in the pre-Broadway tryout of *The World of Jules Feiffer*, directed by Mike Nichols, which folded on the road in 1962; later in 1962, made her Broadway debut as a brassy nightclub singer in the short-lived *Nowhere to Go but Up*; returned to Broadway briefly in the Noel Coward revue *Sweet Potato* (1968) and the musical *The Fig Leaves Are Falling* (1969) and for 100 performances in a revival of the farce *Three Men on a Horse* (1969); in 1971, was cast as Charlotte Haze, the mother of the nymphet, in *Lolita, My Love*, which closed pre-Broadway; following her triumph in *Annie*, starred on Broadway in the musicals *Ballroom* (1978–79) and *Sweeney Todd* (1980); in the latter, succeeded Angela Lansbury as Mrs. Lovett; shared the spotlight with Katharine Hepburn in the comedy *West Side Waltz* in a year-long national tour that ended with a short run on Broadway at the end of 1981; accrued many other stage credits away from Broadway; on television, headed the cast of the four-episode half-hour television situation-comedy *Dorothy*, which ran on the CBS network from August 8 to August 29, 1979; had roles in the motion pictures *Garbo Talks* (1984) and *Midnight in the Garden of Good of Evil* (1997); died in New York City. See *Current Biography* (June) 1984.

Obituary *New York Times* B p11 Nov. 17, 2003

MACKENZIE, GISELE Jan. 10, 1927–Sep. 5, 2003 French-Canadian–born singer; musician; a pop vocalist with a rich contralto voice, perfect pitch, and a distinctive style; was born Marie Marguerite Louise Gisele LaFleche; was trained not in voice but in piano and violin, instruments she played with a masterly touch throughout her career; studied for six years at the Royal Conservatory of Music in Toronto; during World War II, played the violin and sang for military personnel at camps and canteens; in the summer of 1946, was hired as a musician and vocalist by the Canadian bandleader Robert Shuttleworth, whom she had met when he was in the Royal Canadian Navy and who became her first husband and first manager; between the autumn of 1946 and the spring of 1951, sang (often to her own piano accompaniment) on several Canadian Broadcasting Corp. radio programs, including a show called *Meet Gisele*; sang a repertoire characterized by such songs as "J'ai laissé mon coeur," "Piper of Dundee," and the novelty ditty "A Trout No Doubt"; was dubbed "Canada's First Lady of Song"; took her father's middle name as her last name when she began singing on network radio in the U.S., in 1951; following guest spots on Edgar Bergen's and Morton Downey's shows, became a regular on *Club 15*, starring Bob Crosby and the Modernaires, and on *The Mario Lanza Show*, and a guest on *The Eddie Fisher Show*; during the summers of 1952, 1953, and 1954, toured with the comedian Jack Benny; in the autumn of 1953, on Benny's recommendation, filled the vacancy left by the singer June Valli on *Your Hit Parade*, the NBC television network's top-rated Saturday-night song-and-dance show covering the most popular songs of each week; left *Your Hit Parade* to host the half-hour musical/variety television series *The Gisele Mackenzie Show* (NBC, 1957–58), which was produced by Jack Benny's J & M Productions; was a regular on the comedy/variety series *The Sid Caesar Show* (ABC, 1963–64); as an actress, was seen on *Kraft Television Theatre* and in episodes of the television series *Justice*, *MacGiver*, and *Murder, She Wrote*; starred in regional theater for many years; was divorced both from Robert Shuttleworth and from her second husband, Robert Klein, a businessman; died in Burbank, California. See *Current Biography* (November) 1955. — K.D.

Obituary *New York Times* B p7 Sep. 9, 2003

MANCHESTER, WILLIAM Apr. 1, 1922–June 1, 2004 Writer; journalist; biographer; chronicler of powerful political families; novelist; essayist; adjunct professor of history emeritus, Wesleyan University; created a cause célèbre with his book on the assassination of President John F. Kennedy, *Death of a President* (1967); after earning a Purple Heart in combat in World War II and B.A. and M.A. degrees in English at the universities of Massachusetts and Missouri, respectively, was a reporter and correspondent with the *Baltimore Sun* (1947–54) and confidential secretary to H. L. Mencken (1954–56); in 1955, became managing editor of Wesleyan University's publications office; at Wesleyan, became a resident fellow (in 1959), lecturer in English (1968–69), writer in residence (1974–2004), and adjunct professor of history (1979–92); wrote four novels dealing variously with municipal corruption and mystery/espionage: *The City of Anger* (1953), *Shadow of the Monsoon* (1956), *Beard the Lion* (1958), and *The Long Gainer* (1961); published his first book of nonfiction, *Disturber of the Peace,* an authorized biography of H. L. Mencken, in 1951 and his second, *A Rockefeller Family Portrait,* eight years later; in 1962, published *Portrait of a President,* a cloyingly sympathetic study of President Kennedy's first year and a half in office; early in 1964, a few weeks after Kennedy's assassination, was commissioned by the slain president's widow, Jacqueline Kennedy, to write an account of the tragic event; after two years of painstaking research and interviews—including a 10-hour interview with Mrs. Kennedy, the full text of which is under seal until the year 2067—completed the first draft of the manuscript, in March 1966; submitted copies of the draft to Mrs. Kennedy and U.S. Attorney General (later Senator) Robert F. Kennedy, the president's brother (who would himself be assassinated); was at center of controversy when copies also reached other hands, raising eyebrows and hackles around Washington; was confronted by objections from the Kennedys, chiefly regarding the book's flagrant bias against President Lyndon B. Johnson (President Kennedy's successor in the White House), which they feared night harm Robert Kennedy's presidential aspirations; became involved in disputes over serialization rights and other matters; made deletions resulting in, in Manchester's words, "a resolution of misunderstandings"; saw *Death of a President, November 20–November 25, 1963* begin serialization in *Look* magazine early in 1967 and appear in hardcover in March 1967; subsequently, completed work on his book *The Arms of Krupp, 1587–1968,* a history of the German war-weapons manufacturing dynasty; went on to publish *Controversy and Other Essays in Journalism* (1976), the biography of General Douglas MacArthur, *American Caesar* (1978), and *Goodbye Darkness* (1980), a memoir of his wartime experience as a Marine in the Pacific; wrote another book on the Kennedy presidential administration, *One Brief Shining Moment* (1983); began a trilogy on the life and career of Winston Churchill with *The Last Lion: Winston Spencer Churchill: Visions of Glory, 1874–1932* (1983); continued the trilogy with *The Last Lion: Winston Spencer Churchill: Alone, 1932–1940* (1988); before his death, weakened by two strokes following the death of his wife, in 1998, signed an agreement authorizing Paul Reid to finish volume three of the Churchill trilogy, scheduled for publication in 2007; died at his home in Middleton, Connecticut. See *Current Biography* (November) 1967.

Obituary *New York Times* B p10 June 2, 2004

MCCAMBRIDGE, MERCEDES Mar. 17, 1916(?)–Mar. 2, 2004 Actress; brought to her film portrayals of strong and hard-driving women an intense personality and a distinctive sinewy voice that had been honed in radio drama; arguably, never surpassed her Oscar-winning motion-picture debut in the supporting role of Sadie Burke, the campaign manager of the southern political demagogue Willie Stark, in *All the King's Men* (1949), a performance in which, as David Thomson observed, she was "smart and tough and mean" and "spoke her lines with a terrible cursing bitterness"; among other memorable screen performances, played the independent-minded sister of the cattle baron (Rock Hudson) in *Giant* (1956) and won an Oscar nomination for her work, as the moralistic hellion pitted against the town's saloon/gambling-den proprietor (Joan Crawford), in the Freudian Western *Johnny Guitar* (1954); supplied the raspy demonic voice for the soundtrack of *The Exorcist* (1973); most shockingly, played the near-androgynous female leader of a gang of young male sexual marauders in a sequence in Orson Welle's *Touch of Evil* (1958) that somehow escaped the attention of the then-strict censors; was born to Irish Catholic parents in Illinois; after studying drama at Mundelein College, in Chicago, Illinois, in 1936, launched her radio career on network shows, chiefly soap operas, broadcast out of Chicago; in the 1940s, continued that career in Los Angeles and then New York City; regularly performed in the radio plays of Arch Oboler; provided female voices on the thriller/adventure series *I Love a Mystery*; had roles in the spooky *Inner Sanctum* series and such detective and adventure series as *Dick Tracy, Bulldog Drummond,* and *The Thin Man*; played the female lead in the radio adaptation of the stage comedy *Abie's Irish Rose*; frequently co-starred with Orson Welles in the radio plays on Ford Theater; had the title role in the melodramatic sitcom *Big Sister*; in the mid-1940s, ventured abortively into pre-Broadway and Broadway theater; on Broadway, appeared in the successive flops *A Place of Our Own* (1945), *Woman Bites Dog* (1946), and *The Young and the Fair* (1948); after one week, withdrew from the cast of *The Young and the Fair* in order to accept the role of Sadie Burke in *All the King's Men*; remained in Hollywood to star as Liza McStringer, the villain in the whodunit *Lightning Strikes Twice* (1951), and as Connie Carter in the murder mystery *The Scarf* (1951); was cast in the supporting roles of Miss Van Campen in *A Farewell to Arms* (1958), Mrs. Holly in *Suddenly Last Summer* (1959), Mrs. Sarah Wyatt in *Cimarron* (1960), and Sarah Strand in *Angel Baby* (1961); later had roles in the films *Run Home Slow* (1966), *The Counterfeit Killer* (1968), *99 Women* (1969), *Like a Crow on a June Bug* (1974), *Thieves* (1977), *The Concorde: Airport '79* (1979), and *Echoes* (1993); made several television films and played numerous roles in such TV series as *Bonanza, Rawhide,* and *Dr. Kildare*; in returns to the Broadway stage, succeeded Uta Hagen as Martha in *Who's Afraid of Virginia Woolf* in 1964 and Irene Worth as Grandma Kurnitz, the tyrannical matriarch in Neil Simon's comic drama *Lost in Yonkers* in the early 1990s; in her troubled personal life, had two failed marriages, to William Fifield (1939–46) and Fletcher Markle (1950–62); from the first marriage, had a son, John Lawrence Fifield Markle, who in 1987 shot to death his wife, his two young daughters, and himself; wrote two books: *The Two of Us* (1960), an account of her vacation travels with her son when he was a little boy, and *The Quality of Mercy* (1981), her autobiography; achieved sobriety after a long struggle with alcoholism; for many years ran the Livengrin Foundation, an organization devoted to alcoholic rehabilitation; lived in La Jolla, California; died in La Jolla. See *Current Biography* (June) 1964.

Obituary *New York Times* B p10 Mar. 18, 2004

MCMATH, SID June 14, 1912–Oct. 4, 2003 Two-term governor of Arkansas (1949–53); lawyer; a liberal Democrat who presaged the abolition of Jim Crow in his state in the years just preceding the dawn of the civil rights movement; in the U.S. Marines in World War II, was decorated for bravery in combat; after the war, entered politics in Hot Springs, Arkansas, with the aim of breaking the corrupt Democratic political machine of Mayor Leo P. McLaughlin; in 1946, with eight other veterans, formed a slate of reformist Democratic candidates for local offices, elected in its entirety; as the elected prosecuting attorney for Garland and Montgomery counties, closed illegal gambling houses, indicted McLaughlin for malfeasance and several of his associates for election fraud, and made Hot Springs a less attractive haven for gangsters; in the 1948 elections, ran successfully for governor on a relatively progressive, anti-Dixiecrat (segregationist Democrat) ticket, while other Democrats sharing his views won election to the state legislature; was reelected in 1950; as governor, effected improvements in infrastructure and the state's educational system, reforms in its mental-health system, and a rise in the minimum wage; promoted anti-lynching statutes; contributed to the ending of whites-only primary elections in Arkansas and the opening of the state Democratic Party to blacks; appointed blacks to state boards; began the desegregation of the state's medical school; in 1952, lost his bid for a third term; left the governor's mansion under the cloud of allegations (not directly linked to him) of bribery and influence peddling in the highway department; believed that the allegations were instigated by political enemies, especially power companies avenging his promotion of public electric power in rural areas; after leaving office, practiced law in Little Rock; ran unsuccessfully for the U.S. Senate in 1954 and for governor in 1962; was elected president of the International Academy of Trial Lawyers in 1976; wrote the memoir *Promises Kept* (2003); died in Little Rock. See *Current Biography* (March) 1949.

Obituary *New York Times* B p7 Oct. 6, 2003

MCWHIRTER, NORRIS D. Aug. 12, 1925–Apr. 19, 2004 British writer; publisher; broadcaster; co-founder with his late twin brother, Ross McWhirter, of the popular reference book *Guinness World Records*, an annual compilation of superlatives (ranging from such items as "tallest living man," "shortest man ever," and "heaviest person in medical history" to "oldest woman to make a solo parachute jump" and "most prolific serial killer," among myriad others), the international sales of which are exceeded only by those of the Bible, the Koran, and Mao Tse-tung's *Little Red Book*; on British television, was a familiar face as a sports commentator and an authority (at first with his brother) extemporaneously answering questions posed by juvenile audiences on *Record Breakers* (1972–94), a program inspired by the success of *Guinness World Records* (then titled the *Guinness Book of World Records*); was the son of a distinguished Fleet Street newspaperman and publisher; served in the Royal Naval Volunteer Reserve during World War II; following the war, read international relations, economics, and contract law at Ox-

ford University; achieved fame in track and rugby during and following his days at Oxford; was a sports correspondent with a London tabloid, the *Evening Star* (1951–60), and a weekly sports columnist with another London newspaper, the *Observer* (1951–67); became a sports broadcaster with the British Broadcasting Corp., first on radio, then on TV; provided commentary on the BBC's televised coverage of four successive Olympic Games (1960–72); with his brother, founded McWhirter Twins Ltd., a fact-gathering service for advertisers, writers, and publishers, in 1951; three years later, was commissioned by Sir Hugh Beaver, managing director of the Anglo-Irish brewery known as Arthur Guinness Son & Co, to compile a book that would be the final arbiter on superlatives, a reference work that might be used to settle trivia arguments, such as those that sometimes erupt among sports aficionados in pubs; published the first, slim edition of the book (at first titled the *Guinness Book of Superlatives* and subsequently the *Guinness Book of World Records*) in 1955; in succeeding years, published progressively larger editions of what came to be known as *Guinness World Records*, covering hundreds of superlatives (including "fastest frog jump," "fastest climb of Mount Everest," "fastest coconut-tree climb," "smallest dog," "biggest-selling Christmas song," "most poisonous fungi," "longest tennis match," "longest attack of hiccups," and "most one-finger push-ups"); also published a large number of spin-offs, including the *Guinness Book of Answers* (1976), the *Guinness Book of Essential Facts* (1979), and the *Guinness Book of Sports Records* (1980); in 1985, went into semiretirement, turning over the publishing enterprise known as Guinness Superlatives Ltd. to others while retaining the role of advisory editor; returned to active editorship with the *Book of Millennium Records* (1999); meanwhile, had ventured into Conservative politics, although not quite as radically as his brother, who was assassinated by Irish Republican Army gunmen in 1975 after offering a reward of $102,000 for information leading to the conviction of IRA terrorists; with his brother, had founded the Freedom Association, which, among other efforts, helped Prime Minister Margaret Thatcher to muster the courage to challenge what they regarded as the outdated legal privileges of British trade unions; wrote the biography/autobiography *Ross: The Story of a Shared Life* (1976); co-wrote *Treason at Maastricht* (1994), a stinging attack on British involvement in the European Union; died at his home in Kington Langley, Wiltshire, England. See *Current Biography* (November) 1979.

Obituary *New York Times* B p9 Apr. 21, 2004

MILLER, ANN Apr. 12, 1923(?)–Jan. 22, 2004 Dancer; actress; a vivacious performer who danced furioso, 500 taps a minute; with her flamboyant glamour and "million-dollar legs," was dazzling (albeit in the secondary role of "the brassy, good-hearted showgirl," as she observed) in lavish Metro-Goldwyn-Mayer musical films when she was in her 20s and 30s; finally achieved the full stardom she had "yearned for" in Hollywood on the Broadway musical stage in *Sugar Babies* when she was in her 50s; was born Johnnie Lucille Collier; at the age of five, began taking tap-dancing lessons to strengthen her legs after recovering from rickets; after her parents divorced, became a professional dancer in order to support herself and her mother, who was deaf; lying about her age, was dancing in California nightclubs when she was barely pubescent; was discovered by Lucille Ball and the RKO talent scout Benny Rubin when she was dancing at the Bal Tabarin club in San Francisco in 1934; following work as an extra and in bit parts, danced featured numbers in *New Faces of 1937* (1937) and *Radio City Revels* (1938); had her first speaking role in *Stage Door* (1937); played the aspiring ballerina in *You Can't Take It with You* (1938); had supporting roles in the comedy *Room Service* (1938), as Hilda, and the musical comedy *Too Many Girls* (1940), as Pepe; was cast as the female lead in the grade-B Western *Melody Ranch* (opposite Gene Autry) and such low-budget wartime RKO musicals as *Time Out for Rhythm* (1941), *Priorities on Parade* (1942), *Reveille with Beverly* (1943), and *What's Buzzin' Cousin* (1944); as Nadine Hale in *Easter Parade* (1948), her first MGM project, partnered with Fred Astaire and danced the solo number "Shakin' the Blues Away"; contributed spectacularly to the ensemble specialty number "Dance of Fury" in *The Kissing Bandit* (1948); as Claire Huddeson, capped the high spirits of *On the Town* (1949) with her parody of a savage dance ("Prehistoric Man"); as the nightclub performer Bubbles Cassidy in *Lovely to Look At* (1952), displayed excellent comic timing in singing and dancing flirtatiously in the number "I'll Be Hard to Handle" backed by a wolf-whistling male chorus; as Lisa Bellmount in *Small Town Girl* (1953), was showcased by the kaleidoscopic choreographer Busby Berkeley in the number "I Gotta Hear That Beat"; realized her favorite MGM role in Lois Lane, the nightclub dancer in the film version of Cole Porter's *Kiss Me Kate* (1953); as a guest star of *Deep in My Heart* (1954), danced the exhilarating Charleston "It"; tapped to Vincent Youmans's music as Ginger, another nightclub dancer, in *Hit the Deck* (1955); had straight acting roles in two final MGM pictures, released in 1956; by that time had made a total of some 40 movies, including *Tarnished Angel* (1938), *Hit Parade of 1941* (1940), *Go West, Young Lady* (1941), *True to the Army* (1942), *The Thrill of Brazil* (1946), *Watch the Birdie* (1950), *Texas Carnival* (1951), *Two Tickets to Broadway* (1951), *The Opposite Sex* (1956), and *The Great American Pastime* (1956); later made a cameo appearance in *Won Ton Ton, the Dog Who Saved Hollywood* (1976) and had a small role in the film *Mulholland Drive* (2001); found some of her legendary screen performances among those featured in several retrospective films, including *That's Entertainment! III* (1994); made her Broadway debut in 1939 in George White's *Scandals* (the last edition of that revue), in which she stole the show with her big number, "Mexiconga"; during the 1960s, returned to the stage in touring productions of Broadway shows; in 1969, triumphed on Broadway as the fifth successor to Angela Lansbury in the title role in the musical *Mame*; opposite Mickey Rooney, sang, danced, and performed bawdy slapstick in the original production of the hit Broadway revue *Sugar Babies* (1979–82), a nostalgic salute to burlesque and vaudeville; with Rooney, subsequently toured the U.S. in *Sugar Babies* for four and a half

years and took the revue to London's West End in 1989; among numerous appearances on television, sang and danced in a campy big-production ad for Heinz's Great American Soups; was married three times to men of wealth; was unable to marry her one true love, William V. O'Connor (assistant attorney general of California), a divorced, observant Catholic; had romantic liaisons with Louis B. Mayer, Conrad Hilton, and others; with Norma Lee Browning, wrote the autobiography *Miller's High Life* (1972); also wrote, with Maxine Asher, *Tapping into the Force* (1990), about her experiences as a self-proclaimed psychic; believed that she was a reincarnation of Queen Hatshepsut of Egypt; converted to Roman Catholicism on her deathbed; lived in Beverly Hills, California, and had a vacation home in Sedona, Arizona; died at Cedars-Sinai Medical Center in Los Angeles, California. See *Current Biography* (April) 1980.

Obituary *New York Times* A p21 Jan. 23, 2004

MILLER, J. IRWIN May 26, 1909–Aug. 16, 2004 Industrialist; philanthropist; religious-organization official; helped to build the Cummins Engine Co. from a small Columbus, Indiana, manufacturer of diesel engines into a Fortune 500 corporation with recent annual sales of $6.3 billion (2003) and current employee rolls of more than 24,000 worldwide; the corporation now consists of numerous complementary units that design, manufacture, distribute, and service engines and related technologies, including fuel and electrical generation systems; it serves its customers through a dealer/service network of 5,000 facilities and distributor locations in more than 136 countries and territories; in building the company, pursued an equal-employment-opportunity policy and, at the same time, turned Columbus (population circa 30,000) into a showcase for modern architectural design, a place attractive to the families of the young executives, black and white, whom he was recruiting; the architecture critic Paul Goldberger once wrote of Columbus in the *New York Times*, "There is no other place in which a single philanthropist has placed so much faith in architecture as a means to civic improvement"; was born into an affluent family that had holdings in banking and other fields before it invested in the Cummins Engine Co., founded in 1919 by Clessie Cummins, who had been the family's chauffeur; after earning degrees at Yale and Oxford Universities and serving an apprenticeship with a family-owned grocery chain in California, joined the Cummins company as second general manager in 1934; after serving with the U.S. Navy Air Corps in World War II, returned to the company as executive vice president; was president from 1947 to 1951 and chairman of the board from 1951 to 1977; thereafter, chaired the board's executive and finance committees; in 1954, set up the Cummins Engine Foundation to subsidize the fees of architects commissioned by the city to design public buildings, including schools; thereby, and with the example of his personal patronage, inspired others in Columbus to become private patrons of new architecture in the city; among the results are a library designed by I. M. Pei, a shopping center designed by Cesar Pelli, a newspaper building designed by Skidmore, Owings & Merrill, and churches designed by Eliel and Eero Saarinen; was an active layman in the North Christian Church (Disciples of Christ) in Columbus; served as president of the National Council of Churches of Christ in the United States of America from 1960 to 1963; died at his home in Columbus. See *Current Biography* (November) 1961.

Obituary *New York Times* C p13 Aug. 19, 2004

MILOSZ, CZESLAW June 30, 1911–Aug. 14, 2004 Lithuanian-born Polish poet; Nobel laureate; an inspired voice of hope in a post-paradisiacal world; a poet of complex sensibility—a combination of sensuality and spirituality—bred in an idyllic childhood and tempered in the crucible of horrendous world events—including war, the Holocaust, and totalitarian oppression, as well as a wrenching two-decade exile from Poland; in the face of chaos, terror, and loneliness, was driven, as if supernaturally, to write poetry as an alternative to despair—as an instrument of survival; in accepting the Nobel Prize in literature in 1980 (the year before his exile ended), pointed out that "whoever wields power is also able to control language [through] censorship [and] changing the meaning of words" and that he (Milosz), as a poet/survivor, felt mandated by "those who are silent forever" to try to "reconstruct precisely things as they were" and wrestle "the past from fictions and legends"; in his art, as Terrence Des Pres wrote in the Nation, "earned the solution to the most pressing spiritual dilemma today: how to bear the burden of historical consciousness without despair"; grew up chiefly in Vilnius, also known as Vilna (in Russian) and Wilno (in Polish), a Lithuanian borderland region whose beautiful landscapes and diverse cultures (including that of Yiddish-speaking Jews) impressed his young soul indelibly and would provide much of the distinctive, precise imagery of his poetry and contribute to the more enigmatic nature of its symbolism; as a poet, was partly shaped by the seven years he spent as a Catholic schoolboy translating Latin into Polish; began publishing his poetry in 1930, when he was in his second year as a law student at the University of Wilno; was the leader of a literary group of rebellious young "unorthodox Marxists" (his phrase) who published a journal titled *Zagary* and would become known in the history of modern Polish poetry as the avant-garde "Catastrophist school" because of its premonition of a cosmic cataclysm; in 1933, published the first of his many books of poetry, *Poemat o czaie zastyglym* (Poem of a Frozen Time); in 1934–35, studied on a fellowship in Paris, where he formed a close relationship with his uncle Oscar Vladislas de Lubicz Milosz, a diplomat who wrote poetry in French and greatly influenced his intellectual development, deflating his awe of Surrealism and other then-current French literary movements and turning him to disciplined response to his own muse; following one year as a programmer at the Polish Radio affiliate in Lithuania, moved to the network's headquarters in Warsaw, Poland, where he was when, in September 1939, Germany and then the USSR invaded Poland and divided the country between them; remained in Warsaw throughout the Nazi occupation of that city; was active in the Resistance as a contributor to the clandestine press; edited a Resistance anthology of poetry; was profoundly affected by the horrors and sorrows he experienced, including his witnessing the Nazi demolition of Warsaw's Jewish ghetto in 1943; survived the almost complete destruction of the city on Hitler's orders in response to the popular uprising in 1944; after the defeat of Germany, joined the diplomatic service of the Polish People's Republic; was second secretary at the Polish Embassy in Washington, D.C., from 1945 to 1949, when he became cultural attache at the embassy in Paris; after Moscow's control of the Polish government was consolidated in 1947, chafed under the Stalinist insistence on suppressing poetic truth in the names of "historical necessity" and "socialist realism"; deciding not to return to Warsaw, sought and received asylum in France in 1951; later said: "Circumstances fully understandable only to those who lived through the years of Stalinism in Poland, Hungary, or Czechoslovakia made me a reluctant exile"; examined the relationship between the totalitarian state and culture in essays published in the Polish emigre monthly Kultura and elsewhere; brought many of those essays together in *Zniewolony umysl* (1953), published in translation in the U.S. as *The Captive Mind* (1953); that book, the apologia for his defection, shot him to prominence in the West, where, to his consternation, it was exploited by anti-Soviet Cold War propagandists; isolated from his Polish roots, and misunderstood and ostracized by the French intellectual Left (which had not lived under Stalinism), suffered terrible loneliness in exile, to the point of contemplating suicide; in 1960, became a visiting lecturer in Polish literature at the University of California, Berkeley; was professor of Slavic languages and literatures at Berkeley from 1961 to 1978; became a naturalized American citizen in 1970; wrote two novels: *Zdobycle Wladzy* (1953; *The Seizure of Power*, 1955), a fictional companion to *The Captive Mind*, and *Dolina Issy* (1955; *The Issa Valley*, 1981), an elegiac evocation of his childhood and coming of age in Lithuania; combined autobiography with sociopolitical commentary and biographical portraiture of a host of the people great and small he had known in his life in *Rodzina Europa* (1959; *Native Realm: A Search for Self-Definition*, 1968) and *Rok myaliwego* (1990; *A Year of the Hunter* (1994); extended that combination back into history in the alphabetized entries in his encyclopedic "ABC" miscellanies, *Abecadlo Milosza* (1997; *Milosz's ABCs*, 2001) and *Inne Abecadlo* (1998); wrote extensively on Polish literature and compiled several anthologies of Polish poetry; translated into Polish the English of writers from Shakespeare to T. S. Eliot and the French of Simone Weil (who influenced him religiously) and others; also translated several books of the Bible; even after he mastered French and English, wrote his poetry in Polish; published four collections of poems in Polish between 1962 and 1974; few of his poems were available in English translation until Seabury Press published *Selected Poems* in 1973; Allen Lane published his 800-page *New and Collected Poems, 1931–2002* in 2002; also in 2002, Farrar, Straus and Giroux issued his 478-page *To Begin Where I Am: Selected Essays*; was predeceased by two wives and survived by two sons; died at his home in Krakow, Poland. See *Current Biography* (October) 1981.

Obituary *New York Times* p41 Aug. 15, 2004

MOORER, THOMAS H. Feb. 9, 1912–Feb. 5, 2004 U.S. Navy admiral, retired; a member of the old guard who, while staunchly adhering to traditional navy codes, was a leading proponent of military modernization, especially in submarines; during the last years of the Vietnam War, was chief of naval operations (1967–70), the highest position in the navy, and chairman of the Joint Chiefs of Staff (1970–74), the Pentagon's top military officer; after graduating from the U.S. Naval Academy, took flight training at the Naval Air Station in Pensacola, Florida; piloting a twin-engine PBY reconnaissance plane in the Southwest Pacific early in World War II, was wounded and shot down near Australia; received the Purple Heart, the Silver Star, and the Distinguished Flying Cross; later in the war, received the Legion of Merit for his service as an air gunnery and tactical officer with the Atlantic Fleet; after the war, attended the Naval War College and served successively as a naval aviation ordnance test officer, an aircraft carrier operations officer, a plans officer with the Atlantic Fleet, and commanding officer of the USS *Salisbury Sound*; was promoted to rear admiral in 1958; four years later, after directing long range naval objectives at the Pentagon, became commander of the Seventh Fleet, in the rank of vice admiral; in 1964, was promoted to full admiral and named commander in chief of the Pacific Fleet; in addition, was given charge of the Atlantic fleet and NATO's Atlantic command in 1965; supported the controversial 1964 Gulf of Tonkin Resolution, by which Congress gave President Lyndon B. Johnson carte blanche to bomb North Vietnam and commit U.S. ground troops to South Vietnam; in 1965, took charge of the Atlantic fleet and NATO's Atlantic command as chief of naval operations, thus becoming the navy's representative on the Joint Chiefs of Staff; meanwhile, was chafing under the civilian micromanagement of the Vietnam War by President Johnson and Secretary of Defense Robert S. McNamara; felt that his requests for modernization of navy warships and the production of new submarines were given low priority in McNamara's budgeting; grew increasingly frustrated with the administration's pursuit of a policy of containment of the Communist forces in Vietnam by controlled start-and-stop bombing instead of all-out aggressive force aimed at total victory; pressed for the mining of Haiphon harbor, which was finally carried out in 1972; years later, said that without bombing restrictions "we could have polished those clowns off in six months"; as chairman of the Joint Chiefs, was concerned with such matters as arms limitation negotiations with the Soviet Union and the Arab-Israeli war as well as the U.S. withdrawal from Vietnam; in the decades following his retirement in 1974, issued commentaries on military and national security issues on op-ed pages, in broadcasts, and on-line at NewsMax.com; opposed the handover of the Panama Canal to Panama, pursuant to a treaty signed by President Jimmy Carter and effective at midnight December 31, 1999; became more strident in his opposition after Panama leased control of the canal's primary entry and exit ports to Hutchison Whampoa Ltd., a Hong Kong-based company with ties to the People's Republic of China; in November 1999, predicted that the U.S. would eventually have to reclaim the canal by military force; in a 1998 CNN television and *Time* magazine report, was cited as the major independent source confirming allegations that U.S. Special Forces had used lethal Sarin nerve gas against civilians and American defectors in a secret incursion into Laos during the Vietnam War; denied that he had any independent such knowledge and insisted that he had been misrepresented; won a retraction of the story and apologies from CNN and *Time*; died in Bethesda, Maryland. See *Current Biography* (April) 1971.

Obituary New *York Times* A p13 Feb. 7, 2004

MYDANS, CARL M. May 20, 1907–Aug. 16, 2004 Photographer; as a staff member of *Life* magazine throughout its 36 years of existence as a photo-news weekly, set himself apart from other photographers with what the photography curator Marianne Fulton described as "his command of telling gesture and powerful arrangement"; as Richard Lacayo wrote for *Time* magazine, "helped to transform American photojournalism from a source of inert head shots and ceremonious poses into a supple narrative art [chronicling] the darkest moments of a dark century: the Depression, World War II, Korea, and Vietnam"; after taking a degree in journalism at Boston University in 1930, worked on the city desks of several newspapers while privately pursuing an interest in photography; in 1935, was hired by the historical section of the federal Farm Security Administration (at first called the Resettlement Administration), a New Deal agency that also employed such photographers as Walker Evans and Dorothea Lange; in his photographs for that agency, captured the story of a country coping with or crushed by economic crisis in images of the faces of Civilian Conservation Corps workers and oil-field roustabouts as well as Dust Bowl farmers, sharecroppers, migrant workers, and other impoverished rural Americans; "In the FSA, Mydans learned the moral dimension of photography," Richard Lacayo observed. "No eye cast upon the hardships of those years could afterward decline into a tool for pretty picture-making"; joined the staff of *Life* while its first issue was going to press, in November 1936; at *Life*, met and married Shelley Smith, a researcher (and, later, reporter) for the magazine; with his wife, was sent overseas to cover World War II for *Life*, first in Europe and then in the Pacific theater; captured by the Japanese, the couple were interned in camps in Manil and Shanghai for two years, until December 1943; after covering the fighting in Italy and France during 1944, returned to the Pacific to accompany General Douglas MacArthur on his triumphant return to to the Philippines; on January 9, 1945, took one of his best-known photographs, of General MacArthur wading onto the beach at Luzon; later shot such pictures as that of the Japanese surrender aboard the battleship USS *Missouri* in Tokyo Bay in September 1945 and newspaper-reading suburban train commuters absorbed in headline stories of the assassination of President John F. Kennedy in November 1963; remained on the staff of *Life* through its final issue as a weekly publication, in December 1972; published, among other books, a memoir, *More Than Meets the Eye* (1959), *The Violent Peace* (with his wife, 1968), *China: A Visual Adventure* (with Michael Demarest, 1979), and *Carl Mydans, Photojournalist* (1985), a retrospective of his work; died at his home in Larchmont, New York; was predeceased by his wife, Shelley, and survived by several progeny, including his son Seth, a New York Times correspondent. See *Current Biography* (May) 1945.

Obituary *New York Times* A p21 Aug. 18, 2004

NABRIT, SAMUEL M. Feb. 21, 1905–Dec. 30, 2003 Embryologist; marine biologist; university professor; U.S. Atomic Energy commissioner (1966–67); diplomat; grant administrator; a prominent member of one of the most distinguished African-American family dynasties, which included his late brother James Madison Nabrit Jr., a former president of Howard University and one of the three civil rights lawyers who in 1954 won from the U.S. Supreme Court the *Brown v. Board of Education* decision declaring segregated public schools to be unconstitutional; after graduating from Morehouse College, in Atlanta, Georgia, became the first black person to earn a Ph.D. degree (in biology) at Brown University; later became Brown's first black trustee; between 1925 and 1932, while teaching at Morehouse College, spent his summers at the Marine Biological Laboratory at Woods Hole, Massachusetts, conducting research chiefly on the regeneration of the tail fins of fish, the results of which were widely published in scientific journals; while chairing the Biology Department at Morehouse College (1932–47), continued his research at Woods Hole during summers; became a member of the Marine Biological Laboratory Corp. in 1948; was dean of the Graduate School of Arts and Sciences at Atlanta University from 1947 to 1955; was appointed to the National Science Board of the National Science Foundation by President Dwight D. Eisenhower; was president of Texas Southern University in Houston from 1955 to 1966; at that school, maintained a fine balance in handling student unrest, which was erupting into violence on many other campuses at that time; unconditionally supported students involved in sit-ins in their successful effort to end the segregation of public accommodations in Houston; at the same time, cooperated with the Houston mayor's efforts to contain militant agitators; can be viewed as one of the principals in *The Strange Demise of Jim Crow: How Houston Desegregated Its Public Accommodations, 1959–1963* (1997), produced by Thomas Cole and others at the University of Texas; interrupted his presidency of Texas Southern University to serve under President John F. Kennedy as special ambassador to Niger (1960–62); in 1967, founded the Southern Fellowship Fund, a mentoring and funding organization for minority students pursuing advanced degrees; as director (1967–81) of that organization, oversaw the dispensing of $4 million to minority professors to help them gain their doctorates; in 1990, emerged from retirement to serve for 15 months as interim executive director of the Atlanta University Center; in retirement, maintained an office (and a constant presence)

at Morehouse College; died in Atlanta, Georgia. See *Current Biography* (January) 1963.

Obituary *New York Times* B p8 Jan. 6, 2004

NEUSTADT, RICHARD E. June 27, 1919–Nov. 1, 2003 Political scientist; historian; presidential adviser and scholar; earned M.A. and Ph.D. degrees at Harvard University; in 1941, worked briefly as an assistant economist in the U.S. Office of Price Administration; served with the U.S. Navy's Seabees during World War II; after the war, worked at the U.S. Bureau of the Budget for four years; was a policy and administrative adviser in the White House during the last year of President Harry S. Truman's administration, which ended in January 1953; then taught at Cornell University for a year; at Columbia University (1954–65), was a popular professor of government, with standing-room-only class enrollments; in 1960, published his seminal work, *Presidential Power: The Politics of Leadership*, in which he used case studies from the administrations of Presidents Franklin D. Roosevelt, Truman, and Eisenhower in exploring "the classic problem of the man on top: how to be on top in fact as well as in name," a book that became a best-seller when the public learned that John F. Kennedy was reading it; during President Kennedy's administration (1961–63), regularly commuted from Columbia University to Washington to serve as a White House consultant; after Kennedy's assassination, was chosen to direct a proposed political institute (which opened several years later) that was to be connected with the Kennedy Memorial Library at Harvard University and was to offer "non-curricular programs for those holding or seeking elective or appointive posts of leadership in government"; in February 1965, joined the Harvard faculty as professor of government and associate dean of the Graduate School of Public Administration; in collaboration with the economist Thomas Schelling, the statistician Frederick Mosteller, and the decision theorist Howard Raiffa, transformed the graduate school into the John F. Kennedy School of Government, as it became known when the Institute of Politics opened there, in October 1966; updated *Presidential Power* in successive editions, including *Presidential Power and the Modern Presidents* (1990), which covers presidential administrations from Franklin D. Roosevelt to Ronald Reagan; also published, among other books, *Alliance Politics* (1970), *Presidents, Politics, and Analysis* (1986), *Thinking in Time: The Uses of History for Decision-Makers* (with Ernest R. May, 1986), and *Preparing to Be President: The Memos of Richard E. Neustadt* (edited by Charles O. Jones, 2000); in 1987, three years after the death of his first wife, married Shirley Williams, a leader of the Liberal Democrats in the British House of Lords; while maintaining a home on Cape Cod, Massachusetts, established his main residence in Fumeux Pelham, a village in Hertfordshire, England; died at his home in Fumeux Pelham. See *Current Biography* (November) 1968.

Obituary *New York Times* p40 Nov. 2, 2003

NEWTON, HELMUT Oct. 31, 1920–Jan. 23, 2004 German-born fashion, glamour, and celebrity photographer; revolutionized mainstream photography with his obsession with fantasies and fetishes of what he called "the illusion of beauty"; earned the soubriquet "king of kink" and inspired the concept of "porno chic" with his erotically charged black-and-white photos of statuesque nubile "superwomen" (his term), glacially posed, with dark suggestions of sexual domination and/or bondage and other such "sinful" (again his term) implications; was born in Berlin to prosperous Jewish parents; would be influenced professionally by the moral and sexual climate he experienced in Berlin as a pubescent boy, which was, in his words, "as wild as could be"; in 1938, emigrated from Nazi Germany; went to Australia via Singapore, while his parents and his half brother went to South America; in Australia, married the actress and photographer June Browne (a k a Alice Springs); earned his living chiefly by photographing weddings and products for mail-order catalogs until 1952, when his photos began appearing in the Australian edition of the fashion magazine *Vogue*; subsequently, became a contributor to British *Vogue* and several French magazines, including *Jardin des modes*; from 1961 to 1981, made Paris, France, his home base; contributed to *Elle, Marie Claire, Nova, Queen*, and five national versions of *Vogue*; liberated by the shock of a heart attack he suffered in December 1971, began to draw more fully for his inspiration on the Berlin of the early 1930s, the "divine decadence" of which (as Stephen Schiff observed in *Vanity Fair* 16 years later) "permeates the erotic pictures Newton has taken since . . . : the grandiose hotels, so redolent of elaborate prostitution; Marlene Dietrich stockings and garter belts and tuxedos; the Caligari tilt that some of the pictures take; the sadomasochism, stylized in the manner of von Stroheim and George Grosz"; beginning in the late 1970s, shot several hundred portraits of actors, writers, artists, and others, including Salvador Dali (near death, in a silk dressing gown), Paloma Picasso (wearing a monacle), Mickey Rourke (at a urinal), Daryl Hannah (blindfolded), and Claus von Bülow (dressed head to toe in black leather); in the 1980s, was recruited by the magazine editor Tina Brown to contribute regularly to *Vanity Fair* and the *New Yorker*; published, among other collections of photographs, *White Women* (1976), *Sleepless Nights* (1978), *Big Nudes* (1982), *World without Men* (1984), *Portraits* (1987), *Pages from the Glossies* (1998), and the extravagantly outsized *Sumo* (1998), which weighed 26 kilos (57.2 pounds) and sold in Great Britain for more than £600 a copy; wrote a book about his early years, published in Europe as *Autobiographie* (2002) and in the U.S. as *Autobiography* (2003); documented his half-century of marriage to June Browne in *Us and Them* (1999), replete with playful naked photos; with June, lived in Monte Carlo, Monaco, except in winter, which they spent in Los Angeles, California; died in Los Angeles, after losing control of the Cadillac sports-utility vehicle he was driving and crashing into a retaining wall. See *Current Biography* (November) 1991.

Obituary *New York Times* A p12 Jan. 24, 2004

NIKOLAYEV, ANDRIAN Sep. 5, 1929–July 3, 2004 Russian cosmonaut; a record-setting pioneer in the space program launched in the 1960s by what was then the Soviet Union; upon completing service in the Soviet Air Force, in 1960, began cosmonaut training; aboard the spaceship *Vostok III* between August 11 and 15, 1962, made 64 orbits of Earth, a record for endurance in space travel at that time; in 1970, returned to space for the second and final time as commander of the craft *Soyuz 9*, which circled Earth for 18 days; in 1963, married the Soviet cosmonaut Valentina Tereshkova, the first female space traveler, by whom he had one child, a daughter, and from whom he was divorced, in 1982; died in Cheboksary, the capital of his native Chuvash Republic, in Russia. See *Current Biography* (November) 1964.

Obituary *New York Times* A p19 July 7, 2004

O'CONNOR, DONALD Aug. 28, 1925–Sep. 28, 2003 Dancer; singer; actor; an agile and versatile song-and-dance man, expert at comedy-line delivery and comic mugging as well as tap and eccentric dancing; in a long motion-picture career, scored most memorably in dancing the acrobatic "Make 'Em Laugh" number (conceived entirely by him) as Cosmo Brown, the Gene Kelly character's sidekick, in the musical *Singin' in the Rain* (1952); began his career in early childhood as a knockabout vaudevillian, touring the theatrical circuits with "The O'Connor Family" act; learned, as he recalled, to dance "a couple of steps, some triple wings and such," and to improvise on those; in Hollywood in the late 1930s, was cast in several minor juvenile roles; in the early 1940s, graduated to roles in teen musicals, including four in which he shared star billing with Peggy Ryan: *Mr. Big, Chip Off the Old Block, The Merry Monahans*, and *Patrick the Great*; as a conscripted member of the U.S. Army Air Force Special Services, entertained troops from 1944 to 1946; back in Hollywood, co-starred in the musicals *Something in the Wind* (1947), with Deanna Durbin, and *Yes, Sir, That's My Baby* (1949), with Gloria DeHaven; was cast as a bumbling soldier who becomes a war hero with the help of a canny "talking" mule in *Francis* (1949), a box-office hit that spawned an enormously lucrative series of motion pictures; between 1951 and 1955, made five more movies with Francis the Talking Mule: *Francis Goes to the Races, Francis Goes to West Point, Francis Covers the Big Town, Francis Joins the WACs*, and *Francis in the Navy*; finding it "tough being upstaged by a jackass," declined a role in the seventh and last Francis movie, *Francis in the Haunted House*, in which Mickey Rooney replaced him; in 1953, co-starred in *I Love Melvin* (with Debbie Reynolds) and *Call Me Madam* (with Ethel Merman and Vera-Ellen), both of which were choreographed by Robert Alton; testified, "It wasn't until I worked with Gene Kelly and Bob Alton that I started to dance as . . . a total dancer . . . that I started dancing from the waist up, using my arms, my hands, and synchronization in that way"; later, co-starred in the musicals *Walking My Baby Back Home* (1953), *There's No Business Like Show Business* (1954), and *Anything Goes* (1956); played the title role in the biopic *The Buster Keaton Story* (1957) and important supporting roles in *The Wonders of Aladdin* (1961), *Cry for Happy* (1961), and *That Funny Feeling* (1965); returned to the screen in minor roles in *Ragtime* (1981) and *Out to Sea* (1997); on TV, was an alternating host of the hit weekly show *Colgate Comedy Hour* (1951–54) and star of the situation comedy *The Donald O'Connor Show* (1954–55); in 1954, received the National Academy of Television Arts and Sciences' Emmy Award for best male star of a regular series; later made guest appearances on a number of television situation comedies; on Broadway, starred as Albert (opposite Chita Rivera) in the short-lived musical *Bring Back Birdie* in March 1981 and as Cap'n Andy in a revival of the musical *Show Boat* from April to June 1983; also performed in cabaret and regional theater; died at the Motion Picture and Television Fund retirement home and hospital in Woodland Hills, California. See *Current Biography* (May) 1955.

Obituary *New York Times* B p6 Sep. 29, 2003

PAAR, JACK May 1, 1918–Jan. 27, 2004 Television host; actor; humorist; in the late 1950s and early 1960s, was the host—the second in a succession of four—of NBC's still-thriving *The Tonight Show*, the most popular and profitable of television's late-night network talk/variety shows; with his quick wit and mercurial personality, was in Richard Corliss's words "a hot wire in a cool medium," able to keep his dialogues with celebrity guests lively and to keep his audience expecting the unexpected; as a schoolboy, suffered a stammer, which made a career involving public speaking an attractive challenge for him; at 16, dropped out of high school to take a job at a radio station in Jackson, Michigan, where his chores included announcing the outlet's call letters; went on to work as an announcer (and ultimately a comic disc jockey) at radio stations in Indiana, Ohio, Pennsylvania, and New York; with the U.S. Army's Special Services Division, entertained troops as a comedian in the South Pacific during World War II; on network radio programs after the war, filled in for such vacationing hosts as Don McNeill, Jack Benny, and Arthur Godfrey; later briefly hosted a show of his own on the ABC radio network; in Hollywood, supplied the standup humor linking the comedy sketches (excerpted from the RKO studio archives) in the film *Variety Time* (1948); had minor roles in the motion pictures *Easy Living* (1949), *Walk Softly, Stranger* (1950), *Love Nest* (1951), and *Down Among the Shelterng Palms* (1953); in his first network television assignment, hosted the thrice-weekly NBC current-events quiz show *Up to Paar* in 1952; on CBS, hosted the weekly game show *Bank on the Stars* in 1953 and the weekly musical/variety program *The Jack Paar Show* in 1953 and 1954; from August 1954 until June 1955, hosted CBS's daily *Morning Show*; in July 1957, began hosting *The Tonight Show*, which had been launched under Steve Allen as host in 1954 and was retitled *The Jack Paar Tonight Show* from 1958 to the end of Paar's tenure; in the most spectacular of his unpredictable audience shockers, walked off the show when it was being taped on February 11, 1960 in a pique over NBC's censoring a mildly risqué anecdote he had recounted on the previous day's show; returned three weeks later; of his own volition, quit *Tonight* permanently in March 1962; was succeeded by Johnny Carson; from 1962 to 1965, hosted the NBC talk/variety show *The Jack Paar Program* in prime time on Friday

nights; subsequently, briefly, ran his own television station in Poland Springs, Maine; returned to late-night TV as host of *Jack Paar Tonite*, a talk show that aired once a month within ABC's *Wide World of Entertainent* series during 1973; with John Reddy, wrote two autobiographical books, *I Kid You Not* (1960) and *My Sword Is Bent* (1961); in 1965, published a third book, *Three on a Toothbrush* (1965), about his world travels; participated in the production of the video *Jack Paar: As I Was Saying* (1998), consisting of two one-hour tapes from a 1997 PBS television special on him and a third tape with selections from *The Jack Paar Tonight Show* chosen by him or in collaboration with him; died at his home in Greenwich, Connecticut. See *Current Biography* (April) 1959.

Obituary *New York Times* A p23 Jan. 28, 2004

PARK, ROSEMARY Mar. 11, 1907–Apr. 17, 2004 Educator; college administrator; university professor; an important figure in the advancement of women's liberal-arts education; majored in German at Radcliffe College, Harvard University, where she received her B.A. degree in 1928 and her M.A. in 1929; from 1930 to 1932, was an instructor at Wheaton College in Norton, Massachusetts, where her father had been president; received a Ph.D. degree at the University of Cologne in Germany in 1934; was an acting dean at Wheaton in 1934–35; began teaching German at Connecticut College (then called the Connecticut College for Women) in 1935; became chair of Connecticut College's Department of German and acting president of the college in 1945; as president of the college from 1947 to 1962, was an assiduous fundraiser; oversaw the construction of new buildings, including six dormitories, a swimming pool, and an infirmary, costing a total of $10 million; also presided over the growth of the undergraduate body from 700 to more than 1,100; expanded and enriched the curriculum; instituted the college's renowned Summer School of the Dance and American Dance Festival; obtained a charter for the Connecticut College for Men, affording graduate study to 50 nonresident males; was president of Barnard College, the women's undergraduate division at Columbia University in New York City, from 1963 to 1967, when she moved to the University of California at Los Angeles (UCLA), where Milton V. Anastos, whom she had married in 1965, was a professor of Byzantine studies; at UCLA, was a vice chancellor from 1967 to 1970 and a professor of education until her retirement; died in Los Angeles. See *Current Biography* (January) 1964.

Obituary *New York Times* B p7 Apr. 26, 2004

PICKERING, WILLIAM H. Dec. 14, 1910–Mar. 15, 2004 New Zealand–born physicist; electrical engineer; rocket scientist; a pioneer in the U.S. exploration of space; became director of the Jet Propulsion Laboratory at the California Institute of Technology in 1954, when the laboratory was the principal civilian contractor for the U.S. Army; continued directing the JPL for 18 years after it became a NASA facility, pursuant to passage of the National Aeronautics and Space Administration Act of 1958, which founded NASA and separated the military sector from civilian space development (NASA's province); after earning a Ph.D. degree at the California Institute of Technology, in 1936, began teaching physics there; in 1944, joined the JPL as a researcher in telemetry; as chief of the laboratory's guided-missile-electronics division (1951–54), was project manager for Corporal, the first operational missile developed at the JPL; as director of the laboratory, organized a team of scientists assigned the task of quickly matching the space coup scored by the Soviet Union with its launch of the Sputnik satellite in October 1957; with that team, built the first U.S. Earth-orbiting satellite, Explorer I, a slim bullet-shaped satellite, six inches in diameter and five feet long, which was equipped with a radio transmitter and a Geiger counter designed by James Van Allen and which was lifted into orbit on January 31, 1958 by an army Jupiter-C rocket modified by Wernher von Braun; following three Explorer projects, played a central role behind the Ranger and Surveyor robotic landings on the moon (preparing the way for the manned Apollo flights), the flyby of the planet Venus by Mariner 2 in 1962, the photographing of Mars by Mariner 4 in 1965, and the orbiting and mapping of Mars by Mariner 9 in 1971; after retiring from the JPL, in 1976, taught electrical engineering in Saudi Arabia for two years; subsequently, founded and chaired a company manufacturing processed wood chips for the generation of electricity; died at his home in La Cañada Flintridge, Califoria. See *Current Biography* (November) 1958.

Obituary *New York Times* B p9 Mar. 17, 2004

PLIMPTON, GEORGE Mar. 18, 1927–Sep. 26, 2003 Writer; editor; was the editor in chief, since its founding (in Paris in 1953) of the *Paris Review*, a literary quarterly that earned much respect for its fiction and poetry by gifted young writers and for interviews with established authors; more lucratively, was a popular freelance writer, a self-described "participatory journalist" who wrote humorously about his dilettantish excursions into fields beyond his own, chiefly professional sports; was born into blue-blooded privilege, a background reflected in his upper-class-accented speech; concentrating on English literature, was educated at Phillips Exeter Academy, Harvard University, and Cambridge University, where he earned an M.A. degree in 1954; in the late 1950s, persuaded Sidney James, *Sports Illustrated*'s publisher, to subsidize his idea of representing "Mr. Everyman" in a professional baseball setting; before a postseason exhibition All-Star game, pitched to 16 American League and National League hitters, disastrously—an experience he recounted in an article for *Sports Illustrated* and in his book *Out of My League* (1961); in other such misadventures, lost to Archie Moore in boxing, Pancho Gonzalez in tennis, Arnold Palmer in golf, and Arnold Jacoby in bridge; did stints in hockey, as a goalie with the Boston Bruins, in symphonic music, as a percussionist with the New York Philharmonic, and in trapeze acrobatics, as an aerialist with the Clyde Beatty–Cole Brothers Circus; documented his training sessions as a third-string quarterback with the Detroit Lions in his book *Paper Lion* (1963); related anecdotes about golf in *The Bogey Man* (1969), boxing in *Shadow Box*

(1977), and hockey in *Open Net* (1985); in 1983, participated in the planning and execution of the fireworks display for the Brooklyn Bridge's centennial; wrote *Fireworks: A History and Celebration* (1984); as a writer for *Sports Illustrated,* created Sidd Finch, a fictitious Tibetan-raised pitcher with a 168-mph fastball; wrote the novel *The Curious Case of Sidd Finch* (1987); also published, among other books, *One for the Record: The Inside Story of Hank Aaron's Chase for the Home-Run Record* (1974), *The Best of Plimpton* (1990), the biography *Truman Capote* (1997), and *The X Factor: A Quest for Excellence* (1995), about achievement as a psychological motivator; edited many collections of pieces from the *Paris Review* (now based in Manhattan); had roles in several films, including that of a villain in the Western *Rio Lobo* (1970) and a minor part in *Paper Lion* (1968), in which Alan Alda starred as Plimpton; hobnobbed with the likes of President George Bush and the Kennedys; was with Robert F. Kennedy when he was assassinated, in 1968; with his death, in Manhattan, inspired a job description by Cynthia Cotts for the *Village Voice* (October 22–28, 2003): "Wanted: Editor to take over New York–based quarterly magazine of fiction and poetry. Must have impeccable taste, be steeped in the craft of writing and editing, and have met every key literary figure of the last fifty years. Please have natural athletic skills, good manners, and a genuine enthusiasm for life. Be world-famous, witty, unpretentious, admiring of pop stars and complete nobodies, a party animal, experienced fundraiser, and shameless self-promoter. . . . Be tall, handsome, and well-born, with spacious uptown flat that can double as editorial and business offices and party venue." See *Current Biography* (February) 1969. — K.D.

Obituary *New York Times* A p13 Sep. 27, 2003

POUJADE, PIERRE Dec. 1, 1920–Aug. 27, 2003 French right-wing political leader; the namesake of the populist Poujadisme movement and the term "Poujadiste," denoting support for lower-middle-class rebellion against government bureaucracy and the large commercial enterprises perceived to be recipients of preferential treatment by the "État vampire"; in 1953, when he was a municipal council member and the proprietor of a book and stationery shop in the town of Saint Cére in the department of Lot in southwestern France, rallied local shopkeepers, crafts people, and farmers into the formation of the Union de Défense des Commerçants et des Artisans (UDCA), a direct-action tax protest organization that soon began spreading across France and grew within two years into Union et Fraternité Française, a political party representing a provincial nationalism and a traditionalist challenge to what it regarded as the decadence of the Fourth Republic; with undertones of anti-Semitism, denounced with special vituperation the modernizing and decolonizing policies of Prime Minister Pierre Mendes France (June 1954–March 1955), who was Jewish; without running for office himself, campaigned for Poujadiste candidates (including Jean-Marie Le Pen, who would later found the xenophobic, anti-immigrant National Front) in the national election of January 1956, in which they won 12 percent of the votes cast and 52 National Assembly seats (11 of which were subsequently invalidated); became a National Assembly candidate himself in January 1957; suffered an overwhelming defeat, polling only 19,906 of the more than 320,000 votes cast; came to see that the best hope for hastening the end of the Fourth Republic was the return to power of Charles de Gaulle, who had led the Free French forces during World War II and headed the provisional French government in liberated France (1944–45); in 1958, when his party lost all of its parliamentary seats, disbanded it and threw his support behind de Gaulle, who, under a new constitution ratified by referendum, became president of France in December 1958; remained a municipal council member in Saint Cere for many years and president of the UDCA until 1983; modified his views over the decades; was ashamed of having given Le Pen his start in politics; voted for President François Mitterrand in 1981 and President Jacques Chirac in 1995; was appointed by Mitterrand to government advisory panels on economic and social affairs and the development of alternative-energy resources; headed a mission to Romania in 1990; with his wife, ran an advertising agency and a printing company, sold farm produce at discount prices through shops owned by his followers, and developed a holiday center in La Bastide-l'Évêque in the department of Eveyron in southwest France; wrote the book *J'ai choisi le combat*; died in La Bastide-l'Évêque. See *Current Biography* (April) 1956.

Obituary *New York Times* B p9 Aug. 29, 2003

RANDALL, TONY Feb. 26, 1920–May 17, 2004 Actor; a stage, screen, and television performer and personality whose signature style comprised precision in speech, impeccability in taste, smartness in dress and grooming, and droll sardonicism in attitude; first caught the national eye on the live TV situation comedy *Mr. Peepers* (1952–55), with his portrayal of the brashly confident, posturing midwestern high-school history teacher Harvey Weskit, best friend of the meek, ineffectual science teacher Robinson Peepers (Wally Cox); achieved his greatest success on TV in the sitcom *The Odd Couple* (1970–75), in which he played the prim and proper fussbudget Felix Unger, the temperamental opposite of his slovenly apartment mate, Oscar Madison (Jack Klugman); won an Emmy Award for that performance; on the silver screen, scored most memorably in such performances as the title role of the TV ad man in the Madison Avenue satire *Will Success Spoil Rock Hunter?* (1957), the humorously neurotic supporting male characters in the Doris Day/Rock Hudson romantic comedy vehicles *Pillow Talk* (1957), *Lover Come Back* (1961), and *Send Flowers* (1964), and the multiple title roles in the tour-de-force fantasy *The Seven Faces of Dr. Lao* (1964); on Broadway in the mid-1950s, played the alcoholic psychiatric patient in *Oh, Men! Oh, Women!*, and the acerbic journalist, an H. L. Mencken counterpart, in *Inherit the Wind*; sang and danced the lead in the Broadway musical *Oh, Captain!*; founded (1991) and served as artistic director of the National Actors Theater, a Manhattan-based classical repertory company; was born Leonard Rosenberg in Tulsa, Oklahoma; in approaching a career in acting, had to overcome a childhood

stammer; after studying speech and drama at Northwestern University for a year, moved on to the Neighborhood Playhouse School of the Theater in New York City, where he studied acting under Sanford Meisner and movement under Martha Graham; in World War II, served stateside with the U.S. Army Signal Corps; made his New York stage debut Off-Broadway, as Chang Ling in *A Circle of Chalk*, in March 1941; subsequently, had roles in New York stage productions starring Jane Cowl and Ethel Barrymore; after his wartime service, toured (as the stuttering brother) with Katharine Cornell in *The Barretts of Wimpole Street*, in 1947; on Broadway the following year, appeared (as Scarus) with Cornell in *Antony and Cleopatra*; in New York that same year, played Adam in the Garden of Eden comedy *To Tell the Truth*; on radio, performed on Henry Morgan's comedy show and acted in soap operas, including *Portia Faces Life*; from 1949 to 1951, played Reggie York, the British member of a trio of soldiers of fortune turned detectives in the radio adventure serial *I Love a Mystery*; during the golden age of live television drama, in the 1950s, was cast in numerous roles on *Studio One*, *Kraft Television Theater*, *Philco Television Playhouse*, and other drama anthologies; was a frequent guest panelist on the TV quiz show *What's My Line?* during the 1960s; later, was a frequent guest on the late-night TV talk/variety programs of Johnny Carson and David Letterman; in the situation comedy *The Tony Randall Show* (1976–78), played a widowed Philadelphia judge raising two children; in the title role in the TV movie *Sydney Schorr: A Girl's Best Friend* (1981), was cast as a middle-aged commercial artist, homosexual and lonely, who befriends a struggling and pregnant young actress, dissuades her from getting an abortion, and opens his Manhattan apartment to her and her child; starred in the situation-comedy spun from that film, *Love, Sydney* (1981–83), in which the protagonist's sexual orientation became muted; was cast in a total of more than 40 motion pictures, including the theatrical releases *Oh, Men! Oh, Women!* (1957), *No Down Payment* (1957), *Let's Make Love* (1960), *Boys' Night Out* (1962), *Foolin' Around* (1980), and *Down with Love* (2003) and the made-for-TV movie *The Odd Couple: Together Again* (1993); had roles in some of the productions staged by his National Actors Theater, including revivals of *M. Butterfly* (in which he played the Western diplomat infatuated with the Japanese transvestite singer) and *Right You Are*; for many years, trained daily under a vocal coach; in many of his TV appearances, sang quaintly funny pop ditties from the 1920s and 1930s; recorded two albums; was an opera buff and an art collector; was national chairman of the Myasthenia Gravis Association; in 1995, three years after the death of his wife of 54 years, the former Florence Gibbs, married Heather Hanson, an actress 51 years his junior, by whom he had two children; died in Manhattan. See *Current Biography* (January) 1961.

Obituary *New York Times* A p22 May 19, 2004

REAGAN, RONALD Feb. 6, 1911–June 5, 2004 Fortieth president of the U.S. (1981–89); thirty-third governor of California (1967–75); the oldest president ever inaugurated, and the longest lived; "the Great

Communicator"; a personable, affable former motion-picture actor who, on a personal level, was able to charm even his ideological antagonists; championed traditional values and "peace through strength"; echoing the Gospel of Matthew and the Pilgrim leader John Winthrop, envisioned the U.S. as a shining "City on a Hill, the eyes of all people . . . upon us"; domestically, sought to bring "an end to the excessive growth of government bureaucracy and government spending [except on the military] and government taxing"; internationally, departed from the policy of "containment" of Soviet Communism and undertook to destroy the "evil empire"; was the Republican Party's great conservative presidential hope for 16 years before winning election to the presidency in a landslide victory (51 percent of the vote to 41 percent) over Democratic incumbent Jimmy Carter, in 1980; running against Walter Mondale four years later, was reelected by an even greater margin (59 percent of the vote); defeated Mondale in 49 of the 50 states and scored majorities in every bloc of voters save labor unionists, Jews, and African-Americans, according to Paul Johnson in *A History of Modern Times*; early in his first term, sought, with some success, to stimulate the economy with large across-the-board tax cuts; subsequently, modified his so-called "supply side" economic policies (which became generally known as Reaganomics and which were derided by his enemies as "trickle-down economics"), but the reduction in the personal tax rate he set in motion continued, dropping from a high of 70 percent to 28 percent over seven years; during that period, the gross national product, adjusted for inflation, rose 27 percent; reappointed to the chairmanship of the Federal Reserve Bank Paul Volker and named as his successor Alan Greenspan, monetarists whose policies brought under control the ballooning inflation and interest rates inherited from the administrations of President Gerald Ford and President Carter; experienced a surge in popularity as a result of his good-natured response to and plucky recovery from a left-lung wound inflicted by gunfire in an assassination attempt by John W. Hinckley Jr. on a Washington sidewalk on March 30, 1981; in August 1981, fired 11,359 striking members of PATCO, the federal air traffic controllers union, when they failed to obey his order to go back to work; was dubbed the "Teflon president" by some when he emerged relatively unsullied from the Iran-Contra scandal (1986–87), in which his administration was accused of selling arms to Iran for a double purpose—(1) to obtain the release of Americans held hostage by allies of Iran in Lebanon, and (2) to use the profits to fund covert support of the anti-Communist Contra guerrillas in Nicaragua; unfazed by a mounting federal deficit (blamed by him on the Democratic Congress's persistent increases in domestic spending), massively enlarged the national defense budget, forcing the Soviet Union into unsustainable competition in military spending; thus, hastened the implosion of the Soviet system and the winning of the Cold War; meanwhile, had changed the face of Washington–Moscow relations in the warming of his contacts with the Soviet leader Mikhail Gorbachev; with the motto "Trust but verify," negotiated with Gorbachev the INF Treaty eliminating intermediate range missiles from Europe; initiat-

ed negotiations for the START treaty; was born above the general store where his father worked in Tampico, Illinois; earned a B.A. degree in economics and sociology at Eureka College, in Illinois; was a radio sportscaster before launching his successful career as a second-rank leading man in Hollywood in 1937; accrued 52 movie credits, not counting the role of a villain in the made-for-television film *The Killers* (1964); acquired his nickname "the Gipper" from his portrayal of George Gipp, the University of Notre Dame football player who dies young, in *Knute Rockne—All American* (1940); was proudest of the role of Drake McHigh, who loses both his legs in needless surgery, in *King's Row* (1941); in politics, was originally a New Deal Democrat, an admirer of President Franklin D. Roosevelt, whose rhetorical speaking style would influence his own; began to question his political liberalism when, during the first of his two tenures (1949–52, 1959–60) as president of the Screen Actors Guild, he experienced firsthand what some referred to as the "rule-or-ruin" tactics of Communist operatives in Hollywood; without publicly "naming names," cooperated with HUAC (the U.S. House of Representatives Un-American Activities Committee) in its investigation of those operatives; according to the *New York Times*, later supplied names to the FBI; once said, "By 1960, I realized that the real enemy was not big business; it was big government"; hosted the General Electric Theater on TV from 1952 to 1962; switched to the Republican Party in 1962; as governor of California, took a hard line toward political agitators on state-university campuses and the "permissive" administrators who abetted them; by freezing hiring, reduced the size of the state government's bureaucracy; instituted money-saving reforms in welfare programs; was sharply criticized for dismantling the hospitalization of the mentally ill; wrote two autobiographies, *Where's the Rest of Me?* (1965) and *An American Life* (1990, with Robert Lindsey); was survived by his wife, the former Nancy Davis, their two children, Patti and Ron, and an adopted son, Michael, from his earlier marriage to the actress Jane Wyman; was predeceased by his daughter Maureen, from the earlier marriage; died at his home in the Bel Air section of Los Angeles, California. See *Current Biography* (November) 1982.

Obituary *New York Times* p1+ June 6, 2004

REUTHER, VICTOR Jan. 1, 1912–June 3, 2004 Trade unionist; a pioneer labor organizer; with his older brothers Roy and the more famous Walter, played a key role in the birth and growth of the United Automobile Workers, which remained commonly known as the UAW after its transformation into the United Automobile, Aerospace and Agricultural Implement Workers of America; helped his brother Walter (president of the UAW from 1946 until his death, in a plane crash, in 1970) move into and then out of affiliation with the American Federation of Labor–Congress of Industrial Organizations (AFL-CIO, with which it later became affiliated again); was born in Wheeling, West Virginia, five years after his brother Walter's birth; upon graduating from high school, moved to Detroit, Michigan, where he roomed with Walter (then a foreman in the Ford Co. plant) while studying at Wayne University (now Wayne State University); from January 1933 through most of 1935, traveled with Walter throughout Europe, including the Soviet Union, where they worked for 16 months in an auto plant; after returning to Detroit, worked on an assembly line at the Kelsey Hayes Wheel Co. briefly, long enough to enable him to join and begin organizing for the recently founded United Auto Workers; in 1936, helped launch West Detroit Local 174 and was a leader of the first sit-down strike in the Detroit area, following which Local 174 quickly jumped in membership from less than 100 to some 30,000; with his deep, resonant voice, was masterly in his command of the sound truck at the historic, sometimes bloody sit-down strikes at Fisher Body plants in Flint, Michigan (December 1936– February 1937), that resulted in the General Motors Corp.'s recognition of the UAW as a collective-bargaining entity; recognition by Chrysler Motors followed; also played a pivotal role in the unionization of the Ford Motor Co.; joined with his brothers in opposing the UAW's Communist-led extreme leftist faction, which lost the presidency of the organization to Walter Reuther (while retaining control of the executive committee) in the voting at the UAW convention in March 1946; as for himself, emerged from the 1946 convention as the union's education director; removed the Communists who had been using the education office in the battle for control of the union; gathered a group of anti-Communists and gave them intensive training in public speaking and parliamentary law—skills that paid off at the union's November 1947 convention, which elected a complete anti-Communist slate; in the spring of 1949, was shot in an assassination attempt that cost him the sight of his right eye; when he recuperated, moved with his family to Paris, France, with an assignment from the Congress of Industrial Organizations to assist in the rebuilding of the Western European trade unions that had not yet completely recovered from World War II; following his return to the U.S. in the mid-1950s, settled in Washington, D.C., and directed the UAW's department of international affairs until his retirement, in 1972; published a memoir, *The Brothers Reuther and the Story of the UAW* (1976); died in Washington, D.C. See *Current Biography* (December) 1953.

Obituary *New York Times* C p16 June 5, 2004

RHODES, JOHN J. Sep. 18, 1916–Aug. 23, 2003 U.S. congressman from Arizona (1953–83); the first Republican ever elected to the House of Representatives from Arizona; was House minority leader during the last nine years of his tenure; after service with the U.S. Army Air Corps in World War II, opened a law office in Mesa, Arizona, and co-founded the Farm and Home Life Insurance Co.; in Congress, compiled a decidedly conservative voting record; was a member of the powerful House Appropriations Committee and the ranking minority member of that committee's public-works subcommittee; in the latter position, in 1968, helped to guide through Congress the legislation authorizing the construction, at a cost of $4 billion, of the Central Arizona Project, the largest and, according to some sources, most expensive water-conveyance project in American his-

tory, a 336-mile-long system (consisting of dams, pumping plants, pipelines, and other waterworks) delivering 1.5 million acre-feet of Colorado River water from Lake Havasu into the desert area of central and southern Arizona; was a friend of and adviser to Gerald R. Ford, the House minority leader, who became vice president of the U.S. in 1973 and succeeded to the presidency when President Richard M. Nixon resigned under the cloud of the Watergate scandal, in 1974; became minority leader when Ford moved to the White House; in August 1974, was one of the White House trio (the others were Republican senators Hugh Scott and Barry Goldwater) who visited Nixon and helped persuade him to resign rather than face impeachment; wrote the book *The Futile System: How to Unchain Congress and Make the System Work Again* (1976); died at his home in Mesa, Arizona. See *Current Biography* (September) 1976.

Obituary *New York Times* B p9 Aug. 25, 2003

RIEFENSTAHL, LENI Aug. 22, 1902–Sep. 8, 2003 German motion-picture director and producer; photographer; while recognized as one of the most creative figures in the history of world cinema, spent the last half-century of her life trying in vain to escape the shadow of her association with Adolf Hiter and his National Socialist regime; pursued a career in modern dance until she suffered a knee injury in 1924; subsequently, joined the filmmaking team of director Arnold Fanck, playing the heroines in his silent feature films and early talkies—idyllic Wagnerian-style action/nature epics involving skiing, mountain climbing, and other outdoor athleticism—and at the same time learning the fundamentals of her camera work and technique of mise en scène; established her own motion-picture production company in 1931; for her first independent film, chose to star in as well as direct *Das Blaue Licht* (The Blue Light, 1932), based on a romantic Alpine folk tale; soon thereafter, was asked by Hitler to make films about him and his Third Reich once he attained power, which he did in 1933; in that year, shot *Sieg des Glaubens* (Victory of the Faith), a film of a triumphal Nazi rally in Nuremberg, which was officially withdrawn from distribution following the bloody purge of Ernst Roehm and his "Brownshirt" storm troopers; in 1934, used her eye for striking closeups as well as sweeping panoramic views and her editing talent— and the employment of a crew of 120, including 40 cameramen—to evoke the mesmerizing spectacle of goose-stepping Nazi legions, rows upon rows of swastikas, and Hitler's spell-binding charisma in *Triumph des Willens* (Triumph of the Will, 1935), her celebrated documentary sans commentary (but with sound recorded at the event) of the 1934 National Socialist Party congress in Nuremberg; with a crew of 170, including more than 40 cameramen, again applied her innovative techniques—including underwater and slow-motion photography—in capturing the highlights of the 1936 Olympic Games in Berlin in the documentary *Olympische Spiele* (Olympia), widely regarded as her masterpiece; spent 18 months editing the 200 hours of footage taken of the Games, cutting it into two parts, *Fest der Völker* (Festival of Nations, 118 minutes) and *Fest* der Schonheit (Festival of Beauty, 107 minutes), both enhanced by Wagnerian music and both released in 1938; claimed that during World War II she refused a request from Josef Goebbels, the Nazi minister of propaganda, that she make political propaganda films; starred as the Spanish gypsy protagonist in the feature film *Tiefland* (co-directed by her and G. W. Pabst), a nonmusical version of Eugen D'Albert's opera that was completed in 1944 but not released until 10 years later; in 1956, went to Nairobi, Kenya, with the intention of making a film there, a project she canceled when hospitalized following a Land Rover accident; in later visits to Africa, learned the language and customs of the Nuba people in the Sudan; sold color photographs she took in Africa to *Der Stern, Life,* and other magazines; compiled several collections of the photographs, including those published in English as *The Last of the Nuba* (1973), *The People of Kau* (1976), and *Vanishing Africa* (1982); on a final visit to the Sudan in March 2000, was seriously injured in a helicopter crash; meanwhile, had taken up scuba diving when she was in her early 70s; on and off, spent 30 years, until 2002, working as an underwater photographer in the Maldives, in the Indian Ocean; compiled two collections of underwater photographs, published in the U.S. as *Coral Gardens* (1978) and *Wonders Under Water* (1991); in conjunction with her 100th birthday, released the 55-minute documentary film *Underwater Impressions* (2002); wrote a 669-page autobiography, *Memoiren* (1987), translated as *Leni Riefenstahl: A Memoir* (1992); died at her home in Pöcking, south of Munich, Germany. See *Current Biography* (May) 1975.

Obituary *New York Times* C p14 Sep. 10, 2003

RIPLEY, ALEXANDER Jan. 8, 1934–Jan. 10, 2004 Novelist; wrote best-selling historical romances, most often set in the U.S. Old South, the most popular of which has been *Scarlett* (1991), a sequel to Margaret Mitchell's *Gone with the Wind* (1936), the latter of which is said to be the second-ranking bestseller (just behind the Bible) in publishing history, a Civil War/Reconstruction-era saga told from the perspective of the adventurous Scarlett O'Hara, a part-Irish southern belle/plantation mistress; was born Alexandra Braid in Charleston, South Carolina; acquired the name Ripley from the first of her two marriages; after earning a B.A. degree in Russian at Vassar College (on a scholarship from the United Daughters of the Confederacy), worked at a series of jobs, including manuscript reader and publicity director at a New York City publishing house; with her first husband, lived for a time in Florence, Italy; in 1972, under the pseudonym B. K. Ripley, published her first novel, *Who's That Lady in the President's Bed?*, about a female president of the U.S.; in a switch to nonfiction, co-wrote (with Patrick Trese) *Caril* (1974), a biography of *Caril Ann Fugate*, the teenage girlfriend who accompanied Charles Raymond Starkweather on his killing spree across Nebraska and Wyoming farmlands in 1958; in 1981, published her first historical novel, *Charleston*, an epic that begins during the Civil War and ends three decades later; next wrote a sequel, *On Leaving Charleston* (1984); in *The Time Returns* (1985),

imagined a relationship between Lorenzo de Medici and a member of another aristocratic family in Florence during the Italian Renaissance; set her novel *New Orleans Legacy* (1987) in antebellum Louisiana; meanwhile, in 1986, had been contracted by the heirs of Margaret Mitchell and their lawyers to write a continuation of the story of Scarlett O'Hara's on-an-off relationship with Rhett Butler, the third and most dashing of her husbands; with Scarlett, scored a huge popular success while drawing negative assessments from many reviewers, some of whom called the novel a "trashy" book with improbable plotlines and a "toe-curling 'happy' ending"; saw the work translated to television as *Scarlett*, a four-night, eight-hour miniseries broadcast on the CBS network in November 1994; wrote two final novels, *Fields of Gold* (1994), about Virginia tobacco growers, and *A Love Divine* (1997), about the New Testament figure Joseph of Arimathea; died at her home in Richmond, Virginia. See *Current Biography* (March) 1992.

Obituary *New York Times* B p7 Jan. 27, 2004

RITTER, JOHN Sep. 17, 1948–Sep. 11, 2003 Actor; reached the height of his popularity as Jack Tripper, the wacky closet heterosexual sharing an apartment with two attractive, young, single women on the television situation comedy *Three's Company* (ABC, 1977–84), a scrubbed-down-for-TV slapstick pajama farce that was the top-rated sitcom of the 1979–80 season and rode the crest of the ratings throughout its seven-year run; reignited his career in the lead role of the father in the ABC sitcom *8 Simple Rules for Dating My Teenage Daughter*, the most popular ABC comedy series of the 2002–03 season; was one of the two sons of the singing-cowboy movie star Tex Ritter and the actress Dorothy Fay; at the University of Southern California, changed his major from psychology to theater arts; after earning his degree, in 1971, acted in summer stock and regional theater and did stand-up at the Comedy Workshop in Los Angeles; made his television debut in an episode of the police-detective dramatic series *Dan August* in 1971; subsequently, had single-appearance roles on *Kojak, The Mary Tyler Moore Show, M*A*SH, Phyllis,* and *Rhoda,* among other television series, and had the recurring role of the naive reverend Mathew Fordwick on *The Waltons*; for his work in *Three's Company,* received the Emmy Award for outstanding lead actor in a comedy series in 1983–84; starred as San Francisco police detective Harry Hooperman in the situation comedy *Hooperman* (ABC, 1987–89) and as John Hartman, a U.S. Senate chief of staff, in the sitcom *Hearts Afire* (CBS, 1992–95), in which Billy Bob Thornton also had a role, as a Senate aide; in the feature film *Sling Blade* (1996), a tragedy written and directed by Thornton, was cast as a closeted, lonely small-town homosexual, a role written expressly for him by Thornton; later had roles in the motion pictures *Tadpole, Manhood,* and *Bad Santa*; among other TV credits in recent years, was the voice of the title canine in the PBS animated children's series *Clifford the Big Red Dog*; over the years, accrued many credits on the legitimate stage; on Broadway, created the role of Claude Pichon in Neil Simon's *The Dinner Party* in 1980; died in Burbank, California, after collapsing on the set of *8 Simple*

Rules for Dating My Teenage Daughter, the victim of an aortic dissection, a tear in the chief artery carrying blood from the heart. See *Current Biography* (June) 1980.

Obituary *New York Times* C p1+ Sep. 13, 2003

ROCHE, JAMES M. Dec. 16, 1906–June 6, 2004 Corporation executive; joined the General Motors Corp. as a sales statistician in 1927; rose through the ranks of the company to become president in 1965 and chairman of the board two years later; in 1966, issued an apology for GM's attempts to discredit consumer advocate Ralph Nader following Nader's criticism of GM's Corvair as an unsafe vehicle in his book *Unsafe at Any Speed* (1965); "led GM with compassion and grace through some very challenging times," as GM chairman and chief executive Rick Wagoner said following Roche's death; was credited with promoting equal opportunity within General Motors; in 1968, after race riots devastated Detroit, joined with the philanthropist Max Fisher in founding the New Detroit organization to work for the city's recovery; stepped down as chairman of General Motors upon reaching the mandatory retirement age of 65 in 1971; died at his home in Bellair, Florida. See *Current Biography* (February) 1967.

Obituary *New York Times* B p10 June 8, 2004

ROCKEFELLER, LAURANCE S. May 26, 1910–July 11, 2004 Venture capitalist; conservationist; philanthropist; a scion of the Rockefeller financial and philanthropic dynasty; was the third of the five sons of John D. Rockefeller Jr. and the second-to-last surviving grandson of the oil titan John D. Rockefeller Sr., the dynasty's patriarch and modern history's first billionaire (his younger brother David is the last surviving grandson); was described by Robin Winks in his book *Laurence S. Rockefeller: Catalyst for Conservation* (1997) as "the Rockefeller who, in the tradition of grandfather and father, arguably has moved and shaken to the most long-range purpose the preservation of the nation's natural heritage of great historic landscapes"; received a B.A. degree from Princeton University in 1932; after becoming a member of the New York Stock Exchange in the mid-1930s, proceeded to compound his inherited wealth through shrewd and inspired investments in worthwhile projects; in the late 1930s, subsidized the founding of American Airlines; during World War II, was an officer in the U.S. Navy's Bureau of Aeronautics; after the war, served in the New York City Airport Authority (1946–48) and became president of Rockefeller Brothers Inc., an enterprise formed to seek out and finance business projects in such fields as aviation, electronics, and housing; later chaired Rockefeller Center Inc.; in collaboration with his brothers, provided capital to develop resources in Puerto Rico and several Latin American countries through their International Basic Economy Corp.; was a director of such corporations as McDonnell Aircraft, International Nickel of Canada, Olin Mathieson Chemical, and several involved in nuclear energy; through his generous donations of land and influence as a member of federal, state, and local commissions, contributed prodigiously to the Jackson Hole Preserve and the Grand Teton National Park in Wyoming and the Palisades Interstate Park in New York and New Jersey and to the establishment or enlargement of national parks in California, Maine, Vermont, and the Virgin Islands; as the founder of RockResorts Inc., was a pioneering developer of environmentally oriented resort projects from the Caribbean to Hawaii; was a major contributor of funds to the Sloan Kettering Institute (now called the Memorial Sloan-Kettering Cancer Center) and other institutions devoted to cancer care and research; also contributed to organizations promoting the investigation of unidentified flying objects and extraterrestrial life; died at his home in Manhattan. See *Current Biography* (June) 1959.

Obituary *New York Times* B p7 July 12, 2004

ROTH, WILLIAM V. JR. July 22, 1921–Dec. 13, 2003 Five-term Republican U.S. senator from Delaware (1971–2001); two-term U.S. representative (1967–71); the namesake of the tax-sheltered retirement plan known as the Roth IRA, which became effective on January 1, 1998 as a result of passage of the Taxpayer Relief Act of 1997; following military service in World War II and receipt of business and law degrees at Harvard University, joined the legal staff of Hercules Inc., a chemical company in Wilmington, Delaware, with which he became senior counsel; as a congressman, compiled the Catalog of Domestic Assistance Programs, first published in the Congressional Record in 1968 and updated in 1969; in that catalog, listed 1,315 federal-assistance programs that dispensed a total of more than $20 billion a year to state and local governments, nonprofit institutions, and private institutions; in the Senate, established a conservative record; was determined to reduce what he described as "the elephantine tax burdens faced by middle-income taxpayers"; joined forces with a like-minded congressman, Jack F. Kemp of New York, to sponsor a tax-relief proposal that became, in Roth's words, "the centerpiece of President Ronald Reagan's economic recovery program," incorporated into the Economic Recovery Tax Act of 1981, which provided for a three-year series of 5, 10, and 10 percent tax cuts in personal income-tax rates; to encourage retirement investment among all taxpayers (not just the wealthy), created the Roth Individual Retirement Account, which allows an individual meeting certain requirements to deposit front-taxed money into an account in which its growth is thenceforth and forever tax free; chaired the Senate Finance Committee from September 1995 until he left office, in January 2001; in foreign policy, promoted the expansion of NATO into Eastern Europe; was co-chairman of the U.S.-European Union-Slovakia Action Committee; died at Georgetown University Hospital in Washington, D.C. See *Current Biography* (April) 1983.

Obituary *New York Times* B p10 Dec. 15, 2003

SAID, EDWARD W. Nov. 1, 1935–Sep. 24, 2003 Professor of literature at Columbia University; author of books of literary and cultural criticism and of political polemics; a prominent and controversial advocate in the U.S. of the Palestinian cause; was born into an affluent Christian family in Jerusalem in what was then British-mandated Palestine; in 1947, moved with his parents to Cairo, Egypt; in 1951, enrolled at the Mount Harmon School, a prep school in Mount Harmon, Massachusetts; earned a B.A. degree at Princeton University and a Ph.D. at Harvard University; also studied classical piano at the Juilliard School of Music, in Manhattan; wrote music criticism for the *Nation*; joined the faculty of Columbia University as an instructor in the Department of English in 1963; became a full professor at Columbia in 1970; was appointed Parr Professor of English and Comparative Literature in 1977 and Old Dominion Foundation Professor of the Humanities in 1989; in 1966, published his first book, *Joseph Conrad and the Fiction of Autobiography*, an expansion of his doctoral dissertation; in his second book, *Beginnings: Intention and Method* (1975), explored the meaning of modernism in art and literature; established his reputation as a major controversial political polemicist and a hero to many young leftist university teachers and graduate students with his best-known work, *Orientalism* (1978), a seminal document in the establishment of the academic field known as postcolonial studies; in that book, traced the history in the West of what he described as a hostile, clichéd perception ("orientalism") of the Arab/Muslim world, in the "latest phase" of which "the transference of a popular anti-Semitic animus from a Jewish to an Arab target was made smoothly, since the figure was essentially the same"; in *The Question of Palestine* (1979), contended that "in sheer numerical terms, in brute numbers of bodies and property destroyed, there is absolutely nothing to compare between what Zionism has done to Palestinians and what, in retaliation, Palestinians have done to Zionists"; assailed what he viewed as "the hypocrisy of Western . . . journalism and intellectual discourse, which have barely anything to say about Zionist terror" while routinely depicting Arabs as being "synonymous with trouble—rootless, mindless, gratuitous trouble"; in the same vein, wrote *Covering Islam: How the Media and the Experts Determine How We See the Rest of the World* (1981); brought together essays on politics, culture, and literature in *The World, the Text, and the Critic* (1983); co-edited and contributed to *Blaming the Victims* (1988), a collection of essays on the Palestinian question; wrote the text for *After the Last Sky: Palestinian Lives* (1986), illustrated with photographs by Jean Mohr; in *Culture and Imperialism* (1993), pointed out what he saw as the contributions of Joseph Conrad, E. M. Forster, and other British novelists to the cultural legitimization of colonialism; was a member of the Palestine National Council, a parliament-in-exile, from 1977 to 1991; stopped supporting Yasir Arafat, the leader of the Palestine Liberation Organization, in 1993, when Arafat signed the Oslo Accords, which in Said's view made concessions that rendered the prospect of a Palestinian state separate from Israel impractical; thereafter, advocated the creation of a single state in which Jews and Arabs would have equal rights; in his last book, *The Politics of Dispossession* (1994), added to his continued criticism of Western attitudes a scathing attack on the Palestinian leadership; was a friend of Salman Rushdie and a defender of Rushdie against Muslim fundamentalists threatening his life for alleged blasphemy in his novel *The*

Satanic Verses; in 2000, created an international incident when he was photographed throwing a rock toward an Israeli guardhouse on the southern Lebanese border, an act that he described as "a symbolic gesture"; died in Manhattan. See *Current Biography* (November) 1989. — *K.D.*

Obituary *New York Times* A p23 Sep. 26, 2003

SCAVULLO, FRANCESCO Jan. 16, 1921–Jan. 6, 2004 Photographer; exerted an extraordinary influence on modern-day standards of beauty and fashion; with his glitzy and seductive "Cosmo girl" covers for *Cosmopolitan* magazine, launched or accelerated the careers of Farrah Fawcett, Rene Russo, Imam, and other models and helped to create the phenomenon of the iconic "supermodel"; was also known for his idealized portraits of celebrities; "focused on a single task—finding the glamour in any subject—and finessed it for more than fifty years," as Mark Ellwood wrote for the London *Independent* (March 23, 2003); was born on Staten Island, New York City, and grew up in Manhattan, where his father owned the Central Park Casino, an upscale supper club; in the introduction to his first book, *Scavullo on Beauty* (1976), recalled that he was a "very self-conscious" and laconic ("didn't speak") child who thought he was "very ugly" and "only admired attractive people"; in a formative epiphany, was "spellbound" by the luminosity of Greta Garbo as projected on the motion-picture screen in *Queen Christina*, his introduction to "images" and "fantasy," to "total escape into a world of imagination"; with his father's brown box camera (an instrument that liberated him and made him "very bold"), began snapping pictures of his two older sisters and their girlfriends, posing, dressing, and applying makeup to their faces in an effort to make them "look like movie stars"; knew that someday he would "learn how" to "create the transformations [he] wanted to create"; after graduating from high school, worked as a photographer's apprentice at Becker's Studio, a publisher of fashion catalogs, and as assistant to the photographer Horst at *Vogue* magazine, to which he would contribute for many years; in 1948, moved into a converted carriage house (a gift from his father) on Manhattan's Upper East Side that would be his studio and home for the rest of his life; from 1948 through 1950, was a contract photographer with *Seventeen*, a fashion magazine with an adolescent female readership; from *Seventeen*, went to *Town and Country*, where he worked with Tony Mazola and began photographing socialites and celebrities; broke into the pages of *Harper's Bazaar* with a dramatic layout of sophisticated designer gowns in August 1955; also contributed to other women's magazines, among them *Ladies' Home Journal*, *Mademoiselle*, *Glamour*, and *McCall's*; early on, perfected such innovative lighting techniques as shading his models with white umbrellas to achieve a soft, natural daylight effect; contradicting Andy Warhol's acid dismissal of him as "an airbrush queen," insisted that he did not "rely on retouching" ; in 1965, was approached by Helen Gurley Brown, the editor in chief of *Cosmopolitan*, with the proposal that he give that magazine's cover a new look, "sexier" than the covers of other women's magazines without being "vulgar"; shot *Cosmopolitan*'s covers until 1995; from 1972 on, was assisted by his stylist (and life companion) Sean M. Byrnes, who chose the models and supervised the choices for their wardrobes, hair, and makeup; continued to contribute to other magazines, including *Rolling Stone*, *New York*, *Time*, and *Newsweek*; sometimes on commission, photographed an average of 10 subjects a week, including the socialite Gloria Vanderbilt, pop and rock singers (among them Madonna, Diana Ross, Cher, Janis Joplin, Mick Jagger, and Sting), actors and actresses (Elizabeth Taylor, Arnold Schwarzenegger, Paul Newman, and Joanne Woodward, among others), authors (William F. Buckley Jr. and Gore Vidal), the artist Louise Nevelson, the architect Philip Johnson, and the ballet dancer Mikhail Baryshnikov; began making silk-screen portraits in 1989; published eight books of photographs, among them *Scavullo: Photographs, 50 Years* (1997) and *Scavullo Nudes* (2000); is represented in several museums, including the Metropolitan Museum of Art, in New York City, and the Amos Carter Museum in Fort Worth, Texas; died in his Manhattan studio/home. See *Current Biography* (May) 1985.

Obituary *New York Times* C p12 Jan. 7, 2004

SCHOTT, MARGE Aug. 18, 1928–Mar. 2, 2004 Former president and chief executive officer of the Cincinnati Reds professional baseball franchise; businesswoman; philanthropist; the only woman ever to have become majority owner of a Major League Baseball team in her own right (rather than through inheritance); a brash, chain-smoking eccentric whose beneficence, while grand, was oddly pennypinching and whose good works were eclipsed by her notoriety for insensitive rhetoric, including racial and ethnic epithets; was a third-generation German-American, a daughter of Edward Unnewehr, the "very achtung" (her words) millionaire owner of an Ohio company that manufactured plywood; in 1952, married the Cincinnati industrialist Charles Schott; upon her husband's death, in 1968, took control of his business interests, including the largest auto dealership in Ohio, a General Motors franchise; on a lark, bought a limited partnership in the Cincinnati Reds in 1981; three years later, purchased the shares of several other limited partners, thus gaining control of 43 percent of the club and becoming the general partner; considered her purchase of the Reds a "Christmas gift to the people of Cincinnati" because she had feared that the franchise (which was operating in the red) might be sold to buyers from another city; with her management staff (including player/manager Pete Rose until his ouster from baseball, in 1989, for alleged betting on games), was able to build the small-market team that had not won a World Series since the mid-1970s into the world champions of 1990; then proceeded to alienate (partly by her cost-cutting decisions) her valued manager Lou Piniella and general manager Bob Quinn, both of whom left the team in 1992; meanwhile, was being sued (unsuccessfully) by Tim Sabo, a former controller for the Reds, who claimed that he had been wrongfully dismissed for objecting to some of her offensive statements, including use of the world "nigger"; in February 1993, was suspended by Major League Baseball's executive council from day-to-day management of the Reds for the 1993 season and fined $25,000 for "the most base and demeaning type of racial and ethnic stereotyping"; in March 1993, was ordered by the executive council to keep Schottzie 02, one of her two pet St. Bernard dogs, from bothering players in Cinergy Field (a k a Riverfront Stadium); in Mike Bass's book *Marge Schott: Unleashed* (1993), was reported to have called the former Reds marketing director Cal Levy, who disclosed that he had come across a Nazi armband (a war souvenir) in her home, "a beady-eyed Jew"; in May 1996 (when Cincinnati was falling into third place in its National League division), said in a network television interview regarding Adolf Hitler: "When he came in [to power] he was good . . . built tremendous highways and got all the factories going. . . . But he just went too far"; in June 1996, again threatened with suspension by baseball's executive council, voluntarily turned over the day-to-day operations of the Reds to John Allen, the team's controller, through 1998; under pressure from the team's limited owners, sold five and a half of her six and a half shares in the club to a group headed by minority owner Carl Linder for $67 million in 1999; in one of her final acts as principal owner, guaranteed the construction (financed by a half-cent city tax increase approved by Cincinnati voters and by $75 million from the Great American Insurance Co. for naming rights) of a new stadium for the team—the Great American Ball Park, which opened on a site adjacent to Cinergy Field on the riverfront in downtown Cincinnati in March 2003; donated millions of dollars, in total, to the Humane Society, the Cincinnati Zoo, the Cincinnati Children's Hospital, Cincinnati's Dan Beard Boy Scout Council, the Boys & Girls Clubs of Greater Cincinnati, St. Ursula Academy in Walnut Hills, Ohio, and All Saints Church in Kenwood Ohio, among other charities; was remembered by most of those who knew her, from Cincinnati city officials to team associates and players, some black and some Jewish, as "a paradox," a person with "the common touch," "kind-hearted" and "respectful" in "every interpersonal way"; died in Cincinnati. See *Current Biography* (August) 1999.

Obituary *New York Times* C p14 Mar. 3, 2004

SERRANO SÚÑER, RAMÓN Sep. 12, 1901–Sep. 1, 2003 Spanish politician and statesman; as a writer in the Madrid newspaper *El Mundo* eulogized, was "the lawyer who invented the Franquist [Francoist] state," the administrative structure of the fascist totalitarian regime of Generalissimo Francisco Franco, his brother-in-law, a dictatorship that prevailed for four decades, until 1977, two years after Franco's death; at the beginning of his career, practiced law in Saragossa, Spain; in 1933, was elected to the Cortes, the Spanish Parliament; in the midst of the Spanish civil war, joined Franco's insurgent government in Burgos, Spain, as minister of the interior (1938–39); in Madrid, after Franco's victory in the civil war, was minister of press and propaganda (1939–40) and foreign affairs (1940–42); in the latter position, negotiated Spain's World War II "nonbelligerancy" pact with the Axis powers; from 1939 to 1942, was president of the political council of Falange Española

Tradicionalista, the official state political party; merged the Falange into the Movimiento Nacional, a conservative/right wing coalition; left government in 1947; founded Radio Intercontinental and the Spanish state news agency Efe; published an autobiography, a collection of lectures, a collection of essays, and a memoir regarding his diplomatic dealings with Adolf Hitler; died at his home in Madrid. See *Current Biography* (November) 1940.

Obituary *New York Times* B p11 Sep. 4, 2003

SHOEMAKER, WILLIE Aug. 19, 1931–Oct. 12, 2003 Jockey; horse trainer; also known as Bill Shoemaker; the most celebrated jockey of his time, and the most durable; the first to earn a total of more than $100 million in purses for the respective owners of his mounts; the second-leading race winner in history, with 8,833 victories (including 1,009 stakes wins), a mark surpassed by Laffit Pincay Jr. in 1999; in a career spanning an unparalleled 41 years (1949–90), competed in a record 40,352 races and was national champion 15 times; garnered a career total of $123 million in purses (of which he received a small percentage); had a rare, uncanny rapport with his horses, the key to which was a light, relaxed style that belied a strong competitive spirit; rode his first pony on his grandfather Earl Harris's ranch near Abilene, Texas, when he was seven; dropped out of school at 15 to work at the Suzy Q Ranch in Puente, California; within a year, realized that his petite physique (98 pounds and four feet 11 inches at maturity) suited the pursuit of a career as a jockey; exercised horses for a few months at the stables of C. S. Howard at Santa Anita Park; there, met the trainer George Reeves, who, with the jockey Wallace Bailey, introduced him to racing; soon afterward, met the jockey's agent Harry Silbert, who became his close friend and manager; won his first race on April 20, 1949; during his first year as a jockey, was the runner-up for national top jockey honors, with 219 wins; in 1950, tied with Joe Culmone for top honors, with 388 wins; led all jockeys in races won in 1953, 1954, 1958, and 1959; in 1953, won 485 races, a record that stood for 20 years; was the leading money-winner among jockeys in 1951, 1953, 1954, and 1958 through 1964; was never worse than second in races won during the first 14 years of his career and never worse than second in purses from 1953 to 1957; rode three-year-old thoroughbreds to victory in the Kentucky Derby in 1955, 1959, 1965, and 1966, in the Preakness Stakes in 1963 and 1967, and in the Belmont Stakes in 1957, 1959, 1962, 1967, and 1975; won 11 Santa Anita Handicaps, eight Hollywood Gold Cups, four Jockey Club Gold Cups, one San Juan Capistrano Handicap (in 1962), one Arlington Cup Million (in 1981), and one Breeders' Cup Classic (in 1987); after retiring from racing, in 1990, became a horse trainer at Santa Anita Park; in a car accident in 1991, suffered a broken neck, which left him paralyzed from the neck down; confined to a wheelchair, returned to horse training at Santa Anita Park in a supervisory capacity; retired in 1997; with Dan Smith, wrote *The Shoe: Willie Shoemaker's Illustrated Book of Racing* (1976); with Barney Nagler, wrote the autobiography *Shoemaker: America's Greatest Jockey* (1988); also wrote the mystery novels *Stalking Horse*

(1994), *Fire Horse* (1995), and *Dark Horse* (1996); appeared in the TV documentary *Wide Wide World: Sunday Driver* (1956); died at his home in San Marino, California. See *Current Biography* (July) 1966.

Obituary *New York Times* B p8 Oct. 13, 2003

SIMON, PAUL Nov. 28, 1929–Dec. 8, 2003 Democratic congressman from Illinois; historian; a representative and senator whose sartorial trademarks, bow tie and horned-rim glasses, made him easily recognizable; served in the U.S. House of Representatives from 1975 to 1985 and in the U.S. Senate from 1985 to 1997; had previously served in the Illinois state House and Senate; was also a journalist, author, and university teacher; was described by some who knew him on Capitol Hill as "a moralist in politics" who "voted his conscience every time"; described himself as a "pay-as-you-go" Democrat, liberal on social issues but moderate to conservative on fiscal ones; wanted "a government that cares," that "helps people"; promoted federal funding of education at all levels, including student loans, job-training programs, and adult-literacy programs; was a leader in the promotion of foreign-language education; supported campaign-finance reform, gun control, measures to curb depictions of violence on television, assistance to the arts, and aid to "at risk" military veterans, the disabled, and children in need; sponsored the Missing Children Act and was a force behind the creation of the National Center for Missing and Exploited Children; opposed capital punishment, a constitutional amendment for prayer in the public schools, and what he regarded as excessive or ill-advised military spending (including that requested by the administration of President Ronald Reagan for its Strategic Defense Initiative, popularly known as "Star Wars"); voted against Reagan's nomination of Robert H. Bork for the Supreme Court; strongly advocated a balanced federal budget and, to that end, a line-item veto power to enable the president to strike "pork barrel" items from spending bills; was born into a Lutheran missionary family; after studying journalism for two years at Dana College, a small Lutheran institution in Blair, Nebraska, embarked on a career (interrupted by two years of service as an army intelligence agent) as a crusading small-town newspaper publisher/editor; with a bank loan, bought the troubled weekly *Troy Tribune* in Troy, Illinois, in 1948, becoming, at 19, the nation's youngest editor-publisher; went on to acquire a total of 14 newspapers, a chain he ultimately sold, in 1966; convinced that "underworld elements" controlled both major political parties, tried to recruit honest candidates to run for local offices; finally decided to enter elective politics himself; early on, established his practice of providing the electorate with detailed personal financial reports, long before the passage of disclosure laws requiring politicians to do so; following four two-year terms in the Illinois House of Representatives (1955–63), was elected (in 1962 and 1966) to two four-year terms in the Illinois Senate; as a state legislator, was fearless (as he had been as a journalist) in standing up to the criminal syndicate controlling gambling and prostitution in his home district; irritated many of his colleagues when he collaborated on the article "The Illinois Legislature:

A Study in Corruption," published in September 1964 in *Harper's* magazine; in 1968, cutting short his state Senate term, was elected lieutenant governor of Illinois, a position in which he served for four years under a Republican governor, Richard B. Ogilvie; lost a bid for the gubernatorial nomination in the Democratic primary in 1972; during a two-year retreat from politics, taught journalism at Sangamon State University (now the University of Illinois at Springfield) and lectured at the John F. Kennedy School of Government at Harvard University; was elected U.S. representative from the 24th Congressional District (C.D.) in southern Illinois in 1974 and reelected from that district in 1976 and 1978; was elected to Congress for the fourth consecutive time in 1980, when, as a result of redistricting, the numerical designation of the district was changed to the 22d; was reelected from the 22d C.D. in 1982; was elected to his first term in the U.S. Senate in 1984 and his second six years later; in 1988, sought the Democratic presidential nomination, unsuccessfully; chose not to run for a third Senate term in 1996; after leaving government in January 1997, joined the faculty of Southern Illinois University in Carbondale, Illinois, where he taught journalism and political science and founded the Public Policy Institute, a bipartisan think tank; was a major consultant in the drafting of landmark state political-reform legislation, signed into law in Illinois in 2003, which curtailed the influence of lobbyists and government insiders, set limits on the gifts that office holders can accept, and imposed restrictions inimical to the use of tax money for partisan political purposes; wrote a score of books (all unghosted), among them *Lincoln's Preparation for Greatness: The Illinois Legislative Years* (1965), *Once and Future Democrats: Strategies for Change* (1982), *Let's Put America Back to Work* (1987), *Winners and Losers: The 1988 Race for the Presidency—One Candidate's Perspective* (1989), *Advice and Consent: Clarence Thomas, Robert Bork, and the Intriguing History of the Supreme Court's Nomination Battles* (1992), *Tapped Out: The Coming World Crisis in Water and What We Can Do About It* (1998); *P.S.: The Autobiography of Paul Simon* (1999), *Healing America: Values and Vision for the 21st Century* (2003), and *Our Culture of Pandering* (2003); collaborated on books on world hunger and poverty with his first wife, Jeanne (who predeceased him), and his brother, Arthur; endorsed the candidacy of former governor Howard Dean of Vermont for the 2004 Democratic presidential nomination; died in Springfield, Illinois. See *Current Biography* (January) 1988.

Obituary *New York Times* A p29 Dec. 10, 2003

SMITH, JEFF Jan. 22, 1939–July 7, 2004 Chef; clergyman; popular host of the long-running public-television cooking show *The Frugal Gourmet*, until charges of sexual assault led to the end of its run; author of best-selling companion cookbooks to that program; held a B.A. degree in philosophy and sociology from the University of Puget Sound, in Takoma, Washington, and a master of divinity degree from Drew Theological School, in Madison, New Jersey; was ordained a minister in the United Methodist Church in 1965; from 1966 to 1972, was chaplain and assistant professor of religion at the University of Puget Sound, where his most popular course was "Food as Sacrament and Celebration"; in Takoma from 1972 to 1983, ran the Chaplain's Pantry, a restaurant, catering service, and gourmet store where he employed students, many of whom were teenage boys placed through a work-study program at Takoma's Stadium High School; meanwhile, in 1973, began demonstrating cooking in a segment of the weekly television show *Seattle Today* on the local NBC affiliate in Seattle, Washington; in 1983, launched *The Frugal Gourmet,* which aired nationally; as the ebullient host of that weekly program, was seen on 288 PBS affiliate stations with a total audience of more than 15 million for 14 years, until 1997; during that year, was presented with three civil lawsuits filed by eight men claiming that, using "alcohol, coercion, and force," in the words of one of the suits, he sexually assaulted them when they were boys working at the Chaplain's Pantry; corroborative statements were signed by several witnesses; settled the suits out of court; wrote 12 cookbooks, some devoted to American recipes and others to ethnic cuisines; in addition, co-wrote *The Frugal Gourmet's Culinary Handbook* (1991); died in Seattle, Washington. See *Current Biography* (August) 1991.

Obituary *New York Times* B p18 July 10, 2004

SMYLIE, ROBERT E. Oct. 31, 1914–July 17, 2004 Three-term Republican governor of Idaho (1955–67); lawyer; following service with the Coast Guard during World War II, practiced law in Caldwell and Boise, Idaho; in 1947, was appointed asssistant attorney general of Idaho; succeeded Robert Ailshie as attorney general upon Ailshie's death, in November 1947; was elected to a full two-year term as attorney general in 1948; both as attorney general and governor, opposed plans for federal construction of a large multipurpose dam at Hell's Canyon on the Snake River and supported the application of a private utility corporation to build three smaller hydroelectric plants on that river; in 1965, helped assure the passage of a law instituting a state three-cent-per-dollar sales tax; thereby lost favor with many in his core constituency; was defeated in his bid for a fourth term as governor in 1966; with the hotelier Verle Kaiser, wrote *The Idaho Guest Encyclopedia* (circa 1959); wrote an autobiography, *Governor Smylie Remembers* (1998); died at his home in Boise, Idaho. See *Current Biography* (February) 1956.

Obituary *New York Times* B p9 July 20, 2004

SOUZAY, GÉRARD Dec. 8, 1918–Aug. 17, 2004 French opera and concert singer; one of the 20th century's outstanding lyrical baritones, especially esteemed for his feelingful interpretations of art songs and lieder; although limited in vocal size and range, had beautiful tone and was a remarkable stylist, sensitive to a composition's essential thrust and able to convey its poetry and emotion; had few peers as a polished interpreter of such composers as Debussy, Fauré, Poulenc, and Ravel; was equally at ease in the different worlds of Beethoven, Schumann, Schubert, and Hugo Wolf; with recordings of his concert repertoire, won the Grand Prix du Disc several times; was ranked by many aficionados with the less visceral, more intellectual German art-song specialist Dietrich Fischer-Dieskau; in opera, was most at home in roles with an intimate register, such as Purcell's *Aeneas* and Monteverdi's *Orfeo*, but also took on such robust romantic roles as Debussy's Golaud; studied under Pierre Bernac, among others; after graduating from the Paris Conservatory, made his concert debut in 1945; over the following several years, regularly made concert tours of Western Europe; also gave recitals in North Africa; made his New York debut as a concert singer in 1950; during the 1950s constantly toured South America, South Africa, Australia, Japan, and other parts of the world; in 1954, met the young pianist Dalton Baldwin, who became his accompanist and long-term personal associate; on some occasions, was also accompanied by Jacqueline Bonneau; made his operatic debut in Aix-en-Province in 1960; later in the same year, made his American operatic debut with the New York City Opera Company; in 1962, sang at the Rome Opera as well as the Paris Opera; in 1965, made his debut with the Metropolitan Opera as Count Almaviva in *The Marriage of Figaro*; later made operatic appearances in Florence (1966), again in Rome (1974), and in Wiesbaden (1976); included in his operatic repertory the roles of Mercutio in Gounod's *Roméo et Juliette* and Mephisto in Berlioz's *Damnation of Faust*, among others; as a soloist with symphony orchestras, sang under the baton of some of the most eminent conductors in Europe and the U.S.; in his later years, taught at the University of Texas and gave master classes; died at his home in Cap d'Antibes, France. See *Current Biography* (January) 1966.

Obituary *New York Times* C p3 Aug. 19, 2004

SPAHN, WARREN Apr. 23, 1921–Nov. 24, 2003 Professional baseball player; National League pitcher; was a mainstay of the Boston/Milwaukee Braves' pitching staff for two decades; established several major-league records for left-handed pitchers, including games won (363, with 245 losses), innings pitched (5,243 and 2/3) and shutouts (63); also set major-league records for most seasons leading a league in victories (eight) and most seasons leading a league in complete games (nine); shared with the right-hander Christy Mathewson the National League record for most seasons with 20 or more victories (13); was also formidable at the plate, with 35 career home runs, a National League record for a pitcher; was an All Star 14 times; had an unusual delivery, with a high kick of the right leg, which unsettled batters; as a teenager, played first base with the Lake City Athletic Club, a Buffalo, New York, amateur team on which his father was third baseman; switched to pitching at South Park High School in Buffalo; signed with the Boston Braves organization in 1940; pitched with Boston farm teams in the 1940 and 1941 seasons and most of the 1942 season; was called up to Boston late in the 1942 season and appeared in four games with the Braves but was not involved in any decision; following the 1942 season, was drafted for service with the U.S. Army in World War II; in combat in Europe, earned a Purple Heart

and a Bronze Star; in 1946, returned to the Boston roster; in 1947, posted a 21–1 record and led the National League with a 2.33 earned-run average; won 20 or more games in 12 of the following 16 seasons; in 1948, with fellow pitcher Johnny Sain, paced the Braves to their first pennant in 24 years; in the 1948 World Series (which the Braves lost to the Cleveland Indians), won one game and lost one; led the National League in strikeouts pitched in four consecutive seasons (1949–52); pitched with the Braves in Boston until 1953, when the team moved to Milwaukee; at that time, was losing some of the speed of his fastball and began to rely more heavily on the curve, the screwball, the slider, and change-ups; won the Cy Young Award as major-league pitcher of the year in 1957 and was runner-up for the award in each of the following four years; pitched 1–1 in the 1957 World Series, in which the Braves defeated the New York Yankees; went 2–1 in the 1958 Series, which the Braves lost to the Yankees; at the plate, had a .333 batting average in 1958; pitched two no-hitters, one in 1960 and the other in 1961; in the latter year, again had the best ERA in the National League; in 1963, went 23–7; following the 1964 season (when he slipped to a 6–13 win–loss record), was sold to the New York Mets; with the Mets in 1965, went 4–12; in mid-July, was released to the San Francisco Giants, with whom he wrapped up the 1965 season and his major-league pitching career with three wins and four losses; left the majors with a career ERA of 3.09; subsequently pitched in the Mexican League and, in the American minor leagues, was a player/coach with the Tulsa Oilers and a pitching instructor with the Salt Lake Gulls, a California Angels farm team; was elected to the Baseball Hall of Fame in 1973; after retiring from baseball, operated a cattle ranch in Oklahoma; died at his home in Broken Arrow, Oklahoma. See *Current Biography* (May) 1962.

Obituary *New York Times* B p9 Nov. 25, 2003

STANFIELD, ROBERT LORNE Apr. 11, 1914–Dec. 16, 2003 Canadian politician and statesman; former member of Parliament; former leader of the now defunct (as of December 2003) Progressive Conservative Party; was known as "Honest Bob," "a man of integrity and honor" who "radiated moral authority"— "the best prime minister Canada never had"; after serving as premier of the province of Nova Scotia for 11 years, was federal Opposition leader for nine years; as a "Red Tory" with a Burkean view of social policy, personified the Progressive Conservative Party's paradoxical combination of "top hat and overalls"; as his biographer Geoffrey Stevens observed, as quoted in the *Toronto Star* (December 18, 2003), "modernized the Progressive Conservative party, and took it from the shambles it had been under [John G.] Diefenbaker, where it was dominated by a Prairie rump of capital punishment fans, anti-abortionists, and ersatz populists"; made national unity his top priority; in the course of his effort to persuade French-speaking Quebecers not to secede from Canada, participated in French-immersion lessons in Quebec; steadfastly supported official bilingualism; was born into a wealthy Nova Scotia textile-manufacturing family; after earning a law degree at Harvard University, was admitted to the Nova Scotia bar in 1940; became secretary of the provincial Progressive Conservative Party in 1946 and leader of the party in 1949, when he was elected to the provincial House of Assembly; following the election of October 30, 1956, when the Progressive Conservatives won a majority of seats in the provincial House of Assembly, became premier, on November 20, 1956; remained in power through three subsequent elections; as premier, ran a carefully budgeted administration while widening and securing educational and health-care services; formed Industrial Estates Ltd., a group of 10 provincial businessmen mandated to work without government interference "to encourage . . . industrial activity"; with the province of New Brunswick, shared federal funding (from the Progressive Conservative government of John G. Diefenbaker) for the building of thermal-power-generating plants; in 1967, was elected to the Canadian House of Commons, where he assumed leadership of the Progressive Conservative caucus and thus of the Opposition to the Liberal government of Lester Pearson (who had succeeded Diefenbaker in 1963 and would be succeeded by Pierre Elliot Trudeau, a fellow Liberal, in 1968); strongly supported the Liberals' Official Languages Act, passed in 1969 over the opposition of 17 of his own 72-member caucus; barely missed becoming prime minister of Canada in the elections of 1972, when the Progressive Conservatives fell just two seats short of defeating the Liberal government of Pierre Elliot Trudeau, which retained power only through a coalition with the New Democrats; lost to Trudeau by a greater margin in 1974; resigned his leadership of the Progressive Conservative Party in 1976 and his seat in the House of Commons in 1979; subsequently, represented Canada in the Middle East and North Africa; chaired the Commonwealth Foundation from 1987 to 1991; died at Montfort Hospital in Ottawa, Canada, three days after the Progressive Conservative Party merged with the Alliance Party to form the Conservative Party, a less centrist, more populist group than the Progressive Conservatives had been. See Current Biography (December) 1958.

Obituary New York Times C p15 Dec. 19, 2003

STEIG, WILLIAM Nov. 14, 1907–Oct. 3, 2003 Cartoonist; writer; in many of his pen-and-ink drawings for adult readers, reflected a view of human nature influenced at first by the psychoanalytical theories of Sigmund Freud and later by those of Wilhelm Reich, who taught, in the context of his wider anti-fascist theory, that psychological problems stem from repressed sexual energy and who invented the orgone box, an "orgone energy accumulator" (in one of which Steig encased himself daily); also wrote and illustrated (usually with squiggly lines, in pen, ink, and watercolor) some 25 storybooks for children, most of them fantasies with animal protagonists; confessed that he "always despised old people" and "never felt grown up"; was born in New York City to Marxist Jewish immigrant parents; received his art training at the National Academy of Design, in Manhattan; in 1930, began contributing conventional cartoons to magazines, including the New Yorker, with which he ultimately became most closely associated; in total, would publish in the New Yorker 1,600 drawings and 117 covers; in his first New Yorker cartoon, had one prison inmate sayng to another, "My son's incorrigible. I can't do a thing with him"; for several years beginning in 1936, carved small, wooden, humorous sculptures that were exhibited at a Manhattan gallery in 1939; also in 1936, turned from gag cartoons to "symbolic drawings" of neurotic characters drawn from his perception of the way "human beings screw up their lives"—works that the New Yorker at first rejected for being "too personal and not funny enough"; published such drawings in the collections About People (1939), The Lonely Ones (1942), All Embarrassed (1944), The Rejected Lovers (1951), and, years later, in a similar vein, Our Miserable Life (1990); for the New Yorker, executed, among other drawings, a series of cartoons about socially unconditioned, arrogant children (chiefly boys) based on memories of his school days at P.S. 53 in the Bronx; collected those drawings of urban brats in Small Fry (1944); in later decades, made for the New Yorker a series of doodle-like drawings, reminiscent of Picasso, depicting grotesque but benign figures frolicking in Elysian fields; worked in advertising for many years, until he began publishing children's books, in 1968; was awarded the Caldecott Medal for Sylvester and the Magic Pebble (1969), about a donkey who turns into a stone; won Caldecott honors for The Amazing Bone (1976), about the sometimes frightening adventures of a little pig named Pearl; won Newbery honors for Abel's Island (1977), about a mouse marooned on an island, and Doctor De Soto (1983), about a mouse-dentist who cleverly handles a problem patient—a fox with a toothache and an appetite for mice; in 1990, published Shrek!, about an obese green ogre, which was made into an Oscar-winning animated feature cartoon (without the exclamation point in the title) in 2001; also for children, published the collection of cartoons Grown-Ups Get to Do All the Driving (1995); in June 2003 published his last book, When Everybody Wore a Hat, reminiscences of the culture of his childhood; was married four times, the first time to Elizabeth Mead, the sister of the anthropologist Margaret Mead, and the last time to Jeanne Doron, who collaborated with him on several books; died in Boston, Massachusetts. See Current Biography (July) 1944. — K.D.

Obituary New York Times p39 Oct. 5, 2003

STRAIGHT, MICHAEL Sep. 1, 1916–Jan. 4, 2004 Author; former editor and publisher of the journal of opinion the New Republic; former tool of a notorious Soviet spy ring; was the youngest of the three children of parents who had financed the launching of the progressive New Republic in 1914, the investment banker Willard D. Straight (who died in France in World War I) and the heiress Dorothy Payne Whitney Straight (who married Leonard Knight Elmhirst in 1925); received his secondary education at Dartington Hall, a Utopian school run by his mother and her second husband in Totnes, Devon, England; following a year at the London School of Economics, entered Trinity College, Cambridge University, in 1934; as a student of economics at Cambridge (where he earned an M.A. degree), secretly joined the Communist Party; was persuaded by the poet John Corn-ford to infiltrate the Cambridge Union for the party; was elected secretary of the Cambridge Union in 1936 and president of the union in 1937; was recruited into serious espionage by the young Cambridge don Anthony Blount, a clandestine Soviet agent; on instructions from Blount, returned to the U.S. as a Soviet spy; while working as an economist with the U.S. Department of State, wrote economic and political memoranda that he passed on to Soviet intelligence; began to become disillusioned with the Soviet Union when the Nazi-Soviet pact was signed, in August 1939; in 1941, after working with the National Power Policy Committee in the U.S. Department of the Interior (1939–40) and again at the Department of State (1940–41), became editor of the *New Republic*; as editor, turned the journal's editorial policy from neutrality in World War II to involvement on the side of the anti-Fascist forces; during the war, from 1942 to 1945, was stationed with the Army Air Forces in the Midwest; after the war, was publisher of the *New Republic* until 1956; in 1963, was offered a high arts post in the administration of President John F. Kennedy; fearing a background check, sought the counsel of Arthur M. Schlesinger, Jr., a special assistant to the president, who referred him to the U.S. Department of Justice; confessed all to the Federal Bureau of Investigation, which passed on the information to the British MI5, exposing the participants in the Cambridge Soviet spy ring, including Blount, who by then was the curator of Queen Elizabeth's art collection; was deputy chairman of the National Endowment for the Arts from 1966 to 1977; wrote *Trial by Television and Other Encounters* (1979), which included his perspective on the Army-McCarthy hearings, and the memoirs *After Long Silence* (1983) and *On Green Springs Farm* (2004); also wrote the Western novels *Carrington* (1960) and *A Very Small Remnant* (1963); was survived by his three successive wives, including Nina Gore Auchincloss Steers, and several children and grandchildren; died in Chicago, Illinois. See *Current Biography* (August) 1944.

Obituary *New York Times* B p8 Jan. 5, 2004

STRAUS, ROGER W. JR. Jan. 3, 1917–May 25, 2004 Publisher; one of the last of the great independent, hands-on book publishers; co-founded Farrar, Straus and Co., now Farrar, Straus & Giroux, a firm renowned for its fine taste and discernment in international literary fiction, nonfiction, poetry, and juvenalia; presided over the company for more than half a century, a period during which book publishing in general, under corporate influence, became ever more impersonal and crassly commercial; guided his company with a profound regard for literary quality and a serene indifference to accusations of elitism; was born in New York City into a branch of the distinguished Guggenheim family on the maternal side; paternally, was a grandson of Oscar S. Straus, President Theodore Roosevelt's secretary of commerce and labor, the first Jewish person ever named to an American president's Cabinet; received a B.A. degree in journalism at the University of Missouri in 1939; worked as a reporter or editor with several publications; after service in the U.S. Navy in World War II, joined with the veteran publisher John Farrar

to found, in the mid-1940s, the publishing house now known as Farrar, Straus & Giroux; over the following decades, published such writers as Hermann Hesse, T. S. Eliot, Robert Lowell, Isaac Bashevis Singer, Bernard Malamud, Philip Roth, Edmund Wilson, Flannery O'Connor, Alexander Solzhenitsyn, Tom Wolfe, Susan Sontag, Marguerite Yourcenar, Seamus Heaney, Scott Turow, John McPhee, Michael Cunningham, Jonathan Franzen, Shirley Hazzard, and Jeffrey Eugenides—a literary gallery that included scores of Nobel Prize, Pulitzer Prize, and National Book Award winners; in 1994, realizing that he could no longer compete financially with publishing conglomerates, sold controlling interest in Farrar, Straus & Giroux to the German media group Verlagsgruppe Georg von Holtzbrinck, which left him free rein in managing his company; died in Manhattan. See *Current Biography* (August) 1980.

Obituary *New York Times* B p10 May 27, 2004

SUZUKI, ZENKO Jan. 11, 1911–July 19, 2004 Prime minister of Japan (1980–82); a founder of Japan's reigning Liberal Democratic Party (Jiyu-Minshuto); chaired that party's executive council from 1968 to 1980; while pedestrian in his thinking and decision-making, ingratiated himself with the powers that were (chiefly Kakuei Tanaka) as a behind-the-scenes moderator between the party's warring factions; because of his involvement in a vital food industry (fisheries), was not drafted into military service until late in World War II; after the war, was active first in the Socialist Party and then in the Liberal Party; began serving in the Japanese Parliament in 1947; when the Liberals decided to merge with the Democrats in 1955, helped to establish the new Liberal Democratic Party, which drew strong rural support and which, while downplaying ideology, declared itself in favor of private enterprise, the alliance with the U.S., and the extension of Japanese interests in Asia; between 1960 and 1977, held a succession of cabinet portfolios, including postal service and telecommunications, health and welfare, and agriculture, forestry, and fisheries; as prime minister, was notorious for several blunders, the worst of which was his failure to understand the importance of rectifying the whitewashing in Japanese school textbooks of Japan's expeditionary military predations before and during World War II, a lapse that set back China–Japan relations for years; died in Tokyo, Japan; was survived by his son, Shunichi Suzuki, a lobbyist against the moratorium on commercial whale fishing who became minister of the environment in 2002. See *Current Biography* (January) 1981.

Obituary *New York Times* C p13 July 21, 2004

TELLER, EDWARD Jan. 15, 1908–Sep. 9, 2003 Physicist; professor emeritus, University of California; widely regarded as "the father of the hydrogen bomb," a soubriquet he deplored; justified his fierce stance as a scientific Cold Warrior with the explanation that "power should belong to those who do not want to use it"; was born into an assimilated Jewish family in Budapest, Hungary; as a child, demonstrated a precocious mathematical ability, but was pressured by his father to study chemistry as a teenager; subsequently, studied under Werner Heisenberg, a pioneer in quantum mechanics, at the University of Leipzig, Germany, where he earned a Ph.D. degree in theoretical physics in 1930 with a dissertation on the theory of the hydrogen ion; in his postdoctoral work, concentrated on quantum mechanics, especially in its application to physical chemistry; was a research consultant at the University of Göttingen, Germany, from 1931 to 1933, when, with Adolf Hitler's rise to power, it became obvious to him that he had to leave Germany; obtained a Rockefeller Foundation fellowship that enabled him to study for a year under Niels Bohr in the Institute for Theoretical Physics at the University of Copenhagen, Denmark; was a professor of physics at George Washington University, in Washington, D.C., from 1935 to 1941; in the latter year, became an American citizen; at George Washington University, engaged in collaborative research with George Gamow that prepared him for his work in nuclear fission as a member (successively at Columbia University, the University of Chicago, the University of California, and, finally, the Los Alamos National Laboratory in New Mexico) of the Manhattan Project, the top-secret World War II program that created the atomic bombs dropped on the Japanese cities of Hiroshima and Nagasaki in August 1945; all along, was less interested in nuclear fission than in thermonuclear fusion; against the consensus of his colleagues at Los Alamos, urged that the U.S. proceed from the atomic bomb to the building, through thermonuclear fusion, of the hydrogen bomb, an explosive device some 700 times more powerful than the atomic bomb; in 1949, when the Soviet Union detonated its first atomic bomb, helped to persuade President Harry S. Truman to authorize the thermonuclear fusion project that culminated in the detonation at the Eniwetok Atoll, Marshall Islands, in the mid-Pacific in November 1952 of a thermonuclear bomb yielding the explosive equivalent of a million tons of TNT; that same autumn, joined the faculty of the University of California at Berkeley as a professor of physics and co-founded at the University of California at Livermore, under the aegis of the U.S. Atomic Energy Commission, the Lawrence Livermore Laboratory for the purpose of continued atomic research, including thermonuclear; meanwhile, having already alienated his former colleagues at Los Alamos with his dedicated pursuit of the H-bomb, was shunned by many of them after his testimony at a hearing before the Atomic Energy Commission's personnel security board in 1954; contributed significantly to the board's decision to revoke the security clearance of J. Robert Oppenheimer, the director of research at Los Alamos; was associate director of the Lawrence Livermore Laboratory from 1954 to 1958, director from 1958 to 1960, and again associate director from 1960 to 1975; at Livermore, conducted the development of a nuclear bomb small enough to be fired from a submarine; promoted Project Plowshares, devoted to the peaceful use of underground nuclear explosions, for such purposes as blasting for harbor digging and the freeing of oil and natural-gas deposits; more famously, promoted a space-based antimissile system, an idea that in the 1980s inspired the administration of President Ronald Reagan to propose the $30 billion Strategic Defense Initiative, popularly known as "Star Wars," a program dropped by the administration of President Bill Clinton in the 1990s and revived under President George W. Bush in 2001; was senior research fellow at the Hoover Institution at Stanford University from 1975 until his death; was awarded the Presidential Medal of Freedom in July 2003; published a dozen books, including *Better a Shield than a Sword: Perspectives on Defense and Technology* (1987), volumes on the structure of matter, the legacy of Hiroshima, the history and future of energy research, and *Memoirs: A Twentieth-Century Journey in Science and Politics* (2001), written with Judith L. Shoolery; died at his home in Stanford, California. See *Current Biography* (November) 1983. — K.D.

Obituary *New York Times* A p22 Sep. 11, 2003

TISCH, LAURENCE A. Mar. 5, 1923–Nov. 15, 2003 Financier; entrepreneur; a self-made billionaire described in the press as a "contrarian investor," "conglomateur," and "brilliant financial analyst" who focused "on long-term outlooks and long-term values" with a "calculator-and-scalpel style"; co-chairman and former chief executive officer of Loews Corp.; former CEO of CBS Inc. (1986–95); was a precocious learner who went through high school and college in only five years, graduating cum laude from New York University at the age of 18; at 19, earned a master's degree in industry and management at the University of Pennsylvania's Wharton School of Finance and Commerce; with the U.S. Army in World War II, worked as a cryptologist for the Office of Strategic Services, the precursor of the CIA; after the war, with seed money from his parents, purchased a kosher resort hotel in Lakewood, New Jersey; in 1948, was joined in that enterprise by his younger brother, Preston Robert "Bob" Tisch, who was as adept at management as Larry (as Laurence was familiarly known) was at financial manipulations; with Bob, went on to build a hotel empire, acquiring large hotels in Atlantic City, the Catskill Mountains, and Manhattan and constructing the luxurious 780-room Americana Hotel in Bal Harbour, Florida; in 1959, with $65 million in profits from their thriving hotels, began buying into the large chain of aging Loews Theaters (which had dwindling revenues then, at the $100 million level), with an eye on the potential value of the chain's underlying real-estate assets; in January 1961, gained total control of what became the Loews Corp., which over the following four decades would grow into a diversified $70 billion conglomerate; first, sold off some of the unprofitable Loews theaters and steered the corporation into the hotel and motel business; for example, on Loews real-estate sites in Manhattan, built a number of hotels, including the 800-room Summit Hotel and the 2,000-room Americana Hotel (and convention center), as well as apartment buildings; using Loews as a base, went on to acquire such diverse subsidiaries as the cigarette company Lorillard, the property- and casualty-insurance company CNA Financial Corp., the Bulova Watch Co., Diamond Offshore Drilling Inc., and the Texas Gas Transmission Corp.; began investing in CBS Inc. in 1985, when the financially troubled television network was threatened with several hostile takeovers; was invited by CBS executives, as one of them explained, "to take on a substantial share of the company because we felt that having that kind of long-haul commitment from a person like him was in the interest of our shareholders and the country"; within a year, had acquired a 24.9 percent stake in CBS and was a member of its board of directors; in September 1986, became CBS's acting CEO, replacing Thomas H. Wyman, who had alienated the board of directors by broaching sale of CBS to the Coca-Cola Co.; four months later, was unanimously elected CEO by the CBS board; immediately set to work streamlining network operations and cutting costs; fired approximately 1,200 employees and sold off many valuable CBS assets; less experienced at management than at finance, did so with a heavy hand and often summarily; drew criticism within the industry and on Wall Street and heavy flak within CBS itself, especially in CBS News, whose budget he slashed by at least $30 million by dismissing some 200 or more employees, including on-air reporters, and shutting down some national and overseas bureaus, actions that his critics saw as causally related to the news division's drop from first place among the networks in ratings to second, behind ABC News; conceded that he might have avoided the "fiasco" if he had not "mishandled the firings" and "done more of it by attrition"; during his nine years at the CBS helm, oversaw an almost 15 percent annual rise in the network's stock, as he pointed out in 1995, when CBS was sold to the Westinghouse Electric Corp. for $5.4 billion; was CEO of Loews Corp. until 1999, when he was succeeded by his son James; remained co-chairman of the Loews board of directors; was generous in his expenditure of energy and money in such causes as New York University, New York University Medical Center, United Jewish Appeal of Greater New York, the Federation of Jewish Philanthropies, and the Metropolitan Museum of Art; died in New York City, at New York University Medical Center's Tisch Hospital. See *Current Biography* (February) 1987.

Obituary *New York Times* p43 Nov. 16, 2003

TRUMAN, DAVID B. June 1, 1913–Aug. 28, 2003 College and university administrator; was provost of Columbia University when, in the spring of 1968, countercultural and anti–Vietnam War militants led a campus uprising during which students took over six university buildings; acting in place of the absent Grayson L. Kirk, the president of the university, quelled the rebellion by calling in some 1,000 New York City police officers in riot gear, an action that resulted in injuries to 179 students and 37 officers; earned a Ph.D. at the University of Chicago with a dissertation published as "Administrative Decentralization" (1940), a study of the Chicago field offices of the U.S. Department of Agriculture; taught at Bennington College (1939–41) and Cornell University (1941–44); on leaves of absence from Cornell during World War II, did stints of service with the Federal Communications Commission and the Department of Agriculture; during the last year of the war (1944–45), served in the U.S. Navy; after the war, was deputy director of the U.S. Strategic Bombing Survey in the Pacific (1945–46); was a lecturer in government at Harvard University (1946–47) and associate professor of political science at Williams College (1947–51); on a leave of absence from Williams,

was visiting associate professor of government at Columbia University (1950); joined Columbia's faculty as full professor of government in 1951; chaired the department of public law and government at Columbia from 1959 to 1962, when he was named dean of the university's undergraduate college; assumed the dual office of vice president and provost at Columbia in 1967; before the student rebellion of April and May 1968, had an impeccable reputation for good rapport with both students and faculty and was viewed as the heir apparent to Grayson L. Kirk in the university's presidency; regarding the New Left group Students for a Democratic Society, the major force behind the rebellion, said, "They regard the university as a soft spot in a society that they're trying to bring down"; in January 1969, resigned his positions at Columbia to become president of Mount Holyoke College (1969–78); subsequently served as president of the Russell Sage Foundation, a sponsor of research in the social sciences (1978–79); wrote the books *The Government Process: Political Interests and Public Opinion* (1951), *The Congressional Party: A Case Study* (1959), and *The Governmental Process: Political Interests and Public Opinion* (1953); edited *The Congress and America's Future* (1965); died at his home in Sarasota, Florida. See *Current Biography* (June) 1972.

Obituary *New York Times* B p7 Sep. 1, 2003

USTINOV, PETER Apr. 16, 1921–Mar. 28, 2004 British character actor; playwright; screenwriter; producer; director; novelist; short-story writer; a globe-trotting Renaissance man, hirsute and portly in appearance, puckish and urbane in speech and manner, and protean in his brilliant (albeit somewhat untamed, in the opinion of some critics) talent; was fluent in six languages and could communicate in several more; made his stage debut in London in 1938; began appearing in motion pictures in the early 1940s; was nominated for an Academy Award for his supporting portrayal of a strutting, effete Emperor Nero in the film *Quo Vadis?* (1951); won supporting-role Oscars for his performances as the crafty slave dealer Lentulus in *Spartacus* (1960) and the inept jewel thief Arthur Simon Simpson in the caper flick *Topkapi* (1964); in one of his number of multifaceted efforts, directed, co-produced, co-wrote, and played Captain Vere in the film *Billy Budd* (1962); with his gift for mimicry and his cultivated and ready wit as a conversationalist and raconteur, delighted viewers of his many guest appearances on television talk and panel shows, attendees at his after-dinner speeches, and audiences at his solo London stage presentation *An Evening with Peter Ustinov* (1990); was the son of part-Russian parents—his father a journalist and his mother a painter and theatrical designer; attended the Westminster School in London until he was 16; subsequently studied acting at the London Theatre Studio and performed in comic monologues at the Players' Theatre Club in London; in his debut as a playwright, scored a success on the London stage with *House of Regrets* (1942), about an exiled Russian community in England dreaming of a Czarist restoration; followed that up with his plays *Blow Your Own Trumpet* (1943) and *The Banbury Nose* (1944); in the meantime, had joined the British army for World War II service in 1942; co-wrote and acted in the film *The Way Ahead* (1944), a semi-documentary originally intended as a training picture, about the wartime adventures of a platoon of new army recruits; contributed to the writing of, and appeared in, the acclaimed war documentary *The True Glory* (1945); after the war, co-produced, wrote, and directed the film *School for Secrets* (a k a *Secret Flight*, 1946), a drama about the crucial role of radar in the defense of Britain in World War II; on stage, was cast in such London productions as *Crime and Punishment* (1946); wrote, among other plays, *The Indifferent Shepherd* (1948), a Chekhovian portrayal of two clergymen of differing ideals, and *The Love of Four Colonels* (1951), a satire on military officers on both sides of the Cold War that enjoyed a run of hundreds of performances in the West End and went on to continue for 141 performances on Broadway; again spoofed the Cold War in *Romanoff and Juliet* (1956), a hit on both sides of the Atlantic (and played the General of Concordia in the film of that title [1961], which he also directed and produced); wrote a total of some 30 plays, including *No Sign of the Dove* (1953), *Paris Not So Gay* (1958), *The Unknown Soldier and His Wife* (1967), *Halfway Up the Tree* (1967), *Who's Who in Hell* (1974), and *Beethoven's Tenth* (1982); in a motion-picture career spanning six decades, played more than 60 roles, including the protagonist, a clumsy Italian soldier, in *Private Angelo* (1949), a lonely and pompous Prince of Wales in *Beau Brummel* (1954), a waggish Kaptah in *The Egyptian* (1954), the sly escaped convict Jules in *We're No Angels* (1955), the circus master in Lola Montès (1955), the comic idler in the midst of hardworking Australian sheepdrovers in *The Sundowners* (1960), the swindler Marcus Pendleton a k a Caesar Smith in *Hot Millions* (1968), the eccentric Mexican general retaking the Alamo in *Viva Max!* (1969), the bogus physician in *Treasure of Matecumbe* (1976), the sympathetic physician in *Lorenzo's Oil* (1992), and Prince Frederick in *Luther* (2003); starred as Agatha Christie's detective Hercule Poirot in three feature films, *Death on the Nile* (1978), *Evil Under the Sun* (1982), and *Appointment with Death* (1988); also played Poirot in three television specials in the mid-1980s; in total, accrued more than a score of television acting credits, including the voice of the pig Old Major in the animated TV adaptation of *Animal Farm* (1999); received Emmy Awards for his performances (all on NBC) as Dr. Johnson in *Life of Samuel Johnson* in 1957, Socrates in *Barefoot in Athens* during the 1966–67 season, and the country shopkeeper in *A Storm in Summer* during the 1969–70 season; received a Grammy Award for his narration of the concert recording of Prokofiev's *Peter and the Wolf*; also recorded *Peter Ustinov Reads the Orchestra* (1990), among other albums; played the devil for a recording of Igor Stravinsky's *Histoire du Soldat* (1962); lent his voice to such videos as *The Story of Barbar the Little Elephant* (1986) and *Monet: Legacy of Light* (1989) and appeared in such videos as *An Evening with Sir Peter Ustinov* (1996); published the novels *The Loser* (1960), *Krumnagel* (1971), and *Monsieur Rene* (1999) and the collection *Life Is an Operetta and Other Short Stories* (1997), in addition to other short fiction; also wrote the autobiography *Dear Me* (1977) and two additional nonfiction books,

My Russia (1983) and *Peter Ustinov in Russia* (1988); served a term as president of the World Federalist Association (now Citizens for Global Solutions); traveled the world as a goodwill ambassador for UNICEF from 1968 until his death; founded the Ustinov Foundation, an international charity; was awarded the CBE in 1975 and knighted in 1990; died in a clinic near his home in Bursins, Switzerland. See *Current Biography* 1955. — K.D.

Obituary *New York Times* C p14 Mar. 30, 2004

VISCARDI, HENRY JR. May 10, 1912–Apr. 13, 2004 A pioneering advocate for the rights of the handicapped; rehabilitation specialist; business executive; founder of the National Center for Disability Services, a state-supported, tuition-free campus (including a school for children grades kindergarten–12 and job-training and employment services for adults, a combined total of some 4,000 enrollees a year) in Albertson, New York; adhered to the motto, "There are really no disabled people, only people with varying degrees of ability"; was born severely deformed, with legs that were short, twisted stumps; spent most of the first six years of his life confined in New York City hospitals; at the Hospital for Deformities and Joint Diseases, underwent a series of operations that straightened his stumps and made it possible for them to be fitted with orthopedic boots; in succession, dropped out of Fordham University in the Bronx, New York City, and St. John's University School of Law in Queens; beginning in 1933, worked as a clerk in a New York City law firm; subsequently, headed the tax division of the Home Owners' Loan Corp.; in 1938, was introduced by his orthopedic physician, Robert Yanover, to the ingenious Manhattan limb-maker George Dorsch, who fitted him with a pair of prosthetic legs and helped him to acquire the delicate balance needed to use them; with his artificial limbs, stood five feet eight inches, two feet taller than before; during World War II, was a Red Cross field-service officer working with armless and legless war veterans at Fort Dix, New Jersey, and Walter Reed Hospital in Washington, D.C.; in addition, advised military and government agencies on the employment of the disabled and traveled to war plants and civic groups promoting such employment; after the war, was, successively, assistant director of special events and sports with the Mutual Broadcasting System and director of personnel with the Burlington Mills Corp.; married in the late 1940s and became the father of four daughters; in 1949, relinquished the security of his well-paying position with Burlington Mills to agree to the request that he become the first executive director of JOB (an acronym for Just One Break Inc.), formed that year in New York City by Orin Lehman, a World War II amputee, in collaboration with the physician Howard A. Rusk, the businessman and philanthropist Bernard Baruch, and the former first lady Eleanor Roosevelt, for the twin purposes of finding employment for amputees and victims of crippling diseases and of changing prejudices among industrial, business, and labor leaders about hiring the disabled; continued to serve JOB as executive vice president and chairman of the board after founding (with the encouragement of Eleanor Roosevelt and with his own and borrowed money) in a vacant garage in West Hempstead, Long Island, in 1952 Abilities Inc., a small electronics manufacturing plant run by and training and employing physically handicapped men and women, a total of about 50; in the early 1960s, at least partly in response to President John F. Kennedy's concern for the mentally retarded, began training and employing such persons as well; eventually obtained state funding; to accommodate a burgeoning workforce of several hundred and the company's diversification and increasing output, moved his enterprise to Albertson, Long Island; expanded it to include vocational training and job-placement services for adults, a foundation for the study of physiological and psychological problems experienced by employed handicapped persons, and the Henry Viscardi School; named the complex the National Center for Disability Services in 1991; spoke widely to promote efforts to make the "unemployable" employable; wrote several books, including his autobiography, *A Man's Stature* (1952), *Give Us the Tools* (1959), about the establishment and early achievements of Abilities Inc., and *A Laughter in the Lonely Night* (1961), containing the life stories of 15 Abilities Inc. workers; died in Roslyn, New York. See *Current Biography* (December) 1966.

Obituary *New York Times* B p8 Apr. 16, 2004

WASHINGTON, WALTER E. Apr. 15, 1915–Oct. 27, 2003 The first elected mayor of Washington, D.C., in 104 years; was the great-grandson of slaves; at Howard University, received a B.A. degree in public administration and sociology in 1938 and a law degree in 1948; after two decades of varied yeoman service in the National Capital Housing Authority, became director of the authority in 1961; as director, oversaw an increase in low-income housing units in the District of Columbia from 6,000 to 9,000; for the better part of a year, beginning in November 1966, was chairman of the New York City Housing Authority; in September 1967, in a move toward self-government for the District of Columbia, was named by President Lyndon B. Johnson to head the district, which was by then 70 percent black; two months later, assumed the office of commissioner of the district, thus becoming the first black chief executive of a major American city; regularly making the rounds of the city on foot, became known as "the walking mayor"; following the assassination of the Reverend Martin Luther King Jr. in April 1968, when angry young black people began torching inner-city buildings in Washington as in a number of other cities, walked by himself through the streets, urging them, as he recalled, "to go home and help the recovery of people who had been burned out"; was credited with diffusing racial tensions and warding off worse rioting; "was extremely proud of the fact that while there was loss of property, there was no loss of life," as Barbara Franco, the president and CEO of the City Museum of Washington, D.C., has recalled; was reappointed commissioner twice by President Richard M. Nixon; after Congress approved home rule for the district, was elected mayor in 1974; made the transition from appointed commissioner to elected mayor when he was inaugurated, on January 2, 1975; with his moderate style, helped ease the city's passage from full federal control to limited autonomy; opened the formerly all-white district government leadership to African-Americans; moved thousands of the district's poor out of slum buildings and alley dwellings and into public housing; in his low-keyed way, began the enlargement of the black middle class that his successor, Marion Barry, would pursue with his bold opening of business opportunities for blacks through set-asides in city contracts; left office with a surplus of $40 million in the district treasury; lost to Marion Barry in the mayoral election of 1978; remained active in municipal life after leaving office; campaigned for full voting rights for the citizens of the District of Columbia (who at present do not have voting representation in Congress); in his final years, concentrated his energy on the founding of the City Museum of Washington, D.C., which opened in the summer of 2003; died at Howard University Hospital in Washington. See *Current Biography* (July) 1968.

Obituary *New York Times* C p15 Oct. 28, 2003

YASSIN, AHMED 1938(?)–Mar. 22, 2004 Muslim Arab sheik; founder and spiritual leader of Hamas, the militant Palestinian faction responsible for the deaths of an estimated 377 Israeli men , women, and children in at least 425 suicide bombings and other terrorist attacks since September 2000, when the current, second intifada (the Arabic word for "uprising") against Israel began; was born in Askalan in what is now southern Israel; following the Israeli war of independence in 1948, fled with his mother and his siblings to the then–Egyptian-controlled Gaza Strip, where they settled in the squalid Shati refugee camp, near the Mediterranean Sea; diving into the sea from a high rock one day in 1953, hit shallow water and suffered severe damage to his spinal column, resulting in the permanent paralysis of his arms and legs; thenceforth, was confined to a wheelchair; concentrated on the study of language and religion; became a teacher and cleric; fathered a dozen children; after the 1967 Six-Day War, in which Israel won control of the Gaza Strip, the West Bank, and, temporarily, the Golan Heights, devoted himself to strengthening the Muslim Brotherhood in Gaza; in 1973, established the Islamic Center for the purpose of coordinating the social-welfare programs sponsored by brotherhood-affiliated organizations; did not become involved in political and military action against Israel until the early 1980s, when the Muslim Brotherhood was being accused by some militant Palestinians of cooperating with the "Zionist entity" and was losing members to the Fatah, the powerful guerrilla faction of Yasir Arafat's Palestine Liberation Organization; was imprisoned by Israeli authorities on charges of sedition (1984–85); in 1987, when the first intifada erupted in Gaza and the West Bank, founded the Islamic Resistance Movement, which became known by its acronym, Hamas, which means "zeal"; co-drafted the Hamas covenant (1988), which declared, "Israel will exist and continue to exist until Islam will obliterate it, just as it obliterated others before it. . . . There is no solution for the Palestinian problem except Jihad. . . . Israel, Judaism, and Jews challenge Islam and the Muslim people"; was again imprisoned, this time with a life sentence, by the Israelis in 1989, after being found guilty of ordering the kidnapping and killings of two Israelis; was released in 1997 in exchange for two Israelis imprisoned in Jordan; was twice targeted for assassination by the Israelis; in the second attempt, was killed by a missile fired from an Israeli helicopter gunship as he was being wheeled from dawn prayers at a mosque in Gaza City. See *Current Biography* (July) 1998.

Obituary *New York Times* p1+ Mar. 23, 2004

CLASSIFICATION BY PROFESSION—2004

ANTHROPOLOGY
Koff, Clea
Newsom, Lee Ann

ARCHITECTURE
Holl, Steven

ART
Bontecou, Lee
Klein, William
Mortensen, Viggo

BUSINESS
Ashwell, Rachel
Blades, Joan and Boyd, Wes
Bravo, Rose Marie
Breen, Edward D.
Chafee, Lincoln
Dimon, James
Finch, Jennie
Gates, Melinda
Hagel, Chuck
Immelt, Jeffrey R.
Keegan, Robert
Keller, Thomas
Lewis, Kenneth
Nelson, Marilyn Carlson
Potter, Myrtle S.
Saab, Elie
Sanger, Stephen
Schwarzenegger, Arnold
Scott, Tony
Steele, Michael S.
Steward, David L.
Thain, John A.
Waters, Alice
Williams, Armstrong
Witherspoon, Reese
Wright, Will

CONSERVATION
Gruber, Samuel H.

DANCE
Mitha, Tehreema
Ramirez, Tina
Reinking, Ann
Stiefel, Ethan

Wheeldon, Christopher

ECONOMICS
Reinhardt, Uwe E.

EDUCATION
Beers, Rand
Blanco, Kathleen
Brown, Dan
Cox, Lynne
Davidson, Richard J.
Duesberg, Peter H.
Everett, Percival
Farmer, Paul
Finch, Caleb E.
Foner, Eric
Gerberding, Julie Louise
Gruber, Samuel H.
Guillermoprieto, Alma
Harris, Eva
Jagger, Janine
Judson, Olivia
Katz, Jackson
Kilbourne, Jean
Kilpatrick, Kwame M.
Kripke, Saul
Molina, Alfred
Murphy, Mark
Newsom, Lee Ann
Ramirez, Tina
Reinhardt, Uwe E.
Reinking, Ann
Rus, Daniela
Sapolsky, Robert
Thompson, Lonnie
Troutt Powell, Eve
Tull, Tanya
Willis, Deborah

FASHION
Ashwell, Rachel
Bravo, Rose Marie
Hounsou, Djimon
Klein, William
Long, William Ivey
Saab, Elie

FILM
Baitz, Jon Robin
Cedric the Entertainer
Chappelle, Dave
Cooper, Chris
D'Onofrio, Vincent
Fangmeier, Stefen
Firth, Colin
Goldsman, Akiva
Hounsou, Djimon
Katz, Jackson
Keller, Marthe
Kilbourne, Jean
Klein, William
LaFontaine, Don
Long, William Ivey
Ludacris
Madsen, Michael
Malina, Joshua
Martin, George R. R.
McCracken, Craig
Molina, Alfred
Mortensen, Viggo
Murray, Bill
Pekar, Harvey
Reilly, John C.
Reinking, Ann
Ross, Gary
Russell, Kurt
Schwarzenegger, Arnold
Scott, Tony
Stanton, Andrew
Stewart, Jon
Stiefel, Ethan
Theron, Charlize
Tritt, Travis
Witherspoon, Reese
Zellweger, Renée

FINANCE
Lewis, Kenneth
Thain, John A.

GOVERNMENT AND
POLITICS, U.S.
Applebaum, Anne
Beers, Rand
Blanco, Kathleen

Chafee, Lincoln
Coleman, Norman
Cummings, Elijah E.
Edwards, John
Frum, David
Gerberding, Julie Louise
Hagel, Chuck
Hoyer, Steny
Kerry, John
Kilpatrick, Kwame M.
Lee, Barbara
Levin, Carl
Napolitano, Janet
Ross, Gary
Schakowsky, Jan
Schwarzenegger, Arnold
Sebelius, Kathleen
Steele, Michael S.
Williams, Armstrong

JOURNALISM
Applebaum, Anne
Brooks, David
Curry, Ann
Dickerson, Debra
Dickinson, Amy
Frum, David
Garrels, Anne
Guillermoprieto, Alma
Hondros, Chris
Lipinski, Ann Marie
Moss, Adam
Okrent, Daniel
Pitts, Leonard Jr.
Powell, Kevin
Ramos, Jorge
Romenesko, Jim
Troutt Powell, Eve
Williams, Armstrong
Zukerman, Eugenia

LAW
Cummings, Elijah E.
Edwards, John
Farmer-Paellmann, Deadria
Guinier, Lani
Hoyer, Steny
Jones, Elaine
Kennedy, Robert F. Jr.
Kerry, John
Levin, Carl
Ludwig, Ken
Martinez, Vilma
Napolitano, Janet

Steele, Michael S.

LITERATURE
Baitz, Jon Robin
Brown, Dan
Burroughs, Augusten
Everett, Percival
Jones, Edward P.
Martin, George R. R.
Mortensen, Viggo
Navratilova, Martina
Pekar, Harvey
Stewart, Jon
Zukerman, Eugenia

MEDICINE
Farmer, Paul
Finch, Caleb E.
Gerberding, Julie Louise
Groopman, Jerome
Heymann, David L.
Jagger, Janine

MUSIC
Aerosmith
Blythe, Stephanie
Brooks and Dunn
Brown, Dan
Brown, Junior
Chapman, Steven Curtis
Chesney, Kenny
Chieftains
Coldplay
Coleman, Steve
Douglas, Jerry
Harper, Ben
Hill, Andrew
Hunt Lieberson, Lorraine
Jackson, Alan
Keith, Toby
Keller, Marthe
Ludacris
Massive Attack
McBride, Martina
McLaughlin, John
Murphy, Mark
Neptunes
OutKast
Patty, Sandi
Tritt, Travis
Wylde, Zakk
Zukerman, Eugenia

NONFICTION
Akers, Michelle
Applebaum, Anne
Ashwell, Rachel
Blades, Joan and Boyd, Wes
Brooks, David
Burroughs, Augusten
Cox, Lynne
Davidson, Richard J.
Dickerson, Debra
Duesberg, Peter H.
Edwards, John
Farmer, Paul
Finch, Caleb E.
Foner, Eric
Frum, David
Groopman, Jerome
Guinier, Lani
James, Bill
Judson, Olivia
Keller, Thomas
Kennedy, Robert F. Jr.
Kilbourne, Jean
Koff, Clea
Kripke, Saul
Mohammed, W. Deen
Newsom, Lee Ann
Pitts, Leonard Jr.
Powell, Kevin
Ramos, Jorge
Reinhardt, Uwe E.
Romenesko, Jim
Rus, Daniela
Sapolsky, Robert
Schwarzenegger, Arnold
Troutt Powell, Eve
Waters, Alice
Williams, Armstrong
Willis, Deborah
Wilson, Marie C.
Zukerman, Eugenia

ORGANIZATIONS
Blades, Joan and Boyd, Wes
Chafee, Lincoln
Chapman, Steven Curtis
Farmer, Paul
Frum, David
Gruber, Samuel H.
Heymann, David L.
Jones, Elaine
Katz, Jackson
Kennedy, Robert F. Jr.
Lewis, Marvin

Mohammed, W. Deen
Sanger, Stephen
Tridish, Pete
Tull, Tanya
Williams, Armstrong
Wilson, Marie C.

PALEONTOLOGY
Newsom, Lee Ann

PHILANTHROPY
Gates, Melinda
Nelson, Marilyn Carlson

PHILOSOPHY
Kripke, Saul

PHOTOGRAPHY
Hondros, Chris
Klein, William
Simpson, Lorna
Willis, Deborah

PUBLISHING
Moss, Adam
Rubenstein, Atoosa

RADIO
Dickinson, Amy
Pekar, Harvey
Tridish, Pete
Williams, Armstrong

RELIGION
Mohammed, W. Deen
O'Malley, Sean Patrick

SCIENCE
Davidson, Richard J.
Duesberg, Peter H.
Finch, Caleb E.
Gruber, Samuel H.
Harris, Eva
Heymann, David L.
Jagger, Janine
Jin, Deborah
Judson, Olivia
Koff, Clea
Newsom, Lee Ann
Rus, Daniela
Sapolsky, Robert
Spiropulu, Maria
Thompson, Lonnie

SOCIAL ACTIVISM
Blades, Joan and Boyd, Wes
Farmer-Paellmann, Deadria
Farmer, Paul
Gates, Melinda
Harris, Eva
Heymann, David L.
Jones, Elaine
Katz, Jackson
Kennedy, Robert F. Jr.
Kilbourne, Jean
Martinez, Vilma
Mohammed, W. Deen
Navratilova, Martina
O'Malley, Sean Patrick
Schakowsky, Jan
Tridish, Pete
Tull, Tanya
Wilson, Marie C.

SOCIAL SCIENCES
Lee, Barbara
Tull, Tanya

SPORTS
Akers, Michelle
Brady, Tom
Cheeks, Maurice
Cox, Lynne
Croom, Sylvester Jr.
Epstein, Theo
Fawcett, Joy
Finch, Jennie
Gagne, Eric
Gardner, Rulon
Hamm, Paul and Morgan
James, Bill
Keith, Toby
Lewis, Marvin
Lilly, Kristine
Mayweather, Floyd
McKeon, Jack
McNabb, Donovan
Navratilova, Martina
O'Neal, Jermaine
Phelps, Michael
Pujols, Albert
Rampone, Christie
Roddick, Andy
Rose, Jalen
Schwarzenegger, Arnold
Vinatieri, Adam
Wallace, Ben
Wells, David

Woodson, Rod
Wright, Winky
Yagudin, Alexei
Zito, Barry

TECHNOLOGY
Fangmeier, Stefen
Gates, Melinda
Rus, Daniela
Steward, David L.
Wright, Will

TELEVISION
Ashwell, Rachel
Baitz, Jon Robin
Cedric the Entertainer
Chappelle, Dave
Cooper, Chris
Curry, Ann
D'Onofrio, Vincent
Dickinson, Amy
Firth, Colin
Keller, Marthe
Long, William Ivey
Madsen, Michael
Malina, Joshua
Martin, George R. R.
McCracken, Craig
Molina, Alfred
Mortensen, Viggo
Murray, Bill
Navratilova, Martina
Powell, Kevin
Ramos, Jorge
Reinking, Ann
Stewart, Jon
Tritt, Travis
Williams, Armstrong
Witherspoon, Reese
Zellweger, Renée
Zukerman, Eugenia

THEATER
Baitz, Jon Robin
Cooper, Chris
D'Onofrio, Vincent
Falls, Robert
Firth, Colin
Keller, Marthe
Long, William Ivey
Ludwig, Ken
Madsen, Michael
Malina, Joshua
Molina, Alfred

Mortensen, Viggo
Nottage, Lynn
Ramirez, Tina
Reilly, John C.
Reinking, Ann

2001–2004 Index

This is the index to the January 2001–November 2004 issues. It also lists obituaries that appear only in this yearbook. For the index to the 1940–2000 biographies, see Current Biography: Cumulated Index 1940–2000.

Bloomberg, Michael R. Mar 2002
Blount, Winton Malcolm obit Jan 2003
Blur Nov 2003
Blythe, Stephanie Aug 2004
Bocelli, Andrea Jan 2002
Boland, Edward P. obit Feb 2002
Bond, Julian Jul 2001
Bontecou, Lee Mar 2004
Boorstin, Daniel J. obit Yrbk 2004
Borge, Victor obit Mar 2001
Borodina, Olga Feb 2002
Borst, Lyle B. obit Yrbk 2002
Bosch, Juan obit Feb 2002
Boudreau, Lou obit Oct 2001
Bourdon, Rob see Linkin Park
Bowden, Mark Jan 2002
Boyd, John W. Feb 2001
Boyd, Wes see Blades, Joan and Boyd, Wes
Bracken, Eddie obit Feb 2003
Brady, Tom Aug 2004
Bragg, Rick Apr 2002
Brando, Marlon obit Yrbk 2004
Bravo, Rose Marie Jun 2004
Breathitt, Edward T. obit Sep 2004
Breen, Edward D. Jul 2004
Brenly, Bob Apr 2002
Brier, Bob Sep 2002
Brier, Robert see Brier, Bob
Brin, Sergey and Page, Larry Oct 2001
Brinkley, David obit Sep 2003
Brodeur, Martin Nov 2002
Brody, Adrien Jul 2003
Broeg, Bob May 2002
Brokaw, Tom Nov 2002
Bronson, Charles obit Mar 2004
Brooks and Dunn Sep 2004
Brooks, David Apr 2004
Brooks, Gwendolyn obit Feb 2001
Brooks, Kix see Brooks and Dunn
Brooks, Vincent Jun 2003
Brower, David obit Feb 2001
Brown, Aaron Mar 2003
Brown, Charles L. obit Sep 2004
Brown, Claude obit Apr 2002
Brown, Dan May 2004
Brown, Dee obit Mar 2003
Brown, J. Carter obit Yrbk 2002
Brown, Jesse obit Yrbk 2002
Brown, Junior Nov 2004
Brown, Kwame Feb 2002

Brown, Lee P. Sep 2002
Brown, Robert McAfee obit Nov 2001
Brown, Ronald K. May 2002
Browning, John obit Jun 2003
Brueggemann, Ingar Nov 2001
Brumel, Valery obit Jun 2003
Bryant, C. Farris obit Yrbk 2002
Bryson, David see Counting Crows
Buchholz, Horst obit Aug 2003
Buckland, Jon see Coldplay
Buckley, Priscilla L. Apr 2002
Budge, Hamer H. obit Yrbk 2003
Bundy, William P. obit Feb 2001
Bunim, Mary-Ellis see Bunim, Mary-Ellis, and Murray, Jonathan
Bunim, Mary-Ellis obit Yrbk 2004
Bunim, Mary-Ellis, and Murray, Jonathan May 2002
Burford, Anne Gorsuch see Gorsuch, Anne
Burgess, Carter L. obit Yrbk 2002
Burnett, Mark May 2001
Burroughs, Augusten Apr 2004
Burrows, Stephen Nov 2003
Burtt, Ben May 2003
Bush, George W. Aug 2001
Bush, Laura Jun 2001
Bushnell, Candace Nov 2003
Butler, R. Paul see Marcy, Geoffrey W., and Butler, R. Paul

Caballero, Linda see La India
Cactus Jack see Foley, Mick
Calderón, Sila M. Nov 2001
Calle, Sophie May 2001
Camp, John see Sandford, John
Campbell, Viv see Def Leppard
Canin, Ethan Aug 2001
Cannon, Howard W. obit Yrbk 2002
Canty, Brendan see Fugazi
Capriati, Jennifer Nov 2001
Caras, Roger A. obit Jul 2001
Card, Andrew H. Jr. Nov 2003
Carlson, Margaret Nov 2003
Carmona, Richard Jan 2003
Carney, Art obit Yrbk 2004
Carroll-Abbing, J. Patrick obit Nov 2001

Carroll, Vinnette obit Feb 2003
Carter, Benny obit Oct 2003
Carter, Jimmy see Blind Boys of Alabama
Carter, Regina Oct 2003
Carter, Shawn see Jay-Z
Carter, Vince Apr 2002
Cartier-Bresson, Henri obit Yrbk 2004
Cash, Johnny obit Jan 2004
Castle, Barbara obit Yrbk 2002
Castro, Fidel Jun 2001
Cattrall, Kim Jan 2003
Cavanagh, Tom Jun 2003
Cavanna, Betty obit Oct 2001
Cedric the Entertainer Feb 2004
Cela, Camilo José obit Apr 2002
Chaban-Delmas, Jacques obit Feb 2001
Chafee, Lincoln Jan 2004
Chaikin, Joseph obit Yrbk 2003
Champion, Will see Coldplay
Chandrasekhar, Sripati obit Sep 2001
Chao, Elaine L. May 2001
Chapman, Steven Curtis Oct 2004
Chappelle, Dave Jun 2004
Charles, Ray obit Yrbk 2004
Chase, David Mar 2001
Chauncey, Henry obit Mar 2003
Cheeks, Maurice Feb 2004
Cheney, Richard B. Jan 2002
Chesney, Kenny May 2004
Chiang Kai-shek, Mme. see Chiang Mei-Ling
Chiang Mei-Ling obit Mar 2004
Chieftains Mar 2004
Child, Julia obit Nov 2004
Chillida, Eduardo obit Yrbk 2002
Churchland, Patricia S. May 2003
Claremont, Chris Sep 2003
Clemens, Roger Aug 2003
Clinton, Hillary Rodham Jan 2002
Clooney, Rosemary obit Nov 2002
Clowes, Daniel Jan 2002
Clyburn, James E. Oct 2001
Coburn, James obit Feb 2003
Coca, Imogene obit Sep 2001
Cochran, Thad Apr 2002
Cohen, Rob Nov 2002
Cohn, Linda Aug 2002

Colbert, Edwin H. obit Feb 2002
Coldplay May 2004
Coleman, Norman Sep 2004
Coleman, Steve Jul 2004
Collen, Phil see Def Leppard
Collier, Sophia Jul 2002
Collins, Jim Aug 2003
Collins, Patricia Hill Mar 2003
Columbus, Chris Nov 2001
Como, Perry obit Jul 2001
Conable, Barber B. obit Sep 2004
Conneff, Kevin see Chieftains
Connelly, Jennifer Jun 2002
Conner, Nadine obit Aug 2003
Connor, John T. obit Feb 2001
Conway, John Horton Sep 2003
Cook, Richard W. Jul 2003
Cooke, Alistair obit Oct 2004
Coontz, Stephanie Jul 2003
Cooper, Chris Jul 2004
Coppola, Sofia Nov 2003
Corelli, Franco obit Mar 2004
Coulter, Ann Sep 2003
Counsell, Craig Sep 2002
Counting Crows Mar 2003
Cox, Archibald obit Yrbk 2004
Cox, Lynne Sep 2004
Coyne, Wayne see Flaming Lips
Crain, Jeanne obit Sep 2004
Cranston, Alan obit Mar 2001
Creed May 2002
Crick, Francis obit Yrbk 2004
Crittenden, Danielle Jul 2003
Cronyn, Hume obit Yrbk 2003
Croom, Sylvester Jr. Aug 2004
Crosby, John obit Yrbk 2003
Cruz, Celia obit Nov 2003
Cruz, Penelope Jul 2001
Cuban, Mark Mar 2001
Cummings, Elijah E. Feb 2004
Currie, Nancy June 2002
Curry, Ann Jun 2004

Dacre of Glanton, Baron see Trevor-Roper, H. R.
Daddy G see Massive Attack
Daft, Douglas N. May 2001
D'Angelo May 2001
Darling, Sharon May 2003
Davidson, Richard J. Aug 2004
Davis, Benjamin O. Jr. obit Yrbk 2002
Davis, Wade Jan 2003
de Hartog, Jan obit Jan 2003
De Jong, Dola obit Sep 2004

de la Rúa, Fernando Apr 2001
de Meuron, Pierre see Herzog, Jacques, and de Meuron, Pierre
De Sapio, Carmine obit Yrbk 2004
De Valois, Ninette obit Aug 2001
de Varona, Donna Aug 2003
Deakins, Roger May 2001
Dean, Howard Oct 2002
DeBusschere, Dave obit Yrbk 2003
DeCarlo, Dan Aug 2001 obit Mar 2002
Def Leppard Jan 2003
del Naja, Robert see Massive Attack
Del Toro, Benicio Sep 2001
Dellinger, David obit Yrbk 2004
DeLonge, Tom see blink-182
Delson, Brad see Linkin Park
DeMarcus, Jay see Rascal Flatts
DeMille, Nelson Oct 2002
Densen-Gerber, Judianne obit Jul 2003
Destiny's Child Aug 2001
Dickerson, Debra Apr 2004
Dickinson, Amy Apr 2004
Dillon, C. Douglas obit May 2003
Dimon, James Jun 2004
Djerassi, Carl Oct 2001
Djukanovic, Milo Aug 2001
DMX Aug 2003
Donaldson, William Jun 2003
D'Onofrio, Vincent May 2004
Donovan, Carrie obit Feb 2002
Doubilet, David Mar 2003
Douglas, Ashanti see Ashanti
Douglas, Jerry Aug 2004
Douglas, John E. Jul 2001
Drozd, Steven see Flaming Lips
Drucker, Eugene see Emerson String Quartet
Dude Love see Foley, Mick
Duesberg, Peter H. Jun 2004
Dugan, Alan obit Oct 2004
Dunlop, John T. obit Sep 2004
Dunn, Ronnie see Brooks and Dunn
Dunne, John Gregory obit Yrbk 2004
Dunst, Kirsten Oct 2001
Duritz, Adam see Counting Crows
Dutton, Lawrence see Emerson String Quartet

Eban, Abba obit Mar 2003
Ebsen, Buddy obit Yrbk 2003
Eckert, Robert A. Mar 2003
Eddins, William Feb 2002
Edwards, Bob Sep 2001
Edwards, John Oct 2004
Egan, Edward M. Jul 2001
Egan, Jennifer Mar 2002
Eggleston, William Feb 2002
Eiko see Eiko and Koma
Eiko and Koma May 2003
Elizabeth, Queen Mother of Great Britain obit Jun 2002
Elliott, Joe see Def Leppard
Elliott, Sean Apr 2001
Emerson String Quartet Jul 2002
Eminem Jan 2001
Engibous, Thomas J. Oct 2003
Ensler, Eve Aug 2002
Epstein, Samuel S. Aug 2001
Epstein, Theo May 2004
Ericsson-Jackson, Aprille J. Mar 2001
Estenssoro, Victor Paz see Paz Estenssoro, Victor
Etherington, Edwin D. obit Apr 2001
Eugenides, Jeffrey Oct 2003
Eustis, Oskar Oct 2002
Eustis, Paul Jefferson see Eustis, Oskar
Evanovich, Janet Apr 2001
Evans, Dale obit Apr 2001
Evans, Donald L. Nov 2001
Eve Jul 2003
Everett, Percival Sep 2004
Eyadéma, Etienne Gnassingbé Apr 2002
Eyre, Chris May 2003
Eytan, Walter obit Oct 2001

Faber, Sandra Apr 2002
Fallon, Jimmy Jul 2002
Falls, Robert Jan 2004
Fangmeier, Stefen Aug 2004
Farhi, Nicole Nov 2001
Farmer-Paellmann, Deadria Mar 2004
Farmer, Paul Feb 2004
Farrell, Dave see Linkin Park
Farrell, Eileen obit Jun 2002
Farrelly, Bobby see Farrelly, Peter and Bobby
Farrelly, Peter and Bobby Sep 2001
Fast, Howard obit Jul 2003
Fattah, Chaka Sep 2003
Faulk, Marshall Jan 2003
Fawcett, Joy May 2004
Fay, J. Michael Sep 2001
Fay, Martin see Chieftains
Ferré, Luis A. obit Mar 2004

Ferrell, Will Feb 2003
Ferrer, Rafael Jul 2001
Ferris, Timothy Jan 2001
Fey, Tina Apr 2002
Fiedler, Leslie A. obit Yrbk 2003
Finch, Caleb E. Sep 2004
Finch, Jennie Oct 2004
Finckel, David *see* Emerson String Quartet
Firth, Colin Mar 2004
Fishman, Jon *see* Phish
Flaming Lips Oct 2002
Flanagan, Tommy obit Mar 2002
Foer, Jonathan Safran Sep 2002
Foley, Mick Sep 2001
Foner, Eric Aug 2004
Fong, Hiram L. obit Yrbk 2004
Fong-Torres, Ben Aug 2001
Forrest, Vernon Jul 2002
Forsythe, William Feb 2003
Foss, Joseph Jacob obit Yrbk 2003
Fountain, Clarence *see* Blind Boys of Alabama
Fox Quesada, Vicente May 2001
Francis, Arlene obit Sep 2001
Francisco, Don Feb 2001
Frankenheimer, John obit Oct 2002
Franklin, Shirley C. Aug 2002
Franks, Tommy R. Jan 2002
Franzen, Jonathan Sep 2003
Fraser, Brendan Feb 2001
Fredericks, Henry St. Clair *see* Mahal, Taj
Freeman, Orville L. obit Yrbk 2003
Freston, Tom Aug 2003
Friedman, Jane Mar 2001
Frist, Bill Nov 2002
Frum, David Jun 2004
Fugazi Mar 2002
Fukuyama, Francis Jun 2001

Gades, Antonio obit Yrbk 2004
Gagne, Eric Jun 2004
Galinsky, Ellen Oct 2003
Galloway, Joseph L. Sep 2003
Galtieri, Leopoldo obit Yrbk 2003
Gandy, Kim Oct 2001
Garcia, Sergio Mar 2001
Gardner, John W. obit May 2002
Gardner, Rulon Nov 2004
Garfield, Henry *see* Rollins, Henry

Garrels, Anne Mar 2004
Garrison, Deborah Jan 2001
Gary, Willie E. Apr 2001
Garza, Ed Jun 2002
Garzón, Baltasar Mar 2001
Gaskin, Ina May May 2001
Gates, Melinda Feb 2004
Gaubatz, Lynn Feb 2001
Gayle, Helene Jan 2002
Gebel-Williams, Gunther obit Oct 2001
Geis, Bernard obit Mar 2001
Gelb, Leslie H. Jan 2003
Gennaro, Peter obit Feb 2001
Gerberding, Julie Louise Sep 2004
Gerson, Michael Feb 2002
Giannulli, Mossimo Feb 2003
Gibson, Althea obit Feb 2004
Gibson, Charles Sep 2002
Gibson, Mel Aug 2003
Gierek, Edward obit Oct 2001
Gilbreth, Frank B. Jr. obit Jul 2001
Gillingham, Charles *see* Counting Crows
Gillis, John *see* White Stripes
Gilmore, James S. III Jun 2001
Ginzberg, Eli obit Yrbk 2003
Giroud, Françoise obit Jul 2003
Goff, M. Lee Jun 2001
Gold, Thomas obit Yrbk 2004
Goldberg, Bill Apr 2001
Golden, Thelma Sep 2001
Goldman-Rakic, Patricia Feb 2003
Goldovsky, Boris obit Aug 2001
Goldsman, Akiva Sep 2004
Goldsmith, Jerry May 2001 obit Nov 2004
Goldstine, Herman Heine obit Yrbk 2004
Golub, Leon obit Yrbk 2004
Gonzales, Alberto R. Apr 2002
Gonzalez, Henry obit Feb 2001
Good, Mary L. Sep 2001
Good, Robert A. obit Yrbk 2003
Googoosh May 2001
Gordon, Cyrus H. obit Aug 2001
Gordon, Edmund W. Jun 2003
Gordon, Mike *see* Phish
Gorman, R. C. Jan 2001
Gorsuch, Anne obit Yrbk 2004
Gorton, John Grey obit Yrbk 2002

Gottlieb, Melvin B. obit Mar 2001
Gould, Stephen Jay obit Aug 2002
Gourdji, Françoise *see* Giroud, Françoise
Gowers, Timothy Jan 2001
Gowers, William Timothy *see* Gowers, Timothy
Graham, Franklin May 2002
Graham, Katharine obit Oct 2001
Graham, Winston obit Yrbk 2003
Granholm, Jennifer M. Oct 2003
Grasso, Richard Oct 2002
Graves, Morris obit Sep 2001
Gray, Spalding obit Yrbk 2004
Greco, José obit Mar 2001
Green, Adolph obit Mar 2003
Green, Darrell Jan 2001
Green, Tom Oct 2003
Greenberg, Jack M. Nov 2001
Greene, Wallace M. obit Aug 2003
Greenstein, Jesse L. obit Yrbk 2003
Greenwood, Colin *see* Radiohead
Greenwood, Jonny *see* Radiohead
Gregory, Wilton D. Mar 2002
Griffiths, Martha W. obit Yrbk 2003
Grigg, John obit Apr 2002
Grohl, Dave May 2002
Groopman, Jerome Oct 2004
Gruber, Ruth Jun 2001
Gruber, Samuel H. Aug 2004
Grubin, David Aug 2002
Gudmundsdottir, Björk *see* Björk
Guerard, Albert J. obit Mar 2001
Guillermoprieto, Alma Sep 2004
Guinier, Lani Jan 2004
Gunn, Thom obit Yrbk 2004
Gursky, Andreas Jul 2001

Haas, Jonathan Jun 2003
Hacker *see* Hackett, Buddy
Hackett, Buddy obit Oct 2003
Hagel, Chuck Aug 2004
Hagen, Uta obit Yrbk 2004
Hahn, Hilary Sep 2002
Hahn, Joseph *see* Linkin Park
Hailsham of St. Marylebone, Quintin Hogg obit Feb 2002
Hair, Jay D. obit Jan 2003

Halaby, Najeeb E. obit Yrbk 2003
Halasz, Laszlo obit Feb 2002
Hall, Conrad L. obit May 2003
Hall, Deidre Nov 2002
Hall, Gus obit Jan 2001
Hall, Richard Melville *see* Moby
Hall, Steffie *see* Evanovich, Janet
Hamilton, Tom *see* Aerosmith
Hamm, Morgan *see* Hamm, Paul and Morgan
Hamm, Paul *see* Hamm, Paul and Morgan
Hamm, Paul and Morgan Nov 2004
Hammon, Becky Jan 2003
Hampton, Lionel obit Yrbk 2002
Hanna, William obit Sep 2001
Hansen, Liane May 2003
Harden, Marcia Gay Sep 2001
Hardin, Garrett obit Apr 2004
Hargrove, Marion obit Yrbk 2004
Harjo, Joy Aug 2001
Harper, Ben Jan 2004
Harris, Eva Mar 2004
Harris, Richard obit Yrbk 2003
Harrison, George obit Mar 2002
Harrison, Marvin Aug 2001
Harrison, William B. Jr. Mar 2002
Hartke, Vance obit Yrbk 2003
Hartmann, Heidi I. Apr 2003
Haskins, Caryl P. obit Feb 2002
Hass, Robert Feb 2001
Hassenfeld, Alan G. Jul 2003
Hauerwas, Stanley Jun 2003
Hax, Carolyn Nov 2002
Hayes, Bob obit Jan 2003
Haynes, Cornell Jr. *see* Nelly
Haynes, Todd Jul 2003
Headley, Elizabeth *see* Cavanna, Betty
Heath, James R. Oct 2003
Heckart, Eileen obit Mar 2002
Heilbrun, Carolyn G. obit Feb 2004
Heiskell, Andrew obit Yrbk 2003
Helms, Richard obit Yrbk 2003
Henderson, Donald A. Mar 2002
Henderson, Hazel Nov 2003
Henderson, Joe obit Oct 2001
Hendrickson, Sue Oct 2001

Hepburn, Katharine obit Nov 2003
Herblock *see* Block, Herbert L.
Herndon, J. Marvin Nov 2003
Herring, Pendleton obit Yrbk 2004
Herzog, Jacques *see* Herzog, Jacques, and de Meuron, Pierre
Herzog, Jacques, and de Meuron, Pierre Jun 2002
Hewitt, Lleyton Oct 2002
Hewlett, Sylvia Ann Sep 2002
Heyerdahl, Thor obit Yrbk 2002
Heym, Stefan obit Mar 2002
Heymann, David L. Jul 2004
Hicks, Louise Day obit Jun 2004
Higgins, Chester Jr. Jun 2002
Hill, Andrew Apr 2004
Hill, Dulé Jul 2003
Hill, Faith Mar 2001
Hill, George Roy obit Jun 2003
Hill, Grant Jan 2002
Hill, Herbert obit Yrbk 2004
Hillenburg, Stephen Apr 2003
Hiller, Wendy obit Yrbk 2003
Hines, Gregory obit Yrbk 2003
Hines, Jerome obit Jun 2003
Hinojosa, Maria Feb 2001
Hirschfeld, Al obit Jul 2003
Hobson Pilot, Ann May 2003
Hoffman, Philip Seymour May 2001
Hogg, Quintin *see* Hailsham of St. Marylebone, Quintin Hogg
Holden, Betsy Jul 2003
Holl, Steven Jul 2004
Holland, Dave Mar 2003
Holm, Ian Mar 2002
Hondros, Chris Nov 2004
Hong, Hei-Kyung Nov 2003
Hooker, John Lee obit Sep 2001
Hope, Bob obit Yrbk 2003
Hopkins, Bernard Apr 2002
Hopkins, Nancy May 2002
Hoppus, Mark *see* blink-182
Horwich, Frances obit Oct 2001
Hounsfield, Godfrey obit Yrbk 2004
Hounsou, Djimon Aug 2004
Houston, Allan Nov 2003
Howe, Harold II obit Yrbk 2003
Hoyer, Steny Mar 2004
Hoyle, Fred obit Jan 2002

Hughes, Karen Oct 2001
Hugo, Chad *see* Neptunes
Hull, Jane Dee Feb 2002
Hunt Lieberson, Lorraine Jul 2004
Hunter, Kermit obit Sep 2001
Hunter, Kim obit Yrbk 2002

Illich, Ivan obit Yrbk 2003
Immelt, Jeffrey R. Feb 2004
India.Arie Feb 2002
Inkster, Juli Sep 2002
Isbin, Sharon Aug 2003
Istomin, Eugene obit Feb 2004
Ivins, Michael *see* Flaming Lips
Izetbegovic, Alija obit Jun 2004

Ja Rule Jul 2002
Jackman, Hugh Oct 2003
Jackson, Alan Apr 2004
Jackson, Hal Oct 2002
Jackson, Lauren Jun 2003
Jackson, Maynard H. Jr. obit Yrbk 2003
Jackson, Peter Jan 2002
Jackson, Thomas Penfield Jun 2001
Jagger, Janine Apr 2004
Jakes, T.D. Jun 2001
James, Alex *see* Blur
James, Bill Jun 2004
James, Edgerrin Jan 2002
Jarring, Gunnar obit Yrbk 2002
Jarvis, Erich D. May 2003
Jay-Z Aug 2002
Jeffers, Eve Jihan *see* Eve
Jeffords, James Sep 2001
Jenkins, Jerry B. *see* LaHaye, Tim and Jenkins, Jerry B.
Jenkins, Roy obit Yrbk 2003
Jennings, Waylon obit Apr 2002
Jet *see* Urquidez, Benny
Jimenez, Marcos Perez *see* Pérez Jiménez, Marcos
Jin, Deborah Apr 2004
Jobert, Michel obit Yrbk 2002
Johnson, Eddie Bernice Jul 2001
Johnson, Elizabeth A. Nov 2002
Jones, Bobby Jun 2002
Jones, Chipper May 2001
Jones, Chuck obit May 2002
Jones, Edward P. Mar 2004
Jones, Elaine Jun 2004
Jones, Larry Wayne Jr. *see* Jones, Chipper

Jones, Norah May 2003
Jonze, Spike Apr 2003
Joyner, Tom Sep 2002
Judd, Jackie Sep 2002
Judd, Jacqueline Dee *see* Judd, Jackie
Judson, Olivia Jan 2004
Juliana Queen of the Netherlands obit Yrbk 2004

Kabila, Joseph Sep 2001
Kael, Pauline obit Nov 2001
Kainen, Jacob obit Aug 2001
Kamen, Dean Nov 2002
Kane, Joseph Nathan obit Nov 2002
Kani, John Jun 2001
Kann, Peter R. Mar 2003
Kaptur, Marcy Jan 2003
Karbo, Karen May 2001
Karle, Isabella Jan 2003
Karon, Jan Mar 2003
Karsh, Yousuf obit Nov 2002
Karzai, Hamid May 2002
Kase, Toshikazu obit Yrbk 2004
Kass, Leon R. Aug 2002
Katsav, Moshe Feb 2001
Katz, Jackson Jul 2004
Kazan, Elia obit Yrbk 2004
Kcho Aug 2001
Keane, Seán *see* Chieftains
Keegan, Robert Jan 2004
Keener, Catherine Oct 2002
Keeshan, Bob obit Yrbk 2004
Keith, Toby Oct 2004
Kelleher, Herb Jan 2001
Keller, Bill Oct 2003
Keller, Marthe Jul 2004
Keller, Thomas Jun 2004
Kelman, Charles obit Yrbk 2004
Kennedy, Randall Aug 2002
Kennedy, Robert F. Jr. May 2004
Kent, Jeff May 2003
Kentridge, William Oct 2001
Kepes, György obit Mar 2002
Kerr, Clark obit May 2004
Kerr, Jean obit May 2003
Kerr, Mrs. Walter F *see* Kerr, Jean
Kerry, John Sep 2004
Kesey, Ken obit Feb 2002
Ketcham, Hank obit Sep 2001
Keys, Charlene *see* Tweet
Kid Rock Oct 2001
Kidd, Jason May 2002
Kiessling, Laura Aug 2003
Kilbourne, Jean May 2004
Kilpatrick, Kwame M. Apr 2004
King, Alan obit Yrbk 2004

Kittikachorn, Thanom obit Yrbk 2004
Klaus, Josef obit Oct 2001
Kleiber, Carlos obit Yrbk 2004
Klein, Naomi Aug 2003
Klein, William Mar 2004
Knowles, Beyoncé *see* Destiny's Child
Koch, Kenneth obit Yrbk 2002
Koff, Clea Nov 2004
Koizumi, Junichiro Jan 2002
Kolar, Jiri obit Yrbk 2002
Koma *see* Eiko and Koma
Konaré, Alpha Oumar Oct 2001
Koner, Pauline obit Apr 2001
Kopp, Wendy Mar 2003
Kostunica, Vojislav Jan 2001
Kott, Jan obit Mar 2002
Kournikova, Anna Jan 2002
Kramer, Joey *see* Aerosmith
Kramer, Stanley obit May 2001
Krause, David W. Feb 2002
Kreutzberger, Mario *see* Francisco, Don
Kripke, Saul Oct 2004
Krugman, Paul Aug 2001
Kübler-Ross, Elisabeth obit Yrbk 2004
Kushner, Tony Jul 2002
Kyles, Cedric *see* Cedric the Entertainer
Kyprianou, Spyros obit May 2002

La India May 2002
La Russa, Tony Jul 2003
Lacy, Dan obit Nov 2001
LaDuke, Winona Jan 2003
LaFontaine, Don Sep 2004
Lagardère, Jean-Luc obit Aug 2003
LaHaye, Tim *see* LaHaye, Tim and Jenkins, Jerry B.
LaHaye, Tim and Jenkins, Jerry B. Jun 2003
Lally, Joe *see* Fugazi
Landers, Ann obit Nov 2002
Lapidus, Morris obit Apr 2001
Lara, Brian Feb 2001
Lardner, Ring Jr. obit Feb 2001
Lassaw, Ibram obit Yrbk 2004
Lauder, Estée obit Yrbk 2004
Lavigne, Avril Apr 2003
Law, Ty Oct 2002
Le Clercq, Tanaquil obit Mar 2001
Leakey, Meave Jun 2002

Lederer, Esther Pauline *see* Landers, Ann
Lee, Andrea Sep 2003
Lee, Barbara Jun 2004
Lee, Geddy *see* Rush
Lee, Jeanette Oct 2002
Lee, Mrs. John G. *see* Lee, Percy Maxim
Lee, Peggy obit May 2002
Lee, Percy Maxim obit Jan 2003
Lee, Richard C. obit Jun 2003
LeFrak, Samuel J. obit Yrbk 2003
Leibowitz, Jonathan *see* Stewart, Jon
Leiter, Al Aug 2002
Lemmon, Jack obit Oct 2001
Leonard *see* Hackett, Buddy
Leone, Giovanni obit Feb 2002
LeSueur, Larry obit Jun 2003
Letterman, David Oct 2002
Levert, Gerald Oct 2003
Levin, Carl May 2004
LeVox, Gary *see* Rascal Flatts
Levy, Eugene Jan 2002
Lewis, David Levering May 2001
Lewis, David S. Jr. obit Yrbk 2004
Lewis, Flora obit Yrbk 2002
Lewis, John obit Jun 2001
Lewis, Kenneth Apr 2004
Lewis, Marvin Nov 2004
Li, Jet Jun 2001
Li Lian Jie *see* Li, Jet
Libeskind, Daniel Jun 2003
Lifeson, Alex *see* Rush
Lilly, John C. obit Feb 2002
Lilly, Kristine Apr 2004
Lima do Amor, Sisleide *see* Sissi
Lincoln, Abbey Sep 2002
Lincoln, Blanche Lambert Mar 2002
Lindbergh, Anne Morrow obit Apr 2001
Lindgren, Astrid obit Apr 2002
Lindo, Delroy Mar 2001
Lindsay, John V. obit Mar 2001
Lingle, Linda Jun 2003
Link, O. Winston obit Apr 2001
Linkin Park Mar 2002
Lipinski, Ann Marie Jul 2004
Lippold, Richard obit Yrbk 2002
Liu, Lucy Oct 2003
Lloyd, Charles Apr 2002
Locke, Gary Apr 2003

Lomax, Alan obit Oct 2002
London, Julie obit Feb 2001
Long, Russell B. obit Yrbk 2003
Long, William Ivey Mar 2004
López Portillo, José obit Yrbk 2004
Lord, Walter obit Yrbk 2002
Loudon, Dorothy obit Yrbk 2004
Love, John A. obit Apr 2002
Lowell, Mike Sep 2003
Lucas, George May 2002
Ludacris Jun 2004
Ludlum, Robert obit Jul 2001
Ludwig, Ken May 2004
Luns, Joseph M. A. H. obit Yrbk 2002
Lupica, Mike Mar 2001
Lyng, Richard E. obit Jun 2003
Lynne, Shelby Jul 2001

Mac, Bernie Jun 2002
Machado, Alexis Leyva see Kcho
MacKaye, Ian see Fugazi
MacKenzie, Gisele obit Jul 2004
Maddox, Lester obit Yrbk 2003
Madsen, Michael Apr 2004
Magloire, Paul E. obit Nov 2001
Maguire, Tobey Sep 2002
Mahal, Taj Nov 2001
Maki, Fumihiko Jul 2001
Malina, Joshua Apr 2004
Malley, Matt see Counting Crows
Maloney, Carolyn B. Apr 2001
Manchester, William obit Yrbk 2004
Mankind see Foley, Mick
Mann, Emily Jun 2002
Mansfield, Michael J. see Mansfield, Mike
Mansfield, Mike obit Jan 2002
Marcinko, Richard Mar 2001
Marcus, Stanley obit Apr 2002
Marcy, Geoffrey W. see Marcy, Geoffrey W., and Butler, R. Paul
Marcy, Geoffrey W., and Butler, R. Paul Nov 2002
Margaret, Princess of Great Britain obit May 2002
Marlette, Doug Jul 2002
Marshall, Burke obit Yrbk 2003

Marshall, Grant see Massive Attack
Marshall, Rob Jun 2003
Martin, A. J. P. see Martin, Archer
Martin, Archer obit Yrbk 2002
Martin, Chris see Coldplay
Martin, George R. R. Jan 2004
Martin, James S. Jr. obit Yrbk 2002
Martin, Mark Mar 2001
Martinez, Pedro Jun 2001
Martinez, Vilma Jul 2004
Mary Kay see Ash, Mary Kay
Massive Attack Jun 2004
Masters, William H. obit May 2001
Mathers, Marshall see Eminem
Matsui, Connie L. Aug 2002
Matta obit Yrbk 2003
Mauldin, Bill obit Jul 2003
Mauldin, William Henry see Mauldin, Bill
Mays, L. Lowry Aug 2003
Mayweather, Floyd Oct 2004
McBride, Martina Mar 2004
McCambridge, Mercedes obit Yrbk 2004
McCaw, Craig Sep 2001
McCloskey, Robert obit Yrbk 2003
McConnell, Page see Phish
McCracken, Craig Feb 2004
McCrary, Tex obit Yrbk 2003
McDonald, Gabrielle Kirk Oct 2001
McGrady, Tracy Feb 2003
McGraw, Eloise Jarvis obit Mar 2001
McGraw, Phillip Jun 2002
McGraw, Tim Sep 2002
McGreal, Elizabeth see Yates, Elizabeth
McGruder, Aaron Sep 2001
McGuire, Dorothy obit Nov 2001
McIntire, Carl obit Jun 2002
McIntosh, Millicent Carey obit Mar 2001
McKeon, Jack Apr 2004
McKinney, Robert obit Yrbk 2001
McLaughlin, John Feb 2004
McLean, Jackie Mar 2001
McLean, John Lenwood see McLean, Jackie
McMath, Sid obit Jan 2004
McNabb, Donovan Jan 2004
McNally, Andrew 3d obit Feb 2002

McQueen, Alexander Feb 2002
McWhirter, Norris D. obit Yrbk 2004
McWhorter, John H. Feb 2003
Mechem, Edwin L. obit Yrbk 2003
Mendes, Sam Oct 2002
Menken, Alan Jan 2001
Merchant, Natalie Jan 2003
Merton, Robert K. obit Yrbk 2003
Messier, Jean-Marie May 2002
Messing, Debra Aug 2002
Meta, Ilir Feb 2002
Meyer, Cord Jr. obit Aug 2001
Meyer, Edgar Jun 2002
Meyers, Nancy Feb 2002
Michel, Sia Sep 2003
Mickelson, Phil Mar 2002
Middelhoff, Thomas Feb 2001
Miller, Ann obit Yrbk 2004
Miller, J. Irwin obit Yrbk 2004
Miller, Jason obit Yrbk 2001
Miller, John Aug 2003
Miller, Neal obit Jun 2002
Millman, Dan Aug 2002
Milosz, Czeslaw obit Yrbk 2004
Mink, Patsy T. obit Jan 2003
Minner, Ruth Ann Aug 2001
Mirabal, Robert Aug 2002
Mitchell, Dean Aug 2002
Mitha, Tehreema May 2004
Miyazaki, Hayao Apr 2001
Moby Apr 2001
Mohammed, W. Deen Jan 2004
Moiseiwitsch, Tanya obit Jul 2003
Molina, Alfred Feb 2004
Molloy, Matt see Chieftains
Moloney, Paddy see Chieftains
Monk, T. S. Feb 2002
Montresor, Beni obit Feb 2002
Moore, Ann Aug 2003
Moore, Dudley obit Yrbk 2002
Moore, Elisabeth Luce obit Yrbk 2002
Moore, Gordon E. Apr 2002
Moore, Paul Jr. obit Yrbk 2003
Moorer, Thomas H. obit Yrbk 2004
Morella, Constance A. Feb 2001
Morial, Marc Jan 2002
Morris, Errol Feb 2001
Mortensen, Viggo Jun 2004

Moseka, Aminata *see* Lincoln, Abbey

Moses, Bob *see* Moses, Robert P.

Moses, Robert P. Apr 2002

Mosley, Sugar Shane Jan 2001

Mosley, Timothy *see* Timbaland

Moss, Adam Mar 2004

Moss, Frank E. obit Jun 2003

Moten, Etta *see* Barnett, Etta Moten

Moynihan, Daniel Patrick obit Yrbk 2003

Muhammed, Warith Deen *see* Mohammed, W. Deen

Mulcahy, Anne M. Nov 2002

Murkowski, Frank H. Jul 2003

Murphy, Mark Sep 2004

Murray, Bill Sep 2004

Murray, Jonathan *see* Bunim, Mary-Ellis, and Murray, Jonathan

Murray, Jonathan *see* Bunim, Mary-Ellis, and Murray, Jonathan

Murray, Ty May 2002

Musharraf, Pervaiz *see* Musharraf, Pervez

Musharraf, Pervez Mar 2001

Mydans, Carl M. obit Yrbk 2004

Mydans, Shelley Symith obit Aug 2002

Myers, Richard B. Apr 2002

Nabrit, Samuel M. obit Yrbk 2004

Najimy, Kathy Oct 2002

Napolitano, Janet Oct 2004

Narayan, R. K. obit Jul 2001

Nash, Steve Mar 2003

Nason, John W. obit Feb 2002

Nasser, Jacques Apr 2001

Nathan, Robert R. obit Nov 2001

Navratilova, Martina Feb 2004

Ne Win obit Yrbk 2003

Neals, Otto Feb 2003

Neeleman, David Sep 2003

Negroponte, John Apr 2003

Nehru, B. K. obit Feb 2002

Nelly Oct 2002

Nelson, Marilyn Carlson Oct 2004

Neptunes May 2004

Neustadt, Richard E. obit Yrbk 2004

Newman, J. Wilson obit Yrbk 2003

Newsom, Lee Ann Oct 2004

Newton, Helmut obit Yrbk 2004

Nguyen Van Thieu *see* Thieu, Nguyen Van

Nikolayev, Andrian obit Yrbk 2004

Nixon, Agnes Apr 2001

Norton, Gale A. Jun 2001

Nottage, Lynn Nov 2004

Novacek, Michael J. Sep 2002

Nowitzki, Dirk Jun 2002

Nozick, Robert obit Apr 2002

O'Brien, Ed *see* Radiohead

O'Connor, Carroll obit Sep 2001

O'Connor, Donald obit Apr 2004

O'Hair, Madalyn Murray obit Jun 2001

O'Keefe, Sean Jan 2003

Okrent, Daniel Nov 2004

Olin, Lena Jun 2003

Ollila, Jorma Aug 2002

O'Malley, Sean Patrick Jan 2004

O'Neal, Jermaine Jun 2004

O'Neal, Stanley May 2003

O'Neill, Paul H. Jul 2001

O'Reilly, Bill Oct 2003

Orlean, Susan Jun 2003

Orman, Suze May 2003

Ortner, Sherry B. Nov 2002

Osawa, Sandra Sunrising Jan 2001

Osbourne, Sharon Jan 2001

Oudolf, Piet Apr 2003

OutKast Apr 2004

Oz, Mehmet C. Apr 2003

Paar, Jack obit Yrbk 2004

Page, Clarence Jan 2003

Page, Larry *see* Brin, Sergey, and Page, Larry

Paige, Roderick R. Jul 2001

Palmeiro, Rafael Aug 2001

Park, Linda Sue Jun 2002

Park, Rosemary obit Yrbk 2004

Parsons, Richard D. Apr 2003

Pascal, Amy Mar 2002

Patchett, Ann Apr 2003

Patti, Sandi *see* Patty, Sandi

Patton, Antwan *see* OutKast

Patty, Sandi Feb 2004

Pau, Peter Feb 2002

Paulson, Henry M. Jr. Sep 2002

Payne, Alexander Feb 2003

Paz Estenssoro, Victor obit Sep 2001

Pearce, Christie *see* Rampone, Christie

Peart, Neil *see* Rush

Peck, Gregory obit Sep 2003

Pekar, Harvey Jan 2004

Pelosi, Nancy Feb 2003

Pelzer, Dave Mar 2002

Pérez Jiménez, Marcos obit Feb 2002

Perkins, Charles obit Feb 2001

Perle, Richard Jul 2003

Perry, Joe *see* Aerosmith

Person, Houston Jun 2003

Perutz, Max obit Apr 2002

Petersen, Wolfgang Jul 2001

Phelps, Michael Aug 2004

Phillips, Sam Apr 2001

Phillips, Scott *see* Creed

Phillips, William obit Yrbk 2002

Phish Jul 2003

Phoenix *see* Linkin Park

Piano, Renzo Apr 2001

Picciotto, Guy *see* Fugazi

Pickering, William H. obit Yrbk 2004

Pierce, David Hyde Apr 2001

Pierce, John Robinson obit Jun 2002

Pierce, Paul Nov 2002

Pierce, Samuel R. Jr. obit Feb 2001

Pincay, Laffit Sep 2001

Pitt, Harvey Nov 2002

Pitts, Leonard Jr. Oct 2004

Plimpton, George obit Jan 2004

Plimpton, Martha Apr 2002

Poletti, Charles obit Yrbk 2002

Pollitt, Katha Oct 2002

Pomeroy, Wardell B. obit Yrbk 2001

Popeil, Ron Mar 2001

Posey, Parker Mar 2003

Potok, Chaim obit Yrbk 2002

Potter, Myrtle S. Aug 2004

Poujade, Pierre obit Yrbk 2004

Powell, Colin L. Nov 2001

Powell, Kevin Jan 2004

Powell, Michael K. May 2003

Prigogine, Ilya obit Yrbk 2003

Prinze, Freddie Jr. Jan 2003

Pujols, Albert Sep 2004

Pusey, Nathan M. obit Feb 2002

Queloz, Didier Feb 2002

Quine, W. V. obit Mar 2001

Quine, Willard Van Orman *see* Quine, W. V.

Quinn, Anthony obit Sep 2001

Racette, Patricia Feb 2003
Radiohead Jun 2001
Raimi, Sam Jul 2002
Rakic, Patricia Goldman *see* Goldman-Rakic, Patricia
Rall, Ted May 2002
Ralston, Joseph W. Jan 2001
Ramirez, Manny Jun 2002
Ramirez, Tina Nov 2004
Ramos, Jorge Mar 2004
Rampling, Charlotte Jun 2002
Rampone, Christie Oct 2004
Randall, Tony obit Yrbk 2004
Rania Feb 2001
Rascal Flatts Aug 2003
Reagan, Ronald obit Sep 2004
Redgrave, Vanessa Sep 2003
Reeves, Dan Oct 2001
Regan, Donald T. obit Yrbk 2003
Rehnquist, William H. Nov 2003
Reid, Antonio *see* Reid, L. A.
Reid, Harry Mar 2003
Reid, L. A. Aug 2001
Reilly, John C. Oct 2004
Reinhardt, Uwe E. Mar 2004
Reinking, Ann Jun 2004
Reitman, Ivan Mar 2001
Ressler, Robert K. Feb 2002
Reuss, Henry S. obit Mar 2002
Reuther, Victor obit Yrbk 2004
Reynolds, John W. Jr. obit Mar 2002
Reynoso, Cruz Mar 2002
Rhodes, James A. obit Jul 2001
Rhodes, John J. obit Yrbk 2004
Rhyne, Charles S. obit Yrbk 2003
Rice, Condoleezza Apr 2001
Richler, Mordecai obit Oct 2001
Richter, Gerhard Jun 2002
Rickey, George W. obit Yrbk 2002
Ridge, Tom Feb 2001
Riefenstahl, Leni obit Yrbk 2004
Riesman, David obit Yrbk 2002
Riley, Terry Apr 2002
Rimm, Sylvia B. Feb 2002
Rimsza, Skip Jul 2002
Rines, Robert H. Jan 2003
Riopelle, Jean-Paul obit Yrbk 2002

Ripley, Alexander obit Yrbk 2004
Ripley, S. Dillon obit Aug 2001
Ritchie, Robert James *see* Kid Rock
Ritter, John obit Yrbk 2004
Rivers, Larry obit Nov 2002
Robards, Jason Jr. obit Mar 2001
Robb, J. D. *see* Roberts, Nora
Robbins, Anthony *see* Robbins, Tony
Robbins, Frederick C. obit Yrbk 2003
Robbins, Tony Jul 2001
Roberts, Nora Sep 2001
Robinson, Janet L. Mar 2003
Roche, James M. obit Yrbk 2004
Rockefeller, Laurance S. obit Yrbk 2004
Roddick, Andy Jan 2004
Rodriguez, Alex Apr 2003
Rodriguez, Arturo Mar 2001
Rogers, Fred obit Jul 2003
Rogers, William P. obit Mar 2001
Rollins, Edward J. Mar 2001
Rollins, Henry Sep 2001
Romenesko, Jim Feb 2004
Romer, John Jul 2003
Romero, Anthony Jul 2002
Rooney, Joe Don *see* Rascal Flatts
Rose, Jalen Mar 2004
Rose, Jim Mar 2003
Ross, Gary May 2004
Ross, Herbert obit Feb 2002
Ross, Robert Oct 2002
Rostow, Eugene V. obit Yrbk 2003
Rostow, Walt W. obit Jul 2003
Rote, Kyle obit Yrbk 2002
Roth, William V. Jr. obit Yrbk 2004
Rowan, Carl T. obit Jan 2001
Rowland, Kelly *see* Destiny's Child
Rowley, Janet D. Mar 2001
Rowntree, David *see* Blur
Rubenstein, Atoosa Oct 2004
Rule, Ja *see* Ja Rule
Rumsfeld, Donald H. Mar 2002
Rus, Daniela Feb 2004
Rush Feb 2001
Russell, Harold obit Apr 2002
Russell, Kurt Nov 2004
Ryan, George H. Sep 2001
Ryder, Jonathan *see* Ludlum, Robert

Ryer, Jonathan *see* Ludlum, Robert

Saab, Elie Aug 2004
Said, Edward W. obit Feb 2004
Sánchez, David Nov 2001
Sandford, John Mar 2002
Sanger, Stephen Mar 2004
Santos, José Nov 2003
Sapolsky, Robert Jan 2004
Sapp, Warren Sep 2003
Saramago, José Jun 2002
Savage, Rick *see* Def Leppard
Savimbi, Jonas obit Jun 2002
Sayles Belton, Sharon Jan 2001
Scammon, Richard M. obit Sep 2001
Scavullo, Francesco obit Yrbk 2004
Schaap, Phil Sep 2001
Schakowsky, Jan Jul 2004
Schilling, Curt Oct 2001
Schindler, Alexander M. obit Feb 2001
Schlesinger, John obit Yrbk 2003
Schott, Marge obit Yrbk 2004
Schultes, Richard Evans obit Sep 2001
Schwarzenegger, Arnold Aug 2004
Scott, George *see* Blind Boys of Alabama
Scott, Jill Jan 2002
Scott, Tony Nov 2004
Scottoline, Lisa Jul 2001
Scully, Vin Oct 2001
Sears, Martha *see* Sears, William and Martha
Sears, William and Martha Aug 2001
Seau, Junior Sep 2001
Sebelius, Kathleen Nov 2004
Sedaris, Amy Apr 2002
Selway, Phil *see* Radiohead
Senghor, Léopold Sédar obit Mar 2002
Serrano Súñer, Ramón obit Yrbk 2004
Setzer, Philip *see* Emerson String Quartet
Seymour, Lesley Jane Nov 2001
Seymour, Stephanie Oct 2002
Shaheen, Jeanne Jan 2001
Shalhoub, Tony Nov 2002
Shapiro, Irving S. obit Nov 2001
Shapiro, Neal May 2003
Shawcross, Hartley obit Yrbk 2003

Shearer, Harry Jun 2001
Shepherd, Michael *see* Ludlum, Robert
Shinoda, Mike *see* Linkin Park
Shoemaker, Willie obit Apr 2004
Shyamalan, M. Night Mar 2003
Silver, Joel Nov 2003
Simmons, Earl *see* DMX
Simon, Herbert A. obit May 2001
Simon, Paul obit Yrbk 2004
Simone, Nina obit Yrbk 2003
Simpson, Lorna Nov 2004
Sinopoli, Giuseppe obit Sep 2001
Sissi Jun 2001
Slater, Kelly Jul 2001
Slavenska, Mia obit Apr 2003
Smiley, Tavis Apr 2003
Smith, Chesterfield H. obit Yrbk 2003
Smith, Elinor Mar 2001
Smith, Howard K. obit Aug 2002
Smith, Jeff obit Yrbk 2004
Smith, Maggie Jul 2002
Smith, Orin C. Nov 2003
Smylie, Robert E. obit Yrbk 2004
Snead, Sam obit Yrbk 2002
Snow, John Aug 2003
Soffer, Olga Jul 2002
Sothern, Ann obit Aug 2001
Souzay, Gérard obit Yrbk 2004
Spahn, Warren obit Yrbk 2004
Sparks, Nicholas Feb 2001
Spence, Hartzell obit Yrbk 2001
Spencer, John Jan 2001
Spencer, Scott Jul 2003
Spiropulu, Maria May 2004
Spitzer, Eliot Mar 2003
Sprewell, Latrell Feb 2001
St. John, Robert obit Yrbk 2003
Stackhouse, Jerry Nov 2001
Stanfield, Robert Lorne obit Yrbk 2004
Stanley, Kim obit Jan 2002
Stanton, Andrew Feb 2004
Stanton, Bill May 2001
Stapp, Scott *see* Creed
Stargell, Willie obit Sep 2001
Stassen, Harold E. obit May 2001
Steele, Claude M. Feb 2001
Steele, Michael S. Jul 2004
Steig, William obit Apr 2004

Steiger, Rod obit Yrbk 2002
Stein, Benjamin J. Sep 2001
Steingraber, Sandra Sep 2003
Stern, Isaac obit Jan 2002
Stevens, Ted Oct 2001
Steward, David L. Nov 2004
Stewart, Alice obit Yrbk 2002
Stewart, Jon Jul 2004
Stiefel, Ethan Apr 2004
Stoltenberg, Gerhard obit Mar 2002
Stone, W. Clement obit Yrbk 2002
Storr, Anthony obit Sep 2001
Straight, Michael obit Yrbk 2004
Stratton, William G. obit Aug 2001
Straus, Roger W. Jr. obit Yrbk 2004
Streb, Elizabeth Apr 2003
Stroman, Susan Jul 2002
Sucksdorff, Arne obit Sep 2001
Sugar, Bert Randolph Nov 2002
Sullivan, Daniel Feb 2003
Sullivan, Leon H. obit Sep 2001
Summers, Lawrence H. Jul 2002
Sun Wen Apr 2001
Sutherland, Kiefer Mar 2002
Suzuki, Ichiro Jul 2002
Suzuki, Zenko obit Yrbk 2004
Sweeney, Anne Jun 2003
Swinton, Tilda Nov 2001
Syal, Meera Feb 2001

Tajiri, Satoshi Nov 2001
Talley, André Leon Jul 2003
Talmadge, Herman E. obit Jun 2002
Tarter, Jill Cornell Feb 2001
Tartt, Donna Feb 2003
Tauscher, Ellen O. Mar 2001
Taylor, John W. obit Apr 2002
Taylor, Koko Jul 2002
Tejada, Miguel Jun 2003
Teller, Edward obit Sep 2004
Thain, John A. May 2004
Theron, Charlize Nov 2004
Thieu, Nguyen Van obit Jan 2002
Thomas, Dave *see* Thomas, R. David
Thomas, R. David obit Apr 2002
Thompson, Lonnie Jan 2004
Thomson, James A. Nov 2001
Thomson, Meldrim Jr. obit Sep 2001

Thurmond, Strom obit Nov 2003
Thyssen-Bornemisza de Kaszan, Baron Hans Heinrich obit Yrbk 2002
Tice, George A. Nov 2003
Tigerman, Stanley Feb 2001
Timbaland Mar 2003
Tisch, Laurence A. obit Yrbk 2004
Titov, Gherman obit Jan 2001
Tobin, James obit May 2002
Toledo, Alejandro Nov 2001
Toles, Thomas G. *see* Toles, Tom
Toles, Tom Nov 2002
Tremonti, Mark *see* Creed
Trenet, Charles obit Sep 2001
Trenkler, Freddie obit Yrbk 2001
Trevor-Roper, H. R. obit Jul 2003
Tridish, Pete Apr 2004
Trigère, Pauline obit Jul 2002
Tritt, Travis Feb 2004
Trout, Robert obit Jan 2001
Troutt Powell, Eve May 2004
Trudeau, Pierre Elliott obit Jan 2001
Truman, David B. obit Yrbk 2004
Tsui Hark Oct 2001
Tull, Tanya Nov 2004
Tureck, Rosalyn obit Yrbk 2003
Turner, Mark Nov 2002
Turre, Steve Apr 2001
Tweet Nov 2002
Tyler, Steven *see* Aerosmith
Tyson, John H. Aug 2001

Unitas, Johnny obit Yrbk 2002
Uris, Leon obit Yrbk 2003
Urquidez, Benny Nov 2001
Ustinov, Peter obit Aug 2004

Valentine, Bobby Jul 2001
Van den Haag, Ernest obit Jul 2002
Van Exel, Nick Mar 2002
Van Gundy, Jeff May 2001
Vance, Cyrus R. obit Apr 2002
Varnedoe, Kirk obit Yrbk 2003
Verdon, Gwen obit Jan 2001
Vick, Michael Nov 2003
Vickrey, Dan *see* Counting Crows
Vieira, Meredith Apr 2002
Vinatieri, Adam Sep 2004

Viscardi, Henry Jr. obit Yrbk 2004
Voulkos, Peter obit Aug 2002

Wachowski, Andy *see* Wachowski, Andy and Larry
Wachowski, Andy and Larry Sep 2003
Wachowski, Larry *see* Wachowski, Andy and Larry
Walker, Mort Feb 2002
Wall, Art obit Feb 2002
Wallace, Ben Apr 2004
Walsh, John Jul 2001
Walters, Barbara Feb 2003
Walters, Vernon A. obit Jul 2002
Ward, Benjamin obit Yrbk 2002
Ware, David S. Sep 2003
Warnke, Paul C. obit Feb 2002
Washington, Walter E. obit Yrbk 2004
Wasserman, Lew R. obit Yrbk 2002
Waters, Alice Jan 2004
Watkins, Donald Jan 2003
Watkins, Levi Jr. Mar 2003
Watson, Arthel Lane *see* Watson, Doc
Watson, Doc Feb 2003
Waugh, Auberon obit May 2001
Wayans, Marlon *see* Wayans, Shawn and Marlon
Wayans, Shawn and Marlon May 2001
Weaver, Pat obit Yrbk 2002
Weaver, Sylvester *see* Weaver, Pat
Webber, Chris May 2003
Weinrig, Gary Lee *see* Rush
Weiss, Paul obit Yrbk 2002
Weisskopf, Victor F. obit Yrbk 2002
Weitz, John obit Apr 2003
Wek, Alek Jun 2001
Wells, David May 2004
Wellstone, Paul D. obit Yrbk 2003
Welty, Eudora obit Nov 2001
Wesley, Valerie Wilson Jun 2002
Wexler, Jerry Jan 2001

Wheeldon, Christopher Mar 2004
Whitaker, Mark Aug 2003
White, Byron Raymond obit Jul 2002
White, Jack *see* White Stripes
White, Meg *see* White Stripes
White Stripes Sep 2003
Whitehead, Colson Nov 2001
Whitford, Brad *see* Aerosmith
Whitford, Bradley Apr 2003
Whitson, Peggy Sep 2003
Wiggins, James Russell obit Mar 2001
Wilber, Ken Apr 2002
Wilder, Billy obit Yrbk 2002
Wilhelm, Hoyt obit Yrbk 2002
Wilkins, Robert W. obit Yrbk 2003
Williams, Armstrong May 2004
Williams, Harrison A. Jr. obit Mar 2002
Williams, Michelle *see* Destiny's Child
Williams, Pharrell *see* Neptunes
Williams, Serena *see* Williams, Venus and Williams, Serena
Williams, Ted obit Oct 2002
Williams, Venus *see* Williams, Venus and Williams, Serena
Williams, Venus and Williams, Serena Feb 2003
Willingham, Tyrone Nov 2002
Willis, Deborah Sep 2004
Wilson, James Q. Aug 2002
Wilson, Kemmons obit Yrbk 2003
Wilson, Marie C. Sep 2004
Wilson, Owen Feb 2003
Wilson, Sloan obit Yrbk 2003
Winsor, Kathleen obit Yrbk 2003
Winston, Stan Jul 2002
Witherspoon, Reese Jan 2004
Woese, Carl R. Jun 2003
Wojciechowska, Maia obit Yrbk 2002
Wolfe, Julia Oct 2003
Wolff, Maritta M. obit Yrbk 2002
Wolfowitz, Paul Feb 2003
Wong-Staal, Flossie Apr 2001
Wood, Elijah Aug 2002

Woodcock, Leonard obit Apr 2001
Woods, Donald obit Nov 2001
Woodson, Rod Oct 2004
Woodward, Robert F. obit Yrbk 2001
Wooldridge, Anna Marie *see* Lincoln, Abbey
Worth, Irene obit Aug 2002
Wright, Jeffrey May 2002
Wright, Ronald *see* Wright, Winky
Wright, Steven May 2003
Wright, Will Feb 2004
Wright, Winky Jul 2004
Wrynn, Dylan *see* Tridish, Pete
Wylde, Zakk Oct 2004
Wyman, Thomas obit Yrbk 2003

Xenakis, Iannis obit Jul 2001

Yagudin, Alexei Feb 2004
Yashin, Aleksei *see* Yashin, Alexei
Yashin, Alexei Jan 2003
Yassin, Ahmed obit Yrbk 2004
Yates, Elizabeth obit Nov 2001
Yates, Sidney R. obit Jan 2001
Yokich, Stephen P. obit Yrbk 2002
Yorke, Thom *see* Radiohead

Zahn, Paula Feb 2002
Zaillian, Steven Oct 2001
Zambello, Francesca May 2003
Zatopek, Emil obit Feb 2001
Zellweger, Renée Feb 2004
Zerhouni, Elias Oct 2003
Zeta-Jones, Catherine Apr 2003
Zhu Rongji Jul 2001
Ziegler, Ronald L. obit Jul 2003
Zimmer, Hans Mar 2002
Zinni, Anthony C. May 2002
Zito, Barry Jul 2004
Zivojinovich, Alex *see* Rush
Zollar, Jawole Willa Jo Jul 2003
Zorina, Vera obit Yrbk 2003
Zucker, Jeff Jan 2002
Zukerman, Eugenia Jan 2004